Developmental Control in Animals and Plants

edited by C. F. Graham
and P. F. Wareing

SECOND EDITION

BLACKWELL SCIENTIFIC PUBLICATIONS

OXFORD · LONDON · EDINBURGH

BOSTON · PALO ALTO · MELBOURNE

© 1976, 1984 by Blackwell Scientific
Publications
Editorial offices:
Osney Mead, Oxford OX2 0EL
8 John Street, London WC1N 2ES
9 Forrest Road, Edinburgh EH1 2QH
52 Beacon Street, Boston, Massachusetts
    02108, USA
706 Cowper Street, Palo Alto
    California 94301, USA
99 Barry Street, Carlton, Victoria 3053,
    Australia

First published 1976

Second edition 1984

Photoset by Enset Ltd,
Radstock Road, Midsomer Norton,
Bath, Avon
and
Printed and bound in Great Britain
at the Alden Press, Oxford.

DISTRIBUTORS

USA and Canada
    Blackwell Scientific Publications Inc
    PO Box 50009, Palo Alto
    California 94303

Australia
    Blackwell Scientific Book Distributors
    31 Advantage Road, Highett
    Victoria 3190

British Library Cataloguing in Publication Data

Developmental control in animals and plants—
    2nd ed.
    1. Cells
    I. Graham, C.F.   II. Wareing, P.F.
    III. The developmental biology of plants
    and animals.
    574.87′61   QH581.2

    ISBN 0-632-00758-3

Developmental Control in Animals and Plants

Contents

v

The Authors

J.B.L. Bard, MRC *Clinical and Population Cytogenetics Unit, Western General Hospital, Crewe Road, Edinburgh EH4 2XU, U.K.*

J.T. Bonner, *Department of Biology, Princeton University, Princeton, New Jersey 08540, U.S.A.*

A.E. Clarke, *School of Botany, University of Melbourne, Parkville, Victoria 3052, Australia*

I.W. Craig, *Genetics Group, Department of Biochemistry, Oxford University, South Parks Road, Oxford OX1 3QU, U.K.*

A.S.G. Curtis, *Department of Cell Biology, The University, Glasgow G12 8QQ, U.K.*

V. French, *Department of Zoology, University of Edinburgh, West Mains Road, Edinburgh EH9 3JT, U.K.*

C.F. Graham, *Department of Zoology, Oxford University, South Parks Road, Oxford OX1 3PS, U.K.*

B.E.S. Gunning, *Department of Developmental Biology, Research School of Biological Sciences, Australian National University, P.O. Box 475, Canberra A.C.T. 2601, Australia*

M.A. Hall, *Department of Botany and Microbiology, School of Biological Sciences, The University College of Wales, Aberystwyth SY23 3DA, U.K.*

R.E. Keller, *Department of Zoology, University of California, Berkeley, California 94720, U.S.A.*

R.B. Knox, *School of Botany, University of Melbourne, Parkville, Victoria 3052, Australia.*

J.S. Knowland, *Department of Biochemistry, Oxford University, South Parks Road, Oxford OX1 3QU, U.K.*

J.J. Marchalonis, *Department of Biochemistry, Medical University of South Carolina, 171 Ashley Avenue, Charleston, South Carolina 29403, U.S.A.*

A. Miller, *Laboratory of Molecular Biophysics, Department of Zoology, Oxford University, South Parks Road, Oxford OX1 3PS, U.K.*

P.C. Newell, *Department of Biochemistry, Oxford University, South Parks Road, Oxford OX1 3QU, U.K.*

R.W. Old, *Department of Biological Sciences, University of Warwick, Coventry CV4 7AL, U.K.*

J.D. Pitts, *The Beatson Institute for Cancer Research, Wolfson Laboratory for Molecular Pathology, Garscube Estate, Bearsden, Glasgow G61 1B2, U.K.*

L. Saxen, *Department of Pathology, University of Helsinki, SF-00290, Helsinki 29, Finland*

P.F. Wareing, *Department of Botany and Microbiology, School of Biological Sciences, The University College of Wales, Aberystwyth SY23 3DA, U.K.*

G.W. Warr, *Department of Biochemistry, Medical University of South Carolina, 171 Ashley Avenue, Charleston, South Carolina 29403, U.S.A.*

J. Wartiovaara, *Department of Pathology, University of Helsinki, SF-00290, Helsinki 29, Finland*

H.R. Woodland, *Department of Biological Sciences, University of Warwick, Coventry CV4 7AL, U.K.*

Preface to Second Edition

The preparation of a second edition of this book has been the occasion for extensive revision and modification of the original version. About half the chapters are entirely new and the remaining chapters have been re-written or extensively revised. Some of these changes have been necessitated by significant advances in knowledge since the first edition was published, especially in the structure of the eukaryotic genome and the control of gene expression.

However, changes have been made not only to take account of recent advances in knowledge, but also to present a more balanced account and to introduce several new topics. Thus, although the overall structure of the first edition has been retained, some topics previously allocated separate chapters have been dealt with more concisely, making it possible to include new chapters on cell adhesion, patterns of form, position effects and hormonal control in the whole plant.

The same policy has been adopted as in the first edition, namely that the topics selected should be treated in depth, rather than that a comprehensive coverage should be presented at a more general level.

There are now several excellent general textbooks dealing separately with animal or plant development, to which the reader is referred for introductory accounts. This book is intended as a more advanced text and it continues to be unique in attempting to present both animal and plant development at this level.

Our aim has been to draw attention to the similarities and the differences of developmental patterns in animals and plants. At the molecular level the mechanisms of developmental control are probably very similar in animals and plants. However, as the two kingdoms evolved, their organization and patterns of development diverged, reflecting the sedentary, autotrophic mode of life of plants, and the mobile, foraging or predatory habits of most animal species. Consequently, for some topics an integrated treatment for both plants and animals is appropriate, whereas for other topics separate treatments are called for.

If the book renders plant and animal developmental biologists better acquainted with each other's work and concepts, it will have served a useful function.

Part 1
Developmental Processes

Chapter 1.1
Introduction—
Problems of Development
P.F. Wareing and C.F. Graham

The term *development* is used in various senses in biology, but in this book we shall apply it in the broadest sense to the complex changes which an individual organism undergoes in its life cycle from fertilization to death. Development normally involves both quantitative changes, i.e. *growth*, and qualitative changes leading to increased specialization in the various cells, tissues and organs of the body, which we refer to as *differentiation*. The processes leading to and determining the form and structure of the organism are included in the general term *morphogenesis*.

Differentiation can be recognized at various levels of organization, namely at the cell, tissue and organ levels. The use of the term in this way is quite logical since differentiation between tissues and organs simply reflects differentiation which occurred at the cellular level at an earlier stage of development. Development is normally a very orderly process in which one stage follows another in the proper sequence, and at each stage cells which hitherto had shown a common lineage diverge into alternative pathways of differentiation. If such divergence occurs early in development it may lead to subsequent differentiation of whole organs or other major parts of the whole organism, while later the divergence may lead to tissue or cell differentiation.

A central problem of development concerns the nature of the control mechanisms whereby cells of common lineage are caused to diverge into alternative pathways; that is, the problem of the origin of cell heterogeneity, which is the subject of Part 2. Once a group of cells has become committed to a particular pathway of differentiation, it normally becomes very difficult to divert them into another pathway; thus, the developmental potentiality of the cells has become restricted and they are said to have become *determined* along a particular pathway. It might be thought that this restriction of developmental potential reflects a loss of genetic material, i.e. of parts of the genome, during the course of development, but it is now clear that generally the nucleus remains 'pluripotential' and retains the capacity to regenerate a whole organism under certain conditions (see, however, section 1.2.2).

The progressive cell specialization which arises by divergence at successive stages of development would not, of itself, lead to an integrated, whole organism but to a mass of cells which were different in structure and function in different regions, but which did not relate their activities to each other. To achieve integration, there is clearly a need for cells and tissues to be able to communicate and interact with each other in controlled ways. Thus, morphogenesis depends upon cell communication and interaction (Part 4). Moreover, before there can be communication there must be the capacity for recognition between cells. This capacity for recognition is particularly important in animals, in which the cells are potentially motile and if disaggregated can ultimately segregate out again, so that cells of the same type become reassociated together. In plants, most of the cells are non-motile and the need for cell recognition properties is not so evident, but nevertheless we shall see that the capacity for recognition is well developed in certain types of plant cell (Part 3).

Communication between cells can take various forms. Some of these involve short-range interactions, including the induction of differentiation by one type of cell in contiguous cells (Part 3). Such short-range interactions must play a vital role in ensuring the orderly sequence of differentiation in both space and time.

Long-range communication is primarily effected through hormones produced in one part of the organism and acting in a distant part (Part 5). We shall see that hormones probably do not act directly as inducers of differentiation but rather as evocators of the processes leading to differentiation in cells which are already predetermined along certain pathways.

Although for many purposes it is covenient to regard the cell as the unit of differentiation, it is important to recognize that at the subcellular level, organelles such as mitochondria and chloroplasts show their own cycles of development, which are described in detail in Part 6. Moreover, it is self-evident that structural and functional differences between cells must have a molecular basis and that it must be our ultimate aim to describe and understand differentiation in molecular terms.

There are several different aspects of differentiation at the molecular level to be considered. On the one hand, development can be regarded as a problem of programmed sequential gene expression (Part 6). Insofar as gene action is expressed through the synthesis of specific structural and enzyme proteins, this is clearly one field of molecular biology which is vital to a full understanding of development. We know little about the control of gene expression in eukaryotes, but clearly the mechanism whereby the right genes are activated in the right cells at the right time is central to the problem of development. On the other hand, not all aspects of cell organization at the molecular level are enzyme-mediated and therefore directly controlled by the genome. For example, some cellular structures, such as

ribosomes and membranes, exhibit 'self-assembly' and do not require enzymes as catalysts. The extent to which self-assembly plays a role in cell development is also discussed in Part 6.

We shall see that many of these problems of development are common to both plants and animals, particularly at the molecular and sub-cellular levels. At higher levels of organization the problems are not always the same in plants and animals, since the plant cell is enclosed in a rigid wall and is non-motile, whereas this is not the case for animals cells. This basic difference has had profound effects upon the patterns of development of plants and animals. Thus, whereas most animals show a distinct embryonic phase which is terminated by the attainment of the structure of the adult, in plants development is open-ended or 'indeterminate', in that the growing points (apical meristems) of the shoot and root often remain permanently embryonic and capable of further growth and differentiation throughout the life of the plant. On the other hand, the development of organs such as the leaves and fruits is 'closed' and much more analogous to the development of organs in animals. Thus when allowance has been made for these differences in organization of the plant and animal bodies, many of the problems of development are closely analogous in the two groups of organism.

Chapter 1.2
Nucleus and Cytoplasm
P.F. Wareing and C.F. Graham

1.2.1 GENE EXPRESSION AND DEVELOPMENT

J.B.S. Haldane first pointed out as long ago as 1932 [21] that many genes have a specific time of action during development. Nothing was known then about the manner in which gene action is controlled or as to how the correct sequence of gene expression during development is achieved. Today we still have little understanding of the latter problem, but as a result of advances in molecular biology we know a great deal about how the information encoded in the DNA is expressed in the structure of the proteins of the cell. Thus, the concept has arisen that the cell specialization involves the activation of the specific groups of genes which, in turn, control the synthesis of the enzymes and other proteins characteristic of such specialized cells. This is the so-called 'variable gene-activity theory' of cell differentiation.

Our current thinking on gene activation and repression is based upon and conditioned by information gained from studies on micro-organisms. These studies led to the well-known theory of Jacob and Monod, according to which the activity of genes which code for specific enzyme proteins, the so-called *structural genes*, is controlled by other genes referred to as *regulator genes*. A regulator gene forms a cytoplasmic protein called the *repressor*. It is postulated that the initiation of messenger RNA (mRNA) synthesis on the structural gene is controlled by a neighbouring section of DNA called the *operator*, and that the repressor formed by a given gene binds with specific operators, thereby blocking the initiation of mRNA synthesis on the structural gene. A repressor is held to have the property of binding also with certain smaller molecules (metabolites) called the *effectors*. Regulation of mRNA synthesis may be effected by induction or by repression. In induction, the inducing metabolite combines with the repressor to block its interaction with the operator, so that mRNA synthesis on the structural genes can be initiated. In enzyme repression, combination of the repressing metabolite with the repressor *enhances* interaction with the operator (Fig. 1.2.1).

It is not clear how far these concepts derived from studies on bacteria can apply to the control of gene activity in eukaryotic organisms, about which little firm information is available (Part 6). However, the idea that development involves programmed, selective gene activation and repression is an attractive one and provides a useful framework for thinking about selective gene expression. Thus, we are led to the idea that differentiation involves the selective transcription of specific genes, with the release of the corresponding mRNAs into the cytoplasm, where the information they contain is translated into protein synthesis. Selective gene expression may therefore be achieved by control of gene activation at the transcriptional level. However, we shall see that there is evidence that in certain instances the mRNAs may not be translated until some considerable time after their release into the cytoplasm. Thus, the *time* of gene expression may be controlled at the translational level.

Although it is clear that the role of the nucleus in differentiation is paramount, in that the genes are located there and that the coded instructions for protein synthesis they contain is released into the cytoplasm in the form of mRNA, nevertheless the cytoplasm also plays a primary role in determining the time and place of expression of specific genes, i.e. it controls the selective gene expression underlying differentiation.

Some of the best evidence that the cytoplasm may regulate gene expression is provided by studies on the localization within the cytoplasm of certain animal eggs of factors which determine the subsequent pattern of

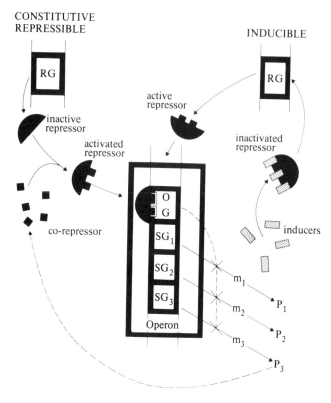

Fig. 1.2.1. A representation of the action of the constitutive repressible and inducible systems of gene regulation. The active and activated repressors produced by the regulator genes (RG) are represented as fitting into the operator gene (OG) of the operon. They then block the transcription of the structural genes (SG) of the operon in producing the mRNAs (m_1, m_2, m_3) which would specify the synthesis of the protein enzymes (P_1, P_2, P_3). One of the enzymes is concerned in activating a repressor in the repressible system. In the inducible system, the inducers are represented as inactivating the repressors by preventing them from fitting the operator genes. From Clowes & Juniper [6].

differentiation of the cells derived from the various regions of the egg during cleavage [57]. These studies are considered in more detail later, in Chapter 2.4. The phenomenon of 'unequal division' in plant cells also shows that the activity of the nucleus is determined by the cytoplasmic environment in which it finds itself (Chapter 2.3).

1.2.2   GENOMIC CHANGES IN DIFFERENTIATION

Advances in molecular biology now make it clear that the cytoplasm could regulate nuclear gene expression by a wide variety of interactions (Chapter 6.4). Alterations in the genome could represent a primary level of control and it is certain that such changes do occur in the development of some organisms.

In development, the nucleus may lose or gain whole chromosomes or parts of chromosomes. For instance, particular chromosomes are eliminated from the somatic cell nuclei of both the gut parasite *Parascaris* and the gall midge *Mayetiola* [2, 17, 32, 51], and DNA sequences are discarded during the differentiation of immunoglobulin-producing cells (Chapter 3.7). Regions of the chromosomes may also be replicated when the rest of the chromosome is not, so that particular genes are disproportionately represented in the cell (Chapter 6.4). These changes are probably irreversible, but there are additional reversible DNA alterations which are now known and these include reorientation of DNA sequences and the movement of sequences to a novel location [1, 34]. Modern DNA-sequencing techniques show that almost any genomic rearrangement is possible, nevertheless there are good biological reasons for believing that irreversible DNA changes do not control the patterns of protein synthesis observed in early developing systems. In general, cell differences do not depend on irreversible genome changes and the differences in protein synthesis between somatic cells result from the regulated transcription and translation of an intact genome.

Nuclear totipotency

Two types of experiment prove that some somatic cells still possess the genes which are necessary to code for the development of a complete, viable individual: these are plant cell culture and nuclear transplant in animals.

There cannot be irreversible changes in the nuclei of plant parenchyma cells, because single parenchyma cells can be manipulated in culture to grow into complete, fertile individuals [53] (Chapter 2.5).

Animal somatic cells cannot so far be manipulated so that they form individuals, and nuclear transplantation has to be employed to demonstrate nuclear totipotency. In this technique, the nucleus of the egg is replaced by the nucleus of another cell. Following this operation, mature individuals have been obtained by implanting the nuclei from the microscopically unspecialized cells of fruit fly, amphibian, and mouse embryos into enucleate eggs of the same species [19, 26a, 27].

So far, it is only in amphibians that nuclei taken from a range of microscopically specialized somatic cells have been tested for their ability to support development. Nuclei from the following donor tissues are known to code for the development of at least swimming tadpoles: intestine, lens, skin, melanophore, kidney tumour (reviewed [20, 39]). The success rate of these experiments is often low, which leaves room for theories about nuclear specializations which may limit the capacity of nuclei to express their totipotency after the operation. However, the fact that the operation can be successful is decisive evidence that irreversible gene loss or re-arrangement is not required for the differentiation of several very distinct cell types. The current view is that a large number of changes in gene expression early in development depend on the interplay between a cytoplasm and a nucleus containing a fixed set of genes each with an unchanging base sequence.

1.2.3 NUCLEAR–CYTOPLASMIC INTERACTIONS

The characters of the cytoplasm are partly determined by previous gene activity and these characters can dominate the activity of nuclei. The general metabolism of nuclei is under cytoplasmic control so that, with nuclear transplantation in Amphibia, it can be shown that somatic cell nuclei are rapidly induced into DNA synthesis and alter their pattern of stable RNA production in response to egg cytoplasm [19]. The cytoplasm of much smaller somatic cells in culture also has this ability to alter DNA and RNA synthesis in introduced nuclei [24]. However, it is cells from early developing systems which most clearly show this persistence of cytoplasmic characters and their domination of nuclear behaviour.

Acetabularia and *Blastocladiella*

Acetabularia has been extensively used for experimental studies on nuclear–cytoplasmic interaction [4, 6, 22, 30, 43, 48]. A plant of *Acetabularia* consists of a single cell of relatively enormous size, 3–5 cm in height, that has a stalk with basal rhizoids by which it is attached to the substratum, while at the apical end there is a hat-shaped 'cap', in which large numbers of gametes are ultimately formed (Fig. 1.2.2). The various species differ in the morphology of the cap, the details of which need not concern us here.

Fig. 1.2.2. Plants of *Acetabularia mediterranea.*

The large size of the cell makes it possible to remove the nucleus and transfer it to another individual of the same or a different species. When the nucleus of one species is transferred into an enucleate cell of another species, the cap that is formed later is characteristic of the species which supplied the nucleus. Grafts can also be carried out between cells of different species, and if the part from one species is nucleate and from the other enucleate, the cap formed resembles more closely the species which supplied the nucleus.

While it is clear that the nucleus ultimately determines the characteristics of the cap and must therefore influence processes occurring in the cytoplasm, the reverse is also true. Thus, division of the nucleus to give large numbers of daughter nuclei normally occurs just before gamete formation, but if the cap is cut off, division of the nucleus does not occur until a new cap is formed.

Although cap formation is ultimately dependent upon influences from the nucleus, the effect of the latter is not immediate and enucleated fragments can continue to function normally for several weeks. Moreover, if the nucleus is removed at a relatively early stage in development, a normal cap can be formed many weeks after removal of the nucleus. Again, if the cell is cut into two to give one part with a nucleus and one without, both parts are capable of regenerating a complete cap. These observations indicate that: (1) all the information necessary for the production of the cap passes from nucleus to cytoplasm long before the cap is normally formed; (2) information for the production of the cap may be present in the cytoplasm without being expressed; (3) the information for the production of the cap is very stable. These conclusions strongly suggest that the nucleus produces stable messenger RNA which is released into the cytoplasm where it can continue to exist for relatively long periods. Several types of evidence support this suggestion.

(1) Cytochemical observations have demonstrated that high-molecular-weight RNA accumulates at the apex of the stalk.

(2) Treatment of the cells with ribonuclease inhibits completely regeneration of both nucleate and enucleate halves so long as it is present in the sea water surrounding the cells, but the inhibition is reversible in the case of nucleate halves and irreversible with enucleate ones.

(3) Treatment with Actinomycin D, which inhibits the transcription of DNA to give mRNA, does not inhibit regeneration in enucleate fragments (which presumably already contain stable RNA), but it does inhibit regeneration of the cap by nucleate fragments, which would presumably be dependent upon the synthesis of new mRNA.

This and other indirect evidence suggest that morphogenesis in *Acetabularia* is dependent on the transcription of nuclear DNA into stable, long-lived mRNA. Moreover, mRNA has, indeed, been isolated from *Acetabularia*, but no one has yet succeeded in isolating and identifying the cap-forming substances and therefore the view that they probably represent mRNAs must be regarded as 'unproven' for the present.

Although cap formation depends upon the presence of stable morphogenetic substances formed in the nucleus, the expression of the genetic information is controlled and effected by regulatory mechanisms in the cytoplasm. The information passed from the nucleus to the cytoplasm can evidently remain unexpressed for several weeks, and the time of cap formation appears to be determined by events that take place in the cytoplasm rather than in the nucleus. Control of morphogenesis therefore appears to be at the translational level.

The formation of the cap involves the net synthesis of protein, the synthesis of specific enzymes and the synthesis of specific polysaccharides. The polysaccharides present in the cell wall of the cap are different from those found in other parts of the cell and cap formation therefore requires the synthesis of specific enzymes required for polysaccharide synthesis. Studies on enzyme synthesis indicate that a high proportion of the proteins of the cell can be found in enucleate cytoplasm, even though their synthesis is under ultimate nuclear control, as has been shown for lactic-acid dehydrogenase. Moreover, not only does the general control of the translation stage in cap formation appear to reside in the cytoplasm, but fine control of the correct sequence of enzyme synthesis appears also to occur at this level. For example, *A. crenulata* contains at least three different phosphatases, having different pH optima (5, 8.5 and 12), all of which are synthesized even in the absence of the nucleus, so that the respective mRNAs coding for their proteins have all been released before removal of the nucleus. Nevertheless, the enzymes active at pH 5 and 8.5 are formed before the one active at pH 12, which only appears a very short time before cap initiation, not only in the whole alga but also in enucleate fragments. The implication is that enzyme synthesis does not occur simultaneously, even if the coordinating messages are released from the nucleus at the same time; the regulation of the sequence of translation, therefore, probably occurs in the cytoplasm.

The conclusion that morphogenesis in *Acetabularia* is directly regulated at the translation stage of protein synthesis, using preformed, long-lived mRNAs, is strongly supported by the results of studies on zoospores of the aquatic fungus *Blastocladiella emersonii* [33, 52]. These zoospores have a single posterior flagellum and the cell is bounded, not by a wall, but by a single continuous membrane. In addition to the usual organelles, these zoospores contain several structures, of which the most conspicuous is the *nuclear cap*, which surrounds the anterior two-thirds of the nucleus, and which contains large numbers of preformed ribosomes.

The zoospores are released into the water from the

parent plant and after a period of free swimming they settle onto a solid substratum and enter a short period of encystment. During encystment the zoospore undergoes a series of rapid and radical changes in structure (Fig. 1.2.3). About 10 min later a small germ tube appears, marking the commencement of germination. Thus, the period of encystment is very short. One of the most striking and important changes during germination is the rapid disorganization of the nuclear cap membrane and the associated release of the enclosed ribosomes, which become dispersed in the cell.

Apart from the morphological changes occurring during encystment and germination, the associated changes in nucleic acid and protein synthesis have been studied using various approaches, including the use of inhibitors of nucleic acid and protein synthesis [31]. Neither inhibition of RNA synthesis with Actinomycin D nor blocking of protein synthesis with cycloheximide

prevents encystment of zoospores, showing that neither of these processes is required for encystment. For further development protein synthesis was necessary, but the cells could develop for 45 minutes after encystment when treated with Actinomycin D, indicating that synthesis of new RNA is not essential up to this stage, even though some mRNA synthesis does occur during these early stages. Since early protein synthesis is not affected significantly by the inhibition of RNA synthesis, it would appear that the ribosomal, transfer and messenger RNAs necessary for it are all present in ungerminated spores.

Polysomes are assembled during the encystment stage. Actinomycin D fails to reduce significantly the early rise in polysome content, and only a trace of new RNA synthesis can be detected during the period of maximum polysome formation. Protein synthesis can be demonstrated by the incorporation of ^{14}C-labelled

ZOOSPORE ENCYSTMENT

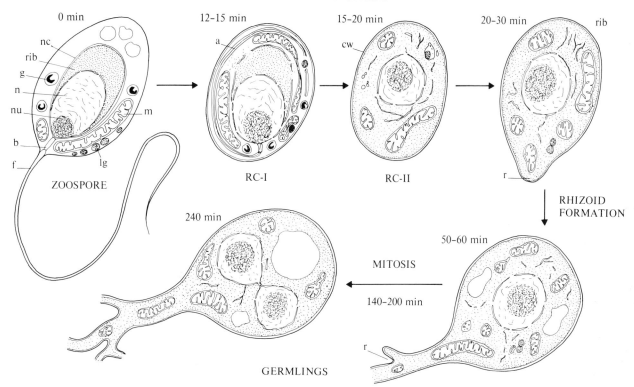

Fig. 1.2.3. Diagrammatic representation of zoospore germination and early development in *Blastocladiella emersonii*. Symbols: b, basal body; g, gamma particle; m, mitochondrion; rib, ribosomes; nc, nuclear cap; nu, nucleolus; n, nucleus; lg, lipid granules; a, flagellar axoneme; cw, cell wall; r, rhizoid; f, flagellum; v, vacuole; RC-I, round cell I; RC-II, round cell II. Kindly supplied by Dr C.L. Leaver.

amino acids at this stage. These results, illustrated in Fig. 1.2.4, show that the rapid formation of polysomes occurs by the attachment of 80S ribosomes released from the nuclear cap to the preformed mRNA molecules, and requires no new RNA synthesis.

Spores treated with Actinomycin D encyst, germinate and continue to develop up to the time when the measurable increase in RNA normally begins, when

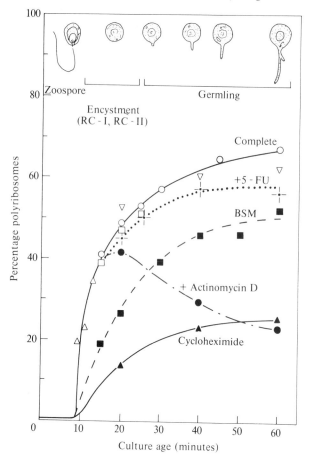

Fig. 1.2.4. The appearance of polysomes during germination and the effects of medium composition and inhibitors. The polysome percentages were determined for cultures germinated under the following conditions: △——△, △——△, ○—○, □——□, complete medium; ■----■, basal salts medium (BSM); +···········+, complete medium with 325 μg ml^{-1} 5-fluorouracil; ●—·—·—●, complete medium with 20 μg ml^{-1} Actinomycin D; ▲——▲, complete medium with 5 μg ml^{-1} cycloheximide. The control cultures in complete medium were grown at cell densities from $1\cdot69\times10^9$ l^{-1} to 3×10^9 l^{-1}; the BSM and inhibitor treated cultures were grown at $2\cdot61\times10^9$–$2\cdot68\times10^9$ cells l^{-1}. From Leaver & Lovett [31].

they stop growing. Cycloheximide inhibits protein synthesis in germinating zoospores. Spores encyst normally, nuclear cap membranes fragment and ribosomes are dispersed normally, but the germ tube does not form. Although germination does not proceed as far as it does in the presence of Actinomycin D, the structural changes associated with encystment apparently require only the protein and RNA formed in the zoospore, which has all the necessary materials for encystment and early germination. However, the later stages of germination and germ tube emergence do appear to require new protein synthesis.

The activation of protein synthesis using pre-existing ribosomes and stored mRNA observed in the germination of zoospores of *Blastocladiella* presents an interesting parallel with animal embryonic systems in which, as we shall see, the utilization of maternal mRNA in early embryonic development seems well established.

Embryonic development and germination

In the previous section we have discussed cases in which a single genome is responsible for the characters of the developing system. The situation is different for plant and animal embryos which are produced from proteins coded by three genomes: those of the mother, the father, and the zygote. The diploid maternal genome is active during oogenesis and forms substances which persist into early development. Its products provide nutrition for the embryo, either by depositing substances directly into the cytoplasm (e.g. yolk [54]; see Chapters 2.2 and 5.5) or by surrounding the embryo with a feeder layer which supplies substances to the developing embryo (e.g. the placenta of mammals).

This genome also controls egg organization and may form substances in the egg which subsequently determine the range of cell types which the embryo can form (e.g. germ plasm of insects; see Part 2). In contrast, substances produced by the diploid paternal genome do not persist far into development. This genome codes for the exine layer of pollen, but the material in this layer remains on the stigma after pollination and makes no further contribution to the young plant (Chapter 3.6); similarly this genome determines sperm structure but most of the extra-nuclear components of sperm dissipate or degenerate soon after fertilization (e.g. mitochondria; see Chapter 6.3). In practice, we can ignore the effects of the diploid paternal genome once syngamy has occurred. The zygote nucleus therefore lies in a cytoplasm whose character was determined by the previous activity of the maternal diploid genome; one of the first problems is to discover the extent to which this cytoplasm controls the functions of the zygote nucleus.

There is good evidence that the early development of amphibians and sea urchins depends on proteins synthesized on mRNA templates provided by the diploid maternal genome. Certainly, early development depends on protein synthesis, since puromycin (a protein-synthesis inhibitor) blocks cleavage. However, if the egg is enucleated or if the nuclear RNA synthesis is inhibited with Actinomycin D, then the egg can still develop up to the early blastula stage. The supply of the mRNA molecules is such that Actinomycin D has no effect on the amount of protein synthesized in early sea urchin embryos. It has been possible to identify the mRNA for microtubular protein (a major component of mitotic spindles) and for histones in the sea urchin egg (see Chapter 6.4). Since these proteins are coded by nuclear genes, these studies prove that mRNA of maternal origin is available for use during early development.

The eggs of Amphibia and sea urchins are similar to the spores of *Blastocladiella* in possessing long-lived mRNA molecules which can be rapidly activated for protein translation when there is an environmental signal, such as fertilization or good germinating conditions, which requires a rapid response from the organism. However, in situations in which the environment is less demanding, eggs may not possess many maternal mRNA molecules. The mammalian egg develops slowly while bathed in the nutrients provided by the mother and it does not appear to possess many maternal mRNA molecules; development can be quickly blocked by RNA-synthesis inhibitors and each cleavage division probably depends on the activity of the zygote genome.

The patterns of RNA and protein synthesis found in sea urchin and amphibian eggs and embryos seem to be paralleled quite closely by the corresponding processes in dormant and germinating seeds. However, whereas in the animal egg we have been considering the changes occurring before and immediately following fertilization, in the case of seeds we are dealing with the changes associated with cessation and renewal of growth of an embryo which, in most cases, has reached a relatively advanced stage of development. Another major area of

differences between the plant and animal systems lies, of course, in the fact that the plant embryo normally undergoes considerable dehydration during ripening of the seed, and frequently it is the imbibition of water by the tissues when the seed is re-wetted which triggers the process of germination, whereas in the majority of animal eggs further development is triggered by fertilization. In both cases, however, we are dealing with the renewal of activity following a period of quiescence.

Metabolism is effectively absent from dry seeds, but when they are placed under favourable conditions of moisture, temperature and aeration there is a rapid increase in metabolic activity, as shown by the re-activation of respiratory pathways and increasing respiration rate. There is no doubt that the early stages of renewal of metabolism involve enzymes already present in the dry seed which become activated by the rehydration of the tissue. On the other hand, amino acid and protein synthesis can be demonstrated soon after the imbibition of the seeds [36, 56], and it has been demonstrated unequivocally that the synthesis of new enzymes occurs [15]. This has been shown for the enzymes isocitratase, α-amylase, protease and peroxidase by demonstrating the incorporation of ^{14}C- or ^{18}O-labelled amino acids into the enzyme protein. A parallel increase in polysomes during germination has been reported for the seeds of a number of species [3, 28, 36]. At the same time an increasing ability of ribosome preparations from germinating seeds to incorporate amino acids into protein in cell-free systems has been reported for the early stages of germination [28].

There is considerable evidence indicating that protein synthesis during early germination is dependent upon mRNA already present in the resting seed [37]. Thus, it has been shown for several species of seed that Actinomycin D does not inhibit protein synthesis and polysome formation during early germination [11, 50]. It was shown for cotton seed that Actinomycin D inhibits incorporation of ^{32}P into polysomes, but has no effect on the incorporation of ^{14}C-labelled amino acids into protein [56]. On the other hand, cycloheximide and puromycin inhibit protein synthesis by germinating seeds [25, 26]. These results suggest that protein synthesis during the early stages of germination does not depend upon parallel RNA synthesis, but is directed by long-lived mRNA present in resting seeds.

If this conclusion is correct, then the question arises as to when this long-lived mRNA is formed. Some evidence on this problem has been obtained from studies on protease in cotton seeds [25, 26]. This enzyme is absent from the resting seed but its activity increases during germination and reaches a maximum after three days. The appearance of the enzyme is completely inhibited by cycloheximide, but is not affected by Actinomycin D. It was shown that ^{14}C-labelled amino acids are incorporated into protease, suggesting synthesis *de novo* of the enzyme.

Developing cotton embryos can be germinated precociously by dissecting them out of the ovules and placing them on a moist substrate, and hence it is possible to determine the time at which transcription of the protease mRNA occurs by precociously germinating embryos at successively younger ages and determining their protease activity. It was found that embryos larger than 85 mg in weight will develop protease in the presence of Actinomycin D, whereas smaller embryos will not do so. The results indicate that when embryos

reach approximately 60 per cent of their final weight, at about 20 days before embryogenesis is complete, mRNA for protease, and presumably for other enzymes necessary for germination, is transcribed in the cotyledons. Since these mRNAs are apparently present in the cotyledons during the last 20 days of embryogenesis, their translation during this time must be inhibited in some manner. Evidence has been obtained that this inhibitor may be abscisic acid, diffusing into the embryo from the ovule wall.

The presence of preformed mRNA, which can be translated *in vitro*, has been demonstrated for wheat embryos [49], radish [13], cotton [23] and rye [42].

1.2.4 GENETICS OF EARLY DEVELOPMENT

The maternal genome codes for the somatic synthesis of products which are deposited in eggs, for the internal

Table 1.2.1. Examples of maternal-effect mutants

Genus	Mutant	Effect	Rescue by	Ref.
Lymnaea pond snail (snails, review [41])	*sinistral*	Altered twist on third cleavage, sinistral shell-coiling in adult	Egg cytoplasm injection	5, 15b
Drosophila fruit fly	*dor**	Death at gastrulation	Egg cytoplasm injection	16, 38
	gs	Absence of primodial germ cells and adults sterile	—	14
	bicaudal	Absence of head region and mirror image duplication of tail	—	10
	mat(3)^{l}*	Arrest at primordial germ cell stage	—	45, 46
Ambystoma Mexican axolotl (review [35])	*nc**	No cleavage	Tubulin injection	44
	o*	Arrest at gastrula stage	Egg cytoplasm injection	7, 8, 9
Mus (review [40])	*T^{hp}*	Death in late development	—	29
	om	Death at implantation	—	55

These examples have in some cases only been analysed from breeding data. Only those marked with an asterisk are known to be germ-line autonomous (see text). The *om* mutant in the mouse exerts its effect even when the embryos are transferred to a wild-type uterus, which shows that it is some feature of egg character which is defective. Those maternal-effect mutants, such as *dor*, *nc*, and *o*, which can be rescued or partially rescued by cytoplasmic injections at the 1-cell stage must have defective egg cytoplasms.

synthesis of substances in the oocyte and megasporocyte of plants prior to meiosis, and for the characters of those somatic tissues which surround and protect the developing embryo. It follows that mutant genes could cause developmental abnormalities by disturbing gene expression in either the maternal somatic tissues or the germ cells.

Maternal-effect mutants

Mutant genes which effect development by any of these three possible routes are loosely called 'maternal-effect mutants' and such mutants have their most obvious effects on development when they are present in the diploid maternal genome and usually have little effect on development when they are present in the paternal diploid genome. Maternal-effect mutants are usually recessive (Table 1.2.1).

The developmental defect may be due either to faulty synthesis in the somatic cells or to faulty internal synthesis in the germ cells, or to both. These possibilities can be distinguished by the following test: primordial germ cells are transplanted from mutant to wild-type mothers. Frequently, these germ cells will develop into eggs, and when they are fertilized they may either develop abnormally, showing that the mutant defect is expressed in the synthetic capacity of the oocyte genome (e.g. *mat(3)* of *Drosophila*), or they may develop normally, which shows that it was the synthetic capacity of the somatic cells which was defective in the mother.

The nature of the defect in the mature mutant egg can also be investigated by attempting to restore normal development by injecting substances from wild-type eggs. Several mutant embryos can be cured of the defect by this procedure, and such rescue experiments again demonstrate that substances found in eggs during oogenesis may have a critical effect only on much later stages of embryogenesis (see section 1.2.3).

There are no known maternal-effect mutants in higher plants. This is probably because the meiotic reduction divisions of the megasporocyte occur before the germ cells grow into the large cell (the megaspore) whose cytoplasmic characters and stores of messenger RNA will contribute to the early embryo's phenotype. The maternal diploid genome is unlikely to have a profound effect on this phenotype since its products will be swamped by substances coded by the haploid nuclei of the megaspore. In contrast, animal germ cell growth occurs before the meiotic reduction divisions and the animal embryo's phenotype is a compound of the activity of the maternal diploid genome and the zygote genome: the maternal diploid genome codes for the characters of early development until the rapidly multiplying embryonic nuclei start to code for proteins which first dilute and then replace the products of the maternal genome.

Most maternal-effect mutants alter early development, presumably because it is only in this early period that maternal gene products cannot be replaced by zygote gene products. However, their influences can persist through development to the adult so that a mutant (*sinistral*) which alters the direction of twist of the third cleavage division of the pond snail also determines the direction of shell coiling of the adult snail and a mutant which alters embryogenesis at the posterior pole of the 500-nuclear-stage fruit fly embryo leads to the development of permanently sterile adults (*gs, grandchildless*).

Extra-embryonic tissues

The fertilized zygote may be surrounded by tissues which are genetically distinct from both the maternal diploid genome and the zygote genome. In higher plants, the nuclei of the nutritive endosperm layer are formed by the fusion of two identical haploid megaspore nuclei and one haploid microspore nucleus and the whole tissue is triploid. In maize, non-disjunction may occur during the divisions of the haploid megaspore nucleus so that the endosperm contains different genes from those of the zygote. Such mosaics can be used to assess the contribution of the endosperm to embryonic development. In the one case in which it has been tested, the endosperm characters had no effect [47], and it is clear that more work is needed to assess the contribution of the different genotypes to the phenotype of the developing plant embryo.

1.2.5 CONCLUSIONS

(1) Early development depends on protein synthesis which occurs on mRNA molecules that were previously coded by the maternal genome.

(2) These mRNA molecules may be long lived and in general such long-lived messages are characteristic of

eggs and seeds which are adapted to rapid growth following an environmental stimulus.

(3) Cytoplasm containing such messages can, without a nucleus, undergo complex sequences of protein synthesis and morphogenesis. These include cap regeneration in the alga *Acetabularia*, and the early cleavages of sea urchin development.

(4) The zygote nucleus interacts with the cytoplasmic characters synthesized under the influence of the maternal genome. A quiescent adult nucleus can be induced into DNA synthesis by egg cytoplasm and its RNA synthesis may also be altered by the interaction. It is also known that regions of egg cytoplasm can elicit the synthesis of histiotypic proteins from the early embryonic nucleus (see Chapter 2.4).

(5) Numerous maternal-effect mutants illustrate the persistence into early development of characters coded by the maternal genome.

(6) The cell-type specific patterns of protein synthesis observed between different cell types of adult plants and animals must, in general, depend on the nucleus reacting to its cytoplasmic environment. The evidence is that many of these pattern differences arise in the absence of irreversible nuclear change (plant culture experiments and nuclear transplants).

1.2.6 REFERENCES

1 Astell C.R., Ahlstrom-Jonasson L., Smith M., Tatchell K., Nasmyth K.A. & Hall B.D. (1981) The sequence of the DNA's coding for the mating type loci of *Saccharomyces cerevisiae*. *Cell*, **27**, 15–23.
2 Bantock C.R. (1970) Experiments on chromosome elimination in the gall midge, *Mayetiola destructor*. *J. Embryol. exp. Morph.*, **24**, 257–286.
3 Barker G.R. & Richer M. (1967) Formation of polysomes in the seed of *Pisum arvense*. *Biochem. J.*, **105**, 1195–201.
4 Bonotto S., Lurquin P. & Mazza A. (1976) Recent advances in the research on the marine alga *Acetabularia*. *Adv. Mar. Biol.*, **14**, 123–150
5 Boycott A.E., Diver C., Garstang S.L. & Turner F.M. (1931) On the inheritance of sinistrality in *Limnaea peregra* (Mollusca, Pulmonata). *Phil. Trans. R. Soc. B.*, **219**, 51–131.
6 Brachet J. (1968) Synthesis of macromolecules and morphogenesis in *Acetabularia*. *Curr. Tops Devl Biol.*, **3**, 1–36.
7 Briggs R. (1972) Further studies on the maternal effect of the *o* gene in the Mexican axolotl. *J. exp. Zool.*, **181**, 271–280.
8 Briggs R. & Cassens G. (1966) Accumulation in the oocyte nucleus of a gene product essential for embryonic development beyond gastrulation. *Proc. natl Acad. Sci., USA*, **55**, 1103–1109.
9 Brothers A.J. (1976) Stable nuclear activation dependent on protein synthesized during oogenesis. *Nature, Lond.*, **260**, 112–115.
10 Bull A.L. (1966) *Bicaudal*, a genetic factor which affects the polarity of the embryo in *Drosophila melanogaster*. *J. exp. Zool.*, **161**, 221–242.
11 Ching T.H. (1972) Metabolism of germinating seeds. In *Seed Biology 2* (Ed. T.T. Kozlowski), pp. 103–218. Academic Press, New York & London.
12 Clowes F.A.L. & Juniper B.E. (1968) *Plant Cells*. Blackwell Scientific Publications, Oxford.
13 Delseny M., Aspart L. & Guitton Y. (1977) Disappearance of stored polyadenylic acid and mRNA during early germination of radish (*Raphanus sativus* L.) embryo axes. *Planta*, **135**, 125–128.
14 Fielding C.J. (1967) Developmental genetics of the mutant grandchildless *Drosophila subobscura*. *J. Embryol. exp. Morph.*, **17**, 375–384.
15 Filner P., Wray J.C. & Varner J.E. (1969) Enzyme induction in higher plants. *Science, N.Y.*, **165**, 358–67.
15b Freeman G. & Lundelius J.W. (1982) The developmental genetics of dextrality and sinistrality in the gastropod *Lymnea peregra*. *Wilhelm Roux' Archiv.*, **191**, 69–83.
16 Garen A. & Gehring W. (1972) Repair of the lethal developmental effect in *deep orange* embryos of *Drosophila* by injection of normal egg cytoplasm. *Proc. natl Acad. Sci., USA*, **69**, 2982–2985.
17 Geyer-Duszyńska I. (1959) Experimental research on chromosome diminution in Cecidomiidae (Diptera). *J. exp. Zool.*, **141**, 391–448.
18 Graham C.F. (1977) Teratocarcinoma cells and normal mouse embryogenesis. In *Concepts in Mammalian Embryogenesis* (Ed. M.I. Sherman), pp. 315–394. MIT Press, Cambridge, Massachusetts.
19 Gurdon J.B. (1974) *The Control of Gene Expression in Animal Development*. Oxford University Press, Oxford.
20 Gurdon J.B. (1976) The pluripotentiality of cell nuclei. In *The Developmental Biology of Plants and Animals*, 1st edn. (Eds C.F. Graham & P.F. Wareing), pp. 55–63. Blackwell Scientific Publications, Oxford.
21 Haldane J.B.S. (1932) The time of action of genes and its bearing on some evolutionary problems. *Amer. Natur.*, **66**, 5–24.
22 Hämmerling J. (1963) Nucleo-cytoplasmic interactions in *Acetabularia* and other cells. *A. Rev. Pl. Physiol.*, **14**, 65–92.
23 Hammett J.R. & Katterman F.R. (1975) Storage and metabolism of poly(adenylic acid)-mRNA in germinating cotton seeds. *Biochemistry*, **14**, 4375–4379.
24 Harris H. (1970) *Cell Fusion*. Oxford University Press, Oxford.
25 Ihle J.N. & Dure L. (1969) Synthesis of a protease in germinating cotton seeds catalysed by masked mRNA synthesized during embryogenesis. *Biochem. biophys. Res. Commun.*, **36**, 705–10.
26 Ihle J.N. & Dure L. (1970) Hormonal regulation of translation inhibition requiring RNA synthesis. *Biochem. biophys. Res. Commun.*, **38**, 995–1001.
26a Illmensee K. (1972) Developmental potencies of nuclei from cleavage preblastoderm and syncytial blastoderm transplanted into unfertilized eggs of *Drosophila melanogaster*. *Wilhelm Roux'. Archiv.*, **170**, 267–298.
27 Illmensee K. & Hoppe P.C. (1981) Nuclear transplantation in *Mus musculus*: developmental potential of nuclei from preimplantation embryos. *Cell*, **23**, 9–18.
28 Jachymczyk W.K. & Cherry J.H. (1968) Studies on mRNA from peanut plants: *in vitro* polyribosome formation and protein synthesis. *Biochim. biophys. Acta*, **157**, 368–77.

29 Johnson D.R. (1975) Further observations on the hairpin-tail ($T^h P$) mutation in the mouse. *Genet. Res.*, **24**, 207–213.

30 Kloppstech K. (1982) Molecular basis of growth and development in *Acetabularia*: a case study. In *Molecular Biology of Plant Development* (Eds H. Smith & D. Grierson). pp. 136–158 Blackwell Scientific Publications, Oxford.

31 Leaver C.L. & Lovett J.S. (1974) An analysis of protein and RNA synthesis during encystment and outgrowth (germination) of *Blastocladiella* zoospores. *Cell Differ.*, **3**, 165–92.

32 Lin M. (1954) The chromosomal cycle of *Parascaris equorum* (*Ascaris megalocephala*): oogenesis and diminution. *Chromosoma*, **6**, 175–198.

33 Lovett J.S. (1975) Growth and differentiation of the water mould *Blastocladiella emersonii*: cytodifferentiation and the role of ribonucleic acid and protein synthesis. *Bact. Rev.*, **39**, 345–404.

34 Mäkelä P.H. & Stocker B.A.D. (1981) Genetics of the bacterial cell surface. In *Genetics as a Tool in Microbiology* (Eds S.W. Glover & D.A. Hopwood), pp. 219–264. 31st Symp. Soc. Gen. Microbiol. Cambridge University Press, Cambridge.

35 Malacinski G.M. & Speight J. (1979) Maternal effect genes in the Mexican axolotl (*Ambystoma mexicanum*). In *Maternal Effects in Development* (Eds D.R. Newth & M. Balls), pp. 241–267. Cambridge University Press, Cambridge.

36 Marcus A. & Feeley J. (1964) Activation of protein synthesis in the imbibition phase of seed germination. *Proc. natl Acad. Sci., USA*, **51**, 1075–79.

37 Marcus A. & Rodaway S. (1982) Nucleic acid and protein synthesis during germination. In *Molecular Biology of Plant Development* (Eds H. Smith & D. Grierson). pp. 337–361. Blackwell Scientific Publications, Oxford.

38 Marsh J.L., Van Deusen E.B., Weischaus E. & Gehring W.J. (1977) Germ line dependence of *deep orange* maternal effect in *Drosophila*. *Devl. Biol.*, **56**, 195–199.

39 McKinnel R.G. (1978) *Cloning, Nuclear Transplantation in Amphibia*. University of Minnesota Press, Minneapolis.

40 McLaren A. (1978) The impact of pre-fertilization events on post-fertilization development in mammals. In *Maternal Effects in Development* (Eds D.R. Newth & M. Balls), pp. 287–320. Cambridge University Press, Cambridge.

41 Murray J. (1975) The genetics of Mollusca. In *Handbook of Genetics* (Ed. R.C. King), **3**, 3–31. Plenum Press, New York and London.

42 Peumans W.J. & Carlier A.R. (1977) Messenger ribonucleoprotein particles in wheat and rye embryos. *In vitro* translation and size distribution. *Planta*, **136**, 195–201.

43 Puiseux-Dao S. (1970) *Acetabularia and Cell Biology*. Logos Press, London.

44 Raff E.C., Brothers A.J. & Raff R. (1976) Microtubule assembly mutant. *Nature, Lond.*, **260**, 615–617.

45 Regenass U. & Bernhard H.P. (1978) Analysis of *Drosophila* maternal effect mutant MAT(3)1 by pole cell transplantation experiments. *Molec. Gen. Genet.*, **164**, 85–91.

46 Rice T.B. & Garen A. (1975) Localized defects of blastoderm formation in maternal effect mutants of *Drosophila*. *Devl. Biol.*, **43**, 277–286.

47 Robertson D.S. (1952) The genotype of the endosperm and embryo as it influences viviparity in maize. *Proc. natl Acad. Sci., USA*, **38**, 580–583.

48 Schweiger H.G. (1976) Nucleocytoplasmic interactions in *Acetabularia*. In *Handbook of Genetics* (Ed. R.C. King), **5**, 451–475. Plenum Press, New York and London.

49 Spiegel S. & Marcus A. (1975) Polyribosome formation in early wheat embryo germination independent of either transcription or polyadenylation. *Nature, Lond.*, **256**, 228–230.

50 Thomas H. (1972) Control mechanisms in the resting seed. In *Viability of Seeds* (Ed. E.H. Roberts), pp. 360–396. Chapman & Hall, London.

51 Tobler H., Smith K.D. & Urpsprung H. (1972) Molecular aspects of chromatin elimination in *Ascaris lumbricoides*. *Devl. Biol.*, **27**, 190–203.

52 Truesdell L.L. & Cantino E.C. (1971) The induction and early events of germination in the zoospore of *Blastocladiella emersonii*. *Curr. Tops. Devl. Biol.*, **6**, 1–44.

53 Vasil V. & Hilderbrandt A.C. (1965) Differentiation of tobacco plants from single isolated cells in microcultures. *Science, N.Y.*, **150**, 889–892.

54 Wallace R.A. & Bergink E.W. (1974) Amphibian vitellogenin: properties, hormonal regulation of hepatic synthesis and ovarian uptake, and conversion to yolk proteins. *Amer. Zool.*, **14**, 1159–75.

55 Wakasugi N. (1974) A genetically determined incompatibility system between spermatozoa and eggs leading to embryonic death in mice. *J. Reprod. Fert.*, **41**, 85–96.

56 Waters L. & Dure L. (1966) Ribonucleic acid synthesis in germinating cotton seeds. *J. molec. Biol.*, **19**, 1–27.

57 Whittaker J.R. (1973) Segregation during ascidian embryogenesis of egg cytoplasmic information for tissue-specific enzyme development. *Proc. natl Acad. Sci., USA*, **70**, 2096–100.

Conclusions to Part 1

This part of the book is concerned with the formation of characters in early developing systems, and it is shown that these characters depend on interactions between the chromosomal genes in the nucleus and the rest of the cell. A more sophisticated treatment of the control of gene expression in development can be found in Chapter 6.4.

Development involves the orderly expression of genes

In all developing systems, different active proteins appear in a sequence and become localized in special regions of the cell or the embryo. We have given examples of this process during cap regeneration in *Acetabularia* (p. 8) and during germination in *Blastocladiella* and in cotton seeds (pp. 10, 11). Numerous examples of this sequential appearance of gene products in development can be found in other parts of this book (Parts 2, 3, 4, 5 and 6).

Gene expression sequences in early development do not involve gene loss

In certain organisms, whole sets of chromosomes are lost early in development, and it is also known that the arrangement of genes within chromosomes can be both reversibly and irreversibly altered during the life of an organism and that these changes can have dramatic effects on gene expression (p. 6). However, the pattern of protein expression in early developing systems does not depend on irreversible gene loss, because nuclei from cells which exhibit different patterns of protein synthesis can still code for the development of the whole organism (nuclear transplantation), and whole plants can be regenerated from cultures derived from single cells (p. 7).

Gene expression may be controlled at different levels

The sequences of protein formation which are observed in early developing systems must therefore depend on the selection of genes for expression. A gene is expressed by coding for the synthesis of a large RNA transcript which is subsequently processed in the nucleus and transferred into the cytoplasm where it is translated into protein. In developing systems, the production of a protein may be controlled at several levels of this process. Nuclear transplant experiments show that egg cytoplasm can select genes for transcription (p. 7) and it is clear from Actinomycin D inhibition of RNA synthesis that selective gene transcription occurs at particular times during the germination of *Blastocladiella* and of cotton seeds (pp. 10, 11).

On the other hand, messenger RNA molecules may lie dormant in the cytoplasm until their translation is evoked by an environmental stimulus. This translational control of gene expression is particularly obvious in the regulated appearance of active proteins during the development of enucleated *Acetabularia* cells and enucleated embryos (pp. 8 and 11). It appears that the availability of genes for subsequent expression as proteins is controlled at the level of transcription in the nucleus, while the time of appearance of active proteins is principally controlled at the level of translation in the cytoplasm.

Extra-nuclear inheritance of characters

Characteristically, early developing systems have long time intervals between the time of transcription and the time of production of active proteins. This lag is probably an adaptation which allows the system to build up populations of mRNA molecules which are available for rapid protein synthesis in response to environmental stimuli such as fertilization and germination (pp. 11 and 12).

Another consequence of this need to change quickly from a quiescent to an active state is that the quiescent cells inherit characters which were formed many hours before; such quiescent cells do not catabolize or dilute out by synthesis the products of ancestral cells as quickly as rapidly dividing active cells. This phenomenon of the persistence of ancestral cell products has been formally shown for mRNA. The genetic consequences of the persistence of this and other previously formed material is that animal eggs inherit characters from the maternal genome which was active during oogenesis. Since this genome segregates at the reduction divisions of meiosis which occur at the completion of oogenesis, it follows that the developmental characters of early animal embryos may depend on genes which are no longer present in the fertilized egg. The analysis of maternal-effect mutants in animals is a clear demonstration of this phenomenon (p. 12). In contrast, in higher plants the meiotic divisions leading to the formation of the large megaspore are followed by three further mitotic divisions during the development of the embryo-sac (p. 44) making it unlikely that the maternal genome will have a direct effect on early plant embryo characters.

Extra-embryonic inheritance of characters

In single-cell organisms such as *Acetabuliaria* and *Blastocladiella,* the cell contains within itself all the genetic information for reproduction. However, eggs of animals depend also on substances formed as proteins in the somatic tissues of the parent organism which are secreted into the developing germ cell (p. 10). Moreover, the walls of the pollen grains of some plant species contain proteins of maternal origin (p. 10). The somatic tissues of the parent may also provide nutrition for the developing seed and for embryos which develop inside egg cases or inside the reproductive tract. These developing systems therefore depend heavily on genes which are expressed by the parental generation (p. 10).

The features of developing systems are characteristically a compound of the products of immediate gene expression and the gene expression which occurs in ancestral and neighbouring cells.

Part 2
Origin and Maintenance of Cell Heterogeneity

Chapter 2.1
Introduction
C.F. Graham

2.1.1 DEVELOPMENT AND LIFE CYCLES

Eggs usually develop from primordial germ cells which are formed from eggs. There is no moment in the production of zygote organization which does not depend in some way on the previous history of the cells and the organisms which contributed to the egg. In Part 2 of the book we artificially break into this evolutionary progression of life cycles to identify apparently decisive events in the development of multicellular organization in individuals.

We examine the extent to which embryonic organization depends on the build-up of membrane and cytoplasmic heterogeneity in single-cell zygotes (Chapter 2.2). Organization also develops and is expressed during the cell divisions of multicellular embryos and meristems; this process is discussed for plant material in Chapter 2.3 and for animal embryos in Chapter 2.4. The major morphogenetic movements and cell interactions of later development are considered in Parts 3, 4 and 5.

2.1.2 ORGANIZED DEVELOPMENT AND THE ENVIRONMENT

We are mainly concerned with the organized development of two kinds of biological system, the fertilized egg and the apical meristem of plants. They can be very different because fertilized eggs are single cells which may develop in isolation, while meristems are cell populations which usually act in contact with cells of the same organism. Nevertheless both systems pose the same problem. How are heterogeneous cell types formed and maintained in orderly arrays?

The cells of the early embryo are ordered in both time and space, and this organization must be implicit in the fertilized egg and its surroundings. Although the organization of the embryo flows from the structure of this single cell, it need not be perfectly described by this structure; the egg divides in an environment of directional influences which may elicit or emphasize its developing asymmetries. Thus the egg of the seaweed *Fucus* is released in the swirling intertidal zone of the marine environment and it tumbles to the bottom, where it sticks; here gravity, light, and neighbouring cells influence its unequal first division which sets the thallus–rhizoid axis of the mature alga (Chapter 2.2). Similarly, the eggs of frogs are shed in haphazard orientations and if these persisted then development would be disturbed, for upended eggs develop confusedly; to avoid this disturbance the fertilized egg rotates so that embryogenesis occurs in a particular orientation to gravity (Chapter 2.2). Thus the structure of the egg expresses organization as it develops surrounded by directional forces and it is only known to be competent to form a normal embryo in the context of such a biased world.

In contrast to the *Fucus* egg and frog egg, which are released into water, many other developing systems are surrounded by egg cases of various shapes or by other living cells. Living cells dominate the environment of many eggs: the early angiosperm embryo divides inside the ovule and numerous animal eggs develop in the female reproductive tract. The organization of embryogenesis is related to the pattern of these surrounding cells. Thus, the part of the plant embryo which will form the shoot is oriented with respect to the structure of the ovule and not to light or gravity, and development is not disturbed when the wind shakes the plant (Chapter 2.3). Similarly, when the uterus of a rat is held upside down, the embryo continues to develop in its normal orientation with respect to the main blood supply of the uterus [1]. In these cases, a zygote or a meristem can receive directional cues from the living environment, and the realization of their structure in organized development might in part depend on these cues.

2.1.3 DEVELOPMENTAL ORGANIZATION IS DIFFERENT FROM GENETIC ORGANIZATION

The structure of the zygote and the meristem therefore impinge on early development in a manner which is different from the way that the structure of messenger ribonucleic acid (mRNA) specifies the primary sequence of amino acids in a protein. The genetic code in mRNA will always operate uniformly in any orientation with respect to light, gravity, the wall of an ovule or the blood vessels of the reproductive tract; it is expressed in disordered solutions of cell sap in a test tube and its message is a line of nucleotides. But cells are designed to develop in response to external signals and to produce a three-dimensional organism which is appropriate to its environment; a plant develops with roots in the soil and shoots in the air and it would not work the other way round. A measure of the difference between developmental and genetic organization is that we are no longer surprised that mRNA molecules from animals are efficiently translated into protein by the cell sap of homogenized wheat seeds but we would be astonished if the frog's egg responded to light in the same way as the *Fucus* egg. Zygotes and meristems are adapted to their respective environments.

The two types of organization also differ in their response to subdivision. Large parts of many early developing systems can be removed and the remnant will form the whole (Chapters 2.3 and 2.4). The organization of genetic information cannot be replaced when parts are removed. Genetic organization describes the primary structure of proteins while developmental organization of zygotes prescribes subsequent embryogenesis. For this reason, developmental organization is less tangible and its nature is the subject of this part of the book.

2.1.4 REFERENCE

1 Alden R.H. (1945) Implantation of the rat egg. 1. Experimental studies of uterine polarity. *J.exp.Zool.*, **100**, 229–235.

Chapter 2.2
Formation of Heterogeneity in Zygotes
C.F. Graham and P.F. Wareing

2.2.1   DEVELOPMENTAL ORGANIZATION

Zygotes usually have distinct ends with components of the cell membrane and internal contents unevenly distributed between these ends. In most species, particular regions of the zygote contribute to different and regular parts of the developing embryo; the zygotes of these species must therefore have sufficient organization to ensure this developmental routine.

The asymmetric arrangement of substances between the ends of zygotes is an aspect of polarity, and zygote structure is frequently described as if it were constructed around vectorial axes and coordinates. Such axes and coordinates have never been observed and so we avoid these terms. Instead we concentrate in this chapter on the nature of developmentally important organization in zygotes and we examine the mechanisms by which it might originate and become located at various sites.

The developmental characters of the zygote in part depend on gene activity during oogenesis, because there are several maternal-effect mutations which act only during oogenesis and which lead to altered or arrested development (see Chapter 1.2). These mutations could either alter a gene product which was necessary for normal development or they could indirectly change the distribution of gene products within the egg. The interpretation is usually not clear and so such mutations have rarely been informative about the mechanisms by which substances become located in various regions of the zygote. Most of the experiments in this chapter are concerned with the cell physiology of zygote organization for development.

Developmental organization builds up in female germ cells at various times in different species. In some species it develops during oogenesis and female meiosis (sections 2.2.2 and 2.2.3). In other species it forms later, during and after fertilization (sections 2.2.4 and 2.2.5). Timing may vary, but there are probably only a small range of mechanisms by which cells can routinely and reliably locate molecules at various sites. In the case of female germ cells, there is evidence that cytoskeletal elements and electric currents are involved in the location of important developmental capacities. However, the analysis of these events is still at a primitive stage when compared to our knowledge of cytoplasmic movements in axons [10, 13] and the membrane movements in lymphocytes [4, 53, 54, 56], and yet the molecular basis of even these well-studied phenomena is rather obscure.

2.2.2   OOGENESIS

The organization of zygotes sometimes appears to originate in the three-dimensional structure of the ovary and the ovule. It is only in the insects that there is direct evidence that developmentally important factors become unevenly distributed in the egg while it is in the ovary, but the phenomenon is almost certainly widespread.

Drosophila (fruit fly) oogenesis

The geometrically organized cell divisions of *Drosophila* oogenesis are described in Fig. 2.2.1. At the completion of these divisions, the oocyte is connected to 15 nurse cells by wide cytoplasmic canals. The contents of the nurse cells stream into the growing oocyte until the nurse cells degenerate and are sealed off by the developing egg case [28, 35]. Sequential histology shows that the end of the oocyte which was previously connected to the nurse cells becomes the anterior end of the egg, the larva, and the adult fly. Further details of insect development can be found in Chapters 2.4 and 3.2.

Polar granules and germ-cell formation

The cytoplasmic capacity to form gametes is layed down in a particular region of the growing oocyte and it is related in time and position to the appearance of polar granules (Fig. 2.2.1). These granules are intermittently associated with ribosomes and mitochondria and they contain a basic protein which is only found in particulate form in these granules [58]. The granules remain near the posterior pole throughout oogenesis and they are eventually incorporated into the germ cells (reviewed [33–35, 55]).

The polar granules of both oocytes and zygotes can be transplanted into other eggs, where they induce the formation of germ cells at other sites [20, 21]. These observations prove that the developmental capacity to form germ cells becomes localized dring oogenesis.

Electric currents and localization

The mechanism by which the polar granules become localized at the posterior pole of the *Drosophila* oocyte is unknown. However, in another insect it has been demonstrated that electric currents move cytoplasmic components in the developing egg. The cercropia moth, *Hyalophora cercropia*, has an ovary which is similar to that of *Drosophila*, except that there are only seven nurse cells which have cytoplasmic canals leading into the oocyte. There is a standing potential difference between the cytoplasm of the oocyte and the nurse cells

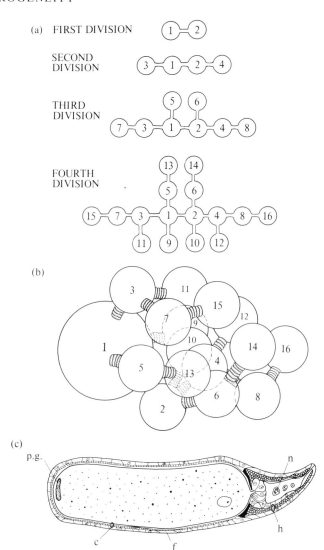

Fig. 2.2.1. Oogenesis in the insect *Drosophila melanogaster*. (a) Cell divisions which form a cluster of 15 nurse cells connected to the oocyte (cell 1) by wide cytoplasmic canals. These are mitotic cell divisions, and the canals are formed by the failure of the cell membranes to separate the daughter cells completely. The meiotic divisions of the oocyte nucleus occur in the mature oocyte and the egg is fertilized during the first meiotic division. (b) Diagram of the three-dimensional arrangement of the 15 nurse cells and growing oocyte (cell 1) at stage 10 of oogenesis. The contents of the nurse cells are flowing into the oocyte through the canals and the oocyte has become the largest cell in the cluster. (c) Drawing of a frontal section of a stage 13 oocyte. The oocyte is now sealed off from the nurse cells by a membrane and the nurse cell nuclei (n) are beginning to degenerate. The somatic follicle cells (f) surround the oocyte and they are synthesizing the chorion (c) and dorsal hairs (h) of the mature egg case. The cloud of polar granules (p.g.) at posterior pole are depicted as a dark band. All figures adapted from King [28], see also [35].

despite a 30 μm wide canal between them. The oocyte is 10 mV positive to the nurse cells, and negatively charged, fluorescein-labelled rabbit serum immuno-globulin injected into the cells will move from nurse cell to oocyte under normal conditions, and in the opposite direction when the current is reversed (reviewed [57]). Further, the direction of migration of injected lysozyme reverses when the charge on the molecule is artificially altered [59]. Thus there is direct evidence that this potential difference can move molecules in and out of the oocyte. What remains unclear is the role of electricity in localizing the polar granules of *Drosophila*; the connection between electric current and developmental capacity in this system is still unknown.

Maternal-effect mutants and localization

There are many known mutations which disrupt the relationship between the oocyte and nurse cells in *Drosophila* [28]; most of these mutations block the formation of viable eggs and it is difficult to know how the defects exert their effects. In contrast, there are many maternal effect mutations which lead to abnormal embryogenesis but which have no known effects on the structure of the ovary. For instance, females homozygous for the mutation *grandchildless* generally produce daughters which are sterile and lack germ cells; nevertheless, the oocytes of these homozygous mothers may contain the normal complement of polar granules in the correct location [5, 34].

The best genetic evidence that the ovary's structure is important in setting up the pattern of subsequent development in *Drosophila* is a maternal-effect mutant called *dicephalic*. Homozygous females tend to produce embryos in which the abdomen is replaced by a mirror image of the head and the thorax; they have two heads, one at each end of the embryo. The oocytes of these homozygous females are like the wild type in that they are connected to 15 nurse cells; however, these nurse cells are separated into two groups at either end of the oocyte. This is the first instance where a specific fault in embryogenesis can be ascribed to a structural rearrangement in the ovary [31, 32, 51]. It remains to be seen what localization is affected by this mutation. The defect may well involve a duplication of material which is usually required for head formation. The presence of such material in the related dipteran *Smittia* has been analysed in considerable detail [27, 50].

2.2.3   MEIOSIS IN THE EGG

The organization of embryos can sometimes be shown to be related to events which occur during the meiotic divisions of the egg nucleus. These meiotic divisions occur after fertilization in a few animals, such as the nemertine *Cerebratulus*; usually animal eggs are fertilized during the first and the second meiotic divisions of the egg nucleus.

The meiotic divisions of the animal egg are frequently unequal and two small polar bodies are formed. These unequal divisions of the egg nucleus often occur in a particular place on the egg surface and this position is presumably related to events which occur during oogenesis; for instance, the polar bodies in Amphibia are produced near the centre of the pigmented animal pole.

The first reason for believing that zygote organization is built up during these meiotic divisions is that visible substances become redistributed in the egg during these divisions. When these redistributions also occur in parthenogenetically activated eggs, without the intervention of the sperm, then we can be certain that they reflect some intrinsic egg organization (e.g in echinoderms [19], and amphibians [1, 3]). The widespread occurrence of such movements suggests that frequently zygote organization develops at this time; however, it is only in a few instances that this has been proved.

Nemertine meiosis

Nemertines are a phylum of bottom-living marine worms. In some, such as *Cerebratulus lacteus*, the embryo first develops into a beautiful ciliated planktonic pilidium larva; the adult is formed from only a few cells in this tiny swimming structure. The value of this species for embryological experiments is that the eggs are shed before the germinal vesicle has broken down in preparation for its meiotic divisions, and it is therefore possible to study the redistribution of developmental capacity within a single cell during meiosis.

The principal features of the pilidium larva are an apical tuft of cilia and a large gut whose lining cells contain high esterase enzyme activity. The capacity to form these two features progressively redistributes to different parts of the egg during meiosis. These redistributions can be demonstrated by cutting eggs across the equator and then allowing the two halves to develop

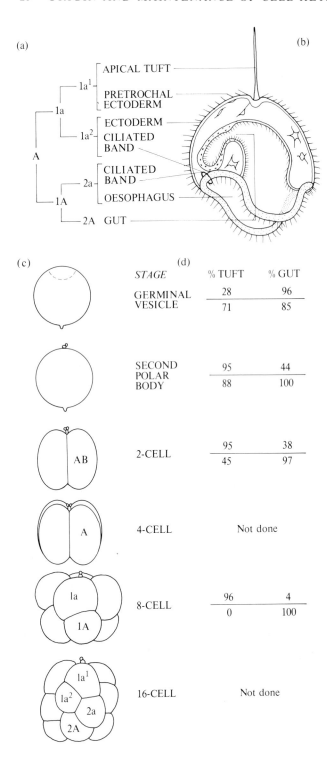

(a)

(b)

APICAL TUFT

1a¹ — PRETROCHAL ECTODERM

1a

ECTODERM

1a² — CILIATED BAND

A

CILIATED BAND

2a — OESOPHAGUS

1A

2A GUT

(c)

(d)

STAGE	% TUFT	% GUT
GERMINAL VESICLE	28	96
	71	85
SECOND POLAR BODY	95	44
	88	100
2-CELL	95	38
	45	97
4-CELL	Not done	
8-CELL	96	4
	0	100
16-CELL	Not done	

AB

A

1a / 1A

1a¹ / 1a² / 2a / 2A

until they display these features (Fig. 2.2.2). Such orientated cuts are possible because the egg nucleus marks the position of the animal pole and there is a small protrusion at the vegetal pole. Initially, almost all the isolated animal halves form gut esterase but they rarely form apical tufts, while by the late 1-cell stage almost all the animal halves form apical tufts and less than half develop gut esterase activity.

There are several reasons for thinking that the female meiotic spindles are involved in the redistribution of these capacities in this single cell. When the spindle of second meiosis is cut out or its structure dissociated with ethyl carbamate, then redistribution is delayed; on the other hand, redistribution is promoted by osmotic conditions which permit extensive spindle growth [6]. These experiments prove that zygote organization develops in time with the events of meiosis and they suggest that the microtubules of the meiotic spindle may move substances around the egg. It is, of course, also possible that the meiotic spindles orient or respond to the direction of action of some other motive force.

Mollusc meiosis

The effect of meiosis on zygote organization has also been studied in the marine gastropod *Limax maximus*. The egg first develops into a free-swimming dispersal larva, the trochophore. The eggs are shed and subsequently fertilized at the completion of second meiosis, and the position on the egg surface at which the second polar body is extruded can be manipulated by pressure.

Fig. 2.2.2. Prelocalization in nemertine development. (a) Cell lineage of *Cerebratulus*. The lineage is drawn from the 4-cell stage and shows the descendants of one cell (the A cell of a 4-cell stage containing cells A, B, C, D; the fate of the other three cells is similar). Each of these four cells gives rise at the 16-cell stage to one cell which will contribute to the apical tuft (1a¹, etc.) and one cell which will contribute to gut esterase activity (2A, etc.). (b) The pilidium larva of *Cerebratulus*. The adult worm is formed from an invagination of a small part of the larval ectoderm. (c) Column showing the cleavage pattern of *Cerebratulus*, viewed from the side. The animal pole with germinal vesicle and polar bodies is at the top and the vegetal pole is marked by a membrane protruberance at the 1-cell stage. (d) Column showing the effect of cutting the egg and embryo across the equator at various stages of development. The figures are the percentage of isolated animal halves (above horizontal line) and the percentage of vegetal halves (below horizontal line) which form either an apical tuft or gut esterase. The animal halves acquire the capacity to form apical tuft and lose the capacity to form gut esterase as development proceeds. (From Freeman [6]).

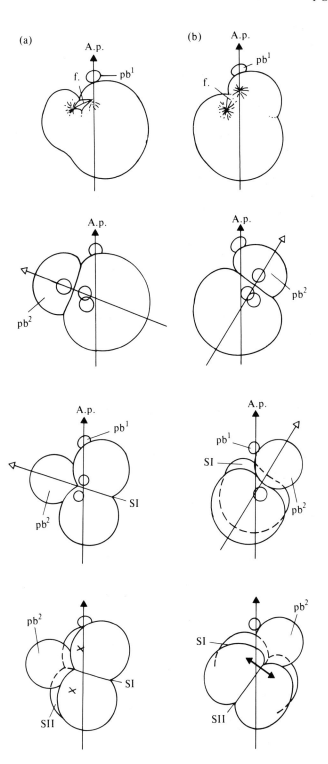

By changing the position of the meiotic spindle, it is possible to show that the cell divisions of subsequent development are arranged around the new position of the meiotic spindle and that they do not follow some earlier organization in the egg (Fig. 2.2.3). In this case there is no evidence that it is the spindle itself, rather than some other local event, which sets up this new pattern of development, but it is certain that the part of the egg which forms the ciliary tuft of the larva is related to the position of the second meiotic spindle.

These two examples show that zygote organization builds up and is in some way dependent on the events of meiosis.

2.2.4 FERTILIZATION

Following fertilization, there are usually major redistributions of material inside the egg. As we have noted, most animal eggs are fertilized during the meiotic divisions of the egg nucleus and it is difficult to decide whether it is sperm entry or the meiotic divisions which are associated with these movements. It is only in the Amphibia, with their very large eggs, that it has so far been possible to prove that substances are organized with respect to the point of sperm entry.

Amphibians

The eggs of amphibians have an obvious dark end (the pigmented animal pole) and a pale end, the yolky vegetal pole, with protein molecules unevenly distributed between the poles [22, 39]. Soon after fertilization, the whole egg rotates so the animal pole is at the top [18].

Fig. 2.2.3. Meiosis in molluscs under compression. The columns illustrate the effect of changing the position of formation of the second polar body by compressing the egg of the marine gastropod *Limax maximus*. The original animal–vegetal axis is indicated by a solid arrow which runs through the animal pole (A.p.), marked by the position of the first polar body (pb^1). (a) Pressure applied only during second polar body formation (pb^2) has moved this polar body to the left of the first polar body; subsequent cleavage planes (SI, SII) are oriented with respect to this position of the second polar body. (b) The second polar body forms beneath, and to the right of, the first polar body under compression and in this case the cleavage planes are orientated to this position of the second polar body. In both cases, a new animal–vegetal axis of development has been created by changing the position of the second polar body (open arrow). In undisturbed development, the second polar body would have formed beside the first polar body and the animal–vegetal organization of development would coincide with that of the egg. (From Guerrier [11, 12].)

Sperm penetration and cytoplasmic distribution

Wherever sperm is locally applied to the animal half of the egg, a sperm penetrates the egg membrane and fertilizes the egg. On the opposite side of the egg, near the equator, a grey crescent forms (Fig. 2.2.4). The point of sperm entry normally controls the position of the grey crescent and the position of the first cleavage plane, which cuts meridionally through the point of sperm entry and the grey crescent. Since this plane roughly divides the egg into a half which will form the left side and a half which will form the right side of the tadpole [17, 40], the point of sperm entry controls the future developmental fate of all parts of the egg.

It is not known how the tiny sperm head directs the development of the large amphibian egg (reviewed [3, 7, 29, 41]). One immediate effect of sperm penetration is the initiation of dark–light waves of reflection at this point [14]; these waves pass across the whole egg and their propagation might be mediated by the local release of calcium, for similar waves of free calcium pass through a fish egg after fertilization [9]. Perhaps the waves elicit the cortical movements which lead to the formation of the grey crescent [14, 45]. The formation of the crescent usually involves the relative movement of egg membrane and attached polar body around the yolk,

but in one species at least it appears that the flow of pigment towards the point of sperm entry may be sufficient to create this paler region in the animal half of the zygote [16].

The sperm head also acts as a nucleating centre for microtubule assembly (microtubules are discussed in Chapters 3.3 and 6.2). Soon after fertilization, the sperm nucleus is at the centre of a radiating array of assembled microtubules (the aster). It is likely that these structures move or guide the movements of cytoplasm inside the zygote, for such movements do not occur in normal activated unfertilized eggs [29], but do occur in activated unfertilized eggs in response to the local injection of microtubule-organizing centres [15, 37, 38], and can be prevented from occurring in fertilized eggs by the application of microtubule-dissociating drugs [38]. It is likely that these cytoplasmic movements are a necessary step in the action of the sperm because when they are re-orientated by gravity then subsequent development follows their new position [7, 29].

Neither the waves of reflectance from the point of sperm entry, nor the microtubule arrays of the aster, nor the displaced cytoplasms, nor the grey crescent itself leaves an indelible imprint on zygote structure [36, 52]. Temperature gradients and the unilateral supply of oxygen will override these events and determine which

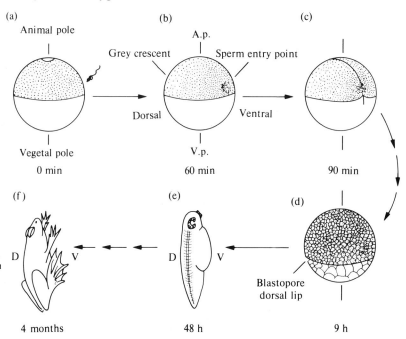

Fig. 2.2.4. Fertilization in Amphibia. This diagram illustrates the normal relationship between the point of sperm entry (a), grey crescent formation (b), the plane of first cleavage (c), the position of the blastopore dorsal lip (d), the tadpole (e) and the adult frog (f). The sperm may enter at any point in the animal half of the egg and future development is orientated with respect to this point, which therefore influences what tissue each part of the egg will form in later development. (After Kirschner *et al.* [29].)

parts of the cleaving embryo will form which parts of the tadpole [8, 30]. The conclusion is that sperm entry sets in train a series of events which mark out the future position of the long axis of the tadpole. None of these asymmetries in zygote structure is itself sufficient to fix this relationship against experimental abuse but in undisturbed development their influence is adequate to prescribe which part of the egg will form which part of the tadpole.

Other phyla

It is generally thought that the point of sperm entry is important in setting up zygote asymmetries in many other phyla (see, for example [19]). Decisive evidence that this is the case is still lacking. It may be of importance that in many animal eggs the point of sperm entry is governed by the sperm canals, which direct the sperm to a particular part of the egg surface and guarantee that sperm influences will be asymmetric in a particular direction with respect to egg structure.

2.2.5   ENVIRONMENTAL CUES

It is useful for research that some zygotes become asymmetric when the microscopic events of meiosis and fertilization are complete. These zygotes may respond to

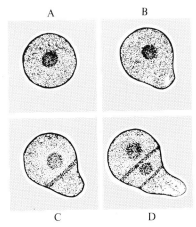

A   B

C   D

Fig. 2.2.5 *Fucus*—polarity and cleavage. Successive stages in the early development of the embryo of the seaweed *Fucus*, at various times after fertilization: A, 4h; B, 16h; C, 18h; D, 26h. In B, a protruberance has formed at the future rhizoid end and fucoidin deposition is localized here. In C, there has been an unequal cleavage (cell wall formation), cutting off the small rhizoid cell from the large thallus cell. In D, further division has occurred. (From Jaffé [23]).

environmental cues which can be imposed on large numbers of eggs simultaneously in a particular direction. It is possible to make a study with these eggs of the biochemical, physiological and cytological changes underlying asymmetry formation.

Algae

The fertilized eggs of certain marine algae, such as the brown seaweed *Fucus*, are initially spherical (review of *Fucus* development in [4b] and [48]. The eggs are released in large numbers and after fertilization they settle onto a solid substratum, where the development of a localized protuberance is the first sign of the formation of a rhizoid by which the young plant becomes attached to a rock or other support. The axis, as indiated by the position of the rhizoid and the orientation of the first mitotic spindle, can be influenced by gradients in various external factors, such as light, heat, pH and osmotic activity [23]. If the fertilized eggs are exposed to unilateral illumination, the shaded side of the cell begins to form a protuberance at about 14h after fertilization. Mitosis takes place so that the axis of the spindle is parallel to the direction of the incident light and a cell wall is formed at right angles to this, cutting off a larger cell which gives rise to the future thallus and a smaller cell which forms the rhizoid (Fig. 2.2.5). External factors such as light can influence this axis up to 8h before the appearance of the rhizoid, and this axis is labile up to 1–3h before the latter event is due, after which the position of emergence of the future rhizoid appears to be irreversibly fixed.

Cell structure

Studies on the ultrastructural changes occurring following the unilateral illumination have shown that 12h after fertilization (before any visible signs of the emergence of the rhizoidal protruberance) the nuclear surface has become asymmetric with finger-like projections radiating towards the site of rhizoid formation [47]. These projections evidently represent membraneous extensions of the nuclear envelope. Mitochondria, ribosomes and fibrillar vesicles are also concentrated in this region of the rhizoidal half of the zygote, which is thus more densely cytoplasmic. These changes can be observed between 11 and 14h after fertilization in zygotes which show no rhizoidal protruberances but yet already have their axes fixed, i.e. at the time when the cell has become determined with respect to the events leading to rhizoid differentiation, but they are not the first signs of axis formation in the developing zygote since it has been shown that, if the cells are plasmolysed, plasmolysis occurs on the shaded side of unilaterally illuminated zygotes within 15 min of exposure to light.

In addition to observable ultrastructural changes described above, there is active conversion of the polysaccharide fucoidan into its sulphated form, fucoidin, as shown by the incorporation of radioactively labelled sulphur (^{35}S) into this fraction. Fucoidan is initially sulphated in all regions of the cell, and it subsequently accumulates and is sulphated near the future rhizoid region of the cell wall 10–14h after fertilization, at which time the axis has become fixed [42]. Germinated embryos show fucoidin localized at the rhizoidal end of the cell. It would appear that fixation of the cell axis is closely associated with the incorporation of fucoidin into the cell wall. The inhibitor cytochalasin B, which may act on the cell surface or plasma membrane, inhibits the determination of axis formation and the localization of fucoidin in the cell wall [48], thus further indicating the close connection between these two processes. However, embryos which are grown in the absence of sulphate can still form a rhizoid even though they are unable to produce sulphated fucoidin [49].

Direction of electric currents

Jaffé [23] has shown that the zygotes of *Fucus* generate electrical currents before and during axis fixation. If about 100 eggs are placed in a capillary tube and illuminated so as to produce rhizoids towards one end of the tube, then this end becomes markedly electronegative. Apparently, each egg drives current through itself and there is evidence that sodium and calcium ions enter at the rhizoidal end and chloride ions at the thallus end. The number of ions so moving is sufficient to account for most of the current measured [26].

Several observations suggest that the current flow is an integral part of the mechanism by which the axis is established. In the related seaweed *Pelvetia*, eggs grown in the dark establish an inward flow of current in a small region of the membrane at 30 min after fertilization. The location of inward flow is initially unstable and moves position, and at this early stage there may be several points of inward current flow. Subsequently, the main region of local current inflow predicts the position of growth of the rhizoid bulge from the cell [43]. Further, the eggs can be first grown with unilateral illumination to establish a point of current entry on the shaded side, and then the illumination shifts to this side. Following the reversal of illumination, two points of current entry can be detected and then current entry is only detected on the new dark side. This rearrangement of the current occurs well before there are any signs of a morphological axis and the observation of two points of current entry before the rearrangement is complete proves that eggs do not simply rotate in response to directional stimuli [43]. Lastly, the axis of the *Fucus* egg can be determined by imposed voltage [2].

Jaffé suggests that the current may help to bring about differentiation as well as axis determination by acting electrophoretically, i.e. by generating a field which may localize negatively charged macromolecules or particles towards the growth point [44]. This idea is supported by the direct observation that receptors for the lectin concanavalin A can be electrophoresed along the membrane of muscle cells in culture [24, 46], and such a mechanism could be responsible for the transport of fucoidin-containing vesicles towards the part of the *Fucus* egg where polysaccharide deposition occurs. This view is supported by the observation that sulphation is required for the polysaccharide to move to one end of the cell and sulphation also increases the net negative charge on the molecule, which might increase its chance of moving by electrophoresis. The presence of electric currents around many eggs and developing systems suggests that mechanisms of this type may be widely used to set up asymmetries along the length of cells in developing systems [25].

Higher plants

The eggs of higher plants usually have their cytoplasmic contents unevenly distributed along the length of the cell (see Fig. 2.3.1). This long axis roughly corresponds to the embryonic axis which runs from the shoot apex to the suspensor. Although it is impossible to prove, it may be that this axis of organization is imposed on the egg during oogenesis, for the relationship between the shoot apex in the embryo and the position of the micropyle in the ovule is invariant.

2.2.6 CONCLUSIONS

(1) The zygotes of animals and plants are usually asymmetric cells.

(2) These asymmetries are related to the organization of the early embryo.

(3) Asymmetries develop in egg cells during oogenesis, female meiosis, fertilization and environmental interactions.

(4) Usually asymmetries are obvious along one length of the cell (e.g. in *Drosophila*, molluscs, nemertines, annelids and algae), while in amphibians, for instance, there is greater detail in the cytoplasmic distributions.

(5) The asymmetries are only known to be decisive in the case of germ-plasm in *Drosophila* oocytes. Usually, they are rough patterns of developmental tendencies which orient subsequent development. Further detailed distributions of developmental capacity build up during cleavage (Chapter 2.4).

(6) The mechanisms of asymmetry formation are not understood in molecular terms. There is persuasive evidence that in some zygotes these asymmetries build up in response to orientated electric currents and microtubular arrays.

2.2.7 REFERENCES

*Useful reviews

1   Benford H.H. & Namenwirth M. (1974) Precocious appearance of gray crescent in heat shocked axolotl eggs. *Devl. Biol.*, **39**, 172–176.

2   Bentrup F.W., Sandon T. & Jaffé L.F. (1967) Induction of polarity in *Fucus* eggs by potassium ion gradients. *Protoplasm*, **64**, 254–266.

*3   Brachet J. (1977) An old enigma: the gray crescent of amphibian eggs. *Curr. Tops. Devl. Biol.*, **11**, 133–186.

4   Bretscher M.S. (1976) Directed lipid flow in cell membranes. *Nature, Lond.*, **206**, 21–23.

4b   Callow M.E., Evans L.V. & Callow J.A. (1982) Molecular basis of growth and development in *Fucus*: a case study. In *Molecular Biology of Plant Development* (Eds H. Smith & D. Grierson). Blackwell Scientific Publications, Oxford.

5   Fielding C.J. (1967) Developmental genetics of the mutant grandchildless of *Drosophila subobscura*. *J. Embryol. exp. Morph.*, **17**, 375–384.

6   Freeman G. (1978) The role of asters in the localization of the factors that specify the apical tuft and the gut of the nemertine *Cerebratulus lacteus*. *J. exp. Zool.*, **206**, 81–107.

7   Gerhart J., Ubbels G., Hara K. & Kirschner M. (1981) A reinvestigation of the role of the grey crescent in axis formation in *Xenopus laevis*. *Nature, Lond.*, **292**, 511–516.

8   Gilchrist F.G. (1928) The effect of a horizontal temperature gradient on the development of the egg of the urodele, *Triturus torosus*. *Physiol. Zoöl.*, **1**, 231–268.

9   Gilkey J.C., Jaffé L.F., Ridgway E.B. & Reynolds G.T. (1978) A free calcium wave traverses the activating egg of the medaka *Oryzias latipes*. *J. Cell Biol.*, **76**, 448–466.

10   Grafstein B. & Forman D.S. (1980) Intracellular transport in neurons. *Physiol. Rev.*, **60**, 1167–1283.

11   Guerrier P. (1970) Les caractères de la segmentation et la détermination de la polarité dorsoventrale dans le développement de quelques Spiralia. I. Les formes a premier clivage égal. *J. Embryol. exp. Morph.*, **23**, 611–637.

12   Guerrier P. (1970) Nouvelles données expérimentales sur la segmentation et l'organogenèse chex *Limax maximus* (Gasteropode pulmone). *Ann. Embryol. & Morphogen.*, **3**, 283–294.

13   Hanson M. & Edstrom, A. (1978) Mitosis inhibitors and axonal transport. *Int. Rev. Cytol.*, Suppl. **7**, 373–402.

14   Hara K. & Tydeman P. (1979) Cinematographic observation of an activation wave (AW) on the locally inseminated egg of *Xenopus laevis*. *Wilhelm Roux' Archiv.*, **186**, 91–94.

15   Heidermann S.R. & Kirschner M.W. (1975) Aster formation in isolated eggs of *Xenopus laevis*: Induction by basal bodies. *J. Cell Biol.*, **67**, 105–117.

16   Herkovits J. & Ubbels G.A. (1979) The ultrastructure of the dorsal yolk-free cytoplasm and immediately surrounding cytoplasm in the symmetrical egg of *Xenopus laevis*. *J. Embryol. exp. Morph.*, **51**, 155–164.

17   Hirose G. & Jacobson M. (1979) Clonal organisation of the central nervous system of the frog. I. Clones stemming from individual blastomeres of the 16-cell and earlier stages. *Devl. Biol.*, **71**, 191–202.

*18   Holtfreter J. & Hamburger V. (1955) Amphibians. In *Analysis of Development* (Eds B.H. Willier P.A. Weiss & V. Hamburger), pp. 230–296. W.B. Saunders, Philadelphia.

19   Hörstadius S. (1973) *Experimental Embryology of Echinoderms*. Oxford University Press, Oxford.

20   Illmensee K. & Mahowald A.P. (1974) Transplantation of posterior pole plasm in *Drosophila*: induction of germ cells in the anterior pole of the egg. *Proc. natl Acad. Sci., USA.*, **71**, 1016–1120.

21   Illmensee K., Mahowald, A.P. & Loomis M.R. (1976) The ontogeny of germ plasm during oogenesis in *Drosophila*. *Devl. Biol.*, **49**, 40–65.

22   Jäckle H. & Eagleson G.W. (1980) Spatial distribution of abundant proteins in oocytes and fertilized eggs of the Mexican axolotl (*Ambystoma mexicanum*). *Devl. Biol.*, **75**, 492–499.

23   Jaffé L.F. (1968) Localization in the developing *Fucus* egg and the general role of localizing currents. *Adv. Morphogen.*, **7**, 295–328.

24   Jaffé L.F. (1977) Electrophoresis along cell membranes. *Nature, Lond.*, **265**, 600–602.

*25   Jaffé L.F. (1979) Control of development by ionic currents. In *Membrane Transduction Mechanisms* (Eds R.A. Cone & J.E. Dowling), pp. 199–231. Raven Press, New York.

26   Jaffé L.F., Robinson K. & Nuccitelli R. (1974) Local cation entry and self electrophoresis as an intracellular localization mechanism. *Ann. N.Y. Acad. Sci.*, **238**, 372–383.

*27   Kalthoff K. (1979) Analysis of a morphogenetic determinant in an insect embryo (*Smittia* Spec. Chironomidae, Diptera). In *Determinants of Spatial Organisation* (Eds S. Subtelny & I.R. Konigsberg), pp. 97–126. Academic Press, New York.

28   King R.C. (1970) *Ovarian Development in Drosophila melanogaster*. Academic Press, New York.

*29   Kirschner M., Gerhart J.C., Hara K. & Ubbels G.A. (1980) Initiation of the cell cycle and establishment of bilateral symmetry in *Xenopus* eggs. In *The Cell Surface: Mediator of Developmental Processes* (Eds S. Subtelny & N.K. Wessels), pp. 187–215. Academic Press, New York.

30   Landström U. & Løvtrup S. (1975) On the determination of the dorsoventral polarity in *Xenopus laevis* embryos. *J. Embryol. exp. Morph.*, 33, 879–895.

31   Lohs-Schardin M. & Sander K. (1976) A dicephalic monster embryo of *Drosophila melanogaster*. *Wilhelm Roux' Archiv.*, 179, 159–162.

32   Lohs-Schardin M. (1982) A *Drosophila* mutant affecting polarity in follicle organization and embryonic patterning. *Wilhelm Roux' Archiv.*, 191, 28–36.

*33   Mahowald A.P. (1977) The germ plasm of *Drosophila*: an experimental system for the analysis of determination. *Amer. Zool.*, 17, 551–563.

34   Mahowald A.P., Caulta J.H. & Gehring W.J. (1979) Ultrastructural studies of oocytes and embryos dervied from female flies carrying the grandchildless mutation in *Drosophila subobscura*. *Devl. Biol.*, 69, 118–132.

*35   Mahowald A.P. & Kambysellis M.P. (1980) Oogenesis. In *The Genetics and Biology of Drosophila, Vol. 2d* (Eds M. Ashburner & T.R.F. Wright), pp. 141–224. Academic Press, New York.

36   Malacinski G.M., Chung H-M. & Asashima M. (1980) The association of primary embryonic organizer activity with the future dorsal side of amphibian eggs and early embryos. *Devl. Biol.*, 77, 449–462.

37   Manes M.E. & Barvieri I. (1977) On the possible role of sperm aster formation in dorsal–ventral polarization and pronuclear migration in the amphibian egg. *J. Embryol. exp. Morph.*, 40, 187–197.

38   Manes M.E. Elinson R.P. & Barvieri F.D. (1978) Formation of amphibian grey crescent: effects of colchicine and cytochalasin B. *Wilhelm Roux' Archiv.*, 185, 99–104.

39   Moen T.L. & Namenwirth M. (1977) The distribution of soluble proteins along the animal–vegetal axis of frogs' eggs. *Devl. Biol.*, 58, 1–10.

40   Nakamura O. & Kishiyama K. (1971) Prospective fates of blastomeres at the 32-cell stage of *Xenopus laevis* embryos. *Proc. Japan. Acad.*, 47, 407–412.

*41   Nieuwkoop P.D. (1977) Origin and establishment of embryonic polar axes in amphibial development. *Curr. Tops. Devl. Biol.*, 11, 133–186.

42   Novotny A.M. & Forman N. (1974) The relationship between changes in cell wall composition and the establishment of polarity in *Fucus* embryos. *Devl. Biol.*, 40, 162–173.

43   Nuccitelli R. (1978) Ooplasmic segregation and secretion in the *Pelvetia* egg is accompanied by a membrane generated electrical current. *Devl. Biol.*, 62, 13–33.

44   Nuccitelli R. & Jaffé L.F. (1974) Spontaneous current pulses through developing fucoid eggs. *Proc. natl Acad. Sci., USA*, 71, 4855–4859.

45   Palecek J., Ubbels G.A. & Rzehak K. (1978) Changes of the external and internal pigment pattern upon fertilization in the egg of *Xenopus laevis*. *J. Embryol. exp. Morph.*, 45, 203–214.

46   Poo M.-M. & Robinson K.R. (1977) Electrophoresis of concanavalin A receptors along the membrane of embryonic muscle cells. *Nature, Lond.*, 265, 602–605.

47   Quatrano R.S. (1972) An ultrastructural study of the determined site of rhizoid formation in *Fucus* zygotes. *Expl Cell Res.*, 70, 1–12.

48   Quatrano R.S. (1973) Separation of processes associated with differentiation of two-celled *Fucus* embryos. *Devl. Biol.*, 30, 209–213.

*49   Quatrano R.S., Brawley S.H. & Hogsett R.E. (1979) The control of the polar deposition of a sulfated polysaccharide in *Fucus* zygotes. In *Determinants of Spatial Organization* (Eds S. Subtelny & I.R. Konigsberg), pp. 77–96. Academic Press, New York.

50   Rau K-G. & Kalthoff K. (1980) Complete reversal of anteroposterior polarity in a centrifuged insect embryo. *Nature, Lond.*, 287, 635–637.

51   Sander K. & Nübler-Jung K. (1981) Polarity and gradients in insect development. In *International Cell Biology, 1980–1981* (Ed. H.G. Schweigen), pp. 497–506. Springer-Verlag, Berlin.

52   Scharf S.R. & Gerhart J.C. (1980) Determination of the dorsal–ventral axis in eggs of *Xenopus laevis*: complete rescue of UV impaired eggs by oblique orientation before cleavage. *Devl. Biol.*, 79, 181–198.

53   Schreiner G.T. & Unanue E.R. (1976) Membrane and cytoplasmic changes in B lymphocytes induced by ligand–surface immunoglobulin interactions. *Adv. Immunol.*, 24, 37–165.

54   Schroit A.J. & Pagano R.E. (1981) Capping of a phospholipid analog in the plasma membrane of lymphocytes. *Cell*, 23, 105–112.

55   Swanson M.M. & Poodry C.A. (1980) Pole cell formation in *Drosophila melanogaster*. *Devl. Biol.*, 75, 419–430.

56   Stern P.L. & Bretscher M.S. (1979) Capping of exogenous Forssman glycolipid on cells. *J. Cell Biol.*, 82, 829–833.

*57   Telfer W.H. (1975) Development and physiology of the oocyte-nurse cell syncytium. *Adv. Insect. Physiol.*, 11, 223–320.

58   Waring G.L., Allis C.D. & Mahowald A.P. (1978) Isolation of polar granules and identification of polar granule specific protein. *Devl. Biol.*, 66, 197–206.

59   Woodruff R.I. & Telfer W.H. (1980) Electrophoresis of proteins in intercellular bridges. *Nature, Lond.*, 286, 84–86.

Chapter 2.3
Patterns of Growth and Differentiation in Plants
P.F. Wareing

2.3.1 UNEQUAL DIVISION AND CELL DIFFERENTIATION

It was seen in Chapter 2.2 that the establishment of the axis of polarity in the *Fucus* egg was associated with an asymmetric distribution within the zygote cell of various cytoplasmic organelles and of certain specific polysaccharide components of the cell wall. The first cell division leads to the formation of a cell wall at right angles to the axis of polarity; this separates a larger cell which becomes the future thallus and a smaller one which gives rise to the rhizoid of the mature seaweed. We must assume that, in addition to the asymmetric distribution of visible constituents of the zygote before division, there is also an asymmetric distribution of certain cytoplasmic 'determinants' which are responsible for the different properties of the two daughter cells.

The nature of these hypothetical determinants is unknown but they could be 'informational' molecules, such as RNA or proteins, which it has been suggested become asymmetrically distributed as a result of electrophoretic movement along the electrical potential gradient within the cell.

Thus, a major aspect of differentiation, the division of the young embryo into future thalloid and rhizoid poles, is established by an unequal division. Unequal or asymmetric divisions play important roles in cell differentiation in all green plants, not only in the first division of the zygote but also in later stages of development. In flowering plants, such as shepherd's purse (*Capsella bursa-pastoris*), the egg is highly polarized, with one-half to one-third of the micropyle end filled with a large vacuole, while the chalazal end contains the nucleus and much of the cytoplasm of this cell (Fig. 2.3.1). Following fertilization the first division is unequal, giving rise to a large vacuolated basal cell and a small terminal cell with densely staining cytoplasm. The future embryo is derived mainly from the terminal cell, while the basal cell forms the suspensor (p. 45).

Unequal divisions appear to play an important role in cell differentiation in later stages of development of higher plants [3]. Some clear examples of unequal division in higher plants are provided by developing stomata in the epidermis of the leaves of grasses and other monocotyledons [15, 17]. The adult stomatal complex of grasses consists of narrow, elongated cells flanked by two subsidiary cells. As a result of more rapid divisions than in the surrounding epidermal cells, rows of small cells are formed. The cytoplasm of a proportion of these cells becomes polarized so that the cytoplasm is denser near the distal ends of the cells. Before the cell divides, the nucleus becomes displaced towards the denser end of the cell and the cytoplasmic vacuoles occupy the other end. The division which follows

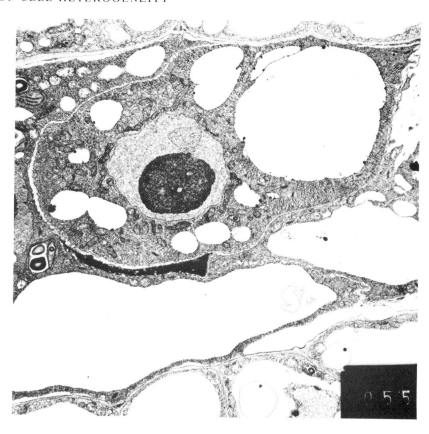

Fig. 2.3.1. Electronmicrograph of the zygote of *Capsella bursa-pastoris* showing marked polarization of the cell, as manifested by the occurrence of the nucleus lying in dense cytoplasm at the micropylar end (left) and a large vacuole at the chalazal end (right). (From Schulz & Jensen [22].)

produces a small distal cell with a smaller, heavily staining nucleus, and a large, more weakly staining proximal cell, the cytoplasm of which rapidly becomes vacuolate (Fig. 2.3.2). The distal cell becomes the guard mother cell and the proximal one becomes a normal epidermal cell. The guard mother cell later divides transversely to form two equal guard cells (Fig. 2.3.3). In this latter division the new cell wall divides the cytoplasm into two similar halves and so no difference between the daughter cells ensues.

A number of analogous examples of unequal division leading to differentiation are found in higher plants. Thus, in the formation of root hairs on the roots of grasses such as *Phleum pratense*, certain elongated cells in the epidermis undergo an unequal division, giving at the distal end a smaller cell with denser protoplasm, and a longer cell at the proximal end [3, 24] (Fig. 2.3.4). The smaller cell forms a protuberance which grows into a root hair, whereas the larger cell remains a normal epidermal cell.

Other examples of unequal division which lead to differentiation are found in the development of the pollen grain, where the pollen mother cell undergoes an unequal division giving rise to the generative nucleus which lies in a region of dense cytoplasm and the vegetative nucleus lying in the remaining volume of the cell (Fig. 2.3.3). The generative nucleus later divides to give the two male gametes, whereas the vegetative nucleus undergoes no further development.

It is clear that unequal division plays an important role in the origin of cell heterogeneity in plants. The essential features of such divisions are that the parent cell first becomes polarized by the establishment of a cytoplasmic gradient in respect of macromolecules or other components, followed by a division in which the mitotic spindle is orientated along the gradient so that the daughter nuclei are located in different cytoplasmic environments.

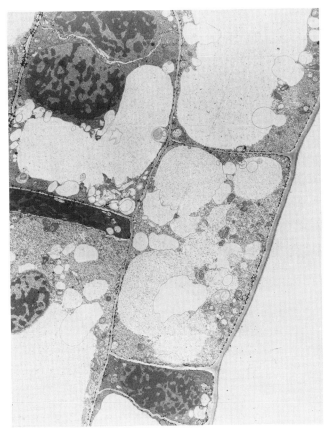

Fig. 2.3.2. Short and long cells in the meristematic region of the internodal epidermis of oat. Note the dense cytoplasm of the short cells, presumptive guard mother cells, and the much greater degree of vacuolation in the long cells. (From Cutter [8]. Photograph by Dr P.B. Kaufman.)

2.3.2 POLARIZED CELL DIVISIONS

The characteristic shape and structure of the various organs of the plant are determined by the planes of cell division and cell enlargement during development. Differences in cell enlargement along various axes will be important in determining the final shape of the organ, especially during the later stages of its development, but the foundations are laid down during the earlier meristematic phase as a result of regulated patterns of cell division. The plane of cell division is determined by the axis of the mitotic spindle and there is evidence that the microtubules may play a vital role in controlling the orientation of the spindle, and hence of the new cell wall, which lies at right angles to this axis [13]. In resting

cells the microtubules lie in the outer cytoplasm, just inside the plasmalemma. In cells which are about to undergo division, a band of microtubules (pre-prophase band) appears in the outer cytoplasm near the longitudinal walls, and at right angles to the axis of the cell, in the mid region (Fig. 2.3.5).

There is strong evidence that the microtubules indirectly determine the orientation of cellulose microfibrils in the cell wall [13]. Thus, if the orientation of the microtubules is disorganized by treatment with colchicine, so is the orientation of the microfibrils. However, the manner in which the orientation of the microfibrils is regulated by that of the microtubules is not understood.

Green and his associates [12] have recently analysed the patterns of reorientation of the planes of cell division which are required when an axial structure, such as a

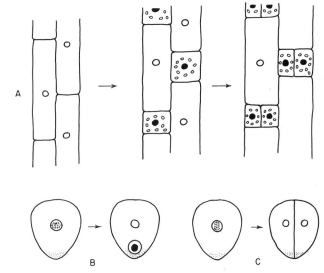

Fig. 2.3.3. A. Unequal division in formation of stomatal guard cells in leaf of a monocotyledonous plant. Epidermal cells undergo unequal division with the formation of a smaller stomatal mother cell (nucleus shaded) and a larger cell (nucleus not shaded). Chloroplasts develop in the stomatal mother cell, which divides again at right angles to the plane of the first division to produce two daughter cells which develop into the guard cells. B, C. Development of pollen grain. B. Normal development. Nucleus divides so that one of the daughter nuclei moves to the region of denser cytoplasm at one end of the cell and becomes one generative nucleus. The other daughter cell nucleus becomes the vegetative nucleus. C. Abnormal development. Nucleus divides at right angles to the normal plane. Daughter nuclei thus remain in the same cytoplasmic environment, and two equal cells are formed, disrupting the further normal development of the pollen grain. (Redrawn from E. Bünning (1958) *Handbuch Protoplasmaforschung*, Vol. VIII, Vienna.)

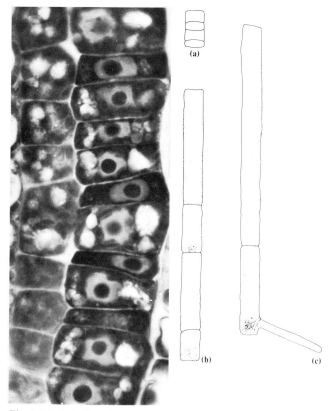

Fig. 2.3.4. Left: Development of root hair initials in root of the grass *Phleum pratense*, at successive stages (a–c). The smaller of the cells formed by unequal division (a) gives rise to the root hair cell. (From Sinnott & Bloch [24]. Right: Formation of trichoblasts (root hair initials) in the root epidermis of *Hydrocharis morsus-ranae*. Unequal division has just given rise in each case to a small cell which is the trichoblast and a larger cell which is the epidermal cell. (From Cutter & Feldman [9].)

stem, forms a lateral organ, such as a leaf, at right angles to it. In the developing stem internode the mitotic spindles are mostly orientated parallel to the long axis of the stem and the developing cells elongate along this axis. Green points out that cell elongation depends upon turgor pressure and can only occur if the side walls of the cell resist the internal pressure exerted on them. The resistance of the side walls depends upon the fact that, in primary cell walls, the cellulose microfibrils are mainly oriented transversely, i.e. at right angles to the long axis of the cell. When a lateral organ is formed, this entails a change in the direction of the mitotic spindles and of the orientation of the microtubules and microfibrils (Fig. 2.3.6). Microscopic studies with polarized light have shown that there is indeed a change in the orientation of the microfibrils in the cell wall when a lateral organ is formed.

Other aspects of polarity

Polarization of the cytoplasm and orientation of the axis of the mitotic spindle are manifestations of a far-reaching polarity of plant cells and tissues which is an essential feature of many aspects of differentiation and morphogenesis in plants [4, 36]. There are many other ways in which this polarity is manifested—for example in the pattern of regeneration of buds and roots from segments of stem or root, in which buds regenerate from the morphologically upper end and roots from the basal end. This polarity is not simply due to gradients of metabolites since, once established, it is normally persistent throughout the life of a given piece of tissue or organ. Moreover, it cannot be changed by reversing the

Fig. 2.3.5. Changes in microtubules at cell division. (From prints supplied by Dr Myron Ledbetter, reproduced from *Symp. Internat. Soc. Cell Biol.*, **6**, 1967.)

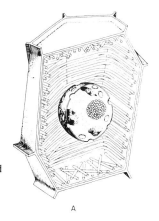

A

B

C

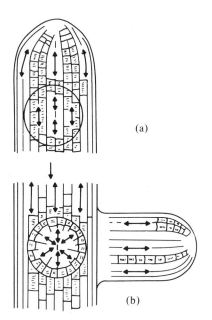

Fig. 2.3.6. Diagram showing the possible arrangement of cellulose microfibrils in the outer wall of the epidermis in a cylindrical plant organ before (a) and after (b) the emergence of a new lateral axis. In (b), the new axis is shown as viewed from the tip (circle on parent axis) and from the side (right). The arrows indicate the direction of expansion of the organs. (From Hardham *et al.* [12].)

2.3.3   PATTERNS OF CELL DIFFERENTIATION IN LOWER PLANTS

Unequal cell divisions are not only characteristic of the early development of plant zygotes, but they are also a regular feature of vegetative growth at the shoot and the root apices in lower plants. The development of these structures can be deduced from histological sections if we assume that these cells do not slip past each other but do maintain orderly arrays as they grow and divide. The growth of the roots and the shoots of lower plants depends on the activity of a single apical cell and all the mature tissues are formed by a few divisions of the daughters of this apical cell.

Shoots

The single apical cell behaves as a stem cell, as is clearly shown in many algae; the apical cell undergoes an unequal division to give a distal daughter, which continues to constitute the apical cell, and a proximal

orientation of a stem cutting, by planting it upside-down.

The polarity of a multicellular tissue appears to reflect the polarity of its constituent cells, as is shown by the fact that after they have been subjected to plasmolysis each constituent cell of the filamentous alga *Cladophora* can regenerate into a nw plant, with a rhizoid forming from the basal end of each cell (Fig. 2.3.7). The structural basis of this polarity of each cell is not known, although it has been assumed that there must be some 'cytoskeleton' within the cytoplasm, based upon the orientation of macromolecules or other subcellular structures such as microfilaments, but this hypothetical cytoskeleton has not yet been identified. Alternatively, the cell polarity may be based upon polarization of the plasma membranes at the end walls of the cell [10]. One of the most important manifestations of cell polarity is seen in the polar movement of the hormone indol-3yl acetic acid ('auxin'), which moves in the plant in a strictly basipetal manner by cell-to-cell transport.

Fig. 2.3.7. Single cell from a filament of *Cladophora* regenerating a thallus from its apical end, and a rhizoid from the basal end. (From A.T. Czaja (1930) *Protoplasma*, **11**, 601.)

daughter which divides several times to give the differentiated tissues of the mature thallus. The apical meristems of mosses and ferns likewise consist of a single large tetrahedral cell, which divides by unequal division and gives rise to daughter cells from each of its three proximal faces in succession (Fig. 2.3.8). The large distal apical daughter of each division continues to divide, whereas the smaller inner cell undergoes only a limited number of divisions before it differentiates.

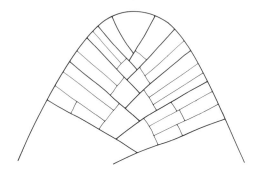

Fig. 2.3.8. Segmentation of tetrahedral apical cell as seen in median section. (From Clowes [5].)

Roots

The most detailed analysis of vegetative growth and development from a single apical cell has been carried out with the roots of the water ferns *Azolla filiculoides* and *A. pinnata* [11]. These ferns grow with their shoots lying flat on the surface of ponds. The shoots branch and each branch produces several sets of leaves before forming roots which grow down into the water; the roots extend out of a sheath of epidermal cells and form rows of root hairs as they grow.

The apical cell of the root, when it is first recognized, has an outer free face and it first divides parallel to this face, cutting off a cell which, by one further division parallel to this face (periclinal) and numerous cell divisions at right angles to it (anticlinal), forms the two-layered root cap. After the first division in this sequence, the apical cell itself takes no further part in the formation of the root cap; it changes its behaviour and only forms tissues in the elongating root proper.

The apical cell now has a curved outer face lying against the root cap and three flat faces against other cells. At each of these proximal faces in turn the apical cell divides, to produce three overlapping daughter cells (Fig. 2.3.9); the pattern of overlap can be seen in transverse section and can be used to find out if the apical cell daughters are being produced in succession to the left or to the right. Since the apical cell only produces daughter cells at these three proximal faces and since each daughter cell gives rise to orderly arrays of cells, each root is divided into three sectors, which are called 'merophytes'. Again, making the assumption that cells do not slip past each other, it is possible to reconstruct the whole development of the root from histological sections. The subsequent divisions of the daughter cells of the apical cell have precise timing and geometry, and the pattern of cell division makes it possible to give a clear description of the lineage of each cell in this orderly array (Fig. 2.3.9).

The principle conclusion from this beautiful study by Gunning and his associates [11] is that the three sequential unequal cell divisions of the apical cell from its three inner faces are decisive in setting up the three 'merophytes' of the mature root. Subsequently, within each merophyte different cell types are exactly located. The neat geometry of this structure may be compared with the pattern of cells in the *Drosophila* cluster of oocytes and nurse cells. In the case of the clusters, the final form of the complex depends on relative cell movement after division (Fig. 2.2.1), while the organization of cells in the roots of *Azolla* derives directly from the planes of cell division.

2.3.4   SHOOT APICAL MERISTEMS*

As we have seen, many lower plants, including various algae, mosses and many ferns, grow by means of a single apical cell. Other lower plants, including the club mosses (*Lycopodium*) and some 'eusporangiate' ferns, have several initial cells, and all seed plants (gymnosperms and angiosperms) grow by apical meristems comprising many cells.

In the seed plants two main layers of cells can be distinguished at the shoot apex: (1) the *tunica* consisting of one or several layers of cells which divide predominantly by anticlinal walls (i.e. perpendicular to the surface), and (2) the central *corpus*, in which divisions are both anticlinal and periclinal (i.e. parallel to the surface) (Fig. 2.3.10). Apart from these broad zones, which can be distinguished solely by the orientation of

*For detailed accounts of plant apical meristems see publications by Clowes [5], Cutter [8], and Wardlaw [34].

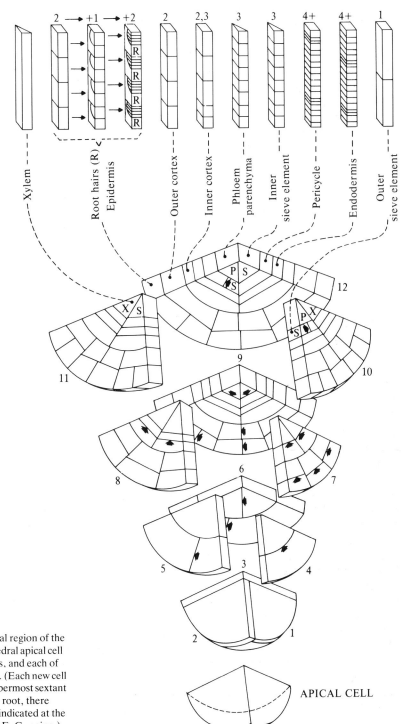

Fig. 2.3.9. Patterns of cell division within the root apical region of the water fern *Azolla pinnata*. Division of the single tetrahedral apical cell cuts off daughter cells from each of its three inner faces, and each of these undergoes a sequence of regular further divisions. (Each new cell wall is indicated by an arrow. Each of the cells in the uppermost sextant is destined to give rise to a specific tissue of the mature root, there being longitudinal files of cells for each such tissue, as indicated at the top of the diagram. (Figure kindly supplied by Prof. B.E. Gunning.)

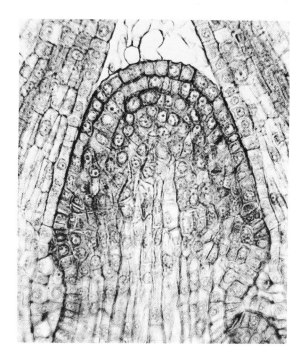

Fig. 2.3.10. Median section through the shoot apical meristem of *Alternanthera philoxeroides*, showing the two-layered tunica overlying the central corpus. (From Cutter [7].)

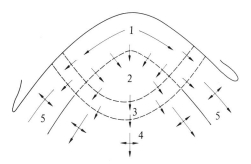

Fig. 2.3.11. Diagram of a median section of the shoot apex of *Chrysanthemum morifolium*: 1, tunica; 2 central mother cell zone; 3, zone of cambial-like cells; 4, rib meristem; 5, peripheral zone. Arrows indicate tissues to which meristematic cells contribute. (From Popham [18].)

the planes of division, other zones may be distinguished in the apices of many species, although in some species not all the zones are present. Those other zones include: (1) the *central mother cells*, (2) *peripheral* or *flank meristems*, and (3) a *central rib meristem* (Fig. 2.3.11). The rate of division in the central mother cell zone is low, but active divisions at the boundary of this zone give rise to the other two zones. There is considerable variation among species in the general shape of the apex and in the number of zones which are recognizable, and yet the apices of all these species produce similar organs, viz. stems, leaves and buds. Thus, it would appear that no special morphogenetic significance can be attached to the various zones recognizable in the shoot apex.

Leaves are initiated in the shoot apical region in a regular pattern which is described below. The leaf primordium is initiated by divisions which commence in a group of cells on the flanks of the apex. These divisions may originate in the outermost layers of the tunica, as in many grasses, or they may occur in deeper layers and may involve both the tunica and the corpus. Thus, the

extent to which the tunica and the corpus are involved in the initiation of leaf primordia varies greatly from species to species, and even within a single species depending upon the nutritional and other conditions under which the plant is growing.

Lateral buds normally originate somewhat later than leaf primordia, again by divisions which begin in a group of cells on the flanks of the apex. As with the leaf initiation, the extent to which these divisions occur in the tunica and the corpus varies greatly from one species to another. As a result of these divisions the bud primordium first develops as a protuberance, which later forms an apical structure similar to that of the main shoot apex of that species.

The siting of leaf primordia

The arrangement of leaf primordia at the shoot apex is normally highly regular and characteristic of the species. A spiral arrangement is very common (Figs 2.3.12 and 13), but other arrangements are frequently found, as when the leaves are arranged (1) alternately on opposite sides of the apex; (2) in opposite pairs, with successive pairs at right angles to each other; or (3) in whorls, when a number of leaves arise around the apex at the same level. These arrangements of leaf primordia are, of course, reflected in the arrangement of the mature leaves on the stem (referred to as *phyllotaxis*).*

In the spiral leaf arrangement, a line drawn from the youngest through successively older primordia constitutes the '*genetic*' or *developmental* spiral. It is a

*For general accounts of phyllotaxis see [5, 19, 20, 23, 37].

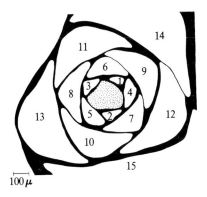

Fig. 2.3.12. Transverse section through the shoot apex of *Saxifraga* showing spiral phyllotaxis. Numbers refer to successively older leaves. (From Clowes [5].)

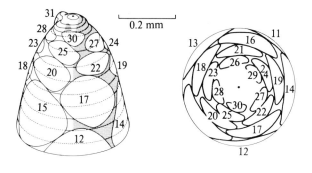

Apical cone   Transverse projection

Fig. 2.3.13. Three-dimensional and transverse projection of the apex of a 15-day-old flax seedling. Dotted lines indicate serial transverse sections. Numbered areas on apical cone represent bases of successive leaf primordia. (From Williams [37].)

logarithmic spiral described by the equation $r = \alpha^{\theta}$, where ρ is the radius, θ is the angle of divergence between two points on the spiral, and α is a constant. This implies that the radius will increase in geometrical progression as it sweeps through successive angles from the starting point.

The angle of divergence between successive primordia varies from species to species and depends upon the density of packing of leaf primordia at the apex; where this is high it approaches the limiting value of 137·5°. Thus, spiral arrangement at a shoot apex can be reproduced by marking points consecutively around a centre at a constant divergence of 137·5° and radially at a distance which increased in geometrical progression. The successive points represent the positions of the leaf

primordia, and a line through them coincides with the genetic spiral.

Clearly, this regular siting of leaf primordia at the shoot apex is an intriguing phenomenon and earlier botanists were fascinated by the mathematical properties of the system. However, here we are concerned primarily with the developmental aspects of phyllotaxis and, in particular, with the problem of what influences operate to regulate the very precise manner in which leaf primordia are sited. Earlier workers were of the opinion that the apex possessed rather mysterious mathematical properties which controlled phyllotaxis. More recent theories, however, are based on the assumption that the regularity of phyllotaxis is partly a problem of geometrical packing of leaf primordia within the shoot apical region, in conjunction with influences from existing primordia on the emergence of new leaf initials.

The first of such theories is the 'available space theory', put forward by van Iterson [14], in which it is postulated that a certain minimum space between existing primordia is necessary before a new primordium can form. If successively older primordia are referred to as P_1, P_2, P_3, etc., and the next primordia to emerge as I_1, I_2, I_3, etc. (in that order), then the regularity of the pattern indicates that I_1 will arise between P_3 and P_5 (Fig. 2.3.14), at an angular divergence from P_1 of approximately 137·5°. It will be seen from Fig. 2.3.13

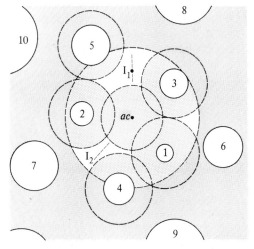

Fig. 2.3.14. The growth centre and field concept as it may apply to the apex of *Dryopteris*. The apex is seen from above. ac, apical cell; 1–9, leaf primordia in order of increasing age; I_1, I_2, position of next primordia to arise. The hypothetical inhibitory fields around the growing primordia are indicated by stippling. (From Wardlaw [32].)

that, as the apex grows, the primordia 'recede' from the centre of the apex and concurrently both the size of the primordia and the space between them increase. Thus, on the available space theory, I_1 appears where it does because a certain minimum free area of the surface of the apex is required before a new primordium can arise, and the region between P_3 and P_5 is the first such area to arise as the growth of the apex proceeds. The theory was tested by M. and R. Snow at Oxford, using elegant surgical techniques on the shoot apex of lupin (*Lupinus albus*) [25]. In one experiment they made cuts in the area in which I_2 would be expected to arise, thereby reducing the free space available, and it was found that no primordium developed in the space, presumably because it was reduced below the minimum area necessary.

An alternative theory was put forward by Schoute [21] who postulated that the centre of a leaf primordium is first determined and that as it grows it produces a substance which inhibits the formation of other primordia within a certain radius, so that new primordia cannot be formed until the distance between neighbouring primordia has increased sufficiently to produce an area which is outside the inhibitory fields of either (Fig. 2.3.14). Thus, according to this theory, the factor controlling the initiation of a primordium is not simply a minimum superficial area between adjacent primordia, but a space which is free from the inhibitory influence of neighbouring primordia.

Evidence tending to support this theory was provided by the experiments of Wardlaw [32]. Using fern apices, in one experiment he isolated the site of I_1 from the neighbouring existing primordia by two radial cuts and found that it then grew *more rapidly* than normally (Fig. 2.3.15), suggesting that it had thereby been released from the inhibitory effects of neighbouring primordia. In further experiments, Wardlaw destroyed the site at which I_1 was due to arise, and found that although this treatment had no effect on the position of I_2 and I_3, it did affect the positioning of I_4 (which would normally be sited between I_1 and P_2), so that it arose nearer the expected I_1 position than is normally the case in the absence of any inhibitory effect from this primordium.

It can be shown from the geometry of the shoot apex that I_1 will arise at a divergence of 137·5° from P_1 if it occurs at a point which divides the angle between P_3 and P_5 in the inverse ratio of their respective ages, i.e. the new primordium is displaced towards the older of the two primordia. The developmental significance of this observation is not clear, but it may indicate that the inhibitory effect of a growing primordium decreases as the primordium increases in age.

For details of the further development of leaves and of differentiation in the stem, the reader is referred to [8]. A detailed discussion of the role of hormones in the differentiation of vascular tissue is given in Chapter 5.3.

2.3.5 ROOT APICES

In certain respects the root apex is a simpler system than the shoot apex, due to the fact that it does not produce lateral organs corresponding to leaves and lateral buds, and secondary roots arise adventitiously at some distance from the apex itself. On the other hand, the root apex produces a cap, whereas no equivalent structure is produced by the shoot apex.

It is possible, by studying the planes of division, to trace the cell lineages within the shoot apical region (Fig. 2.3.16). In this way it ought to be possible to identify the initial cells of the promeristem itself, from which the observed files of cells are derived. Earlier workers interpreted the cell patterns to indicate that the promeristem consisted of two or three layers of initials, from which the main tissue layers of the root (vascular stele, cortex, epidermis and root cap) were held to be derived. However, more recent studies point to a different structure of the promeristem.

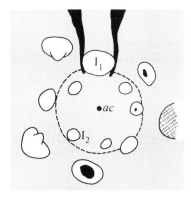

Fig. 2.3.15. The effect of isolating a leaf initial (I_1) by deep radial incisions. The isolated initial has become much larger than the surrounding primordia. (After Wardlaw [32].)

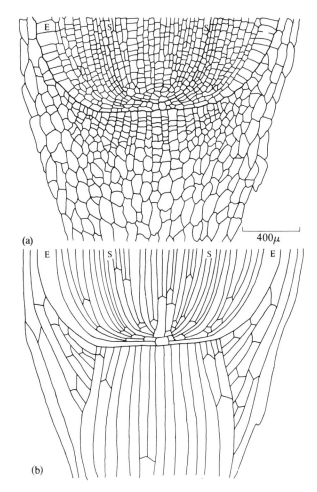

Fig. 2.3.16. (a) Median section of root tip of *Zea mays*. (b) Outline of cell lineages of the same root. E. epidermis: S. outer layer of stele. (From Clowes [5].)

Various approaches, including feeding the roots with tritiated thymidine (the incorporation of which can be used as a measure of DNA synthesis), have indicated that DNA synthesis and mitosis proceed at a much slower rate in a group of cells in the meristem region than in the surrounding cells, and hence this zone has been called the *quiescent centre* [5] (Fig. 2.3.17). The nuclei of the cells in the quiescent centre remain for long periods in the G_1 (pre-synthesis) phase of mitosis, but they appear to be capable of undergoing active mitosis under certain conditions.

Active cell division occurs at the boundary of the quiescent centre and the derivative cells give rise to the

files of cells seen in the older parts of the root. Hence these actively dividing cells are held to be the promeristem, which thus takes the form of an inverted 'cup'. The derived cells give rise to the tissues of the root itself on the proximal side and to the root cap on the distal side.

The quiescent centre varies considerably in size both between species and within the same species, and is often absent in young roots. These fluctuations in size involve corresponding changes in the initial cells, and raise the question as to whether there is a permanent promeristem. However as Clowes [5] states, 'if the promeristem is regarded as a collection of initials lying over the surface of the quiescent centre then the promeristem is not permanent. But there still must be a group of cells from which these initials are derived. At some times they are quiescent and at other times they are meristematic. In this sense then, there is a permanent promeristem'.

The function of the quiescent centre is not known. It has been suggested, however, that the cells of the quiescent centre and of the central zone of shoot meristems represent 'stem cells', i.e. the source from which all other cells, both meristematic and differen-

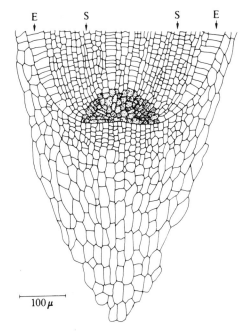

Fig. 2.3.17. Median section of root apex of *Zea mays* with quiescent centre shaded. E. epidermis: S. outer layer of stele. (From Clowes [5].)

tiated, are derived [2]. The 'open-ended' indeterminate pattern of growth in plants by the continued activity of the apical meristems requires that there must be a reservoir of stem cells which remain meristematic indefinitely and which are able to give rise to the other cell types originating in the shoot and root apices. In roots and shoots the cells of the quiescent centre and central zone divide infrequently and may function as stem cells.

The root presents a particularly favourable object for the study of the progress of cell and tissue differentiation, since the successive stages are set out in a linear sequence in passing from the meristem to the older,

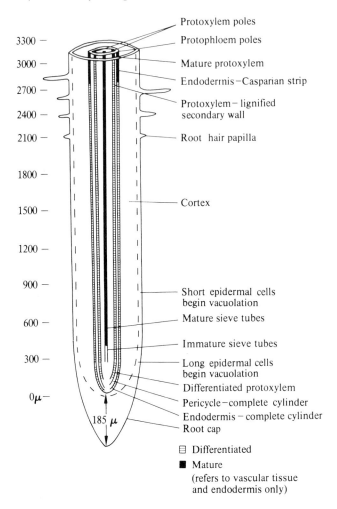

Protoxylem poles
Protophloem poles
Mature protoxylem
Endodermis–Casparian strip
Protoxylem – lignified secondary wall
Root hair papilla

Cortex

Short epidermal cells begin vacuolation
Mature sieve tubes
Immature sieve tubes
Long epidermal cells begin vacuolation
Differentiated protoxylem
Pericycle–complete cylinder
Endodermis – complete cylinder
Root cap

3300
3000
2700
2400
2100
1800
1500
1200
900
600
300
0μ

185 μ

▤ Differentiated
■ Mature
(refers to vascular tissue and endodermis only)

Fig. 2.3.18. Diagram of the root tip of *Sinapis alba*, to illustrate stages of differentiation of various tissues. (From Peterson [16].)

differentiated parts (Fig. 2.3.18; see review by Torrey [29]). The boundary between the central vascular cylinder and the cortex becomes visible immediately behind the region of the promeristem, being recognizable by the difference in size of the cells, which are radially enlarged in the surrounding cylinder of cortical cells. Thus, it is clear that histogenesis may occur at a very short distance from the promeristem itself. The endodermis is recognizable at an early stage, as the innermost layer of the cortex. Similarly, the outermost layer of the central cylinder, the pericycle, is delimited within 100 μm or less of the apical initial region in some roots. The first observable changes to occur in the central cylinder is the blocking out of the future xylem groups by the radial enlargement of certain cells. On the other hand, the first cells to differentiate into mature cells are the sieve elements of the protophloem, which may occur within a distance of 230 μm from the promeristem in slow-growing roots (Fig. 2.3.18).

2.3.6 EMBRYO DEVELOPMENT IN THE FLOWERING PLANT

In the development of the ovule of flowering plants, a large diploid cell (megasporocyte) divides meiotically to produce four haploid megaspores, one of which enlarges and survives while the other three degenerate. The surviving megaspore gives rise to the embryo sac and three successive mitotic divisions of its nucleus give rise to eight haploid nuclei, around which cell walls are formed, one of which is the egg cell (Fig. 2.3.19). The egg cell is polarized insofar as a large vacuole is present towards the micropylar end, and the nucleus and most of the cytoplasm lie towards the chalazal end (see Fig. 2.3.1).

Following pollination and germination of the pollen grain, the generative nucleus of the latter divides to give two haploid male nuclei, one of which fuses with the egg nucleus to form the zygote, while the other fuses with two of the nuclei of the embryo sac to form a triploid nucleus from which the endosperm (nutritive tissue for the embryo) is formed.

As we have seen (p. 33), the first division of the zygote is unequal, and gives rise to a smaller terminal cell with dense cytoplasm which forms most of the future embryo, and a larger, vacuolate basal cell which forms the suspensor (Fig. 2.3.20). In the development of the embryo of *Capsella*, the terminal cell undergoes two

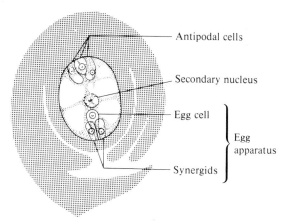

Fig. 2.3.19. The structure of the mature ovule of a flowering plant. (Adapted from A.S. Foster & E.M. Gifford (1974) *Comparative Morphology of Vascular Plants.* W.H. Freeman, San Francisco.)

successive longitudinal divisions, with the plane of the second division at right angles to that of the first, to give four cells; these cells then divide transversely to form eight cells, which constitute the 'octant'. Each octant cell divides to form an outer protodermal cell, which gives

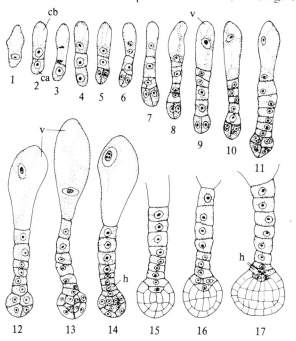

Fig. 2.3.20. Early stages in the development of the embryo of *Capsella bursa-pastoris*. Note the initial unequal division into a larger basal cell (cb) and smaller terminal cell (ca). The basal cell gives rise to the suspensor. (From A. Fahn (1967) *Plant Anatomy*, Pergamon Press, Oxford, adapted from Souèges (1914).)

rise to the future epidermis, and an inner cell. The inner cells continue to divide to form the cotyledons and the hypocotyl.

By several successive transverse divisions, the basal cell gives rise to a row of cells which forms the suspensor, the end cell of which enlarges and becomes sac-like. The suspensor cell nearest the embryo undergoes several divisions to give a group of cells of which the distal ones form the future root cap and epidermis, while the inner ones form the remainder of the radicle.

From the foregoing description it is apparent that of the two cells formed by the first unequal division of the zygote, the basal cell is normally the one nearer the micropyle of the ovule and gives rise to the root end of the ovule, whereas the terminal cell gives rise to the shoot end. Thus, even the very young embryo shows polarity in that it has a 'shoot' end and a 'root' end.

2.3.7 CELL LINEAGES AND DIFFERENTIATION

In the studies on the *Azolla* root described above it was shown that the patterns of cell division leading to the various differentiated cell types are extremely regular, so that the precise cell lineages can be followed in detail. In higher plants, no such regular patterns of division can be identified visually, but by using irradiation with X-rays to induce mutants affecting pigmentation or chlorophyll development in embryos of maize, it has been possible to demonstrate that the patterns of cell division and cell lineages must be much more regular than appears at first sight [6, 26]. Thus, if a maize embryo is X-irradiated at about 36 hours after pollination and then the pattern of leaf and stem pigmentation studied in the mature plant, it is found quite frequently that plants are formed which are half green and half pale. Moreover, the line dividing the two colours runs exactly down the midrib of each leaf and in effect divides the whole plant into bilaterally symmetrical halves. These observations suggest that the two halves of the plant are clonally derived from each of two apical cells in the early development of the maize embryo.

In further studies of this type, mature seeds of maize were X-irradiated and it was found that albino clones frequently contributed to several leaves. Since this frequency was greater than would be expected by chance if each clone had been initiated from different mutant cells, it was probable that several leaves had arisen from

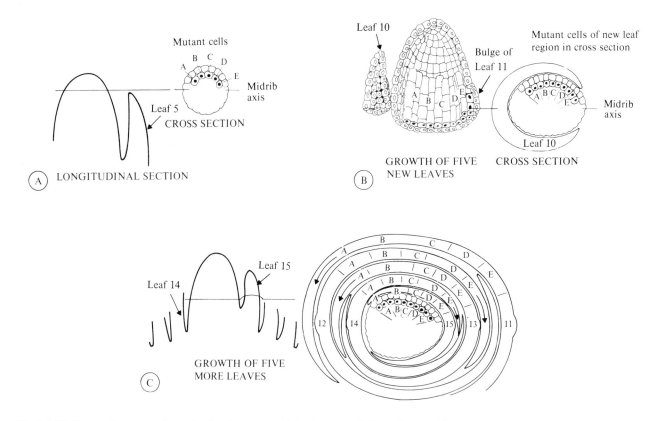

Fig. 2.3.21. Proposed patterns of growth taken by mutant cells in the apical dome during formation of 10 new leaves. (A) Apical dome in dry seed with single mutant cells (A, B, C, D, E), independently induced by gamma rays. (B) Formation of five new leaves with mutant cell files indicated. (C) Further growth to form five additional leaves. The regions of mutant tissue are located diagrammatically in cross section. (From Steffensen [26].)

a group of cells in which one had mutated ('related clones'). In related clones, the width of the mutant clones increases in the later-formed leaves and the clones alternate from one side to the other of successive leaves. Both these observations suggest that the leaves are initiated in accordance with a regular pattern of cell division in the apical meristem (Fig. 2.3.21). The frequency with which albino segments occur is also a measure of the number of cells which contribute to the green parts of each leaf. Calculations suggest that all the leaves of the top half of the plant derive from cells in the upper part of the shoot apex of the embryo (Fig. 2.3.22).

Further studies on the formation of albino sections in plants developing from irradiated seeds strongly suggest that early in the development of the shoot apex the cells which will form the male inflorescence are set aside from the cells which will form the leaves.

These cell lineage studies show that the patterns of cell division in the maize plant are much more regular than

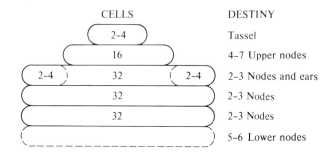

CELLS			DESTINY
	2–4		Tassel
	16		4–7 Upper nodes
2–4	32	2–4	2–3 Nodes and ears
	32		2–3 Nodes
	32		2–3 Nodes
			5–6 Lower nodes

Fig. 2.3.22. Suggested destinies of cells in the shoot apex of the embryo of maize. (From Coe & Neuffer [6].)

had been thought. However, they do not provide any evidence that the distinct clones established in the early development of the plant differ in their developmental potential and are 'pre-programmed' (determined) along separate paths of differentiation, as appears to be the case in certain animal embryos (Chapter 2.4).

The sequence and pattern of cell division during the early development of plant embryos are very regular within a given species. This observation led to the suggestion by earlier plant embryologists that 'each and every cell has a reason for its existence, its origin can be demonstrated and its position is invariably the same. A superfluous cell would seriously upset the harmonious balance.' see [48]. However, as Street [48] has pointed out, the pattern of cell division leading to the development of experimental carrot embryoids (p. 75) is quite different from that in normal zygotic embryos, and yet both structures are equally effective in producing mature plants. Thus, it would seem that the normal regular pattern of cell division in zygotic carrot embryos is not essential for the formation of functional embryos.

There is, in fact, very little evidence that in higher plants lineages of different cell types are established by an initial unequal division followed by 'cloning' of the daughter cells of the unequal division; in most instances, unequal division in higher plants (e.g. in the formation of stomata) is followed by only one or two further equal divisions.

However, it can be seen very clearly in the roots of many species that distinct cell lineages are established very close to the quiescent centre, and that the boundary between cells destined to form the central vascular cylinder and the cortex becomes recognizable very early by the difference in sizes of the cells, which are radially enlarged in the innermost layer of the future cortex According to the 'histogen theory' put forward by Hanstein in 1856, three 'histogens', *dermatogen*, *periblem* and *plerome*, are established in the shoot and root apices of higher plants and are destined to give rise to (i) epidermis, (ii) cortex and (iii) vascular tissue and pith, respectively. When only roots are considered, the histogen concept is still tenable and it is possible that clones of differing developmental potential are established among the cells formed by divisions at the edges of the quiescent centre. However, the formation of leaf traces (vascular tissue) in the developing stem not from 'plerome' but from cortical tissue ('periblem') seems to invalidate the applicability of the histogen concept to the shoot. Experiments are required to test the validity of the histogen concept as applied to roots, but the technical difficulties are considerable.

2.3.8 THE SELF-ORGANIZING PROPERTIES OF APICAL MERISTEMS

Several lines of evidence indicate that shoot and root apices are self-organizing systems. This is almost self-evident from the fact that adventitious buds and roots may arise within parenchymatous tissues of roots and shoots and, in many species, in unorganized callus tissue (p. 74). Moreover, we shall see that adventive 'embryoids' may be developed from liquid suspension cultures of plant cells (Chapter 2.5), and that these embryoids are formed from small groups of a few cells.

Apart from these various examples of organization of apical meristems *de novo*, existing meristems also have the capacity for regeneration if they are cut or damaged. Thus, if the apical region of lupin is divided into four segments by two vertical cuts at right angles, each of these segments is capable of regenerating a complete, normal apex [1]. It has been suggested that the pattern of differentiation at the apex is determined primarily by the pattern of the pre-existing mature tissue, since the procambial strands (primordial vascular tissue) are continuous with the existing vascular tissue and they extend well into the region of the apical meristem in both shoots and roots. However, several types of experiment indicate clearly that the pattern of differentiation in the apical region of both shoots and roots is not controlled by the pre-existing tissues. Thus, when the apical meristem of the fern *Dryopteris* was isolated on a plug by four vertical cuts so that any influence of pre-existing vascular tissue was excluded, the normal phyllotactic sequence of leaf primordia was maintained [31]. A cross section through the plug of pith tissue on which the apex was borne showed that the stele had a quadrangular form, reflecting the shape of the plug (Fig. 2.3.23). In spite of this, the new vascular tissue formed above the plug followed a normal pattern, so that the abnormal form of the vascular tissue in the plug did not affect the normal pattern of vascular differentiation above it, indicating that the fern apex is a self-determining region in this respect.

Experiments on root apices have led to similar conclusions. Thus, if the terminal 0·5 mm of pea root is cut

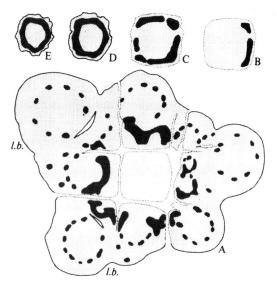

Fig. 2.3.23. The result of isolating the apical meristem of *Dryopteris* by four vertical cuts, as seen in serial transverse sections. The isolated meristem has grown on and has given rise to a short shoot. (A) Section taken near the base of the experimental region, showing the incisions whereby the apex was isolated on a plug of pith tissue. (B–E) Progressively higher sections of the central plug, showing the vascular tissue (black) which has differentiated below the growing apex. (After Wardlaw [31].)

off and cultured on a nutrient medium, instead of the triarch (i.e. three-stranded) xylem formed in normal pea roots, a monarch or diarch condition was found until the root had grown further, when it reverted to the normal triarch condition [27]. Again, if pea roots are de-capitated and allowed to regenerate in the presence of the hormone indol-3yl acetic acid (IAA), the new vascular tissue is hexarch, but if transferred to a medium lacking IAA they ultimately become triarch again [28]. Thus, the pattern of the vascular system of the root appears to be determined by the conditions prevailing with the apical meristem itself and not by the pre-existing vascular tissue.

Similar conclusions are indicated by experiments in which the terminal 2 mm of root tips was cut off and the tip rotated and replaced on the stump of older tissue; it was found that the vascular tissue which later differen-tiates at the tip is out of line with that in the stump. Finally, it has been shown that if root tips are bisected, new apices will regenerate from the two halves.

These various experimental results clearly indicate that apical meristems of higher plants are self-organizing

and self-determining systems [35]. It would seem that the apical meristems represent dynamic systems in a state of equilibrium and that interference with the system, by surgical or other treatments, is counteracted by compensating changes within the system until it reaches the equilibrium configuration.

So far we have considered the problems of differentia-tion in the apical regions of shoots and roots solely as if the solutions could be found in the properties of the individual constituent cells, invoking such factors as polarity and unequal division. However, self-organizing and self-regulating properties suggest that they behave as integrated wholes and, if this is so, the patterns of differentiation of cells and tissues may be regulated by the properties of the meristem as a whole. It is, indeed, possible to construct mathematical models, assuming the occurrence of two 'morphogens' which diffuse at different rates, and to show that in a ring of cells chemical stationary waves would be set up under certain conditions, resulting in a pattern of concentration of the morphogens which could, in turn, lead to a pattern of differentiation [30, 33]. Whether or not this model has any validity, it demonstrates that a system as a whole may show properties which are not expressed by its individual parts; in other words, 'the whole is more than the sum of the parts'.

2.3.9 CONCLUSIONS

We have seen that unequal division marks the first step in the establishment of cell heterogeneity at various stages in the plant life cycle. Where such division occurs in the zygote it results in the establishment of the two main subdivisions of the plant body, viz. thallus and rhizoid in algae and other lower plants, and shoot and root in higher plants. Other examples of unequal division occur in the final stages of development of organs, as in the formation of stomata and trichoblasts.

Unequal division is preceded by a visible polarization of cytoplasmic components within the parent cell, and it seems very probable that there is also a polarization of cytoplasmic determinants which become differentially partitioned between the two daughter cells, so that their subsequent divergent patterns of differentiation are controlled by these factors. If this interpretation is correct, then we seem to have a clear parallel with the 'mosaic' theory for animal embryo development.

This type of developmental control in plants is closely

connected with the phenomenon of polarity (p. 37), since the initial polarization of cytoplasmic components is established either by external factors, such as light or gravity, as in *Fucus* eggs, or by the surrounding maternal tissue in the zygote and stomatal initials in higher plants. Organized development in plants does, indeed, depend entirely upon close control of the orientation of cell division, and where this does not occur we obtain only a disorganized callus. Bünning has epitomized this principle in the aphorism 'no differentiation without polarity'.

Many lower plants, including some algae, bryophytes, most ferns and other vascular cryptogams, have single apical cells which show unequal division, giving rise to a distal (outer) cell which retains its meristematic activity and a proximal (inner) cell whose derivative cells have the capacity for only a limited number of divisions before they differentiate and mature. However, unequal division does not seem to be the primary means of establishing cell heterogeneity in the subsequent stages of differentiation of these lower plants, and in higher plants, in which there is not a single but several apical initial cells, there is no clear evidence for the occurrence of unequal divisions or for their role in the establishment of cell heterogeneity. It would thus appear that we must seek some other origins of cell heterogeneity in the shoot apices of higher plants. The self-organizing properties of the apical meristems of higher plants appear to indicate a more advanced type of organization in which the fates of particular groups of cells are not predetermined by their own intrinsic properties but by the properties of the system as a whole, which controls the pattern of differentiation of its various cellular constituents.

When we consider the types of cell heterogeneity which originate in the shoot apical region, it becomes apparent that it constitutes a zone of *organogenesis*, in which the primordia of stem, leaves and buds are established, and that only at a later stage of development of these organs does heterogeneity arise at the cell and tissue level. We know little about the manner in which different groups of cells become committed along the 'leaf', 'bud' or 'stem' pathways of development, but it would appear that the distinction between corpus and tunica layers plays little or no role in organogenesis. On the other hand, some other zones within the apex (Fig. 2.3.11) may have some morphogenetic significance. Thus, the development of the internode depends upon polarized cell divisions in which the axes of the mitotic spindles are orientated parallel to the main axis of the future stem, and such divisions become apparent earliest in the rib meristem (Fig. 2.3.10).

We have seen that the arrangement of leaf primordia (phyllotaxis) can be related to the geometry of the shoot apex and its pattern of growth. The siting of the new primordium is conditioned by the nearest neighbouring primordia, which appear to be surrounded by inhibitory fields, and the new primordium apparently arises in an area in which these inhibitory effects are absent or minimal.

In the shoot apex, procambial tissue is blocked out in the boundary zone between the rib meristem and the peripheral meristems. However, the further differentiation of vascular tissue in the stem is profoundly influenced by the developing leaf primordia, and there is strong evidence that hormones produced by the young leaves play an essential role in the differentiation of vascular tissue (Chapter 5.3). Thus, several different types of process appear to be involved in the establishment of cell heterogeneity in shoot apices of higher plants.

The situation in root apices appears to be rather simpler, since it is not complicated by the problems associated with the formation of lateral organs, such as leaves and buds (lateral roots are initiated at some distance from the apex in the mature regions of the root). The various tissue zones of the mature root are blocked out at an early stage and differentiating phloem can be recognized at only a short distance from the meristem itself (Fig. 2.3.18). Moreover, cell lineages giving rise to these various tissue zones can be traced back to initial cells at the periphery of the quiescent centre (Fig. 2.3.16). Thus, the old concept of specific histogens destined to give rise to the main tissue zones of the mature root is consistent with the histological evidence and may have some validity for roots, but not for shoots. However, we remain completely ignorant as to the nature of the processes by which cell heterogeneity originates in root apices.

2.3.10   REFERENCES

1 Ball E. (1948) Differentiation in primary shoots of *Lupinus albus* L. and of *Tropaeolum majus* L. *Symp. Soc. exp. Biol.*, **2**, 246–262.
2 Barlow P.W. (1978) The concept of the stem cell in the context of plant growth and development. In *Stem Cells and Tissue Homeostasis* (Eds B.I. Lord C.S. Potten & R.J. Cole), pp. 87–113. Cambridge University Press, London.

3 Bloch R. (1965) Histological foundations of differentiation and development in plants. *Encycl. Plant Physiol.*, **15**(1), 146–188.

4 Bünning E. (1952) Morphogenesis in plants. *Surv. biol. Prog.*, **2**, 105–140.

5 Clowes F.A.L. (1961) *Apical Meristems*. Blackwell Scientific Publications, Oxford.

6 Coe E.H. & Neuffer M.G. (1977) Embryo cells and their destinies in the corn plant. In *The Clonal Basis of Development* (Eds S. Subtelny & I. Sussex), 36th Symposium of the Society for Developmental Biology.

7 Cutter E.G. (1967) Morphogenesis and developmental potentialities of unequal buds. *Phytomorphology*, **17**, 437–445.

8 Cutter E.G. (1971) *Plant Anatomy, Part 2, Organs*. Edward Arnold, London.

9 Cutter E.G. & Feldman L.J. (1970) Trichoblasts in Hydrocharis. I. Origin, differentiation, dimensions and growth. *Am. J. Bot.*, **57**, 190–201.

10 Goldsmith M.H.M. & Ray P.M. (1973) Intracellular localization of the active process in polar transport of auxin. *Planta*, **111**, 297–314.

11 Gunning B.E.S., Hughes J.E. & Hardham A.R. (1978). Formative and proliferative cell divisions, cell differentiation and developmental changes in the meristem of *Azolla roots*. *Planta*, **143**, 121–144.

12 Hardham A.R., Green P.B. & Lang J.M. (1980) Reorganization of cortical microtubules and cellulose deposition during leaf formation in *Graptopetalum paraguayense*. *Planta*, **149**, 181–195.

13 Hepler P.K. & Palevitz B.A. (1974) Microtubules and microfilaments. *A. Rev. Pl. Physiol.*, **25**, 309–362.

14 Van Iterson G. (1907) *Mathematische und Mikroscopisch-Anatomische Studien über Blattstellungen*. G. Fischer, Jena.

15 Kaufman P.B., Petering L.B., Yocum C.S. & Baic D. (1970) Ultrastructural studies on stomata development in internodes of *Avena sativa*. *Am. J. Bot.*, **57**, 33–49.

16 Peterson R.L. (1967) Differentiation and maturation of primary tissues in white mustard root tips. *Can. J. Bot.*, **45**, 319–31.

17 Picket-Heaps J.D. & Northcote D.H. (1966) Cell division in the formation of the stomatal complex of the young leaves of wheat. *J. Cell Sci.*, **1**, 121–28.

18 Popham R.A. (1958) Cytogenesis and zonation in the shoot apex of *Chrysanthemum morifolium*. *Am. J. Bot.*, **45**, 198–206.

19 Richards F.J. (1948) The geometry of phyllotaxis and its origin. *Symp. Soc. exp. Biol.*, **2**, 217–45.

20 Richards F.J. (1951) Phyllotaxis: its quantitative expression and relation to growth in the apex. *Phil. Trans. R. Soc. B*, **235**, 509–64.

21 Schoute J.C. (1913) Beiträge zur Blattstellungslehre. *Recl. Trav. bot. néerl.*, **10**, 153–325.

22 Schultz R. & Jensen W.A. (1968) *Capsella* embryogenesis: The egg, zygote and young embryo. *Am. J. Bot.*, **55**, 807–19.

23 Sinnott E.W. (1960) *Plant Morphogenesis*. McGraw-Hill, New York.

24 Sinnott E.W. & Bloch R. (1939) Cell polarity and differentiation in root hairs. *Proc. natl Acad. Sci., USA*, **26**, 223–27.

25 Snow M. & Snow R. (1933) Experiments on phyllotaxis II. The effect of displacing a primordium. *Phil. Trans. R. Soc. B*, **222**, 363–400.

26 Steffensen D.M. (1968) A reconstruction of cell development in the shoot apex of maize. *Am. J. Bot.*, **55**, 354–369.

27 Torrey J.G. (1955) On determination of vascular patterns during tissue differentiation in excised pea roots. *Am. J. Bot.*, **42**, 183.

28 Torrey J.G. (1957) Auxin control of vascular pattern formation in regenerating pea root meristems grown *in vitro*. *Am. J. Bot.*, **44**, 859.

29 Torrey J.G. (1965) Physiological bases of organization and development in the root. *Encycl. Plant Physiol.*, **15**(1), 1256–1327.

30 Turing A.M. (1952) The chemical basis of morphogenesis. *Phil. Trans. R. Soc. B*, **237**, 37–72.

31 Wardlaw C.W. (1947) Experimental investigation of the shoot apex of *Dryopteris aristata* Druce. *Phil. Trans. R. Soc. B*, **233**, 415–51.

32 Wardlaw C.W. (1949) Experiments on organogenesis in ferns. *Growth* (Suppl.), **13**, 93–131.

33 Wardlaw C.W. (1953) A commentary on Turing's diffusion–reaction theory of morphogenesis. *New Phytol.*, **52**, 40–47.

34 Wardlaw C.W. (1965) The organization of the shoot apex. *Encycl. Plant Physiol.*, **15**(1), 966–1076.

35 Wardlaw C.W. (1965) *Organization and Evolution in Plants*. Longmans, Green & Co., London.

36 Wareing P.F. & Phillips I.D.J. (1981) *Growth and Differentiation in Plants*, 3rd edn. Pergamon Press, Oxford.

37 Williams R.F. (1974) *The Shoot Apex and Leaf Growth—A Study of Quantitative Biology*. Cambridge University Press, London.

Chapter 2.4
Expression of Organization by Animal Zygotes
C.F. Graham

2.4.1 TRANSLATION OF ZYGOTE ORGANIZATION INTO EMBRYO ORGANIZATION

After fertilization and interactions with the environment, most animal zygotes are asymmetric (Chapter 2.2). The problem is to understand how these asymmetries are translated into the organized cell types of the early embryo, each in its place expressing a characteristic range of gene products. It is a problem which has not been adequately solved in any embryo.

It appears that cell division is an essential process in the translation of zygote asymmetries into embryo organization. In rare instances, some elements of morphogenesis and synthesis of tissue specific products can be observed in eggs which do not divide [65, 109, 119] (section 2.4.2); however, the morphogenesis is always inefficient and limited and the expression of differentiated characters is often diffuse and misplaced.

Cell division has at least three functions in the expression of zygote organization. First, it segregates cytoplasmic components with different developmental capacities (section 2.4.2). Secondly, it places cells in different relative positions (section 2.4.3). Thirdly, it creates cells of different relative size (section 2.4.4). In most embryos all three functions are important and proceed together (section 2.4.5).

Cleavage

Animal development starts with cell divisions which divide the zygote's cytoplasm; there is no increase in embryo dry weight and the process is called cleavage. These divisions are timed and oriented, and a set pattern of cell division is often required for normal embryogenesis (Table 2.4.1). The requirement for a set pattern is most frequent in embryos which develop rapidly into feeding organisms. The development of these animals usually depends on preformed capacities in the egg.

Other animals will develop normally when the cleavage pattern is disrupted. This is usually because these embryos have additional mechanisms for placing cells in different relative positions and the embryos' organization principally depends on interactions between these cells. In some embryos it may be necessary to postulate some whole-zygote pattern of organization to explain the transmission of developmental features (see section 2.4.6).

2.4.2 SEGREGATION OF DEVELOPMENTAL CAPACITY

The ability to synthesize products characteristic of different tissues usually becomes restricted to particular

Table 2.4.1. Cleavage patterns and development

Phylum	Genus	Effect of disturbance	Reference
A. DEVELOPMENT ALTERED BY A CHANGED CLEAVAGE PATTERN			
Ctenophora	*Mnemiopsis* (comb jelly)	Altered 2nd or 3rd cleavage plane redistributes cytoplasmic capacities	27. 28
Annelida	*Sabellaria* (reef-building tube worm)	Equalizing 1st cleavage gives two-backed larva without a mouth	42
Mollusca	*Lymnaea* (pond snail)	Change of cleavage plane at 2nd or 3rd cleavage blocks prolonged development	73
		Synchronizing cleavage in each quarter gives radial embryos	3
	Patella (limpet)	Synchrony of macromere divisions gives radial embryos	8
	Dentalium (tusk shell)	Equalizing 1st cleavage gives two-backed larva without a mouth	43
Echinodermata	*Hemicentrous* (sea urchin)	Equalizing 4th cleavage gives larva without a skeleton	110
Chordata	*Styela* (sea squirt)	3rd cleavage under compression gives relocated codifferentiation	120
B. NORMAL DEVELOPMENT AFTER CHANGED CLEAVAGE PATTERN			
Nemertini	*Cerebratulus* (proboscis worm)	Isolated blastomeres	121
Echinodermata	*Paracentrotus* (sea urchin)	Cleavage under pressure. Isolated cells from 4-cell stage	52
	Hemicentrotus (sea urchin)	Unequal 3rd cleavage	60
Chordata	*Rana* (frog)	Cleavage under pressure	72
	Mus (mouse)	Cells rearranged	51

Fig. 2.4.1. Nematode development. Top. Cleavage pattern illustrated for *Caenorhabditis elegans* (a–p). Optical sections of live embryos oriented with the anterior pole to the right, and posterior pole to the left. From the 2-cell stage onwards the dorsal surface is at the top, and the ventral surface is at the bottom. Timing for development at 25°C. Each embryo is about 50 μm long. (After von Ehrenstein & Schierenberg [24, 62].) At 30 min post fertilization, the male and female (right) pronuclei are obvious (a). Within the next 5 min there is a sudden constriction (b), the pronuclei fuse as the egg shortens (c), and the unequal first mitosis occurs (d). At about 45 min post fertilization, the second cleavage begins (e), and it is complete in about 5 min with the daughters of P_1 and AB in new relative positions (f, g, h). The daughter cells of this and subsequent divisions can be read from the lineage diagram (bottom left). In addition the daughter cells of founder cells (e.g. E, MSt, AB) are nominated by their relative position: a, anterior; p, posterior; l, left; r, right. The division of P_1 is also unequal. At 55 min post fertilization, the whole 8-cell stage (solid line towards observer, dotted lines away from observer. (i)). Gastrulation begins at the 26-cell stage (j), and in the wild type the gut precursor cells (Ep and Ea) move to the interior before dividing to give the 44-cell stage seen in optical sections (k, l, m, n). Mutants which alter the relative timing of interior migration and division of the gut precursor cells also disrupt the position of these cells in the embryo at the 44-cell stage and alter subsequent morphogenesis. In one mutant, cell division occurs before migration (o), and in another mutant it occurs during migration (p). See text for significance of these mutants. Bottom left. Cell lineage of the first 150 min of *Caenorhabditis* development at 25°C. This shows that the founder cells of the major tissues of the larval worm have distinct division rates from their origin (cells AB, MSt, E, C, D). The diagram also illustrates the results of cleavage-arrest experiments. When cleavage is arrested at the 2-, 4- and 8-cell stages, then only the underlined cells develop rhabditin granules which are characteristic products of the mature gut cells. (After Deppe, von Ehrenstein & Schierenberg [17, 24]. Experiments of Laufer *et al.* [65].)
Right. The structure of the hermaphrodite adult worm is shown in diagram to illustrate the organs derived from the lineage diagram. The body muscles run in series down the length of the worm and the bulk of body is occupied by the gonad formed by numerous divisions of the four descendants of the P_1 cell which are present in the newly hatched larva. Scale bar = 0.02 mm. (After Schierenberg [24].) The structure of the adult is also illustrated by cross sections across the pharnyx and across the main body of the worm and these are placed near the centre of the figure.

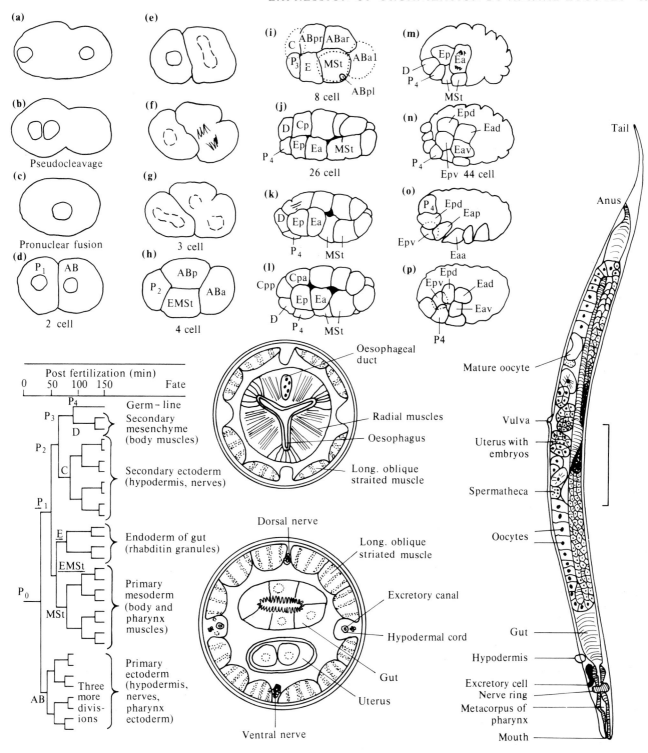

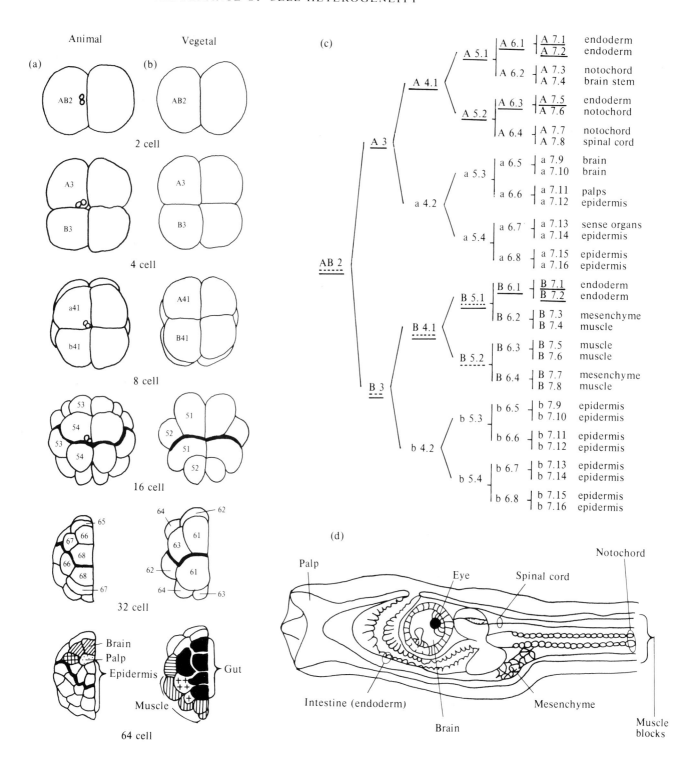

Fig. 2.4.2. Ascidian development. Columns illustrate the cleavage pattern (a) as seen from the animal pole with its polar bodies, or (b) as seen from the vegetal pole. From the 16-cell stage onwards, all cells above the dark line are derivatives of a (animal view) or A (vegetal view), and all cells below the dark line are derivatives of b (animal view) or B (vegetal view). The 32- and 64-cell stages are illustrated for half the embryo. At the 64-cell stage, the following precursors of tadpole organs are indicated: brain (diagonal lines), sense organs including eye (cross hatch), palps (stippling), intestinal endoderm (black), muscle (vertical lines), mesenchyme (crosses), and notochord (horizontal lines). (Based on Ortolani [79, 80].) (c) Lineage diagram

starting from one cell of the 2-cell stage. The diagram also illustrates the results of cleavage arrest experiments. When cleavage is arrested at successive cell stages and the embryo allowed to age, then the underlined cells develop intestine alkaline phosphatase activity and those with dots beneath develop muscle acetylcholinesterase activity. (After Whittaker [117–119]; see also [11, 22, 23].) (d) The structure of the ascidian tadpole with the tail cut off. This shows the organs derived from cells in the lineage diagram. The ascidian tadpole is a brief spasm in the life history of ascidians, and after 24 hours this dispersal stage settles to form the bottom-living marine polyp. (After Berrill [2]; see also [93].)

cell lineages during animal development. This would occur if the cell divisions of early development simply separated by cell membranes the localized capacities of the zygote. In general, it appears that the segregation of capacities is not achieved in this way. Rather, it appears that cell division may actively move capacities in the cytoplasm.

The progressive restriction of developmental capacity during cleavage is most clearly shown by the loss of the ability of cells isolated from progressively older embryos to form whole organisms (Table 2.4.2). These direct experiments do not tell us whether the restriction is due to the diminution of cell size or to the segregation of prelocalized zygote capacities, or to the loss of cell interactions which are required for the development of phenotype. Such objections are avoided when it can be shown that single cells or small groups of cells form fewer cell types when they are transplanted from progressively older embryos into the same site in a host

embryo at one stage of development. So far, only mouse development has been analysed in this way in any detail [34, 35, 100]. These objections can also be avoided when the capacity to form distinctive characteristics of tissue can be visualized in single cells of the intact embryo (see below).

Progressive localization of developmental capacity

In most zygotes, the capacity to form particular features of later embryos is not localized in fine detail. Localization is progressive and it occurs during the cell divisions of meiosis (see Chapter 2.2) and cleavage.

Cleavage arrest

One procedure for studying localization is to arrest cleavage with drugs such as cytochalasin B, and then to allow the embryo to age until the cells express products

Table 2.4.2. Capacity of smallest fragments to form whole embryos

Phylum	Genus	Smallest fragment to form whole	Reference
Ctenophora	*Mnemiopsis* (comb jelly)	Animal and vegetal half of 1-cell-stage	29, 31, 32
Nemertini	*Cerebratulus* (proboscis worm)	Animal and vegetal half of 1-cell-stage	30
Mollusca	*Lymnaea* (aquatic snail)	1 cell of 2-cell stage	73, 116
Echinodermata	*Paracentrotus* (sea urchin)	Meridional half of 1-cell stage Each cell of 4-cell stage	21, 52
	Asterina (star fish)	Each cell of 8-cell stage. 1 cell of 16-cell stage.	16
Chordata	*Cynops* (newt)	Quarter of 1-cell stage.	61
	Mus (mouse)	Half of 1-cell stage.	111
		1 cell of 4-cell stage.	98

characteristic of distinct tissues of later embryos. For instance, embryos arrested at the 2-cell stage will synthesize polypeptides characteristic of the trophoblast and the inner cell mass of the 64-cell mouse blastocyte [82], will produce gut specific granules which usually appear in the 550-cell nematode embryo [65], and will show the enzyme activities normally only expressed by mature muscle, gut and eye of the ascidian tadpole [119]. Clearly cell division beyond the 2-cell stage is not necessary for the expression of these characters and they can be used to follow restriction along cell lineages. The results show that the capacity to produce any one of these characters is restricted to the cells which are the normal precursors of the mature tissue which would normally express that character (Figs 2.4.1 and 2.4.2).

The restriction of these capacities has been shown to depend on the relationship between cell division plane and cytoplasm [120], but the dependence of segregation on cell division may go deeper than this. When large parts of the nematode embryo's cytoplasm and membranes are removed at the 1-, 2- and 4-cell stages, the capacity to form gut is in no way disturbed. It has been suggested that this capacity and other capacities in the zygote must be physically bound to the chromosomes or the mitotic spindle so that the segregation follows the division pattern which is left undisturbed by these large deletions [66]. This explanation of segregation would be special to the nematodes, for segregation usually follows the cytoplasm rather than the nucleus.

Cutting experiments

A second procedure for studying the localization of developmental capacity is to cut the embryo into pieces. Most fertilized eggs can be cut in half in at least one plane, and then one half will form a whole organism (Table 2.4.2); clearly, none of these zygotes contains an immutable plan of embryo organization. We restrict examples to two recent cutting experiments on the eggs of nemertines and ctenophores (Figs 2.2.2. and 2.4.3). These studies both show that developmental capacities are initially diffusely distributed in the zygote and that they subsequently localize, different capacities moving in different directions within the same cell.

Localization by cell division

It is clear from these two types of experiment that the cytoplasms of early embryos are able to express products of distinct cell types of later embryos without proceeding through all the cell divisions which are usually needed to form those cell types. Rather, it is the localization of developmental capacity to particular cell lineages which depends on cell division. It is easy to see how the localization of these capacities could be translated into differential gene expression by a variety of mechanisms; currently, there is no direct evidence about the molecular nature of any one capacity (see Chapter 6.4). What these experiments do demonstrate is that one method for creating cells with different phenotypes is to segregate developmental potential at cell division.

2.4.3   RELATIVE CELL POSITION

Cells are placed in different relative positions by cleavage patterns, and by the subsequent packing together and movements of the daughter cells of such divisions. These cell rearrangements move cytoplasms to novel positions and they are clearly seen in the development of most embryos (Figs 2.4.1, 2.4.3 and 2.4.4).

Relative cell position is known to allow interactions between cells with distinct phenotypes and such interactions are often necessary for early development; when they are blocked, development is limited [52, 112]. Relative cell position also exposes different cells to different environments and the analysis of this phenomenon in the mouse has been particularly informative about the translation of cleavage patterns into differential gene expression.

Mouse development

Early mouse development is illustrated in Fig. 2.4.4. The relative position of cells at the 8- to 16-cell stage appears subsequently to limit their ability to contribute to either the epithelial trophectoderm layer or the inner cell mass of the 64-cell-stage blastocyst [39, 57, 122]. In the 8-cell-stage embryo, cells placed internally tend to contribute to the inner cell mass and eventually to the foetus, while isolated cells or cells placed externally tend only to form parts of the trophectoderm and the placenta [51, 58, 112].

Formation of different relative positions

The cells in the embryo reach different relative positions as a consequence of the cleavage pattern. The division planes which make up this pattern are not fixed in zygote structure; they depend solely on the arrangement of cells surrounding the dividing cell [40, 41]. The positions of the cells are also established as cells flatten against each other after division [68]. The problem is to discover how relative cell position is translated into differential gene expression. During the 8-cell stage, the cells become polarized with a dense concentration of microvilli on the part of the cell exposed to the external medium. The direction of this polarization is also controlled by cell contacts [57, 124, 125]. Division to the 16-cell-stage usually cleaves each single 8-cell-stage blastomere so that one large daughter cell inherits a high concentration of microvilli and is external while the smaller daughter cell has a smoother surface and is located near the centre of the embryo [124].

These distinct phenotypes maintain the position of the internal and external cells: isolated large external microvillar cells will only integrate into the outside layer of the whole 16-cell-stage embryos, while isolated small inside cells rapidly penetrate to its centre [83]. Differential gene expression of the trophectoderm and the inner cell mass of the 64-cell blastocyst could be a direct consequence of the segregation of gene expression regulators at this unequal cell division, but it is more likely that it is cell position which is decisive, for groups of isolated central cells can reform trophectoderm and viable blastocysts [45, 99]. However, in undisturbed development, this polarized unequal cleavage at the 8- to 16-cell-stage creates cells with different phenotypes, and these phenotypes maintain cells in distinct positions. The consequence of these relative positions is differential gene expression, which is thus derived from the cleavage pattern.

2.4.4 RELATIVE CELL SIZE

Almost all animal embryos undergo at least one unequal cell division in their first six cleavages and, where tested, the equalization of these divisions leads to disrupted development (Table 2.4.1). Unequal cell divisions are also a characteristic feature of plant development (see Chapter 2.3). Unequal cell division could be translated into differential gene expression in several ways. It can be a device for disproportionately acquiring localized developmental capacity (a qualitative segregation, e.g. polar lobes of annelids and molluscs [19, 20, 42, 43]; see mouse cell polarization above). Secondly, it may control the phenotype of cells by determining the amount of maternal cytoplasm which they contain and thus the cells inheritance of maternal mRNA molecules and the amounts of oocyte-coded proteins which they synthesize (a quantitative segregation). Thirdly, by creating cells of different relative size, it may change their subsequent packing, movements and relative positions. It is probably relative, rather than absolute, size which is important in these events, because zygotes of very different volumes all develop normally (examples in Table 2.4.2). The possible effects of unequal cell division are only discussed for sea urchins because there has been some attempt at analysis with these embryos.

Sea urchin development

Following fertilization in nearly all species of sea urchin, the first two cleavage divisions are equal and radial, while the third is equatorial and equal (see Figs 2.4.5 and 2.4.6). At the next cleavage, the bottom vegetal cells divide first and unequally to form four large macromeres and four small micromeres at the vegetal pole, while the top four animal cells divide later and give equal-sized mesomeres. This pattern of cell division is not absolutely required for the development of normal larvae, which can also occur after an unequal 3rd cleavage [60], after the cleavage planes have been altered by pressure [52], and after cell isolation at the 2- and 4-cell stages [52]. The common feature of embryos and fragments which survive these treatments and subsequently develop into normal larvae is that they generate cells of different relative size early in embryogenesis.

In the normal development of embryos, the volumes of cells in each layer are very different at the 16-cell stage; in *Arbacia punctulata* the volumes are 13 715 μm^3 for the mesomeres, 20 575 μm^3 for the macromeres, and 5058 μm^3 for the micromeres [54, 55]. Since each cell layer forms a different part of the larva, it is an exciting possibility that cell volume is partly responsible for their differing behaviour. Evidence that this might be the case comes from the observation that equalization of the

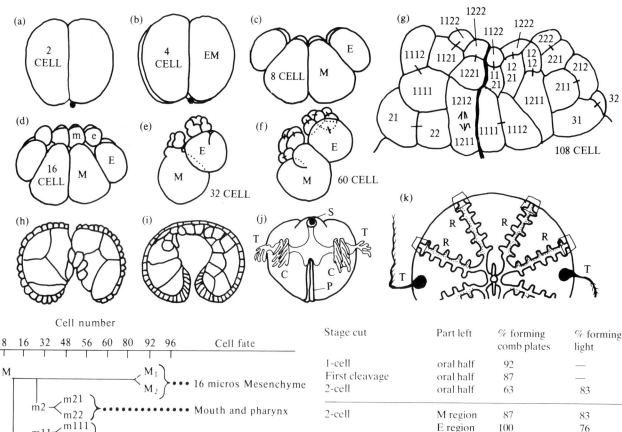

Cell number

8 16 32 48 56 60 80 92 96 — Cell fate

M
- M → M₁, M₂ ••• 16 micros Mesenchyme
  - m2 → m21, m22 ••••••••••• Mouth and pharynx
  - m1 → m11 → m111, m112; m12 → m121, m122 ••••••• Palps near senses

E
- E → E₁, E₂ ••• 8 micros Muscle
  - e3 → e31, e32 ••• Mouth and pharynx
  - e2 → e21 → e211, e212; e22 → e221, e222 •• Unknown
  - e11 → e111 → e1111, e1112; e112 → e1121, e1122 • Comb plates
  - e1 ••••••••••••••••••••••• Sense organs
  - e12 → e121 → e1211, e1212; e112 → e1221, e1222 • Comb plates

Fig. 2.4.3. Ctenophore development. The cleavage pattern for *Mnemiopsis* and *Beröe* illustrated in (a–g). Side views starting at the 2-cell stage with oral (mouth) pole marked by the polar bodies. Cleavage to the 4-cell stage is equal (b), and then there are a series of unequal divisions to give the 8-cell stage (c), and the 16-cell stage (d). Subsequent cleavages are drawn for only one quarter of the embryo and the illustrations are of the division from 32 to 48 cells (e) and of the

Stage cut	Part left	% forming comb plates	% forming light
1-cell	oral half	92	—
First cleavage	oral half	87	—
2-cell	oral half	63	83
2-cell	M region	87	83
	E region	100	76
4-cell	M region	14	100
	E region	100	24

60-cell stage (f). Note the relative cell movements at each division so that by the 108-cell stage (g) the small cells produced by M (left of thick vertical line) and E (right of thick vertical line) have formed a coherent mass. Invagination begins at the oral pole and the late products of E and M form the internal contents of the young larva (sections (h) and (i)). The young larva swims by the glittering beat of eight rows of fused cilia, the comb plates (C), and it catches small prey with contractile tentacles (T). It has a sensory organ (S), mouth (M), and pharynx (P). When viewed from above (k), the diagram shows the eight radial canals (R) with the light-producing organs indicated by stippling. (After Freeman [32] and Yatsu [123].)

Lineage diagram for ctenophores is at the bottom left. (From Ortolani [81].)

The table on the right illustrates the evidence for progressive localization in the ctenophore egg and embryo. When the 1-cell and 2-cell stages are cut across the equator and the aboral halves removed, the nucleated oral halves continue to divide. Between the early 1-cell stage and the 2-cell stage, the capacity of these fragments to form comb plates is greatly reduced; by the 8-cell stage only the E cells with aboral cytoplasm can form these structures.

It is also possible to cut the cells in other directions to ablate those parts whose membranes would exclusively contribute to either the E or the M cell at the 8-cell stage. It is found that the presumptive E region retains the capacity to form comb plates but loses the capacity to form light between the 2- and the 4-cell stages. The reverse is true of the presumptive M region. (After Freeman [27–29]; see also [92].)

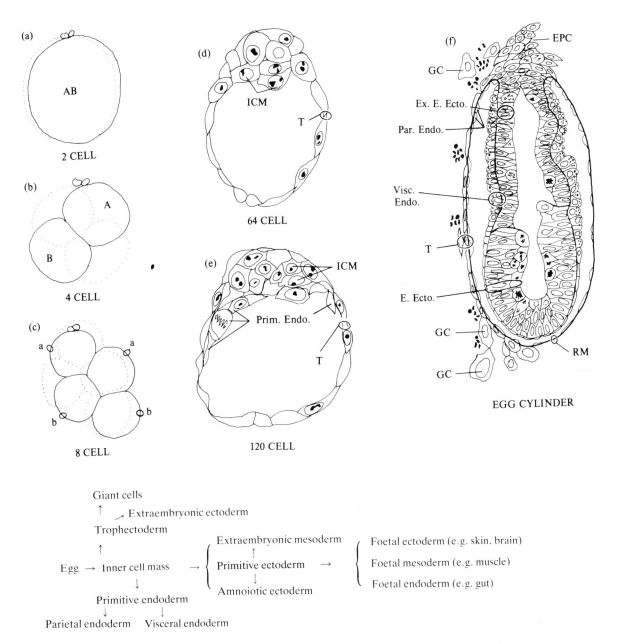

(a) AB

2 CELL

(b) A B

4 CELL

(c) a a b b

8 CELL

(d) ICM T

64 CELL

(e) ICM Prim. Endo. T

120 CELL

(f) EPC GC Ex. E. Ecto. Par. Endo. Visc. Endo. T E. Ecto. GC GC RM

EGG CYLINDER

Giant cells
↑   ↗ Extraembryonic ectoderm
Trophectoderm
        ↑
Egg → Inner cell mass →   { Extraembryonic mesoderm   { Foetal ectoderm (e.g. skin, brain)
                                    ↑
        ↓   Primitive ectoderm   →   Foetal mesoderm (e.g. muscle)
                                    ↓
Primitive endoderm   Amnoiotic ectoderm   Foetal endoderm (e.g. gut)
        ↓   ↓
Parietal endoderm   Visceral endoderm

Fig. 2.4.4. Mammalian development. Drawn for *Mus* (mouse). Whole embryo side views show the equal cleavages to the 8-cell stage during which one cell AB forms four derivatives, a, a, b, b, at the 8-cell stage (a–c). Solid lines are cells towards observer, dotted lines are cells away from observer. The next cleavage is unequal (see text). Subsequent pictures are sections. Cell division is slow and it takes four days to develop the 64-cell blastocyst (d) with its epithelial trophectoderm layer (T) and inner cell mass (ICM). This implants on the wall of the uterus in an asymmetrical manner (e) and the ICM delaminates a surface primitive endoderm layer (Prim. End.). By the seventh day of development, the egg cylinder has developed (f). The trophectoderm has endoreduplicated to form giant cells (GC) which migrate into the uterus stroma and it has divided to form the ectoplacental cone (EPC) and extra-embryonic ectoderm (Ex. E. Ect.). The primitive endoderm has formed the parietal endoderm (Par. End.) which synthesizes basement membrane (RM) and the visceral endoderm which synthesizes alpha foeto-protein (Visc. End.). (The composition of these membranes is discussed in Chapter 3.5.) The whole adult mouse will be formed from the embryonic ectoderm (E. Ecto.) which is a derivative of the inner cell mass. After Gardner [34a, 34b], Graham [39], Rossant & Papaioannou [100] and Smith [106]. The cleavage patterns of the rabbit [44] and monkey [69] are similar. See also [107].

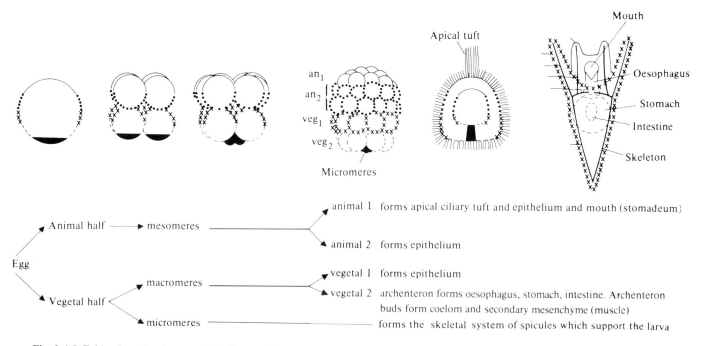

Fig. 2.4.5. Echinoderm development. This diagram illustrates the normal development and cell lineage of the sea urchin *Paracentrotus lividus* from the 1-cell stage to the planktonic pluteus larva. (From Hörstadius [52].)

fourth cleavage leads to embryos which lack skeletal spicules, the normal products of the micromeres formed at this division [110].

Phenotypes of the 16-cell stage

The mesomeres, macromeres and micromeres develop differently when they are isolated from each other. Groups of mesomeres form ciliated hollow spheres, groups of macromeres either form similar structures or they develop into whole larvae, while groups of micromeres do not form any recognizable cell type unless they are cultured with horse serum which evokes spicule formation [60, 78, 108]. After a further two rounds of cleavage, transplantation studies show that the products of these three cell layers have further developmental distinctions [52].

Inheritance of maternal messages

These three cell types of the 16-cell stage also synthesize different quantities of various proteins, although no one protein is exclusively synthesized by one cell type [103, 104, 113]. In each cell type there is a characteristic ratio of histone to non-histone protein synthesis. These differences reflect the relative abundance of the appropriate mRNA molecules and are set up by mRNA synthesis after fertilization [103]. The different ratios can be accounted for by assuming that they depend on both newly synthesized RNA, which is nuclear coded and therefore similar in amount in each cell, and on maternal mRNA, which is unequally inherited by the different cell types because they are the products of unequal cleavage [104]. In addition to this process, there are also further details in the inheritance of maternal RNA by the cell types. The complexity of polyribosomal RNA is similar in each, but the micromeres lack certain maternal RNA transcripts which are found in the other cells [13, 25]. Despite these details, there is good evidence that the pattern of protein synthesis is partly the consequence of unequal cleavage and that this differential inheritance of maternal RNA is a way in

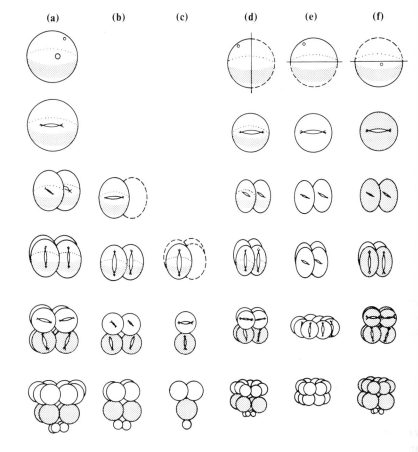

Fig. 2.4.6. Cleavage control in sea urchins. Columns illustrate the results of various treatments on the normal cleavage pattern (a). Cells isolated at the 2- and 4-cell stages divide almost as if they were still part of the whole embryo (b, c), and yet they subsequently generate a spherical blastula which can form a complete larva. Eggs cut in half at the 1-cell stage before fertilization divide like the whole embryo if the fragment contains material from both poles of the egg (d). However, animal halves (e) and vegetal halves (f) have inherently different cleavage patterns, which are similar to their behaviour in the whole embryo. (After Hörstadius [52].)

which unequal cleavage may be translated into differential gene expression [104].

Cleavage control

Cell phenotype at the 16-cell stage, then, partly depends on the control of cleavage plane. Cleavage plane depends on egg structure and the animal and vegetal halves of the egg have distinct cleavage tendencies. The animal half of parthenogenetically activated eggs divides equally, while the vegetal half divides as if it were a whole egg and it has an unequal cell division at the 4th cleavage (Fig. 2.4.6). Fertilization imposes some restraints on cleavage, for meridional halves from unfertilized activated eggs divide as does the whole egg, while similar halves from fertilized eggs do not and only display half the normal pattern (Fig. 2.4.6). From a detailed analysis of cleavage patterns, Hörstadius believes that there are at least three features of the egg

which control the orientation of the cleavage planes:
(1) there are progressive changes in the cytoplasm that control spindle orientation and that alter at various times after fertilization;
(2) there is a region near the vegetal pole which is needed for the unequal division at which the micromeres are formed; and
(3) this region must be activated at a certain time after fertilization.

Asters and cell division

It should, then, be possible to observe the structures which control spindle orientation (see the section on microtubules and cell wall formation in plants, Chapter 2.3). The sea urchin egg does contain beautiful spirals of cytoskeletal elements but the association between these and spindle position is currently unclear [49, 50]. However, the sea urchin embryo has been most useful in analysing the relationship between aster position and the initiation of cleavage furrowing in the cell membrane; such oriented interactions are necessary to ensure cytoplasmic segregation.

A series of neat micromanipulation experiments has shown that the initiation of membrane furrowing depends on an influence emanating from the two mitotic asters, and that the strength of action of this influence is determined by the distance between the two asters and by the distance between the asters and the cell membrane (reviewed [84, 85]). Microtubules are the most obvious structure radiating from asters and it is likely that these convey information from the mitotic spindle to the cell membrane.

If this analysis is correct, then we need to know how the position of the mitotic spindle is controlled. Unfortunately, this is a mystery even though something is understood about the growth of the mitotic spindle (see Chapter 6.2) and about the orientation of tubulin-containing structures in migrating cells (see Chapter 3.3). The causal analysis of early sea urchin development is therefore still limited by the failure to understand the mechanisms which control the cleavage planes and the failure to deduce exactly how such cleavages might be translated into differential gene expression. The cell movements and cell interactions involved in later sea urchin development are discussed in Chapters 3.3 and 4.3.

2.4.5 INTEGRATED DEVELOPMENT

It is likely that the translation of zygote asymmetries into embryo organization depends on an interplay between prelocalization in the zygote (see Chapter 2.2), the fine definition of this localization to particular cell lineages by cell division, the relative cell positions and relative cell sizes set up by unequal cell division, and the cell interactions which follow. So far, we have mainly given single examples of each process. Now it is useful to describe the development of two types of organism where an attempt has been made to analyse several of these events.

Snails and limpets

The molluscs have provided much of the material of classical embryology because their eggs are numerous and their development proceeds through rather rigid cell

lineages and can be reconstructed by fixing successive stages of development.

Oogenesis

Developmental organization builds up in mollusc eggs during oogenesis. The extreme example is the localization of the capacity to form the polar lobe at the vegetal pole [18–20, 115]. In the pond snail *Lymnaea stagnalis*, polar lobes are absent but the egg also contains organization before fertilization. The eggs are released from the ovary in the metaphase of the first meiotic division and during their passage down the genital tract, a pattern of patches of distinct cytoplasm appears. The pattern of these patches resembles the pattern of contacts between the follicle cells and the growing oocyte, and Raven suggests that the follicle cells have 'imprinted' organization of the oocyte [86–90, 114].

The pattern of these patches predicts the position of the vegetal pole of the zygote and the pattern is oriented so that it is possible to make an estimate of the most likely position of the plane of the first cleavage division. Despite this relationship, much of embryo organization builds up during cleavage.

Cleavage patterns

Some invisible feature of egg structure influences the pattern of cleavage. The evidence is genetic. An analysis of the direction of shell coiling in another snail, *Lymnaea peregra*, has shown that it is maternally inherited and therefore transmitted through oocyte structure. Since the direction of shell coiling when viewed from the shell apex exactly corresponds to the direction of twist of the 3rd cleavage division when viewed from the animal pole, it follows that some maternally derived influence controls cleavage direction (Fig. 2.4.7; see [15, 74]).

Cleavage proceeds through a series of regularly oriented and timed divisions. This pattern is probably essential for normal development. First, cells isolated from the 2-cell stage will only form complete larvae if they recapitulate the normal cleavage pattern of the whole embryo [73, 116]. Secondly, lithium ions disturb the pattern and also prevent formation of dorsal–ventral organization in the embryo; the embryos continue to develop into a structure with four identical quadrants of cell arrangement [3]. Lastly, there is evidence that a

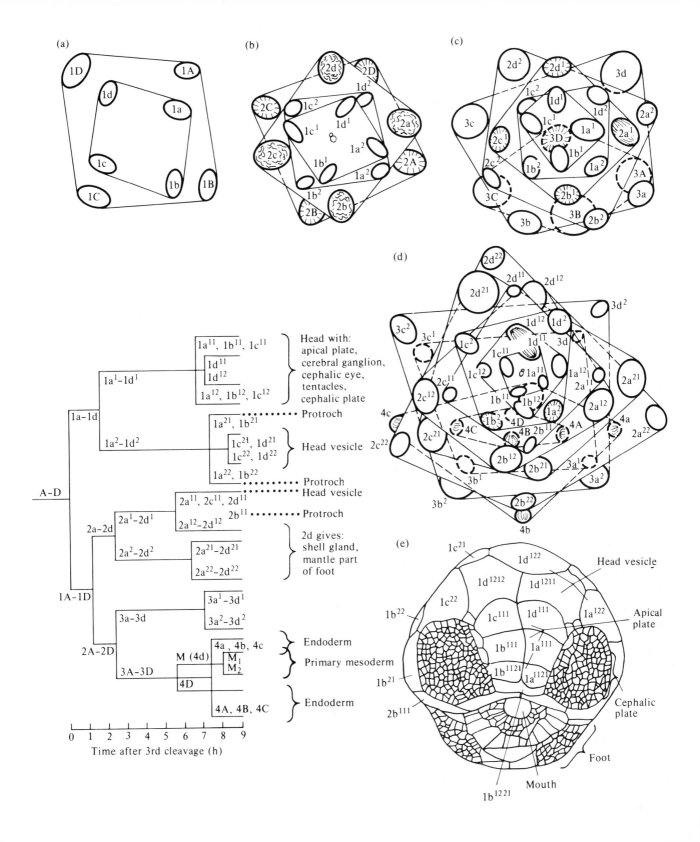

(a)

(b)

(c)

(d)

(e)

1a¹¹, 1b¹¹, 1c¹¹
1a¹-1d¹   1d¹¹
              1d¹²
              1a¹², 1b¹², 1c¹²   } Head with:
                                          apical plate,
                                          cerebral ganglion,
                                          cephalic eye,
                                          tentacles,
                                          cephalic plate

1a-1d

              1a²¹, 1b²¹ ············ Protroch
1a²-1d²   1c²¹, 1d²¹
              1c²², 1d²²   } Head vesicle
              1a²², 1b²² ··········· Protroch
                                     ··········· Head vesicle
A-D
              2a¹¹, 2c¹¹, 2d¹¹
2a¹-2d¹   2b¹¹ ··············· Protroch
2a²-2d²   2a²¹-2d²¹
2a-2d   2a²²-2d²²   } 2d gives:
              2a²²-2d²²   shell gland,
                                        mantle part
                                        of foot

              3a¹-3d¹
3a-3d   3a²-3d²

1A-1D
              4a, 4b, 4c   } Endoderm
2A-2D   M (4d) M₁   } Primary mesoderm
         3A-3D   M₂
              4D
              4A, 4B, 4C   } Endoderm

0 1 2 3 4 5 6 7 8 9
Time after 3rd cleavage (h)

Head vesicle
Apical plate
Cephalic plate
Foot
Mouth

minor change in the pattern will completely alter the dorsal–ventral organization in the embryo.

The best evidence on the function of these cleavage patterns comes from studies on a very similar embryo, that of the marine, rock-living limpet *Patella vulgata*. At the vegetal pole of the 32-cell embryo, there are two cross-furrow cells and two cells which are slightly further from the pole (Fig. 2.4.8).

The arrangement of these cells is inherited from the 4-cell stage. From cell lineage studies, it is known that one of the cross-furrow cells will always form the mesentoblast cell, which will subsequently divide to form most of the internal structures (e.g. muscle) of the larva, apart from the gut. The cross-furrow cell which will form the mesentoblast gradually penetrates into the centre of the embryo during the 32-cell stage, it divides 20 min after its neighbours have completed the next round of division, and it divides unequally to form one large mesentoblast cell at the centre of the embryo and one superficial cell (Fig. 2.4.8). This unequal division defines the dorsal–ventral organization of the embryo; it is for the first time possible to predict which cells will form the left and ventral parts and which will form the right and dorsal parts.

It has been shown that if either of these cross-furrow cells is pricked and killed then the other will take its place [8]. It was very important in the interpretation of these experiments that this substitution should occur in more than fifty per cent of cases because it is not clear which is the normal mesentoblast precursor when killing occurs. This condition was met and it was shown that the new central cell had exactly the same delayed and unequal cell division as its normal counterpart. Additional experiments showed that this asynchrony did not occur if the central cell was prevented from touching and establishing gap junctions with the cells near the animal

pole [63], suggesting that a cell interaction is necessary for initiating division asynchrony; the change probably involves alterations in the length of the G_2 phase of the cell cycle [4, 5]. Nobody knows if one of the cross-furrow cells is usually at an advantage in this movement to the centre. There might be an inherited bias from early oogenesis.

In summary, the zygote inherits developmental tendencies from the oocyte. These include the animal–vegetal organization of the zygote and elements controlling cleavage direction. The expression of dorsal–ventral organization depends absolutely on the pattern of cleavage and on the cell interactions it generates.

Nematode development

In contrast to snails and limpets, whose development has been studied since the earliest days of embryological research, the nematode *Caenorhabditis elegans* is the most recent species available for the analysis of early development. Its cell lineage is described with precision, and it provides a second example of the interplay of localization, segregation by cell division, and cell interactions, in the expression of zygote organization (reviewed [24]). Segregation of capacities in the embryo depends on cell division but does not appear to be localized in fine detail in the zygote (section 2.4.2).

Control of cell division

As the embryo cleaves unequally, so large cells are set aside as founders of distinct tissues in the adult. From their origin, each founder has a distinct rhythm of cell division (see Fig. 2.4.1). The orientation of these divisions depends on cell interactions and intrinsic factors. When one cell is lysed at the 2-cell stage, then the

Fig. 2.4.7. Mollusc development. These diagrams illustrate the relative position of nuclei at successive cleavage stages of *Lymnaea*. The nuclei of corresponding cells in the four quadrants of the embryo are connected by lines to indicate the dextral and sinistral movements of nuclei and cells at each cleavage and the embryo is viewed from the animal pole. At the 8-cell stage (a), the four micromeres (1a–1d) are formed slightly to the right of the four macromeres (1A–1D) when viewed from the animal pole. This clockwise twist corresponds to the direction of coiling in the adult shell when viewed from its apex. The next set of micromeres (2a–2d) are formed to the left of the macromeres to give the 16-cell stage (b), and the next set (3a–3d) are formed to the right of the macromeres (c). At this 24-cell stage, the 3D

cell protrudes to the centre of embryo, occupying the previous cleavage cavity. Here it divides before the other macromeres to give the M cell which will form most of the internal contents of the snail. The contact of 3D with the micromeres 1d¹, 1c² and 1d² is thought to delay their division to give the asymmetric 44-cell stage (d). (From van den Biggelaar [3, 4, 6].)

Bottom left. The timing of division and cell lineage of *Lymnaea*, starting at the 4-cell stage at 22–26°C. The 4-cell stage is reached at about 4 hours after the second polar body is extruded. (From van den Biggelaar [4].)

Part (e) shows the young larva to illustrate the tissues formed from cells in the lineage diagram. (After Raven [87].)

cleavage pattern of the remaining cell alters [65]. In isolation, each cell of the 2-cell stage has a different cleavage pattern showing that there are differences in their intrinsic organization.

Patterns of cleavage can be shown to depend on maternally coded capacities at the slightly later 16–50 cell stage. Two maternal-effect mutants alter the relative timing of cell division and cell migration of the gut precursor cells at this stage and the disarray caused by these mutants depends on the extent to which timing is

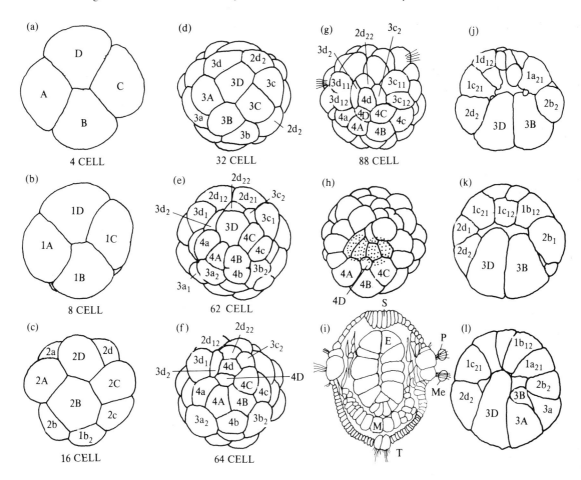

Fig. 2.4.8. Mollusc cleavage. Vegetal pole views of the cleavage pattern of the limpet, *Patella*. At 182 min post fertilization in the 4-cell stage (a) there are two cells which touch at the vegetal pole, and although these are labelled B and D for convenience, there is no means of telling which is which until one of them divides to form the internal contents of the limpet trochophore larva. The lettering of the cells is therefore arbitary until the late 32-cell stage. The two cross furrow cells maintain this cell contact through the dextral and sinistral alternating cleavages to give the 8-cell stage (b), 16-cell stage (c), and 32-cell stage (d), which is reached at 253 min post fertilization. This stage lasts 90 min and during it one cell (now known to be 3D) occupies the central cavity of the embryo, pushes 3A, 3B, and 3C aside, and makes contact with the micromeres. This process is illustrated in sections: (j) at 10 min after the start of the 32-cell stage, (k) 20 min later, (l) 40 min later. The cleavage of 3D is delayed compared to 3A–3C so that there is a definite 62-cell stage (e) before it divides to give a small superficial cell 4D and 4d whose main contents occupy the centre of the 64-cell stage (f). The micromeres in each quadrant now divide asynchronously to give the 88-cell stage (g) and then 4d divides before 4a–4c to form the two internal cells M_1 and M_2 which are indicated by stippling and which will give rise to most of the internal contents of the larva (h). The structure of the trochophore larva is illustrated in cross section. It has a sensory plate (S) and cilia arranged as bands in the protroch (P), metatroch (Me), and telotroch (T) which allow it to swim. Internally there is the gut endoderm (E), and mesoderm (M). (After van den Biggelaar [7, 8].)

The lineage diagram of *Patella* is similar to that of *Lymnaea* (Fig. 2.4.7) although the timing of cleavage is quite different.

altered [71, 102]. The expression of these mutants is temperature sensitive, and it is therefore possible to show that the abnormality only occurs when the actions of the mutant genes are executed at this stage. This coincidence of mutant gene action and the altered cleavage timing suggests that there is a causal relation between cleavage timing and cell allocation.

In summary, normal embryogenesis in *Caenorhabditis elegans* depends on the segregation of capacities (section 2.4.2), and the cleavage pattern depends on inherited tendencies which differ between cells, on maternally coded factors, and on cell interactions. The placement of cells in distinct regions of the 50-cell embryo depends both on the geometry of cleavage and its timing, and on the migration of cells. Embryogenesis flowers from a composite of cellular functions.

2.4.6   ZYGOTES AS DEVELOPMENTAL FIELDS

So far we have discussed early embryogenesis as if it could be explained by a series of local interactions. For many embryologists such an account is inadequate. They object on the practical grounds that such analyses have failed to provide a complete account of the build up of organization in any one embryo. They object on the theoretical grounds that it is limited to think of embryogenesis as a collection of local events when all the parts are within an interacting whole embryo. These embryologists find it more appropriate to think of the embryo as a complete interdependent system (an embryonic field [37]; see also Chapter 2.3 and extensive discussion in Chapter 4.2).

The failure to provide a local cause-and-effect account of embryogenesis is obvious in large developing systems where cell distinctions arise in populations of many cells. Here the failure is discussed for the amphibians and the insect *Drosophila*; it is later described for slime moulds and for insects in general (Chapters 4.2 and 5.2).

Amphibian development

Various asymmetries develop in amphibian eggs during oogenesis and fertilization (see Chapter 2.2.4). There is little evidence for detail in zygote structure because one-quarter of the egg can form a whole tadpole and the only constraint is that a part of the grey crescent should be in the developing nucleated part [9, 61, 75].

Development begins with unequal cell divisions. Dorsal–ventral distinctions may be expressed as early as the 2nd cleavage in some species; the dorsal cells are smaller. Animal–vegetal distinctions are usually first expressed as an unequal supra-equatorial 3rd cleavage; the animal cells are smaller. Subsequently, cells are larger in the vegetal ventral parts when compared to the dorsal animal parts up to the gastrula stage, for in this period all the cells of the embryo complete one round of cell division before any cell starts the next round of division (*Xenopus laevis* [101], *Ambystoma mexicanum* [47]).

Within this rhythm of nearly synchronous divisions, there are local details. Starting at the 4th cleavage, the dorsal animal cells start to divide first, and they continue to initiate new rounds of division ahead of the other cells of the embryo up to the end of the gastrula stage [101].

There is a wealth of information concerning the mechanisms which may control the cell cycles of the amphibian embryo [1, 12, 48, 59, 64]. Unfortunately, there is no direct evidence that either the timing or the inequality of these cleavages is in any way necessary for normal development. Cleavage orientation seems to be irrelevant because flattened embryos with disturbed cleavage planes soon spring back into shape and continue to develop normally when the pressure is released [72]. Perhaps cleavage disorientation never disrupts the inherent radial organization of the embryo which is apparent in the membranes of each blastomere of a normal 16- to 32-cell-stage embryo; each cell is polarized with a non-adhesive crumpled bare external surface and an adhesive internal surface covered with microvilli, concanavalin A receptors and natural lectin receptors [95–97].

Too little is known about local events in these early cells to provide a causal analysis of amphibian embryogenesis. Certainly cells derived from the grey crescent gradually acquire the property of inducing second dorsal–ventral organization and this organization first becomes fixed in the vegetal cells of the blastula [36, 75], but such observations hardly amount to an explanation of development.

It is therefore tempting to treat the zygote as a whole system, the cleavage planes and position of gastrulation of which are the expression of mathematical rules and constraints [38, 126]. Such explanations are intellectually fun and they have the virtue that they are comprehensive. One would like to know if the fields of early

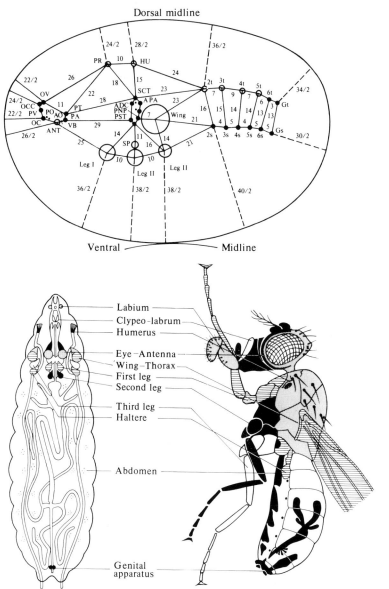

Fig. 2.4.9. Fate mapping in *Drosophila*. The cells of the blastoderm are allocated to the formation of two bodies, that of the larva and that of the adult fly. The progenitor cells of the adult lie in small groups (the imaginal discs) inside the larva (b), and each disc is determined to form discrete structures in the adult (c). Fate mapping depends on creating two populations of genetically different nuclei within the same embryo. This can be achieved in two ways. A common method is to use *Drosophila* stocks in which one of the X chromosomes of female XX embryos is lost from one progeny nucleus at the first mitotic division. If the remaining X chromosome contains a recessive gene, then it will only be expressed by the XO cells and by observing the cells which express this gene it is possible to discover which parts of he larva and fly are formed from each nucleus at the two nuclear stage. It is found that each nucleus usually contributes about half the cells of the body. In most parts of the body the derivatives of each nucleus are in discrete patches and there is a sharp borderline between them: in a few internal organs such as the Malpighian tubules the two populations of cells are known to intermingle.

The borderline between the two populations of cells may cut across any set of adult tissues although there is a tendency for the border to run along the midline and segment edges of adult flies. The explanation of these tendencies appears to be that each side of the adult fly and each segment is formed from a pair of discs which arise far apart in the early embryo and which come together during embryogenesis.

The frequency with which the border falls between larval and adult structures can be used to estimate the distance between the progenitors of these structures at earlier stages of development. An example is given in (a) which is a projection of adult structures onto the right half of the egg at an early stage of development (seen from inside the egg). Distances between structures are indicated in sturts (i.e. the probability in percentage points that the border will fall between the two structures). Dotted lines indicate the distance to the nearest midline measured by dividing in half the number of sturts to the same structure on the other side of the body. Abbreviations: ADC, anterior dorsocentral bristle; AO, anterior orbital bristle; ANP, anterior notopleural bristle; APA, anterior bristle; AO, anterior orbital bristle; APA, anterior postalar bristle; Gt, genital tergite; Gs, genital sternite; HU, humeral bristles; OC, ocellar bristle; OCC, occiput; OV, outer vertical bristle; PA, palp; PNP, posterior notopleural bristle; PO, posterior orbital bristle; PR, proboscis; PT, postorbital bristles; PV, postvertical bristle; SP, sternopleural bristles; VB, vibrisae; 1t, first abdominal tergite; 1s, first abdominal sternite. Data of Hotta and Benzer based on 703 mosaic flies [53]. The problems of fate mapping in this way are discussed in detail elsewhere [33, 56, 67, 127].

A second method of creating two nuclear populations in the embryo is to X-irradiate and to produce mutant cells which express recessive markers by somatic recombination. Irradiation causes cell death and this method can only be used after the embryo is cellular at about the 6000 cell stage. When irradiation is conducted at this time, then some mutant clones may contribute to several discs so that the progeny of one clone may contribute to part of the wing and second leg. When irradiation is conducted later, then the clones are further restricted and it is possible to build up a family tree of clones to derive a lineage map.

embryogenesis which they describe are no more than the expressed capacity of the embryo to spring back into shape after compression. One would also like to know if this capacity is inherent in the radial organization of the membrane domains or whether it depends on the rhythmic cell-shape changes which usually keep time with each cell cycle [46, 59]. The cell shapes and movements of gastrulation are described in Chapter 3.3 and later embryology and tissue interactions of Amphibia are discussed in Chapter 4.3.

Insect development

Insect development provides the second example of an embryogenesis in which distinction of early cell types is thought to build up in response to field phenomena (reviewed in detail in Chapter 4.2). Such a treatment is needed both because it is difficult to provide detailed local explanations and because several maternal-effect mutants and experimental manipulations reorient most of the structures of the embryo as if it were an interacting whole.

The following account of early insect development is based on *Drosophila* species; reviews of the development of other insects can be found in [14]. In early *Drosophila* development, the nuclei initially divide in the egg cytoplasm without cell membranes and they only become surrounded by membranes when they have migrated to the periphery. In *Drosophila melanogaster*, cell walls are formed around the nuclei at the posterior at the 9th cleavage division and the rest of the nuclei are surrounded by membranes four or five divisions later. The nuclear divisions before cell wall formation are organized in space, and this organization is the basis of the fate mapping techniques in the early embryo (see legend to Fig. 2.4.9). These techniques demonstrate that the nuclei of early development are totipotent, as in many other animals and plants (see Chapter 1.2).

Cell wall formation in various parts of the embryo is under the control of maternal genes, for maternal-effect mutants alter cell wall formation in definite localities [91, 94]. There is a direct correlation between the ability to form cell walls early in development and the formation of viable germ cells [26, 70]. Unfortunately, it remains difficult to manipulate cell wall formation experimentally and so it is not clear whether or not the timing or the position of cell wall formation has anything to do with the distinction of cell types in the early embryo.

Fields

The evidence that cell distinctions build up in response to the properties of the whole interacting system comes principally from studies of two maternal-effect mutants. *Bicaudal* is a recessive maternal-effect mutant at a single locus, and homozygous mothers produce embryos which in the extreme state have two posterior ends in mirror-image symmetry; the head is completely missing [10]. A plot of the number of segments involved in this phenomenon suggests that it is the product of gradients running along the length of the egg, and the fact that all structures in the embryo except the germ-plasm are affected by the mutation indicates that the whole somatic organization of the embryo depends on these gradients (reviewed [76]).

Dorsal is also a recessive maternal-effect mutant on a small region of the chromosome, and homozygous mothers produce embryos which only contain dorsal structures; the derivatives of the ventral region of the blastoderm are missing. The embryos do not invaginate and they lack internal organs. This mutant is interpreted as a defect in the dorsal–ventral gradients which are thought normally to specify structures around the circumference of the blastoderm [76, 77].

In both instances, the simplest view is that the *Drosophila* egg normally contains a variety of gradients and that the somatic cells respond to levels of the gradients by expressing distinct features. In both insects and amphibians it has then been necessary to treat the early cell distinctions as field phenomena. Perhaps local explanations will be possible in the future.

2.4.7   CONCLUSIONS

(1) The way in which zygote organization is translated into differential gene expression in the correct location is not understood.

(2) In many animals, the cleavage divisions segregate developmental capacity.

(3) In many embryos, the cleavage divisions place cells in different relative positions and expose the cells to distinct environments.

(4) In many embryos, the cleavage divisions form cells of different relative size which have distinct properties.

(5) In a few embryos, the build-up of cell distinctions appears to depend on interactions across all the cells of the embryo.

2.4.8 REFERENCES

*Indicates useful reviews

1   Benbow R.M., Joenje H., White S.H., Breaux C.B., Krauss M.R., Ford C.C. & Laskey R.A. (1977) Cytoplasmic control of nuclear replication in *Xenopus laevis*. In *International Cell Biology, 1976–77*. (Eds B.R. Brinkley & K.R. Porter), pp. 453–463. Rockefeller University Press, New York.

2   Berrill N.J. (1955) *The Origin of Vertebrates*. Oxford University Press, Oxford.

3   Biggelaar J.A.M. van den (1971) Development of division asynchrony and bilateral symmetry in the first quartet of micromeres in the egg of *Lymnaea. J. Embryol. exp. Morph.*, **26**, 393–399.

4   Biggelaar J.A.M. van den (1971) Timing of the phases of the cell cycle during the period of asynchronous cell division up to the 49-cell stage in *Lymnaea. J. Embryol. exp. Morph.*, **26**, 367–391.

5   Biggelaar, J.A.M. van den (1971) Timing of the phase of the cell cycle with tritiated thymidine and feulgen cytophotometry during the period of synchronous division in *Lymnaea. J. Embryol. exp. Morph.*, **26**, 351–365.

6   Biggelaar J.A.M. van den (1976) Development of dorsoventral polarity preceding the formation of the mesentoblast in *Lymnaea stagnalis. Proc. K. ned. Akad. Wet.*, **C79**, 112–126.

7   Biggelaar J.A.M. van den (1977) Development of dorsoventral polarity and mesentoblast determination in *Patella vulgata. J. Morph.*, **154**, 157–186.

8   Biggelaar J.A.M. van den & Guerrier P. (1979) Dorsoventral polarity and mesentoblast determination as concomitant results of cellular interactions in the mollusc *Patella vulgata. Devl. Biol.*, **68**, 462–471.

*9   Brachet J. (1977) An old enigma: the gray crescent of amphibian eggs. *Curr. Tops Devl. Biol.*, **11**, 133–186.

10 Bull A.L. (1966) *Bicaudal*, a genetic factor which effects the polarity of the embryo in *Drosophila melanogaster. J. exp. Zool*, **161**, 221–242.

11 Catalano G., Eilbeck C., Monroy A. & Paris G. (1979) A model for early segregation of territories in the ascidian egg. In *Cell Lineage, Stem Cells, and Cell Determination*. (Ed. N. le Douarin), pp. 15–28. North-Holland, Amsterdam.

12 Chulitskaia E.V. (1970) Desynchronization of cell divisions in the course of egg cleavage and an attempt at experimental shift of its onset. *J. Embryol. exp. Morph.*, **23**, 359–374.

13 Costantini F.D., Britten R.J. & Davidson E.H. (1980) Message sequences and short repetitive sequences as interspersed in sea urchin egg poly (A)⁺ RNAs. *Nature, Lond.*, **287**, 111–117.

14 Counce S.J. & Waddington C.H. (eds) (1972) *Developmental Systems, Insects*. (Two volumes.) Academic Press, London.

15 Crampton H.E. (1894) Reversal of cleavage in a sinistral gasteropod. *Ann. N.Y. Acad. Sci.*, **8**, 167–170.

16 Dan-Sohkawa M. & Satoh N. (1978) Studies on dwarf larvae developed from isolated blastomeres of the starfish *Asterina pectinifera. J. Emryol. exp. Morph.*, **46**, 171–185.

17 Deppe U., Schierenberg E., Colte T., Krieg C., Schmitt D., Yoder B. & von Ehrenstein G. (1978) Cell lineages of the embryo of the nematode *Caenorhabditis elegans. Proc. natl Acad. Sci., USA*, **75**, 376–380.

*18 Dohmen M.R. & Verdonk N.H. (1979) The ultrastructure and role of the polar lobe in development of molluscs. In *Determin-ants of Spatial Organization* (Eds S. Subtelny & I.R. Konigsberg), pp. 3–27. Academic Press, New York.

19 Dongen C.A.M. van (1976) The development of *Dentalium* with special reference to the significance of the polar lobe. *Proc. K. ned. Akad. Wet.*, **C79**, 245–266.

20 Dongen C.A.M. van & Geilenkirchen W.L.M. (1974) The development of *Dentalium* with special reference to the significance of the polar lobe. *Proc. K. ned. Akad. Wet.*, **C77**, 57–100.

21 Driesch H. (1900) Die isolierten Blastomeren des Echinidenkeimes. *Arch. Entw Mech Org.*, **26**, 361–410.

22 Durante M. (1956) Cholinesterase in the development of *Ciona intestinalis. Experientia*, **12**, 307–308.

23 Durante M. (1957) Cholinesterase in the anterior and posterior hemiembryos of *Ciona intestinalis. Acta Embryol. Morph. exp.*, **1**, 131–133.

*24 Ehrenstein G. von & Schierenberg E. (1980) Cell lineages and development of *Caenorhabditis elegans* and other nematodes. In *Nematodes as Biological Models, Vol. 1, Behavioural and Developmental Models* (Ed. B.M. Zuckerman), pp. 1–71. Academic Press, New York.

25 Ernst S.G., Hough-Evans B.R., Britten R.J. & Davidson E.H. (1980) Limited complexity of the RNA in micromeres of sixteen-cell sea urchin embryos. *Devl. Biol.*, **79**, 119–127.

26 Fielding C.J. (1967) Developmental genetics of the mutant grandchildless *Drosophila subobscura. J. Embryol. exp. Morph.*, **17**, 375–384.

27 Freeman G. (1976a) The effects of altering the position of cleavage planes on the process of localization of developmental potential in ctenophores. *Devl. Biol.*, **51**, 332–337.

28 Freeman G. (1976b) The role of cleavage in the localization of developmental potential in the ctenophore *Mnemiopsis leidyi. Devl. Biol.*, **49**, 143–177.

29 Freeman G. (1977) Establishment of oral–aboral axis in the ctenophore embryo. *J. Embryol. exp. Morph.*, **42**, 237–260.

30 Freeman G. (1978) The role of asters in the localization of the factors that specify the apical tuft and the gut of the nemertine *Cerebratulus lacteus. J. exp. Zool.*, **206**, 81–107.

*31 Freeman G. (1979) The multiple roles which cell division can play in the localization of developmental potential. In *Determinants of Spatial Organization* (Eds S. Subtelny & I.R. Konigsberg), pp. 53–76. Academic Press, New York.

32 Freeman G. & Reynolds G.I. (1973) The development of bioluminescence in the ctenophore *Mnemiopsis leidyi. Devl. Biol.*, **31**, 61–100.

*33 Garcia-Bellido A. & Ripoll P. (1978) Cell lineage and differentiation in *Drosophila*. In *Genetic Mosaics and Cell Differentiation* (Ed. W.J. Gehring), pp. 119–156. Springer-Verlag, Berlin.

*34a Gardner R.L. & Papaioannou V.E. (1975) Differentiation in the trophectoderm and inner cell mass. In *The Early Development of Mammals* (Eds M. Balls & A.E. Wild), pp. 107–132. Cambridge University Press, Cambridge.

34b Gardner R.L. (1982) Investigation of cell lineage and differentiation in the endoderm of the mouse embryo. *J. Embryol. exp. Morph.*, **68**, 175–198.

35 Gardner R.L. & Rossant J. (1979) Investigation of the fate of 4.5 day post-coitum mouse inner cell mass cells by blastocyst injection. *J. Embryol. exp. Morph.*, **52**, 141–152.

36   Gerhart J., Ubbels G., Hara K. & Kirschner M. (1981) A reinvestigation of the role of the grey crescent in axis formation in *Xenopus laevis*. *Nature, Lond.*, **292**, 511–516.

37   Goodwin B.C. (1977) Mechanics, fields, and statistical mechanics in developmental biology. *Proc. R. Soc. Lond. B*, **199**, 404–414.

38   Goodwin B.C. & Trainor L.E.H. (1980) A field description of the cleavage process in embryogenesis. *J. theor. Biol.*, **85**, 757–770.

39   Graham C.F. & Deussen Z.A. (1978) Features of cell lineage in preimplantation mouse development. *J. Embryol. exp. Morph.*, **48**, 53–72.

40   Graham C.F. & Lehtonen E. (1979) Formation and consequences of cell patterns in preimplantation mouse development. *J. Embryol. exp. Morph.*, **49**, 277–294.

41   Graham C.F. & Lehtonen E. (1979) Analysis of cell behaviour in the preimplantation mouse lineage. In *Cell Lineage, Stem Cells and Cell Determination* (Ed. N. le Douarin), pp. 37–47. Elsevier/North-Holland, Amsterdam.

42   Guerrier P. (1970) Les caractères de la segmentation et la détermination de la polarité dorsoventrale dans le développement de quelques *Spiralia*. II. *Sabellaria alveolata* (Annélide polychète). *J. Embryol. exp. Morph.*, **23**, 639–655.

43   Guerrier P., Biggelaar J.A.M. van den, Dongen C.A.M. van & Verdonk N.H. (1978) Significance of the polar lobe for the determination of dorsoventral polarity in *Dentalium vulgare* (da Costa). *Devl. Biol.*, **63**, 233–242.

44   Gulyas B.J. (1975) A re-examination of cleavage patterns in eutherian mammals: rotation of blastomere pairs during cleavage in the rabbit. *J. exp. Zool.*, **193**, 235–248.

45   Handyside A.H. (1978) Time of commitment of inside cells isolated from preimplantation mouse embryos. *J. Embryol. exp. Morph.*, **45**, 37–53.

46   Hara K. (1971) Cinematographic observation of "surface contraction waves" (SCW) during early cleavage of axolotl eggs. *Wilhelm Roux' Archiv.*, **167**, 183–186.

47   Hara K. (1977) The cleavage pattern of the axolotl egg studied by cinematography and cell counting. *Wilhelm Roux' Archiv.*, **181**, 73–87.

48   Harland R.M. & Laskey R.A. (1980) Regulated replication of DNA micro-injected into eggs of *Xenopus laevis*. *Cell*, **21**, 761–771.

49   Harris P., Osborn M. & Weber K. (1980) Distribution of tubulin-containing structures in the egg of the sea urchin *Strongylocentrotus purpuratus* from fertilization through first cleavage. *J. Cell Biol.*, **80**, 211–218.

50   Harris P., Osborn M. & Weber K. (1980) A spiral array of microtubules in the fertilized sea urchin egg cortex examined by indirect immunofluorescence and electron microscopy. *Expl. Cell Res.*, **126**, 227–236.

51   Hillman N.H., Sherman M.I. & Graham C.F. (1972) The effect of spatial arrangement on cell determination during mouse development. *J. Embryol. exp. Morph.*, **28**, 263–278.

*52   Hörstadius S. (1973) *Experimental Embryology of Echinoderms*. Oxford University Press, Oxford.

*53   Hotta Y. & Benzer S. (1973) Mapping behaviour in *Drosophila* mosaics. In *Genetic Mechanisms in Development* (Ed. F.H. Ruddle), pp. 129–167. Academic Press, New York.

54   Hynes, R.O. & Gross P.R. (1970) A method for separating cells from early sea urchin embryos. *Devl. Biol.*, **21**, 383–402.

55   Hynes R.O., Raff R.A. & Gross P.R. (1972) Properties of the three cell types in sixteen-cell sea urchin embryos: Aggregation and micro-tubule protein synthesis. *Devl. Biol.*, **27**, 150–164.

*56   Janning W. (1978) Gynandromorph fate maps in *Drosophila*. In *Genetic Mosaics and Cell Differentiation* (Ed. W.J. Gehring), pp. 1–28. Springer-Verlag, Berlin.

57   Johnson M.H. & Ziomek C. (1981) The foundation of two distinct cell lineages within the mouse morula. *Cell*, **24**, 71–80.

58   Kelly S.J. (1977) Studies on the developmental potential of 4- and 8-cell stage mouse blastomeres. *J. exp. Zool.*, **200**, 365–376.

*59   Kirschner M., Gerhart J.C., Hara K. & Ubbels G.A. (1980) Initiation of the cell cycle and establishment of bilateral symmetry in *Xenopus* eggs. In *The Cell Surface: Mediator of Developmental Processes* (Eds S. Subtelny & N. K. Wessels), pp. 187–215. Academic Press, New York.

60   Kitajima T. & Okazaki K. (1980) Spicule formation *in vitro* by descendants of precocious micromere formed at the 8-cell stage of sea urchin embryo. *Develop. Growth Diff.*, **22**, 265–279.

61   Kobayakawa Y. & Kubota H.Y. (1981) Temporal pattern of cleavage and the onset of gastrulation in amphibian embryos developed from eggs with reduced cytoplasm. *J. Embryol. exp. Morph.*, **62**, 83–94.

62   Kreig G., Cole T., Deppe U., Schierenberg E., Schmitt D., Yoder B. & von Ehrenstein G. (1978) The cellular anatomy of the embryo of *Caenorhabditis elegans*. *Devl. Biol.*, **65**, 193–215.

63   Laat S.W. de, Tertoolen L.G.J., Dorresteijn, A.W.C. & Biggelaar J.A.M. van den (1980) Intercellular patterns are involved in cell determination in early molluscan embryos. *Nature, Lond.*, **287**, 546–548.

64   Landström U., L:.ovtrup-Rein H. & L:.ovtrup S. (1975) Control of cell division and cell differentiation by deoxynucleotides in the early embryo of *Xenopus laevis*. *Cell Differ.*, **4**, 313–325.

65   Laufer J.S., Bazzicalupo P. & Wood W.B. (1980) Segregation of developmental potential in early embryos of *Caenorhabditis elegans*. *Cell*, **19**, 569–577.

66   Laufer J.S. & von Ehrenstein G. (1981) Nematode development after removal of egg cytoplasm: absence of localized unbound determinants. *Science, N.Y.*, **211**, 402–405.

*67   Lawrence P.A. & Morata G. (1976) The compartment hypothesis. In *Insect Development* (Ed. P.A. Lawrence), pp. 132–149. Blackwell Scientific Publications, Oxford.

68   Lehtonen E. (1980) Changes in cell dimensions and intracellular contacts during cleavage-stage cell cycles in mouse embryonic cells. *J. Embryol. exp. Morph.*, **58**, 231–249.

69   Lewis W.H. & Hartmann C.G. (1933) Early cleavage stages of the egg of the monkey (Macau rhesus). *Contr. Embryol. Carneg. Instn.*, **24**, 189–202.

*70   Mahowald A.P. (1977) The germ plasm of *Drosophila*: an experimental system for the analysis of determination. *Amer. Zool.*, **17**, 551–563.

71   Miwa J., Schierenberg E., Miwa S. & von Ehrenstein G. (1980) Genetics and mode of expression of temperature-sensitive mutations arresting embryonic development in *Caenorhabditis elegans*. *Devl. Biol.*, **76**, 160–174.

72   Morgan T.H. (1927) *Experimental Embryology*. Columbia University Press, New York.

73   Morrill J.B., Blair C.A. & Larsen W.J. (1973) Regulative development in the pulmonate gastropod *Lymnaea palustris*, as determined by blastomere deletion experiments. *J. exp. Zool.*, **183**, 47–55.

74   Murray J. (1975) The genetics of Mollusca. In *The Handbook of Genetics*, **3**, 31 (Ed. R.C. King). Plenum Press, New York.

*75   Nieuwkoop P.D. (1977) Origin and establishment of embryonic polar axes in amphibian development. *Curr. Tops Devl. Biol.*, **11**, 133–186.

*76   Nüsslein-Volhard C. (1979) Maternal effect mutations that alter the spatial coordinates of the embryo of *Drosophila melanogaster*. In *Determinants of Spatial Organization* (Eds S. Subtelny & I.R. Konigsberg), pp. 185–211. Academic Press, New York.

77   Nüsslein-Volhard C., Lohs-Schardin M., Sander K. & Cremer C. (1980) A dorso-ventral shift of embryonic primordia in a new maternal-effect mutant of *Drosophila*. *Nature, Lond.*, **283**, 474–476.

78   Okazaki K. (1975) Spicule formation by isolated micromeres of the sea-urchin embryo. *Amer. Zool.*, **15**, 567–581.

79   Ortolani G. (1955) The presumptive territory of the mesoderm in the ascidian germ. *Experientia*, **15**, 445–446.

80   Ortolani G. (1962) Territorio presumptivo del sistema nervoso nelle larvae di ascidie. *Acta Embryol. Morph. exp.*, **5**, 189–198.

81   Ortolani G. (1964) Origine dell'organo apicale e dei derivati mesodermici nello sviluppo embrionale di ctenofori. *Acta Embryol. Morph. exp.*, **7**, 191–200.

82   Pratt H.P.M., Chakraborty J. & Surani. M.A.H. (1981) Molecular and morphological differentiation of the mouse blastocyst after manipulations of compaction using cytochalasin B. *Cell*, **26**, 279–292.

83   Randle B.R. (1982) Cosegregation of monoclonal antibody reactivity and cell behaviour in the mouse pre-implantation embryo. *J. Embryol. exp. Morph.* **10**, 261–278.

*84   Rappaport R. (1974) Cleavage. In *Concepts of Development* (Eds J. Lash & J.R. Whittaker), pp. 76–98. Sinauer, Stamford.

85   Rappaport R. (1975) The biophysics of cleavage and cleavage of geometrically altered cells. In *The Sea Urchin Embryo* (Ed. G. Czihak), pp. 308–332. Springer-Verlag, Berlin.

86   Raven C.P. (1963) The nature and origin of the cortical morphogenetic field in *Lymnaea*. *Devl. Biol.*, **7**, 130–143.

87   Raven C.P. (1966) *Morphogenesis; the Analysis of Molluscan Development*. Pergamon Press, Oxford.

88   Raven C.P. (1967) The distribution of special cytoplasmic differentiation of the egg during cleavage in *Lymnaea stagnalis*. *Devl. Biol.*, **16**, 407–437.

89   Raven C.P. (1972) Determination and direction of spiral coiling in *Lymnaea peregra*. *Acta morph. néerl.-scand.*, **10**, 165–178.

90   Raven C.P. (1974) Further observations on the distribution of cytoplasmic substances among the cleavage cells of *Lymnaea stagnalis*. *J. Embryol. exp. Morph.*, **31**, 37–59.

91   Regenass U. & Bernhard H.P. (1978) Analysis of *Drosophila* maternal effect mutant MAT (3) 1 by pole cell transplantation experiments. *Molec. Gen. Genet.*, **164**, 85–91.

92   Reverberi G. (1971) Ctenophores. In *Experimental Embryology of Marine and Freshwater Invertebrates* (Ed. G. Reverberi), pp. 85–103. North-Holland, Amsterdam.

93   Reverberi G. (1971) Ascidians. In *Experimental Embryology of Marine and Freshwater Invertebrates* (Ed. G. Reverberi), pp. 507–550. North-Holland, Amsterdam.

94   Rice T.B. & Garen A. (1975) Localized defects of blastoderm formation in maternal effect mutants of *Drosophila*. *Devl. Biol.*, **43**, 277–286.

95   Roberson M.M. & Armstrong P.B. (1979) Regional segregation of Con.A receptors on dissociated embryo cells. *Expl. Cell Res.*, **122**, 23–29.

96   Roberson M.M. & Armstrong P.B. (1980) Carbohydrate-binding component of amphibian embryo cell surfaces: restriction to surface regions capable of adhesion. *Proc. natl Acad. Sci, USA*, **77**, 3460–3463.

97   Roberson M.M., Armstrong J. & Armstrong P.B. (1980) Adhesive and non-adhesive membrane domains of amphibian embryo cells. *J. Cell. Sci.*, **44**, 19–31.

98   Rossant J. (1976) Postimplantation development of blastomeres isolated from 4- and 8-cell mouse eggs. *J. Embryol. exp. Morph.*, **36**, 283–290.

99   Rossant J. & Lis W.T. (1979) Potential of isolated mouse inner cell masses to form trophectoderm derivatives *in vivo*. *Devl. Biol.*, **70**, 000–000.

*100 Rossant J. & Papaioannou V.E. (1977) The biology of embryogenesis. In *Concepts in Mammalian Development* (Ed. M.I. Sherman). pp. 1–36. M.I.T. Press, Cambridge, Massachusetts.

101   Satoh N. (1977) Metachronous cleavage and initiation of gastrulation in amphibian embryos. *Devel. Growth Diff.*, **19**, 111–117.

102   Schierenberg E., Miwa J. & von Ehrenstein G. (1980) Cell lineages and developmental defects of temperature-sensitive embryonic arrest mutants in *Caenorhabditis elegans*. *Devl. Biol.*, **76**, 141–159.

103   Senger D.R. & Gross P.R. (1978) Macromolecule synthesis and determination in sea urchin blastomeres at the sixteen-cell stage. *Devl. Biol.*, **65**, 404–415.

104   Senger D.R., Arceci R.J. & Gross P.R. (1978) Histones of sea urchin embryos. Transients in transcription, translation, and the composition of chromatin. *Devl. Biol.*, **65**, 416–425.

105   Smith D.L. & Ecker R.E. (1970) Uterine suppression of biochemical and morphogenetic events in *Rana pipiens*. *Devl. Biol.*, **22**, 622–637.

106   Smith L.J. (1980) Embryonic axis orientation in the mouse and its correlation with blastocyst relationship in the uterus. *J. Embryol. exp. Morph.*, **55**, 257–277.

107   Snell G.D. & Stevens L.C. (1966) Early embryology. In *Biology of the Laboratory Mouse* (Ed. E.L. Green), pp. 205–245. McGraw-Hill, New York.

108   Spiegel M. & Spiegel E.S. (1975) The reaggregation of dissociated embryonic sea urchin eggs. *Amer. Zool.*, **15**, 583–606.

109   Surani M.A.H., Barton S.C. & Burling A. (1980) Differentiation of 2-cell and 8-cell mouse embryos arrested by cytoskeletal inhibitors. *Expl. Cell Res.*, **125**, 275–286.

110   Tanaka Y. (1976) Effects of surfactants on the cleavage and further development of the sea urchin embryo. 1. The inhibition of micromere function at the fourth cleavage. *Devel. Growth Diff.*, **18**, 113–122.

111   Tarkowski A.K. (1976) Haploid mouse blastocysts developed from bisected zygotes. *Nature, Lond.*, **259**, 663–665.

112   Tarkowski A.K. & Wroblewska J. (1967) Development of blastomeres of mouse eggs isolated at the 4- and 8-cell stage. *J. Embryol. exp. Morph.*, **18**, 155–180.

113   Tufaro F. & Brandhorst B.P. (1979) Similarity of proteins

synthesized by isolated blastomeres of early sea urchin embryos. *Devl. Biol.*, **72**, 390–397.

114   Ubbels G.A., Bezem J.J. & Raven C.P. (1969) Analysis of follicle cell patterns in dextral and sinistral *Lymnaea peregra. J. Embryol. exp. Morph.*, **21**, 445–466.

115   Verdonk N.H. (1968) The relation of the two blastomeres to the polar lobe in *Dentalium. J. Embryol. exp. Morph.*, **20**, 101–105.

*116   Verdonk N.H. (1979) Symmetry and asymmetry in the embryonic development of molluscs. In *Pathways in Malacology* (Eds S. van der Spoel, A.C. van Bruggen & J. Lever), pp. 25–45. Scheltema & Holkema, Utrecht.

117   Whittaker J.R. (1973) Segregation during ascidian embyrogenesis of egg cytoplasmic information for tissue-specific enzyme development. *Proc. natl Acad. Sci. USA*, **70**, 2096–2100.

118   Whittaker J.R. (1973) Evidence for localization of RNA templates for alkaline phosphatase in an ascidian egg. *Biol. Bull.*, **145**, 459–460.

*119   Whittaker J.R. (1979) Cytoplasmic determinants of tissue differentiation in the ascidian egg. In *Determinants of Spatial Organization* (Eds S. Subtelny & I.R. Konigsberg), pp. 29–51. Academic Press, New York.

120   Whittaker J.R. (1980) Acetylcholinesterase development in extra cells caused by changing the distribution of myoplasm in ascidian embryos. *J. Embryol. exp. Morph.*, **55**, 343–354.

121   Wilson E.B. (1903) Experiments on cleavage and localization in the nemertine egg. *Arch. EntwMech. Org.*, **16**, 411–460.

122   Wilson I.B., Bolton E. & Cuttler R.H. (1972) Preimplantation differentiation in the mouse egg as revealed by microinjection of vital markers. *J. Embryol. exp. Morph.*, **27**, 467–479.

123   Yatsu N. (1911) Observations and experiments on the ctenophore egg. II. Notes on early cleavage and experiments on cleavage. *Annotnes zool. jap.*, **7**, 333–343.

124   Ziomek C.A. & Johnson M.H. (1980) Cell surface interaction induces polarization of mouse 8-cell blastomeres as compaction. *Cell*, **21**, 935–942.

125   Ziomek C.A. & Johnson M.H. (1981) Properties of polar and apolar cells from the 16-cell mouse morula. *Wilhelm Roux' Archiv.*, **190**, 287–296.

126   Zeeman E.C. (1974) Primary and secondary waves in developmental biology. In *Some Mathematical Questions in Biology*, **6**, 69–161 (also entitled *Lectures in Mathematics in the Life Sciences*, **7**, or *8th Symposium on Mathematical Biology, AAAS San Francisco, 1974*) (Ed. S.A. Levin). American Mathematical Society, Providence, Rhode Island.

127   Zalokar M., Erk I. & Santamaria P. (1980) Distribution of ring-X chromosomes in the blastoderm of gynandromorphic *D. melanogster. Vell*, **19**, 133–141.

Chapter 2.5
Determination and Pluripotentiality
P.F. Wareing and C.F. Graham

2.5.1   INTRODUCTION

Because it is a sequential process, development in a multicellular organism consisting of many different organs and tissue types must, of necessity, involve the divergence of cells or groups of cells of common lineage into contrasting paths of development at successive stages. Since the spatial relations between the various regions of a developing plant or animal embryo must follow a very regular pattern if a normal organism is to result, a particular organ or tissue of the mature organism is likely to be derived from groups of cells occupying a specific part of the embryo in different individuals. In this sense one may say that specific regions of the embryo are destined to form a particular part of the mature organism. This idea was embraced in the statement of Hans Driesch that 'the fate of a cell is a function of its position'. As it stands, this statement might be taken to imply that the pattern of differentiation of any given cell is determined by its position in the organism and that it retains its full developmental potential, so that if it were transferred to another part of the organism it would differentiate in a manner normal for that part. While it does, indeed, appear that many plant cells retain their full developmental potential (section 2.5.2), development in animals appears to involve the progressive restriction of developmental potential, so that most animal cells are no longer capable of forming a whole organism.

Such cells are described as 'determined' if they retain this restriction through many cell generations, and 'determination' is the process by which their developmental potential becomes limited. However, the expression of this restricted developmental potential is profoundly influenced by the environment in which the cell occurs, and can be modified by transferring it to another part of the organism. For instance, the range of cell types formed from the belly ectoderm of the frog gastrula may be extended by transferring it to a new site. Thus, the actual pattern of development is the result of an interaction between the intrinsic potentialities of the cell and influences from its environment. However, as is shown in Chapter 1.2, the restriction of developmental potential in determination is not, in general, accompanied by any irreversible changes in the genome of the cell. Moreover, experiments on plants and animal embryos which are described later in this chapter show that some cells can develop in a specific manner without loss in their developmental potential, so that determination is not the inevitable precondition or consequence of cellular differentiation.

2.5.2   TOTIPOTENCY OF PLANT CELLS

The regenerative capacity of plants is commonplace, as seen in the ancient horticultural practice of vegetative propagation by shoot or root cuttings which develop adventitious roots and/or buds. In shoot cuttings, a callus is frequently formed at the base of the cutting as a result of divisions arising in the cambium, and from such callus, root primordia arise. However, adventitious roots may also be formed in normal tissues of the stem, usually in the pericycle. In root cuttings, both buds roots commonly arise from callus formed from parenchyma in the younger phloem.

The development of aseptic techniques for the culture of isolated callus tissue and liquid cell suspensions has led to striking results concerning the regenerative capacities of plant cells and tissues. For an introduction to this subject see [6, 53] and for a more detailed treatment see [53a]. Callus tissue of many plant species can be cultured aseptically on a nutrient agar (solid) medium containing inorganic salts, sucrose and an organic nitrogen source, together with certain vitamins, such as thiamine, and the plant hormones indol-3yl-acetic acid (IAA) and cytokinin. Liquid cell suspension cultures are obtained by placing pieces of callus tissue in a liquid nutrient medium which is continually agitated or rotated, as a result of which small clumps of cells become detached from the callus and undergo division in suspension. As these suspended clumps of cells grow, they break up into smaller clumps which in turn undergo further growth and so maintain the culture. Liquid cell suspensions tend to have more complex nutrient requirements (probably due to leakage from the cells in a liquid medium) than callus cultures.

Unorganized callus tissue of many plant species can be induced to regenerate buds and/or roots by appropriate manipulation of the composition of the culture medium, especially of the relative concentrations of the IAA and cytokinins supplied. As will be described in Chapter 5.3, the pattern of regeneration of buds and roots by callus tissue derived from tobacco pith is profoundly affected by the relative concentrations of the two hormones—high ratios of auxin to cytokinin promoting regeneration of roots, and low ratios favouring bud regeneration. The shoots developing from the buds later develop roots in some types of callus, so that aseptic techniques have very important practical applications for the vegetative propagation of certain plant species of horticultural and

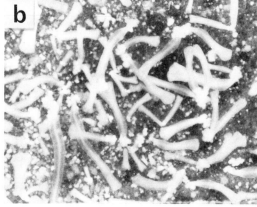

Fig. 2.5.1. Plantlets with integrated root–shoot axis and cotyledons developed in culture from carrot embryoids developing (a) in a callus and (b) in a suspension culture. Note in (b) the presence of plantlets in various stages of development and scattered amongst them the small white cell aggregates in which the embryoids arise. (Photographs by Dr Susan M. Smith. From [48].)

agricultural importance. However, even more spectacular results have been obtained with liquid suspension cultures.

In 1958 Steward [46, 47] found that if liquid suspension cultures of carrot cells were transferred to a solid agar medium containing a reduced concentration of IAA, then large numbers of embryo-like structures were obtained (Fig. 2.5.1), which could be transferred to

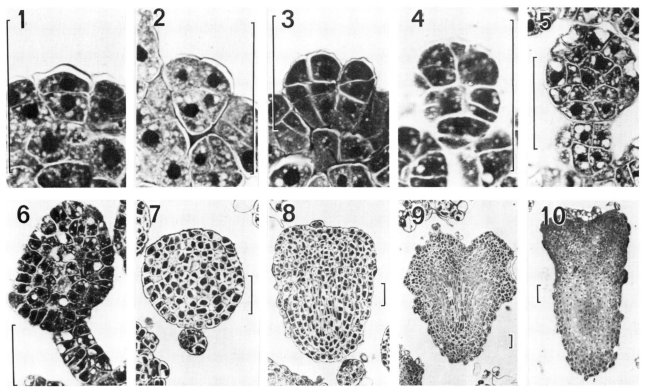

Fig. 2.5.2. Stages in embryo development observed in suspension cultures of a horticultural variety of carrot (*Daucus carota* L.) 1, two-celled stage; 2, four-celled stage; 3, two proembryos, one three-celled and one six-celled; 4, 10–12-celled; 5, globular embryo showing epidermal layer and two-tiered suspensor; 6, later globular stage; 7, fully-developed globular embryo (suspensor still attached) at stage where normally embryos are released from the embryogenic cell aggregates of the culture; 8, young heart-shaped embryo; 9, later heart-shaped embryo showing cotyledonary lobes and beginning of organization of the procambial cylinder; 10, torpedo-shaped embryo. All the above stained with toluidine blue. All scales = 50 μm. (From Street [48]).

soil and which developed into mature plants. Further studies in the early development of the plantlets showed that they originated from embryo-like structures which passed through a number of stages which resembled those of a normal zygotic embryo (p. 45). These embryo-like structures are referred to as *embryoids* or *adventive embryos*. At first it was thought that embryoids formed directly from single cells or aggregates of very few cells. However, subsequently it was shown that they arise from the surface of larger aggregates [24, 28]*. Embryoid development commences with a periclinal division in one of the surface cells and further divisions lead to stages corresponding to the globular, heart-shaped and torpedo phases of normal zygotic embryos (Fig. 2.5.2). The embryoids are uni-

*Nevertheless, whole plants can be regenerated from cultures derived from a single cell (p. 7).

formly polarized, with the root pole towards the centre of the cell clump and the shoot towards the outside.

Embryoids have been obtained with cultures of a considerable range of species. Moreover, embryogenic cultures have been derived from embryo tissue, hypocotyls and stems, storage roots, leaf mesophyll, floral buds and unicellular tissue. The ability of cells derived from such a wide variety of tissues and organs suggests that differentiation of plant cells does not involve any permanent changes in the genome and that all living plant cells are potentially capable of regenerating whole plants, i.e. they retain their totipotency. However, it has to be borne in mind that many attempts which have been made to obtain embryoids from a wide variety of species have proved unsuccessful, so that the generality of assertions concerning the totipotency of all living plant cells is not yet established. Moreover, not all the tissues

Fig. 2.5.3. Embryoids of microspore origin in an anther of *Nicotiana tabacum*. From a thesis for the University of Paris by Brigitte Norreel entitled 'La neoformation d'embryons *in vitro* chez *Daucus carota, Nicotiana tabacum* et *Datura innoxia*', 1971.

of a given species are equally competent to produce embryoids. The most prolific production of carrot embryoids is obtained by culturing a suspension of cells derived from mature carrot embryos.

A further remarkable development has been the production of embryoids from immature anthers cultured on an agar nutrient medium [3, 22]. When this is done, a certain proportion of the pollen mother cells develop into haploid embryoids instead of into pollen grains, so that the anther becomes filled with such embryoids (Fig. 2.5.3)!

Anther cultures are only successful if the anthers are excised after meiosis in the spore mother cells and before the first mitotic division giving rise to the vegetative and generative cells. Once this mitosis has occurred the cells appear to be irreversibly committed to developing into pollen grains.

Normally, the initially uninucleate pollen grains undergo an unequal division to give the larger vegetative cell and the smaller generative cell (p. 34), but in a certain proportion of grains the spindle axis in this division is at right angles to the normal orientation and two *equal* cells result which apparently cannot give rise to functional pollen grains (see Fig. 2.3.3). There is some evidence that experimental embryoids formed in anther culture are derived from pollen grains which have undergone an equal division [50]. Embryogenesis from pollen grains can only be achieved for a limited number of species, including tobacco. In some species the culture of immature anthers results in the production of

haploid callus but not embryoids.

The experimental production of embryoids has led to important practical applications in vegetative propagation and in plant breeding, since it offers great opportunities for rapidly producing large numbers of plants of the same clone. Moreover, the ability to produce haploid plants from anthers, followed by doubling of the chromosome number by colchicine treatment, makes it possible rapidly to obtain completely homozygous plants.

2.5.3 MULTIPOTENCY OF ANIMAL CELLS

We have already noted in Chapter 1.2 that there are no somatic cells in animals which can be induced to re-form a complete individual, and thus there is no animal equivalent of a totipotent plant callus or parenchyma cell. Since the nuclei of many somatic animal cells contain the genes required to code for the development of complete individuals, the implication is that there must be very stable circuits of nuclear–cytoplasmic interactions which hold the phenotypes of somatic cells in particular states. It is likely that it will soon be possible to destabilize these interactions and induce complete development of individuals from the single somatic cells of animals.

At present, we are concerned to show that many animals, like plants, may have an 'open-ended' development so that an individual body may grow from small parts of another complete body [19]. An example of such 'open-ended' development is the asexual reproduction by either budding or fragmentation of such animals as the coelenterate *Hydra* [51], the platyhelminth planarian *Stenostomum* [4, 43], and the annelid worms (reviewed [1]). Other examples of this capacity involve experimental isolation of small parts of an individual. Whole individuals can be formed from a fragment containing one-hundredth of the body size of *Hydra* [51], from a fragment of a planarian containing no more than 10 000 cells [32], from a fragment of a nemertine worm which is 1/200 000 adult size [8], and from at least one particular segment of several annelids which would usually consist of up to 30 segments as adults [1].

Source of cells for regeneration

Regeneration could occur simply by the multiplication of pre-existing cell types which would form the same cell types in the regenerate. Clearly this is not the case. In regenerating planarians, chromosomally marked derivatives of the gonads can contribute to the muscles of the pharynx [21, 42], and grafts of whole muscle (including muscle fibroblasts) can form cartilage, perichondrium, joint connective tissue, subepidermal fibroblasts and muscles in the regenerating amphibian limb [33]. In planarians it is still a possibility that all the cell types of the regenerate are formed from totipotent stem cells, like plant parenchyma cells (section 2.5.2), but there may be limits to the capacity of animal cells to change phenotype; for instance, during amphibian limb regeneration, muscle and cartilage grafts have never been found to contribute to the epidermis of the regenerate [12, 14, 33]. Nevertheless, the multipotentiality of adult animal cells is impressive and the precursors of the haemopoietic system are a good example of the persistence of developmentally multipotential stem cells into the adult (see Chapter 3.7).

Teratomas

The most extreme case of the persistence of multipotential cells in adults is the occurrence of a rare tumour, called a teratoma, which is found in several vertebrates including mouse and man (for recent reviews see [20, 35]). These tumours consist of a variety of cell types such as nerve, pigment cells, muscle, cartilage, bone, tooth and hair. In mouse and man they occur spontaneously in the testis and the ovary and they may be regarded as tumours of primordial germ cells or as tumours of the early embryonic cells, for they can be produced experimentally by grafting either early embryos or embryonic gonads to sites in adults or by culturing early embryos [17]. The stem cell of the tumour is called an embryonal carcinoma cell; it is clearly a multipotential cell because a single embryonal carcinoma cell can form all the somatic cell types found in a teratoma and it can contribute to all tissues of an adult mouse when it is injected into a normal mouse blastocyst [27, 31, 36]. The only known limit on these cells' developmental multipotency is that they cannot readily differentiate into the trophectoderm layer which normally surrounds the developing mouse; without this layer they cannot implant and therefore cannot by themselves develop into an individual organism.

It seems then that during animal development, the ability to develop into complete adults is lost by all cells except the egg. This distinction from plant cells probably does not mean that the two kingdoms develop in fundamentally different ways, but rather that the ecological pressures which demand great powers of regeneration in cropped sessile plants are not such a dominant selective pressure on most animals.

2.5.4 THE STABILITY OF DETERMINATION IN ANIMALS

At present research workers are paying particular attention to two situations in which the stability of determination may be investigated away from the limitations of embryogenesis; these studies have been conducted on transdetermination in the imaginal discs of *Drosophila* and on the expression of differentiated functions by cells in culture.

Transdetermination in imaginal discs

The development of higher insects, such as *Drosophila*, is divided into two quite separate phases. A larva emerges from the egg and after a period of growth transforms during metamorphosis into an adult. This metamorphosis is unlike that of amphibians, which only involves the growth of a few new organs and the resorption of unnecessary structures such as the tail. In contrast, the adult insect is very different from the larva and its progenitor cells lie in small groups (the imaginal discs) inside the larva. At the early blastoderm stage, the cells of the imaginal discs appear to segregate from those which will form the larva, and the disc cells appear to play no part in larval life. During metamorphosis, the larval organs are resorbed and the disc cells start to proliferate and generate the adult structures. Exceptionally, the Malpighian tubules of the larva are retained throughout metamorphosis.

Particular structures of the adult are formed from specific discs (Fig. 2.4.9) in a regular manner. For instance, the external part of the head of the fly is formed from the labial discs, the imaginal cells of the clypeolabrum and the eye antennal discs; these discs occur in pairs as do those which form most of the other parts of the body and it is only the genital apparatus which is formed from a single disc. The cells of different discs look identical under the electron microscope despite the fact that they will subsequently form an astonishing variety of structures including precisely organized chemoreceptors, mechanoreceptors, jointed limbs, wings and the regular array of ommatidia in the compound eye.

It is now known that the morphological uniformity of the disc cells conceals the fact that each disc is determined to form particular adult structures during metamorphosis. The evidence for this view comes from elegant transplantation experiments in which the discs are isolated from one larva and transplanted to the body cavity of another larva. The second larva is allowed to develop into an adult and the transplanted disc will form an adult structure in the body cavity of the fly. It is found that one disc will always form one set of adult structures and that its developmental fate is not controlled by the position which it occupies in the body cavity of the host larva.

Imaginal discs can also be used to study the stability of determination over several years. Such tests are possible because the discs can be propagated without the formation of adult structures. This is achieved by transferring the discs to the body cavity of an adult; here they will never experience the conditions which promote metamorphosis and the development of adult structures. The disc cells normally stop dividing just before the emergence of the adult fly, but in the abdomen of a fly they continue to grow and duplicate and at the end of adult life (two or three weeks), they are dissected out and transferred to a new adult. With this technique it is possible to propagate the discs for many years, and at

any time the state of determination of the disc may be checked by transferring part of it back to a larva, where it is forced to develop adult structures as the host proceeds through metamorphosis (Fig. 2.5.4).

These studies have shown that determination may be stable through many cell generations but that on occasion the cells of the disc may be transdetermined to form a new structure. The transplantation of the male genital disc can serve as an example [23]. The genital disc can be recognized by the structures associated with the anal plate and it was found that these continued to be found in some of the discs for up to 70 transfer generations, that is about three years after the original disc was transferred to the abdomen of a fly. This observation demonstrates that this determination can be inherited for many cell generations. However, at the 6–10th transfer generations new structures began to appear and antennal and leg structures were found in some of the discs. At about the same time discs started to form parts of the wing, and in the 15th transfer generation discs

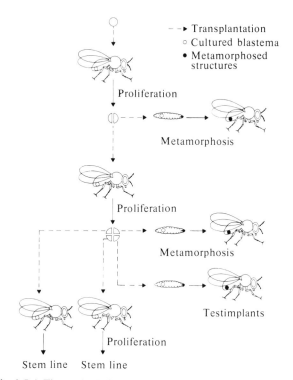

Fig. 2.5.4. The method of culturing and transplanting the imaginal discs of *Drosophila*. The diagram illustrates the method of propagating the discs and testing their state of determination by passing the discs through metamorphosis. (After Gehring [18].)

started regularly to form part of the thorax. The observation of transdetermination clearly demonstrates that determination does not involve an irreversible loss of the ability to form other cell types.

Taken together with the observations on vernalization and phase change in plants (p. 81) we can conclude that cell populations can propagate a state of development over long periods.

Maintenance of cell phenotype by cell interactions

Cell phenotypes are maintained in embryonic and adult animals by tissue interactions. The induction and maintenance of phenotypes by interactions in the embryo are discussed in Chapters 2.4 and 3.5. In the larva and the adult we have already seen that amputation can induce the formation of limb regenerates (see also Chapter 4.2), and this observation implies that these tissues are normally constrained from growing into additional limbs by factors present in unwounded intact limbs. Within tissues, the phenotypes of cells are also dependent on interactions. For instance, the pigmented dorsal iris cells of the eye will transform into crystallin-packed cells of the lens when the inhibitory influence of the original lens is removed (review [7]).

A sophisticated form of such cell interactions occurs in the maintenance of phenotype in mammalian striated muscle. In adult muscles there are fast and slow muscle fibres, and muscles which have predominantly one or the other type of fibre differ not only in the physiology of their contraction characteristics and resistance to fatigue but also in the myosin light chains which they contain (for the structure of myosin see Chapter 6.2). A fast or a slow muscle can be transformed into a muscle of the opposite type by interchanging their nervous supply; during the transition from one type to the other, the population of myosin light chains within individual fibres also changes [41]. These experiments clearly demonstrate that the synthesis of differentiated gene products depends on subtle interactions with other cells.

Expression of differentiated function by cells in culture

Although a cell's full phenotype may only be realized by cell interactions within the whole intact animal, individual cells can both grow and express biochemical products associated with their cell type when cultured on either glass or plastic surfaces. Most animal cells can be maintained in a nutrient solution containing amino acids, buffered salts and glucose with the addition of unknown components in animal serum added at about ten per cent of the volume. In such a medium it is possible to propagate cells which are committed to a particular path of differentiation. For instance, cloned myoblasts may be propagated and then induced to differentiate into striated muscle. It is interesting that the beating muscle formed by such cells only expresses the myosin heavy chain which is characteristic of embryonic muscle [59]. Perhaps no such cell formed in culture can by itself generate the range of phenotypes seen in adults because they lack the necessary interactions; it is certainly the case that the embryonal carcinoma stem cells of mouse teratoma never form as many cell types in culture by themselves as they do when injected back into the blastocyst, where they may experience all the interactions of embryonic development.

The following is a list of some of the differentiated properties which may be retained by cells in culture for over two years: liver cells and albumin synthesis, pigment cells and the synthesis of melanin, nerve cells and the production of acetylcholine, lymphoid cells and the production of immunoglobulins. Cells with these functions have all been cloned and many of these clones continue to express the differentiated function (reviewed by Davidson [11]).

It is important to discover how often a single differentiated cell will form daughter cells which continue, or are able, to synthesize the same differentiated product. This has been investigated with cartilage cells, which synthesize chondroitin sulphate, and with pigment cells, which synthesize melanin. Coon dissociated chick cartilage into single cells and found that more than 98% of these formed colonies which continued to synthesize chondroitin sulphate [9]. Nine of the single cells were grown until they had divided 36 times. During their growth, they were dissociated into single cells on three occasions, and after each dissociation it was found that each of the 200 or more colonies which grew up from these single cells formed chondroitin sulphate. This observation clearly demonstrates that differentiated single cells may inherit their state of determination through many cell generations. He next investigated whether the state of determination was unstable if the expression of the differentiated function was suppressed (chondroitin sulphate not detected). In this case, the cells were grown in a medium with particular protein components which prevented cartilage production and it was shown that after 20 generations the cells could still synthesize chondroitin sulphate if they were returned to normal medium. This observation shows that although a differentiated function may be undetected, the determined state may nevertheless remain stable.

Retention of multipotency by cells in culture

Despite the stability of certain states in cell culture, it is also possible to isolate and maintain cells which are multipotential and which can be induced to differentiate into a wide range of cell types. These cells may be considered to undergo determination as they differentiate and as in plants they provide excellent material for studying the biochemistry of the process.

The earliest embryonic stem cell which can be maintained in this way is the embryonal carcinoma cell of the mouse (section 2.5.3). It can be induced to differentiate into a wide range of cell types by the aggregation of the cells and it can be directed to differentiate into endoderm-like cells by low-density plating and the application of retinoic acid [5, 16, 49]. During the conversion to an endoderm-like cell, the properties of the cells change and the tumourigenic phenotype is transformed into a non-tumourigenic phenotype whose growth depends on the addition to the medium of exogenous growth factors [25, 40]. This stable change in growth properties is similar to the alterations which occur during plant cell habituation (section 2.5.5).

Another case of an unstable state in culture involves pigmented retina cells which can transform into lens cells, as they may also do during lens regeneration in the whole animal (section 2.5.3). Experiments on pigment cells show that in some cases cells may switch their cell type in culture and that determination is not necessarily stable [15]. A population of pigmented cells (99.9% pigmented) was obtained by culturing the pigmented retina of a chick. After a period in culture, a group of pigmented cells was dissociated and the single cells which grew always formed pigmented colonies. However, after the colonies had grown for a period and had been subcultured to new bottles, two of the eight colonies studied started to form groups of organized cells which looked like small lenses. These groups of cells were shown to be synthesizing lens proteins by demonstrating that antibodies prepared against lens fibres reacted with them. These experiments show that a cell synthesizing melanin can give rise to cells synthesizing lens proteins and that determination may be unstable.

The phenotypes of at least one apparently unipotential cell can be dramatically changed by chemical treatment. Fibroblasts can be readily obtained from the embryonic tissues of the mouse by breaking up the tissues with enzymes such as the protease trypsin. These cells can be propagated in culture with a very stable morphology of a spindle-shaped, migratory cell with a bland cytoplasm. After maintaining such a morphology for up to twenty years, such cells can be induced to form striated muscle, cartilage and fat cells by treatment with the nucleic acid base analogue 5-azacytidine [52]. These experiments show that cell phenotype can be destabilized and that a cell can only be regarded as 'determined' in a particular direction under the set of conditions which have been used to test its potential phenotypes.

2.5.5 THE OCCURRENCE AND STABILITY OF DETERMINATION IN PLANTS

The phenomenon of determination has received much less attention in plants than in animals. This is probably because botanists have been fascinated with the 'totipotency' of plant cells. Thus, all cell differentiation is apparently not irreversible in plants, and to this extent it can be argued that restriction in developmental potential is not a necessary consequence of differentiation, although the two processes are often linked in animal development.

However, determination of *organs* appears to occur during normal development in plants, as shown in leaf development [44]. Thus, in the fern apex, leaf primordia arise first, followed later by the axillary bud primordia. The early stages of development are very similar in both leaves and buds (p. 40), but whereas the leaf primordium soon becomes flattened and shows dorsoventrality, the bud remains radially symmetrical. Moreover, the leaf becomes an organ of 'determinate' growth (in the sense that it does not maintain growth indefinitely), whereas the bud is an organ of indeterminate growth, in that it remains potentially capable of unlimited growth. However, at a very early stage of its development the leaf primordium of the fern *Dryopteris* can be induced to develop into a bud by making a deep tangential cut between the shoot apical cell and a very young presumptive leaf primordium [10, 54] (Fig. 2.5.5). With slightly older leaf primordia this

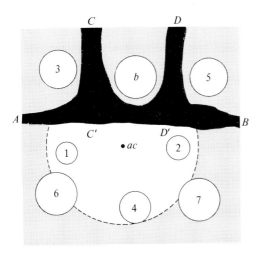

Fig. 2.5.5. *Dryopteris dilatata*. An apex in which the I₁ position has been isolated from the apical cell region (ac) by a deep tangential incision (AB) and from leaf primordia 3 and 5 by radial incisions (CC'', DD''). A bud, b, was formed in what is normally a leaf position (After Wardlaw [54].)

surgical treatment is ineffective and the primordium continues to develop into a leaf.

Determination of leaf primordia has also been studied by removing young leaf primordia of the fern *Osmunda* at different stages of development and transferring them to a sterile culture medium. When the youngest primordia, P_1–P_5, were treated in this way, they developed not as leaves but as shoots which regenerated roots and so formed complete plants [44]. However, progressively older primordia showed an increasing tendency to develop as leaves, and P_{10} always did so [45]. Thus, it appears that very young leaf primordia are not yet irreversibly committed to develop as leaves, but beyond a certain stage they do become determined and when transferred to a culture medium at this stage, they develop into complete, miniature leaves. Thus, although there is good evidence that most living cells of the mature leaf retain the capacity to undergo 'de-differentiation' and to regenerate whole plants, determination of *organs* such as leaves (and probably also flowers) appears to occur during normal development.

It may reasonably be asked how one can have determination of organs without determination of cells. It is possible that the individual cells of leaf primordia suffer no intrinsic restriction of developmental potential and that once the primordium has been channelled into the 'leaf' pathway then the orderly sequence of stages

occurring during leaf development represents a 'chain reaction' in which one developmental stage triggers the next, as has been suggested by Heslop-Harrison for flower development [26]. Whether or not this hypothesis is correct, it is clear that it is possible to construct a model for leaf 'determination' which does not involve a restriction of developmental potential. However, it would appear that other instances of true determination, comparable with the phenomena in animals, do occur in the apical meristems of plants. [55–57].

At first sight it might appear paradoxical to suggest that meristematic cells exhibit determination, since they are usually regarded as the archetype of cells which are totally uncommitted and undifferentiated. However, there are several well-known phenomena in plants which strongly indicate that determination can occur in shoot apical meristems. One of the best-known examples is seen in the phenomenon of *vernalization*. Many plant species are able to initiate flowers only after they have been exposed to chilling temperatures (0–5°C) for several weeks. Biennial plants, which remain vegetative during the first growing season and flower in the following spring, are common examples of species with a chilling requirement for flowering. This induction of flowering by chilling is known as vernalization (reviewed by Purvis [38], Wareing & Phillips [58]).

The 'winter' varieties of cereals such as rye and wheat show very similar behaviour to that of biennial plants, since they will flower in the following summer if sown in the autumn so that they are exposed to a period of chilling during the winter, but they will not flower if they are maintained under warm conditions during the winter. The chilling requirement of winter rye can be met even at the seed stage, since if the seeds are imbibed with water and maintained at 0–5°C for five to six weeks, they will flower in due course if they are planted and maintained under conditions favourable for growth (Fig. 2.5.6).

Flower initiation involves a transformation of the shoot apex from producing leaf primordia to producing flower primordia and this involves a radical reorganization of the structure of the apex. This transformation of the shoot apex to the flowering condition does not occur in rye embryos during the chilling treatment itself, but is only manifested several months and many cell generations later, after the embryo of the seed has grown into a mature plant.

Once the rye plant has become fully vernalized, it appears that the condition is transmitted to all new

Fig. 2.5.6. Effect of vernalization in winter rye. Left: plants from seed chilled at 1°C for six weeks before sowing. Right: plants from seed germinated at 18°C. From O.N. Purvis (1934) *Ann. Bot.*, **48**, 919.

tissues formed subsequently. Thus, if the main shoot apex is removed, so that the lateral shoots are stimulated to grow, and then these are decapitated to stimulate second-order laterals and so on, it is found that even fourth-order laterals are still fully vernalized, although the apices of these laterals were not present at the time of the chilling treatment. Evidently, the vernalized condition is transmitted from a parent cell to its daughters in cell division and it does not appear to be 'diluted' in the process.

In some species, the effects of chilling can be reversed if the embryos or plants are exposed to high temperature (45°C) for several hours immediately after the completion of the chilling treatment, but if the high-temperature treatment is delayed for two days, the reversal of the vernalized state is no longer possible.

The nature of the biochemical changes occurring during vernalization are still completely unknown, but they evidently occur in the cells of the shoot apex itself, since it is possible to vernalize the excised shoot apices of rye embryos if they are placed on a sterile nutrient medium and exposed to chilling temperatures, when they will regenerate into whole plants and ultimately

flower. Whatever the nature of the processes occurring during vernalization, they evidently involve metabolism, since the rye embryos require sugars and an adequate oxygen supply for the chilling treatment to be effective.

Although, in rye, the vernalized state becomes irreversible at a certain stage, in some perennial species, such as the garden chrysanthemum (*C. morifolium*) and Michaelmas daisy (*Aster novi-belgii*), which have a vernalization requirement, the new shoots which emerge from the base of the plant at the end of the growing season require to be vernalized anew before they can initiate flowers in the following summer. Moreover, even with rye the embryos which the vernalized parent plants produce require fresh vernalization, indicating that the changes involved in vernalization must be obliterated during the development of the pollen grains and embryo sacs. Evidently there is a 'slate-cleaning' process during gametogenesis, which wipes out the effects of past vernalization treatment.

The familiar phenomenon of an alternation of free-living gametophyte and sporophyte generations in ferns provides another example of a difference in behaviour of apical meristems which is stable and can be transmitted through many cell generations. Normally the gametophyte is haploid and the sporophyte diploid, but the marked differences in morphology and life cycle between the two generations cannot be attributed to the difference in chromosome number, since it is possible to produce experimentally diploid or even tetraploid gametophytes and haploid sporophytes.

A third example of stable differences in the shoot apical meristems of an individual plant is seen in the phenomenon of phase-change in woody plants (reviewed [13], for a more detailed treatment see [60]). The majority of woody plant species show a distinct *juvenile phase*, lasting from 1 to 30 years, during which they are unable to initiate flowers, but ultimately they attain the *adult* condition which is marked by the ability to form flowers if other conditions are favourable. There are other differences between the two phases affecting a number of vegetative characters, including leaf shape, phyllotaxis, thorniness, etc. A good example of this phenomenon is provided by ivy (*Hedera helix*), in which the base of the vine shows a number of juvenile characters, including palmate leaf shape, whereas the upper part of the vine shows adult characters, including ovate leaves and the capacity to form flowers (Table 2.5.1).

Table 2.5.1. Distinguishing characters of juvenile and adult ivy (*Hedera helix*)

Juvenile characters	Adult characters
Three- or five-lobed, palmate leaves	Entire, ovate leaves
Alternate phyllotaxy	Spiral phyllotaxy
Anthocyanin pigmentation of young leaves and stem	No anthocyanin pigmentation
Stems pubescent	Stems glabrous
Climbing and plagiotropic growth habit	Orthotropic growth habit
Shoots show unlimited growth and lack terminal buds	Shoots show limited growth terminated by buds with scales
Absence of flowering	Presence of flowers

One of the most striking features of this phenomenon is the stability of the two phases. If cuttings are taken from juvenile and adult parts of an ivy vine, they continue for many years to show the characteristic features of the shoots from which they were derived (Fig. 2.5.7). Under natural conditions the juvenile stage ultimately shows the transition to the adult condition, and reversion from the adult to the juvenile phase can be induced in rooted cuttings by various treatments, including growing under fairly high temperatures and treatment with gibberellic acid.

It seems likely that the meristematic cells of juvenile and adult apices of ivy, and of apices of vernalized and unvernalized rye, are themselves determined along the respective pathways of development. Isolated shoot apices of embryos of winter rye can be chilled and will give rise to mature vernalized plants [37]. Very small pieces of the shoot apex of *Citrus*, bearing only three small leaf primordia, can be successfully grafted on to seedling stocks and are found to retain their adult character [34]. Thus, the shoot apical regions themselves can exist in alternative states, but this is still not evidence that the meristem cells themselves are determined, since even these very small excised apices will include some organs (e.g. leaf primordia) or tissues (e.g. procambial tissue) which will have begun differentiation. However, callus cultures derived from juvenile and adult stem tissues grown on the same nutrient medium show differences in their rates of growth and in the fact that 'juvenile' calluses show abundant regeneration of adventitious roots while 'adult' calluses show little capacity for root regeneration. However, such calluses are normally established from mature stem or petiole tissue and may not necessarily reflect differences in the state of determination of meristematic cells in the shoot apices.

Habituation in tissue cultures

The phenomenon known as 'habituation' in plant tissue cultures appears to represent an example of cell deter-

Fig. 2.5.7. Left: plant of juvenile ivy. Right: plant from cutting taken from adult part of parent vine. (Courtesy of Dr V.M. Frydman.)

mination and provides a convenient model system for studies on the molecular basis of determination [30]. Callus cultures derived from pith parenchyma of tobacco require to be supplied with auxin and cytokinin, as well as other basic nutrients, for continued growth in culture. However, when such cultures are subcultured a number of times, they tend to lose the requirement for exogenous auxin and cytokinin and can then be subcultured on a medium lacking these growth substances. That habituation is a property of individual cells is shown by the fact that the cultures from single cells of an habituated callus will continue to grow on a cytokinin-free medium [2].

Callus cultures of tobacco pith can be induced to form buds from which whole plants can be regenerated. When plants were regenerated for habituated callus, and then new callus established from the pith of these plants, the new callus was found to be *cytokinin-requiring* [2, 29]. Thus, the habituated state can be reversed. Moreover, this result indicates that changes occurring during habituation do not affect the genome; rather the changes appear to be 'epigenetic', i.e. they affect gene expression but not the genome itself.

It would appear that the genes coding for the enzymes concerned with cytokinin biosynthesis are not expressed in tobacco pith and that this condition is retained when cell division is induced in pith cells to establish callus cultures (or, alternatively, pith cells may contain enzymes which rapidly degrade or inactivate endogenous cytokinin). However, the genes for cytokinin biosynthesis are evidently still intact in the callus cells, which can in due course become independent of exogenous cytokinin in habituation.

The stability of the differentiated state in plant cells

In plant cells and tissues, cell differences first become clearly manifest with the cessation of cell division and during the process of cell enlargement and maturation. Some of the structural cell differences developed during maturation are visible under the microscope, notably differences affecting the plastids, the cell wall and the endo-membranes. However, it is clear that there are also functional differences between different types of tissue involving various aspects of metabolism, such as photosynthesis and the synthesis of starch, storage proteins and secondary metabolites, just as there are differences in the metabolic capacities of various animal tissues. Although it is taken for granted that plant cells

and tissues differ in their metabolic capacities, there is little precise information on the subject, despite it being known that there are differences between the biosynthetic capacities of shoot and root tissues; thus roots are heterotrophic with respect to certain vitamins, such as thiamine, which are supplied by the shoots; there are also differences between shoots and roots in their capacity for the synthesis of certain amino acids.

Differences in enzyme complements between various tissues imply differences in gene expression; thus differences in gene expression occur not only during the process of cell maturation and differentiation, but are also maintained during the homeostatic state of mature cells and tissues. We have seen (p. 000) that the tissues of various organs (leaf, stem, root, etc.) each possess a unique set of mRNAs comprising the transcripts of thousands of diverse structural genes. There is also evidence for the occurrence of organ-specific antigenic determinants in plants [39]. Stems, leaves, pistils and anthers of *Prunus avium* examined by immunological methods were found to share some antigenic determinants while others were unique to a particular organ. Moreover, callus cells derived from different organs shared some determinants while others were specific. The parental organ determinants were still expressed in callus cells after four subcultures. This observation provides direct evidence for the occurrence of organ-specific antigenic determinants (probably proteins), and also for the continued transmission of certain tissue- or organ-specific characteristics when cell division is induced in mature, differentiated cells. It would appear that the induction of cell division in mature cells does not necessarily completely wipe out the previous selective gene expression of the cells, so that the dividing cells retain some of the characteristics of the parent cells. The requirement for cytokinins and auxin of callus derived from tobacco pith (p. 74) would seem to afford another example of the carry-over of a previously differentiated state to newly dividing cells.

These observations provide good evidence for the 'stability of the differentiated state' in plant cells, comparable with that in animal tissues. However, determination in living plant cells is not completely irreversible, as it appears to be in many animal cells. This reversibility is not incompatible with stability within a certain range of conditions, however. Thus, adult shoots of ivy can be caused to revert to the juvenile phase by high temperature or by the application of high concentrations of gibberellic acid, but in the temperature conditions under which it normally grows the adult phase is remarkably stable. At first sight, the concept of determination might seem incompatible with that of totipotency of plant cells. However, it is not suggested that a given cell is *at the same time* both determined and totipotent, but that before a given mature cell can exhibit totipotency in regeneration, a previous state of determination must be largely or wholly reversed. There are large differences between species in the ability to regenerate adventitious buds or roots, or to form adventive embryos (embryoids) and these interspecific differences may well depend partly upon the readiness with which previous states of determination can be reversed.

Competence in plant cells

The term competence was first applied to the ability of animal cells to respond to induction at certain stages of embryo development. In plant development the term is often used to refer to the ability of different cells to respond in a specific manner to the same hormonal signal. Indeed, the wide spectrum of affects of a growth hormone, such as indol-3yl-acetic acid (IAA), in different tissues of a plant can only be attributed to differences in the competence of the tissue. When used in this sense it is clear that competence is closely allied to determination, to the extent that both terms refer to the situation in which a given tissue is committed to a specific pattern of differentiation in advance of its expression; thus competence represents a special case of determination. At the present time the molecular basis of determination is not known but it may involve specific hormone 'receptors' or receptor-mediated processes.

Where a group of cells showing a specific response to a hormonal signal is strictly localized we may speak of 'target' cells. Examples of such target cells are (1) the cells of the future abscission zone at the base of a leaf petiole which respond in a specific manner to ethylene during leaf senescence, and (2) the cells of the aleurone layer of the barley grain which secrete hydrolytic enzymes in response to gibberellins produced by the embryo.

These examples of target cells appear to represent special cases of differentiation in which the cell is determined with respect to certain hormone-induced processes, but in which the response is delayed. In most types of plant cell, hormone-induced aspects of differentiation occur during cell maturation, but in target cells certain hormone-induced changes are delayed until long after the main phase of maturation has been completed.

It would appear, from the discussion in this and preceding sections, that determination may occur in: (1) cells which are undergoing repeated cell division; (2) cells which are about to undergo maturation and differentiation; (3) resting cells which have undergone differentiation; and (4) target cells which have undergone vacuolation but which are capable of further developmental changes (Fig. 2.5.8).

The stability of root and shoot apical meristems

The division of the plant body into shoot and root originates in the embryo with the establishment of polarity and the initiation of shoot and root apical meristems, which are remarkably stable structures and retain their identity through many cell generations. It is

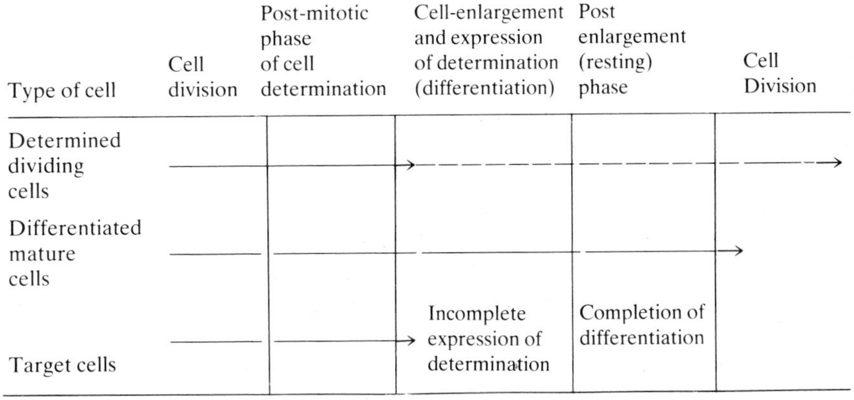

Type of cell	Cell division	Post-mitotic phase of cell determination	Cell-enlargement and expression of determination (differentiation)	Post enlargement (resting) phase	Cell Division
Determined dividing cells	————		——→ - - - - -	————————	————————→
Differentiated mature cells	————			——————→	
Target cells	————		——→ Incomplete expression of determination	Completion of differentiation	

Fig. 2.5.8. Suggested scheme to illustrate differences in the time of expression of determination between various cell types.

very rare for a root apex to be converted directly into a shoot apex or vice versa, although adventitious buds may arise from mature root cells, and adventitious roots may arise in stem tissues. Thus, the question arises as to whether the difference between root and shoot apices is analogous to the differences in states of determination between the apical meristems of juvenile and adult ivy or vernalized and unvernalized rye, that is, whether apical meristems are determined as shoot or root meristems respectively. However, this suggestion is in conflict with the current opinion that cells in the apical meristems of shoots and roots are intrinsically uncommitted with respect to their future differentiation and do not differ from each other in their developmental potential. It is also widely accepted that the apex is a self-organizing region and that the pattern of differentiation occurring in the shoot apical region is controlled by the apex itself, independently of influences from older, differentiated tissues (p. 41). These two current concepts would seem to be mutually incompatible since if we accept both these concepts then the differing properties of the two types of apex must depend solely upon their different structure and organization, and it is then difficult to see how this difference could be maintained so tenaciously.

There would seem to be only two possible alternative hypotheses to account for the stability of the shoot and root apices and the maintenance of the differences between them, namely, either (1) the meristematic cells of the shoot apices are uncommitted, and development into either the shoot or root pathways is controlled by influences from older tissues, or (2) the meristematic cells are intrinsically programmed into either root or shoot channels and are not totally uncommitted, so that the different patterns of organization in shoot and root apices are a consequence of the intrinsic differences in their constituent cells. At the present time it is not possible to resolve this dilemma, since there is evidence to support both hypotheses [56].

2.5.6   CONCLUSIONS

The conclusion from this section on cell determination is that cells may undergo certain changes in their developmental potential during differentiation, and that such changes may be relatively stable. As we have seen, this stability does not usually involve irreversible changes in the genome. Thus nuclei from differentiated cells can code for the normal development of Amphibia (Chapter

2.2), and many cells in an adult plant retain the capacity to form a whole plant (Chapter 2.4). It is also the case that unusual animal cells, called teratocarcinoma cells, are able to form many tissue types after growth in culture for several years (Chapter 2.3). These observations imply that development and differentiation in plants do not require that cells should lose the capacity to repeat the life cycle of the organism, and it is possible that only technical difficulties have prevented similar experiments with animals.

2.5.7   REFERENCES

1 Berrill N.J. (1952) Regeneration and budding in worms. *Biol. Rev.*, **27**, 401–438.
2 Binns A.N. & Meins F. (1972) Habituation of tobacco pith cells for factors promoting cell division is heritable and potentially reversible. *Proc. natl Acad. Sci., USA*, **70**, 2660–2662.
3 Bourgin J.P. & Nitsch J.P. (1967) Obtention de *Nicotiana* haploids à partir d'étamines cultivées *in vitro. Annls Physiol. vég., Paris*, **9**, 377–382.
4 Brondsted H.V. (1969) *Planarian Regeneration*. Pergamon Press, Oxford.
5 Burke D.C., Graham C.F. & Lehman J.M. (1978) Appearance of interferon inducibility and sensitivity during differentiation of murine teratocarcinoma cells *in vitro. Cell*, **13**, 243–248.
6 Butcher D.N. & Ingram D.S. (1976) *Plant Tissue Culture*, Edward Arnold, London.
7 Clayton R.M. (1978) Divergence and convergence in lens cell differentiation: regulation of the specific content of lens fibre cells. In *Stem Cells and Tissue Homeostasis* (Eds B.I. Lord & R.J. Cole), pp. 115–138. Cambridge University Press, Cambridge.
8 Coe W.R. (1929) Regeneration in nemerteans. *J. exp. Zool.*, **54**, 411–459.
9 Coon H.G. (1966) Clonal stability and phenotypic expression of chick cartilage cells *in vitro. Proc. natl Acad. Sci., USA*, **55**, 66–73.
10 Cutter E.G. (1956) Experimental and analytical studies of pteridophytes XXXIII. The experimental induction of buds from leaf primordia in *Dryopteris aristata* Druce. *Ann. Bot.*, **20**, 143–65.
11 Davidson R.L. (1974) Control of expression of differentiated functions in somatic cell hybrids. In *Somatic Cell Hybridization* (Eds R.L. Davidson & F. de la Cruz), pp. 131–150. Raven Press, New York.
12 Desselle J.C. & Gontcharoff M. (1978) Cytophotometric detection of the participation of cartilage grafts in the regeneration of X-rayed Urodele limbs. *Biol. Cell.*, **33**, 45–54.
13 Doorenbos J. (1965) Juvenile and adult phases in woody plants. *Encycl. Plant Physiol.*, **15**(1), 1222–35.
14 Dunis D.A. & Namenwirth M. (1977) The role of grafted skin in the regeneration of X-irradiated axolotl limbs. *Devl. Biol.*, **56**, 97–109.
15 Eguchi G. & Okada J.S. (1973) Differentiation of lens tissue from the progeny of chick retinal pigment cells cultured *in vitro*: a demonstration of a switch in cell type in clonal cell culture. *Proc. natl Acad. Sci., USA*, **70**, 1495–1499.

16 Evans M.J. (1976) Totipotency of animal cells. In *The Developmental Biology of Plants and Animals*, 1st edn. (Eds C.F. Graham & P.F. Wareing), pp. 64–72. Blackwell Scientific Publications, Oxford.

17 Evans M.J. & Kaufman M.H. (1981) Establishment in culture of pluripotential cells from mouse embryos. *Nature, Lond.*, **292**, 154–156.

18 Gehring W. (1972) The stability of the determined state in culture of imaginal disks in *Drosophila*. In *The Biology of Imaginal Disks* (Eds H. Ursprung & R. Nothiger), pp. 35–57. Springer-Verlag, Berlin.

19 Goss R.J. (1969) *Principles of Regeneration*, Academic Press, New York.

20 Graham C.F. (1977) Teratocarcinoma cells and normal mouse embryogenesis. In *Concepts in Mammalian Embryogenesis* (Ed. M.I. Sherman). M.I.T. Press, Cambridge, Massachusetts.

21 Gremigni V. & Miceli C. (1980) Cytophotometric evidence for cell "transdifferentiation" in planarian regeneration. *Wilhelm Roux' Archiv.*, **188**, 107–114.

22 Guha S. & Maheshwari S.C. (1964) *In vitro* production of embryos from anthers of *Datura. Nature, Lond.*, **204**, 497.

23 Hadorn E. (1967) Dynamics of determination. In *Major Problems in Developmental Biology* (Ed. M. Locke), pp. 85–104. Academic Press.

24 Halperin W. & Jensen W.A. (1967) Ultra-structural changes during growth and embryogenesis in carrot cell cultures. *J. Ultrastruct. Res.*, **18**, 428–443.

25 Heath J., Bell S. & Rees A.R. (1981) Appearance of functional insulin receptors during the differentiation of embryonal carcinoma cells. *J. Cell Biol.*, **91**, 293–297.

26 Heslop-Harrison J. (1967) Differentiation. *A. Rev. Pl. Physiol.*, **18**, 325.

27 Illmensee K. & Mintz B. (1976) Totipotency and normal differentiation of single teratocarcinoma cells cloned by injection into blastocysts. *Proc. natl Acad. Sci., USA*, **73**, 549–553.

28 McWilliam A.A., Smith S.M. & Street H.E. (1974) The origin and development of embryoids in suspension cultures of carrot (*Daucus carota*). *Ann. Bot.*, **38**, 243–250.

29 Meins F. (1977) Reversal of the neoplastic state in plants. *Am. J. Path.*, **89**, 687–702.

30 Meins F. & Binns A.N. (1979) Cell determination in plant development. *BioScience*, **29**, 221–225.

31 Mintz B. & Illmensee K. (1975) Normal genetically mosaic mice produced from malignant teratocarcinoma cells. *Proc. natl Acad. Sci., USA*, **72**, 3585–3589.

32 Montgomery J.R. & Coward S.J. (1974) On the minimal size of a planarian capable of regeneration. *Trans. Am. microsc. Soc.*, **93**, 386–391.

33 Namenwirth M. (1974) The inheritance of cell differentiation during limb regeneration in the axolotl. *Devl. Biol.*, **41**, 42–56.

34 Navarro L., Roistacher C.N. & Murashige T. (1975) Improvement of shoot-tip grafting *in vitro* for virus-free citrus. *J. Proc. Am. hort. Soc.*, **100**, 471–479.

35 O'Hare M.J. (1978) Teratomas, neoplasia, differentiation. *Invest. Cell. Path.*, **1**, 39–63.

36 Papaioannou V.E., McBurney M.W. Gardner R.L. & Evans M.J. (1979) Fate of teratocarcinoma cells injected into early mouse embryos. *Nature, Lond.*, **258**, 70–73.

37 Purvis O. (1940) Vernalization of fragments of embryo tissue. *Nature, Lond.*, **145**, 462.

38 Purvis O. (1961) The physiological analysis of 'vernalisation'. *Encycl. Plant Physiol.*, **16**, 76–122.

39 Raff J., Hutchinson J.F., Knox R.B. & Clarke A.E. (1979) Cell recognition: Antigenic determinants of plant organs and their cultured callus cells. *Differentiation.* **12**, 179–186

40 Rees A.R., Adamson E.D. & Graham C.F. (1979) Epidermal growth factor receptors increase during the differentiation of embryonal carcinoma cells. *Nature, Lond.*, **281**, 309–311.

41 Rubinstein N., Mabuchi K., Pepe F., Salmons S., Gergely J. & Sreter F. (1978) Use of type-specific antimyosins to demonstrate the tranformation of individual fibres. *J. Cell Biol.*, **79**, 252–261.

42 Slack J.H.W. (1980) The source of cells for regeneration. *Nature, Lond.*, **286**, 760.

43 Sonnenborn T.M. (1930) Genetic studies on *Stenostomum incandatum* (nov.spec.). *J. exp. Zool.*, **57**, 57–108.

44 Steeves T.A. (1961) A study of the developmental potentialities of excised leaf primordia in sterile culture. *Phytomorphology*, **11**, 346–59.

45 Steeves T.A. & Sussex G.M. (1957) Studies on the development of excised leaves in sterile culture. *Am. J. Bot.*, **44**, 665–73.

46 Steward F.C. (1958) Growth and organized development of cultured cells. III. Interpretation of growth from free cell to carrot plant. *Am. J. Bot.*, **45**, 709–713.

47 Steward F.C., Mapes M.O. & Mears K. (1958) Growth and organized development of cultured cells. II. Organization in cultures grown from freely suspended cells. *Am. J. Bot.*, **47**, 705–708.

48 Street H.E. (1976) Experimental embryogenesis—The totipotency of plant cells. In *The Developmental Biology of Plants and Animals*, 1st edn (Eds. C.F. Graham & P.F. Wareing), pp. 73–90. Blackwell Scientific Publications, Oxford.

49 Strickland S. & Mahdavi V. (1978) The induction of differentiation in teratocarcinoma stem cells by retinoic acid. *Cell*, **15**, 393–403.

50 Sunderland N. (1973) Pollen and anther culture. In *Plant Tissue and Cell Culture* (Ed. H.E. Street), pp. 161–190. Blackwell Scientific Publications, Oxford.

51 Tardent P. (1963) Regeneration in hydrozoa. *Biol. Rev.*, **38**, 293–333.

52 Taylor S.M. & Jones P.A. (1979) Multiple new phenotypes induced in 10T½ and 3T3 cells treated with 5-azacytidine. *Cell*, **17**, 771–779.

53 Thomas E. & Davey M.R. (1975) *From Single Cells to Plants*. Wykeham Publications, London.

53a Tran Thanh Van, K.M. (1981) Control of morphogenesis in *in vitro* cultures. *A. Rev. Pl. Physiol.*, **32**, 291–311.

54 Wardlaw C.W. (1949) Experiments in organogenesis in ferns. *Growth* Suppl., **13**, 93–131.

55 Wareing P.F. (1978) Determination in plant development. *Bot. Mag., Tokyo*, Special Issue, **1**, 3–18.

56 Wareing P.F. (1979) What is the basis of stability of apical meristems? BPGRG Monograph No. 3, *Control of Plant Development*.

57 Wareing P.F. (1982) Determination and related aspects of plant development. In *The Molecular Biology of Plant Development* (Eds H. Smith & D. Grierson), pp. 517–514. Blackwell Scientific Publications, Oxford.

58 Wareing P.F. & Phillips I.D.J. (1981) *Growth and Differentiation in Plants*, 3rd edn. Pergamon Press, Oxford.

59 Whalen R.G., Sell S.M., Butler-Browne G.S., Schwartz K., Bouveret P. & Pinset-Härstrom I. (1981) Three myosin heavy chain isozymes appear sequentially in rat muscle development. *Nature, Lond.*, **292**, 805–809.

60 Zimmerman R.H. (Ed.) (1976) *Symposium on Juvenility in Woody Perennials. Acta Horticulturae*, **56**.

Conclusions to Part 2

This part of the book is concerned with the formation of spatial organization in the developing embryo and plant meristem. The examples are limited to early embryos and organization within meristems while the complexities of large cell populations in late embryos are discussed in Parts 3 and 4 of the book and the hormonal integration of organism development is reviewed in Part 5.

Developing systems are organized in response to directional stimuli

The spatial organization of gene expression in development is usually invariant from one individual to another within the same species. However, early meristematic cells and fertilized eggs do not contain a three-dimensional plan of this organization and they prescribe early development in a completely different way from the description of protein structure which is contained in the genetic code (p. 22).

Thus, the spatial organization of the early *Fucus* embryo is oriented with respect to light, gravity and neighbouring embryos (p. 29), while the position of sperm penetration into the amphibian egg imposes organization on the embryo (p. 28). Clearly, these eggs do not contain an immutable plan of adult structure, but rather they are most unusual cells in that they readily change the organization of their molecular constituents in response to environmental stimuli.

Development of asymmetry in single cells

Frequently, unfertilized eggs of both animals and plants have distinct ends in cell structure. They are often asymmetric cells and this asymmetry is inherited by the developing embryo. The mechanisms by which this asymmetry is generated are usually unclear but the asymmetry is often oriented with respect to the other structures in the ovary or ovule and it may be supposed that these neighbouring cells impose directionality on the growing egg (e.g. *Drosophila*, p. 24; molluscs, p. 26; and higher plants, p. 30).

In other germ cells it is possible to investigate experimentally the formation of asymmetry because it develops after the egg has been shed from the adult organism. There is evidence that the microtubular elements are involved in asymmetry generation during meiosis in nemertines (p. 26), and during fertilization of amphibians (p. 28). In most organisms the primary mechanism remains mysterious, and the alga *Fucus* provides the only example of asymmetry generation which has been studied with a wide variety of techniques. In the fertilized eggs of this and other closely related species of seaweed, the spatial organization of early development is anticipated and controlled by the direction of electric current flow through the egg and it is the orientation of this current flow which first responds to environmental stimuli (pp. 29–30).

Whatever mechanism is involved in forming the distinct ends of eggs, these ends may in rare cases contain organization vital for development. For example, the posterior pole of the *Drosophila* egg inside the ovary contains the organization necessary for viable germ cell formation during subsequent embryogenesis (p. 24). However, it is very unusual for an organism to allocate the control of a vital developmental function to one local region of an egg or meristem. In most eggs, the capacities required for the formation of the variety of embryonic cell types are unevenly distributed between the ends of the egg but they are not localized to small regions (pp. 52–55).

89

Particular parts of early developing systems contribute to particular parts of mature developing systems

It is routine for particular parts of eggs to be enclosed in cells which in undisturbed development regularly contribute to different tissues of the larva and of the adult. In undisturbed development of animals, the cell lineage is usually invariant from one embryo to another within the same species and this phenomenon makes it possible to construct fate maps (Chapter 2.4). Similarly, the cell lineage of the root tip of the water fern *Azolla* may be reconstructed because it is so regular (p. 39).

The uniformity of cell lineage in development must arise from the control of cell division planes and positions. When these cell divisions are disturbed, then embryogenesis may be disrupted (p. 52).

However, the organization of developing systems does not always depend on regular cell lineages. For instance, viable mammals and viable plants can be derived from single cells which do not recapitulate the cell lineages of normal development (pp. 58 and 74). Indeed, it can be shown, both in *Drosophila* (p. 67) and in higher plants, that clones of cells marked in their nuclei at early stages of development can contribute to most or all the tissue types of the adult. Clearly in these organism, the divisions of the early cell lineage have not segregated the capacity to differentiate in a variety of ways.

Lability of developing systems

Even in organisms with a regular cell lineage, the ability of cells to change their developmental potentiality is great. For instance, the developmental potential of early mouse and sea urchin cells can be changed by altering their relative position in the developing embryo (pp. 57 and 60).

There are rather few limitations on the lability of parts of other animal eggs. Isolation and transplantation experiments have identified some regions in the egg which influence the development of neighbouring cells (e.g. the grey crescent in amphibians, p. 66). The effect of these controlling regions is to impose regularity in the embryogenesis of many plants and animals. There is little doubt that some cells in growing plant apices show a degree of lability because their developmental potential can be changed by surgery even though they may be committed, in a general sense, as shoot meristem cells (p. 80).

Developmental systems are able to self-organize

This statement is supported by the evidence that parts of animal embryos are able to form a whole embryo (p. 54), that combined animal embryos can form a single individual (e.g. mouse, p. 55), and that whole plants can regenerate from unorganized cell aggregates and pollen grains (Chapter 2.3). The implication of these findings is that cell heterogeneity arises as a consequence of interactions between the cells of these developing organisms.

Cell heterogeneity by the division of asymmetric cells

It appears that one commonly used method for generating cells with different developmental capacities is the mitotic division of cells with distinct ends so that the original ends segregate into different daughter cells. This process is obvious in the early division of the eggs of *Fucus*, and in the divisions which divide across the animal–vegetal axis of most animal embryos (Chapter 2.4). The division of cells with distinct ends occurs throughout the development of organisms and it is exemplified in adult plants by the cell divisions which produce the guard cells and subsidiary cells of the leaf stomata (p. 35).

It can be shown that developmental capacity segregates in these divisions but the molecular nature of these capacities is usually unclear. In ascidians and nematodes, it is known that the ability to form enzymes characteristic of distinct larval cell types does segregate at early divisions of the embryo and for one enzyme, the alkaline phosphatase characteristic of ascidian larval gut, it is likely that it is the maternal messenger RNA for this molecule which is unequally partitioned between the daughter cells (p. 54). In other cases, it is likely that elements which regulate subsequent transcription are segregating. However, the general importance of cell interactions in the development of adult cell types (Chapters 3.5 and 4.1), suggests that frequently the capacities which are segregating are those that control rather simple cell properties such as adhesion, motility and the ability to form gap junctions (Part 3). It may be that these properties must first lead to progressive cell interactions before the segregated capacity can express itself as differential gene expression. Thus, the division of an asymmetric cell in half may either immediately lead to differential gene expression in its two daughter cells or it may create two cells with distinct phenotypes which interact in different ways with neighbouring cells.

In some instances a parent cell which does not show evidence of asymmetrical distribution of its cytoplasm may undergo division to give two daughter cells of unequal size. It is possible that such unequal cell divisions may give rise to heterogeneous cell types in several ways. On the one hand, the smallest cell formed from an unequal cell division inherits a smaller proportion of the parental cell characters than does the larger cell. This process is thought to be involved in generating the protein-synthetic phenotypes of the three main cell types of the 16-cell sea urchin embryo (p. 58). On the other hand, simply by producing cells of different size the two daughters will pack together in particular ways with each other and with surrounding cells. The beautiful geometry of plant meristems must depend on such processes (p. 38 et seq.) and it is likely that such geometrical considerations are also important during early animal development; the experimental equalization of normally unequal cell divisions frequently alters cell packing (e.g. Table 2.4.1).

Restriction of developmental potential is a progressive process

As embryonic development proceeds so the developmental alternatives of cells in a particular cell lineage become progressively restricted. Thus the cells of the 8-cell mouse embryo can form all parts of the foetus and placenta while at the 64-cell stage, some of the cells can only form the trophoblast part of the placenta while others lack the capacity to form trophoblast. One day later, some of the cells can only form part of the yolk sac, while the other cells have lost this capacity as well (p. 59).

A progressive restriction of developmental potential is also demonstrated by the leaf primordia of the fern *Osmunda* which will regenerate the whole plant if isolated at a very young stage, but with progressively older primordia there is an increasing tendency to form only leaves (p. 80). In this case it is not known whether progressive restriction is a function of the whole organ or whether the constituent cells show an intrinsic restriction of developmental potential.

Stability of developmental restriction

The intrinsic restriction of development can be extremely stable and maintained by cell populations through many rounds of cell division. Thus the imaginal discs of *Drosophila* can be grown in adult flies for long periods and these discs are subsequently usually capable of forming the adult structures to which they were committed by the events of embryogenesis (p. 78). Similarly, the shoot apices of flowering plants can exist in alternative states (as seen in the phase change in *Hedera*, in vernalization, and in the alternation of gametophyte and sporophyte generations), and these alternative states are usually extremely stable and can be transmitted through many cell generations (Chapter 2.5). Such cells may be described as exhibiting a degree of 'determination'.

The transmission of these states may be very stable but it is also potentially changeable. Thus the imaginal discs of *Drosophila* can sometimes transdetermine and form adult structures which are outside their normal developmental range, and heat treatment can alter the vernalized state of some plants (p. 82).

Determination can be shown by single plant and animal cells in culture (pp. 79 and 84). Again these states can be changed by experimental abuse but the implication of these studies on the stability of developmental restriction is that during development very stable circuits of nuclear–cytoplasmic interactions are set up which maintain the phenotype of mature tissues against fluctuations which might otherwise be induced by changing environmental conditions.

Part 3
Cell Communication in
Development

Chapter 3.1
Short-range Interactions in Development
C.F. Graham

3.1.1   INTRODUCTION

It is usual to classify cell interactions into two categories: there are short-range interactions, which depend on close cell apposition, and long-range interactions, which are mediated by diffusible substances which can pass between distant cells. This part of the book is mainly concerned with short-range interactions, and hormone-mediated distant interactions are discussed in Part 5.

Short-range cell interactions are important in early development because they provide the means by which cells can change each other's phenotype without affecting distant cells. Since it is now known that cell allocation and cell determination can occur in cell populations of less than 100 cells in plant and animal embryos, it is clear that there are very local events involved in creating cell distinctions (Chapters 2.2, 2.3 and 2.4). Experiments on these small developing cell populations demonstrate cell interactions between neighbours. Cells removed from developing systems may be able to form many more cell types in isolation than they would have done if they had been left in the intact organism (Chapters 2.3, 2.4 and 2.5). These observations show that cells may be held in check by their neighbours. In contrast, isolated cells may sometimes form fewer phenotypes than they would have done if they had been left in place (Part 2). Clearly, local cell interactions may also extend and enhance the developmental range of a cell in the whole organism.

Here we are concerned with the properties of cells in developing systems and the extent to which apparently simple cell functions, such as adhesion, ionic coupling, locomotion, membrane recognition of other cells and their matrices, are involved in the development of intricate patterns of cell type distribution and maintenance. The morphogenetic consequences of these properties are discussed in the individual chapters and then these properties are put into the context of the whole developing embryo in Chapter 4.3.

3.1.2   PATTERNS OF CELL DISTRIBUTION

Adult animals and plants have their different cell types arranged in an orderly distribution. Several kinds of mechanism could give rise to these patterns. We have already seen that the division pattern of early embryos and plant meristems is both oriented and controlled, and that a disturbance of the division planes alters the pattern of cell distribution later in development (Chapters 2.3 and 2.4). Further, these division patterns, in animal embryos at least, depend on such intimate cell functions as cell adhesion and ionic coupling between the cells. The development of orderly arrays of cells may also be directly dependent on their position either because their formation depends on local interactions such as those which are seen in embryonic induction (Chapter 3.5), or because the cells identify their position in a field of positional information (Chapter 4.2). Certainly, local events must dominate the arrangement of cell types in plant development where the cells are not freely motile.

Animal development is characterized by the relative movement of cell populations so that the final array of tissues is not anticipated in any detail by the distribution of their progenitor cells in the early embryo. The fate maps in Chapter 2.4 illustrate this point, which is further exemplified by a description of the movement of cells in sea urchin, amphibian and fish development (Chapters 3.3 and 4.3).

These relative cell movements are highly patterned, so that the cells usually follow rather fixed routes to their final destination and the time at which a given cell type moves is restricted to a particular developmental stage. The initiation and cessation of movement in such cells does not seem to be due to any irreversible change in cell function, because cells may grow out and spread on plastic or glass surfaces in tissue culture media either before or after the time when they would usually move in the intact embryo.

The importance of cell adhesion and cell locomotion in these movements is obvious. At the simplest level, a cell group may only move by exerting a force against a substrate until the embryo develops a circulatory system which carries cells around the body. Until this time, both adhesion and a locomotory engine are probably needed for movement. It is particularly difficult to disentangle the roles of adhesion and locomotion in the movements of embryogenesis. On the one hand, changes in cell adhesiveness are associated with such movements (Chapter 3.2), and on the other hand, changes in cell locomotion occur in synchrony with these migrations (Chapter 3.3).

It is also clear that in the control of these relative cell movements, the cells behave as if they know where they are. The implication is that cells must be able to distinguish between different substrates, between different surface contacts with other cells and between different circulatory molecules (see following chapters).

3.1.3   INTERACTION MECHANISMS

Transfer of large macromolecules between cells

One cell might be able to control the behaviour of another by transmitting macromolecules such as nucleic acids and proteins. These macromolecules are involved in the control of protein synthesis within a cell and it

would be economical if they were also used in cell-to-cell interactions. However, large molecules do not readily move between cells which are closely linked (Chapter 3.4), and special mechanisms of secretion and endocytosis would be required if large molecules were to be passed between the cells of developing animal systems. Alternatively, there might be cytoplasmic connections but such connections are not found between interacting cells of early animal embryos, although the cells of plant embryos are connected by plasmodesmata. The conclusion is that macromolecular exchange is unlikely to be a general mechanism by which one cell controls the development of another.

Transfer of ions and small molecules between cells

Cells might change the ionic balance in neighbouring cells and in this way alter their development; in some cases it is known that the ionic composition of the medium around the chromosomes may affect their apparent gene activity, and it is therefore interesting that ions are able to move between cells in developing animals and plants. Ion flow between cells can be demonstrated by introducing a pulsed current into one cell and noting the electric potential in neighbouring cells, and it is found that there are low-resistance connections between plant cells joined by plasmodesmata and animal cells linked by gap junctions (Chapter 3.4). The cells of the early embryos of starfish, squid, fish, amphibians and chickens are connected by low-resistance junctions and it is therefore conceivable that ions regularly move between the cells of these embryos and are used to mediate cell interactions.

Release of substances by one cell which interacts with the surface of another

Cells may release chemicals from their cell surface which change the characteristics of adjacent cells. For instance, impulses are transmitted between nerves by one cell releasing acetylcholine which changes the permeability of the neighbouring cell membrane. This impulse transmission is a local event because the acetylcholine is rapidly broken down by the enzyme acetylcholinesterase; it is conceivable that similar types of interaction occur between the cells of developing systems. The only evidence in favour of such a mode of communication is the observation that serotonin, noradrenaline, and acetylcholine are found in developing fish and sea urchin embryos and that analogues and antagonists of these molecules disturb development [1–3]. It is probably premature to decide whether such molecules are used to influence the development of cells inside the embryo.

Interactions between the outsides of cells without molecular exchange

It is known that substances applied to the outside of cells can rapidly change their behaviour. Plant lectins, for instance, can stimulate lymphocytes to divide and form blast cells by acting solely on the cell surface (Chapter 3.6). It seems that moving cells use such interactions to recognize their neighbours and the interactions between pollen and stigma are a particularly clear example of this. Animal cells can recognize each other (Chapters 3.5 and 3.6) and they are presumably using mechanisms similar to those which have been discovered in pollen and stigma.

3.1.4 REFERENCES

1 Buznikov G.A., Chudakova I.V. & Zvezdina N.D. (1964) The role of neurohumours in early embryogenesis. I. Serotonin content of developing embryos of sea urchin and loach. *J. Embryol. exp. Morph.*, **12**, 563–74.
2 Buznikov G.A., Chudakova I.V., Berdysheva L.V. & Vyazmina N.M. (1968) The role of neurohumours in early embryogenesis. II. Acetylcholine and catecholamine content in developing embryos of sea urchin and loach. *J. Embryol. exp. Morph.*, **20**, 119–28.
3 Gustafson T. & Toneby M.I. (1971) How genes control morphogenesis. *Am. Scient.*, **59**, 452–62.

Chapter 3.2
Cell Adhesion
A.S.G. Curtis

3.2.1   INTRODUCTION

The cleavage patterns of early animal embryos are often controlled by adhesive cell interactions (Chapters 2.1 and 2.4), and cell adhesion is also intimately involved in the processes of cell positioning which occur as the cleaved egg is transformed into more complex patterns of structure (Chapters 3.3. and 4.3). In this chapter, I shall describe adhesive structures, evaluate their function in cell adhesion, and then discuss how adhesion may act and be controlled during embryogenesis.

3.2.2   ADHESIVE STRUCTURES

Form of the structures

Zonula adhaerens and general considerations

The cell contacts that form adhesions are frequently unspecialized in nature. This type is termed the zonula adhaerens and this is the only contact structure seen between some cell types (see Fig. 3.2.1). For instance, they are the only contacts found in early stages of chick development [67]. There is a gap of 7 to 30 nm which is

Fig. 3.2.1. Diagrammatic representation of a zonula adhaerens adhesion, shown in cross section. Microfilaments approaching the plasmalemmae are shown in cross section and lengthwise. The gap between the plasmalemmae is about 7–35 nm wide in life. The question of the nature and presence of structure in the gap between the plasmalemmae is discussed in the text.

present between the apposed cell membranes, each darkly stained by osmium tetroxide. Various differing theories as to the nature of this gap, have been put forward. At one extreme, it was suggested [74, 79] that the gap is an artefact, and at another that it is entirely filled with carbohydrate-rich material attached to lipids and proteins in the cell membrane. Both these views seem untenable because it is possible to penetrate the gap with tracers. Brightman [2] permeated ferritin tracer molecules, which can be easily visualized in the electron microscope, down the gaps between live cells. Permeation is exceedingly rapid and all parts of the zonula adhaerens gap were permeable to these molecules. After fixation, the gaps became impermeable to ferritin tracers. These observations suggest that the gap exists in life, that in life it is wider than 9 nm (the diameter of the ferritin molecule), and that little, if any, material other than water and dissolved molecules can fill the gap. However, the phrase 'little, if any' embraces two important alternatives, described in the next paragraph.

Is there a total absence of macromolecular material spanning the gap in the zonula adhaerens? Or is there only an insignificant and unimportant amount of such material? Or is there sufficient material to effect a reasonably strong bond between apposed cells? The correct answer to these questions is not yet known, but it looks as though the answer may well be the remarkably tantalizing one that there is just sufficient macromolecular material to effect a fairly stable adhesion, without appreciably affecting the permeation of tracers such as ferritin.

On occasion, contacts of this type may be complexly involuted, so that the two contacting cells are fitted together like a lock and a key. Such contacts are rare, but they have been seen in some tissues [83]. The effectiveness of such contacts in preventing detachment of the cells presumably will be countered if the two cells are able to make withdrawing movements in the right sequence. In other words, cells that are skilled at unravelling string (withdrawing from the involutions) will be little impeded in detaching such contacts.

More complex contacts are:
(1) The zonula occludens or tight junction (see below).
(2) The macula adhaerens or desmosome (see below).
(3) The septate desmosome.
(4) The gap junction, in which the cells form cytoplasmic connections, as a result of the partial fusion of the cells (see Chapter 3.4).

(5) Incomplete cell divisions which result in cytoplasmic contacts between the daughter cells of each division. One classical example of this is found in the developing spermatids, derived from a single spermatocyte [29], which are all linked by cytoplasmic bridges. Moore [60] pointed out that many such bridges may form as a zygote goes through successive cleavages, and persistent cytoplasmic continuity between daughter cells is observed during mouse cleavage [37]. It is somewhat unclear as to how much this, and the gap junction, contribute to adhesion, but presumably these contacts have a certain strength.

Zonula occludens

The zonula occludens (see Fig. 3.2.2) is a structure which prevents permeation laterally through it of tracers, such as ferritin. This fact and the appearance of the contact in the electron microscope suggest that the pair of cell membranes make very close approaches to each other. These contacts are common in certain regions of the adult (kidney, brain, skin), and they link together the outside cells of the early 32-cell mouse

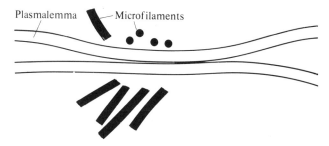

Fig. 3.2.2. Zonula occludens adhesion in cross section. The plasmalemmae approach to within 1 nm and they may be in physical contact. These adhesions often form narrow lines running for considerable distances in the contact between two cells. Protein molecules in the membrane may be aggregated in the region of these contacts.

embryo [24]. Gilula [36] comments that they are frequently present in epithelial cell contacts even early in embryogenesis but there is still insufficient information about their appearance in development.

Macula adhaerens

The macula adhaerens (or desmosome) is apparently a specialized contact structure which is involved in adhesion. Its structure is shown in Fig. 3.2.3. A dense series of specialized filaments of desmin lie in the cytoplasm of each cell in the region close to the specialized contact. The actual structure of the contact itself is still somewhat enigmatic. In sections, longitudinal bands of staining parallel to and between the cell membranes,can be seen, but ferritin tracers can apparently come to lie within these stained bands, which gives rise to doubts about their reality in life. The macula adhaerens is, as its name suggests, 'a spot'; it has close relatives of different geometrical shape—terminal bars and fasciae adherentes. Some authors (Gilula [36], for example) consider that the zonula adhaerens is but a long, linear desmosome. There are still problems concerning the interpretation of the gap in desmosomes and the zonula adhaerens.

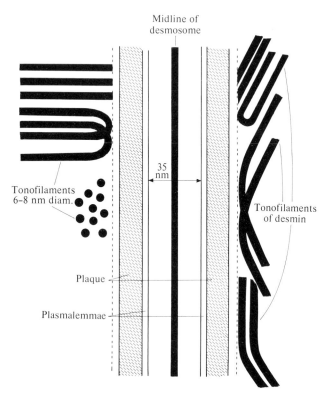

Fig. 3.2.3. Desmosome (macula adhaerens, fascia adhaerens) in cross section. Diagram prepared by Dr C. Skerrow.

Midline of desmosome

Tonofilaments 6–8 nm diam.

35 nm

Tonofilaments of desmin

Plaque

Plasmalemmae

Gap junctions and septate desmosomes

The gap junction formed between cells by the protein elements termed connexons (see Chapter 3.4) may have an adhesive function. Septate desmosomes, found almost exclusively in invertebrates, appear to be a type of occluding junction (Fig. 3.2.4; see Green *et al.* [41]).

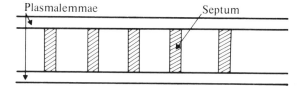

Plasmalemmae   Septum

Fig. 3.2.4. The septate desmosome in cross section: this structure is only seen in invertebrates.

Structures in adhesion

Cell to cell

The evidence that the zonula adhaerens is an adhesive contact comes from the somewhat obvious fact that it is often the only contact found between cells that are clearly adhering. Correlation of this type of contact with the strength of adhesion measured (see section 3.2.3), suggests that these contacts are weakly adhesive [10].

Evidence that the macula adhaerens and the zonula occludens are adhesive structures is somewhat more circumstantial. Macula adhaerens contacts are found to resist breakage when cells shrink in incorrect fixation. This suggests no more than that they may be adhesive structures. The zonula occludens contacts are found mainly in tissues which are difficult to dissociate into single cells. This suggests that they may be strongly adhesive structures in comparison with zonulae adhaerentes (which are easily dissociated either by a variety of chemical techniques or by the activity of the cells themselves (see section 3.2.4)). No technique has yet been introduced which clearly dissects zonulae occludentes. Violent mechanical dispersion of a tissue appears to leave zonulae occludentes intact, because after such treatment an intact cell will carry its own halves of zonulae occludentes, along with the other halves of the zonulae occludentes that have been torn out of the cells that were originally adjacent.

Cell to substrate

Surprisingly few studies have been made of the nature of cell contacts with non-cellular surfaces. In part, this lack must be due to technical difficulties in sectioning materials such as glass. Cornell [5] showed that cells in adhesion with epoxy surfaces, probably covered with adsorbed protein, appear to yield zonula adhaerens type contacts. More recently, Rees *et al.* [68], examining the adhesion of fibroblasts to a variety of surfaces, have produced evidence that a zonula adhaerens structure is produced, with perhaps a complex network of protein within the gap (Fig. 3.2.5). Obviously, it would be interesting to subject such systems to tests on their permeation by tracers such as ferritin. It would also be most interesting to know the structure of artificial adhesions made with reagents such as polylysine, which produce very strong adhesions, comparable in strength with zonula occludens.

Interference reflection microscopy [7] provides a method of measuring the distance between the external membrane of a live cell and the surface to which it is adherent. Thus, in principle, it might distinguish zonulae occludentes from zonulae adhaerentes. Unfortunately, the lateral resolution of the technique is poor. Only the original paper and recent work by Gingell [38] have attempted to use the technique to make measurements of the gap distance. Though the technique would ignore small areas of close contact, such as the classical zonula occludens, it gives a good average measurement over large areas. The author [7] and Gingell [38], established that 10–20 nm gaps can occur in physiological saline between a cell and a substrate to which the cell adheres, and that the dimensions of the gap are sensitive to electrostatic and ionic conditions.

3.2.3 MEASUREMENTS OF ADHESION

It may seem surprising to give consideration to techniques in this book, but an understanding of the methods used in research is particularly important to appreciate the results in this field.

In essence, there are but two techniques of measuring cell adhesion.
(1) Measurement of the forces required to separate cells from a contact.
(2) Measurement of the forces a cell can exert on another cell/surface, to perturb a collision, so that an adhesion results.

Cell separation

The first method has been little used, because a host of problems complicate such measurements. Amongst these are the following.

(i) Uncertainty as to whether the cells separate along their junctions or whether the break-up actually tears through the cell body, which subsequently reseals [85].

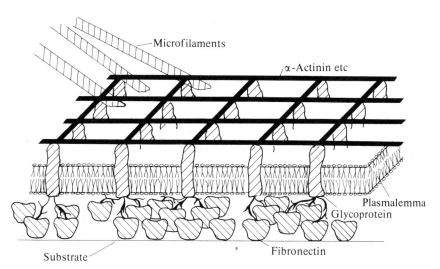

Fig. 3.2.5. Rees's model of an adhesion between a cell and a non-cellular substrate. Fibronectin (LETS) forms a major structural component of this bridging type model. By kind permission of Dr D. Rees and Cambridge University Press.

Microfilaments

α-Actinin etc

Plasmalemma
Glycoprotein

Substrate

Fibronectin

If the latter is the case, measurement of the force required for tissue disruption is not related to any force that may hold cells together. One variation of this technique has been introduced by Steinberg and his co-workers [78]. In this, aggregates or tissue masses of spherical form are deformed under a centrifugal force. The devisers of this technique relate the extent of deformation to the interfacial energy of the cell contacts, and then relate this to adhesiveness. Critics of this theory suspect that the measurement actually includes measurement of other quantities, such as the deformability of the cells or the internal strength and orientation of the cytoskeleton, giving 'grip' to the cell [68].

(ii) Difficulties in deciding whether the description is to be treated as a 'peeling apart' or as normal pull (90° pull) on the adhesive contact areas.

The method has been used to investigate the somewhat simpler case in which cells adhere to a 'plane' surface, such as glass, and are then detached in a gravity or shear field [20, 25, 85]. Results are usually of a qualitative nature.

Cell collision

The second set of methods has been extensively used to investigate cell adhesion, both qualitatively and quantitatively. In essence, a cell suspension is agitated so that aggregates form if the cells are adhesive. Cells are brought into contact by the shear forces induced in the medium by agitation, or in some instances by Brownian movement or by gravitational forces. In most cases, these forces would continue to act and tend to reseparate the cells (Fig. 3.2.6). Thus these measurements are concerned with the process of formation and with the process of break-up of an adhesion.

The actual lifetime of a collision is probably of the order of a millisecond if it is ineffective in producing an adhesion. Thus the process of adhesion takes place to an extent which is sufficient to withstand immediate break-up within this interval. Argument, largely of a speculative nature, has developed as to whether this type of adhesion is entirely identical with that found in a cell adhesion which has persisted for a much longer period. Cell suspensions are usually made by dispersing solid tissues and tissue cultures with one or more of the following agents: collagenase, trypsin, various impure proteases, chelating agents, mechanical agitation, etc. It can be argued that any or all of these techniques modify

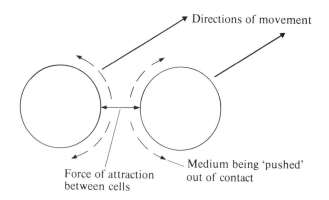

Fig. 3.2.6. Diagram showing the forces acting to bring about or to prevent a cell collision and adhesion with another cell. The left cell is travelling faster than the right one and both are moving in a direction such that the left cell will tend to collide with the right one. This leads to a force tending to cause collision until the particles pass each other, then it induces a re-separating force. Pushing the medium out of the gap between the approaching cells, and pulling it back during re-separation, tends to oppose collision and re-separation. Any force of attraction will perturb the interaction, so that approach is more extensive and re-separation prevented. Analysis of these forces allows calculation and measurement of the forces involved in adhesion. During the approach, the particles rotate as shown.

cell adhesion in unknown and misleading manners.

Four main methods of using this technique to assess cell adhesiveness have been developed. The earliest of these was an end-point assay.

End-point assay

This is the system in which cell suspensions in a shaking flask aggregate into multicellular bodies; its use was pioneered by Moscona [61]. When the diameter of the aggregate ceases to enlarge, it is measured and its size is taken to be a measure of the adhesiveness of the cells. In this simple form there are a number of assumptions made in the use of the techniques and these are rarely if ever tested.

It is assumed that the aggregates cease growing in size because cells are being broken off at the same rate as they are being added; in other words, they are equilibrium aggregates. This has only been tested and found to be so for one cell type [34]. This would lead to the reasonable assumption that aggregate diameter is directly related to adhesiveness. This follows if the adhesiveness of individual cells does not increase with aggregate diameter and if the shearing forces that tend to break up aggregates increase as the square of the aggregate radius.

Another assumption that has not been tested is whether there is a sufficient supply of single cells and small aggregates to allow the aggregates to grow to their equilibrium size. There is also the problem that cells may change their properties during the assay. For instance, it takes 24–48 hours for chick embryonic cells to form aggregates of 2 mm diameter and this time interval is sufficient to permit cells to change their adhesive properties considerably.

When cells from two vertebrate embryonic tissue types are mixed together, it is possible, though not well established, that initially they form aggregates in which the various cell types are in a random arrangement. Over the next 24–48 hours, cells sort out so that one cell type comes to lie as an internal phase while the other is external (see Fig. 3.2.7). Other features of these aggregates are described in section 3.2.5. Tissue type sorting out seems to over-ride species differences in vertebrates. In some sponges [32] and with different slime mould species [33], the aggregates form as initially random or partially random arrangements but may then separate more or less completely into separate species-specific bodies. No systematic investigation has yet been carried out to test whether or not there is a regularity behind the different types of sorting out.

Single-cell aggregation to tissues

A modification of this technique was introduced by Roth and Weston [71] to investigate specificity in adhesion (see section 3.2.5). In this, aggregates or even tissue lumps or sheets are presented with a suspension of cells of the same or different type and the proportions adhering to the aggregates are compared. In most instances (but see Büültjens & Edwards [4]), adhesion with cells of like type is strongly preferred to adhesion with cells of different type.

Kinetics of aggregation

At the moment, the most widely used technique for assessing the adhesiveness of cells is that in which the kinetics of aggregation of a cell suspension are measured. This method was introduced by the author of this chapter [18].

In the simplest form, a cell suspension is shaken and samples are removed over a series of time intervals [26]. The number of single cells and/or aggregates of various sizes is counted. Curves of the type shown in Fig. 3.2.8 are obtained. The more rapid the aggregation, the more adhesive are the cells.

In its simplest form the technique suffers from a number of limitations. The rate of aggregation should be related to the average shear rate in these systems, but the standard deviation in aggregate sizes will be affected primarily by the greatest transient shear rate. Consequently, aggregation will be terminated prematurely and thus measurements will not be linearly related to adhesiveness. The complex flow patterns in flasks shaken on reciprocatory or gyratory shakers will make it difficult to quantify the shear rate on which aggregation depends. Finally, cells of differing sizes or experiments with different cell densities will be very hard to compare. Methods using this approach measure aggregation by

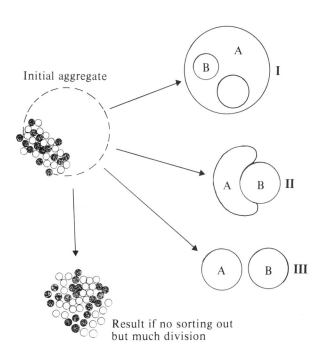

Fig. 3.2.7. Diagram to illustrate the various types of sorting out and patterning that can occur when cells of two types are aggregated together. Aggregates shown in cross section. Cell type A is black, B is white. Aggregates may sort out to type I, where one type encloses the other, or type II, where one cell type partially enclosed another, or to separate bodies, type III. In the absence of sorting out, intense division can produce the appearance of some degree of sorting out (bottom left).

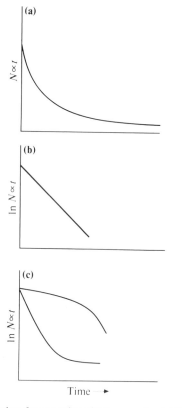

Fig. 3.2.8. Kinetics of aggregation of cell suspension (a) Total number ($N \propto t$) of particles per unit volume (single cells and aggregates of all sizes) plotted against time. (b) Replotting (a) with the total particle concentration expressed logarithmically. The straight line nature of this plot shows that aggregation follows standard kinetics; the gradient of the line is related to the adhesiveness of the cells. (c) Abnormal aggregation kinetics showing changes in adhesion during measurement of non-adhesive cell populations or cells that can form only a small number of adhesions.

direct counting, by image-analysing computer counts, by Coulter counting or, probably least satisfactorily, by optical density.

Kinetics of adhesion: collision efficiency

This approach can be improved by aggregating the cells in a known constant laminar shear flow, as in a Couette viscometer [8]. Here the collision rate, which is dependent on the shear rate, cell size and cell population density, can be evaluated and this compared with the collision rate effective in producing aggregates. The ratio of the effective rate to the absolute rate can be

measured and this, the collision efficiency, gives a reproducible quantitative measurement of adhesion, which is independent of shear rate, cell size and cell population density. The method is rapid, but cannot be used with large cells of high density with existing designs of equipment.

The collision efficiency method has been developed as method for investigating specificity of adhesion [9]. Measurements are made of the adhesiveness of two different cell types and of their mixtures in various proportions of each type. If adhesion is unspecified, the average adhesion of the cells in the mixtures will be the mean of the adhesiveness of each type, separately weighted for their proportions in the mixture. If their adhesion is specific, the adhesion of the mixture will be reduced in a predictable manner because the collisions between unlike cells will be ineffective in producing adhesions. Thus, any mixture of two cell types that each adhere non-specifically and that each have a collision efficiency of 20% will have the same 20% collision efficiency value. If they adhere completely specifically to their own type, the adhesiveness of a 50:50 mixture will be 10%. This method has the advantage that cells do not need to be individually identified, but the disadvantage that a very small proportion of cells showing special behaviour will not be noticed.

3.2.4   CONDITIONS FOR ADHESION OF CELLS

Cell adhesion is affected by a vast variety of substances, by alterations in cell surface structure and by a considerable range of physical conditions. One problem is that adhesion may be produced by a large range of mechanisms. Another problem is that cell biologists rarely know whether the treatment which alters cell adhesion does so within the normal mechanisms used by cells, or whether by accident the cell has been manipulated into some other mechanism of adhesion not used in life. Finally, the reader and the researcher should bear in mind that cells may normally use two or more different mechanisms of adhesion simultaneously; consequently, it may be false to regard all evidence from the viewpoint of someone who looks for but one, universal, mechanism.

However, a mere list of substances and their effects would be of little use to most readers, so that some degree of interpretation will be attempted, dividing the evidence into those conventional sections which groups of workers have usually seen as arguing for one or other particular mechanism of adhesion.

Electrostatic mechanisms

It is well known to physical chemists that surfaces bearing a fixed or adsorbed charge tend to repel the approach of similarly charged surfaces because of the forces of electrostatic repulsion set up as their electrostatic double layers (Gouy–Chapman double layers) begin to overlap [66]. A description of electrostatic forces between atoms can be found in Chapter 6.2. Cell surfaces in physiological saline are negatively charged, and so it might be expected that cell adhesion would be altered by changes in the charge on the cell surface or by conditions which might affect the range of electrostatic repulsion. Curiously, this possibility has only recently been rigorously tested, but there is a large amount of circumstantial evidence that supports the idea that the conditions of electrostatic repulsion acting between two cells may play an important role in determining whether or not an adhesion can form or break up. Cells become less adhesive when the ionic strength of the surrounding medium is lowered, or when divalent cations are removed from the medium. Conversely, replacement of the divalent cations increases adhesion [87], as do treatments which cleave off superficial charged neuraminate [36]. It might be supposed, at first sight, that calcium, magnesium and other divalent cations would have exactly the same extent of effect on the adhesiveness of a particular cell type when used at the same ionic strength. Since some cells adhere better with calcium, and others with magnesium, some scientists concluded that electrostatic forces of repulsion could play little part in controlling cell adhesion. However, this criticism fails to appreciate the physical chemistry of the situation. The different extents of binding of two species of cation by the cell surface and the different sizes of the ions mean that one cation will be more effective in reducing electrostatic forces at a particular concentration than the others. This fact probably dispels doubts about the qualitative evidence in favour of electrostatic forces of repulsion being active in adhesion. Adhesion is diminished by modification of the cell surface with agents that increase surface charge [59].

The rigorous quantitative evidence to establish or destroy the theory that electrostatic forces of repulsion act in cell adhesion requires very careful experiment with cells in systems that are well defined in surface chemical terms. Probably by far the best of the few experiments of this type is one carried out by Gingell [38], in which the detachment of cells from an electrode was studied at various surface potentials with gravity acting as the detaching force. Though some might criticize the artificiality of the system, it shows that electrostatic forces of repulsion can act to detach a cell from a surface.

Titration of cells with a basic polymer flocculates them, presumably because the polymer (polylysine, for example) binds to negative charges on the surface of each cell. Deman and Bruyneel [21] produced an elegant demonstration of the extent of the electrical double layers around each cell. They showed that polylysines of short chainlength (i.e. two residues, and perhaps up to 20 residues) could not flocculate cells, but longer-chain polylysines could do so. This is presumably because those with many residues penetrate through both electrical double layers which kept the cells too far apart for the shorter-chain polymers to act. Brooks and co-workers [3] showed that dextrans (neutral polysaccharide polymers) either flocculate or stabilize, and

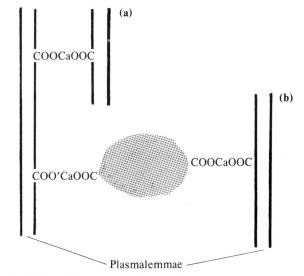

Fig. 3.2.9. Bridging systems. (a) and (b) to illustrate the concept of calcium bridging. In (a) calcium ions are supposed to react with carboxyl groups on either cell surface, and thus link the surfaces together. In (b) calcium bridges are supposed to form between the cell surface and an intervening cement molecule at both ends of the cement molecule.

prevent adhesion of red-cell suspensions depending on the size and concentration of the molecule. Their explanation of the stabilization (prevention of adhesion) is that adsorbed dextran raises the cell-surface potential and that consequently, the forces of repulsion are increased. Flocculation takes place at lower concentrations of dextran because there is a smaller rise in surface potential. The dextrans of higher-molecular weight are more effective than the those of lower-molecular weight in promoting flocculation, probably because they are adsorbed and bridge from one cell to another more effectively (see Fig. 3.2.9). Lower-molecular-weight dextrans are too short to bridge from one cell to another.

Thus there is much evidence that electrostatic forces of repulsion act in tending to prevent cell adhesion at the initial approach of two surfaces, or in actually producing the breaking apart of two surfaces that were in adhesion. Evidence from dissociation studies suggests that only the macula adhaerens and zonula adhaerens structures can be broken up in this way. Alternative theories have been advanced to explain the action of factors such as calcium in terms of calcium bridges [76], but these theories do not explain the whole body of information that is accounted for by the concept that electrostatic forces of repulsion act in controlling whether an adhesion will form or will reseparate. Obviously, this theory cannot account for all experimental results, for there must be some attractive force or system that can at times overcome the forces of repulsion and establish adhesions. The nature or natures of such mechanisms are discussed in the next two sections.

Bridging systems, intercellular cements

Physical chemists use the term 'bridging systems' to describe particle adhesions in which a molecule is adsorbed or bound at one end to one surface and at the other end to a second surface. Biologists will be entirely familiar with one particular bridging system: the use of antibodies to agglutinate cells (see Chapter 3.7). Physical chemists will tend to view bridging systems as those in which flocculation occurs when a soluble bridging agent is added to a particle suspension. Biologists appreciate that there are two manners in which bridging might exist. The bridging molecule might be one which is secreted by cells, as a soluble component and which adsorbs to receptors on the cell surface.

Alternatively, the bridging molecules may be immobilized in the surfaces of the cells, projecting outwards to interact with each other. Theoretical models of these two systems are shown in Fig. 3.2.10. Such systems can be viewed as ones of receptors and bound molecules. The receptors may be mutual receptors for each other.

Although it is easy to produce adhesion by molecules, which obviously provide bridging (e.g. polylysines, plant lectins, and antibodies), these adhesions may be unnatural. It is of interest that all these agents produce adhesions that are far stronger than normal cell adhesions and they may be unlike the adhesions of live cells.

The evidence that cells adhere by some form of bridging system, is as follows.

Action of proteases

Proteases, such as pronase and trypsin, tend to dissociate tissues into individual cells. An obvious, though by no means firm, conclusion from this observation is that some bridging molecule is being degraded. Since these treatments appear to reduce possible electrostatic forces of repulsion, it cannot be argued that proteases simply increase the repulsion between the cells. Explanations other than the destruction of a cementing material have been advanced [19], and it must be pointed out that use of such non-specific agents that can affect many components of the cell membrane makes it hard to interpret these results.

Temperature effects

Many cell types appear to need to be relatively warm in order to adhere and it is supposed that they synthesize new material at the elevated temperature. However, this seems in most cases to be a restriction limited to cells that have been treated with proteases. Are components of the cell surface which are of importance for adhesion being synthesized? Presumably so, but we do not know the function of these molecules. Thus the early argument that this evidence supported a cementing theory of cell adhesion must be regarded with doubt.

Factors stimulating adhesion

Factors can be obtained from cells, which are macromolecular in nature and which stimulate adhesion either

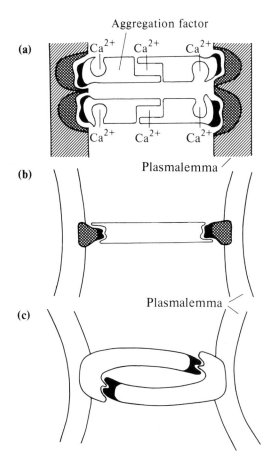

Aggregation factor

(a)

Ca²⁺ Ca²⁺ Ca²⁺

Ca²⁺ Ca²⁺ Ca²⁺

Plasmalemma

(b)

Plasmalemma

(c)

Fig. 3.2.10. Bridging systems continued. (a) A version of the calcium bridge system proposed by Burger (see *Symp. Soc. exp. Biol.*, **32** (1978)) for the adhesion of a species of sponge. The association between the aggregation factor and the cell surface is dependent on some type of carbohydrate interaction, with calcium playing a role in stabilizing the structure of the aggregation factor. The interaction of the two molecules of aggregation factor is depicted as a calcium bridge. Slightly modified from Burger. (b) A receptor–ligand type of bridge in which the receptors on the cell surface bind with a ligand molecule which is at least bivalent. This general model also includes, of course, the structure shown in Fig. 3.2.9 (b). (c) The mutual receptor bridge, in which a single molecular species has both parts of the interaction site and binds to its fellow molecule projecting from an adjacent surface. Bridging systems can be viewed as being either of the receptor–ligand type or of the mutual receptor type. Fig. 3.2.10 (b) and (c) from Burger (ref. above). By kind permission of Dr M.M. Burger and Cambridge University Press.

non-specifically or specifically. The specific aspects of such molecules are considered in detail in section 3.2.5, but it is appropriate to note at this point that another

argument in favour of cementing (bridging) molecules arises from their specificity. If adhesion shows specificity, and one can isolate molecules which confer a similar specificity when added to aggregating cell mixtures, it is tempting to consider that you have isolated the molecule responsible for adhesion. Since these molecules are usually large, sometimes very large, it is natural to think that they must act by bridging between cells. Some examples of such specific and non-specific materials are listed in Table 3.2.1.

The best-characterized material which stimulates adhesion with little specificity is fibronectin [45, 46, 82, 89] (equivalent to LETS (Large External Transformation-Sensitive protein)). This protein has a molecular weight of 440 000 and it is a dimer of two disulphide-bonded 220 000-mol.-wt subunits. It is found on the surface of many mammalian cell types and an equivalent molecule is found on avian cell types. The serum of mammals and birds contains a similar material (Cold Insoluble Globulin or CiG) which appears to have an identical structure to fibronectin except that its subunits are slightly shorter than fibronectin (reviewed [82]). This abbreviation of the molecule appears to reduce its ability to promote cell adhesion when compared with intact fibronectin [89]. This molecule, together with collagen and laminin, is present between cells of the mouse blastocyst; it is localized in all basement membranes at subsequent stages of mouse development; and it is widely distributed in the basement membranes of the early chick embryo (Chapter 3.5). Fibronectin or similar molecules are probably present in all vertebrates. It binds strongly to most types of collagen as well as to proteoglycans. Many cell types, including fibroblasts, myoblasts, hepatocytes and smooth-muscle cells, bind to collagen through fibronectin mediation. Chondrocytes appear to require chondronectin, a two-polypeptide-chain molecule of mol. wt 180 000, while epithelial and endothelial cells appear to have their adhesion to collagen mediated by laminin, an 800 000-mol.-wt glycoprotein. These three proteins and their actions have recently been reviewed by Kleinman *et al.* [50].

Fibronectin binds strongly to glass or polystyrene as well as to collagen. The molecule facilitates the spreading of cells on the surface to which it is adsorbed. A small range of cell types is unreactive, e.g. leucocytes, lymphocytes and macrophages. It is tempting to suggest that these circulating cells are able to be non-adhesive or weakly adhesive because they are unable to react with fibronectin. When adherent cells are torn off a glass or plate substrate they leave behind fragments of their cell surface. Analysis of these fragments by immune fluorescence methods show the presence of fibronectin, actin, myosin, alpha-actinin, and tropomyosin [68] (see Chapters 3.3 and 6.2). This shows that fibronectin is associated with the cytoskeleton and that small pieces of cell surface must have been detached from the cell. The question is just how the fibronectin is packed into the space between the plasmalemma and the substrate. Since fibronectin is bound to surfaces such as glass or tissue-culture plastic, and since it is found attached to cell surfaces, it is tempting to conclude that it forms a bridge between one surface and the other. Rees *et al.* [68] have obtained electron micrographs which suggest that this indeed may be so, but readers will appreciate that clear proof of the actual bridging of the gap by this molecule is still missing. However, objectors to this bridging explanation can in their turn be faced with the question of what alternative mechanism could be responsible. Rees went on to suggest that the fibronectin might be ordered at a spacing of 20 nm, side to side,

which suggests parallels with the Z line in muscle, where actin filaments are anchored. The ordering (putative) of the fibronectin might serve in a similar manner, to anchor actin microfilaments. (See Fig. 3.2.5 for Rees's model of the action of fibronectin in cell adhesion.)

Although it is tempting to ascribe a unique and important role to fibronectin in vertebrate cell adhesion, it should be borne in mind that other proteins (e.g. transferrin) permit cell spreading when adsorbed to glass. The very process of spreading appears to be the recruitment of more and more adhesive patches that are connected appropriately to the cell's cytoskeleton, which thus stretches the cell on to new contacts. Consequently, agents that permit cell-spreading may do so by allowing the establishment of new adhesions or may act by permitting the redeployment and use of the cytoskeleton. However, the spreading of cells on a substrate, so often taken as an indication of an adhesive contact under development, might equally well result from the cell spreading until its adhesive sites are satisfied. If this view is correct, then spreading is an indication of a lack of adhesion. Breakdown of the microfilament bundles internally might allow release of fibronectin from the

Table 3.2.1. Molecules probably involved in ligand–receptor or mutual-receptor recognition systems

Animal	Name given to recognition molecule	Type	Mol. wt	Most effective conc. (μg ml^{-1})	Reference
Sponge					
Microciona prolifera	AF	L	2×10^7	30	Turner [81]
	BP	R	?		
M. parthena	AF	L	2×10^7	—	Turner [81]
	BP	R	?		
Geodia	AF	L	15×10^7	1000	Muller & Zahn [63]
Suberites domuncula	AF	L	5×10^1	—	Muller *et al.* [64]
	BP	R			
Avian					
Neural retina	AF	L?	5×10^1	0.2–1	Hausman & Moscona [43]
Neural retina and brain	AF (CAM)	MR	25×10^1	—	Rutishauser *et al.* [73]
Slime mould					
Dictyostelium discoideum	Discoidins	L	0×10^1	—	Frazier *et al* [30] Rosen & Barondes [70]
	Contact-site antigen	R	8×10^1	—	Muller & Gerisch [62]
Polysphondylium palladium	Pallidin	L	25×10^1	—	Frazier *et al.* [31]

AF = Aggregation-promoting factor
BP = Baseplate
R = Receptor
L = Ligand
MR = Mutual receptor

surface [53]. The concentration of fibronectin in the body fluids means that even if a cell is unable to synthesize this material, all its receptors for this protein will be permanently coated. This presents some problems when we consider that cell movement is perfectly open to normal cells in, for example, conditions of wound repair when fibronectin concentrations must be high; perhaps the abbreviated form of fibronectin found in serum does not irreversibly saturate the receptors. Thus its presence and action do not provide a simple solution to the problem that tissue cells are normally immobile. Adhesions brought about by fibronectin appear to be sensitive to all the agents which affect the adhesion of normal cells. Serum albumin is a protein which appears to inhibit cell adhesion when bound to the surface.

Hughes [45] has shown that a BHK fibroblast requires about 45 000 fibronectin molecules adsorbed to the substrate for adhesion. This is a large number in view of the estimates for the adhesiveness of such cells [10], and argues that the molecules are ineffective bridging agents.

Receptors

Receptors are molecules which bind other molecules with high affinity, so that it is difficult to disrupt the association. Receptors can be detected on cell surfaces and be shown to be associated with adhesive processes. This theme has inspired a number of workers. For instance, Edwards [27] and his co-workers have investigated the surface chemistry of a group of mutant baby hamster kidney cells which are resistant to the toxic action of the ricin lectin (see Chapter 3.6); the ricin lectin binds to galactose and N-acetyl-galactosamine in the oligosaccharides attached to the surface of the cells and so many ricin-resistant mutants have a reduced number of sugars attached to their cell-surface molecules and in this way avoid the toxicity of the lectin. The mutant cells are much less adhesive than the parental cells and there is evidence that the loss of surface galactose is associated with a reduction in adhesiveness.

There is also evidence from another set of experiments that oligosaccharides may be bound by receptors during cell adhesion. Oligosaccharides containing long chains of mannose residues (mannans) are able to inhibit the aggregation of some mouse tumour cells and they also disperse preformed aggregates. One interpretation is that the mannans bind to cell-surface receptors which would usually bind the oligosaccharides on adjacent cells, and in this way the mannans disrupt normal cell adhesion [40].

Many other workers have carried out experiments in which some surface component has been modified or removed more or less specifically and have correlated this with a resulting change in adhesion. Others have obtained membrane fractions which produce cell adhesion. These presumably contain receptors or receptor-binding molecules or binding molecules but it is not known if they promote normal adhesion.

The most elegant demonstration of the involvement of such receptors in adhesion comes from work on slime moulds by Gerisch [35, 62] (the life cycle of slime moulds is described in Chapter 5.2). Aggregating cells of *Dictyostelium discoideum* adhere both side to side and also end to end. The end-to-end adhesion is not dissociated by EDTA whereas the side-to-side adhesion is broken by this agent. Univalent antibody fragments (Fab) against membrane antigens from aggregation-competent cells (i.e. just before aggregation) block adhesion (see Chapter 3.7 for structure of Fab fragments). Fab fragments against membrane antigens from the preceding growth phase block side-to-side adhesion but not end-to-end adhesion. Fab fragments against aggregation-phase membrane antigens block only the end-to-end adhesion (see Fig. 3.2.11). Fab fragments against site A will dissociate aggregates, a result which has been paralleled with Fab fragments of antibodies directed against mammalian embryo cell membranes, which prevent the extensive cell adhesions that usually develop during cleavage in the mouse embryo [47]. Gerisch found about 300 000 contact-site-A receptors per cell. These studies could be taken as evidence for a bridging system, but Gerisch is very careful to point out that it is possible that these sites operate in some more indirect manner to effect adhesion. It should be added that another physical mechanism by which adsorbed molecules might act directly to promote adhesion can now be envisaged, without recourse to cementing hypotheses (see below).

The arguments against the bridging are as follows:
(1) It is difficult to account for the permeation of tracer molecules through a zonula or macula adhaerens adhesion if more than a small number of bridging molecules are present. There is no such difficulty for

occludens adhesions, which are not permeable to tracer molecules, but in these junctions the bridging molecules must be very short to fit in the space available.

(2) The measured strengths of adhesion for both the adhaerens types of adhesion are orders of magnitude lower than the value predicted from the number of sites at which bridging molecules are supposed to act [10]. This discrepancy could be due to the kinetics of making and breaking strong binding contacts but it remains puzzling.

The other difficulty is simply one of lack of evidence; we currently lack information about the structure of the junctions between cells.

Evidence for primary and secondary minimum adhesions and related systems

It will be necessary to devote a short space to describing these models of adhesion, before discussing the evidence.

The theory of the interaction of lyophobic colloids was originally proposed by Deryagin and Landau and by Verwey and Overbeek (DLVO theory). It was pointed out that there were strong reasons for suggesting that this theory might explain features of cell adhesion; the hydrophobic cell membranes, which are covered with charged groups, might well interact by the interplay of the electrostatic forces of repulsion and the electrodynamic force of attraction [6]. In essence, the electrodynamic force of attraction is a long-range force that is most strongly displayed between two particles when their own dielectric constants (related to the atomic and molecular vibrations in their component molecules) are different from those of the intervening space. Early studies had shown that lipid bilayers might stabilize themselves in an aqueous medium at spacings such that gaps of about 10 nm occurred between each layer (see [51] for historical interest, and Chapter 6.2). This stabilization is due to the interplay of the electrodynamic and electrostatic forces and can easily be visualized in Fig. 3.2.12. At great interparticle distances there is a region of attraction because of the long-range nature of the electrodynamic force. At closer approaches there may be an appreciable force of repulsion if the surface charge density or the lack of counter ions in the medium is such that it can be expressed. Under some conditions,

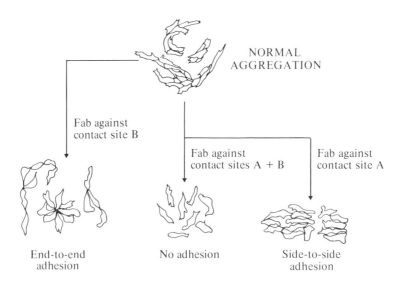

NORMAL
AGGREGATION

Fab against
contact site B

Fab against
contact sites A + B

Fab against
contact site A

End-to-end
adhesion

No adhesion

Side-to-side
adhesion

Fig. 3.2.11. To illustrate the experiment of slime mould adhesion, carried out by Gerisch and his colleagues [35, 62]. Naturally, cells aggregate both side-to-side and end-to-end (see top of diagram). Fab fragments of antibodies directed against the unaggregated growth-phase cells block contact site B, and thus prevent side-to-side cell adhesion. Fab fragments of antibodies directed against aggregation competent phase cells stops adhesion entirely, but when this Fab is adsorbed with growth-phase cells, the activity against contact site A still remains and the cells adhere side-to-side, but not end-to-end (bottom right). By kind permission of Dr G. Gerisch and Cambridge University Press.

particles will not be able to make a closer approach to each other than this secondary minimum of the potential energy diagram (see Fig. 3.2.12). Under other conditions, they will be able, as a result of Brownian motion or other mechanical forces, to make a closer approach and break through the region of repulsion into the primary minimum, where attraction again exceeds repulsion.

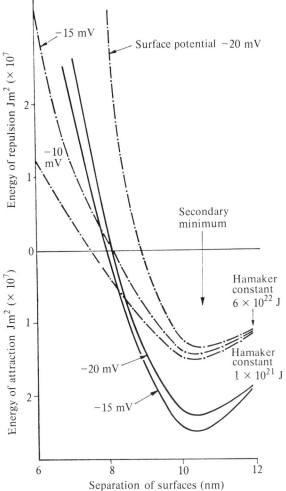

Fig. 3.2.12. Plots of the interaction of cell-like structures according to the DLVO theory showing the secondary minimum in the energy diagram in relation to the distance between plasmalemmae, the surface potential, ionic strength, and the Hamaker constant for the plasmalemmae. Distance between plasmalemmae on abscissa. Energies of interaction on ordinate. Attraction negative, repulsion positive. The primary minimum adhesion corresponds to zero distance of separation and very strong attraction. The secondary minimum of the diagram shows a gap between plasmalemmae and weak attraction, in between this and the primary minimum lies a zone of repulsion.

The appeal of applying this concept to cell adhesion is that it seems to provide an explanation for the existence both of the weak zonula adhaerens adhesion, with the open gap between the cell membranes, and the close, strong zonula occludens adhesion. The first is equated with a secondary minimum adhesion and the second with a primary minimum adhesion. At a subjective level the theory also of course includes all the data mentioned above supporting the action of electrostatic forces of repulsion (see section 3.2.4). The evidence in favour of these theories is as follows.

(1) The dimensions and open nature of the gap in zonula and macula adhaerentes corresponds well to a secondary minimum type of adhesion. The dimensions of the gap, if any, in occludens-type junctions, corresponds to primary minimum expectations.

(2) The measured strengths of adhesion agree well with the expectations for these two types of adhesion [10]. Work by Gingell [80] confirms this in an elegant manner.

(3) Modification of cell adhesion occurs when large changes in the lipid chain length or unsaturation of the cell membrane takes place. This would be expected if electrodynamic forces act in adhesion [14]. Similarly, modification of the dielectric constant of the surrounding medium changes the adhesion of cells in a manner which would be expected if electrodynamic forces act [48].

However, there are difficulties with this theory, despite the fact that a good deal of experimental confirmation has been obtained for it. It is difficult to reconcile the simple DLVO explanation with the evidence that a number of macromolecules, such as fibronectin, effect adhesion so markedly even though their *gross* effect on cell-surface electrostatic properties is so slight. It is also difficult to reconcile this explanation with the evidence that there are a number of cell-surface receptors closely associated with adhesion. A solution to this can be proposed, based on work by Dolowy [23].

Dolowy points out that since most, if not all, of the charge on the cell surface is due to bound groupings, the interaction of two cells as they approach each other is a constant-charge situation. As they approach, the surface potential of each cell rise. This will lead to a marked drop in interfacial tension, which is in turn expressed as a diminution in surface energy and thus as an increase in adhesion. At the moment, the evidence for this is based on theoretical argument. It explains results in which adhesion increased as the surface potential of a substrate was raised. However, this theory is clearly an important improvement to simple DLVO theory. It also explains the mechanisms by which adsorbed molecules may increase adhesion. Adsorbed species may tend to aggregate cell-surface glyco-proteins, thus tending to bare the lipid surface to the intervening medium (or to thin protein or other molecular layers over the lipid) and to increase the electrodynamic forces between the cells. At high concentrations of adsorbed species, presumably the whole surface would be well coated, reducing the adhesion; such behaviour has been reported [3]. The great attraction of this modification of DLVO theory, the work of Dolowy, is that it accounts for the physical situation more completely than the earlier theory, and it provides a good explanation of the means by which macro-molecules can increase adhesion, and for the existence of specific cell-surface receptors connected with adhesion. It avoids the difficulties mentioned above, in reconciling some of the evidence about cell adhesion with the cementing or bridging model.

Discrepant phenomena

Although it is possible to summarize a large amount of the work that has been published in this field under the two headings of those findings that support the bridging hypothesis and those that support a DLVO-type explanation, there are a small number of results which seem to point in quite different directions. Chief amongst these perhaps is the recent finding of Curtis *et al.* [17] that the adhesion of cells to a wide variety of surfaces is related to the number of hydroxyl groups per unit area on these surfaces. Blocking the hydroxyl groups prevents cell adhesion. A simple interpretation of these results is that the hydroxyl groups take part in hydrogen bonding between cell and surface but it is more likely that the hydrogen bonds, if present, form between the surface and serum-derived or cell-secreted proteins, such as fibronectin. It is of interest that the density of hydroxyl groups required is very low, being about one-tenth that of the number of fibronectin molecules. The glycosidic parts of glycoproteins will of course contain similar hydroxyl groups. These results can also be seen as evidence for the action of the DLVO theory, arguing in the following manner. Increasing the number of hydroxyl groups per unit area increases the

wettability of the surface; the resulting change in surface free energy can be seen as a contribution to the DLVO interaction following the modifications to that theory by Dolowy.

We should also remember that the interactions of cells closely resemble in chemical terms the environment discussed by Napper [65] and others in assessing the contributions of enthalpic or entropic destabilization to adhesion. The destabilization they refer to is the adhesion of the surface consequent upon the collapse of an extended filler structure of macromolecules between surfaces. If this type of theory is correct, intercellular materials play a role, not of aiding adhesion, but normally of preventing adhesion by stopping close approach of the plasmalemmae.

3.2.5   SPECIFICITY IN POSITIONING AND ADHESION

Embryological demands

Among one of the main features of animal development are the phases of cell movement during which cell types move from one point in the embryo to another. These movements are described in Chapters 3.3 and 4.3. Such ordered cell migrations lead to patterns of cell disposition which establish much of the final anatomy of the organism.

Cell adhesion must frequently play an important role in the positioning of cells in the embryo (see Chapter 3.1). The simplest argument in favour of this view is that a cell must make and break adhesive contacts if it is to exert a force against the environment and move; adhesion must be regulated by individual cells. It is also the case that the adhesivity of groups of cells in the embryo changes during certain morphogenetic events and there must also be mechanisms which regulate the adhesivity of cell types.

Specific adhesion: evidence and problems

There are a large number of demonstrations that cells can adhere with a greater or lesser degree of specificity. The methods used to establish this are described in section 3.2.3 and examples are provided in Table 3.2.2. The problem is that this specificity could be achieved in two ways: either the mechanism of cell adhesion is specific to particular cell types (specific adhesion) or the adhesivity of particular cell types can be regulated by some mechanism which operates on those particular cell types. Currently, there is no direct evidence that the specificity observed is effected by agents which bond from one cell to another (see section 3.2.4), despite the happy assumption that this must be so.

A number of macromolecules produced by cells have been described which promote adhesion of one cell type specifically (usually their own cell type); see Table 3.2.1

for summary. These are often referred to as aggregation-promoting factors (AFs is a widely used acronym). It is possibly rather dismaying that many of these factors are obtained from cultures which are moribund, or from disaggregation systems in which much cell damage has been done. Possibly one of the most interesting factors is the small glycoprotein macrophage-inhibition (locomotion) factor, produced by mammalian lymphocytes, which specifically increases the adhesion of macro-

Table 3.2.2. Selectivity in the formation of adhesions

Cell types	Technique	Selectivity	Reference
Sponge			
Various species	CA	Species-specific	McClay [56]
Strain types in *Ephydatia*	KAS	Specific control of adhesion	Curtis [9, 11, 12]
Other species	KAS	Non-specific	
Echinoderms, *Lytechinus* and *Tripneusts* embryos	CA	Specific control of adhesion	McClay & Hausman [57]
Embryonic chick tissues			
Neural retina and liver	CA	Tissue specificity	Roth & Weston [72]
	KAS IAC	Tissue specificity under defined conditions only, often not	Curtis [11]
	IAC	Tissus specificity	Elton & Tickle [28]
	CL	Tissue specificity	Walther *et al.* [84]
Neural retina, liver, plue mesencephalon	CA	Tissue specificity	McGuire & Burdick [58]
Neural retina to optic tectum	CT	Ventral retina to dorsal tectum. Dorsal retina to ventral tectum, but low specificity	Marchase [54]
	KAS	No specificity	Jones [49]
Other tissues			
Various embryonic tissues	CA	Tissue specificity	Roth *et al.* [71]
BHK and 3T3	CL	No specificity	Walther *et al.* [84]
Mouse kidney and teratoma	CL	Tissue specificity	Walther *et al.* [84]
Polymorphs, human and calf to endothelia and various cell lines	CL	Preference for endothelia	Hoover [44]
Mouse fibroblasts, different H-2 type	CL	Preference for their own H-2 type	Bartlett & Edidin [1]
Embryonic chick pigmented retina, neural retina and choroid	CL	Choroid collects PRE preferentially	Büültjens & Edwards [4]
Lymphocytes, murine B and T cells	KAS	Specificity under defined conditions, specific	Curtis & de Sousa [16]
Circulating lymphocytes to node beds	CTS	Lymphocytes to high endothelial cells	Stamper & Woodruff [75]

CA = Collecting aggregates
CL = Collecting lawn
CTS = Collecting tissue slice
CT = Collecting tissue surface
IAC = Specificity in initial aggregates
KAS = Kinetic assay of specificity

Table 3.2.3. Fairly well characterized soluble signal molecules acting in cell recognition

Name	Nature	Mol. wt	Biological effects	Reference
Macrophage (locomotion) inhibition factor (MIF) (lymphocyte-derived)	Glycoprotein	15×10^3	Increases adhesion Increases chemotaxis	86
Interaction modulation factors (IMFs)				
B cell	Glycoprotein	35×10^3	Decreases T-cell adhesion Changes lymphocyte distribution	16
T cell	Glycoprotein	35×10^3	Decreases B-cell and leucocyte adhesion Changes lymphocyte distribution	12
Leucocyte (locomotion) inhibition factor (LIF)	Protein	?	Decreases leucocyte adhesion and mobility	12

phages [86]. This factor is secreted by viable, active lymphocytes, and forms one of the group of substances termed the lymphokines [69]. The particular interest of this example is that it is a clear case of one cell type controlling the adhesion of another. Less serendipitous are the aggregation factors described for the species-specific aggregation of sponges: some of these molecules, or even their subunits, are of so great a size that they could not even fit into the zonula adhaerens type contacts found between sponge cells. They have not been seen in electron micrographs of sponge tissue.

Recently, another group of macromolecules has been isolated, or at least detected, which specifically reduce the adhesion of their target cells. There is one exception, which increases adhesion (see Table 3.2.3 for summary). It is clear from this work [12] that these molecules act on particular cell types and that they regulate their adhesion to any kind of surface to which the cell would normally adhere. Thus, these interaction modulation factors (IMFs), as they have been termed [22], specifically reduce the adhesion of the cell to most if not all surfaces, which implies that the actual mechanism is fairly non-specific. This, of course, solves the contradiction that appears to lie between the results which show that cells can adhere to a wide range of surfaces or adsorbed proteins, and the claims that specific mechanisms of adhesion operate. The interaction modulation factors are described more fully later.

Specific adhesion of cells is a concept which has often been applied to explain the positionings that take place during morphogenesis. This hypothesis may be

adequate to explain the accretion of cells to a pre-existing structure, but it does not account for the generation of pattern *de novo*. Yet cells are clearly capable of positioning themselves in precise patterns from random beginnings. This takes place in the sorting out of aggregates and apparently in the normal embryogenesis of the extraordinary annual fish [88], in which the embryos disaggregate to reaggregate later. Steinberg and Curtis [11, 77, 78] have pointed out that such

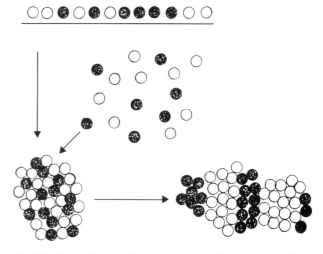

Fig. 3.2.13. An diagram showing the imagined consequences of specific adhesion on sorting out of cells, starting either as cells on a substrate (top left), or as cells in suspension (bottom left). Cells would form aggregates, but although sorting out would occur, no positioning or patterning would result.

positioning behaviour *de novo* cannot be explained in terms of a specific mechanism of adhesion. This point should be appreciated with ease, if you consider an aggregate which initially consists of two cell types in a random arrangement. If the two cell types possess a degree of specificity of adhesion, such that they preferentially adhere to their own type, the results of cell movements will be to sort the cells out, so that larger and larger assemblies of each type will develop, but they will not organize themselves in any pattern simply on the basis of the information provided by a greater or lesser degree of specific adhesion (see Fig. 3.2.13).

Sorting out: hypothesis and results

Differential adhesion

Steinberg [78] made the most important observation that there is a graded hierarchy in sorting-out patterns, so that it is possible to arrange large groups of cell types in a sequences thus any type higher on the list will always sort out in such a way that it ends up external to any cell types lower on the list. This observation implies that there is probably some single, graded property shared by all the tissues in the list, which determines the sorting-out position adopted. In turn, this implication argues against the operation of specific adhesions in sorting-out. Steinberg developed his observation to suggest that the graded property was cell adhesiveness, and that sorting-out resulted from the cells in an initially random mixture exchanging positions until a minimum surface-energy situation was attained. He suggested that since sorting-out patterns are apparently homologous with the patterns of contact adopted by two immiscible oil droplets in a third medium, and since interfacial tensions drive these contacts to their typical resultant patterns, we should expect cells to behave in this way. This theory is termed the 'differential theory of cell positioning'. The theory has been difficult to test; see [42] for discussion. Whether it is correct or not, it makes a number of singularly powerful points against the hypothesis that positioning results from the specific adhesion of cells.

Specific adhesion

The experiment which would go a long way to establishing the concept that positioning is produced by specific adhesion mechanisms would be to isolate a binding molecule, to deplete it from a cell, or to block it specifically, and then to observe deficiencies in the resulting morphogenesis. This result has not yet been obtained. Has the experiment even been tried? It would be necessary first to establish that the molecule actually was involved directly in cell adhesion.

This type of experiment is one which should be attempted in order to provide the real test of any particular theory about cell positioning.

Chemotaxis

The third main hypothesis concerning cell-positioning mechanisms is one of early origin. It suggested that chemotaxis (or perhaps chemokinesis) acts to produce cell positioning. If the mass of cells already contains positioned structures, these might act to either attract or repel certain cell types by positive or negative chemotaxis. If the positioning arises in a random mass of cells, distance from the surface of the aggregate might provide the means of setting up concentration gradients of the chemotaxin, since it will diffuse away into the environment. Concentration gradients in an ordered tissue mass might also be maintained by the destruction of the chemotaxins by one or other cell types. This theory has received little experimental interest until recently, but it is difficult to set up experiments that clearly identify chemotaxis in tissue masses. Matsukuma and Durston [55] have found that the sorting-out of prestalk and prespore cells that occurs during the development of the slime-mould fruiting stage can be modified by application of gradients of cyclic-AMP, a known chemotactic agent (see Chapter 5.2). Since chemotaxis involves changes in adhesion [52] it can be seen as an example of a system in which the level of cell adhesion is specifically controlled. A full theoretical discussion of the possibilities that chemotaxis acts in positioning of cells is given by the author in [12].

Interaction modulation systems

The second hypothesis which suggests that the level of adhesion in cells is controlled by other cells is the interaction modulation factor theory (IMF theory). This (see the beginning of the section) proposes that the interactions between cells are modulated by diffusible factors secreted by other cells. At present, all the interaction modulation molecules discovered have diminished adhesion, with the exception of the macrophage locomotion inhibition factor (MIF). The theory is very closely related to chemotactic theories; both theories propose that adhesion is affected by soluble molecules that bind to the membrane of target cells, modifying their adhesion. The IMF hypothesis (see [12] for a full statement) suggests that the modified cells will tend to leave contacts with cells which diminish their adhesion and will move down a gradient. The movement would probably be chemokinetic rather than chemotactic. It is interesting that the T-cell thymocyte IMF glycoprotein produces chemokinesis in its target cells.

Application of gradients of IMFs from embryonic chick tissues will reverse the sorting-out pattern or even randomize it in mixed aggregates of embryonic chick liver or neural retina [11]. This type of observation goes a long way towards meeting the basic requirement of the tests for any proposed mechanism of morphogenesis that can be put forward, namely that application of, or removal of, the chemical agent supposed to be involved in morphogenesis should radially change the process.

However if we step slightly outside the strictest bounds of developmental biology we come to a system in which probably the best demonstration of the action of these factors in a morphogenetic process has been obtained. Lymphocytes continuously circulate around the body, enter lymph nodes and the spleen and sort into B-cell- and T-cell-rich areas within these organs and then leave them for new sites. They also show considerable preference for location, albeit temporary in other organs, particularly the liver and the lungs (for a good account of this field see de Sousa [22]). Thus lymphocytes show continuous and repeated morphogenetic movements. Curtis and Davies [15] have recently shown that the thymocyte and T lymphocytes release a fragment of one of their histocompatibility antigens (in detail the H-2D antigen) which is very active indeed in controlling and altering this circulation and morphogenesis. Injection of this glycoprotein histocompatibility antigen fragment at nanogram levels into a mouse causes a very extensive release of leucocytes and of B lymphocytes from the spleen. Lymphocytes treated with this histocompatibility product show altered circulation.

The system referred to in the preceding paragraph is relevant also to the question of which genetic loci determine the positioning of tissues. Although a few mutants are known in which cell positioning is abnormal

in some part of the body, we are just starting to identify genes and gene products involved in establishing position. Bodmer (see [13]) has already suggested that the prime function of the histocompatibility system is to determine the various cell interactions that can occur within an organism, and Katz [90] has shown that non-morphogenetic interactions amongst lymphocytes are so controlled. The work described in the preceding paragraph extends experimental result to confirm part of Bodmer's prediction. The suggestion made by Bennett [91] that the T locus (or loci) in the mouse controls cell interactions does not appear to have been borne out in experimental investigation.

3.2.6 CONCLUSIONS

(1) The structures of adhesive contacts are still poorly understood. In adhaerens contacts there is sufficient space for large molecules attached to the cell membrane to effect adhesion between adjacent cells but in occludens contacts there is insufficient space readily to accommodate large molecules protruding from the lipid bilayers of the cell membrane.

(2) It is difficult to measure the adhesion between cells in intact embryos. Consequently, adhesion is measured with disaggregated cells so that measurements will only approximate to the adhesions which occur in undissociated organisms.

(3) The adhesion between cells can be altered by a wide range of agents. The action of these agents can in turn be taken to favour mechanisms of adhesion which either involve electrostatic mechanisms or involve bridging molecules between cells. In practice, several mechanisms of adhesion may be used by a single cell.

(4) A large number of molecules have been isolated from cells which either promote or reduce the adhesion of particular cell types. Currently there is no direct evidence that these molecules effect the adhesive bond between cells.

(5) It is possible, but not certain, that at least some of these molecules act by regulating the adhesivity of particular cell types and that they are not directly involved in the bonding mechanism.

(6) Cell adhesion changes in certain tissues at particular stages of embryogenesis and the regulation of adhesion is an intimate part of the regulation of locomotion.

3.2.7 REFERENCES

1 Bartlett P.F. & Edidin M. (1978) Effect of the H-2 gene complex rates of fibroblast intercellular adhesion. *J. Cell Biol.*, **77**, 377–388.

2 Brightman M.W. (1965) The distribution within the brain of ferritin injected into cerebrospinal fluid compartments. I. *J. Cell Biol.*, **26**, 99–113.

3 Brooks D.E. (1973) The effect of neutral polymers on the electrokinetic potential of cells and other charged particles. IV. *J. Coll. Interface Sci.*, **43**, 714–726.

4 Büültjens T.E.J. & Edwards J.G. (1977) Adhesive selectivity is exhibited *in vitro* by cells from adjacent tissues of the embryonic chick retina. *J. Cell Sci.*, **23**, 101–16.

5 Cornell R. (1969) Cell substrate adhesion during cell culture. *Expl. Cell Res.*, **58**, 289–295.

6 Curtis A.S.G. (1962) Cell contact and adhesion. *Biol. Rev.*, **37**, 82–129.

7 Curtis A.S.G. (1964) The adhesion of cells to glass. A study by interference reflection microscopy. *J. Cell Biol.*, **19**, 199–215.

8 Curtis A.S.G. (1969) The measurement of cell adhesion by an absolute method. *J. Embryol. exp. Morph.*, **22**, 305–325.

9 Curtis A.S.G. (1970) Problems and some solutions in the study of cellular aggregation. *Symp. Zool. Soc. Lond.*, **25**, 335–352.

10 Curtis A.S.G. (1973) Cell adhesion. *Prog. Biophys. Molec. Biol.*, **27**, 317–386.

11 Curtis A.S.G. (1978) Cell positioning. *Receptors and Recognition Ser. B*, **4**, 159–190.

12 Curtis A.S.G. (1978) Cell–cell recognition: positioning and patterning systems. *Symp. Soc. exp. Biol.*, **32**, 51–82.

13 Curtis A.S.G. (1979) The H-2 histocompatibility system and lymphocyte adhesion: interaction modulation factor involvement. *J. Immunogenetics*, **6**, 155–166.

14 Curtis A.S.G., Chandler C. & Picton N. (1975) Cell surface lipids and adhesion. III. *J. Cell Sci.*, **18**, 375–384.

15 Curtis A.S.G. & Davies M. (1982) H-2 antigens released by thymocytes and cell adhesion. *J. Immunogenetics*, **8**, 367–377.

16 Curtis A.S.G. & de Sousa M. (1975) Lymphocyte interactions positioning. *Cell Immunol.*, **19**, 282–297.

17 Curtis A.S.G., Forrester J.V. McInnes C. & Lawrie F. (1984) Hydroxyl groups and cell adhesion. *J. Cell. Biol.*, in press.

18 Curtis A.S.G. & Greaves M.E. (1965) The inhibition of cell aggregation by a pure serum protein. *J. Embryol. exp. Morph.*, **13**, 309–326.

19 Curtis A.S.G. & Hill O. (1979) Cell surface lipids and adhesion. IV. The effects of trypsin in lipid turnover by the plasmalemma. *J. Cell Sci.*, **38**, 283–292.

20 Dan K. (1936) Electrokinetic studies of marine ova. III. *Physiol. Zool.*, **9**, 43–57.

21 Deman J.J. & Bruyneel E.A. (1974) Evidence for long-range electrostatic repulsion between HeLa cells. *Expl. Cell Res.*, **89**, 206–216.

22 de Sousa M. (1978) Ecotaxis, ecotaxopathy and lymphoid malignancy. Terms, facts and predictions. In *Immunopathology of Lymph Neoplasms* (Eds R.A. Good & J. Twomey), pp. 325–359. Plenum Press, New York.

23 Dolowy K. & Holly F.J. (1978) Contribution of interfacial tension changes during cellular interaction to the energy balance. *J. theor. Biol.*, **75**, 373–380.

24 Dubicella T., Albertini D.F., Anderson E. & Biggers J.D. (1975) The pre-implantation mouse embryo: Characterisation of intercellular junctions and their appearance in development. *Devl. Biol.*, **45**, 231–250.

25 Easty G.C., Easty D.M. & Ambrose E.J. (1960) Studies on cellular adhesiveness. *Expl. Cell. Res.*, **19**, 539–548.

26 Edwards J.G. (1973) Intercellular adhesion. In *New Techniques in Biophysics and Cell Biology* (Eds R.H. Pain & B.J. Smith), pp. 1–27. John Wiley & Sons, New York.

27 Edwards J.G., Dysart J. McK. & Hughes R.C. (1978) Cellular adhesiveness reduced in ricin-resistant hamster fibroblasts. *Nature, Lond.*, **264**, 66–68.

28 Elton R.A. & Tickle C.A. (1971) The analysis of spatial distributions in mixed cell populations: a statistical method for detecting sorting out. *J. Embryol. exp. Morph.*, **26**, 135–156.

29 Fawcett D.W. (1961) Intercellular bridges. *Expl. Cell Res. Suppl.* **8**, 174–187.

30 Frazier W.A., Rosen S.D., Reitherman R.W. & Barondes S.H. (1975) Purification and comparison of two developmentally regulated lectins from *Dictyostelium discoideum. J. biol. Chem.*, **250**, 7714–7721.

31 Frazier W.A., Rosen S.D., Reitherman R.W. & Barondes S.H. (1976) Multiple lectins in two species of cellular slime mould. In *Surface Membrane Receptors* (Eds R.A. Bradshaw *et al.*), pp. 57–66. Plenum Press, New York.

32 Galtsoff P.S. (1925) Regeneration after dissociation. I. *J. exp. Zool.*, **42**, 183–222.

33 Garrod D.R., Swan Alma P., Nicol A. & Forman D. (1978) Cellular recognition in slime mould development. *Symp. Soc. exp. Biol.*, **32**, 173–202.

34 Gerisch G. (1968) Cell aggregation and differentiation in *Dictyostelium discoideum. Curr. Tops Devl. Biol.*, **3**, 157–197.

35 Gerisch G., Krelle H., Bozzaro S., Eitle E. & Guggenheim R. (1980) Analysis of cell adhesion in *Dictyostelium* and *Polysphondylium* by the use of *Fab. Brit. Soc. Cell Biol. Symp.*, **3**, (Eds A.S.G. Curtis & J.D. Pitts). Cambridge University Press, Cambridge.

36 Gilula N.B. (1974) Junctions between cells. In *Cell Communication* (Ed. R.P. Cox), pp. 1–29. John Wiley & Sons, New York.

37 Gilula N.B. & Lo C.W. (1979) Gap junctional communication in the pre-implantation mouse embryo. *Cell*, **18**, 399–410.

38 Gingell D. & Todd I. (1980) Red blood cell adhesion. II. Interferometric examination of the interaction with hydrocarbon oil and glass. *J. Cell Sci.*, **41**, 135–149.

39 Gingell D. & Vince S. (1980) A physical theory of cell–cell and cell–substratum interactions. *Symp. Brit. Soc. Cell Biol.*, **3**, 1–37 (Eds A.S.G. Curtis & J.D. Pitts). Cambridge University Press, Cambridge.

40 Grabel L.B., Rosen S.D. & Martin G.R. (1979) Teratocarcinoma stem cells have a cell-surface binding component implicated in cell–cell adhesion. *Cell*, **17**, 477–484.

41 Green C.R., Bergquist P.R. & Bullivant S. (1979) An anastomosing septate junction in endothelial cells of the Phylum Echinodermata. *J. Ultrastruct. Res.*, **68**, 72–80.

42 Harris A.K. (1976) Is cell sorting caused by differences in the work of intercellular adhesion? A critique of the Steinberg hypotheses. *J. theor. Biol.*, **61**, 267–285.

43 Hausman R.E. & Moscona A.A. (1976) Isolation of retina-specific cell aggregating factor from membranes of embryonic neural retina tissue. *Proc. natl Acad. Sci., USA*, **73**, 3594–3598.

44 Hoover R.L. (1978) Modulations of the cell surface and the effects on cellular interactions. *Symp. Soc. exp. Biol.*, **32**, 221–240.

45 Hughes R.C., Pena S.D.J. & Vischer P. (1980) Cell surface glycoproteins in fibroblasts adhesion. *Symp. Brit. Soc. Cell Biol.*, **3**, 329–356 (Eds A.S.G. Curtis & J.D Pitts). Cambridge University Press, Cambridge.

46 Hynes R.O., Ali I.U., Destree A.T., Mautner V., Perkins M.E. Senger D.R., Wagner D.D. & Smith K.K. (1978) A large glycoprotein lost from the surfaces of transformed cells. *Ann. N.Y. Acad. Sci.*, **312**, 317–342.

47 Jacob F. (1978) Mouse teratocarcinoma and mouse embryo. *Proc. R. Soc. Lond. B.*, **201**, 249–270.

48 Jones G.E. (1974) Intercellular adhesion: modification by dielectric properties of the medium. *J. Membrane Biol.*, **16**, 297–312.

49 Jones G.E (1977) Cell disposition and adhesiveness in the developing chick neural retina. *J. Embryol. exp. Morph.*, **40**, 253–258.

50 Kleinman H.K., Klebe R.J. & Martin G.R. (1981) Role of collagenous matrices in the adhesion and growth of cells. *J. Cell Biol.*, **88**, 473–485.

51 Kruyt H.R. (1952) Irreversible systems. In *Colloid Science* (Ed. H.R. Kruyt). Elsevier, Amsterdam.

52 Lackie J.M. & Smith R.P.C. (1980) Interactions of leukocytes and endothelium. *Symp. Brit. Soc. Cell Biol.*, **3**, 235–272 (Eds A.S.G. Curtis & J.D. Pitts). Cambridge University Press, Cambridge.

53 Lloyd D.W. (1979) Fibronectin: a function at the junction. *Nature, Lond.*, **279**, 473–474.

54 Marchase R.B. (1977) Biochemical investigations of retinotectal adhesive specificity. *J. Cell Biol.*, **75**, 237–257.

55 Matsukuma S. & Durston A.J. (1979) Chemotactic cell sorting in *Dictyostelium discoideum*. *J. Embryol. exp. Morph.*, **50**, 243–251.

56 McClay D.R. (1971) An autoradiographic analysis of species specificity during sponge cell reaggregation. *Biol. Bull.*, **141**, 319–330.

57 McClay D.R. & Hausman R.E. (1975) Specificity of cell adhesion: differences between normal and hybrid sea urchin cells. *Devl. Biol.*, **47**, 454–460.

58 McGuire E.J. & Burdick C.L. (1976) Intercellular adhesive selectivity. I. An improved assay for the measurement of embryonic chick intercellular adhesion (liver and other tissues). *J. Cell Biol.*, **68**, 80–89.

59 Mehrishi J.N. (1970) Positively charged amino groups on the surface of normal and cancer cells. *Eur. J. Cancer*, **6**, 127–137.

60 Moore A.R. (1940) Osmotic and structural properties of the blastular wall in *Dendraster excentricus*. *J. exp. Zool.*, **84**, 73–83.

61 Moscona A. & Moscona H. (1952) The dissociation and aggregation of cells from organ rudiments of the early chick embryo. *J. Anat.*, **86**, 287–301.

62 Muller K. & Gerisch G. (1978) A specific glycoprotein as the target site of adhesion blocking Fab in aggregating *Dictyostelium* cells. *Nature, Lond.*, **274**, 445–449.

63 Muller W.E.G. & Zahn R.K. (1973) Purification and characterization of a species-specific aggregation factor in sponges. *Expl. Cell Res.*, **80**, 95–104.

64 Muller W.E.G., Muller I., Zahn R.K. & Kurelec B. (1976) Species-specific aggregation factor in sponges. VI. *J. Cell Sci.*, **21**, 227–241.

65 Napper D.H. (1970) Flocculation studies of stericaly stabilized dispersions. *J. Coll. Interface Sci.*, **32**, 106–114.

66 Overbeek J.Th.G. (1952) The interaction between colloidal particles. In *Colloid Science. Irreversible Systems* (Ed. H.R. Kruyt), pp. 245–277. Elsevier, Amsterdam.

67 Overton J. (1962) Desmosome development in normal and reassociating cells in the early chick blastoderm. *Devl. Biol.*, **4**, 523–548.

68 Rees D.A., Badley R.A., Lloyd C.W., Thom D. & Smith C.G. (1978) Glycoproteins in the recognition of substratum by cultured fibroblasts. *Symp. Soc. exp. Biol.*, **32**, 241–260.

69 Remold H.G., Mednis A.D. & McCarthy P.L. (1979) Studies on MIF and the role of the macrophage associated esterases in the response of the macrophage to MIF. In *Function and Structure of the Immune System* (Eds W. Mullar-Ruchholtz & H.K. Muller-Hermelink), pp. 465–468. Plenum Press, New York.

70 Rosen S.D. & Barondes S.H. (1978) Cell adhesion in cellular slime moulds. *Receptors and Recognition, Ser. B*, **4**, 233–264.

71 Roth S.A. & Weston J.A. (1967) The measurement of intercellular adhesion. *Proc. natl Acad. Sci., USA*, **58**, 974–980.

72 Roth S., McGuire E.J. & McGuire R.S. (1971) An assay for intercellular adhesive specificity. *J. Cell Biol.*, **51**, 525–535.

73 Rutishauser U., Thiery J.P., Brackenbury R., Sela B.A. & Edelman G.M. (1976) Mechanisms of adhesion among cells from neural tissues of the chick embryo. *Proc. natl Acad. Sci., USA*, **73**, 577–581.

74 Sjorstrand F.S. (1962) Critical evaluation of ultrastructural patterns with respect to fixation. In *The Interpretation of Ultrastructure* (Ed. R.J.C. Harris), pp. 47–68. Academic Press, New York.

75 Stamper H.B. Jr. & Woodruff J.J. (1977) An *in vitro* model of lymphocyte homing. I. Characterization of the interaction between thoracic duct lymphocytes and specialized high-endothelial venules of lymph nodes. *J. Immunol.*, **119**, 772–780.

76 Steinberg M.S. (1958) On the chemical bonds between animal cells: a mechanism for type-specific association. *Amer. Natur.*, **92**, 65–82.

77 Steinberg M.S. (1962) On the mechanism of tissue reconstruction by dissociated cells. I. Population kinetics, differential adhesiveness and the absence of directed migration. *Proc. nat. Acad., Wash.*, **48**, 1577–1582.

78 Steinberg M.S. (1978) Cell–cell recognition in multicellular assembly: levels of specificity. *Symp. Soc. exp. Biol.*, **32**, 25–49.

79 Stockenius W. (1963) The molecular structure of lipid-water systems and cell membrane models studied with electron microscopy. In *The Interpretation of Ultrastructure* (Ed. R.J.C. Harris), pp. 349–365. Academic Press, New York.

80 Todd I. & Gingell D. (1980) Red blood cell adhesion. I. Adhesion to oil–water interface. *J. Cell Sci.*, **41**, 125–133.

81 Turner R.S. (1978) Sponge cell adhesions. *Receptors and Recognition, Ser. B*, **4**, 199–232.

82 Vaheri A., Mosher D., Wartiovaara J., Kiski-oja J., Kurkinen M. & Stenman S. (1977) Interactions of fibronectin, a cell-type specific surface-associated glycoprotein. In *Cell Interactions in Differentiation* (Eds M. Karkinen-Jaaskelainen, L. Saxen & L. Weiss), pp. 311–323. Academic Press, London.

83 Waddington C.H., Perry M.M. & Okada E. (1961) 'Membrane knotting' between blastomeres of *Limnea*. *Expl. Cell Res.*, **23**, 631–633.

84 Walther B.T., Ohman R. & Roseman S. (1973) A quantitative assay for intercellular adhesion. *Proc. natl Acad. Sci., USA*, **70**, 1569–1573.

85 Weiss L. (1961) The measurement of cell adhesion. *Expl. Cell Res., Suppl.* **8**, 141–153.

86 Weiss L. & Glaves D. (1975) Effects of migration inhibiting factor(s) on the *in vitro* detachment of macrophages. *J. Immunol.*, **115**, 1362–1365.

87 Wilkins D.J., Ottewill R.H. & Bangham A.D. (1962) On the flocculation of sheep leucocytes. *J. theor. Biol.*, **2**, 165–191.

88 Wourms J.P. (1972) The developmental biology of annual fishes. II. Naturally occurring dispersion and reaggregation of blastomeres during the development of annual fish eggs. *J. exp. Zool.*, **182**, 169–200.

89 Yamada K.M., Olden K. & Pastan I. (1978) Transformation-sensitive cell surface protein: isolation, characterization, and role in cellular morphology and adhesion. *Ann. N.Y. Acad. Sci.*, **312**, 256–277.

90 Katz D.H. (1977) *Lymphocyte Differentiation, Recognition and Regulation*. Academic Press, New York.

91 Bennett D. (1973) The T-locus of the mouse. *Cell*, **6**, 411–454.

Chapter 3.3
Cell Movements in Morphogenesis
R.E. Keller

3.3.1   INTRODUCTION

The central problem of development is to determine what principles and mechanisms govern the replication of an organism. The preformationists imagined that the specificity inherent in replication pre-exists in the form of an encapsulated series of preformed organisms, one inside the next, and that it is manifest by the growth of the last and largest of these at each generation. But in fact metazoans develop by morphogenesis, a process by which a specific and hereditary form and structure is generated from a single cell, the fertilized egg, which does not resemble the adult. The egg, or part of it, undergoes cleavage to form an aggregate of cells, the blastula, which is more or less like the egg in size and shape. The generation of this structure during cleavage has been described for several embryos in Part 2. The accurate and reliable reproduction of a structurally and functionally sound organism from this mass of cells occurs by specific *morphogenetic cell movements*. Each cell may be thought of as having a history of movement in time and space. An analysis of morphogenesis seeks to determine the mechanisms which initiate movements of cells, which constrain them to move along particular paths, and which stop them at the appropriate places.

Such an analysis requires the answers to several questions. Where do cells move? What cellular activities, such as change in cell shape, arrangement, and motile behaviour, bring about these movements? What cellular machinery generates the appropriate mechanical forces and how? How are these movements controlled in extent and direction?

The paths of cell movements have been described, though inadequately, from fate-mapping of several organisms using natural and artificial markers (see [106] and Chapters 2.3 and 2.4). But paths reveal little about mechanisms and control. Most embryos are opaque and thus the cell behaviour bringing about movement has rarely been seen *in vivo*. Likewise, analysis of the factors which control the onset, extent, and direction of cell movements *in vivo* has been difficult, principally because the intact embryo contains a complex array of different cell types. Therefore, much of our knowledge of mechanisms comes from studies of cells cultured on glass or plastic in an artificial medium (*in vitro*) where it is possible to isolate specific cell types, to control the nature of the substratum and the properties of the medium, and to have the cells accessible to experimental manipulation and precise cinemicrographic analysis of behaviour.

3.3.2 MECHANISMS OF CELL MOVEMENT *IN VITRO*

Although it is often taken for granted today, the concept that one could learn something about morphogenesis by observing cell behaviour, or even that morphogenesis has a cellular basis at all, had to be established; these ideas gained substance with the work of pioneers such as Roux [93], Harrison [40, 41], and Holtfreter [46], who first attempted to relate morphogenetic events to behaviour displayed by cells and tissue fragments cultured *in vitro*.

Embryonic cells may be *fibroblastic*, '*amoebocytic*' or *epithelial* in morphology and organization. Fibroblasts are generally stellate, spindle-shaped or dendritic in shape; the amoebocytic type are more rotund. Both types are connected to other cells at small contact areas and are separated by relatively large extracellular spaces. In contrast, epithelial cells are polygonal and adhere by circumferential junctions to form a sheet without appreciable gaps. The first two types of cell appear to move as individual cells or as cell streams and the last are displaced as the result of deformation of the sheet (see [106]). The movement of cells of all types of tissue organization have been studied *in vitro*, particularly a member of the first class, the tissue fibroblast.

Fibroblast movement

The fibroblast can be isolated from a number of embryonic and adult tissues from organs such as heart and kidney. The source tissue is dissociated in calcium- and magnesium-free media or by enzymatic digestion, to yield individual cells. These are washed and cultured in the appropriate medium on glass or tissue-culture plastic. In many cases fibroblasts used in motility studies *in vitro* were probably not moving *in vivo*; others, such as the chick corneal fibroblast (p. 138), were actively moving when cultured.

Spreading

The freshly dissociated fibroblast undergoes changes in morphology and cytoarchitecture during its attachment to, and spreading on, the substratum (Fig. 3.3.1a and b). Initially it is spherical and bears a large number of cylindrical protrusions called *microvilli* on its surface. It also shows hemispherical protrusions called *blebs* which are extended and retracted from the cell surface (blebbing). The cortical region of the cell, including the microvilli but not the blebs, contains a meshwork of electron-dense, 5–7 nm diameter *microfilaments* (Fig. 3.3.1; see also Fig. 3.3.6). After making contact with the substratum, the cell spreads, usually within 10–15 minutes, by extension of a lamellar (flattened-out) region around the cell body (Fig. 3.3.1b). The lamella region bears fewer microvilli than the cell body and when the cell is completely spread the total number of microvilli is decreased. Microvilli appear to serve as a storage mechanism for excess membrane in the rounded cell and contribute this surplus, as needed, when the apparent surface-to-volume ratio increases during spreading [30]. The actual surface area of spread and unspread cells is about the same when microvilli are taken into account.

The fibroblast will not spread or move unless it adheres to the substratum; thus the nature of this adhesion is of great importance (see Chapter 3.2). Interference reflection microscopy, which can be used to estimate the distance between the under side of the cell and the substratum, shows that spread cells make *focal contacts* and *close contacts* with the substratum; these have cell-to-substratum spacings of 10–15 nm and 30 nm respectively [3, 19, 56] (Fig. 3.3.1c, Fig. 3.3.2). Focal contacts seen in interference reflection microscopy correspond to electron-dense adhesion plaques of the plasma membrane seen by electron microscopy, and *microfilament bundles* terminate in these regions [1, 42] (Fig. 3.3.2). Spread cells often have crenelated outlines formed by concave segments between protrusions of the cell margin. If these protrusions are detached from the substratum with a microneedle, the margin retracts, suggesting that the cells adhere to the substratum at these points [39]. When a cell rounds up to divide, its peripheral adhesion sites are revealed by the attached distal ends of *retraction fibres* which are formed as the nonadhering portions of the cell retract (Fig. 3.3.1d). These are often confused with *filopodia*. Filopodia form by extension of the cell surface, not retraction, and often function in moving the cell, whereas retraction fibres do not.

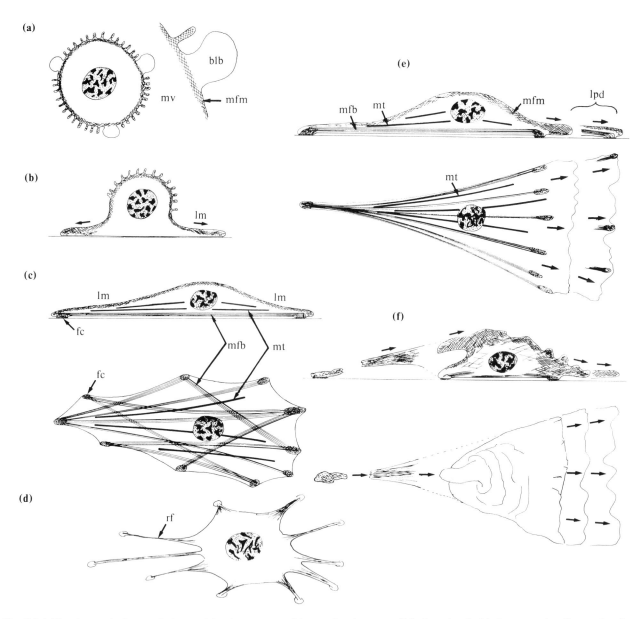

Fig. 3.3.1. The changes in the morphology and the ultrastructure of the tissue fibroblast during spreading (a–c), retraction (d), and locomotion (e, f) *in vitro* are shown diagramatically. The dissociated cell bears microvilli (mv) and blebs (blb) and contains a cortical microfilament meshwork (mfm). The cells spreads by extension of a peripheral lamellar region (lm) (see b, c). The cell is attached to the substratum at focal contacts (fc). Associated with these are microfilament bundles (mfb). Withdrawal of most of the margin toward the cell body, during rounding up prior to division for example, results in the formation of retraction fibres (rf in d). Locomotion occurs by the extension of a lamellipodium (lpd) and its attachment (e) and by retraction of the trailing edge of the cell (f).

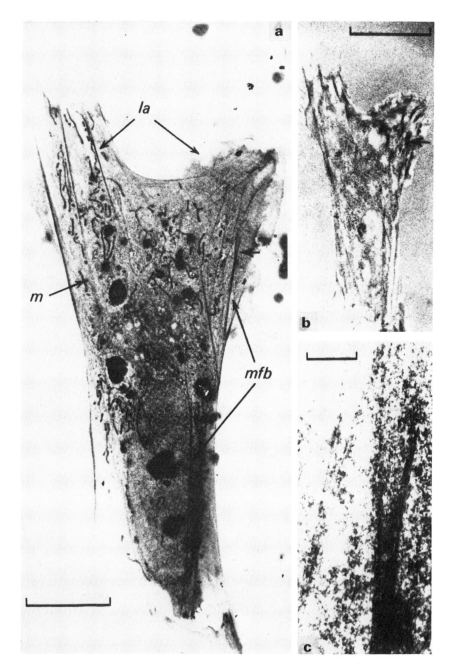

Fig. 3.3.2. A high voltage of electron micrograph of a chick heart fibroblast in primary culture (a) and an interference reflexion micrograph of the same cell (b) shows the relationship of microfilament bundles (mfb; see arrow in a) and focal contacts (black streaks). Grey areas (in b) show close contacts. A high voltage electron micrograph (c) of the lamella (see arrow in a) shows spreading of the microfilament bundle at a focal contact. In (a), section thickness = 1.3 μm, 1000 KV, bar = 10 μm. In (b), bar = 10 μm. In (c), bar = 0.5 μm, 800 KV. The micrographs are reprinted from Heath & Dunn [42], with permission.

Translocation

The fibroblast advances by the extension of a broad, thin (less than 0.5 μm thick) *lamellipodium* beyond the marginal adhesions (focal contacts) where it contacts the substratum and forms new focal contacts (Fig. 3.3.1e). As the lamellipodium advances by repeated extension, the cell is stretched elastically and a 'tail' is formed (Fig. 3.3.1e). The cell is put under increasing tension and finally the tail fractures and retracts to the top of the cell. The adhesion plaque at the trailing edge and a bit of membrane-bound cytoplasm are left on the substratum [19] (Fig. 3.3.1f). After retraction, the cell shows increased blebbing and protrusive activity at the leading edge, usually in the form of rapid extension of the lamellipodium [18] (Fig. 3.3.1f). Lamellipodial extension, cell elongation and tail formation, and trailing edge retraction are repeated, moving the cell forward by the order of 1 μm min^{-1}.

If several competing lamellipodia extend in opposing directions, the cell will not move until one becomes dominant and pulls the cell in that direction. Thus a moving fibroblast is usually elongated in the direction of locomotion, with the dominant lamellipodium at one end and a tail at the other (Fig. 3.3.1). Polarity, expressed as the dominance of a lamellipodium at one side of the cell, depends on the presence of *microtubules* aligned parallel to the long axis of the cell (Fig. 3.3.1c and e). If colchicine (which disrupts microtubules) is added to the culture medium, elongated moving fibroblasts become disc-shaped, like a pancake, and stop moving. Although they show surface motility, it occurs on all sides, and as a result net movement of the cell across the substratum ceases [31, 110]. If cells are plated into media already containing colchicine, they form several lamellipodia and spread in all directions in the fashion of epithelial cells (see p. 126), and thus they fail to translocate [34]. Thus oriented microtubules are not required for spreading on the substratum, but they are necessary to establish a polarity essential for translocation. Other cells, which do not have an elongate form but have a more rounded (amoebocytic) cell body, such as teleost fish gastrula cells (see [107]), vertebrate leucocytes [91], and *Limulus* amoebocytes [6], have few cytoplasmic microtubules and translocate in the presence of colchicine.

The mechanism of lamellipodial extension is poorly understood. The lamellipodium is filled with a meshwork of microfilaments [5, 36] (Fig. 3.3.1e), which decorate with heavy meromyosin and thus undoubtedly contain the contractile protein actin (see p. 128). This meshwork probably serves to support and perhaps to extend the lamellipodium. All activity of the lamellipodium is blocked by cytochalasin B, a drug which disrupts microfilaments [17, 32]. Regions containing a microfilament meshwork contract on incubation of glycerinated cells with ATP [19, 55]. Glycerine destroys the plasma membrane and extracts many proteins from cells but leaves the cytoskeletal–contractile system at least partially intact. Thus the meshwork may be contractile and might function to extend the margin of the cell; it remains unclear how contraction would result in extension. Alternatively, the meshwork might be structural in function (see p. 132) and serve to support a lamellipodium extended by other forces, such as hydrostatic pressure generated by a cortical contraction over the whole cell. Lowering the internal hydrostatic pressure by addition of the osmotically active sugar sorbitol to the culture medium prevents extension of the lamellipodium [24].

Extension of the lamellipodium is often accompanied by *ruffling*. Ruffles are formed on lamellar extensions of the cell margin; they rise up on the upper surface of the cell, move posteriorly toward the nucleus, and flatten into the cell again. These appear in phase-contrast microscopy as dark areas which form, move posteriorly, and disappear (see Fig. 3.3.9, p. 136). Ruffling is associated with, but not necessary for, movement in tissue culture. Cells move under barriers [9], in plasma clots [4] and *in vivo* [8] without ruffling.

Microfilament bundles form in the lamellipodium only after it adheres to the substratum or to another cell, and only in the cytoplasm next to sites of adhesion [42, 43]. This contact-mediated appearance of microfilament bundles may represent alignment of the microfilaments previously arranged in the meshwork, perhaps due to tension generated by a contact-induced contraction of the meshwork itself [19]. Alternatively, it could represent a *contact-mediated assembly* of new microfilaments (see p. 135). In either case, the formation of adhesions at the leading edge of the cell and the associated change in filament organization undoubtedly function to pull the cell forward.

When the tail fractures, it retracts toward the cell body in a biphasic manner. The first phase is rapid and largely, but not completely, independent of energy metabolism. The second phase is slower and completely dependent on metabolic energy. These facts suggest that the first phase is largely an elastic recoil, and that the second phase is an active contraction which may have also contributed to the first phase [19]. A reorganization of microfilaments occurs during tail formation and retraction. Electron microscopy of cells fixed in successive stages of tail formation shows that the filament meshwork gives way to filament bundles as the tail elongates. Polarization microscopy of living cells shows increased birefringence, indicating increased structural alignment. On retraction, the bundles of microfilaments rapidly give way to the meshwork again and the birefringence decreases. Transformation of network to bundles elastically during tail elongation is probably the source of the tension causing the rapid elastic recoil in the first phase of retraction. Contraction, in contrast, occurs when the microfilaments are organized in bundle fashion during the first phase and as a meshwork in the second phase [19].

Tail retraction is intimately related to advance of the leading edge. As the leading edge advances, the total spread area of the cell increases slowly but shows a 10- to 30-fold increase on tail retraction, perhaps because more membrane or cytoplasm is made available to the leading edge or because of release of tension [18]. For this reason, fibroblast locomotion is 'jerky' with alternating periods of rapid and slow advance. Since fibroblasts in their locomotory form show a polarity inherent in having the leading edge opposite the tail, this phenomenon of *retraction-induced spreading* might also have the effect of constantly stimulating locomotory activity at the same end of the cell and thus lead to a persistence in the direction of locomotion. Indeed, when observed over a short time interval (2.5 h), fibroblasts do exhibit such a tendency to move in one direction [33].

Leucocyte movement

The mechanism of locomotion of leucocytes is of particular interest because, unlike the fibroblast, the leucocyte maintains a rounded cell body during movement, it shows cytoplasmic flow, and it moves fast (10 μm min^{-1}) [90, 95]. In these respects leucocytes resemble a variety of the 'amoebocytic' embryonic cells [37, 48, 49, 82, 105]. Leucocytes advance by extension of a thin hyaline lamellipodium, followed by the flow of the granular cytoplasm of the cell body into the lamellipodium [90,

95]. A contractile wave forms near the anterior end of the cell and passes posteriorly with respect to the cell as the cytoplasm flows through it and into the leading lamellipodium (Fig. 3.3.3). The wave remains stationary with respect to the substratum [95]. The cortex contains a meshwork of microfilaments which are actin-like (they decorate with heavy meromyosin in the arrowhead pattern; see p. 128) and thick filaments which are probably myosin [95]. Leucocytes have few cytoplasmic microtubules and, unlike fibroblasts, they do not appear to need them for translocation since they will move in the presence of colchicine at concentrations sufficient to inhibit tubule assembly [91].

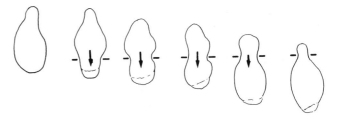

Fig. 3.3.3. Leucocytes often move forward by the formation of a concave segment of the cell surface which remains stationary with respect to the substratum (see the marker bars) while the cytoplasm flows through it (arrows) (see [95]).

Leucocytes move much faster than fibroblasts. This fact and the fact that they maintain a rotund cell body during movement suggest that they detach easily from the substratum. Thus locomotion may be more efficient since less energy is used in detachment. Retraction fibres are formed at the trailing edge but they do not appear to retard the advance of the cell and only a small tail is formed.

Leucocytes show directional locomotion; they are chemotactic. The human leucocyte forms lamellipodia all around its periphery but the cytoplasm flows preferentially into the lamellipodium on the side facing the attractant [90]. In contrast, horse leucocytes form locomotory protrusions more frequently on the side of the cell facing the chemotactic attractant [119].

Epithelial cell movement

Unlike fibroblasts, which adhere to one another only at small contact areas, epithelial cells adhere to one another circumferentially, edge-to-edge, and thus form a cohesive sheet of cells. They form *in vivo* the linings of internal cavities or the exterior of the organism, and they are found as continuous sheets, usually without a margin or free edge. They also show a polarity; the apical or luminal end is characterized by a junctional complex consisting of circumapical tight junctions, which form a physiological barrier, and a subapical band of desmosomes, which bind the cells together (see section 3.2.2, p. 100, and Chapter 3.2). The basal ends do not form specialized junctions of this type but are often attached to a thin layer of extracellular matrix material, the *basal lamina* (basement membranes in the embryo are described in Chapter 3.5).

When a fragment of an epithelial sheet is cultured *in vitro*, its marginal cells attach to the substratum, migrate centrifugally, and thus stretch and spread the sheet [23, 24, 74] (Fig. 3.3.4a). The marginal cells seem to adhere tightly to the substratum. When they are detached by micromanipulation the sheet retracts, suggesting that only marginal adhesions are sufficiently strong to maintain the sheet under tension and in the spread state. The marginal cells show two methods of movement. They may extend a lamellipodium in a fashion similar to a fibroblast, or they may extend their margins by the protrusion of long, apparently rigid microspikes, which wave about and often become attached distally to the substratum some distance from the margin of the cell. The lamellar region of the cell then spreads between these supporting filopodia (Fig. 3.3.4b; see [24]). Epithelial cell lamellipodia contain a microfilament meshwork similar to that seen in the fibroblast. The microspikes contain bundles of microfilaments [24] which apparently form a rigid array and may be capable of supporting a compression load.

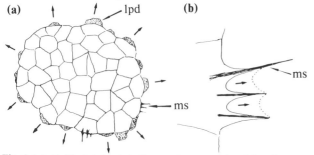

Fig. 3.3.4. Epithelial sheets in tissue culture spread peripherally (arrows) by (a) the motile activities of the marginal cells, which advance by lamellipodia (lpd) similar to those seen in the tissue fibroblast, or (b) by the extension of microspikes (ms) and the movement of the cell margin outward between these supporting microspikes. See [23, 24].

Epithelial cells differ from fibroblasts in their locomotory behaviour in several ways. First, the fibroblast establishes a locomotory polarity in the form of a dominant lamellipodium and thus can translocate as a single cell. In contrast, a single isolated epithelial cell forms lamellipodia in all sectors of its perimeter, which cancel one another in effect, and thus the cell does not translocate. The inability of a single cell to polarize the locomotory machinery may be due to the small number, and perhaps unsuitable arrangement, of cytoplasmic microtubules in epithelial cells. Recall that fibroblasts behave much like single epithelial cells when treated with colchicine. Locomotory polarity of epithelial cells is established by their position in the sheet. Motile activity ceases in the regions of contact between epithelial cells (contact inhibition of cell movement; see p. 135 and Fig. 3.3.9), and thus only the free edges of the marginal cells show motile activity. Thus the locomotory activity is polarized (directed outward) and the epithelial sheet shows its characteristic tendency to spread from any free edge. The fact that colchicine, which disrupts microtubules, has no effect on spreading of epithelial sheets supports the contention that directed movement outward (spreading) is not dependent on microtubules [24]. Epithelial cells form stable edge-to-edge adhesions which survive the tension generated by the outward migration tendencies of the marginal cells, and thus a sheet is maintained with few cells leaving its margin. In contrast, most non-epithelial cells tend to separate after contact (see p. 135).

Most tissue cells in culture show locomotion similar to the fibroblasts, the leucocyte or the epithelial movement described here. Though there are important differences, they all move by some process of extension of a protrusion, its attachment to the substratum, and shortening of the protrusion which pulls the cell body forward or flow of the cell body into the protrusion. Obviously these activities require machinery to generate mechanical force and to provide structural integrity. An understanding of cell motility requires an understanding of the nature and function of this machinery.

3.3.3 MOLECULAR AND ULTRASTRUCTURAL ASPECTS OF CELL MOTILITY

Research in this area has centred on identification and characterization of contractile and cytoskeletal proteins in non-muscle cells and on determination of their structural organization and function during cell movement. Three themes emerge from this research.

(1) Non-muscle cells contain proteins similar to those of the contractile apparatus of muscle.

(2) Contractility in non-muscle cells is based on an actomyosin system similar to that found in muscle.

(3) The organization of the contractile machinery in non-muscle cells is not static, as it is in muscle, but dynamic. It shares components with the cytoskeletal or supporting structure of the cell and is alternately generated from, or reorganized into, the cytoskeleton in a pattern appropriate to the demands of specific motile activities of the cell. The self-assembly properties of many of the molecules involved in cell motility are described in Chapter 6.2.

The sliding filament model of contraction

Muscle and non-muscle contractile machinery show ultrastructural and biochemical similarities in their essential features which suggest that they are based on the same mechanochemical process—the actomyosin sliding filament system. The characteristics of the sliding filament system emerged from extensive electron microscopic X-ray diffraction, and biochemical analysis of striated muscle (see [52] and *Cold Spring Harbor Symp. Quant. Biol.* **37**, 1973, and Chapter 6.2). The contractile apparatus consists of thin (actin) filaments of opposite polarity overlapping both ends of bipolar thick (myosin) filaments. The myosin heads of the thick filaments actively change their angle of attachment to the thin filaments, resulting in increased overlap and thus shortening or contraction of the entire system (Fig. 6.2.6). Thin filaments are composed of at least three major proteins—actin, tropomyosin and troponin (in some types of muscle). Actin in monomer form (G-actin) is a nearly spherical protein, molecular weight 42 000, and about 5.5 nm in diameter. G-actin polymerizes under certain conditions to form thin (about 6.0 nm in diameter) filaments (F-actin). F-actin consists of two polar, parallel strands of actin monomers coiled about one another in a helical array (see [81]). Actin filaments are anchored at one end of the Z disc of the striated muscle sarcomere, or in the plasma membrane of smooth muscle, in a fashion which probably involves a protein, alpha actinin, found in these regions. Tropomyosin is a 35 000-mol.-wt protein consisting of two

polypeptides in an elongate, supercoiled configuration. They are thought to lie in the helical grooves of F-actin filaments, end-to-end, and contraction appears to be regulated in some types of muscle by positioning of the tropomyosins by an aggregate of three proteins, the troponin complex, associated with each tropomyosin. The troponin complex constrains the tropomyosin to lie in the outside region of the grooves in the actin filament, where it prevents the contractile actomyosin interaction. When troponin binds calcium, its conformation changes, tropomyosin falls to its resting position deeper in the grooves, and the cyclical, force-producing actomyosin interaction is allowed to occur. This is called *actin-linked* or *thin-filament regulation* of contraction and is found in vertebrate striated muscle.

The properties and function of the thick filaments reflect the structure of their principal constituent, myosin (see Chapter 6.2 and [72]). Myosin consists of several polypeptides—two heavy chains, each of about 200 000 mol. wt, and several light chains of 18 000–20 000 mol. wt, the number depending on the source of the myosin. Each heavy chain has an alpha-helical region and a globular region. The helical regions of the two chains together form an elongate, rod-like tail about 135 nm long, and the globular regions form the myosin heads. Tryptic digestion cuts myosin into two parts—heavy meromyosin (HMM) and light meromyosin (LMM). HMM consists of the globular heads and the adjacent part of the tail. LMM consists of the remainder of the tail. Papain digestion cleaves myosin into LMM and further divides the HMM into two fragments—a globular head region called heavy meromyosin-subfragment 1 (HMM-S$_1$ or often called S$_1$) and heavy meromyosin-subfragment 2 (HMM-S$_2$). The LMM fragments have a mutual binding region and form aggregates; thus this region is thought to function in binding myosins together in bipolar filaments. The capacity to bind to F-actin and show ATPase activity is associated with the globular head regions of HMM and HMM-S$_1$. The mechanochemical interaction of actin and myosin to produce contraction involves the hydrolysis of ATP by myosin [99], but in the Absence of ATP, myosin and HMM or HMM-S$_1$ form a rigor link as with F-actin. HMM or S$_1$ binding to actin filaments under these conditions forms an arrowhead pattern which is characteristic of actin filaments and also indicates their polarity; the arrowheads point away from the attached end and in the direction of contraction. This fact has been used to

Fig. 3.3.5. Demembranated microvilli of the brush border of chicken intestinal epithelium contains actin filaments which decorate with heavy-meromyosin subfragment 1 (S_1) to form the arrowhead configuration. Note the uniform downward polarity of the filaments. The dense tip material (DT) remains intact in some microvilli. Reprinted from Mooseker M. & Tilney L. (1975) *J. Cell Biol.*, **67**, 725, with permission.

identify actin filaments in non-muscle cells (Fig. 3.3.5).

Several light (polypeptide) chains are associated with the myosin heads. In muscles showing *thick-filament* or *myosin-linked* regulation of contraction, such as scallop muscle, myosin must bind calcium in order to show ATPase activity and to interact with actin to produce a contraction. Calcium binding is controlled by a regulatory light chain which does not bind calcium itself, but is required for calcium regulation of myosin ATPase activity [70].

Contractile proteins in non-muscle cells

A class of proteins, similar to muscle actin, has been identified in non-muscle cells of a variety of organisms, both plant and animal [88]. Non-muscle actin from a variety of sources is similar to muscle actin in molecular weight, amino acid sequence, viscosity, its capacity to polymerize into F-actin filaments, and its activation of myosin ATPase. Ultrastructurally, it shows the same helical structure as muscle actin and it can be decorated with HMM or HMM-S_1 from skeletal muscle to form the characteristic arrowhead pattern [54] (Fig. 3.3.5). Although similar enough to be equivalent in many functions, muscle and non-muscle actin have subtle and perhaps important differences in their amino acid sequence, in their activation of myosin ATPase, and in the conditions under which their polymerization will occur. Non-muscle cells, such as platelets, contain more than one species of actin which differ in their structural and functional properties. Actin may be used as a contractile or structural element [44, 86], and it is possible that different species of actin are specialized for one function or the other.

Myosin is also found in non-muscle cells and functions as a mechanochemical energy transducer in these cells [44, 87, 88]. Non-muscle myosins have ATPase activity which is activated by F-actin; muscle F-actin will activate non-muscle myosin ATPase. Non-muscle myosins are, in general, of the same size, shape, and structure as muscle myosins, and they form bipolar filaments, though much smaller than those formed by muscle myosin [87]. Non-muscle myosin can function in contraction and is indeed a necessary component for contraction in model systems reconstituted from partially purified cell extracts (see p. 133). As with actins, several non-muscle myosins have been found in an organism, and they are undoubtedly products of different genes since their primary structure is different [44].

A tropomyosin-like molecule has been found in non-muscle cells, specifically in brain and in platelets, and a troponin-like component has been found in brain [44]. There is some evidence for both actin-linked and myosin-linked regulation of contraction in non-muscle cells [44] and therefore these molecules may or may not be present or serve a regulatory function in a given cell type. Tropomyosin may have a structural role. In some cells it appears to associate with actin filament bundles, which are thought to serve a cytoskeletal or support function in preference to individual thin filaments, in regions of the cell undergoing contraction [69].

Thus proteins similar to the major proteins of the contractile system of muscle have been identified in non-muscle cells. Their similarities in structure and function to their muscle counterparts suggest that contraction in non-muscle cells occurs by an actomyosin sliding filament system. But non-muscle contractile proteins have not been adequately characterized functionally or biochemically and there are probably important differences in their organization and function in the cell, which are not yet fully appreciated.

Organization of the contractile–cytoskeletal system in non-muscle cells

The contractile proteins of non-muscle cells do not form the stable array of thick and thin filaments found in the sarcomere of striated muscle, but appear to change in organization from minute to minute with changes in cell behaviour and contact (see section 3.3.4). Indeed, they seem to form part of both the contractile and the cytoskeletal systems of the cell. These statements are based on ultrastructural evidence, on immunofluorescent identification and localization studies, and on reconstitution of contractile and cytoskeletal systems from cell extracts. It is important to stress that the arrays of these proteins are frequently observed in fixed cells and that fixation may both polymerize molecules and extract them from the cell. Instances in which the alignment of molecules can be observed in live cells by birefringence (see below) are particularly important in establishing the living arrangement of these molecules.

Microfilament arrays: meshwork and bundles

With electron microscopy of thin sections, 5.0–7.0 nm diameter microfilaments (Fig. 3.3.6) are found in a meshwork pattern in the cortical regions of rounded cells, in the peripheral and lamellar regions of flattened cells, in microvilli and microspikes, and in lamellipodia. These are usually presumed to be actin filaments since, as a class, they decorate with HMM to form the arrowhead pattern characteristic of F-actin. Microfilaments are also found in close-packed, parallel arrays, or microfilament bundles. Microfilament bundles which pass across the substrate side of the cell, near the plasma membrane, and insert on electron-dense regions of the plasma membrane at foci of adhesion to the substratum, are called *stress fibres* [34, 35, 36, 42, 92] (see Fig. 3.3.2). These are found only in well spread cells and were first

observed as dark streaks by phase contrast microscopy. Their association with sites of adhesion and their appearance of being taut suggest that they function in anchoring the cell or perhaps pulling it along the substratum. Also, several minutes after the lamellipodia of two cells contact one another, bundles of microfilaments form in association with the plasma membrane at the site of adhesion, a region which formerly contained only meshwork [43]. The structural relationship of these two patterns of microfilament organization bears on how both of them function.

By studying the organization of microfilaments with polarization microscopy and electron microscopy of cells in several phases of tail retraction, Chen [19] found that microfilament bundles may be formed by tension alignment of the meshwork. The taut, elongated tail of the moving chick heart fibroblast is highly birefringent, indicating the presence of aligned structures, and it is found, by electron microscopy, to contain microfilament bundles. On retraction and release of tension, the bundles give way to a meshwork and birefringence decreases. Furthermore, extending microspikes or lamellipodia are weakly birefringent and electron microscopy shows them to contain the meshwork. But when these protrusions form adhesions to the substratum, they show increased birefringence and alignment of microfilaments into bundles. These facts suggest that tension, possibly generated by contraction of the meshwork itself, aligns the filaments of the meshwork into bundles. Nagai *et al.* [81], studying stretched strands of *Physarum* cytoplasm, also found that tension production correlates with the alignment of filaments. The lamellar region of the fibroblast, which is filled with meshwork, contracts in glycerinated cells treated with ATP [19, 55]. Thus the meshwork can and does contract and if the shortening is resisted, by an adhesion to the substratum for example, tension is generated and alignment occurs. Stress fibres are also able to contract; stress fibre segments, isolated *in situ* with a laser beam, contract on addition of ATP [53]. If contraction in the meshwork or in the bundle or stress fibre is analogous to the sliding filament system of muscle, actin filaments of opposite polarity should be found in association with bipolar myosin filaments. Such an intact sliding filament configuration has not been seen, but this is not surprising since the amount of myosin in non-muscle cells is small, and thick filaments would not be expected frequently in thin sections and, in fact, are rarely seen [87].

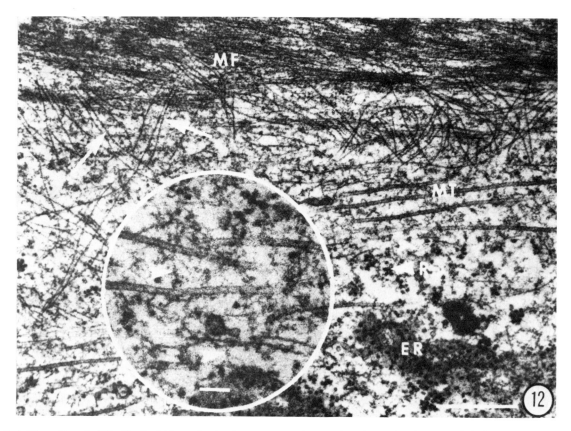

Fig. 3.3.6. A thin section of a WI–38 cell which was fixed and processed as a whole cell, including critical-point drying, before being embedded, sectioned and processed for transmission electron microscopy. Microfilaments (MF) organized as stress fibres, microtubules (MT), and 100 Å (intermediate) filaments (arrows) are shown. The microtrabecular network (pointers in high magnification inset; see [12]), the cisternae of the endoplasmic reticulum (ER), and ribosomes (R) are also shown. Bar = 0.5 μm; inset bar = 0.1 μm. Figure reprinted from Wolosewick & Porter [118], with permission.

Immunofluorescent localization of contractile proteins

Actin, myosin and other proteins associated with the contractile or cytoskeletal structure have been identified and located in fixed cells by immunofluorescent staining. A specific antibody to a contractile protein, usually purified from a muscle source, is prepared and conjugated to a fluorochrome (fluorescein or tetra-methyl rhodamine). The cell must be fixed and then its membrane dissolved and broken up with either acetone or detergent to allow the antibody to penetrate into its internal structures. Fluorescence microscopy is then used to locate the fluorochrome-labelled antibody (IgG) molecules, which bind to a contractile protein similar or identical to the one used to raise the antibody wherever this protein is found in the fixed cell. This is the direct method. In the indirect method, the primary antibody is unlabelled and is located by a second fluorochrome-labelled antibody raised in another organism against the IgG of the species used to raise the primary antibody. Clearly the use of these two methods depends on the assumption that the organization of contractile proteins is not disrupted by these procedures.

In those regions of the cell where electron microscopy shows the microfilament meshwork, which include the lamellar regions of spread cells, microvilli and micro-spikes, there is a diffuse staining with anti-actin and anti-myosin [36, 68, 84, 87] (Fig. 3.3.7). The stress fibres of spread cells show a continuous intense staining with anti-actin and an intense but discontinuous staining with anti-myosin (Fig. 3.3.7d). Myosin is found in the cleavage furrow of dividing cells where an active con-

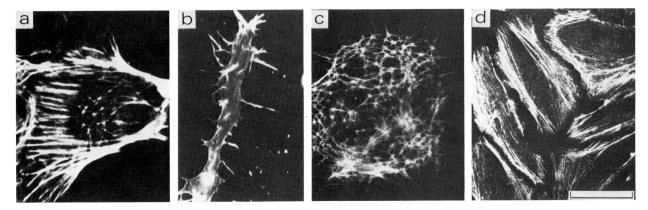

Fig. 3.3.7. (a) A micrograph of a cell of an established cell line of epidermal origin in culture, treated with anti-actin antibody and viewed by indirect immunofluorescence microscopy, shows the actin-containing microfilament bundles and a polygonal network above the nucleus (dark region). (b) Anti-actin staining of a neurite-like extension of a neuroblastoma cell shows actin-containing protrusions of the cell surface. (c) Staining of a cell of the same line as in (a) with anti-myosin shows a polygonal network of myosin-containing structures. Actin appears to be present in the vertices of the network but myosin does not (compare c with a). (d) Staining of myosin in spread HeLa cells with rhodamine-labelled antibody to human platelet myosin rod (direct staining) shows heavy staining of stress fibres or microfilament bundles. (a), (b) and (c) are reprinted from Osborn *et al.* [84], and (d) is reprinted from Pollard *et al.* [87], with permission. (a), (b) and (c) are about 340× and in (d) scale bar = 50 μm.

traction is known to occur [87]. Alpha actinin and tropomyosin show periodic staining in what appear to be alternating, complementary and non-overlapping segments of stress fibres [68]. Alpha actinin is also stained at the insertion of microfilament bundles into the plasma membrane at adhesion sites and at the insertion of filaments into the plasma membrane [78]. In some cells, immunofluorescent staining with either anti-actin or anti-myosin reveals a polygonal network, forming a geodesic cage around the nucleus and sometimes in the peripheral region as well (Fig. 3.3.7a and c). The struts of this cage stain with anti-actin, anti-tropomyosin, and anti-myosin, but the vertices stain only with anti-actin and anti-alpha-actinin. This could mean that the network is made up of segments of actin–tropomyosin filament bundles with associated myosin and these are bound together at the vertices by alpha actinin.

These studies serve to identify and locate the various contractile proteins but can not resolve the precise molecular arrangements because the resolution of the technique is poor. Recently, cytoskeletal and contractile proteins have been identified and located with greater resolution by electromicroscopy of detergent-treated cells in culture, which were incubated with antibody to actin and tubulin labelled with the electron-dense ferritin molecule [113]. Detergent treatment of the cells removes membranes and most organelles but appears to leave most of the cytoskeleton intact. Stereo-electron microscopy of the cytoskeleton shows it to consist of microfilament bundles, microtubules and a lattice of thin (30–40 nm) fibrils. The ferritin-labelled antibody to actin stains the microfilament bundles and the fine lattice-work found throughout the cell. The lattice seen in these detergent-treated cells is similar to the microtrabecular structure of the ground cytoplasm seen in critical-point dried cells with the high-voltage electron microscope [12, 118].

Further development of these techniques may reveal the molecular and ultrastructural arrangement of the contractile–cytoskeletal proteins, but at present the data and concepts gained from conventional electron microscopy of thin sections, from high-voltage electron microscopy of whole cells, and from immunochemical localization experiments have not been integrated into one concept of the dynamic structure of cytoplasm during motility.

Actin insertion on the plasma membrane

High-voltage and conventional electron microscopy show that actin filaments appear to insert on the plasma membrane, particularly at sites of cell–substratum [42] or cell–cell adhesion [43]. Immunofluorescent local-ization studies indicate that alpha actin is found at these insertion sites. Intestinal epithelial cells are a rich source of microvilli because the absorption surface of these cells, the brush border, consists of closely packed microvilli. Mooseker and Tilney (see [78]) found that actin filaments are attached to the plasma membrane of the microvilli of intestinal epithelial cells by an electron-dense material which stains with fluorescent anti-alpha-actinin. When microvilli reform after they have been disrupted by pressure, the dense material appears first and then the actin filaments form from it, suggesting that membrane-associated alpha-actinin-like material may be an assembly site for microfilaments. The micro-filaments decorate *in situ* with HMM, forming arrow-heads pointing uniformly away from the end attached to the plasma membrane, indicating that a contraction would pull on the membrane (Fig. 3.3.5). These facts indicate that actin filaments of non-muscle cells bear the same relationship to the plasma membrane as they do the Z disc in striated muscle. Thus they are in a position to exert force at the cell surface where it can be used to change the shape of the cell or to pull on other cells or the substratum.

Actin filaments in extension

Actin may also be involved in extension or elongation but not through association with myosin. Tilney [101] has shown that an actin-containing amorphous matrix becomes intimately associated with specialized regions of the membrane in the posterior part of the acrosome and the anterior part of the nucleus of the sperm of *Thyone*, a sea cucumber. Eighty-five per cent of this actin is retained in an unpolymerized state by association with two high-molecular-weight proteins. During the acrosomal reaction it polymerizes to form a bundle of filaments in an acrosomal process which extends about 90μm. The polymerization is probably nucleated and directed in the proper direction by a small bundle of filamentous actin already present in the acrosomal material. In *Limulus* sperm, the actin filaments of the extended acrosomal process are bound into a bundle in a hexagonal parallel array by a 55 000-mol.-wt component which binds at or near the myosin-binding site of actin [22]. Thus actin in association with proteins other than myosin can form a structural or cytoskeletal element and most likely generates the force necessary for acrosomal

extension. Although there is no evidence for it now, the possibility that a similar phenomenon might function to extend protrusions in tissue cells should not be overlooked.

Regulation of cytoskeletal organization and contraction

There is evidence that contraction in non-muscle cells requires ATP and is regulated by calcium (see [44] for a review). Hoffman-Berling showed that glycerinated fibroblasts would contract on addition of ATP [45] and that shortening could be reduced by addition of vesicular material from the sarcoplasmic reticulum of muscle which presumably bound up free calcium. Izzard and Izzard [55] demonstrated ATP-dependent, calcium-regulated contraction of naked cytoplasm of the fibro-blast.

Experiments with naked cytoplasm isolated in various physiological solutions show that regulation of con-traction is related to modulation of the physical state of the cytoplasm by changes in the level of Mg-ATP and free calcium. Cytoplasm of free-living amoebae [98] isolated in the absence of calcium and ATP behaves as a viscoelastic solid which consists of thin (actin) filaments and thick (myosin) filaments in a stable rigor linkage. In the absence of calcium and in the absence of ATP, which release the myosin–actin rigor linkage, the cytoplasm is in a relaxed state which shows no viscoelasticity and consists of dissociated actin and myosin filaments. In the presence of ATP and 10^{-6} M calcium, the cytoplasm contracts, and in the presence of 7×10^{-7} M free calcium, it undergoes streaming. Naked cytoplasm can be cycled repeatedly through the stabilized (rigor) state, the relaxed state, and the contractile state by modulating free calcium and ATP concentrations. The naked cyto-plasm of fibroblasts show a similar modulation between stabilized, relaxed and contractile states in response to ATP and calcium.

Investigations of the cytoskeletal and contractile pro-perties of partially purified cytoplasmic extracts of several non-muscle cell types have provided evidence on the molecular composition and organization of the gelated, solated and contractile states of cytoplasm and have indicated some of the physiological parameters regulating the transition from one to the other.

The extracts are typically prepared in the cold (4°C) by homogenizing cells in a low-ionic-strength buffer, centrifuging the homogenate at high speed, and decanting the supernatant which is the crude extract subject to further purification and analysis. Such a crude extract of the slime mould *Dictyostelium* (see [21]) was shown by biochemical analysis to contain actin, myosin and a half-dozen proteins from 28000 to 250000 in molecular weight. On warming to 25°C, this extract forms a solid gel. The gel consists of actin and the 28000- to 250000-mol.-wt proteins which are called *actin-binding proteins* because of their tendency to co-purify with actin. Purified actin even at high concentrations will not form a gel, whereas low concentrations of actin contaminated by these actin-binding proteins will gelate. Myosin is not included in the gel. Gelation will occur in an extract from which myosin has been removed, and under conditions which dissociate the actin–myosin cross-linking which was found in gelated naked cytoplasm of amoebae, discussed above. Electron microscopy shows the gel to consist of amorphous aggregates.

The gel can be solated by several conditions: micromolar calcium concentrations, pH greater than 7.0, mechanical stress, and cold. Solation is accompanied by an increased number of F-actin filaments and a decrease in the number of amorphous aggregates. Regardless of how solation is induced, it results in contraction, but only if myosin is present. If the contracted mass is pelleted by centrifugation and examined biochemically, it is found to contain actin, myosin and a 95000-mol.-wt component. The actin-binding proteins associated with actin in the gel are now found in the supernatant and indeed the gelation activity, as assayed by the ability to form a gel with purified actin, is found in the supernatant. Gelation is calcium-sensitive (it is inhibited by high calcium concentrations). Gelation may regulate contraction by limiting the availability of actin for interaction with myosin since the actin-binding proteins involved in gelation appear to compete with myosin for the available actin (see [21]). The actin-binding protein which cross-links the actin filaments of the acrosomal process of *Limulus* sperm appears to bind at or near the myosin-binding site and may be the factor which prevents myosin binding to these acrosomal filaments (see [22]).

An analysis of sea-urchin egg extracts shows that the actin-binding proteins involved in gelation have different and specific functions [11]. The gel formed by the sea-urchin extract consists of actin, a 58000- and a 220000-mol.-wt component. The purified 58000-mol.-wt protein and actin will form needle-like filaments with a characteristic 11 nm banding pattern, but the 220000-mol.-wt protein is necessary for binding these needles into a gel. The 220000-mol.-wt protein will not form a gel with actin. Furthermore, gelation of these three purified proteins is not inhibited by calcium as it is in the crude extract. This suggests that the calcium-sensitivity of gelation exhibited in this and other systems is mediated by specific components which were removed during purification in this case (see [11]).

These investigations and others [86] show that actin can serve as a structural element when in association with 'actin-binding proteins' to form a gel. It can also serve as a contractile element when associated with myosin. Transition from cytoskeletal to contractile state is regulated by physiological changes in pH, calcium concentration, and mechanical stress. The actin-associated proteins and the nature and conditions regulating their interaction with actin must be studied further. Also, it must be determined whether or to what extent the gelated, solated and contractile states observed and characterized in crude extract preparations reflect cytoplasmic states *in vivo*. Does the gel in these model systems correspond to the cytoskeleton of a cell? How are the gelated, solated and contracted states in crude extracts related to the concepts of cytoplasmic structure and organization gained from the ultrastructural immunochemical localization studies? The sensitivity of cytoplasmic structure to changes in ionic conditions also raises the question of whether the results of these studies reflects the situation *in vivo* or in preparative procedures (see [87]).

Microtubules

Microtubules have been found ubiquitously in eukaryotic cells. They appear as electron-dense, apparently hollow, elongate tubules of variable size, but most commonly about 24 nm in diameter with walls 5 nm thick (see Fig. 3.3.6 and Chapter 6.2). They are found in stable arrays in flagella and cilia and in the cytoplasm in arrays which vary with the shape and motile activity of the cell (cytoplasmic microtubules). Cytoplasmic microtubules are distinguished from mitotic microtubules which form the mitotic spindle and function in the partitioning of chromosomes to daughter cells.

Cytoplasmic microtubules are important in changes in cell shape and in locomotion. They are found aligned parallel to the long axes of elongated cells *in vivo* and *in vitro* (see pp. 130 and 148), and they are thought to function in the extension of some protrusions of the cell surface. In these situations microtubules appear to be rigid rods and by virtue of their resistance to compression or bending they serve a cytoskeletal function. Three mechanisms have been proposed by which microtubules might exert their effect on cell shape: (1) the sliding tubule mechanisms; (2) the cytoplasmic-pumping model; and (3) the force-producing polymerization mechanism. The bases of these models lie in the properties and behaviour of the tubules themselves.

Microtubules consist of 110 000-mol.-wt heterodimers of two related proteins, alpha and beta tubulin, which are similar in molecular weight and electrophoretic behaviour but are products of different genes with different primary structures [89]. These subunits are arrayed in a helical, tubular lattice to form, most commonly, 13 rows of protofilaments which extend the length of the tubule (see Fig. 6.2.9).

In ciliary and flagellar axonemes, microtubules form doublets, with adjacent doublets connected by two rows of arm-like cross bridges of the ATPase protein dynein. Cyclical cross-bridge formation by the dynein arms results in sliding of adjacent doublets [112]. This sliding tubule mechanism produces the force for flagellar and ciliary bending, and it has been suggested as a mechanism by which mitotic tubules control chromosome movement and by which cytoplasmic tubules function in elongation of cells [89].

The cytoplasmic-pumping hypothesis arises from the observation that microtubules appear to serve as a guide and perhaps as movers of particulates in the cytoplasm. An example is the movement of pigment granules in the chromatophores of teleosts [80], and another example is the deposition of material in the plant cell wall (Chapter 2.3). Cytoplasmic particles might be moved along by dynein-like cross bridges which act on the particles rather than on other tubules. Alternatively, the microtubules might serve as a scaffolding for an actomyosin system which moves the particles.

The third mechanism involves the forceful elongation by polymerization of additional subunits to form a longer tubule. There is no direct evidence that polymerization actually produces force, but there is a great interest in polymerization of microtubules since the number, length and orientation of microtubules are of critical importance in their relationship to cell shape and

motility, regardless of how they act. Microtubules are also thought to be important in cytoplasmic segregation in animal eggs and in cell wall depostion in plants (Chapter 2.3 and 2.4).

Much of the research in this area has been done on the mechanism of polymerization and on microtubule-organizing centres [89]. Assemblies of microtubules *in vitro*, similar in structure to those found *in vivo*, occur at a slightly acid or neutral pH, in the presence of magnesium and GTP, and at low calcium concentrations. The sensitivity of polymerization to calcium *in vitro* varies with the magnesium concentration but at least 10^{-5}M is required. Polymerization *in vivo* may be more sensitive, perhaps at intracellular free calcium levels (10^{-6}–10^{-7}M). Calcium may regulate polymerization *in vivo* by a direct effect on the tubules, as it

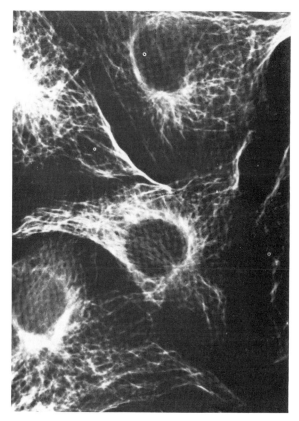

Fig. 3.3.8. Staining of mouse 3T3 cells in culture using a monospecific antibody against tubulin shows radiation of microtubules from a unifocal perinuclear region throughout the cytoplasm. Magnification is about 880×. Reprinted from Osborn *et al.* [84], with permission.

appears to *in vitro*, or its effect may be mediated by the cyclic nucleotides, particularly cyclic adenosine monophosphate (cAMP) [117]. When cAMP levels in CHO cells (cells from Chinese hamster ovary) are raised by treatment with dibutyryl cAMP, these epithelial-like cells elongate into a fibroblastic form and numerous microtubules are found parallel to their newly acquired long axes; this effect is inhibited by high intracellular levels of calcium.

Polymerization *in vivo* of microtubules appears to be associated with amorphous, electron-dense bodies which probably serve as nucleation sites for assembly of microtubules and thus are called microtubule-organizing centres (MTOCs). Localization of microtubules with immunofluorescent labelling of tubulin shows that they often appear to radiate from one or two perinuclear centres (Fig. 3.3.8), and when they re-form after disassembly by cold or colchicine treatment, the microtubules appear to grow from these sites toward the periphery of the cell [84]. There is evidence that assembly of microtubules occurs from either end of the tubule but that the assembly process is polar, in that it occurs three times faster in one direction than in the other. Furthermore, MTOCs appear to be of two types, one type initiating assembly in the fast direction and the other in the slow direction [97]. Thus MTOCs may control rate, as well as direction and site, of assembly.

10 nm (intermediate) filaments

The 10 nm or intermediate filaments are the least-understood fibre-like component of the cytoskeleton. They consist of long rods of variable diameter but intermediate to microfilaments and microtubules in this dimension (usually about 10 nm). 10 nm filaments occur in many cell types. They form a structural element in smooth muscle; they appear as the tonofilaments which insert on desmosomes in epidermal sheets; and they appear in variable numbers in tissue cells in general. It is not clear whether 10 nm filaments appearing in different cell types are structurally and functionally equivalent, though data on the molecular composition and structure of some types are accumulating [51, 96]. The fact that they are anchored to dense bodies on the plasma membrane of smooth muscle, and the fact that they insert in epidermal cells, on the desmosomes which connect these cells to one another, suggest that they might be structural, tension-bearing elements. How-

ever, in tissue culture cells they have a wavey, undulating pattern and do not appear to be taut [84].

3.3.4 CELL BEHAVIOUR *IN VITRO*

An understanding of how cells move alone and what machinery generates the necessary force or provides a structural framework for motility is not sufficient to understand morphogenetic cell movements. Studies of cell behaviour *in vitro* show that motile behaviour of cells is modulated by contact with other cells and by the physical characteristics of the environment. Cell–cell or cell–substrate interactions can affect how a cell moves or whether it moves at all. These interactions can constrain cell movements to specific paths (orientation), and can determine the direction of movement along these paths (directionality). Understanding how these factors operate *in vitro* is an important step in understanding morphogenetic movements *in vivo*, where the environment is replete with opportunities for contact- and substrate-mediated modulations of cell behaviour.

Social or contact-mediated behaviour

Contact inhibition of movement

When a lamellipodium of a fibroblast in culture contacts another cell and forms an adhesion with it, ruffling of the lamellipodium in the region of contact ceases [108] (Fig. 3.3.9), the lamella may retract (*contact retraction*), and the cell stops its advance. A new lamellipodium forms elsewhere, usually on the opposite side of the cell, and never in the region of contact. The cell then moves off in the direction dictated by the new lamellipodium. As it does so, the two cells pull apart. Contact inhibition of motile activity is local and affects only the region of contact [108]. Electron microscopy of cells fixed immediately after contact shows that electron-dense thickenings of the plasma membrane form at the site of adhesion within 20 seconds of contact, and bundles of microfilaments form in the cytoplasm subjacent to the adhesion site within several minutes of contact [43]. The appearance of the filament bundles may be due to a *contact-mediated assembly of filaments*, or it may be due to alignment of pre-existing filaments of the microfilament meshwork by tension resulting from a contact-mediated contraction in the region of contact [19]. In either case, cell–cell contact has an immediate

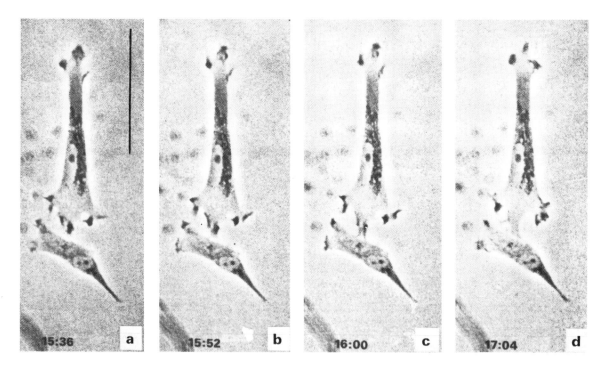

Fig. 3.3.9. An embryonic myoblast translocating toward another cell in culture has just made contact with it (a, b). Ruffling of the leading lamellipodium (phase-dark regions) ceases in the region of contact but continues in other regions of the cell margin (d). Scale in (a) equals 100 μm. Reprinted from Trinkaus *et al.* [108], with permission.

and marked effect on the local organization of the cytoskeletal–contractile machinery. Effects such as these are probably mediated by cell surface constituents (see Chapter 3.2).

Abercrombie and Heaysman [2, 3] demonstrated quantitatively the effect of contact inhibition of movement on the behaviour of populations of cells. When an explant of tissue is placed in culture, cells (fibroblasts) migrate away from the explant in a zone of outgrowth. A statistical analysis showed that this directional migration (away from the explant) is due to contact inhibition of movement. Contact results in local paralysis of motile activity and cessation of movement in that direction. Subsequent motile activity will lead the cell off in another direction. The probability of collisions, and thus cessation and re-direction of movement, increases in regions of high cell population density, and thus there is a net movement of cells from these regions to regions of lower population density. The directionality imparted by contact inhibition applies only to the population; individual cells may be observed moving in any direction.

Epithelial cells also show contact inhibition of movement [23, 73]. Locomotory activity is paralysed in regions of mutual contact and this has the effect of limiting motile activity to the free edges of the marginal cells of the epithelial sheet. Thus the locomotion of these cells is directed outwardly, and the sheet of cells comes under tension and spreads across the substratum (see p. 126).

Contact-induced spreading

If isolated from the sheet, an epithelial cell rounds up, blebs wildly, and will not spread on the substratum or translocate any significant distance. If allowed to contact other epithelial cells, however, it will join the sheet, cease blebbing and spread on the substratum [23, 74, 75]. This behaviour, called *contact-induced spreading*, is displayed by retinal pigment cells of the chick [75], corneal epithelial cells of the chick [23], and teleost fish gastrula cells [105]. It is not clear how contact between two cells changes the behaviour of both toward the substratum.

Contact-coordinated blebbing

There is evidence that the occurrence of protrusive activity can be mediated by contact between cells [107]. *Fundulus* gastrula cells can be induced to bleb by a mechanical stimulus such as poking them with a micro-needle. When these cells are in contact with one another (in a chain of several cells for example), mechanically induced blebbing of the first cell is followed by sequential blebbing of the remaining cells in 80% of cases. It is not known how the stimulus for blebbing is transmitted but these cells are electrically coupled and that may be the signalling mechanism.

Cell alignment and close-packing

Dense cultures of human lung fibroblasts often form two-dimensional parallel arrays of elongate cells with discontinuities where aligned arrays of different orient-ations meet one another [27, 28]. When these cells first attach, spread and move about on the substratum, they show variable morphology and are randomly orientated, but as they proliferate to confluent density they adopt a bipolar, elongate shape and as they move about they form the parallel arrays. These are orientated indepen-dently and thus discontinuities exist between them. These arrays decrease in number with time and the pattern is simplified; this is dependent on cell move-ment. The discontinuities can be assigned appropriate topological indices and the simplification of the pattern may be described topologically [29]. This analysis shows that cells in close-packed arrays do not behave indepen-dently but are influenced in both their shape and orien-tation by global constraints arising from their inter-actions.

This phenomenon may be common *in vivo*. The dermatoglyphic (dermal ridge) pattern on primate foot soles and hand palms show topologically similar aligned arrays and discontinuities [29]. Alignment of elongated cells and the existence of discontinuities between them and adjacent cell groups is common in development and these patterns may arise from similar interactions of close-packed cells.

Substrate-mediated cell behaviour

Contact guidance

Harrison [41] noted that cells in culture tend to align themselves with and move along physical discontinuities in the substratum, such as scratches in the culture dish or a spider's web in the dish. Weiss called this phenomenon 'contact guidance' [114] and it is also referred to as 'substrate guidance'. He found that neurons in culture grow in a pattern which mimics the physical pattern in the environment. They take a circuitous route through the randomly arrayed fibres of a plasma clot, but if the fibres of the clot are aligned by stress, the neurons move along, and parallel to, the oriented fibres. A similar contact guidance may occur *in vivo*. In the Mexican axolotl (the amphibian *Ambystoma*), neural-crest cells migrate from their point of origin dorsal to the neural tube ventrally along fibres of extracellular matrix material aligned in the same direction [71]. Primordial germ cells move dorsally in the dorsal mesentery of the amphibian in a path parallel to the mesentery cells in this region which are already aligned and show stress fibres aligned in the dorsoventral direction [116]. If, in fact, contact guidance does occur in these cases, it only offers an explanation for constraint of cell movements to a path (orientation) but not for movement in a particular direction along that path (directionality).

The mechanism of one type of contact guidance may involve the effect of substratum curvature of the cyto-skeleton. Dunn and Heath [26] hypothesized that linear elements of the locomotory machinery, most likely bundles of microfilaments, cannot form or act effectively when bent. If the shape of the substratum limits the effective length of these elements in a given direction, they form in another direction in which their length is not restricted by curvature. These newly aligned elements will then dominate the locomotory process and shift its direction to correspond to the surface of least curvature. They tested this hypothesis with a time-lapse cinemicrographic and electron microscopic analysis of the behaviour and structure of fibroblasts as they encountered the peak of a prism, shaped like the pitched roof of a house. They found that cells would not cross high ridge angles (16° and 32°) unless they approached at angles far from the perpendicular and thus effectively reduced the bending required to cross to the other side. Furthermore, electron microscopy showed that micro-filament bundles in the leading region of the cell, which had crossed the peak of the ridge, were oriented independently of those in the cell body which had not crossed. Microfilament bundles were disrupted in the part of the cell lying over the peak. These results show that curvature of the surface can alter cell behaviour, probably by a direct mechanical effect on the organization of the cytoskeleton. This mechanism applies only to contact guidance in which the effective surface is relatively large with respect to the cell.

Orientation of the cells on fine fibrils probably has a different, but perhaps related, mechanism [25]. Fibroblasts cultured in an hydrated collagen lattice move along rather than across the fibrils of collagen. Moving across the gaps between one fibre and the next may be less likely than movement along the continuous surface of the fibre. Also, movement from side to side may involve bending since the fibres lie at different levels, whereas movement along a fibre at the same level would require little bending.

Directionality in response to an adhesive gradient

Carter [16] developed a method of varying the cell substratum adhesiveness by vacuum evaporation of the metal palladium on coverslips coated with cellulose acetate. Stencils were used to make fine grid patterns of coated and uncoated surfaces and also gradients in thickness of the metal coating. He found that L-cells, which are mouse fibroblasts grown in culture for many years, accumulate on palladium in preference to cellulose acetate, which he interpreted to mean that the palladium was more adhesive. When placed on a gradient of metal coating, the cells moved up the gradient to the end with the thickest coating of metal. Harris [38] used similar methods, and found that cells accumulate on preferred substrata because they detach more easily from the less-preferred substrata. It appears that locomotory protrusions on the preferred substrata are more difficult to detach and thus are at a competitive advantage when several protrusions are trying to pull the cell in opposing directions. There is no direct evidence that adhesive gradients impart directionality *in vivo* or that particularly adhesive regions trap cells that are wandering about. It has been suggested that accumulation of primary mesenchyme cells in a specific region of the ectodermal wall of the sea-urchin gastrula is due to their entrapment in this region of greater adhesivity (see p. 139).

3.3.5 MECHANISMS OF CELL MOVEMENT *IN VIVO*

The studies *in vitro* discussed above show that different

cell types, such as fibroblasts, leucocytes and epithelial cells, show intrinsic differences in their mechanisms of locomotion. They provide a considerable understanding of machinery used in cell shape changes and motile behaviour. They also show that motility-related cell behaviour is modulated by cell contact and by the substratum. Thus these studies serve as a guide to what factors might affect cell movements *in vivo*. But morphogenetic cell movements must be analysed *in vivo* to determine which of these mechanisms or what new ones actually function in the organism. Knowing what a cell can do under a particular set of conditions *in vitro* does not indicate what it in fact does in the embryo.

Comparison of chick corneal fibroblast movement *in vivo* and *in vitro*

Comparison of the movement of the same cell type *in vivo* and *in vitro* can heighten understanding of movement in both situations. On the sixth day of incubation of the chick embryo, fibroblasts of neural-crest origin migrate into a swollen collagenous matrix lying between the corneal epithelium and the endothelium above the lens. This migration has been studied with transmission and scanning electron microscopy and by time-lapse cinemicrography [8] (see section 4.3.4). The moving corneal fibroblast *in vivo* has a bipolar spindle shape with protrusions at either end that often terminate in branching filopodia. Some cells are pear-shaped and have no protrusion on the trailing edge of the moving cell. Locomotion occurs by flow of cytoplasm into some of the protrusions and not others. The spindle bipolar form and the prevalence of filopodia in fibroblast locomotion *in vivo* appear to be related to their use of the collagen fibrils as a substratum *in vivo*. If these cells are cultured on a plane substratum of glass or plastic, they adopt the morphology typical of a cultured fibroblast with a broad lamellipodium, and they show the same motile behaviour. However, if they are cultured *in vitro*, but on an hydrated collagen lattice much like one found *in vivo*, they adopt the bipolar spindle shape and behaviour seen *in vivo*. It is not just the chemistry of the collagen that is important but the geometry as well. If they are cultured on a flat collagen mat rather than a three-dimensional lattice they again take on a stellate, flattened form with a broad lamellipodium. Thus differences in cell shape and perhaps in locomotory mechanism displayed by cells *in vivo* and *in vitro* can be due to differences in substrata. Cell morphology may also vary *in vivo,* depending on the substratum used. Mesenchymal cells in the anuran tadpole tail have a dendritic shape when moving in the fibrillar meshwork of the tail matrix but become flattened when they move on to the smooth wall of a capillary [20].

Sea urchin gastrulation

The sea urchin embryo is suited well for the study of the cellular basis of morphogenesis. Its transparency and relatively small population of cells make it possible to observe and analyse cell movements *in vivo* with high-resolution light microscopy and time-lapse cinemicrography. Sea urchin gastrulation is discussed in some detail in a later chapter (see section 4.3.4, p. 278). Several points which bear on our understanding of the cellular basis of this process will be discussed here.

Factors affecting primary mesenchyme migration

After leaving the vegetal plate, the primary mesenchyme cells form a loose aggregate at the vegetal pole. The migration of the mesenchyme cells from this aggregate across the wall of the gastrula is reminiscent of the movement of fibroblasts in the zone of outgrowth formed around an explant in culture (see p. 136). This suggests that contact inhibition of movement might function in the dispersal of mesenchyme cells but the event itself was not observed [37]. Mesenchyme cells are obviously not contact-inhibited by the ectodermal cells which they move across. However, they may not make direct contact with these cells but instead attach to the non-cellular basal lamina which covers their basal ends. By a distilled-water treatment, the basal lamina can be isolated as a gastrula-shaped balloon, free of external cells. This balloon contains the mesenchyme cells and spicules formed from them in their normal positions [83].

Primary mesenchyme cell migration appears to be related to changes in extracellular matrix material in several ways. The basal lamina which lines the inner surface of the blastula develops lesions in the region of cell ingression. It is unclear how basal-lamina breakdown and the onset of protrusive activity and ingression of the primary mesenchyme cells are related. Ingression is also correlated with the synthesis of sulphated mucopolysaccharides and their presence on the cell surfaces

[61]. Primary mesenchyme cells selectively incorporate $^{35}SO_4$ into acid mucopolysaccharides prior to their ingression, and histochemical and autoradiographic analyses of sulphate-labelled embryos show these molecules to be found on the cell surfaces. Sea urchins depend on exogenous sulphate sources and when deprived of it in sulphate-free sea water, the primary mesenchyme cells do not ingress and their surfaces are smooth when viewed by scanning electron microscopy, whereas those in normal embryos are roughened by the presence of the matrix material [61]. Mesenchyme cell migration will resume in sulphate-deprived sea urchins when they are returned to sulphated sea water. The synthesis and deposition in the extracellular spaces of sulphated and unsulphated mucopolysaccharides (often called glycosaminoglycans or GAGs) is correlated with the onset of cell movement in frog gastrulation (see p. 146), in corneal fibroblast migration [8] (see section 4.3.4), and in neural crest cell migration [115], but it is not certain how these GAGs might act or if they are necessary for the change in cell behaviour.

The primary mesenchyme cells first become dispersed in an apparently random fashion, but later are found only on the inner surface of specific regions of the gastrular ectoderm in the thickened circumarchenteric region and along the thickened ventral ridges (see section 4.3.4, p. 279(. Filopodial attachment occurs in many regions, but those attached in thickened regions of the ectoderm appear to be more stable under the tension which presumably develops when the filopodia contract and pull the cell forward. Thus the mesenchyme cells may be trapped in what appear to be more adhesive regions, much as fibroblasts accumulate on 'preferred' substrata *in vitro* (see p. 138). There is no direct evidence, however, that any region of the ectoderm is more adhesive and thus 'traps' the mesenchyme cells.

Primary invagination: deformation of a cell sheet

Primary invagination may be viewed as a deformation of a simple monolayer of cells due to changes in cell shape and contact [37]. It is undoubtedly the result of forces generated within the vegetal region by local cell behaviour, rather than arising from global forces generated elsewhere. This region shows the same deformation when isolated from the animal half [76]. What sort of local cell behaviour could bring about invagination? Gustafson and Wolpert suggested that changes in the contact between cells, and between cells and the hyaline layer, generate the necessary forces for primary invagination [37], and they formalized the morphogenetic effects of changes in cell–cell and cell–hyaline-layer contact in a series of models based on simple geometric and mechanical rules (see section on cellular mechanism, p. 280).

Gustafson and Wolpert further suggested that changes in contact between cells or between cell and supporting membrane (hyaline layer) result directly from changes in adhesion. Increased adhesion would lead to increased contact; decreased adhesion would lead to decreased contact. Change in contact would force change in cell shape and thus drive the deformation of the sheet of cells. It is difficult to imagine that these observed changes in cell contact do not involve changes in the positions of cell adhesions and perhaps in their strength as well. There is, however, no direct evidence for change in adhesive strength.

It is possible that the cytoskeleton is also involved in these cell shape changes. Increased cortical tension, perhaps generated by contraction or cortical microfilaments, could force a cell to round up. Constriction of a cell by circumferential microfilaments and the action of aligned arrays of microtubules might force cells to become columnar. Treatment of sea urchins with agents which prevent the assembly (colchicine) or disassembly (D_2O) of microtubules shows that microtubules function in the development of the shape of primary mesenchyme cells [102].

Teleost epiboly

As in the case of the sea urchins, embryos of some species of teleost fish are nearly transparent and therefore it has been possible to describe movements of cells in detail [105]. The egg of *Fundulus heteroclitus*, the killifish, is meroblastic, with cleavage occurring only

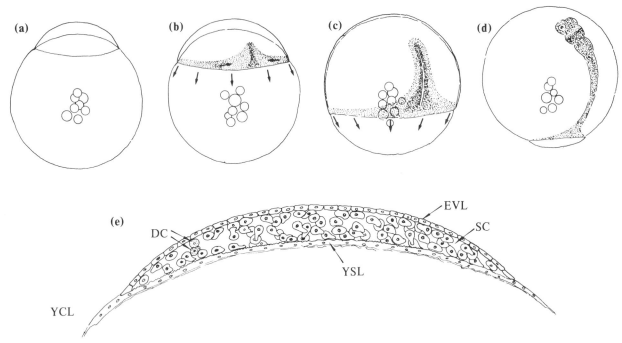

Fig. 3.3.10. The normal development of the teleost *Fundulus heteroclitus* (a–d). Cleavage occurs to form a cellular blastoderm on the larger yolky egg (a). The blastoderm flattens and spreads over the egg during the gastrula stages (arrows in b, c), and concurrently the deep cells (see e) converge dorsally to form the embryonic shield (arrows in shaded area in b, c). The embryo is formed from the deep cells of the embryonic shield (d). A sectional diagram of the early gastrula of *Fundulus* (e) shows that the blastoderm consists of the enveloping layer (EVL) and the yolk syncytial layer (YSL) enclosing a segmentation cavity (SC) which contains the deep cells (DC). The blastoderm is bounded peripherally by the yolk cytoplasmic layer (YCL). Figures a–d were redrawn from Armstrong & Child (1965) *Biol. Bull.*, **128**, 143, and e was redrawn from Lentz & Trinkaus (1967) *J. Cell Biol.*, **32**, 121.

superficially at one pole of the large (2 mm diameter) egg to form a blastodisc (Fig. 3.3.10). When the blastoderm is cleaved into several thousand cells, it consists of a superficial epithelium called the *enveloping layer* (EVL). Beneath the EVL is a loose aggregate of *deep cells* in a cavity called the *segmentation cavity*. The segmentation cavity is bounded below by the *yolk syncytial layer* (YSL), which extends beyond the margins of the disc-like EVL. Peripheral to the YSL is the *yolk cytoplasmic layer* (YCL), which surrounds the remainder of the egg (Fig. 3.3.10).

During gastrulation the EVL and the YSL expand to cover the entire egg (epiboly). As they spread, the segmentation cavity becomes larger and the deep cells begin to move around within it, using the undersurface of the EVL, the YSL or even one another as substrata. As epiboly proceeds, the deep cells move vegetally and dorsally where they form an aggregate known as the *embryonic shield*. The embryo is formed from this aggregate and the EVL forms extra-embryonic structures. Gastrulation in the teleosts studied in detail consists of spreading of the EVL and migration of the deep cells in the segmentation cavity. 'Invagination' or, more correctly, involution does not occur at the margin of the blastoderm (see [7]).

Spreading of the enveloping layer (see [10])

Expansion of the EVL occurs by flattening and spreading of individual cells. EVL cells divide infrequently during expansion and thus division is not significantly involved in spreading. Spreading of the EVL is dependent on its marginal cells being in contact with the YSL. If the EVL is detached by mechanical means, it retracts in the region of detachment and at the same time the YSL accelerates vegetally. The marginal cells of the EVL are connected to the YSL by a complex of tight and close junctions which appear to be stable. Thus the marginal EVL cells do not appear actively to migrate vegetally on the YSL but appear to be passively towed along as the YSL spreads. It is not clear how the YSL spreads, but there are well-developed arrays of microfilaments in the YCL ahead of it, as well as in the YSL and in the EVL cells [10]. These may function in spreading the YSL and the attached EVL vegetally.

Deep-cell movement

In contrast to the cells of the EVL, which appear to be displaced passively as they are stretched by tension generated elsewhere in the embryo, the deep cells move

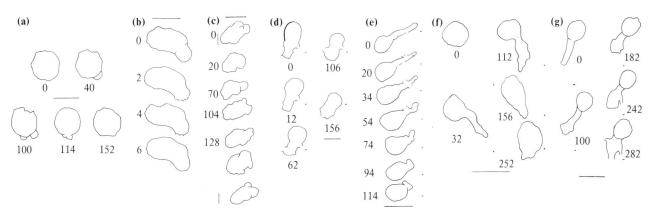

Fig. 3.3.11. A series of tracings from time-lapse movie frames shows the locomotory behaviour of *Fundulus* deep cells. The numbers indicate seconds elapsed. (a) The blebbing characteristic of early blastula deep cells. Bar = 30 μm. (b) In the late blastula stage, blebbing is accompanied by flattening of the bleb on the substratum (the under-surface of the enveloping layer), and scalloping of its margin, suggesting attachment. Bar = 20 μm. (c) A deep cell from the midgastrula stage translocates (with respect to the reference line at the left) by blebbing. Bar = 20 μm. (d) A deep cell translocates without shortening of the leading lamellipodium. Bar = 20 μm. (e) The 'inchworm' type of locomotion, shown here by a midgastrula deep cell, consists of extension of a lobopodium followed by its shortening, which draws the cell body forward. Bar = 30 μm. (f) A midgastrula deep cell advances by shortening of a lobopodium as it extends (32 and 112 seconds). The cell body continues to advance though the protrusion is retracting (112 and 156 seconds). Bar = 30 μm. (g) A deep cell shows lamellipodial advance coincident with its shortening. Bar = 30 μm. Redrawn from Trinkaus [106], with permission.

actively and as individuals. Deep-cell locomotion *in vivo* has been analysed by time-lapse cinemicrography [105]. In the midblastula stage, some of the deep cells show surface activity and by the late blastula stage they are blebbing vigorously and jostling one another about. But this early protrusive activity is not effective in translocation of the cells. In the early gastrula, however, these protrusions become locomotory organelles (Fig. 3.3.11). Instead of retracting without effect, blebs extend to become locomotory protrusions which adhere to the substratum. The cell body is moved forward, either by cytoplasmic flow into the protrusion or by shortening of the protrusion. The cell body may move forward by either of these methods, as the protrusion is being extended or after it has completed extension. The distal end of a protrusion will sometimes flatten on the substratum and form the scalloped or crenated profile characteristic of adherent cells in culture (Fig. 3.3.11).

Deep cells maintain a more or less rotund cell body during locomotion and they move fast, up to 6 μm min^{-1}. In these respects they resemble cultured leucocytes and are different from cultured fibroblasts, which move slowly and are highly spread and flattened (see section 3.3.4). The mechanics of movement of deep cells are similar enough to those of leucocytes to suggest that it also involves cytoplasmic flow.

Deep cells do not appear to be contact-inhibited in their movement, either by one another or by the cells of the EVL or the YSL, since they move on these surfaces and in apparent direct contact with them. It is not known how deep cells are guided vegetally and dorsally to form the embryonic shield.

Changes in adhesiveness and deformability at the onset of movement

As noted above, the onset of deep-cell translocation occurs when protrusions of the cell surface begin to adhere to other cells and thus become effective as organelles of movement. Trinkaus [104] found that deep cells show an increased ability to spread on glass and an increased ability to form aggregates in culture at the time of onset of translocation in the embryo. This suggests an increased ability to make adhesions. At the same time, however, the deep-cell surface becomes more deformable, as measured by an increase in the size of the protrusion which can be drawn from the cell surface by a micropipette under a standard negative pressure [100].

Thus the greater ability to spread, to reaggregate and to move in the embryo may be due to increased stickiness of the cell surface or to greater deformability or to both.

Amphibian gastrulation

Amphibian gastrulation is one of the most fascinating and most studied morphogenetic systems. It is also one of the least well understood, principally because the embryo is opaque and direct observation of cell behaviour has not been possible until recently, and even now only the superficial cells have been studied.

Several mechanisms of gastrulation have been proposed which do not depend on specific details of cell movement or behaviour. Holtfreter [46] concluded that gastrulation is driven by the development of positive and negative affinities between the various tissue types. Later, Townes and Holtfreter showed that amphibian embryonic cells would sort out by type [103]. Steinberg postulated and gathered impressive evidence for the existence of a hierarchy of differences in cell adhesion which would account for sorting-out events in tissue culture and during morphogenetic movements (see section 3.2.5; p. 115).

Holtfreter's model of gastrulation

In a classic series of papers, Holtfreter proposed a mechanism of gastrulation which is based on his acute and perceptive observations of behaviour of cells that he had isolated in culture and on his observations of the structure of dissected, living gastrulae [47–49]. Holtfreter noted that cells of the interior are loosely connected by small knob-like and filiform protrusions. The basal ends of the surface cells are connected to the deep cells by similar protrusions, but their outer ends (apices) are tightly bound together by their common connection to what Holtfreter termed the 'surface coat'. At the onset of gastrulation, the superficial cells in the region of the prospective blastopore become bottle-shaped. Holtfreter isolated and cultured individual bottle cells on a glass substratum in an alkaline culture medium and found that their inner (basal) ends would spread on the substratum and show migratory behaviour, whereas their apical (outer) ends remained unattached to the substratum. Furthermore, alkaline solutions seemed to stimulate locomotory activity in any type of cell. Holtfreter postulated that the alkaline pH of the blastocoel fluid stimulated the bottle cells to migrate into the interior. As they move into the interior, they pull the adjacent parts of the superficial cell sheet in with them since these cells are all connected by the surface coat. Holtfreter found other evidence for the invasive character of the bottle cells. If explanted onto a mass of endoderm, the bottle cells will move into its interior and form a small pit or blastopore on the surface.

However, there are several reasons for thinking that bottle cells play a minor or perhaps different role in gastrulation, the most compelling of which is the fact that in *Xenopus laevis*, the major events of gastrulation proceed in the absence of bottle cells [66]. It is difficult to assign morphogenetic roles to cells in the amphibian embryo when, in fact, nothing is known about what cells actually do during gastrulation. Recently it has been possible to get such information about cell movements during gastrulation in *Xenopus laevis*.

Gastrulation in Xenopus laevis (see [62, 63, 66])

The blastula of *Xenopus*, an anuran amphibian, is double-layered; it consists of a superficial epithelial monolayer of cells and a deep region which is several layers of cells in thickness (Fig. 3.3.12). The superficial layer consists of prospective ectoderm at the animal pole and prospective endoderm in the region bordering the future blastopore, the *marginal zone*, and in the vegetal region (Fig. 3.3.12). All the prospective mesoderm lies as a thick collar in the deep marginal zone.

Gastrulation consists of three basic morphogenetic movements. The lower edge of the mesodermal collar moves vegetally, turns inward, beginning in the dorsal sector of the embryo, and moves in the opposite direction toward the animal pole. This movement is called involution (Fig. 3.3.12e and f). As the involuted material moves toward the animal pole, it moves across and in the opposite direction to the overlying material which has not yet involuted. The discontinuity between the involuted and uninvoluted material is called the *interface* (Fig. 3.3.12). As the mesoderm of the deep layer involutes, the overlying sheet of endoderm, called the *suprablastoporal endoderm*, moves with it. Involution of the deep-layer mesoderm forms the mesodermal mantle and involution of the suprablastoporal endoderm forms the roof of the archenteron. The floor of the archenteron forms from the large mass of subblastoporal endoderm in the vegetal region [62]. This mass is attached at its perimeter to the suprablastoporal endoderm and is carried inside in an in-sinking movement as the suprablastoporal endoderm involutes (Fig. 3.3.12 b–d and e–f).

As deep and superficial cells are removed from the suprablastoporal region (the marginal zone) by involution, others move into this region by *epiboly* (expansion) of the uninvoluted material. Epiboly in the animal region is uniform and proceeds at a slow rate through blastula and gastrula stages [64]. Expansion of the region just above the blastopore (the marginal zone or suprablastoporal region), particularly in the dorsal sector, is anisotropic; it is directed vegetally, toward the site of involution. This movement is called extension. Extension of the marginal zone moves cells vegetally more rapidly than the lip of the blastopore moves ahead, and thus cells are fed over the lip [64]. Accompanying extension of the dorsal marginal zone is *convergence* or narrowing. This region moves a considerable distance along meridian lines toward a point (the site of blastopore closure) on a sphere, and therefore narrowing must take place. Convergence of the marginal zone during extension results in the closing of the blastopore by the end of gastrulation.

It is important to distinguish clearly this process of involution from *invagination* and *ingression*, which are mechanically and geometrically quite different but are often wrongly equated with involution. Invagination occurs by the bending of a cell sheet to form a depression. It occurs during sea urchin gastrulation, but in amphibians it occurs only during the initial formation of the shallow blastoporal groove (Fig. 3.3.12b). The bulk of the depth of the archenteron is formed by involution. Ingression occurs when individual cells leave a cell sheet and move to the interior, such as primary mesenchyme cell ingression in sea urchins.

Cellular behaviour during epiboly

The spreading of the animal region and the marginal zone was described by vital-dye mapping, which yields no information about the cellular events of epiboly. What kind of cell behaviour is associated with epiboly? To answer this question, time-lapse cinemicrography of the superficial cells of the gastrula of *Xenopus* was done with sufficient resolution to identify and trace individual cells through development. Changes in parameters of morphogenetic significance, such as their apical area,

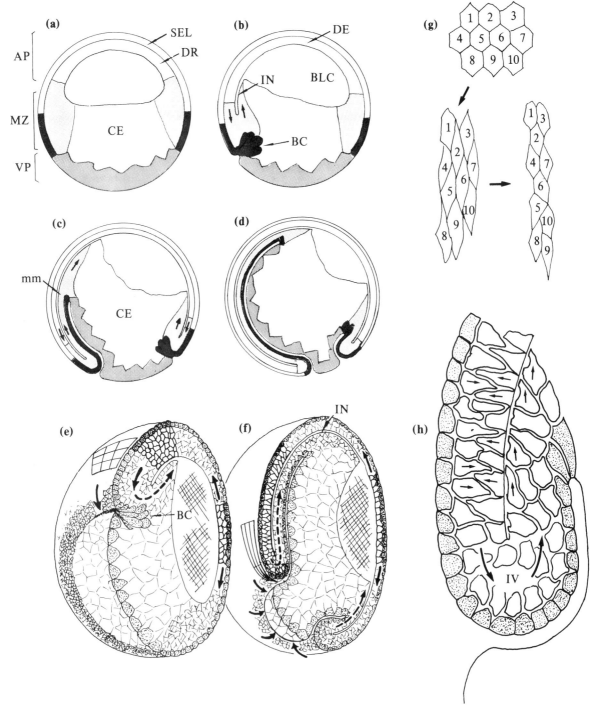

Fig. 3.3.12

their number, their division rate, their shape, and their arrangement, were determined quantitatively [64]. Several conclusions can be drawn from this study. Different regions of the gastrula have characteristic rates of expansion or contraction of the apices of superficial cells, and these changes alone can account for the changes in area observed in vital-dye mapping work [62]. The area increase during epiboly is the result of expansion of the apices of individual superficial cells. Deep cells do not move out into the superficial layer and thus contribute to its increase in area. Secondly, the distortion inherent in the extension and convergence of the dorsal marginal zone occurs by a temporary change in the shape of the cell apices in this region and by cell rearrangement. Cell apices elongate in the direction of

lengthening (extension) of the dorsal marginal zone and they also interdigitate or merge laterally to form a longer and narrower mass (Fig. 3.3.12g). As the rearrangement proceeds, the apices return to their original shape, suggesting that the cell sheet in this area behaves as a viscoelastic system in which the cell apices are stretched elastically by tension in the sheet and then recoil when the tension is relaxed as a result of the rearrangement.

The deep region must also undergo spreading during epiboly, but unfortunately the activities of these deep cells cannot be observed directly because of the opacity of the embryo. One must resort to indirect means. By evaluating several parameters of cell position, arrangement, and shape in scanning electron micrographs of gastrulae fractured midsagitally at several stages of

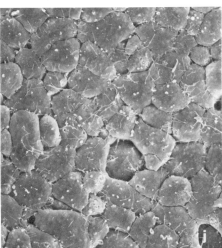

Fig. 3.3.12. The prospective areas and their movements in the *Xenopus* embryo are shown in diagrammatic midsagittal sections of the blastula (a), the early (b), mid (c), and late (d) gastrula stages. The dorsal side is to the left, and the animal pole (AP), the marginal zone (MZ), and the vegetal pole (VP) are indicated. The embryo consists of a superficial epithelial layer (SEL), and a multilayered deep region (DR). The former consists of a band of suprablastoporal endoderm (dark shading), subblastoporal endoderm (medium shading), and superficial ectoderm (unshaded). The deep region consists of a circumblastoporal collar of prospective mesoderm (light shading), which involutes to form the mesodermal mantle (MM), a large mass of central endoderm (CE), and deep ectoderm (DE) in the animal region (unshaded). The involuting mesodermal cells move across the roof of the blastocoel (BLC) forming a discontinuity with the overlying cells which is called the interface (IN in b). Quartering views of midsagitally sectioned early (e) and late (f) gastrulae show the processes of

extension and convergence of the marginal zone in surface view (note the elongation and narrowing of the grid in the dorsal marginal zone) and in sectional view (note heavily outlined cells). Uniform expansion (epiboly) occurs in the animal region (heavily outlined cells). Extension and convergence occur by a temporary increase in the length/width ratio of superficial cells, and by their rearrangement seen in surface view (g). A midsagittal sectional view of the dorsal marginal zone shows the deep cell interdigitation that occurs during extension and convergence. Involution (IV) is followed by transformation of deep cells into a migrating cell-type with a characteristic morphology and arrangement (h). A scanning electron micrograph of the same region (i) and micrographs of the inner surfaces of the interdigitating cells (j) and the involuted cells (k) show this change in morphology and arrangement. Figure i is reprinted from Keller & Schoenwolf [66], with permission.

gastrulation, it was possible to determine that the number of layers of deep cells decreases as epiboly proceeds (see [65]). Several layers of deep cells interdigitate (migrate between one another) to form fewer layers of greater area. Deep cells in the dorsal marginal zone become elongated in the direction of interdigitation and they form numerous protrusions which may be locomotory in function and perhaps actively pull these cells between one another (Fig. 3.3.12).

It is not clear from the evidence available whether the superficial layer, the deep layer, both or neither of them generates the force necessary for spreading (see [65]). Thus the cell behaviour observed in either layer might represent a passive response to stretching forces generated elsewhere, perhaps by the process of involution.

Involution

The motive force for movement of involuted material toward the animal pole and the movement of the un-involuted material vegetally is probably generated, at least in part, along the interface between the two. Protrusions of the involuted cells extend across the interface and attach to the undersurfaces of the uninvoluted cells [66, 82], but there is no direct evidence that these protrusions are locomotory in function.

The mesodermal cells in the deep region undergo a dramatic change in morphology as they involute. Prior to involution they are arrayed in several layers and they participate in the interdigitation of deep cells that occurs during expansion of the marginal zone (Fig. 3.3.12h). Their inner ends are flattened, closely apposed to one another and connected by long, filiform protrusions (Fig. 3.3.12j). After involution, these cells form a loose stream with large intercellular spaces, and numerous protrusions extend outward and contact the uninvoluted cells, which probably serve as a substratum for their migration (Fig. 3.3.12k).

The key to the mechanism of involution lies in this transformation in morphology, and undoubtedly in behaviour as well, of these mesodermal cells in the *deep* region. Superficial cells do not undergo such a transformation but exist as an epithelium before and after involution. Neither do they have access to the interface along which the movement occurs. The bottle cells, which are superficial cells, similarly do not have access to the interface; they are separated from it by the meso-

dermal cell stream. Bottle cells move relatively little with respect to their surrounding cells, a fact not commonly appreciated, and their movement is dependent on the movement of the mesodermal cell stream [66].

Molecular changes correlated with involution

The cells of the dorsal region show an increased cell-surface charge density at the onset of gastrulation, as indicated by the cells' increased rate of migration in an electric field [94]. This may reflect molecular changes in the cell surface. It is also known that involuted cells make and secrete acid mucopolysaccharides into the extracellular species [67] (see also [59]). These materials are made but not secreted in hybrids of *Rana* species which arrest during gastrulation [59]. The onset of morphogenetic movements in the amphibians, as in teleost fish (see p. 140), is correlated with an increased ability of dissociated cells to reaggregate (see [58]).

Neurulation in the newt: the role of change in cell shape and arrangement in deformation of a sheet of cells

In the newt *Tarica torosa*, the behaviour of individual cells and the relationship of this behaviour to the deformation of the neural plate have been studied in detail [13–15, 57]. In this organism, the neural plate consists of a single layer of cells, which is a considerable analytical advantage.

Neurulation in the newt occurs in two phases. First, there is a distortion of a hemispherical sheet of cells, the prospective neural ectoderm located on the dorsal side of the embryo, to form a keyhole-shaped neural plate. Concurrently, the cells of this sheet become columnar; their height increases at the expense of their circumference or cross-sectional area. Second, this thickened, keyhole-shaped plate rolls into a tube, the neural tube (see section 4.3.2 and Fig. 4.3.2). In the process of tube formation, the columnar cells become tapered as their apices shrink. The areal distortion of the neural plate to form the keyhole shape may be due to the cell shape change alone, or other factors might also be required. In order to determine what conditions are necessary and sufficient to bring about the observed behaviour of the neural plate, Jacobson and Gordon [57] did computer simulations of this morphogenetic process. The neural plate was represented by units which could be programmed to shrink in any temporal and spatial pattern. Several simulations of apical shrinkage were tried but none gave the keyhole distortion of the neural plate. However, using simulations of apical shrinkage alone it was possible to generate a pattern of distortion similar to the distortion of the neural plate when isolated in culture without the notochord. This suggests that in addition to cells shrinking in area and becoming columnar in shape, a second force associated with the notochord is necessary to generate the keyhole shape. Neural plates isolated with the notochord attached will elongate and form the proper shape. This suggests that the elongation of the notochord, or an elongation in the medial neural plate induced by the presence of the notochord, is necessary. The simulation was done again but, in addition to the apical shrinkage, the observed extension or elongation of the notochord and the medial neural plate was included. This simulation gave a distortion very similar to that actually observed by time-lapse cinemicrographic tracking of cells in the intact animal. Thus the distortion of the disc-shaped neural plate to form the keyhole configuration can be accounted for by stretching of the medial neural plate due to elongation of the attached notochord. Alternatively, the notochord might not stretch the neural plate mechanically but induce it to elongate by some process within itself.

The evidence indicates that changes in cell shape during neurulation are active and intrinsic to the cells. Holtfreter [50] showed that isolated neural plate cells maintain and even continue their elongation in tissue culture. What cytoskeletal and contractile machinery is responsible for this change in shape? The results of several studies on different organisms pertain to this question (see [60] for a review), particularly those of Burnside on the newt [13, 14]. Electron microscopy shows bundles of microfilaments arrayed in purse-string fashion around the apices of the neural-plate cells (Fig. 3.3.13). Given that these apices constrict, it is likely that these microfilaments are contractile in function. The microfilaments bind heavy meromyosin in the arrowhead configuration and thus are undoubtedly actin-like [85]. There is evidence that apical constriction of neural-plate cells is controlled by calcium. Papaverine, a drug which inhibits the release of bound calcium in the cell, will block neurulation in salamander embryos. Ionophore A23187, which induces movement of calcium across membranes and is thought to release intracellular stores of calcium in this fashion, will counter the effects

of papaverine (see [79]).

Microtubules were found arrayed paraxially in elongated neural-plate cells (Fig. 3.3.13). Microtubules have been associated with the elongation of cells in numerous situations, and several mechanisms of action have been proposed (see p. 134). Burnside's observation that the apical, middle and basal cross-sections of neural-plate cells show the same number of cross-sections of microtubules is consistent with the concept that microtubules actively and forcefully extend by polymerization and thus force the cell to elongate. It is also consistent with the idea that microtubules pump cytoplasm to the ends of the cell and thus cause elongation. It is not consistent with the notion that they bring about elongation by actively sliding past one another (the sliding tubule model), since there would have to be about twice as many cross-sectional views of microtubules in the region of overlap.

Volvox inversion

Volvox is a multicellular eukaryote that undergoes a simple morphogenetic movement of inversion (turning inside-out) in the course of its development. A geometrical, mathematical, and experimental analysis of this process has shown that simple cell shape changes and migration of the intercellular cytoplasmic bridges binding these cells together are necessary and sufficient to produce inversion (see [111]). The *Volvox* embryo consists of a monolayer of about 3000 pear-shaped cells connected to one another laterally by cytoplasmic bridges to form a spheroidal structure enclosed in a tough glycoprotein vesicle (Fig. 3.3.14). The prospective flagellar ends lie to the inside and the chloroplast ends to the outside. This is the reverse of the adult configuration, and inversion is the process by which the embryo turns inside-out to yield the adult pattern.

Inversion begins with the opening of a cross-shaped gap at one end, the phialopore, which has existed since early cleavage but remained closed because of compression of the embryo in the glycoprotein vesicle. It is opened as the perimeter of the embryo decreases and the compression is released by contraction of the cells (Fig. 3.3.14a, d, e). The phialopore can be opened prematurely by eliciting a contraction of the cells with calcium ionophore A23187 in the presence of calcium, or by inducing crenation (shrinkage) of the cells with sucrose or polyethylene glycol.

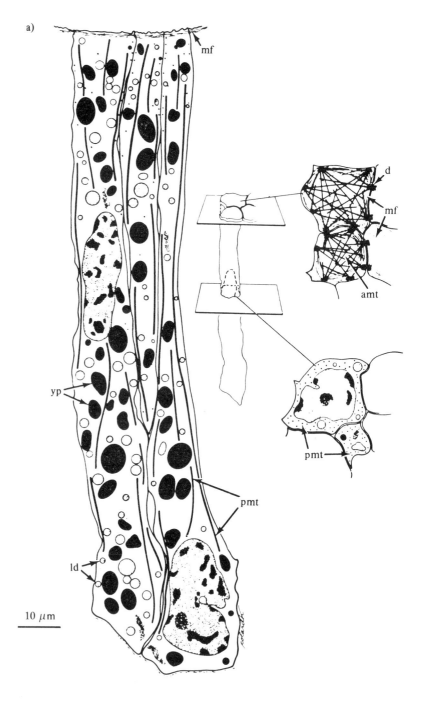

Fig. 3.3.13. (a) Schematic illustrations of the orientation of microfilaments and microtubules in elongating neural plate cells. Numerous microtubules are aligned parallel to the long axis of the cell (paraxial microtubules, pmt). These microtubules are seen in profile in longitudinal section and in cross section in transverse sections of the cell. Just beneath the free surface, microtubules are aligned parallel to the free surface in a layer across the cell apex (apical microtubules, amt). In the same plane with the apical layer of microtubules, 50–70 Å microfilaments (mf) are arranged into a circumferential bundle which encircles the cell apex in purse string fashion. yp, yolk platelet; ld, lipid droplet; d, desmosome. (b) (facing page) Schematic drawing of the orientation of microtubules and microfilaments in a flattening epidermal cell. Beneath the free surface, thicker filaments (70–100 Å in diameter) (f) are arranged into discrete bundles reminiscent of 'tonofibrils'. These bundles of filaments are often seen in continuity with desmosomal filaments and are thought to span the cell from desmosome to desmosome (d). Microtubules (mt) in presumptive epidermal cells appear to be randomly oriented; yp, yolk platelet; ld, lipid droplet. Figures and legend from Burnside [13], with permission.

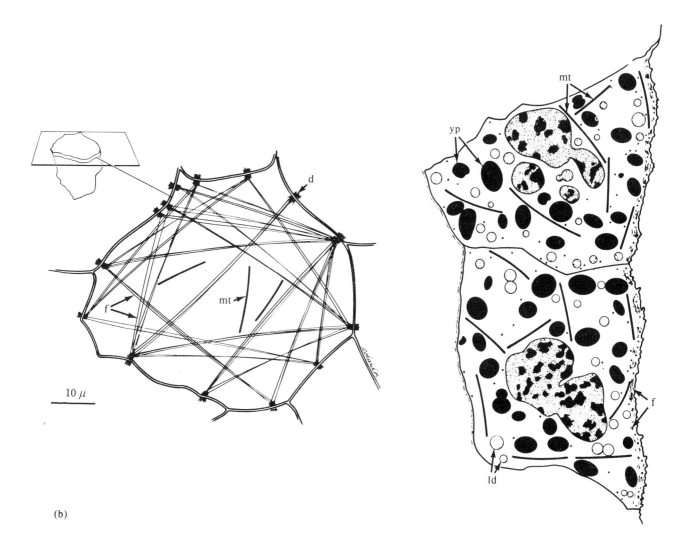

10 μ

(b)

Flask-cell formation

The second and major event in the process of inversion, the generation of a region of negative curvature around the phialopore, begins with the formation of flask- or spindle-shaped cells (Fig. 3.3.14b, f). A wave of negative curvature and flask-cell formation proceeds from the margin of the phialopore toward the opposite pole (Fig. 3.3.14b, c). After passing through the region of negative curvature, the cells become columnar. The transformation from the initial pear shape to the flask shape and finally to the columnar shape, is an auto-

nomous, programmed change which will occur in isolated cells or groups of cells. Therefore, it is more likely to be the cause of inversion rather than an effect of this process. Geometrical analyses [111] showed that flask-cell formation could account for the negative curvature but also predicted that the constriction of the outer ends of the flask cells could not be symmetrical; if it were symmetrical, a purse-string effect would close the phialopore. Indeed, scanning electron microscopy showed that the flask cells in the region of maximum curvature are asymmetric and are thinned only in the direction perpendicular to the circumference of the ring

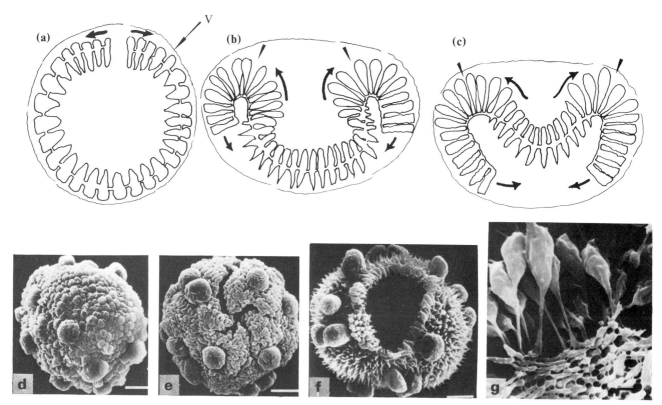

Fig. 3.3.14. Median sections through *Volvox* embryos prior to inversion (a), and during early (b) and middle (c) stages of inversion show diagrammatically the cell shape changes and cytoplasmic bridge migration that produce the region of negative curvature around the phialopore (see pointers in b and c). Note the transformation of the pear-shaped cells (a) to flask-shaped cells (pointers in band, c) and the coincident migration of the cytoplasmic bridges from the midpoints to the chloroplast ends of these cells. The arrows indicate movements of the embryo encased in a glycoprotein vesicle (V). Scanning electron micrographs show the external surfaces of pre-inversion embryos prior to (d) and after (e) phialopore opening and after inversion has just begun (f). A scanning electron micrograph shows the flask-shaped cells and the location of the cytoplasmic bridges and their constricted (chloroplast) ends in the region of maximum negative curvature (g). Note the asymmetry of the constricted ends of the flask cells. The bars in d, e and f = 10 μm and the bar in g = 1 μm. Figures d–g reprinted from Viamontes *et al.* [111], with permission.

of maximum curvature (Fig. 3.3.14g). Disruption of microtubules with colchicine results in the failure of the cells to become flask shaped and inversion is blocked [111]. The microtubules found in these cells appear to be necessary for flask-cell formation and inversion.

Migration of the cytoplasmic bridges

The interconnecting cytoplasmic bridges, which are thought to be produced by incomplete cytokinesis during cleavage, are found at the midpoints of cells not yet in the region of maximum curvature but are found at the outer or chloroplast ends of cells in this region and beyond (Fig. 3.3.14c, g). Movement of the bridges is coincidental with flask-cell formation and mathematical

modelling suggests that the movement of the bridges to the narrow ends of the flask cell (Fig. 3.3.14g) is necessary for the cell shape change to induce the negative curvature efficiently. Treatment of pre-inversion embryos with cytochalasin D (similar to cytochalasin B in its effect on microfilament organization but with less effect on other cell processes) allows transformation of the cells from the pear shape to the flask shape but inhibits the migration of the bridges and inversion. Microtubule disruption will also prevent bridge migration, suggesting that an intact microtubular skeleton is necessary for bridge movement [111].

To summarize, microtubules are necessary and sufficient to produce the cell shape change and necessary but not sufficient to produce bridge migration. Bridge migration requires the function of a cytochalasin-sensitive component, probably microfilaments, though organized arrays of these have not yet been described [111].

Elastic 'snap-through' of the posterior hemisphere

A mechanical and mathematical analysis showed that the mechanical stresses generated as the region of maximum curvature reaches the equator of the embryo should result in an elastic 'snap-through' of the remaining, uninverted (posterior) hemisphere. Indeed, this prediction is supported by the fact that when the wave of cell shape change reaches the equator the rate of inversion increases fivefold and is apparently limited only by the viscoelastic properties of the cells [111]. Furthermore, flask-cell formation continues, and takes about 30 minutes to reach the posterior pole of the embryo, even though inversion is already completed by 'snap-through' in the first four minutes of this period.

These results establish the relationship of cell behaviour to the production of force and the macroscopic distortion of the embryo. This analysis and the fact that there are more than 30 inversionless mutants of *Volvox* should make this system one of the most promising in which the gene activities and regulatory mechanisms underlying morphogenetic cells movements can be studied. Furthermore, the cell shape changes and corresponding deformation of a cell sheet are similar to that seen in several aspects of gastrulation and neurulation in other organisms (such as sea urchin gastrulation and amphibian gastrulation and neurulation) and thus this study should encourage similar analyses of these supposedly more complicated systems.

3.3.6 CELL MOVEMENTS IN MORPHOGENESIS: A PROSPECTUS

The above survey shows some of the technical and conceptual developments at the molecular, cellular and supracellular levels that are carrying the analysis of morphogenetic cell movements into new areas of research and have sharpened the outlines of the problems ahead.

At the molecular level, the structural and mechanical properties of cells are derived from the organization of actin, myosin, tubulin and an assortment of 'associated' proteins which are presently poorly defined but seem to serve as structural modifiers or regulate the organization and function of these primary cytoskeletal proteins. It is the challenge of the future to characterize further these components and their relationships to one another and to determine the conditions regulating their interaction.

At the interface of the molecular or ultrastructural level and the cellular level it is important to learn how the cytoskeletal–contractile system produces force or provides structural support for each specific event in a cell's repertoire of motile behaviour. The fact that the mechanism of a basic motile event like lamellipodial extension is not understood points to the need for this type of work.

It is also important to learn how the cell itself regulates the organization and function of the cytoskeletal–contractile system to produce a cell-type-specific class of motile behaviour, such as fibroblast-specific or epithelial-cell-specific behaviour patterns. This is essential if we are to determine the changes in gene activity that underlie the differentiation of cell-type-specific motility patterns. No less important is the determination of mechanisms by which cell contact- and substratum-induced changes in behaviour occur. Analysis of cell surface components will undoubtedly be important here, since it is at the cell surface that the cell meets the environment, and the plasma membrane shows specialized regions at points of intercellular and cell–substrate contact which also serve as insertion sites of cytoskeletal elements (see section 3.3.2, p. 101).

In the study of cell movements *in vivo* less is known and the work to be done is challenging indeed. Encouragement comes from the recent study of *Volvox* inversion (see p. 150), but this study also draws attention to the fact that much less is known about most morphogenetic systems. Cell behaviour is adequately described for only a few morphogenetic movements and in no other case are the relationships between local cell behaviour, generation of mechanical stress and macroscopic distortion as well defined. In many cases, such as amphibian gastrulation, it is not certain what mechanical forces are involved, what cell populations generate them, or how. From the studies of sea urchin gastrulation, teleost epiboly and newt neurulation it seems that morphogenesis involves local, active, and force-producing behaviour on the part of individual cells, and a global system of mechanical stresses resulting from the interaction of the various regional processes. Future investigations must identify the relevant populations of cells, determine their cell-type-specific patterns of motile behaviour, describe the forces produced by this behaviour and determine how these forces bring about the highly ordered deformations necessary for the reproduction of the organism.

3.3.7 REFERENCES

1 Abercrombie M. & Dunn G.A. (1975) Adhesions of fibroblasts to substratum during contact inhibition observed by interference reflection microscopy. *Expl. Cell Res.*, **92**, 57–62.

2 Abercrombie M. & Heaysman J.E.M. (1953) Observations on the social behavior of cells in tissue culture. I. Speed of movement of chick heart fibroblasts in relation to their mutual contacts. *Expl. Cell Res.*, **5**, 111–131.

3 Abercrombie M. & Heaysman J.E.M. (1954) Observations on the social behavior of cells in tissue culture. II. 'Monolayering' of fibroblasts. *Expl. Cell Res.*, **6**, 293–306.

4 Abercrombie M., Heaysman J.E.M. & Pegrum S.M. (1970) The locomotion of fibroblasts in culture. II. 'Ruffling'. *Expl. Cell Res.*, **60**, 437–444.

5 Abercrombie M., Heaysman J.E.M. & Pegrum S.M. (1971) The locomotion of fibroblasts in culture. IV. Electron microscopy of the leading lamella. *Expl. Cell Res.*, **67**, 359–367.

6 Armstrong P. (1979) Motility of the *Limulus* blood cell. *J. Cell Sci.*, **37**, 169–180.

7 Ballard W. (1973) A new fate map for *Salmo gairdneri. J. exp. Zool.*, **184**, 49–74.

8 Bard J.B.L. & Hay E.D. (1975) The behavior of fibroblasts from the developing cornea. Morphology and movement *in situ* and *in vitro. J. Cell Biol.*, **67**, 400–418.

9 Bell P. (1976) Locomotory behavior, contact inhibition, and pattern formation of 3T3 and polyoma virus transformed 3T3 cells in culture. *J. Cell Biol.*, **74**, 963–982.

10 Betchaku T. & Trinkaus J.P. (1978) Contact relations, surface activity, and cortical microfilaments of marginal cells of the enveloping layer and of the yolk syncytial and yolk cytoplasmic layers of *Fundulus* before and during epiboly. *J. exp. Zool.*, **206**, 381–426.

11 Bryan J. & Kane R. (1978) Separation and interaction of the major components of the sea urchin actin gel. *J. molec. Biol.*, **125**, 207–224.

12 Buckley I. & Porter K.R. (1975) Electron microscopy of critical point dried whole cultured cells. *J. Microsc.*, **104**, 103–120.

13 Burnside B. (1971) Microtubules and microfilaments in newt neurulation. *Devl. Biol.*, **26**, 416–441.

14 Burnside B. (1973) Microtubules and microfilaments in amphibian neurulation. *Amer. Zool.*, **13**, 889–1006.

15 Burnside B. & Jacobson A. (1968) Analysis of morphogenetic movements in the neural plate of the newt *Taricha torosa. Devl. Biol.*, **18**, 537–552.

16 Carter S.B. (1965) Principles of cell motility: The direction of cell movement and cancer invasion. *Nature, Lond.*, **208**, 1183–1187.

17 Carter S.B. (1967) Effects of cytochalasins on mammalian cells. *Nature, Lond.*, **213**, 261–264.

18 Chen W.-T. (1979) Induction of spreading during fibroblast movement. *J. Cell Biol.*, **81**, 684–691.

19 Chen W.-T. (1979) Mechanism of retraction of the trailing edge during fibroblast movement. *J. Cell Biol.*

20 Clark E.R. & Clark E.L. (1925) The development of adventitial (Rouget) cells on the blood capillaries of amphibian larvae. *Am. J. Anat.*, **35**, 329–364.

21 Condellis J. & Taylor D.L. (1977) The contractile basis of amoeboid movement. V. The control of gelation, solation and contraction in extracts from *Dictyostelium discoideum. J. Cell Biol.*, **74**, 901–927.

22 DeRossier D., Mandelkow E. & Silliman A. (1977) Structure of actin-containing filaments from two types of nonmuscle cells. *J. molec. Biol.*, **113**, 679–695.

23 DiPasquale A. (1975) Locomotory activity of epithelial cells in culture. *Expl. Cell Res.*, **94**, 191–215.

24 DiPasquale A. (1975) Locomotion of epithelial cells: Factors involved in extension of the leading edge. *Expl. Cell Res.*, **95**, 425–439.

25 Dunn G. & Ebendal T. (1978) Some aspects of contact guidance. *Zoon*, **6**, 65–68.

26 Dunn G.A. & Heath J.P. (1976) A new hypothesis of contact guidance in tissue cells. *Expl. Cell Res.*, **101**, 1–14.

27 Elsdale T. & Bard J. (1972) Cellular interactions in mass cultures of human diploid fibroblasts. *Nature, Lond.*, **236**, 152–155.

28 Elsdale T. & Bard J. (1972) Collagen substrata for studies on cell behavior, *J. Cell Biol.*, **54**, 626–637.

29 Elsdale T. & Wasoff F. (1976) Fibroblast cultures and dermatoglyphics: The topology of two planar patterns. *Wilhelm Roux' Archiv.*, **180**, 121–147.

30 Erickson G.A. & Trinkaus J.P. (1976) Microvilli and blebs as sources of reserve surface membrane during cell spreading. *Expl. Cell Res.*, **99**, 375–384.

31 Gail M.H. & Boone C.W. (1971) Effect of colcemid on fibroblast motility. *Expl. Cell Res.*, **65**, 221–227.

32 Gail M.H. & Boone C.W. (1971) Cytochalasin effects on BAL/3T3 fibroblasts: dose dependent, reversible alteration of motility and cytoplasmic cleavage. *Expl. Cell Res.*, **68**, 226–228.

33 Gail M.H. & Boone C.W. (1970) The locomotion of mouse fibroblasts in tissue culture. *Biophys. J.*, **10**, 980–993.

34 Goldman R.D. (1971) The role of three cytoplasmic fibres in BHK-21 cell motility. I. Microtubules and the effects of colchicine. *J. Cell Biol.*, **51**, 752–762.

35 Goldman R.D., Berg G., Bushnell A., Chang C.M., Dickerman L., Hopkins N., Miller M.I., Pollack R. & Wang E. (1973) Fibrillar systems in cell motility. In *Locomotion of Tissue Cells. Ciba Foundation Symp.*, **14**, 83–107.

36 Goldman R.D., Lazarides E., Pollack R. & Weber K. (1975) The distribution of actin in non-muscle cells. *Expl. Cell Res.*, **90**, 333–344.

37 Gustafson T. & Wolpert L. (1967) Cellular movement and contact in sea urchin morphogenesis. *Biol. Rev.*, **42**, 442–498.

38 Harris A. (1973) Behavior of cultured cells on substrata of variable adhesiveness. *Expl. Cell Res.*, **77**, 285–297.

39 Harris A. (1973) Location of cellular adhesions to solid substrata. *Devl. Biol.*, **35**, 97–114.

40 Harrison R.G. (1910) The outgrowth of the nerve fiber as a mode of protoplasmic movement. *J. exp. Zool.*, **9**, 787–846.

41 Harrison R.G. (1914) The reaction of embryonic cells to solid structure. *J. exp. Zool.*, **17**, 521–544.

42 Heath J.P. & Dunn G.A. (1978) Cell to substratum contacts of chick heart fibroblasts and their relation to the microfilament

system. A correlated interference-reflexion and high-voltage electron-microscope study. *J. Cell Sci.*, **29**, 197–212.

43 Heaysman J.E.M. & Pegrum S.M. (1973) Early contacts between fibroblasts. An ultrastructural study. *Expl. Cell Res.*, **78**, 71–78.

44 Hitchcock S. (1977) Regulation of motility in nonmuscle cells. *J. Cell Biol.*, **74**, 1–15.

45 Hoffman-Berling H. (1964) Relaxation of fibroblast cells. In *Primitive Motile Systems in Cell Biology* (Eds R.D. Allen & N. Kamiya). Academic Press, New York.

46 Holtfreter J. (1939) Gewabeaffinitat, ein Mittel der embryonalen Formbildung. *Arch. Exp. Zellforsch.*, **23**, 169–209.

47 Holtfreter J. (1943) Properties and function of the surface coat in amphibian embryos. *J. exp. Zool.*, **93**, 251–323.

48 Holtfreter J. (1943) A study of the mechanics of gastrulation: Part I. *J. exp. Zool.*, **94**, 261–318.

49 Holtfreter J. (1944) A study of the mechanics of gastrulation: Part II. *J. exp. Zool.*, **95**, 171–212.

50 Holtfreter J. (1947) Observations on the migration, aggregation, and phagocytosis of embryonic cells. *J. Morph.*, **80**, 25–55.

51 Hubbard B. & Lazarides E. (1979) Copurification of actin and desmin from chicken smooth muscle and their copolymerization *in vitro* to intermediate filaments. *J. Cell Biol.*, **80**, 166–182.

52 Huxley H.E. (1969) The mechanism of muscle contraction. *Science, N.Y.*, **164**, 1356–1366.

53 Isenberg G., Rathke P.C., Hulsman N., Franke W.W. & Wolhfarth-Botterman K.E. (1976) Cytoplasmic actomyosin fibrils in tissue culture cells—direct proof of contractility by visualization of ATP-induced contraction in fibrils isolated by laser microbeam dissection. *Cell Tissue Res.*, **166**, 427–443.

54 Ishikawa B., Bischoff R. & Holtzer H. (1969) Formation of arrowhead complexes with heavy meromyosin in a variety of cell types. *J. Cell Biol.*, **43**, 312–328.

55 Izzard C.S. & Izzard S.L. (1975) Calcium regulation of the contractile state of isolated mammalian fibroblast cytoplasm. *J. Cell Sci.*, **18**, 241–256.

56 Izzard C.S. & Lochner L.R. (1976) Cell-to-substrate contacts in living fibroblasts: An interference reflexion study with an evaluation of the technique. *J. Cell Sci.*, **21**, 129–159.

57 Jacobson A. & Gordon R. (1976) Changes in the shape of the developing vertebrate nervous system analyzed experimentally, mathematically and by computer simulation. *J. exp. Zool.*, **197**, 191–246.

58 Johnson K. (1977) Extracellular matrix synthesis in blastula and gastrula stages of normal and hybrid frog embryos. III. Characterization of galactose- and glucosamine-labelled materials. *J. Cell Sci.*, **25**, 335–354.

59 Johnson K. (1972) The extent of cell contact and the relative frequency of small and large gaps between presumptive mesodermal cells in normal gastrulae of *Rana pipiens* and the arrested gastrulae of the *Rana pipiens×Rana catesbeiana* hybrid. *J. exp. Zool.*, **179**, 227–238.

60 Karfunkel P. (1974) The mechanisms of neural tube formation. *Int. Rev. Cytol.*, **38**, 245–271.

61 Karp G.C. & Solursh M. (1974) Acid mucopolysaccharide metabolism, the cell surface and primary mesenchyme cell activity in the sea urchin embryo. *Devl. Biol.*, **41**, 110–123.

62 Keller R.E. (1975) Vital dye mapping of the gastrula and neurula of *Xenopus laevis*. I. Prospective areas and morphogenetic movements of the superficial layer. *Devl. Biol.*, **42**, 222–241.

63 Keller R.E. (1976) Vital dye mapping of the gastrula and neurula of *Xenopus laevis*. II. Prospective areas and morphogenetic movements of the deep layer. *Devl. Biol.*, **51**, 118–137.

64 Keller R.E. (1978) Time-lapse cinemicrographic analysis of superficial cell behaviour during and prior to gastrulation in *Xenopus laevis*. *J. morph.*, **157**, 223–248.

65 Keller R.E. (1980) The cellular basis of epiboly: An SEM study of deep cell rearrangement during gastrulation in *Xenopus laevis*. Unpublished observations.

66 Keller R.E. & Schoenwolf G. (1977) A scanning electron microscopic study of cellular morphology, contact, and arrangement in the gastrula of *Xenopus laevis*. *Wilhelm Roux' Archiv.*, **182**, 165–186.

67 Kosher R. & Searls R. (1973) Sulfated mucopolysaccharide synthesis during the development of *Rana pipiens*. *Devl. Biol.*, **32**, 50–68.

68 Lazarides E. (1976) Actin, alpha-actinin and tropomyosin interaction in structural organization of actin-filaments in non-muscle cells. *J. Cell Biol.*, **68**, 202–219.

69 Lazarides E. (1977) Two general classes of cytoplasmic actin filaments in tissue culture cells: The role of tropomyosin. In *Cell Shape and Surface Architecture, Proceedings of the ICN–UCLA Symposium* (Eds J.P. Revel, U. Henning & C.F. Fox). Alan Liss, New York.

70 Lehman W., Kendrick-Jones J. & Szent-Gyorgyi A.G. (1973) Myosin-linked regulating systems: Comparative studies. *Cold Spring Harbor Symp. Quant. Biol.*, **37**, 319–330.

71 Löfberg J. & Ahlfors K. (1978) Extracellular matrix organization and early neural crest cell migration in the axolotl embryo. *Zoon*, **6**, 87–101.

72 Lowey S., Slayter H.S., Weeds A.G. & Baker H. (1969) Substructure of the myosin-molecule. I. Subfragments of myosin by enzymic degradation. *J. molec. Biol.*, **42**, 1–29.

73 Middleton C.A. (1972) Contact inhibition of locomotion in cultures of pigmented retina epithelium. *Expl. Cell Res.*, **70**, 91–96.

74 Middleton C.A. (1973) The control of epithelial cell locomotion in tissue culture. In *Locomotion of Tissue Cells, Ciba Foundation Symposium*, **14**, *(new series)*, 251–270. Elsevier/North-Holland, Amsterdam.

75 Middleton C.A. (1976) Contact-induced spreading is a new phenomenon depending on cell contact. *Nature, Lond.*, **259**, 311–313.

76 Moore A.R. & Burt A.S. (1939) On the locus and nature of the forces causing gastrulation in the embryos of *Dendraster excentricus*. *J. exp. Zool.*, **82**, 159–171.

77 Moore P.B., Huxley H.E. & DeRossier D.T. (1970) Three dimensional reconstruction of F-actin thin filaments and decorated thin filaments. *J. molec. Biol.*, **50**, 279–295.

78 Mooseker M. (1976) Actin filament–membrane attachment in the microvilli of intestinal epithelial cells. In *Cell Motility, Book B* (Eds C. Goldman, T. Pollard & J. Rosenbaum). *Cold Spring Harbor Conf. Cell Proliferation*, **3**, 631–650.

79 Moran D. (1976) Action of papaverine and ionophore A23187 on neurulation. *Nature, Lond.*, **261**, 497–499.

80 Murphy D.E. (1975) The mechanisms of microtubule dependent movement of pigment granules in teleost chromatophores. *Ann. N.Y. Acad. Sci.*, **253**, 692–701.

81 Nagai R., Yoshimoto Y., & Kamiya N. (1978) Cyclical pro-

duction of tension force in the plasmodial strand of *Physarum polycephalum* and its relation to microfilament morphology. *J. Cell Sci.*, **33**, 205–225.

82 Nakatsuji J. (1975) Studies on the gastrulation of amphibian embryos: Cell movement during gastrulation in *Xenopus laevis* embryos. *Wilhelm Roux' Archiv.*, **178**, 1–14.

83 Okazaki K. (1975) Normal development to metamorphosis. In *The Sea Urchin Embryo: Biochemistry and Morphogenesis* (Ed. G. Ozihak), pp. 233–266. Springer-Verlag, Berlin.

84 Osborn M., Born T., Kortsch H.W., & Weber K. (1978) Stereo immunofluorescence microscopy: I. Three dimensional arrangement of microfilaments, microtubules and tonofilaments. *Cell*, **14**, 447–488.

85 Perry M. (1975) Microfilaments in the external surface layer of the early amphibian embryo. *J. Embryol. exp. Morph.*, **33**, 127–146.

86 Pollard T. (1976) Cytoskeletal functions of cytoplasmic contractile proteins. *J. Supramolecular Structure*, **5**, 317–334.

87 Pollard T., Fujiwara K., Wiederman R. & Maupin-Szamier P. (1976) Evidence for the role of cytoplasmic actin and myosin in cellular structure and motility. In *Cell Motility, Book B* (Eds R. Goldman, T. Pollard & Rosenbaum). *Cold Spring Harbor Conf. Cell Proliferation*, **3**, 689–724.

88 Pollard T. & Weihung R. (1974) Actin and myosin and cell movement. *Biochemistry*, **2**, 1–65.

89 Raff E. (1979) The control of microtubule assembly *in vivo*. *Int. Rev. Cytol.*, **59**, 1–95.

90 Ramsey W.S. (1972) Locomotion of human polymorphonuclear leucocytes. *Expl. Cell Res.*, **72**, 489–501.

91 Ramsey W.S. & Harris A. (1972) Leucocyte locomotion and its inhibition by antimitotic drugs. *Expl. Cell Res.*, **82**, 262–270.

92 Revel J.P. & Wolken K. (1973) Electron microscope investigations of the underside of cells in culture. *Expl. Cell Res.*, **78**, 1–14.

93 Roux W. (1894) Uber den 'Cytotropismus' der Furchungzellen des Gras-frosches (*Rana fusca*). *Wilhelm Roux' Archiv.*, **1**, 43–68.

94 Schaeffer B., Schaeffer H. & Brick I. (1973) Cell electrophoresis of amphibian blastula and gastrula cells; the relationship of surface charge and morphogenetic movement. *Devl. Biol.*, **34**, 66–76.

95 Senda N., Tamura H., Shibata N., Yoshitake J., Kondo K. & Tanaka K. (1975) The mechanism of the movement of leukocytes. *Expl. Cell Res.*, **91**, 393–407.

96 Starger J.M., Brown W.E., Goldman A.E. & Goldman R.D. (1979) Biochemical amd immunological analysis of rapidly purified 10 nm filaments from baby hamster kidney (BHK-21) cells. *J. Cell Biol.*, **78**, 93–109.

97 Summers K. & Kirschner M. (1979) Characteristics of the polar assembly of microtubules observed by darkfield light microscopy. *J. Cell Biol.*, **83**, 205–217.

98 Taylor D.L. (1976) Motile model systems of amoeboid movement. In *Cell Motility, Book B* (Eds R. Goldman, T. Pollard & J. Rosenbaum). *Cold Spring Harbor Conf. Cell Proliferation*, **3**, 797–821.

99 Taylor E.W. & Sleep J.A. (1976) Mechanism of actomyosin ATPase. In *Cell Motility, Book A* (Eds R. Goldman, T. Pollard & J. Rosenbaum). *Cold Spring Harbor Conf. Cell Proliferation*, **3**, 127–135.

100 Tickle C.A. & Trinkaus J.P. (1973) Change in surface extensibility of *Fundulus* deep cells during early development. *J. Cell Sci.*, **13**, 721–726.

101 Tilney L. (1976) Nonfilamentous aggregates of actin and their association with membranes. In *Cell Motility, Book B* (Eds R. Goldman, T. Pollard & J. Rosenbaum). *Cold Spring Harbor Conf. Cell Proliferation*, **3**, 513–528.

102 Tilney L. & Gibbins J.R. (1969) Microtubules in the formation and development of the primary mesenchyme in *Arbacia punctilata*. II. An experimental analysis of their role in development and maintenance of cell shape. *J. Cell Biol.*, **41**, 227–250.

103 Townes P.L. & Holtfreter J. (1955) Directed movements and selective adhesion of embryonic amphibian cells. *J. exp. Zool.*, **128**, 53–120.

104 Trinkaus J.P. (1963) The cellular basis of *Fundulus* epiboly. Adhesivity of blastula and gastrula cells in culture. *Devl. Biol.*, **7**, 513–532.

105 Trinkaus J.P. (1973) Surface activity and locomotion of *Fundulus* deep cells during blastula and gastrula stages. *Devl. Biol.*, **30**, 68–103.

106 Trinkaus J.P. (1976) On the mechanism of metazoan cell movements. In *The Cell Surface in Animal Embryogenesis and Development* (Eds G. Poste & G.L. Nicolson), pp. 225–329. North Holland, Amsterdam.

107 Trinkaus J.P. (1978) Mediation of cell surface behavior by intercellular contact. *Zoon*, **6**, 51–63.

108 Trinkaus J.P., Betchaku T. & Krulikowski L.S. (1971) Local inhibition of ruffling during contact inhibition of cell movement. *Expl. Cell Res.*, **64**, 291–300.

109 Trinkaus J.P. & Lentz T. (1967) A fine structural study of cytodifferentiation during cleavage, blastula, and gastrula stages of *Fundulus heteroclitus*. *J. Cell Biol.*, **32**, 121–138.

110 Vasiliev J.M., Gelfand I.M., Domina L.V., Ivanova O.Y., Komm S.C. & Olshevskaja L.V. (1970) Effect of colcemid on the locomotory behavior of fibroblasts. *J. Embryol. exp. Morph.*, **24**, 625–640.

111 Viamontes G., Fochtmann L. & Kirk D. (1979) Morphogenesis in *Volvox*: Analysis of critical variables. *Cell*, **17**, 537–550.

112 Warner F. (1976) Cross-bridge mechanisms in ciliary motility: The sliding–bending conversion. *Cell Motility, Book C* (Eds R. Goldman, T. Pollard & J. Rosenbaum). *Cold Spring Harbor Conf. Cell Proliferation*, **3**, 891–914.

113 Webster R.E., Henderson D., Oaborn M. & Weber K. (1978) Three-dimensional electron microscopical visualization of the cytoskeleton of animal cells; immunoferritin identification of actin- and tubulin-containing structures. *Proc. natl Acad. Sci., USA*, **75**, 5511–5515.

114 Weiss P.A. (1945) Experiments on cell and axon orientation *in vitro*: The role of colloidal exudates in tissue organization. *J. exp. Zool.*, **100**, 353–386.

115 Weston J., Derby M.A. & Pintar J.E. (1978) Changes in the extra-cellular environment of neural crest cells during their early migration. *Zoon*, **6**, 103–113.

116 Wylie C., Heasman J., Swan A.P. & Anderton B.H. (1979) Evidence for substrate guidance of primordial germ cells. *Expl. Cell Res.*, **121**, 315–324.

117 Willingham M.C. (1976) Cyclic AMP and cell behavior in cultured cells. *Int. Rev. Cytol.*, **44**, 319–363.

118 Wolosewick J.J. & Porter K.R. (1979) Microtrabecular lattice of the cytoplasmic ground substance. Artifact or reality? *J. Cell Biol.*, **82**, 114–139.

119 Zigmond S. (1978) Chemotaxis by polymorphonuclear leukocytes. *J. Cell Biol.*, **77**, 269–287.

Chapter 3.4
Junctional Communication Between Cells
J.D. Pitts

3.4.1   INTRODUCTION

Animals and plants can be regarded as complex populations of cells which are continually interacting and communicating so that the growth, differentiation and activities of all the cells are coordinated and integrated to meet the demands of the whole organism. This requirement for cell interaction and cell communication is particularly evident during the processes of embryonic development.

Physical and adhesive interactions give shape and structure to tissues and play an important role in controlling various aspects of organogenesis in animals, as described in Chapters 3.2 and 3.3. Communication allows intercellular control of gene expression and modulation of cell functions.

Two forms of cell communication have evolved and both seem to be ubiquitous throughout the plant and animal kingdoms. One involves the secretion of extracellular signal molecules by a cell or a group of cells, and the interaction of these signal molecules with receptors on or in adjacent or distant target cells (see Part 5). The other requires direct contact between the cells and involves the formation of junctions containing aqueous channels which allow the free movement of small ions and molecules between the cytoplasms of coupled cells. The junctional structures joining plants cells are quite different from those joining animal cells, though their permeability and function may be similar. In plants, the junctions are called plasmodesmata while in animals various terms have been applied including gap junction, nexus, communicating junction, permeable junction, low-resistance junction and electrotonic junction. The first of these, although the least informative, is the one most generally used. The term is derived from the appearance of these junctions in the thin-section electron micrographs and it was introduced at a time when the function of the structure was unknown.

This chapter describes the properties of these junctions and discusses current views on their possible functions, both in adult tissues and during embryogenesis.

The discovery of gap junctions and junctional communication

The concept of junctional communication, or the communication between adjacent cells through cytoplasmic bridges or continuities, is a very old one. It was first proposed by botanists nearly a hundred years ago. Several workers noticed structures in stained sections of plants tissues which appeared to connect the cytoplasms of neighbouring cells. Retrospectively, it is clear that the light microscope is unable to resolve what we now recognize as intercellular junctions but it is interesting to follow the thinking of the plant physiologists of the day, concisely summarized by Tangl in 1889 [56] and translated by Carr [3]:

'The observations leave only one correct explanation of the matter; the protoplasmic bodies of the inner cells of the endosperm are united by thin strands passing through connecting ducts in the walls, which put the cells in connection with each other and so unite them as an entity of higher order.'

This idea of the unification of cells through junctional communication was in sharp contrast to the cell theory, which proposed that all living organisms are composed of separate and individual units, but the idea was widely accepted at the time and claims of the existence of animal cell junctions quickly followed. However, the techniques of the day were inadequate to extend the observations, and the idea, common in textbooks at the turn of the century, gradually fell into relative oblivion. It was necessary to await development of the electron microscope, the techniques of electro-physiology and a number of biochemical and genetic methods before the observations could be extended.

Our present knowledge of junctional communication between animal cells comes from three separate lines of investigation. The first was a systematic analysis of tissue sections by electron microscopy to identify membrane specializations at points of contact or close apposition between cells. This led to the description of a large number of such structures but it now seems likely that they are all variations of four basic classes, the desmosome, the adhaerens junction, the tight junction and the gap junction (see Chapter 3.2). Gap junctions are distinguished from tight junctions by the uniform gap of 2 nm which separates the two membranes in the junctional regions. The morphology and structure of these junctions, which contain aqueous channels joining the cytoplasms of the coupled cells, are described in detail below.

The second line of investigation began with the experimental demonstration of electrical transmission (as opposed to chemical transmission) between nerve cells in the crayfish [10]. Such electrical transmission requires a low-resistance pathway between the cytoplasms of the coupled cells and it is necessary to propose a 'junction' which has a specific resistance much lower than that of the normal cell membrane. Subsequent

work [11, 32] showed that low-resistance junctions are not a special characteristic of excitable tissues, but are a common feature of nearly all tissues.

The third line stemmed from an accidental observation [54, 55] that certain mutant animal cells growing in culture lose their mutant phenotype when grown in contact with wild-type cells. This phenotypic modification of mutant cells was subsequently shown to be caused by the transfer of metabolites, to which the normal cell membrane is impermeable, from the wild-type to the mutant cells. Such transfer can only be explained by proposing that intercellular junctions are formed which, unlike the normal membrane, are permeable to the metabolites.

The connection between these different approaches, namely that the gap junction is the structure which allows the free movement of ions and metabolites between coupled cells [16], was suspected for some time because it is the only recognizable membrane specialization always seen between coupled cells. Further evidence supporting the correlation comes from recent work on the structure of the gap junction which provides direct evidence for an aqueous channel passing through each junctional particle. These channels are approximately 2 nm in diameter, which accounts very well for their known permeability.

3.4.2   STRUCTURE OF THE GAP JUNCTION

In thin sections of animal tissues examined by electron microscopy, the gap junction is characterized by a uniform close apposition of the adjacent cell membranes (Fig. 3.4.1a). The gap, the electron-luscent zone between the two bilayers, is 2 nm across and each junctional membrane if 7.5 nm wide, making a total junctional thickness of about 17 nm [48]. If an electron-opaque tracer substance, such as lanthanum hydroxide, is used to fill the extracellular space, the 'gap' is also filled, and as a consequence is more clearly resolved. Further detail is revealed in very occasional glancing sections of such tracer-impregnated junctions, which show a fairly regular array of particles outlined by the tracer. The particles have a diameter of 7–8 nm with a centre-to-centre spacing of 9–10 nm.

The subunit structure of the junction is confirmed by freeze-fracture techniques [14]. The junctions are seen (Figs 3.4.1b and 3.4.2) as aggregates of particles on the

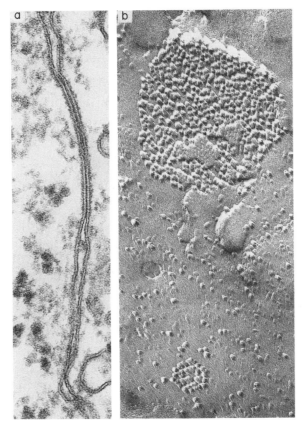

Fig. 3.4.1. The gap junction. (a) Thin section. The intercellular space narrows a barely perceptible gap. (b) Image of a freeze-fractured membrane showing the junctions as aggregates of particles. Magnification in both photographs, ×112 000. Figure taken from Gilula *et al.* [16].

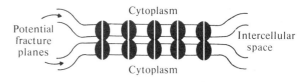

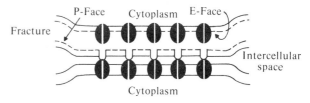

Fig. 3.4.2. Diagrammatic representation of a gap junction (a) showing the intramembranous faces exposed by freeze-fracture (b).

(Fig. 3.4.3). They vary in size from just a few particles to large areas containing several thousand particles and appear to be fairly generally distributed throughout areas of close cell–cell apposition.

The more detailed analysis of gap junction structure requires the isolation and purification of these membrane specializations from animal tissues. They appear not to be attached to the cellular cytoskeleton and therefore appear in the plasma-membrane fraction when this is isolated from other cell components. The disruption of the membranes with mild detergent (such as sarkosyl) does not dissociate the junctions, which can then be purified by centrifugation in sucrose gradients. Isolated junctions can be negatively stained and examined by electron microscopy.

The subunit structure is clearly preserved (Fig. 3.4.4) and dots of stain pick out the channels running through the centre of each particle. The polygonal packing is accentuated in isolated junctions, probably due to loss of phospholipid from the junctional area during the purification procedure. Chemical analysis of purified junctions shows that they contain about equal amounts of protein and lipid, that the lipid has a similar composition to that of the non-junctional membrane and that the proteins contain no detectable carbohydrate (which is unusual for trans-membrane proteins).

Analysis of the protein extracted from isolated junctions shows only one major band in SDS polyacrylamide gels, with an apparent mol. wt of 27 000 [8, 22, 23]. The morphological appearance of isolated

P-face (the inner or cytoplasmic half of the bilayer) with a corresponding pattern of pits in the E-face (the outer or extracellular half of the bilayer). The particles have a uniform size (7–8 nm diameter, as before) and are often packed in polygonal lattices, though the packing is very variable. Sometimes a small depression (about 2 nm in diameter) is seen in the centre of the P-face particles and it has been suggested that this shows the end of the hole or channel running through each particle.

Freeze-fracture analysis not only gives information on the detailed structure of junctions but also reveals something about their size (number of particles per aggregate) and distribution in the lateral membranes

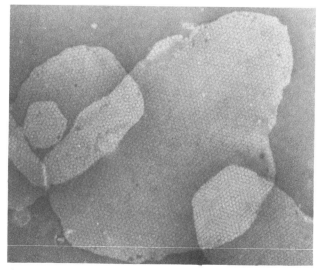

Fig. 3.4.4. Isolated gap junctions, negatively stained with phospho-tungstate. Magnification, ×87 000. Photograph by M.E. Finbow.

junctions is not detectably affected by treatment with trypsin but the 27 000-mol.-wt band disappears and is replaced by another at 11 000. It is not clear yet whether the smaller mol. wt product is a unique peptide or a mixture of two domains of the 27 000-mol.-wt protein which are protected from trypsin action by their inherent structure or by the residual phospholipid.

Isolated junctions have also been analysed by physical methods. The flat structure of the junctions allows them to be centrifuged into organized pellets which can be examined by X-ray diffraction [38]. The results of such analysis, albeit at low resolution, can be interpreted to give the model shown in Fig. 3.4.5. A map of 1.8 nm resolution has been obtained by electron-microscopy of negatively stained junction preparations and is in general agreement with this model, though the latter technique suggests that the six subunits surrounding each channel are twisted at an angle of 14° to the axis of the channel and that the diameter of the channel is somewhat less in the middle than it is at the ends [58, 65].

Most of the analytical work has been carried out on junctions isolated from mouse or rat liver but it seems reasonable to believe from electron microscopy of junctions from a wide variety of tissues that all vertebrate gap junctions are the same. Gap junctions in arthropod tissues, however, are morphologically distinct. The general arrangement of particles in arrays is similar but the particles are larger (about 11 nm in

Fig. 3.4.3. Freeze-fracture image of the membranes of two hepatocytes. The fracture plane in the top left of the photograph exposes the cytoplasmic half (P-face) of the membrane from the cell which would have been below the plane of the page. The fracture plane in the bottom right exposes the extracellular half (E-face) of the membrane from the cell which would have been above the page. The line where the fracture plane jumps from one membrane to the other across the intercellular space runs from bottom left to top right. The intercellular space at the gap junction (right) is reduced to the typical 2 nm. Other gap junctions can be seen. The bands of particles running round the top (apical) edges of these lateral membranes are tight junctions. Magnification, × 35 000. Photograph by D. Goodenough.

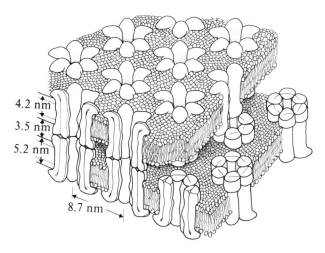

Fig. 3.4.5. Model of a gap junction. Taken from Makowski *et al.* [38].

diameter) and more widely spaced. Permeability studies suggest that the channels are somewhat wider (though this has not yet been confirmed by direct physical analysis), and in freeze-fracture preparations the particles remain associated with the E-face and not the P-face [14].

3.4.3 PERMEABILITY OF THE GAP JUNCTION

Detection of junctional communication by electrophysiological methods

Pathways of low electrical resistance, or low-resistance junctions, were first discovered between nerve cells [10] but, a few years later junctions with the same characteristics were found between non-excitable cells. The apparatus which is used to detect low-resistance junctions is illustrated schematically in Fig. 3.4.6. Salt-filled glass capillaries are inserted by micromanipulation into the cytoplasms of neighbouring cells. The insertion can be followed by microscopy and also electrically, because as the tip of the microelectrode passes through the membrane into the cytoplasm of the cell, the resting potential registers on the oscilloscope. Conveniently, the fluid nature of the membrane results in an automatic 'ion-tight' seal around the tip of the inserted electrode. Current pulses ($2\text{--}4\times10^{-8}$ A, 100–200 ms) are passed into cell A (see Fig. 3.4.6) and the consequent voltage changes which occur in cells A and B are displayed on

the oscilloscope. If the two cells are coupled by low-resistance junctions, similar voltage changes occur in both cells. If the cells are not coupled, the voltage changes occur only in cell A.

The technique gives quantitatively precise information about the voltage changes and the capacitance of the coupled population. The capacitance is calculated from the time constant of the voltage change when current is introduced; because it is the cell membranes which are acting as capacitors, the capacitance is proportional to the total membrane area (i.e. to the number of cells coupled by junctions). The interpretation of the voltage changes in terms of junctional resistance, however, requires a detailed knowledge of the actual circuit. This can lead to uncertainties in all but the most simple cell arrangements.

From resistance measurements in small groups of cells it has been calculated that the junctional membrane

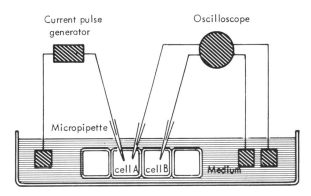

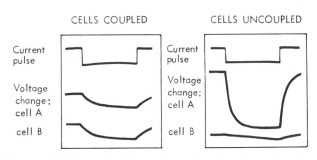

Fig. 3.4.6. The detection of low-resistance junctions. Micro-electrodes are inserted into cells A and B as shown. A current pulse is introduced into cell A and the consequent voltage changes which occur between the cytoplasm of each cell and the surrounding medium are recorded on an oscilloscope. When the cells are coupled by low-resistance junctions, similar voltage changes occur in both cells. When the cells are not coupled, the change in cell A is large, while that in cell B is barely detectable. (After Loewenstein [33].)

conductance is 10^4 times greater than that of the normal cell membrane. If the number of junctional particles (junctional channels) is estimated by morphometric analysis, it can be calculated that each channel has a conductance of 10^{-10} mho [35].

Detection of junctional communication by microinjection of fluorescent probes

The apparatus of the electrophysiologist can also be used to inject molecules into cells. The molecular probes used to detect junctional permeability are normally fluorescent, so they can be located by fluorescence microscopy, and charged, so they can be released from the electrode into the cell by iontophoresis.

If the membrane of the cell is impermeable to the injected probe, the fluorescence will fill the cytoplasm and allow visualization of the shape of the cell. Using the dye fluorescein, Loewenstein and Kanno [36] noticed that when it was injected into cells of the *Drosophila* salivary gland, fluorescence spread to adjacent cells. The movement of fluorescein from cell to cell correlates with the presence of low-resistance junctions and it is now accepted that the dye can pass freely through the junctional channels.

This method for detecting junctional communication with injected fluorescein and other fluorescent dyes (Lucifer yellow, procion yellow) has been extended by Loewenstein and his colleagues [34] to examine the limits of junctional permeability. They have synthesized a series of amino acids, small peptides, sugars and small oligosaccharides labelled with fluorescein, lissamine rhodamine B or dansyl groups and have shown that injected probes with a molecular weight less than about 900 in vertebrate tissues and 1500 in arthropod tissues pass through the junctions, while larger probes remain trapped in the injected cells.

Detection of junctional communication by metabolite exchange

An accidental discovery made by Subak-Sharpe, Bürk and Pitts in 1966 [54, 55] led to the realization that most types of animal cell growing in contact share their pools of intermediate metabolites. The normal cytoplasmic membrane is impermeable to such metabolites and so their exchange between adjacent cells provides a further functional definition of the presence of permeable inter-

cellular junctions. A few cell types do not form these junctions and in experimental systems in tissue culture they provide convenient controls to distinguish junction-mediated transfer from other possible transfer pathways.

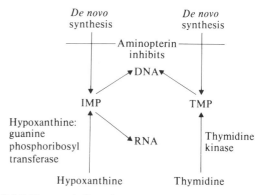

Fig. 3.4.7. The metabolic pathways which leads to the incorporation of hypoxanthine and thymidine into nucleic acid. The pathways of IMP and TMP synthesis *de novo* can be inhibited with aminopterin.

Transfer of nucleotides between cells coupled by junctions was originally demonstrated in culture by using mutant cell lines. Mutant cells lacking the enzyme hypoxanthine : guanine phosphoribosyl-transferase (HGPRT⁻ cells) are unable to incorporate [³H]hypoxanthine into cellular nucleic acid (Fig. 3.4.7). Such mutant cells can therefore be distinguished from wild-type cells after growth in medium containing [³H]hypoxanthine by autoradiography of fixed, acid-washed cultures. When cultured separately, there are no autoradiographic silver grains over the mutant cells, while the wild-type cells are covered with grains and appear black. In mixed cultures of mutant and wild-type cells, in the unusual situation where the two cell types do not form permeable junctions, the two phenotypes are unchanged and the different cells can easily be distinguished (Fig. 3.4.8a). However, in the more common situation, where the two cell types form junctions, grains are found over the mutant cells too (Fig. 3.4.8b). This phenotypic modification of the mutant cells by the wild-type cells depends on cell–cell contact and can pass from wild-type cells through chains or sheets of coupled mutant cells. When the wild-type and mutant cells have different morphologies they can be distinguished in mixed culture (Fig. 3.4.8b), but when the wild-type and mutant are of the same cell type

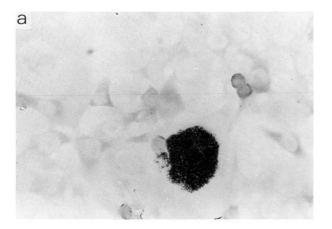

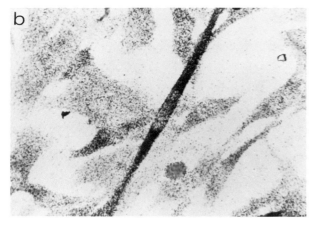

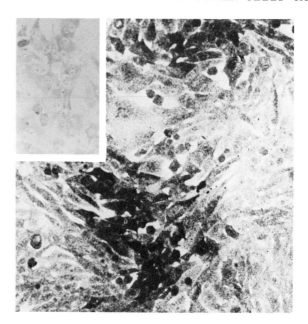

Fig. 3.4.8. (a) Autoradiograph of a wild-type epithelial tumour cell (black cell near centre) and HGPRT⁻ hamster fibroblasts after growth in medium containing [³H]hypoxanthine. The mutant cells, lacking HGPRT, are unable to incorporate the base and do not form permeable junctions with the wild-type cell. They are therefore unlabelled (no grains). (b) Autoradiograph of a wild-type skin fibroblast (long black cell) and the same HGPRT⁻ hamster fibroblasts after growth in the same medium. The mutant cells form junctions with the wild-type and receive [³H]purine nucleotides which they incorporate into their nucleic acid and are therefore labelled (covered with grains). Magnification, × 115.

Fig. 3.4.9. Autoradiograph of a mixed culture containing a few wild-type and many HGPRT⁻ hamster fibroblasts after growth in medium containing [³H]hypoxanthine. The wild-type cells incorporate the labelled base and appear black. Mutant cells receive labelled purine nucleotides through junctions from the wild-type cells. The phenotypic modification of mutant cells adjacent to wild-types is so complete that they are indistinguishable. Mutant cells further away incorporate less than the wild-type cells. Inset: autoradiograph of mutant cells in separate culture but grown in the same labelled medium and processed in the same way. They have not incorporated the [³H]hypoxanthine and are therefore not covered with autoradiographic grains. Magnification, × 83.

phenotypic modification of adjacent cells is so complete that the different cells cannot be distinguished (Fig. 3.4.9).

This complete masking of the mutant phenotype is shown quantitatively by counting grains over individual cells in a 1:1 confluent co-culture of junction-forming HGPRT⁻ and wild-type cells grown in the presence of [³H]hypoxanthine (Fig. 3.4.10a). The complete absence of non-incorporating cells in the mixed culture shows that all the mutant cells interact with the wild-types. However, in similar mixed cultures of cells which do not form junctions (Fig. 3.4.10b) two distinct populations can be identified, one with the mean grain count of the wild-type cells and the other with the mean count of the mutant cells.

The metabolic cooperation seen in these experiments with junction-forming cells might be explained in several ways. It might be due to the transfer of [³H]purine nucleotides from the wild-type to the mutant cells where, because they are beyond the enzyme block, they can be incorporated into mutant-cell nucleic acid. It

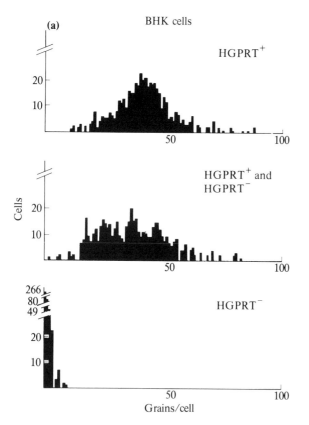

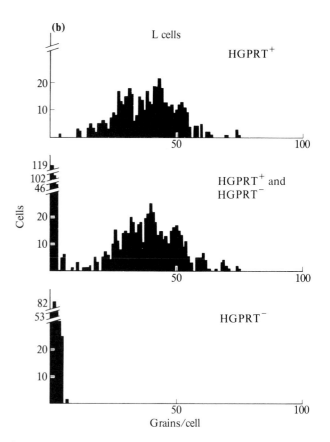

Fig. 3.4.10. (a) Nucleotide transfer between wild-type and mutant cells which form junctions. (b) Absence of nucleotide exchange between cells which do not form junctions. HGPRT⁻ and wild-type cells (hamster fibroblasts in (a), mouse L929 cells in (b)) were grown, either separately or in 1:1 mixed culture, in the presence of [³H]hypoxanthine. After processing for autoradiography, grains were counted over cells selected randomly from each of the cultures. The wild-type cells (upper panels) are all labelled. The mutant cells (lower panels) are unlabelled and have only background levels of grains. In the mixed culture of wild-type and mutant hamster fibroblasts, which form junctions, all the cells are labelled. The mutant phenotype has been eliminated by the transfer of labelled nucleotides through the junctions from the wild-type cells. In the mixed culture of mutant and wild-type L929 cells, which do not form junctions, two populations, one with the mutant phenotype (unlabelled) and the other with the wild-type phenotype (labelled) are seen. Labelled nucleotides have not been transferred. Taken from Pitts [43].

might be due to the transfer of the enzyme HGPRT (or the mRNA or gene, allowing synthesis of the enzyme in the mutant cells). Finally, it might be due to the transfer of labelled nucleic acid.

Enzyme transfer can be ruled out because the mutant cells lose the ability to incorporate hypoxanthine immediately after separation from the wild-type cells [4, 43]. This observation also rules out the possibility of enzyme synthesis in the mutant cells after transfer of informational macromolecules.

Nucleic acid transfer between cells in culture (DNA, RNA, whole chromosomes, whole ribosomes) has been reported from time to time in the literature but more recent work has shown that such transfer is uncommon, if it occurs at all, and anyway could not account for metabolic cooperation.

When mutant cells lacking the enzyme thymidine kinase (TK⁻ cells) are co-cultured with wild-type cells in medium containing [³H]thymidine (in experiments analogous to those shown in Fig. 3.4.10), all the cells, if they form junctions and if they have passed through the DNA-synthetic phase of the cell cycle during the labelling period, are equally labelled. To explain this result in term of labelled nucleic acid transfer would require the equilibration of the DNA among all the cells. Such genetic instability is unknown.

Further evidence for nucleotide transfer and against nucleic-acid transfer comes from experiments using cells pre-labelled with [³H]uridine [47]. When cells (mutant cells are not required for this type of experiment) are grown in the presence of [³H]uridine they will contain labelled uridine, labelled uridine nucleotides and labelled RNA. The labelled uridine (but not the nucleotides or the RNA) can be removed by subsequent washing with unlabelled medium. Such labelled and washed cells are termed 'donor' cells. If donor cells prepared in this way are cultured in unlabelled medium for a further 24 h, the label in the nucleotide pools and in the unstable forms of RNA (heterogeneous nuclear RNA, the turnover of which initially replenishes the radioactivity in the uridine nucleotide pools) is incorporated into metabolically stable forms of RNA (mostly ribosomal RNA

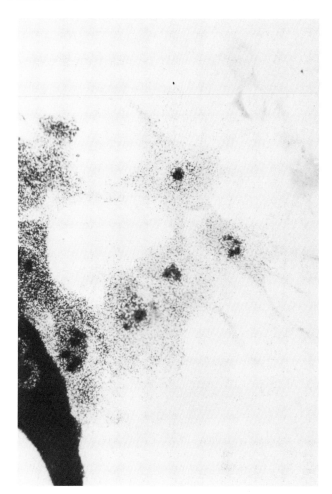

Fig. 3.4.12. Transfer of uridine nucleotides through junctions formed between cells in contact. This autoradiograph shows a gradient of incorporation running from the prelabelled donor cell (see legend to Fig. 3.4.11) through a chain of recipients. Magnification, × 360. Taken from Pitts and Sims [47].

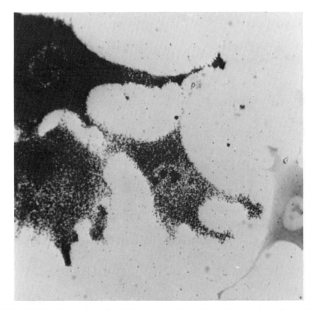

Fig. 3.4.11. Transfer of uridine nucleotides through junctions formed between cells in contact. Donor cells (containing [³H]uridine nucleotides and ³H-labelled RNA) were co-cultured with unlabelled cells. The cultures were then fixed and processed for autoradiography. Labelled nucleotides have been transferred through junctions from the donor cell (black) to recipient cells (speckled) but not to cells not in contact (no grains). Magnification, × 340. Taken from Pitts & Sims [47].

and transfer RNA). Such labelled, washed and chased cells are termed 'chased donor' cells. During the chase period, surprisingly little radioactivity is lost from the cells (in the form of [³H]uridine) so the total activity in the RNA increases.

When donor cells are co-cultured with unlabelled cells, autoradiography shows that labelled components are transferred to cells in contact (Fig. 3.4.11). Contact is required for transfer, and gradients of label are formed through chains of recipient cells in contact with a donor (Fig. 3.4.12). The nucleoli of the recipient cells are heavily labelled and there is a sharp distinction in grain density at the points of contact with donor cells. These features suggest that nucleotides, and not RNA, are transferred from cell to cell.

The suggestion of nucleotide transfer can be confirmed by two simple experiments. The extent of transfer from chased donor cells (Fig. 3.4.13) is much less than that from the unchased donor cells (Fig. 3.4.11) and the reduction in transfer is directly proportional to the fall in radioactivity of the donor-cell nucleotide pools and is quite unrelated to the changes in radioactivity of the donor RNA. Furthermore, when donor cells are co-cultured with unlabelled cells in the presence of actinomycin D, the amount of labelled material found in recipient cells in contact with the donors is greatly reduced (Fig. 3.4.14) compared with the untreated co-cultures (Fig. 3.4.11) and the reduction is exactly equivalent to the extent of inhibition of RNA synthesis by the drug.

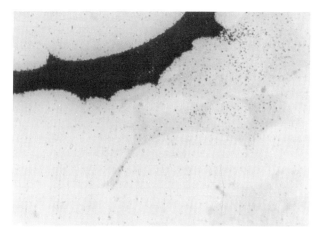

Fig. 3.4.14. RNA is not transferred through junctions. Donor cells (containing [^{3}H]uridine nucleotides and ^{3}H-labelled RNA, cf. Fig. 3.4.11) were co-cultured with unlabelled cells in the presence of Actinomycin D. Nucleotides (but not RNA) are transferred from the donor cell through junctions to the recipient cells but, because of the inhibitor, cannot be incorporated into recipient-cell RNA. ^{3}H-labelled nucleotides are lost from the cells during fixation prior to autoradiography. Magnification, ×340. Taken from Pitts & Sims [47].

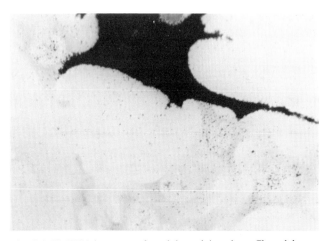

Fig. 3.4.13. RNA is not transferred through junctions. Chased donor cells (containing ^{3}H-labelled RNA, cf. Fig. 3.4.11) were co-cultured with unlabelled cells. The cultures were then fixed and processed for autoradiography. Magnification, ×340. Taken from Pitts & Sims [47].

As with metabolic cooperation between mutant and wild-type cells, uridine nucleotide transfer only occurs between cells which form permeable junctions, and both these methods for detecting junctional communication agree with the results obtained by electrophysiology and by injecting fluorescent probes.

Junctional communication is common in animal tissues

In vivo, most cell types appear to form gap junctions. The evidence for junction formation *in vivo* is mainly morphological but in some cases this has been corroborated by electrophysiology or dye injection. Cells which do not form junctions include skeletal-muscle fibres (not myoblasts), many nerve cells, circulating cells such as red blood cells and lymphocytes and embryonic cells at very early stages in cleavage.

Most cells in tissue culture also form junctions and there is good correlation between observations made *in vivo* and those made in culture. Some cells of tumour origin and of a few established cell lines (which are also tumourigenic) do not form junctions. The best studied of these is the mouse L929 cell line. The origin of the line, which was established more than 30 years ago [51], is obscure in terms of the nature of the cell from which the line arose and it is not clear why it cannot form junctions.

In culture, both cells of a cell pair must have the ability to form junctions before communication can be successfully established [44]. This is consistent with the concept that the junctional channels are formed by the interaction of proteins (junctional precursors) from both cell membranes. In cell hybrids formed by fusing L929 cells with junction-forming cells, the ability to form junctions is dominant [44]. This is consistent with the idea that the L cells lack an active gene-product necessary to form functional channels.

Which cell components pass through junctions?

Microinjection of fluorescent probes has shown that molecules with a molecular weight less than about 900 pass through junctions joining vertebrate cells, while larger molecules do not [9]. Molecular weight is not the best criterion for molecular size, which presumably limits the passage of molecules through the junctional channels; the dimensions of the hydrated species would be better, but as these are generally not known, molecular weight is used as a guide.

The proposed channel diameter of 2 nm is believed to be consistent with such a cut-off point for permeability but without detailed knowledge of the structure (and charge) of the channel lining, it is impossible to predict whether molecules with sizes near the cut-off point will pass through the channels or not. Recent experimental evidence using coupled annelid nerve cells [2] suggests that molecules of similar size and shape (bromo-fluorescein, carboxyfluorescein and aminofluorescein), but with different charges, pass through junctions at different rates, and that molecules which pass slowly can impede the movement of others. This has been interpreted to mean that the channels carry a fixed charge but it is too soon to be certain of this or to predict the effects of such a charge on the permeability of junctions to natural cell components.

The work with synthetic probes on junctional permeability has been confirmed and extended by various experimental procedures which show the intercellular exchange of metabolites, cofactors, ions and low-molecular-weight control molecules in coupled cell populations [7, 28, 29]. The work described above has shown that nucleotides, but not nucleic acids, pass through junctions formed between animal cells in tissue culture. Similar procedures have added sugar phosphates and choline phosphate or CDP-choline to the list of molecules which can pass between coupled cells, and proteins and phospholipids to the list of those which cannot. Intercellular folates can be supplied through junctions to folate-starved cells from unstarved cells, and amino acid auxotrophs can grow normally when

co-cultured with wild-type cells (if both cell types form junctions), by the intercellular transfer of amino acids or amino acid precursors. Cells lacking an active Na^+/K^+ ATPase survive normally when coupled to cells with active pumps, due to exchange of Na^+ and K^+. Different cell types, responding to different hormones which are mediated by the same second messenger, respond to the heterologous hormones in mixed culture, due to the intercellular exchange of cAMP through junctions.

All small molecules which have been examined, representing a broad range of different molecular types, pass through the junctional channels, and it therefore seems reasonable to conclude that junctions are permeable to all low-molecular-weight cytoplasmic components. Near the proposed limit of permeability, the situation becomes less clear; however, cells contain very few molecules in this molecular-weight range. Most molecules are either small enough to pass freely through the junctional channels or are so large that they will clearly remain in the cells where they were synthesized (or in the daughter cells arising by cell division). Only one naturally occurring molecule in the intermediate size range has been examined. The tetraglutamate form of tetrahydrofolate (the active form) has a molecular weight of 960 and does not pass through junctions at a detectable rate, unlike the lower glutamated forms [7]. This is in reasonable agreement with the permeability limit suggested by work with synthetic probes.

Rate of transfer through junctional channels

The estimate of channel conductance (see above) of 10^{-10} mho is similar to that for the ion channel controlled by acetylcholine in the neuromuscular synapse. These channels remain open for about a millisecond and allow about 20 000 sodium ions and an equal number of potassium ions to pass. This gives a rate in excess of 10^7 ions per second per channel for junctional permeability.

Another way of estimating junctional transfer rates is based on the cooperative growth of 1:1 mixed cultures of HGPRT$^-$ and TK$^-$ (junction-forming) cells in HAT medium (medium containing aminopterin, which blocks the pathways of purine nucleotides and dTMP synthesis *de novo*, and which is supplemented with hypoxanthine and thymidine; see Fig. 3.4.7). Neither of these mutant cell types can grow alone in HAT medium, but they grow in the mixed culture because of mutual nucleotide exchange [43]. The HGPRT$^-$ cells make all the dTMP for both cell types and the TK⁻ cells make all the purine nucleotides. From the knowledge of the nucleic acid content of each cell and the division time, the minimum rate of purine nucleotide transfer from the TK⁻ to the HGPRT⁻ cells can be calculated. More than 10^6 nucleotides pass through junctions per second per cell pair. This is only the purine nucleotides; presumably all other small ions and molecules are also moving backwards and forwards at similar rates. This is a huge traffic and it means that macromolecules in cells in coupled populations are in effect all synthesized from common precursor pools which rapidly equilibrate between the cells. The same conclusion can be drawn from the observation that metabolic cooperation results in only one phenotype in mixed cultures, as shown in Fig. 3.4.10a.

It seems likely that similar rates of transfer occur between coupled cells *in vivo*. The Lesch–Nyhan syndrome is an X-linked genetic trait characterized by a variety of neurological disorders and which has been associated with the absence of HGPRT activity. Hemizygous females, because of random X-inactivation, have two populations of cells, one HGPRT⁺ and the other HGPRT⁻, but they appear normal [39]. Purine nucleotide exchange suppresses the HGPRT⁻ phenotype in the half of the cells which are defective when skin cells are examined in culture. Similar phenotypic modification *in vivo* could account for the absence of the disease symptoms.

When considering the functional significance of junctional communication it is important to have some indication of how far molecules might move through coupled populations. In culture, labelled nucleotides can clearly diffuse through several cells before they are incorporated into nucleic acid (Figs 3.4.9 and 3.4.12). Phenotypic modification of cells lacking HGPRT can be detected up to 50 cell diameters away from the wild-type cell (i.e. distances of about 1 mm). More sensitive methods of detection might show diffusion over greater distances than this and molecules which are not fixed (by incorporation into macromolecules) into cells through which they are passing should diffuse further. In the pancreas, it has been shown by electrophysiology that all the cells in an acinus are coupled and, more surprisingly, that cells in adjacent acini are probably coupled too, which means that the acinar cells must also be coupled to the duct cells [24]. When current is injected, similar voltage changes occur in cells more than 100 μm apart and it has been calculated that as many as 500 cells are closely coupled in any one part of pancreatic acinar tissue.

Control of junctional permeability

Junctional communication could, in principle, be controlled either by a mechanism which opened and closed the channels or by a mechanism controlling the formation and breakdown of the junctional structures. Very little is known about the latter processes and there is only indirect evidence to suggest that they are subject to specific control. There is a body of evidence, however, which suggests that the channel permeability is reduced when intracellular calcium concentrations are raised to high levels.

Junction formation between cells brought into contact can be very rapid (functional channels can be detected within minutes) and the process is unaffected by inhibitors of protein synthesis. As mentioned before, both cells must be genetically competent with respect to junction formation, suggesting that both cells contribute protein to the junctional structures. A simple model

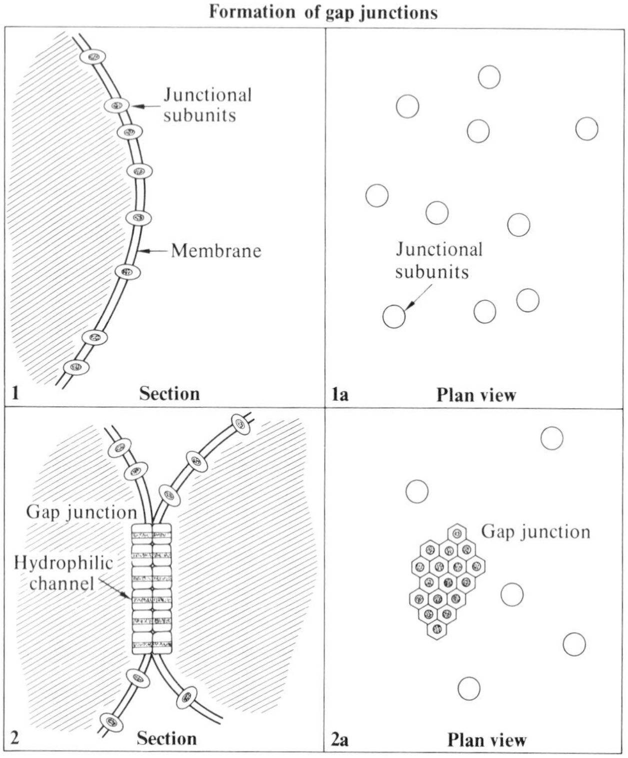

Formation of gap junctions

Fig. 3.4.15. A model for gap junction formation. The upper diagrams show a membrane in section and in plan view, containing junctional channel precursors. Each precursor has a hydrophobic exterior and a hydrophilic core (shaded). The lower diagram shows precursors in adjacent cell membranes interacting to form hydrophilic channels.

consistent with the known facts is illustrated in Fig. 3.4.15 where junctional precursors, present in both cell membranes, interact to form functional channels. The precursor is hypothetical and so far has not been identified either by freeze-fracture, where it is impossible to distinguish putative precursors from other intramembranous particles (they are all about the same size), or by biochemical techniques. If it does exist, it clearly does not contain an open channel connecting the inside and outside of the cell. Some conformational or structural change must occur, opening the channel when the junction forms.

Junction breakdown could occur either by dispersion (the reverse of formation) or by endocytosis of the complete structure into one or other of the coupled cells. The former would require some change in the half channels which reduced their affinity for each other. There is no evidence to suggest that this happens. There is some evidence for the latter process however, as cytoplasmic vesicles with complete gap junctions forming part of their membranes have been observed both in thin-section and freeze-fracture electron micrographs [27].

After partial hepatectomy, the liver begins the process of regeneration, and it has been observed [64] that the mean gap-junctional area between adjacent hepatocytes falls to less than five per cent of the normal value 28 h after surgery, then returns to the normal level 20 h later. Whether this event is a necessary part of the regeneration programme or whether it is simply a consequence of a disturbance in cellular organization caused by the wave of cell division is not known, but it is clear that breakdown and formation do take place and significantly alter the physical extent of junctional interaction. It is possible, however, that these large changes in junctional area are unimportant in functional terms.

A variety of treatments which increase the intracellular Ca^{2+} or H^+ concentration lead to electrical uncoupling and loss of dye transfer [34, 57]. It is difficult to measure intracellular calcium concentrations in the physiological range but in many cases it appears that unusually high concentrations are required to effect uncoupling. The physiological significance of this in these cases is therefore doubtful but reports that acetylcholine and other secretagogues, at concentrations smaller than those required to evoke maximal enzyme secretion, can cause uncoupling between pancreatic acinar cells [24] suggest that the phenomenon

occurs in normal situations and may therefore be functionally important.

Even finer control of junctional permeability has been suggested by Loewenstein and his colleagues [34], who reported that stepwise increases in intracellular calcium concentration produced by microinjection cause progressive decreases in the size of fluorescent probes which can be seen to pass from the injected cells to the surrounding cells. Control of junctional permeability, even in an on–off manner, is a fundamentally important concept and finer control is an attractive extension, but more work is required before it can be said that such control is important *in vivo*.

3.4.4 SPECIFICITY OF JUNCTION FORMATION AND PATTERNS OF COMMUNICATION

Many cell types in culture form junctions with other cells no matter from what tissue or vertebrate species the cells are derived [45]. Human cells form junctions with rodent, avian, amphibian and fish cells, for example, which indicates considerable structural conservation, and hence sequence conservation, of the junctional protein during this part of the evolutionary process. There does, however, appear to be evolutionary divergence at the structural level as well as at the morphological level between junctions of arthropods and those of vertebrates; successful coupling between cells in culture from animals in these different phyla has not been detected.

In vivo, of course, the ordered growth and movement of cells and cell populations (during development for example) means that only certain cells come into contact with cells of a different type (see Chapter 3.3). Do these different cells form junctions and, equally important, do all the cells of the same type in a tissue form a single coupled population or are they divided into compartments of coupled cells with other forms of communication coordinating the activities of the compartments? As yet, these questions cannot be properly answered. Electron microscopy shows that most tissues contain cells coupled by gap junctions but it is very difficult with this technique to show that particular cells are not coupled. The irregularities of the surfaces and the ability of cells to form junctions at the ends of processes confuses the analysis.

Electrical measurements, as mentioned previously,

show widespread and probably non-specific coupling in pancreatic acini and in liver. Very wide-ranging electrical coupling has been demonstrated [19] and it may be that all cells are capable of forming junctions unless they are separated by some physical obstruction.

Basement membranes might appear to provide such obstruction, preventing junctional communication between epithelial and stromal cells. However, it is not known if this is the case, for rat oocytes communicate with follicle cells prior to ovulation and this communication takes place across the zona pellucida. Processes of follicle cells penetrate this layer of matrix material and form junctions with the oocyte which can be detected electrophysiologically by dye injection, and morphologically by freeze-fracture analysis [15]. Cell processes may similarly penetrate basement membranes, though at low frequency as they are not normally seen in thin-section electron micrographs. However, even a low frequency of junction formation could be important functionally.

The discovery of specificity of junctional communication in tissue culture illustrates another possible way in which coupled cell populations could be isolated from each other in vivo. Certain epithelial cell types which form junctions among themselves fail to form junctions, or do so only with low frequency, with fibro-blasts (which in turn form junctions among themselves). However, after prolonged co-culture, junctions can be detected between increasing numbers of heterologous cells in contact and the permeability of these junctions formed between the different cell types is indistinguishable from that of junctions formed between cells of the same type [46]. It appears that the specificity does not lie in the junctional proteins but in some other surface component which affects the frequency with which the cell membranes come sufficiently close together to allow junction formation to occur.

The significance of this specificity is not yet clear. It may be an artefact of cells maintained in culture or, more excitingly, it may be related to developmental compartmentation, the progressive sub-division of an embryo into groups of cells (compartments) which have a common and increasingly restricted developmental fate (see below and Chapter 4.2).

3.4.5 ROLE OF JUNCTIONAL COMMUNICATION IN ANIMAL TISSUES

In contrast to the structure and permeability of gap junctions, which are now reasonably well understood, surprisingly little is known about their functions. They provide pathways for electrotonic coupling in excitable tissues such as heart, but what is their role in non-excitable tissues (where the junctions tend to be larger and more numerous)? It is generally believed that they play a role in coordinating the growth and activities of different cells in tissues, but the evidence for this is entirely circumstantial. An inevitable consequence of junctional permeability is that macromolecules remain in the cells where they were synthesized but metabolites and other small cellular components are shared between all the cells in a coupled population. Experiments described earlier show that this happens in cell populations in culture and there is evidence that it occurs in vivo too. Allophenic mice, created by mixing dissociated blastomeres from two strains with different isozymes of isocitrate dehydrogenase, produce heterologous dimers of the enzyme in skeletal muscle but not in other tissues (e.g. liver, kidney, heart) [40]. This shows that the subunits of the enzyme produced by the two genotypes can mix when cells fuse (in the formation of myotubes) but not in tissues where cells do not fuse, the subunits remaining in the cells where they were made. The sharing of metabolites (purine nucleotides) may be inferred from the normal condition of hemizygous HGPRT$^-$/HGPRT$^+$ mothers of Lesch–Nyhan children described above.

There are various consequences of metabolite exchange. The activity of an enzyme or metabolic pathway which is affected by the intracellular concentration of a precursor or product will be coordinately controlled in coupled populations. In model systems this predicted consequence has been shown to be correct [52]. The activity of the HGPRT pathway (see Fig. 3.4.7) in wild-type cells cultured in medium containing high concentrations of exogenous hypoxanthine, is increased in mixed cultures with HGPRT$^-$ cells if (and only if) the two cell types form junctions. Furthermore, the increased activity of the HGPRT decreases the activity of the pathway of IMP synthesis de novo in both cell types. It seems inevitable that this kind of coordination of metabolic activity will occur in all coupled tissues.

Another consequence of metabolite exchange which has also been characterized in model systems in culture is the creation of cell populations with properties (tissue phenotypes) which are lost when the cells are separated. For example, taking a system described already, neither HGPRT⁻ nor TK⁻ cells grow in HAT medium, but mixed cultures of the two cell types (if they form junctions) grow at the wild-type rate, by mutual nucleotide exchange. Growth in HAT medium is a property of the mixed cultures. In a coupled population, therefore, it is unnecessary for all cells to have all activities so long as collectively they have sufficient of every activity to meet the demands of all the cells. The proportion of the cells which must have any particular activity will depend on the nature of the shared product (metabolite). In the model system described, unequal mixtures of the two cell types (20:1 or 1:20) partially degenerate when they are first placed in HAT medium, but subsequently there is outgrowth of a population dividing at the normal rate and which is morphologically uniform. However, this population is composed of approximately equal numbers of HGPRT⁻ and TK⁻ cells; interdependence results in a self-stabilizing 1:1 mixture.

Do tissues *in vivo* have properties which are characteristic of the tissue but not of the separated cells? There is an example. Oocyte–cumulus complexes (from sheep) incorporate choline, uridine and amino acids into both the oocytes and the cumulus cells, but separated oocytes can only incorporate the amino acids. Incorporation of choline and uridine is a property of oocytes only when they are in the undissociated complexes [41]. It is known that junctions are formed between the two cell types in the complexes, so it is possible to explain the observations in terms of metabolic cooperation.

Junctional communication during embryonic development

There are contradictary reports in the literature about the occurrence of gap junctions in early embryos. Some of the confusion may have arisen because of two special problems associated with these structures. During the early cleavage stages, residual cytoplasmic bridges, which are sometimes hard to detect morphologically, give cytoplasmic continuity and allow ion and dye transfer which may be incorrectly interpreted in terms of junctional communication. Also, the large areas of cell–cell contact may give spurious electrical coupling.

A careful analysis of the early mouse embryo, using electrophysiology, fluorescein injection, horseradish peroxidase injection (to detect cytoplasmic continuity via residual bridges) and electron microscopy, has shown that junctions first appear at the early compaction stage (8-cell embryo [6, 30, 37]). Ionic coupling and dye transfer (which are only seen between sister blastomeres) in earlier embryos are accompanied by peroxidase transfer which indicates the presence of cytoplasmic bridges. At the compaction stage, injected dye spreads to all eight cells but the enzyme only passes to one other cell, again indicating the presence of cytoplasmic bridges between sister blastomeres. Junctional communication between all the cells is retained throughout compaction and during blastocyst development. In the pre-implantation blastocyst, dye injected into trophoblast cells spreads throughout the whole embryo including the inner mass region [30].

The analysis of junctional communication in later embryos in the same global terms is technically more difficult. However, it appears that all the cells in the early trophoblast are still coupled, but in later, more developed embryos, the spread of injected dye becomes progressively more limited [31]. Dye injected into an inner cell spreads throughout the inner cell mass but not to the surrounding trophoblast cells and vice versa. Ionic coupling, however, appears to be maintained between the trophoblast and the inner cell mass at this time, when dye transfer is no longer detected. This difference probably reflects the greater sensitivity of the electrical method for detecting junctional communication, rather than indicating differential permeability. In other words, cells in different parts are coupled by fewer junctional channels than cells in the same part of the embryo. Further restriction of dye transfer occurs in the inner cell mass in embryos which are even more developed; this may suggest that further compartmentation of this incomplete kind is occurring [31].

Similar communication compartments have been observed in insects, in the larval epidermis of *Oncopeltus* and *Calliphora* [60] and in the wing disc of *Drosophila* [62]. The most detailed studies have been made in *Oncopeltus*, where it has been shown that cells on opposite sides of a segmental boundary are coupled electrically and by observable gap junctions but that dye injected into cells adjacent to the boundary only spreads (in detectable amounts) into cells in the same segment. The reduced junctional communication across the

Fig. 3.4.16. Specificity of junctional communication, boundaries and gradients in a model system in culture. Mixtures of rat liver epithelial cells (BRL cells) and fibroblasts (BHK cells) when grown in mixed culture 'sort out' into epithelial islands separated by channels of fibroblasts. The addition of a few cells (BRL or BHK) prelabelled with [³H]uridine (see Fig. 3.4.11) results in junction formation and transfer of labelled nucleotides if the donor cells make contact with recipient cells of the same type. In A a donor BRL cell (black cell) has provided a source of labelled nucleotides for the surrounding BRL cells. The nucleotides have passed through the BRL cells, producing a gradient, but not detectably passed into the BHK cells. Heterologous junction formation (between BRL and BHK cells) occurs only infrequently while homologous junction formation (between BRL and BRL or between BHK and BHK cells) occurs with high frequency. This difference results in an abrupt change in labelled nucleotide concentration (and hence radioactivity seen in the RNA) at the boundary. The gradient from the source cell through the epithelial compartment is exponential. In B the source is a BHK cell so the gradient runs through the fibroblasts and not (detectably) across the boundary into the epithelial compartment.

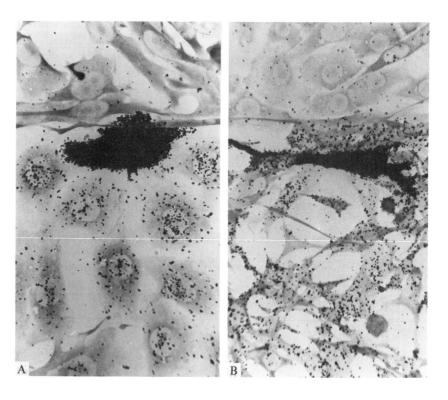

boundary is apparently similar to that seen across the boundaries in mouse embryos (see above). In insects, however, it is possible to relate communication compartments defined by dye injection to developmental compartments defined by cell-marking and genetic techniques (Chapter 4.2). It is not known if specificity of junctional communication (p. 167) is related to developmental compartmentation but model systems in culture (Fig. 3.4.16) have characteristics which at least superficially resemble what is observed *in vivo*.

The onset of junctional coupling at the 8-cell compaction stage of embryonic development in the mouse precedes the 16–32-cell stage, when it is believed that determination first occurs [12], differentiating outer cells, which will become trophoblast, from inner cells, which will become the inner cell mass of the blastocyst. It has been suggested, therefore, that 'inside–outside' positional information could be generated by an intracellular gradient through the coupled cells, perhaps caused by environmental differences (accentuated by the presence of an effective tight-junction network

sealing the spaces between the outer cells) between the inner and outer cells [30].

The production of intracellular gradients in coupled cell populations is an attractive concept in development. In 1970, before junctional communication was generally understood, Crick [5] proposed that a special mechanism which allows the relatively free movement of low-molecular-weight developmental signal molecules (morphogens) from one cell to another must be postulated to explain a variety of observations made in developing systems. Junctional communication offers many of the criteria which must be ascribed to such a special mechanism. Junctions will allow the free movement of such small signal molecules from one cell to another but not to the extracellular fluids. Morphogens could act through populations of 50–100 cells (a few millimetres) and establish gradients over such distances in a few hours. These distances and times are consistent with the hypothetical ideas on developmental signalling (see Chapter 4.2).

The movement of morphogens directly from cell to

cell, rather than through the extracellular fluids, could produce gradients which are independent of the geometry of the interacting cells and which are undisturbed by mixing effects caused by convection or movement (Fig. 3.4.17). Specific formation or breakdown of junctions (or specific control of channel permeability) could produce compartments totally or partially isolated from each other (Fig. 3.4.18) and thus act as a mechanism for developmental organization. These possibilities clearly exist, but in the absence of any identified intracellular morphogens, they must only be treated as such.

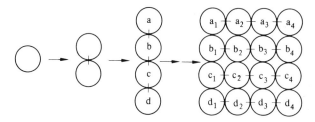

Fig. 3.4.18. Communication compartments could be established if the breakdown and formation of junctions were controlled. For further explanation, see text.

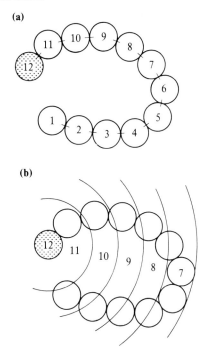

(a)

(b)

Fig. 3.4.17. The movement of molecules from cell to cell through junctions can produce clearly defined concentration gradients, whereas gradients produced by diffusion through extracellular fluids can be more ambiguous and are subject to disturbance by forces which cause fluid movement.

Embryonic induction is a related phenomenon which could also be explained in terms of intercellular signalling via junctional pathways. Specific induction phenomena can be observed *in vitro* and in a study on one such system, the transfer of labelled material was followed, by EM autoradiography, from inducing tissue prelabelled with [³H]uridine to the induced tissue. The earliest incorporation in the induced tissue occurred in the nuclei, particularly in the nucleoli. The data were interpreted either as showing RNA transfer or as showing uridine nucleotide transfer [25]. In light of the more recent studies described in this chapter, uridine nucleotide transfer would appear the more likely explanation and direct evidence for this has since been obtained [20].

It has also been shown [61], using explants of mouse embryonic tissue, that the induction process leading to kidney tubule formation can be correlated with close approaches and contact between cells of the interacting tissues (see Chapter 3.5).

In conclusion, there is no direct evidence to implicate junctional communication in any developmental signalling process. However, junctions are known to occur in most embryonic and adult tissues, so their properties and the possible roles for junctional communication described in this chapter should be remembered by those trying to understand the problems of developmental biology.

3.4.6 JUNCTIONAL COMMUNICATION IN PLANTS

The specializations which have evolved to provide communication between the cytoplasms of adjacent cells in plants are termed plasmodesmata, and are structurally quite different from gap junctions (the structure of plasmodesmata is reviewed in [50]). The large intercellular spaces (150–500 nm) filled with cell-wall material are bridged by tubes of membrane which appear to be continuous with the plasma membranes of the coupled cells (Fig. 3.4.19). The internal diameter of these tubes (25–45 nm) is much larger than that of gap-junctional channels but in most cases the tube is partially blocked by the presence of a central axial structure which passes through the plasmodesmata from

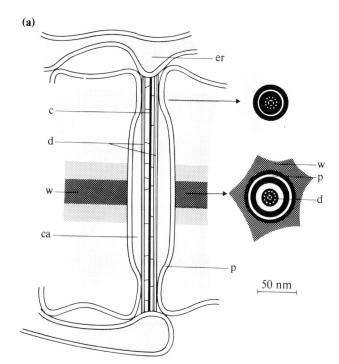

Fig. 3.4.19. (a) Diagram of a simple plasmodesmata in longitudinal and transverse sections based on electron micrographs of plasmodesmata between xylem ray cells of *Salix fragilis* (p, plasma membrane; d, desmotubule; c, central core; ca, cytoplasmic annulus; w, cell wall; er, endoplasmic reticulum). Redrawn from Robards [50]. (b) Transverse section through the same tissue. (c) Longitudinal section through plasmodesmata in the bundle sheath of the cotyledon of *Welwitschia mirabilis*. Micrographs kindly provided by Dr Jean Whatley.

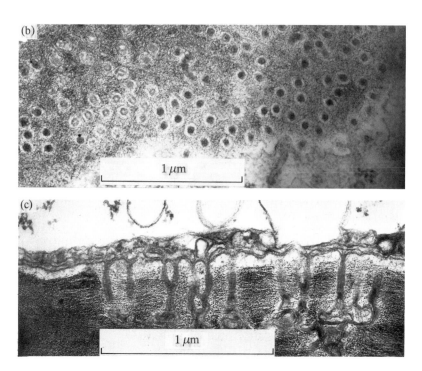

one cytoplasm to the other. This structure, of unknown composition and variable appearance, is called the desmotubule [49] and it, in turn, may have an axial core (Fig. 3.4.19). The core is also of unknown structure and could be an artefact of electron microscopy [50]. The space between the membrane and the desmotubule is called the cytoplasmic annulus and is thought to be the channel providing communication between the cells. It is possible, however, that the desmotubule contains a central pore which could be an alternative or additional channel. The effective cross-section of the cytoplasmic annulus is reduced at both ends by membrane constrictions.

The permeability of plasmodesmata is not yet well defined. The structural information is inadequate for predicting permeability, and permeability measurements have been aimed more at determining fluxes of ions and other small cellular components rather than at determining which components pass through plasmodesmata and which do not.

Various ions, sugars and amino acids and the auxin indole acetic acid have been shown to pass through cells in plant tissues without exchange to the external medium [1, 18] and similar experiments have shown the translocation of fluorescein through the cells of staminal hairs. The cells of several plant tissues have been shown to be electrically coupled [18, 53] and the low-resistance junctions (plasmodesmata) allow the propagation of action potentials between excitable cells [63]. The specific resistance of the intercellular junction is much less than that of the plasma membrane but is very much greater than would be expected from an open-tube structure [18], which is consistent with the presence of the desmotubule suggested by morphological studies.

These studies suggest that, like gap junctions, plasmodesmata allow the indiscriminate passage of small ions and molecules, but data on the movement of larger cell components are less clear. In different studies on different plant tissues it has been shown that injected dyes such as Procion Yellow (mol. wt 550) pass to surrounding cells [18] while Niagra sky blue (mol. wt 961) does not [17]. More recent work by Goodwin, based on the observed intercellular movement of injected fluorescent peptides has now shown that the exclusion limit for junctional permeability is close to a mol.wt of 800 in *Elodea* leaves and 665 in *Silene* stem apices. Other data though, demonstrate the intercellular movement of viruses through plasmodesmata [13]. It is possible, how-

ever, that junctions are modified as a consequence of infection [21] producing syncytia (similar to those produced in some virus-infected animal tissues).

Permeable junctions between animal cells came as a surprise to those who found them, but plant physiologists had never forgotten Tangl's ideas (page 156); ideas which were reinforced by the concept of the symplast introduced in 1930 [42]. The symplast was envisaged as a cytoplasmic network separated by a continuous plasma membrane from the apoplast which, in turn, was thought to be a continuous network of extracellular structures. The evidence for some sort of symplast is now good; the plasmodesmata provide the membrane and cytoplasmic continuity between cells and the permeability studies confirm its extensive nature. Symplastic transport of intracellular components is generally accepted and attempts have been made to determine junctional fluxes for various solutes. The estimates range from 10^{-19} moles per plasmodesmata per second [21] to about 10^3–10^5 molecules per second, a value not unlike the calculated permeabilities of gap junctions (page 165). Transport in plant tissues can be a bulk-flow process or simply diffusive, and in large cells in some tissues, transport may be limited not by the junctions but by the cytoplasmic streaming which delivers the solutes to the junctions [21]. This problem, the restriction of movement of solutes in organized cytoplasm, has not been considered in animal cells.

Apart from transport of metabolites, what functions can be assigned to junctional communication in plants? In one approach [21] to answering this question, the behaviour of cells in the symplast is compared with that of cells isolated from it and with that of cells in the more intimate association of multinucleate syncytia. Isolation, whether natural (as in the formation of reproductive cells) or artificial, brings about a process of dedifferentiation and subsequently processes of embryonic development may begin. Presumably such processes are held in check by the continuity of the cytoplasm (or the plasma membrane) through plasmodesmata. Syncytial organization, on the other hand, suppresses cellular individuality and results in mitotic synchrony. The synchronizing stimuli (division proteins) are presumably restricted to individual cells in the symplast because they do not pass through plasmodesmata. Equivalent signals do not pass through gap junctions in animal tissues but can also produce mitotic synchrony in animal cell cyncytia.

Further comparison between junctional communication in animals and plants is difficult at the present time but as knowledge in the two fields expands, it may prove rewarding.

3.4.7 REFERENCES

1 Arisz W.H. (1969) Intercellular polar transport and the role plasmodesmata in coleoptiles and *Valisneria* leaves. *Acta bot. néerl.*, **18**, 14–38.

2 Brink P.R. & Dewey M.M. (1980) Evidence for fixed charge in the nexus. *Nature, Lond.*, **285**, 101–102.

3 Carr D.J. (1976) Historical perspectives on plasmodesmata. In *Intercellular Communication in Plants: Studies on Plasmodesmata* (Eds B.E.S. Gunning & A.W. Robards), pp. 291–295. Springer-Verlag, Berlin.

4 Cox R.P., Krauss M.R., Balis M.E. & Dancis J. (1970) Evidence for transfer of enzyme product as the basis of metabolic cooperation. *Proc. natl Acad. Sci., USA*, **67**, 1573–1579.

5 Crick F.H.C. (1970) Diffusion in embryogenesis. *Nature, Lond.*, **225**, 420–422.

6 Ducibella J., Albertini D., Anderson E. & Biggars J.D. (1975) The preimplantation mammalian embryo; characterization of intercellular junctions. *Devl. Biol.*, **47**, 231–250.

7 Finbow M.E. & Pitts J.D. (1980) Permeability of junctions between animal cells; transfer of metabolites and a vitamin derived cofactor. *Expl. Cell Res.*, **131**, 1–13.

8 Finbow M.E., Yancey S.B., Johnson R. & Revel J.-P. (1980) Independent lines of evidence suggesting the major gap junctional protein has a M. Wt of 26000. *Proc. natl Acad. Sci., USA*, **77**, 970–974.

9 Flagg-Newton J.L., Simpson I. & Loewenstein W.R. (1979) Permeability of the cell–cell membrane channels in mammalian cell junctions. *Science, N.Y.*, **205**, 404–409.

10 Furshpan E.J. & Potter D.D. (1959) Transmission at giant motor synapses of the crayfish. *J. Physiol.*, **143**, 289–325.

11 Furshpan E.J. & Potter D.D. (1968) Low resistance junctions between cells in embryos and in tissue culture. *Curr. Tops Devl. Biol.*, **3**, 95–127.

12 Gardner R.L. & Rossant J. (1976) Determination during embryogenesis. Ciba Found. Symp. 40. *Embryogenesis in Mammals*, pp. 5–25.

13 Gibbs A. (1976) Viruses and plasmodesmata. In *Intercellular Communication in Plants: Studies on Plasmodesmata* (Eds B.E.S. Gunning & A.W. Robards), pp. 149–164. Springer-Verlag, Berlin.

14 Gilula N.B. (1978) Structure of intercellular junctions. In *Intercellular Junctions and Synapses* (Eds J. Feldman, N.B. Gilula & J.D. Pitts), pp. 1–22. Chapman & Hall, London.

15 Gilula N.B., Epstein M.L. & Beers W.H. (1978) Cell-to-cell communication and ovulation. *J. Cell Biol.*, **78**, 58–75.

16 Gilula N.B., Reeves O.R. & Steinbach A. (1973). Metabolic coupling, ionic coupling and cell contacts. *Nature, Lond.*, **235**, 262–265.

17 Goldsmith N.H.M., Fernandez H.R. & Goldsmith T.H. (1972) Electrical properties of parenchyma cell membranes in the oat coleoptile. *Planta*, **102**, 302–323.

18 Goodwin P.B. (1976) Physiological and electrophysiological evidence for intercellular communication in plant symplast. In *Intercellular Communication in Plants: Studies on Plasmodesmata* (Eds B.E.S. Gunning & A.W. Robards), pp. 121–129. Springer-Verlag, Berlin.

19 Graf J. & Petersen O.H. (1978) Cell membrane potential and resistance in liver. *J. Physiol.*, **284**, 105–126.

20 Grainger R.M. & Wessells N.K. (1974) Does RNA pass from mesenchyme to epithelium during an embryonic tissue interaction? *Proc. natl Acad. Sci., USA*, **71**, 4747–4751.

21 Gunning B.E.S. & Robards A.W. (1976) Current knowledge and outstanding problems. In *Intercellular Communication in Plants* (Eds B.E.S. Gunning & A.W. Robards), pp. 297–311. Springer-Verlag, Berlin.

22 Henderson D., Eibl H. & Weber K. (1979) Structure and biochemistry of mouse hepatic gap junctions. *J. molec. Biol.*, **132**, 193–218.

23 Hertzberg E.L. & Gilula N.B. (1979) Isolation and characterization of gap junctions from rat liver. *J. biol. Chem.*, **254**, 2138–2147.

24 Iwatsuka N. & Petersen O.H. (1978) Electrical coupling and uncoupling in pancreatic acinar cells. *J. Cell Biol.*, **79**, 533–545.

25 Kelley R.O. (1968) An electron microscopic study of chardamesoderm–neurectoderm association in gastrulae of a toad. *J. exp. Zool.*, **172**, 153–180.

26 Laat S.W. de, Barts P.W.J.A. & Bakker M.I. (1976) New membrane formation and intercellular communication in the early *Xenopus* embryo. *J. Membr. Biol.*, **27**, 109–129.

27 Larsen W.J. (1977) Structural diversity of gap junctions. *Tissue Cell*, **9**, 373–394.

28 Lawrence T.S., Beers W.H. & Gilula N.B. (1978) Hormonal stimulation and cell communication in cocultures. *Nature, Lond.*, **272**, 501–506.

29 Ledbetter M.L.S. & Lubin M. (1979) Transfer of potassium. A new measure of cell–cell coupling. *J. Cell Biol.*, **80**, 166–182.

30 Lo C.W. & Gilula N.B. (1979) Gap junctional communication in the preimplantation mouse embryo. *Cell*, **18**, 399–410.

31 Lo C.W. & Gilula N.B. (1979) Gap junctional communication in the postimplantation mouse embryo. *Cell*, **18**, 411–422.

32 Loewenstein W.R. (1966) Permeability of membrane junctions. *Ann. N.Y. Acad. Sci.*, **137**, 441–472.

33 Loewenstein W.R. (1970) Intercellular communication. *Scient. Am.* (May), 79–86.

34 Loewenstein W.R. (1976) Permeable junctions. *Cold Spring Harbor Symp. Quant. Biol.*, **40**, 49–63.

35 Loewenstein W.R. (1977) Permeability of the junctional membrane channel. In *International Cell Biology 1976–77* (Eds B.R. Brinkley & K.R. Porter), pp. 70–82. Rockefeller University Press, New York.

36 Loewenstein W.R. & Kanno Y. (1964) Studies on an epithelial gland junction. *J. Cell Biol.*, **22**, 565–586.

37 Magnuson T., Jacobson J.B. & Stackpole C.W. (1978) Relationship between intercellular permeability and junction organization in the preimplantation mouse embryo. *Devl. Biol.*, **67**, 214–224.

38 Makowski L.D., Caspar L.D., Phillips W.C. & Goodenough D.A.

(1977) Gap junction structures. Analysis of X-ray diffraction data. *J. Cell Biol.*, **74**, 605–628.

39 Migeon B.R., Kaloustian V.M.D., Nyhan W.L., Young W.J. & Childs B. (1968) X-linked HGPRT deficiency: heterozygote has two clonal populations. *Science, N.Y.*, **160**, 425–427.

40 Mintz B. & Baker W.W. (1967) Normal mammalian muscle differentiation and gene control of isocitrate dehydrogenase synthesis. *Proc. natl Acad. Sci., USA*, **58**, 592–598.

41 Moor R.M., Smith M.W. & Dawson R.M.C. (1980) Measurement of intercellular coupling between oocytes and cumulus cells using intracellular markers. *Expl. Cell Res.*, **126**, 15–29.

42 Münch E. (1930) *Die Stoffbewegung in der Pflanze*. Gustav Fischer, Jera.

43 Pitts J.D. (1971) Molecular exchange and growth control in tissue culture. Ciba Found. Symp. *Growth Control in Cell Cultures*, pp. 89–105.

44 Pitts J.D. (1972) Direct interactions between animal cells. In *Lepetit Colloquium on Cell Interactions* (Ed. G. Silvestri), pp. 227–285. North-Holland, Amsterdam.

45 Pitts J.D. (1977) Direct communication between animal cells. In *International Cell Biology 1976–77* (Eds B.R. Brinkley & K.R. Porter), pp. 43–49. Rockefeller University Press, New York.

46 Pitts J.D. & Bürk R.R (1976) Specificity of junctional communication between animal cells. *Nature, Lond.*, **264**, 762–764.

47 Pitts J.D. & Sims J.W. (1977) Permeability of between animal cells; intercellular transfer of nucleotides but not macromolecules. *Expl. Cell Res.*, **104**, 153–163.

48 Revel J.P. & Karnovsky M.J. (1967) Hexagonal array of subunits in intercellular junctions of mouse heart and liver. *J. Cell Biol.*, **33**, 87–12.

49 Robards A.W. (1968) Desmotubule—a plasmodesmatal substructure. *Nature, Lond.*, **218**, 784–786.

50 Robards A.W. (1976) Plasmodesmata in higher plants. In *Intercellular Communication in Plants: Studies on Plasmodesmata* (Eds B.E.S. Gunning & A.W. Robards), pp. 15–58. Springer-Verlag, Berlin.

51 Sanford K.K., Earle W.R. & Likely G.D. (1948) The growth in vitro of single isolated tissue cells. *J. natn Cancer Inst.*, **9**, 229–246.

52 Sheridan J.D., Finbow M.E. & Pitts J.D. (1979) Metabolic interactions between animal cells through permeable intercellular junctions. *Expl. Cell Res.*, **123**, 111–119.

53 Spanswick R.M. (1972) Electrical coupling between cells of higher plants. A direct demonstration of intercellular communication. *Planta*, **102**, 215–227.

54 Subak-Sharpe J.H., Bürk R.R. & Pitts J.D. (1966) Metabolic cooperation by cell–cell transfer between genetically different mammalian cells in tissue culture. *Heredity*, **21**, 342.

55 Subak-Sharpe J.H., Bürk R.R. & Pitts J.D. (1969) Metabolic cooperation between biochemically marked cells in tissue culture. *J. Cell Sci.*, **4**, 353–367.

56 Tangl E. (1879) Ueber offene Communicationen zwischen den Zellen des Endosperms einiger Samen. *Jb. wiss. Bot.*, **12**, 170–190.

57 Turin L. & Warner A.E. (1977) Carbon dioxide reversibly abolishes ionic communication between cells of early amphibian embryo. *Nature, Lond*, **270**, 56–57.

58 Unwin P.N.T. & Zampighi G. (1980) Structure of the junction between communicating cells. *Nature, Lond.*, **283**, 545–549.

59 Warner A.E. & Lawrence P.A. (1973) Electrical coupling across developmental boundaries in insect epidermis. *Nature, Lond.*, **245**, 47–49.

60 Warner A.E. & Lawrence P.A. (1982) Permeability of gap junctions at the segmental border in insect epidermis. *Cell*, **28**, 243–252.

61 Wartiovaara J., Lehtonen E., Nordling S. & Sacen L. (1972) Do membrane filters prevent cell contacts? *Nature, Lond.*, **238**, 407–408.

62 Weir M.P. & Lo C.W. (1982) Gap junctional communication compartments in the *Drosophila* wing disk. *Proc. natl Acad. Sci., USA*, **79**, 3232–3235.

63 Williams S.E. & Spanswick R.M. (1972) Intercellular recordings of the action potentials which mediate the thigmonastic movements of *Drosera*. *Pl. Physiol.* Suppl., **50**, 64.

64 Yee A.G. & Revel J.P. (1978) Loss and reappearance of gap junctions in regenerating liver. *J. Cell Biol.*, **78**, 554–564.

65 Zampighi G. & Unwin P.N.T. (1979) Two forms of isolated gap junctions. *J. molec. Biol.*, **135**, 451–464.

Chapter 3.5
Embryonic Induction
L. Saxen and J. Wartiovaara

3.5.1 DIFFERENTIATION ENTAILS COMMUNICATION BETWEEN CELLS

In this chapter we shall show that the fate of an individual cell is controlled in part by extrinsic factors. In other words, the 'building plan' of an embryo is to be sought for in the organization of tissues and organs rather than on the level of the individual cells. The guiding forces should be found in the constantly changing microenvironment of the cells and the intimate associations of cells with each other. Morphogenetic communication between cells and cell populations may also account for their spatially and temporally synchronized development and the rearrangement of cells required for the creation of a harmoniously built organism.

That such theoretically meaningful *inductive interactions* do occur between adjacent cell populations has repeatedly been demonstrated experimentally, either by surgically separating the cells or the organ anlagen, or

by inserting barriers between them. These measures have affected differentiation, morphogenesis and the maintenance of the differentiated state. Embryonic induction could thus be defined as *communication between cells required for their differentiation, morphogenesis, and maintenance.* The definition does *not* imply that we deal with interacting processes operating through similar mechanisms or leading to similar consequences. It merely states that cells in higher organisms do not develop independently as pre-programmed units but as targets for various extrinsic stimuli. The extrinsic stimuli may include specific determinative signals, less specific permissive conditions and mere nutritional factors required for normogenesis. The search for a unifying concept or a common denominator for the great variety of known (and unknown) interactive processes has caused much confusion in the last 60 years.

On considering the numerous experiments related to embryonic induction, we run into another difficulty. Experiments deal with single developmental events abstracted from the continuous and complicated process of embryogenesis. The cells and tissues to be studied are at various stages of differentiation and might have experienced several interactions before the experiment. The result is that their 'predetermination' and potentialities vary. Besides, the alternative pathways open to them are more or less restricted. It is still premature to make a synthesis out of such fragmentary observations and to extrapolate the results and interpretations to the normal situation *in vivo*. For the present we must be content with the separate examples. However, we should keep in mind that even these simple events, mostly analysed *in vitro*, do not necessarily represent normal conditions. They are to be regarded as model systems which simulate normal development as closely as possible.

3.5.2 NEURAL INDUCTION ILLUSTRATES THE PROBLEMS

'Primary induction' was one of the first inductive interactions to be recognized. It is a process that governs the determinaton and subsequent morphogenesis of the central nervous system (CNS) and we will discuss this process as it occurs in amphibians. We shall use this classic example of induction, in many respects most thoroughly investigated but still only partly understood, for illustrating the basic problems, both solved and unsolved, in the study of inductive tissue interactions (for review, see [42, 49]).

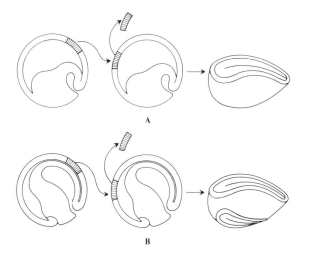

Fig. 3.5.1. Spemann's experiment demonstrating the determination of the presumptive neural plate area. Transplantation at an early gastrula stage (A) leads to normal development, whereas a similar experiment at a late gastrula stage (B) results in the formation of an extra neural plate at the belly side of the donor. (After [41].)

The experiment performed by Spemann some 60 years ago is illustrated in Fig. 3.5.1. It constitutes the basis for studies related to neural induction. When a fragment of the presumptive neural plate of a young amphibian gastrula is transplanted to the ventral surface of a host at the same stage of development, the transplant develops in accordance with its new surroundings (A). When the experiment is performed later, at an advanced gastrula stage, the transplant forms an extra neural plate at its new site (B). This implies that the piece of tissue has been *determined* during the short period between the two stages. The determination is apparently caused by the invaginating mesoderm. The

movement of the mesoderm layers beneath the ectoderm during amphibian gastrulation is described in detail in Chapter 3.3 and the form of the embryo after gastrulation is illustrated in Chapter 4.3. During gastrulation, the mesoderm moves beneath, and interacts with, the ectoderm transplanted in experiment B. This is demonstrated by two further experiments: removal of the mesoderm or prevention of its invagination blocks the development of the central nervous system, and implantation of the mesoderm into another gastrula induces supernumerary structures in the host. If the entire dorsal blastoporal lip of a young gastrula or a combination of certain foreign tissues (e.g. liver and bone marrow from a guinea pig, subsequently called heterogeneous inductors) is implanted into the blastocoel, the competent ectoderm can be induced to form a variety of neural, neuroectodermal, mesodermal and endodermal structures [42, 52].

Observations like this raise questions, most of which appear relevant to many inductive interactions.

— Do specific substances signal each type of induction?
— Is the final result, seen as completed organogenesis, a consequence of a single determinative event or a product of a series of inductive interactions?
— Finally, what are the signal substances, and how do they operate?

Let us start by discussing the first two questions posed above. They will provide the biological framework for the latter part of this chapter, which deals with the complicated and still unsolved problems related to signals, their transmission and their chemical nature.

Neural induction involves more than one signal

Experiments in which various heterogeneous inductors exerting different types of effects on the ectoderm have been employed have led to the hypothesis that there are basically two types of primary responses, neuralization and mesodermalization. Neuralization leads to the formation of cranial neural structures (forebrain and its derivatives, such as the optic cups), whereas mesodermalization culminates in the development of purely mesodermal structures (axial mesoderm, limb, etc.). In order to explain the induction of mid- and caudo-neural structures (hindbrain and its derivatives such as otic vesicles and spinal cord), a hypothesis was put forward that these develop in response to the combined action of the primary neuralizing and mesodermalizing principles

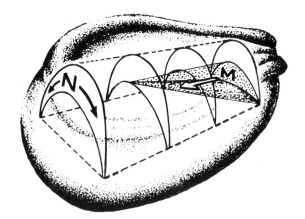

Fig. 3.5.2. The double-gradient hypothesis. Two active principles are postulated, a neuralizing principle, most active in the dorsal mid-line, and a mesodermalizing principle, forming a caudo-cranial gradient. (After [54] and a drawing in [13].)

(Fig. 3.5.2). The hypothesis gets further support from experiments in which two heterogeneous inductors were employed simultaneously, one of them having a neuralizing action and the other inducing mesodermal structures. As expected, such experiments led to the development of secondary hindbrain derivatives and spinal cords and to a reduction of forebrain structures. When the ratio of such neural and predominantly mesodermal inductors was altered in semiquantitative experiments, progressive caudalization of the neural structures was associated with increased relative amounts of the mesodermalizing inductor [41].

Neural induction is a multistep process

Since the combined actions needed for the production of regional specialization of the CNS could not be ascribed to a single inductive event, the following experiment was carried out to discover some of the steps in the inductive process [43] (Fig. 3.5.3). Competent ectodermal cells from an amphibian gastrula were exposed to either of the two heterogeneous inductors, one of them leading to 'pure' neuralization and ultimately to the formation of forebrain structures (guinea-pig liver, A), the other to mesodermal and spinal cord derivatives, but not to hindbrain derivatives (guinea-pig bone marrow, B). After the time required for primary induction (24 h incubation) the inductors were removed and the ectodermal cells were disaggregated to single-cell

suspensions. When the suspensions were allowed to reaggregate, the structures expected were obtained. In culture A the forebrain and eye cups developed, whereas in culture B the spinal cord formed with associated notocord, muscle and kidney tubules. If the two types of induced suspensions of ectodermal cells were thoroughly mixed and cultured as a combined aggregate, hindbrain formations were regularly recovered. It was concluded that these had been determined after the initial period of primary induction, but before the stabilization of the regional determination of the CNS. Finally, presumptive forebrain cells and mesodermal cells taken from the dorsal mid-line of the embryo were disaggregated and combined to simulate

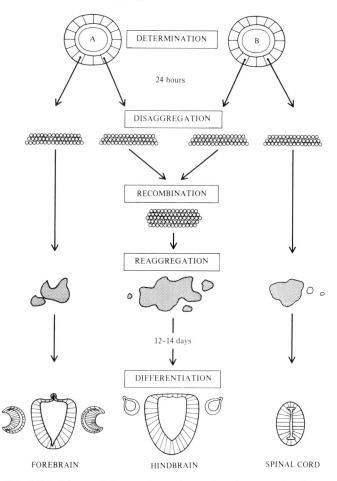

Fig. 3.5.3. Scheme of the experimental procedure demonstrating the two stages, the determination and segregation of the central nervous system [42].

the actual situation *in vivo*. As expected, presumptive forebrain cells from young neurula stages could be 'transformed' to hindbrain and spinal cord structures if cultured in mixed aggregates with mesodermal cells. As a final test, the semiquantitative experiment was repeated, this time with the forebrain and mesodermal cells from young neurulas mixed in different ratios. The results (Fig. 3.5.4) indicated that a gradual increase in the proportion of mesodermal cells resulted in gradual caudalization of the CNS derivatives.

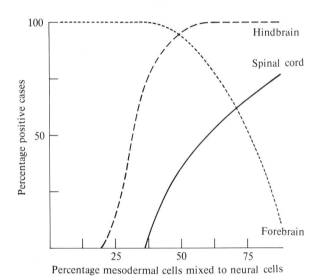

Fig. 3.5.4. Percentage of neural derivatives of various types in a series of experiments in which cells of the axial mesoderm were mixed with neural cells from the prospective forebrain region in different ratios. (After [55].)

This series of experiments provides us with a rough and still over-simplified scheme for the determination and segregation of the CNS. During a short initial phase of interaction with mesodermal cells, the pluripotent ectodermal cells become determined either in a neural or in a mesodermal direction. Without any additional directive influence from the mesoderm, the neuralized cells form forebrain structures. Continued mesodermal influence, however, alters their further morphogenetic course, and they form caudo-neural structures. This secondary type of morphogenetic interaction operates quantitatively, and it is not strictly specific, as the mesenchyme from other sites besides the normal axial region can support the regionalization of the CNS. In conclusion, the induction of the CNS seems to be a multistep process comprising at least specific determinative stimuli and less specific morphogenetic or stabilizing steps. Next we shall have to test whether this scheme is in accordance with what we know of other interactive systems.

3.5.3 EPITHELIO-MESENCHYMAL INTERACTIONS GOVERN ORGANOGENESIS

Many recent studies on the specificity of inductive signals have been performed on model systems for epithelio-mesenchymal interactions, i.e. morphogenetic interactions between differentiating epithelium and its mesenchymal stroma. Although only a few of the many interactive situations studied so far will be described, they all show that the differentiation of the epithelium and mesenchyme is dependent on their interaction. But, as will be seen, such interactions are not necessarily identical in their mechanism and the influence of the mesenchyme varied from determinative, 'directive' actions to entirely non-specific, 'permissive' effects.

Dermal mesenchyme determines epidermal differentiation

The differentiation of the vertebrate epidermis and its derivatives is known to be directed by the underlying mesenchyme. This is another example of a 'directive' influence. When combined experimentally with chick epidermis, the mesenchyme derived from various sources alters epidermal differentiation over the whole range, from the keratinizing, squamous type to the ciliated, cuboidal epithelium [33]. In experiments like this, the regional differences can be demonstrated even within the same embryonic dermis. When dermis from the feather-bearing back is combined with the epidermis of the normally featherless ventral skin, feathers form; whereas the reciprocal combination does not support the development of feathers [44]. Interspecies transplantation experiments between chick and lizard have further elucidated the role of the dermal component [9]. When embryonic lizard epidermis was combined with chick tarsometatarsal dermis, scales of the avian type developed which lacked the reptilian type keratinization. The combination with other chick dermal mesenchyme resulted in partial blocking of scale formation, but the immature scale buds were always

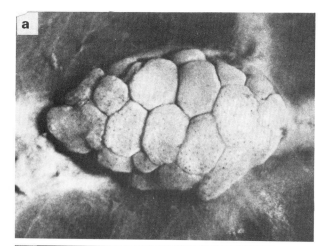

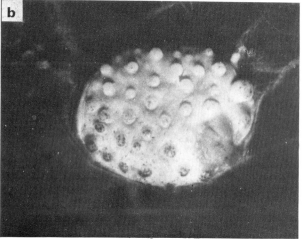

Fig. 3.5.5. Two examples of scale formation in interspecies combination of cutaneous components. (a) 15-day caudal lizard epidermis combined with 9-day tarso-metatarsal chick dermis. The scales are of chick type. (b) 18-day lizard epidermis combined with 7-day dorsal chick dermis. The immature scales show the typical hexagonal feather pattern. (From [9].)

their basal cells are controlled by the dermis throughout adult life. Billingham and Silvers [6, 7] made recombinations of epidermis and dermis from various sites of adult guinea-pig (sole of the foot, ear and trunk). They showed that the type of epidermal morphology was not determined by a stable phenotype of the epidermis but by the dermal mesenchyme. For example, when epidermis from a pigmented area of the ear was transplanted to an unpigmented area in the sole, the transplant remained pigmented but it had the morphological characteristics typical of the sole epidermis.

Tooth morphogenesis provides another example of specific epithelio-mesenchymal interactions deter-

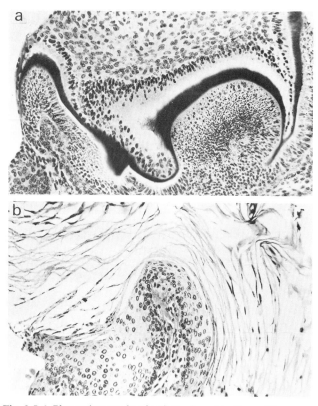

Fig. 3.5.6. Photomicrographs of reciprocal combinations of the epithelium and the mesenchyme of a tooth germ and of non-dentogeneous gingival tissue. (a) Combination of gingival epithelium with mesenchyme from the dental papilla leads to the development of a well-shaped tooth rudiment with differentiated odontoblasts and ameloblasts. The black zone shows predentine secreted by the odontoblasts. (b) Combination of tooth epithelium and gingival mesenchyme shows no dental differentiation. Moreover, the epithelium becomes squamous, displaying strong keratinization. (By courtesy of Dr Irma Thesleff.)

arranged in a pattern typical of the chick (Fig. 3.5.5). The same group of researchers has recently given examples of interspecies transplantations in which not only the morphology of the cutaneous appendage but also its biosynthetic activity was affected by the dermal component [10].

Dermo-epidermal interactions like this are not restricted to the embryonic period. In fact, there is experimental evidence that the maintenance of certain types of epithelium and the continuous differentiation of mining the phenotype of the epithelium [27, 47]. The process is known to be guided by an interaction between the enamel epithelium and the mesenchyme of the dental papilla. The dental papilla ultimately determines the type of tooth formed. The dental mesenchyme was combined with a non-dental epithelium to test its inductive capacity and specificity. The result was well-shaped teeth with differentiated enamel and dental matrices (Fig. 3.5.6).

Glandular mesenchyme supports epithelial morphogenesis

Glandular epithelium regularly interacts with its mesenchymal counterpart. This is a system that has been used in a great variety of experiments. Pancreatic, salivary, mammary, hepatic and many other glandular epithelia have been shown to be morphogenetically dependent on their mesenchymal stroma (for review, see [17, 19]). Unlike the readily modified epidermis discussed above, the glandular epithelium seems to be strictly limited in its developmental alternatives in most instances studied. The pancreatic epithelium is a good example of this. Even at a stage when the gland rudiment is no more than a small stalk, it is not dependent on the presence of the normal pancreas mesenchyme, and it can continue its development if cultured with mesenchyme from almost anywhere in the embryo. Morphogenesis and enzyme synthesis proceed after the combination of this isolated epithelium with a variety of heterologous mesenchymes [11, 37, 38]. Salivary epithelium at a comparable stage is committed in a similar way, but it is much more selective in its mesenchymal requirements as very few mesenchymes tested so far can support its normal branching and adenomere formation [19]. The basis for such variations in the specificity of mesenchymal requirements of these and other glandular epithelia is still unknown. However, most of them respond to the mesenchyme in an all-or-none fashion. The alteration of the morphogenesis of these epithelia by heterologous mesenchyme is rare. The salivary-like branching pattern of the mammary epithelium in combination with the embryonic salivary mesenchyme is possibly the most striking example of this [28].

Parallel with the restriction of their differentiative potentialities, these epithelia gradually acquire independence of the specific mesenchymal influences during embryogenesis. This is shown in the following experiments [37]. An explant of the presumptive pancreatic region of the gut surrounded by its homologous mesenchyme forms pancreatic acini *in vitro* at an early stage and fails to do so if the mesenchyme is removed or replaced by a heterologous mesenchyme. Somewhat later stages of the epithelial anlage still require mesenchymal support, but this becomes less specific. Finally, the epithelium reaches a stage at which the mesenchymal influence can be simulated by high concentrations of embryo extract in the culture medium in the total absence of mesenchymal cells. Comparable phases of interactions of varying specificity have been demonstrated in the development of the liver epithelium [31]. The liver endoderm is determined by the liver–heart mesoderm at the five-somite stage of the chick embryo, and it cannot be replaced by any heterologous mesenchyme. Later, this determined endoderm still requires mesenchymal support in order to become organized into typical liver cords, but now the effect can be simulated by several heterologous mesenchymes.

If experiments on the varying specificity of the inductive interactions are tentatively generalized and simplified, the scheme could be as follows. During embryogenesis, extrinsic influences guide the differentiation of cells and cell populations through various phases. Initially pluripotent cells become determined and their developmental options are restricted. Subsequently, their organization into synchronized structures is governed by less and less specific permissive influences (organogenetic tissue interactions). Finally, stages of increasing stability are reached, and stabilizing influences are replaced by maintenance effects that are supportive in nature and probably act through non-specific channels. Obviously, the scheme is simplified and it needs adjustment when tested with different tissues and organs. For example, the constantly renewed epidermis may represent a target-cell population which never reaches the stable stage of differentiation and, instead of the maintenance effects, requires constant guidance from the underlying dermis. The scheme also emphasizes the great multitude of interactive processes usually lumped under the title 'embryonic induction' and makes it obvious that the various types of interactive mechanisms should be considered separately. This is what we shall do next.

3.5.4 INDUCTIVE COMMUNICATION IS ACHIEVED IN DIFFERENT WAYS

Signal substances are still poorly characterized

The different cases of tissue interactions studied have not so far provided much detailed information about the transmission of inductive stimuli between cells. There have been difficulties in characterizing more closely the signal substances operating in normal development (see p. 188). Until more information is available we must content ourselves with discussing the transmission of inductive stimuli at another level. We can discuss the biological systems studied according to what is known about the distance over which interaction takes place, about the extracellular structures lying between the interacting cells, and about the effects of experimental modifications of the tissue interactions. Various modes of transmission can be postulated. In fact, many of them have been demonstrated in the *in vitro* model systems tested (Table 3.5.1).

Table 3.5.1. Alternative modes of transmission of signal substances.

LONG-RANGE TRANSMISSION (interspace up to 50 000 nm)
  Diffusion
  Matrix interaction

SHORT-RANGE TRANSMISSION (interspace from 5 to 10 nm)
  Exchange of small molecules
  Interaction of surface-associated compounds

Long-range transmission of signals is possible

Neural induction is a good example of a tissue interaction where the need for the physical closeness of the tissues involved has been studied carefully. Spemann's early studies on amphibian embryos dating back to the 1930s already indicated that certain tissues, even if killed, can induce the differentiation of gastrula ectoderm, and this capability can further be transferred to agar in a cell-free form [2]. These experiments gave rise to the idea of transmission of signals by diffusion. This idea gained support from the discovery that purified cell-free extracts can mediate both neural and meso-dermal inductions [48, 50]. Ultrastructural studies showed thereafter that *in vivo* the ectoderm lay well apart from the mesoderm at the time of primary induction [26]. It was also demonstrated that neuralization

could be evoked by the natural inductor tissue across porous filters in the absence of cytoplasmic contacts [39, 55].

The classic lens induction is another recent example of long-range transmission of signal substances. In these experiments a directive effect of the optic vesicle was first demonstrated, as the belly epidermis of a 2-day chick embryo developed lentoids when combined with the natural lens inductor [24]. The model system has also been applied to transfilter experiments. All filter types tested allowed the passage of an inductive trigger, as did the dialysis membrane restricting the size of the passing molecules to 12 000 mol. wt [25].

In many other cases, long-range transmission of an inductive influence is also thought to play a role. The events that can be induced through porous filters include the formation of pancreatic acini and the initiation of cartilage formation in the somites while the vertebral column develops. In these two cases, the responding tissues have already started to differentiate, the induction having a merely supportive function. This was demonstrated by experiments in which the normal inducer had been omitted and the extent of cartilage formation was increased by supplementing the culture medium with cell-free tissue extracts or serum of heterologous origin [16]. These results emphasize the need for caution in interpreting results obtained *in vitro* from induction of differentiation.

Cell contacts mediate inductions

The original object of the transfilter technique, illustrated in Fig. 3.5.7, was to exclude cytoplasmic contacts between interacting tissues. Recent ultra-structural studies have shown that cell processes can penetrate into filters with pore sizes of 0.1 μm or larger and that some earlier data may have to be re-evaluated [59]. The induction of kidney tubulogenesis serves well as an example. It was originally shown that induction took place when the interacting tissues were separated by a Millipore filter, 20–30 μm thick, with an average pore size of 0.45 μm [18]. An inverse relation was found between the pore size and the thickness of the filters across which induction took place. After successful induction, no cytoplasm was found in the 0.1 μm pores of filters less than 18 μm thick. This was thought to mean that transmissible substances were probably involved in the inductive effect. Later on, a minimum pore size of

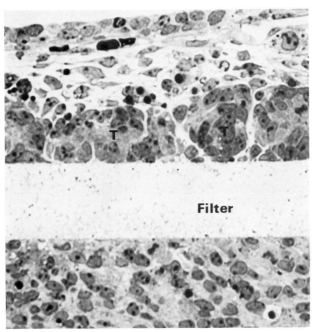

Fig. 3.5.7. Illustration of Grobstein's transfilter method of kidney tubule induction [18]. Metanephrogenic mesenchyme is separated from the adjoining epithelial bud and placed on a filter disc in juxtaposition to a piece of spinal cord tissue sealed to the opposite side with agar. Transfilter induction leads to the formation of kidney tubules (T) in the mesenchyme.

0.15 μm was established for the transmission of tubulogenic induction with Nuclepore filters (which, unlike Millipore filters, have a uniform pore size). Cytoplasmic processes were found to cross the pores of the Nuclepore filters that allowed induction but not in those that restricted it (Fig. 3.5.8). Hence it was apparent that diffusion could no longer be regarded as the only explanation for the transmission of kidney tubulogenesis induction. In fact, induction mediated by cell contacts may be the mechanism most likely to account for this.

Another advantage of the transfilter technique is that the contact between the inducing and responding tissues can be broken whenever wished. It is thus possible to measure the time needed for transmission of the inductive stimulus. The following experiment was performed to extract the actual transfer time from the minimum time for total induction, which consists also of other events such as tissue adaptation to conditions *in vitro*. Kidney mesenchyme was cultured in close proximity to the inducing spinal-cord tissue, with either one or two Millipore filters interposed. After varying periods of time the mesenchyme was removed from the filter and grown alone. With one filter interposed the minimal induction time needed was some 18 h. An additional filter prolonged the required induction time by more than 12 h. The diffusion rates of a number of substances, including virus particles, was then tested with the filters. It was calculated from the diffusion data that the inducing substance would have to be irrationally large in order to satisfy the results of the minimum induction time [36]. More recently, induction has been shown to be a function of the contact area between the interactants and the time of contact. In these studies, Nuclepore filters with varying pore diameters and densities were employed and the response was quantified by counting the tubules (Fig. 3.5.9).

As for transfilter kidney tubulogenesis in general, the transmission of the inductive influence cannot be explained simply by the diffusion of molecules across the interspace. It depends on the cytoplasmic processes extending from the inducing tissue and making contacts with the responding cells. In other systems, direct contacts between interacting cells *in vivo* have been also reported, as in the case of rat submandibular salivary gland [8] and when ameloblasts are determined in the development of the tooth germ [46, 47]. However, it is still an open question whether direct membrane interactions are involved in these cases, or whether the inductive interactions involve cell-surface-associated or pericellular molecules.

The intercellular matrix affects morphogenesis

In most adult organs the epithelial component is separated from the mesenchyme by a layer of extracellular material called basement membrane. Similarly, in developing organs the epithelium is covered by a layer of extracellular material. It is likely that certain components of this material are involved in interactions between neighbouring tissues. The developing embryonic tooth rudiment (p. 180) is a useful model in this respect, especially when studied *in vitro* by the transfilter technique described above.

In the developing tooth, epithelio-mesenchymal interaction takes place between the cells of the enamel-producing epithelium and the dentine-forming mesenchymal cells of the papilla. The two types of cells are separated by a 10–20 μm thick extracellular matrix (Fig.

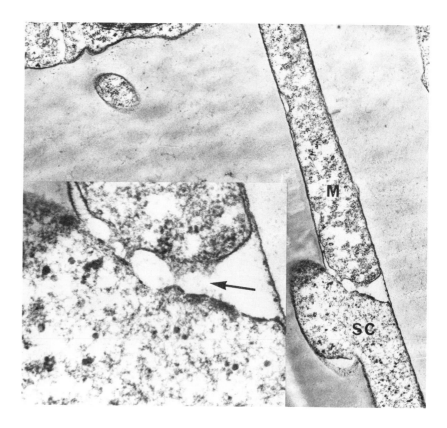

Fig. 3.5.8. Electron micrograph of transfilter kidney tubule induction showing cytoplasmic processes within the 0.5 µm channels of a Nuclepore filter allowing induction. Insert demonstrates the close apposition of a mesenchymal (M) and a spinal cord (SC) process. Magnification, ×17 600, insert ×45 600. (From [60].)

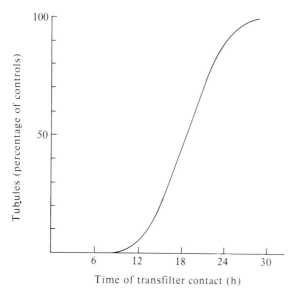

Fig. 3.5.9. Number of tubules in transfilter experiments as a function of contact time. (After [36].)

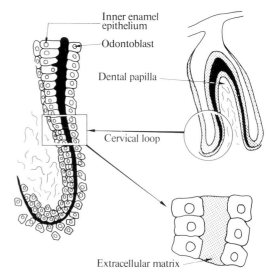

Fig. 3.5.10. Diagram of a developing tooth primordium. Epithelial cells (ameloblasts) are separated from the mesenchymal cells (odontoblasts) by a layer of extracellular material. (After [45].)

3.5.10). If the two interactants are cultured separated by a filter with pores small enough to prevent contact between the cells, no differentiation of mesenchymal cells into odontoblasts takes place [47]. Large-pore filters allowing cell processes to make such contacts do not prevent odontoblast differentiation.

The formation of vertebral cartilage in the chick embryo is another good example of the action of the extracellular matrix in an embryonic cell interaction. In the embryo, some somatic cells migrate away from the main bulk of the somite, which goes on to form the muscle layer beneath the skin and the main muscle blocks of the body (the myotomes); the migratory cells condense around the notocord and neural tube and develop the dense extracellular matrix containing collagen and proteoglycans which is characteristic of adult cartilage cells [35, 56]. If the neural tube and notocord are dissected from the living embryo, then no organized vertebral cartilage is formed and it is therefore reasonable to suppose that the migratory cells must interact with these two organs in order to form cartilage (reviewed in [21]).

Attention has concentrated on the action of the notocord in the induction of vertebral cartilage (reviewed [29]). The notocord is surrounded by a sheath of type-I and type-II collagen; the latter type of collagen is found in adult birds only in cartilage and its presence in the embryonic notocord is surprising (see Chapter 6.2 for the structure of collagen). In culture, the notocord synthesizes and secretes type-II collagen and glycosaminoglycans such as chondroitin sulphate and heparin sulphate. It also secretes proteoglycans which consist of a protein core to which the glycosaminoglycans may be attached. It has been possible to prove that at least two of the secreted products of the notocord can induce chondrogenesis by somite cells. When somites are cultured alone, then no cartilage is formed; when somites are cultured with collagen or with proteoglycans or with both, then cartilage develops.

The biochemical changes in the responding somite cells are slight on a per cell basis. That is, even before this necessary interaction with notocord the migratory somite cells are already synthesizing and secreting glycosaminoglycans, proteoglycans, and collagen; they are said to have a 'chondrogenic bias' in their metabolism because all these syntheses are characteristic of mature cartilage cells, and the effect of the inducer is only to double or so the rate of synthesis of these products [29], although an additional increase in the size

of the sulphated glycosaminoglycans has been reported [30].

The principal effects of the inducer on somites *in vitro* seem to be to increase cell viability, to promote cell division and to increase the proportion of the secreted products which are deposited around the cells. So apparently slight changes in the rate of synthesis of these products can lead to dramatic changes in cell phenotype. The problem with comprehending this system is similar to that encountered with other embryonic inductive interactions. It is difficult to discover whether the collagen and proteoglycan released by the notocord have an immediate and direct action on the metabolism of the migratory cells, or whether the effect of these molecules is indirect and is mediated through an influence on cell viability, cell division, and cell condensation and crowding. The same problem applies, for example, to corneal development, where Meier and Hay [34] have demonstrated that exogenous glycosaminoglycans or collagens stimulate the synthesis of sulphated glycosaminoglycans in the corneal epithelium (cell behaviour during the formation of cornea is described in detail in Chapter 4.3).

From numerous tissue culture experiments it has also become evident that the substratum on which cells grow affects their growth characteristics. Experiments demonstrate that embryonic epidermis requires dermis or collagen as a substratum for morphogenesis to occur *in vitro* [12, 62]. Embryonic muscle differentiation takes place preferentially on a collagen substratum [22]. The effect of collagen on the morphogenesis of salivary gland, ureter bud, corneal epithelium, pancreas and lung have also been described [20, 23, 63, 64]. Again, the role of collagen is not known. It may act in an indirect way, affecting cell adhesion to substratum, which would be required, for example, for secretion of compounds involved in interaction or differentiation [3, 5].

The participation of extracellular material in epithelial morphogenesis has also been studied in the mouse-embryo salivary gland. During the development of the gland, newly synthesized glycosaminoglycans accumulate on the surface of the salivary epithelium, especially at the sites of epithelial branching within the mesenchyme [4]. If the epithelium is separated from the mesenchyme and treated with hyaluronidase and collagenase, the explant loses its lobes and becomes a round mass. Upon further culture in contact with salivary mesenchyme, it resumes its branching morphogenesis

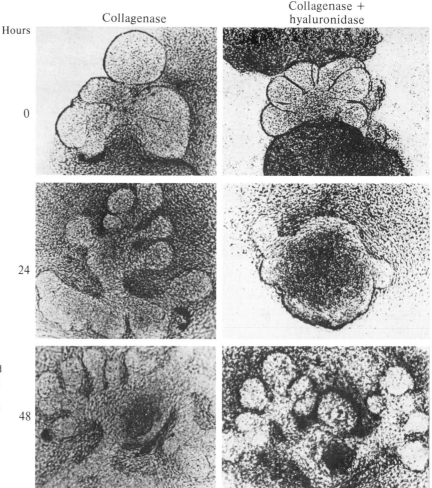

Hours

Collagenase

Collagenase +
hyaluronidase

0

24

48

Fig. 3.5.11. Mouse submandibular salivary gland epithelium shows normal development at 24 and 48 h, after collagenese treatment (0.20 µm/ml) and subsequent cultivation in direct contact with salivary mesenchyme. If hyaluronidase treatment is included, the epithelium rounds up to form a mass which shows formation only at 24 h or cultivation with salivary mesenchyme. During further cultivation normal morphogenesis is acquired. (From [3].)

(Fig. 3.5.11). The glycosaminoglycans are spread evenly over the surface in the rounded mass, but when the branching resumes they concentrate at the sites of branch formation. On the other hand, the distal ends of the branches lose glycosaminoglycans more rapidly than the clefts between the branches, but only in the presence of mesenchyme. The mesenchyme is not itself involved in the synthesis or deposition of the lamina, since the epithelium alone produces an intact lamina. If the epithelium is freed from mesenchyme without enzyme treatment, so that most of the surface mucopolysaccharides remain, it retains its shape and continues its branching morphogenesis if grown in direct combination with fresh mesenchyme. Even if the isolated epithelium is treated with only a low concentration of collagenase, branching continues normally [3].

In summary, the dependence of normal salivary-gland morphogenesis on an intact cell coat at the epithelial surface seems to be attributable to hyaluronidase-sensitive acid mucopolysaccharide protein complexes (proteoglycans). Their mode of action is still unknown. The mesenchyme may, however, influence changes in epithelial morphogenesis by selective remodelling of the glycosaminoglycans of the basal lamina.

It is impressive how early in development extracellular matrix molecules are to be found in the embryo. In the 16-cell, compacted mouse morula (Fig. 3.5.12), a non-collagenous glycoprotein laminin appears intercellularly, lining the cell borders [32, 58]. During the formation of germ layers at and after the blastocyst stage, in addition to laminin, type-IV collagen [1, 32] (Fig. 3.5.13) and fibronectin glycoprotein are deposited

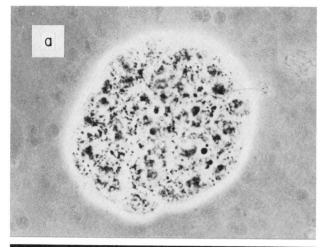

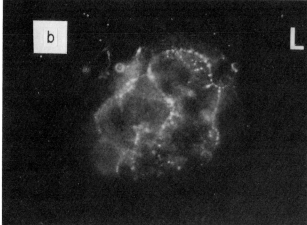

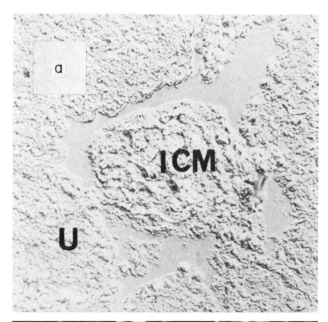

Fig. 3.5.12. A 16- and 32-cell mouse embryo after indirect immunofluorescence staining for extracellular laminin. ×960. From [32]. (a) Phase-contrast view of the formaldehyde-fixed compacted morula with zona pellucida removed. (b) In immunofluorescence, extracellular laminin (L) fluorescence is seen lining cell surface contours of the embryo. The cell lineage of the mouse is illustrated in Chapter 2.4.

in the extracellular matrix between the germ layers [57]. In later stages of development, these matrix components are found in the extra-embryonic membranes and other tissue structures (Fig. 3.5.14). Although it is not known at present what role these molecules play in cellular interactions during early development, the various germ layers and tissue derivatives all seem to have a scaffold of extracellular matrix material that could serve as an adhesive substratum and a morphogenetic frame for tissue organization.

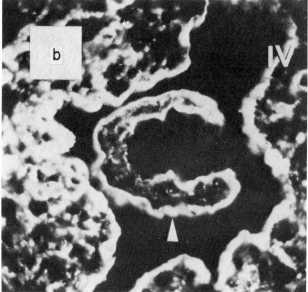

Fig. 3.5.13. Implanting 5-day mouse embryo at early egg cylinder stage stained for type-IV collagen immunofluorescence. ×960. From [32]. (a) Nomarski differential interference contrast micrograph. ICM, inner cell mass; U, uterine wall. (b) In immunofluorescence type-IV collagen staining is seen between ectoderm and endoderm layers of the ICM and in the nascent Reichert's membrane (arrowhead). The basement membrane under uterine epithelium and the uterine mucosal stroma also stain positively.

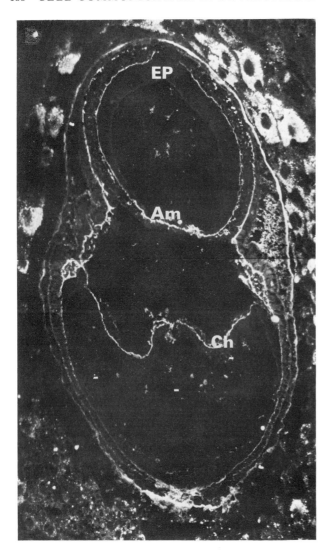

Fig. 3.5.14. Mid-sagittal section of an 8-day mouse embryo after indirect immunofluorescence staining for fibronectin (from [57]). Fibronectin fluorescence is seen between the different germ layers in the embryo proper (EP) and in the extraembryonic membranes including amnion (Am) and chorion (Ch). Magnification, ×450.

3.5.5 MOLECULAR MECHANISMS OF INDUCTION ARE STILL UNKNOWN

From this survey of available data, it appears likely that both specific and less specific substances are involved in embryonic induction. In some cases the signals may be of quantitative significance, controlling, for instance, the amount of specific enzyme synthesis by the develop-

ing pancreatic rudiment [37]. In other cases, the signal may be of qualitative character, causing the appearance of tissue-specific products, as in the case of lens induction [24]. Although the inductive substances involved are not known, it is worth considering three principal categories.

(1) Compounds arranged spatially at the interface between cells leading to the reorientation and re-arrangement of adjacent cells.

(2) Molecules at the cell surface interacting with complementary compounds on the other cell type.

(3) Specific information molecules transmitted from one cell to another.

The possible importance of spatial arrangement and physical forces is illustrated by experiments on embryonic chick epidermis. Differentiation and proliferation are normally controlled in this tissue by the underlying dermal mesenchyme. This mesenchymal effect can be stimulated to a certain extent by a suitable concentration of embryo extract, provided that a physical substrate is available for the basal cells. Such materials as devitalized dermis, collagen gel and Millipore filters have been used with success [12].

The idea of certain 'template' molecules at the surfaces of interacting cells was put forward long ago by Weiss [61], and this system has been shown to operate in various biological interactive processes. Inductive surface interactions may include, for example, antigen–antibody or enzyme–substrate reactions, but so far there is little evidence for their existence. Differentiating cells do show surface specialization detectable as specific affinity for and recognition of like cells (Chapters 3.2 and 4.3). It is conceivable that such complementary specialization for inductive interaction can develop between cells of different types.

Evidence suggestive of the role of surface-associated molecules in inductive tissue interactions has recently been obtained in the kidney model (p. 188). The inter-action is prevented by charged polymers that probably coat the interacting cell surfaces, constituting a molecular barrier between the cells [14]. The inhibition of the synthesis of surface proteoglycans also prevents induction in a reversible manner [15].

Finally, the classic hypothesis of transmissible information molecules should be mentioned. Most complete information about molecules of this kind mimicking normal induction is derived from experiments on primary induction. Tiedemann [49, 50] distinguishes between a 'neural' and a 'vegetalizing' inductor, the latter leading to both mesodermal and endodermal inductions. High concentrations of his purified vegetalizing factor result in endodermal inductions, whereas lower concentrations lead to the mesodermalization of the target cells.

The chemistry of the neuralizing factor, distributed widely in plant and animal tissues, is unknown, but it has been shown to resist both short-term heat treatment and digestion with RNase. The vegetalizing factor has a molecular weight of some 30000, and it is inactivated by heat and by proteolytic enzymes [49, 50]. A recent study suggests an interesting difference in the action of the two factors [50]. When a crude preparation containing both neuralizing and vegetalizing factors is bound covalently to Sepharose beads, the neuralizing action is not affected, while the vegetalizing effect is lost. After the enzymatic cleavage of the Sepharose preparation, the vegetalizing action is, however, fully restored. It is plausible that the vegetalizing factor acts upon the intracellular compartment of the target cells, whereas the neural factor acts upon the receptors of the plasma membrane [51].

3.5.6 REFERENCES

1 Adamson E.D. & Ayers S.E. (1979) The localization and synthesis of some collagen types in developing mouse embryos. *Cell*, **16**, 953–965.
2 Bautzmann H., Holtfreter J., Spemann H. & Mangold O. (1932) Versuche zur Analyse der Induktionsmittel in der Embryonalentwicklung. *Naturwissenschaften*, **20**, 971–974.
3 Bernfield M.R. & Wessells N.K. (1970) Intra- and extracellular control of epithelial morphogenesis. *Devl. Biol. Suppl.*, **4**, 195–249.
4 Bernfield M.R., Banerjee S.D. & Cohn R.H. (1972) Dependence of salivary epithelial morphology and branching morphogenesis upon acid mucopolysaccharide-protein (proteoglycan) at the epithelial surface. *J. Cell Biol.*, **52**, 674–689.
5 Bernfield M.R., Cohn R.H. & Banerjee S.D. (1973) Glycosaminoglycans and epithelial organ formation. *Am. Zool.*, **13**, 1067–1083.
6 Billingham R.E. & Silvers W.K. (1967) Studies on the conservation of epidermal specificities of skin and certain mucosas in adult mammals. *J. exp. Med.*, **125**, 429–446.
7 Billingham R.E. & Silvers W.K. (1968) Dermoepidermal interactions and epithelial specificity. In *Epithelial–Mesenchymal Interactions* (Eds R. Fleischmajer & R.E. Billingham), pp. 252–266. Williams & Wilkins, Baltimore.
8 Cutler L.S. & Chaudhry A.P. (1973) Intercellular contacts at the epithelial-mesenchymal interface during the prenatal development of the rat submandibular gland. *Devl. Biol.*, **33**, 229–240.
9 Dhouailly D. (1975) Formation of cutaneous appendages in dermo-epidermal recombinations between reptiles, birds and mammals. *Wilhelm Roux' Archiv.*, **177**, 323–332.
10 Dhouailly D., Rogers G.E. & Sangal P. (1978) The specification of feather and scale protein synthesis in epidermal–dermal recombinations. *Devl. Biol.*, **65**, 58–68.
11 Dieterlen-Lièvre F. & Hadorn H.B. (1972) Développement des enzymes exocrines dans les bourgeons pancréatiques chez l'embryon de poulet en présence de mésenchymes homologues et hétérologues. *Wilhelm Roux' Archiv.*, **170**, 175–184.
12 Dodson J.W. (1967) The differentiation of epidermis. I. The interrelationship of epidermis and dermis in embryonic chicken skin. *J. Embryol. exp. Morph.*, **17**, 83–105.
13 Ede D.A. (1978) *An Introduction to Developmental Biology*. Blackie, Glasgow.
14 Ekblom P., Nordling S. & Saxén L. (1978) Inhibition of kidney tubule induction by charged polymers. *Cell Differ.*, **7**, 345–353.
15 Ekblom P., Lash J.W., Lehtonen E., Nordling S. & Saxén L. (1979) Inhibition of morphogenetic cell interactions by 6-diazo-5-oxo-norleucine (DON). *Expl. Cell Res*, **121**, 121–126.
16 Ellison M.L. & Lash J.W. (1971) Environmental enhancement of *in vitro* chondrogenesis. *Devl. Biol.*, **26**, 486–496.
17 Fleischmajer R. & Billingham R.E. (1968) *Epithelial-Mesenchymal Interactions*. Williams & Wilkins, Baltimore.
18 Grobstein C. (1956) Transfilter induction of tubules in mouse metanephrogenic mesenchyme. *Expl. Cell Res.*, **10**, 424–440.
19 Grobstein C. (1967) Mechanisms of organogenetic tissue interaction. *Natn. Cancer Inst. Monogr.*, **26**, 279–299.
20 Grobstein C. & Cohen J. (1965) Collagenase: Effect on the morphogenesis of embryonic salivary epithelium in vitro. *Science, N.Y.*, **150**, 626–628.
21 Hall B.K. (1978) *Developmental and Cellular Skeletal Biology*. Academic Press, London.
22 Hauschka S.D. & Konigsberg I.R. (1966) The influence of collagen on the development of muscle clones. *Proc. natl Acad. Sci., USA*, **55**, 119–126.
23 Hay E.D. & Meier S. (1976) Stimulation of corneal differentiation by interaction between cell surface and extracellular matrix. II. Further studies on the nature and site of transfilter "induction". *Devl. Biol.*, **52**, 141–157.
24 Karkinen-Jääskeläinen M. (1978) Permissive and directive interactions in lens induction. *J. Embryol. exp. Morph.*, **44**, 167–179.
25 Karkinen-Jääskeläinen M. (1978) Transfilter lens induction in avian embryo. *Differentiation*, **12**, 31–37.
26 Kelley R.O. (1969) An electron microscopic study of chorda-mesoderm-neurectoderm association in gastrulae of a toad, *Xenopus laevis*. *J. exp. Zool.*, **172**, 153–180.
27 Kollar E.J. & Baird G.R. (1970) Tissue interaction in embryonic mouse tooth germs. II. The inductive role of the dental papilla. *J. Embryol. exp. Morph.*, **24**, 173–186.
28 Kratochwil K. (1969) Organ specificity in mesenchymal induction demonstrated in the embryonic development of the mammary gland of the mouse. *Devl. Biol.*, **20**, 46–71.
29 Lash J.W. & Vasan N.S. (1977) Tissue interactions and extracellular matrix components. In *Cell and Tissue Interactions* (Eds J.W. Lash & M.M. Burger), pp. 101–114. Raven Press, New York.
30 Lash J.W. & Vasan N.S. (1978) Somite chondrogenesis *in vitro*. Stimulation by exogenous extracellular matrix components. *Devl. Biol.*, **66**, 151–171.
31 LeDouarin N. (1964) Induction de l'endoderme pré-hépatique par

le mésoderme de l'aire cardiaque chez l'embryon de poulet. *J. Embryol. exp. Morph.*, **12**, 651–664.

32 Leivo I., Vaheri A., Timpl R. & Wartiovaara J. (1980) Appearance and distribution of collagens and laminin in the early mouse embryo. *Devl. Biol.*, **76**, 100–114.

33 McLoughlin C.B. (1963) Mesenchymal influences on epithelial differentiation. In *Cell Differentiation*. Symposia of the Society for Experimental Biology, No. 17, pp. 359–389. Cambridge University Press, Cambridge.

34 Meier S. & Hay E.D. (1974) Stimulation of extracellular matrix synthesis in the developing cornea by glycosaminoglycans. *Proc. natl Acad. Sci., USA*, **71**, 2310–2313.

35 Muir H. (1977) Structure and function of proteoglycan of cartilage and cell matrix interactions. In *Cell and Tissue Interactions* (Eds J.W. Lash & M.M. Burger). Raven Press, New York.

36 Nordling S., Miettinen H., Wartiovaara J. & Saxén L. (1971) Transmission and spread of embryonic induction. I. Temporal relationships in transfilter induction of kidney tubules in vitro. *J. Embryol. exp. Morph.*, **26**, 231–252.

37 Rutter W.J., Wessells N.K. & Grobstein C. (1964) Control of specific synthesis on the developing pancreas. *Natn. Cancer Inst. Monogr.*, **13**, 51–65.

38 Rutter W.J., Kemp J.D., Bradshaw W.S., Clark W.R., Ronzio R.A. & Sanders T.G. (1968) Regulation of specific protein synthesis in cytodifferentiation. *J. Cell Physiol.*, Suppl. 1, **72**, 1–18.

39 Saxén L. (1961) Transfilter neural induction of amphibian ectoderm. *Devl. Biol.*, **3**, 140–152.

40 Saxén L. & Lehtonen E. (1978) Transfilter induction of kidney tubules as a function of the extent and duration of intercellular contacts. *J. Embryol. exp. Morph.*, **47**, 97–109.

41 Saxén L. & Toivonen S. (1961) The two-gradient hypothesis in primary induction. The combined effect of two types of inductors mixed in different ratios. *J. Embryol. exp. Morph.*, **9**, 514–533.

42 Saxén L. & Toivonen S. (1962) *Primary Embryonic Induction.* Academic Press, London.

43 Saxén L., Toivonen S. & Vainio T. (1964) initial stimulus and subsequent interactions in embryonic induction. *J. Embryol. exp. Morph.*, **12**, 333–338.

44 Sengel P., Dhouailly D. & Kieny M. (1969) Aptitude des constituants cutanés de l'aptérie médioventrale du poulet à former des plumes. *Devl. Biol.*, **19**, 436–446.

45 Slavkin H.C. & Bavetta L.A. (1968) Odontogenic epithelial-mesenchymal interactions *in vitro. J. dent. Res.*, **47**, 779–785.

46 Slavkin H.C. & Bringas P. (1976) Epithelial-mesenchyme interactions during odontogenesis. IV. Morphological evidence for direct heterotypic cell–cell contacts. *Devl. Biol.*, **50**, 428–442.

47 Thesleff I., Lehtonen E., Wartiovaara J. & Saxén L. (1977) Interference of tooth differentiation with interposed filters. *Devl. Biol.*, **58**, 197–203.

48 Tiedemann H. (1971) Extrinsic and intrinsic information transfer in early differentiation of amphibian cells. In *Control Mechanisms of Growth and Differentiation* (Eds D.D. Davies & M. Balls), pp. 223–234. Cambridge University Press, Cambridge.

49 Tiedemann H. (1976) Pattern formation in early developmental stages of amphibian embryos. *J. Embryol. exp. Morph.*, **35**, 437–444.

50 Tiedemann H. (1978) Chemical approach to the inducing agents. In *Organizer. A Milestone of a Half-century from Spemann* (Eds O. Nakamura & S. Toivonen), pp. 91–117. Elsevier/North-Holland, Amsterdam.

51 Tiedemann H. & Born J. (1978) Biological activity of vegetalizing and neuralizing inducing factors after the binding to BAC-Cellulose and CNBr-Sepharose. *Wilhelm Roux' Archiv.*, **184**, 285–299.

52 Toivonen S. (1953) Bone marrow of the guinea-pig as a mesodermal inductor in implantation experiments with embryos of *Triturus. J. Embryol. exp. Morph.*, **1**, 97–104.

53 Toivonen S. & Saxén L. (1955) The simultaneous inducing action of liver and bone marrow of the guinea-pig in implantation and explantation experiments with embryos of *Triturus. Expl. Cell Res.*, Suppl., **3**, 346–357.

54 Toivonen S. & Saxén L. (1968) Morphogenetic interaction of presumptive neural and mesodermal cells mixed in different ratios. *Science, N.Y.*, **159**, 539–540.

55 Toivonen S., Tarin D., Saxén L., Tarin P.J. & Wartiovaara J. (1975) Transfilter studies on neural induction in the newt. *Differentiation*, **4**, 1–7.

56 Trelstad R.L. (1977) Mesenchymal cell polarity and morphogenesis of chick cartilage. *Devl. Biol.*, **59**, 153–163.

57 Wartiovaara J., Leivo I. & Vaheri A. (1979) Expression of the cell surface-associated glycoprotein, fibronectin, in the early mouse embryo. *Devl. Biol.*, **69**, 247–257.

58 Wartiovaara J., Leivo I. & Vaheri A. (1980) Matrix glycoproteins in early mouse development and in differentiation of teratocarcinoma cells. In *The Cell Surface: Mediator of Developmental Processes.* (Eds S. Subtelny & N.K. Wessells), pp. 305–324. Academic Press, New York.

59 Wartiovaara J., Lehtonen E., Nordling S. & Saxén L. (1972) Do membrane filters prevent cell contacts? *Nature, Lond.*, **238**, 407–408.

60 Wartiovaara J., Nordling S., Lehtonen E. & Saxén L. (1974) Transfilter induction of kidney tubules. Correlation with cytoplasmic penetration into Nucleopore filters. *J. Embryol. exp. Morph.*, **31**, 667–682.

61 Weiss P. (1947) The problem of specificity in growth and development. *Yale J. Biol. Med.*, **19**, 235–78.

62 Wessells N.K. (1964) Substrate and nutrient effect upon epidermal basal cell orientation and proliferation *Proc. natl Acad. Sci., USA*, **52**, 252–259.

63 Wessells N.K. & Cohen J.H. (1966) The influence of collagen and embryo extract on the development of pancreatic epithelium. *Expl. Cell Res.*, **43**, 680–684.

64 Wessells N.K. & Cohen J.H. (1968) Effects of collagenase on developing epithelia *in vitro*: lung, ureteric bud, and pancreas. *Devl. Biol.*, **18**, 294–309.

Chapter 3.6
Cell Recognition in Plants
R.B. Knox and A.E. Clarke

3.6.1   INTRODUCTION

Although there are important differences between plant and animal cells the capacity for cell recognition is essential for all living systems. Cell recognition phenomena are both diverse and fundamental; for example sexual reproduction in animals, vascular plants and between different mating types in bacteria and fungi is dependent on recognition of a compatible mating partner. Another example in which the capacity of cells for mutual recognition is dramatically displayed is the growth and development of a multicellular organism. Within each tissue of each organ, the cells are precisely arranged and coordinated to perform particular functions. The development of a characteristic morphology remains one of the most intriguing but yet poorly understood biological phenomena; it undoubtedly depends on a multiplicity of control mechanisms such as temporal and spatial variations in the concentrations of growth factors and hormones (Chapters 5.3 and 5.4) but, for animal tissue at least, it also depends on direct contacts between the surfaces of adjacent cells. The role of cell–cell recognition in development of animal tissues is illustrated by their 'positioning'; that is, the phenomena in which cells take up, maintain or reassume some non-random pattern [11]. For example, embryogenesis involves formation of a disc of cells during the cleavage period. These cells then move and slide into positions characteristic of the embryonic organs. This capacity of embryonic tissues and cells to sort themselves from arbitrary to precise orientations can be illustrated experimentally by watching dissociated embryonic cells sort themselves into organ-specific aggregates (Chapter 3.2).

In plants, differentiation proceeds by a different pattern—the embryo is formed by a series of formative cell divisions and, after seed germination, growth to form the plant occurs at the root and shoot apical meristems (Chapter 2.3). Although there is no requirement for the movement and positioning of embryonic cells, the walls of adjacent cells are in contact and there is a requirement for control over the planes and numbers of cell divisions. The maintenance of the integrity of the organism is demonstrated experimentally by the rejection of stem grafts between unrelated species.

Another situation in which the capacity for cell recognition is apparent is in the defence of cells against invading viruses, bacteria or fungi. For both plants and animals, infection is the exception rather than the rule. There is also a range of symbiotic relationships; for example, between algal and fungal cells in the lichens, between bacteria and higher plants to form root nodules, and between two flowering plants, such as mistletoes and their host plants; all these interactions depend on the capacity of the cells for recognition.

3.6.2   NATURE OF CELL RECOGNITION

Cell recognition is the initial event of cell–cell communication which elicits a defined biochemical, physiological or morphological response. In most cases the chemical basis for these recognition processes remains to be elucidated, but in some systems significant progress has been made. Two principles have emerged. It is generally believed that the cell surface is the transducer of intercellular signals; that is, the receipt and translation of signals is largely a cell-surface phenomenon. Secondly, it is dependent on formation of a molecular complex between the signal and a membrane-bound receptor. The specificity is twofold—it is specific for receipt of a particular signal and for a particular cellular response.

The specific receipt of signals involved in mutual recognition occurs between sterically complementary molecules, rather like enzyme–substrate and antigen–antibody reactions. An enormous variety of chemical signals interact with the corresponding cell-surface receptors and although the existence of an apparently common effect of ligand–receptor binding at the membrane and a cellular response is bound to be an oversimplification, this approach has a logical simplicity from the evolutionary standpoint, and has been expressed in different ways by three Nobel Laureates:

Jacques Monod: 'I am convinced that in the end, only the shape-recognizing and stereospecific binding properties of proteins will provide the key to these phenomena.'

Linus Pauling: 'the complementariness of molecular structure of some sort is responsible for biological specificity in general.'

Sir MacFarlane Burnet: 'all those positive recognitions between cells are readily interpreted as arising from specific union, reversible or irreversible, between chemical groupings on the surface of interacting cells.'

Receipt of signals at the cell surface

There are two general mechanisms by which cell recognition may operate (Fig. 3.6.1). In the first mechanism, it is assumed that the cell surface contains one or more pairs of complementary molecules (Fig. 3.6.1a and b). It is envisaged that at least one partner in the interaction is proteinaceous in nature. One of the most studied examples of this mechanism is the receipt of antigen by specific IgG molecules at the lymphocyte membrane. In another group of cell recognition reactions, the surface receptor is carbohydrate in nature and recognition is mediated by an interaction between the surface carbohydrate and a complementary protein or glycoprotein receptor on the interacting cell surface. For animal cells, the carbohydrate involved in these interactions is believed to be associated with the glycoprotein or glycolipid components of the cell membrane. The receptors for these saccharide components on the interacting cell are either proteins or glycoproteins which belong to a class of molecules known as *lectins*. A particular version of this model is that the recognition depends on the binding of a cell-surface enzyme, a glycosyl transferase, to its substrate on an adjacent cell. The second major mechanism assumes that the cells are bound together by an extracellular multivalent ligand which interacts with receptors on adjacent cells. This model was first derived from investigations of species-specific sorting of sponge cells (Fig. 3.6.1c).

Each version of the model depends on the nature of the membrane components: the glycoproteins, glycolipids and proteins. These components are embedded in the double-lipid bilayer of the membrane. There are two classes of embedded components—the *integral* components, which span the bilayer, and the *peripheral* components, which are those associated with the membrane surface (Fig. 3.6.2). The glycoproteins commonly have an amino acid sequence rich in hydrophobic amino acids, which are embedded in the lipid bilayer. This protein component holds the saccharide components to the outer (extracellular) face—here they are ideally situated for contact and interaction with other cells. An important property of these membrane components is that they can move laterally within the lipid bilayer, but they cannot undergo flip-flop movement. It is also envisaged that there is contact between the integral glycoproteins and the cytoskeletal elements, the micro-

filaments and microtubules. The nature of the saccharide components of the glycoproteins is important in cell–cell recognition, as they hold, or have the

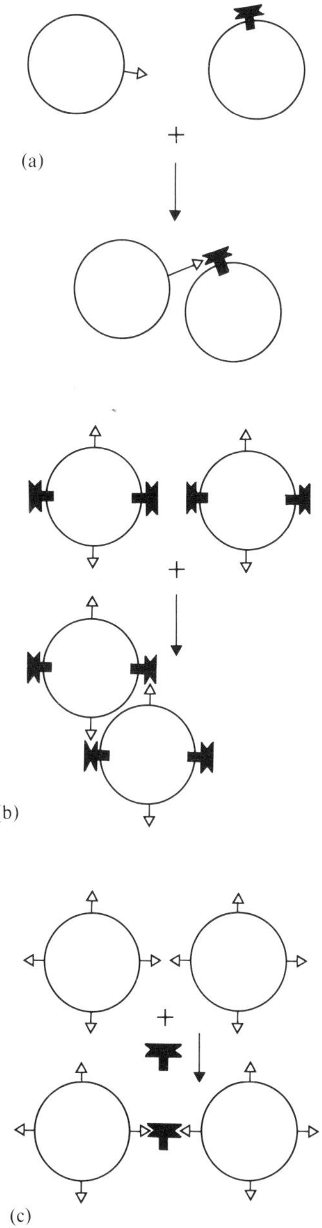

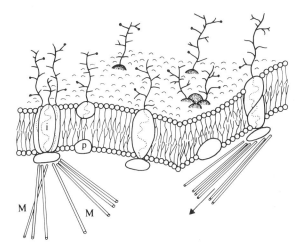

Fig. 3.6.2. Fluid mosaic model of a plasma membrane. The integral components (i) span the lipid bilayer while the peripheral components (p) are associated with the membrane surface. These components are in contact with the cytoskeletal elements, the microtubules (M) and microfilaments. (From Nicholson [2].)

potential to hold, an enormous amount of information in the type and arrangement of the component monosaccharides. Furthermore, at least some of this information can be perceived by complementary carbohydrate-binding proteins on the surface of interacting cells.

We will therefore examine the structure of these glycoproteins and the complementary carbohydrate-binding proteins (lectins) in more detail. There are six major monosaccharides associated with animal membrane glycoproteins: galactose (Gal), mannose (Man), fucose (Fuc), N-acetyl glucosamine (GlcNAc), N-acetyl galactosamine (GalNAc) and sialic acid (or N-acetyl neuraminic acid, NANA). Of these, sialic acid and fucose are found only in terminal positions. There are two major types of linkage between the carbohydrate and protein components of glycoproteins: N-glycosidic linkages between the amide nitrogen of asparagine and N-acetyl glucosamine, and O-glycosidic linkages between the hydroxyl group of serine or threonine and N-acetyl galactosamine (Fig. 3.6.3). The glycoproteins in which the polypeptide chains are linked through GalNAc → Thr/Ser groups are known as 'mucin-type' sugar chains, because they also occur in the major

Fig. 3.6.1. General mechanisms for cell–cell recognition: (a) and (b) involve contact by one or more pairs of sterically complementary molecules. (c) An extracellular multivalent ligand interacts with receptors on adjacent cells.

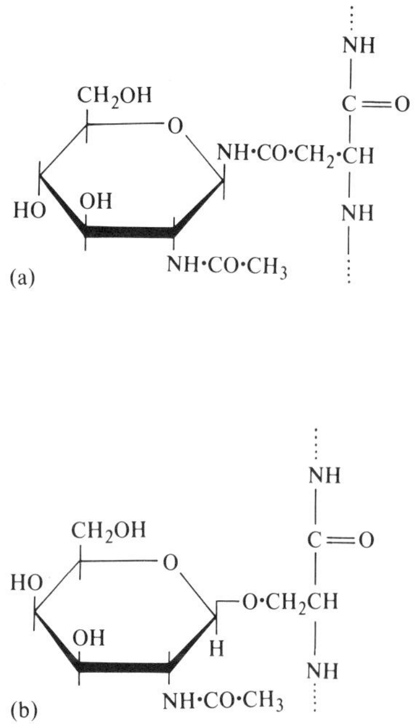

Fig. 3.6.3. The major types of linkage between carbohydrate and protein components of glycoproteins: N-glycosidic linkage between the amide nitrogen of asparagine and N-acetyl glucosamine, and an O-glycosidic linkage between the hydroxyl group of serine or threonine and N-acetyl galactosamine.

carbohydrate components of secreted mucus. The second group linked through GlcNAc → Asn contains three types of carbohydrate chains, 'complex', 'high mannose' and 'hybrid'. The 'complex' type typically contain a 'core' of two N-acetyl glucosamine and three mannose residues; in some cases fucose is associated with the core; there are several outer branches containing varying amounts of N-acetyl glucosamine, galactose and sialic acid (Fig. 3.6.4a). The 'high mannose' group contain only mannose and N-acetyl glucosamine and the same 'core' structure of two N-acetyl glucosamine and three mannose residues (Fig. 3.6.4b). The third, 'hybrid' type contains the same core unit—one substituted in the same way as the 'complex' type and the other substituted with a variable number of mannosyl residues (Fig. 3.6.4c). Variation in the nature of the surface proteins and glycoproteins confers individuality on the cell; thus different cells display different components or markers of identity. Also, cells at different stages of development may display different membrane components. One way this is achieved is by synthesis of new membrane: this process originates in the endoplasmic reticulum, where the protein is synthesized and the core saccharide units are transferred in a block from a lipid (dolichol) carrier. The nascent glycoprotein is then processed as it passes through the Golgi apparatus; other saccharide units are added sequentially from

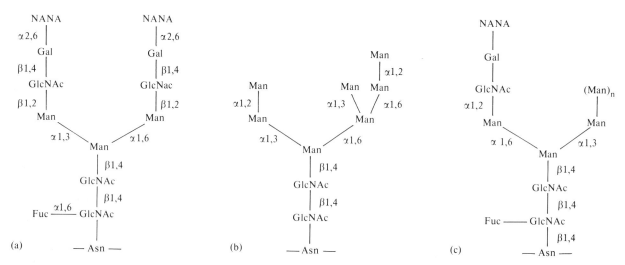

Fig. 3.6.4. Carbohydrate chains of glycoproteins linked through an N-glycosidic linkage to protein. (a) Complex. (b) High mannose. (c) Hybrid.

nucleotide sugars under the control of specific glycosyl transferases, and others are 'trimmed' or hydrolysed from the growing chain until the final form is present in

the vesicles which move through the cytoplasm and fuse with the plasma membrane (Fig. 3.6.5). In this way, the composition of the membrane and its display of markers may vary during the life of the cell [33]. Furthermore, the individual saccharide residues, or sequences of saccharide residues, may be recognized by complementary protein receptors on the interacting cell surface and thus these membrane components, protein, glycoprotein and glycolipid, are involved in cell recognition reactions in animal cells.

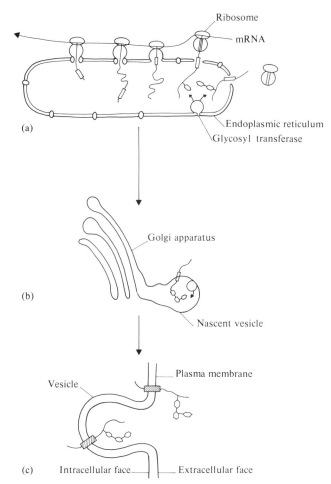

Fig. 3.6.5. Synthesis of membrane glycoproteins. (a) The process commences at the endoplasmic reticulum (e.r.) membrane. The ribosome is attached to the endoplasmic reticulum membrane by a special protein. Translation of messenger RNA occurs and the peptide is detached from the ribosome and discharged into the lumen of the rough endoplasmic reticulum. Oligosaccharide is incorporated into the peptide at this stage and is modified by the action of the glycosyl transferases which are present on the lumen face of the endoplasmic reticulum. (b) The glycoprotein migrates through the Golgi apparatus where elongation and processing of the saccharide continues. (c) The complete glycoprotein is incorporated in a vesicle which moves through the cytoplasm and fuses with the plasma membrane, so that the glycoprotein formed at the lumen of the endomembrane system is displayed at the extracellular face of the plasma membrane. (Adapted from Schachter et al. [33].)

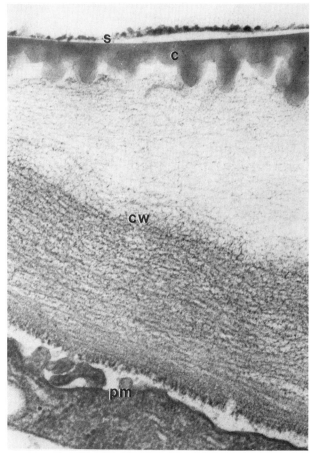

Fig. 3.6.6. Transmission electron micrograph of a stigmatic papilla of *Gladiolus:* The plasma membrane (pm) is overlaid with a cellulosic wall (cw). The microfibrils of the wall are embedded in the matrix. The wall is overlaid with a cuticle (c) which in turn has a layer(s) secreted on the outer face. Extracellular information must pass in some way through the outer cuticular and wall layers to the plasma membrane to ultimately express its effects.

For plant cells, it may well be that the membrane components act in the same way in cell–cell recognition reactions [9, 28]; certainly they have the same general composition and properties as an animal cell membrane, although sialic acid has not been detected in plant membranes. However, there is one major difference— the presence of the cellulosic cell wall which overlays the plasma membrane of plant cells (Fig. 3.6.6). This wall consists of a matrix in which microfibrils of the 1,4 β glucan cellulose are embedded (Fig. 3.6.7). These microfibrils consist of stacks of glucan chains which are precisely aligned and held by hydrogen bonds in crystal-line arrays, about 10 nm in diameter and of variable length, probably up to several hundred nanometres. The composition of the matrix components, the hemicellu-loses and pectins, varies with individual cell types; for

example, the pectins have the general form of a linear polymer of galacturonic acid which is 'kinked' by the presence of 1,2-linked rhamnosyl residues, and which is linked to arabinogalactans. Variations in the degree of methylation of the galacturonic acid, and the number of rhamnosyl residues as well as the number of side branches, occur in different cell types and different plants. There are also wide variations in the nature of the hemicelluloses; for instance, those of monocotyledons are typically arabinoxylans while those of dicotyledons are typically xyloglucans. Other polymers are also usually present and there may be wide variations in the proportions of the component monosaccharides of the individual polymers. Albersheim and his co-workers have suggested that the matrix of the primary cell wall is effectively one large macromolecule, with each of the

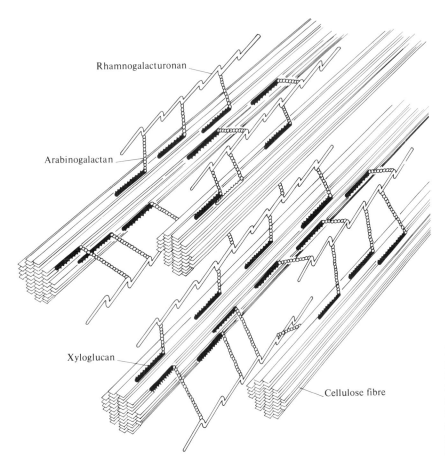

Rhamnogalacturonan

Arabinogalactan

Xyloglucan

Cellulose fibre

Fig. 3.6.7. Model of the primary cell wall. The stacks of cellulose microfibrils are assumed to be linked together in a giant macromolecule by the matrix polysaccharides. The xyloglucan molecules are linked by hydrogen bonds to the cellulose. In turn, the xyloglucans and the pectic polymers (rhamnogalacturonans) are linked together by arabinogalactan chains [8].

individual polysaccharides being linked covalently to another. Furthermore, this giant matrix macromolecule is in turn linked to the cellulose microfibrils by large numbers of hydrogen bonds between the cellulose and hemicelluloses [26]. As the cell matures, the wall composition changes, less pectin is synthesized and the walls may be modified by lignification [30]. Within the individual tissues, the cells are actually in contact with each other via the middle lamella, which contains a high concentration of pectins. This can be demonstrated by the action of pectinases which cause loss of form of the tissue as adhesion between individual cells is lost.

How then could plant cells in contact communicate or exchange information? It is clear that the same direct membrane–membrane contact as occurs in animal cells is not possible for plant cells. However, the walls of the plant cells are essentially porous gels, and molecules of up to 10 nm diameter can pass through the gel matrix of a primary wall of some cells—this is equivalent to a mol. wt of 17 000 for a globular protein or 6500 for a polysaccharide [6]. Thus it is possible that molecular signals could originate from one cell and diffuse through the walls of an adjacent cell to be received at the plasma membrane of a receptor cell. Another possibility is that a message is received at the outer surface of the wall and transmitted in some way by a secondary messenger through the wall. At this stage our information regarding the detailed molecular architecture of the cell wall is insufficient to assess just how likely this possibility may be.

One important way in which membrane–membrane contact is achieved between plant cells is via plasmodesmata. These are extensions of the plasma membrane which penetrate the cell wall and give effective membrane continuity between cells (see Chapter 3.4). These plasmodesmata have an inner structure, the desmotubule, which is apparently a continuity of the endoplasmic reticulum. The numbers of plasmodesmatal connections vary with the stage of development of the tissue, and are certainly involved in the cell–cell communication required for differentiation [19]. However, whether they are also involved in other forms of communication is not known.

Response to receipt of a signal at the cell surface

Both plant and animal cells either directly or indirectly sense their environment through the plasma membrane.

The question now arises of how the complementary molecular interaction at the extracellular face of the membrane is translated to an intracellular signal which ultimately will give an observable response. Several types of secondary events are known which are triggered by specific interactions involving animal cell-surface receptors (Fig. 3.6.8). First of all, there may be migration of bound signal molecules (sometimes referred to as effectors) into clusters or caps. This 'capping' could induce permeability changes in the membrane, and hence changes in the ion concentrations (Fig. 3.6.8a). In some cases there are direct changes in activity of membrane-bound enzymes, such as adenylcyclase, by contact of one region of the integral receptor molecule with the peripheral enzyme (Fig. 3.6.8b). Another possibility is that the 'capping' causes changes in the organization of the underlying cytoskeletal elements, which in turn induces metabolic changes or may lead to internalization of the receptor with its bound signal by endocytosis (Fig. 3.6.8c). The bound signal or effector is in this way transported intracellularly to its site of action, where it may be released [25]. Whether one or more of these mechanisms applies to transmission of signals in plant cells is not known.

3.6.3 LECTINS—MEDIATORS OF INFORMATION?

We have considered in some detail the nature of the carbohydrates of the membrane, we will now examine the nature of the group of molecules which specifically bind carbohydrates, the *lectins*. It is members of this class of molecule which are believed to be involved in cell recognition reactions by complementary interactions with cell-surface saccharides. However, it is only in recent years that lectins have been implicated in these reactions; and this is only one of a number of functions which have been suggested for the lectins. They were, in fact, discovered almost a century ago, but for the next 80 years or so the lectins were really a biological curiosity. In 1960 their potential for interacting with cell-surface saccharides was discovered, and since then there has been an enormous amount of work directed towards understanding their chemical and biological properties.

Characteristics of lectins

Lectins are proteins or glycoproteins which are able to

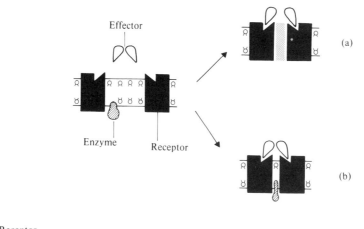

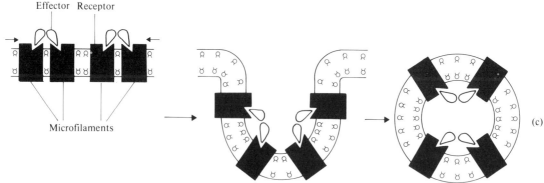

Fig. 3.6.8. Some mechanisms for response of a cell to receipt of an extracellular molecular signal. Binding of a multivalent effector to membrane receptors may cause (a) permeability changes by clustering of receptors; (b) activation of enzymes bound to the membrane; (c) alterations in the cytoskeletal elements; (d) internalization of bound effectors.

bind carbohydrate specifically (for review, see [18]). The binding is non-covalent and reversible, and the carbohydrate is not chemically changed by the interaction with the lectin. The specificity of individual lectins for carbohydrate is usually directed to a single monosaccharide, for example D-mannose or L-fucose, but some lectins have a broader specificity which extends to several structurally related monosaccharides, or to a sequence or series of monosaccharides; on the other hand, they may have a more restricted specificity so that they will only interact with a monosaccharide in a particular sequence of complex oligosaccharides. In most cases though, lectins bind to their complementary monosaccharides whether they occur as free sugars, or as terminal groups in oligosaccharides or complex carbohydrates such as membrane glycoproteins and glycolipids.

Another characteristic feature of lectins is their subunit structure: they usually have two, four or more subunits, each with a carbohydrate-combining site. This allows the lectins to act as effective cross-linking agents and to interact with saccharide-containing macromolecules such as polysaccharides and glycoproteins in solution, to give insoluble aggregates. This reaction resembles an antigen–antibody reaction in that there may be dissolution of the precipitate at regions of excess of either the carbohydrate-containing macromolecule or the lectin. Usually these reactions can be inhibited and often reversed by the presence of specific monosaccharides at the appropriate concentration. Lectins are also able to cross-link cells by interacting with their membrane glycoproteins and glycolipids, causing agglutination (Fig. 3.6.9). Another property which some, but not all, lectins have is a requirement for

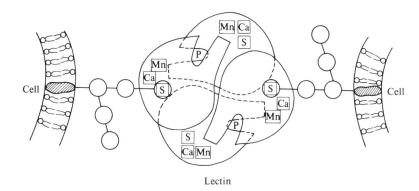

Fig. 3.6.9. Agglutination of cells by Concanavalin A. The multivalent lectin is able to bind to appropriate surface saccharides of different cells, effectively cross linking the cells and causing them to aggregate. Con A is represented in the tetrameric form. Each subunit has a saccharide binding site, S; a hydrophobic pocket, P; and binding sites for Ca^{2+} and Mn^{2+}. The dimensions of each subunit are $42 \times 40 \times 49 Å$. (Adapted from Becker *et al.*[3].)

specific metals for successful saccharide binding and aggregate formation.

Distribution of lectins

Hundreds of lectins have now been described and over 50 have been purified. The early studies showed that they were widely distributed in plants, and that legume seeds were a particularly rich source. Because of this distribution, and their property of agglutinating red blood cells by interacting with the cell-surface saccharides, they became known as 'phytohaemagglutinins'. However, they are now known to occur in animal cells, bacteria and viruses, as well as in both higher and lower plants. Because the lectins can be obtained in good yields from detergent extracts of tissues, they are believed to be integral membrane components, that is, they are in the location appropriate for contact with surface saccharides of another cell. However, this is by no means their sole location; for instance they are present in the cytoplasm of cotyledons of jack bean, in cell walls and in a variety of intracellular membrane components as well [36].

Some defined lectins

A list of some lectins which have been purified and characterized is given in Table 3.6.1. These lectins are not only of interest because they may participate in cell–cell recognition reactions, but they are also extremely useful tools in cell biology for probing the nature and distribution of saccharides at cell surfaces. Because they are so useful, a number of these lectins are available commercially in purified form. They can also be purchased with an FITC (fluorescent) label for investigations at the light microscope level and with a ferritin label for investigations at the electron microscope level. Concanavalin A (Con A) is probably the best known and most widely used of all the lectins. It is found in the jack bean, *Canavalia ensiformis*, in highest concentration in the seeds, at cytoplasmic sites especially common around the starch grains. It can be readily extracted from the seeds and has four subunits, each of mol. wt. 25 500 (Fig. 3.6.9). Con A is a single-chain lectin (identical subunits) and it has many similarities in amino acid sequence to certain other legume lectins, for example to the α-chain of favin. This lectin from *Vicia cracca* consists of two pairs of different subunits, the α and β chains.

Each subunit of Con A has a single saccharide-binding site close to two metal-ion-binding sites (Ca^{2+}, Mn^{2+}). The number of subunits per molecule is pH and temperature dependent. There is also a pocket in the molecule which will bond hydrophobically to suitable molecules (not sugars). Sugar binding is dependent on the presence of the required metal ions. The saccharide-binding sites will accommodate molecules with the α-D-glucopyranose configuration at C3, C4 and C5; that is, it will bind to glucose and mannose but not galactose. Apart from these simple sugars, Con A also binds 1,2α-linked mannosyl residues, either in terminal or non-terminal positions in oligosaccharides. This is important as 1,2-linked mannosyl residues are a common feature of membrane glycoproteins.

Con A will precipitate macromolecules containing appropriate terminal monosaccharide units over a defined concentration range; for example in the Con

Table 3.6.1. Properties of some purified lectins.

Lectin	Source	Inhibitory saccharides	Associated metal ions
Concanavalin A (Con A)	Jack bean (*Canavalia ensiformis*)	α-Man, α-Glc, GlcNAc, 2-substituted mannosyl residues	Mn^{2+}, Ca^{2+}
Garden pea lectin (PSA)	Garden pea (*Pisum sativium*)	Man, Glc, 3-substituted mannosyl residues	Mn^{2+}, Ca^{2+}
Lentil lectin (LcH)	Lentil (*Lens culinaris*)	α-Man, α-Glc, GlcNAc, 2-substituted mannosyl residues (low binding constants)	Mn^{2+}, Ca^{2+}
Bandeiraea simplicifolia lectin (BSL)	*Bandeiraea simplicifolia*	α-Gal	Mg^{2+}, Ca^{2+}
Peanut lectin (PNA)	Peanut (*Arachis hypogea*)	Galβ1,3, GalNAc, α-Gal, GalNH$_2$	
Castor bean lectin (RCA)	Castor bean (*Ricinus communis*) RCA$_i$ RCA$_{ii}$	β-Gal β-Gal, GalNAc	No apparent metal ion requirements
Sophora japonica lectin (SJA)	Japanese pagoda tree (*Sophora japonica*)	β-GalNAc β-Gal	No metals
Soybean lectin (SBA)	Soybean (*Glycine max*)	$\beta\rightarrow$GalNAc $\beta\rightarrow$GalNAc	Mn^{2+}, Ca^{2+}
Lima bean lectin (LBA)	Lima bean (*Phaseolus lunatus*)	GalNAc	Mn^{2+}, Ca^{2+}
Phytohaem-agglutinin (PHA)	Red kidney bean (*Phaseolus vulgaris*)	GalNAc	
Fucose-binding lectin	*Lotus tetragonolobus*	α-L-Fuc	
Ulex europaeus lectin (UEA)	Gorse seed (*Ulex europaeus*) UEA$_I$ UEA$_{II}$	L-Fuc di-N-acetyl-chitobiose	Mn^{2+}, Ca^{2+}
Limulus polyphemus (LPA, limulin)	Horseshoe crab haemolymph (*Limulus polyphemus*)	Sialic acid	Ca^{2+}
Wheatgerm agglutinin (WGA)	Wheat (*Triticum aestivum*)	GlcNAc and its oligosaccharides with sialic acid also present	

A–glycogen precipitation reaction, the precipitate will dissolve in excess of either lectin or glycogen and hence is analogous to an antigen–antibody reaction. The most useful technique for establishing the sugar specificity of the lectins is inhibition with simple sugars. These tests are referred to as hapten-inhibition tests; for example, the precipitation between glycogen and Con A can be inhibited by the haptens glucose and mannose but not galactose.

Agglutination of cells by lectins

It was through the agglutination reaction that lectins were first discovered by Stillmark in 1888 during attempts to discover the cause of toxicity of the castor bean, *Ricinis communis*. This plant is extremely toxic to animals and humans, and some people also suffer a violent contact reaction to the plant. Stillmark took a suspension of red blood cells, mixed them with an extract of castor bean seeds, and observed an immediate clumping or agglutination of the cells. We now know that other mammalian cells such as lymphocytes and sperm, as well as bacteria, fungal spores and plant protoplasts, may also be agglutinated by lectins. This property of being able to agglutinate red blood cells gave the first insight into the saccharide specificity of the lectins. In 1945 Boyd showed that some lectins were blood group specific; for instance, lima bean lectin would agglutinate the cells of people of blood group A but not blood groups O or B. He introduced the term 'lectin' (from the Latin *legere,* to choose) because the lectins were effectively choosing between cells of blood groups A, B and O. Subsequently, other blood-group-specific lectins were found and there is a precise correlation between the saccharide specificity of the lectin and the sequence of sugars on the red blood cell which determine the blood group. This relationship between blood group structure and lectin sugar specificity was resolved by Watkins and Morgan in 1953 [38]. They showed by hapten inhibition tests that the blood group A determinant was N-acetylgalactosamine dependent, and that the O blood group was determined by fucose. The relationship between the terminal saccharide structures of the blood group determinants and haemagglutination by different lectins is shown in Table 3.6.2.

A great spur to work on lectins, and to the notion that lectin–saccharide reactions may be involved in cell recognition, came in 1963 when Joseph Aub made the momentous observation that lectins often preferentially agglutinate malignant cells; that is, the malignant or cancerous cells differ from normal cells in the nature of their cell-surface components. Normally, the receptors and the lectin-binding sites are distributed evenly, but there is patchy or clustered grouping on the surfaces of malignant cells and it is these clusters of receptors which makes the cells so vulnerable to agglutination. Since then, it has been shown that amongst a population of normal cells which are not agglutinated by a particular lectin there may be a few cells which are vulnerable to agglutination; this is due to changes in the cell surface

Table 3.6.2. Relationship between blood group type and agglutinability of red blood cells by lectins.

	Blood group type of cells		Lectin effective in agglutinating cells	
Specificity	Structure of determinant		Source	Monosaccharide specificity
H	Gal$\frac{\beta 1,3\,\text{or}\,4}{}$GlcNAc $\mid\;\alpha 1,2$ Fuc		*Ulex europaeus* (gorse) *Dolichos biflorus*	Fucose Fucose
A	GlcNAc$\frac{\alpha 1,3}{}$Gal$\frac{\beta 1,3\,\text{or}\,4}{}$GlcNAc $\mid\;\alpha 1,2$ Fuc		*Phaseolus lunatus* (lima bean)	N-Acetyl galactosamine
B	Gal$\frac{\alpha 1,3}{}$Gal$\frac{\beta 1,3\,\text{or}\,4}{}$GlcNAc $\mid\;\alpha 1,2$ Fuc		*Banderia simplicifolia*	Galactose

associated with mitotic division. These observations, and the finding that some lectins are mitogenic (induce resting lymphocytes to divide), have led to the suggestion that surface saccharides change during the cell cycle and that saccharide–lectin interactions may be involved in control of growth and differentiation. Another important point is that the surface saccharides of many cell types are able to undergo lateral movement within the plane of the membrane to form patches and caps when treated with lectins; initially, there is an even distribution, which rapidly changes to a patchy distribution at 37°C. Under some conditions, the patches may aggregate to form caps at one pole of the cell. The capping process is apparently energy dependent, while the formation of patches may be due to a simple diffusion. There is evidence that at least some of the receptors involved are connected in some way with the underlying components of the cytoskeletal system, the microtubules and microfilaments.

In summary then:
(i) complex saccharides of the plasma membrane components are oriented to the extracellular face of the membrane;
(ii) specific lectins are known to be present at the plasma membrane;
(iii) sugar and sugar-containing molecules are uniquely sensitive to specific recognition by lectins; this molecular interaction is highly specific and sensitive to structural alteration.

We will now consider how these ideas apply to a number of cell–cell recognition systems.

3.6.4 CELL RECOGNITION SYSTEMS DURING FERTILIZATION IN LOWER PLANTS

Fertilization in algae

The complexity of the events of fertilization increases from the algae up to the flowering plants. Thus, fertilization of algae such as *Chlamydomonas* and *Fucus* occurs in the sea and involves a relatively simple sequence of cell–cell recognition events, namely adhesion resulting in fusion. In flowering plants, fertilization occurs in the ovary, which is deep within the pistil, and the process is physiologically and biochemically much more complex. The algal mating systems fulfil all the criteria for a good experimental system for examining cell–cell recogni-

tion: the cells can be obtained and maintained in large quantities and the recognition phenomena, in this case mating, can be easily monitored and measured in the laboratory. However, whether the principles derived from this relatively simple system can be applied to the more complex mating systems of higher organisms is a question which is viewed cautiously. Gamete fusion in *Chlamydomonas* is the most extensively studied system. This is a unicellular, biflagellate, freshwater alga of the Chlorophyceae. It is isogamous (the gametes are morphologically identical) and dioecious (they are derived from separate plants). The mating reaction proceeds between plus and minus gametes, to form a zygote. Gamete formation from vegetative cells is induced under starvation conditions. Normally, there is no aggregation between vegetative cells or between cells of the same mating type or between gametes of different species. When gametes of the opposite mating type of the same species make contact, they adhere via the tips of their flagella and this is followed by cell fusion. These cells are enclosed by a plasma membrane which is continuous over the surface of the cell body and the flagella.

As these highly specific recognition reactions are mediated by contact at the tips of the flagella, the structure of these regions has been examined in detail. A key finding is that the gametes shed material into the medium which will effectively agglutinate gametes of the opposite mating type. This shed material, known as isoagglutinin, is highly specific, not only for the mating type (+ or −) but also for the species. That is, it is said to have both sex- and species-specific contact capacity. The isoagglutinin from (+) gametes agglutinates (−) gametes of a particular species and vice versa. It is a high-molecular-weight ($c.$ 10^8) material, glycoprotein in nature.

There are differences in the composition and structure of isoagglutinin isolated from different species, although the precise structure is not known. It is believed that the molecules are shed as vesicles from the flagellar surface and are actually membrane fragments. Presumably, if membrane material is being continually shed, it must be continually replaced by biogenesis of membrane from the endomembrane system in the cell body. It may be that changes in flagellar membrane composition occur during the transition from vegetative to sexual cells and that an altered array of membrane components is displayed and shed from the flagellar surface. The precise role of the isoagglutinins in the mating process is not defined. However, further information has been obtained by altering the surface proteins and glycoproteins and examining the effect of this alteration on the mating reaction. For example, addition of Con A at high concentrations promotes isoagglutination of both (+) and (−) gametes. This merely shows that mannosyl and glucosyl groups are present in the cell-surface components. But at low concentrations Con A inhibits the capacity of (+) gametes to agglutinate (−) gametes of the same species, but not vice versa. This indicates that surface α-mannosyl groups of the (+) gametes are involved in the recognition reaction and are masked by the presence of low concentrations of Con A. A similar observation is made when the (+) cells, but not the (−) cells, are treated with α-mannosidase—presumably mannosyl residues are removed enzymically, and because they are normally involved in the recognition reaction, the capacity to agglutinate (−) cells of the same species is lost.

If these surface carbohydrates are involved in the recognition reaction, then a complementary receptor (lectin), either protein or glycoprotein in nature, might be expected to be present on the surface of the (−) cells. This was tested by examining the capacity of the cells for agglutination after treatment with the proteolytic enzyme trypsin. In this case, only the agglutinability of the (−) cells was affected. These observations were made for two species of *Chlamydomonas*, *C. eugametos* and *C. moewusii*, and indicated that in these mating systems recognition may be mediated by an interaction between saccharides and complementary lectins on the flagellar surfaces of different mating types [39]. However, the receptor of the (−) gametes also has a vital carbohydrate component, as contact capacity of the (−) gametes is also destroyed by periodate oxidation and by the action of α-N-acetyl galactosaminidase and α-galactosidase.

One other algal mating system which apparently depends on a saccharide–saccharide binding protein interaction is that of *Fucus*, a member of the brown algae (Fucales). This seaweed is exposed on reefs at low tide, where it is dried in the sun causing release of the eggs and sperm from separate plants. At high tide the gametes are swept into the sea and the motile sperm are attracted chemotactically to eggs by the conjugated octatriene fucoserraten. Fertilization of the large non-motile eggs is highly species-specific and is apparently mediated by attachment of the tip of the anterior flagellum of the sperm to the egg membrane. The plants can be collected and release of gametes induced under laboratory conditions; large numbers of eggs and sperm can be collected separately and conditions for fertilization *in vitro* established. A simple assay for fertilization is appearance of the zygote wall, which gives a characteristic fluorescence with calcofluor, a stain thought to be specific for wall β-glucans. The gametes themselves are naked, i.e. they do not have a wall. The nature and role of the saccharide determinants of the gametes have been explored by examining their capacity to bind a number of lectins [4]. For each lectin, a concentration curve was constructed to distinguish between the possibilities of non-specific or cytotoxic inhibition of fertilization and specific blocking of recognition sites. Two of the lectins tested, Con A and a fucose-binding lectin, effectively inhibited fertilization at low concentration (Table 3.6.3).

Table 3.6.3. Effect of lectins on *in vitro* fertilization of *Fucus* eggs.

Lectin	Specificity	Effect on fertilization
Wheatgerm agglutinin	(GlcNAc)$_2$	No effect up to 0.1 mg.ml^{-1}
Phytohaemagglutinin	GalNAc	Stimulates fertilization at concentrations below 0.1 mg.ml^{-1}
Soybean agglutinin	GalNAc	No effect
Castor bean lectin RC 120	β-Gal	Inhibition at high concentrations (0.1 mg.ml^{-1})
Con A	α-Glc, α Man	Inhibition at low concentrations (0.001 mg.ml^{-1})
Fucose-binding protein	α-L-Fuc	Inhibition at low concentrations (0.001 mg.ml^{-1})

It seems then that Con A and fucose-binding lectin can bind to surface receptors of one of the gametes. The identity of the mating partner involved in lectin binding was then established by pre-incubating both gametes with lower concentrations of the lectins. Below 0.001 mg ml^{-1}, both lectins acted specifically on eggs. Controls in which the lectin was pre-incubated with the hapten sugar confirmed the specificity of the reaction. The implied role of saccharides on the egg cell surface in fertilization was confirmed by observing the effect of specific glycosidases on the reaction. Of a number of glycosidases tested, α-D-mannosidase and α-L-fucosidase were most effective in inhibiting fertilization.

Fertilization in fungi

The initial interactions of mating types in fungi appear in some cases to parallel those for sexual reproduction in the algae. The most detailed study has been for the yeast *Hansenula wingei*. This yeast is constitutive for sexual agglutination and forms aggregates when haploid cells of the opposite mating types, '5-cells' and '21-cells', are mixed. The initial step is the formation of a complex between complementary surface molecules which are distributed evenly over the whole cell wall, allowing a single cell to adhere to several others of the opposite mating type. Thus when cells of different mating types are mixed, they form aggregates of several cells. The sex-specific surface molecules involved are present in the walls and are also secreted into the culture medium. The initial adhesion reaction involves an interaction of the outer 'fuzzy coat' of the mating cells, on which the 5- and 21-factors are presumably situated. Adhesion leads to outgrowth of the contact points, the two walls then fuse and cytoplasmic continuity is established.

Two surface molecules have been isolated, the '5-factor' and the '21-factor'. They are both glycoproteins but have quite different properties (Table 3.6.4).

Table 3.6.4. Comparison of the properties of complementary glycoprotein mating factors from *Hansenula wingei*.

	5-factor	21-factor
Activity	Agglutinates cells of strain 21 and forms a soluble complex with 21f *in vitro*	Inhibits the agglutination activity of 5f by forming a neutralized 5f–21f complex
No. of combining sites	6 or more	1
Molecular weight	Heterogeneous— the sedimentation coefficient varies with the preparation; 160 000	27 000
Composition	Mannan–protein 85% mannose 10% protein 5% phosphate	'High mannose' glycoprotein
Heat stability	Stable	Labile
Sensitivity to mercaptoethanol	Sensitive	Stable

The 5-factor is a heat stable mannoprotein which agglutinates 21-cells. It consists of a glycoprotein core to which several glycopeptide recognition sites are attached by disulphide linkages (Fig. 3.6.10). The linkages are vulnerable to reducing agents; the monovalent glycopeptides are released and these bind to 21-cells without causing agglutination [10]. The 21-factor is

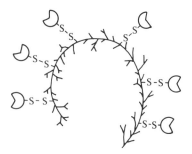

Fig. 3.6.10. Possible structure of the S-agglutinin molecule from *Hansenula wingeii*. The central core is a polypeptide to which a number of monovalent active glycopeptides are attached via disulphide linkages. (From Crandall [10].)

released by trypsinization of 21-cells; it is heat labile, stable to reducing agents and has a low content of carbohydrate, which is mainly mannose. The properties of this glycoprotein are consistent with it being a typical 'high mannose' glycoprotein linked to asparagine. It will bind to 5-agglutinin and neutralize its activity; however, as it is monovalent, it does not agglutinate 5-cells [5].

Molecular species with similar properties have been found to mediate the sexual agglutination of two other yeasts, *Pichia amethionia* and *Saccharomyces kluyveri*; furthermore, the reaction is species-specific, as there is essentially no agglutination in the heterologous reaction.

As a cell recognition phenomenon, this reaction is of particular interest: it is the first we have discussed in which the interacting molecules which mediate a specific recognition reaction are located on the external surface of a cell wall—*they are wall, rather than membrane, components*. It is important to note that the same types of molecules are involved in this reaction as in those we have examined which involve contact at the plasma membrane, i.e. it is an interaction between a glycoprotein and saccharide residues on a complementary macromolecule.

3.6.5 FERTILIZATION IN FLOWERING PLANTS

So far, we have considered sexual interactions in lower plants which are mediated by direct contact between the gametes. For each of the systems described, the biology of the interaction is well understood, and considerable progress has been made in isolating and identifying the molecular species which mediate the specific mating interaction. In the higher plants, the biology of mating is much more complex, and approaches to understanding the molecular basis of the interaction are only just beginning to be made, based on the genetic systems which control sexual reproduction. We will first outline the main features of the male–female recognition system in higher plants, then consider the nature of the surfaces in contact and the approaches which are being taken to define the specificity in molecular terms.

The interacting partners are the pollen and pistil. Pollen grains containing the male gametes are transported, usually by wind currents or by animal vectors, to the female structure, the pistil. Difficulties in approaching the chemical basis of the interaction are compounded by its complexity. The interacting partner on the male side is the pollen grain, the structure which houses the male gametophyte produced by the microspore. Mature pollen grains are usually two-celled, containing a generative cell (which will divide after germination to produce the two sperms) lying within the vegetative cell (p. 34). On the female side, the pistil is parental tissue; the female gametophyte, the embryo sac lying within the ovule, is reached from the receptive surface, the stigma, through the transmitting tissue of the style. The style may be virtually absent in some cases, for example in poppy, or very long, for example in maize (where it forms the silks, which may approach 1 m in length). In compatible mating, the pollen hydrates at the stigma surface of the pistil, and produces a pollen tube which penetrates the stigma surface and grows intercellularly through the style to the embryo sac where fertilization occurs. This involves release of two sperms, one fertilizes the egg and the other fuses with the two nuclei of the central cell to form the primary endosperm nucleus (p. 44). This mode of delivery of the gametes to the ovule through the pollen tube (siphonogamy) gives the plant many more potential points for control of fertilization than are possible in the

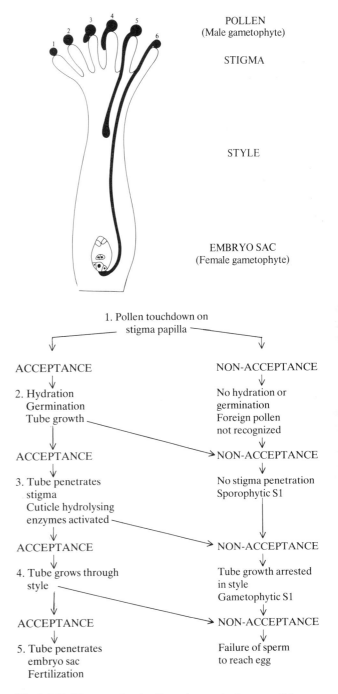

Fig. 3.6.11. Diagrams showing the major events of a compatible pollination of a flowering plant. The possible options leading to incompatibility are indicated by the numbers. (From Clarke & Knox [9].)

direct cell–cell contact of lower plants. These are shown diagrammatically in Fig. 3.6.11.

The specificity of the interactions between pollen and pistil is somewhat different from that involved in fertilization in lower plants. Thus interspecific crosses between flowering plants are only occasionally successful and intergeneric crosses have only rarely been reported. Intraspecific pollinations are usually successful except where specific self-incompatibility genes (S-genes) operate to prevent inbreeding. These systems, in which there may be no morphological difference between the breeding groups, favour out-crossing by preventing successful self-pollination and are known to operate in about 100 of the 300 families of flowering plant.

There are two major types of self-incompatibility that have been genetically defined: (1) gametophytic self-incompatibility, in which the behaviour of the pollen grain is determined by its own genotype, and (2) sporophytic self-incompatibility, in which the behaviour of the pollen is determined by the phenotype of the parent. For both systems, control is usually through a single S-gene locus with multiple alleles; where there is identity of alleles between the two mating partners, the pollination is unsuccessful. In both types of self-incompatibility, the response of the female partner is through the tissues of the stigma and style. In the gametophytic system, the genotype of the individual pollen grain dictates its potential for fertilization—that is, as long as it differs from that of the receptive pistil, the mating will be successful. In the sporophytic system, the mating will only be successful where the genotype of the parent plant from which the pollen was derived, in which dominance of one allele over the other may be expressed, differs from that of the receptive stigma.

Various attempts have been made to understand the basis of recognition in these pollination systems. All the experiments depend on having a satisfactory assay system for successful and unsuccessful pollination and this is often quite difficult to establish. For example, success in self-pollination can be measured by seed set, but the plants need to be grown under controlled conditions, and then seed viability tested. The progress of pollination can be followed by microscopy using such stains as decolorized aniline blue and calcofluor, which stain the pollen tube walls. Using these staining methods, growth of pollen tubes through the style and the distance which incompatible tubes can grow within

the style before they are arrested can be measured (Fig. 3.6.12), usually within a few hours of pollination taking place.

A successful fertilization requires that the viable pollen grain be captured by the stigma, the conditions for germination and pollen tube growth must be

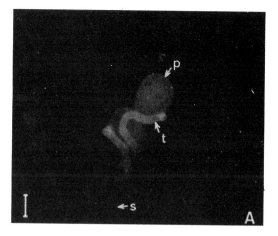

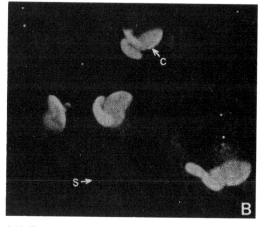

Fig. 3.6.12. Development of pollen tubes and callose formation in compatible and incompatible pollinations of rye. Excised mature stigmas were pollinated by dipping in fresh compatible or incompatible pollen; after 60 min samples were squashed, stained and examined by light or fluorescence microscopy (×900); internal marker = 25 μm. A. Compatible pollen (p) showing the tube growth (t) through the multicellular stigmatic hair (s), stained in decolorized aniline blue and viewed by fluorescence microscopy. B. Incompatible pollen on self stigma (s) showing the comma-shaped deposition of callose (c) which occludes part of the pollen grain and the short pollen tube. Callose is identified by its brilliant yellow fluorescence. (From Vithanage *et al.* [37].)

favourable, the pollen tube tip must reach the embryo sac, and the gametes must be discharged. Success depends on having acceptable matches of the pollen and its tube with the stigma and style at all stages in this sequence of events. If there is mismatch at any point, the mating will not result in fertilization. In some instances, there may be osmotic imbalances between the pollen and stigma surface which prevent the pollen from hydrating and germinating. This type of mismatch certainly produces an effective barrier to fertility, but is not the specific type of cell–cell recognition involving interaction of complementary macromolecules which we have been discussing so far. It is barriers of this kind which probably prevent most foreign pollen (as in many interspecific and intergeneric crosses) from germinating on the stigma surface of a particular species. In the relatively few (c. 4%) instances where this foreign pollen germinates, it may penetrate the stigmatic surface and grow into the style, where it may be inhibited. Rarely is this type of genetically distant mating successful. There does not seem to be a clear-cut relationship between genetic distance of the mating partners and the point of arrest of pollination in these cases.

Self-incompatible matings can also be followed by examining the process of pollen tube growth. In the sporophytic system, tube growth is usually arrested at the stigma surface, and there is a characteristic massive deposition of callose in the inhibited pollen tubes and also in the stigma wall at the point of contact with pollen. This callose can be detected by its brilliant yellow fluorescence with decolorized aniline blue.

In most gametophytic systems, for example wild tomato (*Lycopersicum peruvianum*) or sweet cherry (*Prunus avium*), pollen tube growth proceeds for a certain distance through the style for both compatible and incompatible pollinations. At various intervals along the growing tubes, callose plugs are laid down which effectively seal off the growing tip from the grain. At some stage, characteristic of each species and the environmental conditions, growth of incompatible tubes stops and there may be a massive callose deposition in the tip of the growing tube of the incompatible pollen, whereas compatible tubes grow on to the ovule. For both these systems, the presence of the callose associated with the incompatible pollination, whether in pollen tubes and stigma papillae in the sporophytic systems or in the pollen tube in gametophytic systems, can be used to monitor incompatibility. It is, in fact, such a reliable test that it is used in breeding experiments to establish relationships between compatible cultivars. The precise nature of the callose is not known. Because in one situation (sieve tube callose of grape-vines) the material staining with aniline blue was shown to be 1,3 β-glucan, it has been assumed that a polysaccharide with the same structure is always involved. This is not necessarily so; for example, the aniline-blue-staining callose produced in pollen and tubes in response to self-pollination of rye (*Secale cereale*) contains both 1,3 β and 1,4 β glucosidic linkages [37]. Again, just how callose is formed and what role it plays in the incompatible response is not known. It is detected at the pollen tube tips after growth has ceased, rather than during growth, so that it is probably a secondary response to contact between pollen and stigma or style.

Specific signalling between pollen grains and the female gametophyte is indicated by recent experiments carried out by Deurenberg with *Petunia hybrida* [13]. Specific pollination-induced increases in ribosomal protein synthesis in the ovules have been detected: (1) a primary peak at 9 h (when the pollen tubes are about one-third of the way through the style), and (2) a secondary increase at 18 h which occurs only in cross-pollinated (i.e. compatible) pistils. The first increase is considered to be produced by a primary signal indicating the arrival of pollen tubes, and the second by a further signal indicating the type of pollination, whether it is compatible or not. The existence of the primary signal is also supported by evidence from flower wilting, which is induced when pollen tubes enter the style.

We will now consider the nature of the surfaces in contact which produce these responses—pollen, pollen tubes, stigma surface and stylar tissue.

The pollen wall

The pollen wall is chemically and morphologically complex and often has species-specific or group-specific features (Fig. 3.6.13). The outer wall, the exine, is made of sporopollenin, a polymer of carotenoids and carotenoid esters which is extremely resistant to biodegradation. The underlying wall is the intine, which resembles a typical primary cell wall in having cellulose microfibrils embedded in a gelatinous matrix containing pectins and hemicelluloses. It is markedly thickened at the germinal apertures where the exine is usually absent and the intine protrudes to form the pollen tube on

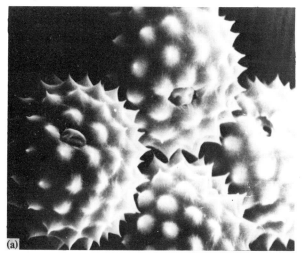

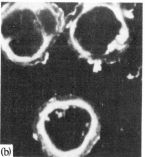

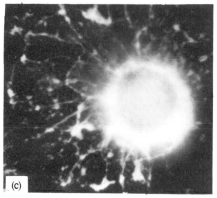

Fig. 3.6.13. The two domains of the pollen grain wall revealed by fluorescent antibody staining of ragweed pollen. (a) shows the appearance of whole grains by scanning electron microscopy, while (b) and (c) show freeze-sectioned grains after treatment with fluorescent-labelled rabbit antibodies to pollen diffusate. In (b), antibody binding to the exine proteins (e) and intine proteins (i) is evident as white areas in the grains which were sectioned within the anthers to avoid diffusion artefacts. In (c), mature dry pollen was freeze-sectioned directly in gelatine medium after exposure to the medium for only 30 s. In this short time, the proteins have diffused from their wall sites and are seen as a halo around the grain (p).

germination. The exine walls contain arcades which may be filled with soluble protein, glycoprotein and lipids derived from the tapetal cells of the anther just before pollen maturation—that is, they are genetically specified by the parental tissue. In contrast, the primary intine wall contains soluble proteins which are specified by the haploid grain itself [22].

The question which is of primary importance when considering the basis of recognition is that of the identity of the points of contact. For the pollen grain, there may be a surface osmiophilic layer. This layer has been detected in ultrastructural studies but has not been studied in detail. It may be important in selecting the conditions for successful pollen growth. Pollen will only germinate either *in vivo* or *in vitro* in a medium of appropriate osmolarity containing particular nutrients. Soon after contact with an appropriate moist surface, the contents of the exine arcades and the soluble components of the intine are released and diffuse out over the contact surface (Fig. 3.6.13). Pollen diffusates contain proteins, glycoproteins, carbohydrates, lipids and pigments. It is these components which are thought to specify the initial recognition events. A second site of interaction is the pollen tube, produced usually by extension growth from the intine layer via one of the germinal apertures. The pollen tube is not always invested by a cell wall in the early stages of germination (for example in pollen of avocado and certain sea-grasses) so there is sometimes the possibility of direct plasma membrane contact with the stigma surface.

The stigma surface

In general, the cells of the stigmatic surface have a typical primary cell wall overlaid with a cuticle. For the 'dry' type of stigma (e.g. cabbage, *Brassica oleracea*), the cells secrete a sticky layer on a cuticular surface when the stigma becomes receptive to pollen (Fig. 3.6.14 a and b). In the 'wet' type of stigma (e.g. lily, *Lilium longiflorum*), the cuticle breaks down when the cells are receptive and there is a massive secretion from the style which accumulates at the stigma surface. The major components of both the stigma surface and style canal of *Lilium* and *Gladiolus* have been isolated; chemically they are arabinogalactans, closely related structurally to plant gums. There are also a range of other components, especially proteins (including the enzyme esterase), glycoproteins and glycolipids [27]. These include glycoproteins of mol. wt. 54500 and 57000 whose presence has been correlated with the expression of the S gene for self-incompatibility in *Brassica*.

The style canal and extracellular stylar material

As pollen tube arrest often occurs in the style canal or in the stylar tissue, it is relevant to consider what we know of molecular species present in these sites. For both *Gladiolus* and *Lilium*, a major component is an arabinogalactan, closely related but not identical with that found at the stigma surface of *Gladiolus* (Fig. 3.6.14c). In the style it is associated covalently with protein, i.e. it is a proteoglycan. For both *Primula* and *Gladiolus*, a lectin (haemagglutinin) has also been identified in these tissues, as have a number of other less well defined components; some enzymes specific to the style transmitting tissue, glucose-6-phosphate dehydrogenase and an isozyme of peroxidase, have been detected in styles of *Nicotiana alata*. However no definite role can yet be attributed to any of these components. Recently, a soluble antigen whose presence is correlated with a particular S-gene product has been isolated from the style of sweet cherry, *Prunus avium*.

Interaction between the stigma surface and pollen components

Attempts to understand the basis of mating in the lower plants have been founded on manipulating the surfaces of the interacting partners and following the effects on mating. For the pollen–stigma interaction, similar approaches have been used—modification of either the stigmatic surface or the pollen diffusate. Studies of this kind have shown the following.

(1) The stigma surface (of dry-type stigmas) is an important barrier to incompatible pollinations. For example, disruption of the stigma chemically (organic

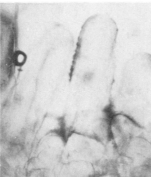
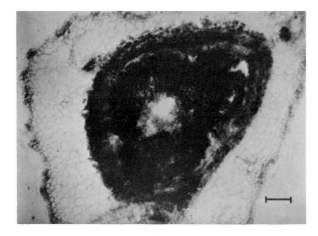
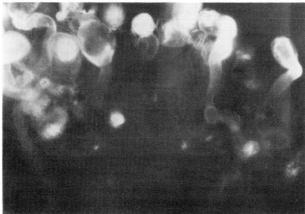

Fig. 3.6.14. Components of the stigma surface and style canal of *Gladiolus*: (a) a secretion containing an arabinogalactan as the major component appears at the surface of the stigmatic papillae when the flower is receptive. This component can be visualized on the surface by its binding to the fluorescent labelled galactosyl binding lectin tridacnin; or (b) to a red dye (artificial β-glycosyl carbohydrate antigen) which specifically binds to arabinogalactans and arabinogalactan proteins [24]; (c) shows material with the same staining properties in the style canal [25]; (d) a squash of *Gladiolus* style 12 h after pollination, showing progress of tube growth by fluorescent staining with aniline blue.

solvents, hexane), physically (heat, mechanical, electrical damage) or enzymically (trypsinization) may disrupt the normal incompatibility barriers [8].

(2) The pollen proteins are important in recognition of incompatible pollen. The incompatibility barriers can be overcome in some cases by mixing normally incompatible pollen with killed compatible pollen or pollen diffusates [24]. Another indication of the possible role of these pollen proteins in recognition is their ability to induce the formation of callose at the stigma surface—callose is deposited in response to application of diffusates of incompatible, but not of compatible pollen [15]. Many airborne pollen grains contain components that are allergenic in man; these proteins and glycoproteins are recognized by specific immunoglobulin E molecules in the responding human cells, but their function in the pollen grain is not known. In one gametophytic system, S-gene products are expressed in the pollen wall proteins; for *Oenothera organensis*, pollen proteins peculiar to particular S-allele groups have been detected immunologically.

(3) In sporophytic self-incompatibility systems (e.g. cabbage, *Brassica oleracea*), the S-gene products are expressed in the stigma, the site of pollen tube arrest. In gametophytic self-incompatibility systems, the S-gene products must be expressed in the transmitting tissue of the style, presumably in the particular part where the growth of the incompatible pollen tube is arrested [21]. Products associated with the expression of a particular S-allele group have been detected immunologically for these systems (e.g. sweet cherry, *Prunus avium*), but precisely how they act to express compatibility is not known. In this system, the S-gene product is extremely soluble and is likely to be secreted into the apoplast system of the transmitting tract. Presumably, there is some receptor for this S-gene product in the pollen tube and the response to such an interaction is ultimately the inhibition of pollen tube growth.

These studies of incompatibility in the pollen–stigma interaction are not yet understood in any detail at the molecular level, but the very fact that such precise incompatibility relationships exist and that they probably depend on an interaction between membrane- or wall-bound molecules and extracellular molecules raises the question as to whether precise interactions of this type (see Fig. 3.6.1c) may be more widespread in plants and occur, for example, in the somatic as well as the sexual tissues.

3.6.6 RECOGNITION BETWEEN SOMATIC CELLS OF FLOWERING PLANTS

Organ transplantation

Grafts between plant organs, like animal transplants, are uncommon in nature, but they provide a system in which the ability to discriminate between self and non-self can be assessed by the reaction between donor and recipient.

In the natural situation, grafts are frequently observed between the roots of trees in stands of the same species (allografts) and among the roots of the same individual (autografts), but are virtually unknown between roots of different species (xenografts). In forests containing predominantly one species, the allografts are likely to be so extensive that plantations of the one species may be effectively one organism joined through the root system. In natural forests there is usually a mixture of different species and genera, and the opportunity for allografting is reduced and autografting predominates. Clearly, this would be a more favourable situation, as extensive allografting may put the whole forest at risk of infection by systemic disease.

In aerial organs of plants, movement usually prevents the sustained contact necessary for union—however, it does occur in some cases, although no systematic studies to establish the taxonomic limitations of grafting partners have been reported. Artificial grafts, on the other hand, have been commonly used for vegetative propagation in horticultural practice through the ages. The shoot or scion in the graft is a desirable cultivar, while the basal rooted stem or stock is a cultivar possessing such qualities as resistance to unfavourable environmental effects. The soft herbaceous plants offer more amenable experimental systems, and it is with plants of this type that the first systematic studies of the sequential cellular changes which occur after grafting have been made. Structural changes which occur at the interface between stem grafts in compatible and incompatible grafts between the tomato and other members of the family Solanaceae have been examined by Yeoman and co-workers [43]. Compatible grafts are those in which the plant will survive, grow and reproduce under normal greenhouse conditions. Incompatible grafts are those which survive only for a limited period. To establish the graft, freshly cut surfaces of the stock and scion are held together tightly at the graft junction so that initial contact is established over the complete area of both faces of the grafting partners. The subsequent events are as follows.

(1) Shrinkage and collapse of cells at the graft junction. This occurs within a few hours and is most pronounced in the peripheral region of the stem, that is, in the cortex and around the vascular bundles. There is less shrinkage in the pith, so that for the first two days only the cells of the pith are in contact.

(2) The cavity created by the cell collapse is filled with some exudate of the plant.

(3) Cells in and around the vascular bundles divide, and the callus cells so produced grow into the space filled with fluid between the stock and the scion. It is these cells, originating from the cut surfaces of the grafting partners, which eventually make contact.

(4) As the cells from opposing surfaces touch, their cell walls dissolve and the plasma membranes come into contact.

The events up to this stage are apparently identical for both compatible and incompatible grafts. The subsequent events for the compatible grafts are differentiation of xylem elements to give continuity between the vascular bundles of stock and scion. For the incompatible graft this development of vascular continuity does not occur. It seems likely then, that the definitive recognition event occurs at step 4, when the plasma membranes of the cells from opposing surfaces make contact.

These cellular events can be followed by measuring development of the strength of the graft. Initially, during the first four days, the strength of the graft is the same for a compatible or an incompatible graft. After four days, the vascular connections start to develop in the compatible grafts and the strength of the graft increases dramatically. However, in the incompatible situation, the strength of the graft continues to depend solely on contacts between cells of the pith, and does not increase with time.

Using this assay, the grafting relationships between members of the Solanaceae have been established. The specificity in stem grafting of plants is not as well defined as it is for organ transplants in animals. In general, there is an acceptance of self (allografts) and grafts from closely related species within the same family (xenografts). Grafts between members of different families, such as between cucumber (*Cucumis sativus*) and runner been (*Phaseolus coccineus*), may produce the initial

union dependent only on cohesion between pith cells, but these grafts do not consolidate by development of

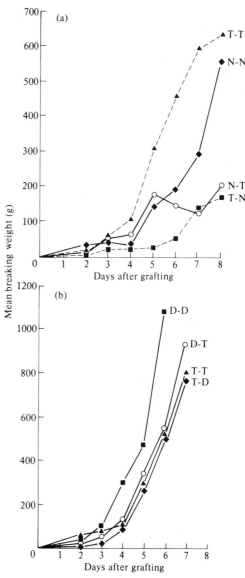

Fig. 3.6.15. (a) Comparison of the increase in breaking weight of autografts of *Lycopersicon* (T–T) and *Nicandra* (N–N) with heterografts of these two species (N–T and T–N). The heterografts of *Nicandra* with tomato never achieve vascular continuity between stock and scion. (b) Comparison of the increase in breaking weight of autografts of *Lycopersicon* (T–T) and *Datura* (D–D) with heterografts of these two species (T–D and D–T). The heterografts of *Datura* with *Lycopersicon* yield viable plants which can be grown successfully for extended periods of time. (From Yeoman Brown [42].)

the vascular tissue and are ultimately incompatible. Within the same family, grafts between closely related species and genera are usually compatible, but those between more distantly related genera are more often incompatible. For example, the tomato (*Lycopersicum esculentum*) forms compatible grafts with the thorn apple (*Datura stramonium*) but not with *Nicandra physaloides* (Fig. 3.6.15).

Another interesting parallel between the grafting situation in animals and plants is the ability of embryonic tissues to accept normally incompatible grafts. For example, grafts of peach stems on to root stocks of two-year-old trees of wild cherry plum, cv Myrobalan, are unsuccessful. However, successful union is achieved if grafts are initiated at the seedling cotyledon stage [20]. This may be analogous to the acceptance of non-self grafts by foetal, but not mature, mammalian tissues.

Cultured callus cells

The callus cells which are produced at the cut ends of the grafting partners can also be produced by explants of various plant organs and taken into sterile culture. The capacity of these callus cells for recognition has been tested by placing clumps of callus initiated from stem explants of seven fruit cultivars together on solid media and observing the growth pattern at the contact zones [16]. Four different responses have been observed.
(1) Adjacent callus cells fail to grow together (score 0).
(2) Adjacent callus cells show slight intermingling at the contact zone, but clumps are easily separated (score 1).
(3) Adjacent clumps grow together but can be separated by force (score 2).
(4) Clumps are completely fused and cannot be separated by force (score 3).

Scores were close to zero in interactions between calli initiated from different families, were slightly higher in interactions between genera within the same family (Rosaceae), and were highest, with values approaching self, between different species of the genus *Malus*. In these cases, the boundary between two pieces of callus could not be detected microscopically. These results suggest that callus cells, which possess a cellulosic wall but are devoid of a cuticle, have some ability to discriminate between self and non-self.

The question now is how the identity of these callus cells is expressed and perceived by other callus cells. We know that plant cells, like animal cells, have characteristic markers of identity which can be detected antigenically for both plant and animal cells. These markers of identity are expressed in cultured as well as parental cells and may also be shed into the culture medium. For example, callus cells from tobacco, corn, *Gladiolus* and the sweet cherry display both species- and organ-specific antigens as well as antigens common to a number of plant organs [31]. Furthermore, at least some of the specific antigens are located at the surface of the plasma membrane, indicating that markers of identity of the plant cells are displayed, as for animal cells, at the plasma membrane. How this information is perceived is a question which is at this stage unresolved. Membrane-bound plant lectins may fulfill this role but to date there is no convincing evidence that this is the case.

Angiosperm parasites

Apart from interactions between cells within an organism, interactions between different organisms can provide striking examples of host-specificity that implicate macromolecular interactions between cells in their control. Epiparasites from land plants may have widely varying host specificity; for example, some species of mistletoe are recorded on more than 300 host species, while others have only one known host. An understanding of the nature of the cells initiating the parasitic interactions has come from ultrastructural studies of the interacting cells. Penetration of the host plant epidermis by the seedling parasite is carried out by a special organ, the endophyte, which adheres to the host surface and produces the intrusive haustorium. In various mistletoes, striking changes occur in the cell wall at the host–endophyte interface; in one species the cell walls appear to fuse, and in another the endophyte cells become octopus-like, with radiating tips that protrude between the host cells. In another case, the cell walls have been eroded and the endophyte and host cells make direct plasma membrane contact, while in other interactions callus-like cells are differentiated at the interface, perhaps as a result of a wound response when the·parasite penetrates the host or perhaps these cells are essential for the intercellular events between host and parasite. This interaction certainly appears to involve initial adhesion followed by an option when host penetration or non-penetration is determined [9].

3.6.7 INTERACTION BETWEEN HIGHER PLANTS AND MICRO-ORGANISMS

Host-specificity of nitrogen-fixing bacteria

One of the most important routes by which atmospheric nitrogen enters the food chain is via the symbiotic association between the Gram-negative bacteria of the genus *Rhizobium* and members of the plant family Leguminosae. For most legumes the primary infection sites are the root hair and the point of emergence of lateral roots, and infection at these sites ultimately results in nodule formation. The association is highly specific; from the diverse microflora of the soil, each species of legume forms an association with a single species of *Rhizobium*, and conversely most species of *Rhizobium* will only infect one legume species. For example, *Rhizobium japonicum*, the soybean symbiont, does not infect the green bean *Phaseolus* or clover (*Trifolium*) and, conversely, the green bean and clover symbionts do not infect soybeans. There is some evidence that the basis for specificity is the interaction between the surface carbohydrates of the bacterial cell and some component of the legume root, possibly a lectin.

The first observations were that soya bean lectin, visualized by a fluorescent label, bound to 22 of 25 strains of *Rhizobium japonicum* which infect soybean, but not to any of 23 strains from five species which infect other legumes but not soybean. Another approach which suggests an association between the legume lectins and the surface polysaccharides of the bacteria was adopted by Albersheim and co-workers. They isolated lectins from four types of legume seeds: Concanavalin A from jack beans, pea lectin, phytohaemagglutinin from red kidney beans and soybean lectin; these lectins were coupled to agarose to make affinity columns. The next step was to isolate the surface lipopolysaccharides from symbionts of the four legumes and test their capacity to bind to the insolubilized lectin (*R. japonicum* for soybeans, *R. leguminosarum* for peas, *R. phaseoli* for red kidney beans). In each case, the lipopolysaccharides from a *Rhizobium* species interacted with the lectin affinity column of its symbiont, but not with the other lectin columns. The evidence suggests that the bacterial lipopolysaccharides of *Rhizobium* species are involved in determining the specificity of symbiosis in legumes. However, other workers have

found that there is no direct correlation between the ability of soybean lectins to bind different *Rhizobium* species and their capacity to nodulate soybeans. Furthermore, it now seems likely that it is the extracellular polysaccharide secreted by the bacteria, rather than the lipopolysaccharides, which may be important in determining nodulation. Thus, a *Rhizobium leguminosarum* mutant which produces very low amounts of extracellular polysaccharides and forms slimeless colonies was unable to nodulate peas effectively. However, the underlying lipopolysaccharides of both the mutant and the wild type were immunologically and chemically identical. Furthermore, the reverted mutant became fully infective [32]. These experiments implicate the surface polysaccharides of the bacteria and the plant lectins, but the precise nature of the initial event is still unresolved.

Plant–pathogen interactions

Plants, like animals, show great variability in their susceptibility to disease. For both, pathogenicity is the exception rather than the rule, and this implies the existence of recognition and defence mechanisms. The basis of many animal diseases caused by infection with micro-organisms is well understood at the molecular level and has allowed design of specific therapeutic agents, such as antibiotics. The molecular basis of plant disease is not so well understood and there is no single plant disease for which the molecular events of infection and response are established.

Plants are susceptible to viral, bacterial and fungal diseases, but the fungal diseases are the most common and damaging of the pathogens. This type of infection usually proceeds with invasion of the plant tissue by the fungal hyphae (Fig. 3.6.16). The symptoms of disease such as wilt are apparent when the hyphae have grown into and blocked the vascular system; in other types of disease, the fungus may produce cell-wall-degrading enzymes, such as pectinases, which cause breakdown of middle lamella and cell walls, causing general tissue destruction. In other cases, the symptoms are caused by specific toxins or hormones produced by the fungus. The infection of a plant by a fungal hypha is analogous to pollination in a number of ways: in each case the host plant tissues are invaded by another plant filament (fungal hypha or pollen tube); growth is from the tip and control of growth may be determined by precise genetic

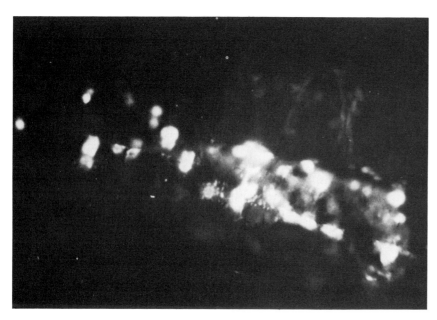

Fig. 3.6.16. Fluorescent micrograph showing infection of root tissue by the fungal pathogen *Phytophthora cinnamomi*. The zoospores are on the outer surface of the root slime, the germ tubes have grown through the slime layer and penetrated the host tissue. One response of the plant to contact with the fungal hyphae is production of callose. The section is stained with aniline blue which stains the fungal cell walls and the plant callose.

relationships of the two plant tissues in contact; furthermore, there are some common responses to incompatibility in the two situations, for example deposition of callose in response to invasion.

The plant has a number of means of resistance against, and devices for protecting itself from, the majority of micro-organisms with which it may interact. Some of these defences are general, in that they provide some protection from infection by a wide range of pathogens, and some are highly specific, being produced in response to attack by a particular pathogen. These responses have developed with the highly specific relationships which result from co-evolution of host and pathogen [35]. Overall, the specificity between host and pathogen exists at a number of different levels, ranging from pathogens with a wide host range to pathogens which are restricted to a single species or even a few genotypes of the host. For example, *Phytophthora cinnamomi*, the cinnamon fungus, is an example of the first type, having a wide host range and causing widespread damage to native forests as well as to horticultural plants; on the other hand, *P. infestans* is highly specific for potatoes and there are precise genetic relationships between the race of the pathogen and the genotype of the host.

The usual interpretation of the co-evolution process is that the hosts are susceptible in the initial state and that resistance results from expression of specific resistance genes which recognize particular pathogen races and initiate defence against infection. If a mutation in a particular fungal race resulted in the capacity for successful infection of a particular host species, the host may eventually counter by producing a corresponding mutation which allows recognition of and defence against the pathogen; this co-evolution of host genes for resistance and pathogen genes for virulence is called the gene-for-gene relationship. Resistance of the plant is due to a group of responses called collectively the hypersensitive response; in this situation, cells in the immediate vicinity of the invading hyphae die and, in so doing, deprive the fungus of the possibility of nutrition from the host. The plant also lays down barriers; for example, cell walls may be lignified and callose is frequently deposited between the plasma membrane and the wall of the host. Also, in some species, phytoalexins, which are microbial toxins, are released, further disrupting the fungal growth [14]. However, these responses themselves are not specific and may be invoked by mechanical wounding as well as by fungal infection. The specificity resides in the recognition event which initiates these responses on contact with the pathogen.

The recognition events in plant–pathogen interactions can be considered in terms of the two cell surfaces in contact which result in the response. There are two separate classes of events: first, the pre-infection events between the fungal spore and the contact surface of the plant, either at the root or leaf; and secondly, the post-infection events between the fungal hyphae and the cell wall of the host plant [34] (Fig. 3.6.16).

There has been very little work on the pre-infection events although, in one instance, *Phytophthora cinnamomi* adhesion is apparently mediated by a lectin–saccharide interaction, the lectin being on the zoospore surface and the saccharide involved being the terminal fucosyl residue on the root slime, which is the first point of contact of plant and pathogen [23].

For the post-infection events, it seems reasonable to suppose that the recognition would occur at contact of the plant and fungal cell surfaces. To test this supposition, fungal cell wall preparations and the secretions of fungal cells in culture have been fractionated to establish identity of the components active in eliciting the phytoalexin response. There are two classes of elicitors: proteins or glycoproteins and polysaccharides. A polypeptide elicitor of the phytoalexin phaseolin produced by the red kidney bean, *Phaseolus bulgaris, was isolated from the fungal pathogen Monilinia fructifolia* in 1969. Since thena glycoprotein elicitor has been detected in *Rhizopus stolonifera* which triggers phytoalexin formation in castor bean. Glucan elicitors have been shown to be produced by a numer of fungal species such as *Phtyopthora megasperma* var *sojae, Collectotrichum lindemutianum* and *P. cinnamomi* [41]. In each case, the elecitor was a branched $1,3\ \beta$ glucan, a structure which is present in amny fungal cell walls as part of the matrix polysaccharide. The simplest structure effective experimentally was a polysaccharide containing 3-linked, 3,6-linked and terminal glucosyl linkages in a ratio of 1:1:1, and of mol. wt. 10000 [2]. The effectiveness of this small, branched carbohydrate in eliciting the response is remarkable and it implicates a plant receptor for this molecule. There is some evidence that such a receptor is present at the plasma membrane, as potato protoplasts are effectively agglutinated by the 3,6 glucan but not by closely related polysaccharides.

However, an interaction of this kind must be general, as phytoalexin production is a general not a specific response, in that it is produced in many plants in response to infection. The molecular mechanisms which underlie the specific gene-for-gene relationships are not known, although it is thought that the avirulence genes of a pathogen code for synthesis or control of factors which, by binding to specific receptors in the plant, activate the plant's defences [12]. It has been suggested that the products of pathogen avirulence genes may be glycosyl transferases which control synthesis of race-specific carbohydrates on the specificity factors.

3.6.8 CONCLUSIONS

From the discussion and examples of cell recognition in plants the following conclusions can be drawn.

(1) The capacity for recognition of other cells, which is expressed in the aggregation of cells of lower organisms, such as the slime moulds and sponges, is also shown by plant cells in the sexual interactions of both the lower and higher plants, and in the interactions of somatic cells of flowering plants, both with other somatic cells and with micro-organisms.

(2) Cell recognition in plants is mediated by interactions between cell-surface and membrane-bound macromolecules. In all the examples for which there is some insight into the molecular basis of recognition, a recurring theme is an interaction between a membrane-bound receptor for a macromolecule which may be present in the contact cell as a component of the membrane or cell wall or as a secreted component.

(3) In many cases the interaction depends on binding between the carbohydrate moiety of a glycoconjugate (glycoprotein or proteoglycan) and a carbohydrate-binding receptor which is either protein or glycoprotein in nature.

(4) Cell recognition in plants results in a defined response. The response may be rejection in a incompatible reaction; for example, self-pollination in a self-incompatible plant results in arrest of pollen tube growth, an incompatible stem graft will be rejected, and an incompatible pathogen will not be able to invade host tissue effectively. Alternatively, the response may be acceptance; for example, acceptance and fertilization of compatible pollen, acceptance and invasion by a compatible pathogen, and acceptance and nodulation by a compatible *Rhizobium* strain.

Studies directed to the understanding of cell recognition phenomenon in plants are now being actively pursued in a number of laboratories throughout the world. We can confidently expect that the many of the questions raised in the text will be answered within the next decade.

3.6.9 REFERENCES

1 Albersheim P. (1975) The walls of growing plant cells. *Scient. Am.*, 80–95.

2 Albersheim P. & Valent B.S. (1978) Host–pathogen interactions in plants. *J. Cell Biol.*, **78**, 627–643.

3 Becker J.W., Reeke G.N., Cunningham B.A. & Edelman G.W. (1976) New evidence on the location of the saccharide-binding site of Concanavalin A. *Nature, Lond.*, **259**, 409–409.

4 Bolwell G.P., Callow J.A., Callow M.E. & Evans L.V. (1979) Fertilization in brown algae. II. Evidence for lectin-sensitive complementary receptors involved in gamete recognition in *Fucus serratus*. *J. Cell Sci.*, **36**, 19–30.

5 Burke D., Mendonca-Previato L. & Ballou C.E. (1980) Cell–Cell recognition in yeast. Purification of *Hansenula wingei* 21-cell sexual agglutination factor and comparison of the factors from three genera. *Proc. natl. Acad. Sci.*, *USA*, **77**, 318–322.

6 Carpita N., Subularse D., Monteginos D. & Delmar D.P. (1979) Determination of the pore size of cell walls of living plant cells. *Science, N.Y.*, **205**, 1144–1147.

7 Clarke A.E., Anderson R. & Stone B.A. (1979) Form and function of arabinogalactans and arabinogalactan proteins. *Phytochemistry*, **18**, 521–540.

8 Clarke A.E. & Knox R.B. (1978) Cell recognition in flowering plants. *Q. Rev. Biol.*, **53**, 3–28.

9 Clarke A.E. & Knox R.B. (1980) Plants and immunity. *Dev. & Comp. Immunol.*, **3**, 571–589.

10 Crandall M. (1978) Mating-type interactions in yeasts. In *Symposium of the Society for Experimental Biology XXXII. Cell–Cell Recognition* (Ed. A.S.G. Curtis), pp. 105–120. Cambridge University Press, London.

11 Curtis A.S.G. (1979) Histocompatibility systems, recognition and cell positioning. *Dev. & Comp. Immunol.*, **3**, 379–387.

12 Day P.R. (1974) *Genetics of Host–Parasite Interactions*. W.H. Freeman, San Francisco.

13 Deurenberg J.J.M. (1976) *In vitro* protein synthesis with polysomes from unpollinated, cross- and self-pollinated *Petunia* ovaries. *Planta*, **128**, 29–33.

14 Deverall B.J. (1977) *Defence Mechanisms of Plants*. Cambridge Monographs in Experimental Biology No. 19. Cambridge University Press, Cambridge.

15 Dickinson H.G. & Lewis D. (1973) The formation of the tryphine coating the pollen grains of *Raphanus* and its properties relating to the self-incompatibility system. *Proc. Roy. Soc. Lond. B*, **184**, 149–165.

16 Fujii T. & Nito M. (1972) Studies on the compatibility of grafting of fruit trees. 1. Callus fusion between root stock and scion. *J. hort. Ass. Japan*, **41**, 1–10.

17 Gleeson P.A. & Clarke A.E. (1980) Comparison of the structures of the major components of the stigma and style secretions of *Gladiolus*: the arabino-3,6-galactans. *Carbohydrate Res.* **83**, 187–192.

18 Goldstein I.J. & Hayes C.E. (1978) The lectins: carbohydrate binding proteins of plants and animals. *Adv. Carbohyd. Chem.*, 128–3401.

19 Gunning B.E.S. & Steer M.W. (1975) *Ultrastructure and the Biology of Plant Cells*. Edward Arnold, London.

20 Herrero J. & Tabuenca M.C. (1969) Incompatibility between stock and scion. X. Behaviour of the peach/myrobalan combination when grafted at the cotyledon stage. *Ann. Aula Dei*, **10**, 937–945.

21 Heslop-Harrison J. (1978) Genetics and physiology of angiosperm incompatibility systems. *Proc. Roy. Soc. Lond. B*, **202**, 73–92.

22 Heslop-Harrison J., Knox R.B., Heslop-Harrison Y. & Mattson O. (1975) Pollen-wall proteins: emission and role in incompatibility responses in biology of the male gamete (Eds J.G. Duckett & P.A. Racey), pp. 181–202. Academic Press, London.

23 Hinch J. & Clarke A.E. (1979) Adhesion of fungal zoospores to root surfaces is mediated by carbohydrate determinants of the root slime. *Physiol. Plant Path*, **16**, 303–307.

24 Howlett B.J., Knox R.B., Paxton J.D. & Heslop-Harrison J. (1975) Pollen-wall proteins: Physicochemical characterization and role in self incompatibility in *Cosmos bipinnatus*. *Proc. Roy. Soc. Lond. B*, **188**, 167–182.

25 Hughes R.C. (1979) Cell surface carbohydrates in relation to receptor activity in glycoconjugate research (Eds J.D. Gregory & R.W. Jeanloz), pp. 985–1005. Academic Press, New York.

26 Keegstra K., Talmadge K.W., Bauer W.D. & Albersheim P. (1973) The structure of plant cell walls III. A model of the walls of suspension—cultured sycamore cells based on the interconnections of the macromolecular components. *Pl. Physiol.*, **51**, 188–196.

27 Knox R.B., Clarke A.E., Harrison S., Smith P. & Marchalonis J.J. (1976) Cell recognition in plants: Determinants of the stigma surface and their pollen interactions. *Proc. natl Acad. Sci., USA*, **73**, 2788.

28 Lamport D. (1980) *Structure and Function of Plant Glycoproteins in the Biochemistry of Plants, Volume 3*, pp. 501–541. Academic Press, New York.

29 Nicholson G.L. (1976) Transmembrane control of the receptors on normal and tumor cells. I Cytoplasmic influence over cell surface components. *Biochim. biophys. Acta*, **457**, 47–108.

30 Northcote D.H. (1977) The synthesis and assembly of plant cell walls: possible control mechanisms. In *The Synthesis, Assembly and Turnover of Cell Surface Components* (Eds G. Poste & G.L. Nicolson). Elsevier/North-Holland, Amsterdam.

31 Raff J.R., Hutchinson J.F., Knox R.B. & Clarke A.E. (1979) Cell recognition: antigenic determinants of plant organs and their cultured callus cells. *Differentiation*, **12**, 179–186.

32 Sanders R.E., Carlson R.W. & Albersheim P. (1978) A *Rhizobium* mutant incapable of nodulation and normal polysaccharide secretion. *Nature, Lond.*, **271**, 240–242.

33 Schachter H., Narasimham S. & Wilson J.R. (1979) The control of glycoprotein synthesis. In *Glycoconjugate Research II* (Eds J.C. Gregory & R.W. Jeanloz). Academic Press, New York.

34 Schmidt E.L. (1979) Initiation of plant root–microbe interactions *A. Rev. Microbiol.*, **33**, 355–376.

35 Sequeira L. (1978) Lectins and their role in host–pathogen specificity. *A. Rev. Phytopathol.*, **16**, 453–81.

36 Sharon N. (1979) Possible functions of lectins in micro-organisms, plants and animals. In *Glycoconjugate Research I*. (Eds J.D. Gregory & R.W. Jeanloz), pp. 458–491. Academic Press, New York.

37 Vithanage H.I.M.V., Gleeson P.A. & Clarke A.E. (1980) Callose: its nature and involvement in self-incompatibility responses in *Secale cereale*. *Planta*, **148**, 498–509.

38 Watkins W.M. (1978) Genetics and biochemistry of some human blood groups. *Proc. Roy. Soc. Lond. B*, **202**, 31–53.

39 Weise L. (1974) Nature of sex-specific glycoprotein agglutinins in *Chlamydomonas. Ann. N.Y. Acad. Sci.*, **234**, 283–295.

40 Wolpert J.S. & Albersheim P. (1976) Host–symbiont interactions 1. The lectins of legumes interact with the O-antigen-containing lipopolysaccharides of their symbiont *Rhizobia. Biochem. biophys. Res. Commun.*, **70**, 729–737.

41 Woodward J.R., Keane P.J. & Stone B.A. (1979) Structures and properties of wilt inducing polysaccharides from *Phytophthora* species.

42 Yeoman M.M. & Brown R. (1976) Implications of the formation of the graft union for organisation in the intact plant. *Ann. Bot.*, **40**, 1265–1276.

43 Yeoman M.M., Kilpatrick D.C., Miedzybrodzka M.B. & Gould A.R. (1978) Cellular interactions during graph for motion in plants, a recognition phenomenon? *Symposium of the Society for Experimental Biology.* XXXII. *Cell–Cell Recognition* (Ed A.S.G. Curtis) pp. 139–159. Cambridge University Press, London.

Chapter 3.7
Cell Recognition in the Immune Response
Gregory W. Warr and
John J. Marchalonis

3.7.1   INTRODUCTION

Cell recognition not only underlies many of the normal developmental and physiological processes of an animal, but it is also vital to the ability of an animal to respond to foreign (i.e. not self) entities which encroach upon its internal environment. In this review, we will briefly outline the basic phenomena of immunity, and then examine what is known of the mechanisms whereby those cells mediating specific immune responses are enabled to recognize foreignness.

Immunity, used colloquially, refers to the resistance of an animal to certain injurious biological agents, which are either infectious (such as micro-organisms) or toxic (generally the secretions of micro-organisms, examples being the tetanus and botulinus exotoxins). However, the immune system can react to many foreign substances which enter the body, including non-pathogens (for example molecules derived from foods, antibiotics, and plant pollens). Responses to this latter class of non-pathogenic molecule are not protective, and can be harmful, as in the case of the allergies such as hay fever, and in the case of auto-immunity, which occurs when an animal recognizes its own tissues and cells as foreign.

The immune system can be considered as consisting of two compartments, sometimes called specific and non-specific. For reasons which will be outlined below, we believe that better terms for these are adaptive and non-adaptive immunity.

Adaptive, acquired or *specific* immunity is manifest as an alteration in the level of response of an animal to an immunogenic (antigenic) stimulus subsequent to an initial exposure to the antigen. This alteration in level of reactivity is specific for the antigen involved. Thus, immunization of an animal or person with diphtheria toxin treated to render it (the toxoid) non-pathogenic results in immunity to the pathogenic effects of infection with diphtheria, but leaves the immunized subject susceptible to other, non-related infectious organisms. Specific, adaptive immune recognition is characteristically found in vertebrates, in which it is associated absolutely with the presence of lymphoid tissues and circulating antibodies [17, 35]. We will consider this immune system, and especially its cellular basis, in greater detail below. In passing, it should be noted that exposure of an animal to an antigen does not always lead to a heightened reactivity. Ignoring cases where the level of reactivity is unchanged (probably because of insufficient antigenic stimulation), the situation can occur where responsiveness is lost. That is, after a first exposure to an antigen, the animal loses all ability to respond to that antigen. It is then referred to as tolerant or paralysed with respect to that antigen. We shall have more to say about this concept later, as it is of interest both theoretically and practically. Unfortunately, the practical applications of tolerance are insufficiently developed to be of current use in clinical organ transplantation, where rejection of the donated organ is still a major problem.

Non-specific or *non-adaptive* immunity occurs in all animals, and results in a rejection of, or reaction against, foreign material which is mediated principally by phago-

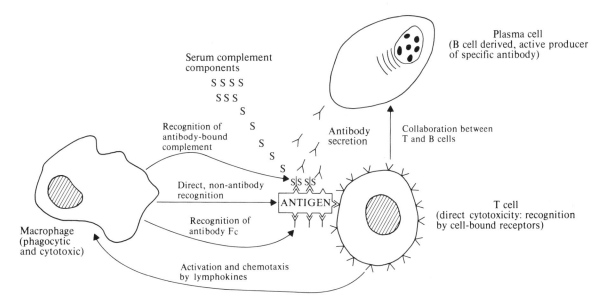

Fig. 3.7.1. Interactions between macrophages, lymphocytes and antigen. This figure shows that macrophages can recognize antigen (e.g. a bacterium) either directly or by means of antibody already attached to the antigen (recognition of antibody Fc). The macrophage also recognizes complement (a complex of serum proteins) that binds to antibody once it has bound to antigen. It is thought that an antibody will bind complement because it undergoes a conformational change upon binding to antigen. This figure also shows that T cells can recognize antigen by direct binding to membrane receptors, whereas

B cells, once they have been triggered by antigen (see text), secrete large quantities of antibody into the body fluid. This antibody reaches antigen by the body's circulatory system and by simple diffusion. The T cell is shown secreting factors that (1) enhance (help) antibody secretion by the B cell (plasma cell) and (2) activate the macrophage metabolically (i.e. increase its mobility and complement of hydrolytic enzymes) and also attract the macrophages to the site of T-cell–antigen interaction.

cytic cells, e.g. macrophages and granulocytes. These cells not only possess intrinsic abilities to recognize foreignness, but, in animals which possess an adaptive immune system (the vertebrates), they can interact with this latter system to provide very efficient functional immunity (Fig. 3.7.1). The mechanisms whereby phago-cytes inherently and directly recognize foreign materials are ill understood, but amongst other things they prob-ably involve carbohydrate–carbohydrate interactions (presumably by hydrogen bonding or other charge inter-actions), lectin-like or glycosyl transferase recognition of carbohydrates, interactions of hydrophobic struc-tures, and chemotactic attraction [31, 36, 37]. Although these reactions obviously have specificity at a molecular level, this is neither (a) of fine specificity, nor (b) adapt-ive, like that of the lymphoid system. One way in which the phagocytic cells interact with the lymphoid system in the expression of immunity is by an ability to recognize (by membrane receptors) the Fc region of antibody once

it has bound to foreign (antigenic) material (Figs 3.7.1, 3.7.2). In addition, these cells can recognize binding of serum complement components to antibody complexed with antigen. The recognition of antibody and com-plement components (some of which have chemotactic properties and some of which have lytic properties) leads to more ready engulfment of the foreign material to which they are bound. The process of making foreign material more susceptible to phagocytic engulfment with antibody (and complement) is termed opsoniza-tion. Lymphocytes can also recruit phagocytic cells, especially macrophages, to aid them in the destruction of foreign material. Certain lymphocytes, termed T cells (defined below), upon recognizing antigen, release mediators (lymphokines) which are chemotactic for macrophages and can also activate them. These acti-vated macrophages are thus attracted to the site of an immune response. The infiltration of lymphocytes and macrophages is typical of certain immune reactions, termed delayed hypersensitivity, such as those seen in response to the tubercle bacillus (*Mycobacterium tuberculosis*).

Although non-adaptive immunity can be enhanced following contact with foreign material (for example the phagocytic capacity of macrophages may be increased), the enhanced activity does not show inherent specificity (i.e. their activity against *all* entities sensed as foreign is enhanced). In the following sections, we consider what is known of cellular recognition and its molecular basis in the well-studied systems of mammalian immunity, and then, by extension of our survey to the poikilothermic vertebrates, we try to draw some simple unifying hypothesis in an area which is still the subject of intense, and largely uncompleted, investigation.

3.7.2 PHENOMENA OF IMMUNITY: SOME MAMMALIAN PATTERNS

The immune response

Following natural or experimental immunization of an animal, immunity can be manifest in a number of ways, but these can all be reduced to two basic mechanisms: (1) the production of serum antibody, and (2) the activities of lymphocytes which can react directly with antigenic materials. Serum antibodies are complex multichain proteins which show exquisite binding specificity for antigen. The basic structure of the antibody molecule is shown in Fig. 3.7.2. The molecule possesses two identical antigen-binding sites at its —NH$_2$ terminal ends, and structures towards the —COOH terminal (or Fc) portion of the molecule which carry out some important non-antigen-specific effector functions. These effector functions include the ability to fix complement and the ability to attach to receptors in the membrane of other cell types, such as macrophages (see Section 3.7.1) and mast cells (the histamine-containing cells which, on reaction of their bound antibody with antigen, release the histamine that gives rise to some of the symptoms of allergies such as hay fever). In addition, the Fc region of the molecule is that part involved in the polymerization which is characteristic of certain immunoglobulin classes. The immunoglobulins of humans are divided into five classes, IgM, IgG, IgA, IgD and IgE (some of which possess subclasses), and some of the simpler properties of these molecules are given in Table 3.7.1.

Cell-mediated immunity, in which the immune lymphocyte reacts directly with the antigen it recognizes, is manifest in a number of ways.

The destruction of cells (cytotoxicity) which is seen when an incompatible tissue or organ graft is being rejected by an animal is a classical example of cell-mediated immunity. Cell-mediated immunity is also characteristically seen with many chronic bacterial infections, and in immunity to some virus infections. Skin hypersensitivity of contact type (delayed-type hypersensitivity [32]), which is often seen in persons exposed to the antigens of *Mycobacteria*, can also occur in animals or persons whose skin has been exposed to certain reactive organic chemicals (e.g. dinitrofluorobenzene) and is a further manifestation of cell-mediated immunity.

Cell-mediated immunity also operates in a number of artificial, experimentally induced situations. For example, the injection of lymphoid cells into an incompatible recipient can result in graft-versus-host disease if matters are arranged so that the recipient is incapable of rejecting the donor cells. Another example is the phenomenon *in vitro* of the mixed lymphocyte reaction. If lymphocytes from two incompatible (for grafting) donors are mixed and co-cultured *in vitro*, their lymphocytes will respond to the foreign stimulus they provide each other by, among other things, entering division.

In recent years, immunologists have begun to understand something about the cellular and molecular events underlying these phenomena. Our knowledge at the present time is reviewed in the following sections.

Clonal selection

For any cell to respond appropriately to its environment, it must be able to receive signals. In the case of the immune system, the signal is in the form of the antigen. Since most antigens are complex macromolecules which are believed not to penetrate to a significant extent the lymphocyte plasma membrane, the view has become prevalent that lymphocytes bear on their membranes specific receptors which can bind to antigen and enable the cell to recognize antigen.

Instructionist theories, such as those of Pauling [23], suggested that the antigen with which a lymphoid cell comes into contact instructs (sterically) the cell which antibody to make. Such theories have become untenable in the light of modern knowledge of the mechanisms of

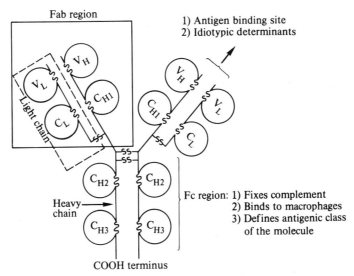

Fig. 3.7.2. Diagrammatic structure of human immunoglobulin IgG. Disulphide bonds are indicated by SS. If all disulphide bonds are reduced to free —SH groups, the molecule is free to fall apart into its four constituent chains. However, the molecule can also be cleaved enzymically, and without reduction some interesting fragments are obtained. Note that only two closely spaced disulphide bonds occur between the two heavy chains. Cleavage by papain occurs —NH$_2$ terminal to these bonds, and the molecule falls apart into an Fc region and two Fab fragments. Alternatively, pepsin cleaves —COOH terminal to these two bonds, and produces a smaller (often degraded) Fc region and two covalently (S—S) linked Fab regions, the so-called (Fab')$_2$ fragment. The Fab fragment is monovalent, and the (Fab')$_2$ fragment divalent. These two fragments are thus very useful to immunochemists because (1) they can determine the effective valency of the antibody, and (2) the Fc piece, which can sometimes do undesirable things like binding to complement or to cell membranes, has been removed.

Table 3.7.1. Classes of human immunoglobulin

Class (isotope)	Chain composition	H-chain molecular weight	Complement-fixing activity	Comments
IgM	$(\mu_2 L_2)_5$	70 000	+	With IgD, the most frequent lymphocyte surface Ig, in the $\mu_2 L_2$ monomeric form
IgG (4 sub-classes)	$\gamma_2 L_2$	53 000	+ (depending on subclass)	Predominant serum class, not frequent as a lymphocyte receptor
IgA	$(\alpha_2 L_2)_2$	65 000	–	The antibody found in secretions (e.g. nasal and gut mucus, saliva, bile)
IgE	$\epsilon_2 L_2$	70 000	–	The mast-cell-bound antibody responsible for reactions of immediate hypersensitivity in allergies such as hay fever.
IgD	$\delta_2 L_2$	70 000	–	The least abundant serum antibody. With IgM, the most frequent lymphocyte surface Ig. Frequently (c. 90%) present on the *same* cell as IgM

The isotype of the Ig molecule is determined by the type of heavy chain it contains. These chains ($\mu, \gamma, \alpha, \epsilon, \delta$) are encoded by separate genes, and therefore differ in primary amino acid sequence as well as in function and antigenic structure. The light (L) chains are of either kappa (κ) or lambda (λ) type, and are likewise encoded by individual genes protein synthesis (see Chapter 6.4). The acceptance of the concept that information generally flows in the direction DNA → RNA → protein makes it impossible to believe that an external signal such as an antigen could control the primary structure of an antibody protein and has led to the conclusion that a lymphocyte possesses preformed receptors for antigen, even before an animal has encountered the antigen in question. Ehrlich suggested that cells have receptors (side chains, as they were termed) with a variety of specificities. He thought that selective reaction of antigen with one of these receptors subsequently led to its loss from the cell, and that the loss was compensated for by the production of a large number of molecules with the same specificity as that of the receptor, which were then secreted. Burnet [5] put forward a simpler version of this idea, known as clonal selection. This has since become accepted dogma

in immunology and, after describing the theory, we shall consider some of the evidence which might be taken to support or contradict it. The theory of clonal selection (shown diagrammatically in Fig. 3.7.3) states that each lymphocyte is precommitted to react with one antigen, and bears receptors which are specific for that antigen (single specificity). Hence, because of the large number of antigens to which an animal can respond (perhaps as high as 10^6), only a few lymphocytes in any one animal will be able to respond to a single antigenic determinant. Thus, for an animal to mount an effective immune response to an antigen, amplification of the response of the few reactive cells is required. This amplification is provided by clonal selection: the antigen reacts with (selects) the specific lymphocyte, and this reaction with antigen leads to repeated division of the lymphocyte, the progeny of which constitute a clone which is expanding under the driving stimulus of the antigen. The theory as expounded by Burnet contained other important ideas, for example that the wide diversity in specificity of lymphocytes was generated by somatic mutation of the genes encoding antibody molecules during development. Another important concept was that the production of self-reactive (auto-immune) cells (forbidden clones) was prevented because, during ontogenetic development, the cells passed through a stage in which they died if confronted with the antigen to which they reacted. Of course, self antigens would be virtually ubiquitous at all times. This explained not only why auto-immunity was uncommon, but also why a tolerant state was easier to induce in the foetal or neo-natal animal, which was immunologically immature (and presumably still at the stage in which cells could be killed, rather than induced to respond, by contact with antigen). Some objections to, or modifications of, these points, i.e. clonal selection, somatic mutation and deletion of auto-reactive clones, will be considered briefly below.

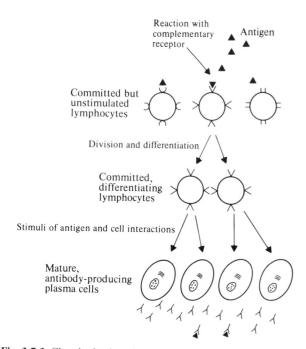

Fig. 3.7.3. Clonal selection of reactive lymphocytes by antigen. In this figure we see the triangular antigen (▲) bind specifically to the middle lymphocyte of the three that have migrated from the bloodstream on to this page. Notice the complementarity between receptors on this cell and antigen. The union of receptor with antigen induces division and differentiation of this lymphocyte when other physiological conditions are met (see text), and the final product is a clone of plasma cells, all derived from the original stimulated cell, and all secreting antibody of identical, triangular specificity.

One cell, one receptor specificity

It has been suggested that clonal distribution of antigen reactivity may not be on a strictly one-to-one basis, on the grounds that not all lymphocytes are restricted to reaction with only one antigen, or the production of only one antibody specificity. The ability of a lymphocyte to recognize antigen is generally assessed by direct observation of antigen-binding cells, the antigen being rendered accessible to study by labelling with a fluorescent group or a radioisotope. In unimmunized animals, the frequency of cells binding any one antigen has been reported to range from the number predicted by clonal selection (about 0.001%) up to around 1%. The interpretation of these results is made difficult because many macromolecular antigens can be 'seen' from many different angles by an antibody, and hence one molecule (for example a serum albumin) may in fact bear dozens of effective, different, antigenic determinants (called epitopes) so one might expect many cells to react with the molecule even when clonal selection occurred. Furthermore, some investigators have reported that a single lymphocyte can bind two antigens. The frequency of these double-antigen-binding cells is usually what might be expected, i.e. the product of the frequencies for each individual antigen. The simplest inference to be drawn from these reports is that a single lymphocyte may possibly, at a certain stage in its life, express receptors of more than one specificity. However, to prove this unequivocally will require a more detailed investigation at the molecular level, a task which is not easy.

There have also been a few reports that an individual antibody-producing cell can produce antibody of more than one specificity. Without detailed discussion of technical points, we will say that the clonal distribution of antigen reactivities among lymphocytes appears to be generally the case, but (a) it may well not be an absolute phenomenon, (b) it is usually, but may not always be, a one cell/one antigen situation, and (c) in any case few people would support the opposing extreme claim that all lymphocytes can recognize all antigens.

Somatic mutation

From recent developments in the study of immunoglobulins, it seems that both somatic mutation and germline encoding of antibody specificities interact to generate the diversity of observed antibody responses.

These observations have included analysis of the variability of immunoglobulin antigen-binding regions in terms of amino acid sequences, and direct studies of the organization of the DNA encoding the immunoglobulins, which are considered later (section 3.7.3).

Deletion of auto-reactive clones

There has been controversy as to whether auto-reactive cells (clones) are deleted from an animal during development of that clone, or whether the reactive cells are present but merely suppressed. The resolution of this issue appears to be that deletion of auto-reactive cells does occur during fetal development, but that suppression of reactive clones is another form of tolerance, of presently undetermined significance, that can be demonstrated in adult animals. Thus, although nearly all the ideas put forward by Burnet have been challenged individually (with varying degrees of success), his theory of clonal selection stands, accepted in broad outline, as the intellectual backbone of cellular immunology.

As will become evident below, other skeletal elements are not so well formed.

Lymphoid heterogeneity and division of function

From observations of the immune status of humans who were genetically deficient in certain lymphoid organs or functions, it became clear that the immune system consisted of at least two compartments, the thymus-derived or processed lymphocytes (T cells) which were responsible for cell-mediated immune reactions, and a second class of lymphocytes responsible for antibody production. These latter cells have been termed B cells, after the Bursa of Fabricius, the organ of origin of these cells in birds. The origin of B cells in mammals is still not entirely defined, but is generally supposed to be in the bone marrow, or more cautiously in some undefined equivalent to the bursa organ. The original clinical observations on humans with selective immune deficiencies resulting from an absence of the thymus (DiGeorge syndrome) or bursa-equivalent function (agammaglobulinaemia) have been reproduced in laboratory rodents and fowls. This has been achieved both by experimental removal of organs such as the thymus, and by the observation of mutants such as the congenitally athymic mouse whose unhappy situation is not improved by an absence of fur, resulting in its being called alternatively the nude mouse.

In mammals and birds, the thymus is essential for the generation of immunological competence, but thymocytes are generally not active in immune processes. However, T cells which have migrated out of the thymus to the peripheral lymphoid organs function in a variety of ways. Not only are they involved in the classical cell-mediated immune reactions, but they collaborate with B cells to bring about efficient production of antibody [21]. In addition, it has been reported that they can act to regulate an immune response by exerting a functional suppressive effect. It is likely that these diverse functions are mediated by distinct subsets of T cells, definable at the moment only by some surface antigenic markers.

Surface markers of lymphocytes

The heterogeneity of lymphocytes can be defined, stud-

ied and taken advantage of not only through functional studies but by virtue of unique differences in the plasma membrane proteins of the functionally distinct populations. It is a generally important concept in developmental biology that cells which look alike by light microscopy may have completely different arrays of molecules on the cell surface. The information below about the diversity of the membranes of cells involved in the immune response may be taken as an indication of the diversity which may subsequently be found in the

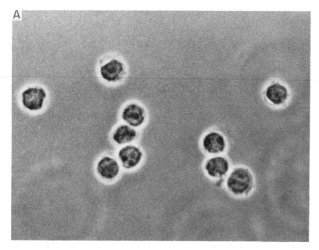

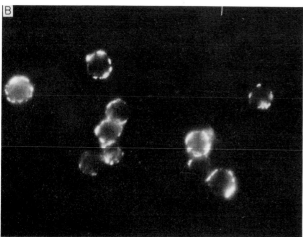

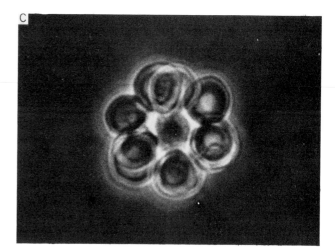

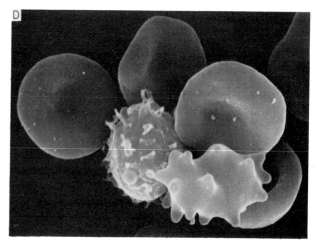

Fig. 3.7.4. Immunofluorescence and erythrocyte rosetting of guinea-pig lymphocytes. Guinea-pig lymphocytes stained with fluorescein-conjugated anti-immunoglobulin antibodies are shown under phase-contrast (A) or fluorescence (B) microscopic examination. Guinea-pig thymocytes rosetting with rabbit erythrocytes are shown under phase-contrast (C) or scanning electron microscopic (D) examination. Note the central lymphocyte surrounded by erythrocytes.

less well studied cell populations of the early embryo. The membrane proteins (or glycoproteins) of lymphocytes are usually studied by immunological means. That is, an antibody is raised to them, and the reaction of antibody with particular cells can be used to identify them (if the reaction of the antibody is traced by virtue of a fluorescent or radioactive group covalently bound to it). Alternatively, the antibody can be used to delete functional lymphocytes bearing the antigen in question by treating with antibody and complement, which then brings about lysis and cell death. Membrane immunofluorescence is illustrated in Fig. 3.7.4 A and B.

Antibodies can be raised by the immunization of genetically different animals with living lymphocytes. Antisera raised in a foreign species are referred to as xenoantisera, and those raised in genetically distinct members of the same species are called alloantisera. One of the most useful markers of T cells in the mouse is the θ alloantigen, now usually termed the Thy.1 antigen. This molecule is a glycoprotein of molecular weight about 23 000, and it is found on thymocytes and peripheral T cells. It is absent from the surface of B cells, but does occur on brain cells, for unknown reasons. No strict equivalent of the Thy.1 antigen is known in humans, although specific xenogeneic anti-T antibodies have been produced. Using xenogeneic antisera to immunoglobulins, usually only B cells, and not T cells, show positive membrane reactions. This criterion has proved a very useful marker for B cells in mammals, but it now appears almost certain that T cells can also bear a type of membrane immunoglobulin. This immunoglobulin can be detected with a varying degree of ease depending on the reagents and techniques used and the species of animal under investigation. Thus, the presence of immunoglobulins in the membrane can be a useful marker for B cells, but it is not absolute.

Many other markers for lymphocytes are available. A series of alloantigens called Ly have been described, and by their use one can define not only T and B cells but apparently also functional subsets of T cells, such as helpers for the antibody response, cytotoxic cells and cells which regulate the immune response (so-called suppressors). In addition, T cells in many mammalian species bear molecules in their membrane which react with various foreign erythrocytes. This reaction can be visualized as rosetting, a cluster of erythrocytes lying around the central lymphocyte (Fig. 3.7.4 C and D). Why this phenomenon should occur is unknown, but it has proved a useful marker. Other surface markers include the presence of receptors for the Fc portion of immunoglobulins or for components (usually C3) of complement. Fc and C receptors usually occur on B cells, but this is not an absolute distinction since some T cells have also been shown to bear Fc receptors.

Cell collaboration in the immune response

The important realization that T and B cells collaborate in the antibody response came from experiments using haptens. Haptens are small, chemically defined groups (such as dinitrophenol) which are antigenic *only* when coupled to a larger, immunogenic molecule, e.g. a protein such as a foreign serum albumin or an invertebrate haemocyanin. Such a molecule is termed the carrier. In order to demonstrate collaboration between T and B cells, use is made of haptens, carriers and cell-transfer systems. In this case, cell transfer means the injection of immunologically competent cells into an animal whose immune system has been destroyed by a high dose of X-irradiation. Transfers are made between genetically identical animals to avoid any possible interference from rejection or other forms of incompatibility.

Suppose that spleen lymphocytes are taken from an animal which has previously been immunized (primed) with a hapten (H) on protein carrier A. If these cells are transferred to an irradiated animal and then tested for their ability to make antibody to hapten H when it is given on carrier protein B, it is found that their response is deficient. However, if cells from an animal primed with A–H (carrier protein A coupled to hapten) are transferred into an irradiated host which receives, at the same time, spleen lymphocytes from a donor primed with the carrier B only (not haptenated), then the cells in the irradiated host collaborate to produce anti-hapten antibody when challenged (immunized) with the hapten on protein carrier B (B–H). It was shown by Mitchison and others [9, 22] that the cells participating in this reaction were, from the carrier-primed donor, T (helper) cells, and from the hapten-primed donor, hapten-reactive B cells, which were the cells that actually produced antibody.

The mechanisms whereby T and B cells interact collaboratively in antibody production are not clear, especially since macrophages are now implicated in this process. At first, it was thought that T cells bound antigen by carrier determinants on their surface, effectively concentrating it so that haptenic determinants could be more readily recognized by B cells. This 'bridging' hypothesis is illustrated in Fig. 3.7.5.

We would like to point out in passing that T and B cells have no inherent power to discriminate between haptens and carriers. In the example cited above, this distinction was made experimentally. In the natural situation, when an animal is immunized with a single molecule, it seems likely that many determinants will be able to act both as carrier groups and as functional analogues of the haptens in the above experiment. Indeed, it has been shown experimentally that by use of the appropriate conditions, haptenic groups can function as carriers.

A development of the bridging theory, taking into account the involvement of macrophages, is also shown in Fig. 3.7.5. This hypothesis suggested that T cells shed specific receptors for antigen, which in turn bound to the macrophage membrane, where they then bound and concentrated antigen for presentation to B cells. These models are included here to illustrate that simple and elegant hypotheses once existed in this area of cellular immunology. For reasons which are too involved to attempt to explain here, but include controversy over the nature of the T-cell receptor and its ability to bind to macrophages, and the involvement, apparently, of a variety of specific and non-specific factors in collabora-

ANTIGEN BRIDGING HYPOTHESIS

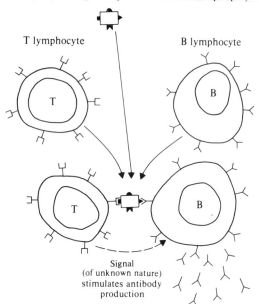

INVOLVEMENT OF THE MACROPHAGE

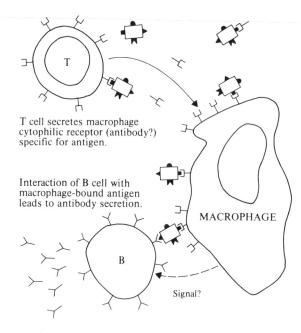

Fig. 3.7.5. Models of cell collaboration in the antibody response. Both these hypothetical schemes depend on the antigen bearing a number of (at least two) individual determinants recognizable by lymphocyte receptors. The antigen bridging hypothesis (shown on the left) suggests that the antigen physically 'cross-links' T and B cells with the right receptor specificity, allowing the T cell to help the B cell to become an active secretor of antibody by the transmission of a signal of unknown nature. This model suffers from the fact that (1) three-body collisions are improbable, and (2) T and B cells have been shown to be able to collaborate without being stuck together. This latter observation was made with the B and T cells separated by a membrane permeable to molecules but impermeable to cells, and further

experiments along these lines showed that macrophages had to be mixed with the B cells and not the T cells. These observations led to the hypothesis demonstrated on the right, in which T cells shed receptors in complexes with antigen, which in turn bind to macrophage membranes. The macrophage thereby acquires a surface coat of antigen which it can present to a B cell of appropriate specificity and so activate it. N.B. As mentioned in the text, neither of these hypotheses is currently considered satisfactory to explain all the observed phenomena of cell collaboration in the antibody response. They should therefore be considered primarily of historical interest, although they also illustrate the sort of concepts with which cellular immunologists operate.

tion, the T/B/macrophage model shown in Fig. 3.7.5 is no longer considered acceptable by many investigators. However, no simple and acceptable model has taken its place, and the molecular nature of cell collaboration remains to be satisfactorily elucidated. Detailed discussions of these problems can be found in the book by Katz [13].

The function of B cells is much easier to investigate and explain. B cells can be considered to be pre-programmed to produce antibody of a given specificity. They are turned on to produce this antibody by a variety of stimuli. Although these stimuli can be nonspecific (i.e. not delivered by antigen) under laboratory conditions, it seems reasonable to assume that in an animal undergoing immune stimulation, these stimuli to the B cell are antigen-related and delivered directly or indirectly via a membrane receptor for that antigen.

The foregoing paragraphs have evaded an issue central to the whole of cellular immunology. What is the nature of the receptor for antigen in the lymphocyte membrane? Perhaps, by taking a reductionist approach, we can find simple underlying mechanisms which will serve as a foundation for clarification of the more complex cellular interactions to be seen in immunology.

Lymphocyte receptors for antigen

Ehrlich's side-chain theory (see p. 222) embodied two important concepts. First, that a cell could recognize antigen by means of a plasma-membrane-bound receptor and, secondly, that the product the cell was stimulated to secrete, as a result of the union of antigen with receptor, was an excess of the particular receptor. This latter point can be stated more simply by the phrase: the receptor equals the secreted product. This is a very appealing concept for the immunologist because the secreted product of the lymphocyte (i.e. immunoglobulin) is the only known class of molecule which possesses the wide variability in antigen-binding properties which is the hallmark of adaptive immunity.

Hence, if we accept the basic principles of the clonal selection theory, we are almost forced to postulate that immunoglobulin is the cell-bound receptor for antigen, for otherwise the lymphocyte would have to possess a second set of molecules (the receptors) with a variability and specificity equivalent to that of the secreted product (the immunoglobulins).

The concept that membrane immunoglobulin is the

lymphocyte receptor for antigen has found wide and ready acceptance in the case of B cells (those cells committed to differentiate into antibody-secreting (plasma) cells), but is disputed for the T-cell lineage.

The reasons for this dispute are many, but some of the more important ones are outlined below.

(1) B cells bear a large amount of membrane immunoglobulin which is readily detected *in situ* by, for example, the direct binding of fluorochrome- or radioisotope-labelled antibody to immunoglobulin (Fig. 3.7.4). In contrast, T-cell membrane immunoglobulin in mammals is usually difficult to detect using these direct-binding techniques. However, as we will discuss later, this observation is not universally true.

(2) T and B cells appear to have different specificity repertoires. In particular, many T-cell reactions seem to be restricted by the nature of the major histocompatibility complex (MHC) antigens present on the surface of the lymphocyte and the target against which its acts. The MHC is considered in the following section.

Major histocompatibility complex (MHC)

This constitutes a so-called multigene family, which in the mouse consists of a large (unspecified) number of loci in a section of chromosome number 17, about 0.5 centimorgans long. The MHC or an equivalent seems to be present in all species of mammals, and most (but not all) other vertebrates. It encodes molecules found on the surface of lymphocytes (and most other nucleated cells) which are the primary antigens recognized as being foreign upon transplantation of cells or tissues to other individuals. These are the so-called histocompatibility antigens. In addition, genes in the MHC code for a number of other products, including the immune-response (Ir) genes. These genes control the level of specific immune responses to a number of antigens. It appears that they do not achieve this by imposing restrictions on recognition of antigen by cells, but that they act at a level (possibly cell collaboration) involving amplification of the immune response. The biology of the murine MHC is reviewed by Klein [15], and the possible involvement of the complex in cell adhesion is discussed in Chapter 3.2.

An example of MHC restriction in immune responses comes in the area of cytotoxic T cells. T cells apparently will recognize and kill virus-infected or hapten-conjugated cells if these cells have the same MHC

222

2

antigens as were present on the virus-infected or hapten-conjugated cell initially used to immunize the T cell.

The requirement for MHC identity is not a universal phenomenon. In some T-cell cytolytic systems, for example against mouse leukaemia virus-infected cells or against some tumour antigens [6], this requirement is absent. Investigators looking at the phenomena of MHC restriction have so far been unable to distinguish between the following two possibilities. First, that T cells recognize antigen in physical association with MHC molecules or, secondly, that T cells recognize simultaneously but independently, using two receptors, antigen and self-MHC molecules.

This is a very brief summary of a huge field of research which is very active at present. Unfortunately, all the activity has failed to produce a clear-cut resolution of the role of the MHC in T-cell recognition. Nevertheless, because of the involvement of the MHC in so many phenomena of immunity, it is impossible to ignore, and some workers have even suggested that MHC products can act as receptors for antigen.

This is not a view that the present authors accept, because there is now a very large body of evidence suggesting that lymphocyte receptors for antigen are immunoglobulin-like on both T and B cells, especially with regard to the possession of the antigen-binding (variable region) portion of the immunoglobulin molecule (see [34] for review). We do not propose to say any more about the MHC in recognition, except that it appears likely that T cells possess immunoglobulin variable region receptors for antigen but, in addition, possess either another receptor (of unknown nature) for MHC molecules, or have their functional expression of immunity (e.g. killing, cell collaboration) dependent upon interactions with or between MHC molecules. The experimental results are not yet clear in this respect. However, we propose to turn now to consideration of an area where the experimental evidence is clearer and simpler to interpret—the occurrence and nature of immunoglobulin on lymphocytes.

The detection of immunoglobulin on lymphocytes

For immunofluorescence, it is standard procedure to isolate immunoglobulin (usually IgG or IgM) from the serum of an animal (for argument, let us say a mouse), and to use it to immunize another species (usually rabbit, goat or sheep). The resulting antiglobulin re-

agent can then be made detectable by labelling the antibody with a fluorochrome or a radioisotope. Upon incubation of mouse lymphocytes with this reagent, and following washing away of unbound material, a membrane reaction can be detected by using a fluorescence microscope as shown in Fig. 3.7.4 (or, in the case of a radioisotope-labelled reagent, by using autoradiography). In practice, this technique is often used in more complex and sensitive ways, and, after appropriate controls have been carried out to establish specificity of binding, a positive membrane reaction can be taken to be indicative of the presence of immunoglobulin on the membrane of the cell being examined. Using this sort of test, workers have been able to identify B cells (in all mammalian species and birds) as being immunoglobulin bearing, while T cells are usually seen as negative. Despite the evidence of the eyes, it appears that this result may be misleading. First, if the membranes of the T cells are solubilized, immunoglobulin determinants are detectable using biochemical techniques under some conditions [16]. This observation led to the suggestion that if immunoglobulin was present on T cells, it might be buried or occluded in the membrane in such a manner that only the functional, antigen-binding (variable) region of the molecule was exposed and that this region would not bind to the usual fluorescent labels which react with the constant part of the molecule. This leads us to the second point, which is that antibodies which are known to react with the antigen-binding (variable) region of immunoglobulin have been shown to (a) bind to T cells, (b) block the binding of antigen by T cells, and (c) induce functional responses (e.g. help or suppression) in T cells [2, 26]. A third observation is that all the lymphocytes (including those of the thymus) are positive for membrane immunoglobulin using rabbit antisera to their serum immunoglobulin in fish, urodele amphibians and larval anuran amphibians. Lymphocytes in these poikilothermic vertebrates have been shown to exhibit functional heterogeneity of T and B cell type (see review [27]), and the presence of immunoglobulin on these cells has been confirmed by both immunofluorescence and biochemical analysis [34].

The relationship of lymphocyte membrane immunoglobulin to the secreted antibody

It has become clear in recent years that the simple concept of 'receptor equals secreted product' does not hold true even for B cells, and in the case of T cells, which have no obvious secreted product, there is a controversy over their possession of immunoglobulin-like receptors. This controversy seems to have established, at least, that T-cell immunoglobulin is not the same as that found in other cells or in serum, although it apparently shares variable regions with serum antibodies.

B cells

B cells provide a simpler case for study than T cells. Everyone agrees that their receptor for antigens is immunoglobulin. However, it appears that membrane immunoglobulin is not quite the same as the secreted product. For example, in most mammals, IgM and IgD are the predomnant classes of immunoglobulin found on lymphocytes (see reviews [11, 33]). In contrast, IgG is the predominant serum class; IgD occurs in serum in a different form from that found on cells. Serum IgM in mammals is a pentamer, consisting of five identical units, each comprised of the basic two heavy and two light chains covalently bonded together (see Fig. 3.7.2). In the membrane of the B cell, the IgM exists as a single unit of this type (i.e. two heavy and two light chains).

Differences demonstrated between B-cell surface IgM and secreted IgM include the mobility of the heavy chain on electrophoresis in polyacrylamide gels in the presence of the detergent sodium dodecyl sulphate (SDS), differences in solubility in the absence of detergent, and differences in buoyant density [18–20].

It has recently been established that the physical basis for these differences resides in the C-terminus of the membane form of the IgM heavy (μ) chain. Compared with the secreted form, the membrane-bound μ chain has a different, longer 'tail'. The normal 20-residue C-terminus of the secreted μ chain is replaced by a different, 41-residue segment which has a high content of uncharged or hydrophobic amino acids [14]. These undoubtedly play a role in the association of the membrane IgM with the lipid bilayer.

T cells

The structure of T-cell immunoglobulin is far from being resolved. There is at present a consensus of opinion that a part of the mammalian T-cell receptor is a polypeptide chain of mol. wt about 68000, which contains the variable region (antigen-binding portion) of the immunoglobulin heavy chain. This knowledge of the nature of the T-cell receptor has been derived from studies of several sorts, involving both functional and biochemical studies. Examples of these are the isolation from antigen-specific T cells of membrane molecules of mol. wt 68000 which can bind to the antigen, and which also bear antigenic markers of the immunoglobulin variable region. In addition, individual antigenic markers of the variable region (idiotypes) can be shown to occur not only on specific molecules of serum antibody and B cells, but also on T cells [2, 26]. Furthermore, genetic studies show that idiotype expression on T cells is linked to known structural genes for the immunoglobulin constant regions, providing further evidence for the immunoglobulin nature of these molecules on T cells [3].

In the case of the 68000-mol.-wt antigen-specific polypeptides isolated from T cells, it is accepted that this heavy chain has a constant region which is probably immunoglobulin in nature, but not of a type previously encountered on B cells or in serum. This conclusion has been reached by a study of its antigenic nature, and by comparison of the peptides produced by chemical or enzymatic cleavage of this molecule with those produced from known immunoglobulin heavy chains. The question of the presence of a light chain on the T-cell antigen receptor is also unresolved, with some investigators reporting its presence, and some its absence. It should be borne in mind that immunochemical studies on serum immunoglobulins have shown that the presence of both heavy- and light-chain variable regions is required for optimal efficiency in binding antigens. Whether or not this observation should lead us to expect a light chain on T-cell immunoglobulin is unclear, but the present authors consider that, on the balance of both theoretical and experimental evidence, T-cell immunoglobulin consists of heavy and light chains. Again, it is possible that the T-cell light chain may not be typical of those found in serum and on B cells.

3.7.3 THE GENETIC BASIS OF IMMUNOGLOBULIN EXPRESSION

The adaptive immune system shows an exquisite ability to discriminate among an almost limitless variety of antigens and, in addition, shows the property of memory, i.e. is a biochemical learning system. As we saw in section 3.7.2, clonal selection is the hypothesis that best explains the observed phnomena. Two questions follow from clonal selection: how is the variety of specificity of antibodies generated, and how does a lymphocyte come to express only one of those specificities? The answers to these questions are not yet completely clear, but recent major advances in our understanding of the molecular genetics of lymphocytes have made much progress.

The generation of diversity

Diversity of the secreted product of lymphocytes (i.e. antibodies) must be underlain by diversity of the DNA encoding the variable (V) region of these antibodies. This much is clear, but for many years immunologists were unable to determine whether or not this diversity pre-existed in the germ-line DNA, or if it was produced during the development of lymphocytes by somatic mutation and recombination or rearrangement. An analysis of protein-sequence data, and the inferences to be drawn about genes from this, did not produce a clear resolution of this issue. However, it now appears that both mechanisms may be operating. For example, gene-counting by nucleic acid hybridization suggests that some light-chain V-region genes are present in very small copy numbers (probably one), whereas analysis by DNA cloning and sequence studies suggests that, for other light chains, a great deal of germ-line variable region diversity exists [30]. Nucleic acid hybridization techniques are detailed in Chapter 6.4. Evidence at the nucleic acid level for somatic rearrangement and mutation has also been presented [1, 4, 12]. We are thus left with the conclusion that the lymphoid system seems to make use of all its available major options for generating diversity in its repertoire of specificities.

Expression of immunoglobulin genes

If we accept that one lymphocyte expresses only one antibody specificity and, as outlined above, that lymphocytes contain in their germ-line more than one variable-region gene, we have to explain how they select only one of these genes for expression. Furthermore, there are two observations on the expression of immunoglobulin that we have to take into account. The first of these is allelic exclusion (the expression, in any one lymphocyte, of the products of only one of the alleles encoding immunoglobulins). Thus, in an animal heterozygous for μ-chain allotypes, we will only be able to detect one allele on any given IgM-bearing cell, although cells bearing each type will occur with roughly equal frequency. Allelic exclusion is easy to understand as part of the

process leading to clonal selection, requiring a restriction of specificities on any given lymphocyte. It seems to be brought about by only one of a pair of chromosomes bearing immunoglobulin genes being selected (at random?) to undergo the sequence of events leading to immunoglobulin expression.

The second observation is a phenomenon termed the 'switch', whereby a cell can express antibody of only one specificity but two isotypes, either simultaneously or sequentially. For example, a cell may produce IgM first, then IgG, both antibodies possessing identical antigen specificity. The obvious implication of this 'switch' is that one variable-region gene can be expressed in combination with two constant-region genes (in this case μ and γ).

As far as we are able to determine, the selection of one variable-region gene for expression by a cell and the subsequent processes of transcription and translation involve quite complex rearrangements of the DNA, and splicing at the level of the primary RNA transcript, before an immunoglobulin polypeptide is synthesized by the cell [1, 4, 8, 12, 24, 25, 28–30].

A simplified hypothesis of these events is outlined for the λ light chain in Fig. 3.7.6. At some stage between the germ-line cell and the committed lymphocyte, the DNA undergoes a rearrangement involving the selection of a variable-region gene and its relocation (translocation) to another region of the chromsosome, where it is much closer to the C-region gene. The existence of the J or joining region (Fig. 3.7.6) should be noted. This J region forms the part of the variable region contiguous with the constant region, but in the embryonic DNA it is associated with the constant region. In the process of the DNA reorganization that occurs during development, the

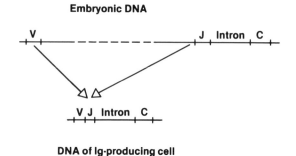

Embryonic DNA

DNA of Ig-producing cell

Fig. 3.7.6. Rearrangement of an immunoglobulin light chain gene during development, to show the J region and non-coding intron. (Based on [4])

DNA encoding the rest of the variable region comes to lie alongside that encoding the J region (Fig. 3.7.6) in the differentiated lymphocyte. It can be appreciated that the J region may not only act as a region for integration and reorganization of immunoglobulin genes, but may also itself contribute to the variability of binding-site repertoires of antibodies. The manner in which this somatic rearrangement of immunoglobulin genes can contribute to the variability of the antibody molecule is particularly well illustrated for the heavy-chain genes [28]. In the case of the heavy chain, there is a sizeable pool of possible V-region genes, but the third hypervariable region is encoded separately (the so-called diversity or D region). Thus the genetic rearrangement that produces the final heavy chain involves the selection of a V region, a D region and a J region, which in the final rearranged gene lie close to, but not contiguous with, the constant (C-region) gene [25], being separated from this by a non-coding stretch of DNA termed an 'intron'. Interestingly enough, the gene encoding the C region is also interrupted by introns. However, these introns occur at 'natural' structural junctions [29], such as those between the three γ heavy chain domains, and at the 'hinge' region (which occurs between the C_{H1} and C_{H2} domains and is believed to provide conformational flexibility in this region). The RNA transcript made from the immunoglobulin heavy- or light-chain gene contains the segments coded for by the introns and by the true coding (exon) stretches. The cytoplasmic form of the messenger RNA is then formed by enzymic splicing [24], and from this the immunoglobulin polypeptide is translated. It is believed that allelic exclusion results from a lack of rearrangement or an abortive rearrangement of immunoglobulin genes on one chromosome. The immunoglobulin class 'switch' from production of IgM to, for example, IgG is believed to involve a further gene rearrangement, in which the complete V-region gene is moved from its position adjacent to the μ-chain gene, and in this case is placed next to the γ-chain gene. The heavy-chain genes all lie in a closely grouped cluster. It is believed that the heavy-chain switch involves the 'looping out', excision and loss of the heavy-chain genes that were between the V region and the new heavy chain with which it is to be associated [8, 28]. In contrast to this, it is believed that the membrane and secreted forms of μ chain (see p. 229) are produced by selective splicing of an mRNA transcript that contains both alternative C termini.

Although the events described here for the immunoglobulin genes, beginning with DNA rearrangements and ending with RNA splicing, may seem remarkably complex, it should be pointed out that interrupted genes and RNA splicing appear to be virtually universal features of eukaryotic gene organization [7, 10] (see Chapter 6.4).

3.7.4 REFERENCES

1 Bernard O., Hozumi N. & Tonegawa S. (1979) Sequences of mouse immunoglobulin light chain genes before and after somatic changes. *Cell*, **15**, 1133–1144.
2 Binz H. & Wigzell H. (1977) Antigen-binding, idiotypic T-lymphocyte receptors. *Contemp. Top. Immunobiol.*, **7**, 113–177.
3 Binz H., Wigzell H. & Bazin H. (1976) T-cell idiotypes are linked to immunoglobulin heavy chain genes. *Nature, Lond.*, **264**, 639–642.
4 Brack C., Hirama M., Lenhard-Schuller R. & Tonegawa S. (1978) A complete immunoglobulin gene is created by somatic recombination. *Cell*, **15**, 1–14.
5 Burnet F.M. (1959) *The Clonal Selection Theory of Acquired Immunity*. Cambridge University Press, London.
6 Burton R.C., Chism S.E. & Warner N.L. (1977) In vitro induction of tumor-specific immunity. III. Lack of requirement for H-2 compatibility in lysis of tumor targets by T cells activated in vitro to oncofetal and plasmacytoms antigens. *J. Immunol.*, **118**, 971–980.
7 Crick F. (1979) Split genes and RNA splicing. *Science, N.Y.*, **204**, 264–271.
8 Dunnick W., Rabbitts T.H. & Milstein C. (1980) An immunoglobulin deletion mutant with implications for the heavy-chain switch and RNA splicing. *Nature, Lond.*, **286**, 669–675.
9 Falkoff R. & Kettman J. (1972) Differential stimulation of precursor cells and carrier-specific thymus-derived cell activity in the in vivo response to heterologous erythrocytes in mice. *J. Immunol.*, **108**, 54–58.
10 Gilbert W. (1978) Why genes in pieces? *Nature, Lond.*, **271**, 501.
11 Goding J.W., Scott D.W. & Layton J.E. (1977) Genetics, cellular expression and function of IgD and IgM receptors. *Immunol. Rev.*, **37**, 152–186.
12 Hozumi N. & Tonegawa S. (1976) Evidence for somatic rearrangement of immunoglobulin genes coding for variable and constant regions. *Proc. natl Acad. Sci., USA*, **73**, 3628–3632.
13 Katz D.H. (1977) *Lymphocyte Differentiation, Recognition and Regulation*. Academic Press, New York.
14 Kehry M, Ewald S., Douglas R., Sibley C., Raschke W., Fambrough D. & Hood L. (1980) The immunoglobulin μ chains of membrane-bound and secreted IgM molecules differ in their C-terminal segments. *Cell*, **21**, 393–406.
15 Klein J. (1975) *Biology of the Mouse Histocompatibility-2 Complex: Principles of Immunogenetics Applied to a Single System*. Springer-Verlag, New York.
16 Marchalonis J.J. (1975) Lymphocyte surface immunoglobulin. *Science, N.Y.*, **190**, 20–29.
17 Marchalonis J.J. (1977) *Immunity in Evolution*. Harvard University Press, Cambridge, Massachusetts.

18 Melcher U., Eidels L. & Uhr J.W. (1975) Are immunoglobulins integral membrane proteins? *Nature, Lond.*, **258**, 343–435.

19 Melcher U. & Uhr J.W. (1976) Cell surface immunoglobulin. XVI. Polypeptide chain structure of mouse IgM and IgD-like molecule. *J. Immunol.*, **116**, 409–415.

20 Melcher U. & Uhr J.W. (1977) Density differences between membrane and secreted immunoglobulins of murine splenocytes. *Biochemistry, N.Y.*, **16**, 154–152.

21 Miller J.F.A.P. (1972) Lymphocyte interactions in antibody responses. *Int. Rev. Cytol.*, **33**, 77–130.

22 Mitchison N.A., Rajewsky K. & Taylor R.B. (1970) Cooperation of antigenic determinants and of cells in the induction of antibodies. In *Developmental Aspects of Antibody Formation and Structure* (Eds J. Sterz & I. Riha), pp. 547–561. Czechoslovak Academy of Sciences, Prague.

23 Pauling L. (1940) A theory of the structure and process of formation of antibodies. *J. Am. chem. Soc.*, **62**, 2643–2657.

24 Rabbitts T.H. (1978) Evidence for splicing of interrupted immunoglobulin variable and constant region sequences in nuclear RNA. *Nature, Lond.*, **275**, 291–296.

25 Rabbitts T.H. & Forster A. (1978) Evidence for noncontiguous variable and constant region genes in both germ line and myeloma DNA. *Cell*, **13**, 319–327.

26 Rajewsky K. & Eichmann K. (1977) Antigens receptors of T helper cells. *Contemp. Top. Immunobiol.*, **7**, 69–112.

27 Ruben L.N. & Edwards B.F. (1980) The phylogeny of the emergence of T–B collaboration in humoral immunity. *Contemp. Top. Immunobiol.*, **9**, 55–89.

28 Sakano H., Maki R., Kurosawa Y., Roeder W. & Tonegawa S. (1980) Two types of somatic recombination are necessary for the generation of complete immunoglobulin heavy-chain genes. *Nature, Lond.*, **286**, 676–683.

29 Sakano H., Rogers J.H., Huppi K., Brack C., Traunecker A., Maki R., Wall R. & Tonegawa S. (1979) Domains and the hinge region of an immunoglobulin heavy chain are encoded in separate DNA segments. *Nature, Lond.*, **277**, 627–633.

30 Seidman J.G., Leder A., Edgell M.H., Polsky F., Tilghmann S.M., Tiemeier D.C. & Leder P. (1978) Multiple related immunoglobulin variable-region genes identified by cloning and sequence analysis. *Proc. natl Acad. Sci., USA*, **75**, 3881–3885.

31 Stossel T.P. (1975) Phagocytosis: recognition and ingestion. *Semin. Hematol.*, **12**, 83–115.

32 Turk J.L. (1975) *Delayed Hypersensitivity.* North-Holland, Amsterdam.

33 Vitetta E.S. & Uhr J.W. (1975) Immunoglobulin receptors revisited. *Science, N.Y.*, **189**, 964–969.

34 Warr G.W. (1979) Membrane immunoglobulins of vertebrate lymphocytes. *Contemp. Top. Immunobiol.*, **9**, 141–170.

35 Warr G.W. & Marchalonis J.J. (1978) Specific immune recognition by lymphocytes: an evolutionary perspective. *Q. Rev. Biol.*, **53**, 225–241.

36 Weir D.M. & Ogmundsdottir H.M. (1977) Non-specific recognition mechanisms by mononuclear phagocytes. *Clin. exp. Immunol.*, **30**, 323–329.

37 Wilkinson P.C. (1976) Recognition and response in mononuclear and granular phagocytes. *Clin. exp. Immunol.*, **25**, 355–366.

Conclusions to Part 3

The equal and unequal mitotic divisions of asymmetric cells form the cell types of early developing systems (Part 2), and as soon as the developing structure contains more than one cell, then the cells may start to interact with each other. This part of the book is concerned with the mechanism of local cell interactions and it also describes the properties of cells which are involved in the generation both of form and of new patterns of cell differentiation. The integration of these properties in the development of complete organisms is discussed in Part 4 of this book, and the coordination of organism development by long-distance diffusible or hormonal interactions is the subject of Part 5.

1. Interaction phenomena

Multicellular organisms must cohere and it is a minimum requirement of most local cell interactions that cells should stick to each other. There are two major methods by which cells interact. On the one hand they may establish or maintain direct cytoplasmic continuity, and on the other hand they may produce molecules on their surface or in their surroundings which influence the behaviour of neighbouring cells, principally by acting on the surface of these neighbours.

The reproduction and development of organisms involve a variety of phenomena where it is clear that one cell type exhibits different reactions when confronted with various other cell types. Thus cells adhere to each other with different affinities (Chapter 3.2), they move differentially on various cellular and matrix substrates (Chapter 3.3), they are induced or fail to be induced into new patterns of gene expression depending on the characters of neighbouring cells (Chapter 3.5). Similarly, pollen grains may be permitted to effect fertilization or not, depending upon 'recognition' reactions between pollen and stigma (Chapter 3.6). The

molecular mechanisms which are responsible for these differential responses are poorly understood, but they are certainly essential for the construction and propagation of most multicellular organisms.

2. Establishment and function of cytoplasmic connections

The sexual reproductive cycles of organisms depend on the capacity of gametes to fuse with each other, and initial cytoplasmic connections lead to complete cytoplasmic intermixing (Chapter 3.6). Here we are principally concerned with small communicating links between the cytoplasms of adjacent cells which allow small molecules to pass between cells without great distortions of shape in the joined cells (Chapter 3.4). Cytoplasmic links may persist between daughter cells after cell division in both animals (p. 169) and plants but characteristically these channels remain open in plant cells for the life of the plant (p. 171 et seq.). Plant plasmodesmata connections are usually between sister cells. In contrast, animal cells make and break cytoplasmic links (gap junctions) as the cells move around the organism and such communicating channels are not obviously restricted by ancestry.

Many different kinds of molecule can pass between the cytoplasms of adjacent cells connected by plasmodesmata and gap junctions; the list includes ions, small hormones such as auxins and cyclic AMP, and metabolites, including sugars. The exclusion properties of plasmodesmata are not fully documented but certainly molecules of molecular weight up to 550 can pass between linked cells and it is likely that the much larger structures of mature viruses can move through these connections during a virus infection (p. 173 et seq.). The permeability of gap junctions between animal cells in culture has been analysed in great detail; these junctions in general permit the indiscriminate exchange of molecules between adjacent cells if their molecular weight does not exceed 1500. However, there is now evidence that some cell types in culture cannot communicate in this way, and that in intact embryos the gap junctions between different cell types are not as freely permeable as they appear to be between like cells. The molecular bases of these restrictions are unclear.

It is therefore likely that if the coordination of early development does depend on these fine cytoplasmic links, then at least in animals the communication must be achieved by the transfer of small molecules, and that large proteins and nucleic acids are not the signals.

3. Interactions at the cell surface

In developing organisms it is often the case that interacting cells are not linked by cytoplasmic connections and it follows that the cells must communicate in other ways. These communicating systems are thought to have two principal components. First, the signal from one cell is thought to form a molecular complex with a membrane-bound receptor on another cell; complex formation is viewed as a steric interaction, similar in kind to the reaction of an enzyme with a substrate or to the other molecular aggregations described in Chapter 6.2. Secondly, the formation of this complex is transduced into an internal cellular response, and secondary signals are evoked by the receipt of the first. This type of communication achieves differential responses by both molecular recognition at the cell surface and by alterations in the state of the responding cell and it is potentially precise and unambiguous. A well-worked analysis of the sophistication of such systems is the display of variable immunoglobulin molecules on the surface of lymphocytes: any one immunoglobulin molecule can only react tightly with one antigenic site and therefore its reaction is limited to the number of different molecules which bear this antigenic site. Usually, a single lymphocyte displays on its surface a single type of immunoglobulin and its reaction is restricted to one antigenic site (Chapter 3.7). In the immune system, the nature of the response can be clearly shown to depend on the state of the responding cell, for T lymphocytes and B lymphocytes show different responses to the same antigen, and this illustrates the second level of response control in this communication system. It must be remembered that the specificity of this system partly depends on the genetic diversity of immunoglobulin genes generated in development, and that this source of molecular variability is probably not available to the other cell-surface molecules displayed in early developing systems (Part 1 and Chapter 6.4).

4. Rapid reactions

In certain biological situations, it is important that two cells should rapidly recognize each other and discriminate in their response. These interactions are most obvious in mating-type reactions in higher plants; in these cases there is evidence that the specificity of the response depends on steric interactions between molecules on or released by the signal cell and molecules on or close to the recipient cell surface (Chapter 3.6).

In these molecular interactions, it is frequently found that the reacting region is a saccharide which is usually displayed on the cell surface bound either to a lipid (glycolipid) or to a protein (glycoprotein). Saccharide sites bind tightly to lectins, which are protein molecules that have different affinities for different sugar chains, and there is evidence that lectins are displayed on the surface of the responding cell. Such sugar–lectin interactions are implicated in the mating of algae and fungi (p. 202 et seq.) and in the aggregation of slime mould amoebae (p. 110 et seq. and p. 298 et seq.). Similar mechanisms may be involved in pollen–stigma interactions, but the nature of the interacting molecular sites is unclear. What is certain is that highly polymorphic single Mendelian gene differences do control the compatibility of pollination in many plant species and this fact suggests that steric molecular interactions control the process.

Certain methods of measuring animal cell adhesion monitor the ability of cells to stick together after a collision and to resist subsequent shearing; they therefore monitor rapid interactions (p. 102 et seq.). In most cases, such studies indicate that adhesion between like cells occurs in preference to adhesion between cells of different types; the molecular mechanism of this specificity is not known.

Rapid reactions between cells of different genotypes in reproductive processes are beginning to be understood in molecular detail, but the responses of genetically identical cells to each other in the developing organism are not yet analysed in sufficient depth.

5. Phenomenology of local interactions in embryogenesis

It is only in a few cases that we can be sure that particular molecules mediate cellular communication in the compact and tight structure of developing embryos. It is therefore important to document the phenomenology of these interactions. For instance, communication between cells which is required for their differentiation, morphogenesis and maintenance may occur by diffusible substances at a small distance (neural induction, p. 182) or it may depend on cell contact (kidney induction, p. 183 and Chapter 3.5). Such observations, and the fact that the local adhesivity of cells can be affected by diffusible substances (p. 114), should make one careful in seeking one single explanation of the specificity of cell interactions in embryogenesis. Indeed it is not clear that cell interactions in embryogenesis require the precision of steric molecular interactions which are seen in the immune system and in mating responses. The specificity of response may be generated by control of cell location and by developmental pre-history setting up states in cells which influence their response.

However, there is one structure, the extracellular matrix, or basement membrane, which can clearly alter embryonic animal cell behaviour in culture and which probably mediates many local cell interactions in intact embryos. Characteristically, such matrices contain collagen, laminin, and long, branched sugar chains attached to a small protein core (proteoglycans) and fibronectin is often associated with the surface of the matrix. Cells have different affinities for such matrices (p. 108), and they move along collagen fibrils in the matrix (p. 188). The extracellular matrix may keep cells apart and thus block the possibility of gap-junction formation (p. 183) and by themselves they may induce the formation of novel cell types within the embryo (e.g. vertebral cartilage and other examples in Chapter 3.6). It is possible that the diversity of collagen molecules (there are at least seven different types of collagen primary sequence) and the variability of the other components of the matrix make up a sufficiently complex aggregate to elicit diverse cell responses in embryogenesis. However, matrices might, like the plant cell wall (p. 197), also contain local concentrations of molecules shed by the cell membrane and have additional molecular detail.

Part 4
Pattern and Form in Development

Chapter 4.1
Introduction
J.B.L. Bard and V. French

4.1.1   TWO SORTS OF CELLULAR PATTERNS

As embryos develop, their cells become organized in ever more complex ways. They divide, move and gradually form the recognizable histological types and patterns of tissues and organs; slowly the embryo acquires the morphology characteristic of its species. In this part of the book, we consider how such cellular patterns arise. In analysing the emergence of organization from an apparently bland embryo, it is helpful to consider two distinct steps [8]: the first is customarily known as *pattern formation* and the second has two aspects, *morphogenesis* and *differentiation*. Pattern formation is the process whereby cells acquire instructions as to how they should change their properties. Differentiation is the acquisition of new properties by cells, while morphogenesis describes the ways in which cells use these properties to build new structures. We can therefore distinguish between two sorts of patterns in embryos: the first is a pattern of developmental fates set up when cells in different parts of the embryo acquire distinct instructions as to how they should develop, and the second is the pattern which the cells subsequently generate. The first sort of pattern is usually invisible under a microscope and its existence has to be inferred; the second is clear in any histological section.

Chapter 4.2 is therefore concerned with the ways in which an embryo or its tissues can acquire regional differences. Chapter 4.3 will examine some of the cellular properties that underlie and characterize morphogenesis. Differentiation, the study of the molecular basis of such properties, is considered in Chapter 6.4. Inevitably, Chapters 4.2 and 4.3 contain only selections from the information available. Over the last century, an enormous body of work has been published on these subjects, which lie at the heart of embryology. In spite of all this research, however, it must be said that complete understanding of both aspects of pattern formation eludes us. Our explanations are incomplete because the phenomena are complex and extremely difficult to investigate experimentally.

4.1.2   ORIGIN OF SPATIAL ORGANIZATION: PREFORMATION AND EPIGENESIS

Since the writings of Aristotle, there have been two distinct views about the development of spatial organization in embryogenesis; these are called preformation and epigenesis [1].

The *preformation* view is that the fertilized egg contains a complete miniature pattern, and that the elements of this pattern grow and develop independently into parts of the adult. The experiments on plant and animal eggs described in Part 2 of this book clearly show that this view is incorrect. However, the preformation view did contain the important idea that the spatial organization for development may be transmitted from one generation to the next through the structure of the fertilized egg; this idea is sustained by the observation that particular parts of the egg form particular parts of the adult in undisturbed development.

The alternate view, *epigenesis,* is that the fertilized

egg has a simpler spatial organization than the adult, and that the embryo gradually becomes more complex with the emergence of new cellular properties. There are now many completely mechanistic models of the ways in which interactions between parts of the egg or early embryo could amplify initial simple heterogeneities to form complex patterns of structure, and these are discussed in Chapter 4.2.

4.1.3 EXPERIMENTAL INVESTIGATION OF PATTERN FORMATION AND MORPHOGENESIS

The first step in analysing development of an embryo is to find out what parts of the egg or early embryo form particular parts of the later embryo or adult; this is the *presumptive fate map* (Chapters 2.3, 2.4, 4.2 and 4.3). It gives descriptive information about normal development but of course this information does not analyse the mechanism by which parts acquire different properties. The major techniques for investigating the time and mechanism by which cells acquire different properties all involve alterations in the spatial relationship of cells; such 'cut and splice' experiments indicate the role of cell interactions in development. Chapter 4.2 discusses such experiments, together with studies of mutations which lead to the formation of abnormal patterns; it then considers some models of how patterns are set up during development.

These models make predictions which can be tested by further experiments but, unfortunately, this approach only gives information at the phenomenological level; it yields indirect clues about actual mechanisms. For several reasons there is little information about the molecular biology of pattern formation: first, developing embryos are very small and the amount of available material is often inadequate for molecular investigations; second, differences must be sought between neighbouring cells and may only be present transiently; third, even if we could show cell–cell differences in, say, the concentrations of some molecule, we would need an independent assay that this molecule had a significant role in pattern formation. There is a further complication: pattern formation probably depends on normal cell–cell contacts and communication and is therefore unlikely to proceed in cell-free systems where this steric aspect would be destroyed. These problems will make it difficult to obtain molecular insights into the mechanisms of pattern formation even when the phenomena are thoroughly understood.

4.1.4 APPROACHES TO MORPHOGENESIS

Morphogenesis is also difficult to study. In this case, the problem is that most embryos are opaque and we cannot see the morphogenesis of organs as it occurs.

There is no comprehensive theory of how organs form. Two distinct lines of thought have, however, stimulated experimental work: the older has emphasized the physical properties of whole tissues while the more recent has concentrated on explaining the morphogenesis of an organ in terms of its constituent cells. An early example of the whole-tissue approach was His' mechanistic explanation of neural tube bending in chick development (see [3] and [5]). His showed that elastic deformations of a rubber tube gave a range of structures that matched those arising from the neural tube. He therefore argued that one could explain the form of this and other tissues in terms of their elastic and mechanical properties. This physical approach was most imaginatively used by D'Arcy Thompson [6]; his classic book makes fascinating reading for anyone interested in the genesis of biological organization.

Over the last half century, the approach of studying morphogenesis from the standpoint of whole tissue has, on the whole, fallen into abeyance, even though some important work has continued to be published. Tuft, for example, has shown that correct amphibian development depends on the embryo being intact, so that water can be pumped from the outside inwards in order to create vesicles [7], and Russian workers continue to emphasize the importance of stress in cellular sheets for generating structures [2]. The majority of contemporary work in morphogenesis, however, seeks explanations at the cellular level and it is fair to credit Roux with being the first to put forward this view, at the end of the nineteenth century. Impressed with the success of classical mechanics in understanding the physical world, he suggested that embryology should be explained in similar terms. He called such a theory *Entwicklungs-mechanik* (developmental mechanics) and emphasized that embryogenesis had to be understood in terms of its 'simple components' rather than in its evolutionary context (see [3] for review).

While Roux' analysis led him to undertake experiments that laid the basis of experimental embryology, he failed to formulate a developmental mechanics and others have been equally unsuccessful. Roux' experimental approach has, however, generated an enormous amount of research about morphogenesis at the cell and tissue level. Some of this work will be reviewed in Chapter 4.3, where the emphasis will be on how tissue formation may be understood in terms of the individual properties of cells. Recently, however, a new method of analysing data, based on computer simulation, has been put forward and this technique may help to coordinate the cell and tissue approaches to morphogenesis. Jacobson and Gordon found that as the neural plate forms in the newt *Triturus*, the superficial ectoderm shrinks and the underlying adherent notochord extends [4]. They were able to simulate these processes on a computer and show that they were sufficient to explain the actual shape changes of the neural plate. This analysis is probably the first quantitative example of a developmental mechanics and the techniques may be applicable elsewhere. Such approaches are of great importance as theoretical analyses of morphogenesis; they provide the only hope that the enormous amount of embryological data in the literature may be integrated and understood.

4.1.5 REFERENCES

1 Baxter A.L. (1976) Edmund B. Wilson as a preformationist: some reasons for his acceptance of the chromosome theory. *J. Hist. Biol.,* **9,** 29–57.
2 Beloussoy L.V., Dorfman J.G. & Cherdantzev V.G (1975) Mechanical stresses and morphological patterns in amphibian embryos. *J. Embryol. exp. Morph.,* **34,** 559–574.
3 Gould S.J. (1977) *Ontogeny and Phylogeny.* Belknap Press, Harvard, Boston.
4 Jacobson A.G. & Gordon R. (1976) Changes in the shape of the developing vertebrate nervous system analysed experimentally, mathematically and by computer simulation. *J. exp. Zool.,* **197,** 191–246.
5 Oppenheimer J. (1967) *Essays in the History of Embryology and Biology.* MIT Press, Cambridge, Massachusetts.
6 Thompson D'A.W. (1966) *On Growth and Form* (Ed. J.T. Bonner). Cambridge University Press, Cambridge.
7 Tuft P. (1965) The uptake and distribution of water in the developing amphibian embryo. *Symp. Soc. exp. Biol.,* **19,** 385–402.
8 Waddington C.H. (1962) *New Patterns in Genetics and Development.* Columbia University Press, New York.

Chapter 4.2
Pattern Formation in Animal Development
V. French

4.2.1 INTRODUCTION

The problem of pattern formation is to understand how cells in different positions in the organism acquire different developmental fates so that they differentiate in patterns, forming tissues and organs rather than random mixtures of cell types.

This chapter will take a general look at the way patterns develop in the animal embryo, and at the evidence that this requires cellular interactions. Three current views will be described of the type of interaction involved in pattern formation, and will be used to interpret the results of surgical and genetical experiments on developing insects.

'Regulative' and 'mosaic' embryos

The detailed spatial organization of the embryo either pre-exists in the egg (*preformation*) or it gradually emerges during development (*epigenesis*: see Chapter 4.1). Some of the first experiments designed to decide between these alternatives were performed in the late nineteenth century by Hans Driesch on the early sea-urchin embryo. After separating the two cells produced by the first cleavage, Driesch found that each cell (which would normally have formed a longitudinal half of the larva) could develop into a complete, normally organized but small larva [12]. Regulation refers to change in the developmental fate of cells after a disturbance, both when the longitudinal fragments produce a normal pattern and when transverse fragments of the early embryo develop into *less* of the larva than they would normally have formed [30, 56] (see Chapter 2.4). These experiments show that the cells of the early embryo gradually acquire their developmental fates through interactions with their neighbours. They will develop differently if they are prevented from interacting or are made to interact with cells that are not normally their neighbours. In Driesch's words, 'the prospective value of any blastula cell is a function of its position in the whole' [12]. At later stages, however, regions develop according to their presumptive fates, even when isolated or grafted elsewhere on the embryo; they are said to be *determined*.

When extirpation and grafting experiments were performed on other sorts of embryos, the results seemed to fall into two distinct categories. Embryos were either 'regulative' (e.g. sea-urchin, amphibian), where cell fate was labile and depended on position within the embryo, or 'mosaic' (e.g. mollusc, annelid worm), where cell fate was fixed and seemed to depend on cytoplasmic determinants localized in different regions of the egg [11]. However, the difference between embryos may lie more in the stage at which interactions cease, than in different basic mechanisms. Thus 'mosaic' embryos can regulate at very early stages [25] and 'regulative' embryos lose their lability in later stages, as the cells become determined [30] (see Chapters 2.2 and 2.4).

Primary and secondary fields

The *field* refers to the region of developing tissue within which regulation can occur [16] (although the term was originally used [70, 71] to describe the interactions involved). The early sea-urchin [30] or amphibian [63] embryo is a single, or *primary field* (Fig. 4.2.1A) until regions become coarsely determined to form particular structures (e.g. the amphibian forelimb). These regions are autonomous *secondary fields* [71], within which regulation can adjust the precise fate of the cells (Fig. 4.2.1b). In many embryos the cells then lose their lability and become finely determined but, in other animals, secondary fields persist after embryonic development and allow appendages to be regenerated by larvae (for example in some insects) and even by adults (some amphibians and crustaceans).

The regulative abilities of embryos show that spatial organization is not preformed, even in classical 'mosaic' eggs [25]. Patterns are built up by interactions occurring during development.

4.2.2 PATTERN FORMATION: INDUCTION, POSITIONAL INFORMATION AND PREPATTERN

Dreisch believed that he had shown the early sea-urchin embryo to be homogeneous—a 'harmonius equipotential system' [12]—and that the emergence of complete spatial organization in an embryonic fragment must be due to a vital force—'entelechy'. Different

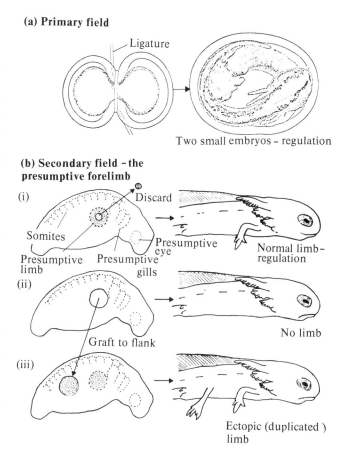

(a) Primary field

Two small embryos – regulation

(b) Secondary field – the presumptive forelimb

Fig. 4.2.1. Primary and secondary fields in the amphibian embryo. **(a)** The primary field. Each longitudinal half of the early embryo can develop into a complete, normally-proportioned but small embryo which subsequently grows to normal size during larval life. (From Spemann [63].) After separation in the transverse plane, neither half of the early embryo develops a complete pattern [50].
(b) A secondary field. When part of the presumptive forelimb is removed (i) the rest regulates to form a normal limb, but when the region is completely removed (ii) no limb forms. Part or all of the presumptive forelimb, grafted to the flank, develops into an ectopic limb which is often duplicated as shown (iii). The region behaves as an independent secondary field: its cells are determined to form a forelimb, but not to form a particular part of it. (From the work of Harrison [26].)

transverse fragments of the embryo form different partial patterns, however, showing that even the early sea-urchin embryo is heterogeneous [30]. A simple heterogeneity in the egg may be the basis for forming complex patterns in the embryo, and there have been three different theoretical approaches to this process of pattern formation. The ideas of *induction, positional information* and *prepattern* each involve two components, the first corresponding to the stimuli that a cell receives from its surroundings, and the second to the cell's response to that information. These two components can be separated experimentally; for example, the *Drosophila* mutant *achaete* lacks specific thoracic bristles because the cells are unable to respond to a normal set of stimuli (Fig. 4.2.2).

We will now consider the three approaches and the ways in which they could account for regulation in primary fields (Fig. 4.2.1a) and the formation of abnormal mutant patterns (Fig. 4.2.2).

Induction

Cells which are already determined to form one embryonic structure may specifically induce or instruct adjacent labile cells to form a different structure [64].

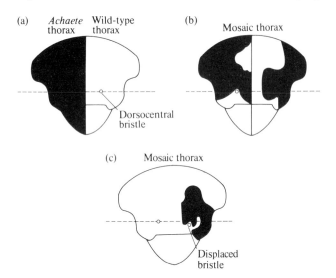

Fig. 4.2.2. Bristle formation in the *Drosophila* mutant *achaete.*
(a) Normal *Drosophila* adults have large dorsocentral bristles at precise positions on the thorax: these are missing in mutant *achaete* flies.
(b) Eggs of particular genotypes produce mosaic flies with normal (white) and *achaete* (black) patches of tissue. In general, the mutation behaves *cell-autonomously:* a bristle is formed on a mosaic thorax if the site is wild type, and is not formed if it is *achaete* (regardless of the genotype of the rest of the thorax). Clearly, bristle sites are defined, even in the *achaete* thorax, but mutant cells cannot respond.
(c) Occasionally a slightly displaced bristle may form on wild-type tissue if the adjacent normal site is *achaete,* so the exact position of a bristle may depend on local interactions (see section 4.2.6). (Taken from Stern [65].)

Hence the formation of a structure (such as a bristle) at a particular site is only dependent on the presence of the neighbouring inducer, and not on overall position in the embryo. If the cells are not competent to respond (for example because of mutation), the structure will not be formed (see Fig. 4.2.2). Induction occurs in the formation of the vertebrate neural plate (see Chapter 3.5), the nose, eyes and ears and the skin appendages [61], but in all these examples the induced patterns depend upon the existence of a corresponding pattern in the inducing tissue layer. Pattern is not *formed* but merely *transferred* from the mesoderm to the ectoderm.

A complex pattern could be generated sequentially within a tissue layer [29] if an initial heterogeneity (the 'organizer' region) induces the formation of a pattern element in neighbouring cells, which then induces the next element to form in their neighbours, and so on (see Fig. 4.2.3a). This mechanism cannot readily explain the formation of a complete set of small pattern elements from half of the primary field (Fig. 4.2.1a), as the size of the pattern elements will depend on how far each inducing signal spreads from the previously formed element. It is not clear how the extent of each induction could vary with the total amount of tissue available.

Positional information

In contrast to the induction approach, the idea of positional information comes directly from Driesch's view that a cell's fate depends on its position in the embryo. Wolpert [73] suggests that no regions are singled out by specific instructions to make particular structures, but rather that a simple map of positional values forms over the field. This map bears no resemblance to the visible pattern which will form later, and it may correspond to a gradient [49], possibly of molecular concentration. A pattern of structures will be formed when the cells interpret their gradient levels according to a code of threshold responses (Fig. 4.2.3b(i)). Wherever a threshold gradient level occurs, those cells will form the appropriate structure. If a mutation renders cells unable to interpret a particular level, the corresponding structure will be missing from the pattern (see Fig. 4.2.2). Pattern regulation after grafting or removal of tissue will result from alterations in the gradient profile and these can be predicted from simple gradient models (see Fig. 4.2.3b(ii)).

If the development of intricate patterns is based upon

(a) Sequential induction

(b) Positional information

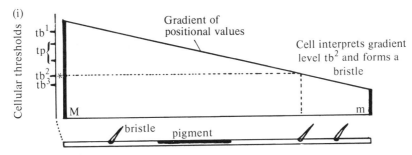

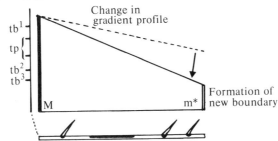

(c) Prepattern

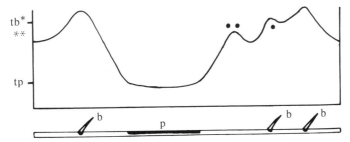

Fig. 4.2.3. Approaches to pattern formation.
(a) Sequential induction. Pattern element A may be induced by a specific signal (a) from the organizer, and then produce another specific signal (b) causing adjacent tissue to form pattern element B. In this way a pattern could be set up sequentially by specific local instructions. A mutation which removes a pattern element (e.g. bristle C) could act by inactivating the spatial cue (**), in which case elements further down the sequence would also be missing, or by preventing the local response (*).
(b) Positional information may be in the form of a gradient (i) of concentration of a diffusible molecule held at maximum and minimum values at two boundaries (M and m). Other gradient models are possible, involving only one boundary or no localized boundaries [23], and gradients need not be of molecular concentration [24]. Cells interpret their gradient levels (positional values) according to a set of

thresholds, e.g. those with values tb^1, tb^2 and tb^3 make bristles. The same gradient may exist in different fields, but the cells interpret it according to other sets of thresholds and hence form different patterns. A viable mutation will remove a bristle by affecting the corresponding threshold (*), rather than removing that gradient value from all fields. Regulation (ii) after removal of tissue will involve changes in gradient profile, and if a boundary has been removed a complete pattern will only be formed if it can be replaced (m^*).
(c) Prepattern. A complex landscape of morphogen concentration may be interpreted according to very simple rules. Bristles (b) may form wherever peaks rise above level tb, and pigmentation (p) may occur wherever levels fall below tp. Mutation may remove a bristle by altering the prepattern (lowering a peak (•)) or raising the threshold (*), and a new bristle may be introduced into the pattern by raising a peak in the prepattern (••) or lowering the threshold (**).

interpretation of simple positional information, such as a gradient, then the interpretation 'code' must be extremely complex. Wolpert [74] argues that the difference between patterns, such as the chick wing and leg, may be due to cells in the different secondary fields interpreting the same simple positional information according to different codes. In other words, positional information may be universal but the interpretation may depend upon how cells were determined earlier in development.

Prepattern

The prepattern approach attributes the visible pattern of cell differentiation to the previous formation of a complex landscape of concentration of a molecular 'morphogen' [65, 62]. Bristles or other prominent pattern elements form in response to peaks in the prepattern, so very simple interpretation of the morphogen landscape gives rise directly to the final pattern (Fig. 4.3.2c. If a mutation raises the cellular threshold for interpretation, pattern elements corresponding to low peaks will be lost (as in *achaete*—see Fig. 4.2.2), while lowering the threshold may introduce new elements into the pattern as previously undetected peaks are 'uncovered' [62].

If interpretation is very simple, corresponding perhaps to a few thresholds, then the formation of complex patterns depends upon the formation of equally complex prepatterns of concentration. Two different patterns, such as the leg and wing, will be formed from correspondingly different prepatterns. Pattern regulation after surgery must result from alterations to the prepattern landscape. A major problem with the prepattern approach is that present models can set up a simple prepattern of regularly repeating peaks [23] but they cannot generate irregular prepatterns corresponding to biological patterns, nor adjust them to the amount of tissue available. There is therefore no way of testing prepattern ideas against the results of grafting or amputation experiments.

Testing models of pattern formation

The induction approach sees a pattern as composed of discrete parts, each of which forms in response to a specific instruction from an adjacent, previously formed part. The positional information approach derives the

pattern from a simple positional map, interpreted by the cells according to a complex set of rules. Finally, the prepattern approach sees the pattern as the direct reflection of a complex landscape of chemical concentration. These three views of pattern formation differ in two respects. First, only positional information predicts that the formation of different patterns will be based on the same set of spatial cues. Following from this, only positional information predicts that most pattern mutants will affect local cellular interpretation rather than the spatial signals, since a defect in the general system of setting up spatial organization is likely to be lethal (pattern mutants will therefore behave cell-autonomously in genetic mosaics—see Fig. 4.2.2). The other approaches predict that different spatial cues (specific induction or specific prepatterns) will exist in each field, so a particular pattern may be abnormal because of changes in these cues or in the cellular response. Secondly, positional information and induction differ in their predictions for some grafting operations (this is explained for specific examples in later sections of this chapter), while it is not possible to derive predictions from prepattern ideas (see above).

We have considered only the simple, most easily contrasted versions of the three approaches (hybrid models are possible—see section 4.2.6) and we will now try to apply them to developing primary and secondary fields in insects. Only in insects can the techniques of experimental embryology (e.g. ligature, grafting, irradiation) be supplemented by those of developmental genetics (e.g. clonal analysis, study of morphogenetic mutants and genetic mosaics). For this reason, recent work on insect development has contributed greatly to our general understanding of pattern formation.

4.2.3 DEVELOPMENT OF A PRIMARY FIELD: INSECT SEGMENT PATTERN

The insect embryo forms from the *germ anlage*, a thickened region of the cellular blastoderm on the ventral side of the egg (Fig. 4.2.4a). The presumptive mesoderm lies in the ventral mid-line, flanked by presumptive ectoderm. The segment pattern is first visible at the *germ band* stage and consists of the head lobes, 3 mouthpart segments, 3 thoracic segments and 8–11 abdominal segments. The eggs of some insects (e.g. Diptera) contain distinct posterior 'pole plasm', from which the germ cells of the adult are formed (see

maternal-effect mutants, so the altered segment pattern depends on the genotype of the ovary rather than the egg, and must therefore be caused by a defect in oogenesis (see Chapter 2.2). Female *bicaudal* mutants produce a range of abnormal embryos, including some with two posterior ends (of from one to five abdominal segments) arranged in mirror symmetry [52]. In *dicephalic* females, nurse cells are frequently found at both poles of the developing oocytes. These eggs either fail to develop or form abnormal embryos, some with two anterior ends (of head, thorax and first abdominal segment) showing mirror symmetry [59].

The polarity of the *Drosophila* egg is normally correlated with the presence of maternal nurse cells anterior to the developing oocyte (Fig. 4.2.4A). In *dicephalic* ovaries the presence of nurse cells at both ends may cause the normal anterior–posterior gradient to be set up in an abnormal, double-anterior form, while *bicaudal* nurse cells may fail to specify an anterior boundary and thus cause the gradient to adopt a double-posterior form.

The development of primary fields: conclusions

The insect segment pattern does not develop as a mosaic of localized determinants and is independent of the 'pole plasm' determinant, since double-abdomen and *bicaudal* embryos have germ cells only in the posterior abdomen [33]. Longitudinal egg fragments regulate to give small complete embryos, while transverse fragments form few large segments unless they contain both egg poles, when they can form small complete patterns. Taken together, the experimental results are incompatible with a mechanism of sequential induction and suggest one or two gradients of positional information set up in the cortex between anterior and posterior poles of the egg. These boundaries are formed in early oogenesis, possibly by the action of surrounding nurse and follicle cells (see Chapters 2.2 and 2.4). At blastoderm stage or later (depending on the species), the gradient levels lead to regions of the blastoderm being determined to form larval segments (and imaginal discs in *Drosophila*). We will now look in the following

---

Fig. 4.2.4. Insect development.
(a) Development of the egg (i) and embryo (ii–v). (i) The immature egg (or oocyte) passes down the ovary surrounded by maternal follicle cells and, in many insects (including Diptera), by nurse cells at the anterior end. Meiosis is completed, the accessory cells die, and the egg is fertilized and laid. (ii) The eggs of many insects (including Diptera) contain distinct pole plasm at the posterior (P) end. The egg nucleus divides many times within the yolk and the daughter nuclei migrate out to the surface layer of cytoplasm. (iii) Nuclei arriving at the posterior pole are enclosed by cell membranes to form the pole cells, and then (iv) cells form in the rest of the surface layer, the blastoderm. Embryonic structures form from the thickened germ anlage on the ventral (V) side of the egg while the dorsal (D) parts of the blastoderm form a temporary covering and also the extra-embryonic membranes (not shown). (v) Segmentation of the germ anlage produces the germ band consisting of anterior extra-embryonic structures (X), the head lobes (A), three mouthpart segments (B), three thoracic segments (C) and 8–11 abdominal segments (D, E). A cross-section of the egg shows that the presumptive mesoderm (solid black) has invaginated along the ventral mid-line (gastrulation) and the embryonic ectoderm (striped) is moving dorsally to enclose eventually the remains of the yolk (dorsal closure). The mesoderm also spreads dorsally and endoderm migrates from anterior and posterior positions, forming the larval gut. Before hatching, the embryo undergoes complex morphogenetic movements within the egg (not shown).
(b) Development of hemimetabolous insects (e.g. Hemiptera, Orthoptera). The first-instar larva hatches from the egg very similar in form to the adult. The epidermis of the legs, abdominal segments

(consisting of dorsal tergites, lateral pleura and ventral sternites) and other areas grows and secretes cuticle before each of the moults to adult stage. Some regions of the dorsal meso- and metathorax (the wing pads) grow considerably in the last larval instar to form the adult wings.
(c) Extreme holometabolous development (e.g. *Drosophila*). The first instar larva is legless and consists of *larval* cells (which do not divide but become very large and polyploid as the larva grows and moults twice to become mature), and *imaginal* cells (which remain diploid). The *imaginal discs* are groups of about 40 cells upwards, which divide through larval life to form invaginated sacs of some 40 000 cells in the mature larva. The disc is connected by a stalk to the surface larval epidermis, which secretes the larval cuticle. There are four discs in each thoracic segment (e.g. the mesothorax has two wing discs and two second leg discs). Each larval abdominal segment contains eight nests of imaginal *histoblast* cells which do not divide, and lie within the larval epidermis, secreting cuticle before each moult. Within the puparium, the imaginal discs evert and spread over the surface as the larval cells die.
Eventually, the imaginal discs join to form the complete head and thorax. The abdominal histoblasts divide rapidly in the pupa and spread to form the abdominal segments as the larval cells die. The imaginal cells then secrete the adult cuticle, and the adult emerges from the pupa. In some holometabolous insects (e.g. Coleoptera, Lepidoptera) the distinction between larval and imaginal cells is less extreme, so that adult legs and abdomen form from the cells of the corresponding larval structures, while the wings form from imaginal discs.

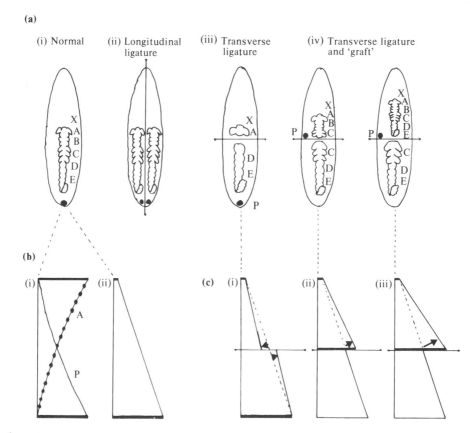

Fig. 4.2.5. Pattern formation in the *Euscelis* egg.
(a) A complete germ band (X–E, see Fig. 4.2.4) is formed in normal eggs (i) and in each longitudinal egg fragment (ii). After transverse ligature at late cleavage stage (iii), five or six head and thoracic segments are formed by either fragment, while ligature at cellular blastoderm stage produces a smaller gap of two or three segments. An anterior fragment containing the posterior pole (p) and ligatured at late cleavage stage produces head and thorax, or a complete germ band (iv).
(b) Gradients in the normal egg. (i) Segments may be formed according to the relative levels of an anterior and a posterior gradient (e.g. the A/P ratio). These gradients may be built up to anterior and posterior maximum values in the time before segment determination. (ii) Alternatively, segments may form according to the absolute level of a single gradient formed between maximum and minimum boundary values (see Fig. 4.2.3b).
(c) The experimental results can be explained by the single-gradient model. After simple ligature (i) the anterior fragment lacks the upper boundary so its gradient levels fall, while those in the posterior fragment rise, resulting in a gap and missing segments. When the anterior fragment contains the upper boundary, levels rise (ii) and a complete steep gradient may be formed (iii). These results may also be explained by the double-gradient model [58].

section at the further development of some of these regions.

4.2.4 DEVELOPMENT OF A SECONDARY FIELD: INSECT ABDOMINAL SEGMENT

Each segment of the insect abdomen forms from a separate population of cells which becomes determined in accordance with its position in the primary field at around blastoderm stage. The segment epidermis grows and secretes cuticle before hatching and before each larval moult (see Fig. 4.2.4). The abdomen bears characteristic cuticular structures (bristles, hairs, folds, etc.), and many grafting experiments suggest that these patterns form in response to a gradient of positional information (see review by Lawrence [38]).

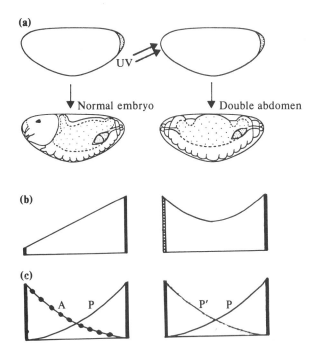

Fig. 4.2.6. Polarity reversal in the *Smittia* egg.

(a) If the egg (or just its anterior tip) is irradiated with U.V. before blastoderm stage, it develops into a symmetrical 'double-abdomen' embryo. Germ cells (stippled) are found only in the ovary of the original posterior abdomen [33].

(b) Single-gradient model interpretation. Irradiation may convert the anterior pole to a maximum boundary value, giving a U-shaped intermediate gradient profile as the levels rise at the anterior end [44]. It is difficult to explain why the same symmetrical pattern is formed regardless of U.V. dose or time of irradiation (between deposition and blastoderm) [32, 33].

(c) Double-gradient model. If the anterior gradient (A) has a U.V.-sensitive component (filled circles), irradiation may convert it to a form (P') very similar to the normal posterior gradient (P). The high gradient levels anteriorly (P') and posteriorly (P) will both cause formation of the posterior end of the embryo [35]. Again, it is difficult to explain why reducing the U.V. dose or the area of egg irradiated should greatly reduce the frequency of double abdomens formed but *not* alter their symmetrical form. This model also fails to explain the formation of symmetrical double-abdomen and double-head embryos after centrifugation [33].

Grafts within the abdominal segment

The dorsal surface (the tergite) of the adult abdominal segment of the bug *Rhodnius* (Hemiptera) bears transverse cuticular folds. This pattern can be altered by grafting squares of larval epidermis into abnormal posi-

tions and orientations [41], as shown in Fig. 4.2.7a. The adult fold pattern is not imposed on labile epidermis at metamorphosis (e.g. by sequential induction from the segment margin), or grafting would have no effect, neither is the pattern rigidly determined within the larval epidermis, or the grafts would produce corresponding, discontinuous adult patterns. The pattern must therefore be carried in the larval epidermis in some form which allows graft/host interactions. The transverse folds cannot depend on side-to-side polarity of the epidermis, since the pattern is characteristically altered by a 180° rotation or a translocation of epidermis to a different level in the A/P axis (Fig. 4.2.7a).

Lawrence [37] and Stumpf [67, 68] suggested that the segment epidermis contains an A/P gradient in concentration of a diffusible molecule which is kept to maximum and minimum values at the segment margins. Folds form perpendicular to the gradient slope, and the gradient is repeated in each segment (since grafts taken from equivalent positions in different segments have similar effects). Rotation or translocation of epidermis will produce sharp discontinuities in the gradient landscape and diffusion will smooth these into hills and hollows, giving the observed concentric 'contour' patterns (Fig. 4.2.7b(i)).

A more complex cuticular pattern, with a prominent transverse ridge, is found on abdominal segments 5, 6 and 7 of the pupa of the wax moth, *Galleria* (Lepidoptera). Stumpf [67] rotated a square of larval epidermis, producing an altered pattern with a deflected transverse ridge and a separate anterior ring of ridge cuticle (Fig. 4.2.8a). This result is readily explained if the ridge is produced at a particular level of the A/P gradient. Stumpf [68] then tested for a segmental gradient in abdominal segment 4, which is covered by uniform cuticle. Epidermis from segment 6 proceeded to make its normal cuticular structures when grafted into an equivalent position on segment 4, but formed other segment 6 structures when put into a non-equivalent position. A graft of posterior origin made more-anterior structures (including the ridge) when grafted to anterior segment 4 (Fig. 4.2.8b) and, reciprocally, a graft from anterior segment 6 formed more-posterior cuticle (including the ridge) when interacting with posterior segment 4. These results lead to the important conclusion that the two segments contain similar gradients but form different patterns because their cells were determined (by their site in the primary field) to

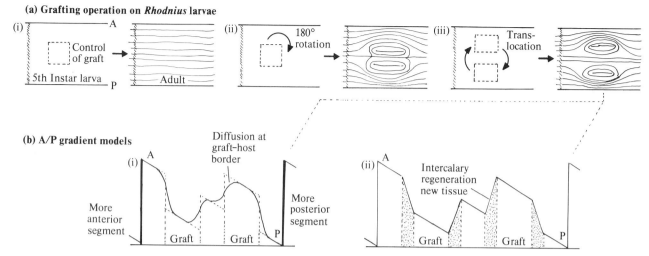

(a) Grafting operation on *Rhodnius* larvae

(i) Control of graft — 5th Instar larva A ... P Adult

(ii) 180° rotation

(iii) Trans-location

(b) A/P gradient models

(i) A — Diffusion at graft-host border — More anterior segment — Graft — Graft — P — More posterior segment

(ii) A — Intercalary regeneration new tissue — Graft — Graft — P

Fig. 4.2.7. The abdominal segment gradient in *Rhodnius*.
(a) Locke's [41] grafting experiments, showing the pattern of adult cuticular folds after (i) a control graft replacing a square of larval epidermis at the same level in the anterior posterior (AP) axis, (ii) 180° rotation and (iii) translocation of anterior and posterior squares.
(b) Schematic anterior–posterior section after the translocation graft

(aiii) showing the effect on the segment gradient. (i) Diffusion model [37, 67] with boundary values maintained at the intersegmental membranes and diffusion occurring elsewhere to smooth the graft/host discontinuities into a hill and a hollow. (ii) Intercalary regeneration model with positional values stable except where growth is stimulated by the disparity between graft and host values.

interpret the positional information in different ways [68].

Grafting experiments [51] on the abdomen of the bug *Dysdercus* (Hemiptera) suggest that confrontation of cells from different A/P levels results in *intercalary regeneration*—a local stimulation of growth to produce new cells with intermediate positional values corresponding to the missing A/P levels. Intercalary regeneration also occurs after similar grafting experiments on insect leg epidermis [5, 14]. The segment gradient may therefore be very stable (except in cells stimulated to divide), rather than being a diffusion gradient maintained by special activities at the segment margins (Fig. 4.2.7b).

Intersegmental margin

If, as suggested by the previous experiments, each abdominal segment is a separate secondary field with a linear A/P gradient of positional information, there must be a discontinuity at each intersegmental margin. Complete removal of the margin will confront very posterior and very anterior levels of successive segments, and would be expected to lead to formation of intermediate gradient levels and hence a region of mid-

segment in reversed A/P orientation. However, this operation leads to regeneration of the intersegmental margin [76], as does grafting together extreme anterior and posterior levels of the same segment (Fig. 4.2.9).

This result suggests that gradient boundaries can be formed when cells with very different positional values are confronted.

Insect abdominal segment: conclusions

Each abdominal segment forms from a region of the primary field, and its epidermis behaves as a secondary field within which growth and the polarity and nature of cuticular structures depend upon cellular interaction. It is extremely difficult to explain the results of the epidermal grafting experiments in terms of sequential induction, and Stumpf's experiments show that the cells of different segments are determined to interpret the same positional cues to form different cuticular patterns. The results of the grafting experiments can be readily interpreted in terms of a gradient of positional information between the anterior and posterior margins of each segment. Confrontation of cells with different gradient levels leads to intercalary regeneration and, in extreme cases, to the formation of gradient boundaries.

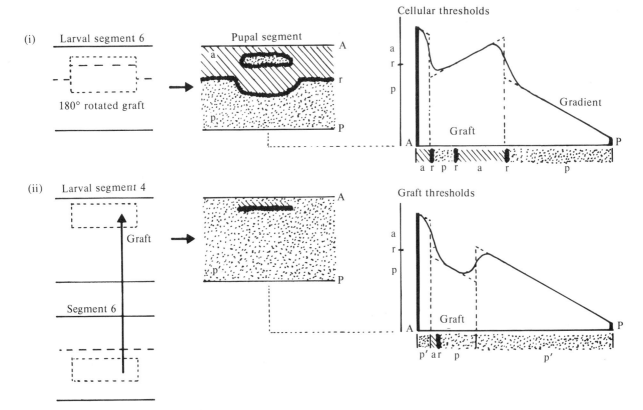

Fig. 4.2.8. Stumpf's grafting experiments on the abdomen of *Galleria*. (a) 180° rotation of segment 6 epidermis including the presumptive ridge (dashed line) disrupts the pupal pattern of anterior cuticle (a), ridge (r) and posterior cuticle (p). A schematic A/P section through the rotated graft shows how the pattern could arise from a diffusion gradient and cellular thresholds for forming a, r and p cuticle. (b) Grafting a region of presumptive posterior epidermis from segment 6 into the anterior of segment 4 (which has a uniform cuticle, p') results in formation of a band of anterior cuticle and a ridge [68]. This is explained if all segments have the same diffusion gradient and graft (segment 6) epidermis forms a, r or p cuticle depending on gradient level, while host (segment 4) epidermis always forms posterior-type (p') cuticle. The gradients in segments 4 and 6 must be the same since the level of the posterior graft rises when moved to anterior host (and the level of an anterior graft falls when moved to posterior host).

We will now consider pattern formation in two dimensions, in the imaginal discs which develop from anterior regions of the primary field in *Drosophila*.

4.2.5 DEVELOPMENT OF SECONDARY FIELDS: IMAGINAL DISCS OF *DROSOPHILA*

The surface epidermis of the adult *Drosophila* head and thorax (including appendages such as antennae, legs, wings and halteres) is formed piecemeal from several *imaginal discs* (Fig. 4.2.4c). These sac-like invaginations form in the embryo, grow during larval life and only evaginate and secrete their complex cuticular patterns at metamorphosis, when the larval epidermis dies. In recent years, pattern formation and cell determination have been extensively studied in imaginal discs (see review by Bryant [7]).

Growth and cell lineage in imaginal discs

The imaginal wing disc consists of just under 40 cells in the newly hatched larva and grows to about 40 000 cells by metamorphosis [43]. If, as was once thought, the disc develops as a mosaic of determined regions, then each early cell will have a fixed lineage and its clone of descendants will form precisely the same patch of cuticle on every fly. This hypothesis can be tested because single

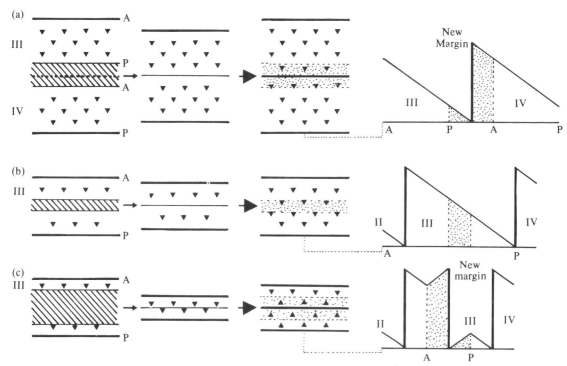

Fig. 4.2.9. Interaction between different anterior–posterior levels in the abdominal segment of *Oncopeltus* [76]. When a small transverse strip (shaded) including the intersegmental margin is removed and the cut edges are grafted together (a) posterior levels of segment III confront anterior levels of segment IV. Tissue is regenerated (stippled) which has normal polarity (triangles show bristle orientation) and contains a regenerated margin. Removal of a small transverse strip within segment III leads to regeneration of missing tissue (b), while removal of a large strip (c) causes regeneration of an area of reversed polarity, containing an ectopic segment margin. In terms of the repeating gradient model of the insect segment, these results suggest that interaction between cells with different gradient levels causes intercalation of intermediate gradient levels (as in Fig. 4.2.7b) but, if the gradient levels are very dissimilar (a, c), new gradient boundaries are formed. Note that the polarity of the region posterior to the ectopic border is not quite as predicted by the gradient model.

early cells can be genetically 'marked' by inducing mitotic recombination. Information about cell lineage obtained by this method is discussed in Chapters 2.3 and 2.4. When many embryos are irradiated at the same stage and the resulting flies examined, two cuticular structures may be in the same clone on one fly but in different clones on another, showing that the disc does not develop by a fixed lineage (Fig. 4.2.9A). This is shown even more dramatically by the use of growth-rate mutations such as *Minute*; a wild-type cell in a slow-growing *Minute* disc produces a far larger clone than normal [19], but the wing is normal in size and pattern (Fig. 4.2.10B).

Clonal analysis does reveal some dramatic lineage restrictions, however, as the developing disc becomes progressively divided into *compartments* [19, 72] with borders which are respected even by the rapidly growing wild-type clones formed in *Minute* discs (see Fig. 4.2.10).

Fate maps and pattern regulation

A mature wing disc metamorphoses *in situ* to give the dorsal and lateral mesothorax, the wing hinge and the wing blade. If the disc is implanted into a host larva, the same structures are formed in a vesicle inside the host fly: the tissue is determined as wing disc. If the two halves of a disc are implanted separately into mature larval hosts, they form complementary halves of the normal set of disc structures. By studying the products of different disc fragments, a detailed fate map can be drawn [6], locating even the presumptive sites of individ-

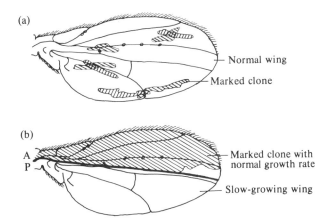

(a)

— Normal wing

— Marked clone

(b)

A
P

— Marked clone with normal growth rate

— Slow-growing wing

Fig. 4.2.10. Cell lineage in the development of the adult mesothorax of *Drosophila*. Irradiation of embryos or larvae heterozygous for a recessive visible mutation like *yellow* will occasionally cause a cell to undergo chromosome rearrangement, so that one of its daughter cells becomes homozygous *yellow*. After growth and metamorphosis the clone of homozygous cells produces a visible patch of yellow cuticle on an otherwise normal fly.
(a) Standard dorsal view of the wing and mesothorax, showing partial overlap between marked clones induced at the same stage in the development of different flies. If the wing developed by a fixed lineage, clones would not overlap (if they developed from different cells in the early disc) or be superimposable (if they formed from the same cell).
(b) A marked clone growing at the normal rate in a slow-growing (*Minute*) wing disc forms far more structures than normal, again showing that lineage is not fixed. Clones never cross a precise line separating anterior (A) and posterior (P) compartments [19].

(c) As the mesothorax develops, new clonal restrictions arise. Clones made at blastoderm stage do not cross to neighbouring thoracic segments (heavy line) nor do they cross between the A and P (shaded) compartments of the segment. After 7 h of embryonic development, clones cannot cross from wing to leg disc derivatives (heavy dashed line). In the wing disc, another compartment border (dotted line) forms in mid-larval life, separating dorsal wing blade and thorax (notum) from ventral wing and lateral thorax (pleura). (Adapted from Garcia-Bellido *et al.* [18] and Steiner [67].)

ual marker bristles (Fig. 4.2.11a). Cells are not determined to form these particular structures, however, since pattern regulation can occur if the fragment is given time to grow before metamorphosis [6].

When ¾ and ¼ fragments of a disc are implanted into adult flies, left for a few days to grow and then re-implanted into larvae [27], the ¼ forms a mirror-image duplicate of its fate-map structures while the ¾ regenerates the missing structures to form a complete pattern (Fig. 4.2.11b). It is likely that new structures are formed from the cut edges and, because any cut edge may be part of a regenerating (¾) *or* a duplicating (¼) fragment, the new pattern elements cannot be added by sequential induction from a cut edge.

Pattern regulation depends on interaction between the cut edges, which do indeed rapidly heal together [55]. Furthermore, two different fragments, which would each duplicate if implanted, can interact when mixed together [27], to form an intercalary regenerate

(Fig. 4.2.10c). These results and those from comparable grafting experiments on cockroach legs [5, 14] have led to the polar-coordinate model [8, 16] of pattern regulation (see Fig. 4.2.12).

One of the most intriguing aspects of secondary fields concerns their initial formation from a region of the primary field. There are indications that pattern *formation* and growth in the early disc occur by the same mechanism as pattern *regulation* in mature disc fragments. Studies of the duplications and deletions resulting from damage to embryonic and early larval discs suggest that the field (of 10–40 cells) already has the same organization of positional information as the mature disc, and undergoes intercalary regeneration in the same way [4, 15]. If a few of the peripheral positional values of the disc are derived from the primary field, their interaction will lead to growth and intercalation of values through larval life [7], until the pattern is complete (Fig. 4.2.12c).

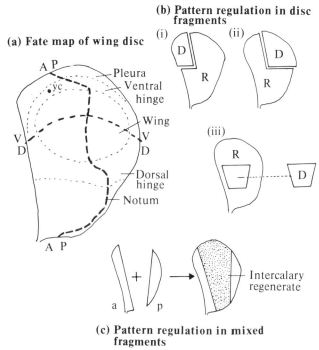

(a) Fate map of wing disc

(b) Pattern regulation in disc fragments

(c) Pattern regulation in mixed fragments

Fig. 4.2.11. Pattern regulation in the wing disc.
(a) Fate map of the mature wing disc derived from implanting specific fragments into mature larval hosts. The full fate map [6] has 30–40 precisely located marker structures such as yc, the 'yellow club'. A/P and D/V compartment borders are drawn onto the fate map.
(b) When fragments are given a period of growth in an intermediate adult host before being forced to metamorphose, they can undergo pattern regulation. (i) The ¼ sector duplicates (D) its portion of the fate map (including yc), and the ¾ sector regenerates (R) missing structures (including yc). (ii) The three other ¼ sectors also duplicate while the corresponding ¾ fragments regenerate. (iii) The centre of the disc duplicates while the periphery regenerates.
(c) Diagrammatic representation of the result of mixing together two small segments (a and p) each of which duplicates when cultured alone. Other parts of the pattern are formed by intercalary regeneration and during this process the A/P border can be crossed (e.g. cells from the anterior fragment a can form structures in the P compartment). Similarly, when dorsal (notum) and lateral (pleura) fragments are mixed together intercalary regeneration occurs, forming hinge and wing structures.

Development of different imaginal discs: genes, determination and pattern

Studies of homoeotic mutants suggest that different imaginal discs form their characteristic patterns in response to the same set of positional cues, interpreted differently because of differences in gene activity.

Homoeotic mutations cause the structures of one disc to be completely or partially replaced by those normally formed from another disc. For instance, an *Antennapaedia* fly has parts of the antenna replaced by ectopic mesothoracic leg structures. The replacement of structures is position-specific [54] with, for example, cells of the second antennal segment always giving trochanter when they transform (Fig. 4.2.13a). Another homoeotic mutation, *bithorax*, transforms anterior metathorax (with haltere and third leg) into anterior mesothorax (with wing and second leg). Clones of *bithorax* induced in a normal haltere disc form position-specific wing structures, resulting in the formation of a chimeric appendage, and they do this even if induced late in larval life, long after the wing/haltere determination decision was taken on the blastoderm [46].

Taken together, these results indicate that head and thoracic discs develop from the same map of positional information, but this is interpreted according to the determination of the disc cells (e.g. 'wing' or 'haltere', 'leg' or 'antenna'). This conclusion is strongly supported by regeneration experiments [2] where specific fragments of wing and haltere discs were mixed and then implanted into adult hosts. The dorsal (notum) fragment of the wing disc interacted with lateral wing disc (as in Fig. 4.2.11c) or with lateral haltere disc and formed in intercalary regenerate, while *no* intercalary regeneration occurred between the notum and the dorsal fragment of the haltere disc. Similar results were obtained from other combinations of fragments, suggesting that homologous regions of the two discs have the same positional values.

The results from ligaturing the egg (section 4.2.3) show that discs are determined from the primary field at around blastoderm stage, and the lineage restriction found by clonal analysis (Fig. 4.2.10c) is consistent with this conclusion. The results from the homoeotic studies indicate that determination involves setting up different patterns of gene activity in the different presumptive discs. More specifically, it has been suggested that determination involves turning on particular switch genes, termed 'selector genes' [17, 47], in each disc. Thus the wild-type allele *Antennapaedia⁺* is turned on in the antenna disc and *bithorax⁺* in the haltere disc. Determination may depend on continued gene activity, so if a haltere disc cell becomes homozygous (through mitotic recombination) for the mutant allele *bithorax*, gene activity is lost and the clone reverts to wing-type

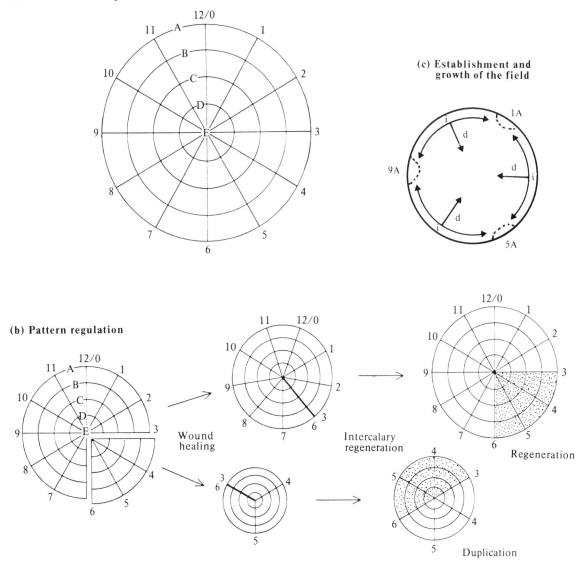

(a) Mature secondary field

(c) Establishment and growth of the field

(b) Pattern regulation

Wound healing

Intercalary regeneration

Regeneration

Duplication

Fig. 4.2.12. The polar-coordinate model [8, 16] of pattern regulation in imaginal discs.
(a) Positional information in the disc may be specified by two components: a circumferential positional value in the continuous sequence 0–12 which runs around the disc, and a proximal–distal value in the radial sequence A–E. The model suggests two rules governing cellular interaction. (1) *Intercalary regeneration by the shortest route*: when cells with non-adjacent values in either sequence (0–12 or A–E) come into contact, local growth is stimulated and the shortest set of intermediate values is formed in the new tissue. (2) *Distalization*: if intercalated cells have positional values identical to those of adjacent cells, then the new cells adopt a more distal value.
(b) Pattern regulation in disc fragments. ¼ and ¾ sectors heal their cut edges together [55] and this will result in growth and intercalary regeneration by the shortest route to form values 4 and 5 (rather than values 2, 1, 12, 11, 10, 9, 8 and 7) duplicating the values already present in the ¼ and regenerating those missing from the ¾ fragment.

Intercalary regeneration and distalization account for the behaviour of the central and peripheral fragments (Fig. 4.2.11b), as the healing of a complete circumference will generate new circles of cells with more distal values [8]. The two sequences of positional values (A–E and 0–12) may be in the form of gradients, but a circumferential gradient will have a discontinuous 'boundary' region where maximum and minimum values are adjacent (e.g. at 12/0). Intercalary regeneration between positions 10 and 2, for instance, will only follow the 'shortest route' (11, 12/0, 1) if confrontation between values differing than six units results in boundary formation (see Fig. 4.2.10).
(c) Growth of the disc. If the disc first forms from the primary field as a small number of cells with 'wing disc' determination and a few proximal values, intercalary regeneration (i) and distalization (d) will generate the missing positional values through larval life. A mature disc should contain the complete field and cease growing (unless it is injured); in general, this is observed [7].

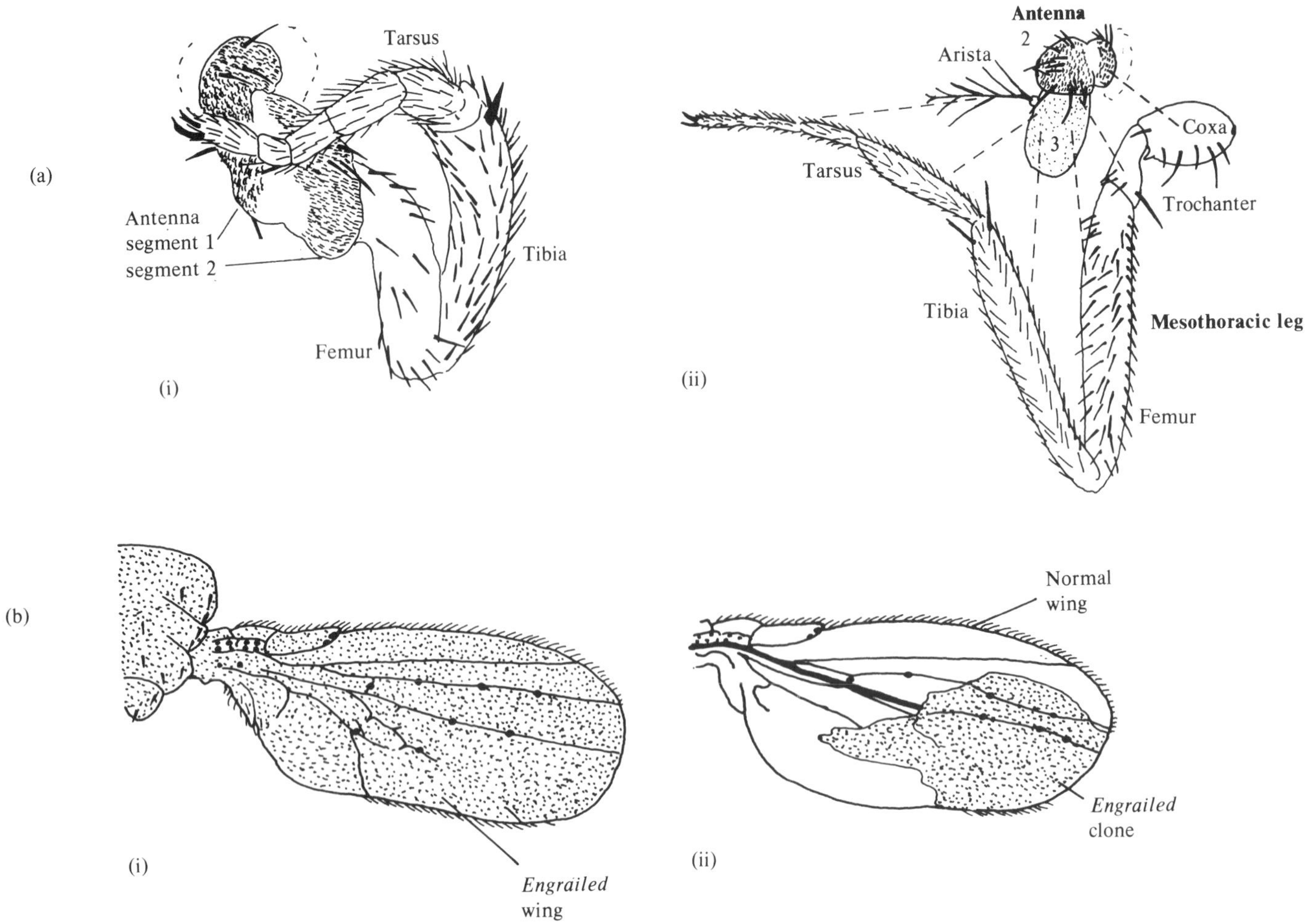

Fig. 4.2.13. Homoeotic mutants and positional information in imaginal discs.

(a) *Antennapaedia* transforms parts of the antenna into parts of the leg, so that a chimeric appendage is formed (i). The transformation is variable in extent and position-specific, so a correspondence map can be drawn between the two appendages (ii). This indicates that leg and antenna discs have the same positional information and that some mutant antenna disc cells switch to leg-type interpretation. (From [54] and [66].)

(b) (i) The mutation *engrailed* transforms parts of the posterior compartment of the wing (but not the thorax) into a fair copy of the anterior pattern. (ii) An *engrailed* clone in the posterior compartment of a wild-type wing also forms anterior structures, and can cross the border into the anterior compartment, while an anterior *engrailed* clone forms normal anterior structures and respects the border with wild-type posterior cells. These results suggest that the positional information may be the same in anterior and posterior compartments, but interpreted differently because the wild-type allele of *engrailed* is active only in the posterior compartment [18, 39].

interpretation of positional information. The same recombination event would not influence an antenna disc cell because its *bithorax+* gene is not active anyway.

Furthermore, the development of compartments (Fig. 4.2.10c) may represent a progressive subdivision of each disc into determined regions with particular combinations of selector genes active [17, 47]. One such selector gene may be *engrailed+*, since it appears to be active in the posterior but not the anterior compartment of the wing disc, and the *engrailed* mutation causes a partial posterior-to-anterior transformation in some regions of the disc [39] (Fig. 4.2.13b). This indicates that the A and P compartments may have similar positional information and normally form different patterns because the *engrailed* gene is only active in the P compartment [39]. Further compartment borders might form at particular positions as the larval disc is subdivided into dorsal and ventral compartments, presumably with equivalent positional information and differing in the activity of another (unknown) selector gene [17]. In this way a particular compartment in a particular disc would be defined by a combinatorial code of the states of a few selector genes.

At present, there seem to be several difficulties in relating selector genes and lineage compartments to other information on pattern formation within discs. First, the *engrailed* studies suggest that the A and P compartments are differently determined fields of positional information in mirror symmetry, but the mutation produces only a partial anterior transformation in the posterior wing blade and hinge, and a similar minor effect on the tarsus of the first leg, and it has no effect on the other posterior regions of these discs. Pattern regulation studies on the wing disc [6] (Fig. 4.2.11) and the leg disc [1] show that the disc responds as a single asymmetrical field. Also, the property of coming from the A or the P compartment does not fit the usual definition of 'determination', since cells can form structures of the other compartment during pattern regulation [1, 28]. Hence compartments do not appear to correspond to fields and may not be regions of differently determined cells [34]. Secondly, the selector-gene hypothesis is simple and attractive but the evidence is not compelling for the state of activity of a single switch gene being sufficient to define two compartments within a disc, or to define two discs. The fact that cells of one disc can change their determination to that characteristic of another disc (e.g. haltere disc cells change to 'wing') when one gene (*bithorax*) loses activity during larval development, does not logically prove that the controlling difference between 'haltere' and 'wing' cells lies in the 'on' or 'off' state of this gene. Determination may involve complex gene-control circuits with few stable states, and transition may be caused in a number of ways [35]. For example, the antenna-to-leg change can be produced by *Antennapaedia*, by other homoeotic mutants, or by culturing wild-type disc fragments in adult hosts [36].

Imaginal disc development: conclusions

The various imaginal discs develop from differently determined regions of the primary field and their determination depends upon continued gene activity. The discs behave as secondary fields through larval life and form different complex cuticular patterns, apparently in response to the same positional information. Growth of the disc and pattern regulation in mature disc fragments can both be interpreted in terms of the polar coordinate model. During development, imaginal discs become divided into lineage compartments. Since these do not seem to be equivalent to fields and may not be differently determined (as they can be transgressed during pattern regulation), their function is at present rather unclear.

4.2.6 DISCUSSION

Pattern formation in the insect epidermis

Of the three approaches described in section 4.2.2, that of positional information has been most successful in explaining pattern formation and regulation in the insect epidermis. There is no evidence in favour of sequential induction, since all the grafting experiments show that patterns are generated in primary and secondary fields by *interaction* rather than by the specific *action* of a determined pattern element on neighbouring tissue (see the egg posterior pole graft (Fig. 4.2.5) and the regulation of imaginal disc fragments (Fig. 4.2.11)). Studies of *Drosophila* homoeotic mutants such as *Antennapaedia* (Fig. 4.2.13) or *bithorax* indicate that different visible patterns can form from the same set of spatial cues, and this important conclusion also follows from grafting experiments between different abdominal segments (Fig. 4.2.8). These experiments provide strong evidence against models where specific inductions or prepattern peaks lead to the formation of a corresponding set of pattern elements (see section 4.2.2). Furthermore, as predicted by a simple and universal map of positional information, pattern mutants (such as *achaete*, Fig. 4.2.2) behave cell-autonomously in genetic mosaics (with minor exceptions—see below) and are therefore effects on local cellular response.

The experimental results which we have considered in sections 4.2.3–4.2.5 therefore suggest that the major features of insect epidermal patterns form by interpretation of a simple map of positional information. There are indications, however, that other mechanisms are involved in developing the details of cuticular patterns. For instance, pattern elements can have local inductive or inhibitory effects.

The slightly displaced bristles sometimes found in *Drosophila* wild-type/*achaete* mosaics (Fig. 4.2.2c) may indicate that the positional information in an area of tissue around the normal site allows bristle formation but the peripheral region is normally inhibited by the bristle differentiating in the centre [62]. When the central site is covered by *achaete* tissue, a peripheral cell

(a)

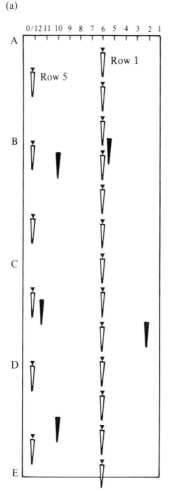

(b)

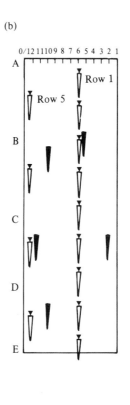

Fig. 4.2.14. Diagram of some features of the bristle patterns of the first tarsal segment of the mesothoracic leg of normal and starved *Drosophila*. (From Held [28].) The cylindrical segment is shown split and opened out.

The normal segment (a) bears eight longitudinal rows of bristles with bracts (triangles) and each row has a characteristic number and spacing of bristles—only rows 5 and 1 are shown. There are also five bractless bristles in characteristic positions.

After starvation during late larval stages, the flies are considerably smaller than normal, and the tarsal segment has approximately 25%

fewer cells down its length and around its circumference (b). The eight longitudinal rows and five bractless bristles are found in (more or less) *normal relative positions*, indicating the presence of a regulating system of positional information (labelled 0–12 and A–E in accordance with Fig. 4.2.12). However, within each row, bristles occur with the *normal spacing*: a normal number of cells separate the bristles. Hence the row bristles are positioned by a different, non-regulating mechanism. In addition, other evidence [7] suggests that the bracts are induced by adjacent bristles.

is free to form the bristle. Similar effects may occur on the abdominal segments of many hemimetabolous insects where the bristles are fairly evenly spaced but not in a precise pattern. As the insect grows between moults, the bristles become more widely spaced and new ones form between them, as if the bristles are spaced by local inhibition (see Lawrence [38]).

Several different mechanisms may be involved in forming a pattern, as shown by bristle patterns on the mesothoracic first tarsal segment of normal and small (starved) *Drosophila* (Fig. 4.2.14). It is clear that the position and identity of the longitudinal rows and the position of the isolated bractless bristles is set by positional information which can regulate for differences in size [28]. However, *within* each row some mechanism such as local inhibition maintains the characteristic spacing of bristles [28]. In addition, the bristles in the rows appear to induce neighbouring proximal cells to form small bracts (see Bryant [7]).

Insects and other animals

Many aspects of cellular structure and biochemistry have been highly conserved during evolution and, similarly, many of the mechanisms of pattern formation may occur throughout the animal kingdom [74]. Many of the results and conclusions from work on insects have parallels in other systems. For example, the behaviour of the primary field after fragmentation and grafting is very similar in early insect (Fig. 4.2.5), amphibian (Fig. 4.2.1a and [50]) and sea urchin [30] embryos. In chicks and amphibians, the primary field splits into different secondary fields, such as the presumptive limbs (Fig. 4.2.1b). We know little about determination in vertebrate limbs and there are no clear homoeotic mutations, but grafting experiments indicate that the fore- and hindlimb fields contain the same positional information.

The polar-coordinate model (Fig. 4.2.12) can be applied to developing insect and vertebrate limbs [8, 16, 31], encouraging us to think in terms of universal models for pattern formation. In both insects and vertebrates, the results of experiments on regulation of limb fields and regeneration of larval limbs suggest that basic cellular properties of intercalation and distalization may be involved in forming the pattern and responding to a disturbance at any developmental stage [15, 16]. We have only considered pattern formation in one or two dimensions within the insect epidermis. However, it

may be generally true of animal development that patterns are formed within cell sheets and three-dimensional structures are subsequently built up by morphogenetic movements (see Chapter 4.3) and secondary interactions (such as induction—see Chapter 3.5) between cell layers [16].

Nonetheless, this chapter cannot give a complete picture of animal pattern formation by just looking at insect epidermis (fruitful experimental system though it has been in recent years), and other aspects of the problem have been stressed in work on other systems. We therefore recommend reviews of recent work on the amphibian egg [50], the mammalian egg [20], hydra [22], ciliate protozoa [13], the chick limb [75], amphibian limb regeneration [8], somite formation [9], and the formation of nerve connections in invertebrates [3] and in the amphibian visual system [21].

Models and mechanisms

The results of most experiments on pattern formation and regulation support *gradient* models of positional information (Figs 4.2.5–4.2.10) with rules concerning the results of interaction between different gradient levels and the circumstances in which new boundaries may be formed. It must be stressed, however, that we have only considered very simple models (which are usually not adequate to account for all details of the experimental results) and we have made an absolute distinction between induction, positional information (with a very simple map, e.g. a gradient) and prepattern (with very simple interpretation, e.g. one threshold). To understand the formation of patterns, particularly those consisting of a large number of repeating units such as insect segments or vertebrate somites, it may be necessary to develop dynamic models in which time as well as space is important [9] and which involve both positional information and sequential induction [33] or a prepattern.

Although we know a great deal about the molecular events involved in cell differentiation (see Chapter 6.4), we have very little information at this level about the preceding process of pattern formation which causes cells to become committed to particular paths of differentiation. We are still searching for satisfactory models with formal rules by which we can understand the behaviour of developing tissues, and which give clues about the molecular mechanisms of pattern formation. For example, the diffusion and intercalary regeneration models of the insect abdominal segment (Fig. 4.2.7b) or the chick limb [31, 75] make very different suggestions about the nature of positional information and the ways in which cells interact. The selector-gene hypothesis [17, 47] and alternative views [34, 35] suggest different mechanisms by which positional information can influence gene activity and lead to 'determination'. Some progress has been made in formulating models of gradients [45] and in their interpretation [40, 42] in terms of known biochemical processes (such as diffusion, enzyme inhibition and activation) and this approach may eventually bring together the phenomenology of the embryologist and the molecular mechanisms of the cell biologist.

It is relatively straightforward to model 'positional information' as a diffusible gradient and 'interpretation' as effects on gene activity, but there are other possibilities. Ciliate protozoa have complex surface patterns which depend on heritable spatial information which is partly independent of their genome [13]. Since pattern regulation and local induction can occur within the one cell with streaming cytoplasm and central nucleus, cell membranes are strongly implicated as sites of the molecular interactions generating positional cues and, in some cases, interpreting them [13].

Pattern formation is the most intriguing and elusive aspect of development. Many of the basic ideas (and experimental methods) were introduced a long time ago [12, 26, 49, 71] but we are gradually building up a more extensive and precise knowledge of the phenomena, proposing more specific and testable models, and just beginning to speculate about molecular mechanisms.

4.2.7   REFERENCES

1 Abbott L., Karpen G. & Schubiger G. (1981) Compartmental restrictions and blastema formation during pattern regulation in *Drosophila* imaginal leg discs. *Devl. Biol.*, **87**, 64–75.

2 Adler P.N. (1979) Position-specific interaction between cells of the imaginal wing and haltere discs of *Drosophila melanogaster*. *Devl. Biol.*, **70**, 262–267.

3 Anderson H., Edwards J.S. & Palka J. (1980) Developmental neurobiology of invertebrates. *Annu. Rev. Neurosci.*, **3**, 97–139.

4 Bownes M. (1975) Adult deficiencies and duplications of head and thoracic structures resulting from microcautery of blastoderm stage *Drosophila* embryos. *J. Embryol. exp. Morph.*, **34**, 33–54.

5 Bohn H. (1970) Interkalare Regeneration und segmentale Gradienten bei den Extremitäten von *Leucophaea*—Larven

(Blattaria) I Femur und Tibia. *Wilhelm Roux' Archiv.*, **165**, 303–340.

6 Bryant P.J. (1975) Pattern formation in the imaginal wing disc of *Drosophila melanogaster*: fate map, regeneration and duplication. *J. exp. Zool.*, **193**, 49–78.

7 Bryant P.J. (1979) Pattern formation in imaginal discs. In *Genetics and Biology of Drosophila* Vol. 2c, (Eds T.R.F. Wright & M. Ashburner), pp. 230–335. Academic Press, New York.

8 Bryant S.V., French V. & Bryant P.J. (1981) Distal regeneration and symmetry. *Science, N.Y.*, **212**, 993–1002.

9 Cooke J. (1981) The problem of periodic patterns in embryos. *Phil. Trans. R. Soc. B*, **295**, 509–524.

10 Cooke J. (1982) The relation between scale and the completeness of pattern in vertebrate embryogenesis; models and experiments. *Amer. Zool.* **22**, 91–104.

11 Davidson E.H. (1977) *Gene Activity in Early Development*, 2nd edn. Academic Press, New York.

12 Driesch H. (1908) *The Science and Philosophy of the Organism*. A. & C. Black, London.

13 Frankel J. (1979) An analysis of cell-surface patterning in *Tetrahymena*. In *Determinants of Spatial Organisation* (Eds S. Subtelny & I.R. Konigsberg), pp. 215–246. Academic Press, New York.

14 French V. (1978) Intercalary regeneration around the circumference of the cockroach leg. *J. Embryol. exp. Morph.*, **47**, 53–84.

15 French V. (1981) Pattern regulation and regeneration. *Phil. Trans. R. Soc. B.*, **295**, 601–617.

16 French V., Bryant P. & Bryant S. (1976) Pattern regulation in epimorphic fields. *Science, N.Y.*, **193**, 969–981.

17 Garcia-Bellido A. (1975) Genetic control of wing disc development in *Drosophila*. In *Cell Patterning*. Ciba Foundation Symp. **29**, pp. 161–182. A.S.P. Amsterdam.

18 Garcia-Bellido A., Lawrence P.A. & Morata G. (1979) Compartments in animal development. *Scient. Am.*, **241**, 102–110.

19 Garcia-Bellido A., Ripoll P. & Morata G. (1973) Developmental compartmentalization of the wing disc of *Drosophila*. *Nature, New Biol.*, **245**, 251–253.

20 Gardner R.L. (1978) The relationship between cell lineage and differentiation in the early mouse embryo. In *Genetic Mosaics and Cell Differentiation* (Ed. W.J. Gehring), pp. 97–118. Springer-Verlag, Berlin & New York.

21 Gaze R.M. (1978) The problem of specificity in the formation of nerve connections. In *Specificity of Embryological Interactions (Receptors and Recognition, Series B, Vol. 4)* (Ed. D.R. Garrod), pp. 53–93. Chapman & Hall, London.

22 Gierer A. (1977) Biological features and physical concepts of pattern formation exemplified by hydra. *Curr. Tops. Devl. Biol.*, **11**, 17–59.

23 Gierer A. & Meinhardt H. (1972) A theory of biological pattern formation. *Kybernetik*, **12**, 30–39.

24 Goodwin B.C. & Cohen H.M. (1969) A phase-shift model for the spatial and temporal organisation of developing systems. *J. theor. Biol.*, **25**, 49–107.

25 Guerrier P. & van den Biggelaar J.A.M. (1979) Intracellular activation and cell intractions in so-called mosaic embryos. In *Cell Lineage, Stem Cells and Cell Determination*, SERM Symp. **10** (Ed. N. Le Dourin). North Holland, Amsterdam.

26 Harrison R. (1918) Experiments on the development of the fore-

limb of *Amblystoma*, a self-differentiating equipotential system. *J. exp. Zool.*, **25**, 413–461.

27 Haynie J.L. & Bryant P.J. (1976) Intercalary regeneration in imaginal wing disk of *Drosophila melanogaster. Nature, Lond.*, **259**, 659–662.

28 Held L.I. (1979) Pattern as a function of cell number and cell size on the second-leg basitarsus of *Drosophila. Wilhelm Roux' Archiv.*, **187**, 105–127.

29 Horder T.J. (1976) Pattern formation in animal embryos. In *The Developmental Biology of Plants and Animals*, 1st edn. (Eds C.F. Graham & P.F. Wareing), pp. 169–197. Blackwell Scientific Publications, Oxford.

30 Hörstadius S. (1973) *Experimental Embryology of Echinoderms.* Clarendon Press, Oxford.

31 Iten L. & Murphy D. (1980) Pattern regulation in the embryonic chick limb: supernumerary limb formation with anterior (non-Z.P.A.) limb bud tissue. *Devl. Biol.*, **75**, 373–385.

32 Kalthoff K. (1978) Pattern formation in early insect embryogenesis —data calling for modification of a recent model. *J. Cell Sci.*, **29**, 1–15.

33 Kalthoff K. (1979) Analysis of a morphogenetic determinant in an insect embryo (*Smittia* spec, Chironomidae, Diptera). In *Determinants of Spatial Organisation* (Eds S. Subtedny & I.R. Konigsberg), pp. 97–125. Academic Press, New York.

34 Karlsson J. (1983) Homeotic genes and the function of compartments in *Drosophila. Devl. Biol.* (in press).

35 Kauffman S.A. (1971) Gene regulation networks: a theory for their global structure and behaviours. *Curr. Tops. Devl. Biol.*, **6**, 145–182.

36 Kauffman S.A. (1973) Control circuits for determination and transdetermination. *Science, N.Y.*, **181**, 310–318.

37 Lawrence P.A. (1966) Gradients in the insect segment: the orientation of hairs in the milkweed bug *Oncopeltus fasciatus. J. exp. Biol.*, **44**, 607–620.

38 Lawrence P.A. (1973) The development of spatial patterns in the integument of insects. In *Developmental Systems: Insects. Vol. 2.* (Eds S.J. Counce & C.H. Waddington), pp. 157–209. Academic Press, London.

39 Lawrence P.A. & Morata G. (1976) Compartments in the wing of *Drosophila*: A study of the *engrailed* gene. *Devl. Biol.*, **50**, 321–337.

40 Lewis J., Slack J.M.W. & Wolpert L. (1977) Thresholds in development. *J. theor. Biol.*, **65**, 576–590.

41 Locke M. (1959) The cuticular pattern in an insect, *Rhodnius prolixus* Stal. *J. exp. Biol.*, **36**, 459–477.

42 MacWilliams H.K. & Papageorgiou S. (1978) A model of gradient interpretation based on morphogen binding. *J. theor. Biol.*, **72**, 385–411.

43 Madhavan M.M. & Schneiderman H.A. (1977) Histological analysis of the dynamics of growth of imaginal discs and histoblast nests during larval development of *Drosophila melanogaster. Wilhelm Roux' Archiv.*, **183**, 269–305.

44 Meinhardt H. (1977) A model of pattern formation in insect embryogenesis. *J. Cell Sci.*, **23**, 117–139.

45 Meinhardt H. (1978) Models for the ontogenetic development of higher organisms. *Rev. Physiol. Biochem. Pharmacol.*, **80**, 47–104.

46 Morata G. & Garcia-Bellido A. (1976) Developmental analysis of some mutants of the bithorax system of *Drosophila. Wilhelm Roux' Archiv.*, **179**, 125–143.

47 Morata G. & Lawrence P.A. (1977) Homoeotic genes, compartments and cell determination in *Drosophila. Nature, Lond.*, **265**, 211–216.

48 Morata G. & Lawrence P.A. (1978) Anterior and posterior compartments in the head of *Drosophila. Nature, Lond.*, **274**, 473–474.

49 Morgan T.H. (1901) *Regeneration.* Macmillan, New York.

50 Nieuwkoop P. (1969) The formation of the mesoderm in Urodelean Amphibians. I Induction by the endoderm. *Wilhelm Roux' Archiv.*, **162**, 341–373.

51 Nübler-Jung K. (1977) Pattern stability in the insect segment. I. Pattern reconstitution by intercalary regeneration and cell sorting in *Dysdercus intermedius* Dist. *Wilhelm Roux' Archiv.*, **183**, 17–40.

52 Nusslein-Volhard C. (1977) Genetic analysis of pattern formation in the embryo of *Drosophila melanogaster.* Characterisation of the maternal-effect mutant *bicaudal. Wilhelm Roux' Archiv.*, **183**, 249–268.

53 Nusslein-Volhard C. (1979) Maternal effect mutations that alter the spatial coordinates of the embryo of *Drosophila melanogaster.* In *Determinants of Spatial Organisation* (Eds S. Subtelny & I.R. Konigsberg), pp.185–211. Academic Press, New York.

54 Postlethwaite J.H. & Schneiderman H.A. (1971) Pattern formation and determination in the antenna of the homoeotic mutant *Antennapedia* of *Drosophila melanogaster. Devl. Biol.*, **25**, 606–640.

55 Reinhardt C.A., Hodgkin N.M. & Bryant P.J. (1977) Wound healing in the imaginal discs of *Drosophila.* I. Scanning electron microscopy of normal and healing wing discs. *Devl. Biol.*, **60**, 238–257.

56 Sander K. (1971) Pattern formation in longitudinal halves of leaf hopper eggs (Homoptera) and some remarks on the definition of "Embryonic regulation". *Wilhelm Roux' Archiv.*, **167**, 336–352.

57 Sander K. (1975) Pattern specification in the insect embryo. In *Cell Patterning.* Ciba Foundation Symp. **29**, pp. 241–263. A.S.P. Amsterdam.

58 Sander K. (1976) Formation of the basic body pattern in insect embryogenesis. *Adv. Insect Physiol.*, **12**, 125–238.

59 Sander K. & Nübler-Jung K. (1981). Polarity and gradients in insect development. In *International Cell Biology 1980–1981* (Ed. H. Schweiger), pp. 497–506. Springer-Verlag, Berlin.

60 Schubiger G. & Wood W.J. (1977) Determination during early embryogenesis in *Drosophila melanogaster. Amer. Zool.*, **17**, 565–576.

61 Sengel P. (1975) Feather pattern development. In *Cell Patterning.* Ciba Foundation Symp. **29**, pp. 51–70. A.S.P. Amsterdam.

62 Sondhi K.C. (1961) The biological foundations of animal pattern. *Q. Rev. Biol.*, **38**, 289–327.

63 Spemann H. (1938) *Embryonic Development and Induction.* Yale University Press, New Haven.

64 Steiner E. (1976) Establishment of compartments in the developing leg imaginal discs of *Drosophila melanogaster. Wilhelm Roux' Archiv.*, **180**, 9–30.

65 Stern C. (1968) *Genetic Mosaics and Other Essays.* Harvard University Press, Cambridge, Massachusetts.

66 Stocker R., Edwards J.S., Palka J. & Schubiger G. (1976) Projection of sensory neurons from a homoeotic mutant appendage,

Antennapedia, in *Drosophila melanogaster. Devl. Biol.,* **52,** 210–220.

67 Stumpf H. (1966) Mechanisms by which cells estimate their location within the body. *Nature, Lond.,* **212,** 430–431.

68 Stumpf H. (1968) Further studies on gradient-dependent diversification in the pupal cuticle of *Galleria mellonella. J. exp. Biol.,* **49,** 49–60.

69 Tank P. & Holder N. (1981) Pattern regulation in the regenerating limb of Urodele amphibians. *Q. Rev. Biol.,* **56,** 113–142.

70 Waddington C.H. (1967) Fields and gradients. In *Major Problems in Developmental Biology* (Ed. M. Locke), pp. 105–124. Academic Press, New York.

71 Weiss P. (1939) *Principles of Development.* Holt, Reinhart &

Winston, New York.

72 Wieschaus E. & Gehring W. (1976) Clonal analysis of primordial disc cells in the early embryo *Drosophila melanogaster. Devl. Biol.,* **50,** 249–263.

73 Wolpert L. (1969) Positional information and the spatial pattern of cellular differentiation. *J. theor. Biol.,* **25,** 1–47.

74 Wolpert L. (1971) Positional information and pattern formation. *Curr. Tops. Devl. Biol.,* **6,** 183–224.

75 Wolpert L., Lewis J. & Summerbell D. (1975) Morphogenesis of the vertebrate limb. In *Cell Patterning.* Ciba Foundation Symp. **29,** pp. 95–130. A.S.P. Amsterdam.

76 Wright D. & Lawrence P.A. (1981) Regeneration of the segment boundary in *Oncopeltus. Devl. Biol.,* **85,** 317–327.

Chapter 4.3
The Cellular Origins of Tissue Organization in Animals
J.B.L. Bard

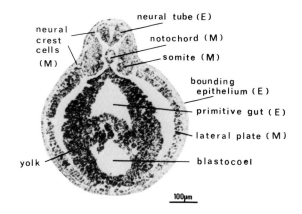

Fig. 4.3.1. A transverse section of a stage 21 *Xenopus* embryo showing the epithelial and mesenchymal structures that form in the early embryo. This specimen was fixed in gluteraldehyde which causes differential shrinking, so that the different tissues are more separated here than they were in the original embryo. E, epithelium; M, mesenchyme. ×85.

4.3.1   INTRODUCTION

No one who has looked down a microscope at sections of, say, a *Xenopus* embryo at the tail-bud stage can fail to be impressed by the exquisite cellular organization that has developed from the simple blastula in less than a day (Fig. 4.3.1). There is evidence of tubules, vesicles and bounding membranes made up of monolayer epithelial cells and between them are mesenchymal masses and space-filling connective tissue. The way in which cells cooperate to build such structures in embryos is called *morphogenesis*, and this chapter will concentrate, in particular, on the various individual and social properties that cells use as they generate organization in tissues.

To do this, an outline will be given of the formation of some of the structures of early embryos (section 4.3.2) followed by a summary of what is known about the morphogenetic abilities of the two major cell types in the early embryo, the epithelia and the mesenchyme (section 4.3.3). Next, two examples of morphogenesis whose cellular basis is well understood—gastrulation in the sea urchin and the formation of the cornea of the avian eye—are examined in detail, so as to show how cells actually use their properties when building tissues (section 4.3.4). Finally, an attempt is made to integrate many of the disparate facts to build up a coherent approach to morphogenesis (section 4.3.5).

The reader will note that the discussion of each aspect of cell behaviour is brief as the functional significance of each property in its embryological context is concentrated upon, rather than the experiments that have established it or the molecular mechanisms that underpin it. These aspects are covered by Chapter 3.3 and by references to the literature. The references themselves are divided into two groups: the first set [1–5] contains general texts on embryology and organogenesis; the second includes detailed reviews and specialized research articles. The reader is, in particular, referred to Balinsky [1] for basic embryological information, to Trinkaus [4] for a detailed review of cell movement in morphogenesis and to Wessells [5] for an introduction to current studies in organogenesis.

4.3.2 DEVELOPMENT OF EMBRYONIC ORGANIZATION

The post-neurula *Xenopus* embryo

In this section, some of the events that take place during the early stages of development will be examined so as to highlight some of the problems of morphogenesis. To set the scene, a description will be given of a frog embryo at the early tail-bud stage, that is after gastrulation and neurulation have occurred (Fig. 4.3.1); the cellular organization of each part of the embryo is then examined and its morphogenesis considered. We shall see that while developmental events are relatively simple to describe, the morphogenetic mechanisms underlying them must be extremely complex.

At the tail-bud stage, the *Xenopus* embryo has a clearly defined polarity with a head at the anterior end and an undifferentiated mesenchymal mass at the tail; the whole embryo is bounded by an epithelium. Inside, there are three major longitudinal tissues. Nearest the dorsal surface is the neural tube, which was formed from the external epithelium (Fig. 4.3.2); this tube is broad anteriorly and narrows towards the tail. Subjacent to this is the mesenchymal notochord, formed by the elongation of cells determined at the blastula stage [1], and below the notochord is the tube of the primitive gut, another epithelium.

In the language of classical embryology [1], the neural tube is called 'ectoderm' as it comes from the dorsal region of the egg, the notochord is called 'mesoderm' as it is derived from the middle of the egg and the gut is 'endoderm', being from the basal region of the egg. These names are important in the context of cell lineages, but are irrelevant if we wish to consider cell properties, for each region can give rise to a range of cell types. Ectoderm, which is initially epithelial-like, can also give rise to mesenchymal and nerve cells; mesoderm, the major source of mesenchymal cells, can also become epithelia (as in kidney tubules or the cells lining blood vessels), while endoderm, which is frequently epithelial, can differentiate to more specialized cells such as the parenchymal cells of the liver (for a detailed review of the abilities of each germ layer see Balinsky [1]).

These geographical terms will therefore not be used to describe post-gastrula cells, which will be considered instead as epithelial- or mesenchymal-like irrespective of their origin unless they have differentiated to a more specialized state. It is a characteristic of development that cells in different regions gradually aquire distinct properties: lens and cornea were originally adjacent pieces of skin epithelium while bone and cartilage derive from a single piece of limb mesenchyme.

Returning to the embryo, it can be seen that there are, on either side of three central organs, two groups of mesenchymal cells. Adjacent to the notochord are the somites (see Fig. 4.3.3) while neural crest cells extend laterally from the top of the neural tube. The neural crest cells budded off the neural ridge (see below) while the somitic mesenchyme moved to its position during gastrulation. The ventral part of the embryo contains yolk-bearing cells that surround the blastopore and are descended from the endodermal region of the egg. It is worth noting that the relative size of each tissue remains constant irrespective of embryo size and even, to a reasonable approximation, irrespective of the relative amounts of each cell type in the blastula [92].

Some basic morphogenetic movements

Although other organisms may form their tissue in a somewhat different order or arrangement [1], the basic organization of the *Xenopus* embryo is common to all vertebrates, as are the morphogenetic movements that generate it. Without doubt, the most important of these is gastrulation, whereby cells at the vegetal pole of the blastula move or fold inwards and form the gut. As the cellular movements of amphibian gastrulation have

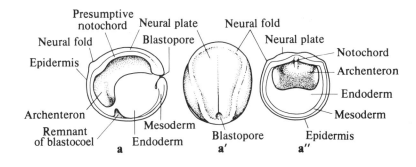

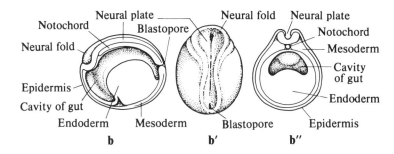

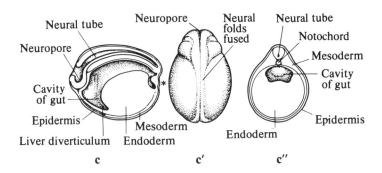

Fig. 4.3.2. Drawings of the neurulation of a frog embryo at **(a)** early **(b)** middle and **(c)** late stages. Left, median plane; centre, dorsal view; right, transverse section of anterior part of embryo. The asterisk in (c) shows where the anal canal will break through. (From Balinsky [1].)

already been described in detail (Chapter 3.3), we shall leave detailed consideration of this process until later when it is examined in the sea urchin. In this section, we will concentrate on tne events that cause the dorsal surface of the embryo to fold into the neural tube and that cause the tail to extend. This latter process derives from the behaviour of the notochord, which forms from a group of mesenchymal cells determined at the blastula stage and which moves just below the dorsal ectoderm during gastrulation. These cells extend to form a long, narrow cylinder that in turn causes the embryo to extend. The notochord also plays an important role in neural tube formation but, as we shall see, its extension is just one component of a complex series of events. It

should be pointed out that the formation of one tissue affecting the development of a second is common in embryogenesis and usually complicates the study of any single aspect of morphogenesis.

The generation of the neural tube is one of the most dramatic events of amphibian development and follows the induction of the surface epithelium (ectoderm) by the underlying mesenchyme (chordamesoderm) brought into contact with it during gastrulation (see also Chapter 3.5). The first stage of neural tube formation is the appearance of an oval ridge on the dorsal surface of the embryo, extending from the head to the blastopore (Fig. 4.3.2), the area enclosing the ridge being called the neural plate. Over a period of a few hours, its posterior

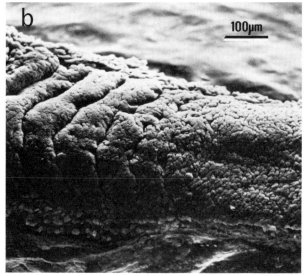

Fig. 4.3.3. The somites of a *Rana* embryo. **(a)** Light micrograph of a fixed embryo with the skin epithelium removed to show the somites. ×28. (Courtesy of Dr T. Elsdale.) **(b)** Scanning electron micrograph showing the cellular organization of the somites and the border between segmented and undifferentiated mesenchyme. The mechanism behind this segmentation remains obscure but it is known [74] that somites form sequentially from front to back. Even if a neurula is bisected before somitogenesis, the posterior half still forms somites when expected. This experiment shows that the wave of somite determination is kinetic, i.e. that it depends on a timing mechanism rather than on the transport of information down the embryo. ×120.

region narrows so that the neural plate takes on a keyhole shape. The ridges on either side then come together, meet, and seal to form a tube that sinks below the surface epithelium and detaches from it.

Neural tube formation has been studied most carefully in the newt *Tarica torosa* [54] and one aspect in particular is now understood: the mechanisms that cause the oval neural plate to become key-holed. Two coupled events appear to be responsible for the change: first, the cells of the overlying epithelium undergo programmed shrinkage, which causes the cells to change from cuboidal to columnar and results in a decrease in surface area. Secondly, the underlying notochord, which adheres to the epithelium, extends causing anterior movement of the overlying cells and the formation of the keyhole shape. The evidence for this mechanism comes in part from traditional morphological observations and in part from computer simulations. Jacobson and Gordon [54] showed that if a sheet of cells were programmed to shrink in an appropriate way and were subjected to the force of an extending adherent notochord, not only would the appropriate shape be generated but the cell movements would mimic those actually observed in time-lapse studies; no simpler mechanisms would generate observed changes. Thus it is clear that the processes of epithelial shrinkage and notochord extension appear necessary and sufficient to generate the change in neural plate shape[1].

As the two ridges fold over to meet, further shape changes take place in the neural plate cells: they contract at the apical ends to become flask shaped and it is likely that the forces that change cell shapes are also responsible for the bending of the ridges. Evidence is now accumulating that it is the contraction of microfilaments and the elongation of microtubules [22, 63] within the cells that are responsible for the shape changes (see Chapter 3.3). The mechanisms responsible for the adhesions between the ridges which form the tube and the breaking of the tubes' adhesion to the adjacent epithelium as it sinks into the mesenchyme remain to be elucidated, although Jacobson has pointed out that elastic forces within the sheet may play a role in tube formation [53].

The mechanisms responsible for the morphogenesis and differentiation of the two major, transitory mesenchymal tissues in the tail-bud embryo, the neural crest cells and the somites, also remain obscure. The neural crest cells, which originate in the ridges of the neural

[1] Note added in proof. This analysis has to be re-examined in the light of recent work showing that axial extension will occur when the notochord is lacking or defective [105].

plate, migrate laterally to the flank and anteriorly to the head, eventually giving rise to pigment, nerve, fibroblastic, osteoblastic, and even epithelial, cells [61, 72]. While they migrate, the somites form: as the tail-bud extends, a wave of determination passes down the mesenchyme adjacent to the neural tube causing the cell mass to segment into some 40 pairs of somites [74] (see [15] for a description of morphogenesis in the chick). Each somite can be considered as containing at least three regions, known as the myotome, the sclerotome and the dermatome. The somites are transitory structures and each region breaks down: the myotome becomes body musculature; the sclerotome, the vertebrae; and the dermatome, the dermis of the skin. Again, nothing is known of the mechanisms responsible for either the differentiation or the morphogenesis of these structures.

By the time that the cells of the neural crest and the somites have completed their migrations, much of the basic form of the embryo has been achieved and the cells are in appropriate positions for their terminal differentiations. Three types of events now occur: epithelia aquire functional properties, mesenchyme differentiates into bone, cartilage, connective tissue and muscle, while epithelia and mesenchyme interact to form structures that neither alone can generate [1]. It is at this stage that tissues take on their final organization (see [3] for review) and that it becomes relatively easy to grow embryonic cells in culture and to study those properties which are necessary for morphogenesis.

4.3.3 MORPHOGENETIC PROPERTIES OF CELLS

We now consider some of the cellular abilities (the nuts and the bolts) underlying morphogenesis in the early embryo. This section therefore summarizes the individual and social properties of mesenchymal cells and epithelial cells, and the interactions between them. The discussion of each property will centre on its role in tissue building, and will, at times, be speculative as it is attempted to show how particular cell behaviours might be relevant to animal morphogenesis. Work on simple organisms is excluded from this chapter, but important examples of their cellular morphogenesis discussed elsewhere are the sorting out of mixed sponge-cell aggregates (Chapter 3.2 and [88]) and the development of the cellular slime moulds (Chapter 5.2 and [58]).

Individual properties of fibroblasts

The term mesenchyme is used as a general label for the precursor of a range of cell types such as fibroblasts, cartilage cells and osteoblasts all of which make connective tissue, associate in three-dimensional masses and are, initially at least, motile. In early embryos, they are identified by being found between epithelial sheets

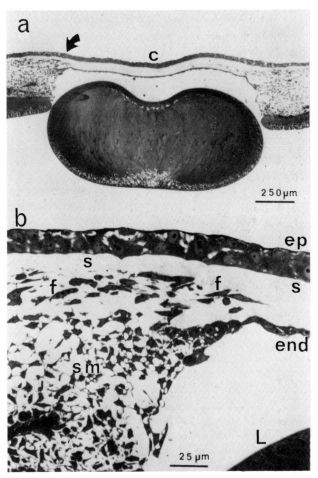

Fig. 4.3.4. Light micrographs of a 6-day-old chick cornea. **(a)** Low power, the cornea (c) is a double layer of cells with a cell-free stroma between them that is being invaded by peripheral cells subjacent to the external epithelium. ×42. **(b)** A region of (a) (arrow) enlarged to show the external bipolar morphology of the invading fibroblasts (f) as they migrate into the stroma (s) between the epithelium (ep) and the endothelium (end), and the stellate, immobile mesenchyme (sm) at the side of the cornea. ×410.

[46]. In this section, we shall concentrate on the fibroblast, the most closely studied of the mesenchymal cell types as it is the easiest to isolate and culture.

Morphology and movement of fibroblasts

The shape of a fibroblast *in vivo* depends on its environment and its motility. The sedentary cell in loose connective tissue (Fig. 4.3.4) is frequently stellate, having a cell body with many processes that adhere to local matrix. In contrast, the motile fibroblast, as seen in the developing chick cornea, is elongated, alternating between a bipolar and a pear-shaped body. The leading edge possesses long, thin processes that are in constant movement, making and breaking adhesions [12]. The trailing edge first elongates, as it adheres to matrix while the cell body advances, and then rounds up as this adhesion breaks under stress, to give a pear-shaped morphology (Chapter 3.3). Typical rates of movement of single cells *in vivo* are about 1 μm per minute. It is interesting to note that cultured fibroblasts move at a similar rate even though they show a very different morphology, having a flattened body and a high ruffling membrane on the leading edge [51] (see Chapter 3.3 and [60, 75] for discussion of the mechanisms of cell movement).

Cell movement is central to morphogenesis, but it has to be directed to ensure that migrating cells end up in appropriate locations. The simplest way of achieving this is for the embryo to set up routes that are defined by tissue geometry. This may involve channelling the cells between set boundaries (as in the migration of the corneal endothelium—see later) or along the cellular equivalent of railway tracks. The ability of cells to align along such features (e.g. collagen bundles *in vivo* and scratches on glass *in vitro*) is known as *contact guidance* [93, 94] (see Chapter 3.3). This mechanism probably accounts for the orthogonal alignment of fibroblasts in the collagen stroma (see later) and it is a possible explanation of the migration of nerve and pigment cells along blood vessels and the posterial migration of the Wolffian duct [86]. Another surface property that can direct cell movement is a *gradient of adhesion*: cells are found to migrate *in vitro* from points of low to points of high adhesivity [25, 45] (see Chapter 3.2 and 3.3); such a gradient is thought to exist on the inner surface of the sea urchin blastula (see later). Concentration gradients can also direct cell movement, but only one example of such

chemotaxis appears to have been demonstrated in an embryo so far. In the newt skin, there is a spaced but random arrangement of pigment cells that have migrated from the neural crest. When cultured normally these cells cohere, but when cultured under a coverslip or in a capillary tube, they repel one another [90]. The accepted explanation of this behaviour is that the cells secrete a molecule, as yet unisolated, that at high concentrations causes cells to separate and show negative chemotaxis. It is of note that in some species of newt the pigment cells later migrate laterally to form a stripe, now perhaps under the influence of positive chemotaxis; such cells also lose the ability to repel one another *in vitro* [89]. The best-known example of positive chemotaxis is, of course, the role of cyclic AMP in *Dictyostelium* aggregation [58] (see Chapter 5.2).

Synthesis of matrix

Perhaps the most important property of mesenchyme, once the migrations of early embryogenesis have taken place, is its ability to synthesize the materials of connective tissue matrix. Each cell type that differentiates from early mesenchyme secretes a somewhat different range of molecules, but they all make collagen, glycosaminoglycans (GAGs) and glycoproteins. Collagen is the major non-cellular component of bone, skin, tendon, eye and basal lamina (see later) and is found in a range of genetically distinct forms (see [20, 69] for review). Type I collagen, the most common, self-assembles to form fibrils of around 100 nm in diameter and of great length, that have a characteristic 64 nm periodicity (see Fig. 4.3.12b), enabling them to be easily recognized in the transmission electron microscope (TEM) (see Chapter 6.2 for assembly of collagen). Type II collagen is found in cartilage, Type III in dermis and arterial wall and Type IV in basement lamina [9]. It is now becoming clear that the different collagen types can play an important role in determining cell function and adhesion in development [57].

A major task of mesenchyme, as yet not understood, is the deposition of particular arrangements of collagen: fibrils that are apparently very similar may be laid down randomly in the skin, in elongated bundles in tendon, and in orthogonal layers in the cornea [52]. This last structure is particularly interesting as it is laid down, not by mesenchyme, but by an epithelium [49]; the only other major collagenous structure laid down by epithelium is the basement lamina. It is of note that collagen, once laid down, can also be removed as tissues are remodelled. The classic example of this is the loss of the amphibian tail during metamorphosis where posterior connective tissue is degraded following the production of a collagenase [98].

Glycosaminoglycans are very large, highly charged chains of repeating disaccharides (most frequently uronic acid and hexosamine) with carboxyl and/or sulphate groups which usually have some attached proteins [82]. A most important property of GAGs is that they bind water and can swell to occupy a domain around 10^4 times larger than the molecule itself. This swelling will exert considerable pressure on tissues and seems to be responsible for cell-free spaces in certain organs [11]. The appearance of hyaluronic acid in the chick embryo, for example, correlates with an increase in the cell-free space near the head and appears to permit the subsequent migration of neural crest cells [76]. It now seems likely that GAGs also play a role in the control of differentiation [30], as well as being an important component of the basement membrane [42]. The significance of most glycoproteins, which frequently contain polymers of sialic acid, remains unclear in the context of development. However, fibronectin (or LETS protein), whose presence can be demonstrated by fluorescent antibody and whose appearance in embryos often correlates with developmental change [102] is now under intense investigation (e.g. [59]). It seems to play a role in cell adhesion [102].

Collective properties of fibroblasts

While the isolated fibroblast is a convenient object for study *in vitro;* it is rarely found in tissues, for mesenchymal cells usually occur in aggregates and move in streams [4]. In this section, we consider the additional properties shown by fibroblasts when they interact with their neighbours and, as before, look for morphogenetic examples where these properties may be of significance.

Contact inhibition of movement

The best-known interaction between isolated fibroblasts occurs when one moving cell meets another. On contact, membrane activity ceases and each cell stops moving. After a while, another part of the cell becomes active and the cell moves off in a new direction (see Chapter

3.3). This phenomenon has been observed between pairs of cells on plastic [6], in three-dimensional collagen lattices and in the corneal stroma [12] and is called *contact inhibition of movement (CIM);* it is shown by normal cells but not by many tumour or transformed cells.

The significance of this phenomenon remains unclear *in vivo,* but it can be seen to have at least two important effects. First it can serve to stabilize a tissue: in a fibroblast mass, cells not on the periphery are surrounded by other cells and the CIM interaction will allow them to keep one another in a relatively quiescent state. Provided the mass is bounded by a barrier impermeable to fibroblasts, peripheral cells will also remain immobile. It should not, however, be thought that CIM maintains total immobility: time-lapse studies of dense cultures *in vitro* show that there are always some residual movements [34] and, in mixed aggregates including marked cells, the position of cells can be seen to have changed after a few days [7, 8]. A second role can be invoked for CIM. Consider again the bound mesenchymal mass. Were one part of the surrounding barrier to break down, peripheral cells would be free to migrate away from the mass and the CIM would ensure that the flow of cells would be directed away from the mass [6]. Such movements occur in wound healing [39] and in corneal morphogenesis [13].

One puzzling feature of cell behaviour in embryos is that some mesenchymal cells seem subject to CIM while others do not. Neural crest cells, for example, are apparently able to migrate over or through other cell types without being constrained by them. Abercrombie has pointed out that migrating cells *in vivo* may be insulated to some extent from other cells by connective tissue and that a contact interaction between different cell types need not inhibit movement [6]. However, the cues by which cells become motile or differentiate between an inhibiting and a neutral contact remain unknown.

Pattern formation by fibroblasts in vitro

In dense monolayer cultures, fibroblasts take up an extended bipolar morphology and form close side-to-side adhesions which lead to unexpectedly complex patterns [34] (Fig. 4.3.5a); similar organization can sometimes be seen in tissue sections. The cultured cells divide to give a series of patchworks of stable parallel

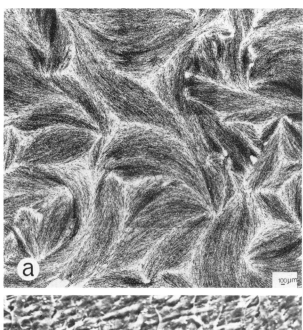

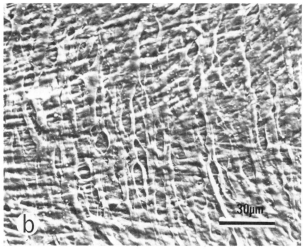

Fig. 4.3.5. Fibroblast patterns *in vitro*: (a) Light micrograph of a fixed dish of human embryonic lung fibroblasts cultured in the presence of collagenase; this enzyme stops multilayering. The cells form small, monolayer, parallel arrays with distinct borders between them. ×10. (Courtesy of Dr T. Elsdale.) (b) Scanning electron micrograph of multilayering, human embryonic, lung fibroblasts with orthogonal morphology. This particular organization probably derives from the fact that orthogonal overgrowth places minimal mechanical stress on the underlying cells. If an overlying cell is at any other angle to underlying fibroblasts, its contractions will pull on the adhesions of the substratum cells and thus serve to disrupt the culture. If, however, the overlying cell is at 90° to underlying ones, its contractions will only compress them and will cause no disruption to substratum adhesions. This orthogonal arrangement is, therefore, relatively stable. ×500.

arrays that eventually meet at borders across which cells do not migrate. Topological constraints, imposed both by the elongated cell morphology and the boundaries of the culture, restrict the ways in which the patchworks can meet and the resulting patterns bear a formal similarity to those of fingerprints [36]. The significance here of this work is its demonstration that organization can arise from no more than cell morphology and the boundaries of tissue. When cultured embryonic fibroblasts are allowed to grow beyond a monolayer [34], the superconfluent cells extend over the parallel arrays of basal cells in positions orthogonal to them (Fig. 4.3.5b); they thus form three-dimensional masses *in vitro* as well as *in vivo*.

Growth and growth regulation

In the early stages of development cells divide rapidly, but, once gastrulation is complete, the embryo as a whole grows relatively slowly. There is evidence that locally-rapid cell division is an important factor in morphogenesis and the best-studied example is the elongation of the chick limb: distal mesenchyme subjacent to the apical ectoderm ridge (AER) divides rapidly, whereas more proximal mesenchyme grows relatively slowly [80]. It is known that the behaviour of this growth zone is controlled by the AER, for its removal slows the growth of distal mesenchyme [24, 80]. Another important example of differential cell division occurs in bone formation [70].

One possible mechanism for slowing down fibroblasts from their maximal growth rates has been studied in cultured cells, where mitotic rate decreases as cell density increases; this phenomenon has been called *density-dependent* growth or *contact inhibition* of growth [79]. While the details of the mechanism remain unknown, it is possible to see how it can regulate growth *in vivo*. As cell density increases, growth rates will slow down; if more space becomes available through, perhaps, the synthesis of GAGs which swell, cell density will be lowered and mitotic rates increased to restore the *status ante quo*. In general, however, we do not know how mesenchymal growth rates are controlled *in vivo*.

Cell death

While growth often gives rise to the development of new tissues, the detailed moulding of the final form sometimes results from the opposite process, cell death, which creates gaps. The phenomenon has been studied most carefully in the limb where, for example, cells die in the areas between presumptive digits [77]. Cell death also occurs in joint formation and in the genesis of the retina [41].

Cell condensations

Initially-uniform mesenchyme may form local aggregations whose cell density is higher than that of the surrounding tissue. The formation of such condensations is an early step in the development of bone, cartilage and muscle in limb mesoderm (Fig. 4.3.6) and of feather papillae in chick skin [95]. While we do not know

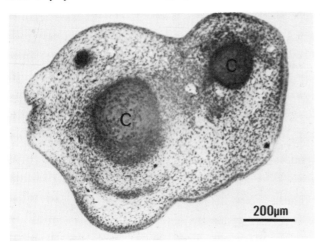

Fig. 4.3.6. A section of a 5-day-old chick leg showing cartilage condensations (C) in the mesenchyme. ×67.

the mechanisms determining the positions of condensations, the local increase in density could be achieved by differential mitosis, cell movement or local increases in adhesivity (see Chapter 3.2).

Epithelia

The second major cellular component of early embryos are the epithelia. These cells are virtually always found aggregated in sheets rather than as individuals. The few cases where individual epithelial cells do leave a cell sheet reflect a major change in the properties of those cells. (Consider the formation of the neural crest cells in Amphibia or the budding off of the primary

mesenchyme in the sea urchin (see later).) Even in the adult, it is rare for normal, functioning cells to leave an epithelium and occurrence of this reflects either turnover and loss of cells (as in the skin or gut) or a diseased state (cells migrate away from the pigmented epithelium of the retina in the disease *retinitis pigmentosa*). In considering the role of epithelia in morphogenesis, we must therefore concentrate on their social properties within the sheet.

Morphology

In early embryos, cells in epithelial sheets tend to be either cuboidal or columnar in shape and have a polygonal cross-section [2]. After the neurula stage, the sheets usually have one surface that does not adhere to other cells: it may either face the exterior world, as in the case of the skin ectoderm, or bound a vesicle or tube. Indeed, this polarized monolayer morphology defines an epithelium [46] and is usually maintained throughout development (exceptions are skin, gut and retinal epithelia which eventually stratify [2]). The other surface usually borders mesenchyme or connective tissue. At the interface between the two cell types is a basal membrane that is made, in part at least, by the epithelium and that ensures the coherence of the sheet [9]. This basal lamina contains Type IV collagen, GAGs and glycoprotein [42, 56].

Adhesions between epithelial cells

While it is easy to break up mesenchymal tissue into single cells by incubating it with enzymes, epithelial cells are harder to separate as there are strong bonds between them. The specific adhesions between these cells are well documented (see Chapters 3.2 and 3.4, and [2]). They include desmosomes (*maculae adhaerentes*) and *zonulae adhaerentes*, which are localized regions of adhesions that 'weld' cells together; *zonulae occludentes*, that seem to stop the leakage of material through gaps between cells [26]; and gap junctions, which permit the passage of electric currents and the diffusion of small molecules (mol. wt. around 1000) between cells.

While these adhesions are localized, there are also more general regions of adhesivity that seem to extend over much of the cell membrane; the modulation of the strength of these adhesions appears to be an important factor in morphogenesis. At one extreme, they may weaken sufficiently to let cells break away from the epithelial sheet (e.g. neural crest). At a lesser level, cells may detach from one another while still remaining in contact with the basal membrane. This seems to occur in that area of the retina that will become the ciliary body, and certainly facilitates the bending of the underlying pigmented retinal epithelium (see legend to Fig. 4.3.8 for a more detailed analysis). It is also possible for the adhesions to increase in strength [16]. Assuming that the shape of a cell results from the equilibrium between membrane tensions and intercellular adhesions [44], such strengthening will cause cuboidal cells to become columnar, provided that the basal lamina decreases in size (Fig. 4.3.7). It is worth noting that cell shapes will

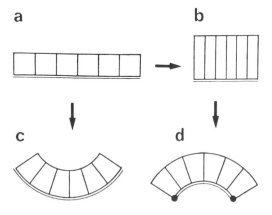

Fig. 4.3.7. A model illustrating the effect of cell adhesion on epithelial morphology. If the adhesions between cuboidal epithelial cells (a) increase in strength and the basement membrane remains of fixed length, the epithelium bends convexly as cells increase their area of contact (c). If, however, the basement membrane can fold or shrink and the intercellular adhesions increase, the epithelium becomes columnar (b). If, in turn, the cells of a columnar epithelium weaken their adhesions (so that the cells can round up) while the basement membrane remains fixed at its ends, then the epithelium becomes concave (d). (From Gustafson & Wolpert [44].)

also change if the organization of the constituent micro-filaments and microtubules alters (see Chapter 3.3 and [22, 23]).

Bending of epithelial sheets

An important morphogenetic property of epithelia is their ability to bend, and one explanation for this has been put forward by Gustafson and Wolpert [44]. They analysed the effect of strengthening or weakening the adhesions between epithelial cells *while maintaining the size of the underlying basal membrane*. They showed that, if the adhesions were to increase in strength, the epithelium would bend to give a convex lamina, whereas if they weakened, the lamina would become concave (Fig. 4.3.7). They invoked these properties to explain part of sea urchin morphogenesis (see later) and it is easy to see that local changes in adhesions could also explain, for example, aspects of the generation of the neural tube, lens formation and the budding off of the primary brain vesicles [1].

There is a further possible mechanism whereby an epithelium could bend—it could buckle. Were an epithelium programmed to grow so that it became larger than the area to which it adhered, one could envisage the epithelium buckling and so reducing its effective surface area (see [40] for a physical analysis). One case where this mechanism might operate is in the generation of the ciliary body (see Fig. 4.3.8 for more details), another is neurulation [86].

Movement

The movement of an unbounded epithelial sheet is relatively rare. In embryos, the best-known example of such a movement is the epiboly of chicks and fishes (the spread of the blastoderm disc over the yolk; see Chapter 3.3), while in adults it occurs in the healing of skin wounds [39]. Epithelial movement is easiest to study in culture, where leading cells possess ruffling activity and pull the rest of the sheet. Such epithelia show *contact inhibition of movement* in that, when two epithelia meet, the leading cells cease ruffling and the epithelia coalesce to form a single sheet [68]. The significance of this for normal wound healing is obvious [39].

A more common epithelial movement *in vivo* is that of the bounded sheet which invades another tissue. A well-studied example of this is the formation of the salivary gland, where epithelial tubules colonize mesenchyme. This organ can be grown in culture and its growth can be followed using time-lapse cinemicrography [5, 19]. As the primitive epithelial tubules extend into the mesenchyme, they are in constant movement, part of the impetus for which is localized cell division. Another aspect of the movement of the sheet is the local blebbing activity which occurs at the top of the tubule; branching points seem to arise at the clefts between such blebs. In the epithelium, branching is marked by microfilament

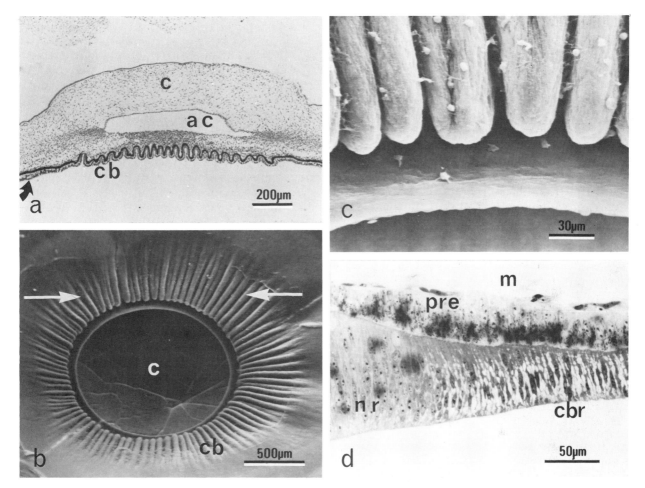

Fig. 4.3.8. The bending of the pigmented retinal epithelium (pre) in the formation of the ciliary body of the eye. (**a**) A light micrograph of a section of a 7-day-old chick eye (cut transverse to the arrows in b) showing the cornea (c), the anterior chamber (ac) and the folded epithelium of the ciliary body (cb). The arrow shows the region of the eye photographed in d. (×54.) (**b**) A scanning electron micrograph showing an interior view of the front of a 7-day-old chick eye whose lens has been removed (×32.5). The radial folds of the ciliary body are strikingly clear. (**c**) A high-power scanning electron micrograph of the 7-day-old ciliary body showing the detailed morphology of the bending epithelium (×400). (**d**) A light micrograph of the 7-day retina showing the border (arrow in a) between the ciliary body retina (cbr) and the neural retina (nr). It can be seen that in the neural retina the cells make strong side-to-side adhesions while in the ciliary body retina, the cells have detached from one another while still adhering to the pigmental retinal epithelium. This tissue is a single continuous sheet and it is clear that it is this epithelium rather than the neural retina that bends, an event probably facilitated by the loss of adhesions between the cbr cells. (×300.) (Note added in proof. It has now been shown that the mechanism driving ciliary body morphogenesis is buckling caused by differential growth—see Bard J.B.L. & Ross A.S. (1982) *Devl. Biol.,* **92,** 73–86, 87–96.)

organization. In the mesenchyme, the positions of such branch points can be recognized by the fact that collagen and GAGs are preferentially deposited there. These depositions may constrain and stabilize the spread of the epithelium [19].

Tensions in cell sheets

Many epithelia are under considerable strain; if a cut is made in them the gap immediately widens [17, 86]. The source of the tension may be external (the cells may pump water into an adjacent vesicle, or GAGs which bind water may swell and exert a pressure [87]) or internal (microfilaments attached to the cell surface may contract—as cytocholasin B breaks down microfilament organization [96], this latter mechanism may easily be tested). The functional significance of these tensions remains to be elucidated in full, but some uses are now clear: they seem to play a role in the formation of curvature [17], in providing a stimulus for epithelial division (see below), and in closing the neural tube [22, 53, 71]. An interesting sidelight on this has been provided by Selman [78]. He measured the contractile forces exerted by the closing amphibian neural ridges (around 4×10^{-2} dynes) and the fraction of the embryo's total energy production required to complete closure. As this fraction was 6×10^{-6}, it is extremely unlikely that available energy will provide a constraint on this or any other morphogenetic movement.

Growth

Epithelial cell division is sometimes localized, as in the case of the salivary gland, and may also be under the control of specific epithelial growth factors [43]. An important need for epithelial growth arises, however, as the embryo enlarges—the epithelia bounding vesicles must also enlarge and the skin epithelium extend. It is not immediately clear whether the growth of the epithelia is intrinsic or dependent on the growth of adjacent mesenchyme. Some evidence that the latter alternative is correct comes from experiments on cultured epithelia. Here, it has been found that monolayer epithelia grow only until available substratum has been colonized [32] and, moreover, that the larger is the epithelial cell, the more likely it is to divide [103]. In the context of the skin epithelium, for example, these results mean that if the mesenchyme grows, the overlying epithelial cells will enlarge to maintain coverage and then divide to give smaller cells which will temporarily be quiescent.

In the case of smaller vesicles, however, we have to explain why the growth of mesenchyme does not crush them. We can speculate that the polarized epithelia maintain a hydrostatic pressure [87] which, presumably, they can control in order to regulate their growth: a higher pressure will encourage cell enlargement, and hence growth.

Self-assembly of epithelia

It is now becoming clear that much of the information required for epithelia to organize themselves into tubules, a particularly common and important morphogenetic event, resides in the epithelial cells themselves. Two model systems demonstrate this nicely. A line of rat mammary-tumour epithelial cells grown on collagen gels can generate a complex structure that includes branching hollow tubes which sometimes show the bulbous ends characteristic of mammary glands [18]. Even more interesting are the results of Folkman and his co-workers on the behaviour of capillary endothelium cells *in vitro*. A few such cells can divide to give rise to a culture that forms new hollow capillaries capable of branching; even individual cells form rings [37]. For this to happen, two conditions have to be satisfied; first, the cells have to be grown on collagen or gelatin and, secondly, the culture has to include what appears to be a specific mitotic activator for endothelial cells, the angiogenesis factor [38]. This substance is necessary *in vivo* if tumours are to form blood supplies and may, in turn, prove important in controlling tumour growth. It is as yet unclear whether or not this substance has any morphogenetic role other than stimulating growth. In other systems, such specific factors are important: mammary-gland morphogenesis *in vitro*, for example, requires hormones if the epithelia are to separate from the mesenchymal cells [91]. Neither such simple chemical factors nor the distinct morphogenetic abilities are, however, enough to specify the form that more complex systems possess. In, for example, the generation of ducted glands, which are mainly composed of epithelia and mesenchymal cells, it is the latter cells that are responsible for determining the details of the organization of the epithelial tubules [99]; it is therefore to the cellular interactions between the two cell types that we now turn.

Epithelia–mesenchyme interactions

The morphogenetic processes that occur when epithelia and mesenchyme come together to form a tissue that neither can form separately are both interesting and important. This tissue-forming interaction is called *induction* (see Chapter 3.5) and salivary gland formation is a particularly well-studied case of this process. A further unusual example occurs in the formation of the

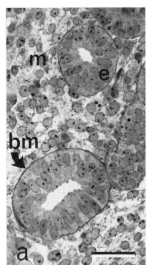
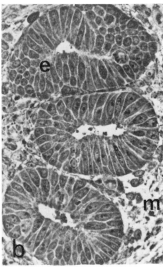

Fig. 4.3.9. Sections of kidney cells. **(a)** A bright-field micrograph of a section of an intact 12-day-old mouse embryonic kidney showing epithelial tubules (e) in a mesenchymal matrix (m). **(b)** A phase micrograph of a section of an aggregate of kidney cells that have sorted themselves out to form epithelial tubules or vesicles in a mesenchymal matrix (From Medoff & Gross [65].) The only obvious difference between the two tissues is that in the original kidney, the epithelia have a well-developed basement membrane (bm). ×580.

kidney tubules, where mesenchyme differentiates locally into epithelia which form tubules that convolute and drain into the nephric duct [1]. Such morphogenesis highlights a problem that underlies many of the structures that have been considered: what properties permit mesenchyme to aggregate into three-dimensional masses while epithelia are usually restricted to open or closed sheets (Fig. 4.3.9a)? Two lines of research using cultured cells have been followed in order to obtain information about these properties: first, aggregates of the two cell types have been made so that the extent to which cells maintain their abilities in unusual environments can be examined and, secondly, the ability of one cell type to use the other as a substratum for spreading has been investigated.

Aggregate studies

It has been well known for many years [84] that if cells of different embryological regions are removed from the embryo, made into single cell type suspensions and then recombined in aggregates, the cell types will sort out

(Fig. 4.3.9b). In the case of aggregates of epithelia and mesenchyme, the epithelia make either bounding membranes or vesicles while the mesenchyme forms a homogeneous mass [65]. Such experiments show that the cells can maintain their functions after disruption and culturing.

To explain sorting out, mechanisms based on differential cell adhesions, specific adhesions and timing (see Chapter 3.2 for review) have been put forward, but none of these mechanisms is generally accepted as being correct for all tissues. In the context of morphogenesis *in vivo* we cannot be sure that such studies have great relevance as cells are very rarely, if ever, required to sort out from random aggregates. It is, however, clear that cells cohere preferentially to their own cell type and Trinkaus [4, 86] has pointed out that one role for such an ability would be to stabilize cellular organization once it had formed. Another use would be to ensure that a cell that had moved by accident or experiment to an inappropriate area would return to its correct region [21].

Cell spreading properties

Insight into the functional interactions responsible for the organization of epithelia and mesenchyme has come from studying how rounded cells of one type can spread on both classes of cultured cells. It is now established that the upper surface of an adhering epithelium that was a monolayer *in vivo* cannot be spread upon by either epithelial or fibroblastic cells [10, 31, 35] (Fig. 4.3.10a and b). In sharp contrast, both cell types will adhere to and spread on dense fibroblast cultures, and epithelial sheets will migrate across such cultures [35]. If the cells possess the properties *in vivo* that they show *in vitro*, then the reason why epithelia are found as monolayers with one free surface is that this latter surface is unacceptable as a substratum. This property differentiates epithelia from fibroblasts, which can spread on one another (Fig. 4.3.5b). The molecular basis for this difference remains unclear, but collagen fibrils, which are synthesized by fibroblasts but not by epithelia, may play a role in aiding adhesion and spreading [34].

The significance of these results for morphogenesis can be seen when one considers which geometric structures can satisfy the cell spreading properties. A little thought shows that the only possibilities are that the epithelia form bounding membranes, vesicles and tubes around and within mesenchymal masses (Fig. 4.3.10c).

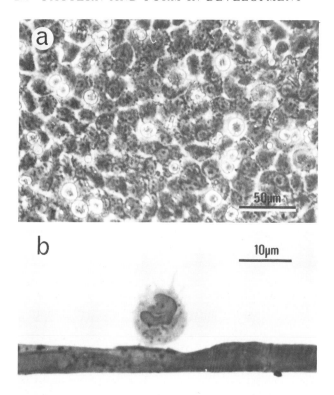

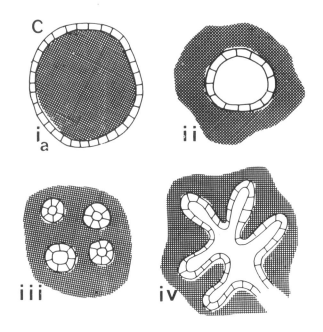

(c) A diagram to illustrate the family of forms of monolayer epithelia and 3-D mesenchyme (hatched): the epithelium forms (i) a bounding membrane, (ii) an internal vesicle, (iii) isolated vesicles and (iv) a set of continuous ducted tubules. (From Elsdale & Bard [34].)

Fig. 4.3.10. (a) Phase micrograph of superconfluent epithelial cells formed by plating epithelial cells onto a spread monolayer; the additional cells remain rounded. ×300. (b) A section of a human kidney outgrowth showing a rounded fibroblast or epithelial cell that has not spread on the underlying epithelium (From Bard [10]). ×1400.

The experiments do not, however, give any clues as to which of these structures might arise in any particular case. In developing tissues, further information beyond cell properties must be provided to specify which of the possible organizations should occur (see later).

4.3.4 MORPHOGENETIC CASE STUDIES

In the previous section, many of the cell properties that can play a role in organogenesis were described. We now examine two examples of tissue formation that have been sufficiently well investigated to show us how the cells actually use their properties in morphogenesis; we shall first consider gastrulation in the sea urchin and then consider the construction of the chick cornea. Both tissues are composed of epithelia and mesenchyme and

we shall see that, as the tissues develop, both cell types appear to use many of the properties that we have considered earlier. In each case, the formation of the tissue is first described, and this is followed by examination of particular events which illustrate the morphogenetic abilities of cells.

Gastrulation in the sea urchin

The most important morphogenetic movements in embryogenesis are those that turn the blastula into the gastrula. In this process, cells on the periphery of the blastula move inside, and eventually form the primitive gut. While most embryos are too opaque for the processes of gastrulation to be followed at the cellular level, the sea urchin provides a fortunate exception to the general rule. Its transparency permitted Gustafson, Wolpert and other workers to film gastrulation using time-lapse cinemicrography, a technique which allowed detailed observations of individual cell behaviour (see [44] for the detailed review from which the basis for this summary is taken).

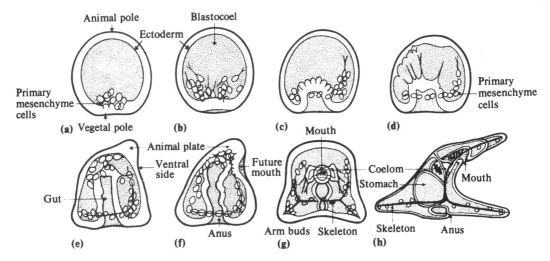

Fig. 4.3.11. Some stages in the early development of the sea urchin embryo. Primary mesenchymal cells leave the vegetal pole (a, b) and take up distinct positions around the embryo (c). At this time, gastrulation starts as the cells at the vegetal pole invaginate (c) and throw out pseudopods (d) that adhere to the region of the animal pole and then contract (e), pulling the cells to the future mouth region at the animal plate which curves and thickens (e, f). The skeleton then grows (g, h) causing the embryo to take up a roughly tetrahedal morphology. (From Wolpert & Gustafson [101].)

Normal development

Before gastrulation takes place, the sea urchin blastula is a hollow sphere whose wall is a monolayer sheet—an epithelium—containing about 1000 cells adhering to an external hyaline membrane and with an interior basement membrane surrounding a central space, the blastocoel. The processes that we will consider are those which cause this blastula to develop a gut and a skeleton and to turn into a roughly tetrahedron-shaped larva (Fig. 4.3.11).

The first event in this development is a pulsatory movement at the vegetal pole of the blastula that results in some 40 cells becoming columnar, breaking septate junctions with their neighbours, and finally leaving the cell wall (Fig. 4.3.11a and b). These departing cells are known as the primary mesenchyme and will eventually form the skeleton (there are, therefore, similarities between these cells and those of the neural crest in chicks and frogs). When they have detached, the cells extend long (c. 30 μm), thin (c. 0.5 μm) contractile processes in, apparently, all directions; if a process adheres to the blastula wall, its contraction pulls the cells towards the point of attachment. Each cell continues to throw out processes whose activity is dependent on the presence of microtubules [81]. These processes continue to make and break adhesions and eventually the primary mesenchymal cells take up a characteristic pattern on the wall of the blastula. Over the next few hours, they lay down a skeleton whose shape follows the pattern of the primary mesenchyme.

A second set of events also takes place at the vegetal pole of the embryo: while remaining in a coherent sheet, the basal cells first pulsate and appear to round up and then detach themselves from the hyaline membrane while still maintaining contact with one another through desmosomes. This pulsation leads, over about three hours, to an invagination that extends about one-third of the way across the embryo (Fig. 4.3.11c and d). After a short quiescent period, the invaginated cells again become active, throwing out long processes that adhere preferentially to a region on the wall near the animal pole. The processes contract and pull the tip of the invaginated region across the blastocoel so that a tube forms which makes contact with the future mouth region, which itself invaginates a little to meet the tip (Fig. 4.3.11e and f). Soon after contact between the two regions has been made, the mouth and presumptive gut fuse.

The final stages in larval genesis are the changes in embryonic shape that turn a sphere into a tetrahedron. First, the animal pole and regions of the vegetal pole of the blastula cell sheet thicken and bend outwards. The primary mesenchyme then lays down long, thin skeletal spicules which distend the epithelium so that it eventually forms the final shape.

Cellular mechanisms

The mesenchymal cells that are determined to form the skeleton undergo a range of activities as they first break their adhesions to neighbouring cells, then throw out long, contractile processes that adhere to the blastula wall and eventually cooperate to build spicules. Little is known about the cues that initiate each of these steps or of the way in which the adhesion points on the cell membrane are activated, apart from the fact that the presence of sulphated GAGs is necessary for primary mesenchymal ingression [55]. Gustafson and Wolpert have, however, examined the way in which the primary cells reach their appropriate positions. They found that the cells initially adhere to an area greater than that of their final arrangement. Their processes continue to be active after these first adhesions have formed and move the cells to regions where the most stable contacts form. This turns out to be the region where the epithelium thickens and where there are probably increased intracellular adhesions [101]. In the light of Carter's experiments [25], it is possible that there are gradients of adhesivity on the internal wall of the blastula and that cells migrate to the points of maximum adhesion; even here they continue to throw out processes and so are capable of responding to any further change in local adhesivity [25].

Almost all of the morphogenetic changes that take place in the epithelial sheet of the blastula during gastrulation can be explained in terms of alterations in the adhesions between cells. The vegetal cells initially pulsate and then break contacts with the hyaline membrane and weaken adhesions to their neighbours, while maintaining septate links; we have seen earlier that this will result in the cell sheet bending away from the hyaline membrane. The next stage of gastrulation, gut formation, seems to follow two simultaneous events: the *observed* pseudopodal activity of cells at the tip of the invagination and the *inferred* adhesivity changes in the area of the presumptive mouth. These last changes must be complex: presumptive mouth cells appear to lose their adhesion to the membrane (and appear to be pulled inwards by the contracting filopodia), lessen their

adhesions to neighbours and change the surface facing the interior so that the processes of invaginating cells will stick preferentially to them. Next, the shape of the epithelia alters when the animal pole and part of the vegetal pole increase their curvature. These last changes would be expected were the cells in this region simply to increase their adhesions to one another; Gustafson and Wolpert noted that, as this explanation predicts, the blastula wall thickens in areas of increased curvature (Fig. 4.3.11e).

The major events underlying sea urchin gastrulation thus seem to be the programming of each cell of the blastula as to exactly how its local adhesions will change with time. The mechanisms responsible for setting up the spatial pattern of instructions and for initiating each temporal event in the sequence remain unknown. The elucidation of such mechanisms is one of the major and most difficult problems in developmental biology (see Chapter 4.2).

The avian cornea

We now consider how a tissue is laid down in a developing vertebrate after the basic framework of the embryo has formed. The cornea is, in fact, one of the simplest such tissues: it arises from the skin epithelium and ultimately has two important physiological properties, it is transparent and it is bent so that it acts as a lens. Anatomically, the adult cornea contains a series of layers (Fig. 4.3.12c). Proceeding from the outside inwards, these are: a thin cell layer (the periderm), a multilayered epithelium, a band of densely packed collagen (Bowman's membrane), a thick layer (the stroma) containing fibroblasts, collagen in orthogonal bundles (Fig. 4.3.12c), GAGs and other proteins, a thin network of protein and GAG fibres (Descemet's membrane) and an internal endothelium responsible, in the adult, for maintaining the appropriate amount of water in the stroma. This last factor controls the transparency of the cornea, for excess water increases the spacing between collagen bundles and decreases the transparency which depends on these bundles acting as a diffraction grating [64].

There are a surprisingly large number of processes necessary to form the adult cornea and only the major morphogenetic events that occur over the three weeks between fertilization and hatching will be described, omitting many of the known biochemical changes. A

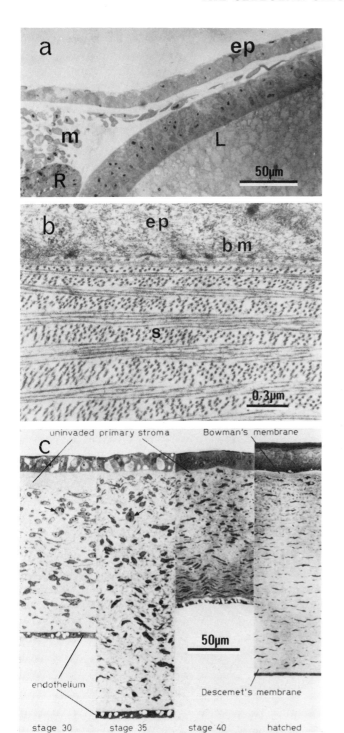

detailed examination of some aspects of the cellular basis of corneal morphogenesis will then be given and finally mention made of some problems that remain to be investigated.

Corneal development

In the first two days or so after fertilization, the chick embryo reaches the early tail-bud stage. In the head, eye vesicles extend from the brain region of the neural tube to reach the skin epithelium, in which they induce an invagination that buds off and becomes the lens. The epithelium overlying the lens becomes the cornea and its initial development may be induced by the lens itself [47].

Day 3: The epithelium anterior to the lens starts to lay down a primary stroma (Fig. 4.3.12b) of thin (*c.* 20 nm) collagen fibrils in layers of parallel bundles [49]. The orientation of each layer is 90° to that above and below it [85]. The epithelium continues to lay down such orthogonal bundles of collagen virtually until hatching. Fibronectin is present between the lens and the presumptive cornea and also in the surrounding mesenchyme [59].

Day 4: Mesenchymal cells from the neural crest [72], which had reached the side of the eye at around day 2, migrate as individuals from the side of the eye between the lens and the corneal stroma to form a confluent monolayer, the endothelium [13] (Fig. 4.3.12a). A GAG-containing matrix appears between the endothelium and the lens [11, 13].

Day 5: The endothelial cells cohere to form a sheet with fibronectin on its basal surface which detaches from the lens as more matrix appears between lens and cornea. The space filled by the matrix becomes the anterior chamber of the eye (Fig. 4.3.4); as the matrix swells over the next few days, it forces the cornea to bend outward.

Fig. 4.3.12. A A light micrograph of a section showing cells migrating between the cornea and lens of a 3-day-old chick eye to form the endothelium. ×300. **(b)** A transmission electron-micrograph showing the orthogonal arrangement of the collagen bundles in the 6-day-old chick corneal stroma (s). The collagen is synthesized in the epithelium (ep) and secreted through the basement membrane (bm) to the stroma where it assembles to form fibrils. ×38 400. **(c)** Light micrographs showing how the chick cornea swells, contracts and grows between stage 30 (7 days) and hatching. ×280. (From Hay & Revel [50].)

It is interesting to note that this curvature is mainly responsible for the refractive power of the eye; the lens only plays a subsidiary role. Light striking this curved surface is bent by the difference in refractive index between air and cornea and is roughly focused on to the retina.

Day 6: The endothelial cells differentiate to form an epithelium with cilia and with microvilli at cell borders which then secretes hyaluronic acid into the stroma, causing it to swell [66] (Fig. 4.3.12c). As this happens, fibroblasts which had migrated from the neural crest invade the swollen collagen (Fig. 4.3.4). They move in radially (Fig. 4.3.13a) and colonize all of the stroma except the region just subjacent to the epithelium, which remains unswollen [50].

Days 7–8: The fibroblasts align along the collagen fibrils to form orthogonal arrays (Fig. 4.3.13b) and deposit more collagen on the primary stroma, thereby increasing bundle size; they also deposit GAGs and fibronectin. This further deposition continues for at least another week [14]; the large bundles are known as secondary stroma.

Day 9: The epithelium which had been laying down orthogonal bundles of collagen changes the orientation of successive layers so that each is only rotated through about 85° with respect to the underlying layer. An anticlockwise twist outwards is thus seen in the layers of both eyes [85].

Days 12–13: The epithelium multilayers [73] (Fig. 4.3.12c).

Days 15–16: Hyaluronidase, secreted by the endothelium under the influence of the thyroid [28], is released into the stroma causing its hyaluronic acid to be degraded and the stroma to condense (Fig. 4.3.12c) and become transparent [83]. Matrix disappears from the anterior chamber and the fibronectin within the stroma is also lost, with that adjacent to endothelium disappearing first [59].

Day 21: The chick hatches with a functional cornea.

Many of the phenomena in this list have been subjected to detailed analysis (see [48] for review). Here, we consider three major events in corneal morphogenesis.

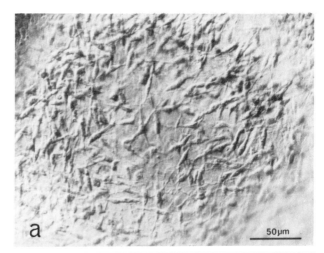
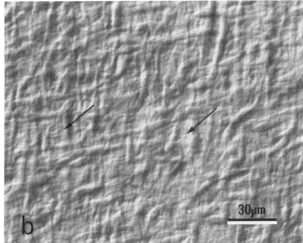

Fig. 4.3.13. (a) A Nomarski micrograph of a section through a 6-day-old chick cornea showing the radial invasion of fibroblasts from the periphery of the cornea inwards. ×280. **(b)** A Nomarski micrograph of a section through a 10-day-old chick cornea showing the orthogonal arrangement of collagen bundles (arrow) and fibroblasts. ×450. (From Bard & Higginson [14].)

Endothelial morphogenesis (day 4)

The neural crest cells which form the endothelium as they migrate between lens and cornea make what is probably the simplest tissue in any multicellular organism, a circular monolayer, c. 5 mm in diameter, containing only a few hundred cells. Here, we need concern ourselves only with how such migrating cells actually form the monolayer and there are two obvious mechanisms that could be responsible [13]. First, the cells might display *contact inhibition of movement* as they migrate and so be unable to move over one another; a second possibility is that, while the cells *could* multilayer, the small space between lens and cornea limits cell movements.

A simple experiment tests these possibilities: if the lens is removed while the cells are migrating, more space is provided for the cells and the geometric constraint on their movement is taken away. The CIM mechanism predicts that a monolayer should still form, while the steric hindrance model predicts multilayering. The experiment has been performed *in vivo* [104] and *in vitro*

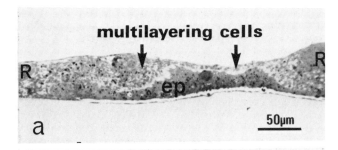

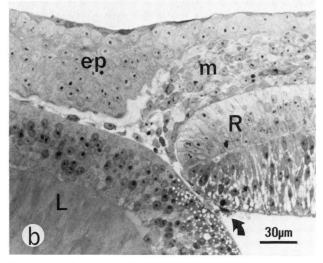

Fig. 4.3.14. Micrographs of sections of experimental 4-day-old corneas. (**a**) A cornea cultured without lens on a millipore filter. Endothelial cells have migrated from the retinal areas (R) across the epithelium (ep) and have multilayered. ×230. (**b**) A cultured anterior eye whose lens was partially removed. The lens (L) has remade its adhesion to the retina (R) but mesenchymal cells (m) have insinuated themselves between the tissues and are migrating out on the retina (arrow). ×335. (From Bard *et al.* [13].)

[13] and, in both cases, the mesenchymal cells multilayer (Fig. 4.3.14a). Even if the lens is only partially removed, migrating cells move through the gap and colonize the back of the retina (Fig. 4.3.14b). It is clear that the cells can move anywhere but are restrained in the embryo by physical constraints; CIM thus seems to play no role in generating monolayer morphology.

Fibroblast migration (day 6)

The late-migrating, neural crest fibroblasts that colonize the swollen stroma of the cornea migrate radially into the eye but within a day or so have aligned along the orthogonal collagen bundles of the stroma (Fig. 4.3.13b). There are thus two questions to ask: what initiates radial colonization and how do the cells change their alignment?

The answer to the first question probably has two components: the swelling of the hyaluronic-acid-containing stroma permits migration (note that unswollen anterior stroma is not invaded (Figs 4.3.4 and 4.3.12c)) and CIM between leading and trailing fibroblasts ensures that the leading cells invade the stroma. The mechanism for the later alignment of the cells along collagen bundles is certainly *contact guidance*. We can speculate that the reason why the original movement was not along these bundles is because they were either too thin (*c.* 0.2 μm [14]) or too weak; it is only after further collagen has been deposited on them that they enlarge sufficiently to be able to provide an acceptable aligning substratum for fibroblasts.

Morphogenetic role of GAGs

In corneal development, there are two important events that are controlled by GAGs: the swelling and contraction of the corneal stroma and the formation of the anterior chamber. The first is controlled by the production and destruction of hyaluronic acid, while the second is mediated by a complex matrix that contains hyaluronic acid, chondroitin sulphate, protein and other substances [11]. In both cases, the swelling is caused by the hydrostatic pressure exerted by the GAGs as they bind water. The pressure from the swelling of the anterior chamber matrix is probably responsible for the initial curvature of the cornea. A similar event takes place in the posterior chamber of the eye where hydrostatic pressure produces the correct shape: Coulombre [27] showed that if a small tube were inserted through the retina to reduce any pressure, the eye did not enlarge properly. The exact role of fibronectin remains unclear but, in endothelium formation, it is likely to stabilize the adhesions of the migrating cells.

Remaining problems

Even though a great deal is known about corneal development, there remain several important phenomena to be explained. We know virtually nothing, for example, about how each morphogenetic event is initiated. At the cellular level the behaviour of the epithelium remains mysterious: neither its multilayering nor its deposition of collagen is understood. In the latter case, it appears that the whole epithelium acts in synchrony as successive collagen layers are laid down. The only clue to the morphogenesis of this exquisite organization is that GAG production appears to play a role [29]. As it is this orthogonal organization that appears responsible for the transparency of the cornea, it might be said that we know almost everything about corneal morphogenesis except the one factor that matters!

4.3.5 AN INTEGRATED APPROACH TO MORPHOGENESIS

Although there is an enormous range of tissue structures in the animal world, they are composed of relatively few cell types. The major problems in morphogenesis are, therefore, to account both for the cellular organization of each individual tissue and for the great diversity in tissue structures. Wolpert has argued that the differences between structures containing different organizations of apparently identical cell types arise from pattern-formation mechanisms [100] (Chapter 4.2). While there must be considerable truth in this view, it cannot be a complete explanation. We have seen in corneal development, for example, that it is the routes available to migrating cells, rather than their initial pattern of determination, that control their final arrangement. Any analysis of morphogenesis must therefore incorporate more than pattern formation and its consequent cellular differentiation.

With this consideration in mind, one can now examine what other aspects there are to tissue formation and how the whole process should be viewed. Perhaps the

simplest way to analyse morphogenesis is to ascribe to it, in the first instance at least, three stages: a beginning, a middle and an end. Morphogenesis begins when participating cells acquire appropriate initial organization and properties (1a, see below) and are given the stimulus to use them (1b). The middle might be called the dynamic stage; it involves cells changing their relative positions (2a), a change subject to the constraints of their environment (2b). The end point (3) is reached when the cells achieve a new stable arrangement, one from which they have no incentive to move.[2] In this final section, we shall examine briefly each of these facets to see how individual cell properties can contribute to morphogenesis and will use, as a main example, the formation of the corneal endothelium.

1a: The initial organization

In the first stage of morphogenesis, the participating cells must reach appropriate initial positions and acquire any new properties that they will need. In the case of endothelial morphogenesis, neural crest cells must be present at the periphery of the cornea and be primed to move. While this instance is relatively simple, others may be more complex. Consider the behaviour of the primary mesenchyme in the sea-urchin embryo: the cells at the vegetal pole break adhesions to their neighbours and then become motile, while cells at the central region of the blastula acquire interior surfaces that seem particularly adhesive for the long processes which the mesenchyme cells will put out. The mechanisms of spatial differentiation by which the participating cells acquire their properties are not our immediate concern. We can, however, envisage that cells may differentiate either in accordance with positional-information cues or as instructed by segregated material that was present in the original egg (see Chapter 4.2).

---

[2]The mathematically inclined reader will note that this approach to investigating morphogenesis is analogous to solving a dynamic problem based on differential equations in classical physics. To do this, one first specifies the differential equations describing the general physical laws that apply to the problem and then solves them subject to the constraints of the initial and boundary conditions which define that particular problem. The solution of the equations shows how the system changes over time and usually reaches a new stable equilibrium.

1b: The starting signal

Morphogenesis may start as soon as cells have differentiated, but primed cells frequently require a change in their environment before they can become active. Endothelial cells, for example, migrate from the neural crest and reach the corneal periphery on the third day after fertilization; they are then held up and only start moving again a day later. In general, the cues that initiate morphogenesis are not known, but enough information is available to point to possible signals that could perform this role. The four most obvious are: the availability of new substrata, the breakdown of a physical barrier, the making of contact between primed tissues, and a change in the concentration of some molecule. Newly available substratum, for example, will encourage potentially motile cells to invade it; thus the swelling of chick corneal stroma allows peripheral fibroblasts to colonize it [48]. New substrata may also become available if a constraining barrier such as a basal lamina breaks down: we can speculate that this mechanism explains the migration of cells from somites. Contact between tissues primed to develop is the stimulus for inductive interactions [67] (see Chapter 3.5), even though the exact role of the contact interaction between the two cell types remains obscure. The last mechanism, a rapid change in the concentration of some molecule, is, superficially, the simplest initiating cue for morphogenesis. In several well-known examples, the molecule is a hormone: the availability of nerve growth factor stimulates axon growth [62] and thyroxin causes corneal condensation in the chick [28] and tail resorption in metamorphosing amphibia [98]. However, as these signals originate outside of the cells that participate in morphogenesis, we are left with the question of what stimulates hormone production (see Part 5), a question that is, in general, still unanswered.

2a: Cell dynamics

The essential and most obvious characteristic of all morphogenesis is that cells change their position with respect to one another. In the case of endothelium formation, we have seen that this is achieved by migration, but mesenchyme and epithelia have other morphogenetic properties as well (see section 4.3.3). Cells may change their shape and their adhesions to one another, sheets may bend, processes may extend and

contract, and there may be differential cell growth and death. These last two have to be precisely controlled by the cells, but the properties which involve movement and which are the most widespread in morphogeneis seem to reflect relatively unconstrained activity by cells; they can, in principle, move in any direction and throw out processes at random. If the bending of a cell sheet in caused by changes in adhesion, this too is undirected. As morphogenesis has to result in the production of well-defined organization, any random cellular activity has to be channelled and controlled by other factors.

2b: Boundaries and other constraints

The constraints that guide active cells from one level of organization to another play a crucial role in morphogenesis, but have not, as yet, been given the attention that they merit. The simplest of them is the physical boundary that encourages migrating cells to move in one direction rather than another. In the case of endothelial formation, the anterior unswollen stroma and posterior lens capsule constrain migrating cells to move between them (Fig. 4.2.12a). External constraints can have other effects on cells: a basal lamina of fixed length can control the extent to which adhesion changes will allow an epithelial sheet to bend (Fig. 4.3.7), while a solid boundary may dictate the organization of nearby cells by constraining their orientation (consider the patterns formed by fibroblasts *in vitro* [36]).

The simple boundary does no more than restrict cell movement passively; a more direct interaction occurs when geometric features in the environment control the movement of individual cells. Aligned fibrils may, for example, direct cell movement through *contact guidance*; consider the fibroblasts being organized by the orthogonal arrays of collagen in the 10-day-old cornea (Fig. 4.3.13b). A *gradient of adhesion* achieves a similar result in a different way; it forces a cell which is throwing out processes at random to reach the point of maximum adhesivity. The best-known example of this seems to occur in sea urchin morphogenesis.

Constraints on individual cells can also come from surrounding cells of the same type. The mechanisms are partly geometric, one cell cannot migrate through another, and partly active, *contact inhibition of movement* specifically encourages movement away from the aggregate (as in the colonization of the corneal stroma by fibroblasts [12]. While CIM is effective only through physical contact, the same effect at a distance can be sustained through negative chemotaxis (as in the repulsion of amphibian pigment cells [90]). Although these examples of local organization directing random cellular activity are by no means comprehensive, they serve to emphasize how important are constraints in determining the final organization of cells.

3: Stopping morphogenesis

At some point in the development of a tissue, the new organization has formed and cell activity need go on no longer. One might imagine that there is some part of the embryo monitoring progress and that it sends a signal instructing all participating cells to cease activity. There is, however, no evidence to support this view and it is far more likely that the tissue and the constituent cells themselves stop further activity, either through cell interactions or through boundary constraints.

Endothelial cells in the cornea appear to stop moving when there is no further space to be colonized and to become quiescent when their density is great enough for CIM to operate. Note that while CIM is not responsible for monolayer morphology here, it could well play this secondary role. Another interaction which would be expected to stop cell activity is the making of adhesions: when the two ridges of the neural tube meet and seal, the new adhesion will stop the independent movement of either ridge. The boundary of a tissue can also restrict movement: an inelastic basal laminar, for example, will permit only a certain amount of epithelial bending. Indeed, cells may restrict their own activity by making such a membrane. The constraint may, on the other hand, come from within the tissue rather than from its periphery. As a tissue ages, for example, it may become impermeable to cell movement: the migration of young neural crest cells transplanted to old embryos is attenuated [97].

These essentially static mechanisms all stop cell activity. There is, however, a second type of stability which ensures that any movement of a cell away from the equilibrium organization is followed by a return of that cell to its initial position. This type of stability is analogous to that found in mechanical systems (consider the movement of a ball at the bottom of a bowl). A clear example in the biological world is the movement of the primary mesenchyme cells of the sea urchin blastula from the vegetal pole to the circumferential region.

When the cells reach the position of apparent maximum adhesion, they do not cease movement but continue to extend processes. These do not move the cells away from the equilibrium position but leave them able to respond to any further change in the environment [44]. Such dynamic stability also occurs in cultured fibroblasts; small cellular movements allow the cells to form a pattern from initially random organization and this pattern is stable to any further movements of the cells (for a comparison of these biological patterns with those formed in the physical world by random movements in so-called 'inherently precise machines' see [33]). A further example of this type of stability is provided by the mechanism responsible for the sorting-out of cells from mixed aggregates. If a cell should arrive at an inappropriate position by accident, the sorting-out mechanism will ensure that it returns to its correct tissue [21]. This dynamic stability thus provides continuous monitoring of tissue organization.

Viewing morphogenesis as a series of distinct steps is a simple approach, perhaps too simple: very often it is not possible to distinguish between two stages of morphogenesis and, frequently, a single cell property may fill more than one role. Nevertheless, by focusing attention on the different aspects of morphogenesis we can at least to begin to understand some of the most complex and intractable problems in animal development.

4.3.6 SUMMARY

(1) Two major types of cells take part in the morphogenesis of early embryos: mesenchyme and epithelia. Mesenchyme cells aggregate in three-dimensional masses while epithelia are usually restricted to monolayer sheets, one surface of which cannot be adhered to by other cells.

(2) The extracellular matrix of collagen and glycosaminoglycans (GAGs) plays a significant role in many cases of tissue contruction. In particular, the swelling of GAGs as they bind water creates new spaces that permit morphogenesis to take place.

(3) The individual cell properties necessary for morphogenesis are mainly dynamic and involve movement, selective adhesion, growth and contact interactions; many of these properties are shown by cells in culture.

(4) While the cellular basis of the morphogenesis of many tissues remains too complex to investigate, con-

siderable progress has been made in elucidating how cells use their properties to build such simple tissues as the sea urchin gastrula and the chick cornea.

(5) The guiding principle behind morphogenesis is that, once cells have received instructions as to how they should differentiate and the appropriate stimulus to initiate activity, they use their dynamic properties to form new structures. Many of these properties reflect essentially random activity by the cell and this activity is directed, constrained and usually terminated by the cell's immediate environment.

4.3.7   REFERENCES

*General reviews

*1 Balinsky B.I. (1975) *An Introduction to Embryology* (4th edn.). W.B. Saunders, Philadelphia.

*2 Bloom W. & Fawcett D.W. (1975) *A Textbook of Histology* (10th edn.). W.B. Saunders, Philadelphia.

*3 DeHaan R.L. & Ursprung H. (Eds) (1965) *Organogenesis*. Holt, Rinehart & Winston, New York.

*4 Trinkaus J.B. (1976) On the mechanism of metazoan cell movements. In *The Cell Surface in Animal Embryogenesis and Development*, (Eds G. Poste & G.L. Nicolson), pp. 225–329. Elsevier/North-Holland, Amsterdam.

*5 Wessels N.K. (1977) *Tissue Interactions and Development*. W.A. Benajmin, California.

6 Abercrombie M. (1967) Contact inhibition: the phenomenon and its biological implications. *In vitro*, **26**, 249–261.

7 Armstrong P.B. & Armstrong M.T. (1973) Are cells in solid tissues immobile? Mesonephric mesenchyme studied *in vitro*. *Devl. Biol.*, **35**, 187–209.

8 Armstrong M.T. & Armstrong P.B. (1978) Cell motility in fibroblast aggregates. *J. Cell Sci.*, **33**, 37–52.

9 Bannerjee S.D., Cohn R.H. & Bernfield M.R. (1977) Basal lamina of embryonic salivary epithelia. *J. Cell Biol.*, **73**, 445–463.

10 Bard J.B.L. (1979) Epithelial-fibroblastic organisation in cultures grown from human embryonic kidney: its significance for morphogenesis *in vivo*. *J. Cell Sci.*, **39**, 291–298.

11 Bard J.B.L. & Abbot A.S. (1979) Matrices containing glycosaminoglycans in the developing anterior chambers of chick and *Xenopus* embryonic eyes. *Devl. Biol.*, **68**, 472–486.

12 Bard J.B.L. & Hay E.D. (1975) The behaviour of fibroblasts from the developing avian cornea. Morphology and movement *in situ* and *in vitro*. *J. Cell Biol.*, **67**, 400–418.

13 Bard J.B.L., Hay E.D. & Meller S.M. (1975) Formation of the endothelium of the avian cornea: a study of cell movement *in vivo*. *Devl. Biol.*, **42**, 334–361.

14 Bard J.B.L. & Higginson K. (1977) Fibroblast–collagen interactions in the formation of the secondary stroma of the chick cornea. *J. Cell Biol.*, **74**, 816–827.

15 Bellairs R. (1979) The mechanism of somite segmentation in the chick embryo. *J. Embryol. exp. Morph.*, **51**, 227–243.

16 Bellairs R., Curtis A.S.G. & Sanders E.J. (1978) Cell adhesiveness and embryonic differentiation. *J. Embryol. exp. Morph.*, **46**, 207–213.

17 Beloussov L.V., Dorfman J.G. & Cherdantzev V.G. (1975) Mechanical stresses and morphological patterns in amphibian embryos. *J. Embryol. exp. Morph.*, **34**, 559–574.

18 Bennett D.C. (1980) Morphogenesis of branching tubules in cultures of cloned mammary epithelial cells. *Nature, Lond.*, **285**, 657–659.

19 Bernfield M.R., Bannerjee S.D. & Cohn R.H. (1972) Dependence of salivary epithelial morphology and branching morphogenesis upon acid mucopolysaccharide-protein (proteoglycan) at the epithelial surface. *J. Cell Biol.*, **52**, 674–689.

20 Bornstein P. & Sage H. (1980) Structurally distinct collagen types. *A. Rev. Biochem.*, **49**, 957–1003.

21 Boucaut J.C. (1974) Etude autoradiographique de la distribution de cellules embryonnair isolées, Transplantees dans la blastocele chez *Pleurodeles waltlii* Michah. *Ann. Embryol. & Morphogen.*, **7**, 7–50.

22 Burnside B. (1971) Microtubules and microfilaments in newt neurulation. *Devl. Biol.*, **26**, 416–441.

23 Byers B. & Porter K. (1964) Oriented microtubules in elongating cells of the developing lens rudiment after induction. *Proc. natl Acad. Sci., USA*, **52**, 1091–1099.

24 Cairns J.M. (1975) The function of the ectodermal apical ridge and distinctive characteristics of adjacent distal mesoderm in the avian wing-bud. *J. Embryol. exp. Morph.*, **34**, 155–169.

25 Carter S.B. (1965) Principles of cell motility: the direction of cell movement and cancer invasion. *Nature, Lond.*, **208**, 1183–1187.

26 Claude P. & Goodenough D.A. (1973) Fracture faces of *zonulae occludentes* from "tight" and "leaky" epithelia. *J. Cell Biol.*, **58**, 390–400.

27 Coulombre A.J. (1964) Problems in corneal morphogenesis. *Adv. Morph.*, **4**, 81–109.

28 Coulombre A.J. & Coulombre J.L. (1964) Corneal development III. The role of the thyroid in dehydration and the development of transparency. *Expl. Eye Res.*, **3**, 105–114.

29 Coulombre J.L. & Coulombre A.J. (1975) Corneal development V. Treatment of five-day-old embryos of domestic fowl with 6-diazol-5-oxo-L-norleucine (DON). *Devl. Biol.*, **45**, 291–303.

30 Derby M.A. (1978) Analysis of glycosaminoglycans within the extracellular environment encountered by migrating neural crest cells. *Devl. Biol.*, **66**, 321–336.

31 DiPasquale A. & Bell P.B. Jr (1974) The upper cell surface: its inability to support active cell movement in culture. *J. Cell Biol.*, **62**, 198–214.

32 Dulbecco R. & Elkington J. (1973) Conditions limiting multiplication of fibroblastic and epithelial cells in dense cultures. *Nature, Lond.*, **246**, 197–203.

33 Elsdale T.R. (1969) Pattern formation and homeostasis. In CIBA Found. Symp. *Homeostatic Regulators* (eds G.E.W. Wolstenholme & J. Knight), pp. 291–303. J. & A. Churchill, London.

34 Elsdale T.R. & Bard J.B.L. (1972) Cellular interactions in mass cultures of human diploid fibroblasts. *Nature, Lond.*, **236**, 152–155.

35 Elsdale T.R. & Bard J.B.L. (1974) Cellular interaction in morphogenesis of epithelial-mesenchymal systems. *J. Cell Biol.*, **63**, 343–349.

36 Elsdale T.R. & Wasoff F. (1976) Fibroblast cultures and dermatoglyphics: the topology of two planar patterns. *Wilhelm Roux' Archiv.*, **180**, 121–147.

37 Folkman J. & Haudenschild C. (1980) Angiogenesis *in vitro*. *Nature, Lond.*, **288**, 551–556.

38 Folkman J., Merler E., Abernathy C. & Williams G. (1971) Isolation of a tumour factor responsible for angiogenesis. *J. exp. Med.*, **133**, 275–288.

39 Gabbiani G. & Montendon D. (1977) Reparative processes in mammalian wound healing: the role of contractile phenomena. *Int. Rev. Cytol.*, **48**, 187–219.

40 Gierer A. (1977) Physical aspects of tissue evagination and biological form. *Q. Rev. Biophys.*, **10**, 529–593.

41 Glucksman A. (1951) Cell deaths in normal vertebrate ontogeny. *Biol. Rev.*, **26**, 59–86.

42 Gordon J.R. & Bernfield M.R. (1980) The basal lamina of the postnatal mammary epithelium contains glycosaminoglycans in a precise ultra-structural organisation. *Devl. Biol.*, **74**, 118–135.

43 Gospodarowicz D. & Moran J.S. (1976) Growth factors in mammalian cell cultures. *A. Rev. Biochem.*, **45**, 531–558.

44 Gustafson T. & Wolpert L. (1967) Cellular movement and contact in sea urchin morphogenesis. *Biol. Rev.*, **42**, 442–498.

45 Harris A. (1973) Behaviour of cultured cells on substrata of variable adhesiveness. *Expl. Cell Res.*, **77**, 285–297.

46 Hay E.D. (1968) Organisation and fine structure of epithelium and mesenchyme in the developing chick embryo. In *Epithelial–Mesenchymal Interactions* (Eds R. Fleischmajer & R.E. Billingham), pp. 31–55. Williams & Wilkins, Baltimore.

47 Hay E.D. (1977) Cell–matrix interaction in embryonic induction. In *International Cell Biology* (Eds B.R. Brinkley & K.R. Porter), pp. 50–57. Rockefeller University Press, New York.

48 Hay E.D. (1980) Development of the vertebrate cornea. *Int. Rev. Cytol.*, **63**, 263–322.

49 Hay E.D. & Dodson J.W. (1973) Secretion of collagen by corneal epithelium. *J. Cell Biol.*, **57**, 190–213.

50 Hay E.D. & Revel J.-P. (1969) *Fine Structure of the Developing Avian Cornea*. Karger, Basel.

51 Ingram V.M. (1969) A side view of moving fibroblasts. *Nature, Lond.*, **232**, 641–644.

52 Jackson S.F. (1968) The morphogenesis of collagen. In *Treatise on Collagen*, **2b** (Ed. B.S. Gould), pp. 1–66. Academic Press, London.

53 Jacobson A.G. (1978) Some forces that shape the nervous system. *Zoon*, **6**, 13–21.

54 Jacobson A.G. & Gordon R. (1976) Changes in the shape of the developing vertebrate nervous system analysed experimentally, mathematically and by computer simulation. *J. exp. Zool.*, **197**, 191–246.

55 Karp G.C. & Solursh M. (1974) Acid mucopolysaccharide metabolism, the cell surface and primary mesenchyme cell activity in the sea urchin embryo. *Devl. Biol.*, **41**, 110–123.

56 Kefalides N.A., Alper R. & Clark C.C. (1979) Biochemistry and metoblism of basement membranes. *Int. Rev. Cytol.*, **61**, 167–228.

57 Kleinman H.K. *et al.* (1980) Collagenous matrices as determinants of cell function. In *Immunochemistry of Collagen* (Ed. H. Furthmayr). CRC Press, Florida.

58 Konijn T.M., Barkley D.S., Chang Y.Y. & Bonner J.T. (1968) Cyclic AMP: a naturally occurring acrasin in the cellular slime molds. *Ann. Nat.*, **102**, 225–233.

59 Kurkinen M., Alitalo K., Vaheri A., Stenman S. & Saxon L. (1979) Fibronectin in the development of the embryonic chick eye. *Devl. Biol.*, **69**, 589–600.

60 Lazarides E. & Revel J.-P. (1979) The molecular basis of cell movement. *Scient. Ann.*, **240**(5), 88–100.

61 Le Lièvre C.S. & Le Douarin N.M. (1975) Mesenchymal derivatives of the neural crest: analysis of chimaeric quail and chick embryos. *J. Embryol. exp. Morph.*, **34**, 125–154.

62 Levi-Montalcini R. & Angeletti P.V. (1965) The action of nerve growth factor on sensory and sympathetic cells. In *Organogenesis* (Eds R.L. De Haan & H. Ursprung), pp. 187–198. Holt, Rinehart & Winston, New York.

53 Lofberg J. & Jacobson C.O. (1974) Effect of vinblastine sulphate, colchicine and guanosine triphosphate on cell morphogenesis during amphibian neurulation. *Zoon*, **2**, 85–98.

64 Maurice D.M. (1957) The structure and transparency of the cornea. *J. Physiol.*, **136**, 263–286.

65 Medoff J. & Gross J. (1971) *In vitro* aggregation of mixed embryonic kidney and nerve cells. *J. Cell Biol.*, **50**, 457–468.

66 Meier S. & Hay E.D. (1973) Synthesis of sulfated glycosaminoglycans by embryonic corneal epithelium. *Devl. Biol.*, **35**, 318–333.

67 Meier S. & Hay E.D. (1975) Stimulation of corneal differentiation by interaction between cell surface and extracellular matrix. I. Morphogenetic analysis of transfilter "induction". *J. Cell Biol.*, **66**, 275–291.

68 Middleton C.A. (1973) The control of epithelial cell locomotion in tissue culture. In *Locomotion of Tissue Cells* (Eds R. Porter & D.W. Fitzsimmons), pp. 251–262. Elsevier/North-Holland, Amsterdam.

69 Miller E.J. (1976) Biochemical characteristics and biological significance of the genetically-distinct collagens. *Mol. & Cell Biochem.* **13**, 165–192.

70 Moffett B.C. (1965) The morphogenesis of joints. In *Organogenesis* (Eds R.L. De Haan & H. Ursprung), pp. 204–215. Holt, Rinehart & Winston, New York.

71 Morriss G.M. & New D.A.T. (1979) Effect of oxygen concentration on morphogenesis of cranial neural folds and neural crest in cultured rat embryos. *J. Embryol. exp. Morph.*, **54**, 17–35.

72 Noden D.M. (1978) Interactions directing the migration and cytodifferentiation of avian neural crest cells. In *Specificity of Embryological Interactions* (Ed. D.R. Garrod), pp. 5–49. Chapman & Hall, London.

73 Nutall R.P. (1976) Epithelial stratification in the developing chick cornea. *J. exp. Zool.*, **198**, 185–192.

74 Pearson M. & Elsdale T.R. (1979) Somitogenesis in amphibian embryos. 1. Experimental evidence for an interaction between two temporal factors in the specification of somite pattern. *J. Embryol. exp. Morph.*, **51**, 27–50.

75 Porter K.R. (1973) Microtubules in intracellular locomotion. In *Locomotion of Tissue Cells* (Eds R. Porter & D.W. Fitzsimmons), pp. 149–166. Elsevier/North-Holland, Amsterdam.

76 Pratt R.M., Larsen M.A. & Johnston M.C. (1975) Migration of cranial neural crest cells in a cell-free hyaluronate-rich matrix. *Devl. Biol.*, **44**, 298–305.

77 Saunders J.W. (1966) Death in embryonic systems. *Science, N.Y.*, **154**, 604–612.

78 Selman G. (1958) The forces producing neural closure in amphibia. *J. Embryol. exp. Morph.*, **6**, 448–465.

79 Stoker M.G.P. & Rubin H. (1967) Density-dependent inhibition of cell growth in culture. *Nature, Lond.*, **215**, 171–172.

80 Summerbell D. (1977) Reduction of the rate of outgrowth, cell density and cell division following removal of the apical ectodermal ridge of the chick limb bud. *J. Embryol. exp. Morph.*, **40**, 1–21.

81 Tilney L.G. & Gibbons J.R. (1969) Microtubules in the formation and development of the primary mesenchyme in *Arbacia punctata* II. *J. Cell Biol.*, **41**, 227–250.

82 Toole B.P. (1976) Morphogenetic role of glycosaminoglycans (acid mucopolysaccharides) in brain and other tissues. In *Neuronal Recognition* (Ed. S.H. Barondes), pp. 275–329. Plenum Press, New York.

83 Toole B.P. & Trelstad R.L. (1971) Hyaluronate production and removal during corneal development in the chick. *Devl. Biol.*, **26**, 28–35.

84 Townes P.L. & Holtfreter J. (1955) Directed movements and selective adhesion of embryonic amphibian cells. *J. exp. Zool.*, **128**, 53–120.

85 Trelstad R.L. & Coulombre A.J. (1971) Morphogenesis of the collagenous stroma of the chick cornea. *J. Cell Biol.*, **50**, 840–858.

86 Trinkaus J.P. (1965) Mechanisms of morphogenetic movements. In *Organogenesis* (Eds R.L. De Haan & H. Ursprung), pp. 55–104. Holt, Rinehard & Winston, New York.

87 Tuft P. (1965) The uptake and distribution of water in the developing amphibian embryo. *Symp. Soc. exp. Biol.*, **19**, 385–402.

88 Turner R.S. (1978) Sponge cell adhesion. In *Specificity of Embryological Interactions* (Ed. D.R. Garrod), pp. 201–232. Chapman & Hall, London.

89 Twitty V.C. (1945) The development analysis of specific pigment patterns. *J. exp. Zool.*, **100**, 141–178.

90 Twitty V.C. & Niu N.C. (1948) Causal analysis of chromatophore migration. *J. exp. Zool.*, **108**, 405–437.

91 Visser A.S., de Haas W.R.E., Kox C. & Prop A. (1972) Hormone effect on primary cell cultures of mouse mammary gland. *Expl. Cell Res.*, **72**, 516–519.

92 Waddington C.H. (1938) Regulation of amphibian gastrulae with added ectoderm. *J. exp. Biol.*, **15**, 377–381.

93 Weiss P. (1945) Experiments on cell and axon orientation *in vitro*: the role of colloidal exudates in tissue organisation. *J. exp. Zool.*, **100**, 353–386.

94 Weiss P.A. (1961) Guiding principles in cell locomotion and aggregation. *Expl. Cell Res.*, Suppl.**8**, 260–281.

95 Wessells N.K. (1965) Morphology and proliferation during early feather development. *Devl. Biol.*, **12**, 131–153.

96 Wessels N.K., Spooner B.S., Ash J.F., Bradley M.O., Luduena M.A., Taylor E.L., Wrenn J.T. & Yamada K.M. (1971) Microfilaments in cellular and developmental processes. *Science, N.Y.*, **171**, 135–143.

97 Weston J.A. & Butler S.L. (1966) Temporal factors affecting localisation of neural crest cells in the chicken embryo. *Devl. Biol.*, **14**, 246–266.

98 Woessner J.F. Jr (1968) Biological mechanisms of collagen resorption. In *Treatise on Collagen*, **2b** (Ed. B.S. Gould), pp. 254–330. Academic Press, London.

99 Wolff E. (1968) Specific interactions between tissues during organogenesis. *Curr. Tops Devl. Biol.*, **3**, 65–94.

100 Wolpert L. (1969) Positional information and the spatial pattern of cellular differentiation. *J. theor. Biol.*, **25**, 1–47.

101 Wolpert L. & Gustafson T. (1967) Cell movement and cell contact in sea urchin morphogenesis. *Endeavour*, **26**, 85–90.

102 Yamada K.M. & Olden K. (1978) Fibronectins—adhesive glycoproteins of cell surface and blood. *Nature, Lond.*, **275**, 179–184.

103 Zetterberg A. & Auer G. (1970) Proliferative activity and cytochemical properties of nuclear chromatin related to local cell density of epithelial cells. *Expl. Cell Res.*, **62**, 262–270.

104 Zinn K.M. (1970) Changes in corneal ultrastructure resulting from early lens removal in the developing chick embryo. *Invest. Ophthal.*, **9**, 165–182.

105 Malacinsk G.M. & Woo Youn B. (1981) Neural plate morphogenesis and axial stretching in "notochord defective" *Xenopus laevis* embryos. *Devl. Biol.*, **88**, 352–357.

Conclusions to Part 4

This part of the book is concerned with the build up of patterns of cell types in late developing animal embryos and it follows directly from the initiation of the spatial organization of gene expression which is found in the early embryo and which is discussed in Parts 1 and 2 of the book.

1. Cell properties into cell patterns

The interacting properties of cells are described in Part 3 of the book and many of the features of animal embryogenesis flow from these possibilities for inter-action and the intrinsic properties of the epithelial and mesenchyme phenotypes, which constitute the two dominant phenotypes of embryonic cells (Chapter 4.3). The activities of cells which are required for morpho-genesis are mainly dynamic and involve movement, selective adhesion, growth, and contact interactions. Individual cells of either phenotype display these pro-perties, but the expression of these properties in embryogenesis is constrained and terminated by the cell's immediate environment.

2. Pattern formation

Pattern formation in the embryos can be regarded as the process whereby cells acquire instructions as to how they should change their properties. Several theories are discussed in Chapter 4.2. The simplest view is that once the early cell types are formed, they proceed through a sequence of embryonic inductions of the kind described in Chapter 3.5. This explanation is inadequate for the purely practical reason that nobody has provided a complete explanation in terms of embryonic induction for the build up of organization in any complex organism. It is also unsatisfactory because so many patterns appear to involve interactions across the complete embryo (see also Chapter 2.4) or across the primordia of limbs and organs.

Theories which seek to explain pattern formation in whole embryos or in primordia can be divided into two main classes. Positional-information theories suggest that cells interpret their position in a field, such as a gradient of a morphogen, and that they respond dif-ferentially to levels in the field. The idea is that the field is simple (e.g. concentration of a substance in a gradient) and that the variety of responses elicited (interpretation) is discriminatory and subtle. In contrast, prepattern theories suppose that the initial field is complicated with, for instance, a pattern of peaks and troughs in the concentration of a substance. The realization of this prepattern and its expression might only depend on the capacity of cells to respond to threshold peaks of concen-trations.

The results of many experiments can be interpreted in terms of gradient models of positional information, with rules governing the interactions with different gradient levels and the circumstances in which new boundaries may be formed. However, the simple models discussed in Chapter 4.2 are usually inadequate to account for all experimental results and much more needs to be dis-covered and explained.

Part 5
Hormones in Development

Chapter 5.1
Hormones in Development

P.F. Wareing

5.1.1 GENERAL ASPECTS OF HORMONAL CONTROL

This section of the book is primarily concerned with studies on substances produced in one part of a developing organism which are transported or move to other parts where they exert their effects. The effects of these substances on development do not depend on a close association between the producing and the responding cells. For simplicity these substances will be called hormones, but it should be noted that in addition to well-known plant and animal hormones, such as indole-3-acetic acid (IAA) and thyroxine, these substances also include cyclic AMP (adenosine 3′, 5′-monophosphate) and ammonia, which are normally not considered as hormones. Moreover, in plants hormonal control does not always involve long-distance transport, since temporal variation in hormone levels may occur within the same cells and tissues which respond to the hormone, as with the tissues of plant embryos in which changes in gibberellin levels occur in response to dormancy-breaking treatments (p. 346); but it is difficult to say that in such cases we are not dealing with hormonal control, since the same types of growth substance, such as gibberellins, which are modulated in the embryo, are considered as normal hormones in the whole plant. However, we need not become too involved in the semantics of the term 'hormone', which for convenience we shall apply in a broad sense to a variety of substances which appear to play a role in the regulation of development.

In this section we consider the role of hormones in development in very different types of organism, viz. slime moulds, vertebrates and insects, and higher plants. Despite this wide biological diversity, there are close analogies in the problems posed and in the general features of hormonal control in all the types of organism considered.

Hormones provide one of the means whereby coordination of development is achieved, both in space and in time (p. 331). Spatial coordination is often concerned with coordinating the growth or activities of cell populations or organs within the organism as a whole. Temporal coordination often involves a developmental switch, as in the metamorphosis of insects or amphibians, or in the transition of the plant from the vegetative to the flowering phase.

Problems of coordination occur at different levels of organization, viz. molecular and subcellular, cell population and tissue, and whole organism. Thus, the problems of coordination are very diverse, and hormones play a correspondingly wide range of roles, as will become abundantly apparent from the examples to be discussed.

5.1.2 HORMONES AND CELL DETERMINATION

A constantly recurring question is whether hormones control the determination of different cell types or whether they stimulate the expression of differences in developmental potential in cells which are already determined. That is, does exposure to hormones decide for the cell what state of determination it will adopt or do hormones simply make a cell express a state of determination which it has already acquired independently of hormone action (p. 349)? This question indicates that two distinct situations can be envisaged in which hormones might play a role in the establishment of cell differences.

(1) Situations in which hormones are required for the expression of differentiation, but where cell differences in various parts of the organism are not dependent upon variations in hormone levels, but upon differences in the states of determination of the target cells. Numerous examples of this situation will be cited, and it is particularly characteristic of the major types of plant hormone that they each evoke a wide spectrum of responses in different parts of the plant, indicating that the type of response is controlled by the pre-programming of the different 'target' tissues and not by the hormone itself. Similar wide-ranging effects of a single hormone are seen in animals, as in the wide diversity of effects occurring during the metamorphosis of amphibians in response to thyroxine (p. 361). However, in general, animal hormones evoke more specific responses and their sites of action (target cells) are more limited than those of plant hormones.

(2) Situations in which differences in the expression of differentiation appear not to be due to the pre-programming of the cells, but are regulated by spatial or temporal variations in hormone concentration. In a few instances the hormones may affect the state of cell determination, but more frequently they do not alter the state of determination but modulate the expression of differentiation. An example in which a hormone appears to act as a cell determinant is seen in some strains of the slime mould *Dictyostelium*, the cells of which can be forced to form microcysts (spores) by exposure to physiological concentrations of ammonia

(Chapter 5.2). In the absence of ammonia the amoebae would have formed a fruiting body with stalk and spore cells, and it appears that all the cells are forced to follow one path of development and that, in this instance, ammonia is a cell-type determinant.

The 'head-forming' activator of *Hydra* (p. 362) seems to be capable of inducing cell determination (p. 363), but whether it can be regarded as a 'hormone' seems doubtful, and it may be more comparable with the factors involved in embryonic induction (Chapter 3.5).

In other instances it is difficult to decide whether the effect of a hormone on differentiation is brought about by a change in the state of determination or whether the hormone is simply affecting the *expression* of differentiation. However, in the frog *Xenopus* it seems clear that the induction of vitellogenin by thyroxine depends upon changes occurring in liver cells during metamorphosis and that the hormone can only stimulate the production of vitellogenin in liver cells of adult frogs which are 'competent' to do so (p. 357). Thus, thyroxine appears to be affecting the expression of changes which the liver cells undergo during metamorphosis.

At first sight, the induction by IAA of highly differentiated vascular tissue in hitherto unspecialized parenchymatous tissue in plants (p. 315) would seem to afford another example of hormonal control of cell-type determination. However, although IAA is necessary for normal differentiation of xylem tissue this response can only be elicited in cells arising on the inner side of the cambium, and differentiation into xylem and phloem appears to be predetermined by a radial polarity within the cambial region (p. 321). Thus, the hormone appears to be stimulating differentiation in determined cells, although the development *de novo* of a vascular strand as a whole appears to be hormonally controlled.

Again, in the hormonal induction of buds and roots in undifferentiated callus tissue we do not seem to be dealing with the direct induction of specific cell types, but rather with the initiation of shoot apical meristems and root meristems as organized wholes, from which specific cell types arise later in a normal (but unknown) manner.

5.1.3 HORMONES AND THE EXPRESSION OF DIFFERENTIATION

An example from plants in which hormones seem clearly to act by regulating the expression of differentiation is provided by dioecious species (which bear male and female flowers on separate plants) such as hemp (*Cannabis sativa*), and with those monoecious species such as cucumber (*Cucumis sativa*) and squash (*Cucurbita pepo*) where the male and female organs, although on the same plant, are borne in separate, distinct flowers. Application of auxins to male hemp plants leads to the formation of female flowers and the same treatment results in an increased ratio of female to male flowers in squash. In organ culture experiments it has been shown that young flower primordia of cucumbers excised from nodes which would normally have formed male flowers can be induced to develop into female flowers if treated with auxin (indole-3-acetic acid).

The young flower primordia in these dioecious species are very similar for both male and female flowers, and both types contain both stamen and pistil primordia, but during further development primordia of one or other of these organs fail to develop so that the mature flower is unisexual. The effect of hormones is to influence the relative development of the stamen and pistil primordia. Thus, the hormones appear to act by affecting the *expression* of differentiation in the two types of primordia, which are themselves presumably 'determined' as stamens or pistil.

Ethylene has similar effects to auxin in experiments such as those described above and since application of auxins to plants often leads to enhanced ethylene production it has been suggested that the effects of auxin in these systems are in fact mediated by the gaseous hormone. Gibberellins on the other hand tend to increase the ratio of male to female flowers and, indeed, in certain lines of cucumber which usually produce only female flowers, application of gibberellins leads to the formation of functional male flowers. The few studies so far carried out on endogenous hormone levels in plants showing these effects suggest that sex expression is effected by balance between endogenous auxins and gibberellins, since in plants showing predominantly male characteristics gibberellin levels are high, whereas wholly female plants tend to have high auxin levels.

Similarly the differentiation of functional ovaries and testes can be controlled by altering the hormone concentration in the water in which amphibian embryos and larvae are reared (reviewed [1]). In these experiments it seems that the hormone has a direct effect on the somatic tissues of the gonad and that it only indirectly influences the sex of the germ cells. The primordial germ

cells of *Xenopus laevis* are labile and will form sperm when transplanted to a male host and eggs when transplanted to a female host, whatever their genetic sex [2]. It seems that it is the sexual nature of the gonad in which the germ cells take up residence which determines whether they form sperm or eggs. The somatic tissues of the gonad are similar in male and female embryos during early development, and consist of an outer cortex surrounding an inner medulla. During ovarian development the cortex proliferates and contains the germ cells while the testes develop by proliferation of the medulla which encloses the germ cells. The hormones induce the proliferation and differentiation of either the cortex or the medulla and thus indirectly determine the cell type which the primordial germ cells will form.

5.1.4 THE MODE OF ACTION OF HORMONES IN DEVELOPMENT

Insofar as differentiation involves selective gene expression, hormones which control differentiation must act by regulating gene expression. Since we still do not fully understand how gene expression, in general, is regulated in eukaryotes, it is not yet possible to determine how hormonal control of gene expression is achieved.

The most detailed information at present available relates to the mode of action of steroid hormones in animals; these bind with a cytoplasmic protein 'receptor' and the hormone/receptor complex then enters the nucleus where it becomes attached to the chromatin and regulates the expression of specific genes (p. 352). Our knowledge of how plant hormones act is much less complete, but there is increasing evidence that they also bind with specific receptors (p. 322).

Most animal hormones appear to act at the transcriptional level, independently of whether they act as determinants of differentiation or regulate gene expression in already determined cells. Information as to the level at which plant hormones act is less precise, but there is evidence that the production of α-amylase in germinating barley grains is regulated at the transcriptional level (p. 327). On the other hand, many responses to plant hormones involve the regulation of *growth*, rather than differentiation, and in some cases control appears to be at a post-transcriptional level, such as translation or enzyme activation.

The molecular basis of determination is still unknown.

It might be thought that the synthesis of hormone receptors would be one of the first signs of determination in a cell. This attractive idea appears to be incorrect in at least one case. The liver enzyme tyrosine amino transferase (TAT) can be induced in fetal liver by cyclic AMP at least two days in development before it can be induced by the hormones glucagon and cortisone. This suggests that liver cells are predetermined to synthesize TAT before they have the receptors required to respond to these hormones [3]. It remains to be seen whether hormone-induced structures are also predetermined to develop in a particular way before they are able to respond to a hormone.

5.1.5 HORMONES AS COORDINATORS WITHIN THE ORGANISM AS A WHOLE

Although hormones do not appear to act as determinants of specific cell types, they do seem to play an important role as coordinators of growth and development within the organism as a whole. This is well illustrated in the critical role of thyroxine in controlling metamorphosis in amphibian tadpoles, where a very wide range of tissues undergo fundamental changes in direct response to the hormone (p. 361). A similar situation appears to be the case in insect metamorphosis. Here the hormone ecdysone triggers all the changes involved in moulting, while the levels of juvenile hormone direct the morphological and biochemical results of the moult. High levels of juvenile hormone yield larval moults; low levels, larva to pupa transformation; and in the absence of juvenile hormone, hemimetabolous larvae and holometabolous pupae form adults. Thus these two hormones direct the overall organization of the insect [4].

The transition from the vegetative to the flowering condition in plants also involves a radical change in the structure of the shoot apical meristems and frequently in the plant as a whole, since when an apical meristem changes from the vegetative to the reproductive condi-

tion it loses its capacity for unlimited growth and becomes a structure of determinate growth, as a result of which it ceases to produce leaves and produces a flower or inflorescence. In many species this transition is controlled by environmental factors, such as seasonal variations in daylength or winter chilling temperatures (p. 342). There is much experimental evidence suggesting that daylength changes are detected by the leaves, although the response occurs in the shoot apices. Hence some sort of a signal must be transmitted from the leaves to the apices under inductive conditions which stimulates the apex to undergo the transition from the vegetative to the reproductive condition. Although there is much circumstantial evidence that this signal is of a hormonal nature, so far attempts to isolate the hypothetical 'flower hormone' have proved unsuccessful. Gibberellins have been found to stimulate flowering in a number of species, but in most species flowering does not appear to be regulated by endogenous gibberellins (p. 345).

Apart from the hormonal control of such major switches in the life cycle as metamorphosis or entry into the flowering phase, hormones play an important coordinating role within the organism as a whole, as seen in the development of secondary sex characters in animals and coordination of growth of the different regions of the plant body, for example in the stimulation of growth in the maternal tissue of fruits, following pollination and development of the embryo.

5.1.6 REFERENCES

1 Burns R.K. (1961) Role of hormones in the differentiation of sex. In *Sex and Internal Secretions*, 1 (Ed. W.C. Young), pp. 76–158. Williams & Wilkins, Baltimore.

2 Blackler A.W. (1966) Embryonic sex cells of amphibia. In *Advances in Reproductive Physiology*, I (Ed. A. McLaren), pp. 1–28. Logos and Academic Press.

3 Greengard O. (1971) Enzymic differentiation in mammalian liver. *Essays in Biochemistry*, **7**, 159–205.

4 Willis J.H. (1974) Morphogenetic action of insect hormones. *Rev. Ent.*, **19**, 97–115.

Chapter 5.2
Signalling Systems in *Dictyostelium*

J.T. Bonner and P.C. Newell

5.2.1   INTRODUCTION

It may be helpful to illustrate communication systems in development by picking one example and examining it in some depth. The cellular slime moulds, and especially the species *Dictyostelium discoideum* which was discovered by K.B. Raper in the 1930s, have become popular organisms for the study of development. The reasons for this popularity are not hard to find.

(1) In the first place, they have a remarkably simple life history in which there is differentiation into only two cell types: stalk cells and spores.

(2) They are very easy to grow in the laboratory on solidified media or in liquid culture with a bacterial food source. Certain strains will also grow without bacteria in axenic media or in a defined minimal medium.

(3) Part of their life cycle takes place on a surface, and therefore is two-dimensional, making experimental analysis that much easier.

(4) They have both a parasexual and a sexual system and therefore it is possible to do genetics.

(5) Finally, they are eukaryotes and therefore presumably any information they divulge in our experi-ments has a good chance of applying to the development of other higher animals and plants.

The life cycle of *Dictyostelium discoideum*, which takes roughly four days in the laboratory, is in itself curious and unusual. The cellular slime moulds differ from other soil amoeba in this respect; most other soil amoebae (e.g. *Hartmanella* and *Acanthamoeba*) form cysts by encapsulating individually in a resistant cellulose wall, while the slime moulds come together in aggregates and form communal fruiting bodies. In the case of *Dictyostelium* (by which we will mean *Dictyo-*

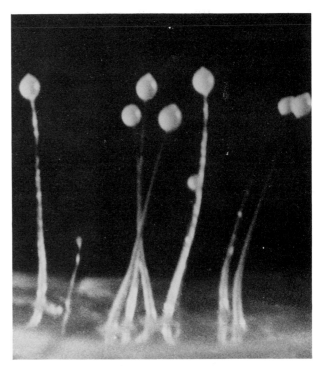

Fig. 5.2.1. Mature fruiting bodies of *Dictyostelium discoideum*.

stelium discoideum) there may be from a few hundred up to hundreds of thousands of amoebae in a large fruiting body. But 'large' is relative and a hundred thousand cells will only produce a fruiting body a few millimetres high which consists of a delicate stalk made up of large vacuole cells (Fig. 5.2.1). At the tip of the stalk there is a lemon-shaped mass of cells, each one of which is an encapsulated spore, similar to the cysts of the solitary amoebae. In nature these small fruiting bodies project into interstices in the soil or into the small cavities between sticks and leaves in humus. It is presumed that gathering the spores in one large mass provides an effective means of dispersal and that this is its adaptive advantage. But this is a subject which, in itself, is poorly understood and in need of further investigation.

A new generation can easily be started from one spore. Normally, the amoebae are grown on a suitable bacterial food source. (*Escherichia coli* and *Klebsiella aerogenes* are the most commonly used food organisms.) It is possible to grow up the bacteria beforehand and add spores to the bacteria, or the two can grow in a medium that will support the growth of the bacteria which, in turn, supplies the feeding and dividing amoebae. The growth can take place either in liquid culture or on the surface of a solid medium and numerous permutations are possible [6, 40]; however, development beyond the amoeboid stage requires a surface covered with a water film.

On an agar surface the amoebae begin the morphogenetic phase of their life cycle. The cells double their rate of locomotion for a brief period, after which they become very sluggish. Certain groups of cells appear to become focal points and begin to attract other cells. The cells soon pour in and form streams that branch outward (Fig. 5.2.2).

In time-lapse motion pictures, and in photographs using dark field optics of confluent lawns of amoebae, the process is very dramatic. The amoebae can be seen to move inward intermittently in response to pulses of chemoattractant that are emitted by the aggregation centres every few minutes. These pulses of attraction are relayed rapidly outwards from the centre in the form of concentric or spiral waves that travel at up to 8 μm s^{-1} while the amoebae move inwards with a velocity of about 0.2 μm s^{-1} (Fig. 5.2.3).

Once the cells are collected into a mass, this begins to push upwards and then falls sideways on the substratum producing a migrating slug (or 'pseudoplasmodium')

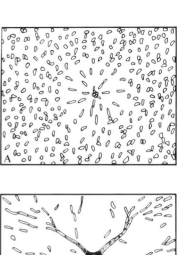

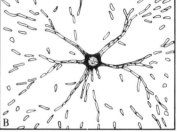

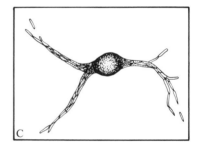

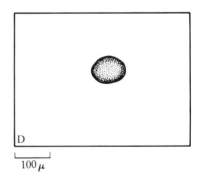

100 μ

Fig. 5.2.2. Four drawings (semi-diagrammatic) of successive stages of aggregation in *Dictyostelium*. At such a low population density the pattern of relaying fields shown in Fig. 5.2.3 are not discernible.

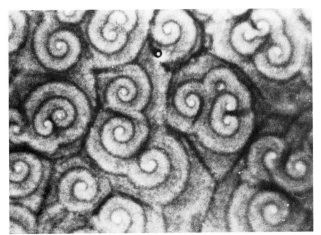

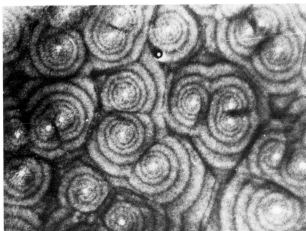

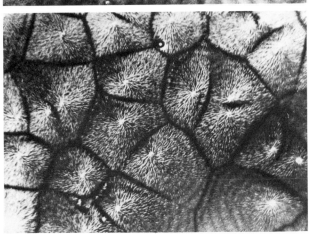

(Fig. 5.2.4). This slug has remarkable properties: it is extraordinarily sensitive to environmental conditions and will go toward light of extremely low intensity and move towards or away from very weak sources of heat (depending on the absolute temperature).

The duration of the migration period is also sensitive to environmental conditions; it will be brought to an end by a very slight drop in the ambient humidity and an increase in overhead illumination. The slug rights itself and stalk formation now begins on the anterior end of the cell mass. Large vacuolate cells appear and these are pushed down through the cell mass to form the base of the stalk. Soon the whole mass rises into the air as the stalk cells move on to the tip and become incorporated into the stalk. The stalk itself is made up of a tapering cellulose cylinder which is secreted by the prestalk cells before they enter into the stalk and become vacuolate and eventually die. As the stalk elongates, so the posterior mass of prespore cells differentiates into spores and it slowly rises with the stalk so that it ends up at the apex (Fig. 5.2.4).

As in an annual plant, maturity means quiescence; there is no change until one of the spores germinates to start a new generation. In this case, the period of active development includes the entire life cycle.

What we have described is the asexual reproduction. It has been shown that the cellular slime moulds are capable of parasexual reproduction and that by this

Fig. 5.2.3. Relaying fields seen in confluent lawns of starving *D. discoideum* amoebae on an agar surface. The same area of the agar surface was photographed with a dark field optical system at 18 min (top frame), 39 min (middle frame) and 75 min (bottom frame) after the initiation of signal relaying. Each picture encloses an area of *c.* 2 cm × 3 cm. The signals emanate from the aggregation centres (which are seen as white dots) at a frequency that increases from approximately one wave every 6 min (top) to one every 2–3 min (middle). The dark and light bands result from a change in the refractive index that makes moving cells appear bright and stationary cells dark, under these optical conditions [2, 31]. Eventually the uniform distribution of amoebae breaks up into a series of streams through which the wave pattern is less discernible (bottom frame). The strain shown here (NP377) has a particularly long (bright) movement period that makes the band pattern particularly amenable for analysis [62]. Although most of the relaying fields show a spiral wave pattern it may be noticed that a concentric relaying field is present in the upper frame (at a position one-third of the distance from the top and right margins). This field is later overrun by the adjacent spiralling fields (middle and bottom frames). Although concentric waves are commonly seen under certain conditions, they tend to show slower and initially more variable signalling frequencies and are often dominated by the faster and more regular spiralling centres.

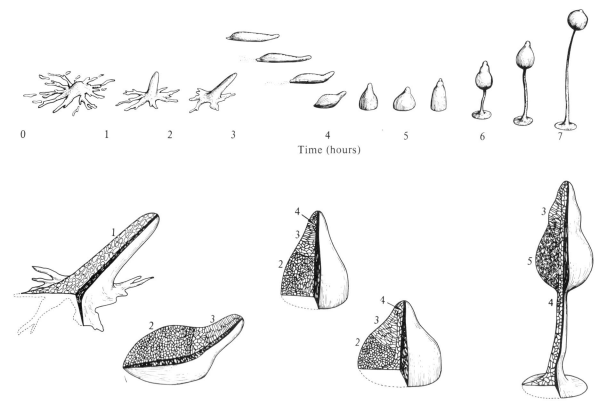

Time (hours)

Fig. 5.2.4. Development in *Dictyostelium discoideum*. Above: The aggregation, migration, and culmination stages shown in an approximate time scale. Below: Cutaway diagrams to show the cellular structure of different stages. 1, Undifferentiated cells at the end of aggregation; 2, prespore cells; 3, prestalk cells; 4, mature stalk cells; 5, mature spores. (Drawing by J.L. Howard, courtesy of the *Scientific American*.)

means it is possible to obtain genetic recombination [53]. A recent development is the discovery of true sexuality. Some time ago, Blaskovics and Raper described macrocysts which appear during aggregation in some species of cellular slime moulds. It is now evident that these macrocysts contain zygotes that probably undergo meiosis [12, 20, 42]. *Dictyostelium discoideum* appears to be heterothallic, that is, it has two mating types. If two of the standard laboratory strains of opposite type are mixed, they will produce macrocysts that remain dormant for many months before germinating to liberate haploid amoebae once more.

5.2.2   EVIDENCE FOR DIFFERENT SIGNALS

We will be concerned entirely with chemical signals,

which are the only kind that have been demonstrated in the cellular slime moulds. Already a surprising number of different kinds of chemical signals are known. For some, we simply have evidence of their existence, but no clue as to their chemical nature. We know some of the chemical details of others, but we still lack a great deal of important information.

The signals could be classified in a number of ways. For instance, one could separate the signals which control or direct cell movement from those that are responsible for differentiation. Our method will be to discuss what is known about signalling for each stage of development; it will be a life-history classification. One virtue of this system is that the life cycle begins with cells which communicate and are separate from one another; then the cells come together in a cell mass and signal to one another while in intimate contact; and finally, when the cell masses are developing there is a communication between these masses by what we might think of as a 'social' chemical hormone system.

Signals in spore germination

In *Dictyostelium*, as with many fungi and other plants, a higher percentage of spores germinate when the spores are sparsely sown rather than in a dense concentration. This inhibition of germination can be removed if the spores are carefully washed and, furthermore, if the washings of spores is concentrated it will greatly inhibit spore germination [6, 14]. The structure of the inhibitor has been found from NMR and mass spectrometry to be a 3-amino, 3-carboxy, propyl derivative of isopentenyl adenine and has been given the name 'discadenine' [1]. Presumably this autoinhibition prevents excess germination in dense spore populations and could serve as a mechanism to prevent germination in the sorus. Moreover, since only a few amoebae are needed to produce a new generation it is obviously good strategy not to germinate all one's spores if there is an excess of spores at any one time. In contrast, the spores are stimulated to germinate in the presence of substances associated with food, namely amino acids [14].

Signals in feeding or vegetative amoebae

If amoebae are put in a concentrated drop on the surface of agar, they will spread and move away from the drop. This could be by random motion of the amoebae (similar to the diffusion of ions away from a salt crystal placed in water) or there could be a repellent produced by the amoebae which causes them to move away from one another (negative chemotaxis). There are two lines of evidence to support the latter hypothesis. One is an unpublished experiment of E.W. Samuel in which he deposited a concentrated mass of amoebae on a small square of cellophane. He placed this near a few vegetative amoebae on an agar surface and they oriented away from the square; if he then moved the square 90° to one side of the amoebae, they changed their direction through 90° and again moved away. Another test was suggested by Lee Segal: if the movement is similar to diffusion, then the distance that the amoebae moved away from the drop would fall off as the square root of time, while if there is a repellent it would be linear with time. Actual measurements show a linear relation-

ship, again supporting the idea of a repellent, as do a number of more recent experiments [9].

Unfortunately, we have no idea of the chemical nature of the repellent. We do know that substances which are given off by bacteria (such as folic acid) attract amoebae. However, this is not a morphogenetic signalling system but rather a mechanism whereby the amoebae can locate their food. When the food is all gone, or when there is an even distribution of food over the surface, then the amoebae are evenly spaced, presumably by this cell repulsion signal which acts at a distance between cells. Such a mechanism will make for even, efficient grazing in the presence of food, and an effective searching mechanism in the absence of food.

Signals between aggregating amoebae

The mechanism of aggregation has been the primary concern of many investigations for some years. The first clear indication that it was a chemotaxis was a key experiment of Runyon [6]. He showed that if one placed an aggregation centre on one side of a dialysis membrane, and sensitive amoebae on the other side, then the amoebae were attracted to the point opposite the aggregation centre. He suggested that this was chemotaxis effected by a small molecule which could get through the cellophane membrane. This conclusion was supported by other evidence [4], but attraction to acrasin (as the attractant is called) was not proved until the work of Shaffer [6, 67]. He developed a test in which he sandwiched some sensitive pre-aggregation amoebae under a small block of agar on a glass slide, and then repeatedly added water containing acrasin (by taking drops of water from around aggregating centres in another dish) to the edge of this agar block. In a matter of minutes the amoebae under the block streamed to the edge. He also showed that the substance broke down readily, for if he lengthened the interval between additions of acrasin to the edge of the block, no attraction occurred. Subsequently, he showed that this was because there is an enzyme, an acrasinase, that destroys the activity of the attractant.

In the 1950s and early 1960s there was a great wave of activity in various laboratories to discover the chemical nature of acrasin but none succeeded. Part of the difficulty was that the Shaffer test was inconvenient as an assay of acrasin in chemical analysis. Independently,

Konijn and Bonner and colleagues devised assays for acrasin that worked on essentially the same principle [8]. A drop of cells was placed on agar containing a test substance and if it had acrasin activity, the cells worked away from the drop, further and more rapidly than in the control. It is presumed that this happens because the cells produce a large amount of acrasinase which diffuses into the agar around the drop and removes all the acrasin from that area. The outer edge of amoebae are therefore in a gradient of acrasin which is more concentrated further from the drop. Since the cells are positively chemotactic, they will go up a concentration gradient and therefore spread rapidly away from the drop. Using this improved assay it was shown that the acrasin for *Dictyostelium* is cyclic AMP (cAMP), the cells at the aggregation stage being extraordinarily sensitive to this nucleotide—the optimum concentration is 100 nM. The acrasinase of Shaffer was shown to be an extracellular phosphodiesterase that specifically degrades cAMP to 5'AMP, a compound devoid of any chemotactic activity.

The pulsatile nature of the signalling system was deduced from time-lapse films of starving amoebae aggregating in waves on agar surfaces (Fig. 5.2.3). The first to appreciate the possible significance of these waves was Shaffer, who suggested that acrasin did not necessarily distribute itself in one big gradient, but that when the cells were still separate each amoeba produced a pulse of acrasin and orientated the next amoeba by producing a small, local gradient [66]. He presumed that the presence of acrasin stimulates a cell to make its own pulse of acrasin and that subsequently each cell goes into an insensitive refractory period, a model which closely parallels the transmission of impulses in nerves or in the hearts of animals. The idea has been subsequently pursued by Cohen and Robertson [13], who argue on the basis of some interesting theoretical considerations that not only aggregation but all aspects of development, including the pattern of differentiation, are governed by these waves.

Although such two-dimensional spiral or concentric waves have been observed by a number of workers over many years, the major advances in understanding the biochemical basis of this pulsatile process occurred only

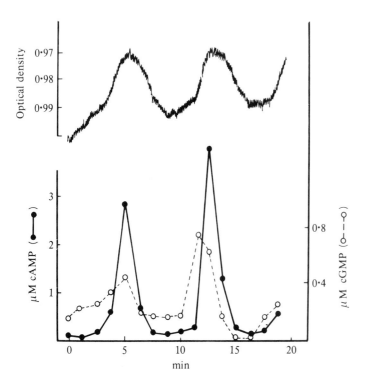

Fig. 5.2.5. Oscillations of cAMP and cGMP concentrations in starving amoebae suspended in a spectrophotometer cuvette. Samples taken at intervals and assayed for cAMP and cGMP show that the concentrations of these nucleotides oscillate in phase with the oscillation of optical density (upper trace) that monitors changes in shape of the amoebae. (Redrawn from Wurster *et al.* [73].)

after Gerisch and Hess adapted the system to suspension culture. The technique that they devised employed a high population density of starving amoebae in an oxygenated spectrophotometer cuvette that was monitored for its absorbance at 405 nm. It was discovered that after several hours of starvation these amoebae showed rhythmic changes in optical density that had a similar periodicity to the waves seen with amoebae on agar [25] (Fig. 5.2.5). Generally, an initial series of spikes was recorded which was gradually followed by more sinusoidal oscillations. The spike amplitude was roughly 2% of the background absorbance and the manner in which the amplitude decreased with increasing wavelength of the incident light suggested that the observed effects were due to light-scattering changes resulting from changes in amoebal shape. This technique, which apparently allowed a synchronous entrainment of the chemotactic process, enabled Gerisch and co-workers to assay the concentration of cAMP and the activity of the cAMP-forming enzyme adenylate cyclase at precisely controlled times during oscillation cycle [27, 61]. Their results clearly indicated that the activity of adenylate cyclase and the internal and external concentrations of cAMP oscillated in phase with the absorbance changes seen with the same amoebae (Fig. 5.2.5). To see rhythmic changes of this nature implies the existence of an internal oscillator in at least some of the amoebae but the nature of such an oscillator is as yet obscure. A possibly important observation, however, was that the redox stage of the cytochrome chain in the mitochondria oscillated in phase with the oscillating absorbance trace [25]. The frequency of the observed oscillations of absorbance and of adenylate cyclase activity are not rigidly coupled to such an oscillator, however, because externally applied pulses of cAMP (of about 10 nM) could change the phase of the absorbance oscillation, and continuous addition of cAMP inhibited the oscillation altogether.

In order to send a pulsatile signal from the aggregation centre to the outer extremities of the aggregation field, a system of relay must operate. This can be demonstrated by supplying tiny pulses of cAMP from hollow electrode needles to starving amoebae on agar [28, 59] but it may also be conveniently seen with the cuvette technique. If small (10 nM) amounts of cAMP are added to starving amoebal suspensions, they can be seen to react by producing a sharp spike followed by a slower wave in their absorbance trace (Fig. 5.2.6). The spike may be

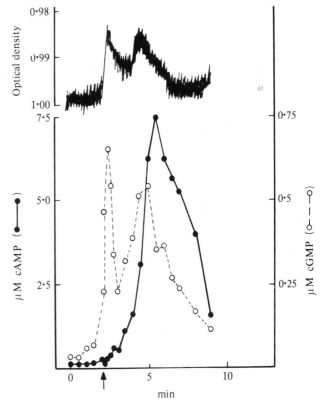

Fig. 5.2.6. The relay response to an exogenous pulse of cAMP shown by starving amoebae in a spectrophotometer cuvette. A small pulse of cAMP (at the time shown by the arrow) evokes a spike followed by a slower wave in the optical density trace and a biphasic increase in the cGMP concentration. The cAMP concentration is seen to rise later and to be correlated with the second peak in the optical density trace. (Redrawn from Wurster *et al.* [73].)

accounted for by a rapid shape change of the amoebae in reaction to the added cAMP pulse and, from assay of the cuvette contents for cAMP, the subsequent slower wave can be correlated with a period of synthesis of cAMP [60].

In order to sense such a relayed pulse, the amoebae possess receptors situated on the outer surface of their plasma membrane [44]. The properties of these receptors, which are highly specific for cAMP, have been found to resemble mammalian hormone receptors in a number of ways [52]. Detailed analysis of the association of the cAMP with the receptors (using Scatchard plots) has revealed that the receptors show affinity that varies with the concentration of cAMP [30,

49], a phenomenon seen with several peptide hormones and thought to be due to interactions between subunits of the receptor or to interactions between the receptor and its effector in the plasma membrane. Desensitization, which again is a feature of a number of hormone systems, is also seen with *Dictyostelium* cAMP receptors such that after prolonged exposure to high cAMP concentrations the number of active receptors is found to be markedly reduced [37].

The link between the cAMP receptor and the adenylate cyclase enzyme is presently a matter for speculation. Although a physical link between the receptor on the outer face of the plasma membrane and the adenylate cyclase (shown from histological data to be on the inner face of this membrane) is not definitely ruled out, it seems more likely from the timing of the response that a second messenger is involved. Two candidates for this role are cGMP [46, 73] and Ca^{2+} ions [72]. The concentrations of both of these molecular species have been observed to change after cAMP binding. A tiny peak of cGMP is produced by the enzyme guanylate cyclase a few seconds after cAMP molecules bind to their receptors and another peak is formed at the time of the secondary wave of absorbance (Fig. 5.2.6). A similar peak is also to be noticed in autonomously oscillating cell suspensions (Fig. 5.2.5). The rapid formation of these peaks of cGMP suggests that it may bring about chemotaxis and possibly cause the activation of adenylate cyclase. Changes in Ca^{2+} ions have been seen as a transient inward movement within a few seconds of cAMP binding to the receptors. From other systems where Ca^{2+} ions play an important role in chemotaxis (such as bacteria [29] or *Paramecium* [50]) this finding is highly suggestive of a role for Ca^{2+} ions as secondary messengers in the process of signal relay or chemotaxis. Although the role in relay may be questioned because of the apparent lack of any effect of externally applied Ca^{2+} chelators such as EGTA on the cAMP-induced absorbance changes in the cuvette system, the possibility of a role for Ca^{2+} in chemotaxis is supported by the finding that the amoebal actomyosin is sensitive to Ca^{2+} activation [48].

The inability of high steady-state levels of cAMP to stimulate chemotaxis has suggested to a number of workers that it is a *change* in cAMP receptor occupancy that is important for the amoebae to sense. A perfusion technique recently described by Devreotes, Derstine and Steck [18] has enabled this hypothesis to be rigorously tested. With a special apparatus that can constantly bathe amoebae with fresh buffer containing varying concentrations of cAMP, these workers have shown that only an increment in cAMP concentration brings about stimulation of adenylate cyclase. Furthermore, this process shows the characteristics of adaptation to static cAMP concentrations, which seems analogous to the adaptation seen in other sensory systems [19].

It is almost certainly in order to avoid the possibility that the cAMP concentration might rise to saturating levels and so block any further response that the amoebae produce phosphodiesterase enzymes which rapidly split cAMP into the inactive 5′ AMP. One form of phosphodiesterase is membrane bound [45, 57] and shows complex kinetics that enable it to degrade cAMP rapidly over a very wide concentration range. Another form is excreted as a soluble enzyme. The significance of this soluble form is puzzling, as some isolates of *Dictyostelium* that aggregate normally produce and excrete an inhibitory protein inactivating the extracellular phosphodiesterase soon after it is liberated. It may be significant that the synthesis of this inhibitor is itself apparently inhibited by the presence of large amounts of cAMP [36, 71, 74]. The need for the phosphodiesterase enzymes is clearly shown by the mutant HPX200 which lacks nearly all phosphodiesterase activity and is totally unable to aggregate unless phosphodiesterase is added to the agar surface on which it is deposited [15].

Besides bringing about orderly chemotaxis of amoebae into collecting centres, the pulses of cAMP also seem to act as a stimulatory system for the onset of development. Cell-surface glycoproteins called Contact sites A, which are considered to be involved in the final cell adhesion, are formed before the amoebae make contact [3]. That the induction of these glycoproteins is probably due to the cAMP pulses can be demonstrated by giving premature pulses of cAMP to amoebae in suspension culture: it is found that the contact sites are formed prematurely. Indeed, certain developmental mutants that produce no contact sites may be induced to do so if given pulses of cAMP every five minutes for a few hours. Continuous application of cAMP is ineffective [16, 17, 26]. The role of cAMP is clearly more than that of a chemotactic agent. Its further involvement as a regulatory agent at even later stages of development is described in the section that follows.

Signalling in multicellular stages

During development of the cellular slime moulds from multicellular aggregates into fruiting bodies containing stalk cells and spores, we may envisage the involvement of three classes of signalling substance. One such class, for example, might be concerned with controlling which of alternative pathways of development is taken by the organism, a second with inducing development in general, without regard to the cell types formed, and a third with inducing the differentiation of specific cell types. Let us now consider these in turn.

Signals controlling developmental pathways

In this class is the substance that can switch developing aggregates of cells from the sorocarp (stalk and spore) forming programme to the alternative 'slug' programme (Fig. 5.2.7). During the slug programme of *D. discoideum*, stalk and spore development is held in abeyance while the organism slowly moves over the substratum in search of a more suitable place to develop. The slug is apparently formed in response to an 'awareness' by the developing aggregate of an overcrowded environment. The substance that induces formation of this migratory stage is a volatile basic substance which is produced by the amoebae and which has recently been identified as NH_3 [55, 64]. The evidence that ammonia is the regulatory agent comes from the finding that not only does the naturally occurring agent show many of the chemical and physical properties of NH_3 but also its action is mimicked by ammonium carbonate at a pH above 7 when added during the appropriate 'decision-making' period. Moreover, the slug stage can be omitted entirely if an NH_3-absorbing chemical reaction system is added to the immediate area surrounding young aggregates. The NH_3, therefore, seems to be acting as a simple, metabolically produced signal, the concentration of which determines the developmental pathway taken.

In the related species of slime mould *Polysphondylium pallidum*, NH_3 seems to have a somewhat similar role at a different stage of development. In this species an additional option is open to the starving amoebae as they can either aggregate and form fruiting bodies as we have described for *Dictyostelium*, or each isolated amoeba can bypass all these stages and immediately encyst (Fig. 5.2.7). These 'microcysts' appear similar in structure to spores except that their cellulose envelope is spherical rather than elliptical. Recently Lonski [39] noticed that if a culture of *Polysphondylium* was very crowded the frequency of microcyst formation increased, but the effect of crowding was totally eliminated by adding activated charcoal to the dish. In a series of experiments, he demonstrated that the crowding effect could be achieved in sparse populations of amoebae by adding physiological concentrations of NH_3 which suggests that this may be the normal signal in nature for operation of the microcyst pathway.

Signals inducing development

Included in the second class of signalling substance is the inductive signal for differentiation into spores and stalk cells. In addition to its actions as a chemoattractant and inducer of early developmental events, there is evidence that cAMP can cause amoebae to transform into typical stalk cells without ever aggregating in the normal way [7, 11]. Until recently, this effect of cAMP was taken to indicate a specific role in inducing stalk cells, but the

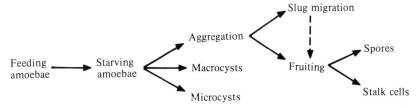

Fig. 5.2.7. Alternative developmental pathways in the cellular slime moulds. In *Dictyostelium* species starvation normally induces the separate amoebae to collect together to form multicellular aggregates. In some species, such as *Polysphondylium pallidum*, appropriate signals produced by the amoebae can bring about direct encystment of the amoebae to form microcysts. Signalling at later stages of the multicellular aggregate can, in *Dictyostelium discoideum*, determine whether a transient, migratory 'slug' stage is formed and whether stalk cells or spores are the final products of the differentiation process (for details see text).

work of Kay, Garrod and Tilly [34] shows that the effect of cAMP is more general. These workers took as a measure of spore formation the number of cells induced to form the 'prespore vacuoles' that are characteristically formed during the course of spore maturation, rather than looking for mature refractile spores as previously. Using this criterion of spore pathway induction they found that both spore and stalk cell development was initiated by added cAMP.

Differentiation of spores differed from that of stalk cells in that the process could not be completed to maturity under these conditions, maturation presumably requiring additional factor(s). It may be deduced that cAMP is a general signal for initiation of development. The concentrations required *in vitro* to produce this effect are high (approximately 1 mM) but, because of the phosphodiesterases surrounding the cells and the impermeability of the amoebal plasma membranes, the amount that actually enters the cell is small and probably within the normal physiological range of cAMP produced endogenously.

The interesting relationship between cAMP and NH_3 may help to explain, at least in part, some of the actions of NH_3 in inducing slug formation. It has been found that NH_3 at physiological concentrations dramatically decreases intracellular cAMP concentrations in starving cell suspensions [65]. Such an effect might explain the lack of further differentiation under conditions favouring formation of migrating slugs. The slug mode is typified by a halting of the programme of developmental enzyme synthesis for the duration of migration [54]. That this lack of enzyme synthesis might result from the influence of NH_3 through its effect on intracellular cAMP levels has gained support from recent work of Kay, who found that while cAMP induced the synthesis of developmentally required enzymes in starving suspensions of amoebae, the addition of ammonia at physiological concentrations successfully antagonized this inductive effect [33]. There would, therefore, seem to be an antagonistic relationship between the levels of ammonia and cAMP that may play an important role in regulating development.

Signals inducing differentiation of specific cell types

An example of this third class of signalling substance is the dialysable factor that specifically induces stalk cells in the presence of cAMP [69, 70]. It was found that

although cAMP could induce stalk cell formation in monolayers of isolated cells, the number so induced was directly proportional to the population density. The more widely the cells were separated, the fewer stalk cells were formed. Using cellophane membranes to separate cell layers at different densities, Town and co-workers were able to show that cells at high density on one side of the membrane were able very efficiently to help cells at low density on the other side to develop into stalk cells in the presence of cAMP. The diffusible factor responsible has so far only been partially characterized, but from its sensitivity to glycosidases and lectin affinity, it appears to require the integrity of an oligosaccharide group that contains sialic acid, L-fucose and N-acetylgalactosamine [70].

The specific factor required for spore induction (again in the presence of cAMP) apparently differs from the stalk-specific factor in that it is not freely diffusible across cellophane membranes and can only act when cells are in close proximity to each other [34]. Unless it acts by very localized diffusion that is difficult to detect by the cellophane membrane technique, this signalling system may represent an entirely different system from those previously considered. It is possible that the signalling molecule in this case remains on the external surface of the cells producing it and has effects only on those cells immediately adjacent.

The problem of pattern formation in the multicellular aggregate

Once the cells come together in a mass, it becomes increasingly difficult to analyse signalling systems. This is regrettable because some of the most interesting features of development take place at this stage. Here we will consider the way in which a regular division of the slug occurs so that the ratio between the number of anterior prestalk cells and posterior prespore cells remains constant. But before we look for models of signalling mechanisms to account for this phenomenon, it is worth considering what is known about development of the migrating slug.

Using histochemical techniques, the cells initially appear uniform, but later the anterior cells become larger and have different staining properties [6]. If cells are stained with a vital dye before aggregation, they will first form uniformly coloured slugs which later, after a period of migration, turn darker at the anterior end and blanch at the posterior end. Furthermore, this difference, which can be revealed with vital dyes in living slugs, corresponds to the prespore and prestalk regions shown in the histological work.

Extensive studies have been done examining the proportion of stalk cells to spore cells [6]. These have involved a variety of different methods and they have been done both by measuring the final differentiated state and the prestalk and prespore cell in the slugs. It is, of course, possible to achieve a rather extraordinary range in size, since size depends upon the number of amoebae that enter an aggregate. The result of these painstaking experiments is that in all species examined there is a proportional relationship between the number of stalk and spore cells. In *Dictyostelium discoideum* the relation is not quite linear (it is allometric) although the percentage stalk or spore mass is roughly constant whether the slug consists of a few cells or hundreds of thousands of cells. This rule applies under normal growth conditions (but see below).

There is now compelling evidence that cells sort out and rearrange themselves within the slug; they do not keep to the positions which they occupy immediately after aggregation. We will not pursue here all the lines of evidence except to point out that Takeuchi showed in an early study that if he made antibodies to spores (by injecting spore suspensions into rabbits) and then he conjugated these antispore sera with a fluorescent compound, he could stain amoebae at different stages of development. Different amoebae contained different amounts of spore antigens before aggregation and, shortly after aggregation, *all* the cells with spore macromolecules ended up in the posterior (prespore) region, while the anterior (prestalk) region had nothing but cells without any fluorescence. This was so despite the fact that a short time previously, during aggregation, the cells that fluoresced were randomly distributed [8].

This type of result has been confirmed more recently by Garrod and Foreman using aggregates in the form of balls of cells in aerated buffer solutions (rather than on agar surfaces). Fluorescent antisera prepared against spores were found to show up in 'prespore vesicles' (structures formed by developing spores) in a random pattern initially, and only later did the fluorescence sort out into distinctly staining and non-staining areas [24].

Another experiment of interest in this connection is one that shows that the normally fixed proportion of stalk cells and spores can, in fact, be shifted by certain growth conditions. Garrod and Ashworth [23] showed using a mutant of *Dictyostelium* that can be grown axenically that if this is grown with excess glucose in the medium, there is a larger percentage of spores. They then mixed glucose-grown cells (which were marked with a radioactive label) and unmarked cells which were grown without glucose, and they found that the glucose-grown cells had a tendency to become spores and the cells grown in minimal medium to become stalk cells.

These are some of the observations; now we want to speculate on what kinds of signals could be operating in the cell mass to account for the proportional development of the spore and stalk cell regions. It is often a basic premise that there must be some kind of gradient inside the slug and that this gradient somehow ends up in two discontinuous regions, so regulated that their ratio is the same regardless of the size of the slug. One very obvious possibility is that the gradient is of some morphogen such as cAMP. There is some old evidence for a gradient of cAMP along the slug, although the data are of only an indirect nature [5]. For this reason, a number of laboratories have more recently attempted direct chemical methods of determining differences in the cAMP concentration in various regions of the slug. Their findings support the notion of a cAMP gradient with the highest concentration at the anterior, although the gradient is surprisingly shallow—the tip concentration being only 1.5 times the posterior level [10]. Measurements of the concentration of cell-type-specific inductive substances have not yet been reported.

A gradient is a method of signalling, of imparting spatial information, but before we examine that proposition, we must ask how a gradient could have arisen in the first place. There are at least three types of hypothesis (which are not mutually exclusive). Let us examine each briefly. The simplest notion would be that the tip is the former centre of the aggregate; it is initially the prime source of cAMP and it continues to maintain the dominant position. This hypothesis then is one of a pure concentration gradient of a particular morphogen. The second possibility is a variation of the first which considers the tip of the slug not so much the point of highest concentration of a morphogen, but a pacemaker region. Its dominance is due to its pacemaking ability, and the waves of morphogen production and destruction pass along the slug. Rubin and Robertson [63] favour such a model and believe that it can account for all the observed phenomena, including the division line between prestalk and prespore cells. Finally, one could speculate that the sorting out of the cells might itself be of key importance in setting up the gradient. One could assume that the pre-aggregation cells have a range of adhesive properties and they in some way sort out by 'differential adhesion', as proposed by Steinberg [68] for the mechanism of sorting-out in vertebrate embryos. The cells form a gradient and this gradient is not only one of adhesion between cells, but there could be numerous other gradients, including spore proteins, cAMP production, energy storage, and so forth, which could exist along the axis of the slug.

However, in any one of these hypotheses we have not said enough; we have not said precisely how a gradient turns into a fixed proportion of prestalk and prespore zones regardless of the size of the cell mass. To emphasize the importance of this, let us consider one more fact. Raper [8] showed many years ago that if a slug was cut into pieces, then each piece could eventually produce a normally proportioned, miniature fruiting body. This means that any portion of the slug, and of the gradient within the slug, is capable of giving the correct proportions. That is, it is capable of regulation. The spore macromolecules of Takeuchi, then, are not fixed, but reversible; one can isolate a part of a slug that normally would give all spores, and cause the prespore cells in the anterior end to turn into prestalk cells. The seemingly inescapable conclusion is that there must be some sort of polar signal that is sent forwards or backwards (or both) in the slug, that must carry information.

Unfortunately, we do not know what the nature of the signal might be. Again, we do have hypotheses. One is that the waves or pulses could, making various assumptions, manage to be such a signal. Another intriguing model has been devised by McMahon [47]. He suggests that each cell, which is known to be arranged in a polar fashion during aggregation, and therefore presumably in the slug, has a different set of enzymes at opposite ends. He assumed that at one end there might be enzymes which when activated by contact-sensing molecules on the cell surface would synthesize a morphogen, and at the other there could be similarly activated enzymes for destroying the morphogen. Again, making some further reasonable assumptions, he showed that the distribution of morphogen would soon become discontinuous in such a system—high in the anterior end and low in the posterior end—and that the boundary between the two

would be very sharp. Furthermore, the position of the boundary in the cell mass would depend on the size and shape of the whole mass, hence accounting for regulation. Finally, another model which is particularly attractive and which fits many of the known facts is the Gierer-Meinhardt reaction-diffusion model [43]. It will be of enormous importance to the problem of development in general to find out what the actual mechanism might be, for proportional development is the rule rather than the exception in the development of all organisms.

Not all the signals within the multicellular mass are merely concerned with the division between spore and stalk cell. There are innumerable other details of the shape of the final fruiting body that need signals in order for them to be perfectly achieved in the same fashion in successive generations. But, unfortunately, we know nothing of the mechanisms or the signals; they simply have not been investigated. Here are a few examples of the kind of controlled phenomena that need analysis: all the control mechanisms for the movements of the cells during stalk formation and the rising of the sorus into the air; the control mechanism for the deposit of the tapering stalk, not only its secretion by the prestalk cells, but also the control of its taper; the control of the formation of the basal disc. One could easily add to this list.

Signals between mating types: gamones

There is evidence that a sex hormone, or 'gamone', is produced by strains of one of the two *D. discoideum* mating types and stimulates macrocyst formation in strains of the other mating type [41, 56]. This relationship is not reciprocal in that the gamone is only formed by one of the strains involved. The system is therefore rather simpler than that of the water mould *Achlya* [58], where a sequential induction between the mating strains occurs. At the moment there is some conflicting evidence as to whether the gamone is dialysable and even volatile [38], and whether or not cells need to be in contact for the transmission of the effect. Although such studies are so far only at a preliminary stage, they do indicate the existence of another signalling system in the cellular slime moulds that has yet to be explored.

Signals between multicellular masses

If one examines the locations of centres of aggregation

on a culture dish, it is obvious that their distribution is non-random (Fig. 5.2.3). This can, furthermore, be verified by simple measurements of the distances to the nearest neighbours and by application of appropriate statistical tests. It turns out there are a number of reasons why there is a non-random distribution and all of the reasons involve signals in one form or another.

The simplest reason is that as aggregation chemotaxis begins so certain areas will soon have fewer amoebae than others, and in these sparse regions new centres are less likely to form. Here the signal is simply acrasin chemotaxis. This is undoubtedly related to instability phenomena which have been emphasized by Keller and Segal [35]. Because of changes in (i) the amount of acrasin secreted; (ii) the sensitivity to acrasin; and (iii) the change in rate of the random motility of the cells, a uniform distribution of acrasin-producing cells will break up into a series of hills and valleys and these will appear in some regular, non-random pattern.

Another factor which inhibits secondary centres from forming near the primary ones is the fact that if a centre is in a steep gradient of acrasin, it will disintegrate [8]. In other words, even if a centre did arise by accident in a zone close to another centre, it would be overruled.

It would seem that these mechanisms would be sufficient to assure non-random spacing of centres, but in fact there appears to be an additional special mechanism to assure non-random spacing. There is a considerable amount of evidence that a centre gives off a substance which inhibits other centres from forming in the near neighbourhood. In *Dictyostelium*, there is evidence that the substance is volatile, for if two layers of cells are opposed on agar surfaces separated by an air space, the centres from one surface will inhibit the centres on the opposite surface. The first suspicion was that the volatile signal might be CO_2, but Feit [21] repeated the experiment with the layers of cells at different ages and put the culture dishes both upside-down and right-side-up. That is, the advanced cells with their centres already established were either on the 'floor' of the culture dishes or on the 'ceiling'. The centre inhibition effect was very much greater when the older centres were on the 'floor'; clearly, the volatile substance was lighter than air and therefore could not be CO_2. Feit suggested it might be ammonia, and Lonski [39] has demonstrated in some detail that NH_3 will produce this effect in concentrations equivalent to those which the organism is known to produce.

There is the interesting related question of why such great pains should be taken to insure a non-random distribution of centres. One presumes that it is again closely related to the effectiveness of spore dispersal. Previously, we suggested that this might be the adaptive advantage of collective masses of spores borne on stalks, and now we are adding the suggestion that it is important to have the spore masses effectively spaced. It is possible to show some further signal-mediated controls which support this contention.

In very sparse populations of amoebae of *Dictyostelium,* where minute fruiting bodies are produced, there is no migration and, therefore, the location of a centre is also the location of a fruiting body. But in dense populations, the aggregation cell mass goes through a period of migration which can totally alter the pattern of distribution of cell masses and therefore the distribution of the fruiting bodies. The point has been made that the migrating slugs move towards light and heat, mechanisms which again must help in producing more effective dispersal by placing the cell masses in optimal positions. There is still another spacing mechanism operating by signals between cell masses that further ensures the optimal spacing of the spore masses (or sori) in the air. Its existence was first appreciated when two cell masses about to culminate (that is, rise into the air to form fruiting bodies) were pushed close together and it was noted that they tended to veer away from one another as they rose into the air. It was subsequently shown that the rising cell masses produce a volatile substance which repels any neighbouring cell mass. The evidence for this came from a series of observations, the most convincing of which was to place a small piece of activated charcoal near the cell mass, in which case the stalk would curve right over towards the charcoal. It is presumed that the charcoal actively absorbs the volatile repellent and, therefore, there is less of it on the charcoal side, which results in its movement toward the charcoal (Fig. 5.2.8). One result of this volatile signal is that the sori are kept far apart as they are raised above the substratum.

Besides the signalling between rising cell masses, this volatile repellent serves another important function. It is responsible for the orientation of the fruiting body with respect to the substratum. For many years it was a puzzle why very small fruiting bodies should always grow at right angles to the substratum, regardless of its orientation. The correct explanation appears to be that the highest concentration of the repellent is retained near the substratum. The repellent is diluted away from the substratum and the fruiting body therefore grows in this direction.

This idea can be tested a number of ways. If the cell mass is covered with mineral oil, fruiting will occur up into the oil, but the shape of the stalk will be utterly convoluted and disoriented. A cell mass can be placed at the bottom of a crack of agar or at the base of an agar cliff and, no matter what the location, the sorus will eventually lie mid-way between the walls. One can even put the cell mass on the edge of a right-angle agar cliff, and the stalk will jut out so that it is exactly 135° from the top and the side of the cliff (Fig. 5.2.9).

Nothing is known concerning the chemical nature of the volatile signal. Lonski (unpublished) made some analyses, using gas chromatography, of what substances are given off by culminating *Dictyostelium*, and he found (besides CO_2 and NH_3) ethane, ethanol, acetaldehyde, and ethylene. Any one of these could be active; this is an important project for future experiments.

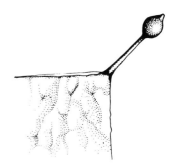

Fig. 5.2.9. A fruiting body of *Dictyostelium* rising on the edge of an agar block. (Drawing by K. Zachariah.)

5.2.3 CONCLUSIONS

The cellular slime moulds have many of the characteristics of the development of higher animals, and at the same time they have some very conspicuous advantages as experimental organisms. Development in general consists of a signalling system out of which comes a consistent pattern from one generation to the next. All the substances of the organism are ultimately produced by the DNA of the nucleus, but even in a spore which begins a generation, many of the proteins and, in fact, all the molecules and internal structure of the spore cell were manufactured in one of the preceding cycles. Each generation begins with at least a cell. This has an active nucleus and an active cytoplasmic metabolic machinery which is ready for and capable of the synthesis of all manner of substances as development unfolds. Development involves not only the synthesis of the proteins and the other substances, but also the timing of the synthesis and the spacing of the products of synthesis. Since the chemical reactions are mutually interdependent, that is the product of one may affect the outcome of another, the production, timing and spacing of the substances to produce an adult rely utterly upon the exchange of signals. In fact, as we have seen, the entire development of *Dictyostelium* can be analysed in terms of the signalling systems. These signals pass between parts of the cytoplasm of a cell, between cells, and even between cell masses. Furthermore, signals pass from any one of these levels to another so that all the levels are in constant communication. This means a remarkable variety of signals are involved in the development of even so simple an organism as *Dictyostelium*. But this intricate network of multilevel signals is precisely what

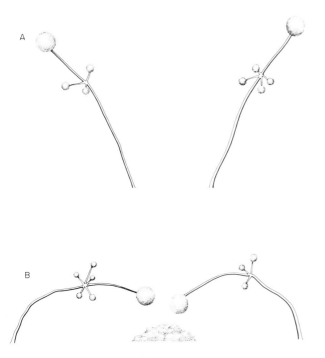

Fig. 5.2.8. A, Two fruiting bodies of *Polysphondylium pallidum* bending away from each other. B, Two similar fruiting bodies bending towards some activated charcoal. (After a drawing by R. Gillmor.)

produces consistent form from one generation to the next in a multicellular organism.

Note added in proof. The interested reader will find the following new book helpful as an up-to-date review of work on the cellular slime moulds: Loomis W.F., ed. (1982) *Development in Dictyostelium*. Academic Press, New York.

5.2.4 REFERENCES

*Indicates a review

1 Abe H., Uchiyama M., Tanaka Y. & Saito H. (1976) Structure of discadenine, a spore germination inhibitor from the cellular slime mold *Dictyostelium discoideum*. *Tetrahedron Lett.*, 1976, 3807–3810.

2 Alcântara F. & Monk M. (1974) Signal propagation during aggregation in the slime mould *Dictyostelium discoideum*. *J. gen. Microbiol.*, **85**, 321–334.

3 Beug H., Katz F.E. & Gerisch G. (1973) Dynamics of antigenic membrane sites relating to cell aggregation in *Dictyostelium discoideum*. *J. Cell Biol.*, **56**, 647–658.

4 Bonner J.T. (1947) Evidence for the formation of cell aggregates by chemotaxis in the development of the slime mold *Dictyostelium discoideum*. *J. exp. Zool.*, **106**, 1–26.

5 Bonner J.T. (1949) The demonstration of acrasin in the later stages of the development of the slime mold *Dictyostelium discoideum*. *J. exp. Zool.*, **110**, 259–271.

* 6 Bonner J.T. (1967) *The Cellular Slime Molds*, 2nd edn. Princeton University Press, Princeton, New Jersey.

7 Bonner J.T. (1970) Induction of stalk cell differentiation by cyclic AMP in the cellular slime mold *Dictyostelium discoideum*. *Proc. natl Acad. Sci., USA*, **65**, 110–113.

* 8 Bonner J.T. (1971) Aggregation and differentiation in the cellular slime molds. *A. Rev. Microbiol.*, **25**, 75–92.

* 9 Bonner J.T. (1977) Some aspects of chemotaxis using the cellular slime molds as an example. *Mycologia*, **69**, 443–159.

10 Brenner M. (1977) Cyclic AMP gradient in migrating pseudoplasmodia of the cellular slime mold *Dictyostelium discoideum*. *J. biol. Chem.*, **252**, 4073–4077.

11 Chia W.K. (1975) Induction of stalk cell differentiation by cyclic AMP in a susceptible variant of *Dictyostelium discoideum*. *Devl. Biol.*, **44**, 239–252.

12 Clark M.A., Francis D. & Eisenberg R. (1973) Mating types in cellular slime molds. *Biochem. biophys. Res. Commun.*, **52**, 672–678.

13 Cohen M.H. & Robertson A. (1971) Wave propagation in the early stages of aggregation of cellular slime molds. *J. Theor. Biol.*, **31**, 101–118.

14 Cotter D.A. & Raper K.B. (1966) Spore germination in *Dictyostelium discoideum*. *Proc. natl Acad. Sci., USA*, **56**, 880–887.

15 Darmon M., Barra J. & Brachet P. (1978) The rule of phosphodiesterase in aggregation of *Dictyostelium discoideum*. *J. Cell Sci.*, **31**, 233–243.

16 Darmon M., Barrand P., Brachet P., Klein C. & Pereira da Silva L. (1977) Phenotypic suppression of morphogenetic mutants of *Dictyostelium discoideum*. *Devl. Biol.*, **58**, 174–184.

17 Darmon M., Brachet P. & Pereira da Silva L.H. (1975) Chemotactic signals induce cell differentiation in *Dictyostelium discoideum*. *Proc. natl Acad. Sci., USA*, **72**, 3163–3166.

18 Devreotes P.N., Derstine P.L. & Steck T. (1979) Cyclic AMP relay in *Dictyostelium discoideum*. 1. A technique to monitor responses to controlled stimuli. *J. Cell Biol.*, **80**, 291–299.

19 Devreotes P.N. & Steck T.L. (1979) Cyclic AMP relay in *Dictyostelium discoideum*. 2. Requirements for the initiation and termination of the response. *J. Cell Biol.*, **80**, 300–309.

20 Erdos G.W., Raper K.B. & Vogen L.K. (1975) Sexuality in the cellular slime mold *Dictyostelium giganteum*. *Proc. natl Acad. Sci., USA*, **72**, 970–973.

21 Feit I.N. (1969) Unpublished Ph.D. thesis, Princeton University.

22 Filosa M.F. & Dengler R.E. (1972) Ultrastructure of macrocyst formation in the cellular slime mold *Dictyostelium mucoroides*. *Devl. Biol.*, **29**, 1–16.

*23 Garrod D. & Ashworth J.M. (1973) Development of the cellular slime mold *Dictyostelium discoideum*. In *Microbial Differentiation* (Eds J.M. Ashworth & J.E. Smith), *Symp. Soc. Gen. Microbiol.*, **23**, 407–435.

24 Garrod D.R. & Forman D. (1977) Pattern formation in the absence of polarity in *Dictyostelium discoideum*. *Nature, Lond.*, **265**, 144–146.

25 Gerisch G. & Hess B. (1974) Cyclic AMP controlled oscillations in suspended *Dictyostelium* cells: Their relation of morphogenetic cell interactions. *Proc. natl Acad. Sci., USA*, **71**, 2118–2122.

26 Gerisch G., Fromm H., Huesgen A. & Wick U. (1975) Control of cell-contact sites by cAMP pulses in differentiating *Dictyostelium* cells. *Nature, Lond.*, **255**, 547–549.

27 Gerisch G. & Wick U. (1975) Intracellular oscillations and release of cyclic AMP from *Dictyostelium* cells. *Biochem. biophys. Res. Commun.*, **65**, 364–370.

28 Gingle A.R. & Robertson A. (1976) The development of the relaying competence in *Dictyostelium discoideum*. *J. Cell Sci.*, **20**, 21–27.

*29 Goy M.F. & Springer M.S. (1978) In search of the linkage between receptor and response: The role of a protein methylation reaction in bacterial chemotaxis. In *Taxis and Behaviour, Receptors and Recognition, Series B* (Ed. G.L. Hazelbauer), **5**, 1–34.

30 Green A.A. & Newell P.C. (1975) Evidence for the existence of two types of cAMP binding sites in aggregating cells of *Dictyostelium discoideum*. *Cell*, **6**, 129–136.

31 Gross J.D., Peacey M.J. & Trevan D.J. (1976) Signal emission and signal propagation during early aggregation in *Dictyostelium discoideum*. *J. Cell Sci.*, **22**, 645–656.

32 Grutsch J.F. & Robertson A. (1978) The cAMP signal from *Dictyostelium discoideum* amoebae. *Devl. Biol.*, **66**, 285–293.

33 Kay R.R. (1979) Gene expression in *Dictyostelium discoideum*: mutually antagonistic roles of cAMP and ammonia. *J. Embryol. exp. Morph*, **52**, 171–182.

34 Kay R.R., Garrod D. & Tilly R. (1978) Requirement for cell differentiation in *Dictyostelium discoideum*. *Nature, Lond.*, **271**, 58–60.

35 Keller E.F. & Segal L.A. (1970) Initiation of slime mold aggre-

gation viewed as an instability. *J. theor. Biol.*, **26**, 399–415.

36 Klein C. & Darmon M. (1977) Effects of cAMP pulses on adenylate cyclase and the phosphodiesterase inhibitor of *Dictyostelium discoideum*. *Nature, Lond.*, **268**, 76–78.

37 Klein C. & Juliani M.H. (1977) cAMP-induced changes in cAMP binding sites on *Dictyostelium discoideum* amoebae. *Cell*, **10**, 329–335.

38 Lewis K.E. & O'Day D.H. (1977) Sex hormone of *Dictyostelium discoideum* is volatile. *Nature, Lond.*, **268**, 730–731.

39 Lonski J. (1976) The effect of ammonia on fruiting body size and microcyst formation in the cellular slime molds. *Devl. Biol.*, **51**, 158–165.

*40 Loomis W.F. (1975) *Dictyostelium discoideum: A developmental system*. Academic Press, New York.

41 Machac M.A. & Bonner J.T. (1975) Evidence for a sex hormone in *Dictyostelium discoideum*. *J. Bacteriol.*, **24**, 1624–1625.

42 MacInnes M.A. & Francis D. (1974) Meiosis in *Dictyostelium mucoroides*. *Nature, Lond.*, **251**, 321–324.

*43 MacWilliams H.K. & Bonner J.T. (1979) The prestalk–prespore pattern in cellular slime molds. *Differentiation*, **14**, 1–22.

44 Malchow D. & Gerisch G. (1974) Short-term binding and hydrolysis of cAMP by aggregating *Dictyostelium* cells. *Proc. natl Acad. Sci., USA*, **71**, 2423–2427.

45 Malchow D., Nagele B., Schwarz H. & Gerisch G. (1972) Membrane bound cAMP phosphodiesterase in chemotactically responding cells of *Dictyostelium discoideum*. *Eur. J. Biochem.*, **28**, 136–142.

46 Mato J.M., Krens F.A., van Haastert P.J.M. & Konijn T.M. (1977) cAMP-dependent cyclic GMP accumulation in *Dictyostelium discoideum*. *Proc. natl Acad. Sci., USA*, **74**, 2348–2351.

47 McMahon D. (1973) A cell-contact model for cellular position determination in development. *Proc. natl Acad. Sci., USA*, **70**, 2396–2400.

48 Mockrin S.C. & Spudich J.A. (1976) Calcium control of actin-activated myosin adenosine triphosphatase from *Dictyostelium discoideum*. *Proc. natl Acad. Sci., USA*, **73**, 2321–2325.

49 Mullens I.A. & Newell P.C. (1978) cAMP binding to cell surface receptors of *Dictyostelium*. *Differentiation*, **10**, 171–176.

*50 Nelson D.L. & Kung C. (1978) Behaviour of *Paramecium*: chemical, physiological and genetic studies. In *Receptors and Recognition, Series B* (Ed. G.L. Hazelbauer), **5**, 75–100. Chapman & Hall, London.

*51 Newell P.C. (1971) The development of the cellular slime mold *Dictyostelium discoideum*: A model system for the study of cellular differentiation. In *Essays in Biochemistry* (Eds P.N. Campbell & F. Dickens), **7**, 87–126. Academic Press, New York and London.

*52 Newell P.C. (1978) Cellular communication during aggregation of *Dictyostelium*. The Second Fleming Lecture. *J. gen. Microbiol.*, **104**, 1–13.

*53 Newell P.C. (1978) Genetics of the cellular slime molds. *A. Rev. Genet.*, **12**, 69–93.

54 Newell P.C. & Sussman M. (1970) Regulation of enzyme synthesis by slime mold cell assemblies embarked upon alternative developmental programs. *J. molec. Biol.*, **49**, 627–637.

55 Newell P.C., Telser A. & Sussman M. (1969) Alternative developmental pathways determined by environmental conditions in the cellular slime mold. *J. Bact.*, **100**, 763–768.

56 O'Day D.H. & Lewis K.E. (1975) Diffusible mating-type factors induce macrocyst development in *Dictyostelium discoideum*. *Nature, Lond.*, **754**, 431–432.

57 Pannbacker R.G. & Bravard L.J. (1972) Phosphodiesterase in *Dictyostelium discoideum* and the chemotactic response to cAMP. *Science, N.Y.*, **175**, 1014–1015.

58 Raper J.R. (1951) Sexual hormones in *Achlya*. *Am. Scient.*, **39**, 110–120.

59 Robertson A., Drage D.J. & Cohen M.H. (1972) Control of aggregation in *Dictyostelium discoideum* by an external periodic pulse of cAMP. *Science, N.Y.*, **175**, 333–335.

60 Roos W. & Gerisch G. (1976) Receptor mediated adenylate cyclase in *Dictyostelium discoideum*. *F.E.B.S. Letters*, **68**, 170–172.

61 Roos W., Scheidegger C. & Gerisch G. (1977) Adenylate cyclase activity oscillations as signals for cell-aggregation in *Dictyostelium discoideum*. *Nature, Lond.*, **266**, 259–261.

62 Ross F.M. & Newell P.C. (1981) Streamers: Chemotactic mutants of *Dictyostelium discoideum* with altered cyclic GMP metabolism. *J. Gen. Microbiol*, **127**, 339–350.

63 Rubin J. & Robertson A. (1975) Tip of *Dictyostelium discoideum* pseudoplasmodium as an organiser. *J. Embryol. exp. Morph.*, **33**, 227–241.

64 Schindler J. & Sussman M. (1977) Ammonia determines choice of morphogenetic pathways in *Dictyostelium discoideum*. *J. molec. Biol.*, **116**, 161–169.

65 Schindler J. & Sussman M. (1979) Inhibition by ammonia of cAMP accumulation in *Dictyostelium discoideum*. Its significance for the regulation of morphogenesis. *Dev. Genet.*, **1**, 13–20.

66 Shaffer B.M. (1957) Aspects of aggregation in cellular slime molds. *Am. Nat.*, **91**, 19–35.

67 Shaffer B.M. (1962) The Acrasina. *Adv. Morphogen.*, **2**, 109–182; (1964) **3**, 301–322.

68 Steinberg M.S. (1970) Does differential adhesion govern self-assembly processes in histogenesis? Equilibrium configurations and the emergence of a hierarchy among populations of embryonic cells. *J. exp. Zool.*, **173**, 395–434.

69 Town C., Gross J. & Kay R. (1976) Cell differentiation without morphogenesis in *Dictyostelium discoideum*. *Nature, Lond.*, **262**, 717–719.

70 Town C. & Stanford E. (1979) An oligosaccharide-containing factor that induces differentiation in *Dictyostelium discoideum*. *Proc. natl Acad. Sci., USA*, **76**, 308–312.

71 Tsang A.S. & Coukell M.B. (1977) The regulation of cAMP phosphodiesterase and its specific inhibition by cAMP in *Dictyostelium*. *Cell Differ.*, **6**, 75–84.

72 Wick U., Malchow D. & Gerisch G. (1978) cAMP stimulated calcium influx into aggregating cells of *Dictyostelium discoideum*. *Cell Biol. Int. Rep.*, **2**, 71–79.

73 Wurster B., Schubiger K., Wick U. & Gerisch G. (1977) Cyclic GMP in *Dictyostelium*: Oscillations and pulses in response to folic acid and cAMP signals. *F.E.B.S. Letters*, **76**, 141–44.

74 Yeh R.P., Chan F.K. & Coukell M.B. (1978) Independent regulation of the extra-cellular cAMP phosphodiesterase inhibitor system and membrane differentiation by exogenous cAMP in *Dictyostelium discoideum*. *Devl. Biol.*, **66**, 361–374.

Chapter 5.3
Hormones and Plant Development: Cellular and Molecular Aspects
M.A. Hall

5.3.1   INTRODUCTION

In considering the hormonal control of growth and differentiation in plants, it is necessary to distinguish control at the cell and tissue levels from that at the whole-plant level of organization. At the whole-plant level, hormonal control is largely concerned with the overall coordination of the growth of several potential meristematic regions, including the vascular cambium, axillary buds and lateral roots, and developing flowers, fruits and storage organs. Some general aspects of control within the whole plant will be considered in the following chapter. In the present chapter we are primarily concerned with hormonal control at the cell, tissue and molecular levels, in both growth and differentiation. Growth substances are essential for both cell division and cell enlargement and we shall discuss some aspects of their roles in these processes.

The possible roles of growth substances in differentiation presents a more difficult problem and a major issue is whether growth substances control the pattern of differentiation or whether they simply permit the expression of cell differences which are already established as states of determination. Representatives of the five main groups of plant growth substances are shown in Table 5.3.1, along with an abridged list of their effects. Since each class of growth substance evokes a wide variety of responses in different parts of the plant, it would appear that, in general, the pattern of response must depend upon the pre-programming of the different organs and tissues of the plant and not on the growth substances themselves. However, in considering hormone responses at the whole-plant level we are dealing with responses by established, organized target tissues and organs of various types, whereas the point at issue here is whether or not growth substances control the establishment of cell and tissue differences in cells which previously were uncommitted.

Evidence was presented in Chapter 2.5 that the meristematic cells can be determined, and that the expression of a state of determination normally occurs during cell enlargement and maturation, but can be delayed until a later stage in target cells, and is still retained in mature, differentiated cells showing biochemical differentiation'. Hormones are evidently involved in the expression of differentiation, not only in cells undergoing enlargement but also in target cells, as in the abscission layer (in response to ethylene) or the barley aleurone layer (in response to gibberellin).

In the present chapter we shall consider first the evidence that hormones may regulate the pattern of differentiation in uncommitted (undetermined) cells. In approaching this problem, it seems appropriate first to consider hormonal effects on systems whose future pattern of differentiation might be expected to be least determined—namely meristematic tissue or callus which has undergone a degree of de-differentiation.

In the second part of the chapter, we shall consider

Table 5.3.1. Involvement of hormones in plant growth and development. A tick indicates that the hormone in question has been shown to affect the process in some way, although not necessarily in all instances.

Type of hormone (showing a representative example of each class)		Cell elongation	Cell division	Induction of primary vascular tissue	Induction of secondary vascular tissue	Root and shoot initiation	Breaking of seed dormancy	Senescence	Abscission of flowers fruits and leaves	Fruit growth	Sex expression	Control of stomatal aperture
Auxins Indole-3-acetic acid (IAA)		✓	✓	✓	✓	✓	✓	✓	✓	✓	✓	
Gibberelins Gibberellic acid (GA₃)		✓	✓		✓	✓	✓	✓	✓	✓	✓	
Cytokinins Zeatin			✓	✓	✓	✓	✓	✓	✓	✓		✓
Inhibitors Absciscic acid (ABA)		✓					✓	✓	✓	✓		✓
Ethylene		✓	✓			✓	✓	✓	✓	✓	✓	

certain molecular aspects of hormone action, including (a) the evidence for hormone receptors in plants, (b) the mode of action of IAA in stimulating cell enlargement, and (c) the mode of action of gibberellic acid in stimulating the production of an enzyme, α-amylase, in an already differentiated tissue, the aleurone layer of the barley grain.

The treatment given in this chapter is necessarily brief but several comprehensive surveys of the whole range of hormonal effects in plants are to be found in the literature [1, 13, 14, 25, 27].

5.3.2 ROOT AND SHOOT INITIATION

Shortly after the recognition of kinetin as a growth-regulating substance involved in the control of cell division in tobacco stem callus cultures, Skoog and Miller [21] discovered that, in the same type of culture, manipulation of the ratio of auxin to kinetin in the growth medium resulted in different patterns of development. If both auxin and kinetin levels were high or low, the cultures grew as amorphous, undifferentiated masses of callus. On the other hand, a high auxin/

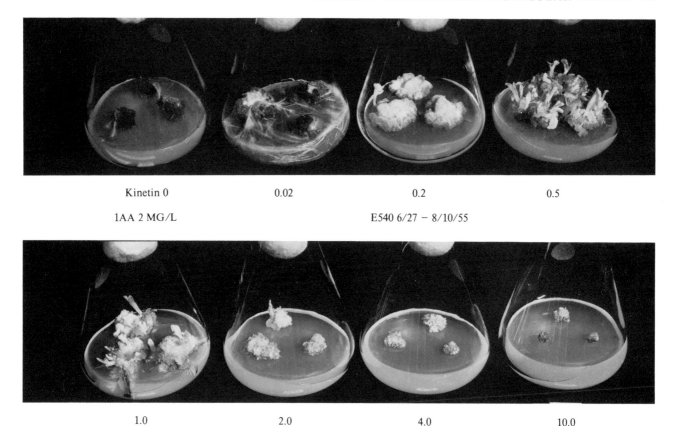

Kinetin 0   0.02   0.2   0.5

1AA 2 MG/L   E540 6/27 − 8/10/55

1.0   2.0   4.0   10.0

Fig. 5.3.1. Effect of indole-3-acetic acid (IAA) and kinetin on growth and organ formation in 44-day-old tobacco callus culture grown on nutrient agar. A range of concentrations of kinetin were used by all cultures contained IAA at a concentration of $2\,mg\,l^{-1}$. Reprinted from *Symp. Soc. exp. Biol.*, **11**, (1957). Photograph kindly supplied by Professor F. Skoog.

kinetin ratio led to the induction of roots in the callus, and a low ratio caused shoots to be produced (Fig. 5.3.1). Since the cells of such cultures are apparently identical and may be diverted into either of two different pathways of development merely by altering the ratio of one hormone to another, it seems likely that, in this case at least, the hormones themselves alone determine the pattern. Of course, Skoog and Miller also found that root and shoot initiation could be modified by other substances, such as sugars and amino acids, in association with particular hormonal concentrations, but these effects were quantitative rather than qualitative.

A somewhat analogous situation has been observed in the regeneration of roots and shoots from segments of *Taraxacum* and *Cichorium* rhizomes. In these experiments, wherever the segments were cut, meristematic areas were initiated and these differentiated pre-dominantly into roots or shoots depending on whether they appeared on the morphologically lower or upper ends respectively. Here again is an example of morphologically identical tissues entering different developmental pathways depending on their position in relation to the cut.

This early work also showed that endogenous auxins tended to accumulate at the morphologically lower ends of the tissue and further that the treatment of the segments with indole-butyric acid (a synthetic auxin) led to initiation of roots at both ends. Later, Vardjan and Nitsch [23] investigated the same system and showed that although the changes in auxins and cytokinins after cutting were complex, nevertheless the alterations in their levels were such that a much higher auxin/cytokinin ratio occurred in the lower ends than in the upper ends of the cuttings (Fig. 5.3.2). The observed

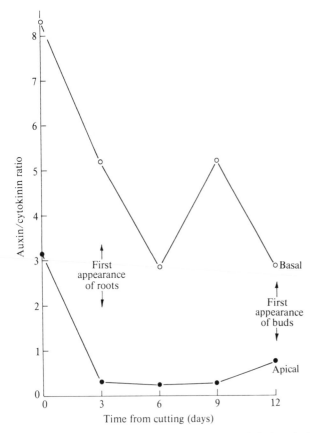

Fig. 5.3.2. Quantitative variations in auxin/cytokinin ratio in the apical and basal zones of *Cichorium* root cuttings during regeneration of roots and shoots. Adapted from J.P. Nitsch (1967) In *Wachstums Regulatoren bei Pflanzen*, Rostock.

redistribution of auxins and cytokinins in this system reflects what we know about the transport of these substances about the plant. Thus plant tissue usually shows a basipetal polarity with respect to auxins (that is, movement is predominantly from the apex towards the base), whereas cytokinins—which appear to be principally synthesized in root tissue—move in the opposite direction.

5.3.3 INDUCTION OF VASCULAR TISSUE

In callus

It has been known for some time that hormones are involved in the induction of vascular tissue. Thus, both

Camus, and Wetmore and Sorokin, showed that grafting a bud into *Syringa* callus tissue led to the formation of xylem in the callus (Fig. 5.3.3). Later, Wetmore and Rier [26] demonstrated that the same effect could be achieved by application of auxin and sucrose at discrete points in the callus, suggesting that these were the factors transmitted by the bud which are responsible for vascularization. In both systems the pattern of development was similar, that is, nodules of actively dividing cells were initiated at fairly precise but different distances from the bud or point of auxin/sucrose application; in addition, a few nodules always flanked the cuts themselves. It is significant that variations in the absolute amounts of auxin and sucrose and their relative concentrations markedly affected the induction of nodules and their subsequent pattern of development.

Variation of IAA concentration above 2.9×10^{-7}M did not appear to affect the type of differentiation, but whereas at all concentrations a ring of nodules appeared, the diameter of this ring increased with increasing concentration. Since *Syringa* callus does not show polar transport of auxins, the point at which differentiation occurs is presumably related to a specific auxin concentration; indeed, similar subsequent work

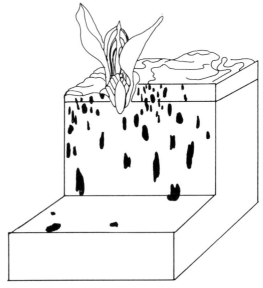

Fig. 5.3.3 Induction of vascular tissue in *Syringa* callus. An apex of *Syringa* bearing two to three leaf primordia was grafted into a block of callus. After 54 days the block was sectioned. Vascular regeneration is shown by dark bands. From R.H. Wetmore & S. Sorokin (1955) *J. Arnold Arboretum*, **36.**

by Jeffs and Northcote [11] showed that both auxin and sugar moved along diffusion gradients in callus and that the concentrations of auxin and sucrose at which differentiation occurred in *Phaseolus vulgaris* callus were 1.4×10^{-7}M and 2.2×10^{-2}M respectively. In all cases phloem forms to the outside of the xylem, which many workers have taken to mean that a lower concentration of IAA favours phloem induction. In addition, sugar concentration appears to determine the pattern of development. Extensive differentiation of both xylem and phloem occurs at 5.8×10^{-2}M sucrose, with lower concentration of sugar favouring xylem differentiatin and higher concentration favouring phloem. Where, instead of an agar block, micropipettes containing sugar and auxin were inserted into *Syringa* callus blocks, a continuous ring of xylem and phloem separated by an organized meristem was produced (Fig. 5.3.4).

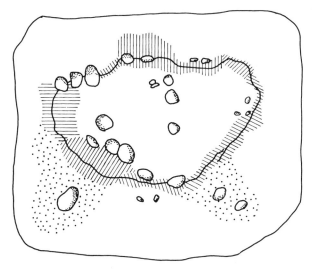

Fig. 5.3.4. Diagrammatic interpretation of a transverse section through a block of *Syringa* callus taken 450 μm below the point of application of an agar block containing 4% sucrose and 0.5 mg l^{-1} NAA (naphthalene acetic acid) after 54 days. Nodules are represented by irregular small circles, the cambium by a black line and cellular regions laid down by cambial activity by radially placed parallel lines. Areas of haphazard mitotic activity are shown by stippling. From R.H. Wetmore & J.P. Rier (1963) *Amer. J. Bot,* **50**.

Thus, as in root and shoot initiation, here is a situation where the pattern of a cell's development appears to be controlled solely by the effect of two extrinsic factors. Also, since the same cells will either remain as undifferentiated callus or become meristematic and later develop into phloem or xylem, it seems unlikely that they are predetermined to respond in a specific way. Other growth regulators can also influence the pattern of development in callus cultures. Thus cytokinins can increase the number of tracheary elements and the extent of lignin production in several different types of callus. This appears to be due, at least in part, to a stimulating effect of the hormone on the activity of the enzyme phenylalanine ammonia lyase, leading to increased availability of phenylpropanoid lignin precursors. Both ABA and GA$_3$ may inhibit such cytokinin-stimulated xylogenesis.

It should be noted that in the type of experiment just described, the xylem tissue which is formed is abnormal in that the cells are isodiametric. It has been suggested that this is due to the fact that in the growing plant the apical region (probably the main source of auxin for the uppermost internode) is constantly moving away from any one point in the stem, so that any given cell behind it will receive a gradually decreasing amount of auxin. Since the optimal auxin concentration for elongation is usually much higher than that for vascularization, we would expect the former process to occur nearer to the apex than the latter. Indeed, in experiments with callus where micropipettes containing auxin are inserted in the tissue, some cell elongation does occur near the point of insertion. Such findings demonstrate that in the intact plant there is a carefully defined developmental sequence depending on auxin concentration, namely, elongation followed by vascularization, which is achieved, at least in part, by having a moving source of auxin production. It should be noted, however, that these conclusions are not necessarily valid in woody plants both because nearly isodiametric ray cells may develop into tracheids in such plants and also because free IAA levels in association with differentiating xylem in conifers are several fold higher than those reported in other tissues or organs [19].

Because of the important role played by sugar in vascular induction, Jeffs and Northcote have investigated the effect of different sugars upon this process in *Phaseolus* callus. They were able to show that, of the 15 sugars tested, only sucrose, trehalose and maltose induced organized nodules and xylem and, of the remainder, only cellobiose, lactose, glucose and fructose, and the last two combined, produced xylem but not nodules. Sucrose does not therefore appear to be necessary merely as an energy source—glucose would be just as effective in this respect and certainly it can replace sucrose as the energy source in maintaining callus cultures. Further, there appears to be a requirement for a specific glycosidic configuration in that sucrose, trehalose and maltose have an α-glucosyl residue at the non-reducing end. Such specificity would imply an interaction with a specific binding site. Torrey has noted a similar dependence on sucrose for the induction of xylem strands in roots.

In intact plants

It seems logical to continue this discussion with a consideration of vascular regeneration or induction in an intact plant, since it does not follow that these processes show the same characteristics there as in undifferentiated callus. The pattern of vascular development in any one higher plant may differ very substantially from that in another. Can this development of pattern be controlled solely by the hormone system, or do other systems of organization take part? It is inappropriate to deal extensively with this question here except insofar as it relates to the question of the extent to which hormones are determining development, and we must take this to include not only the qualitative nature of the tissue produced but also the pattern in which it becomes arranged.

It has been known for some time that IAA is an important factor in the regeneration of vascular bundles after wounding. Thus, Jacobs showed that removal of young leaves above a wound inhibited xylem regeneration but that supplying IAA to the petiole of such an excised leaf overcame this effect. LaMotte and Jacobs later showed that similar systems were operative for phloem regeneration (the pattern of this type of regeneration is shown in Fig. 5.3.5).

Further studies by Jacobs and his collaborators [7, 8], mainly using *Coleus* tissue, showed that there was also an excellent correlation between the rate of normal xylem and phloem differentiation and the rate of auxin production by the leaf which that vascular strand would serve. These workers also demonstrated that, in addition to the normal basipetal development, some development of xylem strands occurred acropetally (i.e. towards the apex) from the next lower internode and this is in agreement with their demonstration of a small acropetal movement of auxin in *Coleus*. It was also observed that the developing basipetal and acropetal

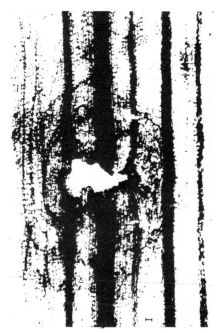

Fig. 5.3.5. Phloem regeneration around a wound made seven days earlier in one side of an internode of *Coleus blumei*. The wound (centre, triangular-shaped light area) severed three phloem bundles. Photograph kindly supplied by Dr C.W. LaMotte.

strands did not always meet directly but usually ceased development as they reached the same level, at which point the intervening parenchyma cells differentiated into xylem elements, thus joining the two strands (Fig. 5.3.6). In addition, it was found that parenchyma cells required approximately ten times more auxin in order to differentiate into xylem elements during regeneration experiments than did procambial tissue in normal development. It is suggested that this provides a mechanism for the selection of which cells will vascularize, in that only where a localized increase in auxin concentration occurs—for example due to the interruption of normal translocation by wounding—will cortical tissue differentiate into xylem. The formation of bridges between basipetally and acropetally developing strands can be explained in the same way if these strands are transporting auxin, as Jacobs suggests.

It is interesting to compare this work with that of Sachs [17, 18], who has studied the effect of IAA upon the induction of vascular tissue in pea plants. Using a variety of elegant surgical techniques, he was able to show that vascular strands from buds connected preferentially to other xylem strands from buds which were previously removed. He demonstrated a similar effect in roots with differential application of auxin apically and laterally. Thus where vascular strands were induced to form by a lateral application of auxin, these joined the vascular cylinder at a wide angle if the latter was not supplied with the auxin and at an acute angle if it was so supplied (Fig. 5.3.7). In other words, vascular strands well supplied with auxin tend to repel other strands whilst those deficient in auxin tend to attract them. This observation would account, at least in part, for the patterns of vascular arrangement which may be observed. For example, it would explain the presence of leaf gaps in the primary body as being due to inhibition

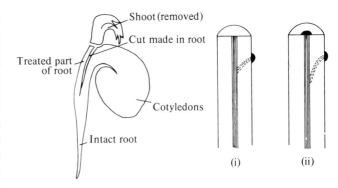

Fig. 5.3.7. Experimental induction of xylem by auxin in pea roots. Left. Diagram of three-day-old pea seedlings showed the cuts made to separate the part of the root used for experiments. Right. Treated in face view. (i) Auxin applied laterally only. (ii) Auxin applied laterally and at the apex. The dotted line shows newly formed xylem. From T. Sachs (1968) *Ann. Bot.*, **32.**

by the leaf strands of a basipetally developing vascular strand within the stem, which would be well supplied with auxin during leaf expansion (see Fig. 5.3.8). Sachs also showed that repulsion of an induced strand by another strand well supplied with auxin only occurred if the latter was supplied with a higher concentration of auxin than the former, suggesting that repulsion was not due to a supra-optimal concentration of auxin in the vicinity of the main strand. He explains repulsion by supposing that vascular elements well supplied with auxin induce longitudinal polarity in the tissue adjacent

Fig. 5.3.6. Longitudinal section through a stem of *Coleus blumei* showing acropetally (A) and basipetally (B) developing vascular strands joined by vascularized parenchyma tissue (C). From C.E. LaMotte & W.P. Jacobs (1962) *Stain Technol.*, **27,** 63–73. Photograph kindly supplied by Dr C.E. LaMotte.

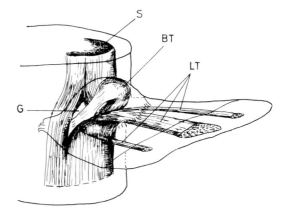

Fig. 5.3.8. Diagram of nodal region of *Phlox* showing stele (S), bud trace (BT), leaf traces (LT) and leaf gap (G). After Miller & Wetmore from Eames & McDaniels (1947) *An Introduction to Plant Anatomy*, 2nd edn. McGraw-Hill.

to them, so that auxin in a neighbouring induced strand cannot pass at right angles through such cells and cause xylem formation by so doing. 'Attraction' is explained in an analogous fashion by auxin-deficient vascular tissue acting as a sink for auxin from an attached strand.

Sachs integrates his findings in a general hypothesis suggesting that, once formed, vascular tissue offers a preferred pathway for the movement of the inducing stimulus; this is another way of saying that the tissue becomes polarized, at least with respect to auxin transport. He further suggests that this polarity can be imposed on adjacent tissues.

The mechanism whereby growth regulators initiate cell division and subsequent differentiation are obscure. A number of workers have reported stimulatory effects of auxin, cytokinin and other growth regulators upon DNA synthesis in tissues or tissue cultures where the hormones initiate cell division and subsequent vascularization; in many cases, hormone treatment results in polyploid cells.

Considerable controversy surrounds the question of whether cell division need necessarily precede the formation of tracheary elements. This question is unresolved but it has been suggested that the stage of the cell cycle at which hormone treatment is given determines whether a cell will develop directly into a tracheary element or whether cell division will be necessary [3].

We can summarize the work described in this section by observing that auxin may be a limiting factor in the induction of vascular tissue in both callus tissue and in higher plants. However, whereas in callus the auxin clearly determines the site of vascular induction and appears to influence (in association with sucrose) the type of tissue formed, in the intact plant constraints are imposed on the locus of induction. These constraints appear to derive partly from the nature of the cells themselves and partly from their polarity and the polarity of adjacent tissues.

It should also be noted that here, as in callus, other growth regulators (particularly cytokinins and gibberellins) may be involved in phloem and xylem differentiation.

5.3.4 INDUCTION OF SECONDARY THICKENING

We have so far only considered the role of hormones in the control of primary tissue formation, but it is now well established that these substances are involved in the formation of secondary tissues, in particular secondary vascular tissue.

It has long been known that the appearance of developing buds on deciduous trees in the spring is accompanied by the onset of cambial division in the trunk and differentiation of the cells produced by this cambial activity. This observation, together with work indicating that developing buds are rich sources of hormones, led a number of workers to suggest that these substances were involved in the initiation of cambial activity. The work of Wareing et al. [24] on this subject showed that apical application of hormone mixtures to disbudded shoots of Acer pseudoplatanus led to cambial division and the differentiation of xylem and phloem. When IAA was applied alone, isolated areas of xylem differentiation were observed. With gibberellic acid alone, there was extensive division internal to the cambium but the newly formed tissue did not differentiate. The effect of the two hormones applied together was to cause extensive cambial division and differentiation into xylem elements. Some division also occurred to the outside of the cambium with this treatment (Fig. 5.3.9). Further studies with IAA and GA_3, alone or in different combinations, indicated that both hormones were required for normal development of xylem and phloem but that little or no phloem differentiation occurred with IAA alone and vice versa for xylem and GA_3. Similar observations were made with herbaceous plants. Cytokinins also appear to play a role in secondary thickening since they can enhance both xylem and phloem differentiation in conifers.

Clearly these results resemble many of the findings on the induction of primary vascular tissues, and it seems that, in the main, hormonal application leads both to cambial division and to determination of the cambial derivatives, whether we are considering primary or secondary vascular tissue formation. Nevertheless, whereas in callus tissue hormone treatment not only stimulates cambial division but also initiates the cambium itself, in secondary thickening we are often dealing with a pre-existent cambial zone, and the different aspects introduced by this additional factor are well illustrated by the work of Siebers [20] with hypocotyl tissue of Rincinus communis.

These studies showed that when blocks of interfascicular tissue were removed from the hypocotyls and then replaced in the inverse direction not only did the interfascicular cambium form in the same layer of cells but, furthermore, its derivatives differentiated into xylem on the outside and phloem on the inside (Fig. 5.3.10). Plugs of pith parenchyma inserted in place of interfascicular tissue only showed differentiation, and then to a very slight extent, when the outer cells of the graft had formed wound tissue, i.e. when they had de-differentiated to some extent. Siebers' conclusion, which seems inescapable, is that the cells in which the interfascicular cambium will arise are already determined at the stage of formation of the primary meristem ring, not only in their position but also in the fate of the products of that division—that is, they exhibit a radial polarity.

Although space does not permit discussion of other work on this subject it is important to realize that normal development appears to depend on a very complex interaction of factors and that the whole range of plant hormones, as well as sucrose and other sugars, appear to play significant determinative roles (cf. Table 5.3.1). It is not yet clear whether the wide range of responses observed represent real differences in the requirements of specific plants or organs, or whether they relate to differing levels of particular hormones within such tissue so that the determinative factor depends on that hormone in shortest supply.

5.3.5   CONTROL AT THE MOLECULAR LEVEL

While the work described so far has been useful in establishing that hormones can induce differentiation, it tells us little about the nature of the controls exercised by hormones at the subcellular or molecular level which underly determination. In point of fact not much work

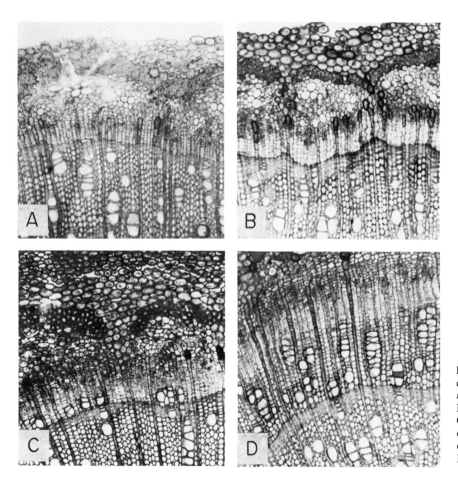

Fig. 5.3.9. Effect of auxin and gibberellin on cambial activity in disbudded poplar (*Populus robusta*) twigs. A. Untreated control. B. Treated with gibberellin (GA) only. C. treated with indole-3-acetic acid (IAA) only. D. Treated with IAA + GA in combination. Photographs supplied by Professor P.F. Wareing.

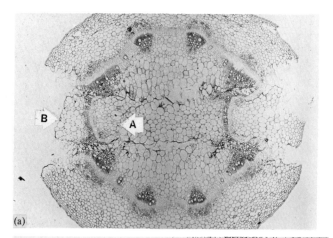

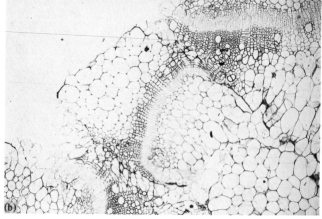

Fig. 5.3.10. (a) Transverse section through 17-day-old hypocotyl of *Ricinus communis* with an inverted plug of interfascicular tissue (BA) 10 days after inversion. At the time of inversion the seedling showed no signs of secondary growth. (b) Detail of (a) showing inverted tissue block and surrounding tissue. Note the inverted position of the xylem. Photographs kindly supplied by Dr A.M. Siebers.

has been performed on these aspects of differentiating systems. On the other hand, there is a wealth of information about the biochemical changes effected by hormones in systems where cell division and/or maturation are not involved. Before discussing this type of work, however, it is appropriate to go back to first principles in hormone physiology and biochemistry and consider some recent results in a relatively new area.

Hormone receptors

It is clear that any hormone, whether in plants or animals, must interact with some component in the cell in order to bring about a change in the extent or direction of growth and development. However, although the presence of such cellular components—termed 'receptors'—has always been assumed by developmental physiologists, much more progress has been made in characterizing them in animals than in plants. The lack of such progress in plants relative to that in animals reflects, at least in part, differences in the nature of plant and animal hormones. Thus, whereas many animal hormones have specific sites of production and specific 'target' cells or tissues, and in general each brings about a rather limited range of responses, as we have already seen (cf. Table 5.3.1), a single plant hormone may be produced and may have its effects in many different cells, tissues and organs and is capable of effecting a bewildering variety of responses. Equally, unlike the situation in animals, the effect of a plant hormone may be quite different at different stages of ontogeny. If the receptor concept is valid, therefore, we might expect that the type of response of a particular cell or tissue to a plant hormone would be dependent on the nature and distribution of receptors within the target. Hence one might expect to find a number of different receptors for the same hormone in different parts of the plant or even in the same part. Alternatively, one or very few types of receptor may be involved but the interaction between the receptor and the process it controls may differ depending on its location.

Quite apart from these conceptual difficulties, there are others of a more technical nature which it is inappropriate to discuss here, but despite this, some progress in the area of hormone receptors in plants has been made.

Thus, it has been shown that cell-free preparations from maize coleoptiles will reversibly bind auxins (see [4] for a review of this work). However, since no one has so far been able to show that the interaction brings about a change in any metabolic process it might well be asked what criteria can be used to establish whether these so-called 'binding sites' (for there are at least two) are, in fact, functional receptors. The same, of course, follows for other binding sites for cytokinins and ethylene which have been isolated.

In the first place it must be shown that the binding site is not, in fact, an enzyme involved with the metabolism of the hormone—that it is not, for example, IAA oxidase in the case of auxins. Clearly, since such enzymes must interact with the hormone in order to metabolize it, they must also have a specific site at which interaction can take place, and this site will have a high affinity and specificity for the hormone. It has been shown satisfactorily that the systems studied so far are not enzymes which degrade the hormone. The second criterion is that the site must show specificity for the hormone in question. This facet can be investigated by examining the effect of physiologically active and inactive structural analogues of the hormone on the equilibrium between the hormone and the binding site. Ideally, the effect of a particular analogue should be proportional to its biological effectiveness, but this is not always so. For example, in the case of one of the auxin-binding sites referred to above, only active auxins such as IAA and 2,4D and auxin transport inhibitors such as TIBA competitively inhibit the binding of NAA to the site, whereas in the case of the other site the inactive auxin analogue benzoic acid also inhibits. On the other hand, in the case of an ethylene-binding site isolated from *Phaseolus vulgaris* cotyledons, physiologically active structural analogues of ethylene, such as propylene, vinyl chloride and acetylene, compete with the natural hormone, whereas physiologically inactive structural analogues such as ethane and propane do not. Moreover, the comparative ability of the active analogues to compete with ethylene at the binding site is proportional to their effectiveness in mimicking the effects of ethylene in developmental systems such as leaf abscission.

The other important criterion which must be established is whether the binding site has a high affinity for the hormone. Here one can apply the same sort of reasoning as is used when the specificity of an enzyme for a particular substrate is being considered. Thus, if the interaction of the hormone with the receptor is a single one-to-one reaction on a molecular basis, we would expect the dissociation constant of the hormone/binding-site complex (K_D) to be similar to the concentration at which the hormone has its half-optimal effect on a developmental process in the system under study. From the equation:

$$K_D = \frac{[\text{Conc of free hormone}][\text{Conc of free binding site}]}{[\text{Conc of hormone:binding site complex}]}$$

(where these are the values at equilibrium)

we can see that where the free-hormone concentration is equal to the K_D, the receptor will be 50% saturated. Of course, it is assumed in hormone receptor studies that the magnitude of the developmental response is directly proportional to the amount of hormone/binding-site complex, which may not be the case.

In any event, the theory seems to hold up rather well in the systems studied so far. Thus the dissociation constants for the auxin-binding sites referred to above are about $1.5 = 10^{-7}$M and $1.6 = 10^{-6}$M for NAA; the latter compares quite well with the concentration of this auxin which induces half-optimal cell extension in maize coleoptiles. Equally, the ethylene-binding site in *Phaseolus* has a K_D of 6×10^{-10}M compared to threshold, half-maximal and saturation concentrations of ethylene in most developmental systems of 4.5×10^{-11}, 4.5×10^{-10} and $4.5 = 10^{-9}$M (0.01, 0.1 and 1.0 μl.1^{-1} air respectively).

The binding sites so far examined in any detail appear to be attached to subcellular organelles. Thus the two auxin-binding sites from maize appear to be present on the membranes of the endoplasmic reticulum and the plasmalemma respectively. It has been suggested that the latter site is perhaps involved in polar auxin transport. All the evidence to date on the various sites indicates that they are probably proteins since they are heat labile and binding activity is destroyed by treatment with proteolytic enzymes. Indeed, some attempts have already been made to identify the amino acids present in the vicinity of one of the auxin-binding sites.

A further characteristic of plant hormones is that the concentration range over which they effect an increased response sometimes covers three to four orders of magnitude, or even more. For example, in the barley aleurone system described below (p. 325) there is a nearly linear response—in terms of the amount of α-amylase released—over a concentration range of GA_3 from 1.4×10^{-10}M to 1.4×10^{-6}M. In animal systems the range is often much smaller. The linearity of the response over four decades of concentration implies that as the concentration of hormone rises it becomes increasingly ineffective. We do not know the reasons behind this behaviour but one possibility is that plant hormone receptors exhibit 'negative cooperativity'— i.e. their affinity for the hormone decreases with an increase in its concentration.

It now appears that the distribution of receptors for specific hormones may be quite rigidly demarcated. Thus in a series of papers Osborne and her co-workers (see [15]) have demonstrated the existence of a defined zone of 'target' cells for ethylene in abscission zones of petioles (p. 335). While the existence of such 'target' cells might have been expected, nevertheless the fact that they can be characterized and distinguished from nearby cells provides circumstantial evidence for the restriction of specific receptors to specific areas.

It would be unwise at this time to pursue consideration of these systems further, since the field is developing very rapidly. Nevertheless, such knowledge as we have already opens up many interesting possibilities, and these will be further discussed below.

Mode of action of auxin

It must be clear to the reader that the amount of information we have on hormone receptors is relatively sparse and, as mentioned above, no one has yet demonstrated a link between such a receptor and a hormone-controlled response. It is self-evident that whatever the basic mode of action of hormones, the system controlled by the hormone–receptor complex must be one which is capable of causing amplification, since a given response involves, directly or indirectly, a number of processes. For this reason and because the effects of hormones, particularly in differentiation, clearly involve the participation of many metabolic processes, workers in the field have tended to suppose that control is exercised via nucleic acids or proteins. The literature is replete with studies on the effects of growth regulators on the behaviour and metabolism of all forms of nucleic acids,

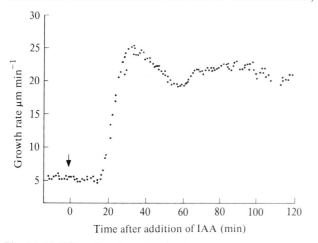

Fig. 5.3.11. Effect of auxin on the growth rate of light-grown pea epicotyl segments. Segments were soaked for 110 min in 20 mM tris-maleate buffer pH 6.1 and 30 μM indole-3-acetic acid was then added (at arrow). (Penny *et al.* (1972) *J. exp. Bot.*, **23**.)

on enzymes and so on. Indeed, it is probably true to say that almost every known metabolic process has been studied in this respect.

However, merely that a particular process is affected by hormone application does not prove that the process is directly controlled by the hormone. As an example one could point to the stimulation by auxin of water uptake by coleoptile sections. Thus it is now clear that the water uptake is a consequence of the growth induced by auxin, and is not its cause (see also below, p. 325). Because many research workers have failed to make the distinction referred to above, much of the work concerned with hormonal effects on metabolic processes has done little to further our understanding of the basic mechanisms of action of hormones. On the other hand, in some systems great advances have been made.

One such system which has proved fruitful for work on the molecular basis of hormone action is that concerned with the control of elongation in segments of stems or coleoptiles. Such stems are usually growing quite rapidly prior to their excision but their growth rate drops dramatically after the segments are cut. Subsequent addition of auxin at a suitable concentration accelerates growth after a lag period of usually 10–20 min (Fig. 5.3.11). If the auxin is removed, the growth rate again falls rapidly. It can thus be said that here the hormone is merely acting to maintain a steady state by restarting a process interrupted by excision (and, by implication, by interruption of a supply of the hormone from the apical region). Moreover, either some of the products of the hormone's action must be unstable or they must be continuously produced, which process in turn must be dependent on the continued presence of hormone–receptor complex. It is also worth noting that here we are dealing with a process which is already organized and which merely responds to the hormonal signal.

It is known that auxin treatment leads to a change in the chemical and physical properties of the cell wall which causes cell wall 'loosening', thus allowing turgor-driven extension. How is this change in properties brought about?

Early work showed that inhibitors of the synthesis of nucleic acids and proteins also inhibited cell elongation. However, the demonstration of the short lag period between auxin application and the acceleration of growth (Fig. 5.3.11) makes it unlikely that an effect on transcription is involved, and further observations that inhibitors of nucleic acid synthesis do not, in general, reduce the length of the lag period suggested that while nucleic acid synthesis may be necessary for continued extension, it is not directly involved in its re-initiation.

It has been known for more than 40 years that a reduction in the pH of the incubation medium leads to an almost instantaneous, albeit transitory, increase in the elongation rate of stem and coleoptile segments. This, together with the demonstration by Jacobs and Ray [9] that, very soon after its application, auxin

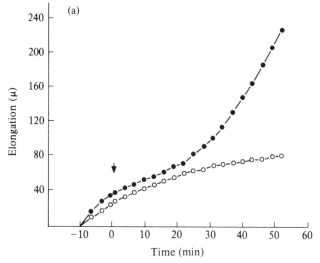

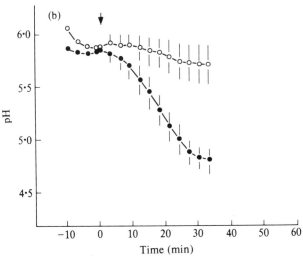

Fig. 5.3.12. (a,b). Comparison of auxin-induced decrease in free space pH (as measured by a pH microelectrode inserted into the tissue) with auxin-induced increase in elongation rate in *Zea* coleoptiles. 20μM IAA (●) or 1 mM phosphate-citrate buffer pH 6 (○) added at arrow. Jacobs & Ray [20].

increases the activity of an outwardly directed proton pump in *Zea* coleoptiles (see Fig. 5.3.12), led to the formulation of the 'acid growth' hypothesis of auxin action. This suggests that a drop in the pH of the cell wall brought about by the increased activity of the auxin-controlled proton pump activates an enzyme or enzymes cleaving and/or re-forming glycosidic linkages in the cell wall. The drop in pH may also affect the properties of the cell wall macromolecules other than by an effect on enzymes. In this hypothesis, the hydrogen ions extruded into the cell wall could be seen as 'second messengers' between the site of auxin action and the site of wall loosening, in much the same way that cyclic AMP functions in many animal systems.

It has now been demonstrated (a) that increased proton extrusion can be detected in auxin-treated tissues *prior* to the recommencement of extension (Fig. 5.3.12), and (b) that treatment of tissue segments at low pH results in changes in cell wall polymers similar, if not identical, to those occurring in auxin-treated segments. It is assumed that the enzymes effecting these changes have pH optima close to that obtaining when auxin-induced acidification is operating. The existence of such a mechanism would account for the rapidity of the effect of low pH on cell extension.

If the acid growth hypothesis is indeed valid, then the auxin effect is apparently a relatively simple one. The energy input for proton-pumping systems appears to derive from redox processes or ATPase, and it is not difficult to postulate how such processes might be accelerated by a change in the conformation of, for example, an ATPase, brought about by an interaction with auxin. The enzyme systems involved would probably have to be intimately associated with the auxin receptor or might indeed be different parts of the same molecule. Such a hypothesis would fit in rather well with the time scale for the induction of the auxin response.

The possibility that auxin acts in cell elongation in the way described above is supported by the demonstration that a very similar system appears to operate in stomata, although the end result is different. Here, abscisic acid induces closure of the stomata and this appears to be due to a specific inhibition by the hormone of a proton pump. This inhibition leads to a very rapid efflux of potassium from the stomatal guard cells (see [16]).

Considerable controversy still surrounds the problem of cell elongation, however. Thus inhibitors of protein synthesis, such as cycloheximide, not only affect the rate of elongation but also affect the length of the lag period before auxin takes its effect. This effect has been attributed to the existence of a 'growth-limiting protein' (GLP) which turns over rapidly. At first sight it is difficult to see how such a protein could effect the sort of system postulated in the acid growth hypothesis, although it has been proposed that if the transport of the protons from the cytoplasm to the cell wall is effected via transport in membrane-bounded vesicles, a requirement for protein synthesis might be expected. Other studies using isolated plasmalemma vesicles treated with auxin have shown the release of a transcription factor that stimulates RNA polymerase *in vitro*. The effect is very rapid and although it has not been related to a specific process involved in growth, its possible significance in this connection cannot be disregarded.

Some of these anomalies can be resolved if one suggests that auxin-controlled proton extrusion represents only one process, albeit probably the first, affected by auxin in controlling the re-initiation of growth, and that many others are also involved. Indeed, since acid-induced growth is only of a very transitory nature, other processes must be involved; in any case, it is clear that there is much more than the cleavage of glycosidic linkages to continued growth and that polysaccharide and protein synthesis must also be involved.

If this is the case, then we must ask which of these other processes are directly affected by auxin and which are controlled by more indirect means. It has been shown that at least one enzyme, β-glucan synthetase, increases in activity within 15–20 minutes of auxin application and this effect appears to involve the activation of preformed enzyme. Stimulations of the synthesis of all species of RNA have been reported in segments induced to elongate by application of auxin, but it is not clear whether this is a direct consequence of auxin action or, indeed, whether this increased synthesis is necessary for growth. Certainly, most of the auxin-induced synthesis of rRNA can be inhibited by treatment with fluorouracil without any effect on growth.

Mode of action of gibberellins

Another system which has received considerable attention is barley aleurone tissue. The aleurone layer, which is present in the seeds of all cereals, surrounds the endosperm and has a very characteristic appearance. The cells have very thick walls and contain prominent

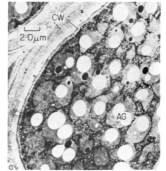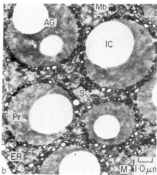

Fig. 5.3.13. (a, b) Section through imbibed wheat aleurone tissue fixed in KMnO₃. CW, wall; AG, aleurone grains; Pr, protein; Mb, microbody (glyoxysome); IC, internal cavity (electron transparent zone probably left by loss of protein–carbohydrate complex during fixing/sectioning); S, spherosome; M, mitochondria; ER, short segments of endoplasmic reticulum.

structures termed 'aleurone grains' (see Fig. 5.3.13). Now it has been shown that many of the enzymes which bring about the mobilization of the endosperm reserves are secreted by the aleurone layer and that the secretion of these enzymes is initiated by some factor emanating from the embryo. Later work indicated that this factor was likely to be a gibberellin.

The first enzyme to be examined in detail was α-amylase. The time course of the development of its activity in the aleurone layers and its release into the medium is illustrated in Fig. 5.3.14. In addition to α-amylase, a number of other enzymes appear in response to treatment with GA₃, namely protease, ribonuclease, β1→3 glucanase, 1→4 xylanase, acid phosphatase, isocitratase and malate synthetase. It is now established that at least the α-amylase and protease components arise as a consequence of protein synthesis *de novo*. This was a major advance but still leaves many questions on the mode of action of the hormone unanswered, since there are numerous possible points at which control of enzyme synthesis might be exercised. Subsequent attempts to define the primary site of the GA₃ effect have taken one of two approaches, namely (a) studies on the kinetics of enzyme production and release, especially in relation to the effects of 'specific' inhibitors of protein and nucleic acid synthesis, and (b) investigations of changes in various macromolecular components in the aleurone layer, in particular nucleic acids.

Given the right conditions, inhibitors of protein and

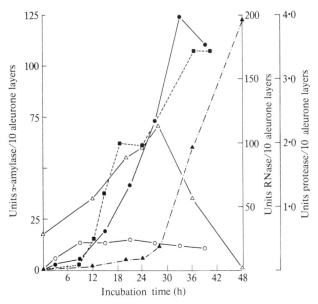

Fig. 5.3.14. Time course of synthesis and release of α-amylase, protease and ribonuclease from barley aleurone layers during incubation in gibberellic acid; α-amylase: in aleurone layers (o), in medium(•); protease: in medium (■); ribonuclease: in aleurone layers (Δ), in medium (▲). Adapted from J.E. Varner & G.R. Chandra (1964) *Proc. natl Acad. Sci., USA*, **52**; J.V. Jacobsen & J.E. Varner (1967) *Plant Physiol.*, **42**; M.J. Chrispeels & J.E. Varner (1967) *Plant Physiol.*, **42**.

nucleic acid biosynthesis will inhibit α-amylase production. Nevertheless, whereas cycloheximide (an inhibitor of protein turnover), 6-methyl purine, azaadenine and bromouracil (inhibitors of RNA synthesis) inhibit α-amylase synthesis even if added some time after the addition of GA_3, actinomycin D does not affect production of the enzyme if added 8 h after GA_3, even though it does inhibit RNA synthesis if supplied at this time. Since actinomycin specifically inhibits DNA-dependent RNA synthesis, this seems to indicate that such a process (i.e. transcription) is only important in the early phases of GA_3 action and implies that the product(s) of transcription—presumably mRNA coding for α-amylase—is relatively stable. On the other hand, the results with the other inhibitors suggest that there is a continuous requirement for other processes involving nucleic acid and protein synthesis. This is not in itself surprising since, clearly, synthesis of other species of RNA and the functioning of the protein-synthesizing machinery would be necessary for the continued production of α-amylase. What is rather more surprising is that the

activity of at least some of these other processes is also controlled by GA_3. This was demonstrated by the observation that there is a continuous requirement for GA_3 and a rapid decrease in enzyme production results from washing the aleurone layers free of the hormone—even 15 h after GA_3 is first applied (5.3.15).

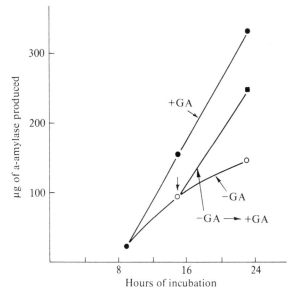

Fig. 5.3.15. Effects of gibberellic acid (GA_3), added and removed at different times, upon production of α-amylase by barley aleurone layers. All aleurone layers incubated for 7 h in 0.5 μm GA_3, then either in GA_3 for a further 16 h (•), or GA_3 removed by four consecutive 30 min rinses (O), or GA_3 added back at 15 h (■). From M.J. Chrispeels & E. Varner (1967) *Plant Physiol.*, **42**.

Other growth regulators are also capable of affecting the synthesis and release of α-amylase and of these the effects of ABA are the best documented. ABA inhibits the GA_3-induced formation of α-amylase without significantly affecting amino acid incorporation into total protein and only slightly depressing RNA synthesis. Application of cordicepin (an inhibitor of RNA synthesis) with or immediately after ABA application caused α-amylase synthesis to be sustained or restored respectively. This appears to suggest that the ABA effect is dependent upon continuous synthesis of a short-lived RNA. The effect of ABA is highly specific and does not affect substrate induction of nitrate reductase in this system, even when α-amylase activity is inhibited by about 90%. It is also notable that both ethylene and cytokinins can overcome the inhibitory effects of ABA.

The results with inhibitors of nucleic acid and protein synthesis are consistent with the hypothesis that the expression of the GA_3 effect involves the synthesis of enzyme-specific RNA molecules. Zwar and Jacobsen [28] showed that GA_3 does not enhance accumulation of precursors into total RNA, nor is the specific activity or amount of total RNA changed. Nevertheless, it was shown that the time course of α-amylase synthesis is paralleled by the appearance of a specific RNA fraction having some of the characteristics of mRNA. The appearance of this 'GA-RNA', as it was termed, was inhibited to much the same extent as α-amylase by actinomycin D, whereas fluorouracil, which halved the incorporation of radioactive RNA precursors in rRNA, had no effect on α-amylase or GA-RNA. ABA supplied simultaneously with GA_3 eliminated synthesis of both α-amylase and GA-RNA. Later work [5, 10] showed that GA_3 enhanced the rate of incorporation of labelled precursors into poly(A) RNA. This poly(A) RNA was shown to contain the mRNA for α-amylase.

Using techniques permitting translation *in vitro* of isolated mRNA, Higgins *et al.* [5] have shown that while the spectrum of translation products does not change markedly, there is a marked and progressive increase in the amount of a polypeptide later identified as amylase. The level of this mRNA is very low in hydrated tissue and begins to increase 2–4 h after GA_3 addition, reaching a maximum of 16–20% of the total translatable mRNA at about 15 h. ABA appears to act by inhibiting the accumulation of the mRNA for α-amylase [6].

This work appears to indicate that amylase synthesis is regulated by the level of mRNA, but how the level of the mRNA is controlled is still unclear. On the other hand, work demonstrating that the efficiency of translation of mRNA increases with time of incubation in GA_3 indicates that other constraints on α-amylase synthesis also exist.

A picture thus begins to emerge of the sites at which GA_3 exerts its effect in barley aleurone, but interpretation is complicated by the fact that all the other classes of hormone appear to be involved in the mobilization of the endosperm reserves. Thus Laidman and his co-workers [12] have shown that cytokinins, probably derived from the endosperm itself, initiate mobilization of at least part of the triglyceride reserves and promote retention of macronutrient mineral ions in the aleurone tissue. IAA in association with glutamine appears to control mobilization of another part of the triglyceride reserves, induces neutral lipase activity and activates phytase (which degrades phytin).

We thus have a situation in this one system where (a) individual hormones control several processes, and (b) particular processes may be controlled by interactions between different hormones. The implications of this will be further discussed below.

There are clear parallels between growth stimulation by auxin and the barley aleurone system, despite the fact that in one case we are dealing with an effect on a growing system and in the other with an effect on the metabolic activities of mature cells. Thus, in both cases there are a multiplicity of processes controlled directly or indirectly by a single hormone. The resemblance becomes even more striking when it is pointed out that other hormones may affect the extent or indeed the direction of cell extension. Furthermore, there exist systems where growth may be controlled by more than one hormone independently. For example, in *Ranunculus sceleratus* growth may be induced by both auxin and ethylene. An attempt to rationalize these diverse effects will be made in the concluding section.

5.3.6 CONCLUSIONS

Is it possible to come to any conclusions as to the role of hormones in either the channeling of plant tissues into particular pathways of development or in the initiation of predetermined events? It seems appropriate to consider this question at two levels. In the first instance it seems likely that hormones, often in association with other substances, are capable of initiating meristematic areas. It is also clear that the subsequent differentiation of cells produced by such meristems may also be controlled by hormonal stimuli, although in this case the hormones may only represent the signal for cells to develop in ways for which they are already programmed. Thus, the observed distribution of phloem centrifugal to the xylem would be a consequence of the presence of a radial polarity with respect to hormonal sensitivity in the cambium and not directly of hormone concentration on the cells derived from it, although part of the determinative process in cambium formation might involve induction of a radial polarity with respect to the transport of hormones or other substances, thus affecting the supply of these factors to the cambial derivatives on either side. Since single cells in suspension culture can be induced to differentiate into xylem elements by application of cytokinin and auxin, it would appear that cells do not require to be programmed to respond in this way but rather that their position may determine what balance of hormones they will receive.

Similar hypotheses could account for the induction of primary vascular tissue in the work of both Sachs and Jacobs. Thus both workers observed that the promeristematic tissues or those adjacent to the vascular cylinder vascularize preferentially, which again might be due either to inherent polarity or to sensitivity. Experimentally induced vascularization in cortical tissue is perhaps not entirely analogous to the situation in callus, although it is significant that higher concentrations of auxin are required in the former case than in the latter, whether applied artificially or derived from an expanding leaf. In any case, regeneration after wounding presumably represents a homeostatic mechanism such that tissue only vascularizes when normal conditions are disturbed, and we cannot exclude the possibility that cortical tissue is programmed to respond to auxin in this way when a certain concentration is exceeded. This would apply equally to vascular strands from expanding leaves.

Hypotheses such as those outlined above do not explain how the observed changes are brought about at the molecular level. In the foregoing section we saw that plant hormones appear to be able to exert their effects at almost all levels of organization, on many processes in the same system and, further, that more than one hormone may be involved in the mediation of the same process in the same or different systems. In barley aleurone at least part of the effect of GA_3 appears to be mediated at the transcriptional level, and it is hard to imagine how the auxin/cytokinin effects on root and shoot initiation in callus (p. 314) could be brought about other than by some similar mechanism. At the other end of the scale, the effects on the activity of proton pumps and enzyme activation in elongating tissue seem to involve rather simpler mechanisms although, here again, more complex processes are probably affected in the control of growth overall.

It seems to the author that the only logical conclusion which we can come to is that the presence of a multitude of the receptors referred to above (p. 322) is required to explain not only how the plethora of developmental processes are controlled by relatively few hormones, but also to account for the multitude of control points which may be affected by a single growth regulator whether in one system or in many. In some of the cases where effects appear to be only indirectly controlled by hormones or where more than one system is affected, it is possible that the coordination of several processes is brought about by control, via a hormone, of the activities of 'integrator' genes, as proposed by Britten and Davidson [2].

If, however, there are so many receptors, why have so few been isolated? In part at least, this may be a technical problem—most receptors so far isolated are only present at concentrations of a few picomoles per gram fresh weight, which makes their detection very difficult. Equally, until we can relate a receptor to a specific metabolic process, we are relying on studies of chemical equilibria to characterize the receptor systems. It is quite possible, therefore, where only one or two specific binding sites with defined dissociation constants appear to be involved, that we are in fact studying many receptors with one or two groups of broadly similar dissociation constants.

We do not yet have any real idea how hormonal interactions are effected. In a number of cases, for example the effect of ABA on GA-induced α-amylase formation, we know at least some of the processes which are affected, but there is insufficient information to generalize. Clearly, the mechanisms of antagonistic or synergistic effects need not be different in kind from those outlined above. For example, different hormones might attach to the same receptor molecule (although it is unlikely that they would do so at the same site, since their structures are so different) and hence modify its behaviour, or attach to different receptors, bringing about metabolic changes which are antagonistic or otherwise.

Another aspect of the problem relates to the difference between the types of hormonal response. We emphasized earlier that in some systems, such as root and shoot initiation, hormones appear to determine patterns of development, whilst in most other cases the target tissue is programmed to respond to a particular hormonal stimulus. In the light of the general hypothesis of hormone action outlined above, the latter type could be explained in terms of specific receptors being synthesized at appropriate times by the changing transcription of the genome during normal ontogeny, and hence being present in the appropriate tissue at the appropriate time. Such a mechanism would also involve coordination with other controls on hormone synthesis and/or transport, so that an appropriate concentration of hormone was present at the right time.

On the other hand, root and shoot development seems to imply that hormones can not only interact with specific receptors but may, in some cases, actually induce the formation of other receptors. In fact, there is no logical reason why this should not be the case. After all, receptors are probably proteins and we know that hormones can affect transcription and protein synthesis. We might add that the implication is that some receptors are 'constitutive'—in the same sense as the word is used of certain proteins in bacterial genetics—whereas others are 'inducible', sometimes by hormones, sometimes in other ways.

We are approaching the stage where, in a few cases at least, an understanding of the mechanisms whereby hormones bring about their effects at the molecular level is beginning to emerge. Indeed, some considerable progress has been made since the first edition of this book was published. Nevertheless, the situation is still far from clear in most cases, and even in the well-documented systems we possess only the outline of events. Much now depends on technological developments, but it is not unrealistic to predict that if progress with plant hormones takes the same direction and proceeds at the same rate as with animal hormones, then within the next decade we will see a hormone–receptor system linked to the control of a metabolic process. If this can be achieved then we may have the first real key to the fundamental mode of action of plant hormones.

5.3.7 REFERENCES

1 Audus L.J. (1973) *Plant Growth Substances*, 3rd edn. Leonard Hill, London.
2 Britten R.J. & Davidson E.H. (1969) Gene regulation for higher cells: A theory. *Science, N.Y.*, **165**, 349–357.
3 Dodds J.H. (1979) Is cell cycle activity necessary for xylem cell differentiation? *What's new in Pl. Physiol.*, **10**,(4).
4 Dodds J.H. & Hall M.A. (1980) Plant hormone receptors. *Sci. Progr., Oxf.*, **66**, 513–535.
5 Higgins T.J.V., Zwar J.A. & Jacobsen J.V. (1976) Gibberellic acid enhances the level of translatable mRNA for α-amylase in barley aleurone layers. *Nature, Lond.*, **260**, 166–169.
6 Higgins T.J.V., Zwar J.A. & Jacobsen J.V. (1977) Hormonal control of the level of translatable mRNA for α-amylase in barley aleurone layers. In *Acides Nucleiques et Synthèse des Protéines chez les Végétaux* (Eds J.H. Weil & L. Bogorad), pp. 481–486, C.N.R.S.
7 Jacobs W.P. (1952) The role of auxin in differentiation of xylem around a wound. *Am. J. Bot.*, **39**, 301–309.
8 Jacobs W.P. & Morrow, I.B. (1957) A quantitative study of xylem development in the vegetative shoot apex of *Coleus*. *Am. J. Bot.*, **44**, 823–842.
9 Jacobs M. & Ray P.M. (1976) Rapid auxin-induced decrease in free space pH and its relationship to auxin-induced growth in maize and pea. *Pl. Physiol.*, **58**, 203–209.
10 Jacobsen J.V. & Zwar J.A. (1974) Gibberellic acid and RNA synthesis in barley aleurone layers: metabolism of rRNA and tRNA and of RNA containing polyadenylic acid sequences. *Aust. J. Plant Physiol.*, **1**, 343–356.
11 Jeffs R.A. & Northcote D.M. (1967) The influence of indole-3-yl acetic acid and sugar on the pattern of induced differentiation in plant tissue culture. *J. Cell Sci.*, **2**, 77–88.
12 Laidman D.L., Colborne A.J., Doig R.I. & Varty K. (1974) The multiplicity of induction systems in wheat aleurone tissue. In *Mechanisms of Regulation of Plant Growth* (Eds R.L. Bieleski, A.R. Ferguson & M.M. Cresswell). Bull. R. Soc. No. 2, *12*.
13 Leopold A.C. (1964) *Plant Growth and Development*. McGraw-Hill, New York.
14 Macmillan J. (Ed.) (1980) *Encyclopaedia of Plant Physiology N.S. 9 Hormonal regulation of development I*. Springer-Verlag, Berlin.
15 Osborne D.J. (1977) Ethylene and target cells in the growth of plants. *Sci. Progr., Oxf.*, **64**, 51–63.
16 Raschke K. (1977) The stomatal turgor mechanism and its responses to CO_2 and abscisic acid: observations and hypothesis. In *Regulation of Cell Membrane Activities in Plants* (Eds E. Marrè & O. Ciferri), pp. 173–183. North-Holland, Amsterdam.
17 Sachs T. (1968) The role of the root in the induction of xylem differentiation in peas. *Ann. Bot.*, **32**, 97–117.
18 Sachs T. (1968) On the determination of vascular tissue in peas. *Ann. Bot.*, **32**, 781–790.
19 Savidge R.A. & Wareing P.F. (1981) Plant growth regulators and the differentiation of vascular elements. In *Xylem Cell Development* (Ed. J.R. Barnett). Castle House Publications, London.
20 Siebers A.M. (1971) Initiation of radial polarity in the interfascicular cambium of *Ricinus communis* L. *Acta. bot. néerl.*, **20**, 211–220.
21 Skoog F. & Miller C.O. (1957) Chemical regulation of growth and organ formation in plant tissues cultures in vitro. *Symp. Soc. exp. Biol.*, **11**, 118–131.
22 Torrey J.G. (1963) Cellular patterns in developing roots. *Symp. Soc. exp. Biol.*, **17**, 285–314.
23 Vardjan M. & Nitsch J.P. (1961) La régénération chez *Cichorium endiva* L. étude des auxines et des 'kinines' endogènes. *Bull. Soc. Biol. France*, **108**, 363–374.
24 Wareing P.F., Hanney C.E.A. & Digby J. (1964) The role of endogenous hormones in cambial activity and xylem differentiation. In *The Formation of Wood in Forest Trees* (Ed. M.H. Zimmerman), pp. 324–344. Academic Press, New York.
25 Wareing P.F. & Phillips I.D.J. (1981) *Growth and Differentiation in Plants*, 3rd edn. Pergamon Press.
26 Wetmore R.H. & Rier J.P. (1963) Experimental induction of vascular tissues in callus of angiosperms. *Am. J. Bot.*, **50**, 418–430.
27 Wilkins M.B. (Ed.) (1969) *Physiology of Plant Growth and Development*. McGraw-Hill, London.
28 Zwar J.A. & Jacobsen J.V. (1972) A correlation between an RNA fraction selectively labelled in the presence of GA and amylase synthesis in barley aleurone layers. *Pl. Physiol.*, **49**, 1000–1004.

Chapter 5.4
Hormones and Plant Development: Coordination and Control in the Whole Plant and Analogies with Insect Development
P.F. Wareing

5.4.1   INTRODUCTION

As we have seen (Chapter 2.3), the initiation and differentiation of organs and tissues occurs mainly during the meristematic phase, in cells which are undergoing division in shoot and root apices and in flower primordia. The dimensions of apical meristems and flower primordia are small (usually of the order of 1–2 mm or less) and control of cell division and determination is required over only short distances. The indeterminate pattern of growth in higher plants by the continued activity of apical meristems leads to the gradual accretion of mature tissue in the older parts of the plant body, while meristematic activity is maintained at the shoot and root apices. However, potential meristematic regions still remain in the older parts of the plant in (1) the vascular cambium, (2) the axillary buds and lateral roots and (3) developing flowers and fruits. Hence there is a need for a control system to coordinate activities in these various growth regions, but the distances involved are greater, often by several orders of magnitude, than in the meristematic regions, and this coordination is, in the main, effected through the hormone system of the plant.

Apart from the need for coordination between the different parts of the plant, its development involves an orderly succession of phases during its life cycle, including germination and vegetative growth, flowering and fruiting, and senescence and dormancy. This orderly sequence of changes, which may be referred to as ontogeny, must also involve control systems to ensure coordination in *time*. Thus, development of the whole plant entails both *spatial* and *temporal* coordination, although the distinction between these two concepts is not always sharply defined [20].

Control systems may be either *autogenous* (i.e. their operation is generated within the organism itself) or *environmental* (operated by external factors). Since environmental conditions do not normally vary appreciably within the different parts of the shoot system, spatial coordination is, in general, effected through the autogenous control systems, although the pattern of spatial integration may be *modified* by environmental factors. Temporal coordination involves both autogenous and environmental controls. Thus, the succession of orderly changes seen during the development of a leaf or a flower must be controlled autogenously. On the other hand, the synchronization of the plant lifecycle with seasonal climatic changes through a vernalization or daylength requirement (p. 342) is an example of the environmental control of temporal coordination. It is now clear that hormones play a paramount role in co-ordinating growth and differentiation in the whole plant.

In order to fall within the traditional definition of a hormone, a substance must be released from the cells in which it is formed and produce an effect in other cells, i.e. the sites of production and action must be separate and movement of the hormone is necessary. Moreover, to effect control the supply of hormone must be capable of spatial or temporal modulation. These criteria apparently are met in various aspects of spatial co-ordination involving auxin, such as apical dominance and cambial activity (section 5.4.2). However, there is less evidence that the criteria are met by the other major classes of endogenous growth substances (gibberellins, cytokinins, abscisic acid, ethylene), since there is no conclusive evidence that their production is localized in specific regions of the plant, or that other regions depend upon the supply of these substances which are produced elsewhere, although leaves may be dependent on the supply of cytokinins from the roots. (For this reason it is better to use the term *growth substance* where the criteria for a hormone are not met.) Thus endo-genous growth substances, other than auxin, cannot be said to fulfill strictly the criteria for the definition of a hormone. On the other hand, there is considerable evidence that the temporal modulation of levels of gibberellins and cytokinins is important in the control of dormancy in buds and seeds (p. 346), and in other processes. Thus growth substances play essential roles in both spatial and temporal coordination in the whole plant. We shall discuss some examples of the role of growth substances in both autogenous and environ-mental control of development. (For more extensive accounts of this subject see [4, 17, 21].)

5.4.2 HORMONES AND AUTOGENOUS REGULATION OF DEVELOPMENT

Spatial coordination

Two of the clearest examples of the role of hormones in spatial coordination are provided by secondary thicken-ing (as a result of cambial activity) in stems, and the correlative inhibition of buds. In many dicotyledons, as the plant increases in height, the stem increases in diameter so that it is normally able to meet the increased bending stresses to which it is subjected. Thus, diameter growth is coordinated with height growth. This increase in diameter is achieved by the activity of the cambium, which forms a cylindrical meristem in the stem and produces secondary xylem and phloem.

Correlative inhibition refers to the complete or partial inhibition of lateral buds which is commonly observed in the shoots of many species. These lateral buds remain inhibited in the presence of the main shoot apical meri-stem, but if the latter is removed or destroyed, the uppermost one or two buds are stimulated to grow out and assume 'apical dominance'. Thus the outgrowth of lateral buds is under tight control in the shoots of many species.

Even before the discovery of plant hormones, it had been well established that both cambial activity and correlative inhibition are controlled by 'influences' emanating from young leaves in the shoot apical region and in expanding tree buds, and that these influences appeared to move in a strictly basipetal manner. It is now clear that in cambial activity the primary stimulus arising in the buds is indole-3-acetic acid (IAA), which can replace the effects of the buds when they are removed (p. 319).

Similarly, the outgrowth of lateral buds following removal of the main shoot apex is inhibited if IAA is applied, in solution or in lanolin, to the decapitated stump. After nearly 50 years of study of the problem, it is still uncertain how endogenous IAA, produced in the shoot apical region and transported basipetally in the stem, inhibits the growth of the lateral buds, and although many hypotheses have been put forward, the matter remains unresolved [12]. It would appear that IAA interacts with cytokinins, and possibly abscisic acid, in regulating apical dominance.

Another phenomenon which appears to be controlled by the basipetal transport of IAA in the stem is the formation of adventitious roots at the base of stem cuttings. It is well known that application of IAA or synthetic auxins promotes root initiation, and the natural production of roots at the base of stem cuttings is probably due to the accumulation of endogenous IAA there.

Although several other groups of endogenous growth substances undoubtedly play important roles in various aspects of shoot growth and differentiation, it appears to be primarily IAA which is the hormone involved in spatial coordination, by virtue of its strictly polar pattern of transport [20]. The polar transport of IAA is an active process and when a stem segment is placed with its basal end upon a block of agar, IAA can be accumulated in the receiver block against a concentration gradient and electrical charge. Therefore, when IAA is transported basipetally from the shoot apical region it is not moving in response to a metabolic demand, but plays an active, determining role in the occurrence of cell division and differentiation in the cambial region and in the inhibition of lateral buds. Polar movement of IAA apparently involves cell-to-cell transport, and although it appears to occur in or near the phloem in woody stems, it does not appear to take place in the sieve tubes, but possibly in the cambium or differentiating cambial derivatives. The precise mechanism of the polar transport is still a matter of dispute.

The transport of other classes of growth substances, gibberellins, cytokinins and abscisic acid, appears to be apolar and may occur in both the xylem and the phloem.

So far, we have been considering aspects of coordination within the shoot as a whole which are dependent upon the basipetal transport of IAA. There are other aspects of autogenous control in which growth substances appear to play a key role, but which do not apparently involve polar transport of IAA. There is a vast literature on this subject and we shall confine the account to three examples illustrating temporal control, viz. fruit development, flower senescence and leaf abscission.

Hormones and fruit development

The early growth of the ovary during flower development involves cell division but little cell vacuolation. In many species, cell division ceases at or shortly after anthesis (flower opening) and the subsequent growth of the fruit following pollination is primarily due to cell enlargement rather than to an increase in cell number. However, in some species (e.g. apple) cell division may continue for a time after pollination has occurred. The ovary ceases growth at about the time of anthesis, and further growth takes place only if pollination is effected. Successful pollination is followed by rapid growth of the ovary and fruit development begins. The start of ovule growth and withering of stamens and petals marks the

start of fruit development and this phase is referred to as *fruit set*. The process of pollination, whether or not it is followed by fertilization, is apparently sufficient to cause an initial stimulation of growth in the ovary and other parts of the fruit.

The stimulating effect of pollen on ovary growth appears to be due to the auxin which it contains. Indeed, in a number of species, fruit set can be induced in the absence of pollination by applying IAA or synthetic auxins to the stigmas. In this way, the development of seedless fruits can be induced in tomato, pepper, tobacco and a number of other species.

Although pollination may stimulate the initial swelling of the fruit, in most species further development of the fruit depends upon the presence of developing seeds, and hence can only occur when fertilization is effected. In many fruits the final size is correlated with the number of seeds it contains.

Fig. 5.4.1. Correlation between achene development and receptacle growth in strawberry. A: only one fertilized achene present; B: three fertilized achenes present; C: *left*, control fruit; *right*, fruit with three vertical rows of achenes. D: *left*, fruit with two rows of achenes; *right*, control fruit. E: three strawberries of the same age; *left*, control; *middle*, all achenes removed and receptacle smeared with lanolin paste; *right*, all achenes removed and receptacle smeared with lanolin paste containing 100 ppm of the auxin β-naphthoxyacetic acid. (Original print supplied by the late Dr J.P. Nitsch. From *Amer. J. Bot.*, **37**, 211–215, 1950.)

Developing seeds are rich sources of auxin, which apparently moves from the seeds to the surrounding maternal fruit tissues, the growth of which is apparently dependent upon a continued supply of auxin from the seeds. This is well illustrated by experiments with strawberry, in which development of the succulent receptacle tissue is prevented by removal of the developing 'seeds' (achenes); application of synthetic auxin to flowers from which the achenes have been removed causes the growth of the receptacle tissue and the production of seedless 'fruits' [9] (Fig. 5.4.1).

Although there is good evidence indicating the role of auxins in fruit set and development, other growth substances also appear to be involved. Thus in some species, such as cherries and peaches, seedless fruits can be induced by application of gibberellin but not auxins, while in apple seedless fruits can be induced by applying a mixture of auxin, gibberellin and cytokinin. It is significant, therefore, that developing seeds contain high levels of each of these three classes of endogenous growth substances.

Flower senescence

The death of whole plants or of individual organs, such as leaves, flowers and fruits, is preceded by a phase of senescence, which is the final phase in development that leads to cellular breakdown and death. The phenomenon of senescence is complex and a detailed discussion is unnecessary for the present purpose. We shall therefore discuss only examples in which hormonal control seems well established.

The petals and corolla of flowers are normally quite short-lived and their death is preceded by senescence of the tissues. A detailed study of senescence has been carried out on the corollas of the morning glory (*Ipomoea tricolor*) [5, 7]. As in the senescence of other organs, including leaves, senescence of the flowers is accompanied by rapid falls in the levels of protein, RNA and DNA. The breakdown of nucleic acids is accompanied by large increases in the activity of RNase and DNase. On the other hand, there is no significant increase in proteinase activity during senescence. It would appear that many hydrolytic enzymes in plant tissues are 'compartmentalized', i.e. they are located in certain 'lytic' compartments within the cell and thus are separated from other cell constituents. Protein breakdown probably results when the proteinases in the lytic

compartments are brought into contact with the cell proteins, either by transfer of proteins across the boundary membranes of the lytic compartments or by the breakdown of these membranes, releasing the hydrolytic enzymes.

Ethylene appears to play an important role in the senescence of the flowers of morning glory. During the normal senescence of the corolla there is active ethylene production, and premature senescence can be induced in open flowers by exposing them to exogenous ethylene. Hence, exogenous ethylene stimulates the tissues to produce endogenous ethylene, by an apparently 'autocatalytic' process. However, exogenous ethylene is not effective in stimulating senescence or endogenous ethylene production before the flowers have opened, indicating that some other 'ageing' processes control the changes in sensitivity to exogenous ethylene. The ageing processes appear to involve changes in the permeability of membranes separating components of the ethylene-generating system, whereby an increased permeability of the membranes leads to the mixing of formerly separated components of the ethylene-generating system and so to ethylene production. It is suggested that exogenous ethylene hastens the loss of cellular compartmentation and hence the production of endogenous ethylene.

The functional significance of endogenous ethylene production would seem to lie in the synchronization of senescence in all the cells of a given tissue mass—the different types of cell in a given tissue mass would probably not senesce synchronously, but 'because of its unique capacity to induce both senescence and its own synthesis, ethylene originating from a few cells that age precociously could trigger the remaining tissues in a fruit or flower to enter the senescent phase, thereby integrating the ageing of the whole organ' [5].

Leaf abscission

Senescence of organs, such as flowers, fruits and leaves is usually followed by their shedding, as the result of the formation of an *abscission layer* at the base of the petiole or peduncle. Generally, before the shedding occurs the organ undergoes senescence.

Senescence in a plant organ, such as a leaf, normally commences in its distal parts and spreads to the proximal regions. The last cells to undergo senescence are those situated immediately adjacent to the future abscission layer, and at this stage the separation zone is often clearly visible as a yellow/green junction.

In leaves, auxin produced in the blade and transported basipetally in the petiole appears to *inhibit* the formation of an abscission layer, but if the supply of auxin declines, either as a result of senescence of the leaf tissue or by removal of the blade, conditions promoting the abscission process are created. A similar situation holds for fruits, where a decline in the supply of auxin from the fruit may occur because fertilization has failed to take place or, later in the season, because the developing seeds have attained full maturity.

Ethylene also plays a paramount role in the regulation of abscission. Abscission of leaves can be induced experimentally by exposing them to ethylene vapour, and ethylene produced during leaf senescence also plays an essential role in natural abscission. A detailed study of leaf abscission in dwarf bean (*Phaseolus vulgaris*) [11, 24] has shown that the cells on the distal and proximal sides of the abscission layer differ in their response to auxin and ethylene. The cells of the petiole on the distal side enlarge in response to auxin, but senesce in response to ethylene. By contrast, the cells on the proximal side of the abscission layer enlarge, and do not senesce, in response to ethylene (Fig. 5.4.2). When the leaf senesces, the ethylene produced stimulates the cells on the proximal side of the abscission layer to enlarge and at the same time these show increased nucleic acid and protein synthesis. They also secrete wall-degrading enzymes, including endopolygalacturonase and cellulase, which degrade the walls of the adjacent layer of senescing cells, thus creating a zone of weakness leading to separation and shedding of the leaf. Thus, endogenous ethylene plays a coordinating role, whereby leaf senescence is accompanied by the formation of an abscission layer and shedding of the leaf, a good example of the involvement of a growth substance in temporal coordination.

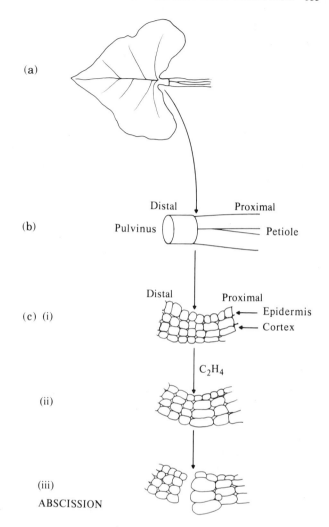

Fig. 5.4.2. Leaf abscission in *Phaseolus vulgaris*. (a) Primary leaf. (b) Abscission zone at junction of pulvinus and petiole. (c) i–iii Details of cells at abscission zone showing position of specialized cells that enlarge in response to ethylene. (Adapted from M. Wright & D.J. Osborne [24].)

5.4.3 HORMONES AND THE ENVIRONMENTAL CONTROL OF PLANT DEVELOPMENT

Introduction

By contrast with animals, plants show a high degree of plasticity in response to environmental conditions. Most plant species are profoundly modified by environmental influences such as light, temperature, water supply and mineral nutrition, and thus show a higher degree of phenotypic plasticity than do most animals. This greater plasticity is partly, though not entirely, a consequence of the 'open-ended' mode of growth of plants by apical meristems of the shoot and root, which are frequently capable of unlimited growth. This plasticity involves both quantitative effects, such as stem height, leaf growth and the degree of branching, and qualitative effects, such as flower initiation. A major factor rendering plants especially subject to environmental conditions is their sedentary habit. Thus whereas most animals are mobile and can often take action to avoid the effects of adverse conditions, plants are, in general, unable to take such action and must become adapted to resist environmental stresses.

In considering the effects of environmental factors upon plant development, it is useful to distinguish between the following.

(a) *Direct effects* of stress factors, such as low temperature, upon plant tissues. The effects are non-adaptive, as exemplified by the damage caused by freezing temperatures on the cells of frost-tender plants.

(b) *Programmed responses* of the plant to an environmental stimulus, such as light or gravity, as in phototropism and gravitropism. The change in the environment serves as a signal and the plant responds in an active and 'programmed' manner.

The programmed responses of plants are both *short-term*, as in phototropism, and *long-term*, as in the adaptation of plants to seasonal climatic changes. Outside the humid tropics, land plants are normally subjected to annual alternations of summer and winter or of wet and dry seasons. In temperate regions the alternation of summer and winter has a profound effect on the annual growth cycles of many plant species, the majority of which show a corresponding alternation of active and dormant phases which are synchronized with the seasonal climatic changes. There are frequently morphological differences between the active and dormant phases, so that many plant species show a *phased* annual life cycle.

Photomorphogenesis

Studies over the past 30 years have led to remarkable advances in our understanding of the role of light in plant development. The term *photomorphogenesis* is applied to the effects of short-term, non-periodic variations in light conditions on plant development. These effects are to be distinguished from responses to day length, in which time measurement is an essential feature, as indicated by the importance of the length of the dark period (p. 343).

A major advance in our understanding of photomorphogenesis arose from studies on the responses of a light-sensitive variety of lettuce seed. This type of seed shows little germination in the dark at 25°C, but germinates well if exposed to a short period of illumination. The most effective region of the spectrum for the promotion of germination is in the red (maximum effectiveness at 660 nm), with a subsidiary peak in the blue. Far-red (maximum at 730 nm) radiation does not promote germination but inhibits it. The effects of red (R) and far-red (FR) radiation are mutually antagonistic and if lettuce seed is exposed to R and FR radiation alternately, whether or not the seed germinates depends on the nature of the last irradiation (Table 5.4.1). Thus each succeeding irradiation reverses the effect of the

Table 5.4.1. Control of lettuce seed germination by red and far-red light (from Borthwick *et al.* (1952) *Proc. natl Acad. Sci. USA*, **38**, 662–666.

Irradiation	Percentage germination
Red	70
Red/Far-red	6
Red/Far-red/Red	74
Red/Far-red/Red/Far-red	6
Red/Far-red/Red/Far-red/Red	76
Red/Far-red/Red/Far-red/Red/Far-red	7
Red/Far-red/Red/Far-red/Red/Far-red/Red	81
Red/Far-red/Red/Far-red/Red/Far-red/Red/Far-red	7

preceding treatment. It was postulated, therefore, that these effects imply the existence of a photoreceptor in the tissues of the seed which can exist in two alternative states, a red-absorbing form (P_r) and a far-red absorbing form (P_{fr}), and that each is capable of being reversibly converted into the other, as symbolized in the equation:

$$P_r \underset{\text{Far-red}}{\overset{\text{Red}}{\rightleftharpoons}} P_{fr}$$

Subsequently, it was possible to isolate from plant tissues a protein fraction which showed reversible changes in its absorption spectrum (Fig. 5.4.3) following exposure to R and FR and which was called *phytochrome*. Phytochrome has been obtained in a highly purified form and the protein fraction has been found to have a molecular weight of 120 000. The chromophore is a tetrapyrrole compound related to the phycocyanin pigments found in the blue-green algae. There is still some uncertainty as to the nature of the intramolecular

*For more general account of this subject see Smith [16], Kendrew & Frankland [6] and Vince-Prue [18].

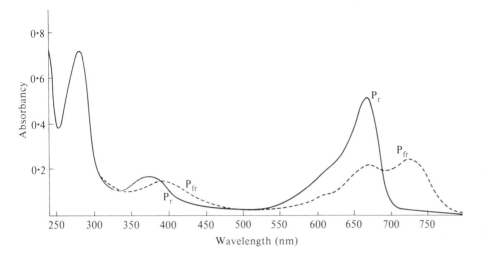

Fig. 5.4.3. The absorption spectrum of pure large rye phytochrome in the P_r and P_{fr} form. Note that P_{fr} in this case actually means an equilibrium mixture of 80% P_{fr} and 20% P_r, thus the absorption spectrum has a large shoulder in the red region. (After Rice & Briggs [13].)

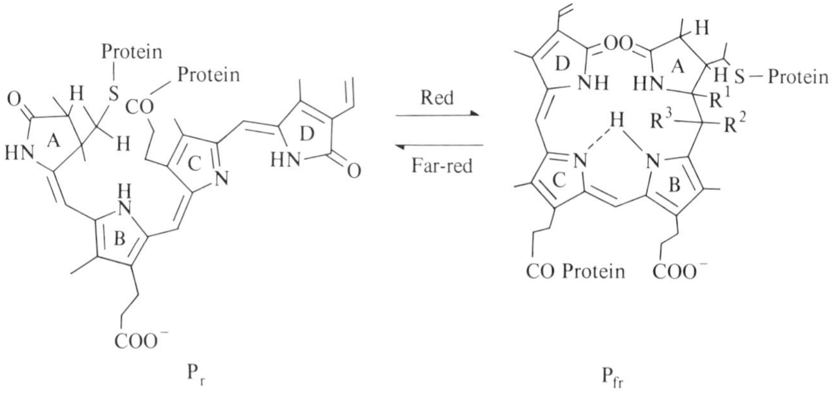

Fig. 5.4.4. Suggested changes within the chromophore of phytochrome occurring during photoconversion. (Courtesy of Prof. W. Rüdiger & Prof. H. Scheer.)

changes undergone by the chromophore when exposed to R or FR but one suggestion is illustrated in Fig. 5.4.4.

A wide range of plant responses have been found to exhibit R/FR reversibility, and this type of response is so characteristic of a phytochrome-controlled process that where it occurs it can be taken to indicate the involvement of phytochrome. It has thus become apparent that phytochrome is present in all green plants, including the green algae, and that it is involved in a number of very diverse processes (Table 5.4.2). These various light-controlled responses involving phytochrome are grouped under the general term *photomorphogenesis*. It is now clear that phytochrome acts as a sensing device whereby the plant is able to detect and measure variations in the quality, intensity and duration of the light regime under which it grows, and thereby plays a key role in the adaptation of the plant to its environment.

Studies have been carried out on changes in phytochrome in plant tissue in relation to growth responses. In dark grown, etiolated seedlings the phytochrome is present entirely in the P_r form, but on exposure to red light about 80% of the total phytochrome is converted to P_{fr}. If the plant is maintained in darkness the level of P_{fr} gradually declines and the level of P_r increases again; in a few tissues, such as cauliflower heads, these changes

Table 5.4.2. Processes that are known to be under photomorphogenic control (after Smith [105]).

NON-VASCULAR LOWER PLANTS	ANGIOSPERMAE (cont.)
Spore germination	Leaf area increase
Cell number per protonema	Coleoptile elongation
Thallus growth rate	Hypocotyl hook opening
Chloroplast size	Leaflet movement (photonasty)
Chloroplast division	Geotropic reactivity
Chloroplast movement	Phototopic reactivity
	Root initiation
	Leaf primordia initiation
PTERIDOPHYTA	Leaf dry weight
Spore germination	Seedling protein content
Rhizoid growth	Cytoplasmic viscosity
Filament growth	Sucrose translocation
Filament differentiation	Starch degradation
	Anthocyanin synthesis
	Flavonoid synthesis
GYMNOSPERMAE	Chlorophyll synthesis
Seed germination	Ascorbic acid synthesis
Hypocotyl hook formation	Various enzyme activities
Stem extension growth	Gibberellin formation/release
	Cytokinin formation/release
	Auxin metabolism
ANGIOSPERMAE	Polysome formation
Seed germination	Membrane permeability to water
Plant height (growth rate)	ATP/ADP conversion
Leaf number increase	Electric potential establishment

are due to the 'dark reversion' of the P_{fr} to the P_r form, but in most tissues such reversion does not seem to occur, and the decline in P_{fr} is apparently due to its destruction. At the same time there is continuing formation of new P_r in many plant tissues. The P_r form appears to be relatively stable, whereas the P_{fr} form is labile. P_{fr} is apparently the active form and appears to initiate the various processes controlled by phytochrome. These various stages of phytochrome interconversion, synthesis and destruction may be summarised as follows:

$$\text{Dark synthesis} \rightarrow P_r \underset{\text{Far-red}}{\overset{\text{Red}}{\rightleftharpoons}} P_{fr} \quad \begin{array}{l} \text{Biological action} \\ \text{Destruction} \end{array}$$

Several observations suggest that phytochrome may act by affecting the properties of cell membranes. For example, if excised roots of barley are placed in a glass beaker in a solution containing ATP, magnesium ions and ascorbic acid, they immediately adhere to the glass when exposed to R light. If they are then exposed to FR

they are released. This effect has been shown to be due to changes in the electrical potential of the root surface, which in turn reflect changes in membrane permeability.

Exposure to R light has also been shown to result in rapid changes in electrical potential in several organs. For example, exposure of etiolated coleoptiles to R light causes the tip to become more electropositive with respect to the base within 15 seconds. If coleoptiles which have been exposed to R light are returned to darkness, the electrical potential returns to the original level in a few minutes, after which FR causes a further decrease in potential, again with a lag of 15 seconds.

Other experimental evidence indicates that phytochrome conversion affects the permeability of cell membranes to electrolytes. The leaflets of the sensitive plant, *Mimosa pudica*, show 'sleep' movements and start closing within one minute on transfer from light to darkness. This movement is under phytochrome control, being inhibited by FR. Similar movement occurs in *Albizzia julibrissin* and is due to changes in the turgor of the pulvini at the bases of the leaflets. Exposure to R and FR affects the rapid exchange of potassium ions between the pulvini and the surrounding cells, indicating that phytochrome is controlling the permeability properties of the cell membranes.

Although the primary mode of action of phytochrome appears to involve changes in membrane permeability, there is good evidence that the secondary effects of phytochrome conversion involve enzyme-controlled processes. Exposure to R light leads to increased activity of a wide range of enzymes. Thus, in pea seedlings R light increases the activity of phenylalanine ammonia lyase (PAL), which catalyses the removal of ammonia from phenylalanine to give cinnamic acid. In this instance R appears to lead to activation of pre-existing enzyme, rather than to new enzyme synthesis, but in other tissues phytochrome appears to control the synthesis of ascorbic acid oxidase. Irradiation of etiolated bean leaves with R light leads to marked increases in polyribosomes within one hour, suggesting that the treatment results in increased availability of messenger RNA.

There is some evidence that some of the growth responses controlled by phytochrome are mediated via changes in endogenous hormone levels. Exposure to R light results in rapid increases in the levels of extractable gibberellins and cytokinins in seeds and in etiolated and green leaves. Thus, exposure to 5 min of R light causes

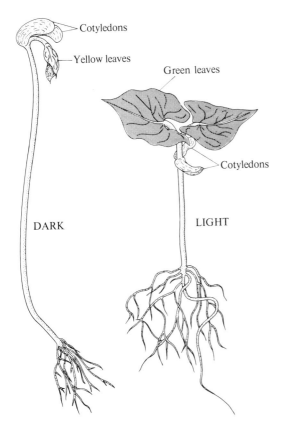

Fig. 5.4.5. Dark grown and light grown bean plants showing the developmental effects of light; (left) bean seedling which has been sown in darkness and grown in darkness for six days; (right) a genetically almost identical bean seedling which has been grown for six days under high-intensity white fluorescent light.

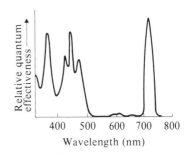

Fig. 5.4.6. A detailed action spectrum for the high-energy inhibition of hypocotyl extension in lettuce seedlings. (After Hartmann [42].)

marked increases in gibberellins in etiolated barley and wheat leaves, and in cytokinin levels in *Rumex* seeds and leaves of polar (*Populus robusta*). Moreover, cell-free preparations from barley leaves containing etioplasts show similar changes in gibberellins in response to R light to those in intact leaves, indicating that the etioplasts are the site of the phytochrome-controlled processes affecting gibberellin levels.

The characteristic features of etiolated shoots of plants grown in complete darkness (viz. pronounced internode elongation, reduced leaf development, lack of chlorophyll) can be greatly reduced by exposing them to quite short periods (e.g. 5 min) of R light each day, and the effect of R can be reversed by FR, indicating the

involvement of phytochrome. However, the appearance of shoots exposed to only short periods of low-intensity R light in this way is still far from 'normal', and in order to obtain the typical appearance of shoots grown in natural daylight it is necessary to expose the shoots to several hours of daylight at high intensity each day (Fig. 5.4.5).

Work on white mustard seedlings showed that whereas short periods of FR at low intensity reversed the effect of R, longer periods of FR produced the same effects as R, i.e. they reduced the characteristic symptoms of etiolation by causing expansion of the cotyledons, reduction of hypocotyl extension and the development of anthocyanin. Moreover, whereas the effects of short periods of R reached saturation at quite low intensities, the effects of longer periods of FR continued to increase as the intensity was increased to high levels. Hence these effects were said to involve a 'High Irradiance Reaction' (HIR).

Action spectra for the HIR show major peaks in the FR at 710–730 nm, and in the blue region (Fig. 5.4.6). At first it was thought that the HIR must involve a separate photoreceptor, other than phytochrome. However, later studies have indicated that HIR effects in the FR region are mediated via phytochrome. When lettuce hypocotyl tissues are exposed to FR, 3% of the total phytochrome remains in the P_{fr} form. This is because the absorption spectra of P_r and P_{fr} overlap (Fig. 5.4.3), so that when tissue is exposed to FR, a 'photostationary state' is reached, in which an equilibrium between photoconversion of P_{fr} to P_r and the reverse reaction is achieved. It was shown that the effects of the HIR could be simulated by irradiating tissues with mixtures of R and FR at various intensities and varying proportions such that 3% of the total phytochrome was present in the P_{fr} form. Thus it appears that phytochrome is the photoreceptor for the high-irradiance FR effects.

However, there is evidence that the effects in the blue region of the action spectrum for the HIR involve a different photoreceptor, possibly a flavin related to the photoreceptor for phototropism in both green plants and fungi.

From the evidence presented above, it seems that the HIR of phytochrome is involved in 'de-etiolation' effects, i.e. in the normal development of green shoots, under natural conditions. Under natural conditions plants are not, of course, subjected to monochromatic R and FR, and normal daylight (containing both R and FR) will induce a photostationary state in which a significant proportion of the total phytochrome will be in the P_{fr} form.

The phytochrome system confers on plants the ability to sense the quality of the light and their environment. Where plants occur at high density, both in natural vegetation and in planted crops, they tend to shade each other and hence to modify the light environment for the shaded plants. Natural vegetation contains approximately equal quantum flux densities of R and FR, but because chlorophyll absorbs strongly in the red region, the light within a leaf canopy will contain a much higher proportion of FR than does normal daylight [3] (Fig. 5.4.7).

Recent studies [8] have shown that the proportion of R to FR (R/FR ratio) has a marked effect on stem elongation of many plants, since it will affect the proportion of the total phytochrome which is present in the P_{fr} form (denoted by the symbol Φ). In experiments with *Chenopodium album*, plants were grown under various light sources which provided varying proportions of R and FR, so that the value of Φ could be varied, and parallel measurements were made upon stem elongation of the plants (Fig. 5.4.8). It was found that there was a

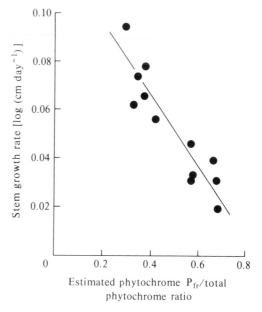

Fig. 5.4.8. Relationship between extension growth and phytochrome photoequilibrium (Φ) in *Chenopodium album*. (From Morgan & Smith [8].)

linear relationship between the logarithm of stem extension rate and the value of Φ, indicating that stem elongation is controlled by the phytochrome system and that phytochrome, through the establishment of various values of Φ, allows plants to monitor the spectral distribution of natural radiation within a leaf canopy. When a plant is in a dense canopy, in which there is a low R/FR ratio, it will tend to elongate and this will confer an

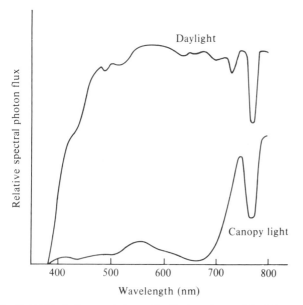

Fig. 5.4.7. Typical spectral photon distribution of natural daylight and daylight filtered through vegetation canopy. (From Holmes & Smith [3].)

advantage on it in the fierce competition for light which occurs within dense natural vegetation or crop stands. Since stem elongation involves endogenous hormones, especially auxin and gibberellin, it would seem probable that the responses to varying values of Φ may be mediated by modulation of endogenous growth substance levels. At present there is no direct experimental information on this matter, but it would seem significant that the abnormally short stem internodes of tomato plants grown under fluorescent lamps (and therefore with a low value of FR) can be rendered normal by application of gibberellic acid to the plants.

The initiation of the flowering phase

The transition from the vegetative to the reproductive phase involves a radical change in the organization and behaviour of one or more shoot apical meristems from a structure which is actively producing leaf and stem primordia to one which produces flower primordia, and at the same time the capacity for unlimited growth is

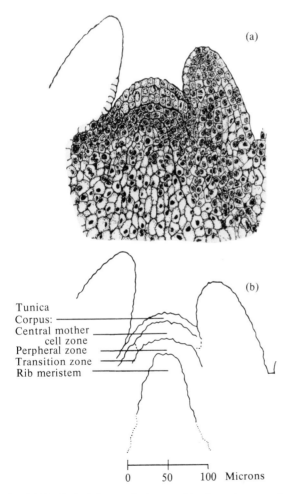

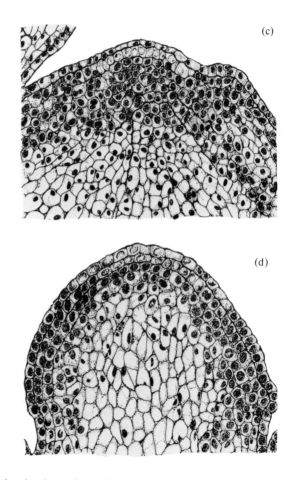

Tunica
Corpus:
Central mother
    cell zone
Perpheral zone
Transition zone
Rib meristem

0   50   100   Microns

Fig. 5.4.9. Histological changes during transition from the vegetative to the reproductive condition in *Xanthium strumarium*. (a) Median section through vegetative apex. (b) Diagram showing zonation of a. (c) Beginning of the transition to the floral bud. (d) Floral stage, showing the meristematic mantle overlying the enlarged rib meristem. (From F.B. Salisbury, *The Flowering Process,* Pergamon Press, Oxford, 1963.)

lost. Flower initiation commences with active cell division in the region between the central zone and the rib meristem and extends upwards into the central zone and outwards to the flanks (Fig. 5.4.9). At the same time there is reduced division in the rib meristem and the cells of the pith become vacuolated. As a result of these changes the surface layers of the apex become transformed into a 'mantle' of actively dividing cells overlying a central core. The mantle gives rise to the bracts and to one or more flower primordia, depending on whether a single flower or an inflorescence is formed. As a result of this radical change in organization, the apex loses its capacity for indefinite growth and gives rise to a flower, which is a structure of determinate growth.

In the subsequent development of the flower the various parts (calyx, petals, stamens, pistil) are initiated in succession (Fig. 5.4.10). The initiation and early development of the various parts are very similar to those of leaves, although the patterns of development diverge later. The stamen arises as a small protuberance and as it enlarges it gradually assumes the four-lobed form of the mature anther.

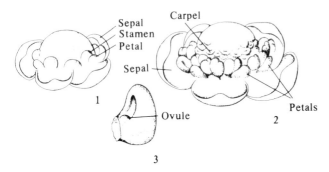

Fig. 5.4.10. Development of the flower in *Ranunculus trilobus*. 1 & 2. Stages in the development of the entire flower. 3. Developing carpel. (Adapted from Payer, *Traité d'Organogénie Comparée de la Fleur*. Paris, 1857. Reprinted from A. Fahn, *Plant Anatomy*, Pergamon Press, Oxford, 1967.)

In flowers with an apocarpous gynoecium, i.e. with free carpels, the first stage of carpel development is the appearance of a rounded primordium similar to that of other flower parts. This primordium elongates and a depression appears in the tip. As a result of further unequal growth each carpel adopts a horseshoe form and, as it elongates, its margins meet and fuse. In flowers with a syncarpous gynoecium, the carpels may arise

independently at first and fuse later, or they may be already joined from the earliest stages.

Photoperiodism

In some species, such as many arable weeds, flowering may occur at any time of the year, provided conditions are favourable for growth. By contrast, it is common knowledge that many other species are markedly seasonal in their flowering times. Such plant species must synchronize their life cycle with the annual cycle of climatic changes. In temperate climates several factors show seasonal trends, including temperature, light and, to a lesser extent, rainfall. We have already seen (p. 81) that in some species flower initiation depends upon exposure to winter chilling (vernalization), and such species include biennials and many spring-flowering plants. However, the environmental factor which varies in the most predictable manner is daylength, and in a wide range of organisms, including not only plants but also insects and vertebrates, the annual life cycle is controlled by seasonal changes in daylength, a phenomenon known as *photoperiodism*. (For more extensive accounts of photoperiodism in plants see Vince-Prue [18] and Wareing & Phillips [21].)

Daylength affects many aspects of growth and development in plants, but among the most striking effects are those on flowering. In some species flowering is promoted by short days (short-day plants), in others by long days (long-day plants), while many other species are relatively insensitive to variations in daylength and are said to be day-neutral. In general, short-day plants are either plants of tropical or subtropical regions (e.g. sugar cane, rice, soybeans) or autumn-flowering species of temperate regions (e.g. the garden chrysanthemum), whereas long-day plants are summer-flowering species of temperate regions. Many vegetative processes are also affected by daylength, such as stem extension in many long-day plants, and runner development in strawberries (a long-day response.) Tuber formation in potatoes and Jerusalem artichoke is promoted by short days, while bulb formation in onion is promoted by long days.

Our knowledge of the biochemical and physiological processes underlying and controlling photoperiodic responses in plants is still very incomplete but certain general facts about the light and dark processes are known.

In short-day plants flowering depends upon a regular alternation of light and dark. Under normal 24-hour cycles of day and night, the requirement for a minimum quantity of light arises primarily from the need for a certain daily amount of photosynthesis, no doubt necessary for the maintenance of the normal metabolism of the leaf. The length of the light period is, in general, not critical, and the primary factor controlling flowering is the length of the dark period—short-day plants require to be exposed to a certain minimum period of unbroken darkness in each daily cycle, known as the *critical dark period*. Hence, short-day plants would be more appropriately called 'long-night plants'.

To be effective, the dark period must be continuous, and interruption by as little as 1 min of light will nullify the effect of the dark period and prevent flowering in some short-day plants. This 'night-break' effect evidently involves phytochrome, since it has been shown that the most effective region of the spectrum in inhibiting flowering is in the red, and the effect of an R night-break can be reversed by FR. At the end of the main light period a high proportion of the phytochrome will be present in the P_{fr} form, but the levels of P_{fr} will decline fairly rapidly during darkness, due to degradation or reversion to P_r. However, if a short exposure to R light is given after several hours of darkness, high levels of P_{fr} will be restored (Fig. 5.4.11), with inhibitory effects on the flower-promoting processes, which apparently require low P_{fr} levels.

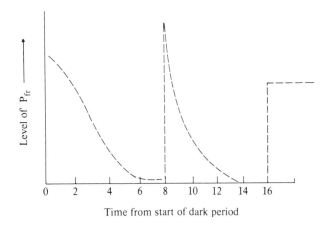

Fig. 5.4.11. Postulated variations in levels of phytochrome P_{fr} in leaves during a dark period which has been interrupted by a short exposure ('night-break') to red light.

The nature of the process controlling the length of the critical dark period for a given species or variety of plant is not known, but is has been postulated that the time-measuring process involves an 'internal clock'. There is considerable evidence that time measurement is achieved through endogenous 'circadian' rhythms, but the problem is complex and controversial.

By contrast with short-day plants, long-day plants flower most rapidly under continuous light, and they have no requirement for a daily dark period. On the other hand, long dark periods are *inhibitory* to flowering in long-day plants. As in short-day plants, the inhibitory effect of a long dark period may be nullified by a short light interruption; that is, a night-break *promotes* flowering in long-day plants. Thus the responses of long-day plants may be regarded as the 'mirror image' of those of short-day plants (Fig. 5.4.12).

Although flower initiation occurs at the shoot apices, the flowering responses of short-day and long-day plants are controlled by the daylength conditions to which *leaves* are exposed. Flower initiation must therefore involve the transmission of some stimulus from the leaves to the shoot apices under flower-inducing daylength conditions and there is convincing evidence that this stimulus is of an hormonal nature (p. 344).

Current ideas regarding the sequence of events controlling flowering in short day plants may be summarized as follows:

←Photoperiod→←————Dark period————→
Photosynthesis | Decay of P_{fr} | Time measuring | Flower
                                     process   hormone
                                                  synthesis

Vernalization

Since the discovery that flower initiation in cereals, such as winter rye and winter wheat, depends on exposure to a period of chilling (p. 81), it has become clear that a considerable number of spring-flowering species require a period of chilling for flowering, including both biennials [e.g. beet (*Beta vulgaris*), celery (*Apium graveolus*), cabbages and other cultivated *Brassica* species, foxglove (*Digitalis purpurea*)], and perennials [e.g. primrose (*Primula vulgaris*), violets (*Viola* spp.) and Michaelmas daisies (*Aster* spp.), certain varieties of garden chrysanthemum and various grasses, including perennial rye-grass (*Lolium perenne*)]. Thus the posses-

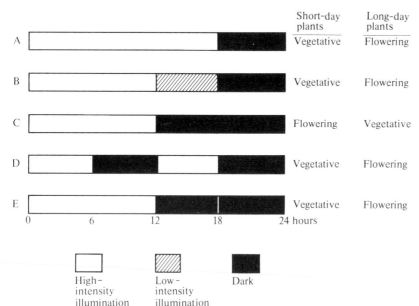

Fig. 5.4.12. Summary of responses of short-day and long-day plants to various photoperiodic regimes.

sion of a vernalization requirement is another means whereby the plant life cycle is synchronized with climatic changes and ensures that flowering does not occur before the winter is past.

Unvernalized plants can be induced to flower in various types of grafting experiment. Thus, if a leaf from a vernalized plant of the biennial variety of henbane is grafted on to an unvernalized stock of the same variety, the latter is induced to flower without chilling. A similar response can be obtained by grafting leaves of *Petunia* or tobacco on to unvernalized henbane, indicating the involvement of some transmissible flowering stimulus. However, in other cases it has not proved possible to obtain transmission of a flowering stimulus from vernalized to unvernalized plants by grafting. Thus, when the tip of an unvernalized radish plant was grafted on to a vernalized one, flowering did not occur. This result is consistent with the conclusion that the vernalized state (as opposed to a flowering stimulus) is only transmitted through cell division, i.e. by cell lineage (p. 82).

Growth substances and flowering

We have seen (p. 343) that, in photoperiodically sensi-
tive plants, the flowering response depends upon the daylength conditions to which the leaves are exposed, although flower initiation occurs at the shoot apices. This observation suggests that a flowering stimulus is produced in the leaves under inductive conditions and is transmitted to the shoot apices, where it causes the transformation to the flowering condition. This conclusion is strongly supported by the results of various grafting experiments. Thus, if flowering and non-flowering plants of *Xanthium pennsylvanicum* (a short-day plant) are grafted together under long-day conditions, the non-flowering plant will be induced to flower even though it has never been exposed to short days. Again, if the tops of *Xanthium* plants growing under long days are grafted on to plants which have been exposed to short days, the long-day scions will initiate flowers. In further experiments, single leaves of 'donor' plants of *Xanthium* exposed to short days were grafted on to 'receptor' plants kept under long days, which were thereby induced to flower under long days.

Transmission of a flowering stimulus by grafting can also be demonstrated for long-day species. Moreover, it would appear that the flowering stimulus is identical in short-day and long-day species, as the following experiment [25] indicates. It is possible to graft together plants of *Kalanchoë blossfeldiana* (a short-day species) and *Sedum spectabile* (a long-day species). If vegetative shoots of *Sedum* are taken from plants growing under short-day conditions and grafted on to *Kalanchoë* under short-day, not only do the stocks of the latter flower, but so too does the *Sedum*, which will not itself flower under short days. Conversely, if vegetative shoots of *Kalanchoë* are taken from plants growing under long days and grafted on to *Sedum* growing under these conditions, again both stock and scion will flower. These experiments suggest that the flowering stimulus is identical in both short-day species and long-day species.

Although the circumstantial evidence for the existence of flower hormones is very strong, repeated attempts to extract a specific flower hormone from short-day plants have nearly always given negative results.

A number of reasons can be suggested for the failure to isolate the flower hormone, such as:
(1) it is unstable and is destroyed during extraction and purification;
(2) it is a macromolecule, such as a protein or nucleic acid, and is not soluble in common organic solvents;
(3) flowering is not controlled by a single substance, but depends upon the interaction of two or more substances.

Numerous attempts have been made to induce flowering by applying exogenous growth hormones, and the greatest success has been achieved with gibberellins. Gibberellic acid (GA_3) will induce flowering of a number of long-day species maintained under short days. Long-day species which respond to GA_3 are typically plants which have a rosette habit (i.e. with short internodes) under short-day conditions. When GA_3 is applied to such plants growing under short days, there is a very marked stimulation of internode extension and this process is accompanied by flowering.

A number of species which normally require vernalizing before flower initiation can occur can also be induced to flower by external application of GA_3 (Table 5.4.3). Thus, in these species GA_3 apparently replaces the chilling requirement.

The question thus arises as to whether endogenous gibberellins are not the 'flower hormone' in long-day species and those with a vernalization requirement. Thus, it might be postulated that in long-day plants growing under short days the level of endogenous gibberellins is too low for flowering, and that the effect of long days is to raise the level of endogenous

Table 5.4.3. Species showing flowering under non-inductive conditions in response to applied gibberellic acid (GA_3).

Long-day plants	Plants with a chilling requirement
Chicory (*Cichorium endivia*)	Celery (*Apium graveolens*)
Lettuce (*Lactuca sativa*)	Sugar beet (*Beta vulgaris*
Poppy (*Papaver somniferum*)	Cabbage (*Brassica oleracea*)
Petunia (*Petunia hybrida*)	Carrot (*Daucus carota*)
Radish (*Raphanus sativus*)	Foxglove (*Digitalis purpurea*)
Spinach (*Spinacia oleracea*)	Forget-me-not (*Myosotis alpestris*)

gibberellins to the threshold necessary for flowering. However, there is considerable evidence against the hypothesis that flowering in long-day plants and species with a vernalization requirement is regulated by gibberellins, including the following observations:
(1) as we have seen, there is evidence that the flowering stimulus is identical in both long-day and short-day species, and yet gibberellins are ineffective in inducing flowering in most short-day plants;
(2) not all long day plants or species with a chilling requirement can be induced to flower by application of gibberellins;
(3) several observations suggest that the primary effect of applied gibberellins is stem elongation, while flower initiation is a secondary effect.

Application of other growth substances, including auxins, cytokinins, abscisic acid and ethylene has been reported to promote flowering in various species but, in the majority of short-day plants and in some long-day plants, flowering cannot be induced by any combination of the known major groups of growth substances. Hence, we cannot at present account for the flowering behaviour of the majority of species in terms of an interaction between known growth substances, and yet all attempts to extract a specific flower hormone have been unsuccessful. It would appear that we have adopted an oversimplified approach to the problem in assuming that flowering is controlled by a single, specific hormone.

The dormancy phase

In many species adapted to regions with warm summers and cold winters the annual life cycle alternates between active and dormant phases, the plant being more resistant to freezing temperatures and associated stresses when it is dormant. A variety of organs show dormancy, including many seeds, buds of woody plants, tubers, rhizomes, bulbs and corms.

In the dormant state, growth is temporarily arrested; this arrest may be due to conditions unfavourable for growth, such as drought or low temperature, so we speak of *imposed dormancy*. However, buds or seeds may also fail to grow even under conditions which are normally favourable for growth; in such cases the dormant state arises from causes within the tissue of the dormant organ itself, when we speak of *innate dormancy*.

The seedlings of many tree species are sensitive to daylength, and grow actively under long days but cease growth and form resting buds under short days. Thus the onset of bud dormancy in young trees of poplar, willow and birch is due to shortening natural days in the autumn. However, not all woody species are similarly sensitive to photoperiod.

When bud dormancy has been fully induced by short days it is not possible, in most species, to induce the resumption of growth by then exposing the plants to long days. In most woody species dormant buds need to be exposed to several weeks of chilling temperatures (0–5°C) before they are able to resume growth when transferred to warmer conditions.

Several types of dormancy are found in seeds, including a form of dormancy which is normally overcome by chilling. Thus seeds of apple, peach and rose will not germinate immediately after they are shed in the autumn if they are placed under warm, moist conditions, but if they remain exposed to normal outdoor temperatures during the winter they will readily germinate in the spring.

There is much evidence to suggest that dormancy in buds and seeds with a chilling requirement is mediated through endogenous hormones. Application of exogenous gibberellin will stimulate the growth of buds and germination of seeds of many species which normally have a chilling requirement. In other species, cytokinins are effective in overcoming dormancy, where gibberellins are not. It has been shown that endogenous gibberellin and/or cytokinin levels increase in buds or seeds of several species in response to chilling treatments. However, it seems probable that growth is actively blocked in dormant tissues and that dormancy is not simply due to the absence of growth-promoting hormones. Thus dormancy may also involve growth-inhibiting substances such as abscisic acid, which inhibits bud growth and germination of seeds. Dormancy control may therefore involve an interaction between growth promoters, such as gibberellins and cytokinins, and inhibitors, such as abscisic acid. However, the subject is a complex one and there is evidence which conflicts with this hypothesis, as well as other evidence which is consistent with it [10, 22].

5.4.4 EFFECTS OF DAYLENGTH AND TEMPERATURE ON INSECT LIFE CYCLES

There are remarkable analogies between the responses of plants and those of certain insects to seasonal change in daylength and temperature. Many of the seasonal cycles of activity in animals, including insects, crustacea, birds, reptiles and mammals, are controlled by photoperiod.

In insects, survival during the winter or a dry season depends upon their entering a state of dormancy, as it does in many plant species. In temperate latitudes most insects become active in the spring and enter a state of dormancy in the autumn, as winter approaches. As in some plants, the state of inactivity may be *directly* imposed by adverse conditions and recovery occurs as soon as more favourable conditions return. This environmentally imposed state of inactivity is referred to as *quiescence* and is analogous to 'imposed dormancy' in plants. On the other hand, insects may enter the state of *diapause,* which has been described as an 'actively induced' state of reduced metabolism and activity, not brought about directly by adverse conditions but by environmental changes that act as 'signals' of the approach of unfavourable conditions, but that are not, in themselves, adverse. The most important of these environmental signals are seasonal changes in daylength. Thus, diapause corresponds to innate or true dormancy in plants.

In some species of insect, diapause is controlled by an autogenous mechanism and is genetically determined, but in other species the onset of diapause is induced by short days in the autumn. Insects which are active in the winter and which aestivate in summer show opposite responses and in these species diapause is induced by long days. There is considerable variation among insect species in the stage of the life cycle at which diapause is entered, and it may occur at the egg, larval, nymphal or adult stage.

In a few species the termination of diapause is controlled by increasing daylength in the spring but in most it depends upon a period of chilling or a change in temperature. Thus, the analogies between the effects of photoperiod and temperature on bud dormancy in woody plants and on diapause in many insects are very close. (For more extensive accounts of the control of the insect life cycle by daylength and temperature and of hormonal control of insect development see Saunders [15] and Wigglesworth [23].)

As well as diapause, other aspects of the insect life cycle may be controlled by daylength changes. Seasonal morphological forms occur in a wide range of insect groups and in most cases photoperiod is the controlling factor. Summer forms of butterflies, short-winged bugs and aphids are produced in response to long days in the summer, while short days promote the appearance of winged sexual forms which become dormant or, in aphids, lay diapausing eggs.

Seasonal polymorphism is widespread in the Homoptera, including leafhoppers (Cicadellidae), white flies (Aleyrodidae) and aphids, the most complex seasonal cycles occurring in the latter. Most temperate species of aphids reproduce during the summer as a series of viviparous, parthenogenetic females, which may be winged or wingless; these produce sexual forms as the daylength shortens in the autumn. The fertilized females generally deposit eggs which overwinter.

As in short-day plants, the responses of some insects to photoperiod are determined primarily by the length of the dark period, but in others the duration of both the dark and light phases is important. In many species there is a critical length of photoperiod above which, in summer-active species, the insects are active and grow, develop or reproduce, and below which they become dormant. In many insects the critical photoperiod is quite sharply delimited, and a difference in length of photoperiod of one hour can determine whether a population occurs in the active or dormant phase. However, there is considerable variation in the shape of the photoperiodic response curves for different species. Moreover, the responses of a given species are modified by various factors, including temperature and diet. In most species which are summer-active, high temperatures act in the same direction as long days in repressing diapause, whereas low temperatures and short days promote diapause.

In the majority of species of insect which are sensitive to photoperiod the most active part of the spectrum is the blue–green (350–510 nm), but there is considerable diversity between species, and in a few sensitivity extends into the red. The nature of the photoreceptors is not known.

Time measurement in insect photoperiodism has been extensively studied and two types of model have been proposed:
(1) it is postulated that the night length is measured by a non-oscillatory timer or 'hourglass';
(2) it is suggested that a circadian rhythm in photoperiodic sensitivity is involved, as suggested for plants (p. 343). At the present time there is evidence for both types of 'clock' and the problem remains unresolved.

The effects of photoperiod on diapause and other aspects of the life cycle are mediated through the hormone system of the insect. Insect growth and morphogenesis are closely associated with the moulting cycle. Larval moulting is regulated by the neuro-endocrine hormones derived from the neurosecretory cells of the brain, which control two endocrine glands, the *corpora allata* and the *prothoracic* glands. Brain hormones can stimulate the *corpora allata* either to synthesize or to inhibit the secretion of juvenile hormone (JH), while prothoracic glands are stimulated to secrete *ecdysone*, the moulting hormone. The brain hormone (also known as 'activation hormone') has not yet been isolated and identified.

Juvenile hormone (JH) is present in high concentrations during the larval stages, which are maintained by JH inhibiting the expression of adult characters. When the *corpora allata* cease to secrete JH, or secrete it only in small amounts, metamorphosis from the larval to the adult stage takes place. JH has been shown to consist of isoprenoid compounds related to the alcohol farnesol. Four closely related compounds have been extracted from blood, all of which are epoxy derivatives of farnesenic acid.

The concentration of ecdysone, a steroid, fluctuates during the larval stages, reaching a peak just before a moult. Secretion of ecdysone from prothoracic glands is dependent upon continued stimulation by the brain hormone, even after the prothoracic glands have begun to secrete. In the hornworm, *Manduca*, larval moulting is stimulated by JH, accompanied by a surge of ecdysone. JH is present later during the deposition of pupal cuticle. If JH is not present, the cuticle proceeds to the adult form.

Diapause is also under hormonal control. In response to diapause-inducing photoperiods, the neurosecretory cells of the brain fail to release the brain hormone, so that the prothoracic glands do not produce ecdysone. In the butterfly *Pieris brassicae*, long photoperiods act directly on the brain itself to maintain secretion of the brain homone and so prevent the onset of diapause; by contrast, a short photoperiod promotes the onset of pupal diapause.

Reproduction, like growth, may show diapause. The cause of reproductive diapause is the inactivation of the brain neurosecretory cells controlling the *corpora allata;* inactive *corpora allata* result in the absence of JH and suppression of the ovaries. In larval diapause, on the other hand, JH levels are quite high. In the Colorado beetle, the induction of reproductive diapause is a short-day response; JH falls to a very low value during short-day-induced diapause, but rises again with long daylength.

Although the mechanisms underlying the photoperiodic control of the life cycles of insects and woody plants are clearly very different, nevertheless from a functional standpoint the analogies between the phenomena in the two very different types of organism are very striking, especially in relation to the roles of daylength and chilling temperatures in controlling diapause in insects and dormancy in plants.

5.4.7 REFERENCES

1 Fahn A. (1967) *Plant Anatomy.* Pergamon Press, Oxford.
2 Hartmann K.M. (1967) Ein Wirkungsspektrum der Photomorphogenese der Hochernergie Bedingungen und seiner Interpretation auf der Basis des Phytochroms. (Hypokotylwachstumshemmung bei *Lactuca sativa* L.). *Z. Naturf.*, **22b**, 1172–1175.
3 Holmes M.G. & Smith H. (1977) The function of phytochrome in the natural environment. II. The influence of vegetation canopies on the spectral energy distribution of natural daylight. *Phytochem. and Photobiol.*, **25**, 539–545.
4 Jacobs W.P. (1979) *Plant Hormones and Plant Development.* Cambridge University Press, London.
5 Kende H. & Hanson A.D. (1977) On the role of ethylene in ageing. In *Plant Growth Regulation* (Ed. P.E. Pilet), pp. 172–180. Springer-Verlag, Berlin.
6 Kendrew R.E. & Frankland B. (1983) *Phytochrome and Plant Growth,* 2nd edn. Edward Arnold, London.
7 Mathile Ph. (1975) *The Lytic Compartment in Plant Cells.* Springer-Verlag, Vienna and New York.
8 Morgan D.C. & Smith H. (1978) The relationship between phytochrome photoequilibrium and development in light grown *Chenopodium album* L. *Planta*, **142**, 187–193.
9 Nitsch J.P. (1950) Growth and morphogenesis of the strawberry as related to auxin. *Am. J. Bot.*, **37**, 211–215.
10 Nooden L.D. & Weber J.A. (1978) Environmental and hormonal control of dormancy in terminal buds of plants. In *Dormancy and Developmental Arrest* (Ed. E.M. Clutter). Academic Press, New York.
11 Osborne D.J. (1977) Ethylene and target cells in the growth of plants. *Sci. Progr., Oxf.,* **64**, 51–63.
12 Phillips I.D.J. (1975) Apical dominance. *A. Rev. Pl. Physiol.*, **26**, 341–367.
13 Rice H.V. & Briggs W.R. (1973) Partial characterization of oat and rye phytochrome. *Plant Physiol.*, **51**, 927–938.
14 Salisbury F.B. (1963) *The Flowering Process.* Pergamon Press, Oxford.
15 Saunders D.S. (1979) *Insect Clocks.* Pergamon Press, Oxford.
16 Smith H. (1975) *Phytochrome and Photomorphogenesis.* McGraw-Hill, London.
17 Thimann K.V. (1977) *Hormone Action in the Whole Life of Plants.* University of Massachusetts Press, Amherst.
18 Vince-Prue D. (1975) *Photoperiodism in Plants.* McGraw-Hill, London.
19 Wangermann E. (1974) The pathway of transport of applied indolyl-acetic acid through internode segments. *New Phytol.*, **73**, 623–636.
20 Wareing P.F. (1977) Growth substances and integration in the whole plant. *Symp. Soc. exp. Biol.*, **31**, 337–365.
21 Wareing P.F. & Phillips I.D.J. (1981) *Growth and Differentiation in Plants,* 3rd edn. Pergamon Press, Oxford.
22 Wareing P.F. & Phillips I.D.J. (1983) ABA in bud dormancy and apical dominance. In *Abscisic Acid* (Ed. F.T. Addicott). Praeger Publishers, New York.
23 Wigglesworth V.B. (1970) *Insect Hormones.* Oliver & Boyd, Edinburgh.
24 Wright M. & Osborne D.J. (1974) Abscission in *Phaseolus vulgaris.* The positional differentiation and ethylene-induced expansion growth of specialized cells. *Planta*, **120**, 163–170.
25 Zeevart J.A.D. (1958) *Flower Formation as Studied by Grafting.* H. Veenman & Zonen, Wageningen.

Chapter 5.5
Hormones and Animal Development
J.S. Knowland

5.5.1   INTRODUCTION

Any discussion of the part that hormones play in development always raises the question of what is meant by a hormone. A simple answer is that any substance released from one part of an organism which, by influencing the behaviour of cells elsewhere, controls or coordinates the overall development of the organism, can be called a developmental hormone. This definition means that some substances which are not usually thought of as hormones can be regarded as hormones in this particular sense. Cyclic AMP, for example, which because of its wide distribution in cells would not be classified as a hormone by traditional physiological criteria, plays a vital role in cell aggregation in slime moulds and behaves as a hormone in that context (Chapter 5.2). Developmental hormones, then, could be defined as agents which regulate developmentally important events.

A fundamental problem in assessing the importance of hormones in regulating development is that of measuring the amounts present, which is obviously of central importance in any attempt to show that a developmental event is controlled by an identifiable hormone. In the few cases where clear effects have been shown, the physiological concentration of hormone responsible is typically very low, about 10^{-9}M, which shows how sensitive the detection methods employed must be. The most promising approach to the difficulty is to develop radioimmunoassays, which are being used to an increasing extent, but even with the sensitivity offered by such methods the problem remains acute.

In assessing the part that hormones play in development, it is important to distinguish between early development, when cells become committed to a restricted line of differentiation, and later development, when cells express their state of determination. Does exposure to hormones decide for the cell what state of determination it will adopt, or do hormones simply make a cell express a state of determination which it has already acquired independently of hormone action? Most well-characterized examples of hormone action seem to fall into the latter category, when hormones initiate a predetermined response, but hormones that control cell determination, and decide what the response will be, may exist as well. From the point of view of differentiation and development, these would be the more important, but only a few possible examples are known.

This chapter deals with some principles of hormone action at four levels. It starts with effects on the genetic activity of cells, passes through effects on cell cytoplasm, goes on to effects on cell populations, and ends with effects on the construction of the whole organism. Thus the subject becomes increasingly complex and, as might be expected, the knowledge available decreases. This contribution is intended only as a very simple guide, and tries to deal with principles rather than details, which are to be found in the original papers cited. It is not comprehensive; I have chosen to concentrate on examples which seem to me to illustrate some important basic principles most clearly.

5.5.2 EFFECTS OF HORMONES ON GENE ACTIVITY

Introduction

The aspect of hormone action which attracts most attention concerns the way in which a single hormone governs the activity of a single gene, or of a group of functionally related genes, in a differentiated cell, and the subject is discussed here because the principles which govern responses to external signals in these relatively simple examples are likely to apply to the more complex case of early embryogenesis. However, such studies have little to do with the actual process of differentiation, because they do not start until after a particular type of differentiated cell, characterized if not defined by the proteins it synthesizes in response to the hormone, has appeared. They are concerned with understanding how a hormone acting from outside the cell selectively activates the transcription of a minute proportion of the genome.

The selection of which genes to activate is extremely accurate—in most cases only a single gene, or a very small number of genes, is activated, while other genes are not affected. The extent of the activation can be immense. Resting frog liver contains five molecules or less of vitellogenin messenger ribonucleic acid (mRNA), while only a few hours after heavy stimulation with oestrogen the number can rise to 10 000 [2]. The great accuracy and the enormous scale of the amplification are two fundamental aspects of hormone action at the genetic level in differentiated cells, and make the study of hormone action unusually attractive for those who are interested in gene control systems (see Chapter 6.4). However, one should remember that genes which are not controlled by hormones may depend on very different mechanisms from those that are, and also that

hormones can have very profound effects on cells without necessarily affecting the activity of their genes [4].

Measurement of gene activity

A question that often arises when hormones and gene activity are discussed is that of whether the gene is active at all in the absence of the hormone. Is the gene always slightly active, so that the hormone should be regarded as merely increasing a pre-existing activity, or is there absolutely no gene activity in the complete absence of the hormone? The question may be important philosophically, but in practice there is little point in asking it, because it cannot be answered properly. It is impossible to say that a gene is totally inactive, or that a hormone is completely absent, because the accuracy of the necessary measurements always has a certain finite limit. It is much more meaningful to compare gene activities before and after exposure to a certain concentration of hormone, and most current work is based on this approach.

Although the phrase 'gene activity' is widely used, it is not particularly easy to define, and it may have different meanings in different contexts. It may refer to the total amount of a single protein that is made in a certain time by a large number of cells, in which case it describes the total activity of a gene in a tissue at the level of protein synthesis. For example, the oviduct of a mature chicken can synthesize up to 2 g of ovalbumin in 24 h [30], giving an idea of the *integrated* activity of all the ovalbumin genes in the oviduct; but it is more useful to use the term to describe the activity of a single gene, either at transcription or at translation. The *absolute activity* of a gene can then be defined as the number of transcripts produced per gene in a given time, or as the number of protein molecules synthesized per gene in the same time [30]. Depending upon the amount of post-transcriptional control, the rate of translation may not be strictly proportional to the rate of transcription, and it is important to keep this in mind. The *differential activity* of a gene is a concept which refers to its own activity relative to that of other genes. It can be defined as the rate at which a gene is transcribed or translated relative to the total rate of transcription or translation. Although it is perhaps a more important concept than the absolute activity of a gene, it is clearly difficult to measure the differential activity of a gene because it is difficult to measure total rates of transcription or translation, and the majority of studies of genes and hormone action are based on absolute activities.

Regulation of ovalbumin synthesis in chicken oviduct

Most hormones that control the amount of a particular protein which is synthesized by a cell appear to do so principally by altering the rate of transcription. There is little clear evidence for significant post-transcriptional effects, although it does seem possible that steroids can stabilize mRNA [31], and that oestradiol, for example, can perhaps modulate the rate of translation of vitello-genin mRNA [13], as well as activate the vitellogenin gene itself. There are not many systems available for studying hormonal regulation of gene activity. A great deal of our knowledge is based on studies of how steroid hormones control protein synthesis in the chick oviduct, which provides one example of how somatic cells can be induced to secrete large quantities of material to be consumed by the developing embryo. The main attri-butes and advantages of this system have been reviewed so many times (e.g. [28–30]) that it is not proposed to explain them in detail here, but the essential features are shown in Figs 5.5.1–5.5.4.

If immature chicks are given very large doses of oestrogen (1 mg a day for several days), enormous changes take place in the magnum of the immature oviduct, which is the part of the oviduct that secretes the white of the chicken egg. A phase of general cell division lasting about four days precedes the formation of tubu-lar gland cells (Fig. 5.5.1) which multiply and start to synthesize lysozyme and ovalbumin. If treatment with oestrogen is stopped after 10 days, the synthesis of lysozyme and ovalbumin gradually declines to zero, but the tubular gland cells remain. They slowly change their appearance when oestrogen is withdrawn (Fig. 5.5.2), but remain responsive to oestrogen, and can be re-stimulated to produce lysozyme and ovalbumin by further treatment with oestrogen. These findings are indicated schematically in Fig. 5.5.3.

Unfortunately, there is no knowledge of how treat-ment with oestrogen induces the formation of tubular gland cells, and indeed there must be some doubt as to whether the method used to produce them, which in-volves persistent treatment with quantities of oestrogen that are much greater than physiological, can accurately reflect the normal mechanism. However, a great deal of work has been done on how oestrogen activates particu-

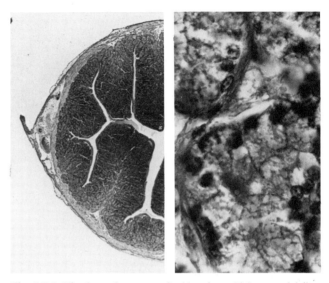

Fig. 5.5.1. Histology of magnum of oviduct from chicks treated daily with oestrogen for 10 days. (a) ×15; (b) ×350. The tubular gland cells contain large numbers of eosinophilic granules and form a characteristic acinar pattern with peripherally placed nuclei which are widely separated in the cells. (Adapted from [27].)

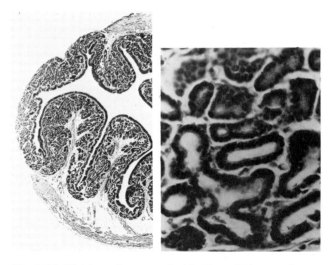

Fig. 5.5.2. Histology of magnum of oviduct from chicks treated initially with oestrogen for 10 days and then untreated for a subsequent 12 days. (a) ×28; (b) ×300. (Adapted from [27].)

lar genes within the tubular gland cells, and it is com-pletely independent of the actual formation of the tubular gland cells. Most of it is based on the model shown in Fig. 5.5.4. Very briefly, it is thought that a

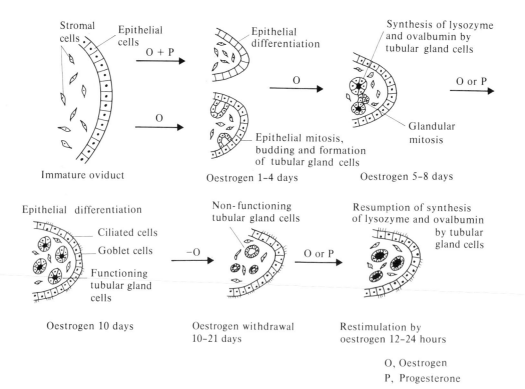

Fig. 5.5.3. Summary of oestrogen–progesterone interaction in the development and function of the tubular gland cells in chick oviduct. (Adapted from [27].)

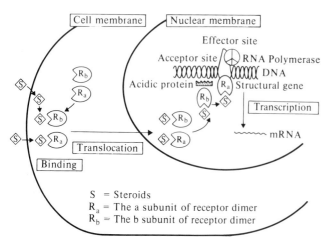

Fig. 5.5.4. Proposed model for steroid hormone action at the genetic level. (Adapted from [9]. See text for details.)

steroid hormone passes freely through the cell membrane and binds to a specific cytoplasmic receptor protein, and that the complex then enters the nucleus, where it binds to particular sites on the chromatin, resulting in the activation of a small number of genes. In principle, it should be possible to isolate and characterize the receptor, to identify the sites on chromatin to which it binds, and, with the aid of *in vitro* systems which imitate the conditions inside the nucleus as closely as possible, to discover how steroid hormones cause such enormous increases in the rate of transcription of particular genes. A lot of progress has been made in this direction, but there is still a great deal to learn about the control of gene activity in the chick oviduct.

One of its outstanding features is that a group of four genes, those for ovalbumin, conalbumin, ovomucoid and lysozyme, seem to be under some kind of coordinate control. Consequently, it has often been suggested that these genes may constitute the eukaryotic equivalent of a bacterial operon. It has been extremely difficult to test the suggestion experimentally because the powerful genetic techniques that have been used so successfully for this purpose in bacterial systems cannot be applied to eukaryotic cells. However, recent advances in techniques for cloning and sequencing DNA, which provide an equally powerful alternative, mean that the organization of the eukaryotic genome can be examined without the need for genetic methods. Not only has it been shown that the base sequences which make up the DNA that codes for ovalbumin are separated from each other by non-coding or intervening sequences (and it is hard to see how any other method could have established this quite unexpected fact), but also that genes with sequences related but not identical to the ovalbumin gene, whose existence had never been suspected before, are present close to the ovalbumin gene itself [10]. The newly discovered genes are transcribed, and appear to be subject to the same hormonal controls as ovalbumin synthesis, but it is not yet known what function they might serve, nor indeed if the transcripts are translated. It seems obvious, however, that further examination, at the molecular level, of genes that are closely linked to the ovalbumin gene will help enormously in the ultimate aim of understanding whether the ovalbumin gene and its relatives and other associated genes do indeed constitute an operon and, if so, how its transcription is controlled by steroid hormones.

Regulation of vitellogenin synthesis in frog liver

The oviduct system is undoubtedly complex, and in recent years a number of alternatives have emerged. One of the most popular depends on the reaction of liver cells to oestrogens. In egg-laying vertebrates, and in many other animals as well, oestrogen induces the synthesis of a protein called vitellogenin, which is the precursor of the main proteins found in egg yolk. It is normally synthesized in female liver, secreted into the bloodstream, taken up by the growing oocytes, and there specifically cleaved to release the insoluble yolk proteins lipovitellin and phosvitin (see Fig. 5.5.5), so that this system too shows how somatic cells can be induced to provide material used in embryogenesis. Its attributes are being reviewed with ever-increasing frequency [20, 34, 46], and it does offer some features which may in time make it even more attractive for detailed analysis than the chick oviduct. Although liver contains several cell types, the population of cells within

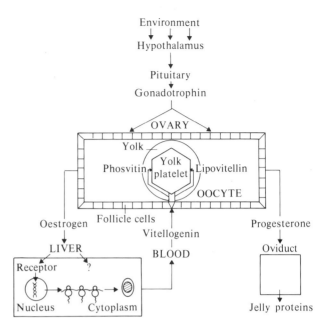

Fig. 5.5.5. Vitellogenesis in *Xenopus laevis*. (Adapted from [46]. See text for details.)

it does not seem to change significantly in response to oestrogen. This contrasts with the oviduct, where oestrogen causes the first appearance and subsequent proliferation of the gland cells that actually synthesize ovalbumin [26, 27].

Male liver responds as effectively as female liver, showing that the vitellogenin gene in the male tissue is just as amenable to activation as the gene in the female liver, even though male liver normally produces no vitellogenin at all. A very important point is that induction can be initiated and sustained *in vitro* as well as *in vivo*. This was first demonstrated in the frog *Xenopus laevis* [49], using organ culture (small cubes of liver incubated in a simple cell culture medium), and has since been achieved with isolated parenchymal cells [50], so that it should be possible to study the whole induction process *in vitro* using only responsive cells. The great advantage of *in vitro* systems is that one can control conditions much more precisely than in living animals, and this is especially important in studying hormone action, because a living animal is far more likely than a cell culture medium to contribute unknown amounts of ill-defined endogenous hormones.

At the molecular level, it is not yet clear whether the

liver system will prove to be simpler than the oviduct system. Until recently it appeared that vitellogenin was the only protein whose synthesis was induced by oestrogen, and that the vitellogenin gene system might therefore be more amenable to detailed analysis than the ovalbumin system. However, it now looks as if the oestrogen receptor which is thought to be involved in activating the vitellogenin gene [54] may also be synthesized in response to oestrogen [55]. A further complication is that there is more than one gene for vitellogenin [48], so it may well be that the system is much more complex than was thought at first. There is one clear disadvantage in that, with a monomer molecular weight of 200 000, vitellogenin is so large that only very little is known about its structure [25, 56], and another in that such a large gene is likely to have very complex sequence organization. Nevertheless, some progress has been made in analysing the mechanism of vitellogenin induction, and the system provides a good illustration of the main features of hormonal control of gene activity.

Properties of receptors for steroid hormones

It was mentioned above that steroid hormones are thought to exert their effects by first binding to receptor molecules. Receptors are proteins found in the tissues which respond to steroid hormones, and have two basic properties which are central to the part they seem to play in activating particular genes. The first is specificity, which describes the range of steroid types to which a given receptor will bind. For example, *Xenopus* liver contains a receptor which is specific for oestrogens. It binds oestradiol-17β, related oestrogenic steroids and also the non-steroidal synthetic oestrogen diethylstilboestrol, but it does not bind progesterone or testosterone at all [54]. The second is affinity, which describes the strength of the binding and is expressed as the dissociation constant of the steroid–receptor complex. The dissociation constant of oestradiol-17β bound to the *Xenopus* liver oestrogen receptor is 0.5×10^{-9}M, which means that if oestradiol-17β is present at a concentration of 0.5×10^{-9}M, half of the receptor will be bound to hormone. The dissociation constant of the same receptor bound to oestriol, a much weaker oestrogen, is 20×10^{-9}M; this means that the concentration of oestriol needed to half-saturate the receptor is forty times higher, or that the affinity of the receptor for

oestriol is forty times less than its affinity for oestradiol-17β [54]. It is important to keep these two concepts, specificity and affinity, separate. It is entirely possible to conceive of a receptor which has equally high affinity for two quite different compounds, in which case it would be described as a receptor with high affinity but low specificity. The oestrogen receptor from *Xenopus* liver, for example, binds oestradiol-17β with high affinity, but it also binds the synthetic anti-oestrogen Tamoxifen with almost equally high affinity, which presumably accounts for the effectiveness of Tamoxifen as an inhibitor of oestrogen-induced vitellogenin synthsis (Langton, Westley & Knowland, unpublished). It is somewhat misleading, therefore, to describe the *Xenopus* liver oestrogen receptor as being entirely *specific* for oestrogens, although among the steroids it is specific for those which are oestrogenic. In practice, however, a receptor that has high affinity for a given steroid is often specific for it as well. Consequently, the term 'specific binding' is frequently used, albeit rather loosely, to mean 'high-affinity binding'; while 'non-specific binding' often really means the low-affinity binding of steroids to proteins other than receptors, and it is helpful to bear this in mind when reading the literature. Low-affinity binding is always encountered in the search for receptors which bind steroids with high affinity, and is due to contaminating plasma and cellular proteins, many of which can bind a wide range of steroids with low affinity.

Distinction between high- and low-affinity binding

Obviously, it is essential to distinguish between high- and low-affinity binding in order to measure the affinity of a steroid for its receptor. The principle is simple, and involves measuring the amount of radioactive steroid that binds to a preparation first by itself and then in the presence of excess non-radioactive steroid. Suppose that a preparation contains a small amount of high-affinity binding which can be ascribed to a specific receptor, and also some low-affinity binding that is due to contaminating proteins. If a small amount of radioactive steroid is added, most of it will bind to the receptor, because that has the highest affinity for the steroid, and only very little will bind to the contaminating proteins. If excess non-radioactive steroid is added at the same time as the radioactive one, the receptor will bind both with equal affinity, and because the non-radioactive steroid is in excess, the high-affinity binding of the radioactive steroid will be virtually eliminated. Therefore the 'suppressible binding', as it is often called, represents the high-affinity binding of the steroid to the receptor. Typically, radioactive steroid is added at concentrations which will saturate the receptor (10^{-9} to 10^{-8}M), and non-radioactive steroid is added at about 10^{-6}M. However, the small amount of radioactive steroid that binds with low affinity to the contaminating proteins will largely persist in the presence of non-radioactive steroid, because both will bind with low affinity to the contaminants, and the low-affinity binding will only be entirely eliminated if a huge excess of unlabelled steroid is used. Therefore the residual, 'non-suppressible' binding represents the low-affinity binding. In this way, the high-affinity binding to the receptor and the low-affinity binding to the contaminating proteins can be distinguished without having to separate physically the receptor from other proteins.

Measurement of binding affinity

In order to calculate the affinity of a receptor for its steroid, it is necessary to measure the amount of steroid bound to the receptor at a range of steroid concentrations, which means that the bound steroid must be distinguished from the free. A variety of methods can be used for this purpose. A common one is based on the ability of charcoal coated with dextran to absorb compounds of low molecular weight, which means that it will absorb free but not protein-bound steroid. In principle, gel filtration can be used to achieve the same end, and in one highly efficient modification of this technique a small column of a hydroxy propylated dextran gel filtration material, Sephadex LH-20, is used to separate receptor-bound oestradiol from the free oestradiol [16]. The receptor-bound oestradiol passes through the column first, while the free oestradiol is retarded, partly because of its low molecular weight and also because it interacts with the hydroxypropyl groups which Sephadex LH-20 contains. This gives a very efficient separation of receptor-bound and free oestradiol. The data obtained at different total oestradiol concentrations can then be analysed by Scatchard's method to calculate the dissociation constant of the receptor–oestradiol complex and also the number of binding sites for oestradiol in the preparation used. An example is given in Fig. 5.5.6, which shows some measurements on the affinity and number of oestradiol receptor sites

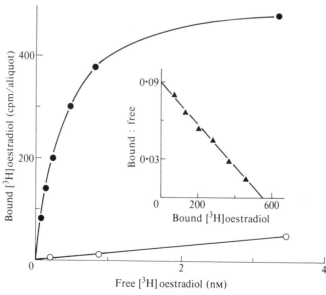

Fig. 5.5.6. Extracts of nuclei from male *Xenopus* liver were incubated with various concentrations of [³H]oestradiol at 0°C for 9 hours, and the bound and free [³H]oestradiol were separated on Sephadex LH-20 columns. ●—● shows the total [³H]oestradiol bound and ○—○ the [³H]oestradiol bound with low affinity. ▲—▲ shows a Scatchard plot of the oestradiol bound with high affinity. This dissociation constant of the oestradiol–receptor complex is $0.5 \pm 0.03 \times 10^{-9}$M, and there are 99 ± 18 binding sites for oestradiol per hepatocyte nucleus. (For further details see [54], from which this figure is reproduced by kind permission of the MIT Press.)

extracted from *Xenopus* liver nuclei [54]. If the number of cells or nuclei used in the preparation is known, then the number of binding sites for oestradiol per cell or per nucleus can be calculated. If one receptor binds one oestradiol molecule, this number equals the number of receptor molecules. In this way it has been shown that nuclei from male *Xenopus* liver contain about 100 oestrogen receptors [54], while axolotl liver nuclei contain about 1000 [24a]. However, nuclei from axolotl liver are about ten times larger, so the concentration of receptors in liver nuclei is about the same in the two species.

Characterization of receptors

An obvious consequence of the high affinity of receptors for their steroids is that receptors are easily saturated, and therefore that very low concentrations of hormone will elicit a response in a tissue that contains a receptor. This explains, at least in part, how very small, physiological concentrations of steroid hormones are able to exert such profound effects on gene activity, while the fact that receptors are restricted to certain tissues means that only those tissues will react to the hormone, although in living animals many, if not all, tissues are normally exposed to the hormone. However, the reason for the high affinity is completely unknown, because receptors have not yet been adequately characterized. One difficulty is that they are found in very small amounts and are therefore difficult to purify, although two methods, affinity chromatography, in which a receptor binds to a column of immobilized steroid [42], and an alternative method, in which a receptor binds to a steroid linked to a soluble polymer of very high molecular weight [18], both offer a way of separating receptors from other proteins. Another fundamental problem is that it is usually impossible to detect a receptor except by virtue of its high-affinity binding to a radioactive steroid, so that any technique which disrupts the binding means that the receptor can no longer be detected. Consequently, although there have been some great advances recently following improvements in purification techniques [32, 40], our knowledge of most steroid receptors is limited to that which can be obtained by non-destructive methods, such as gel filtration and sucrose-gradient centrifugation, which give an idea of the molecular weight. For example, the oestrogen receptor in *Xenopus* liver has a molecular weight of

about 40 000 [54], somewhat lower than the 61 000 reported for the oestrogen receptor in calf uterus [33]. We still do not know, for instance, whether the receptors in tissues that respond in different ways to the same hormone are identical or not. Chicken oviduct responds to oestrogen by making ovalbumin. Chicken liver responds to oestrogen by making vitellogenin. Both tissues contain receptors for oestrogen, but is the oviduct receptor the same as the liver receptor? The answer to this question is important because it may help to explain why the two tissues react differently to the same hormone, but it cannot be given yet. It raises the general question of what dictates the specificity of the response to a steroid hormone. Obviously, the nature of the hormone is a central feature, but it is not clear whether the response of a particular cell is then controlled only by the type of receptor it contains. It has often been suggested that other factors are involved as well, and that the specificity of the response lies partly in the receptor and partly in the site on chromatin to which the steroid–receptor complex binds.

Properties of sites on chromatin to which steriod–receptor complexes bind

The chromatin sites are even less well characterized than the steroid receptors, partly because, as with cytoplasmic receptors, a small number of high-affinity, specific sites may be masked by a huge number of low-affinity, non-specific sites [57]. Under these circumstances it is clearly very difficult to decide what constitutes a high-affinity, specific binding site on chromatin for a steroid–receptor complex, quite apart from the problem of describing the components that confer the specificity on the particular portion of the genome. Nevertheless, there is some evidence that the oestradiol–receptor complex, for example, binds independently to two different sites on chromatin; both to the nu-body, which is that part of the chromatin which contains most of the proteins, and possibly to the linker regions, which are stretches of DNA that connect nu-bodies, either of which could be involved in specific gene transcription [41].

As to what constitutes a specific binding site on chromatin, the two most obvious possibilities are DNA sequence and chromosomal proteins, notably the non-histone proteins. With the rapid advances in cloning techniques and DNA sequence analysis, there seems no reason why the binding sites should not be cloned and studied in great detail, and with the ever-increasing knowledge of the sequence organization of the ovalbumin gene system [10], have come hints of connections between particular sequences and specific binding sites [24c]. There are, also hints that the genetic response to steroid hormones may involve some control by non-histone proteins. A common principle in studying their role is to dissociate inactive and active chromatin partially, to use the components so obtained to reconstitute hybrid chromatin, and then, after adding RNA polymerase, to test the hybrid chromatin for its ability to direct the synthesis of particular messenger RNAs. For example, Tsai *et al.* [47] reconstructed chromatin using non-histone protein extracted from chromatin capable of directing the synthesis of ovalbumin mRNA, and other components extracted from inactive chromatin, and obtained some evidence that the non-histone proteins allow the otherwise inactive ovalbumin gene to be transcribed. However, such *in vitro* systems are very inefficient, so that it is not clear whether the results obtained using them reflect the normal controls that operate *in vivo*. A reliable *in vitro* system should be efficient both quantitatively and qualitatively, which means that it should produce RNA at a rate approximating to that found *in vivo*, and that the transcript should be identical to that made *in vivo*. These are stringent criteria and, with the patterns of transcription of divided genes such as the ovalbumin gene and the modifications of the immediate transcript that follow now known to be distinctly complex, they may be hard to meet. Nevertheless, it is important to bear these points in mind when evaluating results from *in vitro* transcription systems. At the moment it is probably true to say that, unlike translation systems, *in vitro* transcription systems have not yet developed to the point where they can provide really reliable information about the details of the controls that operate, but that the strong indications that non-histone proteins are involved are correct.

Development and the construction of gene control systems

As pointed out earlier, most work on the hormonal control of genetic activity is not really directly related to development, but one aspect that is concerns the way in which the control systems are built up during the dif-ferentiation of the tissues in which they operate. Obviously, a complete understanding of how the control systems are constructed requires a complete knowledge of all the components they contain, and this ideal has not yet been realized. However, some progress in understanding how control systems are put together can be made without a complete knowledge of all the factors involved, and indeed a developmental analysis may help to identify some of them.

For such an approach it is very helpful to use an organism in which embryonic stages and adults are as easy to obtain and study; this requirement is again met by the frog *Xenopus*. It has been shown that vitellogenin, synthesis of which is so easily induced by oestrogen in liver from adult frogs, cannot be induced at all in liver from tadpoles, and that the transition from uninducibility to inducibility takes place during metamorphosis [17, 19, 24]. The transition is not affected if oestrogen is supplied prematurely, and it also seems fairly certain that the transition is not influenced by the sex of the tadpole. Exactly what does govern the transition is not at all clear, but metamorphosis seems to be required. If metamorphosis is inhibited by rearing tadpoles in water containing chemicals (thiourea or propylthiouracil) which antagonize the normal action of thyroxine, the tadpoles do not complete metamorphosis although they continue to grow in size. The inducible state never appears in such tadpoles [17, 24]. On the other hand, the normal transition from synthesis of tadpole haemoglobin to synthesis of adult haemoglobin does occur [22]. Together, these findings suggest that the haemoglobin transition is related to the age of the tadpoles rather than to developmental stage, while the vitellogenin transition is related to developmental stage and not age. Premature exposure of tadpoles to thyroxine does not confer inducibility at an earlier developmental stage than normal [24], but once the tadpoles have started to go through the premature metamorphosis caused by the treatment with thyroxine, inducibility does appear. This suggests that thyroxine does not confer inducibility directly on tadpole liver, but that inducibility is acquired as a consequence of the metamorphosis which thyroxine brings about.

These findings show that the vitellogenin gene changes from a state in which it cannot be activated at all to one in which its activity is regulated by the supply of oestrogen and that the change occurs during normal development of the liver. It is interesting that the change occurs in both sexes, well before the activity of the vitellogenin gene is actually necessary and, by comparing uninducible with inducible liver, it may be possible to see how the change is brought about and to characterize the factors involved. An obvious suggestion is that the transition is caused by synthesis of the receptor, but it has been found that receptor is already present in uninducible liver [24b], so that the explanation must be more complex. It may, for example, involve changes in non-histone chromatin proteins. It is not clear when receptor is first synthesized or what controls its synthesis. As mentioned earlier, extra receptor is produced in adult frog liver if large doses of oestrogen are given [55], and it may be that low levels of receptor appear during tadpole development as a result of endogenous synthesis of low levels of oestrogen. Unfortunately, there are no accurate data on oestrogen levels in *Xenopus* at early stages of development, although it is clear that even very early embryos have the ability to metabolize some steroids [1], so that it is impossible to evaluate this possibility, and as yet there have been no comparisons of chromosomal proteins in uninducible and inducible liver. However, the general approach of studying the construction of control systems as well as what they consist of should eventually help in understanding what part hormones play in the differentiation of tissues in which hormones control gene activity.

5.5.3   EFFECTS OF HORMONES ON THE CYTOPLASM

Introduction

Although the previous section was principally concerned with effects of steroid hormones on gene activity, the same hormones certainly have important effects on the cytoplasm of the cells they affect. For example, oestrogen increases the amount of rough endoplasmic reticulum in liver cells from male frogs [11]. Secreted proteins such as vitellogenin are synthesized on rough endoplasmic reticulum, so this change is clearly appropriate for the synthesis of vitellogenin. There are also other effects. The parenchymal cells increase their lipid content, becoming lighter in consequence. As vitellogenin is secreted with quite a lot of lipid non-covalently bound to it, this change too equips the cell for a high rate of vitellogenin synthesis. However, the parenchymal liver cells do not irreversibly change their

function as a result of oestrogen treatment—they simply express a latent gene and adapt their cytoplasm to suit the changing gene expression . When oestrogen is withdrawn, vitellogenin synthesis stops and the parenchymal cells revert to normal, albeit slowly [50].

There are many other examples where hormones adjust cellular activities without permanently altering the cell. The action of adrenalin in muscle results in a rapid increase in the breakdown of glycogen, releasing energy for muscular contraction. Insulin causes cells to take up glucose from the blood. In such cases the cells that respond to the hormone are only transiently affected by it. From the point of view of development, it is more important to concentrate on examples where a cell is permanently altered by exposure to a hormone. In the case outlined below, a hormone irreversibly converts one type of cell into another, and does so principally by affecting the cytoplasm.

Oocyte maturation and the production of eggs

Mature frog oocytes are converted into eggs by progesterone, a process known as maturation, and the conversion represents an enormous change of function. The oocyte is arrested at the prophase of the first meiotic division. Vitellogenin, amino acids and most other small molecules can enter the oocyte, which has a very stable structure and develops in the ovary over a long period of time to a state where it responds to progesterone. Progesterone brings about the first division of meiosis and the ejection of the first polar body. The egg so formed is impermeable to just about everything except sperm, and is a very unstable cell. If it is not fertilized within an hour or so of leaving the female body, it degenerates. Big changes in the pattern of protein synthesis also accompany the conversion of an oocyte into an egg [3, 8], and are probably due to changes in the pattern of translation. How is it that a simple steroid hormone can cause such profound and irreversible changes in the state of a cell? Some progress has been made in answering this question, but a great deal still remains to be learned [4].

One striking feature is that progesterone is not the only steroid which can trigger the conversion of an oocyte into an egg. Many other, unrelated steroids will do so as well if they are supplied at high enough concentration, and this lack of specificity is in sharp contrast to gene activation by steroids, where in most cases only one type of steroid is effective. It clearly suggests that the response is not mediated by factors analogous to the receptors involved in gene activation, but by a very different mechanism. Very little is known about the interaction of steroids with oocytes, but some kind of receptor in the surface membrane is probably involved. If so, it appears that a loaded receptor is all that is required for oocyte maturation to occur; it does not matter which of a variety of steroids the 'receptor' is loaded with. The site of progesterone action is probably closely linked to the structure of the oocyte membrane because progesterone is effective only if it is supplied to the exterior of the oocyte—injected progesterone has no effect, while a progesterone analogue, covalently linked to a polymer which cannot enter oocytes, remains active. It also seems that the oocyte nucleus is not required for the action of progesterone because many of the events associated with maturation occur in enucleated oocytes [44], although under normal circumstances one of the effects of progesterone is to bring about the first meiotic division of the oocyte nucleus; indeed the breakdown of the oocyte nucleus or 'germinal vesicle', which is detectable in the black animal pole as the appearance of a white spot, is used as a convenient index of oocyte maturation.

Oocytes mature *in vitro* 5–8 hours after treatment with progesterone. Maturation is brought about by a 'maturation-promoting factor', which is synthesized in oocyte cytoplasm in response to progesterone. This factor can to some extent be separated from other cytoplasmic material and is sensitive to proteases [51]. If it is injected into oocytes which have not been treated with progesterone, it causes them to mature, and the level of the factor in the injected oocytes rises to that found in progesterone-treated oocytes. This process of self-amplification is closely connected with protein phosphorylation, which appears to be necessary for the factor to bring about maturation [23], but the precise mechanism of maturation is still very obscure. One very interesting observation is that a maturation-promoting factor can also be found in the cytoplasm of early embryos [52]. Early embryos are very useful for studying more closely the connection between the factor and cell division because, unlike oocytes, embryonic cells divide; and, more importantly, cells in early embryos divide synchronously. In this way it has been shown that the level of maturation-promoting factor fluctuates during the cell cycle, with the highest activity being found in cells which are just about to divide. It may well be,

therefore, that the factor, or a class of factors with similar properties, is of general importance in controlling cell division, and is not restricted to the conversion of an oocyte into an egg. In this connection it is important to remember that whatever the details of the part played by progesterone in initiating the conversion of an oocyte into an egg may be, the response is predetermined. The oocyte can only give rise to an egg; it cannot form any other kind of cell. There are, however, cases where hormones have a deeper influence on cells and not only affect their division but also dictate the kind of cell that is formed. In this way hormones can exert some control over the composition of a cell population. This is an enormous subject, and very poorly understood, but some of the principles are outlined below.

5.5.4 EFFECTS OF HORMONES ON CELL POPULATIONS

Introduction

An enormous number of diverse effects of hormones on cell populations have been described, but from the point of view of development surprisingly few are at all well characterized, let alone understood. Consequently, it is difficult to put forward any general rules, but it may be helpful to draw attention to a few guiding principles. For example, it is important to distinguish between quantitative and qualitative aspects. Under the first heading come factors that control the number of cells in a population, while the second includes effects that influence the type of cell formed in a population.

Quantitative aspects

Many examples are known in which hormones cause an increase in the number of cells in a mixed population. In the immature chick, oestrogen first stimulates general cell division in the oviduct, before tubular gland cells appear [26, 27]. This can be seen as a contribution by a hormone to the development of a functioning tissue, because a similar increase takes place when a female chicken develops naturally into an egg-laying hen. The first influence that the hormone has on the tissue is directly related to its ultimate function as a provider of large amounts of ovalbumin, but it is clearly a quantitative one. No new cell types are produced to begin with; there is simply an increase in the total number of cells.

It is often assumed that this effect of oestrogen on cell division is a direct one, analogous to its effect on gene activity, but the experimental findings must be interpreted with caution. It is commonly found that what appears to be a direct effect of a hormone is actually mediated indirectly, the original hormone first affecting some other tissue in the organism which in turn releases a factor that is directly responsible for the observed effect. Growth hormone, for example, which accelerates cell division in growing bones, almost certainly does not affect the cells directly but acts by stimulating liver or kidney cells to release somatomedins, which do increase the rate of division in the bone cells [45]. It is obviously extremely difficult to disentangle the interactions between tissues in a whole animal, and cell cultures are invaluable here.

One approach [43] is based on measuring the response of cells grown in culture *either* to oestrogen directly *or* to extracts prepared from tissues which have first been exposed to oestrogen in a living animal. Three cell lines were used: one from a rat mammary tumour, one from a rat pituitary tumour, and one from a hamster kidney tumour. They all require oestrogen for optimal growth as tumours in living animals, but oestrogen does not cause an increase in cell number when the cells are grown as cultures *in vitro*. However, extracts (high-speed supernatants of homogenates) of some tissues taken from living rats that have been chronically stimulated with oestrogen do stimulate cell division in the tumour cells grown in culture. Furthermore, these extracts do not stimulate mitosis in cells whose growth is never affected by oestrogen. For example, the extract prepared from rat uterus stimulates growth of all three of the oestrogen-responsive cell lines, but has no effect on cells which do not require oestrogen for growth in the whole animal. These findings suggest that oestrogen accelerates division of responsive cells not directly but indirectly, by first causing another tissue, such as the uterus, to release a factor which in turn affects the cells in question.

It remains to be seen whether a similar mechanism may apply to the early multiplication of cells in the oviduct. If it does, and the factor responsible and its origin can be identified, there is no reason why it too should not be called a hormone. The oviduct would still be thought of as a target tissue for oestrogen, but the direct effect of oestrogen would be confined to gene activation, and should be obtainable in cell cultures. Cell proliferation in the oviduct would be an indirect

consequence of treating the living animal with oestrogen, the new hormone being the factor directly responsible. At the moment this remains pure speculation, but it does underline the importance of developing *in vitro* systems if diverse effects of a hormone on a single tissue are to be thoroughly understood.

Qualitative aspects

In addition to the examples outlined so far, there are clear cases in which hormones can manipulate cell populations by deciding between alternative kinds of progeny cell that can be produced from dividing cells. This is very different from the predetermined conversion of one cell type into another by a hormone trigger, as in oocyte maturation in which there is no choice as to the variety of cell produced. A striking example is that of 'sex determination', which has been quite well studied in Amphibia, particularly in *Xenopus*.

The term 'sex determination' does not refer to genetic sex, which is decided by chromosomal constitution, but to phenotypic or functional sex, which is defined by whether a gonad produces sperm or eggs. It has been known for a long time that the ratio of functional males to females in the progeny of amphibian matings can be affected by a variety of environmental factors such as temperature, but much more dramatic effects can be found if early embryos are exposed to sex hormones. If *Xenopus* embryos are grown from an early stage with oestrogen always present in their water, almost 100% of them develop as functional females, although approximately half are, of course, genotypic males [14]. A 'sex-reversed' male obtained in this way has the normal male genotype, but a functional ovary, which can produce eggs. *Xenopus* males have two identical sex chromosomes and are designated ZZ, while females have two dissimilar sex chromosomes and are designated ZW [53]. A sex-reversed male is genetically ZZ and, because it lays eggs, can be mated with a normal male, also ZZ. The progeny of such a mating will be exclusively ZZ and therefore genetically male. If reared under normal conditions, the progeny will all be functionally male as well, so that once a sex-reversed male has been identified, there is a method of ensuring that all future progeny are male in both senses. This has some practical value for those who need large numbers of male frogs, for example for studies on vitellogenin synthesis.

Sex-reversal in the female to male direction has been

attempted by growing embryos in androgens, but the results are less successful. It can, however, be achieved in either direction by transplanting primordial germ cells into either a male or a female host [6]. This shows that the primordial germ cells of either genetic sex are labile and can form either spermatogonia or oogonia depending on their environment. Unfortunately, it is not precisely clear how the environment exerts its effect. The simplest explanation is that female sex hormones somehow instruct the primordial germ cells to form oogonia, while male sex hormones direct them to form spermatogonia. However, the results from the transplant experiments suggest that the immediate instructions may not be carried by the hormones themselves. The sex hormones may command the somatic tissues of the gonad in which the primordial germ cells develop to issue the instructions. If this is the case, then it constitutes another example of hormones exerting an effect on a cell population indirectly rather than directly, perhaps via another factor, but it does not contradict the general point that where a choice exists in the type of cell that can be formed from a precursor cell, the outcome may be decided by hormones. In this case the consequence of the hormone action is that one type of cell population is established instead of another, while the rest of the organism is not affected. There, are, however, examples where hormones have much wider effects, and to some extent control the construction of the whole organism.

5.5.5 EFFECTS OF HORMONES ON DEVELOPMENT AND CONSTRUCTION OF THE WHOLE ORGANISM

Metamorphosis

The most widely discussed example of an effect of a hormone on morphology is that of metamorphosis, which has been studied mainly in Amphibia and insects. In Amphibia, metamorphosis is initiated by thyroid hormones, and is accompanied by an enormous number of biochemical and morphological changes [5]. The changes range from gene activation, resulting in the synthesis of new enzymes, to proliferation of particular cells, leading to the appearance of new structures such as the limbs. It is most unlikely that such a wide range of responses could all be specified exclusively by thyroid hormones, which once again seem to trigger pre-

determined responses that are characteristic of the cells in question. Thus, particular tissues always act in the same way during metamorphosis and continue to do so even if they are removed from their normal position and grafted on to a tissue that reacts differently. A developing limb in a tadpole, for example, continues to develop and grow normally if it is transplanted to the tail, which is resorbed during metamorphosis. It is not clear how different cells become determined to react in different ways to thyroid hormones, but it seems that the determined state is established early in development, long before thyroid hormone is actually released from the thyroid gland, because many of the changes that are characteristic of metamorphosis can be obtained at unusually early stages of development if embryos are exposed to thyroid hormones. This emphasizes the fact that thyroid hormones alter morphology through effects on previously determined cells, and are almost certainly not involved in establishing the determined state.

Analysis of metamorphosis in insects has progressed rather further, chiefly because insects develop very much faster than Amphibia, but is still poorly understood. The steroid hormone ecdysone is clearly involved in many aspects of insect growth and development, and its role in initiating predetermined responses may be analogous to that of thyroid hormones in amphibian metamorphosis. Apart from the greater speed of insect development, there is the enormous advantage that genetic techniques can be employed as well as biochemical ones. By constructing developmental mutants, that is, mutants which develop no further than a certain stage, and then measuring the endogenous level of ecdysone and testing the effects of exogenous ecdysone, it is possible to define the developmental processes that depend on ecdysone and to analyse the mechanism of ecdysone action in greater detail. This principle has been well known for some time, but has only recently been adopted, partly because it requires a sensitive assay for low levels of ecdysone, which is now available in the form of a radioimmunoassay. One approach [15] uses temperature-sensitive mutants of *Drosophila*, which develop normally at one temperature (20°C) but arrest if grown at a higher temperature (29°C). Such mutants are especially valuable because the effect of the mutation can be obtained at will simply by altering the temperature. In one mutant, *ecd*[1], the developmental failures found at the restrictive temperature are consistently associated with ecdysone deficiency, suggesting that lack of ecdysone is the cause of particular defects. These experiments do not themselves give information as to how ecdysone might act, but they have now been extended to examination of transcription and translation of particular genes for which clones are available [21]. These studies should lead to a clearer understanding of how genes whose operation is essential for particular developmental stages are regulated. Once again, however, this kind of work is principally directed at finding out how certain genes are regulated at transcription and translation. It still remains to be seen whether cell determination is controlled in this way, or whether the developmental fate of cells, and subsequently the construction of an organism, is decided in some other way.

The last part of this chapter outlines one case in which the overall construction of an organism does seem to be profoundly influenced by a relatively simple substance that could be called a hormone, whose primary effect is probably on cell determination.

Morphogenesis

Although considerable changes in morphology accompany metamorphosis in Amphibia and insects, the changes affect a very large number of different cell types in different ways, and occur very late in the development of the organism when a great deal of differentiation has already taken place. Studies on how hormones might affect morphology really need much simpler systems, in which fewer changes occur. Another requirement, if morphological changes are eventually to be connected with biochemical changes at the cellular level, is some sort of assay for a morphological change. It is not particularly easy to think of quantitative assays based on morphological changes. How, for example, does one express numerically the degree to which a certain structure is formed? A number of experiments on these lines are based on regeneration of particular structures, where it is sometimes possible to express the amount of regeneration in simple quantitative terms. Both requirements, for a simple cellular system and a workable assay of morphological change, are provided by the coelenterate *Hydra*.

A *morphogen in* Hydra

If large numbers of *Hydra* are disaggregated with citrate, and the cells reaggregated at random by centri-

fuging them together in 0.5 mm diameter tubes, then heads appear in the aggregate so formed [36]. Aggregates made from the gastric region of *Hydra* form heads only rarely, while aggregates consisting of 90% gastric cells and 10% head cells form heads much more frequently. The heads appear at random, suggesting that a head can form wherever a 'nucleus' of head-forming activity lies, and that head cells are mainly responsible for the activity. Schaller has shown that a substance, known as the 'head activator', can be extracted from *Hydra*, and that more activity is found in the head and budding regions than elsewhere [35, 39]. The head activator promotes the regeneration of heads and tentacles in decapitated *Hydra*, and so by counting the increase in the rate of regeneration of heads and tentacles after treatment it is possible to put morphogenesis on a quantitative basis. This assay has been used in the partial purification of the head activator. Head activator is extracted from large numbers of *Hydra* by sonication, acetic acid extraction, gel filtration and ion-exchange chromatography, giving a recovery of 60% of starting activity and purification of over 500 000 times, meaning that its activity per weight of material increases by this amount. It is insensitive to nucleases but destroyed by proteases, is heat-stable, and seems to have a molecular weight of about 1000. All these properties are consistent with the material being a small peptide, 6–10 amino acids long. Assuming a molecular weight of 1000, the material is active at 10^{-10}M, which is in very sharp contrast to the many non-specific effects on morphology that are known, such as those of metal ions, which typically have to be present at 10^{-3}M or more to have an effect. The activator is therefore a candidate for a true morphogen, because it exerts its effects on morphogenesis at exceedingly low concentrations. It could also be thought of as a hormone which effects morphogenesis.

How the morphogen influences Hydra *cells*

One major obstacle to progress in studying the activator is that *Hydra* contains so little of it, but there is some knowledge of how it induces head formation during *Hydra* morphogenesis. It has two main effects. The first, quantitative effect, is to increase the division rate of the proliferating cells by reducing the length of the G_2 phase of the cell cycle. The second, qualitative and more complex effect is to increase the formation of nerve cells at the expense of nematocytes [37, 38]. It is this aspect which is important from the point of view of cell determination.

Nerve cells and nematocytes, which perform completely different functions, are derived from the same immediate source [12]. Figure 5.5.7 shows the cell lineage, which was deduced [12] by first labelling the dividing stem cells with tritiated thymidine and then following the formation of labelled nerve cells and nematocytes, each of which has a characteristic appearance. There is a pool of dividing stem cells. One stem cell divides to form two, one of which returns to the pool. The other divides again to form two interstitial cells. If this pair of interstitial cells divides again, the progeny always form nematocytes, seen in nests of 2^n cells, where n can be 2, 3, 4 or 5. If the pair of interstitial cells does not divide again, it inevitably differentiates into two nerve cells. The decision to enter the nematocyte pathway, which requires further division, or the nerve cell pathway, in which further division is prohibited, is taken during the division of one of the two stem cells to form two interstitials. The head activator seems to exert its effect just before or during the S phase of this cell division, and somehow causes the immediately post-S-phase cells to enter the nerve cell pathway. Thus only cells that have passed through S phase, which can be distinguished from those that have not by giving the cell population a short pulse of [^{3}H]thymidine at an earlier stage to label the post-S-phase cells, can form nerve cells when activator is supplied. Again, if cells that have completed the S phase are eliminated by first treating the population with nitrogen mustard, which kills cells as they pass through the S phase, the number of nerve cells that form when activator is then supplied is greatly reduced. How the activator works is completely unknown, but the experiments do show that a relatively simple substance can do more than initiate a predetermined response; it can decide which of alternative pathways of differentiation cells are to enter [7]. It is effects such as these which must be studied if the part played by hormones in cell determination and morphogenesis is to be understood.

5.5.6 CONCLUSIONS

The principal conclusion to be drawn from this brief survey of the part that hormones play in animal development is that while knowledge of how hormones activate

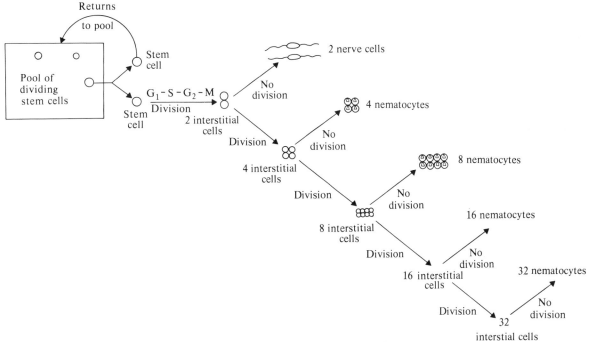

Fig. 5.5.7. Formation of nerve cells and nematocytes in *Hydra*. (Based on [12]. See text for explanation.)

particular genes or sets of genes has progressed to a point where some at least of the factors involved have been identified, knowledge of how hormones may control cell determination or differentiation is still very limited. It is especially important in this context to distinguish between the possibility that a hormone may simply act as a trigger to initiate a predetermined response and the possibility that it may decide what the response is to be. The conversion of oocytes into eggs by progesterone provides a clear example of the first possibility, and the formation of either spermatogonia or oogonia from primordial germ cells illustrates the second. It is also important to remember that the mechanism by which hormones influence cell determination and differentiation may not be the same as the mechanisms by which they activate particular genes. Oestrogen, which activates the ovalbumin and related genes in tubular gland cells in chick oviduct, also stimulates the cell division which leads to the formation of tubular gland cells, but there is no particular reason to suppose that these two independent effects operate by similar mechanisms. However, experimental approaches to the study of hormones and cellular development have undoubtedly been strongly influenced by the results from the study of hormones and gene activation, and this may be one reason why so little progress has been made towards understanding the hormonal control of development.

5.4.7 REFERENCES

1 Antila E. (1977) Early steroid metabolism in *Xenopus laevis*, *Rana temporaria* and *Triturus vulgaris* embryos. *Differentiation*, **8**, 71–77.

2 Baker H.J. & Shapiro D.J. (1977) Kinetics of estrogen induction of *Xenopus laevis* vitellogenin messenger RNA as measured by hybridization to complementary RNA. *J. biol. Chem.*, **252**, 8428–8434.

3 Ballantine J.E.M., Woodland H.R. & Sturgess E.A. (1979) Changes in protein synthesis during the development of *Xenopus laevis*. *J. Embryol. exp. Morph.*, **51**, 137–153.

4 Baulieu E.-E., Godeau F., Schorderet M. & Schorderet-Slatkine S. (1978) Steroid induced meiotic division in *Xenopus laevis* oocytes: surface and calcium. *Nature, Lond.*, **275**, 593–598.

5 Beckingham-Smith K. & Tata J.R. (1976) The hormonal control of amphibian metamorphosis. In *The Developmental Biology of Plants and Animals*, 1st edn. (Eds C.F. Graham & P.F. Wareing), pp. 232–245. Blackwell Scientific Publications, Oxford.

6 Blackler A.W. (1965) Germ-cell transfer and sex ratio in *Xenopus laevis*. *J. Embryol. exp. Morph.*, **13**, 51–61.

7 Bode H.R. & David C.N. (1978) Regulation of a multipotent stem cell, the interstitial cell of Hydra. *Prog. biophys. molec. Biol.*, **33**, 189–206.

8 Bravo R. & Knowland J. (1979) Classes of proteins synthesized in oocytes, eggs, embryos, and differentiated tissues of *Xenopus laevis*. *Differentiation*, **1**, 101–108.

9 Buller R.E., Schwartz R.J., Schrader W.T. & O'Malley B.W. (1976) Progesterone-binding components of chick oviduct. *In vivo* effect of receptor subunits on gene transcription. *J. biol. Chem.*, **251**, 5178–5186.

10 Carey N. (1979) Unsuspected relatives of the ovalbumin gene. *Nature, Lond.*, **279**, 101–102.

11 Clemens M.J. (1974) The regulation of egg yolk protein synthesis by steroid hormones. *Prog. biophys. molec. Biol.*, **28**, 71–107.

12 David C.N. & Gierer A. (1974) Cell cycle kinetics and development of *Hydra attenuata*. III. Nerve and nematocyte differentiation. *J. Cell Sci.*, **16**, 359–375.

13 Farmer S.R., Henshaw E.C., Berridge M.V. & Tata J.R. (1978) Translation of *Xenopus* vitellogenin mRNA during primary and secondary induction. *Nature, Lond.*, **273**, 401–403.

14 Gallien L. (1956) Inversion expérimentale du sexe chez un anoure inférieur *Xenopus laevis* Daudin. Analyse des conséquences génétiques. *Bull. biol. Fr. Belg.*, **90**, 163–173.

15 Garen A., Kauver L. & Lepesant J.-A. (1977) Roles of ecdysone in *Drosophila* development. *Proc. natl Acad. Sci., USA*, **74**, 5099–5103.

16 Ginsburg M., Greenstein B.D., MacLusky N.J., Morris I.D. & Thomas P.J. (1974) An improved method for the study of high-affinity steroid binding: oestradiol binding in brain and pituitary. *Steroids*, **23**, 773–792.

17 Huber S., Ryffel G.U. & Weber R. (1979) Thyroid hormone induces competence for oestrogen-dependent vitellogenin synthesis in developing *Xenopus laevis* liver. *Nature, Lond.*, **278**, 65–67.

18 Hubert P., Mešter J., Dellacherie E., Neel J. & Baulieu E.-E. (1978) Soluble biospecific macromolecule for purification of estrogen receptor. *Proc. natl Acad. Sci., USA*, **75**, 3143–3147.

19 Knowland J. (1978) Induction of vitellogenin synthesis in *Xenopus laevis* tadpoles. *Differentiation*, **12**, 47–51.

20 Knowland J. & Westley B. (1979) The control of vitellogenin synthesis by estrogen in *Xenopus laevis* and conversion of vitellogenin into yolk proteins. In *Maternal Effects in Development, Symposium of the British Society for Developmental Biology* (Eds D.R. Newth & M. Balls), pp. 111–126. Cambridge University Press, Cambridge.

21 Lepesant J.A., Kejzlarova-Lepesant J. & Garen A. (1978) Ecdysone-inducible functions of larval fat bodies in *Drosophila*. *Proc. natl Acad. Sci., USA*, **75**, 5570–5574.

22 Maclean N. & Turner S. (1976) Adult haemoglobin in developmentally retarded tadpoles of *Xenopus laevis*. *J. Embryol. exp. Morph.*, **35**, 261–266.

23 Maller J., Wu M. & Gerhart J.C. (1977) Changes in protein phosphorylation accompanying maturation of *Xenopus laevis* oocytes. *Devl. Biol.*, **58**, 295–312.

24 May F.E.B. & Knowland J. (1980) The rôle of thyroxine in the transition of vitellogenin synthesis from noninducibility to inducibility during metamorphosis in *Xenopus laevis*. *Devl. Biol.*, **77**, 419–430.

24a May F.E.B., Westley B.R. & Knowland J. (1981) Vitellogenin synthesis and characterisation of the liver estrogen receptor in the neotenous salamander *Ambystoma mexicanum*. *Devl. Biol.*, **82**, 350–357.

24b May F.E.B. & Knowland J. (1981) Oestrogen receptor levels and vitellogenein synthesis density development of *Xenopus laevis*. *Nature, Lond.*, **292**, 853–855.

24c Mulvihill E.R., Le Pennec, J.-P. & Chambon P. (1982) Chicken oviduct progesterone receptor: Location of specific region of high-affinity binding in cloned DNA fragments of hormone-responsive genes. *Cell*, **28**, 621–632.

25 Ohlendorf D.H., Barberash G.R., Trout A., Kent C. & Banaszak L.J. (1977) Lipid and polypeptide components of the crystalline yolk system from *Xenopus laevis*. *J. biol. Chem.*, **252**, 7992–8001.

26 Oka T. & Schimke R.T. (1969) Interaction of estrogen and progesterone in chick oviduct development. I. Antagonistic action of progesterone on estrogen-induced proliferation and differentiation of tubular gland cells. *J. Cell Biol.*, **41**, 816–831.

27 Oka T. & Schimke R.T. (1969) Interaction of estrogen and progesterone in chick oviduct development. II. Effects of estrogen and progesterone on tubular gland cell function. *J. Cell Biol.*, **43**, 123–137.

28 O'Malley B.W. & Schrader W.T. (1976) The receptors of steroid hormones. *Scient. Am.*, **234**, (2), 32–43.

29 O'Malley B.W., Tsai M.-J., Tsai S.Y. & Towle H.C. (1977) Regulation of gene expression in chick oviduct. *Cold Spring Harbor Symp. Quant. Biol.*, **42**, 605–615.

30 Palmiter R.D. (1975) Quantitation of parameters that determine the rate of ovalbumin synthesis. *Cell*, **4**, 189–197.

31 Palmiter R.D. & Carey N.H. (1974) Rapid inactivation of ovalbumin messenger ribonucleic acid after acute withdrawal of estrogen. *Proc. natl Acad. Sci., USA*, **71**, 2357–2361.

32 Popp R.A., Foresman K.R., Wise L.D. & Daniel J.C., Jr (1978) Amino acid sequence of a progesterone-binding protein. *Proc. natl Acad. Sci., USA*, **75**, 5516–5519.

33 Puca G.A., Nola E., Sica V. & Bresciani F. (1971) Estrogen-binding proteins of calf uterus. Partial purification and preliminary characterization of two cytoplasmic proteins. *Biochemistry, N.Y.*, **10**, 3769–3780.

34 Ryffel G.U. (1978) Synthesis of vitellogenin, an attractive model for investigating hormone-induced gene activation. *Mol. cell. Endocrinol.*, **12**, 237–246.

35 Schaller H.C. (1973) Isolation and characterisation of a low-molecular-weight substance activating head and bud formation in Hydra. *J. Embryol. exp. Morph.*, **29**, 27–38.

36 Schaller H.C. (1975) Head activator controls head formation in reaggregated cells of Hydra. *Cell Differ.*, **4**, 265–272.

37 Schaller H.C. (1976) Action of the head activator as a growth hormone in Hydra. *Cell Differ.*, **5**, 1–11.

38 Schaller H.C. (1976) Action of the head activator on the determination of interstitial cells in Hydra. *Cell. Differ.*, **5**, 13–20.

39 Schaller H.C. & Gierer A. (1973) Distribution of the head-activating substance in Hydra and its localization in membranous particles in nerve cells. *J. Embryol. exp. Morph.*, **29**, 39–52.

40 Schrader W.T., Kuhn R.W. & O'Malley B.W. (1977) Progesterone-binding components of chick oviduct. Receptor B subunit protein purified to apparent homogeneity from laying hen oviducts. *J. biol. Chem.*, **252**, 299–307.

41 Senior M.B. & Frankel F.R. (1978) Evidence for two kinds of chromatin binding sites for the estradiol–receptor complex. *Cell*, **14**, 857–863.

42 Sica V., Nola E., Parikh I., Puca G.A. & Cuatrecasas P. (1973) Purification of oestradiol receptors by affinity chromatography. *Nature, New Biol.*, **244**, 36–39.

43 Sirbasku D.A. (1978) Estrogen induction of growth factors specific for hormone-responsive mammary, pituitary, and kidney tumor cells. *Proc. natl Acad. Sci., USA*, **75**, 3786–3790.

44 Smith L.D. & Ecker R.E. (1971) The interaction of steroids with *Rana pipiens* oocytes in the induction of maturation. *Devl. Biol.*, **25**, 232–247.

45 Tanner J.M. (1972) Human growth hormone. *Nature, Lond.*, **237**, 433–439.

46 Tata J.R. (1976) The expression of the vitellogenin gene. *Cell*, **9**, 1–14.

47 Tsai S.Y., Tsai M.-J., Harris S.E. & O'Malley B.W. (1976) Effects of estrogen on gene expression in the chick oviduct. *J. biol. Chem.*, **251**, 6475–6478.

48 Wahli W., Dawid I.B., Wyler T., Jaggi R.B., Weber R. & Ryffel G.U. (1979) Vitellogenin in *Xenopus laevis* is encoded in a small family of genes. *Cell*, **16**, 535–549.

49 Wangh L.J. & Knowland J. (1975) Synthesis of vitellogenin in cultures of male and female frog liver regulated by estradiol treatment *in vitro*. *Proc. natl Acad. Sci., USA*, **72**, 3172–3175.

50 Wangh L.J., Osborne J.A., Hentschel C.C. & Tilly R. (1979) Parenchymal cells purified from *Xenopus* liver and maintained in primary culture synthesize vitellogenin in response to estradiol-17β and serum albumin in response to dexamethasone. *Devl. Biol.*, **70**, 479–499.

51 Wasserman W.J. & Masui Y. (1976) A cytoplasmic factor promoting oocyte maturation: its extraction and preliminary characterization. *Science, N.Y.*, **191**, 1266–1268.

52 Wasserman W.J. & Smith L.D. (1978) The cyclic behaviour of a cytoplasmic factor controlling nuclear membrane breakdown. *J. Cell Biol.*, **78**, R15–R21.

53 Weiler C. & Ohno S. (1962) Cytological confirmation of female heterogamety in the African water frog (*Xenopus laevis*). *Cytogenetics*, **1**, 217–223.

54 Westley B. & Knowland J. (1978) An estrogen receptor from *Xenopus laevis* liver possibly connected with vitellogenin synthesis. *Cell*, **15**, 367–374.

55 Westley B. & Knowland J. (1979) Estrogen causes a rapid, large and prolonged rise in the level of nuclear estrogen receptor in *Xenopus laevis* liver. *Biochem biophys. Res. Commun.*, **88**, 1167–1172.

56 Wiley H.S. & Wallace R.A (1978) Three different molecular weight forms of the vitellogenin peptide from *Xenopus laevis*. *Biochem. biophys. Res. Commun.*, **85**, 153–159.

57 Yamomoto K.R. & Alberts B. (1975) The interaction of estradiol-receptor protein with the genome: an argument for the existence of undetected specific sites. *Cell*, **4**, 301–310.

Note: This chapter is based mainly on work published before 1980 and includes very little published since then.

Conclusions to Part 5

1. Chemical signals in slime moulds

The overriding importance of chemical signals in the control of development is abundantly illustrated by studies on the slime mould, *Dictyostelium*, in which a remarkable variety of signals is involved throughout the life cycle. These signals pass between different parts of the cell, between cells and between cell masses, and all levels of organization are in constant communication.

The problems of coordination and control of development in *Dictyostelium* show many analogies with those of development in higher animals and plants, so that the slime moulds provide useful models for the study of general problems of development. In animals, as in *Dictyostelium*, hormones can be seen to act at different levels, viz. at the molecular and intracellular levels, on cell populations and on the development of the whole organism.

2. Hormones coordinate developmental changes

As well as the short-range interactions between cells and tissues discussed in Part 3, development also requires the coordination of changes occurring in different parts of the organism. In animals such long-range interactions generally depend on the movement of substances ('hormones') through the organism which initiate changes in different tissues, as in the wide range of changes occurring during amphibian metamorphosis in response to thyroxine. The situation in plants is modified by the constraints imposed by the presence of cell walls, so that hormones can generally affect development only during the growth phase in the meristematic regions of the plant. Nevertheless, hormones are of overriding importance as coordinators of development between different parts of the plant, at the cell, tissue and organ levels. Thus correlation between the development of a leaf and its vascular connections is ensured by the circumstance that development of the vascular tissue is stimulated by IAA produced in the growing leaf itself.

Hormones also appear to play an essential role in developmental responses to environmental factors, as in the induction of metamorphosis in insects and of flowering in plants by seasonal changes in daylength and temperature.

3. Hormones usually do not determine cell type but induce developmental changes in already determined cells

Hormones often elicit growth and differentiation in pre-existing tissues without inducing new cell types. These hormones can control whether flowering plants and amphibians have male or female reproductive organs by stimulating the growth of either male or female primordia in ambisexual organisms. The multiple effects of each type of plant hormone (p. 314) clearly indicate that the specificity of the response must lie in the 'programming' of the target tissue. Thus, gibberellic acid may cause flowering, germination or α-amylase production in different organs and tissues. Again, the normal production of xylem on the inner side of the cambium in response to IAA can be changed if a sector of cambial tissue is reversed in its orientation, suggesting that the derivative cells on the normally inner side are predetermined to produce xylem (p. 315).

There are other cases when hormones set up the necessary conditions for the formation of new cell types. Cyclic AMP is required for the aggregation of some slime moulds and without aggregation the cells will not differentiate unless they are exposed to special conditions; the hormone is therefore a necessary condition for the subsequent stalk and spore cell development.

4. In rare cases hormones may be direct cell type determinants

A key question is whether or not hormones control the establishment of cell and tissue differences in cells which previously were uncommitted. In other words, do hormones decide what state of determination a cell will adopt, or do hormones make a cell express a state of determination which it has already acquired?

In a few cases it has been shown that cells may become determined and differentiate by the direct action of a hormone. Thus, physiological concentrations of ammonia will induce 100 per cent spore formation in sparse cultures of the slime mould *Polysphondylium*, and there is also evidence that this may be the normal signal for spore formation in this species. The production of vascular tissue in parenchymatous cortical tissue by applied IAA would also seem to provide an example of induction of differentiation by a hormone in plant cells not predetermined to follow this pattern. Another example of differentiation induced by hormones is the regeneration of organized bud and root primordia in undifferentiated callus tissue by appropriate concentrations of IAA and kinetin; this is apparently an example of organogenesis induced by hormones, but the specific cell types formed by the meristems are probably not determined by hormones.

5. Mechanism of hormone action

In many cases hormones induce changes in RNA metabolism and in some instances the hormone is thought to exert this effect by binding to the chromatin in association with a hormone receptor (e.g. in the binding of oestradiol-17β with a protein in the liver of *Xenopus*). This change in RNA metabolism is followed by the massive synthesis of particular proteins (e.g. α-amylase in barley seeds, ovalbumin in chicken oviduct and vitellogenin in *Xenopus* liver), and it is likely that the synthesis of messenger RNAs for these proteins are induced by the hormones.

It should be noted that hormones may also have a direct effect outside the cell nucleus. There is evidence that the initial action of IAA on plant cell extension and the induction of movement in aggregating slime moulds by cAMP do not immediately depend on the action of the nucleus.

In several examples, the pattern of development appears to be controlled by changes in hormone concentration; thus in amphibians the different stages of metamorphosis appear to be controlled by the levels of thyroxine. There are several examples from plants, in which the pattern of differentiation is markedly affected by the relative concentrations of two different types of hormone, as in bud and root regeneration in callus tissue, and the production of xylem and phloem by the cambium.

Part 6
Molecular Biology of Development

Chapter 6.1
Limits of Molecular Biology

C.F. Graham

6.1.1　HISTORY AND DEVELOPMENT

This part of the book is concerned with the molecular biology of developing systems and the aim is to discover the extent to which the properties of these systems are constrained and derived from the properties of the genetic material and of the proteins whose primary structure is coded in the genes.

There are limits to any molecular explanation of the properties of developing systems. Many of these limits are set by the history of the Earth and the history of evolution. For instance, if one wishes to know why certain elements are abundant in developing organisms on Earth, then the answer depends both on the properties of the elements and on their availability to organisms during evolution; the availability of the elements depends on the cosmological events which occurred during the formation of the Earth [7].

The history of evolution also constrains developing systems. It has been argued that the use of one out of a number of genetic codes does not depend on the efficiency of one over another, but rather on some frozen accident in which the exploitation of one code happened to occur first in evolution; at the time when this code had become tuned to accurate expression and replication the other possible codes might still be experimenting with these functions, and in a competitive environment at this stage of their evolution they would be at a selective disadvantage [1]. It is a cold thought that an understanding of both the elements in developing systems and the genetic code which controls their use may depend on historical events which in the absence of their repetition are unlikely to be the subject of scientific study.

Development itself has evolutionary constraints which are difficult to decipher. Much of eighteenth and nineteenth century embryology was concerned with assessing the relatedness between the early developing forms of different organisms. Various clever and devious theories stimulated this study, but one prevalent idea was that early stages of development represented a basic and simple plan of the adult organism and that a comparison of such basic plans would provide a reliable guide to the evolutionary connections between organisms [3]. It is an idea which has persisted into the late twentieth century to coexist with attempts to explain the commonness of form of early development in terms of the physical forces which operate on oil droplets or soap bubbles or as derivatives of mathematical rules and constraints [2, 5]. It remains a possibility that the form of early developing systems principally depends on the selective living and inanimate environment which existed during the early evolution of different animal and plant phyla, and that once adopted, a particular mechanism of development became efficient at forming multicellular organisms and excluded other forms of development simply because it had evolved first. Perhaps one should be unimpressed by any of these arguments when it is known that multicellular organisms can develop either from spores, or from eggs, or from plant cells in culture, or from the coming together of the individual cells of the slime mould amoeba. The diversity of developmental devices suggests that many are possible and that the use of one over another mechanism may be no more than the immediate consequence of selective pressures which operate now in the living world.

6.1.2 INHERITANCE OF DEVELOPMENTAL CHARACTERS

It is clear that even in short spans of time, the characters of a developing system are more subtle than the mere expression of its genes and that these characters could not be directly deduced from a knowledge of the base sequence of these genes. For instance, the expression of one or other X chromosome in the membranes which surround a developing mouse embryo depends on whether the X chromosome was inherited from the mother or the father, and the mechanism which achieves this control of gene expression is unlikely to involve changes in base sequence [6].

More immediately, the characters of developing systems depend on messenger RNA synthesized from the maternal genome as well as that coded by the zygote genome and so a developing system inherits characters quite independent of the activities of its own genome (Chapters 1.2 and 6.4).

Within the developing system, the expression of the genes is regulated and the expression of these genes depends on their environment (Chapter 6.4). The gene environment depends on the organization of inherited cytoplasmic characters which flows from the experience of ancestral life cycles, and once again the characters of the system do not simply derive from a knowledge of the molecular biology of gene regulation.

It might be supposed that a protein, once synthesized from a genetic code, would simply effect its action. However, protein molecules characteristically assemble into multimolecular aggregates and these aggregates have properties which are not present in the individual parts. Further, the regulation of the assembly depends on the environment both inside and outside the organism and therefore it is constrained by the previous activity of ancestors of the organism. The assembly may only be efficient if the parts are presented in order, again leaving room for the intervention of environmental cues (Chapter 6.2). The assembly may also depend on pre-existing structures, as appears to be the case in the assembly of thylakoids (Chapter 6.3). The important conclusion is that a gene product when produced does not simply and directly determine the developing organism's character. It frequently interacts with inherited pre-existing characters and conditions [4].

6.1.3 ADVANTAGES OF MOLECULAR BIOLOGY

Although molecular biology will never be able to explain the properties of developing systems in terms of the properties of its constituent atoms and molecules, it does provide the most revolutionary and practically useful techniques for studying development. The explanation of this paradox is that an ability to analyse the bricks and mortar of development has permitted biologists to discover new phenomena which would not have been anticipated by studying the gross biochemistry, physiology and morphology of development. These discoveries include the properties of molecules and their environment which are involved in building filaments which inside the cell are involved in locomotion and which outside the cell are involved in embryonic induction (Chapters 6.2, 3.3, 3.5). They include techniques of DNA sequencing and characterization which have allowed a direct analysis of the inheritance of characters from previous generations, such as the mitochondria and messenger RNA (Chapters 6.3 and 6.4). They include the analysis of gene structure which has revealed 'split' genes and controlling sequences which are likely to be the places where the environment of genes evokes this regulated expression (Chapter 6.4). The subsequent chapters in Part 6 record recent advances in an area of learning in which most remains to be discovered.

6.1.4 REFERENCES

1 Crick F.H.C. (1968) The origin of the genetic code. *J. molec. Biol.*, **38**, 367–380.
2 Goodwin B.C. & Trainor L.E.H. (1980) A field description of the cleavage process in embryogenesis. *J. theor, Biol.*, **85**, 757–770.
3 Gould S.J. (1977) *Ontogeny and Phylogeny*. Belknap, Harvard.
4 Monod J. (1972) *Chance and Necessity*. Collins, London.
5 Morgan T.H. (1927) *Experimental Embryology*. Columbia University Press, New York.
6 Papaioannou V.E. & West J.D. (1981) Relationship between the parental origin of the X chromosomes, embryonic cell lineage and X chromosome expression in mice. *Genet. Res.*, **37**, 183–197.
7 Williams R.J.P. (1981) Natural selection of the chemical elements. *Proc. R. Soc. Lond. B.*, **213**, 361–397.

Chapter 6.2
Self-Assembly

A. Miller

6.2.1 INTRODUCTION

The aim of molecular biology is to account for the properties of biological organisms in terms of the properties of their constituent atoms and molecules. It is a programme of reductionism. Since the sciences of the behaviour of matter are chemistry and physics, the goal is to describe the physico-chemical processes which correspond to the behaviour of organisms. Note the use of the word 'correspond' in the previous sentence rather than 'give rise'. The latter would imply a causal priority of the atomic level over the macroscopic level which discussions of reductionism show could be premature. Another point worth emphasis is that the reduction of properties of organisms to properties of atoms is unlikely to be complete as a matter of principle rather than practicality [106, 108]. Even the most extensive example of reduction of one theory to another, viz. thermodynamics to molecular kinetic theory, leaves a residuum. Furthermore, the aspects of natural phenomena under study demand concepts for their analysis appropriate to the level at which the study is carried out. There is a hierarchy of levels in time and space within which scientific studies may be conducted and the relations between the levels in the hierarchy are not simple one-to-one relations [89]. The thick myofilaments of muscle have properties which cannot be ascribed to their molecular components as individuals. As will be described later, it is likely that the myosin molecules have an amino acid sequence (derived from the order of the nucleotides in the gene coding for the myosin) which dictates the geometrical relation between myosin molecules when they assemble into myofilaments so that the form of the myofilament originates in the structure of the molecule. However, in the myofilament there emerge properties of symmetry and directed force development of which the individual myosin molecules are devoid. This is an elementary example chosen to illustrate what is not a trivial point. As many biologists would wish to emphasize, there are properties of organisms which cannot be reduced to properties of their constituent atoms and molecules as individual components. This is not to say that a full account at the atomic or molecular level is not possible, but such an account alone is not an exhaustive account of the properties of the organism. When the molecules act as assemblies, these assemblies, while composed only of atoms and molecules, are capable of functions which the individual constituents are not, and so in molecular biology there will be, in addition to physics and chemistry, concepts involving the spatio-temporal organization of the macromolecular structures.

The point of this chapter is to explore the extent to which the development of an organism occurs by a process of self-assembly. The aim is a restricted one; the question at issue is whether the component parts of an organism have, by themselves, the potential spontaneously to aggregate with the relationships that result in the organism. To what extent is the final form of an enzyme, cell organelle or larger structure a consequence of its component parts? Is it a property of the parts to aggregate in this way as an expression of their regular behaviour? What are the conditions required to enable them to aggregate thus? Is it possible to understand the aggregation of the parts in terms of physical forces? To what extent may the demand of biological usefulness supplement the minimization of free energy as a factor in understanding biological structures? By posing these restricted questions we may see to what extent self-assembly is a useful concept in discussing the formation of biological structures.

The question of self-assembly may be raised at various levels in the organism. Does molecular folding occur by self-assembly and do molecules then self-assemble to form higher levels of aggregation such as filaments, membranes and organelles? We may then ask if these structures self-assemble to yield cells and finally whether cells self-assemble to make tissues. We shall start with the long polymer molecules—proteins, nucleic acids and lipids. This is not quite arbitrary though there is a sense in which self-assembly occurs before this level. Atoms may be regarded as the product of the self-assembly of more elementary particles which exist in highly symmetrical states of low energy. Small molecules are similarly stable states of the aggregation of atoms. Experiments on the prebiotic synthesis of amino acids and sugars show that when energy in a variety of forms is introduced into certain gaseous mixtures of small molecules, common monomers of biology are formed (e.g. [99]). We will exclude discussion of these from self-assembly because of the high energies involved and, in particular, because of the breaking and making of many covalent bonds. We shall also exclude, on grounds of high energy, the self-assembly of coacervates and microspheres (e.g. [44]) which occurs when mixtures of polypeptides are heated. The self-assembly under discussion is the kind that could occur in living animals. Thus, extremes of energy are not permitted. A start will be made at the molecular level and the aim will be to see how far up the hierarchy of levels of organization the concept of self-assembly is appropriate.

A further point about self-assembly that requires clarification is the interpretation of 'self'. Once more we deliberately side-step the philosophical questions of the extent to which the concepts of physics, such as force, energy, length and mass, which are estimated by operations involving the behaviour of matter, can be described as properties of the parts of organisms. The only aspect considered here will be the experimental question, 'Can the parts alone aggregate to form the organism or a more complex part of it?'. Even at this stage it is necessary to delimit further the self-assembly under consideration. Kellenberger [42] has suggested that the general process of whereby a biological structure takes its shape be called morphopoesis. He then defines morphopoesis of the first level as that in which the only subunits which take part in the assembly process are those which will themselves form part of the completed structure. *This will be the meaning of self-assembly in this chapter.* It rules out cases where spatial information is imposed externally by a template which is not itself part of the final structure. It also excludes systems where other subunits such as enzymes are required to effect some of the steps in assembly. If thoroughly followed, this definition of self-assembly would also exclude the participation of solvent molecules, and so small molecules and ions, such as water, small anions and cations, are arbitrarily discounted as subunits when the assembly of macromolecules is being considered.

We are thus left with a very elementary definition of self-assembly as a process in which macromolecules and larger units either fold or aggregate into specific structures by themselves in aqueous solutions of small molecules. Our basic question is, 'How far does this kind of self-assembly occur in the development of organisms?'.

A model for the type of self-assembly we shall discuss is crystallization. When the environmental conditions are right, crystallization occurs spontaneously and the resultant microscopic symmetry of the crystal is a direct consequence of the intermolecular interactions. To deal with biological materials however we must have a broad understanding of crystallization, which led Bernal [13] to introduce the term 'generalized crystallography'. We are not only interested in the regular three-dimensional lattices but also in the linear arrays of identical interactions which form helices, and the two-dimensional arrays comprising the closed surfaces of the regular solids. It was pointed out by Crane [26] and Caspar and Klug [18] that the high symmetry of helical polymers and icosahedral viruses makes it likely that these structures arise by self-assembly. In self-assembly two subunits may interact with an energetically favourable interaction. If a third subunit is added and can adopt the same relation to the second as the second to the first, then a highly symmetrical structure will result. A symmetry operation is one which usually involves rotation, translation or reflection of an object and the result of the operation is to leave the object indistinguishable from its initial state [139]. Symmetry, therefore, depends on equivalence within the object and self-assembly depends on equivalent intersubunit interaction. Equivalence results from there being a favoured, low-energy interaction between the assembling or assembled units. At the molecular level a distinguishing feature is that subunits are *precisely* identical, so symmetrical relationships can be precisely obeyed. In this chapter we shall survey some examples of self-assembly at the molecular level and it will now be obvious that we may expect the symmetrical filaments and spheres to form by self-assembly.

There is one aspect of self-assembly in biology which distinguishes it sharply from crystallization; this is that in biology there exists *controlled* self-assembly. Control implies that the self-assembly is a step within an ordered system of reactions. It is not enough to understand the physics and chemistry of the aggregation of molecules involved in the self-assembly. It is essential to see how these aggregations (disaggregations and modification of aggregates) are integrated into the network of spatially and temporally ordered reactions that occur in organisms. Two types of questions are raised by this. The first of these is the question of 'switching' [17]. How are aggregates of molecules switched from one type to the other? Can this be accounted for in terms of medium-dependent conformational changes in the monomers within the aggregates? The second question is about the dynamics of networks of reactions. Once the physico-chemical reactions in the formation and modulation of biological organelles are understood, can we give an analysis of the ensemble of interacting reaction pathways? A successful systems analysis is not sufficient by itself. Systems analysis is often applied to biological problems but with a 'black-box' assumption about the mechanism of the steps in the system. A valid account of self-assembly requires that the systems analysis be based on a physico-chemical understanding of the individual steps in the system. In this article we deal only with the self-assembly of organelles and how

organelles may be switched from one state to another to provide controlled assembly.

Self-assembly has already been discussed by Bernal [13], Calvin [16], and Kushner [74], and in symposia edited by Wolstenholme and O'Connor [140], Allen [3], Hayashi and Szent-Györgi [56], Engström and Strandberg [42] and Timasheff and Fasman [133]. In this chapter we will try to give an up-to-date account of the available evidence. Since a large number of topics has to be covered, references will only be to key papers and to recent reviews which could be consulted for more detailed information.

A discussion of the function of the molecules which are described will be found in the chapters on cell adhesion (Chapter 3.2), cell locomotion (Chapter 3.3), embryonic induction (Chapter 3.5), and the cellular origins of tissue organization (Chapter 4.3).

6.2.2 MOLECULAR FOLDING

Protein molecules crystallize and this implies that each molecule is folded into the same three-dimensional conformation. It is possible to ask whether this conformation can arise spontaneously or whether it requires some external information to fold correctly. At the level of molecular folding it is now widely accepted that the three-dimensional structure of the molecule is determined by the sequence of amino acid residues. At present the basis of this view is almost entirely experimental with only partial indication of the physical principles behind the protein folding, and we shall now review some of this evidence.

Helix–coil transitions

Many homo-polypeptides (polymers of a single type of amino acid) will take up the regular α-helical conformation in aqueous solution. There is a conformation which results in the main chain of the polypeptide following the locus of a helix of pitch 0.54 nm with a 0.15 nm axial translation between adjacent amino acids (Fig. 6.2.1). Clearly, the relation between neighbours in this helix is energetically favourable. That this is so has been demonstrated in a number of ways. Ramachandran *et al.* [110] pointed out that the relation between neighbouring amino acids in a polypeptide chain with planar peptide groups could be represented by two angles ϕ, ψ (see Fig. 6.2.2). The definitions of ϕ and ψ

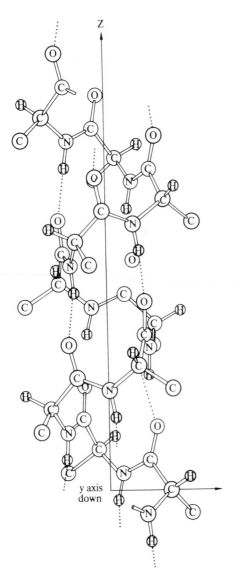

Fig. 6.2.1. The α-helix conformation of a polypeptide chain. This is a right-handed helix of pitch 0.54 nm with an axial shift of 0.15 nm between adjacent amino acid residues.

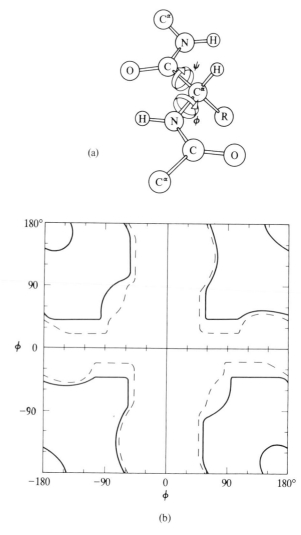

Fig. 6.2.2. Diagram to show the angles ϕ and ψ which relate neighbouring amino acids in a polypeptide chain.

recommended by the IUPAC-IUB Commission [66] is used here. Wooden space-filling molecular models may be used to show that if one assumes that atoms could not approach each other more closely than the van der Waals' distance*, then the possible (ϕ, ψ) values are severely limited and occur in about five patches in

*See facing page.

the (ϕ, ψ) plot. This exercise was repeated by Liquori [79], who used Lennard-Jones potential functions* to represent the molecular interactions and showed quantitatively that there were five minima in the energy contours for poly-L-alanine. The lowest minimum from Liquori's calculations occur at the (ϕ, ψ) values in the α-helix. Hence the common occurrence to the α-helix can be understood and deviations from it have to be explained.

In studies on polyglutamic acid, Doty *et al.* [35] had shown the α-helix arrangement in solution existed at pH values when the carboxylic groups were uncharged, but the helix gave way to a random coil at pH values where the groups were charged. Mutual repulsion between the similarly charged acid groups is obviously causing the helix to unfold. Similarly poly-L-lysine was examined [5] and it was found that the optical rotation at neutral pH was 100° more negative than that at pH 12. Now the extent of optical rotation has been used as a measure of helix content. The change in optical rotation occurred over a pH range between 1 and pH 10, the pK value of the amine group. The values of the optical rotation indicate that polylysine is helical when the amino group is uncharged, but when it is charged by the uptake of a proton at low pH the molecule unfolds. Raising the pH brings about α-helical formation again. In 1M salt solution plus buffer, this transition is moved to a lower pH, presumably because the ionic solvent decreases the charge–charge repulsions which unfold the helix.

Another factor which can cause destabilization of the α-helix is bulky side chains. For this reason valine and isoleucine do not form α-helices. Work on the conformation adopted by sequential polypeptides [45] has shown the increasing destabilization of the α-helix by progressively increasing the fraction of valine in poly(Glu–Val).

Hence, it is reasonable to conclude that the nature of the side chains, which is often determined by the solution medium, does enable polypeptide chains to self-assemble into a specific conformation.

Coiled-coils

In addition to determining the helical parameters of a polypeptide chain, the particular sequence of amino acid residues has now been clearly associated with the way in which the polypeptide chain may interact with other chains. This is evident in the relatively simple case of fibrous proteins where there is a regularity of sorts along the polypeptide chain.

Collagen

In collagen, glycine occurs as every third residue for the whole of the collagen molecule (1014 residues plus two teleopeptides without this regularity, accounting for an additional 41 residues—see summary in [59]). There is also a high fraction of proline and hydroxyproline residues in collagen and the effect of proline in a polypeptide chain is to make ϕ equal $-70°$. Thus a single chain folds up as a helix with approximately three residues per turn. This results in all the glycine residues occurring approximately above each other on one side of the helix. The collagen molecule is then formed when three such single chains come together parallel, with their glycine edges in contact; the individual helices must be twisted about each other so as to bring the glycines exactly above each other to form the core of a three-strand rope. Sequential polypeptides (Gly—Pro—Hyp)$_n$ and (Gly—Pro—Pro)$_n$ adopt a collagen-like conformation [4, 134].

The three-strand collagen molecule can be broken down by heat treatment to form a gelatin. This collagen–gelatin transition is accompanied by a loss of order and the original collagen molecule of molecular weight 300 000 breaks down to monomers of molecular weight 100 000, the so-called α-chains. The complete amino acid sequence of a single α-chain has been determined (see summary in [59]) and for 1014 residues glycine

---

*For an uncharged atom it is possible to estimate a so-called van der Waals' radius. The sum of the van der Waals' radii of two atoms is frequently used to evaluate the contact distance between the atoms. Two physical interactions are involved. One is the force of *repulsion* between the negatively charged electron clouds of the atoms. This force, frequently termed the Born repulsion force, varies as l/r^{12}, where r is the distance between the atomic centres. The other has a more complex origin and is a force of *attraction*. Two permanent dipoles have a residual force of attraction between them. Atoms with equal numbers of positive and negative charges in nucleus and electron cloud respectively have no permanent dipole when the electron positions are averaged over time. However, a 'snapshot' of an atom would reveal an instantaneous dipole and London calculated that the average effect of interactions of these instantaneous atomic dipoles was an *attractive* force proportional to l/r^6 (London attractive forces).

The force arises because one instantaneous dipole induces a dipole in the other atom. Experimentally, the force may be estimated by measurement of the dispersive affect induced in rays of light. This is because they depend on *induced* dipoles and hence the polarizability of atoms. This, in turn, determines their effect on the refractive index of light. The combined effect of the Born *repulsive* force and the London dispersion *attractive* forces was calculated by Lennard-Jones to give an expression for the energy of interactions as $(a/r^{12}-b/r^6)$. The value of this expression is very large when r is small (less than 0.01 nm) indicating that a large amount of energy would be required to bring atoms as close as this. However, an energy minimum does exist around r values of 0.3–0.4 nm and this corresponds to the van der Waals' distance. The van der Waals' radius of an atom determines the atomic volume which was assumed by van der Waal in his modification of the perfect gas equation. For details, see a standard text such as [118].

occurs in every third position, as essential factor for the adoption of the collagen fold. Gelatin may be renatured by cooling and triple-helical molecules are reformed. This has been demonstrated by the fact that stretched gelatin yields an X-ray diffraction pattern similar to native collagen [50] and infra-red studies show the reappearance of the N-H stretching frequency characteristic of collagen when gelatin gels are cooled [113]. The primary sequence thus determines the molecular interaction between the three α-chains to form a collagen molecule.

Alpha proteins of muscle

A similar situation has been shown to exist in the α-proteins of muscle. In 1953, Crick [29] suggested that the X-ray diffraction pattern of the α-proteins could be accounted for by a structure in which two (or three) α-helices coiled around each other to form a two-strand coiled-coil. He further suggested that this supercoiling might be brought about if the apolar amino acid residues were arranged in a regular way such that they lay on a long-pitch helix round the outside of an α-helix. Two such α-helices could then twist around each other so as to bring the apolar helices into contact in the centre of the two-strand rope. Coiling the α-helices would straighten out the apolar helices so that they met in a line along the core of the two-strand rope. X-ray evidence for the two-strand structure was proved for paramyosin [21] and (for two or three strands) α-keratin [46], and Woods [141] showed that a tropomyosin molecule could be dissociated in 8M urea into two chains of equal molecular weight. Elegant confirmation of Crick's suggestion has now come from studies on the amino acid sequence of tropomyosin [57]. The sequence of amino acids for about one-half of the tropomyosin molecule has been determined and it has been shown that apolar residues occur regularly along the chain. When the chain is plotted in the α-helical conformation, the apolar residues trace out a helix of about the pitch of the coiled coil required by Crick (see Fig. 6.2.3). Once again the sequence of the amino acids clearly determines the molecular interactions and thus directs the construction of the tropomyosin molecule.

Alpha keratin

In α-keratin, the molecular arrangement is more com-

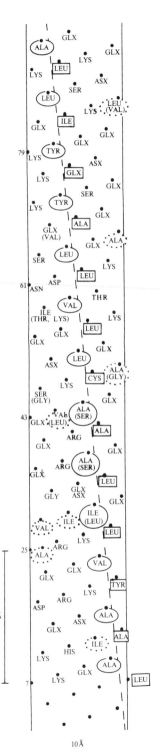

Fig. 6.2.3. A radial projection of the amino acids in tropomyosin in the α-helical conformation. This projection is made by drawing radii through each amino acid residue and making their intersection on a cylindrical sheet concentric with and surrounding the α-helix. The cylindrical sheet is then cut along a line parallel to the helix axis and opened into a flat sheet.

plicated. Microfibrils of diameter 8 nm are embedded in a matrix of proteins which have a high sulphur content. There is no clear evidence of regular structure in the matrix, but the low-sulphur proteins which form the microfibrils have the α-protein or coiled-coil conformation. The amino acid sequence of the low-sulphur proteins also shows the heptapeptide regularity which was discovered in tropomyosin [100]. A similar situation exists in the fibrinogen molecule. This has regions of 'coiled-coil' structure separated by domains of a different structure. The 'coiled-coil' regions display the heptapeptide regularity [34].

Globular proteins

The globular proteins are more complex than the fibrous proteins in that they are not mainly regular in structure and the geometric relations between nearest neighbours in the polypeptide chain are not identical, so the chain does not adopt a regular helical conformation for the whole of its length like collagen or the α-proteins. However, the globular proteins do have the common features that, though the main polypeptide chain follows an irregular course, it usually winds up in a compact manner with roughly spherical or ellipsoidal shape. The fact that globular proteins crystallize implies that the molecules have adopted a precisely identical three-dimensional structure, though at room temperatures these structures could still have substantial energy fluctuations within the molecule [27] (Fig. 6.2.4).

The self-assembly of a molecule into its three-dimensional structure from an unfolded state was first clearly demonstrated with ribonuclease [43]. The ribonuclease molecule contains four disulphide bonds. When these bonds are broken by reducing the sulphydryl groups, the molecule will unfold with accompanying loss of enzyme activity. There are over one hundred theoretical ways in which the eight reduced half-cysteine residues could recombine, but in an oxidizing environment the molecule refolds to form the original structure in high yield with full enzyme activity.

Other globular proteins have since been denatured by various means and renatured to restore structure and activity. Sometimes heating followed by cooling can effect the transitions. Thus the primary structure is sufficient to determine the tertiary structure of globular as well as fibrous proteins.

Because of the increased complexity of the situation,

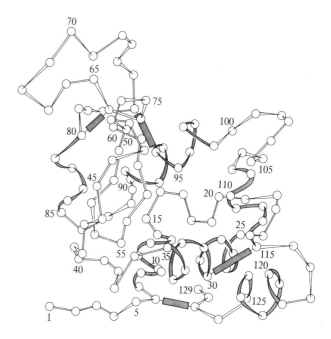

Fig. 6.2.4. Schematic drawing of the main chain of lysozyme. (By W.L. Bragg, from Blake *et al.* (1965) *Nature, Lond.*, **206**, 757–763.)

it is not so easy to see why globular proteins adopt the three-dimensional structure that they do. However, the same general feature of apolar residues occupying the interior of the molecule applies here as in fibrous proteins. In some cases it is possible to see why certain amino acids residues are essential for the preservation of a given tertiary structure. For example, only glycine in cytochrome *c* could permit the shortish chain to encompass the prosthetic group. In general, however, it is more difficult to understand the folding mechanism. The most recent experiments and ideas on how some globular proteins fold have been reviewed [48, 78]. A basic question is whether or not the molecule folds up as it comes off the ribosome. This is made unlikely by the observation that a peptide consisting of the first twenty amino acids of ribonuclease appears to take up no definite tertiary conformation. Presumably then, the whole molecule is required to stabilize the native structure. This idea is supported by the work of Anfinsen and colleagues on staphylococcal nuclease. The bond following amino acid 126 can be split to give a polypeptide containing amino acids 1–126 from the amino terminal end of the molecule. This is 85% of the molecule and it is found to possess no definite structure and to lack catalytic activity. Other experiments reveal that fragment 6–48 will react with 49–149 to yield an active enzyme. Thus nearly all of the protein is required for it to take up the 'native' conformation.

Experiments on staphylococcal nuclease by Jardetzky and co-workers have provided information about the steps by which the protein folds into its native conformation. Proton magnetic resonance is used to probe the conformation of recognizable residues in the polypeptide chain. Jardetzky finds that when the molecule is converted from a 'random coil' to a specific tertiary structure by varying the pH, the change does not take place in one step. Fragments of the molecule 'click' into the native conformation one by one and it has been possible to suggest a sequence of steps by which the random coil adopts the native conformation. Anfinsen believes that the kinetic folding and unfolding of the molecule will result in transitory 'native' fragments which may interact with each other to form a nucleus for the folding of the rest of the molecule.

It is now clear from the large number of protein structure determinations by X-ray crystallography that most globular proteins consist of two or more well-defined domains. Amino acids which are close to each other in the in the amino acid sequence also tend to be close to each other in the three-dimensional structure. However, in enzymes the active site is composed of atoms which usually come from more than one domain. Intriguing observations have emerged. There is a tendency for specific three-dimensional structures to be maintained with different amino acid sequences. These amino acid sequences are frequently homologous and this may appear unsurprising, but in some cases no obvious relation at all can be detected between sequences which have the same three-dimensional structure.

We may conclude then that the mechanism of the folding of globular proteins certainly conforms to our requirements for self-assembly. The primary sequences alone, in the appropriate solvent conditions, is sufficient to determine the unique and complex manner in which the polypeptide chain will fold. However, it also appears that nearly all of the molecule is required for the folding process and the stability of the unique tertiary structure depends on the interaction of virtually the whole molecule. At present it seems unlikely that the molecule folds up simply from one end to the other and we are far from understanding the physics of protein folding. This is not surprising in view of the fact that the physics of folding of polyethylene is still a topic of active research. Levine *et al.* [78] put it thus:

'It appears that the sequence controls the energetics and kinetics (dynamics) of a series of conformations and depends on the environment in which the protein sits. That is to say, in the language of statistical thermodynamics, that the sequence controls the partition function of the protein'.

For our purpose we note that the form adopted by the molecule is determined by the amino acid sequence and hence, by derivation, from the sequence of the bases in the DNA coding for the protein (Chapter 6.4).

6.2.3 MOLECULAR AGGREGATION— (1) LIKE MOLECULES

Once macromolecules such as proteins have folded into their native conformation it is possible to ask if this tertiary structure is sufficient to determine the arrangement which these molecules will adopt in the next level of the structural hierarchy, in structures such as fibres, organelles, membranes and viruses. This is frequently the main point at which self-assembly of biological materials is discussed (see, for example, [74]) but it is obviously one of a series of levels.

Many biological structures are, in fact, composed of identical subunits assembled, like bricks, to form a larger structure. The genetic advantage of this was recognized early [30]. The DNA need only be long enough to specify one subunit.

Well-established examples are available of self-assembly of long molecules to form fibrous structures.

Collagen

Collagen is a fibrous molecule which is a major component of basement membranes. It appears very early in the development of some species (e.g. in mice at the 64-cell stage, Chapter 3.5). It is a substrate to which cells adhere (Chapter 3.2), and on which cells move in embryogenesis (Chapters 3.3 and 4.3). In later development it forms a large part by weight of all connective tissues, but particularly bone, cartilage and tendons.

Collagen molecules may be separated from connective tissue by extraction with salt at low temperatures or at acid pH at room temperatures. The so-called collagen molecules obtained are 300 nm long and 1.5 nm in diameter with the triple-helical structure described in the section on coiled-coils above. A solution of collagen may be reprecipitated and the precipitate examined in the electron microscope. This reveals fibrils with a 67 nm periodic banding pattern indistinguishable from the fibrils isolated from native tendons. It is clear that the structure of the molecule is sufficient to define the mode of molecular packing in the fibril.

In native tendons the molecules are held together by covalent bands formed between modified lysine residues (see [135] for review). The lysine is oxidized enzymatically to allysyl residues which have aldehyde groups. These then cross-link covalently. Covalent cross-linking is not essential for fibril formation since banded fibrils may be reconstituted from collagen in which the conversion of lysine to aldehyde is prevented, and the molecular arrangement in such rat tail tendon is

the same by X-ray diffraction as that in native tendon (Miller & Parry, unpublished).

Some understanding of the kind of interactions that might be responsible for specifying the molecular packing in collagen comes from studies of the amino acid sequence [59].

The primary sequence of one α-chain is now known from the pooled results of various workers. If two such linear sequences are laid alongside each other, it is possible to estimate by rather crude criteria how the intermolecular interaction would vary as the sequences are moved past each other. The interaction is scored by assigning $+1$ when two oppositely charged residues are within range of each other and $+1$ when two apolar residues are within range. These estimates reveal a periodicity of 67 nm (or 234 residues) in the intermolecular interactions, which tallies well with structural information available by X-ray diffraction and electron

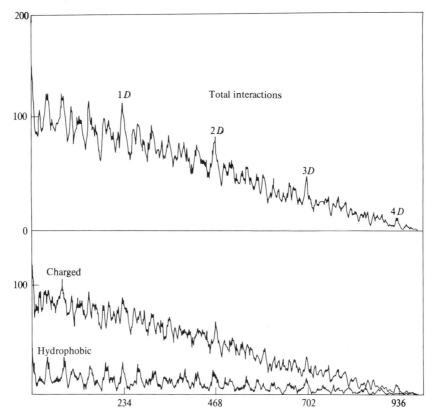

Fig. 6.2.5. A computer plot of the number of hydrophobic and charge interactions and their total between two collagen molecules (on the ordinate) as a function of the stagger between them. The stagger (on the abscissa) is measured in residues. See [22].

microscopy (see Fig. 6.2.5). The main implication for our purposes is that this periodicity emerges from the amino acid sequence alone, thus it is possible to give a chemical account of the origins of the self-assembly of the molecules. We also note that the most clearly defined periodicity is followed by the large apolar residues. The hydrophobic interactions are shown to be important in molecular aggregation just as they were in molecular folding.

The collagen molecule can be precipitated from solution to yield other regular polymorphic structures which are not usually observed in native collagen. One of these, the so-called SLS form in which the neighbouring molecules are lined up in parallel register with each other, is readily understood since it occurs in the presence of ATP. The diphosphate could be thought of as bridging similarly charged residues. Other polymorphic forms have symmetric periodicities and this indicates that the molecules are assembling in antiparallel array. The relative stagger between the molecules in these symmetric structures has also been shown to involve regular interaction between polar residues [36]. Thus in collagen we begin to understand the origins of molecular specificity which determines the different ways in which the molecules may self-assemble. Note that additional molecules intervene to predispose the collagen to assemble in particular arrays.

Muscle

Muscle afford an excellent example of a series of levels of order, all of which are essential for the biological function of contractility which involves transduction of the chemical energy from the hydrolysis of ATP into mechanical work.

In striated muscle, single fibres of diameter 70 μm have a regular banded appearance of period 2–3 μm. In electronmicrographs of longitudinal sections through muscle fibres, this banding is seen as due to the in register arrangement of myofibrils of about 1 μm diameter. Each longitudinal unit of length of 2–3 μm is termed a sarcomere. When muscle shortens, the sarcomeres shorten by the same fraction and this has been accounted for by two sets of filaments sliding between each other [60, 61] (Fig. 6.2.6). The thick filaments are in the centre of the sarcomere and the thin filaments originate from the Z-disc and interpenetrate between the thick filaments. Thus muscle shortening

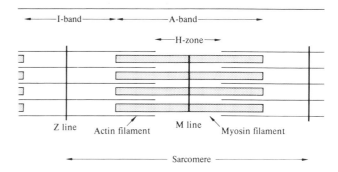

Fig. 6.2.6. A diagram of the arrangement of thick and thin filaments in a sarcomere of striated muscle.

occurs by the filaments sliding between each other without themselves changing length. Cross bridges have been visualized in the electron microscope, and shown by this method and X-ray diffraction to originate from the thick filaments (see review in [62]). A suggested mechanism for muscle contraction is that the cross bridges interact cyclically with the thin filaments and pull them into the centre of the sarcomere, thus shortening the sarcomere and hence the whole myofibril.

Myosin

A satisfying illustration of self-assembly is provided by studies on the molecular packing within the thick filaments. The thick filaments are composed largely of the protein myosin. This molecule is about 150 nm long and consists of a α-helical rod of length 135 nm to which is attached a globular, enzymatically active head [63, 81] (Fig. 6.2.7).

Myosin molecules may be dissolved from thick filaments by solutions of high ionic strength (0.6M). When the ionic strength of such myosin solutions is lowered, it was observed with the electron microscope that the molecules reaggregated to form rodlets [67]. A detailed study of this reaggregation process and the structures of the aggregates was made by H.E. Huxley

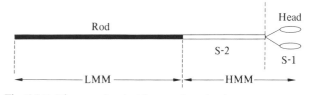

Fig. 6.2.7. Diagram of part of the myosin molecule.

[63]. The spindle-shaped aggregates were very similar in appearance to the thick filaments of muscle, though they exhibited a wide variation in length, in contrast with the precisely equivalent filaments in muscle. However, the synthetic filaments were always polarized about their centre. The centre of each synthetic filament differed from the rest of the length in that it did not have rough projections on the surface but was relatively smooth. This so-called 'bare zone' in the centre of the synthetic filaments was observed to be of a fairly constant length, 150–200 nm. The projections from the rest of the filament surface were presumed to be the globular heads of myosin molecules.

Huxley's [63] results suggest that the assembly of thick filaments takes place in two stages (Fig. 6.2.8). First, myosin molecules came together pointing in opposite directions with the rod portions overlapping. This accounted for the constant length 'bare zone' in the centre of the filament. The ability of myosin to form antiparallel dimers has been supported by Harrington et al. [54] on the basis of high-speed sedimentation equilibrium studies of myosin association. More detailed study of the antiparallel interaction of myosin by electron microscopy has revealed that myosin molecules and rods are able to form antiparallel segments in vitro with overlap lengths of 130, 90 and 43 nm [55] (for a review see [22]). These studies reveal that, in vitro, distinct modes of antiparallel packing of myosin rods are possible.

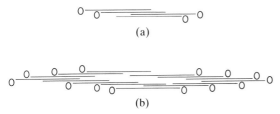

Fig. 6.2.8. Two stages in self-assembly of myosin molecules to form synthetic thick filaments. (a) Molecules assemble rod-to-rod pointing in opposite directions to form a nucleus. (b) The nucleus grows in both directions by the aggregation of myosin molecules pointing in the same direction to form a bipolar thick filament.

The second stage of thick-filament assembly follows the first when the nucleating antiparallel segments ('bare zones') are elongated by the parallel interaction of rods on opposite sides of the segment (Fig. 6.2.8b). Myosin molecules in opposite halves of the filament point in opposite directions but molecules in the same half point

in the same direction. Compound segments of myosin rods have also been shown in vitro to form both polar and bipolar patterns [69]. As Huxley [63] pointed out, this bipolar symmetry of synthetic thick filaments is a design feature essential for the functioning of the sliding filament model of muscle contraction, where thin filaments are moved in opposite directions in opposite halves of a sarcomere. Huxley [63] further demonstrated that the thin filaments are polar when interacted with globular portions of myosin and that they too point in opposite directions in opposite halves of a sarcomere. Huxley's work shows that the thick filament design features are a consequence of the self-assembling properties of the myosin molecule.

Once again, we note that, as with the collagen molecule, the myosin molecule is capable of polymorphism in which the modes of molecular interaction are distinct. The question arises as to whether all of these modes are utilized in vivo, and Harrison et al. [55] have proposed a scheme for the molecular arrangement in the thick filament which does involve a number of the distinct molecular contacts. It may also be possible to generate varieties of filament structures by modulation of the same set of modes of molecular contacts. Sobieszek [123] has shown that myosin from vertebrate smooth muscle may be reprecipitated to yield long filaments that have no central 'bare zone' but rather a 'bare zone' is located on one side at the ends of the filament. A possible interpretation is that these filaments are formed by association of small bipolar units such as myosin dimers. These filaments have a clear 14 nm axial periodicity which is taken as a visualization of myosin heads.

In summary, the thick filaments of muscles are known to have different symmetries but it is likely that they are all based on similar interactions of myosin molecules. A general model for thick-filament structure has been suggested by Squire [124–126], in which the myosin contacts are closely similar. It is worth noting, however, that other factors are likely to be involved in determining thick-filament architecture. Though the shapes of myosin molecules isolated from different kinds of muscle are closely similar, there are known variations in other properties such as solubility, ATPase activity and presence of low-molecular-weight components. Furthermore, it has been established that there is another major protein constituent of the thick filaments, the so-called C-protein [97], which appears to be regularly arranged with the periodicity of the myosin heads. Sequence information on the myosin molecule will help to elucidate the determining features in the self-assembly of myofilaments.

Paramyosin

A special type of thick filament occurs in certain non-striated muscles of molluscs; this is the paramyosin-rich 'catch' muscle of the oyster adductor and the anterior byssus retractor of mussels. Filaments are of diameter 10–150 nm, in other words about 4–6 times that of the thick filaments of vertebrate striated muscle. Myosin occurs as a macromolecular veneer on the surface of these filaments while the rest of the filament is composed of the protein paramyosin. This is rod shaped, some 130 nm long, having the two-strand coiled-α-helix structure of the α-proteins, and is devoid of enzymic activity. The detailed molecular arrangement of the paramyosin within these filaments has been investigated [39, 40].

Paramyosin may be precipitated *in vitro* and reconstituted filaments with various banding patterns are observed by electron microscopy, indicating the ability of paramyosin to make different polymorphic structures. As in the case of myosin, these polymorphic forms and the bipolar structure point to different modes of packing of the paramyosin molecule. One of the polymorphic patterns has the symmetry of the native pattern and closely similar periodicities; it may be constructed by appropriate arrangement of other observed polymorphic aggregates and Cohen *et al.* [23] conclude that it is likely that the thick filaments of catch muscle are formed by self-assembly of paramyosin molecules. They also suggest that polymorphism indicates that the different modes of molecular bonding are likely to have closely similar energies and it is not unlikely that dynamic transitions between some of these states are important in certain contractile functions, such as 'catch' in which the muscle can develop tension for prolonged periods. Paramyosin is now known to occur quite generally. It has been isolated from insect flight muscle [15] and the suggestion has been made that it is a core for the myosin containing elements in certain muscles.

Tropomyosin

The muscle protein tropomyosin offers a particularly clear example in which it is possible to relate the amino acid sequence to the three-dimensional molecular arrangement in muscle filaments. Tropomyosin occurs on the thin myofilaments where it lies in the groove of the two-fold actin helix [97]. Each tropomyosin molecule is about 40 nm long and entirely composed of two-strand coiled-coil with the α-protein structure. As pointed out in the section on coiled-coils, the apolar amino acids are distributed so that an apolar core of the two-strand coiled-coil is formed (Fig. 6.2.3). If attention is now concentrated on the apolar residues not in the core, it is noted [88, 101] that they occur at axial intervals of 2.7 nm. Remarkably, 2.7 nm is the axial separation between the globular actin monomers in the actin two-strand helix. Hence, the amino acid sequence in tropomyosin, in addition to promoting the formation of a two-strand coiled-coil, will further facilitate a specific interaction between actin and tropomyosin. This actin–tropomyosin matching has now been shown to exist in considerable detail [24].

It is clear then that the muscle proteins self-assemble in the same way as the proteins of connective tissue. The primary sequence (the distribution of apolar residues) determines how the two molecular chains fold together to produce a two-strand rope. These ropes then self-assemble to produce higher level structures, namely the thick and thin myofilaments, which have design properties appropriate to the biological function of contractility.

Cytoplasmic filaments

It has been recognized for a long time by electron microscopists that the cytoplasm of a cell is replete with assemblies of thin filaments. These filaments appear to be directly involved in cell locomotion and to act as cytoskeletons within cells (Chapter 3.3). It is only recently, however, that detailed structural studies have been made on many of these filaments and that their biochemistry has been carefully investigated. There is evidence that all of these filaments can form by self-assembly but there is also evidence in each case that a different molecule may be involved in the control or switching on and off of the assembly [80]. Some sort of pattern is emerging amongst this plethora of filaments and the present situation will be summarized here. The muscle proteins, principally actin and myosin but not excluding some of the others, occur widely in non-muscle motile systems [75]. Myosin and actin are involved in non-muscle cell motility, while actin alone forms filaments which comprise the cytoskeleton, in particular the so-called 'stress fibres' and the furrow encircling a cell before division. Actin filaments are thin, having a diameter of about 6 nm. A second set of filaments are the much thicker microtubules of diameter about 24 nm which, like actin, are part of the cyto-skeleton and participate in cell division, when they comprise the mitotic spindle. Finally, a third set, termed intermediate filaments, of diameter around 10 nm have been recognized. These in turn are of at least five different types in higher eukaryotic cells but all appear to be concerned with directing and constraining the structures of cytoplasmic space in a way that is appropriate to the differentiated state of the cell [76]. It also appears that an extracellular filamentous network composed of the protein fibronectin exists on the cell surface. These extracellular filaments may even be continuous with some of the internal filament arrays and they are involved in cell adhesion and probably in cell–cell interaction (Chapter 3.2). If they are continuous with the internal fibres, this may provide a mechanism for relaying information across the cell boundary. This ensemble of fine filaments of different types plays an exceedingly important part in cell movement, division and differentation and cell–cell interaction. Here we shall consider their relevance to our concern with self-assembly.

Microtubules

Considerable interest now centres on the structure and function of microtubules, since it has been shown that they occur widely in eukaryotic cells. It is of great importance to understand the formation and the dissolution of microtubules within cells. They appear to be intimately involved in the segregation of morphogenetic substances in the one-cell egg and they may organize the cell divisions of developing systems (Chapters 2.2, 2.3, 2.4). The term microtubule was first introduced by Slautterback [120] with reference to the tubules in cytoplasm but the term took on a wider significance when tubules with apparently identical structures were found in a wide range of situations. It is well known that the cilia and flagella of eukaryotic cells are more complex than the flagella of bacteria; they possess a $9+2$ arrangement of fibre 'doublets' and it is now well established that each fibre has a microtubular structure.

Microtubules have been found in plant cells, and tails of spermatozoa, mitotic spindles, axopodial fibres which project from the surface of various protozoa, and as neurotubules of nerve fibres. They have been associated with cytoplasmic streaming, with directing the flow of materials such as synaptic vesicles within cells and with imparting asymmetry to cell shape. Reviews have been provided by Porter [109], Stephens [127, 129] and Dustin [37].

The accepted relationship between these microtubules is based on a common structure (Fig. 6.2.9). The cylindrical appearance shows a diameter of about 24 nm.

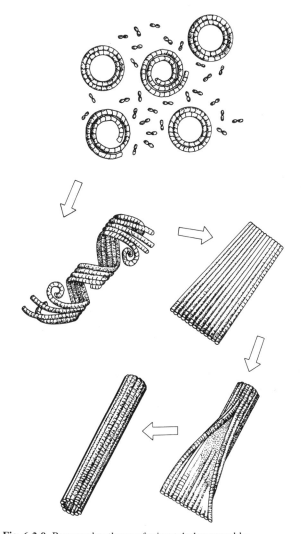

Fig. 6.2.9. Proposed pathway of microtubular assembly.

In electron micrographs of transverse cross sections through microtubules they are observed to consist of a ring of 12–13 subunits evenly distributed round the circumference, suggesting a bundle of 12–13 protofilaments. The sensitivity of this appearance to the tilt of the specimen from normal to the electron beam precluded the possibility that the protofilaments followed a helical path and indicated that they were oriented parallel to the microtubular axis. Electron micrographs of longitudinal sections through the structures revealed that the protofilaments have a 4 nm axial periodicity and are spaced about 5 nm apart around the microtubule circumference. X-ray diffraction studies on wet and dry preparations of orientated gels of sea urchin flagellar outer fibre doublets indicate a half-staggered surface lattice of 4 nm × 5.3 nm in the wet state. This is consistent with a 12- or 13-fold rotational symmetry for the microtubule. On drying, the lateral register of the surface lattice is lost and the structure diffracts as a ring of protofilaments each with a 4 nm axial periodicity. This indicates the importance of protofilaments as stable assemblies; support of this comes from electron microscopy reported below. In the electron microscope, an 8 nm axial periodicity is sometimes observed and this may be related to dimerization of 4 nm subunits, also discussed below.

A microtubular protein was characterized by Renaud *et al.* [111, 112] from ciliary outer fibre doublets. The protein migrated as a single band on acrylamide gel electrophoresis. The molecular weight of the monomer is about 60 000 and it can readily exist as a dimer. Mohri [93] compared the amino acid composition of the microtubule protein with that of the muscle proteins actin, myosin and tropomyosin and also with that of flagellin, the protein from bacterial flagella. In agreement with previous findings, Mohri found the amino acid composition of the microtubular protein resembled that of actin, but he considered that they were sufficiently different to justify the name 'tubulin' for the former. This suggestion has proved appropriate. Differences in properties of tubulins are well known and have led to a suggestion that there are four kinds of tubulin from A-outer fibres, B-outer fibres, central fibres and cytoplasmic microtubules [8, 9], but at present a complete, consistent classification has not been achieved.

Self-assembly of microtubules has been studied at various levels. Before microtubules were recognized in mitotic spindles, Inoue [64, 65] had noted the dependence of birefringence of the spindles on temperature. On lowering the temperature, birefringence disappears, but it reappears on raising the temperature again. Similar behaviour has been observed in the axopods of the heliozoon *Actinosphaerium* [109]. Axopods are spikes about 500 μm in length that project from the spherical surface of the protozoan and they possess a highly birefringent axoneme running along the central core. The axonemes consist of microtubules [70]. When *Actinosphaerium* is exposed to low temperature [132] the birefringence of the axoneme disappears. Electron micrographs of sections through axonemes in this condition revealed that the microtubules had disassembled, leaving amorphous material. On raising the temperature, the axopods resumed their normal appearance and the birefringence returned. These observations clearly suggest that microtubules are capable of self-assembly, though the steps involved are not obvious. Furthermore, the temperature dependence of the polymerized structure is similar to that of tobacco mosaic virus, where polymerization is also an endothermic reaction. All microtubules, however, do not show the same temperature dependence as mitotic spindles and heliozoan axonemes. The outer fibres of cilia and flagella do not dissociate in the cold.

Behaviour suggestive of self-assembly was more difficult to observe with the outer fibres. Some degree of reconstitution of parts of microtubules was achieved by Gibbons [51, 52], who was able to remove the 'projections' from the outer fibres of a cilium and show that this was accompanied by disappearance of the ATPase activity. The 'projections' could be added back on to the outer fibres with some restoration of response to ATP.

Attempts to reconstitute microtubules from tubulin were not at first successful; however, a more satisfying demonstration of self-assembly of microtubules was finally provided by Stephens [128]. He obtained the 60 000-mol.-wt tubulin monomer from the sperm tail of the sea urchin by treatment with the detergent Sarkosyl. This mild treatment was followed by simple dilution and addition of salt and resulted in the reassociation of tubulin into several fibrous forms, some closely similar in appearance to the original microtubules. Just as fibrous actin contains adeninediphosphate (ADP), so microtubules contain guaninediphosphate (GDP), though whether the polymerization of microtubules, like that of actin, is dependent on dephosphorylation is not yet clear. Stephens found that small protein aggregates of about 100 nm in size were essential for nucleation of polymerization; if these were centrifuged off, only random aggregates were found. In the absence of magnesium the polymerized forms were ribbons which could aggregate into clusters. When diluted in the presence of 0.1 M magnesium chloride [127, 128] Sarkosyl solutions of tubulin yielded microtubules, so demonstrating that magnesium is required for protofilaments to aggregate into microtubules.

Tubulin and its association properties also resemble the muscle proteins myosin, paramyosin and tropomyosin in exhibiting polymorphism which can be controlled by the species of the medium [122]. It is particularly important for our purpose of enquiring into the role of self-assembly in the development of organisms to note its occurrence in microtubules, since these structures appear to play a part in shaping the cell, in determining the asymmetry of an organism, and thus in influencing the possible geometric congruences or incongruences with neighbouring bodies. The ability of microtubules to dissociate and associate rapidly and to respond to environmental changes with modifications of form obviously provide a mechanism for translating minute alterations in concentrations of fluid media into dynamic and novel macroscopic effects. The extent to which this mechanism is used in vivo remains to be investigated, but the evidence described in this section leaves no doubt that the tubulin molecules are sufficient to determine their own self-assembly into biologically functional microtubules. However, other molecules termed microtubule accessory proteins (MAPs) may be of critical importance in controlling the assembly of microtubules [142, 122] and in deciding where and when microtubules grow in the cytoplasm. One important feature of microtubule structure is that they are inherently polar. It can be shown that this polarity has an effect on the rate of tubulin assembly at either end [131]. Further, when assembly is initiated by polar structures, such as the base of a bacterial flagellum, then growth occurs preferentially at one end [11, 12].

To summarize the discussion so far, we can say that aggregation of collagen molecules to form fibrils is beginning to be understood in terms of amino acids along each molecule. This is not yet the case for the aggregation of myosin or tubulin, but both of these molecules clearly demonstrate self-assembly and also show that a range of different types of aggregation can

occur in vivo. We can then ask how the different modes of aggregation are controlled in vivo. Does the solvent play a part or is a different mechanism operative? Different modes of aggregation do occur in the same solvent conditions. An observation on muscle that may be significant for the assembly of molecules in vivo is that the muscle cell proteins are synthesized by polyribosomes lined up in the growing muscle [2]. In the case of differentiating muscle cells of certain insects and the development of the muscle filaments, there is strong evidence for a concerted role of the microtubules and the myofilament array [7]. It may be that during the process of differentiation the microtubule array is acting to direct and orient the developing thick myofilaments. Thus the final structure might be governed both by the self-assembly properties of the molecules and their mode of synthesis.

Actin filaments

Actin is found in the cytoplasm of eukaryotic cells. The monomer is a globular protein which is capable of ATP-dependent polymerization to form 6 nm diameter actin filaments. These actin filaments along with additional regulatory proteins form the thin filaments of striated muscle. They are also involved in non-muscle cell motility. However, they occur most frequently as arrays of thin filaments in the cytoskeleton. These actin filament arrays are probably attached at some points to the cell membrane and they can polymerize and depolymerize rapidly. Accessory proteins, distinct from the regulatory proteins of striated muscle, may be involved in the control of these actin arrays and of the type of arrays which are formed. There is evidence that the aggregates of actin microfilaments in cells are in some way associated with fibronectin on the cell surface (Chapter 3.2).

Intermediate filaments

These are a polymorphic class of cytoplasmic filaments distinct from microtubules and actin. They are capable of polymerization and depolymerization like microtubules and actin but it may be that this is controlled by a proteolytic mechanism. Intermediate filaments have been reviewed recently [76]. The diameter is usually 8–10 nm, which is 'intermediate' between that of actin and microtubules, but it is now clear that this term has been used to cover several quite different types of filament. At least five different types are recognizable— keratin, desmin, vimentin, neurofilaments and glial filaments. Desmin filaments can be disaggregated into a monomer protein and reconstituted into filaments similar to desmin filaments *in vivo*. Desmin has been shown to occur at the periphery of the Z-discs of striated muscles and to form an interconnecting network across the muscle fibre. It is proposed that desmin is instrumental in aligning the muscle sarcomers in register to produce the striated appearance of skeletal muscle and also in maintaining this alignment. Desmin may even function in the biogenesis of the T-SR membrane system in muscle. Vimentin is also capable of assembly and disassembly. It is suggested that vimentin filaments are tightly associated with the cell nucleus, possibly ensuring its location within the cell.

Lazarides [76] summarizes by describing this class of five intermediate filaments as mechanical integrators of cellular space. They appear to function principally in cell differentiation. The three kinds of filaments, microtubules, actin and 'intermediate filaments', can all, to different degrees of precision, be said to form by self-assembly. However we see that the self-assembly does not exactly conform to Kellenberger's [42] 'morphopoesis of the first type'. Other protein molecules are involved in switching filament assembly on or off, or deciding between types of assembly, and it is not always clear that these accessory molecules remain on the finished assembly. What is becoming clear, is the physical chemistry of some of these assemblies and disassemblies.

Bacterial flagella

Flagella are fine fibres that adhere to the outside of many cell surfaces and by actively rotating are probably the source of a primitive cell motility (Fig. 6.2.10). Bacterial flagella are frequently about 14 nm in diameter and they may be dissociated by heat or acid pH into monomers of the protein flagellin of molecular weight about 40000 [1]. Flagellin lacks ATPase activity [95]. The structure of bacterial flagella has been determined by electron-microscopy and X-ray diffraction [19, 20, 82, 83]. The subunits are arranged on a set of co-axial helices or on rows parallel to the flagellar axis. The periodicity of the structure projected on to the flagellar axis is 5.2 nm. In the electron microscope, the appearance is of about

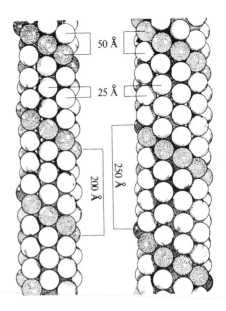

Fig. 6.2.10. Models of a bacterial flagellum.

eight to ten rows of subunits. X-ray diffraction studies on reconstituted filaments formed from flagellin show that they have a similar structure to the original flagella.

Bacterial flagellar movement, previously thought to involve moving waves of perturbation in the flagellum [72], is now understood to involve an intricate rotatory mechanism like a wheel [10, 98], in which the wavy flagellum is rotated about the axis of the wave.

Asakura and co-workers [6] have studied the reconstitution of the flagella of the bacterium *Salmonella*. The flagella have a wavy appearance. A mutant form is also wavy but with a wavelength about half that of the normal form. Seeds of the normal flagella will stimulate flagella assembly when placed in a solution of mutant flagellin and the resultant flagella will have a mutant wavelength; similarly when a solution of normal flagellin is seeded with a fragment of a mutant flagellum, growth of flagella results but they have the wavelength of the normal form. Either form can seed either type of growth, but the wavelength of the resulting flagella is determined by the monomer rather than the initiating seed.

We conclude that not only do we have another example of self-assembly in bacterial flagella, but also a particularly clear indication that the form of the flagellum is determined by the flagellin molecule. Seeding may be useful in starting self-assembly but it is not able to alter the normal mode of interaction of the molecules.

6.2.4 MOLECULAR AGGREGATION— (2) UNLIKE MOLECULES

Most of the original ideas about the assembly of unlike molecules into aggregates come from studies on the formation of viruses. Here we deal with more poorly characterized assemblies of molecules in ribosomes and membranes, because of their important roles in development. None of the systems is yet comprehensible at the atomic level, but often some idea is available of the sort of chemical reactions which are involved. The discovery of accessory molecules promises a way towards understanding how these processes are controlled in the cell and the whole problem is then pushed to the level of asking for a description of total network of molecular interactions within a cell and how this changes with time. The important step forward is that this 'systems analysis' is continuous with the molecular mechanisms. The units in the network are discoverable physico-chemical interactions and not 'black boxes'. Further progress is hindered by the sheer complexity of the problem and the technical difficulties in obtaining information about dynamic systems at the molecular level (see discussion in Chapter 3.3).

Ribosomes

Ribosomes occur in virtually all types of cells, where they comprise part of the machinery of protein synthesis (Chapter 6.4). Most assembly studies have been conducted with bacterial ribosomes, which are discussed below. The general structure of ribosomes is well known—they are made up of two subunits, a large one that sediments in the ultracentrifuge at 50S and another smaller one at 30S in animal cells. The complete ribosome sediments at 70S. The molecular weights of the 50S and 30S subunits are 1.8×10^6 and 0.7×10^6 respectively, and they are readily dissociated from the 70S particle by lowering the concentration of magnesium ions from 10^{-2}M to 10^{-4}M. The ribosome consists of 60% ribonucleic acid and 40% protein by weight. The 50S subunit contains two RNA molecules, one 23S and a smaller 5S as well as 34 different proteins; the 30S subunit contains only one RNA molecule sedimenting at 16S and 23 different proteins. Here we shall describe some of the

evidence concerning the extent to which the 70S ribosome may be formed spontaneously by self-assembly from RNA and proteins.

It has been suggested [84, 85] that the 30S and 50S subunits do not come together spontaneously but require ribosomal RNA (rRNA) and transfer RNA (tRNA). Thus they probably come together for protein synthesis but dissociate again when this is completed.

While the 50S and 30S particles are stable they will dissociate on centrifugation in caesium chloride into proteins and 'core particles' which are ribonucleoproteins. These core 'particles' can reassemble with the split proteins to yield 50S and 30S subunits which, in turn, may be joined to yield functional 70S ribosomes. The 'core particles' are inactive and are only reactivated if reassembled with their own split proteins.

More detailed analyses of these subunits and their constituents has been carried out by Nomura and his colleagues [96]. They have shown that some of the split proteins are essential for certain functions such as binding mRNA or tRNA or amino acid incorporation; others are not essential but stimulatory.

Traub and Nomura [136] have shown that a 23S core particle (derived from a 30S ribosomal particle) may be dissociated into free 16S rRNA plus core protein (CP30S). A functionally active 30S subunit can then be assembled from the 16S rRNA and the mixture of ribosomal proteins. This reassembly is a specific reconstitution. The above reconstitution was done using ribosomes from *E. coli,* and neither yeast 16S rRNA nor rat liver 16S rRNA can replace *E. coli* rRNA in the reconstitution, nor is degraded *E. coli* rRNA effective. Core protein from 50S subunits (CP50S) cannot effectively replace the CP30S protein used above. Thus the specificity of the RNA and the core protein is demonstrated. It was also shown that streptomycin resistance lies in CP30S.

A similar reconstitution of the 50S subunit proved more difficult. Nomura and Erdman [96] noted that the high temperature apparently required to drive the assembly caused denaturation of the proteins. They therefore selected a thermophilic bacterium, *Bacillus stearothermophilus,* and achieved a successful reconstitution of a 50S subunit from their rRNA and protein. Maruta *et al.* [86] investigated the conditions for reassembly of *E. coli* 50S subunits and showed that previous attempts at reconstitution had probably failed because of denaturation of the proteins. They designed a method to avoid denaturation and obtained successful reconstitution of 50S subunits of *E. coli*. They confirmed that though reconstitution of 30S subunit is not dependent on 50S, the reverse is not true, and they established the necessity for the 5S rRNA in the 50S reassembly.

These studies were taken a stage further in an ambitious project [92] to map the sequence of steps by which the 30S subunit of *E. coli* was assembled. The method was to take each of some 20 proteins and test them separately for binding to the 16S rRNA.

The binding tested was rather specific, since coulombic forces were decreased by using high-ionic-strength solutions. While this has the advantage of preventing non-specific electrostatic binding of basic proteins to RNA, it may also inhibit specific electrostatic interactions which are important *in vivo*. Only three proteins (termed 4a, 4b and 14) bind strongly and most showed no binding, so those binding were taken to be the first added to rRNA when the 30S subunit is assembling. The 18 non-binding proteins were then tested for binding to complexes of rRNA and 4a, 4b and 14 proteins. Three showed up as strong binders (5, 9 and 10a) while the other 15 did not bind. This technique was continued to reveal the sequence of binding of all the proteins to 16S rRNA and their interdependence of binding. The method is based on consideration that if protein B will not bind until protein A does, then protein B must follow protein A into the complex.

Mizushima and Nomura [92] conclude that they have established the topology of interprotein contacts in the complete ribosome. Experiments are underway in an attempt to determine the three-dimensional molecular arrangement in ribosomes (see, for example, [41]) and it will be of interest to observe developments in this exciting field.

For the purpose of our argument we must summarize. There appears to be good evidence that the final form of a 30S or 50S subunit is a consequence of the identity of the constituent rRNA and protein molecules. Reconstitution takes place by self-assembly and the temperature dependence of some reactions suggest that hydrophobic interactions may be involved [74]. A ribosome is a fairly complex organelle and takes part in the highly integrated process of protein synthesis. It is interesting that self-assembly can lead to structures with this demanding complexity and that this involves self-assembly of a large number of different protein components. The importance of a proper sequence of addition is also evident. It

implies that for the rapid assembly of ribosomes which occurs *in vivo* in a few seconds, the protein must be presented to the assembling ribosome in the correct order. In other words temporal presentation of the parts assists self-assembly.

Membranes

Membranes form the outer coats of cells and of parts of cells. Their functions can be complex and range from simple physical support to those of a selectively permeable barrier. Their proper function is central to many biological systems. The basic membrane structure is formed by a combination of phospholipid with protein. Phospholipids form bilayers in which the phospholipid molecules are arranged on a two-dimensional lattice with the molecular axis normal to the plane of the layer. In one layer the molecules are parallel and in register, so that all the phosphate groups are on one side of the layer; on the other side are the fatty acid ends of the lipid molecules. Thus a single layer has one side apolar and the other highly charged. Two such layers adhere with their apolar faces in contact, to form a bilayer. The existence of the bilayer structure in phospholipids and membranes has been well established by X-ray diffraction. Lecithin layers can be stacked together and the X-ray diffraction pattern from the stacks has a series of reflections which are orders of approximately 4.8 nm. The intensities of these orders are consistent with a bilayer structure. Stacks of lecithin bilayers have been studied by varying the charge on the layer surface and observing the effects on the inter-bilayer spacing in various solvents. This suggests that they are stabilized by a sensitive force balance.

Membranes contain varying ratios of lipid to protein and, as yet, the exact nature of the interaction of the protein with the lipid bilayer is not known. However, there is good evidence from X-ray diffraction and electron microscopy that the protein molecules in some membranes are regularly arranged on a lattice in the plane of the membrane [14, 53]. When membranes are delipidated with phospholipase, ethanol or ether, the basic structure frequently remains, suggesting that the proteins are important in membrane stabilization. When the proteins are digested by enzymes the membrane frequently collapses [104]. There are many experiments which suggest that complex lipoprotein systems such as mitochrondria will self-assemble from smaller units.

Certainly, the lipid bilayer readily forms by self-assembly.

In many biological tissues such as keratin [47], muscle (Miller, unpublished), and collagen [91], X-ray diffraction patterns show reflections which index on 4.8 nm. These are of variable character and appear to become more intense as the tissue keratinizes or gets older. Pollard *et al.* [104] noted that preparations of chromaffin granules showed a similar set of reflections of variable intensity. This may indicate that as membranes break down, the phospholipids may readily recrystallize as bilayers by themselves.

Many reasonable suggestions have been made to the effect that cells may adhere by relatively simple physical forces (electrostatic and van der Waals' forces) which may be estimated from some familiarity with the membrane structure [31–33, 102] (see Chapter 3.2). It has also been suggested that the different compositions of cells in terms of protein and sugar molecules may eventually account for specificity of cell recognition [68]. This topic is at present under development since regular progress is being made in our understanding of membrane structure, the physical forces themselves and the phenomena of cellular recognition. If these speculations are confirmed then the concept of self-assembly even in its simplest form may be sufficient to account for interactions between cells and open the way for formalization of theories of development at this level [105].

6.2.5 CONCLUSIONS

In this survey we have considered examples of self-assembly of various biological structures. Self-assembly is defined here as a mechanism in which only the constituents of the final structure take part in the assembly process. By constituents we mean mainly macromolecular subunits and not water molecules or other small solvent ions. This type of self-assembly occurs at several levels and is well exemplified by the proteins. The order of amino acids in a protein (its primary structure) is determined by the order of nucleotides in the DNA of the gene coding for the protein. The first level of self-assembly is the adoption of a secondary structure by the protein. This is a regular coiling of the molecule to form a helix such as the α-helix or collagen triple helix. Both of these helices are determined by the primary sequence of the protein but the actual structure can also be affected by the solvent conditions. A second level of

self-assembly is when a protein molecule folds into an irregular three-dimensional tertiary structure. While the actual course of the main polypeptide chain is irregular in such structures, the tertiary structures of all molecules of a given protein are identical under the same conditions. Yet another level of self-assembly is when two fibrous molecules, such as myosin, coil about each other to form a two-strand coiled α-helix. In tropomyosin this is now seen to be due to a regularity in the positioning of apolar amino acid side chains in the single α-helices, so once more the self-assembly is determined by the primary sequence of the protein. In the case of the collagen molecules of connective tissue, self-assembly of the molecules into native-like fibrils is well known. The origin of this is now known to lie in the amino acid sequence. Where the recognition process between these long molecules is due to like–like interactions, it seems possible to state a general principle which relates the symmetry of the molecule to the symmetry of the aggregate. If two molecules are related by a given symmetry operation in the aggregate, then the molecule itself will contain that same symmetry element in at least quasiform. Thus the collagen molecules, which are staggered axially by a distance D in the fibril, themselves have a quasi-D-period in their apolar residues. It is likely that the role of the solvent is to control the symmetry of the interacting residues on the molecule and thus to control the symmetry of the aggregate. Thus the fibrous proteins have proved valuable in providing examples of a situation where biological specificity, and hence self-assembly, may be understood in terms of physicochemical interactions between molecules of known structure. Collagen may be the first example where all of the processes can be understood from the molecular level, through molecular folding and molecular aggregation, to aggregation of fibrils into tissues of known biological function.

Self-assembly of globular subunits also takes place to yield specific aggregates. Globular protein subunits comprise flagella, microtubules, viruses and ribosomes and while it is not as easy at present in these cases to recognize the origins of these interactions in the amino acid sequence, it is likely that similar principles will operate as in the fibrous systems and in haemoglobin, which was the first molecule to be understood at this level.

We see then that self-assembly according to our simple definition certainly occurs up to the level of cell organelles and some animal tissues, and this despite the fact that some of these, such as muscle, are intracellular and others, such as collagen, are extracellular. It is also difficult in the case of intracellular systems to detect the effect of the surrounding organization of the cell, but *in vitro* experiments help to clarify which assembly mechanisms are, at least in principle, capable of self-assembly. We may then inquire whether the particular organization within the cell serves to enhance assembly rates or not. Frequently, a complex system involving templates may be converted to one which meets our simple definition by considering a larger 'aggregate' which includes previous aggregates plus templates, etc., so there are examples where the question of self-assembly can become purely semantic and unhelpful. However, the value of the simple definition is that where a system does conform to it, then it can be possible to trace an unbroken line of causal steps from the gene to the form of the aggregate. This is obviously of considerable significance for our understanding of development and something close to that situation may soon exist for the extracellular connective tissues of metazoans. For interactions between cells, it may be that the architecture of molecular packing on the cell surface, which is possibly a self-assembling system, will in turn provide the platform for a rationalization of cellular recognition processes. But this has not been demonstrated yet. It is necessary to have a grasp of the properties of the elementary parts in order to interpret completely an experiment in terms of self-assembly.

If this chapter had resulted in a purely molecular physico-chemical account of all of the processes in and between cells, then our original goal would be realized. This account would include descriptions of the switching mechanisms whereby accessory or regulatory molecules control the state of aggregation or the form of aggregation of the assemblies of monomeric units. In some cases, the pH or ionic strength of the medium may be sufficient to define the state of the 'switch'. Thus we would have a molecular mechanism for how biological organisms develop, for cell division and differentiation, and for specific physiological mechanisms such as vision, muscle contraction, connective tissue plasticity and so on. There would still be required a sort of flow chart describing how all these dynamic, reversible, interconnecting reactions were related in space and time. The enterprise of giving a 'total account' of say, an organism, should be possible in principle (except that the principles

of network and systems theory may require further development to deal with actual biological systems). In practice, the sheer complexity of biological organisms may mean that the 'total account' is not readily realized.

In addition the present technical difficulties involved in elucidating these structures are so great that simply the time involved in investigating one structure after another would make the goal rather distant. The conclusion of this discussion is that the systems so far investigated indicate the kind of answers that can be expected when we inquire how biological development is controlled at the molecular level. In some cases the extent of our knowledge may be such that the organisms can be manipulated intelligently. In other cases, such as genetic engineering, it is salutary to recall that the ability to control can run well ahead of a physico-chemical understanding of the system.

6.2.6   REFERENCES

1 Abran D. & Koffer H. (1964) *In vitro* formation of flagella-like filaments and other structures from flagellin. *J. molec. Biol.*, **9**, 168.
2 Allen E.R. & Pepe F. (1965) Ultrastructure of developing muscle cells in chick embryo. *Am. J. Anat.*, **116**, 115.
3 Allen J.M. (Ed.) (1967) *Molecular Organisation and Biological Function.* Harper & Row, New York.
4 Andreeva N.S., Millionova M.I. & Chirgadzi Y.N. (1963). In *Aspects of Protein Structure* (Ed. G.N. Ramachandran), p. 137. Academic Press, New York.
5 Applequist J. & Doty P. (1962) α-helix formation in poly-E-carbenzoxy-L-lysine and poly-L-lysine. In *Polyamino Acids, Polypeptides and Proteins* (Ed. M.A. Stahlman), p. 161. University of Wisconsin Press, Madison, Wisconsin.
6 Asakura S., Eguchi G. & Iino I. (1966) *Salmonella* flagella *in vitro* reconstruction and overall shapes of flagellar filaments. *J. molec. Biol.*, **16**, 302.
7 Auber J. (1969) La myofibrillogèse du muscle strié. I. Insectes. *J. Microsc.*, **8**, 197–232.
8 Behnke O. & Forer A. (1967) Evidence for four classes of microtubules in individual cells. *J. Cell Sci.*, **2**, 169.
9 Behnke O. (1967) Incomplete microtubules observed in mammalian blood platelets during microtubule polymerization. *J. Cell Biol.*, **34**, 697.
10 Berg H.C. (1974) Dynamic properties of bacterial flagellar motors. *Nature, Lond.*, **249**, 77–79.
11 Bergen L.G. & Borisy G.G. (1980) Head to tail polymerization of microtubules *in vitro*. *J. Cell Biol.*, **84**, 141–150.
12 Bergen L.G., Kuriyama R. & Borisy G.G. (1980) Polarity of microtubules nucleated by centrosomes and chromosomes of Chinese hamster ovary cells *in vitro*. *J. Cell Biol,.* **84**, 151–159.
13 Bernal J.D. (1967) *The Origin of Life.* Weidenfeld & Nicholson, London.

14 Blaurock A.E. & Stoeckenius W. (1971) Structure of the purple membrane. *Nature, Lond.*, **233**, 152.

15 Bullard B., Luke B. & Winkelman L. (1973) The paramyosin of insect flight muscle. *J. molec. Biol.*, **75**, 359.

16 Calvin M. (1969) *Chemical Evolution.* Oxford University Press, Oxford.

17 Caspar D.L.D. (1976) In *Structure–Function Relationships of Proteins.* Proc. Third John Innes Symp., p. 85. Elsevier, Amsterdam.

18 Caspar D.L.D. & Klug A. (1962) The structural principles of viruses. *Cold Spring Harbor Symp. Quant. Biol.*, **27**, 1.

19 Champness J.N. & Lowy J. (1968) Structure of bacterial flagella. In *Symposium on Fibrous Proteins* (Ed. W.G. Crewther), p. 106. Butterworths, London.

20 Champness J.N. (1971) X-ray and optical diffraction studies of bacterial flagella. *J. molec. Biol.*, **56**, 295.

21 Cohen C. & Holmes K.C. (1963) X-ray diffraction evidence for α-helical coiled-coils in native muscle. *J. molec. Biol.*, **6**, 423.

22 Cohen C. & Szent-Györgyi A.G. (1971) Assembly of myosin filaments and the structure of molluscan "catch" muscles. In *Contractility of Muscle Cells and Related Processes* (Ed. R.J. Podolsky), pp. 123–136. Prentice-Hall, Engelwood Cliffs, New Jersey.

23 Cohen C., Szent-Györgyi A. & Kendrick-Jones J. (1971) Paramyosin and the filaments of molluscan "catch" muscles. *J. molec. Biol.*, **56**, 223.

24 Cohen C. (1975) The protein switch of muscle contraction. *Scient. Am.*, November.

25 Cooper A. (1976) Thermodynamic fluctuations in protein molecules. *Proc. natl Acad. Sci., USA*, **73**, 2740.

26 Crane H.R. (1950) Principles and problems of biological growth. *Scient. Hon. Lond.*, **70**, 376–390.

27 Creighton T.E. (1978) Experimental studies in protein folding. *Prog. biophys. molec. Biol.*, **33**, 231–296.

28 Crewther W.G. (1976) *Proceedings of 5th International Wool Textile Research Conference, Aachen*, Vol. 1, p. 1.

29 Crick F.H.C. (1953) The fourier transfer of a coiled-coil. *Acta crystallogr.*, **6**, 685.

30 Crick F.H.C. & Watson J.D. (1956) Structure of small viruses. *Nature, Lond.*, **177**, 473.

31 Curtis A.S.G. (1966) Cell adhesion. *Sci. Progr. Oxf.*, **54**, 61–86.

32 Curtis A.S.G. (1967) *The Cell Surface.* Academic Press, London.

33 Curtis A.S.G. (1972) Intra- and inter-membrane interactions on the cell surface. *Sub-cell. Biochem.*, **1**, 179–196.

34 Doolittle R.F., Goldbaum D.M. & Doolittle L.R. (1978) Designation of sequence involved in the 'coiled-coil' interdomainal connections in fibrinogen-construction of an atomic scale model. *J. molec. Biol.*, **120**, 311–325.

35 Doty P., Wada A., Yang J.T. & Blout E.R. (1957) Polypeptides VIII. Molecular configurations of poly-L-glutamic acid in water-dioxane solution. *J. Polym. Sci.*, **23**, 851.

36 Doyle B.B., Hulmes D.J.S., Miller A., Parry D.A.D., Piez K.A. & Woodhead-Galloway J. (1974) A D-periodic narrow filament in collagen. *Proc. Roy. Soc. Lond. B*, **186**, 67–74.

37 Dustin P. (1978) *Microtubules.* Springer-Verlag, Berlin.

38 Elliott A. & Lowy J. (1970) A model for the coarse structure of paramyosin filaments. *J. molec. Biol.*, **53**, 181.

39 Elliott A. (1971) Direct demonstration of the helical nature of

paramyosin filaments. *Phil. Trans. R. Soc. B*, **261**, 197.

40 Elliott A. (1979) Structure of molluscan thick filaments. *J. molec. Biol.*, **132**, 323–341.

41 Engelman D.M. & Moore P.B. (1972) A new method for the determination of biological quarternary structure by neutron scattering. *Proc. natl Acad. Sci., USA*, **69**, 1997.

42 Engstrom A. & Strandberg B. (Eds) (1969) *Nobel Symposium No. 11 on Symmetry and Function of Biological Systems at the Macromolecular Level.* John Wiley & Sons, New York.

43 Epstein C.J., Goldberger R.F. & Anfinsen C.B. (1963) A genetic control of tertiary protein structure. *Cold Spring Harbor Symp. Quant. Biol.*, **28**, 439.

44 Fox S.J. & Dose K. (1972) *Molecular Evolution and the Origin of Life.* W.H. Freeman, Reading.

45 Fraser R.D.B., Harrap B.S., Macrae T.P., Stewart F.H.C. & Suzuki E. (1965) Sequential polypeptides containing L-valyl and α-methyl-L-glutamyl residues. *J. molec. Biol.*, **12**, 482.

46 Fraser R.D.B., Macrae T.P. & Miller A. (1965) X-ray diffraction patterns of α-fibrous proteins. *J. molec. Biol.*, **14**, 432.

47 Fraser R.D.B., Macrae T.P., Rodger G.E. & Filshie B.K. (1963) Lipids in keratinised tissue. *J. molec. Biol.*, **7**, 90.

48 Freedman R. (1973) What makes proteins fold? *New Scient.*, **58**, 560–563.

49 Gerhart J.C. & Schachman H.K. (1965) Distinct subunits for the regulation of catalytic activity of aspartic transcarboxylase. *Biochemistry*, **4**, 1054.

50 Gerngross O. & Katz J.R. (1926) Uber die Herstellunf sehr stark gedehnter Gelarinepräparate und darein Röntgendiagramm. Gellatin und Kollagen. *Kolloid Zh.*, **39**, 181.

51 Gibbons I.R. (1965) Chemical dissection of cilia. *Arch. Biol.*, **76**, 317.

52 Gibbons I.R. (1967) In *Formation and Fate of Cell Organelles* (Ed. K.B. Warren), p. 99. Academic Press, New York.

53 Goodenough D.A. & Stoeckenius W. (1971) The isolation of mouse hepatic gap junctions. *J. Cell Biol.*, **54**, 646.

54 Harrington W.F., Burke M. & Barton J.C. (1972) Association of myosin to form contractile systems. *Cold Spring Harbor Symp. Quant. Biol.*, **37**, 77.

55 Harrison R.G., Lowey S. & Cohen C. (1971) Assembly of myosin. *J. molec. Biol.*, **59**, 531.

56 Hayashi T. & Szent-Györgyi A.G. (Eds) (1966) *Molecular Architecture in Cell Physiology.* Prentice-Hall, Engelwood Cliffs, New Jersey.

57 Hodges R.S., Sodek J., Smillie L.B. & Jurasek L. (1972) Tropomyosin: amino-acid sequence and coiled-coil structure. *Cold Spring Harbor Symp. Quant. Biol.*, **37**, 299.

58 Hull D. (1974) *Philosophy of Biological Science.* Prentice-Hall, Engelwood Cliffs, New Jersey.

59 Hulmes D.J.S., Miller A., Parry D.A.D., Piez K.A. & Woodhead-Galloway J. (1973) Analysis of the primary structure of collagen for the origins of molecular packing. *J. molec. Biol.*, **79**, 137.

60 Huxley A.F. & Niedergerke R. (1954) Structural changes in muscle during contraction. *Nature, Lond.*, **173**, 971.

61 Huxley H.E. & Hanson J. (1954) Changes in the cross-striations of muscle during contraction and stretch and their structural interpretation. *Nature, Lond.*, **173**, 973.

62 Huxley H.E. (1969) The mechanisms of muscle contraction. *Science, N.Y.*, **164**, 1356.

63 Huxley H.E. (1963) Electron microscopic studies on the structure of natural and synthetic protein filaments from striated muscle. *J. molec. Biol.*, **7**, 281.

64 Inoue S. (1952) Effects of temperature on the birefringence of mitotic spindles. *Bull. Biol.*, **103**, 316.

65 Inoue S. (1952) The effect of colchicine on the microscopic and submicroscopic structure of the mitotic spindle. *Expl. Cell Res.* Suppl. **2**, 405.

66 IUPAC-IUB, Commission on Biochemical Nomenclature (1970) *J. molec. Biol.*, **52**, 1.

67 Jakus M.A. & Hall C.E. (1947) Studies of actin and myosin. *J. biol. Chem.*, **167**, 705.

68 Jehle H. (1970) Bilateral symmetry in morphogenesis of embryos. *Bull. Am. phys. Soc. Ser.*, **11**, 15 (11), 1335.

69 Kendrick-Jones J., Szent-Györgyi A.G. & Cohen C. (1971) Segments from vertebrate smooth muscle myosin rods. *J. molec. Biol.*, **59**, 527.

70 Kitching J.A. (1964) The axopods of the sun animalcule *Actinophyrs sol* (Heliozoa). In *Primitive Motile Systems in Cell Biology* (Eds R.D. Allen & N. Kamiya), p. 445. Academic Press, New York.

71 Klotz I.M. (1971) in Ref. 133, p. 55.

72 Klug A. (1967) In *Formation and Fate of Cell Organelles* (Ed. K.B. Warren), p. 1. Academic Press, New York.

73 Koestler A. & Smythies J.R. (Eds) (1969) *Beyond Reductionism.* Hutchinson, London.

74 Kushner D.J. (1969) Self assembly. *Bact. Rev.*, **33**, 302.

75 Lazarides E. & Revel J.P. (1979) The molecular basis of cell movement. *Scient. Am.*, May, 88.

76 Lazarides E. (1980) Intermediate filaments as mechanical interpreter of cellular space. *Nature, Lond.*, **283**, 249.

77 Leadbetter M.C. & Porter K.R. (1963) A "microtubule" in plant cell fine structure. *J. Cell Biol.*, **19**, 239.

78 Levine B.A., Moore G.R., Ratcliffe R. & Williams R.J.P. (1979) Nucleic magnetic resonance studies of the solution structure of proteins. *Int. Rev. Biochem.*, **24A**, 77–141.

79 Liquori A.M. (1966) In Ref. 140, p. 40.

80 Lloyd C. (1979) Fibronectin: a function at the junction. *Nature, Lond.*, **279**, 473.

81 Lowey S., Slater H.S., Weeds A.G. & Baker H. (1969) Substructure of the myosin molecule. *J. molec. Biol.*, **42**, 1.

82 Lowy J. & Hanson E.J. (1965) Electron microscopic studies of bacterial flagella. *J. molec. Biol.*, **11**, 293.

83 Lowy J. & Spencer M. (1968) Structure and function of bacterial flagella. *Symp. Soc. exp. Biol.*, **22**, 215–236.

84 Mangiarotti G. & Schlessinger D. (1967) Polyribosome metabolism in *E. coli. J. molec. Biol.*, **29**, 395.

85 Mangiarotti G., Apirion D., Schlessinger D. & Silengo L. (1968) Biosynthetic precurors of 30S and 50S ribosomal particles in *E. coli. Biochemistry*, **7**, 456–472.

86 Maruta E., Tsuchiya T. & Mizuno D. (1971) *In vitro* reassembly of functionally active 50S ribosomal particles from ribosomal proteins and RNAs of *E. coli. J. molec. Biol.*, **61**, 123.

87 Matthew B.M. & Berhard S. (1973) Structure and symmetry of oligomeric enzymes. *A. Rev. biophys. bioeng.*, **2**, 257.

88 McLaughlan A.D. & Stewart M. (1976) The 14-fold periodicity in α-tropomyosin and the interaction with actin. *J. molec. Biol.*, **103**, 271–298.

89 Medawar P. (1974) A geometric model of reduction and emergence. In *Studies in the Philosophy of Biology* (Eds F.J. Ayala & T. Dobzhansky), p. 57. University of California Press, Berkeley.

90 Medawar P.B. & Medawar J. (1978) *The Life Science*, Ch. 22. Granada, St Albans.

91 Miller A. & Wray J.S. (1971) Molecular packing in collagen. *Nature, Lond.*, **230**, 437.

92 Mizushima S. & Nomura M. (1970) Assembly mapping of 30S ribosomal proteins from *E. coli. Nature, Lond.*, **226**, 1214.

93 Mohri H. (1968) Amino-acid composition of "tubulin" constituting microtubules of sperm flagella. *Nature, Lond.*, **217**, 1053.

94 Nagel E. (1961) *The Structure of Science*, pp. 336–397. Routledge & Kegan Paul, London.

95 Newton B.A. & Kerridge D. (1965) Flagellar and ciliary movement in microorganisms. *Symp. Soc. gen. Microbiol.*, **15**, 220–247.

96 Nomura M. & Erdmann V.A. (1970) Reconstruction of 50S ribosomal subunits from dissociated molecular components. *Nature, Lond.*, **228**, 744.

97 Offer G. (1972) C-protein and the periodicity in the thick filaments of vertebrate striated muscle. *Cold Spring Harbor Symp. Quant. Biol.*, **37**, 87.

98 Omoto C.K. & Kung C. (1979) The pair of central tubules rotate during ciliary beat in *Paramecium. Nature, Lond.*, **279**, 532–534.

99 Orgel L.E. (1973) *The Origins of Life.* Chapman & Hall, London.

100 Parry D.A.D., Crewther W.G., Fraser R.D.B. & Macrae T.P. (1977) Structure of α-keratin: structural implications of the amino-acid sequences of the type I and type II chain segments. *J. molec. Biol.*, **113**, 9.

101 Parry D.A.D. (1975) Analysis of the primary sequence of α-tropomyosin from rabbit skeletal muscle. *J. molec. Biol.*, **98**, 519.

102 Parsegian V.A. (1973) Long range physical forces in biology. *A. Rev. biophys. bioeng.*, **2**, 221.

103 See for example Perutz M.F. (1971) Haemoglobin: the molecular lung. *New Scient.*, **50**, 676–679.

104 Pollard H., Miller A. & Cox H. (1973) Structure of chromaffin granule membranes. *J. supramol. Struct.*, **1**, 295–306.

105 Pollard E.C. (1973) The control of cell growth. In *Cell Biology in Medicine* (Ed. E.E. Bittar), p. 357. John Wiley & Sons, London.

106 Popper K. Scientific reduction and the essential incompleteness of all Science. In *Studies in the Philosophy of Biology* (Eds F.J. Ayala & T. Dobzhansky). University of California Press, Berkeley.

107 Popper K. & Eccles J. (1977) *The Self and its Brain.* Springer-Verlag, Berlin.

108 Popper K. (1972) *Objective Knowledge.* Oxford University Press, Oxford.

109 Porter K.R. (1966) In Ref. 140, p. 308.

*110 Ramachandran G.N., Ramakrishnan C. & Sasisekharan V. (1963) Stereo-chemistry of polypeptides chain configurations. *J. molec. Biol.*, **7**, 95.

111 Renaud F.L., Rowe A.J. & Gibbons I.R. (1966) Some properties of the protein forming the outer fibers of cilia. *J. Cell Biol.*, **31**, 92A.

112 Renaud F.L., Rowe A.J. & Gibbons I.R. (1968) Some properties of the protein forming the outer fibers of cilia. *J. Cell Biol.*, **36**, 79.

113 Robinson C. & Bott M.J. (1951) Optical rotation and chain folding in synthetic polypeptides and gelatin. *Nature, Lond.*, **168**, 325.

114 Ruse M. (1973) *The Philosophy of Biology.* Hutchinson University Library, Atlantic Highlands, New Jersey.

115 Schaffner K. (1967) Approaches to Reduction. *Philosophy Sci.*, **34**, 137–147.

116 Schaffner K. (1969) The Watson–Crick model and reductionism. *Br. J. Phil. Sci.*, **20**, 325–348.

117 Schultz G.E. & Schirmer R.H. (1979) *Principles of Protein-Structure.* Springer-Verlag, Berlin.

118 Sebera D.K. (1964) *Electronic Structure and Chemical Bonding*, Ch. 11. Blaisdell Publishing Company, New York.

119 Segrest J.P. & Cunningham L.W. (1971) Tropocollagen: molecular basis for fibrillar aggregation. *Nature, New Biol.*, **19**, 239.

120 Slautterback D.B. (1963) Cytoplasmic microtubules. *J. Cell Biol.*, **18**, 367–388.

121 Smith J.W. (1968) Molecular patterns in native collagen. *Nature, Lond.*, **219**, 157–158.

122 Snyder J.A. & McIntosh J.R. (1976) Biochemistry and physiology of microtubules. *A. Rev. Biochem.*, **45**, 699.

123 Sobieszek A. (1972) Crossbridges of self-assembled smooth muscle myosin filaments. *J. molec. Biol.*, **70**, 741.

124 Squire J.M. (1971) General model of myosin filament structure I. *Nature, Lond.*, **233**, 475.

125 Squire J.M. (1972) General model of myosin filament structure II. *J. molec. Biol.*, **72**, 125.

126 Squire J.M. (1973) General model of myosin filament structure III. *J. molec. Biol.*, **77**, 291.

127 Stephens R.E. (1971) In Ref. 133, p. 355.

128 Stepphens R.E. (1968) Reassociation of microtubule protein. *J. molec. Biol.*, **33**, 517.

129 Stephens R.E. (1969) Factors influencing the polymerisation of outer fibre microtubule protein. *Q. Rev. Biophys.*, **1**, 377.

130 Stewart M. & McLauchlan A.D. (1975) Fourteen actin bonding sites on tropomyosin. *Nature, Lond.*, **257**, 331–333.

131 Summers K. & Kirschner M.W. (1979) Characteristics of the polar assembly and disassembly of microtubules observed *in vitro* by darkfield microscopy. *J. Cell Biol.*, **83**, 205–217.

132 Tilney L.G. & Porter K.R. (1967) Studies on the microtubules in Heliozoa. *J. Cell Biol.*, **34**, 327.

133 Timasheff S.N. & Fasman G.D. (Eds) (1971) *Biological Macromolecules* Vol. *5A*. Dekker, New York.

134 Traub W., Yonath A. & Segal D.M. (1969) On the molecular structure of collagen. *Nature, Lond.*, **221**, 914.

135 Traub W. & Piez K.A. (1971) Chemistry and structure of collagen. *Adv. Protein Chem.*, **25**, 243–352.

136 Traub P. & Nomura M. (1968) Structure and function of *E. coli* ribosome V. *Proc. natl Acad. Sci., USA*, **59**, 777.

137 Van Holde K.E. & Van Bruggen E.F.J. (1971) in Ref. 133, p. 1.

138 Waddington C. (1977) *Tools of Thought.* Paladin, St Albans.

139 Weyl H. (1952) *Symmetry.* Princeton University Press, Princeton, New Jersey.

140 Wolstenholme G.E.W. & O'Connor M. (Eds) (1966) *Principles of Biomolecular Organisation.* Churchill, London.

141 Woods E.F. (1967) Molecular weight and subunit structure of tropomyosin B. *J. biol. Chem.*, **242**, 2859–2871.

142 Timasheff S.N. & Grisham L.M. (1980) *In vitro* assembly of cytoplasmic microtubules. *A. Rev. Biochem.*, **49**, 565–591.

Chapter 6.3
The Structure and Function of Chloroplasts and Mitochondria
B.E.S. Gunning and I.W. Craig

6.3.1   INTRODUCTION

There are several reasons why the study of subcellular organelles is important in developmental biology. Although they are comparatively small biological structures, they cannot be formed as a result of self-assembly processes alone, and they therefore indicate the limits of self-assembly as an explanation of the form of develop-

ing systems (Chapter 6.2). They also demonstrate the dependence of cytoplasmic structures on nuclear activity, even though mitochondria and chloroplasts contain their own DNA. In addition, chloroplasts and mitochondria are involved in providing energy essential for developing systems.

This chapter is concerned with the way in which these complex structures develop and are maintained. Although functionally quite distinct, a superficial comparison of the structure of mitochondria and chloroplasts shows many parallels. Some of the more obvious similarities should become apparent in the following brief description of their basic morphology.

Mitochondria

Mitochondria consist of two membrane bags, one enclosed within the other. The inner membrane is folded into characteristic invaginations known as cristae. Although the exact number and form of these vary from one tissue to another, they appear to be built on a common plan. Except where the cristae fold inwards, the contour of the inner membrane closely follows that of the bounding membrane. The two membranes are separated by a gap which extends into the cristae (the intracristal space). The compartment inside the inner membrane is called the matrix (Fig. 6.3.1). The overall dimensions of mitochondria are also extremely variable, depending on tissue type, stage of development and physiological conditions; a 'typical' mitochondrion has dimensions of $1-2~\mu m \times 0.5~\mu m$ and it is similar in size to a bacterium such as *Escherichia coli*.

Chloroplasts

Chloroplasts and related organelles exhibit a wide range of differentiated forms which reflect a variety of

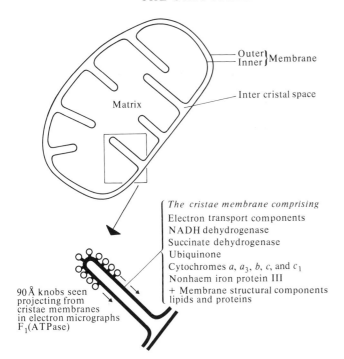

Outer ⎱ Membrane
Inner ⎰

Inter cristal space

Matrix

The cristae membrane comprising

Electron transport components
NADH dehydrogenase
Succinate dehydrogenase
Ubiquinone
Cytochromes a, a_3, b, c, and c_1
Nonhaem iron protein III
+ Membrane structural components
lipids and proteins

90 Å knobs seen
projecting from
cristae membranes
in electron micrographs
F_1(ATPase)

Fig. 6.3.1. Diagram of the basic mitochondrial structure, illustrating the suggested localization of soluble enzymes (in the matrix) and of the electron transport components which are primarily associated with the inner membrane. Other enzymes, e.g. monoamine oxidase, are found in preparations of the outer membrane (see [7, 74]).

specialized functions, such as photosynthesis and the storage of starch (see section 6.3.3). Mature chloroplasts, like mitochondria, vary in size and shape [62]. In higher plants they generally appear as elongated discs, with a long axis of 3–10 μm. They are enclosed by a double membrane structure, called the envelope, which is about 30 μm in total width. Inside the envelope of

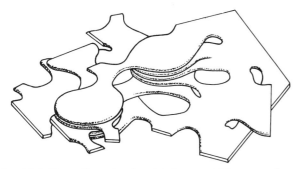

Fig. 6.3.2. Three-dimensional model of grana with inter-granal connections. From [113], by permission.

mature chloroplasts are to be found further membrane structures which form the basis of the photosynthetic apparatus—the thylakoids. Each of these forms a flattened sac-like structure with sealed ends (Fig. 6.3.2).

Several thylakoids may be stacked on top of each other, forming a structure which has been compared with a pile of hollow pennies. However, the individual membrane discs or thylakoids extend further than their own discrete pile and link up in a very complex fashion with other thylakoid stacks [81]. The non-membrane part of the chloroplast is known as the stroma, and it appears in electron micrographs as a granular substance. Thus the only architectural difference between mitochondria and chloroplasts lies in the greater complexity of the internal membrane system of the chloroplast. The chloroplast stroma corresponds to the mitochondrial matrix; the intrathylakoid space to the intracristal space.

6.3.2 MOLECULAR BIOLOGY OF ORGANELLES

Organelle DNA

Both mitochondria and chloroplasts contain DNA and the contribution of this DNA to the regulation of organelle development has become the subject of extensive discussions and investigations.

The overwhelming evidence for the presence of DNA in organelles has accumulated from two major approaches: electron microscopy and biochemistry.

Obviously, one of the main problems to be overcome in these types of investigation is that of confusing the DNA in organelle preparations with nuclear DNA. However, it turns out that organelle DNA can frequently be distinguished from nuclear DNA by base compositional differences as shown by equilibrium centrifugation in caesium chloride. Furthermore, in many cases, the DNA of chloroplasts and mitochondria has been shown to be circular (see Table 6.3.1).

It has been possible to make very precise estimates of the amount of coding information available to the organelle using the type of analysis described in Chapter 6.4. Typically, the genome size is estimated by a comparison of the second-order rate constant for the reassociation of the organelle DNA with those obtained for DNA samples of known molecular weight, e.g. that of the bacteriophages T4 and λ (see Chapter 6.4).

Table 6.3.1 The DNA of mitochondria and chloroplasts.

	Length (μm)	Form	Approximate molecular weight*
Mitochondria from:			
Most animal cells	5	Circles	10^7
Tetrahymena	15–18	Linear	$3.0–3.5 \times 10^7$
Yeast (*Saccharomyces*)	25	Circles	5×10^7
Plants (pea)	30–35	Circles	$6–7 \times 10^7$
Chloroplasts from:			
Euglena	44	Circles	8×10^7
Spinach	45	Circles	9×10^7
Corn	38	Circles	8×10^7

Many organelle genomes were first thought to be linear and were only found to be circular when improved extraction techniques became available.
* Estimates from contour length analysis agree quite well with those obtained from renaturation experiments, see text and [14, 21, 44].

Fortunately, the estimates from this type of study agree quite well with calculations based on the assumption that the contour length of circular genomes seen in electron micrography represents the entire unique sequence length of the organelle genome. In general, this type of analysis also indicates that all of the organelle DNA molecules in an organism are identical (as many as 10^{17} mitochondrial DNA molecules in a single human) and that there are no major gene repetitions in mitochondrial DNA. In chloroplasts, although most of the genome is unique, two or three copies of the region specifying the ribosomal RNA may be present in tandem duplications or as an inverted repeat. These conclusions are based principally on evidence from the analysis of restriction endonuclease digests [14, 21, 56].

Given the amount of organelle-specific DNA available, one can get an estimate of how many proteins could be coded for within the organelle, assuming as a rough guide that 500 base pairs are needed to code for a protein of molecular weight about 20000. A study of the data presented in Table 6.3.2 shows that informational content of mitochondria and chloroplast DNA is severely restricted. Even these calculations of the number of proteins which could be coded for are maximum estimates because a considerable fraction of mitochondrial DNA (and a lesser fraction of chloroplast DNA) is necessary to provide a template for ribosomal and transfer RNA (next section).

Table 6.3.2. The genome size of organelle DNA estimated from renaturation kinetics.

	Estimated genome size (daltons)*	Reference
Mitochondria from:		
Guinea pig	1.1×10^7	[19]
Yeast	5.0×10^7	[19]
Pea	7.4×10^7	[87]
Chloroplasts from:		
Euglena	1.8×10^8	[147]
Lettuce	1.4×10^8	[161]
Tobacco	1.9×10^8	[152]
Chlamydomonas	2.0×10^8	[11]

*A molecular weight of 10^7 daltons corresponds to about 15 000 base pairs.

In several cases the estimates of genome size estimated from renaturation kinetics compare extremely well with those derived from electron microscopic observations, although with chloroplast DNA the figures derived from renaturation data are, in general, larger than the estimates from contour length analysis. To obtain a genome size from renaturation kinetics the second-order rate constant for the renaturation is determined for the organelle DNA under investigation and a molecular weight for the unique sequence length derived by comparison with the rate constants determined for the DNAs of known molecular weight, e.g. the phages λ or T4. Precise estimates are difficult to obtain because of minor variations probably resulting from differences in base composition (see [19]).

Protein synthesis components

When techniques for isolating relatively pure and un-damaged organelles became available, it was shown that isolated chloroplasts and mitochondria could incorporate radioactive amino acids into protein [7, 25, 62, 117]. This suggested that they contained the necessary machinery for protein synthesis, such as ribosomes, ribosomal RNA (rRNA), transfer RNA (tRNA) and aminoacyl tRNA synthetases.

Many studies have shown that organelle ribosomes differ in size from those of the cytoplasm (Table 6.3.3) and bear a superficial similarity to those of bacteria and blue-green algae. They also differ in their interaction with a variety of drugs. Drugs which inhibit protein synthesis can be divided into three main groups (see Table 6.3.4). It can be seen that some inhibitors have a very wide spectrum of action and presumably affect some stage in protein synthesis common to all ribosome-mediated protein synthesis. Puromycin, for example,

Table 6.3.3. The sizes of ribosomes from prokaryotes, organelles and eukaryotic cell cytoplasm.

Source	Sedimentation value	References
Bacteria	70S	[107]
Blue-green algae	70S	[36, 107]
Eukaryotic cytoplasm	80S	[83]
Mitochondria from:		
Fungi	70–80S	[25, 44]
Animal cells e.g. *HeLa*	55–60S	[25, 44]
Chloroplasts	70–80S	[25, 44]

The sedimentation values presented are approximate. Ribosomes from prokaryotes and eukaryotic cytoplasm are conventionally described as belonging to a 70S or 80S class, respectively. In fact, the average value determined by Taylor and Storck [107] for 25 bacteria was 68.4S.

acts as an aminoacyl tRNA analogue. Other types of inhibitor appear to differentiate between the ribosomes of eukaryote cytoplasm and prokaryotes.

By this criterion of drug sensitivity, the organelle ribosomes seem to resemble those found in bacteria and blue-green algae. Nevertheless, it is important to exercise caution in pressing the analogies between prokaryotic and organelle ribosomes too far. Although the mitochondrial ribosomes of mammalian cells have extremely low sedimentation values, they actually con-tain more proteins than *E. coli* ribosomes. It is the presence of these which alters significantly the buoyant density of the ribosomes and results in a low rate of sedimentation [25].

The results from a very large number of studies indicate that most mitochondrial proteins are encoded by nuclear genes, that they are synthesized by the ribosomes in the cytoplasm, and that they must there-fore be transported subsequently into the organelle (see later). Although the chloroplasts have more genetic potential, a large proportion of their components are similarly dependent on nuclear information and cyto-plasmic protein synthesis.

What then is the role of the extranuclear genetic information of mitochondria and chloroplasts in direct-ing organelle biogenesis in cellular development?

The role of organelle DNA

It has been established that organelles synthesize tran-scripts corresponding to messenger, ribosomal and transfer classes of RNA.

Organelle ribosomes like those of bacteria contain many different proteins [77] and three major classes of RNA which will be referred to as 'heavy' (18S–23S), 'light' (12S–16S) and a much smaller, 5S species. The last is present in ribosomes of bacteria, chloroplasts and plant mitochondria but absent from ribosomes of yeast

Table 6.3.4. The effect of various inhibitors on protein synthesis in different systems.

	Bacteria	Eukaryotic cytoplasm	Yeast mitochondria	Animal mitochondria	Chloroplasts
Antibiotic inhibitor:					
Puromycin	+	+	+	+	+
Cycloheximide	–	+	–	–	–
Emetine	–	+		–	
Chloramphenicol	+	–	+	+	+
Erythromycin	+	–	+	–?	+
Streptomycin	+	–	+	–	+

Symbols
+ Inhibition of protein synthesis.
– No inhibition of protein synthesis at the dose range found to block protein synthesis in other systems. If used at high doses, many of the inhibitors can effect protein synthesis in most systems, often by an indirect mechanism. For additional information on inhibitors which act differently on mitochondrial protein synthesis in yeast and animal cells, see [44].

or animal mitochondria [14, 22, 25, 44, 95]. The technique of DNA/RNA hydribization makes it possible to discover whether the various organelle ribosomal RNAs are coded for by nuclear or organelle DNA. In all cases examined, from mitochondria of human cells to tobacco plant chloroplasts, the available evidence indicates that organelles code for their own rRNA. Hybridization of saturating quantities of rRNA species with organelle DNA indicates that, whereas mitochondrial genomes contain a single gene copy for the 'heavy' and 'light' RNA types, chloroplast genomes may contain two or, in some cases, three copies of the sequences corresponding to 16S, 23S and 5S RNA. In *Zea mays* the rRNA genes lie within an inverted repeat comprising about 15% of the total circular genome [14, 22, 25, 44]. The exact size of the organelle rRNAs varies somewhat. Ribosomal RNA components of animal cell mitochondria are about half the molecular weight of the equivalent species found in yeast mitochondria and in plant chloroplasts, where they appear to be of similar sizes to those found in bacteria and blue-green algae.

In contrast to the RNA components of the ribosome, the vast majority of organelle ribosomal proteins are made in the cytoplasm and are probably not coded for by the organelle genome. Kuntzel [64], for example, has studied the effect of either chloramphenicol or cyclo-heximide on the incorporation of labelled amino acids into mitochondrial ribosomal proteins of *Neurospora* and found that the inhibitor of cytoplasmic protein synthesis (i.e. cycloheximide) reduced the labelling by 97%, whereas chloramphenicol had little or no effect. More recent studies have largely confirmed these observations for most of these ribosomal proteins, although there are exceptions (in *Neurospora* and *Chlamydomonas*) [20, 65].

The genetic origin of the transfer RNAs which are necessary for protein synthesis can also be examined directly by the techniques of DNA/RNA hybridization. In chloroplasts and in the mitochondria of fungi there are enough regions homologous with 4S (presumed transfer) RNA to provide for at least one type of tRNA for each amino acid [14, 22, 44]; however, it would appear that insufficient tRNA species are present to enable all 61 sense codons to be read if the tRNA/codon interactions follow the patterns predicted by Crick's wobble hypothesis. Even fewer (about 22) tRNA genes have been found for the mitochondrial DNA from mammalian cells [44]. The conclusion that the codon/

anticodon interactions in mitochondria must differ significantly from those generally observed has been confirmed dramatically by the recent demonstration of a different genetic code in these organelles [9, 69]. UGA codes for tryptophan in human mitochondria rather than acting as a termination (stop) codon and AUA may code for methionine instead of isoleucine. The code in yeast mitochondria also utilizes UGA for trytophan. There is some speculation that the unusual features may represent a more primitive genetic code.

It is possible to establish the relative positions of some tRNA genes on the organelle genome by tagging the molecules with the electron-dense molecule ferritin and visualizing the sites of hybridization in the electron microscope. Employing this elegant procedure, twelve sites have been detected on one strand of human mitochondrial DNA and seven sites on the other, the strands having been separated first by denaturation and purified by CsCl centrifugation [4].

Less is known about the origin of other components necessary for efficient protein synthesis, such as the factors required in the initiation and elongation steps of peptide synthesis. However, it is known that organelles require *N*-formylmethionine tRNA to initiate protein synthesis, as do prokaryotic organisms [25, 95, 117].

It appears that most of the additional components for mitochondrial protein synthesis are provided by the cytoplasm. The same holds for the RNA and DNA polymerase activities which have been shown to be present in isolated organelles (see Table 6.3.5).

Organelles in different organisms show quite large variation in their potential to provide for themselves (in terms of DNA content). Nevertheless, even in the chloroplast, which has the most genetic potential, extensive cooperation with the remainder of the cell is essential to provide even for a complete protein-synthesizing apparatus.

Components made on organelle ribosomes

In order to understand the process of development at the subcellular level, it is necessary to know which organelle proteins are synthesized *in situ* and which are transported in from the exterior. The following section describes attempts to discover where organelle components other than nucleic acids are synthesized in the cell, using genetic and biochemical techniques.

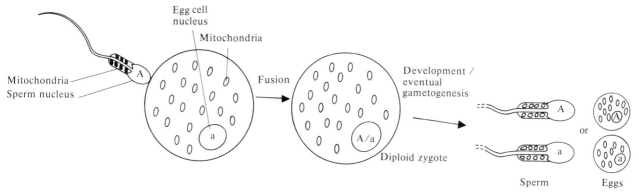

Fig. 6.3.3. Diagrammatic representation of maternal inheritance of mitochondria in animals. Although the mitochondria in the sperm mid-piece may penetrate the egg cell, their descendants have not been detected in the developed offspring (see text). They are possibly degraded [106] and in any case would be vastly outnumbered by the maternally derived organelles.

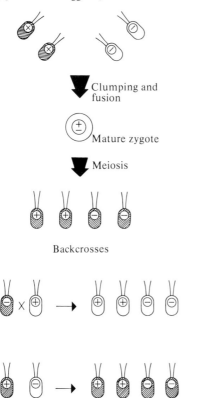

Fig. 6.3.4. Uniparental inheritance of streptomycin resistance in the unicellular alga *Chlamydomonas reinhardtii*. + and − refer to mating type determinants controlled by nuclear genes and which therefore segregate 2:2 in the four meiotic products of the zygote. (Normally only the zygote stage in *Chlamydomonas* is diploid.) Streptomycin resistance (shaded cytoplasm) in the progeny is usually the same as that present in the + mating type parent. See text and [97] for possible explanation.

Information from genetic studies

It was once thought that nuclear chromosomes might hold a master copy of the organelle genome which could be replicated and transferred to the cytoplasm at some stage during development. This suggestion has little experimental support (see above). Furthermore, the existence of traits which effect organelles and which are transmitted by genetic factors in the cytoplasm strongly argues for the independent nature of the information in organelles. A consideration of the nature of male and female gametes and the processes leading to zygote production in higher plants and animals demonstrates the way in which cytoplasmic inheritance can be distinguished from the Mendelian segregation of nuclear genes.

The female gamete usually provides the bulk of the zygote cytoplasm, whereas the cytoplasmic contribution from the male gamete is very small. Sperm may introduce several mitochondria into the eggs of mammals. The fate of these mitochondria has been carefully studied in only a few species; serial electron microscopy suggests that these mitochondria degenerate during early development [106]. In situations where the maternal and paternal mitochondrial DNA (mitDNA) can be distinguished by hybridization or by the pattern of restriction enzyme cleavage (e.g. in interspecies crosses or, as in the case of man, by making use of polymorphisms for restriction enzyme target sites) only maternal-type mitDNA had been detected in the offspring [37, 43b, 55]. Early development is therefore dominated by the complement of organelles present in the female gamete cytoplasm. Genetic determinants which are present in organelles and which influence organelle traits are transmitted more or less exclusively through the female line (see Fig. 6.3.3). Any factor transmitted in this way shows 'maternal inheritance'.

The situation in microorganisms such as yeast and unicellular algae is less straightforward. In the majority of cases, although some traits affecting organelles are transmitted uniparentally in that the offspring resemble only one of the parental types (see Fig. 6.3.4), the contribution to the zygote of cytoplasm both from parental type of gametes is equal. One might therefore expect the progeny to show traits resembling both parents. A possible explanation for this enigma has been suggested by Sager and Lane for maternally inherited chloroplast traits in *Chlamydomonas* [97]. They proposed that the plastid genome of one mating type, although initially present, is broken down soon after fusion of the plastids (which occurs in the zygote), possibly by a mechanism analogous to the modification and restriction of DNA found in bacteria.

In plants, many of the observations can be accounted for by complete elimination of plastids from one or other of the gametes. This has long been known, e.g. for *Spirogyra* (see [62]), and is also thought to occur in the male gametes in certain flowering plants. Indeed, no plastids have been found in male gametes in any species of higher plant so far given a thorough examination [59]. Nevertheless, transmission of plastid mutations through the male gamete is well documented for *Pelargonium* [108]. Examples of fern and bryophyte male sperm are known which possess plastids, but which lose them just prior to fertilization [82]. In any case, it does not follow that all organelles derived from the male and female gametes will survive to contribute to the embryo. In certain gymnosperms a spatial segregation is maintained within the zygote, and it is held that the 'female' plastids degenerate [28, 29, 32].

It is thus possible for one gamete to lose its plastids but, even where this occurs, the continuity of plastids is assured by their presence in the cytoplasm of the other gamete. A convincing demonstration of such continuity comes from long-term breeding experiments in the genus *Oenothera*, in which one subgenus consists of a number of species formed as a result of combinations of five types of plastid genome and six types of nuclear genome. Since a given type of plastid genome can be recovered unchanged after many successive generations of existence combined with a given type of nucleus, it

follows that the plastids carrying that particular genome retained their individuality and were never lost [39, 102].

The most important conclusion to be drawn from the available work on plastid and mitochondrial genetics and the ultrastructure of male and female gametes is that there is no need to hypothesize a *de novo* origin for organelles.

Identification of a cytoplasmically inherited trait affecting organelles does not rigorously establish that the relevant gene(s) are present in organelle DNA. However, the bulk of evidence, both circumstantial and direct, supports this hypothesis.

A cytoplasmic pattern of inheritance has enabled a variety of organelle-coded functions to be identified. Mutations in organelle DNA may confer resistance to antibiotics which normally inhibit organelle protein synthesis or electron transport. Other mutations may result in organelles deficient in either of these two processes.

Biochemical investigations of organelle autonomy in vivo and in vitro

The alternative approach to that of genetics in seeking to establish the role of organelle genomes during development is less rigorous, but more widely applicable. It depends on the assumption that the proteins made within the organelle (on organelle ribosomes) are gene products of the chloroplast or mitochondrial DNA. Analysis of such proteins can be carried out by following the incorporation of labelled amino acids into proteins of isolated organelles and using electrophoresis or other techniques to separate the labelled polypeptides. Recent estimates suggest that intact, isolated chloroplasts may synthesize as many as 80 soluble proteins and 12 membrane proteins (see [14]).

Alternatively, studies can be done on intact cells by *selectively* blocking cytoplasmic protein synthesis with the drug cycloheximide. Incorporation of amino acids can be followed as with the isolated organelle. Both approaches have disadvantages and, unless combined with the use of transcription inhibitors, they do not distinguish between proteins made in response to messages of nuclear origin which may be taken up by organelles and those directed by RNA made on organelle genome. Nevertheless, both approaches give similar results, which are consistent generally with data from genetic studies.

Two of the most interesting facts which emerge from the data compiled in Table 6.3.5 (which combines information from a variety of sources) are as follows:

(1) Key enzymes which are necessary for the exploitation of the genetic information within the organelle (DNA and RNA polymerases) are coded for by the nucleus.

(2) Even those products apparently coded for by the organelle (e.g. rRNA, tRNA, subunits of cytochrome oxidase, cytochrome *b*, ATPase and ribulose bisphosphate carboxylase) are not functional by themselves but have to cooperate with additional components from the cytoplasm (e.g. ribosomal proteins, tRNA synthetases, other enzyme subunits) for activity. This suggests that a tight interdependence of the organelle and cytoplasmic systems must operate during development. Exceptions to this generalization exist and are discussed in a later section.

Very recently, an international venture has been undertaken in collecting and characterizing a vast number of cytoplasmically inherited mutants of yeast having deficiences in electron transport or resistance to known inhibitors of the electron transfer chain. This has led to the identification of several sites on the mitochondrial genome which are the presumptive structural genes for cytochrome *b* and cytochrome oxidase subunits. Sophisticated genetic studies have provided a fairly complex picture of the genetic organization in the region of these genes and suggest that the structural genes for cytochrome *b* and cytochrome oxidase subunit 1 are not continuous but exist as several coding regions (exons) interspersed with other sequences (introns) [105].

Localization mechanisms for organelle components

One of the puzzling features of organelle biogenesis is that although some components are manufactured internally, clearly the majority of proteins must come in from the cytoplasm. Therefore, the problem is how these components find their way to their specific subcellular sites. An additional complexity is posed by the observation that several mitochondrial enzymes (e.g. malate dehydrogenase) have cytoplasmic equivalents. So two forms of protein exist in the cell, both having similar catalytic properties, yet one of these is found almost exclusively in the mitochondria, the other in the cytoplasm. How this compartmentalization is achieved

Table 6.3.5. Probable origin of major organelle components.

Mitochondrial components	Origin
DNA polymerase	Cytoplasm
RNA polymerase	Cytoplasm
Ribosomes	
(a) ribosomal RNA	Organelle
(b) most, if not all,	
ribosomal proteins	Cytoplasm
Cytochrome oxidase	
subunits I–III	Organelle
subunits IV–VII	Cytoplasm
Cytochrome b (apoprotein)	Organelle
Cytochrome c	Cytoplasm
ATPase	
F_1	Cytoplasm
OSCP	Cytoplasm
Membrane proteins	Organelle
Transfer (4S) RNA	Organelle

Chloroplast components	
DNA polymerase	Cytoplasm
RNA polymerase	Cytoplasm
Cytoplasm	
Ribosomes	
(a) ribosomal RNA	Organelle
(b) most ribosomal proteins	Cytoplasm
Ribulose bisphosphate carboxylase	
large subunit	Organelle
small subunit	Cytoplasm
Some thylakoid membrane proteins	
associated with ATPase and photo-	
systems I and II	Organelle

The evidence for the origin of particular components is discussed in the text. Nucleic acid hybridization studies provide unequivocal evidence for localization of rRNA and tRNA genes to the organelle genome. The origin of many protein components has been deduced from their site of synthesis (on organelle or cytoplasmic ribosomes). The isolation of extrachromosomally inherited mutations affecting these components and, more recently, the direct sequencing of mitochondrial DNA, has generally confirmed the existence of coding sequences for such components in the organelle genomes.

when both are nuclear gene products and synthesized on cytoplasmic ribosomes is not clear. In man, genetic studies indicate that the two malate dehydrogenases are coded for by genes on different chromosomes [115]; however, the electrophoretically distinguishable mitochondrial and cytoplasmic forms of fumarate hydratase are apparently derived from the same gene product, yet end up in different subcellular compartments [35, 43].

There are two attractive suggestions that could account for localization. Both have some experimental support. One possibility is that proteins destined for inclusion within the organelle are synthesized with, or acquire by modification, specific physico-chemical properties. These, it is thought, enable recognition and specific uptake at the organelle membrane barrier. The specificity might result from a particular distribution of hydrophobic and hydrophilic residues, or by addition of a particular carbohydrate group.

There is some evidence that a localization mechanism similar to this may hold for lysosomal enzymes which are normally involved in mobilizing carbohydrate storage products. In a rare human disease, several of the lysosomal enzymes are unable to associate properly and integrate with the organelle. Furthermore, they apparently lack specific carbohydrate residues normally associated with the functional enzyme [52]. There are also instances of apparent structural-gene mutations resulting in the localization of the altered enzyme at a different subcellular site, e.g. β glucuronidase in mice [79], malate dehydrogenase in *Neurospora* [73].

It has also become apparent that, at least in the case of the cytoplasmically synthesized smaller subunit of ribulose bisphosphate carboxylase (in plants), proteolytic cleavage is associated with subcellular localization [101].

The second suggestion is that the proteins which eventually find their way into organelles are manufactured on a class of cytoplasmic ribosome which binds to the organelle surface membrane. It is envisaged that during synthesis the proteins are directed into the organelle, perhaps in an analogous way to the production of proteins made for 'export' on the ribosome-studded endoplasmic reticulum. There is now fairly extensive evidence in support of the suggestion made by Blobel and others, that proteins destined for transfer into membrane vesicles *en route* to the cell membrane for export have a particular configuration of amino acids at the N-terminal end, which acts as a signal for membrane attachment and penetration [17]. In spite of the apparent difficulties a mechanism of this sort might have in injecting a growing polypeptide chain through both

outer membranes, there is circumstantial evidence for this type of mechanism from the electron microscope and from biochemical studies, which suggest the existence of a group of ribosomes in yeast which appear to associate specifically with the outer membrane at regions where the two membranes are closely adpressed [61].

6.3.3 DEVELOPMENT AND BIOGENESIS OF CHLOROPLASTS

The variety of forms

The term plastid embraces a variety of differentiated organelle forms (see Figs 6.3.5–6.3.8). We therefore have to consider not only problems concerned with origin and continuity of chloroplasts but also problems concerned with the development of a wide range of plastid-type organelles, differing in structure and function.

The simplest member of the plastid family is the *proplastid*. Proplastids are small, though usually slightly larger than mitochondria (Fig. 6.3.5). They are transmitted through cell division and reproduction and are capable of developing into other types of plastid during cell differentiation. They thus act as a plastid stem-line. In general, meristematic cells contain proplastids. As the products of cell division differentiate, so too do their plastids. The types that may appear include *chloroplasts, etioplasts, amyloplasts, chromoplasts* and *leucoplasts*. Chloroplasts are usually green, with photosynthetic functions; etioplasts develop where chloroplast formation is partially blocked by lack of light; amyloplasts store starch in bulk; chromoplasts are pigmented but are not green and non-photosynthetic; leucoplasts contain little pigment, and this category embraces a fairly heterogeneous assemblage of sub-types, each one within limits typical of the cell in which it is found.

The following sections describe aspects of the development of chloroplasts and etioplasts after a brief consideration of the origin and continuity of the lineage.

Origin and continuity

There are very few plant cells that lack plastids. An exception is mentioned on p. 402. Meristems of higher plants have, in general, between 10 and 100 proplastids per cell, and a balance is maintained between the rate of

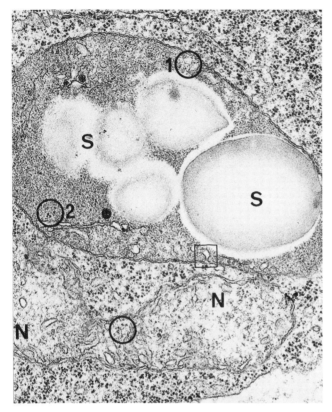

Fig. 6.3.5. Proplastid (upper right) and mitochondrion (lower) in a root tip cell (*Vicia faba*). The proplastid displays several of the general features of plastids: double envelope, nucleoid area (e.g. circle 1) ribosomes (e.g. small granules in circle 2) and plastoglobuli (large dense granules). It also contains some starch (S) and a rudimentary internal membrane system, in parts continuous with the inner membrane of the envelope (square). Three nucleoid areas (N) appear in this particular section of the mitochondrion. Its ribosomes, e.g. in circle, like those of the proplastid, can be seen to be smaller than the surrounding cytoplasmic ribosomes.

cell division and the rate of plastid multiplication. It is, however, one aspect of the differentiation of certain cell types for this balance to become altered. In cases such as the formation of photosynthetic leaf mesophyll tissue, plastid division continues long after cell division has ceased, and the population per cell may rise to several hundred [89]. Contrasting with the behaviour of the mesophyll, the plastid population remains at a much lower level in the epidermal cells of the leaf and usually consists of leucoplasts that are, compared with the mesophyll chloroplasts, poorly developed.

It is common for chloroplasts to have genomes present in multiple copies as judged by estimation of the number of nucleoid areas (se Fig. 6.3.7, p. 408) present in them [51], of the extent of incorporation of labelled precursors into DNA [49], and of the amount of DNA present [50]. It seems that the larger the chloroplast the more likely it is to be 'polyploid'. There can be several copies of the plastid DNA per nucleoid, and several nucleoids per plastid [63]. Mitochondria too can have more than one nucleoid area [75] (Fig. 6.3.5), but the assumption of the extensively poly-nucleoid condition in chloroplasts in a leaf cell does not, it seems, necessarily go along with parallel phenomena in the mitochondria of the same cells [63].

The consequences of the polyploidization of plastids, or at any rate of chloroplasts, are many. For instance, although there may be only two genes coding for ribosomal RNA in each copy of the plastid genome [14], by the time the numbers in the population are taken into account the total number of rRNA organelle genes per cell can rival that in the nucleus.

It has been estimated that in *Vicia faba* green leaves, the number of plastid ribosomes approximately equals the number of cytoplasmic ribosomes [42]. Fairly similar figures are available for *Chlamydomonas* chloroplasts and cytoplasm [23].

Plastid multiplication often occurs in association with increases in nuclear DNA, and in sugar beet it can be shown that at least four of the nine nuclear chromosomes carry genes which, if present in three rather than the usual two copies, will lead to plastid population growth [27]. The cessation of plastid multiplication and a reduction in plastid numbers per cell must certainly be controlled and there is evidence for nuclear, hormonal and environmental factors being involved.

In lower plants, a reduction from many chloroplasts to a single chloroplast per cell has often been reported for cells that are participating in formation of gametes or even in a vegetative reproductive process [26]. For example, in the moss *Polytrichum*, formation of sporogenous cells involves reduction to one chloroplast per cell; following this, mitosis and chloroplast fission keep pace, each of the progeny receiving one nucleus and one chloroplast. Then, control of plastid division is altered just prior to meiosis in the spore mother cells. Four plastids are produced instead of the usual two, so that the four haploid spores that arise following meiosis each receive one plastid. When the spore germinates,

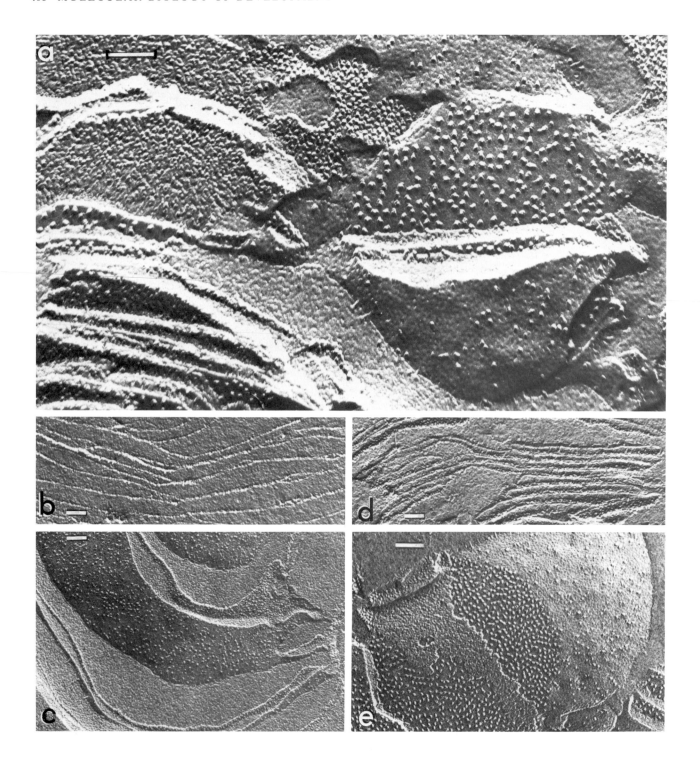

the control system has again altered, and the multi-chloroplast condition is resumed [80]. It has been observed that three processes can contribute to reduction in plastid numbers. One is fusion of plastids, another is cell division without accompanying plastid division [26], and the third is breakdown of entire chloroplasts, including their DNA [70]. It would be of great interest to know whether the reduction in numbers is accompanied by a simplification of the plastid DNA to only a single copy per plastid, for this would mean that the plants arising from the uniplastid spores (or other cells) are genetically uniform with respect to their plastids.

Development of the internal membrane system

Like other differentiated forms of plastid, chloroplasts arise from proplastids. Plastid multiplication may proceed during the developmental processes; indeed, most of the increase in the population during maturation of mesophyll cells seems to occur amongst young chloroplasts, rather than at the proplastid stage [19, 53, 90].

Chloroplast development includes many synthetic steps involving both nuclear and plastid genomes. Undoubtedly, the change that is most obvious is the formation of the chlorophyll-bearing system of internal membranes. The few fragments of membrane that are present in proplastids (Fig. 6.3.5) first enlarge to form more extensive flattened sacs, or *primary thylakoids,* and then the complex system of *grana* develops upon this foundation.

Self-assembly

Complex though it is, the membrane system of the chloroplast has a certain ability to *self-assemble*. If chloroplast membranes are isolated and suspended in an organic buffer, the partitions very largely fall apart [1, 5, 15, 57] (Fig. 6.3.6). The intricately interconnected system becomes a series of concentric single thylakoid surfaces, with few or no grana surviving. Although measurements have not been made, it is likely that this is merely a change in architecture without membrane loss. The significance from the point of view of development is not so much this experiment, but its sequel—that of adding salts (divalent cations are best). An extraordinary event takes place. Many grana reappear. It is not claimed that the original membrane system is re-created, but the conclusion that chloroplast internal membranes can self-assemble into small grana, given a suitable ionic environment, seems justified. Fig. 6.3.6 illustrates this experiment. Other examples of self-assembly are given in Chapter 6.2. Studies by freeze-etching show that when the original partitions are broken down, their large particles disperse, and when partitions are re-formed, one of the events is the reaggregation of the large particles (Fig. 6.3.6). The large particles probably consist of chlorophyll–protein complexes that 'harvest' light energy via photosystem II. The smaller particles seen in the inter-granum membranes (Fig. 6.3.6) are probably the corresponding reaction centres for photosystem I.

The actual process of granum development in young

Fig. 6.3.6. Substructure of chloroplast membranes, and their ability to 'self-assemble', studied by freeze-etching.
(a) Portions of two grana in a spinach chloroplast that was rapidly frozen, and fractured while frozen. The membranes that were exposed along the fracture were then shadow-cast so that their surface topography could be visualized by means of electron microscopy. The various types of particle are thought to correspond to light-harvesting complexes of chlorophyll, protein, and lipid. The large particles exposed in the right-hand granum stack back onto the intra-thylakoid space, and correlate with the distribution of photosystem 2 activity in the chloroplast. They are restricted to the grana, unlike the smaller particles that are visible in the left-hand granum, which are present in the unstacked inter-granum thylakoids as well, and which are in that part of the membrane that backs onto the chloroplast stroma. These smaller particles correlate with the distribution of photosystem 1 actvity. The smooth expanses between the particles probably represent areas of exposed lipid bilayer. × 110 000.

(b, c) Spinach thylakoids freeze-fractured after the chloroplasts had been suspended in a low-salt tricine buffer for 1 h. The grana have become unstacked and the thylakoids now occur as large, usually single, sheets, seen in (b) in edge-on profile, and in (c) in face view. The large particles are now uniformly distributed, but both they and the smaller particles have remained in their respective halves of the membrane (see (a)). Also the total number of each category of particle remains the same.
(d, e) Spinach thylakoids as in (b) and (c) but 1 h after addition of divalent cations (2 mM $MgCl_2$). The edge-on fracture view (d) shows that the thylakoids have restacked into grana, and the face view (e) shows that most of the large particles have re-segregated to their original *in vivo* positions, as in (a).

Micrographs kindly provided by Dr L.A. Staehelin; (a), (c), (d), (e) from Staehelin, Armond & Miller (1976) *Brookhaven Symp. Biol,* **28,** 278–315; (b) from Staehelin (1976) *J. Cell Biol,* **71,** 136–158.

All scale markers 0.1 μm.

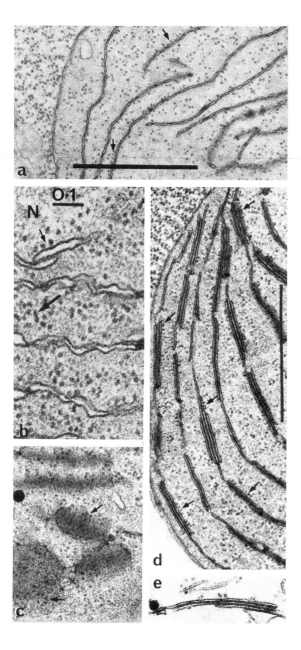

chloroplasts is less dramatic, but presumably involves elements of the self-assembly reactions discovered in the test-tube experiments described above. Primary thylakoids do not form grana if they are suspended in low-salt buffer and then given salt. Evidently they lack materials that are needed in order to form partitions [1]. *In vivo,* such materials soon arise. A primary thylakoid produces an evagination in the form of a small pouch (Fig. 6.3.7). This grows out over the surface of the parent. Its growth ceases when it has attained the shape and diameter of a granum disc—that is, when a granum consisting of two loculi and one intervening partition has been formed. The term spirocyclic growth describes subsequent events [112]. Further pouches protrude and grow out over the first granum disc. Each new disc is connected to the underlying disc or to the primary thylakoid at the point where its evagination commenced, and these channels of interconnection, if they are to generate a final form as shown in Fig. 6.3.2, must lie in a helix. Eventually, a stack of discs, all connected to a helically ascending fret, is produced. The growth process cannot, however, end there. Mature grana have multiple frets, and each disc has multiple fret connections around its periphery [81]. Clearly, in order to establish these, there must be considerable fusions between existing discs and locally growing frets. It may be that establishment of a mature and relatively symmetrical granum is a slow process involving numerous adjustments, many of which can be imagined as occurring automatically if it is remembered that, in general, symmetry and stability go together. The more order, or 'repeating units' of structure, in the system, the less

Fig. 6.3.7. 'Rough thylakoids' in oat chloroplasts developing from etioplasts. In early stages of greening, the thylakoids dispersing from the prolamellar body are perforated, but are 'smooth', although ribosomes and probably polyribosomes are present in the stroma.
(a) Slightly later, the perforations have healed, and ribosome chains lie on the developing thylakoids (e.g. arrows) and free in the stroma.
(b) After the lag period of greening has ended, the first granum discs and partitions appear, and polyribosomes are seen free in the stroma as irregular chains (e.g. large arrows) or tight helices (star), as well as on the thylakoids (e.g. small arrows). N = Nucleoid area. (c, d) By this stage, granum formation is about half complete. The stroma–granum interface, with its associated ribosome chains (e.g. arrows) is seen in profile (d) and face (c) views. (e) Ribosomes remain attached to the young grana even when the chloroplast is broken and the stroma allowed to disperse. Note that in (a), (c) and (d), no ribosomes are seen associated with the chloroplast envelopes. (b) reproduced by permission from [64].

information the nuclear and plastid genomes need in order to produce and maintain it (see Chapter 6.2). Thus, development adjustments which maximize symmetry will be favoured.

Many environmental factors influence the final form of the thylakoid system. Amongst those that affect the size and shapes of grana are: light quality, light intensity, the photoperiod, the CO_2 supply, and the supply of mineral nutrients, especially forms of nitrogen (see [62]).

Molecular aspects

Turning from the gross conformation of the chloroplast membranes to their development in terms of molecular composition, it seems that the operations involved are similar to those known to occur in the formation of other cell membranes, such as the intermitochondrial membrane and the endoplasmic reticulum [103]. In none of these membranes does the cell manufacture all of the necessary molecular species and then assemble them into an instantly functional membrane. Rather, the various types of molecule are added in a multi-step sequence, akin to constructing a mosaic one colour at a time, until the final pattern is completed. In order to detect this type of membrane growth it has been necessary to find material in which the thylakoid systems of large numbers of cells and chloroplasts are developed synchronously. Mutant algal cells triggered to develop by an abrupt alteration of the nutrient regime have proved valuable, as have populations of etioplasts induced to develop towards the chloroplast condition by switching on the light [78, 84].

When the thylakoids are being extended rapidly, the microscopist can see (Fig. 6.3.7), and the biochemist can isolate, polyribosomes attached to the membranes [31, 33, 72]. Treatment with puromycin, which releases nascent proteins from polyribosomes, leaves the proteins that were being assembled at the time of treatment attached to the thylakoids [33, 72]. A process of synthesis and direct incorporation of protein into the growing membrane is inferred. Polyribosomes also occur free in the stroma of chloroplasts (Fig. 6.3.5), which suggests that developing plastids contain different classes of messenger RNA molecules and possess a means of determining whether their translation shall occur free or membrane bound.

The most reasonable inference from modern work on thylakoid development is that the component molecular

species are added independently, and probably not in any strongly localized region of the membrane surface [45]. Direct observations of *Spirogyra* and *Nitella* chloroplasts suggest that they grow along their length [46].

It is clear that nuclear and plastid genomes collaborate with one another in chloroplast development. Thylakoid assembly is known to involve materials coded for by both genetic systems. The same applies, though at the *intra*molecular level of protein subunits rather than the *inter*molecular level of thylakoids, to the enzyme ribulose bisphosphate carboxylase (see section 6.3.2), which is accumulated in bulk in chloroplasts as they are formed [98, 104], and which consists of two subunits. The large subunit, consisting of polypeptides each of mol. wt 50000–60000, is synthesized within the chloroplast, using plastid mRNA coded for by plastid DNA. The small subunit, consisting of polypeptides in the size range 12000–20000, is synthesized on cytoplasmic ribosomes by translation of cytoplasmic mRNA that is in turn derived from nuclear DNA. Clearly, the genetic and synthetic systems for these two subunits must operate in harmony.

The small-subunit polypeptide is first made as a precursor molecule which has a molecular weight 4000 higher than the final molecule. The precursor, which has been synthesized *in vitro*, has been supplied to isolated intact chloroplasts, whereupon it is taken in, its extra portion removed, and the residue combined with large-subunit protein in the stroma. The precursor from the alga *Chlamydomonas* is not processed by pea or spinach chloroplasts, whereas the two higher plant chloroplasts can accept and process precursor from each other and, in *in vitro* experiments, produce an enzyme that is indistinguishable from that formed *in vivo* [101].

The large subunit is made within the chloroplast. By fragmenting chloroplast DNA with restriction enzymes and transcribing and translating the products in *in vitro* protein-synthesizing reaction mixtures, it has been found that in *Zea mays* there is a single copy of the gene for the large-subunit polypeptide in the circular DNA molecule of the chloroplast [13]. By contrast, there are two copies of each of the genes for chloroplast rRNA molecules (16S, 23S and 5S) [14].

Chloroplast differentiation

One of the most interesting findings is the relationship between cell differentiation and organelle differentiation. *Zea mays* is one of a number of plants which possess the 'C-4 pathway' of photosynthesis, which involves two sorts of chloroplast. One type, found in the mesophyll cells, does not contain ribulose bisphosphate carboxylase. The other type, found in the cells of the sheath that surrounds the vascular bundles of the leaf, does contain the enzyme. Here then are two classes of chloroplast. Does cell differentiation, and the associated chloroplast differentiation, result from or lead to changes in the genetic make-up of the chloroplast? The answer appears to be no. The gene for the ribulose bisphosphate carboxylase large subunit exists in the chloroplasts of the mesophyll cells as well as in those of the bundle sheath cells [110]. The latter have much more mRNA for the subunit than the former [67], so the two

types of chloroplast have a developmental difference in the extent of transcription (or possibly in the rate of destruction of transcribed mRNA).

What is not yet understood is the switching system that, in the course of cell differentiation, must operate to control the development of the different types of chloroplast. One example will suffice to show the order of complexity that can be anticipated [54]. In the *y-1* mutant of *Chlamydomonas reinhardtii*, a major polypeptide of the thylakoid membranes is made on cytoplasmic ribosomes (as judged by the sensitivity of its synthesis to inhibitors specific to this class of ribosome). Despite its extra-chloroplast site of production, its manufacture seems to be geared to the synthesis of chlorophyll within the chloroplast. It is thought that a protein made in the chloroplast on chloroplast ribosomes regulates the activity of the gene coding for the thylakoid polypeptide. The regulatory protein is, in turn, influenced by the rate at which chlorophyll is formed, perhaps by interaction with a precursor of the pigment. The harmonious end result is that the membrane protein is made when chlorophyll is being made.

Formation of etioplasts

Formation of etioplasts is to some extent an atypical process, conspicuous only when tissues that would otherwise become green and photosynthetic are forced to develop, or *etiolate*, in darkness. Then, a quasi-crystalline array of membrane in the form of interconnected branched tubules appears within the plastid (Fig. 6.3.8), in place of grana and frets. Because the array of tubules metamorphoses into more conventional thylakoids upon illumination, it is known as the *prolamellar body*. Its production is emphasized during growth in darkness, but darkness is not obligatory, for some appear at low light intensity in leaves [48, 94].

Most types of prolamellar body are based upon regularly interconnected, tetrahedrally branched, membranous tubules [75] (Fig. 6.3.8). Unless the etioplasts have been exposed at some time to light, the prolamellar body carries not chlorophyll but its immediate precursor, protochlorophyllide *a*, which undergoes a rapid photochemical reduction to chlorophyllide *a* upon illumination of a dark-grown leaf. Somewhat more slowly, esterification with phytol then gives rise to chlorophyll *a* in a light-independent reaction. These processes are part of the conversion of etioplasts to

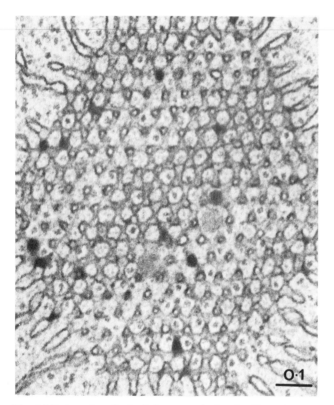

Fig. 6.3.8. A prolamellar body in an oat etioplast. In this particular example, the body was in the form of a hexagonal prism, here sectioned close to the (0001) plane, and made up of tetrahedrally branched tubules interconnected in the same geometrical relationship as the zinc and sulphur atoms in the mineral wurtzite. The plastid stroma, including many ribosomes, penetrates between the tubules. Reproduced, by permission, from [47].

chloroplasts, to be considered again below. While still in the dark, the protochlorophyllide *a* is associated with a large protein, the protochlorophyll holochrome. Some calculations suggest that the holochrome molecules, each about 10 nm in diameter, that occur in a prolamellar body would cover an area approximately equal to the area of membrane that is present [60]. Whether the protein, with its pigment, does in fact exist in a monolayer in or on the membrane remains to be seen. One point of interest in relation to earlier discussions of *self-assembly* is that prolamellar bodies can be isolated and fractionated. A lipid–protein complex obtained from them is capable of assembling *in vitro* into branched tubules, and it seems that it is the lipid component that confers this ability to assemble, for it is not abolished by digestion with protease.

Etioplasts contain neither as much pigment nor as much membrane as chloroplasts. Plastid development is thus not only diverted into the morphologically distinct etioplast condition, but is also held in check. There is considerable evidence that the supply of δ-aminolaevulinic acid is the limiting factor. This compound is the first biosynthetic intermediate unique to the tetrapyrrole pathway that leads to the synthesis of both chlorophylls and haems [11, 12]. If it is supplied to etioplasts in leaves, their content of protochlorophyllide is increased, though the addition may not have the same photochemical properties as the original content. In other words, giving an exogenous supply of the precursor overcomes the check that is imposed upon protochlorophyll synthesis. Normally, after a certain amount of development in darkness, during which δ-aminolaevulinic acid is produced and is converted to protochlorophyllide, the pathway is closed down. Illumination will then reopen it. The enzyme, or enzymes, that produces δ-aminolaevulinic acid is relatively unstable, compared with others operating between this compound and protochlorophyllide itself (see [11]). The analysis of a number of mutants of barley plants in which the normal repression system does not function, so that unusually large amounts of protochlorophyllide accumulate, indicates that several nuclear genes operate to provide a control system governing δ-aminolaevulinic acid formation [76, 116]. Most probably, the controls act at the level of gene transcription, on the principle that if new enzyme is not continually produced by gene transcription and then translation, the instability of the enzyme will bring the biosynthetic process to a halt.

The first event of the 'greening process' that converts the etioplast to the chloroplast is the rapid photoreduction of protochlorophyllide *a*. Except in very humid conditions [2], there is then a lag period, lasting a few hours, before rapid synthesis of chlorophylls and thylakoid membrane starts. The initial chlorophyllide *a* becomes phytylated, and the prolamellar body gradually loses its symmetry during the lag period. The tubular form of membrane metamorphoses into a series of relatively flat primary thylakoids, which at first are perforated and devoid of partitions. The perforations disappear (Fig. 6.3.7a), and granum formation, shown in its earliest stages in Fig. 6.3.7b, commences coincident with net synthesis of new chlorophylls, the enzymes producing δ-aminolaevulinic acid having been derepressed. The mechanics of granum formation have already been described for chloroplasts developing from proplastids, and are probably similar during greening. The light-harvesting chlorophyll–protein complexes that can be visualized using freeze etching gradually increase in size during greening until they reach the mature dimensions shown in Fig. 6.3.6. Biochemical analyses show the concomitant development of photochemical activity and the addition of the coupling factor for phosphorylation. Thus, morphological and biochemical developments proceed hand in hand.

6.3.4 DEVELOPMENT AND BIOGENESIS OF MITOCHONDRIA

In this section, particular attention will be given to the morphological and biochemical changes which accompany the development and proliferation of mitochondria in a variety of situations.

Development of mitochondria in yeast

Wild-type yeast *Saccharomyces* are facultative anaerobes. They are able to grow, in the absence of oxygen, on a carbon source such as glucose, which can yield energy by fermentation pathways. In this situation, the mitochondria are redundant as far as oxygen-linked electron transport requirements are concerned. Even in aerobic conditions, as long as a rich supplement of glucose is provided, the cells rely on the fermentative pathways, largely to the exclusion of mitochondrial function. High levels of glucose thus leads to a reduction in respiratory activity—the Crabtree effect.

Mitochondria under conditions of glucose repression or in absence of oxygen, when they are non-functional in terms of electron transport, also exhibit considerable structural changes from those normally observed. It was thought at first that mitochondria disappeared altogether under these conditions. More recently it has become recognized that, although extremely reduced in structure, mitochondrial equivalents are present; these are referred to as *promitochondria* [100]. Cells containing inactive and structurally deficient organelles may have the same DNA content (10–20% of total cell DNA) as those cells possessing structurally well developed and active mitochondria. Promitochondria serve as the developmental precursors of fully functional mitochondria and there is no reason to believe that mature mitochondria arise *de novo* in aerobically respiring cells. (Note that clear distinction should be borne in mind between yeast which are deficient in mitochondrial profiles because of damage to the organelle DNA (petites) and those resulting from reversible changes in metabolic status.)

Organelle development induced by aeration

In yeast, the changes which occur on a shift from anaerobic conditions are rapid. Within a few hours the promitochondrial precursors develop into forms that are indistinguishable cytologically from normal mitochondria. Even after one hour of oxygenation, some internal membrane organization can be seen in the dense granular matrix of the glutaraldehyde prefixed cells. The proliferation of internal membranes continues and the granular matrix disperses, so that by three hours the formation of cristae appears similar to that of aerobically grown cells [111].

The structural changes occur in parallel with the appearance of a functional organelle protein-synthesizing system and electron transport capability. Some low level of protein-synthetic activity may be present in promitochondria, particularly if a lipid supplement is provided. In the experiments on the oxygen adaptation of glucose-grown anaerobic yeast, the level of mitochondrial protein synthesis (chloramphenicol sensitive) increased dramatically after three hours of treatment, reaching one-quarter that of aerobically grown cells. Whereas promitochondria retain only vestiges of the functional, coupled-electron transport system (having only cytochrome b_1 and oligomycin-sensitive ATPase

(see later)), after two hours' aeration the presence of cytochromes c and b could be detected spectroscopically, to be followed shortly afterwards (3h) by cytochromes a and a_3.

The fatty-acid composition of the mitochondria also alters radically during the early stages of adaptation, the most notable effects being an increase in long-chain unsaturated fatty acids and a concomitant decrease in the percentage of short-chain fatty acids. The absolute necessity for unsaturated fatty acids in mitochondrial development has been shown by withholding these from a mutant which required a supplement of unsaturated fatty acids for growth. Respiratory adaptation will not take place unless a further addition is made to the medium [66].

Although some disagreement may exist concerning the extent of dedifferentiation and differentiation on anaerobic/aerobic switching, it is clear that the expression and proliferation of mitochondria is built up on a scaffold of existing precursors. It has been shown by selective radioactive tagging of the promitochondria (^{14}C-labelled leucine + cycloheximide) that it indeed these precursors which give rise to functional organelles [88].

Development of insect sarcosomes

In animal cells there are no examples which exactly parallel the development of mitochondria from promitochondria seen in yeast. However, rapid increases in size and respiratory capacity occur at various selected times of development. In flying insects, for example, the enormous energy requirements of active flight muscles are provided by grossly enlarged mitochondria called sarcosomes, which have extensively developed inner-membrane structures.

In locusts, the major development of the flight muscle sarcosomes occurs during a period of about eight days on either side of the imaginal moult, the final moult which results in the mature adult. In this time period it has been estimated that the mitochondrial membranes increase by a factor of 40-fold (see [74]). This proliferation of membrane is associated with parallel increases in enzyme activities associated with cristae and matrix. However, at all stages, even in the very early muscle precursors (eight days before moulting), the structures exhibit the characteristics of respiratory-competent mitochondria. Thus developmental change is not from inactive to active but rather a rapid expansion based on functionally competent precursors. During this time period the mitochondria expand from about 1.5 μm long and 0.3 μm wide to mature sarcosomes about 6.0 μm long and 1 μm wide. It is interesting to note that in this case increasing demand for energy-yielding oxidative processes are met by increases in size, rather than in number of organelles.

Similar observations have been made for other insects [16]. In *Lucilia cuprina*, the Australian sheep blowfly, the volume of the mitochondria increases by about 10-fold during the period immediately before and after the

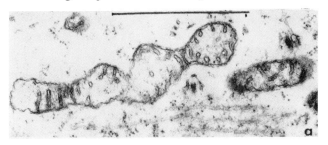

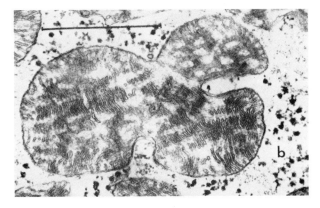

Fig. 6.3.9. Electron micrographs showing the structural development of blowfly sarcosomes. (a) In developing flight muscle three days before emergence. (b) At emergence. (c) Five days post-emergence. (Longitudinal sections; the bar on each print represents 1 μ.) Reproduced from [16] with permission.

pupal hatch (eclosion) (Fig. 6.3.9). Clearly, this period represents a time of intensive biosynthetic activity and it has been shown that a rapid increase in the contribution of both mitochondrial and cytoplasmic protein synthesis to the expanding organelle occurs at this stage. It is now recognized that the structural and biochemical changes represent the synthesis of new material rather than a redeployment and modification of existing proteins, lipids, etc.

Mitochondria and the developing embryo

Mitochondria serve a vital role during early development by providing energy through respiratory activity. It is apparent that this requirement of the developing embryo is met by the activation and later proliferation of a large organelle population which has been accumulated by the oocyte. A massive stockpiling of mitochondrial material occurs during oogenesis in many organisms and in some cases, e.g. in *Xenopus laevis*, the mature oocyte may contain more mitochondrial DNA than nuclear DNA [30]. The densely packed organelles form a structure below the nucleus which is readily visible under the light microscope (see [8]). A similar build-up of mitochondria occurs during oocyte formation in mammals. Estimates suggest that each mouse oocyte contains about 3 pg (*c.* 10^5 molecules) of mitochondrial DNA and 6–8 pg of nuclear DNA [87].

The accumulation of mitochondrial DNA in oocytes occurs in the absence of nuclear DNA replication, indicating that the two processes are controlled independently during oogenesis. After fertilization, nuclear DNA division begins and continues for some time before the initiation of organelle replication. In *Xenopus*, mitochondrial DNA replication does not get underway until fairly late in development, at the swimming tadpole stage, 50–65 h after fertilization [30]. In mammals also, mitochondrial DNA replication is absent during early stages (up to the blastocyst) [65]; however, the existing mitochondria become metabolically much more active, as evidenced by the expansion of their inner membranes. The mitochondria of oocytes and early embryonic stages (2–4-cell stages) have a dense matrix and poorly developed, randomly orientated cristae, but by middle–late blastocyst stage the cristae are much better developed and organized [86]. Concomitant with the activation and proliferation of inner membranes is a rapid increase in the mitochondrial ribosome population, as would be expected from their role in production of inner-membrane proteins. Detailed investigations have shown that in late embryonic (and post-embryonic) rat liver cells, the specific activities of several key mitochondrial components (e.g. cytochrome oxidase, succinate dehydrogenase and succinate cytochrome c reductase) all increase together relative to the amount of cardiolipin [58]. As this latter compound is a lipid exclusive to the mitochondrial inner membrane, it would seem that activation or insertion of electron-transport components into pre-existing membranes can occur.

Inhibitors of mitochondrial function, such as ethidium bromide (which blocks mitochondrial transcription) and chloramphenicol (which blocks protein synthesis), have little effect on overall development up to the blastocyst stage [86]. It is unlikely, therefore, that mitochondria export components or information essential for early embryogenesis.

There is evidence to suggest that the block on mitochondrial replication which follows the extensive build-up during oogenesis and which persists through the early stages of embryonic development is controlled negatively by the nucleus. The effect of the nucleus on mitochondrial activity can be relatively easily examined in sea urchin eggs. Replication has been monitored by following the uptake of radioactive thymidine into mitochondrial DNA, either in normal eggs or in the enucleated portions of eggs which can be obtained by centrifuging the eggs under appropriate conditions. In the absence of the nucleus, parthenogenetic stimulation (mock fertilization) results in a burst of replicative activity which is not observed in whole (nucleated) eggs treated similarly [92]. This suggests that the presence of the nucleus in the latter acts as a check in some way on mitochondrial DNA replication.

In summary then, mitochondria serve a vital role during embryogenesis in providing energy through respiratory activity. The developing embryo meets this demand by activation and, later, proliferation of existing organelles originally contributed by the oocyte. In some animals very large quantities of mitochondrial DNA and protein are present in the zygote and can thus act as a reserve which is progressively diluted out until active replication and mitochondrial protein synthesis get underway.

Transcription of mitochondrial DNA occurs very early in embryogenesis in some species, one of the probable products being ribosomal RNA, as rapid increases in mitochondrial ribosomes also occurs. In those species where mitochondrial activity (respiration and RNA synthesis) shows early stimulation, the mitochondria show alterations in morphology, the most characteristic changes being the appearance and proliferation of cristae. Exactly this type of behaviour would be expected to provide the energy necessary for rapid cell division and differentiation. Analogous changes can be seen in other tissues when switching from a relatively inactive state to one dependent on increased respiratory activity.

Coordination between mitochondrial and cytoplasmic protein synthesis

Before concluding this section on mitochondrial biogenesis, there is one aspect which must be discussed because of its relevance to the interaction between organelle and cytoplasmic protein-synthesizing systems. Several mitochondrial enzyme complexes (see Fig. 6.3.1) contain components made by both systems, as we have also seen to be the case for chloroplast ribulose bisphosphate carboxylase (section 6.3.2). Cytochrome oxidase and ATPase are made from several subunits, some of which are made on cytoplasmic ribosomes and some on organelle ribosomes. In this type of situation, one might anticipate a close harmony in the two synthetic systems, which would ensure a balanced production of subunits. It is not surprising to find that particular attention has been centred on the biogenesis of these complexes.

One of the most informative studies of this type has been done on the ATPase of yeast (see [44, 109]). The normal ATPase activity of the mitochondria is sensitive to the inhibitor oligomycin (or rutamycin). This property is retained by the complex, even after being solubilized by detergent treatment. Enzyme purified in this way has been shown to consist of 9–10 different polypeptides. On further fractionation, the main ATPase can be separated into three major components. These are:

(1) *F₁ ATPase (hydrolytic activity).* Not sensitive to oligomycin. Five polypeptides, all synthesized in cytoplasm.

(2) *Oligomycin-sensitivity-conferring protein (OSCP).* Acts as a bridge between F_1 ATPase and membranes. Synthesized in cytoplasm.

(3) *ATPase-associated proteins of inner membrane.* These can be thought of as the part of the membrane to which the ATPase activity is attached. Four polypeptides, which are made on mitochondrial ribosomes.

The whole complex can be reconstituted from the ATPase, the OSCP and the membrane fraction. It appears that the OSCP itself does not act as the oligomycin target site, but serves to couple the ATPase to the membrane, which does contain an oligomycin-binding site.

During mitochondrial development in yeast which has been switched from anaerobic to aerobic conditions, the activity in oligomycin-sensitive ATPase doubles in 2 h. If chloramphenicol is added, no increase is observed. However, what is of particular relevance is that ATPase activity corresponding to the expected increase is found free in the cell sap. This part of the complex is apparently made there, as inhibitors of cytoplasmic protein synthesis (cycloheximide) prevent the accumulation. If the block on mitochondrial protein synthesis is now removed, the ATPase activity is incorporated into the mitochondria. Therefore, in the short term at least, there is apparently a disruption of the expected stoichiometric production of ATPase-complex components, showing non-obligatory coupling of the two pathways.

Cytochrome oxidase in yeast is made from seven polypeptides, the three largest being made in the mitochondria and the four small subunits by cytoplasmic ribosomes. Many mutants lacking functional cytochrome oxidase have been obtained, some of which result from alterations to nuclear genes and some from alterations to mitochondrial genes. In petites lacking functional mitochondrial DNA, three large subunits normally synthesized in the organelle are missing and although the four subunits continue to be manufactured in the cytoplasm, they are unable to integrate correctly and remain only loosely associated with the inner membrane [99]. This again illustrates the requirement for organelle gene products to enable the correct assembly and functioning of nuclear-coded components.

Rather surprising results have been obtained from the analysis of some nuclear-coded mutants with defects in cytochrome oxidase activity. They have been found to lack at least one of the mitochondrially made subunits, yet still retain a complete set of those made in the cytoplasm [99]. These, however, fail to assemble correctly with the remaining membrane components.

Observations such as these further emphasize the important role of mitochondrial gene products in the assembly of components made in the cytoplasm and further indicate a complex pattern of interactions in which defects in nuclear genes have profound effects on the expression of proteins made within the organelle.

6.3.5 REPLICATION OF ORGANELLES

In the early stages of embryogenesis, in the formation of insect flight muscle sarcosomes, and in the development of respiratory activity of adapting yeast, a requirement for increased mitochondrial function is met by further elaboration of existing structures. However, in actively dividing cells which already contain mature mitochondria there is an obvious need to increase the number of organelles to keep pace with cell division.

Synthesis of DNA in organelles has been studied in detail and most reports indicate that the replication mechanism is similar to that of bacteria and higher organisms to the extent that it proceeds semi-conservatively (see [44, 95]).

A fascinating series of electron micrographs showing the intermediate steps in the replication of DNA in the mitochondria of tissue culture cells has been published. The process seems to be partly discontinuous, in that the synthesis proceeds from one point on the circular genome, a daughter strand being first formed on one parental strand but not on the other. There is no apparent synthesis on the second parental strand until the replicating fork on the first strand has progressed some way round the circle [93]. After initiation, the second daughter strand is synthesized in the opposite direction (Fig. 6.3.10).

It is more difficult to demonstrate division of the whole organelles, even using electron microscopy. The main problem is the interpretation of what the apparently discrete organelles seen in sections actually represent. Are they really independent of one another and not interconnected in some way?

This is a difficult point to establish without resorting to the tedious process of building up a composite picture from serial sections. When this has been done, the results show that in many cases the organelles (mitochondria in particular) may assume a quite complicated branching structure inside the cell [47]. Nevertheless, fission of the organelle is presumed to provide the mechanism for the approximate portioning of mito-

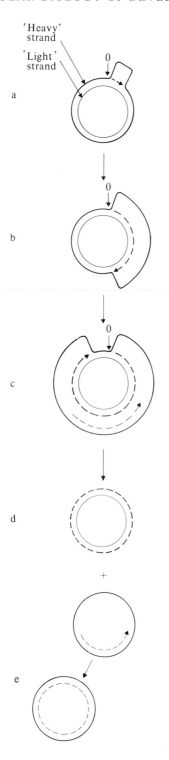

'Heavy' strand

'Light' strand

chondria and chloroplasts at cell division. Although this is sometimes difficult to demonstrate unequivocally in some higher plants and animals, there is abundant evidence for this type of process in other systems.

Micromonas is a simple flagellate which possesses a single mitochondrion and a single chloroplast, each of which divides by fission at cell division [71]. Chloroplast division by fission has also been recorded by time-lapse photography in the giant internodal cells of the alga *Nitella* [46]. Nevertheless, it should be borne in mind that the organelles, which appear as discrete bodies in the light microscope, may have interconnections not visible at this level of resolution. Even so, if one accepts that *de novo* synthesis does not occur, it is obvious that organelle division and separation must take place at some stage in rapidly dividing cells to maintain un-depleted populations of chloroplasts and mitochondria.

There is strong biochemical evidence that mitochondria found in the bread mould *Neurospora* are descendants of pre-existing structures. *Neurospora* is a convenient organism for genetic studies and many auxotrophic strains have been isolated. One of these requires choline for growth. Choline is incorporated, eventually as lecithin, into the mitochondrial membranes. When *Neurospora* was grown in radioactive choline until half way through the logarithmic phase of growth and then grown for a further three generations on non-labelled supplement, it was found in radioautograms that nearly all of the mitochondria were labelled [68]. This would be expected if the new mitochondria were formed by division of pre-existing structures, as the radioactive membrane component would be shared out between them. Whereas if new mitochondria were made more or less from scratch, only those assembled during the early stages would contain the label. The newly synthesized mitochondria would contain only the unlabelled choline.

Organelle turnover

The observation that many cells (e.g. those of the liver) exist for up to 4–5 months raises the question of

Fig. 6.3.10. Diagram of the model for mitochondrial DNA replication in mouse cells, proposed by Robberson *et al.* Note the asynchronous replication of the heavy and light strand. Separation of the parental strands (d) yields one completely replicated molecule and one (comprising the parental heavy strand with an incomplete progeny light strand) which finishes replication later. From [93] with permission.

organelle stability. Once made, do they remain active indefinitely, or are the component parts turned over? As the vast bulk of cellular protein is apparently 'turned over' in four weeks and the mitochondria represent up to 25% of this total, it is apparent that they are also recycled. Originally, it was thought that the mitochondria were broken down and resynthesized as a whole. However, although exact turnover rates are difficult to establish, application of a double-labelling procedure have indicated that the outer membrane in rat liver is more rapidly recycled than the inner membrane [38]. This suggests that some asynchrony may exist in the production (and/or integration) of organelle components, as has been noted previously for mitochondrial and cytoplasmic synthesis of ATPase or cytochrome oxidase subunits. This may well indicate a requirement for sequential assembly of some parts of the organelle. The overall process could, therefore, be thought of as an erection and expansion of a basic mitochondrial scaffold, followed by integration of other components from the cytoplasm to provide the structurally organized assembly of respiratory 'enzymes' necessary for efficient electron transport coupled to the production of ATP.

6.3.6 PROBLEMS RAISED BY THE PRESENCE OF MULTIPLE COPIES OF ORGANELLE DNA

As we have seen, mitochondria and chloroplasts contain DNA coding for rRNA, tRNAs and some proteins associated with the organelle membranes. Apart from direct hybridization studies, one of the most convincing ways of showing that a particular function is coded for by the organelle DNA is likely to result from genetic analysis. For this reason, a wide variety of mutagenic treatments have been employed in an attempt to generate identifiable alterations in the organelle which can be linked genetically to the organelle genome. Yeast and *Chlamydomonas* have, in particular, been subjected to intensive investigations of this kind and some of the resulting types of organelle mutant have been discussed in the text of this chapter.

Consideration of the unique sequence of organelle DNA and the total amount present per cell indicate that yeast and animal cells have between 20 and several hundred copies of mitochondrial DNA per cell. Multiplicity also exists in the case of chloroplast DNA. *Chlamydomonas,* although having only one structurally

discrete chloroplast, appears to possess multiple copies of chloroplast DNA. Thus, for any mutation in the organelle DNA to be effective, it must either occur in all copies or be able to exert its effect in the presence of excess copies of the normal wild type. Continued duplication of the mutant DNA copy and its subsequent partitioning among the progeny organelles may generate an organelle containing only mutant DNA copies. This in turn may provide further progeny which, after random segregation and cell division, could give rise to a line of cells entirely populated by mutant organelles. In plants this may generate mutant sectors in the leaves. This and other aspects of the production and occurrence of variegation (many variegations are in fact due to nuclear mutations) are discussed fully elsewhere [44, 62, 108].

6.3.7 CONCLUSIONS

(1) There are basic similarities in the structural organizations of mitochondria and chloroplasts. Both have extensive membrane proliferations folded, or packaged, into characteristic shapes. Many of the complex enzymes and electron-transport components concerned with energy production, either by photosynthesis or by respiration, are intimately associated with these membranes. Other enzymes and metabolic intermediates are found in the fluid-filled spaces (matrix or stroma) and can be liberated by gentle disruption of the organelle. The internal structures of both organelles are separated from the rest of the cell by a bounding membrane.

(2) The high degree of structural organization necessary for efficient energy generation may pose particular problems in developing systems.

(3) The final structure of organelles results from a cooperation between two genetic systems, that of the organelle itself and that of the nucleus.

(4) Mitochondria and chloroplasts contain their own independent protein-synthesizing systems, which can be distinguished from those in the cytoplasm of animal or plant cells by their different sensitivities to a range of antibiotic inhibitors. The isolated organelles can also incorporate amino acids into protein.

(5) Biochemical and genetic data have been used independently, or in cooperation, to identify the range of components manufactured in organelles—rRNA, tRNA and a restricted spectrum of membrane-

associated proteins are thought to be coded for by organelle DNA.

(6) Most of the components identified cannot operate independently but have to cooperate with cytoplasmically made (nuclear-coded) components before becoming fully functional. Many electron-transport complexes are compounded from subunits derived from both organelle and nuclear genetic systems.

(7) One of the most dramatic changes which occurs during chloroplast development from the precursor proplastid is the proliferation of the chlorophyll-bearing internal membrane system. Although achieving a rather complex final architecture, there is some evidence that this results in some part from the self-assembly properties of the membrane components.

(8) Other types of plastid may develop from the precursor proplastid. The actual developmental pathway taken depends on the interaction of environmental and nuclear factors. In contrast to the observations on differentiation at the cellular level, most if not all of the various plastid types are interconvertible.

(9) The development of mitochondria from less developed precursors has been described in two systems: (a) the appearance of active mitochondria in yeast adapting from a fermentation-based energy production to one based on aerobic respiration; (b) the formation, in insect flight muscle, of elongate sarcosomes which are the equivalents, both structurally and functionally, of giant mitochondria.

(10) Studies on the mitochondria in developing embryos indicate that the oocytes contain a stockpile of these organelles, which achieve functional status after fertilization and are subsequently distributed between the rapidly dividing cells of the early embryo. Replication of mitochondrial DNA is not observed until the original population is considerably diluted out.

(11) Taken together, the information from a wide variety of studies indicates that new organelles are not formed *de novo*, but result from the elaboration of existing precursors or by division of mature organelles. The synthesis of the various mitochondrial and chloroplast components in development appears to be coordinated under normal conditions although, in some cases, products of cytoplasmic protein synthesis destined for organelle inclusion may accumulate (until sufficient sites for integration are produced).

(12) The genetics of organelles is complicated, not only by the presence of many individual organelles in each cell, but also in many cases by the existence of multiple genome copies in each plastid or mitochondrion.

6.3.8 REFERENCES

1 Akoyunoglou G. & Argyroudi Akoyunoglou J. (1974) Reconstitution of grana thylakoids in spinach chloroplasts. *F.E.B.S. Letters*, **42** (2), 135–140.

2 Alberti R.S., Thornber J.P. & Naylor A.W. (1972) Time of appearance of photosystems I and II in chloroplasts of greening jack bean leaves. *J. exp. Bot.*, **23**, 1060–1069.

3 Aloni Y. & Attardi G. (1971) Expression of the mitochondrial genome in HeLa cells. IV. Titration of mitochondrial genes for 16S, 12S and 4S RNA. *J. molec. Biol.*, **55**, 271–276.

4 Angerer L., Davidson N., Murphy W., Lynch D. & Attardi G. (1976) An electron microscope study of the relative positions of the 4S and ribosomal RNA genes in HeLa cell mitochondrial DNA. *Cell*, **9**, 81–90.

5 Armond P.A., Staehlin L.A. & Arntzen C.J. (1977) Spatial relationships of photosystem I, photosystem II, and the light harvesting complex in chloroplast membranes. *J. Cell Biol.*, **73**, 400–418.

6 Arntzen C.J., Dilley R.A. & Crane F.L. (1969) A comparison of chloroplast membrane surfaces visualized by freeze etch and negative staining techniques. *J. Cell Biol.*, **243**, 16–31.

7 Ashwell M. & Work T.S. (1970) The biogenesis of mitochondria. *A. Rev. Biochem.*, **39**, 251–290.

8 Balinsky B.I. (1970) *An Introduction to Embryology*, 3rd edn. W.B. Saunders, Philadelphia.

9 Barrell B.G., Bankier A.T. & Drouin J. (1979) A different genetic code in human mitochondria. *Nature, Lond.*, **282**, 189–194.

10 Bastia D., Chiang K.-S., Swift H. & Siersma P. (1971) Heterogeneity, complexity and repetition of the chloroplast DNA of *Chlamydomonas reinhardtii. Proc. natl Acad. Sci., USA*, **68**, 1159–1161.

11 Beale S.I. & Castelfranco P.A. (1974) The biosynthesis of δ-aminolevulinic acid in higher plants. I. Accumulation of δ-aminolevulinic acid in greening plant tissues. *Pl. Physiol.*, **53**, 291–296.

12 Beale S.I. & Castelfranco P.A. (1974) The biosynthesis of δ-aminolevulinic acid in higher plants. II. Formation of ^{14}C-aminolevulinic acid from labelled precursors in greening plant tissues. *Pl. Physiol.*, **53**, 297–303.

13 Bedbrook J.R., Coen D.M., Beaton A.R., Bogorad L. & Rich A. (1979) Location of the single gene for the large subunit of ribulose bisphosphate carboxylase on the maize chloroplast chromosome. *J. biol. Chem.*, **254**, 905–910.

14 Bedbrook J.R. & Kolodner R. (1979) The structure of chloroplast DNA. *A. Rev. Pl. Physiol.*, **30**, 593–620.

15 Berg S., Dodge S., Krogmann D.W. & Dilley R.A. (1974) Chloroplast grana membrane carboxyl groups: their involvement in membrane association. *Pl. Physiol.*, **53**, 619–627.

16 Birt L.M. (1971) Structural and enzymic development of blowfly mitochondria and chloroplasts. In *Autonomy and Biogenesis of Mitochondria and Chloroplasts* (Eds N.K. Boardman, A.W. Linnane & R.M. Smillie), pp. 130–139. North Holland, Amsterdam.

17 Blobel G. & Dobberstein, B. (1975) Transfer of proteins across membranes. *J. Cell Biol.*, **67**, 835–851.

18 Boardman N.K. (1977) *Encyclopedia of Plant Physiology* (Eds A. Pirson & M.H. Zimmerman), Vol. 5. Photosynthesis I (Eds A. Trebst & M. Auron), pp. 583–600. Springer-Verlag, Berlin, Heidelberg, New York.

19 Boasson R., Bonner J.J. & Laetsch W.M. (1972) Induction and regulation of chloroplast replication in mature tobacco leaf tissue. *Pl. Physiol.*, **49**, 97–101.

20 Bogorad L. (1975) Evolution of organelles and eukaryotic genomes. *Science, N.Y.*, **188**, 891–898.

21 Borst P. (1977) Structure and function of mitochondrial DNA. In *International Cell Biology, 1976–1977* (Eds B.R. Brinkley & K.R. Porter), pp. 237–244. Rockefeller University Press, New York.

22 Borst P. & Grivell L.A. (1978) The mitochondrial genome of yeast. *Cell*, **15**, 705–723.

23 Bourque D.P., Boynton J.E. & Gillham N.W. (1971) Studies on the structure and cellular location of various ribosome and ribosomal RNA species in the green alga *Chlamydomonas reinhardtii*. *J. Cell Sci.*, **8**, 153–183.

24 Bucher, Th. (1965) In *Aspects of Insect Biochemistry* (Ed. T.W. Goodwin), p. 15. Academic Press, London.

25 Buetow D.E. & Wood M.M. (1978) The mitochondrial translation system. *Sub-cell. biochem.*, **5**, 1–85.

26 Burr F.A. (1969) Reduction in chloroplast number during gametophytic regeneration in *Megaceros flagellaris*. *Bryologist*, **72**, 200–209.

27 Butterfass T. (1973) Control of plastid division by means of nuclear DNA amount. *Protoplasma*, **76**, 167 195.

28 Camefort H. (1968) Cytologie de la fécondation et de la proembryogénèses chez quelques Gymnospermes. *Bull. Soc. bot., Fr.*, **115**, 137–160.

29 Camefort H. (1969) Fécondation et proembryogénèses chez les Abiétacées (notion de néocytoplasme). *Rev. Cytol. Biol. vég.*, **32**, 253–271.

30 Chase J.W. & David I. (1972) Biogenesis of mitochondria during *Xenopus laevis* development. *Devl. Biol.*, **27**, 504–518.

31 Chen J.L. & Wildman S.G. (1970) 'Free' and membrane-bound ribosomes, and nature of products formed by isolated tobacco chloroplasts incubated for protein synthesis. *Biochim. biophys. Acta.*, **209**, 207–219.

32 Chesnoy L. (1969) Sur la participation du gamète mâle à la constitution du cytoplasme de l'embryon chez le *Biota orientalis*. *Rev. Cytol. Biol. vég.*, **32**, 273–294.

33 Chua N.H., Blobel G. Siekevitz P. & Palade G.E. (1973) Attachment of chloroplast polysomes to thylakoid membranes in *Chlamydomonas reinhardtii*. *Proc. natl Acad. Sci., USA*, **70**, 1554–1558.

34 Coen D.M., Bedbrook J.R., Bogorad L. & Rich A. (1977) Maize chloroplast DNA fragment encoding the large subunit of ribulose bisphosphate carboxylase. *Proc. natl Acad. Sci., USA*, **74**, 5487–5491.

35 Craig I., Tolley E. & Bobrow M. (1976) Mitochondrial and cytoplasmic forms of fumarate hydratase assigned to chromosome I. Third International Workshop on Human Gene Mapping. *Birth Defects* original article series XII, 7, pp. 118–121. The National Foundation, New York.

36 Craig I.W. & Carr N.G. (1968) Ribosomes from the blue-green alga *Anabaena variabilis*. *Arch. Microbiol.*, **62**, 167–177.

37 Dawid I. & Blackler A.W. (1972) Maternal and cytoplasmic inheritance of mitochondrial DNA in *Xenopus*. *Devl. Biol.*, **29**, 152–161.

38 De Bernard B., Getz G.S. & Rabinowitz M. (1969) The turnover of the protein of the inner and outer mitochondrial membrane of rat liver. *Biochim. biophys. Acta.* **193**, 58–63.

39 Diers L. (1970) Origin of plastids: cytological results and interpretations including some genetical aspects. *Symp. Soc. exp. Biol.*, **24**, 129–145.

40 Dixon H., Kellerman G.M. & Linnane A.W. (1972) The effects of Mikamycin, Carbomycin, Spiramycin, Erythromycin and Paromomycin on growth and respiration of HeLa cells. *Archs Biochem. Biophys.*, **152**, 869–875.

41 Douce R. (1974) Site of biosynthesis of galactolipids in spinach chloroplasts. *Science, N.Y.*, **183**, 852–853.

42 Dyer T.A. & Miller R.H. (1971) Leaf nucleic acids I. Characteristics and role in the differentiation of plastids. *J. exp. Bot.*, **22**, 125–136.

43 Edwards Y.H. & Hopkinson D.A. (1978) The genetic determination of fumarase isozymes in human tissues. *Ann. Human Genetics*, **42**, 303–313.

44 Gilham N.W. (1978) *Organelle Heredity*. Raven Press, New York.

45 Goldberg I. & Ohad I. (1970) Biogenesis of chloroplast membranes. V. A radioautographic study of membrane growth in a mutant of *Chlamydomonas reinhardtii* y-1. *J. Cell Biol.*, **44**, 572–591.

46 Green P.B. (1964) Cinematic observations on the growth and division of chloroplasts in *Nitella*. *Am. J. Bot.*, **51**, 334–342.

47 Gunning B.E.S. & Steer M. (1975) *Ultrastructure and the Biology of Plant Cells*. Edward Arnold, London.

48 Henningsen K.W. & Boynton J.E. (1970) Macromolecular physiology of plastids. VII. Pigment and membrane formation in plastids of barley greening under low light intensity. *J. Cell Biol.*, **44**, 290–304.

49 Herrmann R.G. (1970) Multiple amounts of DNA related to the size of chloroplasts. I. An autoradiographic study. *Planta*, **90**, 80–96.

50 Herrmann R.G. (1970) Anzahl und Anordnung der genetischen Einheiten (Chloroplastengenome) in Chloroplasten. *Ber. dt. bot. Ges.*, **83**, 359–361.

51 Herrmann R.G. & Kowallik K.V. (1970) Multiple amounts of DNA related to the size of chloroplasts. II. Comparison of electron-microscope and autoradiographic data. *Protoplasma*, **69**, 365–372.

52 Hickman S. & Neufeld E.F. (1972) A hypothesis for I-cell disease: defective hydrolases that do not enter lysosomes. *Biochem. biophys. Res. Commun.*, **49**, 992–999.

53 Honda S.I., Hongladarom-Honda T. & Kwanyeum P. (1971) Interpretations on chloroplast reproduction derived from correlations between cells and chloroplasts. *Planta*, **97**, 1–15.

54 Hoober J.K. & Stegeman W.J. (1973) Control of the synthesis of a major polypeptide of chloroplast membranes in *Chlamydomonas reinhardi*. *J. Cell Biol.*, **56**, 1–12.

55 Hutchinson C.A., Newbold J.E., Potter S.S. & Edgell M.H. (1974) Maternal inheritance of mammalian mitochondrial DNA. *Nature, Lond.*, **251**, 536–538.

56 INC–UCLA Symposia on Molecular and Cellular Biology, Vol. XV (1979) *Extrachromosomal DNA* (Eds D.J. Cummings, P. Borst, I.B. Dawid, S.M. Weissmann & C.F. Fox).

57 Izawa S. & Good N.E. (1966) Effects of salts and electron transport on the conformation of isolated chloroplasts. II. Electron microscopy. *Pl. Physiol.*, **41**, 544–552.

58 Jakovic S., Haddock J., Getz G.S., Rabinowitz M. & Swift H. (1971) Mitochondrial development in liver of foetal and newborn rats. *Biochem. J.*, **121**, 341–347.

59 Jensen W.A. (1974) Reproduction in flowering plants. In *Dynamic Aspects of Plant Ultrastructure* (Ed. A.W. Robards), pp. 481–503. McGraw-Hill, Maidenhead.

60 Kahn A. (1968) Developmental physiology of bean leaf plastids. II. Negative contrast electron microscopy of tubular membranes in prolamellar bodies. *Pl. Physiol.*, **43**, 1769–1780.

61 Kellems R.E. & Butow R.A. (1972) Cytoplasmic 80S ribosomes associated with yeast mitochondria. *J. biol. Chem.*, **249**, 3297–3303.

62 Kirk J.T.O. & Tilney-Bassett R.A.E. (1978) *The Plastids*, 2nd edn. Elsevier, Amsterdam.

63 Kowallik K.V. & Herrmann R.G. (1972) Variable amounts of DNA related to the size of chloroplasts. IV. Three-dimensional arrangement of DNA in fully differentiated chloroplasts of *Beta vulgaris* L. *J. Cell Sci.*, **11**, 357–377.

64 Kuntzel H. (1969) Proteins of mitochondrial and cytoplasmic ribosomes of *Neurospora crassa*. *Nature, Lond.*, **222**, 142–146.

65 Lambowitz A.M., Chua N.-H. & Luck D.J.L. (1976) Mitochondrial assembly in *Neurospora*, site of synthesis of *mit* ribosomal proteins and studies on the *poky* mutant. *J. molec. Biol.*, **107**, 223–253.

66 Levin B. (1972) In *Membrane Molecular Biology* (Eds C.F. Fox & A. Keith), pp. 386–438. Sinauer, Sunderland, Massachusetts.

67 Link G., Coen D.M. & Bogorad L. (1978) Differential expression of the gene for the large subunit of ribulose biphosphate carboxylase in maize leaf cell types. *Cell*, **15**, 725–731.

68 Luck D.J.L. (1973) Formation of mitochondria in *Neurospora crassa*. A quantitative radioautographic study. *J. Cell Biol.*, **16**, 483–499.

69 Macino G., Coruzzi G., Nobrega F.G., Li, M & Tzagoloff A. (1979) Use of the UGA terminator as a tryptophan codon in yeast mitochondria. *Proc. natl Acad. Sci., USA*, **76**, 3784–3785.

70 Manning J.E. & Richards O.C. (1972) Synthesis and turnover of *Euglena gracilis* nuclear and chloroplast deoxyribonucleic acid. *Biochemistry*, **11**, 2036–2043.

71 Manton I. (1959) Electron microscopical observations on a very small flagellate: the problem of *Chromulina pusilla* Buchter. *J. mar. biol. Ass. U.K.*, **38**, 319–333.

72 Margulies M.M. & Michaels A. (1974) Ribosomes bound to chloroplast membranes in *Chlamydomonas reinhardtii*. *J. Cell Biol.*, **60**, 65–77.

73 Munkres K.D., Benviste K., Gorski J. & Zuiches C.A. (1970) Genetically induced subcellular mislocation of *Neurospora crassa* mitochondrial malate dehydrogenase E.C.1.1.1.37. *Proc. natl Acad. Sci., USA*, **67**, 263–270.

74 Munn E.A. (1974) *The Structure of Mitochondria*. Academic Press, London.

75 Nass M.M.K. (1969) Mitochondrial DNA. I. Intramitochondrial distribution and structural relations of single and double-length circular DNA. *J. molec. Biol.*, **42**, 521–528.

76 Nielsen O.F. (1974) Photoconversion and regeneration of active protochlorophyll(ide) in mutants defective in the regulation of chlorophyll synthesis. *Archs Biochem. Biophys.*, **160**, 430–439.

77 Nomura M. (1970) Bacterial ribosome. *Bact. Rev.*, **34**, 228–277.

78 Ohad I. (1972) Biogenesis and modulation in chloroplast membranes. In *Role of Membranes in Secretory Processes* (Eds L. Bolis, R.D. Keynes & W. Wilbrandt), pp. 24–51. North Holland, Amsterdam.

79 Paigen K. (1971) In *Enzyme Synthesis and Degradation in Mammalian Systems* (Ed. C. Rechcigl), pp. 1–46. Karger, Basel.

80 Paolillo D.J. (1969) The plastids of *Polytrichum*. III. The sporogenous cells. *Cytologia*, **34**, 133–144.

81 Paolillo D.J. (1970) The three-dimensional arrangement of intergranal lamellae in chloroplasts. *J. Cell Sci.*, **6**, 243–255.

82 Paolillo D.J. (1974) Motile male gametes of plants. In *Dynamic Aspects of Plant Ultrastructure* (Ed. A.W. Robards), pp. 504–531. McGraw-Hill, Maidenhead.

83 Petermann M.L. (1964) *The Physical and Chemical properties of Ribosomes*. Elsevier, Amsterdam.

84 De Petrocellis B., Siekevitz P. & Palade G.E. (1970) Changes in chemical composition of thylakoid membranes during greening of the γ-1 mutant of *Chlamydomonas reinhardtii*. *J. Cell Biol.*, **44**, 618–634.

85 Piko L. (1970) Synthesis of macromolecules in early mouse embryo cultured *in vitro*. 1: RNA, DNA and a polysaccharide component. *Devl. Biol.*, **21**, 257–279.

86 Piko L. & Chase D.G. (1973) Role of the mitochondrial genome during early development in mice. *J. Cell Biol.*, **58**, 358–378.

87 Piko L. & Matsumoto, L. (1976) Number of mitochondria and some properties of mitochondrial DNA in the mouse egg. *Devl. Biol.*, **49**, 1–10.

88 Plattner H., Salpeter M., Saltzgaber J., Rouslin W. & Schatz G. (1971) Promitochondria of anaerobically grown yeast. In *Autonomy and Biogenesis of Mitochondria and Chloroplasts* (Eds N.K. Boardman, A.W. Linnane & R.M. Smillie), pp. 175–184. North Holland, Amsterdam..

89 Possingham J.V. & Saurer W. (1969) Changes in chloroplast number per cell during leaf development in spinach. *Planta*, **86**, 186–194.

90 Possingham J.V. & Smith J.W. (1972) Factors affecting chloroplast replication in spinach. *J. exp. Bot.*, **23**, 1050–1059.

91 Poynton R.O. & McKemmie E. (1976) The assembly of cytochrome *c* oxidase from *Saccharomyces cerevisiae*. In *Genetics and Biogenesis of Chloroplasts and Mitochondria* (Eds. T. Bucher, W. Neupert, W. Sebald & S. Werner), pp. 207–214. North Holland, Amsterdam.

92 Rinaldi A.M., De Leo G., Arzone A., Salcher I., Storace A. & Mutolo V. (1979) Biochemical and electron microscopic evidence that the cell nucleus negatively controls mitochondrial genome activity in early sea urchin development. *Proc. natl Acad. Sci., USA*, **76**, 1916–1920.

93 Robberson D.L., Kasamatsu H., & Vinograd J. (1972) Replication of mitochondrial DNA. Circular replicative intermediates in mouse I cells. *Proc. natl Acad. Sci., USA*, **69**, 737–741.

94 Rosinski J. & Rosen W.G. (1972) Chloroplast development: fine structure and chlorophyll synthesis. *Q. Rev. Biol.*, **47**, 160–191.

95 Sager R. (1972) *Cytoplasmic Genes and Organelles*. Academic Press, New York.

96 Sager R. (1975) Patterns of inheritance of organelle genomes: Molecular basis and evolutionary significance. In *Genetics and Biogenesis of Mitochondria and Chloroplasts* (Eds C.W. Birky, P.S. Perlman & T.J. Byers). Ohio State University Press, Columbus.

97 Sager R. & Lane D. (1972) Molecular basis for maternal inheritance *Proc. natl Acad. Sci., USA*, **69**, 2410–2413.

98 Sakano K., Kung S.D. & Wildman S.G. (1974) Identification of several chloroplast DNA genes which code for the large subunit of *Nicotiana* fraction I proteins. *Molec. Gen. Genet.*, **130**, 91–97.

99 Saltzgaber J., Cabral F., Birchmeier W., Kohler C., Frey T. & Schatz G. (1977) The assembly of mitochondria. In *International Cell Biology, 1976–1977* (Eds B.R. Brinkley & K.R. Porter), pp. 256–263. Rockefeller University Press, New York.

100 Schatz G. (1965) Subcellular particles carrying mitochondrial enzymes in anaerobically grown cells of *Saccharomyces cerevisiae. Biochim. biophys. Acta.* **96**, 342–345.

101 Schmidt G.W. & Chua N-H. (1978) *In vitro* transport of ribulose 1,5-bisphosphate carboxylase small subunits into chloroplasts and assembly into the whole enzyme. *J. Cell Biol.*, **79**, 321a.

102 Schotz F. (1970) Effects of the disharmony between genome and plastome on the differentiation of the thylakoid system in *Oenothera. Symp. Soc. exp. Biol.*, **24**, 39–54.

103 Siekevitz P. (1972) Biological membranes: the dynamics of their organization. *A. Rev. Physiol.*, **34**, 117–139.

104 Singh S. & Wildman S.G. (1973) Chloroplast DNA codes for the ribulose diphosphate carboxylase catalytic site on fraction I proteins of *Nicotiana* species. *Molec. Gen. Genet.*, **124**, 187–196.

105 Slonimski P.P. *et al.* (1978) Mosaic organization and expression of the mitochondrial DNA region controlling cytochrome *c* reductase and oxidase. III. A model of structure and function. In *Biochemistry and Genetics of Yeast* (Eds M. Bacilla, B.L. Horecker & A.O.M. Stoppani). Academic Press, New York.

106 Szollosi D. (1965) The fate of middle-piece mitochondria in the rat egg. *J. exp. Zool.*, **159**, 367–378.

107 Taylor M.M. & Storck R. (1964) Uniqueness of bacterial ribosomes. *Proc. natl Acad. Sci., USA*, **52**, 958–965.

108 Tilney-Bassett R.A.E. (1975) Genetics of variegated plants. In *Genetics and Biogenesis of Mitochondria and Chloroplasts* (Eds C.W. Birky, P.S. Perlman & T.J. Byers). Ohio State University Press, Columbus.

109 Tzagoloff A., Macino G. & Sebald W. (1979) Mitochondrial genes and translation products. *Am. Rev. Biochem.*, 419–441.

110 Walbot V. (1978) The dimorphic chloroplasts of the C_4 plant *Paricum maximum* contain identical genomes. *Cell*, **11**, 729–737.

111 Watson K., Haslam J.M., Veitch B. & Linnane A.W. (1971) Mitochondrial precursors in anaerobically grown yeast. In *Autonomy and Biogenesis of Mitochondria and Chloroplasts* (Eds N.K. Boardman, A.W. Linnane & R.M. Smillie), pp. 162–174. North Holland, Amsterdam.

112 Wehrmeyer W. (1964) Zur Klärung der strukturellen Variabilität der Chloroplastengrana des Spinats in Profil und Aufsicht. *Planta*, **62**, 272–293.

113 Wehrmeyer W. (1964) Über Membranbildungprozesse im Chloroplasten. *Planta*, **63**, 13–30.

114 Williams K.L., Smith E., Shaw D.C. & Birt L.M. (1972) Studies of the levels and synthesis of cytochrome *c* during adult development of the blowfly *Lucilia cuprina. J. biol. Chem.*, **247**, 6024–6030.

115 van Heyningen V., Craig I.W. & Bodmer W.F. (1973) Genetic control of mitochondrial enzymes in human mouse somatic cell hybrids. *Nature, Lond.*, **242**, 509–512.

116 von Wettstein D., Kahn A., Nielsen O.F. & Gough S. (1974) Genetic regulation of chlorophyll synthesis analysed with mutants in barley. *Science, N.Y.*, **184**, 800–802.

117 Whitton B.A., Carr N.G. & Craig I.W. (1971) A comparison of the fine structure and nucleic acid biochemistry of chloroplasts and blue-green algae. *Protoplasma*, **72**, 325–357.

Chapter 6.4
Gene Expression in Animal Development
H.R. Woodland and R.W. Old

6.4.1   INTRODUCTION

All cellular activities are conducted, directly or indirectly, through proteins, and are therefore under ultimate genetic control. Developmental biologists have found it useful to classify developmental phenomena into distinct groups, for example cytodifferentiation, morphogenesis and pattern formation [466]. All of these processes must be mediated by proteins and hence must be expressed by the action of gene products. For example, the formation of patterns is often explained in terms of gradients of small molecules or ions (see Parts 2, 3 and 4). These gradients must be established and maintained by structures such as ion pumps, and their interpretation presumably involves receptors, comparable to those which mediate hormone effects. All known ion pumps and receptors are proteins; as far as we know they are encoded by genes just like other proteins. At present, most of our rapidly growing knowledge of the molecular basis of gene expression concerns genes like those encoding ovalbumin and haemoglobin. These are major proteins characteristic of particular differentiated states, rather than proteins causing cells to differentiate in special ways. However, both types of gene are likely to be regulated through similar molecular mechanisms, and a knowledge of the way in which the former behave is likely to be very helpful in unravelling the behaviour of the latter.

The aim of this chapter is to summarize our present knowledge of the way in which gene expression leads differentiating cells to acquire different populations of protein molecules. We assume that the reader has a working knowledge of basic molecular biology and of gene manipulation techniques. Reference books which provide a suitable background are by Watson [445] and by Old and Primrose [323]. Most of what we write will concern those proteins which are the ultimate consequence of cell differentiation, but in the last section we describe how it is now possible to begin a study of the genes which actually control the commitment of cells to particular pathways of differentiation.

6.4.2   THE VARIABLE GENE ACTIVITY THEORY OF DEVELOPMENT

How do cells acquire their characteristic complements of proteins? It must be because different sets of genes are expressed in particular places at particular times. This could happen in one of two ways.

(a) Cells of different types might contain different sets of genes.

(b) All cells might contain the same genes, but regulate their expression so that different sets are active in cells with different differentiated phenotypes.

In most organisms possibility (a) can be excluded. The most telling evidence comes from nuclear transplantation (Chapter 1.2) and from the redifferentiation of specialized cells (Chapter 2.5). Clearly, the nucleus of a skin cell can only programme the development of a tadpole if it contains functional copies of every gene necessary to form the variety of cells present in this organism. Thus explanation (a) does not provide a general explanation of cytodifferentiation.

Similar conclusions have been reached from less incisive biochemical experiments. For example, McCarthy and Hoyer [272] conducted experiments in which the hybridization of embryonic mouse DNA to itself was competed with DNA from the nuclei of a variety of differentiated mouse cells, as well as with DNA from embryos. Loss of sequences in any tissues should reveal itself by failure to prevent all of the self-hybridization of the embryonic DNA. In fact all of the DNAs were equally effective in competition. Although this experiment indicates that the DNAs had identical composition, its sensitivity was limited by the fact that a total DNA preparation includes highly reiterated sequences as well as sequences in single copies. An experiment of this design actually shows that there is little change in the repeated sequences and no loss or amplification of *large numbers* of different single-copy sequences. In order to find out about single-copy sequences this approach has since been refined by using purified single-copy DNA in place of total DNA (see [99]). Changes in DNA sequence composition have never been detected, but the possibility that a few sequences (5–10%) are lost can never be excluded. In addition, experiments of this design cannot exclude the possibility that the same sequences are present but are rearranged.

A more precise, if more limited, approach to this problem is to analyse the number and structure of chosen genes in different tissues. Thus liver and blood cells contain the same number of globin genes [42], and each globin gene always has the same structure in a given individual [220]. Amongst many genes examined in this

way only immunoglobulin genes have been found to change (see section 6.4.4 and Chapter 3.7), and even here the rearrangements of the genes occur after the cell has committed itself to the complex pathways of lymphocyte differentiation. Thus analysis of the gene sequence has shown that genes encoding the major products of specialized cells do not change in a way that might have caused this specialization. They do not exclude the possibility that there are changes to a few, as yet unidentified, genes that actually control differentiation. If such changes occur they must be reversible or inconsequential, at least in those differentiated cells or nuclei which can be shown to be pluripotential.

A last, and much quoted, source of evidence for genomic constancy is the polytene chromosome of dipteran flies. The banding pattern of these highly endoduplicated chromosomes accurately reflects the relative position of genes. Precisely the same pattern is seen in all differentiated somatic tissues in which these chromosomes are found, whether or not the genes are expressed. The drawback of these observations is that they do not exclude the possibility that there are small changes to the DNA; polytene bands typically contain about 30 000 base pairs (30 kb) of DNA*.

The conclusion from data of this kind is that cell differentiation does not normally involve the loss or irreversible inactivation of crucial genes. Rather, all genes are present and variably expressed in different cells.

6.4.3 SITUATIONS WHERE THE DNA OF CELLS CHANGES DURING DEVELOPMENT

(1) *Total loss of DNA.* Some cells lose their DNA during terminal differentiation, e.g. mammalian erythrocytes, lens cells, plant xylem cells. Clearly, this does not lead to differential gene expression.

(2) *Polyploidy.* Many animal and plant tissues acquire multiple complete sets of chromosomes (e.g. the liver of man, the trophoblast of the mouse). Because all genes

---

*There is a recent report that in *Calliphora erythrocephala* the nurse cells of the oocyte show a banding different from that in somatic cells [355]. There is no evidence that they contain different DNA sequences. Nurse cells are of the germ-cell lineage and the different banding might reflect a fundamentally different pattern of gene expression in germ-line and somatic cells. In other organisms this could be reflected in chromosome elimination and diminution.

are affected equally, it is not relevant to differential gene expression. In addition, it may not be an obligatory part of the differentiated phenotype. Thus hepatocytes may be diploid or polyploid.

(3) *Polyteny* occurs in a number of organisms (many tissues of dipteran flies, the suspensor cells of *Vicia faba* embryos). Like polyploidy it has an equal effect on the vast majority of genes. However, in Diptera the centromeric parts of the chromosomes are not polytene and the nearby ribosomal genes are underrepresented compared to diploid tissues [185, 407]. Furthermore, effects like this can lead to an increase in certain genes. In *Rhynchosciara* [54] more endoreduplication occurs in some regions ('DNA puffs') than in others. Since this is a response to humoral cues and it affects regions of DNA (puffs) that are being transcribed, it therefore affects the transcriptional capacity of the genes concerned. The same kind of amplification of chorion genes occurs in *Drosophila* follicle cells [409].

(4) *Ribosomal gene amplification* occurs on an enormous scale in the oocytes of some animals which lay down vast stores of ribosomes (section 6.4.13).

(5) *Immunoglobulin gene sequences* are rearranged to create the functional light- or heavy-chain genes of immunoglobulins (section 6.4.12).

(6) *DNA loss in somatic cells.* In a number of organisms, dispersed throughout the animal kingdom, parts of or whole chromosomes are lost from somatic cells. This is a visible early manifestation of germ-cell/soma differentiation and provided historically important material for studying the effect of cyoplasmic localization on cell determination. One form of this phenomenon is chromosome diminution, seen in certain nematode worms and most closely studied in Ascaridae, where the germ-line cells contain paired multicentromeric chromosomes. During the early differentiation of somatic cells these break up to give normal monocentromeric chromosomes and two large terminal fragments, which lack centromeres and which are therefore lost. In *Ascaris lumbricoides* 20–30% of the germ-line DNA is lost [156, 309, 417] and as much as 85% is lost in *Parascaris equorum* [309, 371]. Although the conclusion is controversial, it seems that the lost DNA consists entirely of repetitive sequences [371], at least within the limits of detection of sequences which applied in these studies. A somewhat comparable phenomenon is seen in the crustacean *Cyclops* [23, 24].

In midges of the family Cecidomyiidae, whole chromosomes are lost on a vast scale in somatic cells; for example in *Mayetiola destructor* 32 out of 40 chromosomes are lost at the 5th syncytial nuclear division of the embryo [22]. However, at a very crude level of analysis there is no evidence that midge somatic cells lack sequences present in the germ-line [245].

It is a reasonable proposition that in these midges, and in other organisms showing chromosome diminution, the sequences lost are functional during gametogenesis. The eliminated chromosomes of midges seem to synthesize RNA in oocytes [246], but in *Cyclops* and *Ascaris* the germ-line DNA seems always to be heterochromatic [24], and it may therefore play an unknown structural role. The fact that these phenomena occur in such a sporadic way throughout the animal kingdom points to some underlying feature of germ-line/somatic cell differentiation which is only occasionally taken as far as complete loss of DNA. It is possible that in other organisms equivalent sequences are found in the constitutive heterochromatin.

6.4.4   THE ORGANIZATION OF THE GENOME AND THE STRUCTURE OF EUKARYOTIC GENES

The large amount of DNA in many eukaryotic genomes raises the question of whether it all has a function. How much of the DNA encodes proteins? What other sequences, such as regulatory sites, reside in the DNA? The issue is most often expressed in terms of the C-value paradox (the C-value is the quantity of DNA in the haploid genome). For example, the C-values of Amphibia can vary from less than 1 pg to almost 100 pg. Even closely related Amphibia may have greatly different C-values. Where this is not simply the result of polyploidization in recent evolution, the function of the excessive DNA appears puzzling, since it is hard to believe that one amphibian necessarily requires much more genetic information than another. Indeed it is hard to imagine why an amphibian should require over 25 times more than man (C-value = 3.4 pg).

For many years it has been known, through DNA reassociation experiments, that in most eukaryotes only a fraction of the DNA is unique in sequence. At the level of precision obtained in hybridization experiments with populations of mRNA, it has been found that most mRNA is homologous to a small part of this single-copy DNA [80, 155]. Most structural genes therefore occur as

Table 6.4.1. Repetition frequency components of some eukaryotic genomes.

Species	Haploid genome size (bp)	Proportion of genome in component	Repetition frequency	Complexity† of component (bp)
Drosophila	1.4×10^8	70	0.9	1.0×10^8
melanogaster		12	70	2.5×10^5
(fruit fly)		12	24 000	7.2×10^2
		5*		
Strongylocentrotus	8.6×10^8	50	0.9	4.6×10^8
purpuratus		27	10	2.3×10^7
(sea urchin)		19	160	1.0×10^6
		10	6000	1.3×10^3
Xenopus laevis	3.1×10^9	54	1.0	1.0×10^9
(frog)		10	110	2.8×10^6
		31	2000	4.5×10^5
		6	3×10^5	6.3×10^2
		5*		
Mus musculus	2.7×10^9	58	1.6	9.3×10^8
(mouse)		11	150	1.1×10^6
		14	7500	2.9×10^4
		8	3×10^5	4.0×10^2
		2*		
Homo sapiens	3.3×10^9	51	1.8	9.0×10^8
(man)		22	500	7.7×10^5
		13	50 000	4.5×10^3

Data taken from [6], where original references may be found. Asterisk denotes fraction of DNA reassociating very rapidly and may include very highly repetitive sequences and foldback (hairpin) sequences.

†Complexity is defined as total length of different sequences present, usually expressed as base pairs. See also legend to Table 6.4.4.

few or single copies, and repeated sequences are not structural genes. However, a small fraction of the DNA does consist of structural genes which are repetitive, and often these occur in clusters. Genes for histones and ribosomal RNA are repeated. In addition, the β-like globin genes of mammals are organized in a small cluster of genes and pseudogenes which, although dissimilar in many ways to the monotonous repetition of large ribosomal gene clusters, do formally constitute a cluster of related gene sequences.

Repeated sequences, which are therefore almost entirely non-coding, occur in the form of families, with members that are usually similar but not identical. Families may comprise anything from a few members up to hundreds of thousands of members. In many eukaryotes it is found that the genome can be more or less arbitrarily divided into three or more components on the basis of reassociation kinetics: (i) unique sequences, (ii) moderately repetitive sequences, and (iii) highly repetitive sequences (Table 6.4.1). In addition to these, there may be a component which reassociates almost instantaneously. This component includes 'foldback' DNA, i.e. inverted duplications which will form a duplex DNA hairpin by intramolecular base-pairing. With some organisms the division into discrete frequency classes is more arbitrary than with others. Experiments with cloned representatives of repeated sequences of sea urchin DNA show a broad distribution of frequences up to about 10 000 copies. The median repeat family has no more than 100 members.

Some families are characterized by members which are almost identical, other families have members with up to 30% sequence divergence [6, 234, 346, 385]. Very highly repetitive sequences are often composed of a short sequence element (6–50 bases long) arranged in tandem. Such blocks of sequence give rise to 'satellite' DNA, so called because the overall base composition differs from bulk DNA sufficiently to allow it to be separated as a satellite peak or shoulder in density-gradient centrifugation procedures.

What then is the relationship between the large amount of unique DNA in the genome and gene number? There are two types of possible answer. One is that genes occupy a small part of the genome; the remainder of the genome will then include unique as well as repetitive sequences which must serve functions at present largely unknown. An extreme form of this view is that nearly all of this DNA has no informational function at all, but accumulates during the course of evolution simply as a result of its ability to survive and multiply in the absence of strong selection for its removal—'selfish' DNA [111, 325]. The other possible type of answer proposes that genes have a much more complex organization in eukaryotes than that familiar in prokaryotes, so that each gene encompasses much more DNA than that necessary just to encode a polypeptide. Such sequences might take the form of lengthy sequences which are both upstream and downstream of the sequences which code for the protein and which are essential for correct gene transcription and regulation. In addition, it is known that eukaryotic genes often contain internal non-coding intervening sequences or introns which have the effect of spreading the coding regions over a stretch of DNA much longer than that required for coding regions alone. Evidence on these matters come from a wide variety of studies including the organization of repeated sequences, comparisons of corresponding sequences in related organisms so that evolutionary change in the genome can be followed at the molecular level, and studies on the structure and function of particular cloned genes. It appears that in fact both types of answer are correct in accounting for the size of the genome.

Repeated and unique sequence interspersion

Whilst satellite DNA occurs as blocks of tandemly repeated, highly repetitive sequences, most moderately repetitive sequences are interspersed among unique sequences throughout the genome. Detailed reassociation [101] and electron microscopic [83] analyses of DNA from the amphibian *Xenopus* and the sea urchin *Strongylocentrotus purpuratus* [161] have shown that most of the unique sequence DNA occurs in segments averaging about 1 kb in length. Interspersed among these segments are sequence elements of a few hundred bp in length which fall into the mid-repetitive class. This has come to be known as the *Xenopus* 'pattern' or 'short-period pattern' of interspersion and is found in a wide variety of eukaryotes [154].

The fruit fly *Drosophila* and some other, but not all, insects have a different pattern in which stretches of unique DNA are much longer than in *Xenopus*, and the repetitive elements average a few kb in length [92, 288]. Chickens and other birds appear to have an intermediate pattern [114]. The human genome has the short-period pattern of interspersion. Among many other families of repeated sequences in the human genome, one is especially prominent. It is called the 'Alu' family. Houck *et al.* [199] gave it this name on the basis of the following experiments. Human DNA was fragmented to about 2 kb, denatured, allowed to reassociate just long enough for the repeated sequence to anneal, and then treated with the single-strand specific nuclease S1, which digests away all the sequences which have not annealed. When run on agarose gels and stained with ethidium bromide, the remaining duplex DNA gave a band characteristic of fragments about 300 bp long. When treated with restriction endonuclease Alu I, prior to gel electrophoresis, at least one-half of these repeated sequences gave rise to two fragments of about 170 and 120 bp each. Therefore, at least one half of these 300 bp repeated elements belong to a single-sequence family: the Alu family.

The Alu family is estimated to be present in about 300 000 copies, and it is fairly divergent as indicated by the thermal stability of reassociated repeats and by sequencing several of its members [372]. It is interspersed throughout the genome [221]. On average, a representative of the Alu family should occur once every 4000 base pairs throughout the human genome. One large region of the human genome that has been examined in detail for the presence of repeated elements is a 64 kb region containing the β-like globin genes. At least eight Alu repeats were present, together with at least nine other repeats not of the Alu family [137].

A repeat which closely resembles the Alu repeat of man has been found in both mouse and Chinese hamster DNA [221, 243]. It is generally assumed that conservation of a sequence over a long evolutionary period, such as has elapsed since the divergence of rodents and primates, probably indicates that the primary sequence is functionally important. But the functions of these and other middle-repetitive sequence elements remain unclear. However, the resemblance between the Alu repeat and transposable elements may indicate another cause for the apparent conservation, i.e. transmission as a retrovirus-like agent (see below). Whatever their function, there is no doubt that some middle-repetitive sequences are transcribed and can give rise to nuclear and cytoplasmic transcripts. Repetitive sequences may also be transcribed in association with adjacent unique sequences. Several reports have shown that some nuclear RNA is composed of unique DNA transcripts covalently linked to sequences transcribed from repetitive DNA, but the significance of these nuclear transcripts is unknown [88, 127]. Also, in the mature eggs of *Xenopus* and the sea urchin a large part of the poly(A)$^+$ RNA contains interspersed repetitive and unique sequence transcripts covalently linked together. Again, the function of these transcripts is unknown; possibly they are unprocessed pre-mRNA molecules [5, 415]. In the case of a *Xenopus* vitellogenin gene, transcription of linked unique and repetitive sequences must result from the occurrence of repetitive sequences in several introns [375].

Transposable elements

Recent studies on the evolution of genomic DNA have presented a view of the genome as much more variable and dynamic than had previously been suspected [219, 485]. This is partly due to the identification, in *Drosophila melanogaster,* of sequence elements which fall into the middle-repetitive class; these are of defined length [347], have direct terminal repeats [130] and exhibit great variation in frequency and location among different strains [215, 413]. Similar dispersed repetitive elements capable of moving about the genome have been described in yeast [79], and presumably occur in most eukaryotes. Such sequences have been called transposable elements because of their variation in chromosomal location. They can act as insertional mutagens, but it appears that their frequency of transposition is often low on the time-scale of a single gener-

ation, but very high from an evolutionary point of view [150]. A similar type of transposable element has been described, having inverted terminal repeats and showing length variation [348]. It appears that transposable elements make up a considerable fraction of the middle-repetitive sequence in *Drosophila* [485].

Transposable elements have structural similarities with both bacterial transposons [78] and vertebrate endogenous retroviruses [451]. They are often transcribed and can give rise to abundant poly(A)$^+$ RNA [130]. The human Alu repeat resembles a transposable element in that it is often flanked by direct repeats, can be transcribed, and is associated with genome rearrangement, even among different tissues of a single individual [77]. Similarly, short direct repeats have also been found flanking non-functional pseudogenes of three small nuclear RNAs (snRNAs) in the human genome [424]. This is the basis of a model of transposition in which reverse transcription of the RNA leads to duplex DNA copies which insert at novel positions in the genome [218]. Consistent with this model, and others, is the finding of circular duplex DNA copies of the Alu sequence in monkey [244], and human cells [77].

Transposable elements might be involved in gene regulation. The formation of a mature immunoglobulin chain gene from separated sequences involves DNA rearrangement which seems to entail excision of interposed DNA sequence. Other processes that generate diversity, such as antigenic variation of protozoan parasites, may also involve rearrangements. Yeast mating-type conversion is another example of directed rearrangement of DNA sequences to perform a specific function [78]. Whether the resemblance between these rearrangements and movement of transposable elements is merely a formal one, or whether there is a general developmental role for transposable elements remains to be seen. However, the conclusions of section 6.4.2 should be borne in mind. No metazoan gene other than the immunoglobulin genes has been found to undergo rearragement prior to activation, and there are various situations where a cell or nucleus can redifferentiate.

Structure of eukaryotic genes

RNA polymerases

Transcription in the nucleus occurs both in the nucleolus and in the extranucleolar region or nucleoplasm. The genes encoding rRNA are associated with the nucleolus, which is the site of synthesis and processing of rRNA precursor molecules. The enzyme responsible for the transcription of these RNAs is known as RNA polymerase I, and is largely confined to the nucleolus itself. Nucleolar transcription typically accounts for about half of the total transcription in the cell.

RNA polymerase II and III are located in the nucleoplasm. RNA polymerase II is responsible for transcribing genes which encode proteins. It gives rise to a population of transcripts known as heterogeneous nuclear RNA (hnRNA), which includes the nuclear precursors of messenger RNA (mRNA), called pre-mRNA. RNA polymerase II typically accounts for a little under half the total transcriptional activity in the cell. RNA polymerase III accounts for a small proportion of the total transcription, roughly 10%, representing the synthesis of non-coding RNAs such as the 5S RNA of the large ribosomal subunit, and transfer RNA (tRNA). RNA polymerases II and III are also responsible for the synthesis of a number of discrete small RNA species identified in the nucleus and/or cytoplasm as ribonucleoprotein complexes [257, 488]. There is evidence implicating at least one of the small nuclear RNA species in the processing of pre-mRNA [366, 396] (Table 6.4.2; see section below on intron processing).

The three RNA polymerases can be distinguished on the basis of their sensitivity to α-amanitin, an inhibitor isolated from the poisonous mushroom *Amanita phalloides*. In animal cells, the RNA polymerase II is highly sensitive to the inhibitor, whereas RNA polymerase I is essentially insensitive. RNA polymerase III of mammalian and amphibian cells is sensitive to intermediate concentrations, but in insects polymerase III is the most resistant of the three enzymes (Table 6.4.3).

Eukaryotic genes can be categorized into classes I, II or III according to which RNA polymerase is responsible for their transcription. The genes of class II encode the protein molecules of the cell, including the proteins which are expressed in every cell type and those which are developmentally regulated.

Structure of class II genes

It is appropriate here to consider the structural features essential for expression of class II genes. These features

Table 6.4.2. Abundant species of small stable RNAs in mammalian cells.

Species					Class
(a)	(b)	Nucleotides	Localization	snRNA	III
K	7–3	300	Nucleus		+
M	7–2, 1	290	Nucleus and cytoplasm		+
L	7S	280	Nucleus and cytoplasm		+
A	U3	216	Nucleolus	+	
C	U2	188/189	Nucleoplasm	+	
D	U1	165	Nucleoplasm/ hnRNP	+	
F	U4	139	Nucleoplasm	+	
G	U5	118	Nucleoplasm	+	
H	U6	106	Perichromatin granules	+	
4.5S		91–95	Nucleus and cytoplasm		+

It is likely that the small nuclear (sn) RNAs are transcribed by RNA polymerase II, and like other class II transcripts have 5′-capped termini. The nomenclatures are those used by (a) Penman's laboratory, (b) Busch's laboratory. See [488].

Table 6.4.3. RNA polymerases of animal cells.

	RNA pol I	RNA pol II	RNA pol III
Location	Nucleolus	Nucleoplasm	Nucleoplasm
Proportion of cellular transcription	50–70%	20–40%	10%
RNA transcripts	rRNA	hnRNA small stable RNAs	5S RNA, tRNA and other small stable RNAs
α-amanitin sensitivity	Low	High	Intermediate (low: insects)

have been recognized in nucleic acid sequence comparisons between the various class II genes which have been cloned. The functional significance of the sequence features has subsequently been investigated by a variety of approaches in which the effects of *in vitro* gene manipulation of particular sequences are assessed. It is therefore necessary to be able to reintroduce the DNA into a system in which it is transcribed. There are currently three basic approaches: cell-free transcription [255, 287], cell transformation [380], and microinjection into the nucleus of living cells. The last approach has been exploited with cells in tissue culture [9], *Xenopus* oocytes [177], mouse oocytes [58], and mouse eggs [60].

If the regulation of transcription is to be investigated then the system should exhibit the appropriate regulated expression of the gene in unmanipulated form. This is not the case with the *in vitro* transcription systems employed to date. However, there have been major advances with *in vivo* systems. DNA-mediated transformation of tissue culture cells with a normally 'unregulated' mouse dihydrofolate reductase gene (DHFR) that had been fused to a hormonally responsive mouse mammary tumour virus (MMTV) promoter region, resulted in regulation of the DHFR by steroid hormone [256]. In other experiments *in vivo*, injection of fertilized mouse eggs with a thymidine kinase gene fused to the promoter region of the mouse metallo-thionein gene gave appropriate inducible regulation by cadmium [60], and adult mice derived from eggs thus injected displayed regulated, tissue-specific expression [57]. Thus it seems that for defining DNA regions necessary for regulation, the living cell is more faithful than current fractionated *in vitro* systems.

A large number of eukaryotic class II genes, from organisms as diverse as yeasts, plants, insects, Amphibia and man have been shown to be split or discontinuous [52]. The term exon has been defined as a sequence block appearing in mRNA, and the term intron or intervening sequence as a sequence block separating exons. Introns are thus elements splitting regions appearing in mRNA. This definition is based on mRNA sequences rather than simply upon protein-coding sequences because introns can occur in non-translated regions of the message; for example the rat prepro-insulin genes, of which there are two kinds, both contain a 119 bp intron in the 5'-non-coding region of the mRNA [269]. The only higher eukaryotic class II genes which are definitely known not to contain introns are histone genes [186] and some interferon genes [203]. Most mouse brain poly(A)$^+$ RNAs seem to be encoded by split genes and the mouse genome probably contains at least tens of thousands of discontinuous genes [293].

In addition to internal structural features associated with introns, 5' (upstream) and 3' (downstream) conserved structural sequence features have been identified in class II genes. These are shown in Fig. 6.4.1.

Upstream features

Comparison of the 5'-extragenic regions of a large number of class II genes has revealed two conserved sequence elements. The nearest of these is located about 30 bp upstream from the site of initiation of RNA synthesis and is an (A+T)-rich region with a sequence related to the consensus TATA$_A^T$A$_A^T$ (the Goldberg–

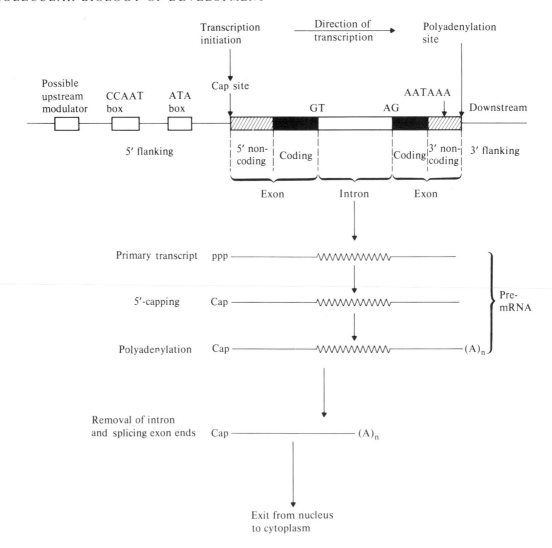

Fig. 6.4.1. Class II gene: showing consensus features. For simplicity, only one intron is shown, there may be over 50 present. Most mRNAs are polyadenylated, but histone mRNA is polyadenylated only in certain situations, e.g. yeast histone mRNA [125] and *Xenopus* oocytes.

Hogness or ATA box) [148, 350]. The second of these conserved sequences is the CCAAT box [31, 115, 186], which is located about 80 bp upstream from the site of initiation of RNA synthesis. There is good evidence that the site of initiation of RNA synthesis is coincident with the site of the 5′-cap on the mature mRNA [90, 349].

These blocks are not the only 5′-regions where homology has been detected in comparisons between at least some genes. The histone genes have a consensus sequence CATTC at the cap site, with transcriptional initiation occurring at the underlined A residue [186].

Downstream features

Many mRNA molecules possess the sequence AAUAAA in the untranslated region near their 3′-end, about 20 nucleotides upstream from the poly(A) segment [350]. Comparison of 3′-extragenic regions of many class II genes has revealed the corresponding AATAAA sequence as the only notable conserved sequence. It has been suggested that this sequence may serve as a signal for polyadenylation. The occurrence of a *Xenopus* histone 4 (H4) cDNA clone which lacks the sequence despite having been derived from a poly-adenylated mRNA, may argue against this [186]. However, this cDNA was derived from poly(A)$^+$ RNA isolated from oocytes, which are unusual in poly-adenylating histone mRNA at all, since histone mRNA is not polyadenylated in other tissues. So oocytes may polyadenylate mRNA promiscuously, in the absence of the normally essential signal.

The histone genes differ from other gene families in that their most impressive homology blocks are located in the downstream region. There are two highly con-served blocks. The block nearer to the termination codon is characterized by extensive dyad symmetry (it is an inverted repeat) [186, 421].

There is uncertainty about the *mechanism* giving rise to the 3'-termini of primary transcripts of class II genes in general, but whatever the situation, these termini must be created by simple termination of RNA synthesis or by an endonucleolytic cleavage, either of which is presumably mediated through recognition of conserved sequence elements (see below).

Functional tests for sequences necessary for correct transcriptional initiation

Several *in vitro* transcription systems are now available which initiate the synthesis of capped transcripts from a variety of viral and cloned cellular class II genes, including genes for differentiated functions [287, 449]. These confirm that the site of initiation is the cap site (see Fig. 6.4.1). Using these *in vitro* systems, combined with deletion and point mutations constructed by gene manipulation techniques, several groups have shown that the ATA box is required for specific initiation of the Adenovirus-2 major late gene [91, 206], the conalbumin gene [444], and the β-globin gene [168]. Thus the ATA box has been functionally equated with the essential sequence of prokaryotic promoters, the 'Pribnow' box [369]. (The term 'promoter' was originally defined with reference to prokaryotes, where it denotes a region of DNA at which RNA polymerase binds and initiates transcription.) In accord with this view is the finding that a small fragment containing the ATA box can be excised from the Adenovirus-2 major late gene and cloned in a bacterial vector where, *in vitro*, it will direct specific initiation of transcription which starts in the foreign,

plasmid sequences about 30 bp downstream from the ATA box [379].

What is the relevance of the *in vitro* experiments to transcription in living cells? Problems in assessing this arise because so few of the experiments have been precisely duplicated in both systems. In agreement with the *in vitro* results, *in vivo* studies with the sea urchin histone gene H2A [165], the simian virus SV40 early region genes [30, 153], and the rabbit β-globin gene [167] show that deletion of sequences downstream from the ATA box result in the initiation of novel transcripts about 30 bp downstream from the ATA box irrespective of the DNA sequences at the actual site of initiation. The normal cap site is therefore not required. But the comparative simplicity of the *in vitro* results is not completely reflected *in vivo* because deletion of the ATA box does not always eliminate transcription *in vivo*. Thus, in the case of the SV40 early genes, deletion does not abolish transcription. However, these new transcripts have heterogeneous 5' ends [30]. Similar results have been observed upon microinjection of a deleted sea urchin H2A gene into *Xenopus* oocyte nuclei. Here, loss of the ATA box resulted in a fivefold downturn in transcription rate, compatible with its promoter role, but a plurality of 5'-termini was generated [165, 166]. Deletion of the ATA box from the β-globin gene prior to transformation of human HeLa cells in a virus vector, resulted in a downturn in trans-cription and a loss of specificity in the initiation site [167]. All of these results point to a function of the ATA box which is additional to any promoter role. The ATA box also selects the precise site of initiation. These results are consistent with the finding that mRNAs of slightly different lengths, with three different 5'-cap sites, are generated from the chicken lysozyme gene in the hen oviduct. This gene has been found to lack the extremely conserved ATA box [162]. The same argument can be made for certain viral genes transcribed by polymerase II which lack clear ATA boxes [18].

Deletion of the CCAAT box usually has little or no effect *in vitro* [91, 168, 206, 444], although it may be required *in vivo* [167, 294]. As for the requirment for regions even further upstream, a variety of observations have been made with various experimental systems with no general rule becoming apparent. Some genes may possess upstream modulators which other genes lack. Most dramatically, sequence manipulation in the region between 184 and 785 bp upstream from the cap site of a sea urchin histone H2A gene could modulate transcription by a factor of 100 in the *Xenopus* oocyte assay [165, 166], but sequences far upstream from the rabbit β-globin gene had little effect in a system based upon SV40-recombinant plasmid DNA introduced into HeLa cells [167]. The H2A gene is only expressed at early developmental stages, but it is not yet known if the sequence identified above is involved in this developmental regulation.

The sequence requirements for specific transcriptional initiation by RNA polymerase II are in marked contrast with the requirements of RNA polymerase III. The 5S RNA and tRNA genes have an essential sequence component, or components, within the transcribed sequence itself. Furthermore, the requirements for initiation on class II genes are also quite different from ribosomal genes (class I) which clearly lack upstream sequences homologous to class II genes.

Termination of transcription?

It is a remarkable observation that the *in vitro* systems which have been applied to studies of transcriptional initiation of class II genes all fail to give termination at specific sites. No studies on newly formed class II transcripts *in vivo* have indicated that synthesis actually stops at the polyadenylation site.

Hofer and Darnell [193] have investigated events at the 3′-terminus of a mouse β-globin gene by analysing nascent transcripts extended and radiolabelled *in vitro* by incubation of isolated nuclei from Friend erythroleukaemia cells (these are cancer cells which can be induced to synthesize haemoglobin). Their results showed that the majority of polymerase II molecules transcribed at least one thousand nucleotides past the polyadenylation site. In order to try to exclude the possibility that their results were a consequence of aberrant transcription in isolated nuclei, other experiments were performed by labelling whole cells for brief periods. It was not expected that it would be possible to duplicate the quantitative experiments done in isolated nuclei, but it was possible to detect RNA labelled *in vivo* homologous to regions downstream from the polyadenylation site, and by labelling for times from 3 to 20 min it was found that the proportion of this RNA fell sharply compared with an intron region of the gene, suggesting a very rapid turnover of the downstream RNA. These authors therefore propose that the transcription of cellular class II genes starts at the cap site and produces primary transcripts beyond the polyadenylation site which are then cut endonucleolytically and polyadenylated. This proposal awaits further confirmation as far as cellular class II genes are concerned, but it is strongly supported by the fact that it does apply to a chicken globin gene [453] and to every mammalian virus mRNA studied so far (see [193] for references).

Alternative transcript initiation and termination sites

Possibilities exist for regulating gene expression not simply by switching transcription on or off, but by altering the site of initiation or the site of termination (however achieved) of the pre-mRNA. Two interesting examples of this type of regulation are known: tissue-specific expression of α-amylase which involves alternative initiation events; and expression of both the membrane-bound and secreted forms of immunoglobulin heavy chains which involves alternative termination events.

Alpha-amylase is an enzyme which digests starch. It is produced in large amounts in the salivary glands and the pancreas, but in much lower amounts in the liver. In the laboratory mouse, a single gene *Amy 1* encodes both the liver and salivary gland amylases, which are identical proteins. A second gene, *Amy 2* encodes pancreatic α-amylase, which has a different primary sequence from the other protein. Young *et al.* [386, 487] have examined the tissue-specific expression of *Amy 1* in liver and salivary gland. The α-amylase mRNAs which accumulate in these two tissues are identical except for their 5′-non-translated sequences. The 5′-terminal 158 nucleotides of the major liver α-amylase mRNA (there are other minor liver transcripts) are unrelated to the 5′-terminal 47 nucleotides of its salivary gland counterpart. By comparing these leader sequences with DNA sequences upstream from the structural gene it was clear that the initial 161 nucleotides of the liver α-amylase mRNA are specified by DNA sequences that lie 4.5 kb upstream from those for the common body of the two mRNAs. In contrast, the 5′-terminal 50 nucleotides of the salivary gland α-amylase mRNA are found 7.5 kb upstream from the sequences shared by the two mRNAs. There are ATA boxes appropriately positioned just upstream from both putative initiation points, suggesting that the alternative mRNAs are obtained by differential initiation. However, it is possible that both transcripts are synthesized in the two cell types and only the mRNA containing the appropriate leader might be exported to the cytoplasm in the relevant tissue. Whatever the mechanism, the uncapped liver-type leader sequence must be part of an intron in the salivary gland transcript (Fig. 6.4.2).

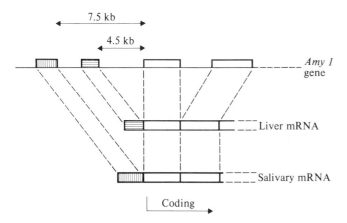

Fig. 6.4.2. Tissue-specific mRNA biosynthesis from the *Amy 1* gene of the mouse [487]. The pattern by which gene sequences are ultimately incorporated into mature salivary gland and liver α-amylase mRNA is shown. Tissue-specific sequences are represented by ▥ = salivary gland; ▤ = liver. Open boxes represent exons shared by both mRNAs. The diagram includes only that portion of the gene which specifies the initial one-quarter of the two mRNAs.

Why should the mouse generate multiple mRNAs from the *Amy 1* gene? It is possible that this is due to the requirements for different concentrations of the same mRNA. Alpha-amylase mRNA accounts for 2% and 0.02% of total polyadenylated mRNA in salivary gland and liver cytoplasm, respectively. This difference may reflect different efficiencies of the two promoters. Alternatively, the rate of RNA processing may differ markedly for the two precursor molecules. It is also possible that there are effects upon translational efficiencies of these two mRNA types which differ so much in their 5'-non-translated leader regions. Finally, it is conceivable that the 5'-non-translated sequences influence mRNA stability.

The B-lymphocyte lineage moves through an orderly series of developmental changes. The involvement of these cells in the immune response is described in Chapter 3.7. Immature B-lymphocytes synthesize IgM-class antibody as a cell-surface antigen receptor. The lymphocytes differentiate further into cells bearing both IgM and IgD on their surface. Subsequently, after stimulation by antigen, the cells differentiate to become plasma cells which either actively secrete IgM or change the class of immunoglobulin secreted to one of the other class (IgG, IgA, IgE) with different functions and distinguished by different heavy chains. The problem which concerns us here is how the switch from membrane-bound to secreted IgM is achieved.

The heavy chains of membrane-bound IgM μ_m are a little larger than those of secreted IgM μ_s. The difference is due to a short extra C-terminal region on the membrane-bound form. The fact that the extra piece is strongly hydrophobic accounts for the association with the plasma membrane. These two forms of heavy chain are encoded by two distinct mRNAs which differ at their 3'-termini and yet which are derived from the same gene. The μ gene, like other active immunoglobulin genes, consists of a number of exons encoding the variable and constant-region domains separated by introns. The 3'-portion of the μ gene has a complex structure such that alternative pathways of RNA processing, subject to developmental control, give rise to the two forms μ_m and μ_s (Fig. 6.4.3). Some early transcripts apparently terminate with poly(A) addition near the 3'-end of the final constant-region domain (C4). Other transcripts can continue through this site to terminate with polyadenylation at a second site. These transcripts undergo two additional splices that connect the C4 domain to two additional exons, M exons, which encode the C-terminus of the μm chain (see [158] for review). This mechanism for dual expression by regulating the events generating 3'-termini may not be restricted to the μ class of heavy chains. Membrane-bound forms of the δ and γ chains of IgD and IgG have been reported, which probably differ from secreted forms through a similar mechanism [84, 281, 365]. As a further complication, dual expression of IgD and IgM may occur by a mechanism involving read-through beyond the M exons into C_δ exons with RNA splicing generating a mature δ mRNA from V and C_δ exons [158].

Intron processing

Splicing must be a highly accurate process, and must ultimately depend upon the sequence of the pre-mRNA. The accuracy is best illustrated by the chicken α-2 collagen gene, which has at least 51 exons that must be

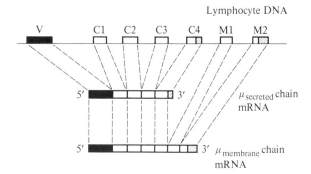

Fig. 6.4.3. Structure of an active immunoglobulin heavy chain (μ) gene. Model for the formation of two different heavy chain mRNAs, one encoding a secreted heavy chain, and the other a membrane-bound heavy chain.

linked precisely because even a one-nucleotide error would alter the reading frame of the message upon translation [479]. The roles of collagen in development are described in Chapter 3.3 and 3.5, and its structure is illustrated in Chapter 6.2. At present the enzymology of the splicing reactions which convert pre-mRNA to mRNA is not well understood. Splicing of tRNA precursors has been studied *in vitro* [235], but this process appears to be different from that acting on pre-mRNA. While the enzymology of pre-mRNA splicing is unclear, we do have information concerning the features of the gene sequence that are essential for splicing to occur.

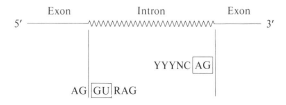

Fig. 6.4.4. Consensus sequences at junctions of pre-mRNA. R, purine; Y, pyrimidine; N, any base.

Sequence comparisons of many splice junctions in many genes have allowed consensus sequences at the site of 5′ splice sites and 3′ splice sites to be deduced [396] (Fig. 6.4.4). In most cases the intron–exon junction of individual splice sites cannot be defined exactly because nucleotides are duplicated at corresponding positions in the 5′- and 3′-sites so that alternative splices could generate the same sequence. However, all cases are consistent with the rule that the

intron begins with GT at its 5′-end and finishes with AG at its 3′-end. This has been called the GT–AG rule. The consensus sequences are clearly very simple, and it is probable that they alone do not define the splice sites.

Processing intermediates have been identified in a variety of systems. It seems that some individual introns may be excised in several steps, e.g. the mouse β-globin mRNA appears to require two stages to excise the large intron [233] and an intron in the chicken α-2 collagen pre-mRNA is apparently removed in multiple steps [14], although proof that the intermediates are genuine, and not the result of abortive pathways, is lacking. Studies on pre-mRNAs with multiple introns, such as the *Xenopus* vitellogenin [376] and chick ovomucoid [321, 418] pre-mRNAs, suggest that there is no absolutely fixed order of removal of introns, although a preferred order may operate for ovomucoid pre-mRNA [418].

The 5′ and 3′ splice sites in pre-mRNA must be brought into close proximity for covalent splicing to occur. It has been suggested that the two splice sites pair bases with another RNA molecule, which could be a structural component of the splicing enzyme(s). Such effector RNAs might be found among the small, stable, nuclear RNAs that are ubiquitous in eukaryotic cells (Table 6.4.2). Evidently, most of the hnRNA in cells is found associated with RNP structures containing such small RNA molecules. Rogers and Wall [366] have shown that the most abundant of these RNAs, U1 snRNA (also called SnD), is complementary to the consensus sequence at splice sites, and hence could hybridize with them so as to stabilize a looped intermediate in splicing.

Splicing and regulation of gene expression

It is tempting to speculate that splicing may be used as a means of controlling cellular gene expression. There is little experimental evidence for this. Nevertheless, infection of undifferentiated mouse teratocarcinoma cells by SV40 does not lead to the production of early mRNAs, and the block appears to lie at the splicing level [394]. After differentiation of the cells has been induced *in vitro*, the block is lifted [393]. Apparently, therefore, despite the fact that transcripts can be spliced in heterologous systems, mechanisms exist for recognizing different introns and modulating their excision. It remains to be shown that the undifferentiated cells fail to splice out any of their own introns. They must have the ability to splice many pre-mRNAs since they make thousands of mRNAs, some of which must be derived from pre-mRNAs containing introns.

The notion that differential splicing can be used to regulate gene expression is borne out by detailed study of mammalian virus transcripts. For example, Adenovirus generates a dazzling spectrum of gene products by differential splicing in combination with the differential use of promoters (reviewed by Ziff [489]).

6.4.5 THE mRNA SPECTRUM IN CELLS

The final intermediate between structural gene and polypeptide is mRNA. One way of gaining an insight into the enormous number of different polypeptides being synthesized in a cell is to analyse the population of mRNAs which direct their synthesis. The techniques of nucleic acid hybridization allow the very complicated populations of mRNA molecules occurring in cells to be analysed. Such a population could comprise over 10 000 mRNA species represented in a whole spectrum of frequencies or abundances. One of the major advantages of analysis by hybridization at the mRNA level is that answers can be obtained to quantitative questions such as the following. How many different polypeptides are encoded in the mRNA of a cell? What is the range of abundancies of the mRNAs, i.e. are some present at only a few copies per cell, and others present at many thousands of copies per cell? To what extent do different tissues share the same mRNAs, and to what extent do they differ in their mRNA populations? Answers to the corresponding questions at the protein level are almost impossible to obtain even with the most highly resolving two-dimensional gel electrophorectic techniques for displaying the population of cellular polypeptides. Hybridization of RNA gives a global analysis in terms of numbers of sequences and abundances of sequences. The two-dimensional gels of polypeptides allow one to look at individual polypeptides in a way which is difficult to integrate into a global picture. The extreme sensitivity of hybridization methods is also noteworthy; transcripts present at a concentration of less than one per cell can be detected and quantified.

Number of polysomal mRNAs

As we have noted previously (section 6.4.4), most mRNAs are derived from non-repetitive DNA

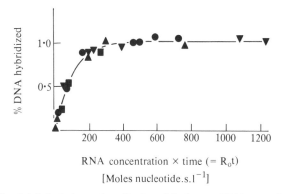

Fig. 6.4.5. Isolation and application of single-copy DNA tracer for measuring mRNA complexity [140]. Note that the single-copy fraction ideally will contain every DNA sequence present in the genome (including repeated sequences), but with each of them reduced to the same frequency which is characteristic of unique sequences.

sequences. Reaction of labelled single-copy denatured DNA with an excess of mRNA should drive the genomic sequences represented in the mRNA population into the hybrid form. The plateau, or saturation point, of such a reaction will therefore be an estimate of the fraction of the single-copy DNA expressed in the mRNA (taking a factor of two into account because only one strand of the DNA is transcribed into message). Single-copy DNA must be used for such an experiment because the reaction of labelled DNA must be exclusively with the excess mRNA, and not with itself in a DNA reassociation reaction. This reassociation reaction of DNA with DNA would occur to a significant extent with repetitive sequences, on the time-scale required for the hybridization of DNA with a complex population of mRNAs. Therefore single-copy sequences are prepared prior to the hybridization experiment by allowing denatured genomic DNA to reassociate with itself to such an extent that only the highly and moderately repetitive sequences can react. This reassociation is then followed by fractionation on hydroxyapatite, which will retain reassociated (partially or totally duplex) DNA, and allow the required single-copy DNA to pass through the column [140] (Fig. 6.4.5).

The sequence complexity of mRNA populations from several sources is given in Table 6.4.4. In the tissues of higher eukaryotes in general, the number of structural genes expressed is found to be around 10 000 to 20 000. Notice also that the number of expressed genes in oocytes is similar for *Xenopus* and *Stronglyocentrotus*,

Table 6.4.4. Total sequence complexity of mRNA populations.

mRNA source	Complexity (kb)	Number of different mRNAs*
S. purpuratus (sea urchin)		
Oocyte total RNA	37000	18500
Blastula polysomal	26000	13000
Gastrula polysomal	17000	8500
Adult intestine polysomal	6000	3000
Xenopus		
Oocyte total RNA	30000	15000
Chick		
liver polysomal	34000	17000

*Assuming average mRNA size of 2000 nucleotides [42]
References: sea urchin [142, 143, 202]; *Xenopus* [100]; chick [15]

The complexity of a nucleic acid is the total length of different sequences present. It is usually expressed as number of bases, but daltons or other units may be used. Suppose for example, that an RNA population consists of 100 molecules of sequence 'A', 10 molecules of sequence 'B' and 1 molecule each of sequences 'C', 'D' and 'E'. If each molecule in our example is 2000 nucleotides in length, then the complexity is the sum of the different sequences (i.e. A+B+C+D+E), $5 \times 2000 = 10$ kb. In practice, complexity is determined experimentally by nucleic acid hybridization, and then used to estimate the number of different types of RNA present. The term 'abundance' denotes the number of representatives of each type of RNA in the population. In the example, sequence 'A' is ten times more abundant than sequence 'B', and 100 times more abundant than sequence 'D'.

despite a fourfold difference in genome size. A comparison of mRNA complexities between oocytes of the newt *Triturus* and *Xenopus* gives a similar equivalence, despite a 10-fold difference in genome size [261]. These observations give a quantitative dimension to our previously intuitive appreciation of the C-value paradox. Larger genomes do not necessarily express higher numbers of structural genes. Table 6.4.4 also shows that during the development of the sea urchin there is a reduction in the complexity of the mRNA.

What is the range of mRNA abundances in the cell?

An approach to answering this question has been established by Bishop *et al.* [41]. First, an mRNA population is used to direct the synthesis of radiolabelled cDNA by the enzyme reverse transcriptase. The cDNA is isolated from the template mRNA, and then placed in a hybridization reaction with a large excess of the same mRNA preparation from which it had been synthesized. All of the tracer cDNA should eventually be driven into hybrid form. A kinetic treatment of this reaction is given by Davidson [99], but without giving a mathematical

discussion here it should be obvious that if an mRNA species is highly abundant in the population then its corresponding cDNA sequence will account for a correspondingly large fraction of the tracer radioactivity. The hybridization of this cDNA species, driven by the abundant mRNA, will be rapid, much faster than the reaction of non-abundant sequences. The slowest reacting component in such an analysis will be made up of a large number of different scarce cDNAs. Their large number will be reflected in the fact that they form a significant percentage of the tracer radiolabel, even though individually they are scarce. This component therefore represents (through their large number) a high sequence complexity because many different sequences are present. An analysis of this kind, called an R_0t analysis (see Fig. 6.4.6), therefore reveals abundance classes in the mRNA population, and can be used to determine the sequence complexities represented by each class.

There are several limitations to this type of analysis. (i) It can only readily be applied to poly(A)$^+$ RNA, because only this can be primed simply with oligo(dT), for reverse transcription.

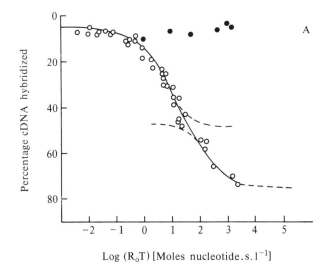

Log (R_0T) [Moles nucleotide.s.l^{-1}]

Fig. 6.4.6. Abundance classes in a mRNA population from mouse embryos. Hybridization of cDNA with homologous mouse embryo poly(A) RNA [484]. The reaction covers a wide range of log R_0T units and therefore cannot be represented by a single abundance class. The data have therefore been resolved into the minimum number of components necessary to describe adequately the complete reaction. These components are shown in by broken lines, and it is clear that the reaction requires a minimum of two abundance components (each hybridizes over about 2.5 log R_0T units, which is characteristic of a single component).

(ii) The analysis depends upon the assumption that the cDNA population accurately reflects the poly(A)$^+$ RNA population.

(iii) For estimating total sequence complexity it may be unreliable, because this value is largely due to the slowest reacting class, and the size of this class can be uncertain if unreacting DNA remains at the end of the reaction (in practice, a significant proportion—perhaps 10 or 15%—remains unreacted, even after prolonged incubation). Estimates of total sequence complexity are therefore best obtained using a single-copy DNA tracer in the way described previously.

Table 6.4.5 summarizes data from three typical systems. Usually, more or less discrete mRNA abundance classes can be observed, the components being assigned somewhat arbitrarily on the basis of using the minimum number of them for a reasonable fit to the data. Also, a wide range of abundances is observed in any cell type or tissue. The abundances may differ by 1000-fold. Note that there can be a very complex class of mRNAs which are present at only a few copies per cell. This is a very important observation, because it suggests that many cellular proteins are themselves scarce. What is the significance of this? Two extreme views are possible.

(i) Regulation of gene expression is rather imprecise, so that genes are not completely turned off but merely turned down to a very low level of expression. In other words control is leaky.

(ii) Regulation is indeed precise, proteins are carefully regulated at this level of expression, which need not be so very low since one mRNA molecule can synthesize one polypeptide about every 3 s, amounting to some 30 000 polypeptide molecules per day, assuming of course that the mRNA is very stable.

Evidence in favour of the second view has been

Table 6.4.5. Abundance classes of typical mRNA populations.

Source	Complexity (kb) of each class	Number of mRNAs	Abundance (molecules/cell)
Mouse liver cytoplasmic poly(A)$^+$	17	9	12 000
	1400	700	300
	23 000	11 500	15
Mouse embryo polysomal poly(A)$^+$	840	420	—
	20 000	10 000	—
Chick oviduct polysomal poly(A)$^+$	2	1	100 000
	14	7	4000
	25 000	12 500	5

References: mouse tissues [484]; chick oviduct [15]

presented by Galau *et al.* [141]. Data regarding the rates of synthesis of 40 rodent liver proteins were collated from the literature. Estimates of the rates of synthesis were then made either on the basis of known steady-state protein concentrations and turnover rates or, more directly, from measurements of the fraction of total protein synthesis accounted for by the protein in question. Making conventional assumptions about the rates of polypeptide synthesis on mammalian polysomes and the stability of mRNA, the authors concluded that many of proteins would require steady-state mRNA concentrations in the range of only 1–30 copies per cell. Several of these proteins are of the 'household' type, i.e. they are common to all cells because they perform a basic undifferentiated cellular function. Significantly, several of the proteins requiring only a low-abundance mRNA are known to be expressed histospecifically. Certain of these proteins are even under physiological control, e.g. acetyl CoA carboxylase drops to a level 10-fold lower than normal in rats switched to a high-fat diet. All of these observations make a convincing case for regarding the expression of low-abundance mRNA as being non-leaky.

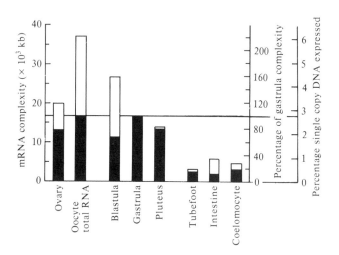

Fig. 6.4.7. Structural gene sets active in embryos and adult tissues of the sea urchin [142]. The solid portion of each bar indicates the amount of single-copy sequence shared between gastrula mRNA and the RNA preparation listed along the abscissa. The open portions show the amount of single-copy sequence present in the various RNAs studied but absent from gastrula mRNA. The total complexity of each RNA is indicated by the overall height of each bar.

How much overlap is there between mRNA populations in different cell types?

All of the cell types in an organism are expected to have a proportion of their mRNA populations in common, since all cells will contain mRNA populations which code for ubiquitous household functions. It is important to know not only how cell types resemble one another, but also to gain a quantitative appreciation of how they differ in their RNA populations. The most comprehensive studies of this kind, and related studies concerning nuclear RNA populations, have been made in the sea urchin *Strongylocentrotus purpuratus*. The morphology of various stages of sea urchin development is illustrated in Figs 2.4.5 and 4.3.11. In an important series of experiments, Galau *et al.* [142] compared the structural gene sets which are active in sea urchin adult and embryo tissues. First, a single-copy, radiolabelled, genomic DNA was prepared. By hybridizing this DNA with gastrula mRNA, a (mDNA) tracer was prepared which could be reacted with mRNA from other embryos and tissues. Similarly, single-copy DNA which was totally devoid of gastrula message sequences, was prepared and reacted with the various mRNAs (Fig. 6.4.7). The sequence complexity of the reacting mRNA could then be calculated as described previously.

Large differences in the extent of both mDNA and null mDNA reaction with the various mRNAs were observed, indicating that in each state of differentiation a distinct set of structural genes is being expressed, generally characterized by several thousand specific sequences (abbreviations described in legend to Fig. 6.4.7). A relatively small set of mRNAs, the complexity of which is about 2100 kb, i.e. about 1000 mRNA types, appears to be shared by the tissues studied. There was a steady decline in mRNA complexity with differentiation into adult tissues. In fact these tissues showed complexities as low as any known in eukaryotes. Sequences expressed in the gastrula continued to be a large part of the mRNA population at subsequent stages. All of the mRNAs in the gastrula are present in the oocyte, although most of the gastrula mRNAs are not maternally inherited but are products of embryonic transcription [143]. Some sequences are present in oocyte and gastrula but are missing in the intervening blastula. Similar results, substantiating these conclusions, have been obtained in further studies using mDNA and null-DNA sequences derived from oocyte mRNA [202].

These experiments also revealed new gene expression in the blastula, which is turned off again by the gastrula. The conclusions from both these studies refer mainly to the low-abundance class of mRNAs which, because of their high complexity, contribute most to the single-copy DNA probes used. A study was therefore undertaken to determine whether the specificity of the embryo transcripts extends to moderately and highly abundant mRNAs [482]. In these experiments, a large set of cloned pluteus stage cDNAs were analysed by hybridization with radioactive cDNA made from cytoplasmic poly(A)$^+$ RNA of pluteus embryos and adult coelomocytes (these are circulatory cells in the adult body cavity). More than 85% of the moderately abundant embryo transcripts were below the limit of detection of about one copy per cell in coelomocytes. However, the most abundant pluteus transcripts were frequently also abundant in the coelomocytes. A major overall conclusion from these investigations of sea urchin development is that there is an evident reduction in the numbers of genes expressed with increasing specialization towards the adult tissues.

If the relationship between the mRNA populations of the embryo and adult tissues which is revealed by these investigations holds for all of the other adult tissues in the sea urchin, then it is possible to set the overall complexity of mRNA sequences ever expressed in this organism at about 50 000 kb. This would set the total number of different structural genes at about 25 000, and account for no more than a few per cent of the total sequence complexity of the genome.

6.4.6 LEVELS AT WHICH GENE EXPRESSION MAY BE REGULATED

The pathway from gene to phenotype is potentially very complex, with many steps at which regulatory mechanisms could operate. Subdivision of the pathway can be introduced almost indefinitely, but an attempt has been made in Fig. 6.4.8 to identify and classify major stages of the pathway, any of which could be affected differentially, hence leading to regulation of gene expression. Compared with prokaryotes, eukaryotes have an important extra area for control which arises from the compartmentalization of the cell into nucleus and cytoplasm; there is ample opportunity for post-transcriptional nuclear events to mediate regulation prior to translation. In prokaryotes, translation and transcription are often intimately coupled.

In the following sections of this chapter, the contribution to development and differentiation of regulation at each of these steps will be discussed in turn.

6.4.7 CONTROL OF GENE ACTIVITY THROUGH PROTEIN STABILITY AND DEPLOYMENT

With the exception of those genes that do not encode proteins (e.g. rRNA and tRNA genes), genes do not exert any phenotypic effect on the cell until the proteins they encode perform their function in the cell. There may be a delay in a protein performing its role once it is made and its activity may be continuously controlled by other agents. Even when proteins have become functional, the time that they remain active depends on their stability. These are the levels of genetic regulation furthest removed from transcription.

Protein stability

Protein stability has been most intensively studied in rat liver [387]. Selected data are shown in Table 6.4.6. Proteins in this tissue decay with first-order kinetics (i.e. protein molecules always have a finite chance of decay—they do not age) and their half-lives vary by factors of at least 40-fold. Moreover, their rates of degradation may change. Thus the level of these enzymes, many of which

Table 6.4.6. Protein stability in rat liver.

Enzyme	$t_{1/2}$
Arginase	4–5 days
L-α-glycerophosphate dehydrogenase	4 days
Urocanase	3.5 days
Histidine	2.5 days
Cytochrome P$_{450}$	2 days
Serine dehydratase	20 hours
Ornithine transaminase	20 hours
3-phosphoglycerate dehydrogenase	15 hours
Glucokinase	12 hours
Tyrosine transaminase	1.5 hours
δ-aminolaevulinate synthetase	1 hour

Selected data from Schimke & Doyle [285], from which source references may be obtained

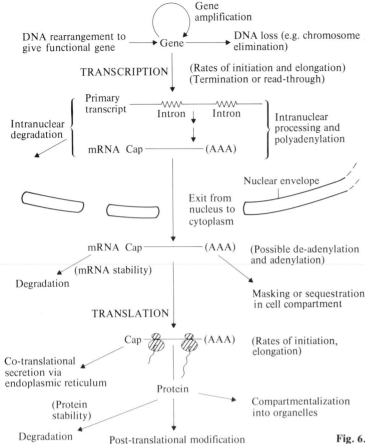

Fig. 6.4.8. Possible points of regulation on gene-to-phenotype pathway of class II nuclear genes.

are hepatocyte-specific, depends as much on degradation as it does on synthesis. However there is no suggestion that restriction of any protein to a particular type of differentiated cell is ever determined by protein stability.

Changes in protein activity and deployment

Some proteins are made as inactive precursors and are only later converted to an active form. An example is tyrosinase (tyrosine-DOPA oxidase), an enzyme mainly found in neural cells and in derivatives of the neural crest. It is involved in melanin and catecholamine synthesis and is first synthesized in an inactive form in frog neurulae, and it is not activated by proteolytic cleavage until some hours later [32].

There are other well-known mechanisms for activating enzyme molecules, for example phosphorylation.

These may also be used for continuous regulation of enzymic activity. Examples of pathways controlled in this way (e.g. glycogen metabolism) are to be found in standard biochemical textbooks.

Another important feature of protein synthesis in development is that proteins are often made long before they are required, and this applies particularly to proteins stored in oogenesis. Important examples of such stored proteins are those used to construct nuclei. In most animals the first phase of development involves rapid cell division and therefore very large supplies of nuclear constituents are required. One solution to the problem of rapidly providing these constituents is to store the proteins during oogenesis. This strategy is adopted by the frog *Xenopus*, which divides to form 30 000 cells in the first 9 h of development. The oocyte stockpiles sufficient histone to assemble about 20 000 of these nuclei [1,470]. It also contains sufficient RNA polymerase to support transcription to the tail-bud tadpole stage (c. 100000 cells) [363]. Both histones and RNA polymerase are stored in the large nucleus of the oocyte. It may be that many other proteins are stored in a similar fashion. If so, it would be interesting to know if any become unevenly distributed in the early embryo. This would make them good candidates for agents controlling early events in pattern formation (see Chapter 4.3).

In *Xenopus*, histones are also made on stored mRNA (see section 6.4.8). This alternative to storage of the protein is emphasized in other organisms. For example sea urchin eggs contain enough histone to assemble only 32 nuclei [344]; the rest is provided through mobilization of stored mRNA and extensive gene transcription. In *Drosophila* there is a large store of histones in the egg [313, 314], as well as a very large pool of stored histone mRNA [8]. Like *Xenopus*, both sea urchins and *Drosophila* also store RNA polymerases [230, 364], but in *Drosophila* the store is located in the cytoplasm, not the nucleus. Even mammalian embryos, where cleavage is not rapid, have been reported to store at least one histone [442] (H4, although see [290]).

Thus nuclear proteins are stored during oogenesis for future use in assembling nuclei in later development, even though this may not be the only source of these proteins. Exactly the same is true of certain microfilament and microtubule proteins required for cell division (these proteins are described in Chapters 3.3 and 6.2). This has been known for many years, since various noxious treatments cause the cytoplasms of unfertilized eggs to fill up with asters (radiating, assembled microtubules). In sea urchins' and frogs' eggs, tubulin represents about 1% of soluble protein [338, 352, 404], and it is also abundant in mammalian eggs [390].

6.4.8 TRANSLATIONAL CONTROL

There are situations in which the rate at which various proteins are made in living cells does not correspond to the relative abundance of different kinds of mRNA within the cells. Moreover, translation of these mRNAs *in vitro* shows that they have unchanged intrinsic ability to be translated. This is the empirical recognition of the phenomenon of translational control.

Translational control may be achieved by one of two extreme mechanisms, or by a combination of them.

(i) Changing translational efficiency

Here all mRNAs of a given type have an equal chance of translation at any given moment. Control is exerted by varying the efficiency of this translation. It may occur in one or both of two ways: (a) by changing the rate at which ribosomes move along the mRNA, and thus the rate of elongating the growing polypeptide (*elongation rate*), or (b) by changing the rate at which ribosomes bind to mRNAs, and thus the rate of initiating new polypeptide chains (*initiation rate*). If either (a) or (b) happens independently, the average polysome size will change; if the rate of initiation increases, so will the polysome size, while if the elongation rate increases then the polysome size will decrease. This is shown in Fig. 6.4.9.

(ii) Storage of mRNA

A fraction of the mRNA may be stored, and a fraction translated. The efficiency with which the active fraction is translated (i.e. the initiation and elongation rates) could always be the same, it is the size of the translated fraction which changes.

Significance of translational control

The most obvious reason for the existence of control at the translational level, either of all or of particular mRNAs, is to increase the rate of protein synthesis faster than might be possible by transcriptional means, or to decrease it more rapidly or specifically than could be achieved by mRNA degradation. The clearest situation in which translational control is employed to increase protein synthesis is in the early development of animals, particularly those with large eggs and/or rapid development.

We can illustrate why this should be so by considering one moderately large, rapidly developing zygote, that of the frog *Xenopus laevis*. (The morphological stages of amphibian development can be found in Figs. 3.3.12 and 4.3.2.) This is 1.2–1.3 mm in diameter, and a 1 μl egg develops to a 30000 cell gastrula in about 10 hours at 21°C. Let us try to work out how rapidly the synthesis of a protein, constituting 2% of total protein synthesis, can be regulated by new transcription if the gene concerned is represented by a single gene in the haploid genome.

The total rate of protein synthesis in the fertilized egg

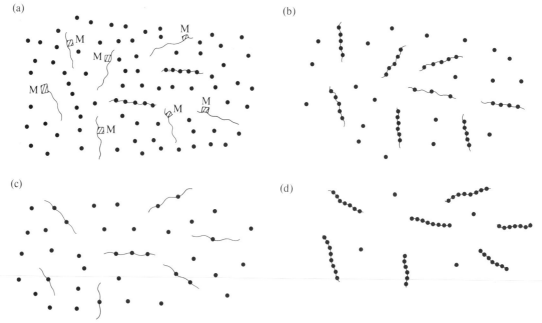

Fig. 6.4.9. Translational control according to the mechanisms outlined in section 6.4.8. A protein of globin size is used as an example. Typically there are about 5–6 ribosomes per mRNA. (a and b) Control by mechanism 1—translation of only part of the mRNA pool. In (a) translation of most mRNAs is blocked by a masking protein M. However, a few mRNAs lack M and are loaded with more than five ribosomes. In (b) the masking protein is removed and all of the mRNAs have recruited ribosomes. (c) Control by reduction of the rate of polypeptide initiation. Ribosomes bind to mRNAs infrequently, but traverse the mRNAs at normal rate. Thus the average polysome size is reduced. (d) Control by reduction in the rate of elongation. The effect is exactly opposite to that in (c). mRNAs become very heavily loaded with ribosomes.

may be calculated from its content of polysomes (120 ng rRNA in polysomes [469]). This is about 30 ng protein h^{-1*} and about 2.7 ng mRNA is needed to sustain this rate†. This means that 54 pg of an mRNA is needed to encode 2% of total protein synthesis.

---

* The rate of protein synthesis is calculated from the number of active ribosomes and a polypeptide elongation rate of one peptide bond s^{-1}. Rate of protein synthesis = no. of active ribosomes × rate of peptide bond formation × mol. wt of an amino acid ÷ Avogadro's number; i.e. $(4 \times 10^{10}) \times 1 \times 120 \div (6 \times 10^{23}) = 0.8 \times 10^{-11}$ g s^{-1} or 29 ng h^{-1}.

† The number of active ribosomes is given by: mass of rRNA × Avogadro's number ÷ mol. wt rRNA, i.e. $(120 \times 10^{-9}$ g$) \times (6 \times 10^{23}) \div (1.8 \times 10^{6}) = 4 \times 10^{10}$. A typical mRNA, like globin mRNA (mol. wt 200 000) carries an average of five ribosomes, both in a reticulocyte and an oocyte [262], i.e. 4×10^{4} daltons per ribosome. Thus the mass of mRNAs translated will be $(4 \times 10^{10}) \times (4 \times 10^{4}) \div$ Avogadro's number = 2.7×10^{-9} g or 2.7 ng.

† A polymerase would complete an mRNA molecule once every $100 \div 15$ s = 6.7 s. Let us take as an example a gene making an mRNA of about 200 000 mol. wt. On the two genes of a diploid cell $(2 \times 10^{5}) \times 2 \div 6.7 = 0.6 \times 10^{5}$ daltons could be made per second. Dividing by Avogadro's number (6×10^{23}) we get 10^{-19} g s^{-1}. Thus the time needed to make 54 pg is $54 \times 10^{-12} \div 10^{-19}$ s = 54×10^{7} s = 6250 days.

How long would a diploid cell take to manufacture this amount? In oocytes, RNA polymerases are typically about 100 base pairs apart on the DNA [302] and elongate RNA at about 15 nucleotides s^{-1} [7]. It may be calculated that a diploid zygote would need about 6000 days to complete the task. It is possible that polymerases could be as close as 50 base pairs apart and elongate as fast as 30 nucleotides s^{-1}, but even then the zygote would need 1500 days to make the RNA.

Clearly, transcriptional control is out of the question for any protein making up a measurable proportion of protein synthesis. In order to control a 2% protein over a reasonable time scale, like 3 h, solely by transcriptional means, there would have to be enormous reiteration of the genes, say about 50 000-fold, depending on the size of the protein. It is a corollary of this argument that such transcriptional control is entirely feasible when 50 000 cells have been formed, that is, by the neurula stage.

This calculation is not entirely hypothetical. For example, individual histones make up as much as 2% of protein synthesis in *Xenopus* zygotes, though their genes are reiterated 50- to 100-fold. It is thus not surprising that their synthesis is controlled at the translational level [469] (see below).

Xenopus represents a relatively extreme example, although there are many animals with larger eggs. Other animals have smaller eggs and contain commensurately less mRNA. Table 6.4.7 shows the polyadenylated RNA content of some representative eggs. We calculated above that it would take the zygote of Xenopus about 6000 days to make the mRNA for a protein representing 2% of protein synthesis and encoded by a single copy gene. Ignoring factors like temperature differences, this converts to about 100 days for Drosophila, 10 days for the sea urchin and 1 day for the mouse. Only in the last is transcriptional control really feasible, and the higher body temperature means that less than 10 h would be needed, i.e. a period shorter than one cell cycle in these slowly dividing organisms. Even so, as we shall see, translational control is important during the first two cell cycles in the mouse.

Table 6.4.7. Polyadenylated RNA contents of unfertilized eggs.

Organism	Poly(A$^+$) RNA per egg (pg)	Reference
Xenopus	40 000	See text
Drosophila	4500	8
S. purpuratus	50–100	99
Mouse	7	(Calculated from [343])

Fruiting body formation in Acetabularia provides a situation that is exactly analogous to the eggs of animals. In both, the low nucleus-to-cytoplasm ratio is presumably the reason why translational control is so important (see Chapter 1.2).

Translational control of overall protein synthetic rate

Sea urchins

The sea urchin egg has a prominent place in the study of translational control because it was the first, and in many ways is still one of the most dramatic examples of such effects [207, 311]. In sea urchins the oocyte undergoes its reduction division in the ovary, and the free, haploid eggs remain there in a dormant state until the appropriate environmental conditions cause their release.

Fertilization ends dormancy through a complex battery of changes, some, such as increased respiration rate, increased Ca^{2+} concentration and increased pH, occurring within 1 min of fertilization, and others occurring more slowly [122]. Superficially at least, one of the 'late responses' is a 10- to 100-fold increase in the rate of protein synthesis [121, 192, 207, 208, 311, 354]. The cause of this increase excited early speculation long before the detailed mechanism of protein synthesis was known. Even now a complete explanation of the effect is still awaited, but it is clear that it involves translational control of a maternal store of mRNA. This was clearly shown by Denny and Tyler [104], who found that the increase occurred in artificially activated, non-nucleated fragments of eggs. Thus the transcription of nuclear genes could not have produced the effect. In any case it can be calculated that the single nucleus of the unfertilized egg contains insufficient genes to increase protein synthesis by the amount and in the time that is observed. Recent measurements indicate that most of the RNA made in eggs is in fact mitochondrial, the mitochondrial DNA content of an egg being far higher than that in the nucleus [106, 373]. Even this quantity of RNA is too small in amount to cause the increase in protein synthesis. Further, inhibitors of mitochondrial RNA synthesis have no effect on the increase in protein synthesis rate and the proteins made in the eggs are not in the main mitochondrial.

Ballinger and Hunt [21] summarized the problem of identifying the cause of the increased protein synthesis as follows: 'it has been estimated that over 200 different components participate in protein synthesis; any of these components might be inactive or unavailable in unfertilized eggs'. One empirical approach has been to search for differences between the various components of the protein synthetic machinery in fertilized and unfertilized eggs. Very often, changes have been identified. However, this does not prove that these changes actually cause the increase in protein synthesis; they could be its consequence, or might even be incidental. A second, and more productive, approach has been to measure the efficiency of protein synthesis in intact eggs [50, 208]. This distinguishes the two main methods of translational control mentioned above, i.e. restricting the fraction of the mRNA which is available for translation on the one hand, and changing the efficiency of translation on the other. Measurements of translational efficiency were first reported by Humphreys [208, 209].

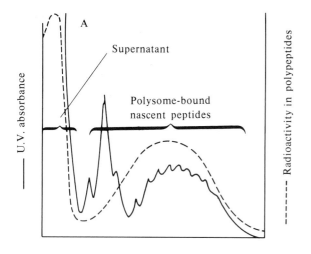

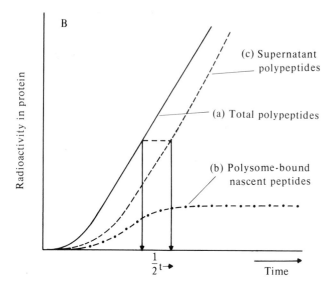

Fig. 6.4.10. Determination of polypeptide elongation rate by the method of Fan and Penman [126]. A: Embryos are incubated with radioactive amino acids for various times, fractionated on sucrose gradients and the radioactivity in nascent polypeptides bound to polysomes determined, as well as that of completed chains released into the supernatant fraction. B: These data are plotted as shown. At equilibrium the separation of curves (a) and (c) along the abscissa represents the time it takes the average amino acid in a nascent chain to complete its passage along the mRNA, i.e. half the total transit time of the ribosome across the mRNA.

Certain of his experiments were technically flawed, though giving essentially the correct conclusions. They have recently been repeated and refined [50, 191].

The first important observation made by these workers was that the size distribution of polysomes (i.e. number of ribosomes per average mRNA) is the same in unfertilized and fertilized eggs. Figure 6.4.9 shows that if the protein synthetic rate rises solely by an increase in the rate of polypeptide initiation, the polysome size increases; whereas if the rate of nascent peptide elongation rises, the polysome size decreases. A constant polysome size during an increase in protein synthetic rate of 10- to 100-fold can have one of two explanations.

(i) The rates of initiation or elongation rise, but are exactly counteracted by a change in the average size of polypeptide synthesized (an increase in the former case, and a decrease in the latter).

(ii) The rate of initiation and elongation could increase in precise concert, the effect of one on polysome size negating that of the other.

Possibility (i) has been eliminated by measuring the size of newly synthesized polypeptides before and after fertilization, either by analysing them using sucrose gradient centrifugation [208] or by SDS gel electrophoresis [50]. There is no significant change.

Possibility (ii) can be approached by measuring the rate of elongation. The two methods used were in excellent agreement [50, 191]. One is shown in Fig. 6.4.10. It was deduced that the ribosomes of the fertilized egg elongate polypeptides 2–2.5 times faster than those of unfertilized eggs. Since the polysomes remain the same size, the initiation rate must also rise by this factor. Thus possibility (ii) is correct, but since the rise in elongation rate is so small, it can account for only 2- to 2.5-fold of the 10- to 100-fold increase in the rate of protein synthesis which actually occurs after fertilization*. The remainder must come from the translation of mRNAs which were previously untranslatable. This increase in translated mRNA was measured directly by Humphreys [209]. It is sufficiently large to explain completely the observed increase in the rate of protein synthesis. Recently Raff *et al.* [351] designed a computer model to describe these changes. When the

---

*It might be thought that the two factors should be multiplied, but this is not so. If the rate of elongation rises, the effect is only to decrease commensurately the number of ribosomes per mRNA, unless free ribosomes are rate limiting. Except in the latter case, only changes in initiation affect the rate of protein synthesis.

observed rate of mRNA mobilization, the ribosomal transit time and the kinetics of change of radioactive amino acid pool specific activity were inserted into it, the model precisely fitted the kinetics of increase in protein-synthetic rate monitored in amino acid incorporation experiments.

An interesting prediction of this model is that the changes causing the increase in the rate of protein synthesis must occur within 0–2 min of fertilization, in spite of the fact that the increase takes 30 min and has been classified as a 'slow' response to fertilization [122]. The reason that it takes so long to accelerate the rate of protein synthesis is that elongation is very slow at the temperature of sea urchin eggs (16.5°C in these experiments). Since it takes about 20 min for ribosomes to traverse an mRNA, it takes at least this long for mRNAs to become fully loaded with ribosomes.

What agent brings about the increase in protein synthesis? This question may be divided into two parts: (a) what physiological effects link fertilization to the protein-synthetic apparatus? and (b) what changes in this apparatus cause the mobilization of stored mRNA and the increases in elongation and initiation rates?

The answer to question (a) seems to reside, at least in part, in a rapid rise in pH from 6.9 to 7.4 which occurs after fertilization [398]. Some evidence that this brings about the increase in protein synthesis comes from experiments with intact eggs. Thus it is possible to raise the intracellular pH of the unfertilized egg by incubation with NH_4Cl, because NH_3 enters the egg. This treatment alone activates protein synthesis, but not many of the other changes of fertilization. Conversely the rate of protein synthesis falls when the pH of fertilized eggs is lowered with CH_3COONa (see [463] for references). There is also evidence from cell-free systems that links pH change to protein synthesis. Winkler and Steinhardt [463] made a crude protein-synthetic system from unfertilized eggs, and found that it could be reversibly activated by raising the pH. However, the increase of rate was never to the same high level seen in extracts of fertilized eggs. Thus, it seems likely that the increase in pH is a major factor controlling protein synthesis, but that other changes are also necessary.

The complete answer to question (b) is still uncertain. The reason for the mobilization of the stored mRNA is probably that in unfertilized eggs it is inactivated by 'masking' proteins, i.e. proteins bound to the mRNA. This 'masked' message hypothesis [408] has been given

weight by more recent observations [214, 222], which indicate that the untranslated mRNPs of unfertilized eggs differ from those of polysomes in their ability to stimulate protein synthesis in a cell-free system. Unlike the latter, they need unphysiological ion concentrations for efficient translation. Since the mRNAs isolated from the two types of particle behave identically in the cell-free system, it must be the protein component which confers their different translatabilities.*

The reason for the increase in rate of initiation and elongation is more uncertain. A large number of components of the protein-synthetic apparatus change at fertilization. For example, one of the proteins of the small ribosomal subunit (rp 31) becomes heavily phosphorylated, through the disappearance of a phosphatase activity [21]. Although this happens in a wide variety of situations where the rate of protein synthesis increases, it is not clear that the phosphorylation is ever the direct cause of the increase. However, it has been shown that unfertilized egg ribosomes are less efficient at translating globin mRNA than those of fertilized eggs [98]. Other possible agents producing this effect are a large protein associated with unfertilized egg ribosomes [422] and a protein associated with unfertilized egg ribosomes that inhibited binding of amino-acyl-tRNA by embryo ribosomes [295]. These are all effects on the ribosome, but there have also been reports of change in elongation factors. Thus Felicetti et al. [128] reported that the activities of eIF1 and eIF2 increase within 2 min of fertilization. The list of these changes could be continued, but what is critically needed now are experiments capable of identifying which changes produce the twofold increase in protein-synthetic efficiency.

The phenomena outlined above undoubtedly play an important role in activating of the unfertilized egg, but a very important question concerns the specificity of the process. Are different mRNAs handled differently during the increase in rate of protein synthesis or is the rate of synthesis of every protein increased by the same factor? One approach to this matter is to examine the proteins made before and after fertilization using two-dimensional gel electrophoresis, the method giving the highest resolution available for the global analysis of proteins. By these means Brandhorst [49] was able to resolve 400 proteins made in fertilized eggs and only a

*Footnote added in proof. Recent experiments (Moon et al. (1982) Devl. Biol. **93**, 284–403) have shown these experiments to be invalid and have thus thrown the concept of protein masking into doubt.

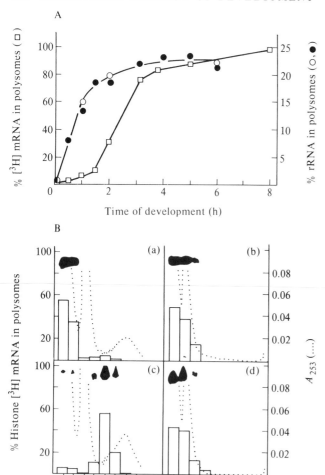

Fig. 6.4.11. A. Delayed appearance of histone [³H]mRNA after fertilization of sea urchin (*Strongylocentrotus purpuratus*) embryos. The origin is the time of fertilization. The increase in percentage rRNA in polysomes shows the mobilization of the bulk of mRNAs into polysomes; this begins immediately and plateaus after about 2h. On the other hand the mobilization of ³H-labelled histone mRNA scarcely starts for 105 minutes, and plateaus after about 4h. [³H]mRNA was measured by hybridization of filter-bound polysomal RNA to a cloned sea urchin gene (see B).
B. The untranslated [³H]mRNA is not bound to polysomes. Homogenized 1h (a and b) and 3.75h (c and d) embryos were centrifuged on sucrose gradients to reveal polysomes (A_{253} trace). Portions were spotted on to a nitrocellulose filter, hybridized to radioactive ³H-labelled gene sequences and autoradiographed. The dark patches in the upper part of each figure show the hybridization, which is quantified in the histogram. Clearly [³H]mRNA is in the supernatant of 1h embryos (a) and in polysomes in 3.75h embryos (c). Parts b and d confirm that the mRNA is present in embryos. The homogenate was treated with EDTA, which dissociates ribosomes thus releasing mRNA into the supernatant. (From [458].)

very few were not detected before fertilization. Thus the vast bulk of the increase in protein synthesis results from more rapid synthesis of proteins made previously at low rates. It is, however, incorrect to say that no individual mRNAs are handled differently from the bulk, since one class at least, the histone mRNAs, show a delayed increase in their translation [159, 458] (Fig. 6.4.11). The rate of elongation of nascent histone chains is constant during this period [159], as is the polysome size [159, 458]. Thus the increase in rate of histone synthesis must result from the release of stored histone mRNA from an untranslatable state and, since this release is delayed relative to typical mRNAs, different classes of mRNAs must be mobilized via distinct mechanisms.

Other organisms

The activation of protein synthesis seen in sea urchins is unusual in its abruptness. Similar examples are found in true dormancy situations, such as the germination of seeds and the hatching of *Artemia salina* 'eggs' (which are in fact arrested gastrulae of this attractive brine shrimp). In both these examples, hydration is the primary stimulus. In most developmental systems there is a much less pronounced increase in protein synthesis at fertilization, although over a long time-scale the rate changes may be just as great. An example is provided by amphibians. The rate of protein synthesis is low in amphibian oocytes [403] and only 1–2% of the ribosomes are engaged in polysomes at any given time [469].

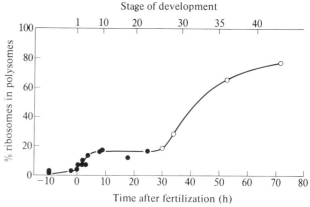

Fig. 6.4.12. Mobilization of stored ribosomes in *Xenopus laevis* development (23°C). The stages of development on the upper abscissa are taken from Nieuwkoop and Faber [317]. −10 hours is the full-grown oocyte, before progesterone induces it to become an egg (maturation) [469].

There is a several-fold increase in the rate of protein synthesis at maturation [443] and only a further 1.5-fold increase at fertilization [403], and these changes are paralleled by the increase in polysome content [469]. It is not until the late blastula stage, roughly 10 h after fertilization, that 15% of the ribosomes are engaged in protein synthesis [469] (Fig. 6.4.12). Thus the amphibian takes 10 h to reach the level achieved in 2 h by sea urchins. The mechanism of the increase has recently been investigated by Richter *et al.* [356], using the same kinds of approach described above for sea urchins, and again it seems that increased availability of mRNA, not increased efficiency of translation, is responsible.

Similar behaviour is seen in a range of marine invertebrates (see [99] for detailed examples). For example, in the surf clam, *Spisula solidissima*, maturation of the oocyte is triggered by fertilization and is accompanied by an abrupt increase in protein synthesis, but its magnitude is small, the polysome content increasing by only twofold [28, 131]. In all examples, increases in protein synthesis are associated with increases in polysome content, so the mobilization of stored mRNA, rather than changes in protein-synthetic efficiency, is almost certainly the main process involved.

Mammals might be considered the organisms least likely to show this pattern of behaviour. The small size, high temperature and slow divisions of their eggs would suggest that direct nuclear control of protein synthesis should be possible. However, only 19% of their ribosomes are present in polysomes in the oocyte, more than in amphibians but there is still a substantial reserve of protein-synthetic capacity [17]. The stored ribosomes may be incapable of protein synthesis at this time and apparently they are only slowly mobilized after fertilization [123]. Of course, mammals have evolved from ancestors with large external eggs and they appear not to have forgotten that they were once reptiles! It is not surprising that they retain some of the biochemical features of these ancestors, just as they retain many of the morphological features of their development (e.g. primitive streak gastrulation).

Translational control of specific proteins

The fact that the majority of organisms do not show large, abrupt changes in the overall rate of protein synthesis does not mean that important translational control events do not occur. It is often found that there are switches in the types of proteins made, and that these are not dependent on new gene transcription.

A good example is provided by mammals (the morphology of early mammalian development is illustrated in Fig. 2.4.4). The 2-cell mammalian embryo shows the abundant synthesis of a number of proteins only slowly made in oocytes, including a group of 35 000 mol. wt polypeptides. These accelerate synthesis as usual when mRNA transcription is blocked with α-amanatin [51] and in enucleated eggs [340]. It is therefore not surprising to find that their mRNAs were already present in the unfertilized egg, as judged by the translation of purified, deproteinized RNA *in vitro* [51, 81, 389].

The molecular basis of this delayed mobilization of specific maternal mRNAs has been more thoroughly examined in other organisms. In the last section we mentioned experiments on untranslated mRNP particles in sea urchins which indicated, though did not rigorously prove, that the protein component was responsible for their failure to translate. We also mentioned that the stored histone mRNA was delayed in its mobilization relative to average mRNAs. Presumably, the protein component of the mRNPs was responsible for this delay.

A similar situation exists in *Spisula*. It will be recalled that a modest increase of protein synthesis occurs at fertilization in this organism, but this masks considerable changes in the relative amounts of proteins made. In particular, the synthesis of three proteins that were scarcely made in the oocyte becomes very rapid [370]. Pure RNA made from the pre- and post-fertilization stages programmes the synthesis of identical proteins when added to a rabbit reticulocyte cell-free system. The mRNAs encoding these proteins are present as untranslated mRNPs in the unfertilized eggs, and these mRNPs cannot be translated by the reticulocyte system. This was shown by mixing the reticulocyte system with lightly centrifuged supernatants from *Spisula* embryos at various stages of development; the proteins made corresponded to those seen in the intact embryos of the appropriate stage. Mixing oocyte and unfertilized egg extracts in different proportions before adding them to the cell-free system resulted in synthesis of oocyte and unfertilized-egg proteins in the same proportions. This suggests that oocytes do not contain factors that inhibit the synthesis of proteins specific to the fertilized egg, but rather that the egg mRNAs have inhibitors bound to them. Since the untranslated mRNA is known to be bound to protein, it seems very likely that this protein inhibits the translation of the mRNA. Experimentally, this inhibition can be relieved by deproteinization of the particles with phenol plus detergents, but in the fertilized egg some more gentle and discriminating process must obviously operate. An agent like a protein kinase is a good candidate [282]. It could well be imagined that introducing negative phosphate groups on to a protein could dissociate it from an RNA. If so, there must be several kinases or some other such means of activating various mRNAs at different times.

Another developing system in which translational control shows specificity is in the regulation of histone synthesis during *Xenopus laevis* development [1, 470]. Figure 6.4.13 shows that the rate of nucleosomal-core (non-H1) histone synthesis rises about 50-fold during oocyte maturation and a further two- to threefold during development through the blastula (stages 7–9) to the gastrula stage (stages 10–12). The synthesis of histone H1 also rises, but this is delayed until the morula stage (stages 6–7). These changes are all the results of translational control. This can be shown in a number of

ways. First, Actinomycin D fails to inhibit the rise in core nucleosomal histone synthesis at maturation, and the rise also occurs in enucleated oocytes [2]. Secondly, histone mRNA levels, measured by translation *in vitro*, remain roughly the same during the entire period [374]. Thirdly, it is possible to use interspecific hybrids to show that the rise in H1 histone synthesis seen in the blastula results from the mobilization of stored maternal mRNA [472].

The third experimental approach will be described in detail because it has other uses; for example, we will use it to show how long amphibian maternal mRNA persists to programme early development (section 6.4.9). It relies on the observation that the H1 histones of *Xenopus laevis* and *X. borealis* can be separated by electrophoresis, and that the two species form a fully viable hybrid. When a *Xenopus laevis* egg is fertilized with a *Xenopus borealis* sperm it is therefore possible to determine when new H1 gene action becomes detectable, i.e. when the paternal type of H1 first appears (there can be no significant mRNA store in a sperm). This occurred at the 1000–10000 cell blastula stage, about 6 h after fertilization, and it is the earliest stage at

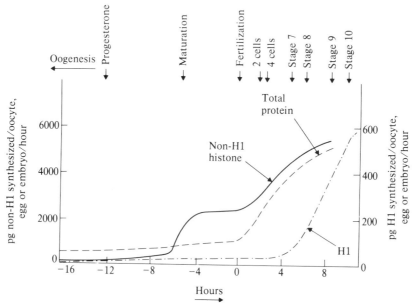

Fig. 6.4.13. Changes in the rate of histone synthesis in *Xenopus laevis* development. The period covered is from oogenesis, a period of 6 or more months, to gastrulation, when 30 000 cells are present. The total protein synthetic rate is computed from the polysome content and is shown on an arbitrary scale. Its approximate value can be judged from the observation that about 10% of protein synthesis in the unfertilized egg is histone [470].

which there would be enough genes for the paternal H1 protein to be detected, bearing in mind the calculations described in the first part of this section. However, histones are made before this and are of the maternal type. Proof that this is not the result of activation of the maternal before the paternal genes was obtained as follows. The *X. laevis* egg was fertilized with an *X. borealis* sperm, and then U.V.-irradiated at the animal pole. This destroyed the *X. laevis* nucleus and hence all of the *X. laevis* H1 genes. The developing androgenetic haploid embryo therefore had genes exclusively of the *X. borealis* type and stored mRNA which was wholly of the *X. laevis* type. Therefore, any *X. borealis* H1 histone that was made must have been the result of new gene transcription, and any *X. laevis* H1 histone must have been made on the stored maternal mRNAs. It was found that the first H1 histone made was exclusively of the maternal type (see Fig. 6.4.14). This shows that the rise in H1 synthesis at the early blastula stage (Fig. 6.4.13) is fuelled by stored maternal mRNA.

Control of protein synthesis by differential mRNA translatibility

Reticulocytes contain more α-globin than β-globin mRNA, yet they make approximately equal amounts of the two globins [267]. This is because the α-globin mRNA is less efficient in binding ribosomes to initiate new polypeptide chains than is the β-globin mRNA. This is a conclusion based on the observation that α-globin is made on smaller polysomes than β-globin, although the proteins are similar in size [213] and elongation of the polypeptides occurs at the same rate [212] (the argument is the same as that presented in Fig. 6.4.9). This seems a peculiar situation, but the lower efficiency of α-globin chain initiation might have evolved to compensate for the fact that there are two α-globin genes, compared to one of β. Equal transcription of these produces an imbalance of mRNA.

Lodish [266] pointed out that if two mRNAs differ in their efficiency of polypeptide initiation, changing the overall rate of initiation or elongation will change the proportions of the two proteins that are made. He illustrated this with experiments on α- and β-globin. Thus, lowering the overall rate of initiation reduces the proportion of α-globin made, and reducing the rate of elongation increases it. There is no reason to believe that the ratios of the two globins is ever naturally controlled

in this way, indeed it is hard to see what purpose it would serve. However, other proteins might be, especially since in early development there are changes in the general efficiency of protein synthesis (last section). An effect like this has been described by Alton and Lodish [3] in the morphogenesis of *Dictyostelium discoideum*. During the first minutes of differentiation the efficiency of polypeptide initiation falls drastically. At the same time synthesis of five polypeptides ceases, even though their mRNAs persist in a form translatable *in vitro*. It is likely that the reason for this fall is that the mRNAs show relatively poor initiation. However, most of the changes in protein synthesis during later differentiation are actually produced by changed mRNA content [4].

mRNA-specific changes in protein synthesis that are not involved in cell differentiation

There are a number of situations where there are dramatic translational control effects which have no direct role in differentiation, even though they may occur in differentiating cells.

One of these concerns histone synthesis in cultured animal cells and may occur wherever cell division is of comparatively high rate. In these conditions most histone synthesis is restricted to the S phase of the cell division cycle, and if DNA synthesis is inhibited, histone mRNA rapidly disappears from the polysomes [231]. Exactly the same happens in yeast [188]. Although cell-free systems have been made in order to investigate this effect further [53], extracts of normal and inhibited cells had the same capacity to translate histone mRNA, so the control system does not survive the extraction procedures.

This is not true in the second situation, which is the effect of heat shock on *Drosophila*. In section 6.4.11 we describe how heat shock brings about a dramatic change in the proteins made by all *Drosophila* cells and tissues, partly through the transcription of a number of specific genes. However, the dramatic initial change in protein synthesis is produced by halting translation of the bulk of cellular mRNAs, which cease binding ribosomes and persist undegraded in the cell [306]. Cell-free systems made from normal cells translate normal mRNAs and those of the heat-shock genes equally well, but the latter are preferred by an extract of heat-shocked cells [412]. The factor responsible seems to be bound to ribosomes [341].

Does translational control ever determine the proteins made by a differentiated cell?

Hypothetically, one extreme type of cell differentiation is that in which each and every cell receives all possible mRNAs but translates only those appropriate to its specialized state. There is no evidence for this, even in a partial form, although it is not formally possible to show that it *never* occurs.

If this type of translational control existed it would mean that the ability to translate particular kinds of mRNAs would appear during the differentiation of particular types of cell. Evidence against this has been obtained by injecting oocytes or eggs of *Xenopus* with mRNAs encoding proteins characteristic of specialized cells [174, 253]; in every case the mRNA was translated. Thus oocytes or eggs injected with globin mRNA translate it efficiently, making globin for a protracted period (over 2 weeks in the case of the oocyte [176]); this globin is a substantial proportion of protein made. Fertilized eggs continue to make globin as they develop, even when they have become swimming tadpoles [180], and globin is made in regions that have differentiated into nonerythroid cells [475]. Not only does the capacity to translate specialized mRNAs exist before differentiation but so does the ability to modify the polypeptide in the appropriate way (e.g. to cleave it, phosphorylate or acetylate it [253]) and to transport it to the appropriate site in the cell, for example in order to secrete it [87, 423].

All of these experiments argue against the fundamental importance of translational control in determining the direction of cell differentiation. There are, however, situations in which mRNAs encoding specialized proteins have been reported as being made some time before their translation begins. For example, Robbins and Heywood [359], who studied the differentiation of myoblasts to form skeletal muscle, found that myosin mRNA was stored for a short time, and that its translation became rapid when the myoblasts fused. Processes like this appear to control the timing of translation and not the population of cells that make a particular protein. It is possible that the mechanism is similar to that of mRNA storage in oocyte.

One situation in which post-transcriptional mechanisms appear to control the synthesis of a cell-specific protein in early development is in ascidians [459]. As indicated in Fig. 2.4.2, alkaline phosphatase appears specifically in the endoderm cells, and it appears in cells of this lineage even when RNA synthesis is blocked with a variety of inhibitors. The mechanism remains to be established, but it is likely that it involves storage of the mRNA and its segregation to the appropriate cells. If so, true translational control is not the mechanism which actually restricts alkaline phosphatase synthesis to endodermal cells. Nevertheless, it is very important to find out if there is segregation of stored mRNAs to cells of different lineages. It has been reported that the micromeres of 16-cell sea urchin embryos contain different mRNA populations from the rest of the embryo [124, 362]. Localization is one possible explanation of this phenomenon, but its significance is unclear, since micromeres and other cells seem to synthesize the same 1000 most abundant polypeptides [420].

6.4.9   CONTROL OF PROTEIN SYNTHESIS THROUGH mRNA STABILITY

mRNA stability during terminal differentiation

The proteins synthesized by cells will not reflect rates of gene transcription unless all mRNAs have the same stability. There is evidence that this is not the case.

A good example is provided by red blood cell differentiation. In its later stages the non-nucleated mammalian reticulocyte synthesizes little but haemoglobin, but this is not true of young reticulocytes. In the latter a protein of mol. wt 64 000 called I constitutes 10% of the protein which is synthesized, and its synthesis is not detectable in late reticulocytes. Since translatable protein I mRNAs are not detectable and the cell lacks a nucleus, it follows that protein I mRNA must be less stable than the mRNA encoding globin [268]. A similar conclusion has been reached regarding β- and δ-globin mRNAs [467]. In adult human erythrocytes the ratio of β- to δ-globin content is 40:1. This is not because β mRNA is translated much more efficiently than δ mRNA or because little δ mRNA is transcribed, but mainly because δ mRNA is less stable. This is known because younger reticulocytes contain more δ mRNA.

There is also evidence that the relative stability of mRNAs can change during differentiation. This happens in red blood cells, at least as judged by the Friend-cell model system [270]. Similar hints of changes in the stability of mRNAs in differentiating slime moulds are seen when their development is perturbed [285]. When *Dictyostelium* amoebae aggregate, they synthesize a set of 2500 mRNAs specific to aggregated cells, as well as retaining about 4500 present before. Both have half-lives of at least 3 h, but if the cells are artificially disaggregated then the former disappear with a half-life of 25–40 min, whereas the conserved RNAs remain. Directly analogous is the way that ovalbumin mRNA disappears from the oviduct when oestrogen is withdrawn [326]. Effects like these have frequently been found when searched for, and thus must have ubiquitous effects on the protein composition of differentiated cells.

Stability of mRNA in early development

Stability of mRNA also affects the protein-synthetic capacity of the early embryo. A simple question that may be asked is how this stability affects the time that maternal mRNA persists to influence early development.

The stability of stored maternal histone H1 mRNA in *Xenopus* embryos may be deduced from the experiment shown in Fig. 6.4.14. It will be recalled from section 6.4.8 that in androgenetic haploid embryos of *Xenopus laevis* (♀) and *Xenopus borealis* (♂), newly synthesized H1 mRNA directs only the synthesis of *X. borealis* H1

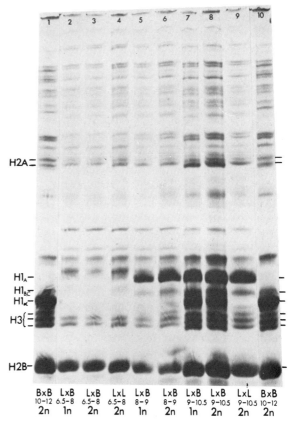

Fig. 6.4.14. H1 histone gene expression in hybrids of *Xenopus laevis* (L) × *X. borealis* (B). The Figure shows electrophoresis on Triton/acetic acid/urea gels. H1$_{A,B,C}$ are *X. laevis* H1 histones and H1α is *X. borealis*. The 1n embryos were prepared by UV irradiating the *laevis* eggs soon after irradiation with *borealis* sperm, thus destroying the *laevis* nucleus. In these embryos *X. laevis* H1 histone is made on stored maternal mRNA and *X. borealis* on newly-synthesized mRNA. The stage of development is shown at the bottom of the track. H1 synthesis is indetectable till the blastula stage (st 8). Paternal gene expression is in full swing at gastrulation (st 10), as is translation of the stored *laevis* mRNA. The synthesis of the maternal H1 disappears in the hybrid haploid mid-gastrula (st 11–12). From [472].

histone, whereas stored maternal H1 mRNA directs only that of *X. laevis* H1. Figure 6.4.14 shows that, whereas in the early blastula most of the H1 was made on stored templates, by the mid-gastrula (stage 11) translation of stored, maternal H1 mRNA was not detected. This almost certainly means that the maternal H1 mRNA had been destroyed by this stage, about a dozen hours after fertilization [472]. In normal adult cells, histone mRNA is degraded at the end of each S phase [336]. It is possible that this pattern of stability, quite different from that seen at earlier stages, becomes established in the gastrula. Other histone mRNAs probably behave in the same way as H1, although in frogs they have been studied only by micro-injecting sea urchin histone mRNAs into oocytes or fertilized eggs [476, 477]. These studies showed a half-life of about 3 h, quite independent of the cell cycle. The same pattern of stability is found in sea urchins [315, 462] and in *Drosophila* [8]. In the latter, the stability of histone mRNA falls even further as development proceeds. Mouse embryos are likely to provide an exception, since histone synthesis is tightly coupled to DNA synthesis in the 2-day (16-cell) embryo [290]. However, as we shall see below, the stored maternal mRNA is lost by the 2-cell stage, so the crucial experiments here should be done on 1-cell embryos.

However, it must not be thought that all mRNAs are as unstable as those encoding histones. In identical experiments to those in which maternal H1 mRNA was shown to disappear by the mid-gastrula stage of *Xenopus*, Woodland and Ballantine [471] found that another maternal mRNA persisted to the late neurula stage. Applying an entirely different strategy to another frog, *Engystomops pustulosus*, Hough *et al.* [201] showed that radioactive maternal messenger-like RNA synthesized during the lampbrush stage of oogenesis survived to the tadpole stage. Unfortunately, there is no evidence that this was mRNA, but the result still emphasizes that in early developmental stages RNAs can have different stabilities, and therefore that this must be taken into account when attempting to correlate transcription and protein synthesis. In sea urchins, half of the oocyte mRNA sequence types are still represented in the gastrula, even though they are continuously degraded. This is because they are replaced by further synthesis [143]. Here the stabilities of different mRNAs may be similar [315]. If this is correct, then it is the rates of transcription, processing and exit of finished

mRNA from the nucleus that determine mRNA levels in the cytoplasm.

In the mouse the stored maternal mRNA disappears by the end of the 2-cell stage, and this probably applies to every sort of mRNA. Thus enucleated embryos [340] or those treated with α-amanitin [223] cease protein synthesis at the end of this stage, and the content of poly(A)$^+$ RNA and poly(A) is minimal in untreated embryos [17, 258, 343]. Even globin mRNA, which is very stable when injected into *Xenopus* embryos [180], ceases globin synthesis at the 2-cell stage when injected into the mouse egg [59].

Disappearance of maternal mRNA at the 2-cell stage seems 'early' when judged by morphology. But the second division occurs 35 h after fertilization, when *Xenopus* would be a tail-bud tadpole and the sea urchin a swimming gastrula.

6.4.10 SELECTIVE PROCESSING OF TRANSCRIPTS AND THEIR TRANSPORT FROM THE NUCLEUS

In section 6.4.5 the results were presented of measurements of the complexity and abundance classes of mRNA populations. A number of important conclusions were drawn about the spectrum of mRNAs appearing in cells at different stages of development and in various differentiated states. Among these conclusions it was noted that during development of the sea urchin the spectrum of expressed genes is clearly specific for each stage and tissue, but the overlap between these different spectra of mRNA populations is considerable.

In searching for the mechanism by which these differences in the mRNA populations arise, we have two further extreme possibilities to consider. (i) Does the mRNA spectrum in the cell simply reflect control of gene transcription? (ii) Is there in fact no transcriptional control, all genes being transcribed in all cells, with regulation operating by selection of some transcripts for processing and export to the cytoplasm, and the remaining transcripts being degraded within the nucleus?

It has been known for many years that most of the newly synthesized hnRNA is broken down in the nucleus and never reaches the cytoplasm [181]. The significance of this in distinguishing between the two possibilities was for a long time problematical because

Table 6.4.8. Minimum primary transcript size compared with mRNA size for various class II genes.

Gene	mRNA size (nucleotides)	Minimum primary transcript size (nucleotides)	Ratio	Ref.
β-globin (rabbit)	589	1295	2.2	425
β-globin major (mouse)	620	1382	2.2	416
Rat preproinsulin I	443	562	1.3	269
Rat preproinsulin II	443	1061	2.4	269
Chick ovalbumin	1859	7500	4.0	360
Chick ovomucoid	883	5600	6.3	82
Chick lysozyme	620	3700	6.0	20
Chick pro-α 2 collagen	5000	38 000	7.6	479
Xenopus vitellogenin A1	6300	21 000	3.3	437
Xenopus vitellogenin A2	6300	16 000	2.5	437
Mouse dihydrofolate reductase	1600	42 000	26	322

the relationship between mRNA and pre-mRNA was not understood. The questions of whether hnRNA contained any pre-mRNA molecules longer than mature mRNA aroused considerable contention. This was complicated by the finding that putative long pre-mRNA molecules appeared to bear a 5′-cap and 3′poly(A), both of which were evidently conserved in mature mRNA. The situation was greatly clarified by the discovery of discontinuous genes. We now know that there are indeed long pre-mRNA molecules; they may be very much longer than the mature mRNA (Table 6.4.8). Processing of these pre-mRNAs by excision and subsequent degradation of intron sequences must account for at least a large part of the turnover of hnRNA. But the question remains as to whether this is sufficient to account for all of the turnover of newly transcribed sequences in hnRNA, or whether there is yet a component of that turnover which arises from possibility (ii). We should bear in mind the finding that in sea urchin embryos (blastula, gastrula), for example, the proportion of newly synthesized hnRNA converted to mRNA is only about 4% by mass, and should compare this with the ratios in Table 6.4.8 (admittedly, these ratios may be biased by the nature of the genes investigated in detail to date).

Complexity of hnRNA

The complexity of hnRNA can be determined by a variety of approaches. Just as with poly(A)$^+$-mRNA, cDNA reverse transcripts derived from nuclear poly(A)$^+$ RNA can be used as tracer in an RNA-driven R_0t analysis [151] and, just as with poly(A)$^+$-mRNA, this approach is subject to the limitations previously described (see section 6.4.5). A more satisfactory approach uses single-copy DNA as tracer in an RNA-driven reaction [200]. Experiments with both approaches lead to estimates, in a variety of cells, of the hnRNA complexity that are about five to ten times greater than the complexity of the polysomal mRNA in the same cells. In sea urchin embryos 28.5% of the sequence complexity of the genome is represented in the nuclear RNA [200], compared with only about 2.8% represented in polysomal mRNA [140], and all of the sequences present in mRNA are present in the hnRNA population [464].

Control by post-transcriptional selection for export to cytoplasm

The fact that the hnRNA complexity is so much higher

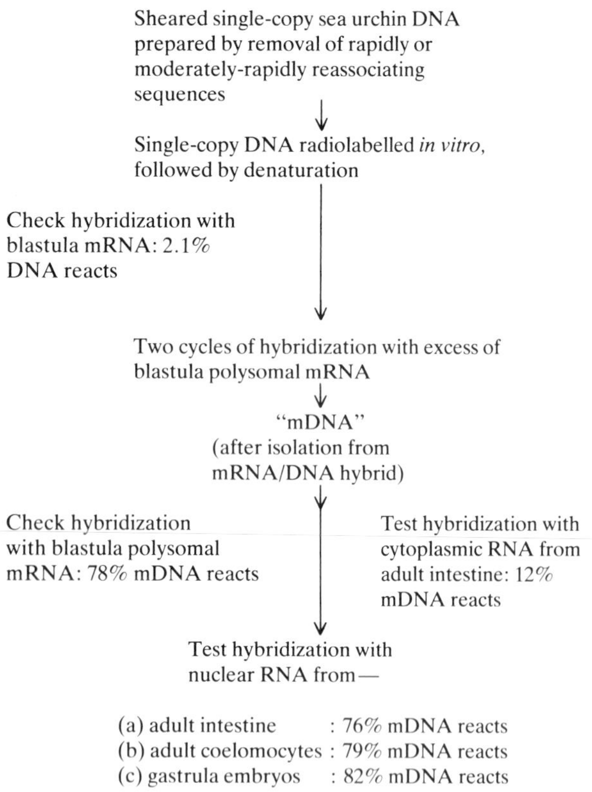

Sheared single-copy sea urchin DNA
prepared by removal of rapidly or
moderately-rapidly reassociating
sequences

↓

Single-copy DNA radiolabelled *in vitro*,
followed by denaturation

Check hybridization with
blastula mRNA: 2.1%
DNA reacts

↓

Two cycles of hybridization with excess of
blastula polysomal mRNA

↓

"mDNA"
(after isolation from
mRNA/DNA hybrid)

Check hybridization
with blastula polysomal
mRNA: 78% mDNA reacts

Test hybridization with
cytoplasmic RNA from
adult intestine: 12%
mDNA reacts

↓

Test hybridization with
nuclear RNA from—

(a) adult intestine   : 76% mDNA reacts
(b) adult coelomocytes : 79% mDNA reacts
(c) gastrula embryos   : 82% mDNA reacts

Fig. 6.4.15. Sea urchin embryo mRNA sequences are expressed in nuclear RNA of adult tissues not expressing the mRNA in their cytoplasms [464].

than that of polysomal RNA is of course un-expected. The crucial question remains as to whether any of the difference is accountable to possibility (ii), outlined above. According to the studies by Galau *et al.* [142] and Hough-Evans *et al.* [202] mentioned in section 6.4.5 during the discussion of mRNA populations, only a minor fraction of the sea urchin embryo mRNA set is expressed in the mRNA of three adult tissues. Wold *et al.* [464] built on these observations in making the following critical test. They asked if message sequences are present in nuclear RNA, not only in tissues which utilize these messages in their polysomes, but also in tissues which do not. A radioactive single-copy DNA tracer highly enriched for sequences complementary to blastula embryo RNA was prepared and used to detect nuclear transcripts in various adult tissues. The results show that virtually all of the blastula mRNA sequences are indeed present in the nuclear RNAs of mature

tissues (see Fig. 6.4.15). This series of results therefore suggests that control of sea urchin gene expression occurs at least partially by post-transcriptional selection of transcripts for export to the cytoplasm.

How does the selection occur? At the present time we do not know. In section 6.4.4 three examples of possible selective processing events have already been described: selective removal of introns in undifferentiated terato-carcinomas, possible selective processing to generate membrane-bound and secreted IgM heavy chains, and possible selective processing of α-amalyase transcripts. Whether any of these can be thought of as prototypes for generally applicable mechanisms remains to be seen.

A word of caution is necessary lest we unjustifiably generalize from the results of investigations of sea urchin development. The strategy of their development, as we have seen for the adult tissues tested, is to reduce drastically the number of polysomally expressed genes with increasing specialization of the tissues (Table 6.4.4; Fig. 6.4.7), and this is brought about by post-transcriptional selection. Equally comprehensive investigations of RNA populations in mammalian development have not been undertaken, but there is an apparent difference from sea urchin development in that there is not a generalized reduction in mRNA complexity with increasing specialization. Mammalian liver, for example, is composed of relatively few cell types (the majority are parenchymal cells, also called hepato-cytes), but mouse liver has a mRNA complexity of 21 000 kb, equivalent to about 10 500 mRNA types. In the next section, evidence will be presented for trans-criptional control of at least the class of moderately abundant mouse liver-specific mRNAs.

6.4.11 REGULATION OF TRANSCRIPTION

From evidence presented in preceeding sections it has been possible to conclude the following.
(i) Certain structural genes for 'household' functions appear to be transcribed in all cell types and are present in the mRNA of all cell types.
(ii) In sea urchin development, the experimental system which has been investigated most thoroughly in this context, some structural genes appear to be transcribed in all cell types, but are expressed in the polysomes of only some cell types.

In this section first we present evidence for the following additional conclusion.

(iii) Certain genes are actively transcribed only in tissues which are also expressing them in polysomal mRNA. They are not transcribed in other tissues. In other words, these genes are under transcriptional regulation.

This evidence comes mostly from analysing transcription of highly abundant or moderately abundant mRNAs in terminally differentiated cells. Before reviewing this evidence, it is worth noting that there are sequences in the genome which are invariably non-transcribed. The most often quoted examples are satellite sequences, even although transcription of certain satellite sequences has been detected in two exceptional cases, both occurring in lampbrush chromosomes of amphibian oocytes [107, 431]. It has been suggested that the transcriptional units of lampbrush chromosomes, which are exceptionally long (often 10 μm of loop axis, equivalent to 33 kbp assuming a packing ratio of 1.1:1 for DNA in the chromatin), are abnormal in resulting from a general extended relaxation of transcriptional termination. In the case of the satellite 1 sequences of the amphibian *Notophthalmus* there is evidence that transcription of the satellite is a consequence of read-through from adjacent histone-gene clusters [107]. In view of the notion, discussed previously, that termination may generally be a process occurring well downstream from polyadenylation sites, it might be valid to regard transcription in lampbrush chromosomes as exhibiting an extreme manifestation of this general phenomenon. We do not even know the significance of transcription in lampbrush chromosomes [5, 415]. This transcription is very active, with RNA polymerase molecules densely packed on the chromatin [5, 190], and yet it is evident that the mRNA which accumulates in oogenesis is made predominantly at stages preceeding maximum lampbrush transcriptional activity [368].

Observations of differential gene transcription in polytene chromosomes

In the salivary glands and other tissues of dipteran flies, especially in the larval stages, interphase chromosomes are displayed in an enlarged form in which they are much longer and thicker than metaphase chromosomes. This is a consequence of repeated endoreduplication of the interphase chromosomes in such a way that the many hundreds or (thousands) of chromatin strands remain in lateral register. In addition, the homologous pairs are synapsed. A manifestation of the maintenance of the lateral register of the chromosomes is the appearance of a distinctive pattern of bands in cytological preparations of these polytene chromosomes.

The number of bands in *D. melanogaster* polytene chromosomes is open to dispute, being dependent upon the level of resolution employed and the appearance of doublets, etc., but the figure usually quoted is about 5000 bands per genome [55]. Most of the DNA, estimates varying between 95% and 70% [26, 249], is in the bands, giving an estimate of about 30 kbp of DNA per band per haploid genome. Even before the band pattern of polytene chromosomes had been studied in detail, very conspicuous thickenings were observed in polytene chromosomes of *Chironomus*, where the thickenings are called Balbiani rings after their discoverer. In fact polytene chromosomes in all cells can form thickenings. This is the result of local decondensation of the chromatin, and may not always be so spectacular as Balbiani rings. These sites are known as puffs.

The correspondence between decondensed chromatin at puff sites and the sites of active RNA synthesis was demonstrated by Pelling [333] and Ritossa [358], who exposed salivary glands to the radioactive RNA precursor [³H]uridine and subsequently autoradiographed cytological preparations of the polytene chromosomes. The appearance of puffs can be prevented by actinomycin or α-amanitin, although regression of previously established puffs does not always follow such treatment [11].

The pattern of puffing is tissue- and stage-specific, as first shown by Beerman in *Chironomus* [25]. Some puffs only appear in certain tissues and there is a temporal series of changes during larval development. In *Drosophila*, most of the puffs are in fact stage-specific [12]. In addition, some puffs appear in response to environmental stimuli, such as heat shock (for review see [13]).

In view of the correspondence between RNA synthesis and the appearance of puffs, it would seem reasonable to suggest that the changes observed in the puffing pattern reveal gene regulation at the transcriptional level. This conclusion has been reinforced by studies of the heat shock response with cloned probes. Cloned DNA sequences which encode proteins induced by heat shock have been shown to hybridize with the corresponding mRNAs present in polysomes after heat shock, and to hybridize *in situ* to polytene chromosomes at the loci where puffs are induced by heat shock [195]. Thus the connection between transcription at these loci and the appearance of heat-shock proteins has been confirmed, giving a very clear demonstration of transcriptional regulation of the heat-shock response. This level of control operates in conjunction with translational control described previously in section 6.4.8.

Transcriptional control of gene activity, as revealed by changes in the puffing pattern of polytene chromosomes, is evident in the striking increases in puffing activity which occur around the time of larval moults (ecdysis). In the Diptera, moulting is under humoral control by ecdysone and juvenile hormone. In the presence of juvenile hormone, ecdysone release from the prothoracic glands results in the moults which characteristically separate larval instar stages. In the absence of juvenile hormone, which is produced by the corpora allata, the ecdysone triggers a more dramatic final moult leading to metamorphosis into the immobile pupa.

The role of ecdysone in causing changes in puffing has been demonstrated by injecting pure ecdysone into intermoult larvae. Puffs were induced at sites which normally are active just before moulting. Some of these puffs were induced very rapidly, within 15 minutes of hormone injection, while others appeared after a delay of several hours [86]. A similar biphasic pattern was observed when isolated salivary glands were incubated with ecdysone [10]. It has been suggested that the hormone has a rather direct effect upon transcription at the loci where puffing is so rapidly induced. Such a suggestion is consistent with findings on the mode of action of other steroid hormones, which are known to bind to intracellular receptor proteins and enter the nucleus (Chapter 5.5) Gronemyer and Pongs elegantly demonstrated that the ecdysone-induced genes are directly activated (presumably by such a receptor complex) when they used immunofluorescence of an anti-ecdysone antibody to visualize the hormone specifically bound to puffs [164]. Puffs which are induced after a delay may be dependent upon gene products of the early loci.

Transcriptional regulation in vertebrate cells

In the nuclei of differentiated vertebrate cells there are no cytological manifestations of the transcription of individual genes as dramatic as the puffing of polytene chromosomes. Evidence of other kinds must be sought, and this evidence is most easily obtained by examining the expression of genes which are subject to spectacular changes in activity, i.e. genes which give rise to highly abundant mRNA in expressing tissue. Examples of such gene products are globin in red blood cells, the ovalbumin and conalbumin components of egg white in the stimulated chicken oviduct, and vitellogenin in the artificially stimulated liver of male *Xenopus*. In non-expressing tissues there is no mRNA for these differentiated products present in the cytoplasm.

One approach towards assessing whether such genes are under transcriptional regulation is to examine nuclear RNA from expressing and non-expressing tissues. Can gene transcripts be detected in the nucleus even if there are no mRNA molecules in the cytoplasm of non-expressing cells? Highly radioactive cloned DNA hybridization probes are available for detecting such nuclear transcripts. In general, using such radioactive probes to detect transcripts in nuclear RNA, it has been concluded that the steady-state concentration of the specific gene transcripts in the nuclei of non-expressing tissues is very low or below the limits of detection (which is less than one transcript per cell) [19, 170, 367].

The observation of a very low steady-state concentration of a gene transcript does not, however, prove that the gene is not being transcribed. There is the possibility that the gene is transcribed actively with the resulting transcript being very rapidly degraded. A different type of assay has therefore been employed. Groudine and Weintraub [170] decided to determine whether bound RNA polymerases could be detected on globin genes of non-expressing chicken cells. The non-expressing cells in these experiments were in fact precursor red cells. Nuclei were isolated from the precursor cells and from primitive erythroblasts synthesizing embryonic globin chains. Radioactive triphosphates were added to the nuclei, and the bound RNA polymerase molecules were allowed to elongate for 50–100 bases (1–2 min of synthesis *in vitro*). The synthesized RNA was isolated and then hybridized to a Southern blot of cloned embryonic β-globin DNA. Under comparable conditions, there was marked hybridization of the coding regions of the globin DNA with RNA synthesized by red cell nuclei, but no detectable hybridization with RNA synthesized by precursor cell nuclei. If rapid degradation were to be invoked as an explanation for these results, it would have to operate in isolated nuclei such that the globin transcripts have an improbably brief half-life of much less than 1 min. Therefore, it can be concluded that the globin gene in the non-expressing cells is transcriptionally dormant, with no bound RNA polymerase.

Are these results, obtained with a chicken globin gene, generally applicable? Using an approach similar to that of Groudine and Weintraub, it has been shown that a large set of cloned cDNA sequences, complementary to mRNA found only in mouse liver, hybridize to labelled RNA synthesized in isolated nuclei from liver only, but not to labelled RNA synthesized in isolated nuclei from other tissues [105]. These cloned cDNAs were, however, derived from abundant mRNAs, so that at present it cannot be concluded that transcriptional regulation operates for the majority of tissue- or stage-specific class II genes. The majority of these genes give rise to the low-abundance, complex class of mRNAs. As we have seen previously, regulation of this class of mRNAs involves a post-transcriptional mechanism in the development of the sea urchin. Thus it appears that both transcriptional and post-transcriptional nuclear mechanisms have been exploited in Nature for the control of differentiation and development.

6.4.12 WHAT MAKES GENES TRANSCRIPTIONALLY ACTIVE?

From evidence presented in preceding sections we have seen that a major part of gene regulation operates at the transcriptional level, and that this is especially true for genes encoding abundant proteins in terminally differentiated cells. In this section we discuss experiments designed to identify events that are at least necessary, if not sufficient, for the transcriptional activation of gene expression.

DNA rearrangement

Rearrangement of the DNA sequence in a eukaryotic genome can occur in a variety of ways which are essentially random in their effects. Transposition of transposable elements is an example of such a change. However, some DNA rearrangements are non-random in their location, may be restricted to particular stages of development or tissues, and are associated with gene activation. To date, the immunoglobulin genes provide the only known example in metazoan organisms of such

a directed rearrangement (see sub-section on transposable elements).

Individual antibody-producing lymphocytes synthesize a single type of functional light chain and a single type of functional heavy chain, which together form immunoglobulin molecules containing a pair of each type of chain (Fig. 6.4.16). Each heavy and light chain contains two functionally and structurally distinct regions; an amino-terminal variable (V) region that binds to antigen, and a constant (C) region responsible for immunological effector functions such as interaction with complement. The antigen-binding specificity is determined by the particular amino acid sequences of the variable regions of the heavy and light chains.

The genes for the expressed light and heavy chains are created by somatic rearrangement of separate germ-line gene segments (reviewed in [158]). These rearrangements are tissue-specific: they occur only in the lymphocyte cell-lineage. In the light-chain gene families, DNA rearrangement joins a V_L gene segment, encoding approximately the first 98 amino acids of the variable region, to a J_L gene segment, which encodes the remaining approximately 13 amino acids of the variable region. The germ-line DNA between V and J is deleted. The DNA between VJ and C is retained and forms an intron which is transcribed and ultimately removed from the pre-mRNA (Fig. 6.4.16). In contrast to the bipartite structure of a light-chain V gene, a complete heavy-chain V gene is formed by joining three DNA segments—V_H (approximately 99 codons), D (1–15 codons) and J_H (approximately 15 codons). The assembly of this complete heavy-chain V gene by two joining events also occurs by deletion of intervening germ-line DNA. The complex rearrangements of the regions have a crucial role in expanding the repertoire of antigen specificities beyond those that could be inherited in the germ-line.

In addition to these rearrangements, during differentiation of the B-lymphocyte to become a plasma cell, one heavy-chain C_μ gene may be substituted for another (C_γ, C_α, C_ϵ) without affecting the $V_H/D/J_H$ combination. This heavy-chain class switching involves a second type of rearrangement, utilizing tandemly repeated 'switch' sequences upstream from the C_H genes. By switching the heavy-chain constant regions in this way, immunoglobulins with the same antigen specificity, but different effector functions, are generated during the immune response.

(a)

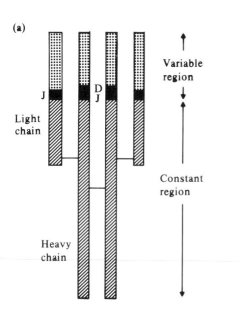

Variable region

Constant region

Light chain

Heavy chain

J

D J

Fig. 6.4.16.
(a) Schematic representation of an immunoglobulin molecule.
(b) The arrangement of immunoglobulin genes in mouse germ-line DNA. Note that each region may contain one or more introns which are NOT SHOWN.
There are 5 major classes of immunoglobulin (IgM, IgD, IgG, IgA, IgE). Some of these classes can be subdivided further, depending upon the animal species. In the mouse there are four IgG subclasses. Each class or subclass is distinguished by the nature of its heavy chain, designated by the corresponding Greek letter. Light chains are of two types, kappa and lambda, which can occur in all classes of immunoglobulin. In the diagram the kappa and lambda genes are drawn to the same scale. The heavy chain family is drawn to a different scale, with one region shown expanded. Distances are in kb. JHψ is a pseudo-J segment.
(c) Translocation of a kappa variable region gene during lymphocyte development. Note that there are multiple V$_\kappa$ and J$_\kappa$ segments.
(d) Switch in the class of heavy chain expressed from μ to α.
Adapted from Gough [158].

(b)

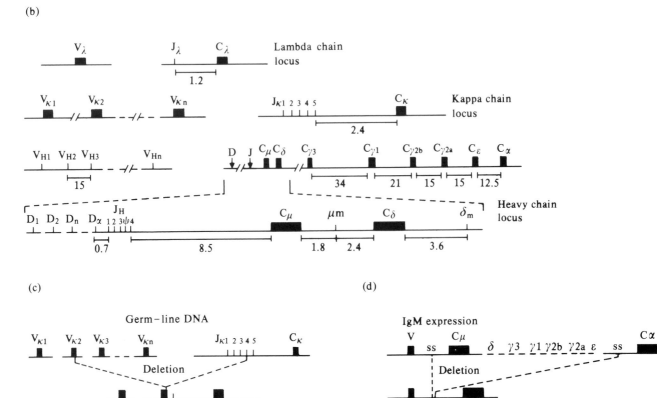

These rearrangements are, of course, essential for correct expression of the immunoglobulin genes, but do they play a key role in activation of the genes? Clues to this may come from a study of the phenomenon called allelic exclusion. This is apparent in the immunoglobulin system because each B cell expresses only one (i.e. either a maternal or paternal) antibody allele for a particular antibody polypeptide. The simplest explanation for allelic exclusion is that in individual B cells, gene-activating rearrangements can occur once only and hence affect only one of the two homologous chromosomes. However, antibody-gene rearrangements can occur on both homologous chromosomes, with only one rearrangement being productive in the sense of giving rise to a functional polypeptide [112]. There is presently some uncertainty about the transcription and nature of the rearrangements of the excluded allele; it appears that transcriptional activation is independent of gene rearrangement [337], but is closely correlated with the local methylation state of the DNA (next section, Table 6.4.9).

DNA methylation—regulatory signal in eukaryotic gene expression?

The genomic DNAs of most organisms contain modified bases. The only modified base found in higher eukaryotes is 5-methyl-cytosine (5 mC) (although other modified bases may be present in minute quantities); this results from the direct enzymatic transfer of the methyl group of S-adenosyl-methionine to cytosine residues already present in DNA. The frequency of occurrence of the methylated derivative relative to the unmethylated base in DNA varies over a wide range. It is 0.17 mole % in some insects, 2–8% in mammals and as high as 50% in some higher plants. Notably, *Drosophila* DNA appears to contain very few, if any, methylated cytosine residues [405].

In animal cells, most but not all of the 5 mC occurs in the dinucleotide sequence 5'-CG-3', with typically 50–70% of all such dinucleotides modified in any particular cell [426]. Furthermore, each methylated site contains two methyl groups symmetrically positioned on both complementary strands ($^5_G{}^{mC\text{-}G}_{\text{-}5mC}$). An indication of the occurrence within the genome of methylated and unmethylated CG can be obtained with restriction enzymes. This approach depends upon the chance discovery by Waalwijk and Flavell [435] that the

restriction endonuclease pair Hpa II and Msp I are isoschizomers and cleave the target sequence CCGG. These authors also made the important discovery that when the internal C-residue of the sequence is modified to CC̊GG by methylation, the endonuclease Hpa II cannot cut it, whereas the Msp I enzyme is indifferent to this modification and does cut it. The availability of this pair of isoschizomers makes possible the mapping of such methylated sites within the genome, as follows. Genomic DNA is cleaved either with Msp I or Hpa II and the resulting restriction fragments are separated on an appropriate gel electrophoresis system and transferred to nitrocellulose filters using the Southern blot technique [406]. By hybridizing these filters with highly radiolabelled cloned DNA probes, the fragmentation in and around specific gene sequences can be determined, and by comparison of the patterns obtained with the two enzymes, conclusions can be drawn about the state of methylation at all these CCGG sites. Of course, not all CG sites occur within the sequence CCGG, so that only a subset of potential methylation sites can be studied with this pair of isoschizomers. At present, the Hpa II/Msp I isoschizomeric pair is the only one available for detection of methylation in the way just described. However, several other restriction endonucleases are known which have target sequences including CG and which are sensitive to methylation of the C-residue. Using such enzymes, the distribution of methylated sites in and around a specific sequence can be studied by comparing digests of genomic DNA (visualized by probing Southern blots) with digests of the pure sequence cloned in *E. coli* (and therefore not methylated at these sites).

Undermethylation and gene activity

The application of restriction endonucleases gave the first support for the notion that DNA methylation in eukaryotes exerts a regulatory role in gene expression. In particular, numerous studies have shown a strong correlation between undermethylation and gene activation. For example, there is a tissue-specific association of undermethylation with activity of globin genes, the chicken ovalbumin gene and the expression of the J chain during B cell differentiation. On the other hand, abundant methylated sites are apparent in the DNA of sperm and early embryos (see Table 6.4.9.)

The study, by Groudine and Weintraub [170] of the

Table 6.4.9. Correlation of undermethylation and gene activity.

Gene(s)	Organism	Tissue or cell-type in which gene is active and undermethylated relative to other cells	Ref.
Globin	Friend erythroleukaemia cell (mouse)	Induction of differentiation	85
Globin	Rabbit	Red blood cell	397, 435
Globin	Man	Red blood cell	426
Globin	Chicken	Red blood cell	274, 453
Globin	Chicken	Embryonic red blood cell v. precursor cell	170
Ovalbumin	Chicken	Hormone-stimulated oviduct	283, 247
X (associated with ovalbumin)	Chicken	Hormone-stimulated oviduct	283
Y (associated with ovalbumin)	Chicken	Hormone-stimulated oviduct	283
Conalbumin	Chicken	Hormone-stimulated oviduct Undermethylation correlates with DNase I sensitivity	247
J chain*	Mouse	Cell lines representing antigen-stimulated lymphocytes	483
Cγ2b heavy chain	Mouse	Cell lines expressing IgG 2b	483
Ribosomal RNA	Mouse	Liver; heavily methylated and unmethylated genes present, but only unmethylated genes in chromatin sensitive to DNAse I	37
Ribosomal RNA	*Xenopus*	Loss of rDNA methylation in embryogenesis correlates with (presumed) onset of ribosomal gene activity	38, 34

*IgM antibody assembles into pentamers. This assembly requires a small protein, the J chain, which is incorporated in the ratio of one J chain to five IgM subunits. The J chain should not be confused with the J section of the variable region of light and heavy immunoglobulin chains.

activation of globin genes during chicken development is especially illustrative because a variety of approaches were adopted in studying events during the stages at which the genes become active. Haemoglobin first appears in the developing chick blastoderm at 35 h of development, in the primitive line of erythroid cells that appear as the blood islands of the area vasculosa. Red-cell precursors can be isolated from the presumptive red-cell-forming region of the embryo at 20–23 h of development, and these precursors were the subject of analysis in three ways.

(a) It was already known that the precursor cells contained less than 0.1 copy of globin RNA per cell. This had been determined using cloned hybridization probes labelled at very high specific radioactivity. The authors decided to extend this observation, asking whether bound RNA polymerases could be detected on the globin genes by adding radioactive triphosphates to isolated nuclei and then allowing bound polymerase to elongate existing RNA chains. Globin transcripts were assayed by hybridization to cloned globin DNA sequences. No transcripts were observed from precursor cell nuclei under conditions where red-cell nuclei gave a strongly positive result. This excludes the possibility that the globin genes were making previously undetected transcripts, e.g. very unstable or very heterogeneous in size.

(b) No DNase-I-hypersensitive site near the embryonic β-globin gene was apparent in the chromatin of precursor cell nuclei, whereas a hypersensitive site was readily detectable in the 5-day (embryonic) red-cell lineage (see section below on structure of active chromosomal regions).

(c) Finally, methylation at the CCGG sequences around the globin genes was analysed. In the case of active adult chicken globin genes in red cells these sites in globin-coding regions are entirely unmethylated, whereas sites in adjacent non-coding regions are heavily methylated [170]. The sites associated with the embryonic β-globin coding region were found to be more extensively methylated in precursor cells than in the erythroblasts of 5-day embryos which express the gene. In later developmental red cells, where this gene is not expressed, the sites are methylated. This reappearance of methylated embryonic genes in red cells at later developmental stages does not, however, necessarily imply a mechanism for the re-methylation of the DNA, since it is likely that the cells expressing adult genes are derived from precursor cells of a different lineage which never expresses embryonic globin genes. As expected, the adult α-globin genes and β-globin genes are highly methylated in precursor cells. These experiments therefore show not only a strong association between undermethylation and gene activity *per se*, but also uphold the association with other correlates of gene activity (see next section).

Methylation patterns and their inheritance

It is important to understand the mechanisms both for establishing methylation patterns in the genome and for their subsequent maintenance or loss. Riggs [357] and, independently, Holliday and Pugh [194] hypothesized that a methylation pattern, once established in somatic cells, could be inherited by progeny cells. They proposed that methylation of both DNA strands at CG sequences could be the result of a methylase which acts only at half-methylated sites as they arise upon semi-conservative replication of the DNA. Through the action of this 'maintenance' methylase, methylated sites would remain methylated, and unmethylated sites would remain unmethylated and hence the pattern of methylation would be clonally inherited.

Direct evidence for the passive maintenance of methylation patterns comes from studies involving the techniques of DNA-mediated transformation of cultured mammalian cells [345, 411, 461]. DNA molecules were methylated *in vitro* by the bacterial modification methylase M. Hpa II, which methylates the internal cytosine residues of the duplex CCGG sequence, and then these DNA molecules and their unmethylated controls were transferred into growing cells. Many generations later the methylation of the transforming DNAs, which had become integrated into the host chromosome, was examined by restriction endonuclease digestion and Southern blotting. Bacteriophage $\emptyset$X174 RF DNA, bacterial plasmid pBR322 DNA, the cloned thymidine-kinase gene from chicken and the cloned herpes-virus thymidine-kinase gene were used for the experiments. It was found that there was inheritance of the methylation patterns, except in some sites in the two thymidine-kinase genes. However, there had been selection for expression of these genes so that selection may have been imposed for loss of methylation.

The number and variety of cases in which undermethylation and transcriptional activity are correlated make a compelling case for a causal connection. But is undermethylation involved in permitting transcription, or is it a consequence of the conformational changes in chromatin which accompany transcription? In order to distinguish between these two possibilities a number of *in vitro* studies have been performed. Thus fragments of Adenovirus DNA have been methylated *in vitro* by M. Hpa II and microinjected into the nucleus of *Xenopus* oocytes, whereupon the synthesis of Adenovirus-2-specific RNA was monitored [428, 429]. The results provide direct evidence for the notion that methylation causes transcriptional inactivation.

The process of demethylation is not understood, but two mechanisms can be envisaged. Either methylation of the daughter DNA strand following DNA replication is inhibited (replicative demethylation), or methyl groups (or methylated bases) are removed enzymatically (enzymatic demethylation). The demethylation event need only occur once in each cell lineage in view of the evidence for clonal inheritance of the pattern by progeny cells. Thus a picture emerges of a master pattern of methylation existing in the germ-line cells and subsequently in the zygote. This is maintained intact in the germ-line for transmission to the next generation, but passed on to somatic cells in varying degrees according to a programme of demethylation. If demethylation occurs by the replicative mechanism, then DNA replication is a necessary prerequisite for gene activation. Such a requirement has been observed in a number of developmental systems [170, 196]. Some random loss of methylation might also be expected to result from an occasional failure of the maintenance methylase. This would result in a variable methylation pattern, which has been observed in some cell types. This picture implies that *de novo* methylation need not occur. Studies with DNA-mediated transformation using unmethylated DNA do indicate that *de novo* methylation is relatively infrequent [345, 411, 461]. Additionally, it has been found that there is very little or no methylation of Adenovirus-2 DNA in productively infected human cells, or of Adenovirus-12 DNA in abortively infected BHK21 cells [109, 430], so that either *de novo* methylation is rare in uninfected mammalian cells or the viruses have a mechanism for avoiding methylation. There is no doubt, however, that *de novo* methylation can occur, since it has been shown that both Adenovirus-2 and Adenovirus-12 DNAs can be extensively methylated when they are integrated into the genome of transformed cells [109]. Indeed, DNA methylases have been isolated from eukaryotic cells, but their biochemistry, and their substrate specificities in particular, are only just beginning to be characterized in detail.

Consistent with the picture of programmed demethylation during differentiation is the finding that 5-azacytidine is a potent agent affecting differentiation or gene expression in a number of experimental systems. The analogue carries a nitrogen atom at the 5-position of the pyrimidine ring and so when incorporated into eukaryotic DNA [225] it leads to a site which cannot be methylated. It has been found that 5-azacytidine induces myotube formation in mouse embryonic fibroblast cultures [89, 224], causes transcriptional activation of endogenous retrovirus loci in chick cells [169] and induces endogenous C-type virus formation in several mouse cell lines [318].

DNA methylation in the germ-line

In general, vertebrate genes are maximally methylated in sperm. Methylation in the DNA of the egg is difficult to study but indirect evidence [38] suggests that egg DNA may also be maximally methylated. As outlined above, a simple explanation of many observations would involve maximal methylation in the germ-line at all times. It would then be necessary for germ cells to be set aside during development before demethylation takes place. An alternative explanation would involve changes in methylation in germ-line cells with a mechanism for re-establishing or correcting the pattern during gametogenesis. Both explanations are compatible with the available observations. However, there are interesting consequences of the first explanation which are amenable to experimental test. These have been discussed by Bird [38] in the context of ribosomal-gene methylation.

In view of the correlations between hypomethylation and transcription, the question arises as to how germ cell DNA can be transcribed in gametogenesis (as it clearly must be, for example, in the lampbrush chromosomes of amphibian oocytes). The full answer to this problem is not clear but perhaps ribosomal genes have evolved a special mechanism. Thus in Amphibia it may be the case that fully methylated ribosomal genes in germ cell chromosomes are not transcribed whereas the extrachromosomal rDNA genes are active. Evidence for this comes from the following observations. The amplified rDNA appears in both sexes when there are only 9 to 16 primordial germ cells [228] and it persists during spermatogonial and oogonial multiplication [146, 329]. In oocytes a second, much larger wave of amplification subsequently occurs giving rise to extrachromosomal rDNA which is known to be hypomethylated. In *Triturus*, which has methylated chromosomal rDNA [36], Morgan *et al.* [308] found clearly detectable transcription at the amplified nucleoli, but the chromosomal sites of rDNA in the same nucleus showed no evidence of transcription. A test of this hypothesis may be provided by *Plethodon cinereus*, in which both the chromosomal and extrachromosomal rDNA appear to be active in oogenesis [434]. One would predict that in this organism the chromosomal rDNA is not highly methylated. (Ribosomal gene amplification is discussed in section 6.4.13.)

Concluding remarks on DNA methylation

In the foregoing discussion, clear examples have been presented of the involvement of methylation in transcriptional regulation of gene expression. However, the correlation between hypomethylation and activation does not hold invariably in all systems. Some notable instances will therefore conclude this section.

Early in embryonic development, one of the two X chromosomes is inactivated in the somatic cells of normal female mammals. It has been proposed that DNA methylation may play a role in this event [194, 357]. Experiments have been reported in which 5-azacytidine was shown to cause reactivation of HGPRTase located on an inactivated human X chromosome in a mouse–human somatic cell hybrid [307]. However, recent experiments with normal human fibroblasts have given no evidence for derepression of the inactive X upon treatment with the analogue. In addition, by using cloned DNA fragments unique to the X chromosome as hybridization probes in a restriction endonuclease analysis of methylation, it was concluded that overall methylation of the X chromosome is not the mechanism of inactivation [465].

The *Xenopus* 5S genes can be highly methylated as well as being transcriptionally active. Oogenetic 5S genes from somatic cells can be transcribed, despite their heavy methylation [296], when injected into oocyte nuclei [66, 241]. On the assumption that rapid demethylation of the injected DNA does not occur, then either methylation is irrelevant to the regulation of these genes or oocytes can override the effect of methylation that normally prevents transcription of these genes in somatic cells.

Finally, in *Drosophila*, no methylation has been detected at a very large number of Hpa II sites. In most tissues, at least, methylation is absent or very rare [405]. This implies that other mechanisms for achieving the same regulatory ends as methylation may be operating. Similarly, although sea urchin DNA has methylated and unmethylated regions, it appears that genes fall into the unmethylated component whether expressed or not—a component which remains constant from sperm through to differentiated tissues [39].

There is evidence that methylation of cytosine residues in DNA may fundamentally alter the structure of the double helix by favouring the transition from the B form to the Z form (left-handed DNA) [27]. There has been speculation that the B–Z transition is involved in gene regulation, and that the role of methylation in regulation is mediated through this transition. Antibodies against DNA in the Z-configuration have demonstrated clearly the occurrence of Z-DNA in the interband regions of *Drosophila* polytene chromosomes [320]. In *Drosophila*, 10–30% of the DNA is thought to be localized in the interband regions, but the precise relationship between the interbands and genes is unclear. It is not known if genes occur in bands, interbands or both. If *Drosophila* DNA lacks methyl groups it would appear that the B–Z transition in this organism must be controlled by a mechanism other than methylation, such as binding of proteins or small negatively charged molecules like spermidine, or through supercoiling. However, it is possible that the polytene chromosomes are a special case because, in contrast to restriction analysis of total *Drosophila* DNA, immunological techniques have revealed 5-methylcytosine in the polytene chromosomes [113].

Structure of active chromosomal regions

In recent years the structure of bulk chromatin has been revealed in some detail. It is now well known that DNA is usually wrapped around an octamer of two each of the four histones H2A, H2B, H3 and H4, forming a repeating structure containing approximately 200 base pairs of DNA. The histone octamers, or nucleosomes, are cross-linked by another histone, H1, to give a close-packed fibre, 10 nm in diameter, which is usually coiled upon itself to generate a 25 nm fibre in which the DNA is folded so that its length is reduced fivefold compared to free, extended, B-form DNA. This 25 nm fibre may be further folded to give higher orders of structure, the most compact of which is the metaphase chromosome, with a packing ratio of 5000–10000. There is no space here to discuss the generalities of chromatin structure; the reader is referred to the many excellent reviews which now exist (e.g. [129, 242, 261, 273]). However, we must consider possible special features of transcribed regions of the DNA in order to find out why some genes are active and others inactive.

Although methylation of cytosines may play a part in making genes active (see above), it is generally believed that the proteins associated with the DNA play the major role in this process. How do they do this? The first questions to be answered concern the basic structure of these active regions. In a given cell most DNA is inactive, and thus it is the structure of inactive DNA which is revealed when bulk chromatin is studied. Is active DNA organized into nucleosomes? If so, are these nucleosomes like those in inactive regions? These questions are by no means easy to approach and at present there are no definitive answers [292]. The main problem is obtaining active genes. Although a bulk, transcriptionally enriched chromatin fraction may be purified [157], rapid advances would be made if it were possible to isolate particular genes in an active and an inactive state, and in amounts sufficient for conventional chemical and physical analysis. Since a single gene represents only a millionth of the total chromatin this is not feasible, except to a limited extent for certain amplified genes like the ribosomal genes of amphibian oocytes and the protozoan *Tetrahymena* [189, 226, 227]. However, two other major approaches are viable; first, in certain favourable circumstances particular genes may be examined with the electron microscope and, secondly, chromatin may be digested with nucleases and DNA fragments from specific genes detected by electrophoresis followed by blot hybridization (cf. methylation).

Electron micrograph examination of active genes

The electron microscope gives two types of information. First it enables nucleosomes to be seen as 11–13 nm particles. However, the possibility that other proteins could give a similar structure must be borne in mind. Secondly, if a gene can be identified, its length in chromatin may be compared with that of the naked DNA. Typical nucleosomal DNA in the 25 nm fibre shows a packing ratio of about five. Unfortunately, interpretation of the data is not straightforward [292], because the technique of Miller usually used for spreading chromatin prior to EM examination partially unwinds the DNA, converting the 25 nm to the 10 nm fibre giving packing ratios of 1.6–2.5 (references in [292]). This makes interpretations of ratios in the range 1.1–2.0 uncertain.

The first necessity of the EM approach is to be able to recognize the gene. This has restricted the technique to only a few genes, of which ribosomal genes are the chief example. The regular, tandem repetition of these genes in very long series, coupled with their very high density of RNA polymerase I molecules bearing nascent rRNA chains, facilitates their ready recognition (Fig. 6.4.24; section 6.4.13). A variety of ribosomal genes yield packing ratios of about 1.1. Globular structures are usually present on them but, since they all bear nascent RNA chains, they must be polymerase molecules, not nucleosomes. In the early stages of amphibian oogenesis the amplified ribosomal genes are inactive (see section 6.4.13), but they may still be recognized because the extrachromosomal genes are present in extrachromosomal nucleoli and sometimes as small circles. In this state the genes are packed with typical nucleosomes [382]. Thus loss of nucleosomes seems to be prerequisite for activity of ribosomal genes; it is not, however, a sufficient cause of this activity. For example, Foe [133] found loss of nucleosomes from the ribosomal genes of *Oncopeltus* embryos some time prior to the activation of rRNA synthesis (section 6.4.13), and it is also possible to see naked, untranscribed genes in amphibian oocytes [382, 384].

Exactly the same techniques yield similar results when genes are examined that are densely packed with polymerase II. For example, the lateral loops of lampbrush chromosomes in amphibian oocytes [382], *Drosophila* embryonic cells [277] and one defined gene, that of silk fibroin [278], all failed to give visible evidence of nucleosomes. The DNA packing ratio in fibroin genes was 1.1, similar to that seen in ribosomal genes examined by the same methods. In other tissues, genes could be seen, but not identified, so packing ratios were not calculable.

Where genes have lower frequencies of transcription by polymerase II, nucleosome-like bodies may be seen between the transcription complexes [292], and in the case of *Drosophila* embryos, active genes react with antibodies against histone H3 and H4 [276]. It therefore seems that infrequent nucleosomes are present on submaximally transcribed genes, and this conclusion is supported by measurements of packing ratios in defined genes of *Chironomus* polytene chromosomes [252].

Dissection of active genes with micrococcal nuclease

Various nucleases may be used to dissect chromatin [261], but the most frequent are micrococcal nuclease and pancreatic DNase I. The property of micrococcal nuclease which makes it especially useful is that DNA wound round the nucleosome is relatively protected from its attack, but it cuts chromatin between the nucleosomes, allowing their purification by methods such as sucrose density-gradient centrifugation. Alternatively, the digested DNA may be purified and analysed by electrophoresis. If the digest is partial, a characteristic ladder of protected DNA fragments is seen (Fig. 6.4.17). This DNA may be blot-transferred and hybridized to pure gene probes, thus revealing the propensity of given genes to be cut by nuclease, the size of the fragments indicating the arrangement of nucleo-

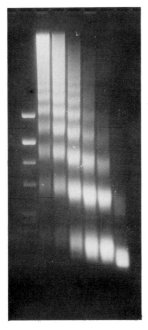

Fig. 6.4.17. Nucleosomes revealed by micrococcal nuclease digestion. *Xenopus* erythrocyte nuclei were digested for increasing lengths of time, left to right, with nuclease. The purified DNA was electrophoresed on agarose gels and revealed by staining with ethidium bromide. With short digestion a ladder of repeats is revealed, showing that nucleosomes evenly spaced along the DNA. With longer digestion all regions between nucleosomes are cut, so only the monomer DNA fragment is seen. The smallest DNA fragment gets progressively smaller with increased digestion because the region of DNA between nucleosomes is only partially protected. The left hand track shows molecular weight markers. (Photograph by Dr Vaughan Hilder.)

somes on them. Studies of this kind show that nucleosomes may have different spacing in different tissues and that particular genes can differ from the bulk. For example, Humphries *et al.* [211] found that nucleosomes are spaced 175 bp apart on *Xenopus laevis* oocyte-type 5S genes in both blood and liver cells, whereas bulk DNA shows repeats of 189 and 178 bp, in the respective tissues. However, there is little evidence that these differences in spacing relate to transcription. For example, in calf thymus nuclei the average repeat length is the same on transcribed and non-transcribed regions of DNA such as satellite [248, 263]. This is not inconsistent with the EM data, since nucleosomes can be seen on sub-maximally transcribed genes. However, Bellard *et al.* [29] found that both globin and ovalbumin genes in

chick oviduct were digested by micrococcal nuclease as if they were complexed with nucleosomes. This is surprising, because the ovalbumin genes are believed to be transcribed very rapidly in this tissue. There are a number of ways in which this information could be reconciled with the EM data. One possibility is that proteins other than nucleosomes (e.g. DNA gyrase [264]) could protect a fragment of about 145 bp. Another is that there may be enough room between polymerases to accommodate several nucleosomes. Whatever the answer to this problem, there is also evidence that the nucleosome structure of active genes must be different from that in inactive regions of the genome. Even digestion with micrococcal nuclease suggests this, since it digests the ovalbumin genes of chick oviduct faster than globin genes in the same tissue [29] (see also [292], for discussion of this point). This kinetic approach has been more revealingly applied using DNase I.

Preferential digestion of active genes by DNase I

The most useful property of DNase I is that it selectively digests transcribed regions of DNA. In a typical experiment, nuclei or chromatin are prepared from a particular organ or cell type, the first examples described being chicken erythrocytes [452] and oviduct [149]. These are lightly digested with DNase I and the chromatin or nuclei centrifuged into a pellet, leaving digested chromatin in the supernatant. Enzyme levels and incubation times are chosen such that 5–20% of the DNA is solubilized. The pellet is washed, DNA purified from it and its sequence composition examined by hybridization to selected probes. A typical result, from chick oviduct, is shown in Fig. 6.4.18. When 90% of total DNA remains in the pellet, only 40% of expressed ovalbumin gene sequences, but over 90% of the unexpressed globin sequences, are present. Not only are highly transcribed genes preferentially attacked by DNase I, those encoding rare mRNAs, and therefore transcribed less frequently, are equally susceptible (Fig. 6.4.18). As would be predicted, the differential sensitivity of globin and ovalbumin genes is exactly reversed in the erythroblast. It is noteworthy that it was the adult-type globin genes that were hypersensitive in adult erythrocytes; those encoding embryonic globins were neither preferentially digested nor expressed.

Many genes have now been examined in this way, and

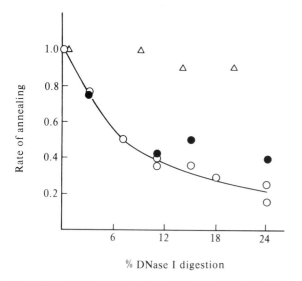

Fig. 6.4.18. Rates at which DNase I digests DNA in chick oviduct nuclei. The rate of annealing is a measure of the proportions of particular DNAs left undigested at particular times, and is obtained by hybridization of the undigested DNA (proportion total DNA solubilization is shown on the abscissa) to cDNAs. △ globin genes, ○ ovalbumin genes, ● genes encoding diverse, rare mRNAs. (From Garel *et al.*[149].)

in every case the rule that active genes are preferentially digested by DNase I, has always held. Further, the region of sensitivity can extend thousands of bases either side of the transcribed region of the gene, although these outer regions may be of sensitivity intermediate between coding and non-transcribed regions [410]. DNase sensitivity therefore seems to be a *prerequisite* for transcription. However, it may not be a *sufficient* condition, since a number of 'inactive' genes have been reported to be DNase I sensitive (see [292]). For example, adult globin genes are hypersensitive in 18-day chick embryos [452], as are γ-globin genes in adult sheep bone marrow [486], yet neither type of cell contains their mRNAs. These results must be treated with caution, since genes transcribed at very low rates are just as sensitive to digestion as those transcribed very frequently (see above). It is thus important to know if sensitive, but 'inactive' genes are absolutely inactive.

DNase I also digests specific sites in chromatin

Figure 6.4.19 shows the analysis of a hypothetical gene by probing Southern blot transfers of DNA digested with restriction enzymes. In this case, the DNA was derived from nuclei which were first very lightly digested with DNase I (the DNase levels are lower than those employed to solubilize whole regions of active DNA; see previous section). Experiments like this (review by Elgin [116]) reveal specific sites that are hypersensitive to DNase. The reason that they are seen is that double-strand cuts seem to be introduced into the DNA at these sites, whereas DNase I normally introduces single-strand nicks; the latter are mostly not revealed when DNA is electrophoresed in a double-stranded state. If pure DNA is digested with DNase these hypersensitive sites are not observed. Thus other molecules (presumably proteins) must be associated with it and make specific points highly accessible to nuclease attack. It is possible that molecules other than DNase I also experience this increased accessibility; these could include polymerases and proteins with regulatory functions, for example hormone receptors or molecules that control cell determination.

Are hypersensitive sites relevant to transcription? Digestions of the same gene in different tissues often reveal the presence of extra hypersensitive sites where it is active. A good example is provided by chicken globin genes (Fig. 6.4.20), where the hypersensitive sites are correlated with transcription. It may be no coincidence that they are mostly located near the 5'-end of the genes, that is, near the point where transcription starts. Similar sites have been found in a number of other genes [116], though they are not always associated with expression. For example, they are found near *Drosophila melanogaster* heat-shock genes in both heat-shocked cells, where the genes are intensely active, and in normal cells, in which their transcripts have not been detected [232. 480]. This is, however, unusual among current reports. More typical is the rat preproinsulin II gene [481]. Here a region of hypersensitivity is found at the 5'-end of the gene in a pancreatic beta-cell which makes insulin, but it is absent from liver, spleen, kidney and brain. Curiously there is a DNase-I-hypersensitive site at the 3'-end of the gene in liver cells, but not in other tissues, including cells making insulin.

Further evidence that these sites are important for regulating gene activity comes from studies of DNA viruses like SV40 and Polyoma. The minichromosome of SV40 is preferentially attacked by nuclease near promoters of transcription and the origin of replication [187, 392, 432, 438].

At present it remains an unproved hypothesis that the

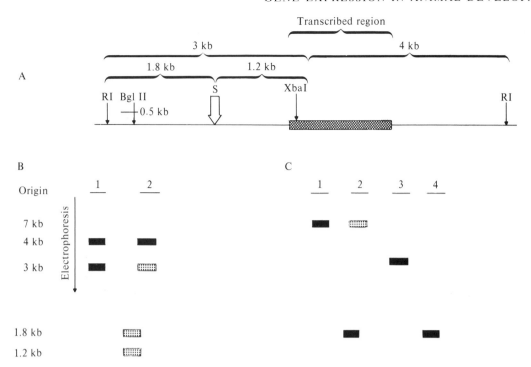

Fig. 6.4.19. Detection and mapping of sites hypersensitive to DNase I.
A. Shows a hypothetical gene (thick line) with its surrounding regions.
These regions contain one hypersensitive site, S.
B. Track 1. Total DNA has been double digested with the restriction
enzymes Eco RI and Xba I. The DNA was electrophoresed and
probed with a radioactive cloned probe representing the entire region
between the two Eco RI sites. As expected two fragments of 3 and 4 kb
hybridize.
Track 2. Nuclei are lightly digested with DNase I before processing,
as for track I. The 3 kb band becomes lighter and two new bands of 1.8
and 1.2 kb appear. This indicates that double-strand cuts are readily
introduced in the 3 kb fragment, but it does not show if they are 1.8 or
1.2 kb from the left-hand Eco RI site.

C. Track 1. Total genomic DNA is digested with Eco RI and probed
with a small radioactive DNA fragment representing the region
between the left-hand Eco RI site and a neighbouring Bgl II site. The
whole RI to RI fragment is revealed, measuring 7 kb.
Track 2. The procedure of track C 1 is repeated after light DNase I
digestion. An extra band is seen at 1.8 kb.
Tracks 3 and 4. The experiment is the same as in C, 1 and 2, except that
the restriction enzymes used were Eco RI and Xba I in combination.
Only the 3 kb fragment is seen because the probe represents only the
left-hand region of the 3 kb fragment.
The method of C is called the indirect end-labelling technique [312],
first applied to this problem by Wu [480]. It shows that the hypersensitive site must be 1.8 kb from the left-hand Eco RI site.

accessibility experienced by DNase I at hypersensitive
sites is there, not to accelerate nuclease digestion,
but to allow the binding of polymerases or regulatory molecules, and that it results from the presence
of special proteins in this region. The fact that
hypersensitive DNA is sometimes found when a gene is
inactive is not inconsistent with this idea; these could be
regions where molecules will bind to make the gene
active. What the proteins responsible may be, and what
regulatory molecules bind to these sites, is still a total
mystery.

What makes whole regions of chromatin sensitive to DNase I?

We concluded above that the whole region of DNA that
is transcribed is especially sensitive to DNase I. This is
a phenomenon that is distinct to the specific hypersensitive sites around transcribed regions described in
the last section. *A priori*, it seems likely that general
hypersensitivity is produced by the presence of proteins;
one approach to identifying the cause of hypersensitivity
is to treat chromatin in ways that remove protein classes

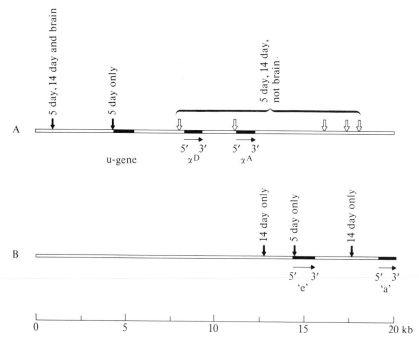

Fig. 6.4.20. DNase I hypersensitive sites in chicken globin genes.
A. The α-globin gene region of the chicken. α^D and α^A are expressed in both embryonic and adult red blood cells [75]. u is an embryonic gene, probably $\alpha\pi$ [108], and is not expressed in adult cells. The arrows show DNase I hypersensitive sites in brain, in embryonic (5 day) and adult (14 day) red blood cells (Redrawn from Weintraub *et al.* [453].)
B. A β-globin cluster. 'e' is an embryonic and 'a' is an adult embryonic gene. The DNase I hypersensitive sites in brain were not tested. (Redrawn from Stalder *et al.* [410].)

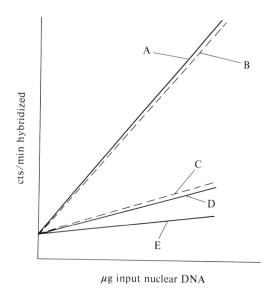

Fig. 6.4.21. Factors responsible for DNase I sensitivity of globin genes. Nuclei or chromatin were digested with DNase I so that 10–15% was rendered acid-soluble. The globin gene concentration in the remaining DNA was estimated by hybridization to a constant amount (10^1 cts/min) of globin cDNA. The linearity of hybridization (ordinate) with increasing input of digested DNA (abscissa) shows that the globin genes were saturated and hence the cts/min hybridized are directly proportional to the gene concentration. Other details are given in the text.
A. 0.35 M NaCl-washed chromatin not reconstituted.
B. 0.35 M NaCl-washed chromatin reconstituted with trypsin-treated 0.35 M eluate.
C. 0.35 M NaCl-washed chromatin reconstituted with 0.35 06M NaCl eluate.
D. 0.35 M NaCl-washed chromatin reconstituted with the 10% trichloroacetic acid soluble, 25% trichloroacetic acid insoluble components of the 0.35 M NaCl eluate.
E. Unwashed nuclei.
Data of Weisbrod and Weintraub [455].

and thus test if hypersensitivity is also lost. This approach was successfully applied by Weisbrod and Weintraub [455] to globin genes.

Chromatin was prepared from chicken erythrocytes and washed with 0.35 M NaCl, which removes many non-histone proteins. The chromatin was then tested for sensitivity of the globin gene to DNase I by solution hybridization to cDNA prepared from globin mRNA. The results are shown in Fig. 6.4.21. In untreated nuclei or chromatin, the globin gene is hypersensitive to DNase I, but when chromatin is washed with 0.35 M NaCl, DNase sensitivity is lost. This change is reversible; when washed chromatin is mixed with 0.35 M NaCl eluate and dialysed back to physiological ionic strength the sensitivity of the globin gene is regained. The agent(s) responsible is sensitive to trypsin and must therefore include protein in its active ingredients. It is soluble in 10% trichloroacetic acid but not in 25% trichloroacetic acid, and when this fraction is analysed by electrophoresis it is found to contain two main proteins, corresponding to high-mobility group proteins 14 and 17 (HMG 14 and 17). These proteins are ubiquitous so, as one might expect, the HMG 14 and 17 proteins of brain can restore the sensitivity of globin genes in washed erythrocyte chromatin, but they have no effect on the globin genes of brain chromatin. It therefore appears that HMG 14 and 17 are probably necessary for the DNase-I sensitivity of transcribed globin genes, but that *some other agent* remains bound to the chromatin and induces them to bind to active chromatin. Of course, many genes other than those encoding globin are DNase-sensitive in the erythrocyte; in fact this is true of most or all of the genes encoding hererogeneous nuclear RNA. The sensitivity of these is also associated with the presence of HMG protein 14 or 17 [454]. Whether the same conclusion is true of all genes in all tissues is controversial, and will be discussed briefly later.

HMG proteins are a group of acid-soluble proteins with high contents of both basic and acidic amino acids. HMG 17 has been sequenced [440]. It is 89 amino acids in length and its N-terminal half is rich in basic amino acids; of the first 58 amino acids 22 are lysine or arginine. In contrast the C-terminus has an overall negative charge. It may be surmised that the basic half interacts with DNA, and the acidic half with histones. HMG 14 has a similar structure [439].

Do HMG 14 and 17 perform different functions in establishing the DNase-I sensitivity of globin genes?

Weisbrod *et al.* [454] found that they were individually just as capable of restoring DNase sensitivity to salt-washed globin genes, to an expressed, integrated chicken virus gene and to the spectrum of genes encoding total nuclear RNA. Although these experiments do not rule out the possibility that some sub-set of nuclear genes is associated exclusively with HMG 17, or that effects *in vivo* are more subtle that those *in vitro,* at present it seems likely that HMG 14 and 17 are to a large extent interchangeable in their effects.

Do HMG 14 and 17 bind to all regions of an active globin gene, or only to part? Weisbrod *et al.* [454] isolated mononucleosomes from micrococcal nuclease limit digest and showed that all of the transcribed globin gene present in this fraction was sensitive to DNase I. This sensitivity was lost when HMG 14 and 17 were removed, and regained when they were replaced. The same question has also been approached in a somewhat different way. HMG 14 and 17 were bound to a solid support and made into an affinity column. When HMG 14 and 17 depleted mononucleosomes were passed through this column it was shown that the nucleosomes that were derived from active chromatin bind to the column. Thus when erythroblasts were used as the source of chromatin these nucleosomes included the entire transcribed, DNase-sensitive region of the chicken α-globin gene [456]. This shows that pieces of DNA associated with individual nucleosomes have the property of binding HMG 14 and 17, as well as of DNase I sensitivity; this property is therefore not the result of some higher-order structure in chromosome organization. Furthermore, it is characteristic of the entire transcribed region, not just small parts of it. This is consistent with the observation that full DNase I sensitivity is reached when one in 20 nucleosomes binds an HMG molecule, because this roughly corresponds to the proportion of the genome transcribed [454].

The work of Weintraub and his associates is comparable to that of several other groups of workers using various tissues, such as trout testis [260]. However, not all reported results fit simply with the idea that HMG 14 and 17 are found in active regions of chromatin and that they are the direct reason for DNase hypersensitivity (see review by Mathis *et al.* [292]). There are a variety of methods, other than HMG 14 and 17 columns, of preparing active fractions of chromatin, for example DNase II digestion, followed by Mg^{2+} precipitation of the active fraction [157]. It can be asked if the active fraction prepared by these methods is greatly enriched for HMG 14 and 17. Not all workers have found this to be the case [292]. For example, Gabrielli *et al.* [138] studied cultured mouse cells and found HMG 14 only in the active fraction, whereas the much more abundant HMG 17 was present in both fractions but preponderantly in that which was inactive. Various other examples could be provided; satellite sequences are not transcribed, but seem to be associated with HMG 14 and 17 [259, 291]; nucleosomes containing ovalbumin genes may be washed with 0.6 M NaCl (when HMGs should be lost) and still retain a measure of their DNase sensitivity [395].

On the whole, the current view is that HMG 14 and 17 are major factors, if not the only ones, in inducing DNase I sensitivity in chromatin, especially of certain genes, like those encoding globin. However, even for these there is as yet no direct evidence that these HMG proteins *cause* transcription. Nevertheless, the correlation between DNase I sensitivity and transcription is so strong that a causal relationship between these phenomena is the basis of an excellent working hypothesis. Accepting this forces us to ask what makes HMG 14 and 17 bind to particular regions of chromatin. In answering this we might hope to move a step nearer to finding why genes become active. Weisbrod and Weintraub [455] reported that HMG 14 and 17 could restore DNase sensitivity to chromatin washed with NaCl concentration as high as 1M. This means that specific sites remain when all histones other than H3 and H4, as well as other detectable proteins, have been removed. Thus either the H3 and H4 have special features, like methylation, acetylation or phosphorylation, not found on other molecules, or the DNA must contain special features (such as unmethylated bases), or there must be trace proteins or RNA molecules that have not yet been detected.

If a protein is bound exclusively to a single-copy gene should we expect to find it in say, a vertebrate chromatin preparation? A simple calculation shows that if this protein were of 40 000 molecular weight, then 1 kg of DNA in the form of chromatin would contain only 20 μg of the protein! This is a pessimistic calculation, since each gene cannot have its own, exclusive, regulatory protein. Even so, the problems of detecting proteins like this are formidable. It should be easier to detect such proteins by functional assays or by binding to specific, cloned DNAs than by standard purification techniques. This approach is described in the next section.

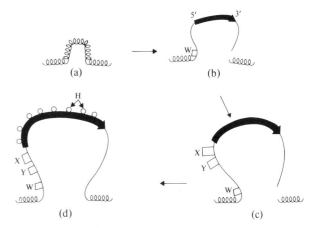

Fig. 6.4.22. Model for alterations in chromatin structure during gene activation (based partly on Stalder *et al.* [410]).
(a) In cells which do not express a gene, its DNA is highly condensed, highly methylated and relatively resistant to DNase I.
(b) A factor or factors, W, bind to the gene and cause it to open out. The transcribed region is marked by the thick arrow.
(c) Agents X and Y bind near the 5' end of the gene. These might cause demethylation of certain sites or change the conformation of the gene to give a DNase I hypersensitive sites.
(d) In some way the events of c cause a propagated change in the nucleosomes of the gene such that they bind HMG 14 and 17 (H). This makes the whole gene very DNase I sensitive.

The events of (d) and (e) cause RNA polymerase to bind to the gene and begin transcription. It is possible that the events of (c) cause the first polymerase to bind and its passage along the molecule causes HMG binding.

To conclude this section we present a simple model for gene activation (Fig. 6.4.22), based mainly on the ideas of Stalder *et al.* [410]. It must be remembered that the evidence is controversial and may apply only to a few genes, like globin. Perhaps it would be surprising if a single type of mechanism was involved in the activation of all genes. Most of the critical events in this scheme are unknown. For example, it has been suggested that high levels of histone acetylation are the cause of HMG binding and of gene transcription. Although elevated levels of histone acetylation may cause more extensive gene transcription and DNase I sensitivity, most of the nucleosomes on active genes do not have highly acetylated histones (see review by Mathis *et al.* [292]). It is always possible that histone acetylation is an early event in gene activation, but that this acetylation is later lost. The most important blanks in our knowledge are the hypothetical proteins X and Y which cause specific transcription to begin. These are the subject of the next section.

Regulatory proteins binding to specific DNA sequences

Histones and HMG proteins do not bind to specific DNA sequences. However, the high precision of gene regulation demands that such molecules exist (e.g. the hypothetical proteins W, X and Y in Fig. 6.4.22; it is also possible that these molecules are RNA, or even RNAs coupled to proteins). As we pointed out in the last section, they might be present in very small amounts in chromatin. Very sensitive methods are therefore necessary for their detection, unless much larger amounts exist in the cell than are bound to chromatin. (This may well be true, since single genes are low in concentration in cells and DNA-binding proteins have a finite non-specific binding constant to any DNA sequence. Quite large numbers of molecules may therefore be needed to saturate specific-binding sites. Even so, very discriminating assays will be necessary to pick the regulatory protein out of the much higher background of cellular protein than exists in a chromatin preparation.) Two main approaches have been used to detect these proteins; one is to find proteins that modify transcription *in vitro* and the other is to search for DNA-binding proteins.

Transcription assays

If transcription assays are to be useful they must be efficient, transcribe exactly the same regions of whole genes that are transcribed in whole cells, and be sensitive to putative regulatory agents. Eukaryotic RNA polymerase III fulfils at least the first two of these requirements and the analysis of factors affecting its transcription of 5S rRNA genes shines out as a solitary beacon in this field. These experiments will be described later (section 6.4.13). Crude cell extracts have recently been used to transcribe pure, cloned genes with polymerase II, but no regulation is evident. These systems will transcribe cell-specific genes, like globin, even though the same genes were not transcribed in the cells from which the extract was made (see section 6.4.4). Thus, either regulatory factors were lost in preparing the system, or the pure DNA added to it does not reproduce the properties of genes that are present in chromosomes in intact cells.

Another approach has been to use purified chromatin, often with added *E. coli* RNA polymerase. Under these circumstances some measure of specific transcription has often been reported. A development of this approach was to dissociate this chromatin and then try to reassemble it in a way that retained the supposed specificity [152]. Unfortunately, the whole basis of this approach is highly questionable, especially as regards supposed specific transcription by *E. coli* polymerase [152, 460]. Since there is no evidence that experiments of this type have produced results that are both relevant and valid, we will not discuss them further.

A recent application of *E. coli* polymerase to transcribing isolated *Drosophila* nuclei has yielded very interesting results [93, 94]. Cloned heat-shock genes were used to detect homologous transcripts in diploid nuclei from heat-shocked cells to which *E. coli* polymerase was added, and these were found in far higher abundance than in nuclei from normal cells. Furthermore, a protein component in extracts of heat-shocked cells was able to induce normal nuclei to behave like those that were from the heat-shock cells. However, the actual transcripts were from a region upstream of the start of transcription, and not from the region normally transcribed by *Drosophila* RNA polymerase II. Thus the *E. coli* polymerase was revealing accessibility of sites in a way exactly analogous to DNase I digestion, and the experiments are not directly relevant to normal transcriptions. However, they do provide an assay for factors which affect the activity of heat-shock genes.

DNA-binding proteins

Any protein which binds to specific DNA sequences is an excellent candidate for gene regulation. In order to be detected in conventional assays the proteins must retain binding activity through isolation procedures that are often very harsh, and they must be capable of binding to pure DNA, a structure that does not normally exist in the living cell. Nevertheless, a number of specific DNA-binding proteins have been detected. Several methods have been used, often in combination, to do this.

(1) Total DNA is bound to cellulose and used to construct an affinity column. Protein is passed through this and the bound fraction of general DNA-binding proteins submitted to further fractionation.

(2) Many proteins bind to nitrocellulose filters. It is therefore possible to assay for DNA-binding proteins, purified by other means, by mixing them with a pure, cloned, radioactive DNA and passing the mixture

through a filter. If a protein binds to the DNA, the latter remains bound to the filter and its radioactivity may be detected. In the absence of binding, the DNA passes through.

(3) Proteins may be electrophoresed and transferred to nitrocellulose filters. This filter may then be incubated with a radioactive DNA probe to reveal binding to a specific protein bound to the filter. This procedure is an analogue of the analysis of DNA restriction fragments after Southern blot transfer [48].

Approach (1) gives a great mixture of proteins, only a fraction of which bind to specific DNA sequences. This therefore can only be used as a first step in a purification procedure. Nor is procedure (2) straightforward, because proteins which bind to specific sequences are usually outnumbered by non-specific binding proteins which compete with them for the specific binding sites. It may therefore be necessary to devise competition assays to detect specific binding [205, 447]. A notable success of these approaches was in characterizing the DNA which bound to DB-2, a protein from the unfertilized eggs of *Drosophila* which was purified by DNA–cellulose affinity chromatography and iso-electric focussing [447]. This was mixed with a library of plasmids containing genomic fragments from *Drosophila* and passed through a nitrocellulose filter. The bound plasmids were enriched in sequences binding to DB-2. These were transformed into *E. coli*, cloned again and the procedure repeated several times. Finally, two plasmids were obtained which bound specifically to DB-2. One was shown to hybridize to a single band on chromosome 3. It is instructive that 2 kg of unfertilized eggs yielded 2 g of total DNA-binding protein and 5 μg of DB-2. If the recovery was 10% there would be 150–1500 molecules per egg.

Approaches of the sort outlined above have also yielded proteins binding to *Drosophila* satellite DNA [205], to *Drosophila* nucleolar DNA [448] and to *Drosophila* heat-shock genes [216]. In no case has an effect on transcription been demonstrated (the protein binding to heat-shock genes was present in both normal and heat-shocked cells). Even so, this approach would seem to have considerable potential for isolating regulatory proteins.

6.4.13 REGULATION OF RIBOSOMAL RNA GENE TRANSCRIPTION

The major RNAs of cells are tRNA and the four RNA molecules of the ribosome (5s, 5.8S, 18S and 28S rRNA). These were the first molecules the synthesis of which was studied in development, largely because, unlike individual mRNAs, they were sufficiently abundant to be purified by entirely physical means. Their genes are also highly reiterated in animal and plant genomes, which means that they were available in sufficient quantities for effective study before the advent of gene cloning techniques. Older work, as well as newer studies using cloning, have given considerable information about these genes and their regulation. Less is known about tRNA than the other RNAs, partly because there are over 40 types of tRNA in the cell, so we will concentrate here on the ribosomal RNAs. More is known about their synthesis in pre-organogenetic embryos than any other RNA, with a possible exception of histone mRNA.

Apart from the bulk of literature on the subject, rRNA is important for a number of reasons. First, it has been claimed that its transcription is regulated in development, yet it has been extremely difficult to prove this conclusively. The same problems apply to study of changes in the activity of any gene, the products of which are already present in large amounts. We believe that it is important and instructive for the student of molecular embryology to consider these problems in detail. Secondly, methods of transcribing isolated ribosomal genes are being developed and should be capable of detecting regulatory factors. It is important to know the result of this regulation *in vivo* to appreciate the biological context in which these factors operate.

Genes of 5S RNA are important because the mechanism of their regulation is already partially worked out, a statement that cannot be made of other eukaryotic chromosomal genes. For this reason we also consider 5S RNA genes in detail.

28S, 18S and 5.8S rRNA synthesis in post-fertilization development

These rRNAs are made on tandemly reiterated genes as a large precursor, which is cleaved to give the mature rRNA molecules (Fig. 6.4.23). The literature contains numerous claims that rRNA genes show dramatic changes in activity during development, and also counter-claims that this is untrue. We will begin our review of the evidence with developing insects, because here we have the clearest case for a dramatic change in the efficiency of ribosomal-gene transcription.

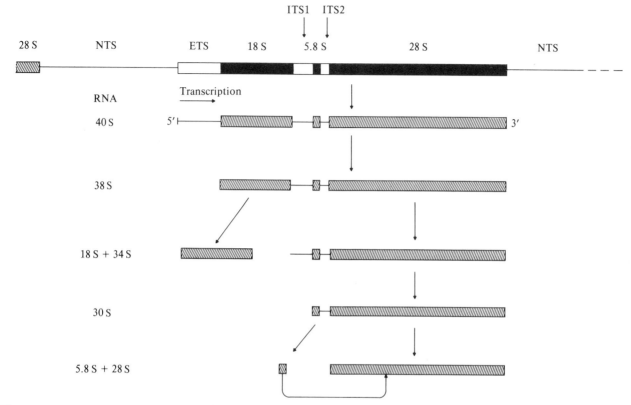

Fig. 6.4.23. Transcription of a eukaryotic rRNA gene. The example shown is *Xenopus laevis* [46, 47], but other eukaryotic rRNAs are made in a similar fashion. The genes are found in tandemly repeated arrays (450–800 in *Xenopus laevis* [73, 441]). All of the region, except the non-transcribed spacer (NTS), is transcribed to give a single 40S precursor RNA. This is progressively cleaved by endonucleases to give mature 18S, 28S and 5.8S rRNA molecules and the external (ETS) and internal (ITS) transcribed spacers are lost. The 5.8S rRNA is base paired to the central region of the 28S molecule. During synthesis the molecule is progressively methylated [279] and associates with proteins, the 18S rRNA forming the 40S sub-ribosomal particle and the 28S plus 5.8S the 60S particle. In mammals the precursor is larger (45S) because there are larger amounts of transcribed spacer.

Insects

Initial experiments on *Drosophila* and *Oncopeltus* (the milkweed beetle) were of a strictly biochemical nature. Embryos were incubated or injected with radioactive precursors and the amount of isotope that was incorporated into the various major RNA species was determined [183, 265]. In *Drosophila* it was concluded that rRNA synthesis began at the time of cellular blastoderm formation, that is immediately after the syncytial stage, the analogue of cleavage in other embryos. This was also the first time at which synthesis of other types of RNA was detected, although it is now known that histone-mRNA synthesis accelerates about

1 h earlier [8]. In *Oncopeltus*, rRNA synthesis was reported to start somewhat later, at the mid germ-band stage, and to be preceded by the synthesis of RNA of other types. As we shall see when considering sea urchins and amphibians, drawing conclusions of this type from such biochemical experiments on early embryos is fraught with problems. However, in insects these have been circumvented by using an entirely different approach—direct examination of the genes.

The rRNA genes are surrounded by relatively short non-transcribed regions of DNA, and the individual unit is tandemly repeated many times (Fig. 6.4.23). When actively transcribing genes are spread and examined with the electron microscope, they are seen as fir-tree-

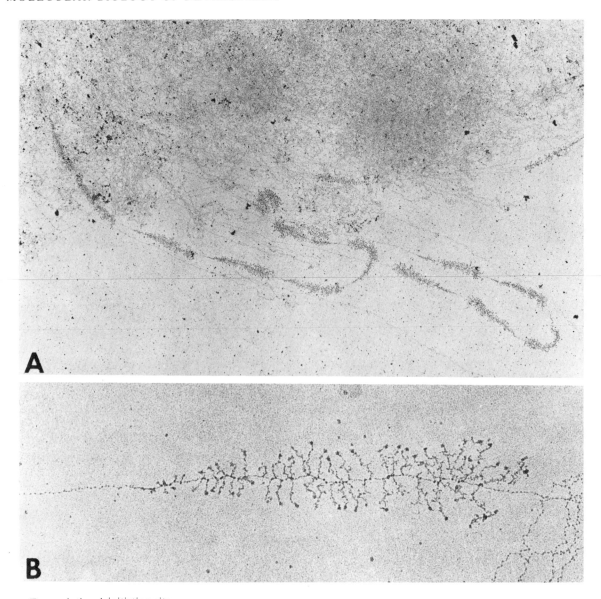

Transcriptional initiation site

Nascent transcripts

Transcript release site

(C)

like structures, stacked one next to the other, the side branches representing the progressively longer 40S pre-rRNA transcripts attached to an RNA polymerase molecule progressing along the gene (Fig. 6.4.24). They can be identified because the fir-tree structures are repeated with the periodicity that is characteristic of the tandemly repeated ribosomal genes. In *Drosophila* these structures are visible at the cellular blastoderm stage [277]. They are absent during the cell division preceding this, that is, just before plamsa membranes surround the nuclei to form the blastoderm. Other types of transcriptional unit also become abundant at this stage, although a few may also be seen during the syncytial stage. Thus, as indicated by earlier biochemical evidence, in *Drosophila*, rRNA genes become active at the inception of the cellular blastoderm stage, coincident with an increase in general RNA synthesis. In *Oncopeltus* the data are similar except that rRNA transcription complexes appear a little later, at the germ-band stage [133]. Measurement of the length of the active ribosomal genes indicates that their activation involves unfolding them from nucleosomes. It is particularly interesting that in *Oncopeltus* this unfolding precedes the transcription of the ribosomal gene, i.e. it is likely that some agent appears at the germ-band stage causing the genes to unfold; some second change at a slightly later stage permits RNA polymerase I molecules to transcribe the genes. This second change could be an alteration in the gene or in the polymerase, and if it were reversible it could be used by the cell to modulate the rate of rRNA synthesis. Evidence that this occurs comes from observation of the structure of ribosomal transcription units during later stages of development [133]. At this time the rate of rRNA synthesis per cell falls off [183] and some ribosomal genes may be seen as untranscribed structures in the unfolded state.

Sea urchins

In sea urchins there is a wealth of data derived from the incorporation of radioactive nucleosides. In order to relate information of this type to the rate of ribosomal transcription, it is necessary to have information of four types.

(1) An accurate measurement of the amount of radioactive precursor incorporated into the class of RNA molecule under study. This measurement can be difficult if there is a high background of heterogeneous RNA synthesis.

(2) An estimate of the direct precursor specific activity. Thus if [^{3}H]uridine is used as an RNA precursor, it must enter the cells concerned and be converted to [^{3}H]UTP before it will label RNA molecules. For a given rate of RNA synthesis the amount of incorporation will depend on the amount of [^{3}H]UTP present and also on the amount of non-radioactive UTP (i.e. the UTP specific activity); if the latter was halved while the amount of [^{3}H]UTP remained constant, the rate of incorporation of radioactivity into RNA would double when the absolute rate of RNA synthesis remained constant. Thus it is imperative to measure the precursor specific activity.

(3) The stability of the RNA must be known. Whenever this has been measured, rRNA has been found to be stable compared to the time-scale on which experiments are conducted. This parameter is therefore usually ignored.

(4) The number of genes making the RNA must be known. Usually this remains constant per cell (though not for RNA in amphibian oocytes, see below), so the relevant figure is the number of nuclei or cells per embryo. Obviously, there are very few nuclei in early embryos. It may therefore be difficult to detect gene activity in early development, even if the genes are very active.

Account has now been taken of these factors in sea urchin embryos. Initial studies failed to reveal rRNA synthesis before the late blastula/early gastrula stage (see [99]). Emerson and Humphreys [118] showed that this might result from its masking by the unusually large

Fig. 6.4.24. Active ribosomal genes made visible: ribosomal transcription units from 68 h (neurula stage) *Oncopeltus fasciatus* embryos. (A) Region of dispersed chromatin at a nuclear periphery. In this electron micrograph there are 16 or more ribosomal transcription units that are associated with fibres (and that therefore are interpreted as having been transcriptionally active at the time of preparation). The fibre-free spacers that flank ribosomal transcription units are heterogeneous in length. (B) Detail of a ribosomal transcription unit from a 68 h embryo (not the same preparation as in A). The chromatin morphology of the transcription unit is not clearly visible because of the presence of fibres (nascent transcripts). The spacer chromatin is beaded. Preparations shown in A and B were stained with phosphotungstic acid (pH 2.5, unadjusted), but not platinum-shadowed. Scale bar indicates 1 μm. (C) Interpretative drawing of B. (From [133].)

amount of heterogeneous RNA made by blastula nuclei. Two estimates of rRNA synthesis at the blastula stage are now available and indicate that each blastula nucleus make rRNA just as fast as later-stage embryos. The more direct is that of Griffith *et al.* [163], who increased the sensitivity of their uridine-incorporation studies by hybridization of the newly made RNA to cloned ribosomal genes. A second approach was adopted by Surrey *et al.* [414], who made ingenious use of the fact that rRNA molecules are much more densely methylated than other high-molecular-weight RNAs and the sequences methylated are different. They estimated rates of rRNA synthesis by measuring the transfer of [^{3}H]methyl groups from a pool of S-adenosyl methionine of known specific activity to [^{3}H]methyl oligonucleotides characteristic of rRNA. Both groups of workers found that about 2000 rRNA transcripts per cell per hour were made in blastulae and gastrulae. There is also a suggestion from both groups that rRNA synthesis progresses at much the same rate at the 32-cell stage. This needs confirmation, especially since Ruderman and Schmidt [373] failed to detect rRNA synthesis in eggs, under conditions where histone mRNA synthesis was easily seen. It is important to know about these early stages because in terms of cell division rate the blastula of sea urchins is like the gastrula of amphibians and the cellular blastoderm of insects. The quiescent rRNA genes in the syncytial stages of insects are found at a stage more analogous to the cleaving morula of the sea urchin.

Thus at all stages from blastula to feeding, sea urchin cells make rRNA at about 1000–4000 mols h^{-1}. Humphreys [210] and Galau *et al.* [143] pointed out that this is a very low rate, less than 10 transcripts per hour per gene, since each diploid cell contains 100–500 ribosomal genes [163, 330]. It is about 100 times lower than the maximum theoretical rate of synthesis which is seen in oogenesis of the sea urchin [163]. The low rate in blastulae and gastrulae is confirmed by electron microscope observations of ribosomal genes [76]. An efficient rate of transcription does not appear until the pluteus larvae are fed [210]. It may therefore be argued that the genes are essentially repressed till the pluteus stage, and their previous transcription may represent no more than leaky repression. If this is true it could legitimately be argued that sea urchins control their rRNA genes, somewhat like insects, that they activate them in the larva, and that this increase is analogous to the activation seen in the *Drosophila* blastoderm embryo.

Amphibians

There is still controversy about the regulation of rRNA genes in amphibian embryos. The amphibian most closely studied is *Xenopus laevis,* where the strategy adopted in incorporation studies must differ from that in sea urchins, because the embryos are impermeable to all normal nucleic acid precursors except CO_2. Labelling has therefore been either by microinjection of nucleosides or nucleoside triphosphates into the egg or the embryo, by incubation with $H^{14}CO_3^-$, or by injecting $^{32}PO_4$ into the peritoneum of the female prior to ovulation. This last strategy was adopted by Brown and Littna [68–71]. Figure 6.4.25 shows the result obtained in studies of this kind. It is correct to conclude that rRNA synthesis cannot be detected before the blastula stage, but not that it is absent. Brown and Littna [70] provided data on pool specific activities in similar experiments, which enabled Davidson [99] to conclude that they could not have detected rRNA synthesis in the blastula, even if it had occurred at the same rate as in the neurula. He applied similar arguments to dismiss a range of experiments using injection techniques [172, 236, 474]. It is not particularly valuable to discuss these experiments now, since they have been superseded by more recent work. However, it is worth mentioning some older data of a different kind. In these experiments radioactive uridine was injected into embryos and the incorporation into RNA measured by autoradiographic examination of sectioned nuclei [16, 179]. Changes in cell number are irrelevant using this method, just as for the electron microscope studies of other embryos mentioned above. Prior to the 1000-cell stage (early blastula), nuclei are totally unlabelled, but subsequently they show heavy incorporation of label into RNA. Study of neurula stages shows heavy incorporation into RNA at a stage at which rRNA is the major product. Since it is known that [^{3}H]uridine is efficiently converted into [^{3}H] UTP in eggs [468], rRNA synthesis would have been detectable in cleaving embryos and early blastulae if it had occurred. This means that cleavage nuclei make little rRNA compared to neurulae. These experiments do not, however, tell us if the very active RNA synthesis of the late blastula includes ribosomal-gene transcription.

It has been argued that the absence of a definitive nucleolus at all stages before the gastrula shows that rRNA synthesis is also absent [61, 184]. A counter argument to this is that blastulae of sea urchin, now

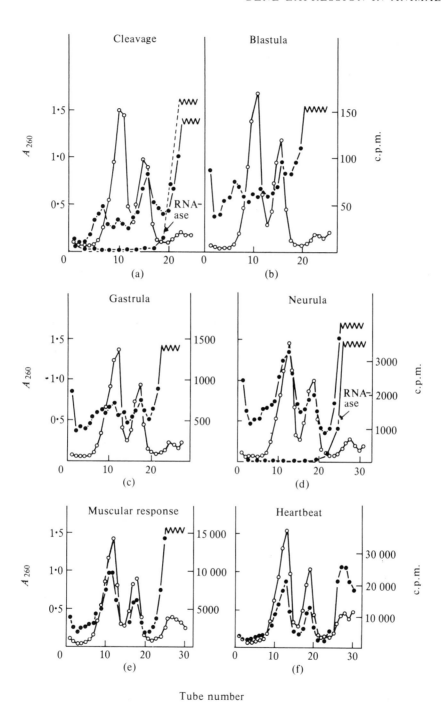

Fig. 6.4.25. RNA synthesis in embryos of *Xenopus laevis*. Eggs were labelled with $^{32}PO_4$ by injecting it into the peritoneum of the female before ovulation. The extracted RNA was centrifuged on sucrose gradients (right to left); the major RNAs may be seen by their UV absorbance (O—O), 28S rRNA being the left-hand peak and 18S the right; the radioactivity (●—●) shows newly-synthesized RNA [69].

known to be making rRNA, lack definitive nucleoli, and that apparent nucleoli may be induced by inhibiting DNA synthesis with fluorodeoxyuridine [119]. It is argued that typical nucleolar morphology is prevented by the rapid cell division of cleavage stages. This argument carries weight, but the cell cycle of *Xenopus* embryos slows down some time before definitive nucleoli appear [160], and sea urchins are in any case showing extremely low rates of rRNA synthesis, even when their genes were said to be activated and definitive nucleoli appear (see above). As we shall see below, this low rate does not apply in *Xenopus* neurulae.

Davidson [99] has reworked Brown and Littna's [70] data to show that the *Xenopus* tail-bud embryo makes rRNA at a rate of only 200 mols cell^{-1} min^{-1}. Since 940 genes are present per diploid cell [73] this is a rate of only 0.2 mols gene^{-1} min^{-1}. However, at this temperature a maximally active gene, like those found in the oocyte, has polymerase molecules 100 nucleotides apart [303], elongating at 15 nucleotides s^{-1} [7]. Each gene therefore makes one 40S rRNA precursor every $100 \div 15 = 7$ s. This implies that *Xenopus* neurula rRNA genes are almost inactive—but is this really true?

A more recent study is that of Nakahashi and Yamana [310]. They labelled *Xenopus* embryos with H^{11}CO$_3{}^{-}$, determined pool specific activities of nucleotide triphosphates, and estimated incorporation into rRNA by gel electrophoresis. The results are shown in Table 6.4.10. In the gastrula on average each ribosomal gene makes 3.5 mols min^{-1}, or one per 17 s. An identical result is

obtained by reworking the data of Shiokawa *et al.* [399], who labelled disaggregated neurula cells with [^{3}H]uridine. A third method of measuring the rate of rRNA synthesis is by the incorporation of [^{3}H]methyl groups, just as done by Surrey *et al.* [414] for sea urchin embryos. With this methodology Shiokawa *et al.* [400] arrive at a rate of 0.7 mols gene^{-1} min^{-1}, about one-twelfth of the theoretical maximal rate. It is not clear why this value is less than that obtained by ^{11}CO$_2$ or uridine labelling, but in any case it seems that ribosomal-gene transcription is more efficient than earlier data suggested (one-fortieth of the theoretical maximum). EM observations of the type described above indicate that all ribosomal genes are never maximally active in any cell. Miller and Knowland [301] showed that *Xenopus* neurulae with 35% of the normal ribosomal-gene content make rRNA at reduced rates and die as tadpoles. However, when they have 50% they compensate by raising the rate of rRNA synthesis per gene and survive. It is hard to explain these results if transcription is unusually inefficient.

When does rRNA synthesis start? One quantitative approach to this problem is shown in Table 6.4.10, partly discussed already. This appears to demonstrate a marked activation of rRNA synthesis at gastrulation. However, it is possible to take issue with the authors over the low value that they obtain in blastulae. When computing the rate of synthesis per cell, they divide the rate of rRNA synthesis/embryo by 11 000, the number of cells present at the *end* of the labelling period. They

Table 6.4.10. Rates of rRNA synthesis in *Xenopus laevis* embryos. (Data partly recalculated from Nakahashi and Yamana [310]).

Stages	Morphological stage	Rate of rRNA synthesis (ng/embryo/h)	DNA content	Rate of rRNA synthesis in terms of DNA content (pg/ng DNA/h)	Molecules rRNA* made per ribosomal gene per min
6–9	Morula/blastula	0.28	70	4.0	0.14
9–10	Blastula/gastrula	3.88	110	35.3	1.2
10–11	Early gastrula	8.35	175	47.7	1.6
11–12	Late gastrula	25.1	250	100.4	3.5

*This number is obtained as follows, taking the late gastrula as an example. 100 pg/h rRNA is made per ng DNA. A diploid cell contains 6 pg DNA and about half will have doubled their DNA, thus containing about 9 pg DNA. Therefore rRNA will be made at a rate of 0.9 pg/cell/h. This may be converted to molecules by: mass in grams $\div$ molecular weight $\times$ Avogadro's number, i.e. $(0.9 \times 10^{-12}) \times (1.8 \times 10^{6}) \times 6 \times 10^{23}) = 3 \times 10^{5}$ pre-mRNA molecules. Each cell contains 940×1.5 rRNA genes (half are in G$_2$). Thus each average gene makes $(3 \times 10^{5}) \div (940 \times 1.5) = 210$ pre-rRNA molecules/h or 3.5/min.

should actually use a much smaller number than this, because so few cells were present at the start of incubation. This would bring the rate of synthesis into line with that in the gastrula. More recently Shiokawa *et al.* [400] used C^3H_3 labelling over shorter time intervals to measure rRNA synthesis in blastulae. They concluded that rRNA synthesis was absent in morulae, begins in the early blastula and proceeds maximally, on a per-cell basis, from the mid-blastula stage onwards. The negative morula result was obtained using the same number of cells as at later stages, and so seems to be valid. The authors also conclude that the rate of rRNA synthesis per *nucleolated* cell remains constant, i.e. the activation of ribosomal genes occurs by increasing the proportion of cells which make rRNA. It seems that the endoderm

cells are the last to commence detectable rRNA synthesis [132, 299, 402, 436, 474].

The extensive research effort surveyed above suggests, on balance, that the ribosomal genes are inactive or of low activity in the early cleaving embryo, that they become active during the blastula stage, and that this activation is somewhat delayed in endoderm cells.

rRNA synthesis in amphibian oogenesis

In general, eggs are unusually large cells and are provided with the material to carry out normal metabolism in proportion to their mass, not their content of genes. This poses severe problems for ribosome syn-

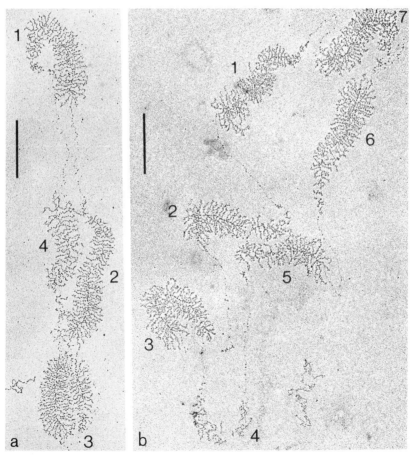

Fig. 6.4.26. Transcription on amplified circles of rDNA in oocytes of *Triturus alpestris*, spread with the Miller technique. In (a) four and in (b) seven active ribosomal genes may be seen. All are fully active, except in 4 (b). (a) × 19 000; (b) × 20 000. Scales = 1 μm. (From [383].)

thesis in species with large eggs. For example, the egg of *Xenopus* contains 4 μg of rRNA [66], or 10^{12} ribosomes. The oocyte contains a 4C amount of DNA, which includes 1880 ribosomal genes [73]. Since each gene makes only one rRNA molecule per 7 s (see above), it would take the oocyte $10^{12} \times 7 \div 1880$ s to synthesize its rRNA. This is 3.7×10^9 s or 117 years! Clearly some other mechanism is employed; this mechanism is selective amplification of the ribosomal genes.

rDNA amplification occurs in a wide variety of organisms, including amphibians, fish, some insects, echiuroid worms, molluscs and crustaceans. It may be absent in a number of organisms, such as starfish [433]. These have small eggs and do not need to accumulate as many ribosomes as amphibians, for example. Amplification has been most studied in the amphibian *Xenopus* [63, 145, 275].

The oocytes of *Xenopus* contain about 1500 extra-chromosomal nucleoli [334], each containing several hundred ribosomal genes (Fig. 6.4.26). In total there are $1.5–2.5 \times 10^6$ ribosomal genes in an oocyte [334], a 1000-fold amplification over the chromosomal ribosomal genes. Since the mass of this DNA is 30 pg, compared to 13 pg total chromosomal DNA, most of the nuclear DNA in an oocyte is ribosomal.

The amplification begins in pre-meiotic oogonia [228], but the bulk occurs at the pachytene stage [144, 328, 427]. It is known that amplification is regulated, in the sense that the same final rDNA level is used whatever the starting number of chromosomal genes, because an animal heterozygous for the deletion of the ribosomal genes contains half of the normal amount of chromosomal rDNA [441], but the typical number of extra-

chromosomal amplified ribosomal genes [334]. This is not surprising since a single gene is chosen for amplification, and in each oocyte the major gene chosen differs [33]. Apparently the choice is not wholly at random [457] and in hybrids between *Xenopus laevis* and *X. borealis* it is always the *laevis* rDNA that is amplified [62]. The amplified ribosomal genes exist as episome-like, circular molecules containing a few, or even hundreds, of ribosomal genes. They replicate by a rolling circle mechanism from other circles [35, 204, 361]. The way that the first circular molecule is replicated from the chromosome is unknown. Parallels with the production of viruses from chromosomally integrated proviral sequences may be drawn, and may or may not be realistic.

The ribosomal genes are regulated in a unique fashion in amphibian oogenesis. During pre-vitellogenic oocyte growth they are scarcely active, whereas the other major classes of RNA are made at high rates. The most thorough quantitative study has been that of Scheer *et al.* [383] on *Triturus alpestris*, where the rate of rRNA synthesis peaks in early vitellogenic oocytes and falls off again at the end of oocyte growth (Table 6.4.11). The situation is similar in seasonal frogs [419], but in laboratory *Xenopus* there is not necessarily a fall at the end of oogenesis [251]. The changes in rate of rRNA synthesis shown in Table 6.4.11 seem mainly to be brought about by the number of polymerases active at a given stage, i.e. the rate of elongation does not seem to change very much, rather it is the rate with which polymerase I molecules initiate new chains which is the important variable. The effect of changing elongation and initiation rates is exactly comparable to that in polysome

Table 6.4.11. Relative rates of rRNA synthesis compared with polymerase molecules transcribing amplified ribosomal genes in *Triturus alpestris* oocytes. (Data from Scheer *et al.* [383].)

Oocyte stage (diameter)	Relative rates of synthesis of stable rRNA (variation in brackets)	Mean number of growing rRNA molecules per ribosomal gene	Relative transcriptional activity
Previtellogenic (0.3 mm)	0.013% (0.01–0.04)	3.3	3
Vitellogenic (0.8–1.0 mm)	100%	117	100
Full-grown (1.6–2.8 mm)	12.9% (0.7–14.0)	17	15

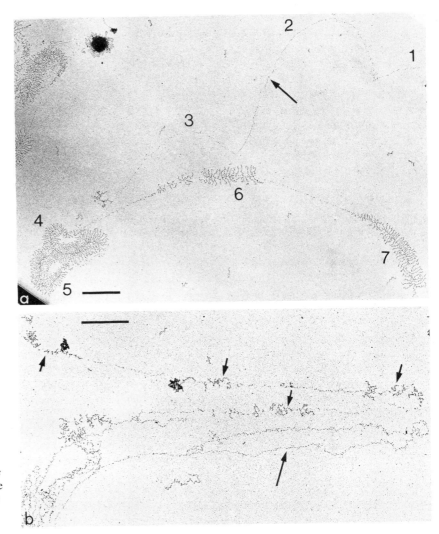

Fig. 6.4.27. Variable transcription of adjacent amplified ribosomal genes in oocytes of *Triturus alpestris*. In (a) a series of inactive genes (1–3) lie next to four very active genes (4–7). In (b) there are inactive genes (lower arrow) adjacent to genes with sparse transcripts. (From [383].)

size in protein synthesis (see Fig. 6.4.9). When individual ribosomal genes were examined (Fig. 6.4.27) the surprising conclusion was reached that ribosomal genes behave heterogeneously when the rate of rRNA synthesis changes. At maximal rates of rRNA synthesis, over 90% of the genes are heavily packed with polymerases; at other stages this packing must be reduced. All of the possibilities are shown in Fig. 6.4.27, and all were observed in full-grown and pre-vitellogenic

oocytes. The reason for the variability is not known, but one explanation is that there is a limited availability of a factor which binds reversibly to rRNA genes and then permits transcription. Its loss could produce absence of transcription (Fig. 6.4.28), interruptions of transcriptions or widely spaced transcripts. It is also possible that individual genes vary in their affinity for polymerase or other molecules effecting transcription. It should be remembered that excess supplies of RNA polymerase I

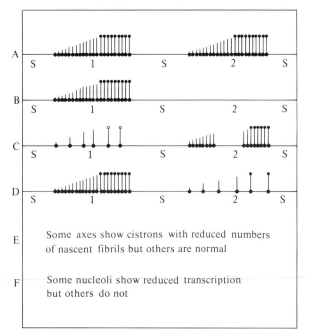

Some axes show cistrons with reduced numbers
of nascent fibrils but others are normal

Some nucleoli show reduced transcription
but others do not

Fig. 6.4.28. Diagrammatic representation of the various ways in which changes in RNA polymerase initiation can reduce the maximal rate of synthesis shown in A. Actual cistrons are shown in Fig.6.4.22. (From [383].)

are present during all of these stages [363]. Heterogeneity in the behaviour of individual ribosomal genes was also noted in insects [133, 277] and sea urchins [76].

Factors controlling rRNA synthesis in amphibian development

What agents control the activity of rRNA genes during development? Available data exist only for amphibians, so we will restrict our discussion to them and begin with more general biological features of this regulation.

The first important point is that the ribosomal genes become active at a stage when their product is not essential for the embryo. When embryos are homozygous for the deletion of all of their ribosomal genes (O-*nu* mutant) they develop for ten days (19°C) in the absence of rRNA synthesis [65]. Only as the tadpoles approach feeding do they become abnormal. Thus the embryos can develop using only their stored ribosomes. Moreover, though rRNA synthesis is intense at the neurula stage, only about 20% of the ribosomes are actually active at any given moment, i.e. are present in

polysomes [469] (Fig. 6.4.12). It could be argued that the newly synthesized ribosomes represent a special subclass, but they actually seem to equilibrate with the stored ribosome pool [399, 469]. Thus ribosomal genes do not seem to be regulated in any simple way in response to changes in the availability of their end product.

However this does not mean that they are not regulated at all. Tadpoles heterozygous for the O-*nu* mutation contain half of the normal number of rRNA genes, yet seem to make the normal amount of rRNA (relative to tRNA) [65, 238]. This is an unusual example of dosage compensation in an autosomal gene of animals. When the number of genes falls below 35% of the diploid value there are insufficient for compensation and the animal dies [301].

The simplest explanation of the activation of rRNA synthesis is that it occurs according to a cue in the developmental programme which is totally unrelated to ribosome usage. Just this kind of gene control is found in developing slime moulds [316]. When amoebae aggregate to form a fruiting body they synthesize a fixed amount (a 'quantum') of a number of enzymes, such as UDPG-pyrophosphorylase. If the cells are disaggregated and allowed to aggregate anew they produce a second quantum of enzyme, thus doubling their content of the enzyme. This process can be repeated a number of times. Clearly, enzyme synthesis is not controlled by enzyme content.

What is known of the factors that control rRNA genes in development? It is known that they exist in the cytoplasm and can change the activity of ribosomal genes in nuclei from various cells. Thus neurula cell nuclei, which synthesize rRNA, have been transplanted into enucleated eggs and it was claimed that they switched off rRNA synthesis and began it again at the appropriate stage [175]. These experiments are subject to all the objections raised by Davidson [99] as far as inability to detect rRNA synthesis is concerned (see previous section). However autoradiography of individual nuclei showed that in egg cytoplasm there was no detectable RNA synthesis. This necessarily includes rRNA (see previous section). When transplanted, the rRNA genes must therefore be reduced in activity and subsequently activated by the neurula stage. It has also been shown that oocyte cytoplasm is capable of inducing RNA synthesis in previously inactive blastula nuclei [174, 178]. Since prominent nucleoli appear, it can safely be presumed that rRNA is made [173]. The activating substances show species-specificity in that *X. borealis* rRNA genes show delayed activation in *X. laevis* cytoplasm [198]. There are also interchromosomal effects, since *X. borealis* rRNA genes are inefficiently expressed in *X. laevis* × *X. borealis* hybrids [198].

What is the nature of the substances which control rRNA synthesis? Are eggs and cleaving embryos deficient in an activator of rRNA genes, or do they contain an inhibitor? One approach to these questions has been that of Shiokawa and Yamana [401]. They showed that blastula cells release a low-molecular-weight factor which inhibits rRNA synthesis (relative to tRNA) when added to neurula cells. This result has been confirmed by Laskey *et al.* [255]. The main further evidence that this inhibitor is of relevance to the intact embryo is that the agent disappears from ectoderm cells before endoderm [436], correlating with the delayed acceleration of rRNA synthesis in the latter.

Another approach has been to attempt to reproduce the results obtained with transplanted nuclei by adding cytoplasmic extracts to isolated nuclei [95]. It was found that the previously active ribosomal genes of cultured cells were stimulated to make more rRNA by extracts of oocytes and gastrulae but inhibited by extracts of eggs and blastulae. Thus the cytoplasmic extracts caused nuclei to behave like nuclei normally found in the cells from which the extracts were made. A stimulatory protein factor(s) seemed to produce the effects [96], but it has yet to be proved that it affects rRNA genes *in vivo*.

Thus, although early embryos provide unique material for identifying agents that control rRNA synthesis, progress has been slow to date. The recent development of *in vitro* transcription systems for cloned rRNA genes [171, 298] encourages hope that progress will soon accelerate and will emulate what has been achieved for 5S genes (see below).

rRNA synthesis in other embryos

Various strategies of ribosome production are adopted by embryos of other types. The reader is referred to the review of Davidson [99]. Mouse embryos provide the situation which is, at first impression, most unlike any description above. Here rRNA is already the major class of rRNA made in 4-cell embryos [117, 342, 473]. This rate represents a considerable acceleration over that at the 2-cell stage [473], although rRNA may be made in

small amounts in 2-cell embryos [237]. In rabbits rRNA synthesis is apparent by the 16-cell stage [284, 388]. It might be thought that the acceleration in rRNA synthesis in 4-cell mouse embryos is 'early' compared to *Drosophila* or *Xenopus*, and so it is in terms of *stage*. But the 4-cell mouse embryo is already two days old—in other words rRNA synthesis is unusually late accelerating in mice.

Regulation of 5S rRNA genes

The genes for 5S rRNA

A single 5S rRNA molecule is included in all ribosomes, except those of animal mitochondria. As one might expect, in typical cells long-term isotope-incorporation studies reveal equal net synthesis of 5S, 5.8S, 18S and 28S rRNA. Since the last three are located on the same precursor RNA molecule it is easy to see how their synthesis is regulated coordinately, yet the 5S genes are located elsewhere in the genome and must be regulated separately. It is possible to go further in explaining their regulation than it is for any other eukaryotic gene, so we will consider them in some detail. Since most information is available for *Xenopus laevis* and *X. borealis*** we will restrict ourselves to these organisms.

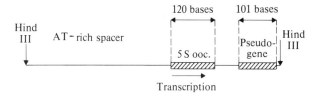

Fig. 6.4.29. The repeat unit of the *Xenopus laevis* oocyte 5S gene, as defined by Hind III restriction sites (from [217]). About 21 000 such units are tandemly repeated at the telomeres of most of the chromosomes [327].

The first studies of the sequence of 5S RNA in the oocytes and somatic cells of *Xenopus laevis* showed that the genes encoding them had different sequences [136, 446]. More recent data concerning both *X. laevis* and *borealis* genes indicate that the somatic 5S gene differs from the major gene expressed in oocytes by six bases out of the 120 total [135, 240]. In addition, there are also

---

*N.B. In papers up to 1977, *Xenopus borealis* was misidentified as *X. mülleri* [64].

minor variants of these oocyte genes [135, 339]. The clustered major oocyte 5S genes of *X. laevis* are composed of a repeating unit including one 5S pseudogene for each 5S gene (Fig. 6.4.29). The pseudogene contains only the first 101 bases of a 5S gene [217] and, although its transcription has not been detected, this possibility cannot be excluded [297]. A similar pseudogene structure is seen in *X. borealis* [240]. In *Xenopus laevis* there are about 21 000 oocyte-specific genes and 400 specific to somatic cells [339]; in *X. borealis* there are 9000 oocyte and 700 somatic genes [72, 110]. The 5S genes of *Xenopus* have recently been reviewed by Korn [239].

Programme of 5S rRNA synthesis in oogenesis

Since 5S genes are not amplified in the oocyte [63] there will be about 80 000 chromosomal genes present (four times the haploid value). On the other hand the oocyte has 1.5–2.5×10^6 amplified 18S and 28S genes. The way that the oocyte produces enough 5S rRNA is by transcribing the 5S genes for much longer than the 18S and 28S genes. As pointed out above, 18S and 28S rRNA accumulation is very slow until the onset of vitellogenesis. Then, under the unusual circumstance of partial ovariectomy, the oocyte can accumulate its 10^{12} ribosomes in as little as a month [381]. In contrast, 5S synthesis is rapid from the beginning of oogenesis, and half of the eventual 5S complement is accumulated by the onset of vitellogenesis [134, 280].

This uncoupling of 5S synthesis from that of 18S and 28S rRNA is unusual, but not unique. In mammalian tissue culture cells the latter may be inhibited with low doses of Actinomycin D while 5S is unaffected [335]. Similar uncoupling occurs during mitosis [491]. In *Xenopus*, 5S synthesis is also uncoupled in the blastula, since it occurs before rRNA synthesis becomes detectable. Further the anucleolate mutant makes 5S RNA though it lacks 18S and 28S rRNA genes [300].

What happens to excess 5S RNA that is not incorporated into ribosomes? In all cells except young oocytes it seems to be degraded [300, 335], and this is also true in large oocytes, where Miller and Melton [297] reported that injected 5S RNA was degraded with a half-life of 4 h. In a much ignored paper, Denis and Wegnez [103] reported that the reason somatic 5S RNA did not accumulate in oocytes was not that the genes were inactive, but rather that the RNA failed to enter ribosomes or 42S particles (see below) and that it was then degraded. Although degradation might play a small part in ensuring that the ribosomes of somatic cells contain only somatic 5S RNA, the data of Korn and Gurdon [241] show that unless 5S RNA can have an extremely short half-life in *Xenopus* cells, the main reason must be that the oocyte 5S genes are scarcely active compared to the somatic genes. Why is 5S RNA stable in young oocytes, even though it does not enter ribosomes? About half of it is combined with a 40 000-molecular-weight protein to form a 7S particle [341] and the other half is combined with tRNA and two proteins (mol. wt 40 000 and 54 000) in a 42S particle [102, 134]. None of these proteins corresponds to that with which 5S RNA is complexed in a ribosome [341]. One function of the proteins in the 7S and 42S particles may be to stabilize the 5S RNA. The other, as we shall see, is to stimulate 5S RNA synthesis.

Gene sequences involved in transcription of 5S genes

Like tRNA genes, 5S genes are transcribed by polymerase III. This enzyme has turned out to have amazingly different DNA template requirements from those seen in genes transcribed by polymerase II (section 6.4.4).

The study of 5S transcription has been enormously facilitated by the efficiency with which polymerase III functions in cell-free systems. However, one of the initial approaches was to inject 5S DNA into the nucleus of *Xenopus* oocytes [66, 67]. This has the advantage that the intracellular fate of transcripts can readily be studied, and the situation is more likely to correspond to normality than can be expected of all cell-free systems. Related to the intact oocyte system is one using homogenized, isolated oocyte nuclei [40]. Lastly, there are a number of systems based on supernatants of homogenized whole cells, either oocyte, egg or somatic [450]. All show correct initiation and termination of transcription on a variety of polymerase III genes.

Preconceptions based upon our experience of other genes would suggest that sequences required to initiate transcription would be before and around the 5′-terminus of the gene. However, the deletion of the entire 5′ prelude to the 5S gene has no effect on its transcription *in vitro* [377]. The construction of deletions was performed as shown in Fig. 6.4.30. These deletions may be extended into the transcribed gene itself with no effect on transcription except, naturally enough, that the

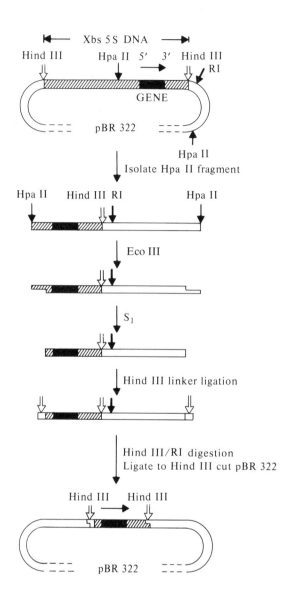

RNA made may be shorter than usual if the deletion is small or includes vector sequences if it is large. Once the deletion passes beyond about residues 50–55 of the gene, transcription vanishes (Fig. 6.4.31). A similar approach was then used to prepare deletions extending in the other direction, from the 3′-end of the gene [45]. When bases on the 5′-side of residue 80–83 was deleted, correct initiation was lost. Thus the region between

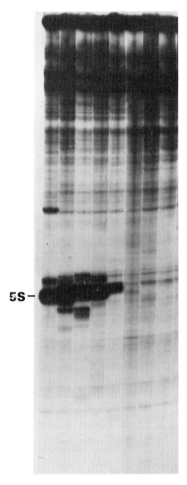

Fig. 6.4.30. Manufacture of deletion mutants of 5S genes (from [377]). The gene is cloned in the bacterial plasmid pBR322. Part of the gene, linked to part of the vector, is isolated by digestion with HpaII. The piece of vector is important because both ends are digested by exonuclease III, but the 3′ end of the gene is shielded by vector sequences and the partly digested vector piece removed at a later stage. The single-stranded ends left by Eco III are trimmed off with S1 nuclease, then Hind III linkers are ligated on to the end. The gene is digested with Hind III, thus removing the 3′ vector region and the DNA is religated into the Hind III site of pBR322. The DNA may now be grown up after transfection into *E. coli*.

Fig. 6.4.31. The central region of the 5S RNA gene is necessary for its transcription. Deletion mutants of the 5′ end of a cloned *X. borealis* 5S gene were prepared as shown in Fig. 6.4.30. They were transcribed in an oocyte extract and the 5S RNA made was analysed by electrophoresis. Track 1, intact gene; 2, the first 3 bases deleted; 3, first 28 bases deleted; 4, first 47 bases deleted; 5, first 63 bases deleted; 6, first 65 bases deleted; 7, 125 bases deleted; 8, plasmid vector alone. Transcription of the 5S gene cases when bases beyond about 50 are lost. (From [377].)

A. Pure DNA

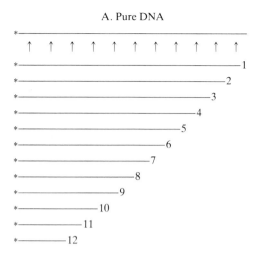

B. DNA binding protein

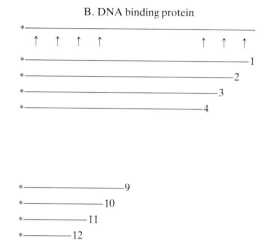

C. Electrophoresis
   samples

	A	B
↓		
1	—	—
2	—	—
3	—	—
4	—	—
5	—	
6	—	
7	—	
8	—	
9	—	—
10	—	—
12	—	—

D

Xbs1

bases 50–55 and 80–83 control the normal initiation of 5S RNA molecules (Fig. 6.4.31). The importance of this region was confirmed by cloning isolated bases 41–87 into a bacterial plasmid; the plasmid now became transcribable by polymerase III from a site in its own sequence [45].

The deletion mutants have also been used to define the sequences needed for efficient termination. These seem to be four T residues, surrounded by GC-rich sequences. 5S RNA ends in the centre of the four Ts [44].

A comparable study of the transcription of tRNA genes has been made by Galli *et al.* [147], who found that two blocks of internal sequence are necessary for transcription.

Control of 5S RNA synthesis

While extracts of oocytes transcribe 5S genes accurately and well, extracts of eggs do not. This observation enabled Engelke *et al.* [120] to identify a component of oocytes that permitted egg extracts to restore this ability. Oocyte extracts were fractionated and added to a transcription system containing 5S DNA and egg extract. A single oocyte polypeptide (TFIIIA), of molecular weight about 40000, produced accurate transcription of 5S RNA by binding to the central region of the 5S gene. This was shown through DNase-I protection experiments, the so-called 'footprinting technique', which is outlined in Fig. 6.4.32. The protein covers approximately residues 45–96, in other words, a region slightly larger than that previously shown to control normal initiation [45]. The use of the deletion mutants described in the last section confirmed that these

sequences were necessary for binding of the protein as well as its transcription [378].

It will be recalled that the 5S RNA of small oocytes is bound to a protein of molecular weight about 40000, either in 7S or 42S particles (see above). That of the 7S, but not the 42S, particle turns out to be the same as the protein which binds to the gene [197, 331]. Thus it has been proposed that this protein has two functions: to stabilize the 5S RNA before incorporation into the ribosome and to stimulate its transcription. A simple feedback control of 5S RNA synthesis was suggested by the observation that added free 5S RNA inhibited 5S RNA transcription in an oocyte cell-free system [331], presumably by binding the protein. The situation may not be this simple, however, since added 7S and 42S particles have been reported to be just as efficient at stimulating transcription as the pure protein [197, 331]. It would help to resolve this problem if the relative affinities of the protein for the gene and RNA were to be determined.

Nevertheless, the high rate of 5S RNA synthesis in young oocytes almost certainly results from their high content of free TFIIIA, and its disappearance accounts for the absence of 5S RNA synthesis in the egg [120, 332, 378]. Genes for tRNA do not require TFIIIA for transcription [120].

How is transcription regulated in somatic cells? It seems that a similar protein is involved, but that it is slightly larger than that in oocytes (42000 molecular weight) [332]. The two proteins are antigenically related.

Unfortunately, the discovery of these proteins has not shed great light on the means by which somatic cells and oocytes make different 5S RNAs. Cloned oocyte and

---

Fig. 6.4.32. Location of site on DNA to which a protein binds, using the foot-printing method [139]. (A) A pure DNA fragment is labelled at one end and digested with DNase to a limited extent. After denaturation this generates the 10 radioactive fragments shown below, each 1 bp longer or shorter than the next. The right-hand fragments exist, but will not be radioactive and therefore will not be seen. (B) The same procedure is followed after binding a protein to the DNA. Some nucleotides will be inaccessible to DNase and therefore some fragments will be missing. (C) The two DNAs are fractionated by electrophoresis, then the fragments revealed by autoradiography. Clearly sites 5–8 are missing, so the protein must bind here. Since these sites represent individual bp, the binding site can now be located on the DNA sequence. (D) An actual experiment of this type, using 5S genes. The tracks show a gel electrophoretogram of *Xenopus borealis* somatic 5S genes (Xbs1), with the positions of bases 47 to 96 marked on the left, and the intervening bases shown by the horizontal lines. Track 2 shows pure DNA cleaved with DNase I to give a ladder of bases. In the other tracks the following components were added before the DNase. Track 1, pure factor TF IIIA; track 3, pure RNA polymerase III plus TF IIIA; track 4, pure RNA polymerase III; track 5, unfertilized egg extract (which lacks TF IIIA), plus RNA polymerase III, plus TF IIIA; track 6, unfertilized egg extract, plus RNA polymerase III. It is concluded that nucleotides 45–92 are protected from DNase attack by TF IIIA. Several cuts can occur in this region, however (see small arrows), and must represent small regions of the DNA exposed in the complex with TF IIIA (D from [120]).

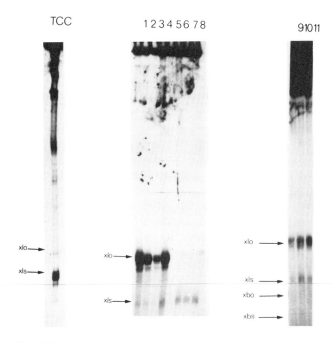

TCC   1 2 3 4 5 6 7 8   9 10 11

xlo→   xlo→   xlo→
xls→   xls→
     xls→   xbo→
             xbs→

Fig. 6.4.33. Reactivation of 5S genes in nuclei injected into oocytes. The nuclei of *Xenopus laevis* cultured kidney cells were injected into the oocyte nuclei of *X. borealis*. Newly synthesized 5S RNA was labelled with $[\alpha - {}^{32}P]$GTP, extracted and analysed by electrophoresis, so as to separate *Xenopus laevis* somatic (xls) and ovary (xlo) 5S RNA, and *Xenopus borealis* somatic (xbs) and ovary (xbo) 5S RNA. TCC: the 5S RNA made in *X. laevis* cultured kidney cells. Lanes 1–4: kidney cell nuclei injected into oocytes from a female that reactivates oocyte 5S genes. Lanes 5–8: the same, but this female does not activate ovary 5S genes. Lanes 9–11: as lanes 1–4, but here the positions of *X. borealis* 5S RNAs may be seen, showing that 5S synthesis by the oocyte's own genes was scarcely enough to be detected in the experiment. (From [241].)

somatic genes are transcribed equally well in injected oocytes, oocyte extracts and somatic cell extracts. Further, although TFIIIA does have a fourfold higher affinity for somatic than oocyte 5S genes, it is the same whether the factor is from oocytes or somatic cells [478] and there is a 1000-fold change in the ratio of oocyte to somatic 5S RNA during development [241]. Other possible explanations, which may or may not involve TFIIIA, have been discussed by Korn and Gurdon [241] and Wormington *et al.* [332]. A different way to unravel the control mechanisms responsible has been suggested by experiments in which whole nuclei are injected into oocytes.

Korn and Gurdon [241] injected *Xenopus laevis* erythrocyte or tissue culture nuclei into the nuclei of full-grown *Xenopus borealis* oocytes. The 5S RNA that they made was analysed on a gel electrophoresis system in which *X. laevis* and *X. borealis* somatic and oocyte RNAs can all be resolved from one another (Fig. 6.4.33). It was found that in the oocytes of certain females, efficient transcription of somatic 5S continued in the tissue-culture cell nuclei, and it was reactivated in the previously inactive erythrocyte nuclei. In other females the oocyte-specific 5S genes were reactivated in both types of nuclei (Fig. 6.4.33). The reactivation occur only if the nuclei are injected into the nucleus, rather than the cytoplasm of the oocyte, so the factor(s) responsible are presumably in the oocyte nucleus. The fact that some oocytes did not activate the oocyte genes enables tests to be made of the agent that they lack. Injection of the 7S particle and the 5S-RNA-binding protein had no effect, so these do not seem to be responsible. Stripping nuclei of much of their proteins by washing with 0.35 M NaCl solutions gave activity of oocyte-type 5S genes in the oocytes of inactivating females. Thus the factor in reactivating females may work by removing inhibitory proteins from the oocyte-type 5S genes.

In summary, 5S genes seem to be transcribed in response to a factor which binds to them. The 5S RNA can exert feedback control by binding this factor, but in early oogenesis the vast amounts of the factor that are present (15% of total protein), cause the excess production of 5S RNA. The main remaining mystery is the way in which the oocyte and somatic genes are separately regulated.

6.4.14 THE MOLECULAR BIOLOGY OF GENES THAT REGULATE DEVELOPMENT

So far our account has been wholly concerned with genes the expression of which is a consequence of differentiation, not its cause. There is no plausible, scientific explanation of development that does not invoke a central role of gene products. This may be through cell-surface receptors or chromatin proteins. It may even be through localized mRNA molecules, as is implied by studies of the maternally programmed coordinates for establishing the antero-posterior axis in insects [229]. Virtually nothing is known about these genes, indeed very few have even been identified, yet clearly this is an objective of the greatest importance.

In this section we describe modern molecular biological procedures which may help us to unravel the properties and behaviour of such genes and even to identify them in the first place.

The analysis of regulation starting from a mutant with abnormal development

If it is possible to isolate a mutation affecting any complex biological phenomenon, including those in development, it is possible to adopt the strategy shown in Fig. 6.4.34 to dissect its mode of action. We will consider each step in turn, showing that each is possible, though not necessarily straightforward.

(1) The key to this strategy is to obtain developmental mutants affecting the mechanism of cell differentiation. Few exist outside *Drosophila*.

(2) It is then necessary to map it genetically to establish its relation to other genetic markers and its location on the chromosomes. It is vital to map the gene as accurately as possible to ease the problems of steps 3 and 4.

Fig. 6.4.34. Strategy for identifying the molecular mechanism of action of a gene with unknown products.

1. Obtain developmental mutant

2. Map position of gene

3. Identify cloned fragment which is derived from sequence near the wild-type gene

4. Walk along the chromosome from one overlapping cloned sequence to another until gene is reached

5. Sequence normal gene

6. Determine sequence of abnormal allelles

7. Use *in situ* hybridization to sectioned embryos to locate cells containing the mRNA

8. Use hybridization to cloned gene to isolate mRNA made by the gene

9. Translate mRNA *in vitro* to identify the protein encoded

10. Examine proteins made by embryos to find time the protein is made and its location

11. Make monoclonal antibody against the protein to identify its location and mode of action

(3) It is likely that cloned DNA sequences will exist that have been mapped to specific sites on the genome. It should be possible to find a cloned sequence (located by *in situ* hybridization or by its genetic function) which is near to the gene under study.

(4) Starting from the already cloned DNA fragments it is then possible to 'walk along the chromosome' in the direction of the regulatory gene. The procedure is to use the DNA fragment to screen a library of recombinants containing the whole genome or the relevant chromosome in order to locate a sequence that overlaps it. The bacteria containing this sequence may be grown up and the recombinant sequence used for the next step of the walk. The procedure is outlined in Fig. 6.4.35, and further details may be found elsewhere [286, 323].

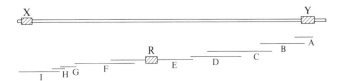

Fig. 6.4.35. Isolation of cloned DNA from a mapped gene by chromosome walking. Suppose that an interesting phenomenon in development has been associated with a particular gene X. Although its mode of action and structure is unknown it has been mapped near to gene Y, from which a cloned DNA fragment A has already been isolated. It is possible to screen a suitable chromosomal DNA library (one containing fragments that should overlap A, i.e. either made with a different restriction enzyme, or made from DNA partially digested with the same enzyme) to find a clone B which overlaps A. This can be used to isolate clone C and so on until clone I is isolated and contains part or all of gene X. At each step it is necessary to check that the walk is in the correct direction. It is also necessary to side-step repeated sequences, like R on fragment E, which could cause a leap to distant regions of the genome. This could be done by isolating the left hand part of fragment E and using this as the probe. In *Drosophila* gene X would be localised to a specific band of polytene chromosomes. By *in situ* hybridization the location of I in this band may be established.

In most situations the distance to be walked will be large, but in a genetically well-defined organism deletions and inversions may be available to reduce it. However, the magnitude of the walks should not be underestimated. A vertebrate chromosome typically contains about 10^8 bp of DNA. At present it would be difficult to imagine a good laboratory walking more than, say, 5000 bp per week. At this rate it would take 20 000 weeks, or 400 years, to walk from one end to the other! Few vertebrate chromosomes have more than 50 genes mapped onto them, so on average it would take 8 years to walk from one to the next, unless deletions were employed. Nevertheless, by adopting subtleties in the approach or by using *Drosophila*, it should be possible to obtain sequences which cover the developmental gene of interest, although knowing when one has arrived might be a problem. Even in *Drosophila* few genes are mapped within limits of 30 000 bp.

(5 and 6) Once the gene is cloned, it may be sequenced. All of the possible proteins encoded may then be deduced. Clues as to the function of the locus may be obtained by isolating and sequencing mutant alleles of the gene.

(7) Sub-clones representing the coding sequences of the gene may be used to probe sections of embryos to locate the mRNA and hence find where the gene is expressed. The same probe can be used to quantify this expression and to establish its timing in development.

(8 and 9) The cloned gene may be used to isolate mRNA by hybridization. This can then be translated *in vitro* and the protein or proteins encoded by the gene identified.

(10) It may be possible to identify this protein in extracts of whole embryos, for example by comparing two-dimensional gel electrophoretograms of proteins labelled *in vivo* with those obtained at step 9.

(11) The protein may be used to obtain a monoclonal antibody, a specific and immortal reagent to identify the protein in future [304, 305]. Finding the location and time of synthesis of the protein may give clues as to its function. The antibody may also be useful to probe this more directly. For example, it may be possible to incubate differentiating cells with it and observe its effects on differentiation [56]; alternatively the antibody or its mRNA may be injected into the developing cell. Any of these procedures could produce specific effects on cell development which would thus identify the role of the protein in the cell.

This outline shows the enormously powerful techniques now available for analysing complex phenomena in developmental, physiological and behavioural sciences. They are more than a pipe dream. Hogness and his colleagues (unpublished results summarized by Marx [289]) have adopted just this strategy to isolate the *bithorax* gene sequences of *Drosophila melanogaster*, a gene the product of which is believed to be involved in the decoding of oogenetically established positional information used for segment determination. There has already been considerable mapping and sequencing of

normal and abnormal *bithorax* sequences and an mRNA has been identified which is one of the products of the *bithorax* gene complex. There is no doubt that experiments like these are about to produce an explosion in our knowledge of cell differentiation in *Drosophila*.

The analysis of regulation where no mutant exists

The main drawback to analysing cell differentiation in most animals is that so few mutations affecting the regulation of cell determination have been identified, and even then genetic mapping is at low resolution. Without these, the strategy described above has limited usefulness. However, most of the steps outlined in Fig. 6.4.34. are reversible, even if this reversal is not easy. Thus it is possible to construct a reverse strategy from a monoclonal antibody to obtain a developmental gene. The problem is obviously that of selecting interesting monoclonal antibodies. This is not out of the question; it should be possible to identify cells or cell constituents where regulatory proteins are likely to be abundant (perhaps bound to particular genes or on the surface of cells). The monoclonal antibody technique can be used in a way analogous to 'shot-gun' gene cloning. Antibodies can be raised against a mixture of antigens, then the spleen lymphocytes fused to myeloma cells in the usual way to produce hybridomas, which are grown up individually. This yields a library of cells, each producing a single antibody. These can then be screened for reaction with proteins of developmental interest, for example they might be screened on or in whole cells or embryos for interference with differentiation. This strategy is anything but straightforward, but if it works in any given case it will lead directly into the heart of the molecular control of cell differentiation.

6.4.15 CONCLUDING REMARKS

Development may be viewed as varying patterns of gene activity in differentiating, proliferating cells. The first phase is oogenesis, in which intense gene activity over an extended period builds up a very large cell, the ovum, with vast stocks of proteins, RNAs and other molecules. The next phase of development, starting at fertilization, involves the utilization of these stores and does not depend on further gene expression. Usually, this is a phase of extremely rapid cell division.

The time when new gene activity may first be detected

varies from the 2-cell stage in mammals to early blastula stages in many other organisms. Usually, the first steps in cell determination are found at around this time (for example, endoderm/ectoderm differentiation in amphibians). However, it is not known whether new gene expression is necessary for the first steps in this process. It is possible that determination is controlled by unevenly distributed regulatory molecules, which function by turning on different genes in different cells and hence introduce different patterns of gene expression. On the other hand, the early events of determination may involve unevenly distributed molecules which do not act directly through the genome, and patterns of gene expression may only change much later. Whatever happens it is clear that gene expression eventually does change because different later cells contain different complements of proteins and mRNAs.

Although we now know a great deal about the structure of genes, we still do not know what makes them active. However, considerable advances are being made in this area as the compositions of genes in active and inactive states are worked out. We also do not know how genes fit together into hierarchies of control. It seems likely that some of the higher control elements in these hierarchies are agents controlling the overall pattern of gene expression in specialized cells, i.e. their differentiated state. Recent technical advances in molecular biology and immunology suggest that some of these agents may soon be identified.

6.4.16 REFERENCES

1 Adamson E.D. & Woodland H.R. (1974) Histone synthesis in early amphibian development: histone and DNA syntheses are not co-ordinated. *J. molec. Biol.*, **88**, 263–285.

2 Adamson E.D. & Woodland H.R. (1977) Changes in the rate of histone synthesis during oocyte maturation and very early development of *Xenopus laevis*. *Devl. Biol.*, **57**, 136–149.

3 Alton T.H. & Lodish H.F. (1977) Translational control of protein synthesis during the early stages of differentiation of the slime mould *Dictyostelium discoideum*. *Cell*, **12**, 301–310.

4 Alton T.H. & Lodish H.F. (1977) Developmental changes in messenger RNAs and protein synthesis in *Dictyostelium discoideum*. *Devl. Biol.*, **60**, 180–206.

5 Anderson D.M., Richter J.D., Chamberlin M.E., Price D.H., Britten R.J., Smith L.D. & Davidson E.H. (1982) Sequence organization of the poly(A) RNA synthesized and accumulated in lampbrush chromosome stage *Xenopus laevis* oocytes. *J. molec. Biol.*, **155**, 281–309.

6 Anderson D.M., Scheller R.H., Posakony J.W., McAllister L.B., Trabert S.G., Beall C., Britten R.J. & Davidson E.H.

(1981) Repetitive sequences of the sea urchin genome. Distribution of members of specific repetitive families. *J. molec. Biol.*, **145**, 5–28.

7 Anderson D.M. & Smith L.D. (1978) Patterns of synthesis and accumulation of heterogeneous RNA in lampbrush stage oocytes of *Xenopus laevis* (Daudin). *Devl. Biol.*, **67**, 274–285.

8 Anderson K.V. & Lengyel J.A. (1980) Changing rates of histone mRNA synthesis and turnover in *Drosophila* embryos. *Cell*, **21**, 717–727.

9 Anderson W.F. & Diacumakos E.G. (1981) Genetic engineering in mammalian cells. *Scient. Am.*, **245**, 60–93.

10 Ashburner M. (1972) Patterns of puffing activity in the salivary gland chromosomes of *Drosophila*. VI induction by ecdysone in salivary glands of *D. melanogaster* cultured *in vitro*. *Chromosoma*, **38**, 255–282.

11 Ashburner M. (1972) Ecdysone induction of puffing in polytene chromosomes of *D. melanogaster*. Effects of inhibitors of RNA synthesis. *Expl. Cell Res.*, **71**, 433–440.

12 Ashburner M. (1973) Temporal control of puffing activity in polytene chromosomes. *Cold Spring Harbor Symp. Quant. Biol.*, **38**, 655–662.

13 Ashburner M. & Bonner J.J. (1979) The induction of gene activity in *Drosophila* by heat shock. *Cell*, **17**, 241–254.

14 Avvedimento V.E., Vogeli G., Yamada Y., Maizel J.V., Pastan I. & de Combrugghe B. (1980) Correlation between splicing sites within an intron and their sequence complementarity with U1RNA. *Cell*, **21**, 689–696.

15 Axel R., Feigelson P. & Schultz G. (1976) Analysis of the complexity and diversity of mRNA from chicken oviduct and liver. *Cell*, **7**, 247–254.

16 Bachvarova R. & Davidson E.H. (1966) Nuclear activation at the onset of amphibian gastrulation. *J. exp. Zool.*, **163**, 285–295.

17 Bachvarova R. & De Leon V. (1977) Stored and polysomal ribosomes of mouse ova. *Devl. Biol.*, **58**, 248–254.

18 Baker C.C., Herisse J., Courtois G., Galibert F. & Ziff E. (1979) Messenger RNA for the Ad2 DNA binding protein: DNA sequences encoding the first leader and heterogeneity at the mRNA 5′ end. *Cell*, **18**, 569–580.

19 Baker H.J. & Shapiro D.J. (1977) Kinetics of estrogen induction of *X. laevis* vitellogenin mRNA as measured by hybridization to cDNA. *J. biol. Chem.*, **252**, 8428–8434.

20 Baldacci P., Royal A., Cami B., Perrin F., Krust A., Garapin A. & Kourilsky P. (1979) Isolation of the lysozyme gene of chicken. *Nucl. Acids Res.*, **6**, 2667–2681.

21 Ballinger D.G. & Hunt T. (1981) Fertilization of sea urchin eggs is accompanied by 40S ribosomal subunit phosphorylation. *Devl. Biol.*, **87**, 277–285.

22 Bantock C.R. (1970) Experiments on chromosome elimination in the gall midge *Mayetiola destructor*. *J. Embryol. exp. Morph.*, **24**, 257–286.

23 Beerman S. (1966) A quantitative study of chromatin diminution in embryonic mitoses of *Cyclops furcifer*. *Genetics*, **54**, 567–576.

24 Beerman S. (1977) The diminution of heterochromatic chromosomal segments in *Cyclops* (Crustacea, Copepoda). *Chromosoma*, **60**, 297–344.

25 Beerman W. (1952) Chromomerrenkonstanz und spezifische Modifikationen der Chromosomenstruktur in der Entwicklung und Organ Differenzierung von *C. tentans*. *Chromosoma*, **5**, 139–198.

26 Beerman W. (1972) Chrommeres and genes. In *Results and Problems in Cell Differentiation, 4* (Eds W. Beerman, J. Reinert & H. Ursprung.) Springer-Verlag, New York.

27 Behe M. & Felsenfeld G. (1981) Effects of methylation on a synthetic polynucleotide: the B–Z transition in poly (dG-m^{5}dC).poly(dG-m^{5}dC). *Proc. natl Acad. Sci., USA,* **78,** 1619–1623.

28 Bell E. & Reeder R. (1967) The effect of fertilization on protein synthesis in the egg of the surf clam, *Spisula solidissima. Biochim. biophys. Acta,* **142,** 500–511.

29 Bellard M., Gannon F. & Chambon P. (1977) Nucleosome structure. III. The structure and transcriptional activity of the chromatin containing the ovalbumin and globin genes in chick oviduct nuclei. *Cold Spring Harbor Symp. Quant. Biol.,* **42,** 779–791.

30 Benoist C. & Chambon P. (1981) *In vivo* sequence requirements of the SV40 early promoter region. *Nature, Lond.,* **290,** 304–310.

31 Benoist C., O'Hare K., Breathnach R. & Chambon P. (1980) The ovalbumin gene-sequence of putative control regions. *Nucl. Acids Res.,* **8,** 127–142.

32 Benson S.C. & Triplett E.L. (1974) The synthesis and activity of tyrosinase during development of the frog *Rana pipiens. Devl. Biol.,* **40,** 270–282.

33 Bird A.P. (1977) A study of early events in ribosomal gene amplification. *Cold Spring Harbor Symp. Quant. Biol.,* **42,** 1179–1183.

34 Bird A.P. (1978) Use of restriction enzymes to study eukaryotic DNA methylation: II. The symmetry of methylated sites supports semi-conservative copying of the methylation pattern. *J. molec. Biol.,* **118,** 49–60.

35 Bird A.P., Rogers E. & Birnstiel M.L. (1973) Is gene amplification RNA directed? *Nature, New Biol.,* **242,** 226–230.

36 Bird A.P. & Taggart M.H. (1980) Variable patterns of total DNA and rDNA methylation in animals. *Nucl. Acids Res.,* **8,** 1485–1497.

37 Bird A.P., Taggart M.H. & Gehring C.A. (1981) Methylated and unmethylated ribosomal RNA genes in the mouse. *J. molec. Biol.,* **152,** 1–17.

38 Bird A.P., Taggart M. & Macleod D. (1981) Loss of rDNA methylation accompanies the onset of ribosomal gene activity in early development of *X. laevis. Cell,* **26,** 381–390.

39 Bird A.P., Taggart M.H. & Smith B.A. (1979) Methylated and unmethylated DNA compartments in the sea urchin genome. *Cell,* **17,** 889–901.

40 Birkenmeier E.H., Brown D.D. & Jordan E. (1978) A nuclear extract of *Xenopus laevis* oocytes that accurately transcribes 5S RNA genes. *Cell,* **15,** 1077–1086.

41 Bishop J.O., Morton J.C., Rosbash M. & Richardson M. (1974) Three abundance classes in HeLa cell mRNA.*Nature, Lond.,* **250,** 199–203.

42 Bishop J.O. & Rosbash M. (1973) Reiteration frequency of duck haemoglobin genes. *Nature, New Biol.,* **241,** 204–207.

43 Bishop J.O., Rosbash M. & Evans D. (1974) Polynucleotide sequences in eukaryotic DNA and RNA that form ribonuclease-resistant complexes with poly-U. *J. molec. Biol.,* **85,** 75–86.

44 Bogenhagen D.F. & Brown D.D. (1981) Nucleotide sequences in Xenopus 5S DNA required for termination of transcription. *Cell,* **24,** 261–270.

45 Bogenhagen D.F., Sakonju S. & Brown D.D. (1980) A control region in the center of the 5S gene directs specific initiation of transcription: II. The 3′ border of the region. *Cell,* **19,** 27–35.

46 Boseley P.G., Moss T., Machler M., Portmann R. & Birnstiel M.L. (1979) Sequence organization of the spacer DNA in a ribosomal gene unit of *Xenopus laevis. Cell,* **17,** 19–31.

47 Boseley P.G., Tuyno A. & Birnstiel M.L. (1978) Mapping of *Xenopus laevis* 5.8S rDNA by restriction and DNA sequencing. *Nucl. Acids Res.,* **5,** 1121–1137.

48 Bowen B., Steinberg J., Laemmli U.K. & Weintraub H. (1980) The detection of DNA-binding proteins by protein blotting. *Nucl. Acids Res.,* **8,** 1–20.

49 Brandhorst B.P. (1976) Two-dimensional gel patterns of protein synthesis before and after fertilization of sea urchin eggs. *Devl. Biol.,* **52,** 310–317.

50 Brandis J.W. & Raff R.A. (1978) Translation of oogenetic mRNA in sea urchin eggs and early embryos. Demonstration of a change in translational efficiency following fertilization. *Devl. Biol.,* **67,** 99–113.

51 Braude P.R., Pelham H., Flach G. & Lobatto R. (1979) Post-transcriptional control in the early mouse embryo. *Nature, Lond.,* **282,** 102–105.

52 Breathnach R. & Chambon P. (1981) Eukaryotic split genes. *A. Rev. Biochem.,* **50,** 349–383.

53 Breindl M. & Gallwitz D. (1974) On the translational control of histone synthesis. Quantitation of biologically active histone mRNA from synchronized HeLa cells and its translation in different cell-free systems. *Eur. J. Biochem.,* **45,** 91–97.

54 Breuer M.E. & Pavan C. (1955) Behavior of polytene chromosomes of *Rhynchosciara angelae* at different stages of larval development. *Chromosoma,* **7,** 371–386.

55 Bridges C.B. (1938) A revised map of the salivary gland X chromosome of *D. melanogaster. J. Hered.,* **29,** 11–13.

56 Brink N.G., Spragg J.H. & Roberts D.B. (1981) The binding of antibodies to *Drosophila* embryonic cells and their effect on *in vitro* cell differentiation. *Cell Differ.,* **10,** 183–191.

57 Brinster R.L., Chen H.Y., Trumbauer M., Senear A.W., Warren R. & Palmiter R.D. (1982) Somatic expression of Herpes thymidine kinase in mice following injection of a fusion gene into eggs. *Cell,* **27,** 223–231.

58 Brinster R.L., Chen H.Y. & Trumbauer M.E. (1981) Mouse oocytes transcribe injected Xenopus 5S RNA gene. *Science, N.Y.,* **211,** 396–398.

59 Brinster R.L., Chen H.Y., Trumbauer M.E. & Avarbock M.R. (1980) Translation of globin messenger RNA by the mouse ovum. *Nature, Lond.,* **283,** 499–501.

60 Brinster R.L., Chen H.Y., Warren R., Sarthy A. & Palmiter R.D. (1982) Regulation of metallothionein—thymidine kinase fusion plasmids injected into mouse eggs. *Nature, Lond.,* **296,** 39–42.

61 Brown D.D. (1966) The nucleolus and synthesis of ribosomal RNA during oogenesis and embryogenesis of *Xenopus laevis. Natn Cancer Inst. Monogr.,* **23,** 297–309.

62 Brown D.D. & Blackler A.W. (1972) Gene amplification proceeds by a chromosome copy mechanism. *J. molec. Biol.,* **63,** 75–83.

63 Brown D.D. & Dawid I. (1968) Specific gene amplification in oocytes. *Science, N.Y.,* **160,** 272–280.

64 Brown D.D., Dawid I.B. & Reeder R.H. (1977) *Xenopus borealis* misidentified as *Xenopus mulleri. Devl. Biol.*, **59**, 266–267.

65 Brown D.D. & Gurdon J.B. (1964) Absence of ribosomal RNA synthesis in the anucleolate mutant of *Xenopus laevis. Proc. natl Acad. Sci., USA*, **51**, 139–146.

66 Brown D.D. & Gurdon J.B. (1977) High fidelity transcription of 5S DNA injected into *Xenopus* oocytes. *Proc. natl Acad. Sci., USA*, **74**, 2064–2068.

67 Brown D.D. & Gurdon J.B. (1978) Cloned single repeating units of 5S DNA direct accurate transcription of 5S RNA when injected into *Xenopus* oocytes. *Proc. natl Acad. Sci., USA*, **75**, 2849–2853.

68 Brown D.D. & Littna E. (1964) RNA synthesis during the development of *Xenopus laevis*, the South African Clawed Toad. *J. molec. Biol.*, **8**, 669–687.

69 Brown D.D. & Littna E. (1964) Variations in the synthesis of stable RNAs during oogenesis and development of *Xenopus laevis. J. molec. Biol.*, **8**, 688–695.

70 Brown D.D. & Littna E. (1966) Synthesis and accumulation of DNA-like RNA during embryogenesis of *Xenopus laevis. J. molec. Biol.*, **20**, 81–94.

71 Brown D.D. & Littna E. (1966) Synthesis and accumulation of low molecular weight RNA during embryogenesis of *Xenopus laevis. J. molec. Biol.*, **20**, 95–112.

72 Brown D.D. & Sugimoto K. (1973) 5S DNA of *Xenopus laevis* and *Xenopus mülleri*: evolution of a gene family. *J. molec. Biol.*, **78**, 397–415.

73 Brown D.D. & Weber C.S. (1968) Gene linkage by RNA/DNA hybridization. II. Arrangement of the redundant gene sequences for 28S and 18S rRNA. *J. molec. Biol.*, **34**, 681–697.

74 Brown D.D., Wensink P.C. & Jordan E. (1971) Purification and some characterization of 5S DNA from *Xenopus laevis. Proc. natl. Acad. Sci., USA*, **68**, 3175–3179.

75 Brown J.L. & Ingram U.M. (1974) Structural studies in chick embryonic hemoglobins. *J. biol. Chem.*, **249**, 3960–3972.

76 Busby S. & Bakken A.H. (1980) Transcription in developing sea urchins: electron microscopic analysis of cleavage, gastrula and prism stages. *Chromosoma*, **79**, 85–104.

77 Calabretta B., Robberson D.L., Barrera-Saldana H.A., Lambrou T.P. & Saunders G.F. (1982) Genome instability in a region of human DNA enriched in Alu repeat sequences. *Nature, Lond.*, **296**, 219–225.

78 Calos M.P. & Miller J.H. (1980) Transposable elements. *Cell*, **20**, 579–595.

79 Cameron J.R., Loh E.Y. & Davis R.W. (1979) Evidence for transposition of dispersed repetitive DNA families in yeast. *Cell*, **16**, 739–751.

80 Campo M.S. & Bishop J.O. (1974) Two classes of messenger RNA in cultured rat cells: repetitive sequence transcripts and unique sequence transcripts. *J. molec. Biol.*, **90**, 649–664.

81 Cascio S.M. & Wassarman P.M. (1982) Program of early development in the mammal: post-transcriptional control of a class of proteins synthesized by mouse oocytes and early embryos. *Devl. Biol.*, **89**, 397–408.

82 Catterall J.F., Steui J.P., Lai E.C., Woo S.L.C., Mace M.L., Means A.R. & O'Malley B.W. (1979) The ovomucoid gene contains at least six intervening sequences. *Nature, Lond.*, **278**, 323–327.

83 Chamberlin M.E., Britten R.J. & Davidson E.H. (1975) Sequence organization in *Xenopus* DNA studied by the electron microscope. *J. molec. Biol.*, **96**, 317–333.

84 Cheng H-L., Blattner F.R., Fitzmaurice L., Mushinski J.F. & Tucker P.W. (1982) Structure of genes for membrane and secreted murine IgD heavy chains. *Nature, Lond.*, **296**, 410–415.

85 Christman J.K., Weich N., Schoenbrun B., Schniederman N. & Acs, G. (1980) Hypomethylation of DNA during differentiation of Friend erythroleukemia cells. *J. Cell Biol.*, **86**, 366–370.

86 Clever U. (1966) Puffing in giant chromosomes of Diptera and the mechanism of its control. In *The Nucleohistones* (Eds J. Bonner & P. Tso). Holden-Day, San Francisco.

87 Colman A. & Morser J. (1979) Export of proteins from oocytes of *Xenopus laevis. Cell*, **17**, 517–526.

88 Constantini F.D., Britten R.J. & Davidson E.H. (1980) Message sequences and short repetitive sequences are interspersed in sea urchin egg poly(A)$^+$ RNAs. *Nature, Lond.*, **287**, 111–117.

89 Constantinides P.G., Jones P.A. & Gevers W. (1977) Functional striated muscle cells from non-myoblast precursors following 5-azacytidine treatment. *Nature, Lond.*, **267**, 364–366.

90 Contreras R. & Fiers W. (1981) Initiation of transcription by RNA polymerase II in permeable, SV40-infected or noninfected, CV1 cells; evidence for multiple promotors of SV40 late transcription. *Nucl. Acids Res.*, **9**, 215–236.

91 Corden J., Wasylyk B., Buchwalder A., Sassone-Corsi P., Kedinger C. & Chapman P. (1980) Promoter sequences of eukaryotic protein-coding genes. *Science, N.Y.*, **209**, 1406–1414.

92 Crain W.R., Davidson E.H. & Britten R.J. (1976) Contrasting patterns of DNA sequence arrangement in *Apis mellifera* (honeybee) and *Musca domestica* (housefly). *Chromosoma*, **59**, 1–12.

93 Craine B.L. & Kornberg T. (1981) Transcription of the major *Drosophila* heat-shock genes *in vitro. Biochemistry*, **20**, 6584–6588.

94 Craine B.L. & Kornberg T. (1981) Activation of the major Drosophila heat-shock genes *in vitro. Cell*, **25**, 671–681.

95 Crampton J.M. & Woodland H.R. (1979) A cell-free assay system for the analysis of changes in RNA synthesis during the development of *Xenopus laevis. Devl. Biol.*, **70**, 453–466.

96 Crampton J.M. & Woodland H.R. (1979) Isolation from *Xenopus laevis* embryonic cells of a factor which stimulates ribosomal RNA synthesis by isolated nuclei. *Devl. Biol.*, **70**, 467–478.

97 Crippa M. (1970) Regulatory factor for the transcription of the ribosomal RNA genes in amphibian oocytes. *Nature, Lond.*, **227**, 1138–1140.

98 Danilchik M.V. & Hille M.B. (1981) Sea urchin egg and embryo ribosomes: differences in translational activity in a cell-free system. *Devl. Biol.*, **84**, 291–298.

99 Davidson E.H. (1976) *Gene Activity in Early Development*, 2nd edn. Academic Press, New York.

100 Davidson E.H. & Hough B.R. (1971) Genetic information in oocyte RNA. *J. molec. Biol.*, **56**, 491–506.

101 Davidson E.H., Hough B.R., Amenson C.S. & Britten R.J. (1973) General interspersion of repetitive with nonrepetitive sequence elements in the DNA of *Xenopus. J. molec. Biol.*, **77**, 1–24.

102 Denis H. & Mairy M. (1972) Recherches biochimiques sur

l'oogénèse. 2. Distribution intracellulaire du RNA dans les petits oocytes de *Xenopus laevis*. *Eur. J. Biochem.*, **25**, 524–534.

103 Denis H. & Wagnez M. (1977) Biochemical research on oogenesis. Oocytes of *Xenopus laevis* synthesize but do not accumulate 5S RNA of somatic type. *Devl. Biol.*, **58**, 212–217.

104 Denny P.C. & Tyler A. (1964) Activation of protein biosynthesis in non-nucleate fragments of sea urchin eggs. *Biochem. biophys. Res. Commun.*, **14**, 245–249.

105 Derman E., Krauter K., Walling L., Weinberger C., Ray M. & Darnell J.E. (1981) Transcriptional control in the production of liver-specific mRNAs. *Cell*, **23**, 731–739.

106 Devlin R. (1976) Mitochondrial poly(A) RNA synthesis during early sea urchin development. *Devl. Biol.*, **50**, 443–456.

107 Diaz M.O., Barsacchi-Pilone G., Mahon K.A. & Gall J.G. (1981) Transcripts from both strands of a satellite DNA occur on lampbrush chromosome loops of the newt *Notophthalmus*. *Cell*, **24**, 649–659.

108 Dodgson J.B. & Engel J.D. (1980) Analysis of the closely linked adult chicken α-globin genes in recombinant DNAs. *Proc. natl Acad. Sci., USA*, **77**, 2597–2599.

109 Doerfler W. (1981) Review article. DNA methylation—a regulatory signal in eukaryotic gene expression *J. gen. Virol.*, **57**, 1–20.

110 Doering J. (1976) Characterization of new 5S DNA from *X. mulleri. Carnegie Inst. Washington Yearbook*, **75**, 15–16.

111 Doolittle W.F. & Sapienza C. (1980) Selfish genes, the phenotype paradigm and genome evolution. *Nature, Lond.*, **284**, 601–603.

112 Early P. & Hood L. (1981) Allelic exclusion and nonproductive immunoglobulin gene rearrangements. Minireview. *Cell*, **24**, 1–3.

113 Eastman E.M., Goodman R.M., Erlanger B.F. & Miller O.J. (1980) 5′-methylcytosine in the DNA of the polytene chromosomes of the Diptera *Sciara coprophila, Drosophila melanogaster* and *D. persimilis. Chromosoma*, **79**, 225–239.

114 Eden F.C. (1980) A cloned chicken DNA fragment includes two repeated DNA sequences with remarkably different genomic organizations. *J. biol. Chem.*, **255**, 4854–4863.

115 Efstratiadis A., Posakony J.W., Maniatis T., Lawn R.M., O'Connell C., Spritz R.A., DeRiel J.K., Forget B.G., Weissman S.M., Slightom J.L., Blechl A.E., Smithies O., Baralle F.E., Shoulders C.C. & Proudfoot N.J. (1980) The structure and evolution of the human β-globin gene family. *Cell*, **21**, 653–668.

116 Elgin S.C. (1981) DNAase I-hypersensitive sites of chromatin. *Cell*, **27**, 413–415.

117 Ellem K.A.O. & Gwatkin R.B.L. (1968) Patterns of nucleic acid synthesis in the early mouse embryo. *Devl. Biol.*, **18**, 311–330.

118 Emerson C.P. & Humphreys T. (1970) Regulation of DNA-like RNA and the apparent activation of ribosomal RNA synthesis in sea urchin embryos: Quantitative measurements of newly synthesized RNA. *Devl. Biol.*, **23**, 86–112.

119 Emerson C.P. & Humphreys T. (1971) Ribosomal RNA synthesis and the multiple, atypical nucleoli in cleaving embryos. *Science, N.Y.*, **171**, 898–901.

120 Engelke D.R., Ng S.Y., Shastry B.S. & Roeder R.G. (1980) Specific interaction of a purified transcription factor with an internal control region of 5S RNA genes. *Cell*, **19**, 717–728.

121 Epel D. (1967) Protein synthesis in sea urchin eggs: a "late" response to fertilization. *Proc. natl Acad. Sci., USA*, **57**, 899–906.

122 Epel D. (1978) Mechanisms of activation of sperm and egg during fertilization of sea urchin gametes: sperm activation precedes egg activation. *Curr. Tops Devl. Biol.*, **12**, 185–246.

123 Epstein C.J. & Smith S.A. (1973) Amino acid uptake and protein synthesis in preimplantation mouse embryos. *Devl. Biol.*, **33**, 171–184.

124 Ernst S.G., Hough-Evans B.R., Britten R.J. & Davidson E.H. (1980) Limited complexity of the RNA in micromeres of sixteen cell sea urchin embryos. *Devl. Biol.*, **79**, 119–127.

125 Fahrner K., Yarger J. & Hereford L. (1980) Yeast histone mRNA is polyadenylated. *Nucl. Acids Res.*, **8**, 5725–5738.

126 Fan H. & Penman S. (1970) Regulation of protein synthesis in mammalian cells. II. Inhibition of protein synthesis at the level of initiation during mitosis. *J. molec. Biol.*, **50**, 655–670.

127 Federoff N., Wellauer P.K. & Wall R. (1977) Intramolecular duplexes in heterogeneous nuclear RNA from HeLa cells. *Cell*, **10**, 597–610.

128 Felicetti L., Metafora S., Gambino R. & DiMatteo G. (1972) Characterization and activity of the elongation factors T_1 and T_2 in the unfertilized egg and in the early development of sea urchins. *Cell Differ.*, **1**, 265–277.

129 Felsenfeld G. (1978) Chromatin. *Nature, Lond.*, **271**, 115–122.

130 Finnegan D.J., Rubin G.M., Young M.W. & Hogness D.S. (1978) Repeated gene families in *Drosophila melanogaster. Cold Spring Harbor Symp. Quant. Biol.*, **42**, 1053–1063.

131 Firtel R.A. & Monroy A. (1970) Polysomes and RNA synthesis during early development of the surf clam *Spisula solidissima. Devl. Biol.*, **21**, 87–104.

132 Flickinger R.A. (1969) A regional difference in the time of initial synthesis of ribosomal RNA in frog embryos. *Expl. Cell Res.*, **55**, 422–423.

133 Foe V.E. (1978) Modulation of ribosomal RNA synthesis in *Oncopeltus fasciatus*: an electron microscopic study of the relationship between changes in chromatin structure and transcriptional activity. *Cold Spring Harbor Symp. Quant. Biol.*, **42**, 723–740.

134 Ford P.J. (1971) Non-coordinated accumulation and synthesis of 5S ribonucleic acid by ovaries of *Xenopus laevis. Nature, Lond.*, **233**, 561–564.

135 Ford P.J. & Brown R.D. (1976) Sequences of 5S ribosomal RNA from *Xenopus mulleri* and the evolution of 5S gene-coding sequences. *Cell*, **8**, 485–493.

136 Ford P.J. & Southern E.M. (1973) Different sequences for 5S RNA in kidney cells and ovaries of *Xenopus laevis. Nature, New Biol.*, **241**, 7–12.

137 Fritsch E.F., Shen J.C.-K., Lawn R.M. & Maniatis T. (1981) The organization of repetitive sequences in mammalian globin gene clusters. *Cold Spring Harbor Symp. Quant. Biol.*, **45**, 761–776.

138 Gabrielli F., Hancock R. & Faber A.J. (1981) Characterization of a chromatin fraction bearing pulse-labelled RNA. 2. Quantification of histones and high mobility-group proteins. *Eur. J. Biochem.*, **120**, 363–369.

139 Galas D. & Schmitz A. (1978) DNase footprinting: a simple method for the detection of protein–DNA binding specificity. *Nucl. Acids Res.*, **5**, 3157–3170.

140 Galau G.A., Britten R.J. & Davidson E.M. (1974) A measurement of the sequence complexity of polysomal mRNA in sea urchin embryos. *Cell*, **2**, 9–21.

141 Galau G.A., Klein W.H., Britten R.J. & Davidson E.H. (1977)

Significance of rare mRNA sequences in liver. *Archs Biochem. Biophys.* **179**, 584–599.

142 Galau G.A., Klein W.H., Davis M.M., Wold B.J., Britten R.J. & Davidson E.H. (1976) Structural gene sets active in embryos and adult tissues of the sea urchin. *Cell*, **7**, 487–505.

143 Galau G.A., Lipson E.D., Britten R.J. & Davidson E.H. (1977) Synthesis and turnover of polysomal mRNAs in sea urchin embryos. *Cell*, **10**, 415–432.

144 Gall J.G. (1968) Differential synthesis of the genes for ribosomal RNA during amphibian oogenesis. *Proc. natl Acad. Sci., USA*, **60**, 553–560.

145 Gall J.G. (1969) The genes for ribosomal RNA during oogenesis. *Genetics*, **61**, Suppl. 1, 121–132.

146 Gall J.G. & Pardue M.L. (1969) Formation and detection of RNA-DNA hybrid molecules in cytological preparations. *Proc. natl Acad. Sci., USA*, **63**, 378–383.

147 Galli G., Hofstetter H. & Birnstiel M. (1981) Two conserved sequence blocks within eukaryotic tRNA genes are major promoter elements. *Nature, Lond.*, **294**, 626–631.

148 Gannon F., O'Hare K., Perrin F., LePennec J.P., Benoist C., Cochet M., Breathnach R., Royal A., Garapin A., Cami B. & Chambon P. (1979) Organization and sequences at the 5′ end of a cloned complete ovalbumin gene. *Nature, Lond.*, **278**, 428–434.

149 Garel A., Zobu M. & Axel R. (1977) Genes transcribed at diverse rates have a similar conformation in chromatin. *Proc. natl Acad. Sci., USA*, **74**, 4867–4871.

150 Gehring W.J. & Paro R. (1980) Isolation of a hybrid plasmid with homologous sequences to a transposing element of *Drosophila melanogaster*. *Cell*, **19**, 897–904.

151 Getz M.J., Birnie G.D., Young B.D., MacPhail E. & Paul J. (1975) A kinetic estimation of the base sequence complexity of nuclear poly(A)-containing RNA in mouse Friend cells. *Cell*, **4**, 121–130.

152 Gilmour R.S. (1978) Structure and control of the globin gene. In *The Cell Nucleus*, Vol. 6 (Ed. H. Busch), pp. 329–367. Academic Press, New York.

153 Gluzman Y., Sambrook J.F. & Frisque R.J. (1980) Expression of early genes of origin-defective mutants of simian virus 40. *Proc. natl Acad. Sci., USA*, **77**, 3898–3902.

154 Goldberg R.B., Crain W.R., Ruderman J.V., Moore G.P., Barnett T.R., Higgins R.C., Gelfand A., Galau G.A., Britten R.J. & Davidson E.H. (1975) DNA sequence organization in genomes of 5 marine invertebrates. *Chromosoma*, **51**, 225–251.

155 Goldberg R.B., Galau G.A., Britten R.J. & Davidson E.H. (1973) Nonrepetitive DNA sequence representation in sea urchin embryo messenger RNA. *Proc. natl Acad. Sci., USA*, **70**, 3516–3520.

156 Goldstein P. & Straus N.A. (1978) Molecular characterization of *Ascaris suum* DNA and of chromatin diminution. *Expl. Cell Res.*, **116**, 462–466.

157 Gottesfeld J.M. (1977) Methods for fractionation of chromatin into transcriptionally active and inactive segments. *Methods Cell Biol.*, **16**, 421–436.

158 Gough N. (1981) The rearrangements of immunoglobulin genes. *Trends Biochem. Sci.*, **6**, 203–205.

159 Goustin A.S. (1981) Two temporal phases for the control of histone gene activity in cleaving sea urchin embryos (*S. purpuratus*). *Devl. Biol.*, **87**, 163–175.

160 Graham C.F. & Morgan R.W. (1966) Changes in the cell cycle during early amphibian development. *Devl. Biol.*, **14**, 439–460.

161 Graham D.E., Neufeld B.R., Davidson E.H. & Britten R.J. (1974) Interspersion of repetitive and non-repetitive DNA sequences in the sea urchin genome. *Cell*, **1**, 127–137.

162 Grez M., Land H., Giesecke K., Schutz G., Jung A. & Sippel A.E. (1981) Multiple mRNAs are generated from the chicken lysozyme gene. *Cell*, **25**, 743–752.

163 Griffith J.K., Griffith B.B. & Humphreys T. (1981) Regulation of ribosomal RNA synthesis in sea urchin embryos and oocytes. *Devl. Biol.*, **87**, 220–228.

164 Gronemeyer H. & Pongs O. (1980) Localization of ecdysterone on polytene chromosomes of *Drosophila melanogaster*. *Proc. natl Acad. Sci., USA*, **77**, 2108–2112.

165 Grosschedl R. & Birnstiel M.L. (1980) Identification of regulatory sequences in the prelude sequences of an H2A histone gene by the study of specific deletion mutants *in vivo*. *Proc. natl Acad. Sci., USA*, **77**, 1432–1436.

166 Grosschedl R. & Birnstiel M.L. (1980) Spacer DNA sequences upstream of the TATAAATA sequence are essential for promotion of H2A histone gene transcription *in vivo*. *Proc. natl Acad. Sci., USA*, **77**, 7102–7106.

167 Grosveld G.C., de Boer E., Shewmaker C.K. & Flavell R.A. (1982) DNA sequences necessary for transcription of the rabbit β-globin gene *in vivo*. *Nature, Lond.*, **295**, 120–126.

168 Grosveld G.C., Shewmaker C.K., Jat P. & Flavell R.A. (1981) Localization of DNA sequences necessary for transcription of the rabbit β-globin gene *in vitro*. *Cell*, **25**, 215–226.

169 Groudine M., Eisenmann R. & Weintraub H. (1981) Chromatin structure of endogenous retroviral genes and activation by an inhibitor of DNA methylation. *Nature, Lond.*, **292**, 311–317.

170 Groudine M. Weintraub H. (1981) Activation of globin genes during chicken development. *Cell*, **24**, 393–401.

171 Grummt I. (1981) Specific transcription of mouse ribosomal DNA in a cell-free system that mimics control *in vivo*. *Proc. natl Acad. Sci., USA*, **78**, 727–731.

172 Gurdon J.B. (1967) Control of gene activity during the early development of *Xenopus laevis*. In *Heritage from Mendel* (Ed. A. Brink), pp. 203–239. University of Wisconsin Press, Wisconsin.

173 Gurdon J.B. (1968) Changes in somatic nuclei inserted into growing and maturing amphibian oocytes. *J. Embryol. exp. Morph.*, **20**, 401–414.

174 Gurdon J.B. (1974) *The Control of Gene Expression in Animal Development*. Clarendon Press, Oxford.

175 Gurdon J.B. & Brown D.D. (1965) Cytoplasmic regulation of RNA synthesis in developing embryos of *Xenopus laevis*. *J. molec. Biol.*, **12**, 27–35.

176 Gurdon J.B., Lingrel J.B. & Marbaix G. (1973) Message stability in injected frog oocytes: long life of mammalian α and β globin messages. *J. molec. Biol.*, **80**, 539–551.

177 Gurdon J.B. & Melton D.A. (1981) Gene transfer in amphibian eggs and oocytes. *A. Rev. Genet.*, **15**, 189–218.

178 Gurdon J.B. & Woodland H.R. (1968) The cytoplasmic control of nuclear activity in animal development. *Biol. Rev.*, **43**, 233–267.

179 Gurdon J.B. & Woodland H.R. (1969) The influence of the cytoplasm on the nucleus during cell differentiation, with special reference to RNA synthesis during amphibian cleavage. *Proc. Roy. Soc. Lond. B.*, **173**, 99–111.

180 Gurdon J.B., Woodland H.R. & Lingrel J.B. (1974) The translation of mammalian globin mRNA injected into fertilized eggs of *Xenopus laevis*. I. Message stability in development. *Devl. Biol.*, **39**, 125–133.

181 Harris H. (1963) Nuclear RNA. *Progr. Nuc. Acid Res.*, **2**, 20–60.

182 Harris H. (1968) *Nucleus and Cytoplasm*. Clarendon Press, Oxford.

183 Harris S.E. & Forrest H.S. (1967) RNA and DNA synthesis in developing eggs of the milkweed bug *Oncopeltus fasciatus* (Dallas). *Science, N.Y.*, **156**, 1613–1615.

184 Hay E.D. & Gurdon J.B. (1967) Fine structure of the nucleolus in normal and mutant *Xenopus* embryos. *J. Cell Sci.*, **2**, 151–162.

185 Hennig W. & Meer B. (1971) Reduced polyteny of ribosomal cistrons in giant chromosomes of *D. hydei*. *Nature, New Biol.*, **233**, 70–72.

186 Hentschel C.C. & Birnstiel M.C. (1981) The organization and expression of histone gene families. *Cell*, **25**, 301–313.

187 Herbomel P., Saragosti S., Blangy D. & Yaniv M. (1981) Fine structure of the origin-proximal DNAase I-hypersensitive region in wild-type and EC-mutant polyoma. *Cell*, **25**, 651–658.

188 Hereford L.M., Osley M.A., Ludwig J.J. & McLaughlin C.S. (1981) Cell-cycle regulation of yeast histone mRNA. *Cell*, **24**, 367–375.

189 Higashinakagawa T., Wahn H. & Reeder R.H. (1977) Isolation of ribosomal gene chromatin. *Devl. Biol.*, **55**, 374–386.

190 Hill R.S. (1979) A quantitative electron-microscope analysis of chromatin from *Xenopus laevis* lampbrush chromosomes. *J. Cell Sci.*, **40**, 145–169.

191 Hille M.B. & Albero A.A. (1979) Efficiency of protein synthesis after fertilization of sea urchin eggs. *Nature, Lond.*, **278**, 469–471.

192 Hoberman H.D., Metz C.B. & Graff J. (1952) Uptake of deuterium into proteins of fertilized and unfertilized *Arbacia* eggs suspended in heavy water. *J. gen. Physiol.*, **35**, 639–643.

193 Hofer E. & Darnell J.E. (1981) The primary transcription unit of the mouse β-major globin gene. *Cell*, **23**, 585–593.

194 Holliday R. & Pugh J.E. (1975) DNA modification mechanisms and gene activity during development. *Science, N.Y.*, **187**, 226–232.

195 Holmgren R., Livak K., Morimoto R., Freund R. & Meselson M. (1979) Studies of cloned sequences from four *Drosophila* heat shock loci. *Cell*, **18**, 1359–1370.

196 Holtzer H., Rubinstein N., Fellinci S., Yeoh G., Chi, J., Birnbaum J. & Okayama M. (1975) Lineages, quantal cell cycles and the generation of cell diversity. *Q. Rev. Biophys.*, **8**, 523–557.

197 Honda B.M. & Roeder R.G. (1980) Association of a 5S gene transcription factor with 5S RNA and altered levels of the factor during cell differentiation. *Cell*, **22**, 119–126.

198 Honjo T. & Reeder R.H. (1973) Preferential transcription of *Xenopus laevis* ribosomal RNA in interspecies hybrids between *Xenopus laevis* and *Xenopus mulleri*. *J. molec. Biol.*, **80**, 217–228.

199 Houck C.M., Rinehart F.P. & Schmid C.W. (1979) A ubiquitous family of repeated DNA sequences in the human genome. *J. molec. Biol.*, **132**, 289–306.

200 Hough B.R., Smith M.J., Britten R.J. & Davidson E.H. (1975) Sequence complexity of the heterogeneous nuclear RNA in sea-urchin embryos. *Cell*, **5**, 291–299.

201 Hough B.R., Yancey P.H. & Davidson E.H. (1973) Persistence of maternal mRNA in *Engystomops* embryos. *J. exp. Zool.*, **185**, 357–368.

202 Hough-Evans B.R., Wold B.J., Ernst S.G., Britten R.J. & Davidson E.H. (1977) Appearance and persistence of maternal RNA sequences in sea urchin development. *Devl. Biol.*, **60**, 258–277.

203 Houghton M., Jackson I.J., Porter A.G., Doel S.M., Catlin G.H., Barber C. & Carey N.H. (1981) The absence of introns within a human fibroblast interferon gene. *Nucl. Acids Res.*, **9**, 247–266.

204 Hourcade D., Dressler D. & Wolfson J. (1973) The amplification of ribosomal genes involves a rolling circle intermediate. *Proc. natl Acad. Sci., USA*, **70**, 2926–2930.

205 Hsieh T.S. & Brutlag D.L. (1979) A protein that preferentially binds *Drosophila* satellite DNA. *Proc. natl Acad. Sci., USA*, **76**, 726–730.

206 Hu S.L. & Mauley J. (1981) DNA sequence requirement for initiation of transcription *in vitro* from the major late promoter of adenovirus 2. *Proc. natl Acad. Sci., USA*, **78**, 820–824.

207 Hultin T. (1952) Incorporation of N-labelled glycine and alanine into the proteins of developing sea urchin eggs. *Expl Cell Res.*, **3**, 494–496.

208 Humphreys T. (1969) Efficiency of translation of messenger RNA before and after fertilization in sea urchins. *Devl. Biol.*, **20**, 435–458.

209 Humphreys T. (1971) Measurements of messenger RNA entering polysomes upon fertilization of sea urchin eggs. *Devl. Biol.*, **26**, 201–208.

210 Humphreys T. (1973) RNA and protein synthesis during early animal embryogenesis. In *Developmental Regulation. Aspects of Cell Differentiation*. (Ed. S.J. Coward), p. 1. Academic Press, New York.

211 Humphries S.E., Young D. & Carroll D. (1979) Chromatin structure of the 5S RNA genes of *X. laevis*. *Biochemistry*, **18**, 3223–3231.

212 Hunt T. (1974) The control of globin synthesis in rabbit reticulocytes. *Ann. N.Y. Acad. Sci.*, **241**, 223–231.

213 Hunt T., Hunter A.R. & Munro A.J. (1969) Control of haemoglobin synthesis: rate of translation of the messenger RNA for the α and β chain. *J. molec. Biol.*, **43**, 123–133.

214 Ilan J. & Ilan J. (1978) Translation of messenger ribonucleoprotein particles from sea urchin in a cell-free system from unfertilized eggs and product analysis. *Devl. Biol.*, **66**, 375–385.

215 Ilyin Y.V., Tchurikov N.A., Ananiev E.V., Ryskov A.P., Yenikolopov G.N., Limborska S.A., Maleeva N.E., Grozdev V.A. & Georgiev G.P. (1977) Studies on the DNA fragments of mammals and *Drosophila* containing structural genes and adjacent sequences. *Cold Spring Harbor Symp. Quant. Biol.*, **42**, 959–969.

216 Jack R.S., Gehring W.J. & Brack C. (1981) Protein component from *Drosophila* larval nuclei showing sequence specificity for a short region near a major heat-shock protein gene. *Cell*, **24**, 321–331.

217 Jacq C., Miller J.R. & Brownlee G.G. (1977) A pseudogene structure in 5S DNA of *Xenopus laevis*. *Cell*, **12**, 109–120.

218 Jagadeeswaran P., Forget B.G. & Weissman S.M. (1981) Short interspersed repetitive DNA elements in eukaryotes: transposable DNA elements generated by reverse transcription of RNA polymerase III transcripts. *Cell*, **26**, 141–142.

219 Jeffreys A.J. (1981) Recent studies of gene evolution using recombinant DNA. In *Genetic Engineering 2* (Ed R. Williamson). Academic Press, London.

220 Jeffreys A.J. & Flavell R.A. (1977) The rabbit β-globin gene contains a large insert in the coding sequence. *Cell*, **12**, 1097–1108.

221 Jelinek W.R., Toomey T.P., Leuiwand L., Duncan C.H., Biro P.A., Choudary P.V., Weissman S.M., Rubin C.M., Houck C.M., Deininger P.L. & Schmid C.W. (1980) Ubiquitous, interspersed repeated sequences in mammalian genomes. *Proc. natl Acad. Sci., USA*, **77**, 1998–2402.

222 Jenkins N.A., Kaumeyer J.F., Young E.M. & Raff R.A. (1978) A test for masked message: the template activity of messenger ribonucleoprotein particles isolated from sea urchin eggs. *Devl. Biol.*, **63**, 279–298.

223 Johnson M.H. (1981) The molecular and cellular basis of pre-implantation mouse development. *Biol. Rev.*, **56**, 463–498.

224 Jones P.A. & Taylor S.M. (1980) Cellular differentiation, cytidine analogues and DNA methylation. *Cell*, **20**, 85–93.

225 Jones P.A. & Taylor S.M. (1981) Hemimethylated duplex DNAs prepared from 5-azacytidine-treated cells. *Nucl. Acids Res.*, **9**, 2933–2947.

226 Jones R.W. (1978) Preparation of chromatin containing ribosomal deoxyribonucleic acid from macronucleus of *Tetrahymena pyriformis*. *Biochem. J.*, **173**, 145–153.

227 Jones R.W. (1978) Histone composition of a chromatin fraction containing ribosomal deoxyribonucleic acid isolated from macronucleus of *Tetrahymena pyriformis*. *Biochem. J.*, **173**, 155–164.

228 Kalt M.R. & Gall J.G. (1974) Observations of early germ cell development and premeiotic ribosomal DNA amplification in *Xenopus laevis*. *J. Cell Biol.*, **62**, 460–472.

229 Kalthoff K. (1979) Analysis of a morphogenetic determinant in an insect embryo (*Smittia* spec., Chironomidae, Diptera). In *Determinants of Spatial Organization* (Eds S. Subtelny & J.R. Konigsberg), pp. 97–126. Academic Press, New York.

230 Kasteria W.H., Underberg D.A. & Berry S.J. (1981) DNA-dependent cytoplasmic RNA polymerase I and II in insect oocytes. *Devl. Biol.*, **87**, 383–389.

231 Kedes L. (1979) Histone genes and histone messengers. *A. Rev. Biochem.*, **48**, 837–870.

232 Keene M.A., Corces V., Lowenhaupt K. & Elgin S.C.R. (1981) DNase I hypersensitive sites in *Drosophila* chromatin occur at the 5′ ends of regions of transcription. *Proc. natl Acad. Sci., USA*, **78**, 143–146.

233 Kinniburgh A.J. & Ross J. (1979) Processing of the mouse β-globin mRNA precursor: at least two cleavage-ligation reactions are necessary to excise the larger intervening sequence. *Cell*, **17**, 915–921.

234 Klein W.H., Thomas T.L., Lai C., Scheller R.H., Britten R.J. & Davidson E.H. (1978) Characteristics of individual repetitive sequence families in the sea urchin genome studied with cloned repeats. *Cell*, **14**, 889–900.

235 Knapp G., Beckmann J.S., Johnson P.F., Fuhrman S.A. & Abelson J. (1978) Transcription and processing of intervening sequences in yeast tRNA genes. *Cell*, **14**, 221–236.

236 Knowland J.S. (1970) Polyacrylamide gel electrophoresis of nucleic acids synthesized during the early development of *Xenopus laevis* Daudin. *Biochim. biophys. Acta*, **204**, 416–429.

237 Knowland J.S. & Graham C. (1972) RNA synthesis at the two-cell stage of mouse development. *J. Embryol. exp. Morph.*, **27**, 167–176.

238 Knowland J. & Miller L. (1970) Reduction of ribosomal RNA synthesis and ribosomal RNA genes in a mutant of *Xenopus laevis* which organizes only a partial nucleolus. I. Ribosomal RNA synthesis in embryos of different nucleolar types. *J. molec. Biol.*, **53**, 321–328.

239 Korn L.J. (1982) Transcription of *Xenopus* 5S ribosomal RNA genes. *Nature, Lond.*, **295**, 101–105.

240 Korn L.J. & Brown D.D. (1978) Nucleotide sequence of *Xenopus borealis* oocyte 5S DNA: comparison of sequences that flank several related eukaryotic genes. *Cell*, **15**, 1145–1156.

241 Korn L.J. & Gurdon J.B. (1981) The reactivation of developmentally inert 5S genes in somatic nuclei injected with *Xenopus* oocytes. *Nature, Lond.*, **289**, 461–465.

242 Kornberg R.D. (1977) Structure of chromatin. *A. Rev. Biochem.*, **46**, 931–934.

243 Krayev A.S., Kramerov D.A., Skyrabin K.G., Ryskov A.P., Bayev A.A. & Georgiev G.P. (1980) The nucleotide sequence of the ubiquitous repetitive DNA sequence B1 complementary to the most abundant class of mouse fold-back RNA. *Nucl. Acids Res.*, **8**, 1201–1215.

244 Krolewski J.J., Bertelsen A.H., Humayun M.Z. & Rush M.G. (1982) Members of the Alu Family of interspersed repetitive DNA sequences are in the small circular DNA population of monkey cells grown in culture. *J. molec. Biol.*, **154**, 399–415.

245 Kunz W. & Eckhardt R.A. (1974) The chromosomal distribution of satellite DNA in the germ-line and somatic tissues of the gall midge, *Heteropeza pygmaea*. *Chromosoma*, **47**, 1–9.

246 Kunz W., Trepte J. & Bier K. (1970) On the function of germ-line chromosomes in the oogenesis of *Wachtliella persicariae* (Cecidomyiidae). *Chromosoma*, **30**, 180–192.

247 Kuo T., Mandel J. & Chambon P. (1979) DNA methylation: correlation with DNase I sensitivity of chicken ovalbumin and conalbumin chromatin. *Nucl. Acids Res.*, **7**, 2105–2113.

248 Lacy E. & Axel R. (1975) Analysis of DNA of isolated chromatin subunits. *Proc. natl Acad. Sci., USA*, **72**, 3978–3982.

249 Laird C.D. (1980) Structural paradox of polytene chromosomes. *Cell*, **22**, 869–874.

250 Laird C.D., Wilkinson L.E., Foe V.E. & Chooi W.Y. (1976) Analysis of chromatin associated fiber arrays. *Chromosoma*, **58**, 169–192.

251 La Marca M.J., Smith L.D. & Strobel M.C. (1973) Quantitative and qualitative analysis of RNA synthesis in stage 6 and stage 4 oocytes of *Xenopus laevis*. *Devl. Biol.*, **34**, 106–118.

252 Lamb M.M. & Daneholt B. (1979) Characterization of active transcription units in Balbiani rings of *Chironomus tentans*. *Cell*, **17**, 835–848.

253 Lane C.D. (1976) Rabbit hemoglobin from frogs eggs. *Scient. Am.*, **253**, 60–71.

254 Lane C.D., Colman A., Mohun T., Morser J., Champion J., Kourides I., Craig R., Higgins S., James T.C., Applebaum S.W., Ohlsson R.I., Paucha E., Houghton M., Matthews J. & Miflin B.J. (1980) The *Xenopus* oocyte as a surrogate secretory system. The specificity of protein export. *Eur. J. Biochem.*, **111**, 225–235.

255 Laskey R.A., Gerhart J. & Knowland J.S. (1973) Inhibition of ribosomal RNA synthesis in neurula cells by extracts from blastulae of *Xenopus laevis*. *Devl. Biol.*, **33**, 241–247.

256 Lee F., Mulligan R., Berg P. & Ringold G. (1981) Glucocorticoids regulate expression of dihydrofolate reductase cDNA in

mouse mammary tumour virus chimaeric plasmids. *Nature, Lond.*, **294**, 228–232.

257 Lerner M.R. & Steitz J.A. (1981) Snurps and scyrps. *Cell*, **25**, 298–300.

258 Levey I.L., Stull G.B. & Brinster R.L. (1978) Poly(A) and synthesis of polyadenylated RNA in the preimplantation mouse embryo. *Devl. Biol.*, **64**, 140–148.

259 Levinger L., Barsonon J. & Varshavsky A. (1981) Two-dimensional hybridization mapping of nucleosomes. Comparison of DNA and protein patterns. *J. molec. Biol.*, **146**, 287–304.

260 Levy-Wilson B., Wong N.C.W. & Dixon G.H. (1977) Selective association of the trout specific H6 protein with chromatin regions susceptible to DNase I and DNase II: possible location of HMG-T in the spacer region between core nucleosomes. *Proc. natl. Acad. Sci. USA*, **74**, 2810–2814.

261 Lewin B. (1980) *Gene Expression 2*, 2nd edn. Wiley-Interscience, New York.

262 Lingrel J.B. & Woodland H.R. (1974) Initiation does not limit the rate of globin synthesis in message-injected *Xenopus* oocytes. *Eur. J. Biochem.*, **47**, 47–56.

263 Lipchitz L. & Axel R. (1976) Restriction endonuclease cleavage of satellite DNA in intact bovine nuclei. *Cell*, **9**, 355–364.

264 Liu L.F. & Wang J.C. (1978) DNA–DNA gyrase complex: the wrapping of the DNA duplex outside the enzyme. *Cell*, **15**, 979–984.

265 Lockshin R.A. (1966) Insect embryogenesis: macromolecular synthesis during early development. *Science, N.Y.*, **154**, 775–776.

266 Lodish H.F. (1974) Model for the regulation of mRNA translation applied to haemoglobin synthesis. *Nature, Lond.*, **251**, 385–388.

267 Lodish H.F. (1976) Translational control of protein synthesis. *A. Rev. Biochem.*, **45**, 39–72.

268 Lodish H.F. & Small B. (1976) Different lifetimes of reticulocyte messenger RNA. *Cell*, **7**, 59–65.

269 Lomedico P., Rosenthal N., Efstratiadis A., Gilbert W., Kolodner R. & Tizard R. (1979) The structure and evolution of the two nonallelic rat preproinsulin genes. *Cell*, **18**, 545–558.

270 Lowenhaupt K. & Lingrel J.B. (1978) A change in the stability of globin mRNA during the induction of murine erythroleukemia cells. *Cell*, **14**, 337–344.

271 Luse D.S. & Roeder R.G. (1980) Accurate transcription initiation on a purified mouse β-globin DNA fragment in a cell-free system. *Cell*, **20**, 691–699.

272 McCarthy B.J. & Hoyer B.H. (1964) Identity of DNA and diversity of messenger RNA molecules in normal mouse. *Proc. natl Acad. Sci.*, USA, **52**, 915–922.

273 McGhee J.D. & Felsenfeld G. (1980) Nucleosome structure. *A. Rev. Biochem.*, **49**, 1115–1156.

274 McGhee J. & Ginder G.D. (1979) Specific DNA methylation sites in the vicinity of chicken β-globin genes. *Nature, Lond.*, **280**, 419–420.

275 Macgregor H. (1972) The nucleolus and its genes in amphibian oogenesis. *Biol. Rev.*, **47**, 177–210.

276 McKnight S.L., Bustin M. & Miller O.L. (1977) Electron-microscopic analysis of chromosome metabolism in *Drosophila melanogaster* embryo. *Cold Spring Harbor Symp. Quant. Biol.*, **42**, 741–754.

277 McKnight S.L. & Miller O.L. Jr. (1976) Ultrastructural patterns

of RNA synthesis during early embryogenesis of *Drosophila melanogaster*. *Cell*, **8**, 305–319.

278 McKnight S.L., Sullivan N.L. & Miller O.L. (1976) Visualization of the silk fibroin transcription unit and nascent silk fibroin molecules on polyribosomes of *Bombyx mori*. *Progr. Nuc. Acid. Res.*, **19**, 313–318.

279 Maden B.E.H., Hall L.M.C. & Salim M. (1981) Ribosome formation in the eukaryotic nucleolus: recent advances from sequence analysis. In *The Nucleolus*. Society for Experimental Biology. Seminar Series 15. (Eds E.G. Jordan & C.A. Cullis), pp 87–101. Cambridge University Press, Cambridge.

280 Mairy M. & Denis H. (1971) Recherches biochemiques sur l'oogenese. Synthese et accumulation du RNA pendant l'oogenese du crapaud sud-africain *Xenopus laevis*. *Devl. Biol.*, **24**, 143–165.

281 Maki R., Roeder W., Traunecker A., Sidman C., Wabl M., Rascke W. & Tonegawa S. (1981) The role of DNA rearrangement and alternative RNA processing in the expression of immunoglobulin delta genes. *Cell*, **24**, 353–365.

282 Maller J.R. & Krebs E.G. (1977) Progesterone-stimulated meiotic cell division in *Xenopus* oocytes. Inductions by regulatory subunit and inhibition by catalytic subunit of adenosine 3'5' monophosphate dependent protein kinase. *J. biol. Chem.*, **252**, 1712–1718.

283 Mandel I. & Chambon P. (1979) DNA methylation: organ specific variations in the methylation patterns within and around ovalbumin and other chicken genes. *Nucl. Acids Res.*, **7**, 2081–2103.

284 Manes C. (1971) Nucleic acid synthesis in preimplantation rabbit embryos. II. Delayed synthesis of ribosomal RNA. *J. exp. Zool.* **176**, 87–96.

285 Margiarotti G., Lefebvre P. & Lodish H.F. (1982) Differences in the stability of developmentally regulated mRNAs in aggregated and disaggregated *Dictyostelium discoideum* cells. *Devl. Biol.*, **89**, 82–91.

286 Maniatis T., Hardison R.C., Lacy E., Lauer J., O'Connell C. & Quon D. (1978) The isolation of structural genes from libraries of eucaryotic DNA. *Cell*, **15**, 687–701.

287 Manley J.L., Fire A., Cano A., Sharp P.A. & Gefler M.L. (1980) DNA-dependent transcription of adenovirus genes in a soluble whole-cell extract. *Proc. natl Acad. Sci., USA*, **77**, 3855–3859.

288 Manning J.E., Schmid C.W. & Davidson N. (1975) Interspersion of repetitive and non-repetitive DNA sequences in the *Drosophila melanogaster* genome. *Cell*, **4**, 141–155.

289 Marx J.L. (1981) Genes that control development. *Science, N.Y.*, **213**, 1485–1488.

290 Matheson R.C. & Schultz G.A. (1980) Histone synthesis in preimplantation rabbit embryos. *J. exp. Zool.*, **213**, 337–349.

291 Mathew C.G.P., Goodwin G.H. Igo-Kemenes T. & Johns E.W. (1981) The protein composition of rat satellite chromatin. *F.E.B.S. Letters*, **125**, 25–29.

292 Mathis D., Oudet P. & Chambon P. (1980) Structure of transcribing chromatin. *Progr. Nuc. Acid Res.*, **24**, 1–55.

293 Maxwell I.H., Maxwell F. & Hahn W.E. (1980) General occurrence and transcription of intervening sequences in mouse genes expressed via polyadenylated mRNA. *Nucl. Acids Res.*, **8**, 5875–5894.

294 Mellon P., Parker V., Gluzman Y. & Maniatis T. (1981) Identifi-

cation of DNA sequences required for transcription of the human α1-globin gene in a new SV40 host–vector system. *Cell*, **27**, 279–288.

295 Metafora S., Felicetti L. & Gambino R. (1971) The mechanisms of protein synthesis activation after fertilization of sea urchin eggs. *Proc. natl Acad. Sci., USA*, **68**, 600–604.

296 Miller J.R., Cartwright E.M., Brownlee G.G., Federoff N.V. & Brown D.D. (1978) The nucleotide sequence of oocyte 5S DNA in *Xenopus laevis* II. The GC-rich region. *Cell*, **13**, 717–725.

297 Miller J.R. & Melton D.A. (1981) A transcriptionally active pseudogene in *Xenopus laevis* oocyte 5S DNA. *Cell*, **24**, 829–835.

298 Miller K.G. & Sollner-Webb B. (1981) Transcription of mouse rRNA genes by RNA polymerase I *in vitro* and *in vivo* initiation and processing sites. *Cell*, **27**, 165–174.

299 Miller L. (1972) Initiation of the synthesis of ribosomal ribonucleic acid precursor in different regions of frog (*Rana pipiens*) gastrulae. *Biochem. J.*, **127**, 733–735.

300 Miller L. (1974) Metabolism of 5S RNA in the absence of ribosome production. *Cell*, **3**, 275–281.

301 Miller L. & Knowland J. (1972) The number and activity of ribosomal RNA genes in *Xenopus laevis* embryos carrying partial deletions in both nucleolar organizers. *Biochem. Genetics*, **6**, 65–73.

302 Miller O.L. Jr., & Bakken A. (1972) Morphological studies of transcription. *Acta endocr.* Suppl., **168**, 155–177.

303 Miller O.L. Jr., & Beatty B.R. (1969) Extra-chromosomal genes in amphibian oocytes. *Genetics*, Suppl., **61**, 133–143.

304 Milstein C. (1980) Monoclonal antibodies. *Scient. Am.*, **243**(4), 66–74.

305 Milstein C. & Lennox E. (1980) The use of monoclonal antibody techniques in the study of developing cell surfaces. *Curr. Tops Devl. Biol.*, **14**, 1–32.

306 Mirault M.E., Goldschmidt-Clermont M., Moran L., Arrigo A.P. & Tissieres A. (1978) The effect of heat shock on gene expression in *D. melanogaster*. *Cold Spring Harbor Symp. Quant. Biol.*, **42**, 819–827.

307 Mohandas T., Sparkes R.S. & Shapiro L.J. (1980) Reactivation of an inactive human X chromosome: evidence for X inactivation by DNA methylation. *Science, N.Y.*, **211**, 393–396.

308 Morgan G.T., Macgregor H.C. & Colman A. (1980) Multiple ribosomal gene sites revealed by *in situ* hybridization of *Xenopus* rDNA to *Triturus* lampbrush chromosomes. *Chromosoma*, **80**, 309–330.

309 Moritz K.B. & Roth G.E. (1976) Complexity of germ line and somatic DNA in *Ascaris*. *Nature, Lond.*, **259**, 55–57.

310 Nakahashi T. & Yamana K. (1976) Biochemical and cytological examination on the initiation of ribosomal RNA synthesis during gastrulation of *Xenopus laevis*. *Devl. Growth Differ.*, **18**, 329–338.

311 Nakano E. & Monroy A. (1958) Incorporation of ³⁵S-methionine in the cell fractions of sea urchin eggs and embryos. *Expl Cell Res.*, **14**, 236–242.

312 Nedospasov S.A. & Georgiev G.P. (1980) Non-random cleavage of SV-40 DNA in the compact minichromosome and free in solution by micrococcal nuclease. *Biochem. biophys. Res. Commun.*, **92**, 532–539.

313 Nelson T., Hsieh T. S. & Brutlag D. (1979) Extracts of *Drosophila* embryos mediate chromatin assembly *in vitro*. *Proc. natl Acad. Sci., USA*, **76**, 5510–5514.

314 Nelson T., Wiegand R. & Brutlag D. (1981) Ribonucleic acid and other polyanions facilitate chromatin assembly *in vitro*. *Biochemistry*, **20**, 2594–2601.

315 Nemer M., Dubroff L.M. & Graham M. (1975) Properties of sea urchin embryo messenger RNA containing and lacking poly(A). *Cell*, **6**, 171–178.

316 Newell P.C., Franke J. & Sussman M.J. (1972) Regulation of four functionally related enzymes during shifts in the developmental program of *Dictyostelium discoideum*. *J. molec. Biol.*, **63**, 373–382.

317 Nieuwkoop P.D. & Faber J. (1956) *Normal Table of* Xenopus laevis *(Daudin)*. North-Holland, Amsterdam.

318 Niwa O. & Sugahara T. (1981) 5′-Azacytidine induction of mouse endogenous type C virus and suppression of DNA methylation. *Proc. natl Acad. Sci., USA*, **78**, 6290–6294.

319 Noll M. (1974) Subunit structures of chromatin. *Nature, Lond.*, **251**, 249–251.

320 Nordheim A., Pardue M.L., Lafer E.M., Moller A., Stollar B.D. & Rich A. (1981) Antibodies to left-handed Z-DNA bind to interband regions of *Drosophila* polytene chromosomes. *Nature, Lond.*, **294**, 417–422.

321 Nordstrom J.L., Roop D.R., Tsai M-J. & O'Malley B.W. (1979) Identification of potential ovomucoid mRNA precursors in chick oviduct nuclei. *Nature, Lond.*, **278**, 328–331.

322 Nunberg J.H., Kaufman R.J., Chang A.C., Cohen S.N. & Schimke R.T. (1980) Structure and genomic organization of the mouse dihydrofolate reductase gene. *Cell*, **19**, 355–364.

323 Old R.W. & Primrose S.B. (1981) *Principles of Gene Manipulation: An Introduction to Genetic Engineering*, 2nd edn. Blackwell Scientific Publications, Oxford.

324 Olins A.L. & Olins D.E. (1979) Stereo electron microscopy of the 25-nm chromatin fibers in isolated nuclei. *J. Cell Biol.*, **81**, 260–265.

325 Orgel L.E. & Crick F.H.C. (1980) Selfish DNA: the ultimate parasite. *Nature, Lond.*, **284**, 604–606.

326 Palmiter R.D. (1975) Quantitation of parameters that determine the rate of ovalbumin synthesis. *Cell*, **4**, 189–197.

327 Pardue M.L., Brown D.D. & Birnstiel M.L. (1973) Location of the genes for 5S ribosomal RNA in *Xenopus laevis*. *Chromosoma*, **42**, 191–203.

328 Pardue M.L. & Gall J.G. (1969) Molecular hybridization of radioactive DNA to the DNA of cytological preparations. *Proc. natl Acad. Sci., USA*, **64**, 600–604.

329 Pardue M.L. & Gall J.G. (1972) Chromosome structure studied by nucleic acid hybridization in cytological preparations. In *Chromosomes Today 3*, (Eds C.D. Darlington & K.R. Lewis), pp. 47–52. Hafner, New York.

330 Patterson J.B. & Stafford D.W. (1971) Characterization of sea urchin ribosomal satellite deoxyribonucleic acid. *Biochemistry*, **10**, 2775–2779.

331 Pelham H.R.B. & Brown D.D. (1980) A specific transcription factor that can bind either the 5S RNA gene or 5S RNA. *Proc. natl Acad. Sci., USA*, **77**, 4170–4174.

332 Pelham H.R.B., Wormington W.M. & Brown D.D. (1981) Related 5S RNA transcription factors in *Xenopus* oocytes and somatic cells. *Proc. natl Acad. Sci., USA*, **78**, 1760–1764.

333 Pelling C. (1964) Ribonuklein Säure Synthese der riesen Chromosomen. *Chromosoma*, **15**, 71–122.

334 Perkowska E., Macgregor H.C. & Birnsteil M.L. (1968) Gene

amplification in the oocyte nucleus of mutant and wild type *Xenopus laevis. Nature, Lond.*, **217**, 649–650.

335 Perry R.P. & Kelley D.E. (1968) Persistent synthesis of 5S RNA when production of 28S and 18S ribosomal RNA is inhibited by low doses of actinomycin D. *J. Cell Physiol.*, **72**, 235–246.

336 Perry R.P. & Kelley D.E. (1973) Messenger RNA turnover in mouse L cells. *J. molec. Biol.*, **79**, 681–696.

337 Perry R.P., Kelley D.E., Coleclough C., Seidman J.G., Leder P., Tonegawa S., Matthyssens G. & Weigert M. (1980) Transcription of mouse kappa chain genes: implications for allelic exclusion. *Proc. natl Acad. Sci., USA*, **77**, 1937–1941.

338 Pestell R.Q.W. (1975) Microtubule protein synthesis during oogenesis and early embryogenesis in *Xenopus laevis. Biochem. J.*, **145**, 527–534.

339 Peterson R.C., Doering J.L. & Brown D.D. (1980) Characterization of two *Xenopus* somatic 5S DNAs and one minor oocyte-specific 5S DNA. *Cell*, **20**, 131–141.

340 Petzoldt U., Hoppe P.C. & Illmensee K. (1980) Protein synthesis in enucleated, fertilized and unfertilized mouse eggs. *Wilhelm Roux' Archiv.* **189**, 215–219.

341 Picard B. & Wegnez M. (1979) Isolation of a 7S particle from *Xenopus laevis* oocytes. A 5S RNA-protein complex. *Proc. natl Acad. Sci., USA*, **76**, 241–245.

342 Pikó L. (1970) Synthesis of macromolecules in early mouse embryos cultured *in vitro*: RNA, DNA and a polysaccharide component. *Devl. Biol.*, **21**, 257–279.

343 Pikó L. & Clegg K.B. (1982) Quantitative changes in total RNA, total poly(A), and ribosomes in early mouse embryos. *Devl. Biol.*, **89**, 362–378.

344 Poccia D., Salik J. & Krystal G. (1981) Transitions in histone variants of the male pronucleus following fertilization and evidence for a maternal store of the cleavage-stage histones in the sea urchin egg. *Devl. Biol.*, **27**, 287–296.

345 Pollack Y., Stein R., Razin A. & Cedar H. (1980) Methylation of foreign DNA sequences in eukaryotic cells. *Proc. natl Acad. Sci., USA*, **77**, 6463–6467.

346 Posakony J.W., Scheller R.H., Anderson D.M., Britten R.J. & Davidson E.H. (1981) Repetitive sequences of the sea urchin genome III. Nucleotide sequences of cloned repeat elements. *J. molec. Biol.*, **149**, 41–67.

347 Potter S.S., Brorein W.J., Dunsmuir P. & Rubin G.M. (1979) Transposition of elements of the 412, copia and 297 dispersed repeated gene families in *Drosophila. Cell*, **17**, 415–427.

348 Potter S.S., Truett M., Phillips M. & Maher A. (1980) Eucaryotic transposable genetic elements with inverted terminal repeats. *Cell*, **20**, 639–647.

349 Proudfoot N.J. (1979) Eukaryotic promoters? *Nature, Lond.*, **279**, 376.

350 Proudfoot N.J. & Brownlee G.G. (1976) 3' Non-coding region sequences in eukaryotic messenger RNA. *Nature, Lond.*, **263**, 211–214.

351 Raff R.A., Brandis J.W., Huffman C.J., Koch A.L. & Leister D.E. (1981) Protein synthesis as an early response to fertilization of the sea urchin egg: a model. *Devl. Biol.*, **86**, 265–271.

352 Raff R.A. & Kaumeyer J.F. (1973) Soluble microtubule proteins of the sea urchin embryo: partial characterization of the proteins and behaviour of the pool in early development. *Devl. Biol.*, **32**, 309–320.

353 Reeves R. (1978) Nucleosome structure of *Xenopus* oocyte amplified ribosomal genes. *Biochemistry*, **17**, 4908–4915.

354 Regier J.C. & Kafatos F.C. (1977) Absolute rates of protein synthesis in sea urchins with specific activity measurements of radioactive leucine and leucyl-tRNA. *Devl. Biol.*, **57**, 270–283.

355 Ribbert D. (1979) Chromomeres and puffing in experimentally induced polytene chromosomes of *Calliphora erythrocephala. Chromosoma*, **74**, 269–298.

356 Richter J.D., Wasserman W.J. & Smith L.D. (1982) The mechanism for increased protein synthesis during *Xenopus* oocyte maturation. *Devl. Biol.*, **89**, 159–167.

357 Riggs A.D. (1975) X inactivation, differentiation and DNA methylation. *Cytogenet. Cell Genet.*, **14**, 9–25.

358 Ritossa F.M. (1964) Behaviour of RNA and DNA synthesis at the puff level in salivary gland chromosomes of *Drosophila. Expl. Cell Res.*, **36**, 515–523.

359 Robbins J. & Heywood S.M. (1978) Quantification of myosin heavy-chain mRNA during myogenesis. *Eur. J. Biochem.*, **82**, 601–608.

360 Robertson M.A., Staden R., Tanaka Y., Catterall J.F., O'Malley B.W. & Brownlee G.G. (1979) Sequence of three introns in the chick ovalbumin gene. *Nature, Lond.*, **278**, 370–372.

361 Rochaix J.D., Bird A. & Bakken A. (1974) Ribosomal RNA gene amplification by rolling circles. *J. molec. Biol.*, **87**, 473–487.

362 Rodgers W.H. & Gross P.R. (1978) Inhomogeneous distribution of egg RNA sequences in the early embryo. *Cell*, **14**, 279–288.

363 Roeder R.G. (1974) Multiple forms of deoxyribonucleic acid-dependent RNA polymerase in *Xenopus laevis*. Levels of activity during oocyte and embryonic development. *J. biol. Chem.*, **249**, 249–256.

364 Roeder R.G. & Rutter W.J. (1970) Multiple RNA polymerases and RNA synthesis during sea urchin development. *Biochemistry*, **9**, 2543–2553.

365 Rogers J., Choi E., Souza L., Carter C., Word C., Kuehl M., Eisenberg D. & Wall R. (1981) Gene segments encoding transmembrane carboxyl termini of immunoglobulin γ chains. *Cell*, **26**, 19–27.

366 Rogers J. & Wall R. (1980) A mechanism for RNA splicing. *Proc. natl Acad. Sci., USA*, **77**, 1877–1879.

367 Roop D.R., Nordstrom J.L., Tsai S.Y., Tsai M-J. & O'Malley B.W. (1978) Transcription of structural and intervening sequences in the ovalbumin gene and identification of potential ovalbumin mRNA precursor. *Cell*, **15**, 671–685.

368 Rosbash M. & Ford P.J. (1974) Polyadenylic acid containing RNA in *Xenopus laevis* oocytes. *J. molec. Biol.*, **85**, 87–101.

369 Rosenberg M. & Court D. (1979) Regulatory sequences involved in the promotion and termination of RNA transcription. *A. Rev. Genet.*, **13**, 319–353.

370 Rosenthal E.T., Hunt T. & Ruderman J.V. (1980) Selective translation of mRNA controls the pattern of protein synthesis during early development of the surf clam, *Spisula solidissima. Cell*, **20**, 487–494.

371 Roth G.E. (1979) Satellite DNA properties of the germ line limited DNA and the organization of the somatic genomes in the nematodes *Ascaris suum* and *Parascaris equorum. Chromosoma*, **74**, 355–371.

372 Rubin C.M., Houck C.M., Deininger P.L., Friedman T. & Schmid C.W. (1980) Partial nucleotide sequence of the 300-

nucleotide interspersed repeated human DNA sequences. *Nature, Lond.*, **284**, 372–374.

373 Ruderman J.V. & Schmidt M.R. (1981) RNA transcription and translation in sea urchin oocytes and eggs. *Devl. Biol.*, **81**, 220–228.

374 Ruderman J.V., Woodland H.R. & Sturgess E.A. (1979) Modulations of histone messenger RNA during the early development of *Xenopus laevis*. *Devl. Biol.*, **71**, 71–82.

375 Ryffel G.U., Muellener D.B., Wyler T., Wahli W. & Weber R. (1981) Transcription of single-copy vitellogenin gene of *Xenopus* involves expression of middle repetitive DNA. *Nature, Lond.*, **291**, 429–431.

376 Ryffel G.U., Wyler T., Muellener D.B. & Weber R. (1980) Identification, organization and processing intermediates of the putative precursors of *Xenopus* vitellogenin messenger RNA. *Cell*, **19**, 53–61.

377 Sakonju S., Bogenhagen D.F. & Brown D.D. (1980) A control region in the centre of the 5S gene directs specific initiation of transcription: I. The 5′ border of the region. *Cell*, **19**, 13–25.

378 Sakonju S., Brown D.D., Engelke D., Ng S.Y., Shastry B.S. & Roeder R.G. (1981) The binding of a transcription factor to deletion mutants of a 5S ribosomal RNA gene. *Cell*, **23**, 665–669.

379 Sassone-Corsi P., Corden J., Kedinger C. & Chambon P. (1981) Promotion of specific *in vitro* transcription by excised TATA box sequences inserted in a foreign nucleotide environment. *Nucl. Acids Res.*, **9**, 3941–3958.

380 Scangos G. & Ruddle F.H. (1981) Mechanisms and applications of DNA mediated gene transfer in mammalian cells—a review. *Gene*, **14**, 1–10.

381 Scheer U. (1973) Nuclear flow rate of ribosomal RNA and chain growth rate of its precursor during oogenesis of *Xenopus laevis*. *Devl. Biol.*, **30**, 13–28.

382 Scheer U. (1978) Changes of nucleosome frequency in nucleolar and non nucleolar chromatin as a function of transcription: an electron microscopic study. *Cell*, **13**, 535–549.

383 Scheer U., Trendelenburg M.F. & Franke W.W. (1976) Regulation of transcription of genes of ribosomal RNA during amphibian oogenesis, a biochemical and morphological study. *J. Cell Biol.*, **69**, 465–489.

384 Scheer U., Trendelenburg M.F., Krohne G. & Franke W.W. (1977) Lengths and patterns of transcriptional units in the amplified nucleoli of oocytes of *Xenopus laevis*. *Chromosoma*, **60**, 147–167.

385 Scheller R.H., Anderson D.M., Posakony J.W. McAllister L.B., Britten R.J. & Davidson E.H. (1981) Repetitive sequences of the sea urchin genome II. Subfamily structure and evolutionary conservation. *J. molec. Biol.*, **149**, 15–39.

386 Schibler U., Pittet A.C., Young R.A., Hagenbuchle O., Tosi M., Gellman S. & Wellauer P.K. (1982) The mouse α-amylase multigene family. Sequence organization of members expressed in the pancreas, salivary gland and liver. *J. molec. Biol.*, **155**, 247–266.

387 Schimke R.T. & Doyle D. (1970) Control of enzyme levels in animal tissues. *A. Rev. Biochem.*, **39**, 929–976.

388 Schultz G.A. (1973) Characterization of polyribosomes containing newly synthesized messenger RNA in preimplantation rabbit embryos. *Expl. Cell Res.*, **82**, 168–174.

389 Schultz G.A., Clough J.R., Braude P.R., Pelham H.R.B. & Johnson M.H. (1981) A re-examination of messenger RNA populations in the preimplantation mouse embryo. In *Cellular and Molecular Aspects of Implantation* (Eds S.R. Glasser & D.W. Bullock), pp. 137–154. Plenum Press, New York.

390 Schultz R.M., Letourneau G.E. & Wasserman P.M. (1979) Program of early development in the mammal: changes in patterns and absolute rates of tubulin and total protein synthesis during oogenesis and early embryogenesis in the mouse. *Devl. Biol.*, **68**, 341–359.

391 Scott M.P. & Pardue M.L. (1981) Translation and control in lysates of *Drosophila melanogaster* cells. *Proc. natl Acad. Sci., USA*, **78**, 3353–3357.

392 Scott W.A. & Wigmore D.J. (1978) Sites in Simian Virus SV40 chromatin which are preferentially cleaved by endonucleases. *Cell*, **15**, 1511–1518.

393 Segal S. & Khoury G. (1979) Differentiation as a requirement for simian virus 40 gene expression in F-9 embryonal carcinoma cells. *Proc. natl Acad. Sci., USA*, **76**, 5611–5615.

394 Segal S., Levine A.J & Khoury G. (1979) Evidence for non-spliced SV40 RNA in undifferentiated murine teratocarcinoma stem cells. *Nature, Lond.*, **280**, 335–338.

395 Senear A.W. & Palmiter R.D. (1981) Multiple structural features are responsible for the nuclease sensitivity of the active ovalbumin gene. *J. biol. Chem.*, **256**, 1191–1198.

396 Sharp P.A. (1981) Speculations on RNA splicing. *Cell*, **23**, 643–646.

397 Shen C.J. & Maniatis T. (1980) Tissue-specific DNA methylation in a cluster of rabbit β-like globin genes. *Proc. natl Acad. Sci., USA*, **77**, 6634–6638.

398 Shen S.S. & Steinhardt R.A. (1978) Direct measurement of intracellular pH during metabolic derepression at fertilization and ammonia activation of the sea urchin egg. *Nature, Lond.*, **272**, 253–254.

399 Shiokawa K., Misumi Y. & Yamana K. (1981) Mobilization of newly synthesized RNAs into polysomes in *Xenopus laevis* embryos. *Wilhelm Roux' Archiv.*, **190**, 103–110.

400 Shiokawa K., Tashiro K., Misumi Y. & Yamana K. (1981) Non-coordinated synthesis of RNAs in pre-gastrular embryos of *Xenopus laevis*. *Devl. Growth Differ.*, **23**, 589–597.

401 Shiokawa K. & Yamana K. (1967) Inhibitor of ribosomal RNA synthesis in *Xenopus laevis* embryos. *Devl. Biol.*, **16**, 389–406.

402 Shiokawa K. & Yamana K. (1979) Differential initiation of rRNA gene activity in progeny of different blastomeres of early *Xenopus* embryos: evidence for regulated synthesis of rRNA. *Devl. Growth Differ.*, **21**, 501–507.

403 Smith L.D. (1975) Molecular events during oocyte maturation. In *Biochemistry of Animal Development* Vol. 3 (Ed. R. Weber), pp. 1–46. Academic Press, New York.

404 Smith L.D. & Ecker R.E. (1969) Cytoplasmic regulation in early events of amphibian development. In *Canadian Cancer Conference*. Proceedings of the Eighth Canadian Cancer Research Conference, Honey Harbor, Ontario, 1968 (Ed. J.F. Morgan). Pergamon Press, Oxford.

405 Smith S.S. & Thomas C.A. Jr. (1981) The two dimensional restriction analysis of *Drosophila* DNAs: males and females. *Gene*, **13**, 395–408.

406 Southern E.M. (1975) Detection of specific sequences among DNA fragments separated by gel electrophoresis. *J. molec. Biol.*, **98**, 503–517.

407 Spear B.B. & Gall J.G. (1973) Independent control of ribosomal gene replication in polytene chromosomes of *D. melanogaster*. *Proc. natl Acad. Sci., USA*, **70**, 1359–1363.

408 Spirin A.S. (1966) On "masked" forms of messenger RNA in early embryogenesis and in other differentiating systems. *Curr. Tops Devl. Biol.*, **1**, 2–38.

409 Spradling A.C. (1981) The organization and amplification of two chromosomal domains containing *Drosophila* chorion genes. *Cell*, **27**, 193–201.

410 Stalder J., Larsen A., Engel J.D., Dolan M., Groudine M. & Weintraub J. (1980) Tissue-specific DNA cleavages in the globin chromatin domain introduced by DNAase I. *Cell*, **20**, 451–460.

411 Stein R., Gruenbaum Y., Pollack Y., Razin A. & Cedar H. (1982) Clonal inheritance of the pattern of DNA methylation in mouse cells. *Proc. natl Acad. Sci., USA*, **79**, 61–65.

412 Storti R.V., Scott M.P., Rich A. & Pardue M.L. (1980) Translational control of protein synthesis in response to heat shock in *D. melanogaster* cells. *Cell*, **22**, 825–834.

413 Strobel E., Dunsmuir P. & Rubin G.M. (1979) Polymorphisms in the chromosomal locations of elements 412, copia, 297 dispersed repeated gene families in *Drosophila*. *Cell*, **17**, 429–439.

414 Surrey S., Ginzburg I. & Nemer M. (1979) Ribosomal RNA synthesis in pre- and post-gastrula-stage sea urchin embryos. *Devl. Biol.*, **71**, 83–99.

415 Thomas T.L., Posakony J.W., Anderson D.M., Britten R.J. & Davidson E.H. (1981) Molecular structure of maternal RNA. *Chromosoma*, **84**, 319–335.

416 Tiemeier D.C., Tilghman S.M., Polsky F.I., Seidman J.G., Leder A., Edgell M.H. & Leder P. (1978) A comparison of two cloned mouse β-globin genes and their surrounding and intervening sequences. *Cell*, **14**, 237–246.

417 Tobler H., Smith K.D. & Ursprung H. (1972) Molecular aspects of chromatin elimination in *Ascaris lumbricoides*. *Devl. Biol.*, **27**, 190–203.

418 Tsai M.J., Ting A.C., Norstrom J.C., Zimmer W. & O'Malley B.W. (1980) Processing of high molecular weight ovalbumin and ovomucoid precursor RNAs to messenger RNA. *Cell*, **22**, 219–230.

419 Trendelenburg M.F. & McKinnell R.G. (1979) Transcriptionally active and inactive regions of nucleolar chromatin in amplified nucleoli of fully grown oocytes of hibernating frogs, *Rana pipiens* (Amphibia, Anura). *Differentiation*, **15**, 73–95.

420 Tufaro F. & Brandhorst B.P. (1979) Similarity of proteins synthesized by isolated blastomeres of early sea urchin embryos. *Devl. Biol.*, **72**, 390–397.

421 Turner P.C. & Woodland H.R. (1982) H3 and H4 histone cDNA sequences from *Xenopus*: a sequence comparison of H4 genes. *Nucl. Acids Res.*, **10**, 3769–3780.

422 Unsworth B.R. & Kaulenas M.S. (1975) Changes in ribosomal-associated proteins during sea urchin development. *Cell Differ.*, **3**, 21–27.

423 Valle G., Besley J. & Colman A. (1981) Synthesis and secretion of mouse immunoglobulin chains from *Xenopus* oocytes. *Nature, Lond.*, **291**, 338–340.

424 Van Ardsell S.W., Denison R.A., Bernstein L.B., Weiner A.B., Manser T. & Gesteland R.F. (1981) Direct repeats flank three small nuclear RNA pseudogenes in the human genome. *Cell*, **26**, 11–17.

425 Van den Berg J., Van Ooyen A., Mantei N., Schambock A., Grosveld G., Flavell R.A. & Weissmann C. (1978) Comparison of cloned rabbit and mouse β-globin genes showing strong evolutionary divergence of two homologous pairs of introns. *Nature, Lond.*, **276**, 37–43.

426 Van der Ploeg L.H.T. & Flavell R.A. (1980) DNA methylation in human γ δ β-globin locus in erythroid and nonerythroid tissues. *Cell*, **19**, 947–958.

427 Van Gansen P. & Schram A. (1969) Etude des ribosomes et du glycogène des gastrules de *Xenopus laevis* par cytochimie ultrastructurale. *J. Embryol. exp. Morph.*, **22**, 69–98.

428 Vardimon L., Kressmann A., Cedar H., Maechler M. & Doerfler W. (1982) Expression of a cloned adenovirus gene is inhibited by *in vitro* methylation. *Proc. natl Acad. Sci., USA*, **79**, 1073–1077.

429 Vardimon L., Kuhlmann J., Cedar H. & Doerfler W. (1981) Methylation of adenovirus genes in transformed cells and *in vitro*: influence on the regulation of gene expression. *Eur. J. Cell Biol.*, **25**, 13–15.

430 Vardimon L., Neumann R., Kuhlman I., Suffer D. & Doerfler W. (1980) DNA methylation and viral gene expression in adenovirus-transformed and infected cells. *Nucl. Acids Res.*, **8**, 2461–2473.

431 Varley J.M., Macgregor H.C. & Erba H.P. (1980) Satellite DNA is transcribed on lampbrush chromosomes. *Nature, Lond.*, **283**, 686–688.

432 Varshavsky A.J., Sundin O. & Bohn M. (1979) A stretch of "late" SV40 viral DNA about 400 bp long which includes the origin of replication is specifically exposed in SV40 minichromosomes. *Cell*, **16**, 453–466.

433 Vincent W.S., Halvorson H.O., Chen H.-R. & Shin D. (1969) A comparison of ribosomal gene amplification in uni- and multinucleolate oocytes. *Expl. Cell Res.*, **57**, 240–250.

434 Vlad M.T., Macgregor H.C. & Barnett L. (1977) An investigation of some problems concerning nucleolus organizers in salamanders. *Chromosoma*, **59**, 283–299.

435 Waalwijk C. & Flavell R.A. (1978) DNA methylation at a CCGG sequence in the large intron of the rabbit β-globin gene: tissue specific variations. *Nucl. Acids Res.*, **5**, 4631–4641.

436 Wada K., Shiokawa K. & Yamana K. (1968) Inhibitor of ribosomal RNA synthesis in *Xenopus laevis* embryos. I. Changes in activity of the inhibitor during development and its distribution in early gastrulae. *Expl. Cell Res.*, **52**, 252–260.

437 Wahli W. & Dawid I.B. (1980) Isolation of two closely related vitellogenin genes including their flanking regions, from a *Xenopus laevis* gene library. *Proc. natl Acad. Sci., USA*, **77**, 1437–1441.

438 Waldeck W., Fohring B., Chowdury K., Gruss P. & Sauer G. (1978) Origin of DNA replication in papovavirus chromatin is recognized by endogenous endonuclease. *Proc. natl Acad. Sci., USA*, **75**, 5964–5968.

439 Walker J.M., Goodwin G.H. & Johns E.W. (1979) The primary structure of the nucleosome-associated chromosomal protein HMG 14. *F.E.B.S. Letters*, **100**, 394–398.

440 Walker J.M., Hastings J.R. & Johns E.W. (1977) The primary structure of a non-histone chromosomal protein. *Eur. J. Biochem.*, **76**, 461–468.

441 Wallace H. & Birnstiel M.L. (1966) Ribosomal cistrons and the nucleolar organizer. *Biochim. biophys. Acta*, **114**, 296–310.

442 Wassarman P.M. & Mrozak S.C. (1981) Program of early

development in the mammal: synthesis and intracellular migration of histone H4 during oogenesis in the mouse. *Devl. Biol.*, **84**, 364–371.

443 Wasserman W.J., Richter J.D. & Smith L.D. (1982) Protein synthesis during maturation promoting factor and progesterone-induced maturation in *Xenopus* oocytes. *Devl. Biol.*, **89**, 152–158.

444 Wasylyk B., Kedinger C., Corden J., Brison O. & Chambon P. (1980) Specific *in vitro* initiation of transcription on conalbumin and ovalbumin genes and comparison with adenovirous-2 early and late genes. *Nature, Lond.*, **285**, 367–373.

445 Watson J.D. (1975) *Molecular Biology of the Gene*, 3rd edn. Addison-Wesley, London.

446 Wegnez M., Monier R. & Denis H. (1972) Sequence heterogeneity of 5S RNA in *Xenopus laevis*. *F.E.B.S. Letters*, **25**, 13–20.

447 Weideli H., Brack C. & Gehring W.J. (1980) Characterization of *Drosophila* DNA-binding protein DB-2: demonstration of its sequence-specific interaction with DNA. *Proc. natl Acad. Sci., USA*, **77**, 3773–3777.

448 Weideli H., Schedl P., Artavanis-Tsakonas S., Steward R., Yuan R. & Gehring W.J. (1978) Purification of a protein from unfertilized eggs of *Drosophila* with specific affinity for a defined DNA-sequence and cloning of this DNA-sequence in bacterial plasmids. *Cold Spring Harbor Symp. Quant. Biol.*, **42**, 693–700.

449 Weil P.A., Luse D.S., Segall J. & Roeder R.G. (1979) Selective and accurate initiation of transcription at the Ad2 major late promoter in a soluble system dependent on purified RNA polymerase II and DNA. *Cell*, **18**, 469–484.

450 Weil P.A., Segall J., Harris B., Ng S.Y. & Roeder R.G. (1979) Faithful transcription of eukaryotic genes by RNA polymerase III in systems reconstituted with purified DNA templates. *J. biol. Chem.*, **254**, 6163–6173.

451 Weinberg R.A. (1980) Origins and roles of endogenous retroviruses. *Cell*, **22**, 643–644.

452 Weintraub H. & Groudine M. (1976) Chromosomal subunits in active genes have an altered conformation. *Science, N.Y.*, **193**, 846–856.

453 Weintraub H., Larsen A. & Groudine M. (1981) α-globin gene switching during the development of chicken embryos: expression and chromosome structure. *Cell*, **24**, 333–344.

454 Weisbrod S., Groudine M. & Weintraub H. (1980) Interaction of HMG 14 and 17 with actively transcribed genes. *Cell*, **19**, 289–301.

455 Weisbrod S. & Weintraub H. (1979) Isolation of a subclass of nuclear proteins responsible for conferring a DNase I-sensitive structure on globin chromatin. *Proc. natl Acad. Sci., USA*, **76**, 630–634.

456 Weisbrod S. & Weintraub H. (1981) Isolation of actively transcribed nucleosomes using immobilized HMG 14 and 17 and an analysis of α-globin chromatin. *Cell*, **23**, 391–400.

457 Wellauer P.K., Reeder R.H., Dawid I.B. & Brown D.D. (1976) The arrangement of length heterogeneity in repeating units of amplified and chromosomal ribosomal DNA from *Xenopus laevis*. *J. molec. Biol.*, **105**, 487–505.

458 Wells D.E., Showman R.M., Klein W.H. & Raff R.A. (1981) Delayed recruitment of maternal histone H3 mRNA in sea urchin embryos. *Nature, Lond.*, **292**, 477–478.

459 Whittaker J.R. (1977) Segregation during cleavage of a factor determining endodermal alkaline phosphatase development in ascidian embryos. *J. exp. Zool.*, **202**, 139–154.

460 Wickens M.P. & Laskey R.A. (1981) Expression of cloned genes in cell-free systems and in microinjected *Xenopus* oocytes. *Genetic Engineering*, **1**, 103–167.

461 Wigler M.H. (1981) The inheritance of methylation patterns in vertebrates. *Cell*, **24**, 285–286.

462 Wilt F.H., Maxson R.E. & Woodland H.R. (1979) Gene activity in early development, oogenetic and zygotic contributions to mRNA. In *Mechanisms of Cell Change* (Eds J.D. Ebert & T.S. Okada), pp. 71–82. John Wiley & Sons, New York.

463 Winkler M.M. & Steinhardt R.A. (1981) Activation of protein synthesis in a sea urchin cell-free system. *Devl. Biol.*, **84**, 432–439.

464 Wold B.J., Lein W.H., Hough-Evans B.R., Britten R.J. & Davidson E.H. (1978) Sea urchin embryo mRNA sequences expressed in nuclear RNA of adult tissues. *Cell*, **14**, 941–950.

465 Wolf S.F. & Migeon B.R. (1982) Studies of X chromosome DNA methylation in normal human cells. *Nature, Lond.*, **295**, 667–671.

466 Wolpert L. (1971) Positional information and pattern formation. *Curr. Tops Devl. Biol.*, **6**, 183–224.

467 Wood W.G., Old J.M., Roberts A.V.S., Clegg J.B. & Weatherall D.J. (1978) Human globin gene expression: control of β, δ and δβ chain production. *Cell*, **15**, 437–446.

468 Woodland H.R. (1969) The phosphorylation of thymidine by oocytes and eggs of *Xenopus laevis* Daudin. *Biochim. biophys. Acta*, **186**, 1–12.

469 Woodland H.R (1974) Changes in the polysome content of developing *Xenopus laevis* embryos. *Devl. Biol.*, **40**, 90–101.

470 Woodland H.R. (1980) Histone synthesis during the development of *Xenopus*. *F.E.B.S. Letters*, **121**, 1–7.

471 Woodland H.R. & Ballantine J.E.M. (1980) Paternal gene expression in developing hybrid embryos of *Xenopus laevis* and *Xenopus borealis*. *J. Embryol. exp. Morph.*, **60**, 359–372.

472 Woodland H.R., Flynn J.M. & Wyllie A.J. (1979) Utilization of stored mRNA in *Xenopus* embryos and its replacement by newly synthesized transcripts: histone H1 synthesis using interspecies hybrids. *Cell*, **18**, 165–171.

473 Woodland H.R. & Graham C.F. (1969) RNA synthesis during early development of the mouse. *Nature, Lond.*, **221**, 327–332.

474 Woodland H.R. & Gurdon J.B. (1968) The relative rates of synthesis of DNA, sRNA and rRNA in the endodermal region and other parts of *Xenopus laevis* embryos. *J. Embryol. exp. Morph.*, **19**, 363–385.

475 Woodland H.R., Gurdon J.B. & Lingrel J.B. (1974) The translation of mammalian globin mRNA injected into fertilized eggs of *Xenopus laevis*. II. The distribution of globin synthesis in different tissues. *Devl. Biol.*, **39**, 134–140.

476 Woodland H.R. & Wilt F.H. (1980) The functional stability of sea urchin histone mRNA injected into oocytes of *Xenopus laevis*. *Devl. Biol.*, **75**, 199–213.

477 Woodland H.R. & Wilt F.H. (1980) The stability and translation of sea urchin histone mRNA injected into *Xenopus laevis* eggs and developing embryos. *Devl. Biol.*, **75**, 214–221.

478 Wormington W.M., Bogenhagen D.F., Jordan E. & Brown D.D. (1981) A qualitative assay for Xenopus 5S RNA gene transcription *in vitro*. *Cell*, **24**, 809–817.

479 Wozney J., Hanahan D., Tate V., Boedtker H. & Doty P. (1981) Structure of the pro α2(I) collagen gene. *Nature, Lond.*, **294**, 129–135.

480 Wu, C. (1980) The 5' ends of *Drosophila* heat shock genes in chromatin are hypersensitive to DNAase I. *Nature, Lond.*, **286**, 854–860.

481 Wu C. & Gilbert W. (1981) Tissue-specific exposure of chromatin structure at the 5' terminus of the rat preproinsulin gene. *Proc. natl Acad. Sci., USA*, **78**, 1577–1580.

482 Xin J-H., Bandhorst B.P., Britten R.J. & Davidson E.H. (1982) Cloned embryo mRNAs not detectably expressed in sea urchin coelomocytes. *Devl. Biol.*, **89**, 527–531.

483 Yagi M. & Koshland M.E. (1981) Expression of the J chain gene during B cell differentiation is inversely correlated with DNA methylation. *Proc. natl Acad. Sci., USA*, **78**, 4907–4911.

484 Young B.D., Birnie G.D. & Paul J. (1976) Complexity and specificity of polysomal poly(A)$^+$ RNA in mouse tissues. *Biochemistry*, **15**, 2823–2828.

485 Young M.W. (1979) Middle repetitive DNA: A fluid component of the *Drosophila* genome. *Proc. natl Acad. Sci., USA*, **76**, 6274–6278.

486 Young N.S., Benz E.J., Kantor J.A., Kretschmer P. & Nienhuis A.W. (1978) Hemoglobin switching in sheep: only the γ gene is in the active conformation in fetal liver but all the β and γ genes are in the active conformation in bone marrow. *Proc. natl Acad. Sci., USA*, **75**, 5884–5888.

487 Young R.A., Hagenbuchle O. & Schibler U. (1981) A single mouse α-amylase gene specifies two different tissue-specific mRNAs. *Cell*, **23**, 451–458.

488 Zieve G.W. (1981) Two groups of small stable RNAs. *Cell*, **25**, 296–297.

489 Ziff E.B. (1980) Transcription and RNA processing by the DNA tumour viruses. *Nature, Lond.*, **287**, 491–499.

490 Ziff E.B. & Evans R.M. (1978) Coincidence of the promoter and capped 5' terminus of RNA from the adenovirus 2 major late transcription unit. *Cell*, **15**, 1463–1475.

491 Zybler E.A. & Penman S. (1971) Synthesis of 5S and 4S RNA in metaphase arrested HeLa cells. *Science, N.Y.*, **172**, 947–949.

Conclusions to Part 6

This part of the book is concerned with the molecular bits and pieces which are composed into developing, growing and reproducing organisms. It deals with the molecules which are involved in cellular reproduction, cell adhesion, locomotion, and interaction, and which control gene expression, and which provide energy for these processes.

1. Boxes of molecules

Developing systems are not even mixtures of their molecular components; they are not soups. Characteristically, their molecules are arrayed and organized in space and time: molecules aggregate to form multi-molecular complexes (Chapter 6.2), the complexes are built into organelles (Chapter 6.3), and each cellular sack contains a set of organelles. Cells develop distinct phenotypes and are grouped into patterns (Part 4). Development is about boxing of molecules and their reactions and the complete construct transmits cells of the organism through selection and time to form a new generation.

Multicellular organisms propagate by transmitting cells to the next generation; such organelles as mitochondria and nuclei are not infective agents like viruses.

2. Developmental democracy

The control of development is often regarded as a hierarchical process. The genetic material in the DNA molecules of the nucleus, mitochondria and chloroplasts replicates on its templates and codes for all protein synthesis in the cell. Paternal organisms transmit little more than this material to the next generation, and genes are sometimes viewed as controllers of development. They certainly provide the molecular bits and pieces of development but expression of genes is regulated by extra-genetic inheritance and their cellular and ecological environment.

The most remarkable feature in gene expression as a process is that it involves so many stages. In any one cell type, only a proportion of the genes are transcribed, and this set of transcribing genes is different from one cell type to the next (p. 445 *et seq*.). Transcription in development is often associated with a change of state of the chromatin and with the degree of methylation of bases in and around the gene, but it is unclear whether these changes are the cause or consequence of transcription (p. 457 *et seq*.). In the rare case where it has been possible to identify the sequence required for the initiation of transcription (the ribosomal 5S gene), it has been found that a protein binds to this site. Although this observation suggests that eukaryotic gene transcription is regulated by protein–nucleic acid base sequence recognition, the failure to associate the presence of this protein with changes in 5S gene transcription implies that further undiscovered elements are involved (p. 483 *et seq*.).

Transcripts of eukaryotic genes are usually much longer than that part of the gene which codes for a protein, and the primary transcript is edited and spliced into a mature message. Further, there is evidence that the transport of messages from nucleus to cytoplasm may be a regulated process (p. 452). The availability of messages for translation depends both on their stability which is regulated and variable (p. 449 *et seq*.), and on their packaging (p. 443 *et seq*.). The translation of a message depends on the presence of regulating factors (p. 449).

This description of the process of protein synthesis draws attention to the various stages at which components in the cell and its environment may intervene in regulating gene expression, and the possibilities for control at various stages may be a fundamental requirement for integrating gene expression into the other cellular events of development. Developing systems must be able to alter their gene expression in response to such general events as the hydration of a seed and to such subtle events as a confrontation with a particular extracellular matrix (Chapter 3.6).

3. Interplay between nuclear and organelle genes

Nuclear and organelle genes cooperate in developing systems, and provide particularly clear examples of the interdependence of one part of a cell on another.

The protein synthesis which is observed in cell organelles is mediated by products of both nuclear and organelle genes. Despite the fact that organelles may use a distinct genetic code from that of the nucleus and have a special set of transfer RNA genes, components of some elements in protein synthesis are provided by the nucleus (p. 403 *et seq.*). The final structure and function of organelles is a compound of the products of these two sets of genes. Thus the enzymes of the citric acid cycle and electron transport system are principally coded by nuclear genes and the enzymes move into the organelles, while other enzymes, such as cytochrome oxidase and ribulose diphosphate carboxylase, are multi-subunit enzymes with some units coded by the nucleus and others by the organelle genome (p. 403). Clearly, it is at least the cell as a whole which is the unit for transmitting organization from one generation to the next.

Index